ROLEX

Presents

The World of
Professional Golf
Founded by
Mark H. McCormack
2009

sports · entertainment · media

Editor: Bev Norwood
Contributors: Andy Farrell, Doug Ferguson, Donald (Doc) Giffin, Marino Parascenzo

All rights reserved
First published 2009
© IMG Operations, Inc. 2009

Designed and produced by Davis Design

ISBN-13: 978-1-878843-56-2
ISBN-10: 1-878843-56-7

Printed and bound in the United States.

Contents

APPENDIXES

Introduction

Rolex has done so many things over the years that were and are good for golf. Sponsorship of this publication is a prime example. My friends at Rolex, recognizing the historic and research value *The World of Professional Golf* has provided to the game continuously since the middle 1960s, stepped up in 2005 with the support necessary to continue its existence and the service it extends to the world of golf.

I well remember my conversations with my close friend and business manager, the late Mark McCormack, when he outlined his concept of filling a written gap in the game's history with an annual book carrying detailed stories and statistics covering every organized national and international tournament during that particular calendar year. The idea made complete sense to me and I encouraged him to proceed. He did, recruiting a group of talented golf journalists to work with him in producing the first edition that covered the 1966 season worldwide. Its publication has continued and grown in size and scope ever since, keeping pace with the tremendous growth of the game throughout the world.

Mark McCormack passed away in 2003, but his contribution to the historical record of golf did not die. Credit for this goes to IMG executives and others within the organization who considered the book an important continuing tribute to Mark and to Patrick Heiniger and his executive associates at Rolex, whose support has kept the literary chain intact.

Arnold Palmer
Orlando, Florida

Foreword
(Written in 1968)

It has long been my feeling that a sport as compelling as professional golf is deserving of a history, and by history I do not mean an account culled years later from the adjectives and enthusiasms of on-the-spot reports that have then sat in newspaper morgues for decades waiting for some patient drudge to paste them together and call them lore. Such works can be excellent when insight and perspective are added to the research, but this rarely happens. What I am talking about is a running history, a chronology written at the time, which would serve both as a record of the sport and as a commentary upon the sport in any given year—an annual, if you will....

When I embarked on this project two years ago (the first of these annuals was published in Great Britain in 1967), I was repeatedly told that such a compendium of world golf was impossible, that it would be years out of date before it could be assembled and published, that it would be hopelessly expensive to produce and that only the golf fanatic would want a copy anyway. In the last analysis, it was that final stipulation that spurred me on. There must be a lot of golf fanatics, I decided. I can't be the only one. And then one winter day I was sitting in Arnold Palmer's den in Latrobe, Pennsylvania, going through the usual motions of spreading papers around so that Arnold and I could discuss some business project, when Arnold happened to mention that he wanted to collect a copy of each new golf book that was published from now on, in order to build a golf library of his own. "It's really too bad that there isn't a book every year on the pro tour," he said. "Ah," I thought. "Another golf fanatic. That makes two of us." So I decided to do the book. And I have. And I hope you like it. If so, you can join Arnold and me as golf fanatics.

Mark H. McCormack
Cleveland, Ohio
January 1968

Mark H. McCormack
1930 – 2003

In 1960, Mark Hume McCormack shook hands with a young golfer named Arnold Palmer. That historic handshake established a business that would evolve into today's IMG, the world's premier sports and lifestyle marketing and management company —representing hundreds of sports figures, entertainers, models, celebrities, broadcasters, television properties, and prestigious organizations and events around the world. With just a handshake Mark McCormack had invented a global industry.

Sean McManus, President of CBS News and Sports, reflects, "I don't think it's an overstatement to say that like Henry Ford and Bill Gates, Mark McCormack literally created, fostered and led an entirely new worldwide industry. There was no sports marketing before Mark McCormack. Every athlete who's ever appeared in a commercial, or every right holder who sold their rights to anyone, owes a huge debt of gratitude to Mark McCormack."

Mark McCormack's philosophy was simple. "Be the best," he said. "Learn the business and expand by applying what you already know." This philosophy served him well, not only as an entrepreneur and CEO of IMG, but also as an author, a consultant and a confidant to a host of global leaders in the world of business, politics, finance, science, sports and entertainment.

He was among the most-honored entrepreneurs of his time. *Sports Illustrated* recognized him as "The Most Powerful Man in Sports." In 1999, ESPN's Sports Century listed him as one of the century's 10 "Most Influential People in the Business of Sport."

Golf Magazine called McCormack "the most powerful man in golf" and honored him along with Arnold Palmer, Gerald Ford, Dwight D. Eisenhower, Bob Hope and Ben Hogan as one of the 100 all-time "American Heroes of Golf." *Tennis* magazine and *Racquet* magazine named him "the most powerful man in tennis." Tennis legend Billie Jean King believes, "Mark McCormack was the king of sports marketing. He shaped the way all sports are marketed around the world. He was the first in the marketplace, and his influence on the world of sports, particularly his ability to combine athlete representation, property development and television broadcasting, will forever be the standard of the industry."

The London *Sunday Times* listed him as one of the 1000 people who influenced the 20th century. Alastair Cooke on the BBC said simply that "McCormack was the Oracle; the creator of the talent industry, the maker of people famous in their profession famous to the rest of the world and making for them a fortune in the process ... He took on as clients people already famous in their profession as golfer, opera singer, author, footballer, racing car driver, violinist—and from time to time if they needed special help, a prime minister, or even the Pope."

McCormack was honored posthumously by the Golf Writers Association of America with the 2004 William D. Richardson Award, the organization's highest honor, "Given to recognize an individual who has consistently made an outstanding contribution to golf."

Among McCormack's other honors were the 2001 PGA Distinguished Service Award, given to those who have helped perpetuate the values and ideals of the PGA of America. He was also named a Commander of the Royal Order of the Polar Star by the King of Sweden (the highest honor for a person living outside of Sweden) for his contribution to the Nobel Foundation.

Journalist Frank Deford states, "There have been what we love to call dynasties in every sport. IMG has been different. What this one brilliant man, Mark McCormack, created is the only dynasty ever over all sport."

Through IMG, Mark McCormack demonstrated the value of sports and lifestyle activities as effective corporate marketing tools, but more importantly, his lifelong dedication to his vocation—begun with just a simple handshake—brought enjoyment to millions of people worldwide who watch and cheer their heroes and heroines. That is his legacy.

ROLEX

The year 2008 was rich in milestones and memorable events.

Trevor Immelman won the Masters Tournament, joining Gary Player as the second South African golfer to win at Augusta. Lorena Ochoa maintained her No. 1 position in the Rolex Rankings. Annika Sorenstam announced her intention to leave the tour and pursue business and personal interests. The United States regained the Ryder Cup after nine years of European domination.

It was a year that demonstrated the continuity of Rolex's presence in golf, both professional and amateur.

For more than 40 years, since Arnold Palmer became the first Rolex Testimonee in 1967, Rolex has enjoyed relationships with players and developed partnerships in the sport. Gary Player and Jack Nicklaus later joined Arnold Palmer as Rolex Testimonees. They became golf's Big Three.

The list of Rolex Testimonees has grown to include younger prominent players such as Phil Mickelson, Retief Goosen, Luke Donald, Adam Scott, Camilo Villegas and Martin Kaymer.

Rolex is especially proud of its partnerships with the leading golf organizations including the Royal and Ancient Golf Club of St Andrews and the Augusta National Golf Club, the United States Golf Association, the PGA of America, the European Tour, the PGA Tour, the LPGA and all four Major tournaments in both men's and ladies' golf, plus the Ryder Cup, Presidents Cup and Solheim Cup competitions. The support which Rolex extends to amateur golfers completes its involvement in the sport.

Golf is Rolex!

Bruno Meier
Managing Director
Rolex SA

Rolex and Golf

Rolex's association with golf dates from 1967 when Andre Heiniger presented Arnold Palmer with a gold Oyster Perpetual to honor his achievements on the golf course. This marked the beginning of a loyal and privileged relationship, not only with Arnold Palmer and afterwards with two other golfing greats, Gary Player and Jack Nicklaus, but also many of the great talents who have followed them. Rolex has also established relationships with the major organizating bodies of the game.

Sven Holmberg (FEI), Bruno Meier, Sylvie Robert (CSI Lyon), Jean-Noël Bioul, Renato Ruedi

Johnny Storjohann, Bertrand Gros and Gilbert De Meuron

Jean-Claude Killy, Jackie Stewart, Gary Player, Arnold Palmer and Jack Nicklaus

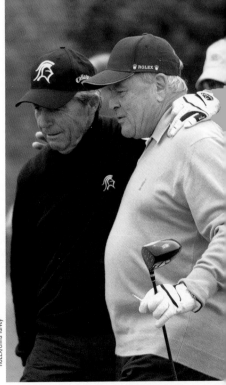

Bertrand Gros and Arnold Palmer

Gary Player and Gérard Bernheim

Rolex's Top 10 of Women's Golf

David Cannon/Getty Images

1. Lorena Ochoa (Mexico) 15.64 points

ROLEX/Chris Turvey

3. Annika Sorenstam (Sweden) 8.90 points

David Cannon/Getty Images

2. Yani Tseng (Taiwan) 9.31 points

Jonathan Ferrey/Getty Images

4. Paula Creamer (USA) 7.93 points

Montana Pritchard/Getty Images

Travis Lindquist/Getty Images

5. Suzann Pettersen (Norway) 7.55 points

Montana Pritchard/Getty Images

7. Cristie Kerr (USA) 5.84 points

6. Ji-Yai Shin (Korea) 7.09 points

ROLEX/Chris Turvey

Scott Halleran/Getty Images

8. Helen Alfredsson (Sweden) 5.73 points

Koichi Kamoshida/Getty Images

9. Angela Stanford (USA) 5.27 points

10. Karrie Webb (Australia) 4.87 points

The Open Championship

Camilo Villegas

Trevor Immelman

Rolex and Sport

Since 1927, Rolex has been associated with the quest for excellence in sport, when it placed a Rolex Oyster on the wrist of a young swimmer, Mercedes Gleitze, as she swam across the English Channel. In 1933, Rolex began to sponsor Himalayan and polar expeditions, including the first successful ascent of Everest by Sir Edmund Hillary in 1953.

Today Rolex supports top sporting and cultural events all over the world. It is present at more than 150 events in the realms of golf, yachting, tennis, equestrian events, motor sports, exploration, culture and the arts, as well as philanthropic awards programs. Because of the commitment and continuity of these relationships, Rolex is seen not only as a sponsor … but as a real partner.

Adam Scott

Phil Mickelson at The Ryder Cup

U.S. Open

The Tour Championship

Annika Sorenstam at the Evian Masters

Lorena Ochoa at the Ricoh Women's British Open

Retief Goosen

Martin Kaymer

Luke Donald

Rolex Rankings

In the year that Annika Sorenstam announced that she would be stepping away from professional golf, Lorena Ochoa showed no sign of relinquishing the world No. 1 position on the Rolex Rankings that she had taken from Sorenstam in 2007.

Ochoa won five of her first six tournaments in 2008, including a major title in the Kraft Nabisco Championship, added two more victories later in the year, and finished with an average of 15.64 in Rolex Rankings points for a lead of more than six points. The Mexican was followed at No. 2 by Yani Tseng, a first-year player from Taiwan who won a major championship in the McDonald's LPGA Championship. Tseng had an average of 9.31.

Sorenstam had four victories for the year and the Swede finished at No. 3 with an average of 8.90.

With four victories, Paula Creamer was the leading player from the United States on the Rolex Rankings, holding fourth place with a 7.93 average. She was one place better on the list than her 2007 finish. Suzann Pettersen of Norway dropped three places during the year to No. 5 in the world with a 7.55 average.

South Korean Ji-Yai Shin was ranked No. 6 with a 7.09 average after winning the Ricoh Women's British Open, Mizuno Classic and the season-ending ADT Championship. She was followed by American Cristie Kerr, down one place to No. 7 with a 5.84 average and Sweden's Helen Alfredsson, up from No. 103 to No. 8 with a 5.73 average. American Angela Stanford (5.27 average) and Australian Karrie Webb (4.87 average) completed the top 10 of the Rolex Rankings for 2008.

Players who fell out of the top 10 of the Rolex Rankings during 2008 were Juli Inkster of the United States (No. 8 to No. 26), Mi Hyun Kim of South Korea (No. 9 to No. 30) and Se Ri Pak of South Korea (No. 10 to No. 31).

The U.S. Women's Open was won by Inbee Park of South Korea, who rose from No. 69 to No. 21 on the Rolex Rankings for the year.

The Rolex Rankings—which was developed at the May 2004 World Congress of Women's Golf—is sanctioned by the five major women's professional golf tours: the Ladies Professional Golf Association (LPGA), Ladies European Tour (LET), Ladies Professional Golfers' Association of Japan (JLPGA), Korea Ladies Professional Golf Association (KLPGA), Australian Ladies Professional Golf (ALPG), and the Ladies' Golf Union (LGU).

The five major golf tours and the LGU developed the rankings and the protocol that governs the ranking while R2IT, an independent software development company, was retained to develop the software and to maintain the rankings on a weekly basis. The official events from all of the tours are taken into account and points are awarded according to the strength of the field, with the exception of the four major championships on the LPGA Tour schedule and the Futures Tour events, which have a fixed points distribution. The players' points averages are determined by taking the number of points awarded over a two-year rolling period and dividing that by the number of tournaments played, with a minimum divisor of 35.

The Rolex Rankings are updated and released following the completion of the previous week's tournaments around the world.

Rolex Rankings
(As of December 31, 2008)

Rank	Player	Country	No. of Events	Average Points	Total Points
1	Lorena Ochoa	Mex	47	15.64	734.89
2	Yani Tseng	Twn	35	9.31	325.98
3	Annika Sorenstam	Swe	41	8.90	364.85
4	Paula Creamer	USA	53	7.93	420.28
5	Suzann Pettersen	Nor	52	7.55	392.42
6	Ji-Yai Shin	Kor	59	7.09	418.52
7	Cristie Kerr	USA	50	5.84	292.16
8	Helen Alfredsson	Swe	39	5.73	223.43
9	Angela Stanford	USA	51	5.27	268.99
10	Karrie Webb	Aus	46	4.87	224.16
11	Seon Hwa Lee	Kor	58	4.56	264.63
12	Yuri Fudoh	Jpn	45	4.42	199.03
13	Jeong Jang	Kor	55	4.26	234.30
14	Momoko Ueda	Jpn	63	4.06	255.99
15	Jee Young Lee	Kor	54	4.06	219.35
16	Maria Hjorth	Swe	55	4.03	221.85
17	Eun-Hee Ji	Kor	57	4.01	228.45
18	Hee-Won Han	Kor	36	3.94	141.81
19	Morgan Pressel	USA	53	3.81	202.14
20	Karen Stupples	Eng	34	3.67	128.52
21	Inbee Park	Kor	57	3.59	204.67
22	Laura Diaz	USA	51	3.54	180.62
23	Angela Park	Bra	56	3.53	197.78
24	Candie Kung	Twn	44	3.48	153.20
25	In-Kyung Kim	Kor	53	3.45	182.78
26	Juli Inkster	USA	39	3.35	130.82
27	Na Yeon Choi	Kor	51	3.33	169.75
28	Sakura Yokomine	Jpn	67	3.32	222.75
29	Katherine Hull	Aus	58	3.28	190.41
30	Mi Hyun Kim	Kor	49	3.16	155.07
31	Se Ri Pak	Kor	43	3.04	130.90
32	Nicole Castrale	USA	50	2.94	146.85
33	Sophie Gustafson	Swe	53	2.90	153.57
34	Song-Hee Kim	Kor	48	2.78	133.45
35	Miho Koga	Jpn	70	2.77	193.76
36	Ai Miyazato	Jpn	54	2.68	144.81
37	Stacy Prammanasudh	USA	48	2.65	127.26
38	Catriona Matthew	Sco	46	2.64	121.38
39	Christina Kim	USA	58	2.60	150.65
40	Mi-Jeong Jeon	Kor	64	2.56	163.74
41	Shiho Oyama	Jpn	58	2.55	147.61
42	Natalie Gulbis	USA	46	2.51	115.64
43	Ji-Hee Lee	Kor	57	2.50	142.75
44	Akiko Fukushima	Jpn	56	2.45	137.20
45	Shi Hyun Ahn	Kor	37	2.42	89.53
46	Brittany Lang	USA	54	2.41	130.35
47	Jane Park	USA	41	2.27	93.23
48	Shanshan Feng	Chn	31	2.13	74.44
49	Yuko Mitsuka	Jpn	62	2.10	130.02
50	Hyun-Ju Shin	Kor	53	2.09	110.75

Rank	Player	Country	No. of Events	Average Points	Total Points
51	Eun-A Lim	Kor	52	1.99	103.30
52	Lindsey Wright	Aus	51	1.99	101.31
53	Ji Young Oh	Kor	52	1.91	99.07
54	Sun Young Yoo	Kor	53	1.91	100.97
55	Shinobu Moromizato	Jpn	66	1.90	125.48
56	Mayu Hattori	Jpn	49	1.85	90.69
57	Meena Lee	Kor	56	1.85	103.64
58	Miki Saiki	Jpn	59	1.85	109.16
59	Hee Young Park	Kor	52	1.84	95.81
60	Bo-Bae Song	Kor	59	1.83	108.02
61	Teresa Lu	Twn	51	1.78	90.87
62	Na Zhang	Chn	48	1.72	82.48
63	Sun Ju Ahn	Kor	44	1.71	75.08
64	Brittany Lincicome	USA	47	1.65	77.40
65	Erina Hara	Jpn	67	1.60	107.35
66	Minea Blomqvist	Fin	51	1.60	81.40
67	Young Kim	Kor	50	1.59	79.45
68	Laura Davies	Eng	64	1.58	101.38
69	Giulia Sergas	Ita	49	1.53	74.83
70	Kristy McPherson	USA	44	1.43	62.84
71	Sarah Lee	Kor	44	1.42	62.54
72	Louise Friberg	Swe	42	1.42	59.65
73	Stacy Lewis	USA	13	1.41	49.29
74	Sherri Steinhauer	USA	40	1.39	55.59
75	Hiromi Mogi	Jpn	68	1.38	94.15
76	Michele Redman	USA	39	1.38	53.91
77	Akane Iijima	Jpn	72	1.38	99.31
78	Ayako Uehara	Jpn	69	1.30	90.00
79	Jimin Kang	Kor	54	1.30	70.33
80	Leta Lindley	USA	45	1.30	58.52
81	Pat Hurst	USA	47	1.29	60.86
82	Midori Yoneyama	Jpn	63	1.28	80.68
83	Allison Fouch	USA	44	1.28	56.26
84	Chie Arimura	Jpn	68	1.25	85.33
85	Jin-Joo Hong	Kor	48	1.23	59.20
86	Reilley Rankin	USA	49	1.21	59.30
87	Amy Yang	Kor	33	1.21	42.25
88	Maiko Wakabayashi	Jpn	47	1.21	56.72
89	Rachel Hetherington	Aus	52	1.19	62.02
90	Wendy Ward	USA	44	1.17	51.60
91	Carin Koch	Swe	46	1.14	52.60
92	Meaghan Francella	USA	49	1.10	53.83
93	H.J. Choi	Kor	57	1.08	61.61
94	Yukari Baba	Jpn	66	1.07	70.75
95	Esther Lee	Kor	69	1.05	72.77
96	Saiki Fujita	Jpn	61	1.03	63.11
97	Linda Wessberg	Swe	50	1.01	50.60
98	Ji-Woo Lee	Kor	62	1.00	61.86
99	Rui Kitada	Jpn	66	0.99	65.60
100	Yun-Jye Wei	Twn	63	0.98	61.96

Rank	Player	Country	No. of Events	Average Points	Total Points
101	Hiroko Yamaguchi	Jpn	70	0.98	68.47
102	Janice Moodie	Sco	50	0.98	48.77
103	Gwladys Nocera	Fra	49	0.97	47.53
104	Na On Min	Kor	46	0.97	44.48
105	Hee Kyung Seo	Kor	47	0.96	45.16
106	Ha-Neul Kim	Kor	45	0.96	43.23
107	Nikki Campbell	Aus	61	0.96	58.38
108	Mie Nakata	Jpn	65	0.95	61.91
109	Heather Young	USA	51	0.91	46.49
110	Birdie Kim	Kor	41	0.88	36.19
111	Hye-Yong Choi	Kor	31	0.87	30.47
112	Il Mi Chung	Kor	58	0.87	50.37
113	Becky Morgan	Wal	49	0.86	42.24
114	Alena Sharp	Can	50	0.85	42.74
115	Irene Cho	USA	42	0.83	34.89
116	Julieta Granada	Par	52	0.82	42.67
117	Namika Omata	Jpn	50	0.82	40.91
118	Gloria Park	Kor	50	0.81	40.68
119	Diana D'Alessio	USA	58	0.81	47.18
120	Amy Hung	Twn	42	0.80	33.39
121	Mhairi McKay	Sco	44	0.79	34.79
122	Yui Kawahara	Jpn	66	0.76	50.41
123	Jill McGill	USA	48	0.76	36.55
124	Sandra Gal	Ger	23	0.76	26.62
125	Kim Hall	USA	46	0.74	33.92
126	Becky Brewerton	Wal	39	0.72	28.19
127	So Yeon Ryu	Kor	26	0.71	25.02
128	Joo Mi Kim	Kor	35	0.71	24.81
129	Kaori Higo	Jpn	55	0.71	38.78
130	So-Hee Kim	Kor	68	0.70	47.39
131	Wendy Doolan	Aus	47	0.70	32.71
132	Charlotte Mayorkas	USA	41	0.69	28.30
133	Martina Eberl	Ger	40	0.68	27.12
134	Katie Futcher	USA	41	0.68	27.71
135	Michiko Hattori	Jpn	59	0.66	39.18
136	Silvia Cavalleri	Ita	44	0.66	29.17
137	Meg Mallon	USA	28	0.66	23.12
138	Marisa Baena	Col	27	0.66	22.97
139	Kyeong Bae	Kor	56	0.66	36.68
140	Mikiyo Nishizuka	Jpn	65	0.65	42.20
141	Yuko Saitoh	Jpn	66	0.65	42.81
142	Hiromi Takesue	Jpn	32	0.64	22.41
143	Lisa Hall	Eng	47	0.64	30.04
144	Kelli Kuehne	USA	42	0.64	26.71
145	Trish Johnson	Eng	38	0.63	23.91
146	Russy Gulyanamitta	Tha	19	0.63	21.90
147	Moira Dunn	USA	47	0.62	29.36
148	Soo-Yun Kang	Kor	49	0.62	30.52
149	Mikaela Parmlid	Swe	41	0.61	25.17
150	Kuniko Maeda	Jpn	68	0.60	41.08

Rank	Player	Country	No. of Events	Average Points	Total Points
151	Ah-Reum Huang	Kor	21	0.60	20.94
152	Hyun-Hee Moon	Kor	40	0.59	23.76
153	Jennifer Rosales	Phl	36	0.59	21.28
154	Tamie Durdin	Aus	59	0.59	34.59
155	Anja Monke	Ger	45	0.58	26.24
156	Sophie Giquel	Fra	43	0.57	24.69
157	Dorothy Delasin	USA	44	0.57	25.23
158	Iben Tinning	Den	33	0.57	19.94
159	Paula Marti	Sp	36	0.57	20.42
160	Karin Sjodin	Swe	49	0.57	27.79
161	Beth Bader	USA	48	0.56	27.07
162	Ran Hong	Kor	47	0.55	25.99
163	Julie Lu	Twn	56	0.55	30.92
164	Liselotte Neumann	Swe	38	0.55	20.84
165	Mayumi Shimomura	Jpn	66	0.55	36.10
166	Nobuko Kizawa	Jpn	69	0.53	36.61
167	Karine Icher	Fra	53	0.53	27.92
168	Melissa Reid	Eng	20	0.53	18.43
169	Yuki Ichinose	Jpn	33	0.52	18.34
170	Kaori Aoyama	Jpn	27	0.51	17.91
171	Bo-Kyung Kim	Kor	43	0.51	21.99
172	Yasuko Satoh	Jpn	64	0.51	32.66
173	Rebecca Hudson	Eng	35	0.51	17.82
174	Mollie Fankhauser	USA	40	0.51	20.24
175	Yun-Joo Jeong	Kor	62	0.50	31.22
176	Jamie Hullett	USA	37	0.50	18.53
177	Michie Ohba	Jpn	55	0.50	27.53
178	Hye-Youn Kim	Kor	28	0.50	17.47
179	Chae-Young Yoon	Kor	36	0.50	17.84
180	Danielle Downey	USA	33	0.49	17.28
181	Sherri Turner	USA	37	0.49	18.19
182	Johanna Head	Eng	45	0.48	21.74
183	Lotta Wahlin	Swe	40	0.48	19.22
184	Keiko Sasaki	Jpn	66	0.48	31.44
185	Joanne Mills	Aus	40	0.47	18.96
186	Louise Stahle	Swe	28	0.47	16.38
187	Heather Daly-Donofrio	USA	34	0.46	16.24
188	Ji-Yeon Han	Kor	54	0.46	25.04
189	Lorie Kane	Can	45	0.46	20.75
190	Carri Wood	USA	46	0.46	21.16
191	Jae-Hee Bae	Kor	58	0.46	26.55
192	Mihoko Takahashi	Jpn	56	0.46	25.54
193	Kumiko Kaneda	Jpn	13	0.46	15.95
194	Toshimi Kimura	Jpn	55	0.45	24.56
195	Yayoi Arasaki	Jpn	57	0.45	25.44
196	Sarah Kemp	Aus	39	0.44	17.32
197	Eva Dahllof	Swe	37	0.44	16.33
198	Anna Rawson	Aus	40	0.43	17.28
199	Seul-A Yoon	Kor	40	0.43	17.09
200	Mihoko Iseri	Jpn	65	0.43	27.70

Official World Golf Ranking
(As of December 31, 2008)

Ranking		Player	Country	Points Average	Total Points	No. of Events	06/07 Points Lost	2008 Points Gained
1	(1)	Tiger Woods	USA	11.97	478.71	40	-732.13	426.24
2	(12)	Sergio Garcia	Sp	8.10	421.34	52	-230.50	408.10
3	(2)	Phil Mickelson	USA	7.03	344.38	49	-351.77	312.68
4	(8)	Padraig Harrington	Ire	6.95	354.44	51	-293.67	330.64
5	(10)	Vijay Singh	Fij	6.65	365.51	55	-301.61	357.24
6	(41)	Robert Karlsson	Swe	5.09	269.61	53	-145.74	269.91
7	(56)	Camilo Villegas	Col	4.90	244.75	50	-103.24	235.14
8	(16)	Henrik Stenson	Swe	4.77	243.06	51	-232.39	256.12
9	(4)	Ernie Els	SAf	4.77	257.28	54	-316.46	196.19
10	(23)	Lee Westwood	Eng	4.73	255.55	54	-165.62	238.05
11	(75)	Anthony Kim	USA	4.45	226.84	51	-96.09	254.94
12	(13)	Geoff Ogilvy	Aus	4.44	213.14	48	-217.38	212.05
13	(3)	Jim Furyk	USA	4.30	210.72	49	-310.61	193.77
14	(92)	Kenny Perry	USA	3.89	198.27	51	-89.38	218.02
15	(5)	Steve Stricker	USA	3.87	174.13	45	-215.47	131.66
16	(24)	Stewart Cink	USA	3.85	188.70	49	-185.60	207.48
17	(7)	Adam Scott	Aus	3.80	171.15	45	-272.77	159.40
18	(9)	K.J. Choi	Kor	3.75	198.50	53	-258.36	158.42
19	(6)	Justin Rose	Eng	3.58	164.66	46	-228.29	81.11
20	(19)	Trevor Immelman	SAf	3.40	180.23	53	-198.79	174.76
21	(35)	Mike Weir	Can	3.35	170.81	51	-119.59	157.63
22	(38)	Miguel A. Jimenez	Sp	3.35	180.72	54	-126.10	169.69
23	(89)	Justin Leonard	USA	3.24	175.19	54	-98.66	188.71
24	(119)	Ben Curtis	USA	3.12	146.78	47	-80.27	157.61
25	(76)	Martin Kaymer	Ger	3.12	171.49	55	-88.76	192.72
26	(22)	Ian Poulter	Eng	3.09	166.81	54	-166.16	131.70
27	(51)	Robert Allenby	Aus	3.06	186.72	61	-136.47	195.67
28	(29)	Tim Clark	SAf	2.99	155.57	52	-110.85	128.82
29	(84)	Ross Fisher	Eng	2.91	151.25	52	-67.79	132.98
30	(28)	Andres Romero	Arg	2.87	149.02	52	-125.77	130.49
31	(17)	Luke Donald	Eng	2.81	115.34	41	-198.88	112.95
32	(39)	Shingo Katayama	Jpn	2.80	156.86	56	-114.73	129.38
33	(106)	Graeme McDowell	NIre	2.77	157.88	57	-86.62	164.65
34	(11)	Rory Sabbatini	SAf	2.76	149.09	54	-205.60	101.58
35	(77)	Jeev Milkha Singh	Ind	2.76	203.92	74	-137.33	212.57
36	(18)	Aaron Baddeley	Aus	2.72	130.46	48	-173.17	94.84
37	(33)	Stephen Ames	Can	2.70	127.09	47	-113.01	122.08
38	(36)	Stuart Appleby	Aus	2.62	149.26	57	-144.19	146.59
39	(232)	Rory McIlroy	NIre	2.58	103.03	40	-23.80	96.42
40	(101)	Oliver Wilson	Eng	2.57	138.90	54	-70.59	130.61
41	(21)	Paul Casey	Eng	2.51	123.08	49	-162.74	112.16
42	(14)	Angel Cabrera	Arg	2.51	125.57	50	-168.59	66.88
43	(44)	Richard Sterne	SAf	2.47	128.18	52	-100.66	110.65
44	(34)	Hunter Mahan	USA	2.44	134.43	55	-126.29	108.70
45	(26)	Retief Goosen	SAf	2.44	131.75	54	-189.19	129.25
46	(15)	Zach Johnson	USA	2.38	114.04	48	-170.03	75.76
47	(46)	Soren Hansen	Den	2.37	125.74	53	-98.39	98.85
48	(45)	Boo Weekley	USA	2.36	127.52	54	-134.09	129.06
49	(171)	Lin Wen-tang	Twn	2.35	93.80	40	-37.16	91.86
50	(69)	Soren Kjeldsen	Den	2.27	131.90	58	-80.85	113.91

( ) Ranking in brackets indicates position as of December 31, 2007.

Ranking		Player	Country	Points Average	Total Points	No. of Events	06/07 Points Lost	2008 Points Gained
51	(150)	Kevin Sutherland	USA	2.26	115.25	51	-68.16	122.00
52	(72)	Prayad Marksaeng	Tha	2.25	144.12	64	-82.01	123.04
53	(59)	Brendan Jones	Aus	2.21	101.50	46	-65.34	74.63
54	(448)	Dudley Hart	USA	2.18	87.22	40	-30.13	102.31
55	(54)	Peter Hanson	Swe	2.17	121.73	56	-81.24	99.01
56	(52)	Rod Pampling	Aus	2.16	129.72	60	-115.25	121.64
57	(31)	Woody Austin	USA	2.13	123.38	58	-130.24	93.63
58	(191)	Mathew Goggin	Aus	2.13	125.50	59	-56.82	128.75
59	(65)	Sean O'Hair	USA	2.12	114.43	54	-110.97	117.66
60	(434)	Ryo Ishikawa	Jpn	2.07	82.90	40	-11.92	79.61
61	(40)	Richard Green	Aus	2.07	91.18	44	-95.07	75.23
62	(61)	Carl Pettersson	Swe	2.03	121.93	60	-112.57	114.99
63	(25)	Scott Verplank	USA	2.01	96.29	48	-123.16	65.57
64	(47)	Brandt Snedeker	USA	1.98	118.90	60	-120.96	100.00
65	(93)	Chad Campbell	USA	1.96	109.57	56	-86.12	116.24
66	(180)	Ryuji Imada	Jpn	1.95	114.82	59	-83.75	136.30
67	(82)	Fredrik Jacobson	Swe	1.94	85.30	44	-58.20	78.58
68	(83)	Charl Schwartzel	SAf	1.92	107.32	56	-94.56	108.41
69	(220)	Azuma Yano	Jpn	1.85	92.37	50	-34.95	87.12
70	(225)	Darren Clarke	NIre	1.84	104.64	57	-46.50	114.62
71	(114)	Rocco Mediate	USA	1.80	88.17	49	-59.01	92.16
72	(155)	James Kingston	SAf	1.79	100.28	56	-51.85	94.05
73	(291)	Alvaro Quiros	Sp	1.77	72.62	41	-23.96	73.32
74	(211)	D.J. Trahan	USA	1.76	102.33	58	-66.60	116.50
75	(208)	J.B. Holmes	USA	1.75	90.90	52	-72.55	118.40
76	(90)	G. Fernandez-Castano	Sp	1.73	91.66	53	-59.36	71.00
77	(68)	Hideto Tanihara	Jpn	1.70	88.32	52	-68.87	70.24
78	(48)	Nick Dougherty	Eng	1.67	86.61	52	-94.17	53.90
79	(177)	Francesco Molinari	Ita	1.66	91.53	55	-49.63	92.29
80	(67)	Davis Love	USA	1.66	73.21	44	-76.25	69.22
81	(116)	Ken Duke	USA	1.65	105.56	64	-73.87	98.21
82	(70)	Pat Perez	USA	1.63	88.09	54	-75.85	84.58
83	(128)	Hiroyuki Fujita	Jpn	1.61	75.62	47	-51.47	63.17
84	(98)	David Smail	NZl	1.60	79.93	50	-55.66	59.28
85	(134)	Bart Bryant	USA	1.58	75.64	48	-78.87	92.98
86	(161)	Peter Hedblom	Swe	1.58	77.15	49	-51.96	78.91
87	(136)	Jeff Quinney	USA	1.57	89.38	57	-88.79	110.08
88	(1032)	Shintaro Kai	Jpn	1.57	65.85	42	-7.87	71.98
89	(50)	Anders Hansen	Den	1.56	76.20	49	-88.03	54.26
90	(534)	Gareth Maybin	NIre	1.54	61.59	40	-10.32	60.69
91	(96)	Thongchai Jaidee	Tha	1.54	90.67	59	-69.23	78.52
92	(111)	Billy Mayfair	USA	1.51	89.19	59	-75.09	82.47
93	(27)	Toru Taniguchi	Jpn	1.51	80.02	53	-111.29	33.49
94	(390)	Hennie Otto	SAf	1.48	59.28	40	-32.03	73.54
95	(37)	Nick OHern	Aus	1.48	82.76	56	-124.64	68.67
96	(689)	Pablo Larrazabal	Sp	1.47	67.72	46	-12.53	73.44
97	(187)	Alexander Noren	Swe	1.47	79.23	54	-45.22	75.60
98	(105)	Paul Goydos	USA	1.46	66.93	46	-73.25	78.15
99	(91)	Steve Flesch	USA	1.45	88.56	61	-82.88	74.53
100	(73)	Heath Slocum	USA	1.43	81.71	57	-91.49	73.96

( ) Ranking in brackets indicates position as of December 31, 2007.

Ranking		Player	Country	Points Average	Total Points	No. of Events	06/07 Points Lost	2008 Points Gained
101	(205)	Ben Crane	USA	1.43	57.19	40	-49.61	72.28
102	(63)	Jerry Kelly	USA	1.43	85.52	60	-108.14	80.77
103	(135)	Gregory Havret	Fra	1.42	78.22	55	-54.24	64.90
104	(207)	Paul McGinley	Ire	1.39	73.42	53	-49.08	76.22
105	(322)	Mark Brown	NZl	1.38	73.30	53	-34.21	86.49
106	(55)	John Senden	Aus	1.38	85.59	62	-114.49	73.86
107	(86)	Liang Wen-chong	Chn	1.37	75.50	55	-78.68	65.44
108	(20)	Niclas Fasth	Swe	1.36	74.59	55	-141.28	37.76
109	(199)	Stephen Marino	USA	1.36	86.72	64	-54.90	96.96
110	(131)	Anthony Wall	Eng	1.35	79.85	59	-61.29	73.26
111	(210)	Brian Gay	USA	1.35	84.80	63	-60.45	92.22
112	(80)	Steve Webster	Eng	1.33	68.02	51	-48.67	45.02
113	(223)	Briny Baird	USA	1.33	80.94	61	-51.79	88.47
114	(182)	Charlie Wi	Kor	1.33	76.87	58	-51.17	73.84
115	(58)	Peter Lonard	Aus	1.32	83.33	63	-91.95	62.95
116	(43)	David Toms	USA	1.32	55.29	42	-97.04	41.86
117	(239)	Scott Strange	Aus	1.30	73.95	57	-45.69	83.10
118	(233)	S.K. Ho	Kor	1.30	58.34	45	-36.86	56.93
119	(124)	Mark Wilson	USA	1.28	69.33	54	-64.61	70.13
120	(298)	Toshinori Muto	Jpn	1.28	60.02	47	-26.17	57.64
121	(57)	Colin Montgomerie	Sco	1.28	65.03	51	-100.28	54.98
122	(143)	Alastair Forsyth	Sco	1.27	66.27	52	-53.86	60.19
123	(1375)	Kevin Streelman	USA	1.27	50.88	40	-6.69	57.57
124	(30)	Arron Oberholser	USA	1.27	50.80	40	-92.87	21.26
125	(107)	Bubba Watson	USA	1.27	69.55	55	-74.93	67.62
126	(138)	Gregory Bourdy	Fra	1.26	68.16	54	-48.71	57.54
127	(1375)	Taco Remkes	Hol	1.25	49.81	40	-4.17	53.97
128	(542)	David Horsey	Eng	1.24	51.87	42	-11.30	52.43
129	(64)	Simon Dyson	Eng	1.24	75.31	61	-94.66	53.90
130	(120)	Daniel Chopra	Swe	1.23	87.56	71	-96.53	86.85
131	(110)	Tomohiro Kondo	Jpn	1.23	55.41	45	-54.12	39.98
132	(277)	Richard Finch	Eng	1.22	75.48	62	-33.50	72.84
133	(849)	Matt Bettencourt	USA	1.21	49.59	41	-3.48	49.54
134	(112)	Louis Oosthuizen	SAf	1.21	61.43	51	-65.83	58.03
135	(202)	Matt Kuchar	USA	1.19	64.15	54	-53.45	68.81
136	(170)	Felipe Aguilar	Chi	1.17	53.57	46	-47.61	52.12
137	(149)	Graeme Storm	Eng	1.15	63.34	55	-60.39	54.92
138	(146)	Taichi Teshima	Jpn	1.15	55.20	48	-47.11	44.50
139	(176)	Koumei Oda	Jpn	1.15	56.22	49	-30.76	41.89
140	(115)	George McNeill	USA	1.14	67.31	59	-46.78	59.24
141	(42)	Charles Howell	USA	1.14	65.95	58	-139.64	60.60
142	(281)	Tommy Armour	USA	1.14	55.63	49	-34.08	60.10
143	(1375)	Dustin Johnson	USA	1.12	44.85	40	-8.33	53.18
144	(49)	Mark Calcavecchia	USA	1.11	58.83	53	-106.75	37.30
145	(201)	David Lynn	Eng	1.11	62.05	56	-40.54	59.69
146	(263)	Mikael Lundberg	Swe	1.10	51.87	47	-23.60	45.49
147	(87)	Jyoti Randhawa	Ind	1.10	58.01	53	-76.33	54.77
148	(247)	Marc Turnesa	USA	1.09	65.60	60	-20.97	59.33
149	(237)	Johnson Wagner	USA	1.09	65.35	60	-52.63	73.82
150	(97)	Markus Brier	Aut	1.09	58.58	54	-62.15	45.77

( ) Ranking in brackets indicates position as of December 31, 2007.

Ranking		Player	Country	Points Average	Total Points	No. of Events	06/07 Points Lost	2008 Points Gained
151	(343)	Thomas Levet	Fra	1.08	49.79	46	-25.64	55.66
152	(219)	Steven Conran	Aus	1.08	48.61	45	-26.42	39.45
153	(144)	Lu Wen-teh	Twn	1.08	43.03	40	-33.23	29.59
154	(142)	Robert-Jan Derksen	Hol	1.08	60.20	56	-53.18	48.73
155	(60)	Jonathan Byrd	USA	1.07	53.65	50	-75.02	45.68
156	(327)	Nicholas Thompson	USA	1.07	73.50	69	-42.24	80.29
157	(53)	Bradley Dredge	Wal	1.06	49.96	47	-77.74	33.18
158	(74)	Ryan Moore	USA	1.06	56.99	54	-79.33	47.88
159	(118)	Dean Wilson	USA	1.06	63.31	60	-82.01	61.92
160	(199)	Thaworn Wiratchant	Tha	1.05	63.18	60	-43.34	54.85
161	(432)	Richie Ramsay	Sco	1.05	45.19	43	-12.26	42.18
162	(129)	Lee Dong-hwan	Kor	1.04	52.13	50	-38.37	39.18
163	(196)	Steve Elkington	Aus	1.04	52.99	51	-44.43	58.63
164	(162)	Tim Herron	USA	1.04	57.07	55	-50.79	51.57
165	(431)	David Gleeson	Aus	1.04	49.77	48	-11.76	46.23
166	(231)	Paul Lawrie	Sco	1.04	56.97	55	-30.00	50.36
167	(165)	David Howell	Eng	1.04	51.74	50	-60.25	59.66
168	(206)	Hidemasa Hoshino	Jpn	1.03	43.31	42	-36.63	42.84
169	(160)	John Bickerton	Eng	1.02	51.12	50	-45.09	41.76
170	(123)	Johan Edfors	Swe	1.02	54.05	53	-70.22	60.09
171	(164)	John Mallinger	USA	1.02	58.97	58	-50.70	57.05
172	(513)	Kenichi Kuboya	Jpn	1.02	48.71	48	-10.91	44.76
173	(359)	John Merrick	USA	1.01	58.59	58	-37.43	68.01
174	(320)	Damien McGrane	Ire	1.00	61.74	62	-41.71	70.48
175	(65)	John Rollins	USA	0.98	56.01	57	-98.19	50.11
175	(541)	Fred Couples	USA	0.98	39.30	40	-23.89	52.38
177	(81)	Lucas Glover	USA	0.98	53.80	55	-87.61	43.90
178	(192)	Jason Bohn	USA	0.97	38.88	40	-49.93	47.09
179	(275)	Peter Lawrie	Ire	0.97	56.34	58	-37.00	58.09
180	(1042)	Noh Seung-yul	Kor	0.96	38.44	40	-9.17	45.94
181	(240)	Michael Allen	USA	0.95	47.51	50	-27.08	41.06
182	(117)	Tom Lehman	USA	0.95	37.96	40	-55.60	35.49
183	(174)	Michael Campbell	NZl	0.94	47.04	50	-46.82	42.83
184	(1253)	Lam Chih Bing	Sin	0.94	38.56	41	-1.44	39.40
185	(100)	Troy Matteson	USA	0.94	52.60	56	-84.81	52.49
186	(163)	Katsumasa Miyamoto	Jpn	0.94	46.91	50	-46.58	38.45
187	(251)	Gary Orr	Sco	0.93	37.34	40	-27.10	37.60
188	(308)	Yasuharu Imano	Jpn	0.93	43.86	47	-17.13	32.78
189	(95)	Nathan Green	Aus	0.93	61.50	66	-91.85	53.93
190	(316)	Steve Lowery	USA	0.93	43.61	47	-43.40	58.64
191	(1375)	Estanislao Goya	Arg	0.92	36.90	40	-6.58	43.47
192	(104)	Thomas Bjorn	Den	0.92	41.46	45	-63.68	30.05
193	(204)	Hiroshi Iwata	Jpn	0.92	45.01	49	-29.24	35.36
194	(1375)	Chris Wood	Eng	0.91	36.52	40	-2.77	39.30
195	(368)	Parker McLachlin	USA	0.91	50.70	56	-30.64	54.16
196	(1068)	Scott Piercy	USA	0.90	36.14	40	-4.09	38.72
197	(403)	Bae Sang-moon	Kor	0.90	36.00	40	-14.20	33.21
198	(109)	Ross McGowan	Eng	0.90	53.06	59	-42.54	39.78
199	(154)	Tom Pernice Jr.	USA	0.90	54.85	61	-74.60	58.54
200	(262)	Greg Chalmers	Aus	0.90	52.12	58	-41.23	54.39

( ) Ranking in brackets indicates position as of December 31, 2007.

Age Groups of Current Top 100 World Ranked Players

Under 25	25-28	29-32	33-36	37-40	41-44	45 & Over
				Mickelson		
				Harrington		
	Garcia			Karlsson		
	Villegas			Els		
	Scott			Furyk		
	Rose			K.J. Choi		
	R. Fisher	Stenson		Weir		
	A. Romero	Ogilvy		Allenby		
	Baddeley	Immelman		J.M. Singh		
	O. Wilson	Curtis	Woods	Appleby		
	Sterne	Poulter	Westwood	Cabrera		
	Mahan	Donald	Cink	Goosen		
	O'Hair	McDowell	Leonard	Hart	Stricker	
	Snedeker	Sabbatini	T. Clark	Pampling	Jimenez	
	Quiros	Casey	Katayama	R. Green	Ames	
	Trahan	Z. Johnson	S. Hansen	Clarke	Sutherland	
	Holmes	P. Hanson	Weekley	Duke	Marksaeng	
	Fdez-Castano	Pettersson	Lin Wen-tang	Fujita	Austin	
	Dougherty	Imada	Kjeldsen	Smail	Verplank	
A. Kim	F. Molinari	Yano	B. Jones	Hedblom	Kingston	
Kaymer	Kai	Tanihara	Goggin	A. Hansen	Love	V. Singh
McIlroy	Maybin	Perez	C. Campbell	Jaidee	Mayfair	K. Perry
Ishikawa	Larrazabal	Quinney	Jacobson	Taniguchi	Goydos	Mediate
Schwartzel	Noren	Otto	Slocum	O'Hern	Flesch	Bt. Bryant

2008 World Ranking Review

Major Movements

Upward				Downward			
	Net Points	Position			Net Points	Position	
Name	Gained	2007	2008	Name	Lost	2007	2008
Sergio Garcia	177	12	2	Tiger Woods	305	1	1
Anthony Kim	158	75	11	Justin Rose	147	6	19
Camilo Villegas	131	56	7	Ernie Els	120	4	9
Kenny Perry	128	92	14	Jim Furyk	116	3	13
Robert Karlsson	124	41	6	Brett Wetterich	116	32	223
Martin Kaymar	103	76	25	Adam Scott	113	7	17
Justin Leonard	90	89	23	Rory Sabbatini	104	11	34
Graeme McDowell	78	106	33	Niclas Fasth	103	20	108
Ben Curtis	77	119	24	Angel Cabrera	101	14	42
Jeev Milkha Singh	75	77	35	K.J. Choi	99	9	18
Rory McIlroy	72	232	39	Zach Johnson	94	15	46
Lee Westwood	72	23	10	Luke Donald	85	17	31
Dudley Hart	72	448	54	Steve Stricker	83	5	15
Mathew Goggin	71	191	58	Charles Howell	79	42	141
Darren Clarke	68	225	70	Aaron Baddeley	78	18	36
Ryo Ishikawa	67	434	60	Toru Taniguchi	77	27	93
Ross Fisher	65	84	29				
Shintaro Kai	64	—	88				
Pablo Larrazabal	60	689	96				
Oliver Wilson	60	101	40				
Vijay Singh	55	10	5				
Lin Wen-tang	54	171	49				

Highest-Rated Events of 2008

	Event	Top 5	Top 15	Top 30	Top 50	Top 100	World Rating Points
			No. of World Ranked Players Participating				World Rating Points
1	PGA Championship	4	14	28	48	93	783
2	U.S. Open Championship	5	15	29	48	69	755
3	Masters Tournament	5	15	30	50	65	738
4	The Open Championship	4	14	27	47	73	669
5	The Players Championship	4	13	28	44	73	713
6	WGC - Accenture Match Play	5	15	30	49	64	728
7	WGC - CA Championship	5	14	29	49	69	729
8	WGC - Bridgestone Invitational	4	14	28	47	63	666
9	The Barclays	4	11	22	38	65	621
10	Deutsche Bank Champ.	4	11	22	38	62	603
11	Northern Trust Open	3	12	20	30	52	546
12	BMW Championship	4	11	22	33	48	518
13	Wachovia Championship	3	10	20	30	53	519
14	BMW PGA Championship	1	3	8	15	35	265
15	Arnold Palmer Invitational	2	6	19	29	50	477
16	Memorial Tournament	3	8	15	25	49	459
17	Buick Invitational	3	7	11	21	43	422
18	FBR Open	2	6	10	21	47	317
19	Verizon Heritage	1	4	10	23	44	362
20	Crowne Plaza Colonial	2	6	10	16	40	357
21	The Tour Championship	3	8	16	21	30	382
22	HSBC Champions	3	8	13	18	30	337
23	PODS Championship	2	3	10	19	41	347
24	Shell Houston Open	3	6	11	17	35	336
25	Dubai Desert Classic	2	4	8	14	31	280
26	Volvo Masters	2	5	8	14	32	276
27	Sony Open	2	7	9	14	31	284
28	Barclays Scottish Open	2	3	8	12	30	268
29	Alfred Dunhill Links	1	5	7	14	28	254
30	Honda Classic	1	7	8	16	34	285
31	AT&T National	0	4	6	17	35	279
32	Mercedes-Benz Championship	2	7	10	18	22	253
33	Commercialbank Qatar Masters	0	3	9	15	30	240
34	Zurich Classic of New Orleans	2	4	7	14	32	260
35	Abu Dhabi Championship	0	2	8	13	26	213
36	EDS Byron Nelson Champ.	0	3	8	12	32	233
37	Stanford St. Jude Champ.	0	3	8	15	25	202
38	AT&T Pebble Beach Pro-Am	1	4	4	10	19	201
39	European Open	0	3	4	7	22	170
40	South African Open Champ.	0	3	6	9	15	145

World Golf Rankings 1968-2008

Year	No. 1	No. 2	No. 3	No. 4	No. 5
1968	Nicklaus	Palmer	Casper	Player	Charles
1969	Nicklaus	Player	Casper	Palmer	Charles
1970	Nicklaus	Player	Casper	Trevino	Charles
1971	Nicklaus	Trevino	Player	Palmer	Casper
1972	Nicklaus	Player	Trevino	Crampton	Palmer
1973	Nicklaus	Weiskopf	Trevino	Player	Crampton
1974	Nicklaus	Miller	Player	Weiskopf	Trevino
1975	Nicklaus	Miller	Weiskopf	Irwin	Player
1976	Nicklaus	Irwin	Miller	Player	Green
1977	Nicklaus	Watson	Green	Irwin	Crenshaw
1978	Watson	Nicklaus	Irwin	Green	Player
1979	Watson	Nicklaus	Irwin	Trevino	Player
1980	Watson	Trevino	Aoki	Crenshaw	Nicklaus
1981	Watson	Rogers	Aoki	Pate	Trevino
1982	Watson	Floyd	Ballesteros	Kite	Stadler
1983	Ballesteros	Watson	Floyd	Norman	Kite
1984	Ballesteros	Watson	Norman	Wadkins	Langer
1985	Ballesteros	Langer	Norman	Watson	Nakajima
1986	Norman	Langer	Ballesteros	Nakajima	Bean
1987	Norman	Ballesteros	Langer	Lyle	Strange
1988	Ballesteros	Norman	Lyle	Faldo	Strange
1989	Norman	Faldo	Ballesteros	Strange	Stewart
1990	Norman	Faldo	Olazabal	Woosnam	Stewart
1991	Woosnam	Faldo	Olazabal	Ballesteros	Norman
1992	Faldo	Couples	Woosnam	Olazabal	Norman
1993	Faldo	Norman	Langer	Price	Couples
1994	Price	Norman	Faldo	Langer	Olazabal
1995	Norman	Price	Langer	Els	Montgomerie
1996	Norman	Lehman	Montgomerie	Els	Couples
1997	Norman	Woods	Price	Els	Love
1998	Woods	O'Meara	Duval	Love	Els
1999	Woods	Duval	Montgomerie	Love	Els
2000	Woods	Els	Duval	Mickelson	Westwood
2001	Woods	Mickelson	Duval	Els	Love
2002	Woods	Mickelson	Els	Garcia	Goosen
2003	Woods	Singh	Els	Love	Furyk
2004	Singh	Woods	Els	Goosen	Mickelson
2005	Woods	Singh	Mickelson	Goosen	Els
2006	Woods	Furyk	Mickelson	Scott	Els
2007	Woods	Mickelson	Furyk	Els	Stricker
2008	Woods	Garcia	Mickelson	Harrington	Singh

(The World of Professional Golf 1968-1985; World Ranking 1986-2008)

Year	No. 6	No. 7	No. 8	No. 9	No. 10
1968	Boros	Coles	Thomson	Beard	Nagle
1969	Beard	Archer	Trevino	Barber	Sikes
1970	Devlin	Coles	Jacklin	Beard	Huggett
1971	Barber	Crampton	Charles	Devlin	Weiskopf
1972	Jacklin	Weiskopf	Oosterhuis	Heard	Devlin
1973	Miller	Oosterhuis	Wadkins	Heard	Brewer
1974	M. Ozaki	Crampton	Irwin	Green	Heard
1975	Green	Trevino	Casper	Crampton	Watson
1976	Watson	Weiskopf	Marsh	Crenshaw	Geiberger
1977	Marsh	Player	Weiskopf	Floyd	Ballesteros
1978	Crenshaw	Marsh	Ballesteros	Trevino	Aoki
1979	Aoki	Green	Crenshaw	Ballesteros	Wadkins
1980	Pate	Ballesteros	Bean	Irwin	Player
1981	Ballesteros	Graham	Crenshaw	Floyd	Lietzke
1982	Pate	Nicklaus	Rogers	Aoki	Strange
1983	Nicklaus	Nakajima	Stadler	Aoki	Wadkins
1984	Faldo	Nakajima	Stadler	Kite	Peete
1985	Wadkins	O'Meara	Strange	Pavin	Sutton
1986	Tway	Sutton	Strange	Stewart	O'Meara
1987	Woosnam	Stewart	Wadkins	McNulty	Crenshaw
1988	Crenshaw	Woosnam	Frost	Azinger	Calcavecchia
1989	Kite	Olazabal	Calcavecchia	Woosnam	Azinger
1990	Azinger	Ballesteros	Kite	McNulty	Calcavecchia
1991	Couples	Langer	Stewart	Azinger	Davis
1992	Langer	Cook	Price	Azinger	Love
1993	Azinger	Woosnam	Kite	Love	Pavin
1994	Els	Couples	Montgomerie	M. Ozaki	Pavin
1995	Pavin	Faldo	Couples	M. Ozaki	Elkington
1996	Faldo	Mickelson	M. Ozaki	Love	O'Meara
1997	Mickelson	Montgomerie	M. Ozaki	Lehman	O'Meara
1998	Price	Montgomerie	Westwood	Singh	Mickelson
1999	Westwood	Singh	Price	Mickelson	O'Meara
2000	Montgomerie	Love	Sutton	Singh	Lehman
2001	Garcia	Toms	Singh	Clarke	Goosen
2002	Toms	Harrington	Singh	Love	Montgomerie
2003	Weir	Goosen	Harrington	Toms	Perry
2004	Harrington	Garcia	Weir	Love	Cink
2005	Garcia	Furyk	Montgomerie	Scott	DiMarco
2006	Goosen	Singh	Harrington	Donald	Ogilvy
2007	Rose	Scott	Harrington	Choi	Singh
2008	Karlsson	Villegas	Stenson	Els	Westwood

World's Winners of 2008

U.S. PGA TOUR

Mercedes-Benz Championship	Daniel Chopra
Sony Open	K.J. Choi
Bob Hope Chrysler Classic	D.J. Trahan
Buick Invitational	Tiger Woods
FBR Open	J.B. Holmes
AT&T Pebble Beach National Pro-Am	Steve Lowery
Northern Trust Open	Phil Mickelson
WGC - Accenture Match Play Championship	Tiger Woods (3)
Mayakoba Golf Classic	Brian Gay
Honda Classic	Ernie Els
PODS Championship	Sean O'Hair
Arnold Palmer Invitational	Tiger Woods (4)
WGC - CA Championship	Geoff Ogilvy
Puerto Rico Open	Greg Kraft
Zurich Classic	Andres Romero
Shell Houston Open	Johnson Wagner
Masters Tournament	Trevor Immelman
Verizon Heritage	Boo Weekley
EDS Byron Nelson Championship	Adam Scott (2)
Wachovia Championship	Anthony Kim
The Players Championship	Sergio Garcia
AT&T Classic	Ryuji Imada
Crowne Plaza Invitational	Phil Mickelson (2)
Memorial Tournament	Kenny Perry
Stanford St. Jude Championship	Justin Leonard
U.S. Open Championship	Tiger Woods (5)
Travelers Championship	Stewart Cink
Buick Open	Kenny Perry (2)
AT&T National	Anthony Kim (2)
John Deere Classic	Kenny Perry (3)
U.S. Bank Championship	Richard S. Johnson
RBC Canadian Open	Chez Reavie
WGC - Bridgestone Invitational	Vijay Singh
Legends Reno-Tahoe Open	Parker McLachlin
PGA Championship	Padraig Harrington (2)
Wyndham Championship	Carl Pettersson

PGA TOUR PLAYOFFS FOR THE FEDEXCUP

The Barclays	Vijay Singh (2)
Deutsche Bank Championship	Vijay Singh (3)
BMW Championship	Camilo Villegas (2)
The Tour Championship	Camilo Villegas (3)

The Ryder Cup	United States
Viking Classic	Will MacKenzie

PGA TOUR FALL SERIES

Turning Stone Resort Championship	Dustin Johnson
Valero Texas Open	Zach Johnson
Justin Timberlake Shriners Hospitals Open	Marc Turnesa
Frys.com Open	Cameron Beckman
Ginn sur Mer Classic	Ryan Palmer
Children's Miracle Network Classic	Davis Love

SPECIAL EVENTS

Tavistock Cup	Isleworth
CVS/Caremark Charity Classic	Bubba Watson/Camilo Villegas
PGA Grand Slam of Golf	Jim Furyk
Callaway Golf Pebble Beach Invitational	Tommy Armour
Del Webb Father/Son Challenge	Larry Nelson/Drew Nelson
Merrill Lynch Shootout	Scott Hoch (3)/Kenny Perry (4)
Chevron World Challenge	Vijay Singh (4)

NATIONWIDE TOUR

Movistar Panama Championship	Scott Dunlap
Mexico Open	Jarrod Lyle
Chitimacha Louisiana Open	Gavin Coles
Livermore Valley Wine Country Championship	Aron Price
Athens Regional Foundation Classic	Robert Damron
Henrico County Open	Greg Chalmers
South Georgia Classic	Bryan DeCorso
Fort Smith Classic	Colt Knost
BMW Charity Pro-Am	David Mathis
Melwood Prince George's County Open	Jeff Klauk
Bank of America Open	Kris Blanks
Rex Hospital Open	Scott Gutschewski
Knoxville Open	Jarrod Lyle (2)
Ford Wayne Gretzky Classic	Justin Hicks
Nationwide Tour Players Cup	Rick Price
Price Cutter Charity Championship	Colt Knost (2)
Nationwide Children's Hospital Invitational	Bill Lunde
Cox Classic	Ryan Hietala
Preferred Health Systems Wichita Open	Scott Piercy
Xerox Classic	Brendon de Jonge
Northeast Pennsylvania Classic	Scott Piercy (2)
Utah Championship	Brendon Todd
Albertsons Boise Open	Chris Tidland
Oregon Classic	Matt Bettencourt
WNB Golf Classic	Marc Leishman
Chattanooga Classic	Arjun Atwal (2)
Miccosukee Championship	D.A. Points
Nationwide Tour Championship	Matt Bettencourt (2)

CANADIAN TOUR

Spring International	Spencer Levin
Stockton Sports Commission Classic	John Ellis
Corona Mazatlan Mexican PGA Championship	John Ellis (2)
Iberostar Riviera Maya Open	Daniel Im
La Loma San Luis Potosi Open	Russell Surber
Times Colonist Open	Daniel Im (2)
Greater Vancouver Charity Classic	Adam Spiers
ATB Financial Classic	Dustin Risdon
Saskatchewan Open	Josh Geary
Telus Edmonton Open	John Ellis (3)
Canadian Tour Players Cup	Wes Heffernan
Desjardins Montreal Open	Graham DeLaet
Jane Rogers Championship of Mississauga	Alex Coe
Seaforth Country Classic	Kent Eger
Canadian Tour Championship	Tom Stankowski

TOUR DE LAS AMERICAS (SOUTH AMERICA)

Abierto Visa del Centro	Estanislao Goya
Abierto Visa de Argentina	Antii Ahokas
Club Colombia Masters	Wil Besseling
Abierto de Chile Visa	Felipe Aguilar (2)
Copa 3 Diamantes	Sebastian Saavedra
TLA Players Championship	Rafael Gomez
Canal i Abierto de Venezuela	Angel Romero
Taurus Abierto de Peru	Alan Wagner
Carlos Franco Invitational	Clodomiro Carranza
Abierto de San Luis	Rafael Gomez (2)
Abierto del Litoral	Andres Romero (2)
De Vicenzo Classic	Paulo Pinto
Sport Frances Open	Rafael Gomez (3)
Torneo de Maestros	Fabian Gomez
Costa Rica Golf Classic	Mauricio Molina

EUROPEAN TOUR

Abu Dhabi Golf Championship	Martin Kaymer
Commercialbank Qatar Masters	Adam Scott
Dubai Desert Classic	Tiger Woods (2)
Madeira Islands Open BPI – Portugal	Alastair Forsyth
MAPFRE Open de Andalucia	Thomas Levet
Estoril Open de Portugal	Gregory Bourdy
Open de Espana	Peter Lawrie
Methorios Capital Italian Open	Hennie Otto
Irish Open	Richard Finch
BMW PGA Championship	Miguel Angel Jimenez
Celtic Manor Wales Open	Scott Strange
Bank Austria GolfOpen	Jeev Milkha Singh
Saint-Omer Open	David Dixon
BMW International Open	Martin Kaymer (2)
Open de France ALSTOM	Pablo Larrazabal
European Open	Ross Fisher
Barclays Scottish Open	Graeme McDowell (2)
The Open Championship	Padraig Harrington
Inteco Russian Open Golf Championship	Mikael Lundberg
SAS Masters	Peter Hanson
KLM Open	Darren Clarke (2)
Johnnie Walker Championship	Gregory Havret
Omega European Masters	Jean-Francois Lucquin
Mercedez-Benz Championship	Robert Karlsson
Quinn Insurance British Masters	Gonzalo Fernandez-Castano
Alfred Dunhill Links Championship	Robert Karlsson (2)
Madrid Masters	Charl Schwartzel
Portugal Masters	Alvaro Quiros
Castello Masters Costa Azahar	Sergio Garcia (2)
Volvo Masters	Soren Kjeldsen

CHALLENGE TOUR

Tusker Kenya Open	Iain Pyman
AGF-Allianz Open Cotes d'Armor Bretagne	Joakim Haeggman
Banque Populaire Moroccan Classic	Michael Hoey
Piemonte Open	Seve Benson
DHL Wroclaw Open	Gary Clark
Oceanico Group Pro-Am Challenge	Alessandro Tadini
Reale Challenge de Espana	Andrew McArthur
SK Golf Challenge	Simon Robinson
Telenet Trophy	David Horsey

Scottish Challenge	Taco Remkes
AGF-Allianz EurOpen de Lyon	David Horsey (2)
Credit Suisse Challenge	Rafael Cabrera Bello
MAN NO Open	Andre Bossert
SWALEC Wales Challenge	Michael McGeady
Challenge of Ireland	Andrew Tampion
Lexus Open	Jeppe Huldahl
Trophee du Golf Club de Geneve	Klas Eriksson
Vodafone Challenge	Richie Ramsay
Ypsilon Golf Challenge	Seve Benson (2)
ECCO Tour Championship	Antti Ahokas (2)
The Dubliner Challenge	Mark Haastrup
Qingdao Golf Open	Gareth Maybin
Kazakhstan Open	Gary Lockerbie
The Dutch Futures	Taco Remkes (2)
AGF-Allianz Golf Open Grand Toulouse	Richie Ramsay (2)
Margara Diehl-Ako Platinum Open	Taco Remkes (3)
Apulia San Domenico Grand Final	Estanislao Goya (2)

ASIAN TOUR

Emaar-MGF Indian Masters	S.S.P. Chowrasia
Enjoy Jakarta Astro Indonesia Open	Felipe Aguilar
SAIL Open	Mark Brown
Johnnie Walker Classic	Mark Brown (2)
Maybank Malaysian Open	Arjun Atwal
Ballantine's Championship	Graeme McDowell
Asian Tour International	Lin Wen-tang
Philippine Open	Angelo Que
Volvo China Open	Damien McGrane
BMW Asian Open	Darren Clarke
GS Caltex Maekyung Open	Hwang Inn-choon
Pine Valley Beijing Open	Hiroyuki Fujita
Bangkok Airways Open	Thaworn Wiratchant
Singha Thailand PGA Championship	Mo Joong-kyung
Worldwide Selangor Masters	Ben Leong
Brunei Open	Rick Kulacz
Pertamina Indonesia President Invitational	Scott Hend
Mercuries Taiwan Masters	Lu Wen-teh (2)
Kolon-Hana Bank Korea Open	Bae Sang-moon
Hero Honda Indian Open	Liang Wen-chong
Midea China Classic	Noh Seung-yul
Macau Open	David Gleeson
Iskandar Johor Open	Retief Goosen
HSBC Champions	Sergio Garcia (3)
Barclays Singapore Open	Jeev Milkha Singh (3)
UBS Hong Kong Open	Lin Wen-tang (2)
Omega Mission Hills World Cup	Robert Karlsson (3)/Henrik Stenson
Hana Bank Vietnam Masters	Thongchai Jaidee
Johnnie Walker Cambodian Open	Thongchai Jaidee (2)
Volvo Masters of Asia	Lam Chih Bing

OMEGA CHINA TOUR

Guangzhou Championship	Zhang Lian-wei
Dell Championship	Li Chao
Kunming Championship	Lu Wen-teh
Shanghai Championship	Hsu Mong-nan
Sofitel Golf Championship	Liao Gui-ming
Luxehills Golf Championship	Tsai Chi-huang
Tianjin Championship	Tsai Chi-huang (2)
Omega Championship	Zhou Jun

JAPAN TOUR

Token Homemate Cup	Katsumasa Miyamoto
Tsuruya Open	S.K. Ho
The Crowns	Tomohiro Kondo
Japan PGA Championship	Shingo Katayama
Munsingwear Open KSB Cup	Hideto Tanihara
Mitsubishi Diamond Cup	Prayad Marksaeng
Mizuno Open Yomiuri Classic	Prayad Marksaeng (2)
UBS Japan Golf Tour Championship	Hidemasa Hoshino
Nagashima Shigeo Invitational	Jeev Milkha Singh (2)
Sun Chlorella Classic	Takuya Taniguchi
Vana H Cup KBC Augusta	Shintaro Kai
Fujisankei Classic	Toyokazu Fujishima
ANA Open	Azuma Yano
Asia-Pacific Panasonic Open	Hideto Tanihara (2)
Coca-Cola Tokai Classic	Toshinori Muto
Canon Open	Makoto Inoue
Japan Open	Shingo Katayama (2)
Bridgestone Open	Azuma Yano (2)
mynavi ABC Championship	Ryo Ishikawa
The Championship by Lexus	S.K. Ho (2)
Mitsui Sumitomo Visa Taiheiyo Masters	Shingo Katayama (3)
Dunlop Phoenix	Prayad Marksaeng (3)
Casio World Open	Koumei Oda
Golf Nippon Series JT Cup	Jeev Milkha Singh (4)

AUSTRALASIAN TOUR

HSBC New Zealand PGA Championship	Darron Stiles
Moonah Classic	Ewan Porter
Sportsbet Australian Masters	Rod Pampling
Cadbury Schweppes Australian PGA	Geoff Ogilvy (2)
Australian Open	Tim Clark

AFRICAN TOURS

Joburg Open	Richard Sterne
Dimension Data Pro-Am	James Kamte
Nashua Masters	Marc Cayeux
Africa Open	Shaun Norris
Vodacom Championship	James Kingston
Telkom PGA Championship	Louis Oosthuizen
Mount Edgecombe Trophy	Mark Murless
Chainama Hills Zambia Open	Tyrone Ferreira
Vodacom Origins of Golf Free State	Dion Fourie
Vodacom Origins of Golf Gauteng	Tyrone van Aswegen
Samsung Royal Swazi Sun Open	Jean Hugo
Nashua Golf Challenge	Keith Horne
Vodacom Origins of Golf Kwazulu Natal	Jean Hugo (2)
Lombard Insurance Classic	Merrick Bremner
SAA Pro-Am Invitational	George Coetzee
Vodacom Origins of Golf Western Cape	Garth Mulroy
Telkom PGA Pro-Am	Merrick Bremner (2)
SunCoast Classic	Jake Roos
Vodacom Origins of Golf Eastern Cape	George Coetzee (2)
Seekers Travel Pro-Am	Trevor Fisher, Jr.
BMG Classic	Doug McGuigan
Metmar Highveld Classic	James Kamte (2)
Vodacom Origins of Golf Final	Jaco Van Zyl
Platinum Classic	Thomas Aiken
MTC Namibia PGA Championship	T.C. Charamba
Hassan II Trophy	Ernie Els (2)

Coca-Cola Championship	Garth Mulroy (2)
Gary Player Invitational	Bobby Lincoln/Garth Mulroy (3)
Nedbank Affinity Cup	Tyrone van Aswegen (2)
Nedbank Golf Challenge	Henrik Stenson (2)
Alfred Dunhill Championship	Richard Sterne (2)
South African Open Championship	Richard Sterne (3)

U.S. LPGA TOUR

SBS Open	Annika Sorenstam
Fields Open	Paula Creamer
HSBC Women's Champions	Lorena Ochoa
MasterCard Classic Honoring Alejo Peralta	Louise Friberg
Safeway International	Lorena Ochoa (2)
Kraft Nabisco Championship	Lorena Ochoa (3)
Corona Championship	Lorena Ochoa (4)
Ginn Open	Lorena Ochoa (5)
Stanford International Pro-Am	Annika Sorenstam (2)
SemGroup Championship	Paula Creamer (2)
Michelob Ultra Open	Annika Sorenstam (3)
Sybase Classic	Lorena Ochoa (6)
LPGA Corning Classic	Leta Lindley
Ginn Tribute Hosted by Annika	Seon Hwa Lee
McDonald's LPGA Championship	Yani Tseng
Wegmans LPGA	Eun-Hee Ji
U.S. Women's Open	Inbee Park
P&G Beauty NW Arkansas Championship	Seon Hwa Lee (2)
Jamie Farr Owens Corning Classic	Paula Creamer (3)
LPGA State Farm Classic	Ji Young Oh
CN Canadian Women's Open	Katherine Hull
Safeway Classic	Cristie Kerr
Bell Micro LPGA Classic	Angela Stanford
Navistar LPGA Classic	Lorena Ochoa (7)
Samsung World Championship	Paula Creamer (4)
Longs Drugs Challenge	In-Kyung Kim
Kapalua LPGA Classic	Morgan Pressel
Grand China Air LPGA	Helen Alfredsson (2)
Hana Bank-Kolon Championship	Candie Kung
Lorena Ochoa Invitational	Angela Stanford (2)
ADT Championship	Ji-Yai Shin (4)
Lexus Cup	International Team

LADIES EUROPEAN TOUR

VCI European Ladies Golf Cup	Trish Johnson/Rebecca Hudson (2)
Catalonia Ladies	Lotta Wahlin
Open de Espana Femenino	Emma Zackrisson
Aberdeen Asset Management Scottish Open	Gwladys Nocera
Garanti American Express Turkish Open	Lotta Wahlin (2)
Deutsche Bank Ladies Swiss Open	Suzann Pettersen
HypoVereinsbank Ladies German Open	Amy Yang
ABN AMRO Ladies Open	Gwladys Nocera (2)
Ladies Open de Portugal	Anne-Lise Caudal
Tenerife Ladies Open	Rebecca Hudson (3)
Oxfordshire Ladies English Open	Rebecca Hudson (4)
AIB Ladies Irish Open	Suzann Pettersen (2)
BMW Ladies Italian Open	Martina Eberl
Evian Masters	Helen Alfredsson
Ricoh Women's British Open	Ji-Yai Shin (2)
Scandinavian TPC Hosted by Annika	Amy Yang (2)
S4/C Wales Ladies Championship of Europe	Lotta Wahlin (3)
SAS Masters	Gwladys Nocera (3)

Finnair Masters   Minea Blomqvist
Nykredit Masters   Martina Eberl (2)
UNIQA Ladies Golf Open   Laura Davies (2)
Goteborg Masters   Gwladys Nocera (4)
Vediorbis Open de France Dames   Anja Monke
Madrid Ladies Masters   Gwladys Nocera (5)
Suzhou Taihu Ladies Open   Annika Sorenstam (4)
Saint Four Ladies Masters   Hee Kyung Seo
Dubai Ladies Masters   Anja Monke (2)

JAPAN LPGA TOUR

Daikin Orchid Ladies   Bo-Bae Song
Accordia Golf Ladies   Yuri Fudoh
Yokohama Tire PRGR Cup   Ji-Yai Shin
Yamaha Ladies Open   Hiroko Yamaguchi
Studio Alice Ladies Open   Hyun-Ju Shin
Life Card Ladies   Yukari Baba
Fujisankei Ladies Classic   Ayako Uehara
Crystal Geyser Ladies   Miho Koga
World Ladies Championship Salonpas Cup   Akiko Fukushima
Vernal Ladies   Eun-A Lim
Chukyo TV Bridgestone Ladies   Ji-Hee Lee
Kosaido Ladies Golf Cup   Akane Iijima
Resort Trust Ladies   Mi-Jeong Jeon
We Love Kobe Suntory Ladies Open   Momoko Ueda
Nichirei PGM Ladies   Yuko Mitsuka
Promise Ladies   Chie Arimura
Belluna Ladies Cup   Hiromi Mogi
Meiji Chocolate Cup   Yuri Fudoh (2)
Stanley Ladies   Akiko Fukushima (2)
Kagome Philanthropy Players Championship   Mi-Jeong Jeon (2)
AXA Ladies   Shinobu Moromizato
NEC Karuizawa 72   Erina Hara
CAT Ladies   Miho Koga (2)
Yonex Ladies   Rui Kitada
Golf 5 Ladies   Saiki Fujita
Japan LPGA Championship   Hyun-Ju Shin (2)
Munsingwear Ladies Tokai Classic   Yuri Fudoh (3)
Miyagi TV Cup Dunlop Ladies Open   Momoko Ueda (2)
Japan Women's Open   Ji-Hee Lee (2)
Sankyo Ladies Open   Maiko Wakabayashi
Fujitsu Ladies   Yuri Fudoh (4)
Masters Golf Club Ladies   Shiho Oyama
Hisako Higuchi IDC Otsuka Ladies   Mayu Hattori
Mizuno Classic   Ji-Yai Shin (3)
Itoen Ladies   Miho Koga (3)
Daioseishi Elleair Ladies Open   Sakura Yokomine
Japan LPGA Tour Championship Ricoh Cup   Miho Koga (4)

AUSTRALIAN LADIES TOUR

LG Bing Lee Women's NSW Open   Laura Davies
MFS Women's Australian Open   Karrie Webb
ANZ Ladies Masters   Lisa Hall

LADIES AFRICAN TOUR

Women's World Cup of Golf   Jennifer Rosales/Dorothy Delasin
WPGA Masters   Rebecca Hudson
Acer Women's South African Open   Julie Tvede
Pam Golding Ladies International   Stacy Bregman
Telkom Women's Classic   Lisa Holm Sorensen
Princess Lalla Meryem Cup   Laura Davies (3)

CHAMPIONS TOUR

MasterCard Championship	Fred Funk
Turtle Bay Championship	Jerry Pate
Allianz Championship	Scott Hoch
ACE Group Classic	Scott Hoch (2)
Toshiba Classic	Bernhard Langer
AT&T Champions Classic	Denis Watson
Ginn Championship Hammock Beach Resort	Bernhard Langer (2)
Cap Cana Championship	Mark Wiebe
Outback Steakhouse Pro-Am	Tom Watson
Liberty Mutual Legends of Golf	Tom Watson (2)/Andy North
FedEx Kinko's Classic	Denis Watson (2)
Regions Charity Classic	Andy Bean
Senior PGA Championship	Jay Haas
Principal Charity Classic	Jay Haas (2)
Bank of America Championship	Jeff Sluman
Commerce Bank Championship	Loren Roberts
Dick's Sporting Goods Open	Eduardo Romero
3M Championship	R.W. Eaks
U.S. Senior Open	Eduardo Romero (2)
JELD-WEN Tradition	Fred Funk (2)
Boeing Classic	Tom Kite
Wal-Mart First Tee Open	Jeff Sluman (2)
Greater Hickory Classic	R.W. Eaks (2)
SAS Championship	Eduardo Romero (3)
Constellation Energy Players Championship	D.A. Weibring
Administaff Small Business Classic	Bernhard Langer (4)
AT&T Championship	John Cook
Charles Schwab Cup Championship	Andy Bean (2)

EUROPEAN SENIOR TOUR

DGM Barbados Open	Bill Longmuir
Azores Senior Open	Stewart Ginn
Parkridge Polish Seniors Championship	Ian Woosnam
Jersey Seniors Classic	Tony Johnstone
Ryder Cup Wales Seniors Open	Peter Mitchell
Irish Seniors Open	Juan Quiros
Russian Seniors Open	Ian Woosnam (2)
The Senior Open Championship	Bruce Vaughan
Bad Ragaz PGA Seniors Open	Carl Mason
De Vere Collection PGA Seniors Championship	Gordon J. Brand
Travis Perkins plc Senior Masters	Gordon J. Brand (2)
Casa Serena Open	Bernhard Langer (3)
Weston Homes PGA International Seniors	Nick Job
Scottish Seniors Open	Peter Mitchell (2)
Lake Garda Italian Seniors Open	Peter Mitchell (3)
OKI Castellon Open - Senior Tour Championship	Sam Torrance

JAPAN SENIOR TOUR

Starts Senior Golf Tournament	Hajime Meshiai
Fancl Classic	Tateo Ozaki
Komatsu Open	Hisashi Nakase
Akira Kobayashi Invitational Sanko Senior	Hajime Meshiai (2)
Japan PGA Senior Championship	Tsukasa Watanabe
Fujifilm Senior Championship	Tsukasa Watanabe (2)
Japan Senior Open Championship	Tsuneyuki Nakajima
Kinojo Senior Open	Isao Aoki
PGA Handa Cup Philanthropy Senior Open	Takashi Miyoshi

Multiple Winners of 2008

PLAYER	WINS	PLAYER	WINS
Lorena Ochoa	7	Akiko Fukushima	2
Gwladys Nocera	5	Fred Funk	2
Tiger Woods	5	Estanislao Goya	2
Paula Creamer	4	Jay Haas	2
Yuri Fudoh	4	Padraig Harrington	2
Rebecca Hudson	4	S.K. Ho	2
Miho Koga	4	David Horsey	2
Bernhard Langer	4	Jean Hugo	2
Kenny Perry	4	Daniel Im	2
Ji-Yai Shin	4	Thongchai Jaidee	2
Jeev Milkha Singh	4	Mi-Jeong Jeon	2
Vijay Singh	4	James Kamte	2
Annika Sorenstam	4	Martin Kaymer	2
Laura Davies	3	Anthony Kim	2
John Ellis	3	Colt Knost	2
Sergio Garcia	3	Ji-Hee Lee	2
Rafael Gomez	3	Seon Hwa Lee	2
Scott Hoch	3	Lin Wen-tang	2
Robert Karlsson	3	Lu Wen-teh	2
Shingo Katayama	3	Jarrod Lyle	2
Prayad Marksaeng	3	Graeme McDowell	2
Peter Mitchell	3	Hajime Meshiai	2
Garth Mulroy	3	Phil Mickelson	2
Taco Remkes	3	Anja Monke	2
Eduardo Romero	3	Geoff Ogilvy	2
Ji-Yai Shin	3	Suzann Pettersen	2
Richard Sterne	3	Scott Piercy	2
Camilo Villegas	3	Richie Ramsay	2
Lotta Wahlin	3	Andres Romero	2
Felipe Aguilar	2	Adam Scott	2
Antti Ahokas	2	Hyun-Ju Shin	2
Helen Alfredsson	2	Jeff Sluman	2
Arjun Atwal	2	Angela Stanford	2
Andy Bean	2	Henrik Stenson	2
Seve Benson	2	Hideto Tanihara	2
Matt Bettencourt	2	Tsai Chi-huang	2
Gordon J. Brand	2	Momoko Ueda	2
Merrick Bremner	2	Tyrone van Aswegen	2
Mark Brown	2	Tsukasa Watanabe	2
Darren Clarke	2	Denis Watson	2
George Coetzee	2	Tom Watson	2
R.W. Eaks	2	Ian Woosnam	2
Martina Eberl	2	Amy Yang	2
Ernie Els	2	Azuma Yano	2

World Money List

This list of the 350 leading money winners in the world of professional golf in 2008 was compiled from the results of men's (excluding seniors) tournaments carried in the Appendixes of this edition. This list includes tournaments with a minimum of 36 holes and four contestants and does not include such competitions as skins games, pro-ams and shootouts.

In the 43 years during which World Money Lists have been compiled, the earnings of the player in the 200th position have risen from a total of $3,326 in 1966 to $767,393 in 2008. The top 200 players in 1966 earned a total of $4,680,287. In 2008, the comparable total was $360,327,697.

The world money list of the International Federation of PGA Tours was used for the official money list events of the U.S. PGA Tour, PGA European Tour, PGA Tour of Japan, Asian Tour, Southern Africa Tour and PGA Tour of Australasia. The conversion rates used for 2008 for other events and other tours were: Euro = US$1.39; Japanese yen = US$0.01; South African rand = US$0.13; Australian dollar = US$0.89; Canadian dollar = US$0.95.

POS.	PLAYER, COUNTRY	TOTAL MONEY
1	Vijay Singh, Fiji	$8,025,128
2	Sergio Garcia, Spain	7,247,459
3	Tiger Woods, USA	6,396,717
4	Kenny Perry, USA	5,812,257
5	Phil Mickelson, USA	5,455,356
6	Padraig Harrington, Ireland	5,421,958
7	Anthony Kim, USA	5,301,661
8	Henrik Stenson, Sweden	5,248,090
9	Robert Karlsson, Sweden	5,241,472
10	Camilo Villegas, Colombia	5,079,698
11	Jim Furyk, USA	4,338,127
12	Stewart Cink, USA	4,118,150
13	Justin Leonard, USA	4,117,778
14	Robert Allenby, Australia	3,832,449
15	Lee Westwood, England	3,639,807
16	Ernie Els, South Africa	3,588,063
17	Miguel Angel Jimenez, Spain	3,510,886
18	Jeev Milkha Singh, India	3,474,894
19	Geoff Ogilvy, Australia	3,368,715
20	Steve Stricker, USA	3,364,411
21	Ryuji Imada, Japan	3,244,061
22	K.J. Choi, Korea	3,211,441
23	Mike Weir, Canada	3,194,896
24	Trevor Immelman, South Africa	3,189,452
25	Graeme McDowell, N. Ireland	3,053,096
26	J.B. Holmes, USA	3,000,843
27	Ben Curtis, USA	2,966,905
28	Boo Weekley, USA	2,848,463
29	Martin Kaymer, Germany	2,764,557
30	Hunter Mahan, USA	2,709,112
31	Adam Scott, Australia	2,649,442
32	Stuart Appleby, Australia	2,628,901

POS.	PLAYER, COUNTRY	TOTAL MONEY
33	Kevin Sutherland, USA	2,583,511
34	Carl Pettersson, Sweden	2,512,538
35	Stephen Ames, Canada	2,469,314
36	Ian Poulter, England	2,451,205
37	Oliver Wilson, England	2,414,008
38	Chad Campbell, USA	2,404,770
39	Ross Fisher, England	2,380,185
40	Andres Romero, Argentina	2,379,681
41	Luke Donald, England	2,353,115
42	D.J. Trahan, USA	2,304,368
43	Ken Duke, USA	2,238,885
44	Dudley Hart, USA	2,218,817
45	Woody Austin, USA	2,216,191
46	Brian Gay, USA	2,205,513
47	Mathew Goggin, Australia	2,167,684
48	Retief Goosen, South Africa	2,159,371
49	Steve Marino, USA	2,122,353
50	Sean O'Hair, USA	2,089,735
51	Pablo Larrazabal, Spain	2,060,870
52	Briny Baird, USA	2,039,808
53	Jeff Quinney, USA	2,006,454
54	Rory Sabbatini, South Africa	1,997,106
55	Tim Clark, South Africa	1,972,927
56	Rod Pampling, Australia	1,947,245
57	Soren Kjeldsen, Denmark	1,937,754
58	Shingo Katayama, Japan	1,932,543
59	Paul Casey, England	1,916,570
60	Davis Love, USA	1,901,362
61	Nicholas Thompson, USA	1,877,529
62	Daniel Chopra, Sweden	1,831,177
63	Dustin Johnson, USA	1,789,895
64	Pat Perez, Uruguay	1,762,388
65	Paul Goydos, USA	1,755,889
66	Billy Mayfair, USA	1,750,683
67	Soren Hansen, Denmark	1,748,942
68	Jerry Kelly, USA	1,744,067
69	Brandt Snedeker, USA	1,738,790
70	Darren Clarke, N. Ireland	1,722,435
71	Bart Bryant, USA	1,718,914
72	Zach Johnson, USA	1,702,454
73	Charlie Wi, Korea	1,684,895
74	Bubba Watson, USA	1,683,523
75	Aaron Baddeley, Australia	1,671,936
76	James Kingston, South Africa	1,663,565
77	Prayad Marksaeng, Thailand	1,658,873
78	Peter Hanson, Sweden	1,648,487
79	Charles Howell, USA	1,619,490
80	Richard Green, Australia	1,604,327
81	Fredrik Jacobson, Sweden	1,596,880
82	Rocco Mediate, USA	1,584,499
83	Mark Wilson, USA	1,578,337
84	Justin Rose, England	1,565,711
85	Tommy Armour, USA	1,561,256

POS.	PLAYER, COUNTRY	TOTAL MONEY
86	Francesco Molinari, Italy	1,534,129
87	Steve Lowery, USA	1,526,205
88	Rory McIlroy, N. Ireland	1,514,568
89	Nick O'Hern, Australia	1,507,412
90	Heath Slocum, USA	1,491,556
91	Ben Crane, USA	1,488,505
92	Ryan Palmer, USA	1,481,638
93	Peter Lonard, Australia	1,470,275
94	Matt Kuchar, USA	1,452,896
95	Chez Reavie, USA	1,450,102
96	Scott Verplank, USA	1,446,967
97	Johnson Wagner, USA	1,435,738
98	Charl Schwartzel, South Africa	1,422,650
99	George McNeill, USA	1,361,532
100	Kevin Streelman, USA	1,352,705
101	Dean Wilson, USA	1,350,002
102	Azuma Yano, Japan	1,349,738
103	Tom Pernice, Jr., USA	1,336,277
104	Marc Turnesa, USA	1,334,270
105	Paul McGinley, Ireland	1,318,339
106	Cameron Beckman, USA	1,312,837
107	John Merrick, USA	1,312,005
108	Parker McLachlin, USA	1,311,839
109	John Senden, Australia	1,308,639
110	Colin Montgomerie, Scotland	1,301,053
111	Alvaro Quiros, Spain	1,298,693
112	Steve Elkington, Australia	1,291,114
113	Steve Flesch, USA	1,277,425
114	Anthony Wall, England	1,274,870
115	Tim Herron, USA	1,251,666
116	Fred Couples, USA	1,251,005
117	Richard Sterne, South Africa	1,237,303
118	Richard Finch, England	1,235,576
119	Ryan Moore, USA	1,214,900
120	Brendan Jones, Australia	1,213,305
121	Troy Matteson, USA	1,212,018
122	Greg Kraft, USA	1,204,559
123	Tim Wilkinson, New Zealand	1,201,569
124	John Mallinger, USA	1,201,433
125	Michael Letzig, USA	1,199,534
126	Gonzalo Fernandez-Castano, Spain	1,193,498
127	Damian McGrane, Ireland	1,180,836
128	Scott Strange, Australia	1,176,866
129	Brian Davis, England	1,167,378
130	Angel Cabrera, Argentina	1,146,259
131	Peter Lawrie, Ireland	1,098,755
132	Peter Hedblom, Sweden	1,094,667
133	Hennie Otto, South Africa	1,087,109
134	Felipe Aguilar, Chile	1,075,746
135	Ryo Ishikawa, Japan	1,074,469
136	Cliff Kresge, USA	1,070,907
137	Gregory Havret, France	1,069,399
138	Alexander Noren, Sweden	1,066,154

POS.	PLAYER, COUNTRY	TOTAL MONEY
139	Hideto Tanihara, Japan	1,061,097
140	David Lynn, England	1,058,059
141	Alex Cejka, Germany	1,053,943
142	Vaughn Taylor, USA	1,053,423
143	Kevin Na, Korea	1,041,059
144	Jonathan Byrd, USA	1,039,584
145	Joe Ogilvie, USA	1,035,831
146	Scott McCarron, USA	1,030,919
147	Gregory Bourdy, France	1,022,856
148	John Rollins, USA	1,015,897
149	Bill Haas, USA	1,000,939
150	S.K. Ho, Korea	1,000,623
151	Liang Wen-chong, China	1,000,580
152	Lucas Glover, USA	998,363
153	Charley Hoffman, USA	996,643
154	David Howell, England	991,265
155	Paul Lawrie, Scotland	988,385
156	Mark Brown, New Zealand	986,538
157	J.J. Henry, USA	983,662
158	Michael Allen, Ireland	981,263
159	Anders Hansen, Denmark	971,126
160	Nathan Green, Australia	964,252
161	Tim Petrovic, USA	963,290
162	Brett Quigley, USA	938,216
163	Simon Dyson, England	924,906
164	Corey Pavin, USA	924,282
165	Oliver Fisher, England	919,031
166	Will MacKenzie, USA	911,194
167	Shintaro Kai, Japan	906,877
168	Bo Van Pelt, USA	903,967
169	Eric Axley, USA	903,065
170	Nick Dougherty, England	892,354
171	Lin Wen-tang, Taiwan	890,808
172	Richard S. Johnson, Sweden	890,667
173	Jeff Overton, USA	890,354
174	Johan Edfors, Sweden	881,701
175	Nick Watney, USA	878,173
176	Jean-Francois Lucquin, France	873,722
177	Jason Bohn, USA	868,786
178	Graeme Storm, England	863,932
179	Thongchai Jaidee, Thailand	862,792
180	Brad Adamonis, USA	862,413
181	Mark Calcavecchia, USA	860,067
182	Martin Laird, Scotland	852,752
183	Thomas Levet, France	843,878
184	Shane Bertsch, USA	841,248
185	Bob Estes, USA	829,395
186	Robert-Jan Derksen, Netherlands	824,277
187	Ignacio Garrido, Spain	813,950
188	Hiroyuki Fujita, Japan	809,630
189	Patrick Sheehan, USA	805,897
190	Jose Manuel Lara, Spain	805,334
191	Joe Durant, USA	802,568

POS.	PLAYER, COUNTRY	TOTAL MONEY
192	Charles Warren, USA	800,694
193	David Toms, USA	799,114
194	Alastair Forsyth, Scotland	793,587
195	Jyoti Randhawa, India	788,535
196	Bob Tway, USA	785,641
197	Matt Jones, Australia	784,026
198	Jason Gore, USA	782,364
199	Markus Brier, Austria	778,550
200	Jason Day, Australia	767,393
201	Mikael Lundberg, Sweden	761,282
202	Jay Williamson, USA	758,623
203	Steve Allan, Australia	756,851
204	Robert Garrigus, USA	756,732
205	Toshinori Muto, Japan	752,337
206	Chris DiMarco, USA	747,046
207	Rich Beem, USA	738,201
208	Steve Webster, England	734,922
209	John Bickerton, England	732,369
210	James Driscoll, USA	708,549
211	Louis Oosthuizen, South Africa	703,400
212	David Smail, New Zealand	703,289
213	Toru Taniguchi, Japan	697,453
214	Gary Orr, Scotland	682,185
215	Arjun Atwal, India	682,182
216	Koumei Oda, Japan	677,016
217	Tom Lehman, USA	676,292
218	David Frost, South Africa	669,681
219	Maarten Lafeber, Netherlands	661,608
220	Kenichi Kuboya, Japan	659,692
221	Hidemasa Hoshino, Japan	651,646
222	Robert Dinwiddie, England	647,451
223	Jesper Parnevik, Sweden	646,635
224	Makoto Inoue, Japan	646,064
225	Martin Erlandsson, Sweden	636,598
226	Scott Sterling, USA	628,022
227	Raphael Jacquelin, France	624,686
228	Stephen Gallacher, Scotland	622,940
229	Niclas Fasth, Sweden	622,462
230	Taichi Teshima, Japan	617,467
231	Michael Campbell, New Zealand	613,662
232	Bradley Dredge, Wales	607,702
233	Katsumasa Miyamoto, Japan	603,058
234	Kevin Stadler, USA	598,792
235	Gavin Coles, Australia	597,003
236	Tomohiro Kondo, Japan	592,763
237	Tag Ridings, USA	589,674
238	Ross McGowan, England	588,470
239	Mark Foster, England	578,530
240	Tommy Gainey, USA	576,691
241	Daisuke Maruyama, Japan	572,579
242	Magnus Carlsson, Sweden	571,282
243	Alejandro Canizares, Spain	566,169
244	Simon Wakefield, England	565,807

POS.	PLAYER, COUNTRY	TOTAL MONEY
245	Thomas Bjorn, Denmark	564,785
246	Simon Khan, England	559,846
247	Lee Dong-hwan, Korea	554,805
248	Frank Lickliter, USA	548,113
249	Todd Hamilton, USA	537,598
250	Pelle Edberg, Sweden	534,939
251	Shigeki Maruyama, Japan	534,601
252	Jarmo Sandelin, Sweden	533,661
253	Rafael Echenique, Argentina	526,773
254	Ricardo Gonzalez, Argentina	526,604
255	S.S.P. Chowrasia, India	525,427
256	Hiroshi Iwata, Japan	524,686
257	Jamie Donaldson, Wales	522,731
258	Y.E. Yang, Korea	518,455
259	Yasuharu Imano, Japan	517,233
260	Takao Nogami, Japan	505,800
261	Andrew McLardy, South Africa	504,435
262	Lee Janzen, USA	500,155
263	John Huston, USA	496,876
264	David Gleeson, Australia	490,344
265	Kaname Yokoo, Japan	490,322
266	Jon Mills, Canada	489,510
267	Chris Stroud, USA	486,233
268	Mark Hensby, Australia	480,483
269	Keiichiro Fukabori, Japan	480,386
270	Marcel Siem, Germany	477,014
271	Chapchai Nirat, Thailand	464,659
272	Arron Oberholser, USA	463,081
273	Greg Chalmers, Australia	461,681
274	Marco Dawson, Germany	460,902
275	Brandt Jobe, USA	459,287
276	Justin Bolli, USA	458,022
277	Gary Murphy, Ireland	457,517
278	Glen Day, USA	454,938
279	Mikko Ilonen, Finland	454,426
280	Michael Jonzon, Sweden	452,976
281	Steven Conran, Australia	452,713
282	Brett Rumford, Australia	452,414
283	Robert Rock, England	448,471
284	Matt Bettencourt, USA	447,863
285	Christian Cevaer, France	446,348
286	Roland Thatcher, USA	445,212
287	Jeff Maggert, USA	444,484
288	Harrison Frazar, USA	444,059
289	Bae Sang-moon, Korea	443,812
290	Brendon de Jonge, Zimbabwe	441,485
291	Paul Broadhurst, England	439,410
292	Casey Wittenberg, USA	439,234
293	Marc Warren, Scotland	437,721
294	Marcus Fraser, Australia	436,796
295	Alvero Velasco, Spain	436,384
296	Chris Riley, USA	433,932
297	Michio Matsumura, Japan	433,620

POS.	PLAYER, COUNTRY	TOTAL MONEY
298	Paul Waring, USA	424,442
299	Jarrod Lyle, Australia	418,266
300	Miles Tunnicliff, England	417,551
301	Philip Archer, England	412,441
302	Jeff Klauk, USA	407,418
303	Kiyoshi Miyazato, Japan	404,201
304	Thaworn Wiratchant, Thailand	399,740
305	Yusaku Miyazato, Japan	399,158
306	D.A. Points, USA	395,426
307	Benn Barham, England	394,339
308	Toyokazu Fujishima, Japan	389,475
309	Carlos Franco, Paraguay	385,261
310	Brenden Pappas, South Africa	384,072
311	Sam Little, England	381,589
312	Nick Flanagan, Australia	379,036
313	Chawalit Plaphol, Thailand	372,654
314	David Dixon, England	372,547
315	Michael Lorenzo-Vera, France	372,118
316	Noh Seung-yul, Korea	371,623
317	Jean Baptiste Gonnet, France	367,634
318	Craig Kanada, USA	363,597
319	Gareth Maybin, N. Ireland	362,008
320	Ryan Armour, USA	354,508
321	Omar Uresti, USA	351,100
322	Takuya Taniguchi, Japan	349,893
323	Colt Knost, USA	348,338
324	Kim Kyung-tae, Korea	345,710
325	Shiv Kapur, India	343,551
326	Bill Lunde, USA	341,446
327	Chad Collins, USA	339,959
328	Doug LaBelle, USA	337,963
329	Patrik Sjoland, Sweden	336,575
330	Greg Owen, England	335,910
331	Craig Parry, Australia	334,390
332	Billy Andrade, USA	330,157
333	Scott Piercy, USA	327,817
334	Darron Stiles, USA	326,602
335	David Horsey, England	326,595
336	Daniel Vancsik, Argentina	326,059
337	Bob Heintz, USA	325,051
338	Peter O'Malley, Australia	324,322
339	Michael Sim, Australia	321,394
340	Toru Suzuki, Japan	316,333
341	J.P. Hayes, USA	312,152
342	Thomas Aiken, South Africa	310,390
343	Fredrik Andersson Hed, Sweden	309,896
344	Akio Sadakata, Japan	308,229
345	Jeff Gove, USA	305,818
346	Kent Jones, USA	304,432
347	Lam Chih Bing, Singapore	302,993
348	Sushi Ishigaki, Japan	302,175
349	Garth Mulroy, South Africa	297,868
350	Francois Delamontagne, France	297,530

World Money List Leaders

YEAR	PLAYER, COUNTRY	TOTAL MONEY
1966	Jack Nicklaus, USA	$168,088
1967	Jack Nicklaus, USA	276,166
1968	Billy Casper, USA	222,436
1969	Frank Beard, USA	186,993
1970	Jack Nicklaus, USA	222,583
1971	Jack Nicklaus, USA	285,897
1972	Jack Nicklaus, USA	341,792
1973	Tom Weiskopf, USA	349,645
1974	Johnny Miller, USA	400,255
1975	Jack Nicklaus, USA	332,610
1976	Jack Nicklaus, USA	316,086
1977	Tom Watson, USA	358,034
1978	Tom Watson, USA	384,388
1979	Tom Watson, USA	506,912
1980	Tom Watson, USA	651,921
1981	Johnny Miller, USA	704,204
1982	Raymond Floyd, USA	738,699
1983	Seve Ballesteros, Spain	686,088
1984	Seve Ballesteros, Spain	688,047
1985	Bernhard Langer, Germany	860,262
1986	Greg Norman, Australia	1,146,584
1987	Ian Woosnam, Wales	1,793,268
1988	Seve Ballesteros, Spain	1,261,275
1989	David Frost, South Africa	1,650,230
1990	Jose Maria Olazabal, Spain	1,633,640
1991	Bernhard Langer, Germany	2,186,700
1992	Nick Faldo, England	2,748,248
1993	Nick Faldo, England	2,825,280
1994	Ernie Els, South Africa	2,862,854
1995	Corey Pavin, USA	2,746,340
1996	Colin Montgomerie, Scotland	3,071,442
1997	Colin Montgomerie, Scotland	3,366,900
1998	Tiger Woods, USA	2,927,946
1999	Tiger Woods, USA	7,681,625
2000	Tiger Woods, USA	11,034,530
2001	Tiger Woods, USA	7,771,562
2002	Tiger Woods, USA	8,292,188
2003	Vijay Singh, Fiji	8,499,611
2004	Vijay Singh, Fiji	11,638,699
2005	Tiger Woods, USA	12,280,404
2006	Tiger Woods, USA	13,325,949
2007	Tiger Woods, USA	12,902,706
2008	Vijay Singh, Fiji	8,025,128

Career World Money List

Here is a list of the 50 leading money winners for their careers through the 2008 season. It includes players active on both the regular and senior tours of the world. The World Money List from this and the 42 previous editions of the annual and a table prepared for a companion book, *The Wonderful World of Professional Golf* (Atheneum, 1973) form the basis for this compilation. Additional figures were taken from official records of major golf associations, although shortcomings in records-keeping outside the United States in the 1950s and 1960s and a few exclusions from U.S. records during those years prevent these figures from being completely accurate, although the careers of virtually all of these top 50 players began after that time. Conversion of foreign currency figures to U.S. dollars is based on average values during the particular years involved.

POS.	PLAYER, COUNTRY	TOTAL MONEY
1	Tiger Woods, USA	$100,358,213
2	Vijay Singh, Fiji	74,091,990
3	Ernie Els, South Africa	67,581,417
4	Phil Mickelson, USA	55,279,998
5	Jim Furyk, USA	46,700,059
6	Davis Love, USA	46,348,835
7	Colin Montgomerie, Scotland	40,286,553
8	Sergio Garcia, Spain	38,976,591
9	Padraig Harrington, Ireland	38,375,852
10	Retief Goosen, South Africa	37,733,466
11	Hale Irwin, USA	35,354,248
12	Bernhard Langer, Germany	33,313,580
13	Nick Price, Zimbabwe	32,995,434
14	David Toms, USA	30,946,767
15	Fred Couples, USA	30,668,852
16	Justin Leonard, USA	29,761,406
17	Kenny Perry, USA	29,622,178
18	Mark Calcavecchia, USA	28,388,363
19	Tom Kite, USA	28,015,571
20	Darren Clarke, N. Ireland	27,709,933
21	Stewart Cink, USA	27,390,979
22	Lee Westwood, England	26,948,123
23	Scott Hoch, USA	26,450,625
24	Stuart Appleby, Australia	26,414,144
25	Fred Funk, USA	26,283,278
26	Adam Scott, Australia	26,244,493
27	Mike Weir, Canada	26,161,280
28	Jose Maria Olazabal, Spain	26,142,717
29	Tom Lehman, USA	26,010,391
30	Jay Haas, USA	25,961,976
31	Gil Morgan, USA	25,860,831
32	Greg Norman, Australia	25,690,380
33	Robert Allenby, Australia	25,139,142
34	Chris DiMarco, USA	24,389,159
35	Tom Watson, USA	24,264,759
36	Loren Roberts, USA	23,356,997
37	Scott Verplank, USA	23,223,231

POS.	PLAYER, COUNTRY	TOTAL MONEY
38	Jeff Sluman, USA	23,121,273
39	K.J. Choi, South Korea	22,686,137
40	Mark O'Meara, USA	22,299,454
41	Masashi Ozaki, Japan	21,883,221
42	Miguel Angel Jimenez, Spain	21,509,258
43	Brad Faxon, USA	21,384,912
44	Craig Stadler, USA	21,167,770
45	Nick Faldo, England	20,670,137
46	Luke Donald, England	20,644,329
47	Raymond Floyd, USA	20,542,999
48	Larry Nelson, USA	20,381,021
49	Shigeki Maruyama, Japan	20,377,005
50	David Duval, USA	20,359,680

These 50 players have won $1,565,469,007 in their careers.

Women's World Money List

This list includes official earnings on the U.S. LPGA Tour, Ladies European Tour, Japan LPGA Tour and Ladies African Tour, along with other winnings in established unofficial events when reliable figures could be obtained.

POS.	PLAYER, COUNTRY	TOTAL MONEY
1	Lorena Ochoa, Mexico	$2,763,193
2	Ji-Yai Shin, Korea	2,175,460
3	Paula Creamer, USA	1,993,172
4	Annika Sorenstam, Sweden	1,923,591
5	Yani Tseng, Taiwan	1,783,336
6	Helen Alfredsson, Sweden	1,483,491
7	Suzann Pettersen, Norway	1,433,180
8	Seon Hwa Lee, Korea	1,218,544
9	Ji-Hee Lee, Korea	1,208,566
10	Miho Koga, Japan	1,208,541
11	Angela Stanford, USA	1,186,836
12	Inbee Park, Korea	1,169,620
13	Cristie Kerr, USA	1,160,922
14	Na Yeon Choi, Korea	1,127,009
15	Jeong Jang, Korea	1,111,347
16	Katherine Hull, Australia	1,106,565
17	Sakura Yokomine, Japan	1,095,712
18	Eun-Hee Ji, Korea	1,047,418
19	Yuri Fudoh, Japan	1,041,412
20	Song-Hee Kim, Korea	1,012,133
21	Akiko Fukushima, Japan	965,007
22	Momoko Ueda, Japan	952,184
23	Karrie Webb, Australia	943,206

POS.	PLAYER, COUNTRY	TOTAL MONEY
24	Mi-Jeong Jeon, Korea	908,507
25	Candie Kung, Taiwan	907,452
26	Angela Park, Brazil	883,218
27	Yuko Mitsuka, Japan	835,560
28	Hee-Won Han, Korea	826,679
29	Laura Diaz, USA	809,541
30	Jee Young Lee, Korea	795,991
31	Karen Stupples, England	778,519
32	In-Kyung Kim, Korea	773,956
33	Shiho Oyama, Japan	764,585
34	Eun-A Lim, Korea	752,438
35	Christina Kim, USA	730,681
36	Morgan Pressel, USA	711,261
37	Shinobu Moromizato, Japan	704,955
38	Hyun-Ju Shin, Korea	699,652
39	Sophie Gustafson, Sweden	692,503
40	Ai Miyazato, Japan	692,190
41	Sun Young Yoo, Korea	688,983
42	Ji Young Oh, Korea	680,225
43	Maria Hjorth, Sweden	664,287
44	Erina Hara, Japan	658,678
45	Nicole Castrale, USA	650,227
46	Bo-Bae Song, Korea	647,199
47	Ayako Uehara, Japan	633,080
48	Jane Park, USA	631,357
49	Brittany Lang, USA	630,294
50	Gwladys Nocera, France	600,031
51	Mayu Hattori, Japan	587,223
52	Miki Saiki, Japan	585,832
53	Meena Lee, Korea	553,090
54	Esther Lee, Korea	549,427
55	Hiromi Mogi, Japan	526,196
56	Akane Iijima, Japan	513,976
57	Teresa Lu, Taiwan	507,618
58	Catriona Matthew, Scotland	503,179
59	Maiko Wakabayashi, Japan	500,575
60	Minea Blomqvist, Finland	484,658
61	Ji-Woo Lee, Korea	476,327
62	Hee Young Park, Korea	474,744
63	Chie Arimura, Japan	473,500
64	Shanshan Feng, China	472,758
65	Stacy Prammanasudh, Thailand	470,612
66	Juli Inkster, USA	460,734
67	Midori Yoneyama, Japan	452,941
68	Lindsey Wright, Australia	447,060
69	Yukari Baba, Japan	441,398
70	Leta Lindley, USA	439,213
71	Mi Hyun Kim, Korea	438,571
72	Hiroko Yamaguchi, Japan	428,472
73	Giulia Sergas, Italy	417,554
74	Kristy McPherson, USA	407,237
75	Louise Friberg, Sweden	406,102
76	Se Ri Pak, Korea	397,393

POS.	PLAYER, COUNTRY	TOTAL MONEY
77	Young Kim, Korea	393,468
78	Allison Fouch, USA	375,345
79	Jimin Kang, Korea	373,365
80	Rui Kitada, Japan	363,442
81	Yun-Jye Wei, Taiwan	357,587
82	Amy Yang, Korea	352,310
83	Martina Eberl, Germany	346,983
84	Jin Joo Hong, Korea	339,534
85	Laura Davies, England	336,636
86	Carin Koch, Sweden	331,667
87	Nikki Campbell, Australia	322,473
88	Natalie Gulbis, USA	318,320
89	Saiki Fujita, Japan	317,195
90	Shi Hyun Ahn, Korea	303,126
91	Anja Monke, Germany	301,092
92	Lotta Wahlin, Sweden	286,706
93	Mie Nakata, Japan	283,290
94	Rebecca Hudson, England	274,468
95	Pat Hurst, USA	271,423
96	Jennifer Rosales, Philippines	268,185
97	Dorothy Delasin, Philippines	260,710
98	H.J. Choi, Korea	259,071
99	Yuko Saitoh, Japan	258,726
100	Paula Marti, Spain	257,641
101	So-Hee Kim, Korea	248,914
102	Diana D'Alessio, USA	244,970
103	Becky Morgan, Wales	237,338
104	Namika Omata, Japan	237,071
105	Michele Redman, USA	234,907
106	Jill McGill, USA	233,792
107	Wendy Ward, USA	229,092
108	Na Zhang, China	225,177
109	Lisa Hall, England	224,415
110	Il Mi Chung, Korea	220,513
111	Tania Elosegui, Spain	213,962
112	Janice Moodie, Scotland	213,074
113	Alena Sharp, Canada	212,458
114	Kaori Higo, Japan	208,074
115	Becky Brewerton, Wales	207,688
116	Yasuko Satoh, Japan	202,728
117	Mayumi Shimomura, Japan	198,578
118	Anne-Lise Caudal, France	198,429
119	Melissa Reid, England	198,141
120	Keiko Sasaki, Japan	195,391
121	Rachel Hetherington, Australia	191,169
122	Heather Young, USA	188,218
123	Michiko Hattori, Japan	186,976
124	Julie Lu, Taiwan	185,137
125	Marianne Skarpnord, Norway	183,477
126	Yui Kawahara, Japan	183,032
127	Ah-Reum Hwang, Korea	182,830
128	Sandra Gal, Germany	181,162
129	Katie Futcher, USA	176,792

POS.	PLAYER, COUNTRY	TOTAL MONEY
130	Irene Cho, USA	176,787
131	Karine Icher, France	176,419
132	Linda Wessberg, Sweden	175,357
133	Kim Hall, USA	175,235
134	Junko Omote, Japan	168,659
135	Veronica Zorzi, Italy	167,993
136	Kyeong Bae, Korea	166,095
137	Mikiyo Nishizuka, Japan	166,013
138	Hiromi Takesue, Japan	165,200
139	Nina Reis, Sweden	162,045
140	Yuki Ichinose, Japan	159,215
141	Kuniko Maeda, Japan	157,080
142	Yayoi Arasaki, Japan	153,980
143	Trish Johnson, England	153,367
144	Soo-Yun Kang, Korea	152,817
145	Michie Ohba, Japan	152,471
146	Joanne Mills, Australia	151,087
147	Johanna Head, England	151,081
148	Mayumi Nakajima, Japan	149,603
149	Ya-Huei Lu, Taiwan	146,730
150	Na On Min, Korea	146,643

Senior World Money List

This list includes official earnings from the world money list of the International Federation of PGA Tours, U.S. Senior PGA Tour, European Seniors Tour and Japan Senior Tour, along with other winnings in established unofficial events when reliable figures could be obtained.

POS.	PLAYER, COUNTRY	TOTAL MONEY
1	Bernhard Langer, Germany	$2,469,032
2	Fred Funk, USA	2,150,714
3	Jay Haas, USA	1,991,726
4	Scott Hoch, USA	1,873,915
5	Jeff Sluman, USA	1,833,443
6	John Cook, USA	1,824,238
7	Loren Roberts, USA	1,674,939
8	Eduardo Romero, Argentina	1,628,021
9	Andy Bean, USA	1,506,789
10	Nick Price, Zimbabwe	1,377,164
11	Tom Kite, USA	1,374,592
12	Lonnie Nielsen, USA	1,224,012
13	Scott Simpson, USA	1,152,226
14	Brad Bryant, USA	1,128,413
15	Mark McNulty, Zimbabwe	1,128,272
16	Denis Watson, Zimbabwe	1,112,580
17	Mark Wiebe, USA	1,061,949

POS.	PLAYER, COUNTRY	TOTAL MONEY
18	D.A. Weibring, USA	1,059,197
19	Gene Jones, USA	1,022,061
20	Tom Watson, USA	977,908
21	Greg Norman, Australia	975,139
22	R.W. Eaks, USA	942,316
23	Tom Jenkins, USA	900,932
24	Bruce Vaughan, USA	832,595
25	Keith Fergus, USA	822,151
26	Joey Sindelar, USA	817,684
27	Craig Stadler, USA	795,732
28	Tim Simpson, USA	782,641
29	David Eger, USA	749,087
30	Joe Ozaki, Japan	713,725
31	Mike Goodes, USA	676,084
32	Bob Gilder, USA	657,283
33	Ian Woosnam, Wales	636,253
34	Tom Purtzer, USA	588,252
35	Gil Morgan, USA	580,406
36	Mark O'Meara, USA	571,588
37	Fulton Allem, South Africa	557,710
38	Dana Quigley, USA	510,195
39	Jim Thorpe, USA	508,332
40	Ben Crenshaw, USA	503,362
41	Morris Hatalsky, USA	493,542
42	Jerry Pate, USA	481,879
43	Bruce Fleisher, USA	477,256
44	Bobby Wadkins, USA	473,499
45	Hajime Meshiai, Japan	466,396
46	Fuzzy Zoeller, USA	463,019
47	Tsukasa Watanabe, Japan	447,530
48	Allen Doyle, USA	441,235
49	Don Pooley, USA	439,866
50	Takashi Miyoshi, Japan	432,993
51	David Edwards, USA	430,974
52	Vicente Fernandez, Argentina	424,075
53	Larry Nelson, USA	423,461
54	Tsuneyuki Nakajima, Japan	417,636
55	Kiyoshi Murota, Japan	395,729
56	Phil Blackmar, USA	383,547
57	Gary Hallberg, USA	382,924
58	Tom McKnight, USA	375,379
59	Gordon J. Brand, England	361,764
60	Dan Forsman, USA	359,631
61	Mark James, England	347,827
62	Hale Irwin, USA	331,447
63	Ron Streck, USA	328,612
64	Mike Reid, USA	324,901
65	Gary Koch, USA	320,629
66	Tateo Ozaki, Japan	309,732
67	John Morse, USA	303,321
68	Peter Mitchell, England	302,308
69	Chip Beck, USA	295,544
70	Sandy Lyle, Scotland	291,530
71	Juan Quiros, Spain	288,108

POS.	PLAYER, COUNTRY	TOTAL MONEY
72	Des Smyth, Ireland	284,786
73	Walter Hall, USA	283,327
74	Bruce Lietzke, USA	277,048
75	Curtis Strange, USA	276,505
76	Larry Mize, USA	275,563
77	Wayne Grady, Australia	270,417
78	John Harris, USA	268,182
79	Masahiro Kuramoto, Japan	259,368
80	Bill Longmuir, Scotland	246,076
81	Nick Job, England	240,129
82	Andy North, USA	230,780
83	Costantino Rocca, Italy	224,616
84	Sam Torrance, Scotland	218,957
85	Carl Mason, England	217,415
86	Katsuyoshi Tomori, Japan	213,595
87	Ronnie Black, USA	212,263
88	Hisashi Nakase, Japan	204,330
89	Katsunari Takahashi, Japan	194,048
90	Mike Hulbert, USA	187,531
91	Kirk Hanefeld, USA	183,747
92	Angel Franco, Paraguay	174,027
93	Domingo Hospital, Spain	173,277
94	Wayne Levi, USA	171,878
95	Dave Stockton, USA	170,040
96	Tony Johnstone, Zimbabwe	165,285
97	Jerry Bruner, USA	164,775
98	James Mason, USA	160,009
99	Boonchu Ruangkit, Thailand	158,699
100	Leonard Thompson, USA	156,827
101	Bob Cameron, England	154,907
102	Luis Carbonetti, Argentina	153,249
103	Ross Drummond, Scotland	147,817
104	Eamonn Darcy, Ireland	146,828
105	Jose Rivero, Spain	144,354
106	Stewart Ginn, Australia	142,090
107	Donnie Hammond, USA	142,003
108	Seiji Ebihara, Japan	137,657
109	Dave Eichelberger, USA	136,643
110	Mike McCullough, USA	135,995
111	Peter Jacobsen, USA	130,476
112	David Merriman, Australia	129,866
113	Gary McCord, USA	129,712
114	Isao Aoki, Japan	127,759
115	Bob Boyd, USA	126,924
116	Rod Spittle, Canada	117,447
117	Tomohiro Maruyama, Japan	114,202
118	Angel Fernandez, Chile	113,417
119	John Chillas, Scotland	113,146
120	Gohei Sato, Japan	112,102
121	Pete Oakley, USA	111,864
122	Denis O'Sullivan, Ireland	111,176
123	Nick Faldo, England	107,000
124	Masami Ito, Japan	106,129
125	Giuseppe Cali, Italy	103,424

1. The Year in Retrospect

Tiger Woods never said winning the Grand Slam would be easy, rather that winning all four majors in the same calendar year was "easily within reason." And with those words, the 2008 season was launched amid high hopes and great expectations, because Woods had spent the better part of a decade doing things that few imagined possible. For reasons no one saw coming, he delivered another amazing chapter that was part fiction and part fantasy, a mixture of tragedy and triumph and, as always, loaded with action and drama.

The record Woods compiled was outstanding by any standards but his. He won 71 percent of the tournaments he played. He never finished worse than fifth place. He won the U.S. Open and joined Jack Nicklaus as the only players to win the career Grand Slam three times over. But what made this year so memorable was not the high rate of winning but the short time he played. Woods took two months off after the Masters to recover from one knee surgery, won the U.S. Open with what amounted to a broken leg, then had reconstructive surgery on his left knee that ended his season in June. He still managed to win five of the seven tournaments he played, the exceptions a runner-up finish at the Masters and fifth place in the WGC - CA Championship.

The only player judged to have a better year was Padraig Harrington by winning the British Open and PGA Championship, the first European to win successive majors in the same season. But even after Harrington was honored as the PGA Tour Player of the Year, he couldn't help but wonder if the vote was based in part on expectations.

"If I had done what Tiger had done this year, I would have won Player of the Year, if you can understand what I'm saying," Harrington said. "It's the baggage he brought into the year and the fact that he is as talented as he is and has done as well as he has that would lead players to look to somebody like myself, who has had an exceptional year. So I think in some ways, the fact that I had an exceptional year has swayed the vote toward me, whereas Tiger's phenomenal year is just what we're used to with Tiger Woods. He tends to have phenomenal years every year."

This was a phenomenal year for only six months, and that might be the best way to size up 2008 — two years in one.

The first was almost entirely devoted to Woods, who played at such a high level that even he conceded it was the best stretch of golf he had ever played. There was even discussion about a perfect season, which was ludicrous to consider except that he kept winning. The winning streak stretched to seven tournaments over seven months, including his Target World Challenge and the Dubai Desert Classic. Turns out that Grand Slam was not easily within reason, for even playing all four majors proved to be too much. It's a wonder Woods even made it through the U.S. Open, for only at year's end did he disclose a left knee so swollen that he couldn't see his knee cap.

The second half of the season became an audition to see who would fill the void left by the world's No. 1 player. Harrington wasted no time at the Open Championship by matching Woods's feat of winning golf's oldest championship in successive years. Woods had won at St. Andrews and Royal Liverpool, while Harrington carved out consecutive entries on the claret jug with victories at Carnoustie and Royal Birkdale. It had been more than a century since a European won the Open in consecutive years, and the Irishman was in a European class by himself by winning the PGA Championship. He was becoming a forgotten figure at Oakland Hills, five over par after two rounds, until a 66-66 finish that broke Sergio Garcia's heart (again).

Harrington owned the majors, but not the spotlight during the second half of the year. Anthony Kim lived up to so much talk about his potential with his second victory of the year in the AT&T National at Congressional; Camilo Villegas helped renew focus on youth when the 26-year-old Colombian won the final two tournaments of the PGA Tour Playoffs for the FedExCup, holding off Kim and Jim Furyk at the BMW Championship, then beating Garcia in a playoff at The Tour Championship. Garcia was a runner-up four times, but he ended a three-year victory drought by winning — in a playoff, of course — at The Players Championship. Vijay Singh also cashed in on Woods's absence, winning the first two FedExCup playoff events and building such an insurmountable lead in the points race that he only needed to walk 18 holes a day and sign for the correct score to take home the $10 million bonus.

While Harrington, Kim, Villegas, Garcia and Singh took center stage, equally noteworthy in the second half of the season where those who were reduced to understudies. Phil Mickelson was No. 2 in the world and seemingly poised to take advantage of Woods recovering from season-ending knee surgery. Despite his 35 victories on the PGA Tour and his three majors, Mickelson had never been No. 1 in the World Ranking, won a Vardon Trophy, a PGA Tour money title nor was voted Player of the Year. He is still waiting.

Mickelson only came close to winning twice, at the WGC - Bridgestone Invitational and The Tour Championship, both times done in by his putting. He missed a 20-foot birdie putt at East Lake to join a playoff at The Tour Championship, and with it lost out in the Vardon Trophy race to Garcia. Ernie Els raised hopes with his victory at the Honda Classic, his first title on U.S. soil in four years, but didn't won another. Jim Furyk failed to win a single tournament; not since 1997 had he failed to hoist a trophy when playing an entire season without injury.

Indeed, this was a year of change. It became a buzzword during the marathon U.S. presidential election, and it was true in golf. Players such as Els, Mickelson, Furyk and even Davis Love, who slipped out of the top 200 in the World Ranking until making a late charge and winning at Disney, suddenly began to look older compared with Kim, Villegas, Garcia and Hunter Mahan, a key American player in the Ryder Cup. Adding to the change was Robert Karlsson, becoming the first Swede to capture the Order of Merit on the European Tour.

Woods noticed it from the comforts of his couch. He was duly impressed with Harrington winning two majors, but the youth really caught his attention. "The way they've played this year, with Anthony and Camilo and Sergio, they've all played well, and it's that generation right behind me. You have the older generation right ahead of me with Phil and Ernie and Furyk. Vijay is one step ahead of that. My generation, guys didn't really do a lot, just because of timing or who knows? But the generation right behind, they're just hitting their stride now."

But at the start of the year, it looked as though nothing had changed. Tiger Woods was still playing, and playing better than ever.

Woods began his 12th full season on the PGA Tour with expectations larger than ever. The only difference is that he created them with a comment on his website when he was asked about the possibility of a Grand Slam. "I think it's easily within reason," he said. This was the same player who in 1997 had said the Grand Slam was a matter of winning the right four tournaments, but at the end of that year said even getting into contention at the four majors was difficult. The renewed confidence came from having done just that. In his previous 12 majors, Woods won five of them and finished among the top five in all but two. Plus, he had ended the 2007 season by winning five of his last six tournaments, the exception a runner-up finish in the Deutsche Bank Championship. Even more telling was swing coach Hank Haney shedding some light on how hard Woods had been working in the off-season. "It's the first time he didn't go skiing," Haney said.

For the fourth straight year, Woods began his season at the Buick Invitational at Torrey Pines, which would host the U.S. Open later in the summer. He opened with 67 on the tough South Course, two strokes out of the lead. A caddie from the group ahead stood behind the 18th green to watch Woods finish and had seen enough. "He just won two tournaments with one round," said the caddie, alluding to the U.S. Open. One round on the North Course later, Woods already had a four-shot lead and the Buick Invitational had become a formality. He stretched the lead to eight shots on Saturday, his eventual margin of victory over Ryuji Imada, who said of his runner-up finish to Woods: "That's almost like winning the tournament." Woods said he was hitting the ball better than he did in 2000, when he won nine times and the final three majors. Finally, people were starting to believe him, and two trips to the desert did little to change anyone's mind.

The first one took place eight times zone away in Dubai, and Woods started the final round four shots out of the lead. Starting with a chip-in for birdie from thick rough, Woods ran off five birdies over his last seven holes for a 65. His approach to the par-five 18th went over the green, and his chip was well short, some 25 feet above the cup. The putt was picking up speed when it disappeared, and Woods punched the air to celebrate his largest comeback in eight years.

The next stop was the high desert of Arizona for the WGC - Accenture Match Play Championship, and it looked as though it would be a short week. Woods faced big-hitting J.B. Holmes in the opening round and was headed toward defeat, trailing by three holes with five to play and unable to rely on his power to intimidate. Then came a birdie on the 14th hole, a mistake by Holmes, and a 20-foot birdie by Woods on the 16th hole to square the match. Holmes was helpless, and Woods all but finished him off with a 35-foot eagle putt on the 17th. He played the second nine in 30 for a 1-up victory. "You're playing the best player in the world, 3 up with five to play," Holmes said. "I just said, 'Don't do anything stupid. Make him beat you.' And he did. What do you do?"

Woods had one other close call against Aaron Baddeley, who twice had putts to win the match on the 18th and 19th holes before Woods put him away with a 13-foot birdie on the 20th hole. The 36-hole final against Stewart Cink felt like the shortest match of all. Woods made 14 birdies in 29 holes, and his 8-and-7 victory was the largest margin in the championship match in the 10-year history of the tournament. "I think maybe we ought to slice him open to see what's inside — maybe nuts and bolts," Cink said.

Woods surpassed Arnold Palmer on the PGA Tour career victory charts with No. 63, and he headed for Bay Hill to perform for the King amid increasing chatter of a perfect season. It was a ludicrous notion, especially in golf, and even Woods pointed out that the difference between playing 16 holes or 117 holes at the Accenture Match Play Championship could have been one putt. Even so, he was 3-for-3 on the season and becoming more dominant by the week.

He once captured the title at the Arnold Palmer Invitational four straight years, but he had gone the next four years failing to crack the top 20 at Palmer's place. Woods shot 66 on a wild Saturday atop the leaderboard that put him in a five-way tie for the lead going into the final round, and he endured an unlikely challenge from Bart Bryant. Woods three-putted for bogey from 10 feet on the 10th hole to fall into a tie, and he never regained the lead until the 18th hole, when he hit a five iron from 164 yards into a stiff breeze to 25 feet. Bryant was in the scoring trailer, waiting to see if there would be a playoff.

Palmer was watching from the side of the green, a glint in his eye indicating he already knew the outcome. The putt was true, but the reaction from Woods was one of his strongest yet. He turned and slammed his cap to the ground, so caught up in the moment that he was puzzled when caddie Steve Williams handed back his cap. Woods said he didn't remember ever taking it off. Bryant never saw the putt. "I heard a big cheer, and I got up and left," he said. "That's why he's Tiger Woods." He had won seven in a row heading to Doral, where Woods was the three-time defending champion. But the Blue Monster delivered a dose of reality, and in a rain-delayed finish on Monday, Woods had to settle for fifth place behind Geoff Ogilvy. It was the end of a streak, right as the majors — the start of a Grand Slam he said was "easily within reason" — were about to begin.

The putts that Woods couldn't seem to miss during the first three months of the season stopped falling at Augusta National, and he was six shots behind going into the final round. Poised for a charge, Woods again failed to take advantage of birdie opportunities and had to settle for a runner-up finish to Trevor Immelman by three shots. The biggest shock came two days after the Masters, when Woods announced he had arthroscopic surgery on his left knee to repair cartilage damage. It was his second operation in five years on that knee, although he was expected to recover in time for the U.S. Open, if not sooner.

Only later did Woods reveal that he suffered a double stress fracture in his left leg while trying to get ready for the Memorial, and that it became a struggle to walk to the bathroom. Doctors said he would need to spend three weeks on crutches, followed by three weeks of rest to let it heal. Hank Haney, his swing coach, was with him that day and saw Woods's resolve. He told the doctor he was playing in the U.S. Open and he was going to win. "And then he started putting on his shoes," Haney said. "He looked at me and said, 'Come on, Hank. We'll just putt today.' He was not going to miss the U.S. Open at Torrey Pines. There just wasn't any discussion."

He played the U.S. Open, and he won. Never mind that lightning bolts of pain shot through his leg unannounced, causing him to wince and stagger, sometimes buckling over and then using the club as a cane. Or that he made four double bogeys during the week, three of them on the opening holes at Torrey Pines. Or that he twice stood over a birdie putt on the 18th green, one from 12 feet in regulation, the other from four feet in the playoff, knowing that if he missed, he would lose the U.S. Open. And perhaps the most amazing part of this victory is that Woods had not walked 18 holes of golf since the final round of the Masters until teeing it up Thursday at the U.S. Open. He wasn't sure he could make 72 holes, and he ended up walking 91 holes — with enough strength left to walk away with a trophy. "I think this is the best ever," Woods said of his 14 majors. "All things considered, I don't know how I ended up in this position, to be honest with you."

Woods missed the first of what turned out to be six title defenses in 2008 at the Wachovia Championship. He missed The Players Championship for the first time in his career. Those two months away from golf proved to be the first window of opportunity for other players to shine, and the first three players to emerge were Anthony Kim, Sergio Garcia and Kenny Perry.

Kim made his PGA Tour debut in the fall of 2006 by tying for second in the Valero Texas Open, and while the street-smart kid from Los Angeles easily made it through the qualifying tournament and retained his tour card with little effort, that became the glaring problem for someone who seemed to have unlimited potential. He spent more time at parties than on the practice range and was on the verge of wasting his talent until a fortuitous meeting with Mark O'Meara during the challenge season. O'Meara, who served as a big brother to Woods when he turned pro, talked to Kim about what it takes to succeed and what it means to be a professional.

The message came through, and Kim showed renewed dedication. He tied for third at the Bob Hope Chrysler Classic, then showed some maturity when he narrowly failed to qualify for the Accenture Match Play Championship. Kim traveled to Arizona as the first alternate, knowing odds were long he would get into the 64-man field. And in the first tournament Woods failed to play after the first knee surgery, Kim blew away a strong field at Quail Hollow to win the Wachovia Championship by five shots for his first victory. He was 22 years of age and determined not to stop there.

Woods pays close attention to everyone, especially those coming up behind him, and such was the case with Kim. During a practice round at the 2007 PGA Championship at Southern Hills, while waiting on the sixth tee for the green to clear, Woods turned and asked out of the blue, "What do you think of Anthony Kim?" Perhaps it was only fitting that Kim stamped his arrival by winning the AT&T National, which Woods hosts at Congressional. Woods was still home in Florida recovering from his second knee surgery when Kim closed with 65 to become the first American under 25 since Woods to win twice in the same season.

There is a flashy side to Kim that Woods never embraced himself, such as the gaudy belt buckles with the initials "AK" that he talks about more than his game. But he is fearless, sets no limits on himself, and appears to appreciate the importance of hard work. Before accepting the trophy, Kim was all smiles with a cell phone plugged into his ear to speak to the tournament host. "He told me to just keep working hard and keep it up, and the sky's the limit, and there's no reason to stop now," Kim said. "I idolized him growing up."

Kim didn't win again the rest of the year, although he challenged for his first major championship at Royal Birkdale, where he tied for seventh, and he had top threes in the final FedExCup playoff events. What made him the most promising young player was the Ryder Cup, where his infectious enthusiasm and fearless play made him the emotional leader of a winning U.S. team. His defining moment was the leadoff singles match against Garcia, a pivotal match for the Americans. On the opening hole, Kim and Garcia each hit their approach shots to about two feet. Walking up to the green, Garcia, a veteran of five Ryder Cups, looked over at Kim and suggested they concede the tap-ins. "Good, good?" Garcia said. "Let's putt them," Kim replied. The tone was set, and Kim was so intent on burying the Spaniard that when the match ended on the 14th hole, 5 and 4, Kim headed for the next tee, unaware that he had won. By year's end, Woods had invited Kim to fill in for him at a corporate clinic.

Kim didn't enjoy the only breakthrough moment at Congressional. Not far from where the likes to Mark McGwire and Roger Clemens testified on performance-enhancing drugs, Tim Clark made PGA Tour history after the first round of the AT&T National when he became the first player to submit a urine sample as part of golf's drug testing program. Drug testing turned into a global effort, endorsed by the World Golf Foundation to encompass the major tours around the world. The PGA Tour spent the first six months educating its players on the list of banned substances, the process and appeals and the penalties. It was met by great resistance during a mandatory meeting at Torrey Pines, mainly from veterans who felt testing was not necessary and the process was humiliating. Charles Howell was among those tested on the first day, and it took some 40 minutes because he was dehydrated from his five-hour round. "I hope Gatorade Tiger passes the test, because I put two bottles in me," Howell quipped. By the end of the year, PGA Tour spokesman Ty Votaw said the fact that the tour made no announcements on a positive test was a pretty good indication that golf tested clean this year. But it did test, and Perry was most annoyed when his name came up twice in three months during random selection.

Perry turned 48 this year, with gray showing up in his hair and a paunch indicating he was closer to the Champions Tour than being any kind of a threat against players half his age. He had not won the previous two years while dealing with nagging injuries that accompany age, and there was no reason to expect anything from him in 2008 except for an exhibition on the calendar called the Ryder Cup, to be played for the first time in his native state of Kentucky. Even as he wiped off mud from his clubs and rust from his game in Honolulu, Perry couldn't stop talking about the Ryder Cup. It was a long shot at his age, but in this respect, few players rose to such an occasion.

There were signs at The Players Championship, when he started the final round one shot out of the lead until shooting 80, and at the AT&T Classic in Atlanta, where he lost in a playoff when his approach to the par-five 18th caromed off a tree and into the water. Perry finally delivered by winning the Memorial, joining Woods as the only three-time winners at Muirfield Village. That sent him on his way toward an unlikely spot on the Ryder Cup team, and he all but clinched it a month later by winning the Buick Open. Two weeks later, Perry won for the third time this season — only Woods won more tournaments in 2008 — in a three-man playoff at the John Deere Classic.

As much attention as he received from where he won, Perry received more for where he didn't even play. After his two-shot victory at the Memorial, he declined to go through U.S. Open qualifying because he didn't want to wear himself out in his pursuit of a Ryder Cup berth. He earned a spot in the British Open through his three victories, but instead of competing in his first major of the year, he played that week in the U.S. Bank Championship in Milwaukee against a field that resembled a Nationwide Tour major. A feel-good story turned sour quickly, as players and the press roasted Perry for skipping one major and being unwilling to qualify for another, especially as great as he was playing. "For 22 years, nobody cared where I was playing," Perry said as he tried to brush off the criticism.

He was stung, but he bit back. Perry wound up playing exactly one round in the majors this year after he had to withdraw from the PGA Championship with an eye injury, but he still made the Ryder Cup team with ease. Perry had played in only one Ryder Cup, losing both matches at Oakland Hills in 2004, and as the matches drew near, he wondered what he was getting himself into. Especially with Woods not around, Perry was becoming the focus of this American team at Valhalla, and he knew it. In the weeks leading up to the matches, he talked about the pressure he had put on himself, after a career in which he often ran from the spotlight. "This is the pinnacle of my career," said a player with 12 victories. "I'm either going to be a hero or goat in the state of Kentucky. I've got way too much at stake for me going out there and playing poorly. I've got to find a way to execute and win matches. That will brand me for the rest of my life."

So what happened in his opening match? He missed a five-foot putt on the 17th hole to win the match, then drove into the water on the 18th hole that allowed Europe to escape with a halve. Perry plugged on, however, splitting his matches on Saturday and then beating Henrik Stenson in Sunday singles, despite feeling pain so severe that he thought his left arm was going to fall off. Perry clinched victory on the 16th green, and in one of the most poignant moments at Valhalla, his 82-year-old father, wearing denim overalls, embraced him on the green. "I figured this was going to define my career," Perry said. "But you know what? It made my career."

Garcia's career remains a work in progress. At the end of year, when Jim Furyk was asked about the host of young challengers to Woods and Garcia's name was mentioned, Furyk sarcastically replied, "Sergio is still in his 20s? Really? When did he start, when he was 12?" It only seems that way because the 28-year-old Spaniard has been so good for so long, and despite never winning a major, he always seems to be part of the mix. Garcia was 19 when he tried to chase down Woods at Medinah in 1999, coming up one shot short in the PGA Championship. He was in the final group with Woods at the 2002 U.S. Open at Bethpage Black, again at Hoylake in the 2006 British Open.

When Woods was out of the picture, Garcia was primed to win at Carnoustie until Harrington beat him in a playoff. And at 28, he already had played in the Ryder Cup five times. That's why it was so hard to believe that he had gone three years and 53 starts on the PGA Tour without winning, and there was scant evidence that would change anytime soon the way he played the first four months of the year. He opened with a tie for seventh in the Qatar Masters, but that was his only top 10. Even more troubling was that he missed the cut in the Masters, the second straight major he had failed to finish. All that changed at The Players Championship.

Typical of his game, he hit the ball better than anyone on the Stadium Course at TPC Sawgrass, only for his putter to hold him back. Tied for the lead late in the third round, he three-putted from 10 feet on the island green 17th, then bogeyed the 18th to fall three shots behind. But he hung around an unlikely leader, Paul Goydos, throughout the final round and never lost hope. Garcia's fortunes turned on the 14th when he rolled in a 45-foot birdie putt for a two-shot swing, then calmly sunk a nervy three-foot par putt on the 17th hole in regulation to stay one shot behind. Standing over a seven-foot par putt on the 18th hole, the kind he has routinely missed, Garcia poured this one in the heart to force a playoff.

Trying to build drama into its major, the PGA Tour opted to start the playoff on the scariest par-three in golf, and Goydos's nine iron to the island came up short enough to splash. Garcia found the green and won the next best thing to a major, which proved to be a major breakthrough for his psyche. Even in the glow of victory, when asked the best thing about winning against the strongest field assembled in golf, Garcia replied: "Not having to listen to you guys." He is ultra sensitive when quizzed about his putting problems, and he felt this was the start of him answering his critics. He had no argument from Goydos, who said: "He's right there on the precipice of great things."

And yet, that's where Garcia stayed — on the precipice. He won twice more in 2008, at the Castello Masters on his home course in Spain and at the HSBC Champions to start Europe's 2009 schedule. But despite his biggest victory on the PGA Tour, his year was marked more by close calls than trophy presentations. He had the lead making the turn in the final round of the PGA Championship, but had to settle for another runner-up finish in a major — to Harrington for the second straight year — when he hit into water on the 16th, missed a four-foot birdie putt on the 17th to fall one shot behind, and could only watch as Harrington holed his 15-foot par putt on the 18th hole to secure victory at Oakland Hills. Two weeks later, he looked like a winner at The Barclays to kick off the FedExCup Playoffs when he drained a 30-foot birdie putt on the first extra hole, only to see Singh make one from about the same length to match him. Garcia found trouble off the tee on the second playoff hole and Singh beat him with a birdie. Then came another playoff loss in the FedExCup finale at The Tour Championship, missing a 20-foot birdie putt for the victory on the 18th hole in regulation, then taking three shots to reach the green on the par-three 18th in the playoff, losing to Camilo Villegas.

Garcia had three victories, but was a runner-up four times. And he remained the best player without a major, with little debate. The only down was the Ryder Cup. Garcia went into Valhalla with a 14-4-2 record, including an 8-0 record in foursomes. But he failed to win a match, sat out a session for the first time in his career, and lost in Sunday singles for the fourth time in five matches.

Even so, Garcia was impossible to ignore, and his steady play took him up to a career-best No. 2 in the World Ranking at the end of the year, making him the top threat to Woods's reign. "I think the next goal is trying to win a major," Garcia said. "Attacking No. 1 probably depends a little bit on how much he (Woods) takes off and if I keep playing well. It's possible, mainly because he's been injured. But we know that as soon as he comes out, he's going to play well and he's going to become quite tough, and he seems to get away from us a little bit. But ... I've never been this close to No. 1, and it's exciting to be there."

Villegas was thrilled to be mentioned in the same breath with other young stars. He was a marketing dream, with his ripped physique and the looks of a young man who looked natural on the cover of a fashion magazine. Villegas was best known for his "Spider-Man" pose on the greens when reading putts, contorting his body horizontal to the ground to read the line, moving as nimble as a cat. But he rarely was a threat to win, and even though he tied for fourth in the PGA Championship, Villegas was not in serious contention.

Stealing a page from Singh, Villegas tried to convince himself that he was among the best putters in golf. And for the final two weeks of the season, he looked like it. Despite a four-putt double bogey in the second round and missing three straight putts inside eight feet in the final round of the BMW Championship at Bellerive Country Club in St. Louis, Villegas closed with 68 for a two-shot victory, his first on the PGA Tour. For an encore, Villegas overcame a five-shot deficit in the final round by making six birdies over the final 11 holes for a four-under 66 in The Tour Championship at East Lake, then beating Garcia with a par in the playoff.

Suddenly, the Colombian was no longer mentioned with Anna Kournikova, instead joining a list of Kim and Garcia as the future of golf. "You can see it two different ways," Villegas said. "My third year on tour, I mean, yes, it took me a little bit longer to win than some guys thought it should have. But at the same time, I look at it right now and I think it's perfect timing. I got better and better every year, and that will be the same goal for next year. I've got a great challenge in front of me. I'll be very excited to just work hard for it."

Hard work has been the hallmark of Singh's career, but there was evidence that his 45-year-old body was breaking down. If it wasn't the nagging injuries, from his shoulder to tendonitis in his left arm, it was the inability to close out victories they way he had routinely done in becoming the PGA Tour's most prolific foreign-born champion. Sometimes, it was simply shocking. Singh was coasting to victory at the AT&T Pebble Beach National Pro-Am, leading by three shots with a sand wedge in his hand from the fairway on the par-five 14th hole. He turned that opportunity into a bogey, made another bogey from the middle of the 15th fairway, bogeyed the 16th from a fairway bunker, and only managed to force a playoff with Steve Lowery with an eight-foot par on the 17th and a birdie on the par-five 18th. Order seemingly restored, Singh promptly found a fairway bunker and lost to a birdie by Lowery, who had not won in seven years. That was Singh's best chance at winning for five months. If his name was found on the leaderboard Sunday, it was a late charge when the tournament was out of reach. And when he missed the cut at the Open Championship, he fell to No. 15 in the World Ranking.

Over the next two months, wearing a wrap on his left arm, Singh suddenly looked as good as new. He captured the PGA Tour money title for the third time in six years, won the FedExCup and its $10 million prize, finished the year with three PGA Tour victories and ended the season at No. 5 in the World Ranking. And the big Fijian might owe it all to a three-and-a-half foot putt at Firestone Country Club.

Singh started the final round of the Bridgestone Invitational in a three-way tie with Mickelson and Lee Westwood, each of whom seemed to seize control at some point during the way. Singh was shaky with the putter, missing 10 times between four and eight feet during the tournament, unable to make anything down the stretch. But he stayed in the lead with a five-foot par on the 17th, and needed only to two-putt from 30 feet on the final hole to capture his first World Golf Championship. Just his luck, he left it three-and-a-half feet short, the length that had haunted him much of the week, if not the year. The ball caught enough of the cup to swirl around the edge and fall, and Singh raised his arms more in relief than celebration for a 32nd victory that moved him ahead of Harry "Lighthorse" Cooper on the all-time list of foreign-born players.

"It puts me in a really good frame of mind going into next week and the rest of the season," Singh said. And with that, he went to Oakland Hills and missed the cut in the PGA Championship, his second straight weekend off in a major. Then he missed another cut at the Wyndham Championship in Greensboro, and it appeared that the Fijian would be one-and-done for the year, especially with The Barclays moving from Westchester Country Club, where Singh had won three times, to Ridgewood Country Club in New Jersey.

Singh was a bust in the inaugural year of the FedExCup Playoffs, missing one cut, not cracking the top 60 in two other tournaments, and picking up his only top 10 when the field was reduced to 30 players. But he hit the ball well and made enough putts at The Barclays to stay in contention, and delivered a putt that ranks among the best of the year on the final hole. For historical purposes, it would be tough to argue that Woods's 12-foot birdie putt on the 72nd hole of the U.S. Open to force a playoff was the best of 2008. Right behind would be any of Harrington's putts on the three closing holes at Oakland Hills that brought him a second straight major.

This was only a FedExCup playoff event, but it was jolting to watch Garcia hole a 30-foot birdie on the first extra hole, tap his chest and look as though he had just won the tournament. "It was almost the same as if you had a putt to win or to tie. Just give it your all," Singh said. "And I did." He matched Garcia's birdie from about the same distance and won with a birdie on the next hole. More birdie putts followed the next week at the Deutsche Bank Championship, and they were equally dramatic, even if not as much was riding on each stroke. Three shots behind going into the final round at the TPC Boston, Singh closed with an eight-under 63 by making putts from everywhere. He took control with a 35-foot birdie on the 13th and finished off the field with a 60-foot birdie putt on the 14th. Just for show, he dropped in another one from 35 feet on the 17th hole for his second straight victory in the Playoffs.

The PGA Tour must have had a difficult time celebrating such a feat, for Singh winning back-to-back in the Playoffs effectively rendered the final two weeks of the FedExCup meaningless. And when Villegas won in St. Louis the following week, Singh's lead in the points race was such that the only way he could not win the FedExCup was to get lost on his way to East Lake, fail to finish one of the four rounds or sign an incorrect scorecard. It was a strange sensation for someone who plays to win. Singh found himself being overly cautious at The Tour Championship, distracted by such a bizarre scenario, and he failed to break par all week. No matter. An hour before a scintillating finish involving Villegas, Kim, Garcia and Mickelson, PGA Tour commissioner Tim Finchem was handing the FedExCup trophy to Singh in front of television cameras tucked away behind the 18th green.

Woods had won the inaugural FedExCup with such ease that he skipped the first tournament and, in hindsight, could have skipped The Tour Championship and still collected $10 million. Trying to inject more drama and create opportunity for more players, the tour revamped the points system in the Playoffs to add 2,000 points to every position. The thinking was that more players would arrive at East Lake with a mathematical chance of capturing the trophy by winning The Tour Championship.

Only after the first week, however, did it become clear that anyone missing the cut had effectively taken himself out of contention. Turns out some of the best golfers in the world are good at math, and not just when it comes to their bank accounts. They figured out that a player who finished 70th two weeks in a row earned more points than someone who missed the cut by one shot and then finished fifth. Essentially, anyone received a 2,000-point bonus for making the cut. "Making a cut isn't anything to be proud of, in my opinion," Furyk said. "Finishing fifth? Now, there's something to be proud of. As we know, two 70ths is better than a fifth and a missed cut. I think we're rewarding mediocrity. I don't like rewarding mediocrity." And with Singh winning the first two weeks, there was no way for anyone to catch him.

The Tour was left with another anti-climactic finish to a competition it once likened to the Super Bowl. And perhaps the most embarrassing of all was that Harrington, the winner of the last two major championships, didn't even qualify for The Tour Championship. By the end of the year, Tour officials were back to the drawing board, giving it three different point structures in three years of the FedExCup.

Just as the FedExCup was ending, the European Tour announced its version of a season-ending bonanza called "The Race to Dubai," which replaced the Order of Merit. Instead of packaging big tournaments at the end of the year and devising a complicated points system, Europe decided to end its season with the $10 million Dubai World Championship (for the top 70 players), then pay out $10 million in bonuses to the top 15 players. Europe even changed its logo, a montage of landmarks from all the countries it plays. It was a big step in competing with the U.S. PGA Tour, and it was lucrative enough that a half-dozen or so regular U.S. members — Kim, Villegas and Ogilvy among them — decided to take up joint membership and compete for the Race to Dubai.

It was quite a turnaround for Europe, which only 18 months earlier met at La Costa during the Accenture Match Play Championship and listened to chief executive George O'Grady tell them that the European Tour was "worth fighting for." The money and top players still congregated on American soil, but this was a big step in leveling the playing field.

The final Order of Merit title went to a Swede for the first time, even though Robert Karlsson didn't win a tournament until September. He quietly worked his way up the World Ranking and the Order of Merit by performing steadily at the majors, recording a tie for eighth at the Masters, a tie for fourth at the U.S. Open and a tie for seventh at the British Open. With a chance to become the only player with top 10s in all the majors this year, Karlsson opened with 68 but finished in a tie for 20th at the PGA Championship.

Even so, Karlsson easily qualified for his second Ryder Cup team, then poured it on with victories in the Mercedes-Benz Championship in Germany and the Alfred Dunhill Links Championship in Scotland. When the season concluded at Valderrama for the Volvo Masters, double major winner Harrington needed to finish at least third to have a chance to catch Karlsson and didn't come close. Karlsson was the toast of Sweden, at least among male golfers, but it was easy to keep the attention in perspective considering he had played most of his career in virtual anonymity. "My caddie said, 'Don't complain. Four years ago, we had problems to get an extra dozen golf balls,'" Karlsson said.

Indeed, it was a banner year in golf for Europe. It made enormous strides with the Race to Dubai, produced two major champions for the first time since 1999, and finished the year with 17 players among the top 50 in the World Ranking, the most of any continent. About the only thing missing from its credentials was a trophy Europe had become accustomed to winning: the Ryder Cup. Europe had won the last three matches, including two straight by record margins of 18½ to 9½. And it was facing an American team that had six rookies and no Tiger, with Woods having to sit this one out while recovering from knee surgery.

But this was a new Ryder Cup in so many ways. Colin Montgomerie was not part of the European side for the first time since 1989, having endured another miserable season that left captain Nick Faldo no options of choosing him. Europe also played without its emotional leader, Darren Clarke, who was left off by Faldo despite winning two tournaments in a span of five months. Instead, Faldo chose Paul Casey and Ian Poulter, the latter on the strength of his runner-up finish at the Open Championship.

The Americans introduced a radical new points system that was orchestrated by captain Paul Azinger. Instead of awarding points on top 10s — deemed an archaic system with so many international players on the U.S. PGA Tour — points were based purely on money, with an emphasis on the current year and the majors. It truly was a stroke of genius by Azinger. He essentially convinced the PGA of America to copy the Presidents Cup system, and it worked so well that Azinger probably could have done with just two captain's picks (he was awarded a record four for the first time, another change in the system).

But he didn't stop there. Azinger then broke his team into three groups, which he called "personality pods," and they stuck together as partners in practice sessions and during the matches. "If we win, I'll go down as having the lowest IQ of any genius who ever lived," Azinger said during the summer.

Genius still requires good putting, and the Americans delivered in that department, too. They had not led after any session since last winning the Ryder Cup in the "Miracle at Brookline" in 1999, but on the opening day at Valhalla, the Americans lost only one of eight matches and grabbed a 5½-to-2½ lead. As much praise as Azinger received, the British press buried Faldo for a series of peculiar decisions. Not only did he leave the popular Clarke off the team, he opted to sit Westwood and Garcia for the first time in their Ryder Cup careers. So ended a streak of 27 straight matches for Westwood, 22 in a row for Garcia. Combined, they had a 27-5-8 record in team play.

Europe clawed back into a contention, trailing 9-7 after a Saturday that might have ranked as the best day in golf all year. There were 86 birdies made in 138 holes spread over eight matches, all crammed into 10 hours of action, perhaps no putter bigger than Steve Stricker making a 15-footer on the final hole to deny Europe another full point. It came down to Sunday singles, and Europe simply didn't have enough left. Kim buried Garcia so badly that when the matched ended on the 14th hole, Kim didn't realize he had a 5-and-4 victory and headed to the next tee. Boo Weekley galloped off the first tee, riding his driver like a toy horse, and defeated rookie Oliver Wilson.

The pivotal match proved to be J.B. Holmes, a Kentucky native with awesome power off the tee, blasting two drives that set up wedges for birdie for a victory over Soren Hansen. That set up the winning point for Furyk, who was conceded his par on the 17th hole against Miguel Angel Jimenez that led to a U.S. celebration that was a long time coming. The final score was 16½ to 11½, the Americans' widest margin since 1981. "This team was more of a European team," Harrington said of the Americans. And they got a European result.

The one place Americans continued to take a beating was on the LPGA Tour, where a dubious streak continued when the season ended at the ADT Championship. It was the 15th consecutive year without an American winning the money title. Paula Creamer won four tournaments and finished second on the money list, but that was merely a footnote to a year dominated by Lorena Ochoa and Annika Sorenstam for vastly different reasons. Ochoa made headlines for winning, Sorenstam for leaving.

During a spring in which hype often trumped reality, Ochoa was talking about a Grand Slam after winning the first one. But just like Woods commanded attention for talk about a Grand Slam (or a perfect season, for that matter), there was ample reason to believe in the Mexican star with her knack to dominate. Ochoa was firmly planted as No. 1 in women's golf when the year began, coming off a season in which she won eight times and was the first woman to surpass $4 million in earnings.

Ochoa stayed in Mexico when the season began, but she made an inspiring 2008 debut by winning the HSBC Women's Championship in Singapore by 11 shots. After failing to win before a home crowd in Mexico, she then ran off four straight victories in impressive fashion, including another double-digit margin of victory.

Most impressive was the Kraft Nabisco Championship, the first major of the year, which Ochoa won by five shots. With a mariachi band playing "Pajarito Lindo," Ochoa and her family took a joyous plunge into the pond surrounding the 18th green at Mission Hills Country Club. "Nothing can stop her," Se Ri Pak said. It was her second straight victory in a major, having won at St. Andrews the previous summer in the Ricoh Women's British Open. And while Ochoa failed in her bid to join Sorenstam and Nancy Lopez with five straight LPGA Tour victories, her mind was clearly on the majors and a Grand Slam. Unlike Woods, she reached first base at the Nabisco and was still circling the bases.

Two rounds into the second major, the McDonald's LPGA Championship, Ochoa had the lead through 36-holes after 65 in the second round at Bulle Rock in which she missed only one fairway and one green. "My best round of the season," she said, and that was a frightening prospect for those trying to stop her. But it all changed in the third round, starting with a three-putt bogey on the opening hole. She stumbled to a 72 and never caught up in the final round. That was the end of her Grand Slam bid. That was the last of her chances in the majors, too, for she never gave herself a good chance at the U.S. Women's Open or Ricoh Women's British Open. Even so, Ochoa won seven times and captured the money title for the third consecutive year. She was the undisputed queen of women's golf, although there were questions at the end of the year how much longer that would last.

The McDonald's LPGA Championship signaled a change in other ways. Sorenstam stood over a 15-foot birdie putt on the 72nd hole to join a playoff, but it came up well short. That was her best chance in the majors this year, but this year was more about saying goodbye than adding to her awesome record as the best woman of her generation.

Sorenstam failed to win on the LPGA Tour last year for the first time since her rookie season in 1994, and she was determined to regain her superiority in women's golf. She certainly made a statement in the season-opener when Sorenstam won the SBS Open at Turtle Bay. She won the Stanford International Pro-Am in Miami, then won her third tournament of the year at the Michelob Ultra Open at Kingsmill for her 72nd career victory, just 16 short of the record held by Kathy Whitworth. No one would have imagined that day it would be her last, or that Sorenstam played that week at Kingsmill knowing she had an important announcement to make the next week.

It was time to retire.

"I have given it all, and it's been fun," Sorenstam said on a Tuesday at the Sybase Classic, an announcement that only those in her inner circle knew about. She was careful the rest of the year not to use what she called the "R-word" — retirement — but she made it clear that it was time to step away as a full-time competitor on a tour that she defined for more than a decade. She won 10 majors to go with her 72 victories on the LPGA Tour, outlasting rivals that included Laura Davies, Karrie Webb, Se Ri Pak and Ochoa, at least for as long as she could. Sorenstam said she would give it her all the rest of the year, but so much energy was taken away from what amounted to a farewell tour the rest of the season. The LPGA Championship was her only serious chance in a major. The only news she made at the U.S. Women's Open was holing a six iron from 199 yards for eagle on the final hole at Interlachen, but that only moved her up to a tie for 24th.

After announcing she was stepping away, Sorenstam went five straight tournaments without cracking the top 10, an anomaly for a player of her caliber and a tour still lacking the depth found in men's golf. She finished out of the top 10 a dozen times in 22 starts on the LPGA Tour. There were simply too many distractions on the course, and she lacked the motivation to work as hard as she once had off the course. At every stop, she was reminded how many tournaments she had left. "To compete at this level, you have to practice, and you have to dedicate yourself full time," she said as the season wound down. "I just don't have that in me anymore." Her last chance to win came at the Lorena Ochoa Invitational in Mexico, where a five-foot putt to force a playoff swirled around the cup and stayed out.

At the ADT Championship, where a victory would have produced yet another money title, Sorenstam missed the weekend cut — then was told her name was drawn for drug testing, denying her one last moment to soak in the adulation of her legion of fans. Her year ended in the Dubai Ladies Classic, and while Sorenstam planned to marry in January, she did not rule out at least one more tournament if the situation allowed.

The rest of the year in women's golf was dominated by Asians in so many ways. Yani Tseng, a 19-year-old from Taiwan, won the McDonald's LPGA Championship, while Inbee Park won the U.S. Women's Open and Ji-Yai Shin captured the Ricoh Women's British Open. Of those victories, none was more significant than Park at the U.S. Women's Open, which revealed the strength of South Korea and the roots that traced to 10 years ago with Pak, perhaps the greatest pioneer of any country in golf.

Park woke up in the middle of the night in South Korea in 1998 when she heard cheering from the living room of her tiny apartment. Her parents were watching Pak become the first player from their country to win the U.S. Women's Open, and Park snuggled between mom and dad to see what the fuss was all about. The next day, she placed her hands around a golf club for the first time. There were 45 players from South Korea on the LPGA Tour this year, and they have won six of the last 20 majors.

Even more impressive than Park winning the U.S. Women's Open at age 19 was Shin winning the Women's British Open, the Mizuno Classic in Japan and then the ADT Championship and its $1 million prize. The 20-year-old Shin, with uncanny accuracy off the tee, will officially be a rookie on the LPGA Tour in 2009.

Asian players, particularly South Korean, made news beyond their trophies, however. In an embarrassing moment for the LPGA Tour, *Golfweek* magazine broke a story about commissioner Carolyn Bivens's plan to require LPGA members to pass an oral evaluation of English skills or face suspension. That brought the LPGA Tour more coverage than when Ochoa was winning four straight tournaments or when Sorenstam announced she was stepping away. The tour was criticized in the media and by political groups for discrimination, and even some of its title sponsors questioned whether this was a good idea. One state senator in California asked the Legislature to determine whether the policy would violate anti-discrimination laws in a state where the LPGA Tour played three times, including a major.

Ultimately, Bivens backed down and said the tour would revise its proposed policy. Among those perplexed by the notion of having to speak English was Angel Cabrera, the 2007 U.S. Open champion from Argentina, who speaks enough to get by. "I remember what (Roberto) de Vicenzo once said to me. 'If you shoot under 70, everybody will understand you. If you don't, they won't want to talk to you anyway,'" Cabrera said.

The beauty of golf is that it ultimately is measured by numbers, not words.

Two majors for Padraig Harrington. A $10 million bonus for Vijay Singh for winning the FedExCup. The 16½ points won by the American team to capture the Ryder Cup. And a U.S. Open victory for Tiger Woods on one good leg.

2. Masters Tournament

It was getting on to eight o'clock in the morning that Thursday, April 10, and Arnold Palmer arrived at the first tee at Augusta National Golf Club to do his duty as honorary starter of the Masters Tournament. The King was 79 years old now, but he had lost nothing. He looked down off the first tee and said: "I have a chance to hit it out of sight this morning."

And so Palmer did, right down the middle of the fairway, into a dense fog, and the 2008 Masters was under way. Which was to say, by contemporary standards in golf, how many shots would Tiger Woods win by? He hadn't won a Masters since 2005 — his fourth — so he was due. Better yet, he had stirred up the golf world early in January when on his website he said that winning the Grand Slam was within reason. In Tiger-speak, to most, that was the equivalent of a prediction. The ensuing hubbub was considerable. But he was giving every sign of being primed. He had come to Augusta with four wins worldwide, and three in four starts on the PGA Tour.

"It's just another week," said Woods. "You have to put whatever happened behind you, whether you won or lost, and it's all about this week."

Interestingly enough, Woods's words would have a 24-karat glow to them at the end of the week, when Trevor Immelman stepped up to have Zach Johnson, the 2007 champion, help him into the green jacket. If anyone had to forget what happened, Immelman was the man. Coming into this Masters, he was remembered — if at all — as the one who had picked up an intestinal parasite in the 2007 Masters, and had to exist and play golf on toast and medication. The bug sapped him, but he played on and tied for 55th. He lost 25 pounds in three weeks, and it took him six weeks to get his strength back.

Then in December, Immelman had to withdraw from a South African tournament because of severe pain across his ribcage. He won the Nedbank Challenge the next week despite the pain. He thought the parasite had returned. But doctors discovered a golf-ball-sized tumor on his diaphragm. He feared the worst as he lay there for two days after surgery, wondering whether it was cancer. He thought of his wife Carminita and their little son Jacob? What would become of them? Then came the report. The tumor was benign. But the episode was a turning point.

"It made me realize," Immelman said, "that golf wasn't my whole life."

This opportunity had been a lifetime in the making for the 28-year-old Immelman, tracing back to his childhood in South Africa, a country whose most famous sporting figure was Gary Player.

Immelman had played beautifully for three days, building a two-stroke advantage over Brandt Snedeker, with Woods lurking six strokes behind. As Immelman pulled away from Augusta National that Saturday evening, he checked the messages on his telephone. One, in particular, caused him to stop.

It was from Player, who had counseled Immelman since he was a child, helping to guide a career that had come to this place. Player was preparing to fly to the Middle East on a business trip but took a moment to offer another bit of encouragement.

"He told me that he believed in me and that I need to believe in myself," Immelman remembered. "He told me I've got to keep my head a little quieter when I putt. He said I'm peeking too soon. He told me to go out there and be strong through adversity because adversity would come and I just had to deal with it.

"I took that all to heart."

A day later, Immelman became the second South African in history to win the Masters, by three strokes over Woods. It had been 30 years since Player's last win at Augusta. The victory also altered Immelman's position among the best of professional golf's new generation of players. He had shown his potential in 2006 when he beat Woods in the Western Open, and with a handful of victories around the world, but capturing the Masters transformed Immelman's place in the game.

First Round

The engaging thing about golf is the slow pace at which it unfolds. Accordingly, it's doubtful that, in a field of 94 players, anyone thought that either Trevor Immelman, the unpretentious South African, or Justin Rose, the forever-young Englishman, would end up winning the Masters after shooting 68s in fairly benign conditions, which tied them for the lead. It is written: You don't win a tournament on the first day. Besides, with Tiger Woods in the field, the primary question is, where is he? The answer this time is that Woods was in a 14-man traffic jam at par 72, four strokes off the lead. Not to worry, Tiger fans. In Woods's four victories, he opened with 70 three times and 74 the other. And this was a quiet 72. "There's really no roars out there anymore, because it's hard to make the eagles and the big birdies," Woods said. "The way the golf course plays now, you don't really shoot low rounds here anymore. You've got to plod along."

Masters officials must have rejoiced on hearing that, because that's precisely what they had in mind with the course changes over the years — not to make Augusta National quiet, but to keep golfers with all that new technology in hand from getting all those eagles and big birdies. If some of the fun had gone out of the Masters, some self-respect had been preserved. This was not some low-scoring tour event.

The course had only minor changes for the 2008 Masters, principally a few yards to the front of the 10th tee and a few at the back left of No. 7 green to allow for some other pin positions. And a few trees were removed at No. 11.

Woods plodded along to 12 straight pars, then from the 13th went bogey-bogey-eagle. The 13th is one of Augusta's four eminently birdie-able par-fives, and so that was an odd place for Woods to make bogey. He hit a four-iron second shot from 215 yards, a pretty routine approach. But the ball bounced off the green and rolled off the back. Then a weak pitch rolled back down to him, and he bogeyed from there. He chipped in for the eagle at the 15th, and when he parred in, it meant he had gone his last 34 Masters holes without a birdie. But he wasn't troubled about the 72 even though he had hit only 11 greens in regulation. "If the weather worsens in the weekend," Woods said, "I'll be right there."

Rose spotted the field two strokes with early bogeys, then spurted to four straight birdies from the sixth, on one-putts of five, 15 and 20 feet and two from 45 feet for the birdie at the eighth. He added birdies at the 12th and 13th, a run of five under par on eight holes. He parred in for his 68.

Of course, Rose, ranked No. 9 in the world, was asked whether he could be the first European since Jose Maria Olazabal in 1999 to win the Masters. "I think there's enough pressure without having to pile all of the pressure of a whole continent on your shoulders," he said.

Immelman had a trouble-free day. That is, he suffered no bogeys and got his 68 from some remarkable iron play. He had one long birdie putt, a 35-footer at No. 9, and the other three were from six, two and five feet. And it seems he had done some prudent homework. He, Rose and Ian Poulter had dropped by Augusta National for practice rounds late in March. "It was kind of like three kids going to your favorite golf course," he said. "It was an awesome couple of days."

Immelman didn't try to lean on his illnesses. "Obviously, my form hasn't been too stellar so far yet this season," he said, asked about his game. "I think I've been struggling through a few things. The results have been pretty frustrating and pretty disappointing. I knew I had to stay patient with myself because I know it's in there somewhere."

Immelman and Rose shared a one-stroke lead on Brandt Snedeker, Brian Bateman and England's Lee Westwood, who tied at 69 through developments at the end of the round. Westwood bogeyed the 17th. Snedeker, 27, in his second Masters, bogeyed the 18th, and Bateman got a birdie at the 18th, one of just three there. Bateman, a Masters rookie, allowed himself a quick peek at the leaderboard at the 16th, just at the time his name was going up for the first time. He turned to his caddie. "Wow, they are showing us some love," he said.

For the Masters, it was an odd leaderboard. Only two golfers among the top 10 had won majors, defending champion Zach Johnson and former U.S. Open champ Jim Furyk, in a tie at 70.

Johnson, who a year ago set up his winning tap-in with an exquisite chip shot at the 18th, had to scramble at the tough 11th and ended up saving par with an eight-foot putt. "That was a round-saver," he said. He flashed a bit of temper when someone suggested he might have been a fluke winner last year. "There's not a surprise guy on the leaderboard," he said. "There's not a surprise guy in the field."

England's Ian Poulter, known as much for his wardrobe as his golf, also shot 70 and did it with a hole-in-one at the 16th. "It's the biggest adrenaline rush I've ever had," Poulter said. It was the 11th ace at No. 16, making it the most aced hole in Masters history.

Among other goings-on in the first round: Two Asian Tour stars made their Masters debut. "I definitely enjoy the feel of the golf course, and the whole ambience," said China's Liang Wen-chong, after a one-birdie 76. He said, given the growth of golf in China, the tournament would be drawing large television audiences. Thailand's Prayad Marksaeng fought through a very sore back for an 82 and insisted he wouldn't withdraw. "That is my pride and I don't think I would do that," he said.

First-Round Leaders: Justin Rose 68, Trevor Immelman 68, Brian Bateman 69, Brandt Snedeker 69, Lee Westwood 69, Ian Poulter 70, Robert Karlsson 70, Zach Johnson 70, Stephen Ames 70, Jim Furyk 70

Second Round

The second round came and went on Friday, and the magic number to make the 36-hole cut, three-over-par 147, left 45 players in the field, and also left some surprising victims in its wake. Gone were two of the game's brightest, Sergio Garcia (72) and Ernie Els (74), along with Aaron Baddeley (73) and England's Luke Donald (75) These were the kinds of names that don't miss cuts.

And if they were surprises, what was to be said of Trevor Immelman, who after the fold of Justin Rose, found himself alone in the lead, one stroke up on Brandt Snedeker. Immelman put together another tidy 68, with only one bogey, for an eight-under 136 total. "I'm thrilled with my play so far," Immelman said. "But there is a very long way to go. I can't sit back and put my feet up."

Immelman three-putted at the par-three sixth hole off a 30-foot putt that went 40 feet past the hole, and two-putted from there for a bogey, his only bogey in the first two rounds. He bracketed that with 10-foot birdies at the fifth and seventh. He passed a big test at the tough 11th, hitting a seven iron to five feet for a birdie. In the first round, it was a six iron to two feet, so he was two-for-two at the most difficult hole on the course.

Oddly enough, Immelman didn't birdie any of the par-five holes and had only one birdie in the first round. And then he closed with two bogeys, the 17th from 15 feet and the 18th from 10 feet. "Anytime you can make a birdie in a major championship, it's like a thrill," Immelman said.

This pretty well sums up Tiger Woods's bumpy 71: At the 18th, he saved par from the 10th fairway. It was a scattering of four birdies and three bogeys that left him at 143, seven strokes off the lead. He seemed to be getting revved up with a birdie at No. 1, his first birdie of the week, but then bogeyed the par-five second, one of the easiest holes on Augusta National. "Seven back on this course, you can make that up," said Woods, and he had proof of that in his trophy case.

On the PGA Tour, Woods won six times after being seven strokes down at the halfway point. At the 18th, he drove into the trees on the right and had to punch out to the 10th fairway. From there, he hit the green, and his ball seemed headed for the hole until it hit Stuart Appleby's ball and stopped, six feet from the hole. And he made that for his par. So seven shots didn't really seem that much.

Fred Couples, the 1992 Masters champion, was just one cut from setting the record of making 24 straight. But he missed his 10-foot birdie putt at the 18th, missed the cut, and remained tied with Gary Player at 23. "To be quite honest with you," Couples said, "I don't consider it that great of a deal."

The lead seemed to be the curse for Justin Rose, and it struck again, only this time earlier. In 2004 he led through the first two rounds, then shot 81 in the third. In 2007, he led the first round, then shot a pair of 75s. This time he ballooned to 78. In a post mortem, it looked even worse. He had hit all 18 fairways, but hit nine greens. He made no birdies and fell victim to the par-five 15th. He hit a wedge into the fronting pond, the next over the green and the next almost back over into the water, and made a triple-bogey eight. "Obviously," Rose said, "it's not going to be the exciting weekend I was looking forward to."

Steve Flesch, age 40, was bidding to become the third left-hander (after Phil Mickelson and Mike Weir) to win the Masters in five years. He outwitted the par-fives for three birdies and an eagle for a bogey-free 67, the low round of the day. An average driver, he planned to lay up at the four par-fives, in the Zach Johnson method of 2007. He did lay up at the second and eighth.

On the second nine, Flesch succumbed to the temptation of good drives. "I thought, 'You can't hit it out here this far and not go for it,'" Flesch told himself. At the 13th, he found himself 234 yards from the flag. "I wanted to hit four iron, but my caddie talked me into hitting three iron," Flesch said. He put the ball two feet from the cup and eagled. "He made the right call, I guess," Flesch conceded. He then birdied the 15th for his 67 and at 139 was three out of the lead, by far his best position in four Masters.

The three lefties, by the way, were the only players in the field without a bogey in the second round. It must have been something in the pollen.

Mickelson, with 68–139, was looking for his "Arnold Palmer" — winning the Masters on even years. Mickelson won his two in 2004 and 2006. "I would love to be in the lead," Mickelson said, "but I would have had to … press the issue at some spots, and I didn't want to do that yet." Still, tied for third after two rounds was better than he was for either of his wins.

Jim Furyk, the former U.S. Open champion, who bogeyed the 18th in the first round, double-bogeyed it this time after hooking his tee shot into some pine straw. The six left him at 73–143, seven strokes off the lead. "Two days in a row — a disappointing finish," Furyk said. For pure excitement, few could match Stephen Ames's 70. He made two birdies and two bogeys on the first nine and then a classic stretch on the second nine, from the 10th — bogey-birdie-birdie-bogey-birdie-par-birdie. "It was a bit up-and-down," Ames said. "But otherwise, it was a solid round."

The final question was, would Trevor Immelman, an unlikely leader of the Masters through 36 holes, feel the pressure on Saturday, in the third round?

Said Immelman: "I feel pressure playing for a hundred bucks against a mate."

Second-Round Leaders: Trevor Immelman 68–136, Brandt Snedeker 68–137, Steve Flesch 67–139, Phil Mickelson 68–139, Ian Poulter 69–139, Stephen Ames 70–140, Paul Casey 69–140, Stewart Cink 69–141, Arron Oberholser 70–141, Mike Weir 68–141

Third Round

If there was to be a sign that this Masters had Trevor Immelman's name stamped all over it from the beginning, it finally showed itself gloriously, like a peacock fanning its tail. It came at the par-five 15th, that great 530-yard temptress with the pond lurking in front, where so many Masters champions have made up so much ground — and others lost ground. Immelman was hanging by a thread, in between. His wedge approach hit the green and was spinning back, heading for the pond, when somehow it stopped on the tight-cut bank. Hanging by a blade of grass, someone said.

Most compared it to Fred Couples's tee shot in the final round at the par-three 12th hole, when he won in 1992, when his ball just hung there until he could arrive and save his par. More precisely, however, Immelman's case was like Jose Maria Olazabal's when he won in 1994. Olazabal's five-iron second shot to the 15th ended up clinging to the bank about a foot above the water and 30 feet from the hole. Olazabal putted from there and made the eagle and went on to beat Tom Lehman.

"That's such a tough shot into the 15th green," Immelman said. "I knew there was a chance it was going into the water. I must say, I couldn't quite believe it when it stayed up. I was extremely fortunate."

Immelman chipped on and saved his par and very possibly his Masters, too. He shot 69 for an 11-under 205 total and at the end led Brandt Snedeker (70) by two, Steve Flesch (69) by three and Paul Casey (69) by four. And then there was Tiger Woods.

The long-awaited move by Woods, such as it was, finally materialized in the third round. He shot 68, his first round in the 60s in 11 rounds, since his 65 in the third round in 2005, when he last won the Masters. He finished the day at 211, six strokes off Immelman's lead, but undaunted. "I put myself right back in the tournament," he said. "This was as high a score as I could have shot today, and if I have a few more putts go in, I'm right there. But I'm still right there, anyways." It was flawless 68, with the lone birdie on the first nine at the second hole, then birdies at the 10th, 13th and 17th.

In terms of ranking and accomplishment, there seemed to be no great obstacles in front of Woods. Immelman was ranked 29th in the world, Casey 34th, Snedeker 44th and Flesch 107th. Flesch had won four times on the PGA Tour, Immelman and Snedeker each once, and Casey eight times on the European Tour. But there were no major titles among them, meaning none of them had come through the pressure of a major championship in the final round.

Immelman committed only his second bogey of the tournament at No. 4, and played the last 11 holes in four under, with birdies at Nos. 8, 13, 14 and 18.

Snedeker, with birdies at the second and eighth, had edged into a one-stroke lead over Immelman through the turn. Then he fell victim to the Amen Corner, bogeying his way through the treacherous bend — a hooked drive at the 11th, a missed green at the 12th and watered approach at the 13th. He held himself together and birdied the next two holes and then the 18th for 70 to sit just two behind Immelman. "If this was Sunday, maybe a little different story on how I react," Snedeker said. "But we've got a lot of golf left to play."

At the 18th, while Phil Mickelson was finishing off the 75 that killed his chances, Steve Flesch, facing a four-foot putt for birdie, turned and looked at the scoreboard. He was checking to see what Tiger Woods had shot, he said. Well, actually he was trying to keep his attention off that four-footer. "If somebody had a coke and a pizza, I might have had a slice of that, too," Flesch said. He knocked in the short putt for a birdie and 69, and at 208 he would end the day just three behind Immelman.

Paul Casey had a wild ride. After a four-birdie first nine for 32, he came in with three bogeys and two birdies for a 69–209. "Today was a day of ups and downs," Casey said. "I take the good out of it. I enjoyed myself out there." In fourth place, he was in his best position in the Masters since a third place in the third round in 2004. Could he forget that he shot 74 in the final round that year?

The third round ended with six players separated by seven strokes, and with the prediction of heavy, blustery winds on Sunday, and two closing thoughts hung over Augusta National:

Said Tiger Woods: "Anything can happen. You can shoot yourself right out of it and you can put yourself right back in it."

Said Trevor Immelman: "I've never had the lead in a major going into the final round. All I can ask of myself is to play as hard as I can and believe in myself."

Third-Round Leaders: Trevor Immelman 69–205, Brandt Snedeker 70–207, Steve Flesch 69–208, Paul Casey 69–209, Tiger Woods 68–211, Stewart Cink 71–212, Zach Johnson 68–214, Boo Weekley 68–214, Padraig Harrington 69–214, Andres Romero 70–214, Robert Karlsson 71–214, Sean O'Hair 71–214, Retief Goosen 72–214, Ian Poulter 75–214, Phil Mickelson 75–214

Fourth Round

The buffeting winds, gusting to 35 miles an hour, did arrive Sunday, and soon, by the process of elimination, Tiger Woods rose almost to the top of the 2008 Masters — almost. Which is to say that all of Trevor Immelman's biggest challengers fell away in the final round, and Woods, with nothing stronger than par 72, ended up in second place by three strokes. And he got that close only because Immelman closed with 75.

There were just four rounds under par, none by contenders — Miguel Angel Jimenez had 68, Heath Slocum, 69, and Nick Watney and Stuart Appleby, 71.

This was Immelman's Masters, and from the start, it turned out. Including a first-round tie with Justin Rose, Immelman became only the fifth wire-to-wire winner in Masters history and the first since Raymond Floyd in 1976.

Immelman bogeyed No. 1 (it was only his third bogey of the tournament), but so did Brandt Snedeker, and he remained two behind. Then Snedeker eagled the second to tie him for the lead. The tie lasted for one hole. Snedeker bogeyed the third to start a steep slide. "I about put myself in the psychiatric ward," Snedeker said. "I went from extreme highs to extreme lows, and that's what you don't want to do around here."

He didn't end up in the psycho ward, but in tears. He pulled his visor down low to cover them. With the eagle, Snedeker suddenly realized that he really could win the Masters while everyone else was being turned away by the strong winds. "I was expecting, hopefully, a good week," he said. "But all in all, if you told me at the beginning of the week, would I have taken a tie for third, I'd say heck, yes, and watch it on television."

Snedeker's game crumbled. "The 13th was probably the pivotal hole," he said. "A great putt on 12. And 13, I had a four iron to that hole, and golly, man, if somebody could tell me how to play that second shot, I'd love to know, because two days in a row I've hit it right in the middle of that damn water." He bogeyed it again, shot 77 and tied for third with Stewart Cink.

Steve Flesch collapsed over the last six holes. He was even par through the 11th, then double-bogeyed the 12th from the water and bogeyed the last four for a 78 and a tie for fifth. "I was trying to make some birdies and got a little too aggressive," he said.

"Had to be the swirling wind," Snedeker said. "You just never felt comfortable."

Woods shot a workaday 72, with three birdies — none of them at the vulnerable par-fives — and three bogeys. He blamed his putting. He missed a short par putt at the fourth, a short birdie putt at the 13th, and he three-putted the 14th. He needed 30 putts in the final round and 130 for the tournament. "I kept dragging the blade," he said. "I wasn't releasing it. I tried to release it, tried to get it going. I've tried to hook my putts, trying to do anything ... I just didn't quite have it this week."

Immelman bogeyed No. 1, and got the stroke back with a birdie from three feet at the fifth. He three-putted the eighth for a bogey and saved par at the 11th after missing the green by 20 yards. He bogeyed the 12th after missing the green, then birdied the 13th for only the second time, this off a wedge to a foot. He hit his tee shot into the water at the par-three 16th and double-bogeyed, and still wasn't in trouble. And then the gods wanted to test him one last time.

"I hit the drive of the week," Immelman said, "into the biggest divot you've ever seen..." From there, the ball could go anywhere. "I just put an eight iron back in my stance and just ripped at it," he said. The shot rivaled Sandy Lyle's seven iron from the fairway bunker in 1988. Immelman's ball ended up just 15 feet from the cup, and he calmly two-putted for a par and 75. This was just his second PGA Tour victory, but his first major.

It's part of Masters lore that you win on the par-fives. Immelman, an average hitter, didn't. He won on four par-fours — Nos. 5, 7, 11 and 18 — plus the par-five 13th. He did not bogey any of these holes, and he played them in 10 under, with 10 birdies and 10 pars.

All that was left was his reaction. He was eloquent in his brevity.

"Here I am, after missing the cut last week — Masters champion," Immelman said. "It's the craziest thing I've ever heard of."

The Final Leaders: Trevor Immelman 75–280, Tiger Woods 72–283, Stewart Cink 72–284, Brandt Snedeker 77–284, Steve Flesch 78–286, Padraig Harrington 72–286, Phil Mickelson 72–286, Miguel Angel Jimenez 68–287, Robert Karlsson 73–287, Andres Romero 73–287

3. U.S. Open Championship

With the United States Open trophy finally in his hands again, Tiger Woods made a statement in his news conference that at the time was very surprising. Not one to exaggerate, Woods told the assembled media: "This is probably the greatest tournament I ever had."

It sounded like what an excitable golf writer or television commentator would say, not the No. 1 golfer in the world.

After all, Woods had produced some mind-boggling performances in major championships, starting in 1997. He won the first of his four Masters by a record 12 strokes with an 18-under-par 270 score, also a record. He won his first U.S. Open in 2000 at Pebble Beach by 15 strokes with a record-equaling 272 total and broke the major championship record for winning margin that Old Tom Morris set in 1862. He won his first Open Championship, also in 2000, at St. Andrews by eight strokes with another scoring record of 19-under-par 269 and became, at age 24, the youngest player to own the career Grand Slam. He finished his amazing 2000 run in the PGA Championship at Valhalla with an 18-under 270 total, then went three extra holes to beat Bob May for his third major title of the year. With his 2001 Masters victory, he became the first to hold all four professional major championships at the same time.

None of that compared to Woods's playoff victory over Rocco Mediate, a 45-year-old journeyman with five career victories, in the 2008 United States Open Championship, played on the Torrey Pines (South) Golf Course in San Diego, California.

Woods provided the perspective two days later when he announced that his 2008 season was over because his left knee required reconstructive surgery. He had competed on a left leg that he had no business putting through the rigors of a golf championship. Not only was Woods suffering from a torn anterior cruciate ligament in his left knee — which he injured nearly a year ago on a training run — but also he had to contend with stress fractures in his left tibia, which were the result of a rehabilitation regimen that proved to be too ambitious following arthroscopic surgery he had after the Masters. He underwent surgery the next week, on June 24, and no timetable was given for his return.

Woods's pursuit of golf's most significant records was put on hold at age 32, in his 12th season on the PGA Tour. He had 14 professional major championships, now within four of the record 18 held by Jack Nicklaus. He had 65 PGA Tour career victories to rank third on the all-time list behind Sam Snead (82) and Nicklaus (73). The U.S. Open victory tied Woods with Bobby Jones for a record nine USGA national championships. For Woods that consisted of three Junior Amateurs, three Amateurs and now three Opens.

The South Course at Torrey Pines was the second municipal facility to host the U.S. Open, following Bethpage State Park in New York in 2002. It was only the fourth U.S. Open course accessible to the public, also following the resort venues of Pebble Beach (since 1972) and Pinehurst (since 1999).

While still a child, before his USGA success, Woods was already making a name for himself at Torrey Pines in the annual Junior World events, having victories in his age groups at eight, nine, 12, 13 and 14. Then at 15 he became the youngest ever to win the USGA Junior Amateur.

He had continued success at Torrey Pines as a professional in the annual PGA Tour event there (Buick Invitational) with six victories, including the last four years. It was his first win of 2008, and he entered the U.S. Open with four titles for the year, including one in Dubai, in six starts.

The U.S. Open was Woods's first tournament since he finished second to Trevor Immelman in the Masters. Two days after that, Woods underwent arthroscopic surgery on his left knee to repair cartilage damage. He had planned to return at the Memorial Tournament but wasn't healthy enough to play a round of golf. Once he arrived at Torrey Pines, he did not hit balls on the range and he limited himself to nine-hole practice sessions.

First Round

The USGA decided for the first time to send the top 12 players in the World Ranking off in four sets of threes, meaning players ranked Nos. 1-3, 4-6, 7-9 and 10-12 would compete alongside one another. With Tiger Woods would be No. 2 Phil Mickelson and No. 3 Adam Scott.

The hometown favorite, the 37-year-old Mickelson was having a chance to win his first U.S. Open on a course he had played as a boy. Like Woods, who was five years younger, Mickelson had won in the Junior World and also three times in the Buick Invitational at Torrey Pines.

Off at 8:06 a.m. before a huge gallery, there were no smiles after they exchanged greetings on the first tee. Woods had worried aloud about his ability to get into the flow of the round and start out decently. Indeed, Woods took double-bogey six on the first hole. He was not sharp, and there were a few grimaces between golf swings, but Woods did not crumble. He carded a one-over-par 72 and was right in the mix. "To make two double bogeys and a three-putt and only be four back, that's a great position to be in, because I know I can clean that up tomorrow," Woods said.

Mickelson, after his 71, and Scott, who shot 73, also had work to do.

Mickelson also had some explaining to do. He played without a driver in his bag — just two years after winning his second Masters using two drivers. "You noticed that I didn't have a driver today, huh?" Mickelson said, grinning. "My game plan was that I only want to hit it a certain distance. I don't really want to hit it past 300 yards on most of the par-fours because it starts running into the rough. And I felt like with the fairways being firm like they were today, all I needed was a three wood on the holes." But he noted that his inability to hit more fairways "kind of defeats the game plan, because now I'm short and crooked."

Scott was possibly even less prepared than Woods after breaking a bone on the outside of his right hand before the Memorial Tournament. Had he not always used the overlapping grip, Scott said he wouldn't have been able to play. Despite the handicap, he hung in there, perhaps because of the company he was keeping.

"I find it a lot easier to focus because I think I've got to be a little more disciplined," the 27-year-old Australian said. "And I felt like I played really well out there today and I really didn't make any putts. So my game didn't feel too bad."

A familiar early U.S. Open storyline was developing at the top of the leaderboard with the emergence of two relatively unknown players, Kevin Streelman and Justin Hicks, claiming first place at three-under 68 for a one-stroke lead over four better-known players — Mediate, 2006 U.S. Open champion Geoff Ogilvy, Stuart Appleby and Eric Axley.

Streelman, age 29, didn't seem intimidated, and perhaps for good reason. Earlier in the year, the PGA Tour rookie was paired with Woods on the weekend at the Buick Invitational, when Woods went on to win for the fourth consecutive time at Torrey Pines. Streelman tied for 29th in the Buick Invitational after shooting 75-77 on the weekend, but he seemed to have found his return to be an uplifting experience. "There was definitely a familiarity effect," Streelman said.

Not everyone was feeling so confident at Torrey Pines. Defending champion Angel Cabrera had quit smoking in the months before the U.S. Open, just as well because Torrey Pines was a non-smoking course. He shot 79. Immelman, the Masters champion, shot 75. Sergio Garcia, winner of The Players Championship, shot 76, as did two-time U.S. Open champion Retief Goosen. Open champion Padraig Harrington shot 78.

And no one failed to notice that Woods was near the top, almost like he had never been gone.

First-Round Leaders: Justin Hicks 68, Kevin Streelman 68, Rocco Mediate 69, Stuart Appleby 69, Eric Axley 69, Geoff Ogilvy 69, amateur Rickie Fowler 70, Robert Karlsson 70, Lee Westwood 70, Robert Allenby 70, Ernie Els 70

Second Round

A 45-foot birdie putt on the 18th hole not only gave Stuart Appleby a one-under 70 and the lead, but also it took out 11 players after 36 holes of the U.S. Open. All players within 10 shots of the lead make the halfway cut, so when Appleby finished at three-under 139, those at eight over par were sent packing.

That stroke aside, nearly all the attention in the second round was focused on Tiger Woods, who put to rest any lingering notions as to whether he or his game were healthy enough to challenge for the title. An inward five-under 30 on a series of medium-length putts gave Woods a three-under 68 and a 140 total, just one stroke off the pace set by Appleby.

Beginning his second round at the 10th hole, Woods opened with a bogey and made the turn in 38. Then he took advantage of a fortunate break after a wayward drive on the first hole, birdied four of five holes in a surprising and mesmerizing dash, and fist-pumped his way into a tie for second place with Rocco Mediate and Robert Karlsson.

"I didn't do anything. I actually just kept patient," Woods said after a round filled with great shots and also shooting pain in his surgically repaired left leg that had him wincing and looking worried at times. "I was trying to get back to even par for the tournament. I was playing the back nine at even par. All of a sudden, they started flying in from everywhere. If I shot three under par on that back nine, that would have put me at even par for the tournament. And I just got a couple more."

Two over par for the day at the turn, Woods pushed his drive far right on the par-four first hole. His ball, however, came to rest near a tree on a trampled down bare lie next to the cart path. He opted not to take a drop, then had to take a careful swing with an eight iron while standing on the cart path in metal spikes. His shot from 157 yards came within 10 feet of the hole, and he drained the putt. That bit of luck and skill started his rally.

"I made some 15- and 20-foot putts and got on a roll that way," said Woods, who converted birdies at the second, fourth, fifth and ninth holes, all from 18 feet or longer except at the last, which was a tap-in after he reached the green in two.

His playing companions had their moments, too, although Phil Mickelson shot 75 and Adam Scott, a second straight 73. Mostly they got stuck in neutral and were reduced to spectators, almost blending into the huge crowd as Woods summoned his Torrey Pines magic.

Woods wasn't the only member of the walking wounded who occupied a prime spot on the leaderboard. Mediate, with his fragile back, was near the top with an even-par 71 that left him tied with Woods and Karlsson at 140. Karlsson, from Sweden, carded his second straight 70. Davis Love, sidelined last autumn by a torn tendon in his left ankle that eventually required surgery, shot 69 for a 141 total. Love was tied for fifth place with Spain's Miguel Angel Jimenez, who carded the low round of the day, a five-under 66, England's Lee Westwood, who shot 71, and D.J. Trahan, who shot 69.

Prominent players who missed the cut included two of the last three U.S. Open winners in Angel Cabrera, the defending champion, and Michael Campbell, the 2005 winner, and 2007 Masters winner Zach Johnson, who was among those knocked out by Appleby's last putt. In all, 80 of the 156 players advanced into the weekend with scores of 149 or better, including Padraig Harrington, the reigning Open champion, who rallied from 78 with a four-under 67. Masters champion Trevor Immelman, who won the 1998 USGA Public Links at Torrey Pines, kept his hopes alive at 73–148, and The Players winner Sergio Garcia shot 70 to come in at 146.

Second-Round Leaders: Stuart Appleby 70–139, Rocco Mediate 71–140, Robert Karlsson 70–140, Tiger Woods 68–140, D.J. Trahan 69–141, Davis Love 69–141, Lee Westwood 71–141, Miguel Angel Jimenez 66–141, Luke Donald 71–142, Robert Allenby 72–142, Geoff Ogilvy 73–142, Ernie Els 72–142, Carl Pettersson 71–142

Third Round

England's Lee Westwood was in the media interview tent, holding the third-round lead in the U.S. Open. He had shot 70 for a 211 total and was two strokes ahead of Tiger Woods, who was still struggling with his aching knee and in trouble again at the 17th hole. Within a few minutes all that changed, and Westwood was being asked how he would try to overtake Woods in the final round.

What happened was swift and stunning. From a scruffy lie in the rough by the 17th green, Woods popped the ball into the hole for an unlikely birdie. At the 18th, a good drive and five-wood shot by Woods set up a downhill 40-foot putt for eagle, his second in a five-hole span. When the ball went in, the crowd went wild, while Woods displayed a tight-lipped smile and slowly but emphatically pumped his right fist.

Recovering from a five-stroke deficit over his final six holes, Woods came in under par, with 70 for a three-under 210 total for a one-shot lead over Westwood. He had trouble with his driver and the soreness in his left leg, yet still managed to post one of the 11 sub-par rounds on an afternoon when the ocean mists wouldn't relinquish their hold over the picturesque landscape.

"That's what it's all about is getting the ball in the hole in as few shots as possible," said Woods, who for the second day in a row had been able to find another gear and initiate a kick to the finish.

"I was just trying to manage my game, stay in there. It's a U.S. Open. Guys are not going to go low. Even though I got off to such a poor start again, I just hung around. I was just trying to get back to even par, either for the tournament or for the day. The day would be great. But even if I finished at even par for the tournament, it wouldn't be a bad thing either. And then, all of a sudden, things started turning."

That left Westwood one stroke behind, while Rocco Mediate, who had one point in the middle of the round held a three-stroke lead, was the last of the three players under par after 72 left him at one-under 212. Geoff Ogilvy shot 72 and D.J. Trahan shot 73, leaving both at one-over 214.

Phil Mickelson had hoped to work his way back toward even par for the championship. Instead, he blew himself out of contention when he suffered a quadruple-bogey nine at the par-five 13th hole, shot 76 and dropped to 222, tied for 47th place.

Woods wasn't much enjoying his round either. The day appeared to belong to others, most notably Mediate, who was playing in the final group with Stuart Appleby, the second-round leader. While Appleby shot 41 on his first nine on his way to 79 for a tie for 19th at 228, Mediate went out in 34 with birdies at the second and fifth holes offsetting his bogey at the third. When he birdied the 10th hole from eight feet, he was four under par and three strokes clear of the field.

Westwood was hanging in, but Woods again made double bogey at the par-four first hole on the way to an outward 37. He was five strokes behind Mediate when he bogeyed the long par-four 12th. Things were looking even bleaker when his drive at the 13th went far right. After taking a free drop for line-of-sight relief, he hit a five iron from 210 yards that stopped on the back of the green, 70 feet from the hole. The double-breaking putt tracked slowly toward the hole and then veered sharply left and in for eagle-three.

"The antics, I saw it all," said Mediate, who had been standing back in the fairway. "Completely out of his mind. The stuff he does is unreal."

Mediate bogeyed the hole, but Woods gave the stroke back at the 14th after a wild drive cost him another bogey. At the 15th, Woods produced another poor swing and lingered on the tee box for a few anxious seconds before carrying on.

"I just keep telling myself that if it grabs me and if I get that shooting pain, I get it, but it's always after impact, so go ahead and just make the proper swing if I can," Woods said. "But if pain hits, pain hits. So be it. It's just pain."

Woods managed to save par at the 15th and again at the 16th, then drove in the rough again at the 17th, from which he began his torrid finish.

Mediate tripped at the 15th when he couldn't get to the green after an errant drive. His third shot from rough bounded over the green into a bunker, and he blasted out and two-putted for double-bogey six to fall to one under par for the championship.

"I made one little mistake and got ripped, but that's what the Open does to you," Mediate said.

Third-Round Leaders: Tiger Woods 70–210, Lee Westwood 70–211, Rocco Mediate 72–212, Geoff Ogilvy 72–214, D.J. Trahan 73–214, Hunter Mahan 69–215, Camilo Villegas 71–215, Robert Allenby 73–215, Miguel Angel Jimenez 74–215, Robert Karlsson 75–215

Fourth Round

His injured leg was hurting worse but Tiger Woods wanted nothing more than to play golf for another day, with the U.S. Open at stake. He had to make a birdie on the par-five 72nd hole to tie Rocco Mediate and send the championship to an 18-hole playoff the next day. The putt was 12 feet, separating Woods from possibly his 14th major title or Mediate, his first.

Setting the scene Woods explained: "The putt was probably about two and a half balls outside right. And the green wasn't very smooth. I kept telling myself, make a pure stroke. If it bounces in or out, so be it, at least I can hold my head up high and hit a pure stroke. I hit it exactly where I wanted it, and it went in."

It bounced along but on the intended line and caught the edge of the hole, swirled to the back corner and then down. Woods responded with vigorous fist pumps with both arms.

"Unbelievable," said Mediate, who watched on television from the scoring room, about 200 yards away. "I knew he would make it. That's what he does."

Mediate, who had to win a playoff in sectional qualifying just to get to the Open, was now the last hurdle for Woods. Mediate shot even-par 71 in the fourth round, and Woods finished with 73 for their 283 totals, one under par.

The fourth round started for Woods with a double bogey, his third of the week on the first hole. That made the leader Lee Westwood, with him in the final group, and Westwood went to the turn one stroke in front of Woods and Mediate and two ahead of 2006 U.S. Open champion Geoff Ogilvy.

Woods took back the lead when he birdied the 11th hole from three feet and Westwood bogeyed the 10th and 12th. Mediate got up and down from a greenside bunker at the 14th just as Woods and Westwood were making bogeys at the par-five 13th. Westwood birdied the 14th after driving the green to end a string of three bogeys in four holes, but Woods had to settle for a par-four. He was running out of holes.

"It looked like I was shooting myself out of the tournament," Woods said. But Mediate pulled his drive at the 15th and bogeyed to drop back to one under par. Then Woods also missed the fairway at the 15th, took bogey and slid back to even par, tied with Westwood.

Many observers had figured that the 18th hole, at 527 yards and reachable for much of the field in the final round, would swing the championship. With a one-stroke lead, Mediate could put two strokes between himself and the two in the final group if he could somehow make a birdie. He drove in the fairway and laid up to 106 yards for his third shot. But he struck it too firmly and watched it settle 30 feet above the hole. His first putt never threatened the hole and he tapped in for par. There was nothing more he could do.

"I did the absolute best that I could. I have nothing left right now. I'm toast," said Mediate.

The final two were back on the 18th tee. Westwood pulled his shot into the left fairway bunker and Woods pushed his into the right bunker. Both laid up, but Woods hit his into the right rough with a nine iron out of a perfect lie. He spun and swung his club in anger and frustration.

Westwood, like Mediate, powered his approach 25 feet past the hole. He had to settle for par and 73 for a 284 total, one stroke too many. That left Woods, with 95 yards to the front edge of the green and 101 yards to the hole. He took his 60-degree wedge for the shot, to plow through the thick kikuyu grass. "It came out perfectly," Woods said, leaving him that 12-foot putt.

It was reminiscent of the nine-foot birdie putt Woods had to convert on the 72nd hole of the 2000 PGA Championship to continue in a playoff at Valhalla. "It feels very similar to what Valhalla felt like," Woods said. "If I didn't make that putt, I don't get to keep playing. At best, I gave myself a chance to win the tournament tomorrow. And that's all I can ask for."

There was relish in his voice when Mediate said: "I'm playing against a monster tomorrow morning. I've got to get excited to play. I get to play against the best player that ever played. I want to see what happens against the man. Whatever happens, happens. I'm happy that I'm here and I will give it everything I have and see what we do."

It should be noted that Phil Mickelson, the hometown favorite, enjoyed his best round with 68 and tied for 18th place at 290.

The Final Leaders: Rocco Mediate 71–283, Tiger Woods 73–283, Lee Westwood 73–284, Robert Karlsson 71–286, D.J. Trahan 72–286, Carl Pettersson 68–287, John Merrick 71–287, Miguel Angel Jimenez 72–287, Heath Slocum 65–288, Eric Axley 69–288, Brandt Snedeker 71–288, Camilo Villegas 73–288, Geoff Ogilvy 74–288

Playoff

With a crowd of about 25,000 in tow, Tiger Woods, age 32, and Rocco Mediate, trying to become the oldest U.S. Open champion at 45 years, six months, matched wits, shots and pained expressions.

Woods appeared to seize firm control when he birdied the sixth and seventh holes to erase an early bogey and get to one under par, while Mediate, looking uneasy, bogeyed the fifth after a poor bunker shot, three-putted the par-five ninth from 18 feet for bogey, and took five for another bogey at the 10th hole. The margin was three shots.

Mediate appeared spent. But then Woods, uncharacteristically, provided an opening. He bogeyed the 11th after driving in a bunker. Then he bogeyed the 12th the same way. Seeing a thin layer of hope, Mediate rattled off three straight birdies, only one of which Woods could match.

"All of a sudden bang, bang, bang, I pick up three, four shots, and in a few holes, I'm one up," Mediate said.

It was just that fast. Mediate converted a five-footer at the par-five 13th to match Woods's birdie and then got up and down for a second birdie after driving to the front edge of the green at the 14th. At the 15th, a curling 20-foot putt went down for his third birdie in a row.

They matched pars on the 16th and 17th, then on the 18th, Woods had a 45-foot eagle chance which he left four feet from the hole. Mediate then had a 20-foot putt for a birdie and the victory. "I said to myself, 'You've waited your whole life for this putt, just don't lag it,'" Mediate said.

He didn't, but he didn't have the line and it ran three feet past.

They were tied after 18 holes with even-par 71s and went on to sudden death at the par-four seventh hole. Mediate hooked his drive into the left fairway bunker and found an awkward lie. He missed the green with his second shot from 284 yards, then had a chip to 18 feet past the hole. He missed, and Woods won with a par. "Great fight," Woods told Mediate as they embraced.

"Obviously, I would have loved to win," Mediate said. "I don't know what else to say. They wanted a show. They got one. I never quit. I never quit. I've been beaten a few times and came back, and I got what I wanted. I got a chance to beat the best player in the world. And I came up just a touch short. Nothing he does amazes me."

Woods was no less confounded by an outcome that eventually ended in his favor. "All things considered, I don't know how I ended up in this position, to be honest with you," Woods said. "It was a long week. There was a lot of doubt, a lot of questions going into the week. And here we are 91 holes later.

"I'm glad I'm done. I really don't feel like playing anymore."

4. The Open Championship

As they walked down the 18th fairway on Sunday, Padraig Harrington turned to Greg Norman and said: "I'm sorry it isn't your story that is being told this evening."

Norman led the 137th Open Championship by two strokes entering the final round at Royal Birkdale Golf Club, but Harrington emerged as the champion by four strokes, becoming the first European to successfully defend the title in more than 100 years (since James Braid won in 1905 and 1906). In doing so Harrington turned back the 53-year-old Norman's quixotic run to become the oldest champion, a record that had stood since 1867, when Old Tom Morris won at the age of 46.

The Great White Shark of 1980s and 1990s fame, and the winner of this championship in 1986 and 1993, had not played competitive golf since May and had not led a major championship since the 1996 Masters, which was notable for the most spectacular collapse in a career that had included dramatic losses in all four majors.

Norman became the sentimental favorite over the four days on the English coast near Southport. The Australian also was on honeymoon with his new wife, the former tennis star Chris Evert. "It would have been a fantastic story," Harrington said. "Greg has been a great champion, and you know, another win at this time in his career would have been the icing on the cake."

Instead, Harrington played the final six holes in four under par, including an eagle on the 17th hole, for a round of 69, one under par, and a total of 283, three over par. A late charge by Ian Poulter resulted in 69 and a 287 total for second place. Norman shot 77 and tied for third at 289 with Henrik Stenson, who finished in 71. Jim Furyk and amateur Chris Wood tied for sixth place at 290, ahead of a group of nine at 292 including past Open champions Ben Curtis and Ernie Els, who had started with 78 and 80, respectively.

"Obviously I'm disappointed," said Norman, frowning for the first time in what had been a magical week. "That would be an understatement to say I was disappointed. But it was a tough day today."

Four days of howling winds, and often rain, made Royal Birkdale, a 7,173-yard, par-70 course, play to a stroke average of 74.9 for the week. But Harrington played three stunning approach shots — for birdie at the 13th hole, for eagle at the 17th, and for par at the last — before being called forward to collect the silver claret jug once more.

"I'm holding on to this," Harrington, age 36, told the crowd at the 18th green as he cradled the trophy. "I had a great year as Open champion, so much so I didn't want to give it back (at the beginning of the week)," the Irishman said. "It's a little shinier than I remember. They obviously cleaned it up nicely. I'm looking forward to getting it back in its rightful spot on the breakfast table."

Harrington added: "I never put last year down as an isolated event. I felt I was going to win another one, but it's come around quicker than I thought.

Never at any stage, or if I did I stopped myself, did I think about what it means to win a second Open. Obviously winning a major puts you in a special club. Winning two of them puts you in a new club altogether."

There were many differences between this and the victory at Carnoustie, in Scotland, a year earlier. His wins were with Tiger Woods in 2007 and without Tiger this time. He started with a six-stroke deficit in 2007 and went out in the final pairing this time. He stumbled into a playoff in 2007 and raced away this time. He won by someone else's misfortune in 2007 (when Sergio Garcia missed a putt to win) and removed luck from the equation all together this time.

"There is a different satisfaction this year," Harrington said. "Last year was a great high, it was a great thrill, and it was exciting and unexpected, and I was on top of the world when I won.

"This year is more satisfying. I feel more accomplished. It was the first time I was in the last group of a major on Sunday. It's a different pressure, it's a different stress, and to shoot under par and come through all that and by a few shots will give me a lot more confidence."

First Round

On the first day of the Open Championship, Royal Birkdale had very little in common with Torrey Pines, venue for the U.S. Open a month earlier, except that both were by the sea. Far from the warm sunshine of California, Royal Birkdale was wet, cold and windy. Summer it was not. But Rocco Mediate was there, just as he was at Torrey Pines while battling for 91 holes before losing to Tiger Woods.

Woods was finished for the year, but Mediate was back at the top of the leaderboard, posting 69, one under par, with birdies on the last two holes. The affable 45-year-old American journeyman was tied for the lead with the Irishman Graeme McDowell, the surprise first-round leader at Hoylake two years ago, and Australia's Robert Allenby, who both followed Mediate and both also birdied the last two holes.

"Great day, fun, insane," Mediate said. "I have no explanation for that whatsoever, no idea why that happened. The guys this morning had it the worst. Those conditions were unbelievable. Then the rain stopped, and it was easier this afternoon, for sure. I was fortunate today."

The morning starters were battered by 30-mile-an-hour gusts and sheets of rain that soaked through rain suits and numbed the fingers, hands and feet. The stroke average for those who finished play before noon was 77.81. For those who finished later, it was 74.49.

Behind the three leaders were three players with even-par 70s. They were another American veteran, Bart Bryant, and two more Australians, Adam Scott, who bogeyed two of the last three holes, and two-time past Open champion Greg Norman.

Generally, the course set-up was praised. "I think this is the best Open I've ever played in," Norman said. "I think the golf course has been set up by the R&A about the fairest and toughest I've seen. It doesn't favor one particular player or style of player. It's very well balanced and gives an opportunity to everyone to put a number on the board."

Struggling with injured fingers that went numb, past Open champion

Sandy Lyle withdrew after playing 10 holes in 11 over par. Rich Beem, also injured, withdrew after playing nine holes in 12 over.

Vijay Singh had 80, as did the other two in his group, Hunter Mahan and Reinier Saxton, the British Amateur champion from the Netherlands. Ernie Els also had 80, his worst score ever in the Open. He was even par after five holes but unraveled with three sixes in a row from the 14th for triple bogey, bogey and double bogey. Phil Mickelson took triple bogey at the sixth on his way to 79.

Past Open champion Ben Curtis and Lee Westbrook started badly but kept battling. Curtis started seven, six and finished with 78. Westbrook went out in 40 but came back in 35 for his 75.

Royal Birkdale's 1983 winner and a five-time Open champion, Tom Watson, at 58 the oldest man in the field, shot 74, the same score as playing companion Justin Rose, returning to the scene of his amazing performance 10 years ago, when he tied for fourth place as an amateur.

Rose got plenty of attention entering the championship, as did defending champion Padraig Harrington and Sergio Garcia, the runner-up at Carnoustie last year and now the betting favorite. Garcia shot 72 and Harrington posted 74 despite a right wrist injured in practice the previous Saturday.

Harrington had played nine holes Tuesday in practice, but after two shots on Wednesday, he went in for treatment. Later he simply walked the second nine. His physiotherapist convinced Harrington that he could do no more damage, so the decision was made to play whatever the pain. There were a few twinges while warming up on the range, but the real test would be playing out of the rough.

That test would come at the very first hole, and there were more visits to the rough than he would have liked on the opening few holes, but he turned that into a positive. "I was apprehensive going onto the course about hitting from the rough," Harrington said. "Of course, that's what I managed to do over the first four or five holes, but when it didn't hurt, I started to become more relaxed. After seven or eight holes, I wasn't thinking about it at all."

First-Round Leaders: Rocco Mediate 69, Graeme McDowell 69, Robert Allenby 69, Greg Norman 70, Adam Scott 70, Bart Bryant 70, Retief Goosen 71, Mike Weir 71, Jim Furyk 71, Gregory Havret 71, Fredrik Jacobson 71, Peter Hanson 71, Simon Wakefield 71, Anthony Wall 71

Second Round

Even though K.J. Choi came in around dinner time with 67 to take the halfway lead at 139, one under par, the second round belonged to Greg Norman, who at breakfast time had holed an improbable birdie putt from 45 feet on the first green and who had gone to lunch as the clubhouse leader.

With two rounds of even-par 70, Norman had withstood the vicious combination of wind and rain that had buffeted the coast for two days and — until Choi passed him by one stroke — was the only player to win the battle against the tough, old links course.

Norman was one stroke ahead of 26-year-old Camilo Villegas, the promising Colombian player who had eight birdies, including five straight to close out his round of 65.

At two-over-par 142 was a group of seven that included the three co-leaders from the first round — Rocco Mediate, Graeme McDowell and Robert Allenby, each of whom shot 73 in the second round — and also David Duval, the former world No. 1 who had slipped to a tie for No. 1087. Duval shot 69. Also bunched at 142 were defending champion Padraig Harrington, Jim Furyk and Open rookie Alexander Noren of Sweden. And Sergio Garcia slipped to 73 and 145.

With all these subplots battling for attention, Norman, the 1986 and 1993 Open champion who now spends more time playing tennis with his wife than competitive golf, stole the spotlight. He had not won an official professional event in 10 years, but here he was acknowledging a thunderous reception on the 18th green.

"Of course you feel like you are you're stepping back in time," acknowledged Norman, who was No. 1 in the world for a total of 331 weeks between September 1986 and January 1998. "My expectations were almost nil coming in, to tell you the truth. I hadn't played a lot of golf. Expectations are still realistically low, and I have to be that way, too, because I can't sit here and say, 'Okay, it's great, I'm playing well and I'm doing it.

"Well, I am playing well, I am doing it, but I still haven't been there for a long time."

Norman's last real shot at a major championship was in 1996, when he went into the final round of the Masters with a six-stroke lead, shot 78, and lost by five strokes to Nick Faldo.

After the birdie on the first hole, Norman was tied with the three first-round leaders. He tangled with the rough both left and right on the sixth and took a double-bogey six, but he hit back with birdies on the next two holes. A four iron from 181 yards finished 25 feet away at the par-three seventh, and he followed that putt with another putt from 15 feet at the eighth. Then there was a long stretch of par golf, interrupted only by his bogey-six at the 17th.

The conditions were better than in the first round, with rain only in brief showers and the wind not quite so strong. Again, the morning starters had the worst of it, so the field was beginning to even out.

Of the opening-day leaders, Mediate shared the lead with Norman until making a double bogey at the 11th, and after a bogey-six at the 17th, finished in style by hitting an eight iron to six inches for a birdie at the last hole. McDowell dropped out of the lead with a bogey at the second and posted three more bogeys before regaining his rhythm with a wonderful shot on the 16th hole, a three iron from 180 yards into the wind to five feet for a birdie. Allenby continued that pattern. He bogeyed the first two holes but then birdied two of the last four, joining Mediate and McDowell with 73.

After bogeys on the first two holes, Villegas was eight over par for the championship and in danger of missing the cut. Birdies at the fourth, fifth and ninth put the Colombian out in 33. Then after bogeying the 13th, he finished with five birdies in a row for his 65. It was an astonishing sequence. He started by hitting a five iron to 16 feet at the par-three 14th, then had a pitch-and-putt birdie at the par-five 15th with a nine iron to six feet. Then came a five iron to 17 feet at the 16th, a greenside bunker shot to three feet at the par-five 17th, and a 25-foot putt at the last.

The cut fell at nine over par, and among those to miss were past Open champions Paul Lawrie, Mark O'Meara, Tom Watson and John Daly, and major winners Vijay Singh, Geoff Ogilvy and Angel Cabrera. Ernie Els made the cut on the number with 69, 11 better than in the fist round, as did Paul Casey. Ben Curtis, with 69, and Phil Mickelson, after 68, were at seven over. Colin Montgomerie came in with 36 for 75 that kept him alive at eight over.

If keeping mistakes to a minimum was the key, then Choi was the man. He had only one bogey on his card of 67. Only Mickelson and Soren Hansen, who also broke par with 69, could say the same. Choi's dropped shot came at the first, and from then on the Korean was immaculate. He hit a nine iron to a foot for a birdie at the third, then ground out the pars. His run to the top of the leaderboard began with a 20-foot birdie putt on the 13th, then a two-putt birdie from 30 feet at the 17th and another birdie from 25 feet at the final hole.

"Today was probably my best round I ever played in the Open," Choi said.

Choi was not the only player to finish strongly in the late afternoon. Harrington went out in 34, then bogeyed the 10th and 11th holes to be six over par. He then was four under par for the last four holes, starting with a wedge to six feet at the 15th. He hit a five iron for his second shot on the 17th and holed from 30 feet for an eagle, and on the 18th, he hit a nine iron from 183 yards to five feet and holed that putt.

Second-Round Leaders: K.J. Choi 67–139, Greg Norman 70–140, Camilo Villegas 65–141, Rocco Mediate 73–142, Graeme McDowell 73–142, Jim Furyk 71–142, Robert Allenby 73–142, Alexander Noren 70–142, Padraig Harrington 68–142, David Duval 69–142

Third Round

The wind was at its strongest in the third round, gusting up to 50 miles an hour at times, which meant that thinking about anything other than how to navigate the links of Royal Birkdale would have been disastrous. As the cliché demanded, players had to focus on one shot at a time. It worked for some, and in particular, for Greg Norman and Padraig Harrington.

At the age of 53, Norman ended as the oldest leader ever in an Open Championship, while Harrington put himself into position to become the first European for more than 100 years to defend the Open title.

It was warmer and dry, at least, and the R&A had placed the hole locations on flatter parts of the greens and moved the tees forward on three holes. It was an extremely difficult day for everyone and best scores were even-par 70 by four players. Norman shot 72 for a 54-hole total of 212, two over par, the highest score for a third-round leader in half a century.

"I would put it in the top three hardest rounds I've ever played under the circumstances," said Norman, whose closest pursuers were Harrington and the second-round leader, K.J. Choi, both at 214. Harrington shot 72 and Choi, 75. "I've played under tougher weather conditions, but under the circumstances, the third round of a major championship and on the Royal Birkdale golf course, it was just brutal today."

David Duval began the round three strokes out of the lead and shot 83 after starting with a triple bogey. Nine players scored 80 or higher, and the average score was 75.76, almost six strokes over par. Camilo Villegas started in third place but shot himself out of contention with 79. Rocco Mediate fell back with the first of his two 76s on the weekend.

Simon Wakefield was alone in fourth place at 215 after one of the four rounds of 70. Ben Curtis, the 2003 Open champion, started the day tied for 38th place, shot 70, and moved up to a tie for fifth at 217 with Anthony Kim, Ross Fisher and Alexander Noren. Henrik Stenson's 70 tied him for ninth, and Davis Love returned the other 70, rising to a tie for 15th after making the cut on the number, tied for 69th.

When Choi, after five pars, drove into a pot bunker at the sixth and took a double bogey, no one was under par and no one would be again this week. Choi marveled at Norman's shot-making ability. "He's a very imaginative player," said the Korean, "more imaginative than me."

Norman was relying on all his experience to find his way around the course. At the fifth hole he hit a five iron onto the green from only 120 yards. "The yardage was mentioned to me, but I didn't pay attention to it," Norman explained. "I already saw the shot that I knew I had to play to get close to the hole."

Elsewhere, there was Norman's seven iron from 104 yards, and at the 17th he found the green with a second shot of 209 yards played with a six iron that started out over the grandstand to the left of the green. He came back from a double bogey at the 10th with a 12-foot birdie putt on the 14th, and nearly eagled the 17th with a 25-foot putt that stopped just short. As a closing gesture, Norman grazed the edge of the hole with a birdie chip after missing the 18th green, electrifying the grandstands with a vintage jolt from the Great White Shark.

"I'm sure there are players probably saying, 'My God, what's he doing there?'" Norman said. "But I've played golf before. I've played successful golf before."

Norman had not done so for a while, and he almost did not here. While he and Chris Evert were honeymooning the previous week at Skibo Castle in Scotland, he told her he was thinking about not playing because he was not prepared. Evert told him he ought to use the event as preparation for the next week's Senior British Open at Troon. He decided she was right, and went on to hit practice balls and recall swing thoughts.

Now Norman was standing close to one of the most remarkable achievements in golf history, but he did not need to be reminded of the biggest flaw in his career record, that he had failed to win six of the seven times he had the 54-hole lead in a major championship.

Third-Round Leaders: Greg Norman 72–212, Padraig Harrington 72–214, K.J. Choi 75–214, Simon Wakefield 70–215, Ben Curtis 70–217, Ross Fisher 71–217, Anthony Kim 71–217, Alexander Noren 75–217, Henrik Stenson 70–218, Graeme Storm 72–218, Chris Wood 73–218, Ian Poulter 75–218, Robert Allenby 76–218, Rocco Mediate 76–218

Fourth Round

Greg Norman's two-stroke overnight lead evaporated after he bogeyed the first three holes to fall behind Harrington, who went on making his pars, having found the pace of the greens. His superb touch helped with long two-putts at the fifth and sixth holes, while Norman dropped another shot at the sixth.

Up ahead, only one player was making a move, the amateur Chris Wood. He made birdies at the seventh and ninth. Although Wood never got closer than within three of the lead, he was then tied for third place.

Harrington missed the green at the par-three seventh for his first bogey, but then he bogeyed the next two holes. With Norman making three pars to be out in 38 to Harrington's 37, suddenly Norman was back in the lead by one.

A crucial moment arrived at the 10th hole. Norman was in trouble, struggling in vain to save par, but when Harrington's birdie attempt ran four feet past the hole, suddenly Harrington was in trouble too. He faced a tricky return putt on one of the most exposed greens on the course. He made it, but had to watch it all the way to the hole. "That putt really settled him down," Norman said.

Wood's moment came to an end with three bogeys in a row from the 11th, but he went on to tie for fifth, the best finish for an amateur in the Open since Justin Rose tied for fourth at Royal Birkdale in 1998. "It's been the week of my life," Wood said. The support I've had from my family and friends, everyone at the golf club, and all the gallery was fantastic." Wood finished at 10 over par, four strokes ahead of Thomas Sherreard for the silver medal awarded to the low amateur completing 72 holes.

Playing alongside Wood, Ian Poulter seemed to be inspired by the energy and attention their pairing was receiving. After bogeys at two of the first three holes, birdies at the ninth and 11th got him back to eight over and within three of the lead. He missed a fine chance from five feet at the 13th and also failed to birdie the par-five 15th, but as Harrington slipped back, Poulter was now only one behind. Poulter holed from 18 feet at the 16th and now was tied for the lead.

Poulter missed a birdie effort from eight feet at the 17th, while back at the 13th Harrington was finding his form just at the right time. Harrington's approach from 229 yards with a five iron finished 15 feet away, and he holed the putt. Norman made his third bogey in four holes, and Harrington led by one over Poulter.

Next Poulter needed to get safely past the 18th, and did so only with a 20-foot putt for par. "It was such as great buzz all around the whole back nine," said Poulter, whose 69 put him at seven over. "I don't think I have enjoyed a week as much as this. I've done my best and it wasn't quite enough. Hats off to Patrick. Going back-to-back is very impressive. But I'll be back for lots more of this." So, too, would Henrik Stenson, who closed with 71 to tie for third at nine over.

Back at the par-five 15th, Harrington two-putted for his four and Norman claimed his only birdie of the day. After they both parred the 16th, it was evident that Harrington was more worried about Norman, three behind, than Poulter, two shots behind in the clubhouse. Harrington's caddie asked if he wanted to lay up on the par-five 17th. He had his favorite five wood in his hands, seeing the 249 yards ahead. "I was worried if I laid up and made par, it would be giving Greg a chance to get within one of me with an eagle," Harrington said.

His stroke was so pure that Harrington's caddie said "Good shot" while the ball was still in the air, and Harrington punched the air when the result was confirmed that his ball was three feet from the hole. Norman found trouble but made his par, while Harrington holed out for eagle, and then hit a three wood off the 18th tee. "Once I hit that, I knew I'd won the Open," Harrington said. For good measure, he hit a five-iron approach that almost went in, but by then he was already enjoying the champion's ovation. He took two putts for his 69 and 283 total, and Norman finished with 77 for 289 to tie Stenson for third place.

Harrington and his caddie, Ronan Flood, enjoyed the walk to the finish, which they had not been able to do the previous year because the championship ended in a playoff. "What a great experience it is to come down the 18th at the Open on the weekend with the stands full, and it's even more special when you're winning the Open," Harrington said. "The only experience that could beat it in a dramatic sense is actually holing a putt to win the Open. But there is no more comfortable or pleasurable feeling than having a four-shot lead and knowing your work is done."

The Final Leaders: Padraig Harrington 69–283, Ian Poulter 69–287, Henrik Stenson 71–289, Greg Norman 77–289, Jim Furyk 71–290, Chris Wood 72–290, David Howell 67–292, Robert Karlsson 69–292, Ernie Els 69–292, Paul Casey 70–292, Stephen Ames 71–292, Steve Stricker 73–292, Robert Allenby 74–292, Anthony Kim 75–292, Ben Curtis 75–292

5. PGA Championship

This was the 90th PGA Championship, but a few were suggesting it might go into the record books as the Asterisk PGA. It was a measure of Tiger Woods's presence in golf that he dominated tournaments even when he wasn't playing in them. Woods, winner of four PGA Championships in his 11 visits, including the last in 2007, sat this one out, recuperating from knee surgery. The big question was, as one media representative put it: "Casual golf fans will look at this tournament much like the (British) Open and say Tiger Woods isn't here, so what does it matter?"

The question, in one form or another, was directed at many of the players as they arrived at Oakland Hills Country Club in Bloomfield Township, Michigan, a suburb of Detroit. It was especially meaningful to Padraig Harrington. He won the 2007 Open Championship in Britain with Woods in the field, then won again a few weeks earlier, but this time without Woods in the field. There was a hint of contempt in the question: Was a victory without Woods in the field tainted? Harrington fielded it with grace and bite.

"I've got to say Jack Nicklaus didn't play in the Open Championship either, neither did Arnold Palmer or Ben Hogan," Harrington said. "So you can only win the tournament you're playing in, you can only win the week you're playing, and you can only beat the field there."

Harrington would do exactly all those things that week, and when he walked away with the PGA Championship trophy the following Sunday, he wasn't wearing an asterisk. And the course he won it on didn't carry an asterisk, either.

The famed — or notorious — South Course at Oakland Hills was the "monster" of Ben Hogan fame. Oakland Hills was revamped for the 1951 U.S. Open by Robert Trent Jones to meet the challenge of improved golf clubs and balls. Jones lengthened the course and in general toughened it from the original Donald Ross creation. When Hogan had finally won, he uttered that famous line: "I'm glad I brought this course, this monster, to its knees."

If anyone had an edge at Oakland Hills, it was the Europeans who whipped the Americans there in the 2004 Ryder Cup. Among the veterans of that European frolic were Sergio Garcia and Lee Westwood, who each went 4-0-1, Harrington, 4-1, and the ever-present Colin Montgomerie, 3-1. But that was 2004. This was the new Oakland Hills. The club summoned another Jones — Rees, a son of Trent — to rearm the course against modern equipment. Jones added bunkers, grew rough, and lengthened the par-70 course to 7,445 yards. What occupied golfers most wasn't the absence of Woods but the presence of this new monster.

"It's frustrating when you stand on par-threes and you're aiming for a greenside bunker because you know that's the only way you can make par," said England's Ian Poulter. Another Englishman was more graphic. "They are sucking the fun out of the championships when you set it up like that," Westwood said. The PGA was noted for providing the most user-friendly courses of all of the four majors. But the players thought they had stepped into a U.S. Open here. Oakland Hills was at its toughest for the first two rounds, playing to an average of 74.85 strokes. There were only 13 rounds under par. The PGA relented after the 36-hole cut, watering some areas and cutting rough to three inches in the landing areas. Heavy rains did the rest. The final two rounds averaged at 73.18, and there were 19 rounds under par.

First Round

Every golf tournament has its surprises. This PGA Championship opened with bunches, chief among them Sweden's Robert Karlsson and India's Jeev Milkha Singh. They shared the first-round lead with 68s, two under par.

Karlsson, the 6-foot-5 blond who spent a lot of time trying to sort out the psychology of the game, was the only man in the field who had finished in the top 10 in the previous three majors, tying for eighth in the Masters, fourth in the U.S. Open and seventh in the Open Championship. This time, he was a candidate for an early departure. At the first hole, he bounced his second shot over the green and double-bogeyed. "Just made a bit of stupidity," he said. But he birdied the next three holes and birdied five overall on the first nine and shot 68.

Singh was almost flying blind at Oakland Hills. A sore ankle limited his practice, but he still shot 68. He bogeyed the first hole, but eagled the par-five second when his four-iron second shot caromed off the greenside slope and stopped five feet from the hole. His chances in the PGA? "It depends on how the ankle holds up," he said.

The first round was interrupted late Thursday afternoon by frightening skies, then was resumed about 7 p.m., and then falling darkness left 18 players to finish Friday morning. Among them was Argentina's Andres Romero, who finished par-bogey for 69, one shot off the lead. "I didn't hit the rough very often," said Romero, "and when I hit from the rough, I made the putt, which was good."

Sergio Garcia, the boy hero of the 1999 PGA Championship, as runner-up to Tiger Woods, opened with a solid 69. He was sailing along, with birdies at the sixth and 13th holes, but bogeyed the 18th, which was to become the fire-breathing dragon of the championship. But that wasn't the only trap. "Like, for example, on No. 9 today," he said. "It's almost stupid to go for that pin. The room for error is like three feet. I decided to hit a good, solid shot to the middle of the green and try to make three a different way."

Among others likely to succeed: Phil Mickelson, the 2005 PGA champion, bogeyed his first two holes and battled back for 70. "Everybody is going to make bogeys," Mickelson said. "If you can just keep your round around par, you're going to be in the tournament."

Adam Scott, always highly regarded, shot 77, and Vijay Singh, a two-time champion and fresh from winning the Bridgestone Invitational, labored for 76.

Among the up-and-coming, Anthony Kim, age 23, in his second PGA, shot a dramatic 70. It included three bogeys in four holes going into the turn and a spectacular eagle off a 350-yard drive at the second hole (his 11th). And

Colombia's Camilo Villegas, age 26, playing in his third PGA, went five over par in five holes but also eagled the second hole and shot 74.

Harrington shot 71, but looked anything but a winner. He birdied the first three holes, then sputtered the rest of the way, scattering five bogeys and one other birdie. "The score is good," he said. "I have to sit down and get that into my head. It's all about staying patient for the first three days."

If this PGA needed more spice, it got it from the chase for the Ryder Cup. This was the final event for Americans to earn points for the automatic eight berths and also an excellent chance for others to impress Paul Azinger, who would fill the final four spots with his captain's picks. At the moment, however, Azinger, the 1993 PGA champion, was a competitor himself, and after opening with 72, he would go on to finish tied for 63rd.

Then there was the other kind of surprise. Lee Westwood, the leading European Tour money winner, who tied for second in the Bridgestone Invitational a week earlier and was solo third in the U.S. Open in June, shot 77. "Standing on the 17th tee, I asked my caddie if he could hear the sea," Westwood said. "I was sure I could hear my holiday calling. But I hung in there." (But not well enough. He would shoot 78 in the second round and head for his holiday.)

First-Round Leaders: Robert Karlsson 68, Jeev Milkha Singh 68, Andres Romero 69, Ken Duke 69, Sergio Garcia 69, Billy Mayfair 69, Sean O'Hair 69, Phil Mickelson 70, Brian Gay 70, Michael Allen 70, Anthony Kim 70

Second Round

The 36-hole cut came in at 148, a generous eight over par, and left some big names high and dry. Vijay Singh, a two-time winner this year, was the most surprising victim. He shot another 76, including a five-putt six at the par-three ninth hole. Masters champion Trevor Immelman double-bogeyed the first hole and also shot 76. Scott Verplank had two double bogeys and shot 77. Stewart Cink, the American Ryder Cup points leader, left after 76. Hunter Mahan suffered a triple bogey and two doubles and shot a whopping 81. Colin Montgomerie at 45 was no longer a favorite, but who could believe he would shoot 84. "I got off to a bad start," said Monty, "and kept it going."

Jeev Milkha Singh and Karlsson seemed about to join them. Karlsson bogeyed his first four holes, on his way to 77, and Singh bogeyed four of his last six before the turn and shot 74. Oakland Hills had to be reined in. It would take a strong hand.

That hand belonged to J.B. Holmes, age 26, the very heavy hitter from Kentucky, who shot his way into the lead despite some wayward tee shots. In the first round, he had hit only six fairways and a mere five greens in regulation, and shot 71. In the second round, he improved to nine fairways and 14 greens, and shot 69, for a one-under 139, the only player under par at the halfway point. "I'm hitting the ball really well," Holmes said. "If I make a few more putts, if I can hit it like I did today..." The key to his third round was the three straight birdies from the par-five 12th. There he chipped to four feet, holed an eight-footer at the par-three 13th, then a 25-footer at the 14th. He drove the green at the sixth — playing at 300 yards — and two-putted from 40 feet. Even so, he joined in the chorus of complaints.

"There are a lot of holes that are almost unplayable," Holmes said. "I don't think that's real fair when you hit good shots and in some cases you get penalized for them."

Three players bunched up in the second round, just a stroke behind him at par 140: Ben Curtis, Justin Rose and Charlie Wi. Curtis and Rose shot 67s, the day's low. A bunkered tee shot at the par-three third hole cost Curtis his only bogey. Three of his four birdies came off sharp putting, from 10, 30 and 10 feet. At the 12th? "Got lucky," Curtis said. He missed the fairway 30 yards to the right but ended up in flattened grass. He hit a three iron into a front bunker and got up and down. "The putting was better," Curtis said. "No three-putts."

The highlight of Rose's day, awkwardly enough, was a bogey at the 18th (his ninth hole). He bunkered his tee shot, got plugged in another bunker, hacked out into the fairway, hit a seven iron to eight feet, and holed the putt for five. "That was a really key point in my round," Rose said. Toss in birdies at the 12th and 15th holes, and two more coming home, including a wedge to two feet at his 13th (the fourth).

Charlie Wi, best known on the Nationwide Tour, was playing in his first PGA Championship — in fact, his first major. Wi shot a nicely balanced 70 — a bogey at the fifth hole, a double bogey at the eighth, and three birdies. "I'm very excited about being near the lead," Wi said. "I want to see how I handle myself and see what the pressure feels like."

David Toms, the 2001 PGA champion, turned back the odds and moved into contention at 69–141, two strokes off the lead, despite his age, 41, and a chronic bad back. "It flares up from time to time, but I don't want to use that as an excuse," Toms said. Things looked promising for Sergio Garcia until he four-putted the par-three 17th from 50 feet for five and a 73–142 total. "I just hope I got rid of my bad moments today," he said.

The storyline included Rocco Mediate, a hero of the U.S. Open. He shot 74 and was at 147, eight strokes off the lead, in danger of missing the cut, but delighted just to be finished. "Very glad," Mediate said. "Very glad." Brandt Snedeker (71–142) echoed Mediate's relief. "Brutal, absolutely brutal," said Snedeker.

Phil Mickelson bogeyed three of his last five holes for 73–143 and was troubled by his short game. "It's hard to say if my technique or feel is bad, or if just the shot is tough," he said.

Padraig Harrington also was puzzled. He rattled around for four-over 74, with five bogeys (and one offsetting birdie) down his last seven holes. "I'm still having a hangover after winning (the Open Championship)," he said. Now he was five strokes behind Holmes. "I've run out of steam. I'm just losing my focus and can't keep my mind quiet."

Second-Round Leaders: J.B. Holmes 68–139, Charlie Wi 70–140, Ben Curtis 67–140, Justin Rose 67–140, David Toms 69–141, Henrik Stenson 70–141, Angel Cabrera 72–142, Brandt Snedeker 71–142, Jeev Milkha Singh 74–142, Aaron Baddeley 71–142, Ken Duke 73–142, Sergio Garcia 73–142, Sean O'Hair 69–142

Third Round

A torrential rain swept into Oakland Hills Saturday. Play was finished for the day about 2 p.m., leaving most of the field to complete the third round on Sunday morning. For the six leaders, it meant playing 36 holes. David Toms and Henrik Stenson would tee off at 7:20 a.m., followed by Ben Curtis and Justin Rose, then J.B. Holmes and Charlie Wi. That leaderboard amounted to a changing of the guard in golf.

Consider first that some big names had been swept away by the cut — Vijay Singh, Stewart Cink and Scott Verplank. Other big names were back in the pack. Phil Mickelson, for one, wasn't an immediate threat, and Padraig Harrington was lurking back there with Sergio Garcia.

Of the 25 players who completed the third round on Saturday, Andres Romero was the only one to break par, and he did it with fireworks, tying the Oakland Hills course record with 65 that included two bogeys. Suddenly, he was a contender, at two-over 212, four strokes off the lead. "I played an excellent round — almost perfect," Romero said through an interpreter. He can explode like that. He did it at the 2007 Open Championship, making 10 birdies in 16 holes in the final round. An ill-advised two iron out of dense rough killed his chances.

Now Romero had to contemplate that temper-driven 78 he had shot the day before. "Yesterday, I finished very mad with my round," he admitted. A quadruple-bogey eight will do that to a man. At the 16th, he hit his nine iron twice and both shots spun back into the water. Then he double-bogeyed the 18th.

Ben Curtis, who started with 73-67, turned an early Sunday start into a bumpy but rewarding morning — two birdies, a bogey, two more birdies, then a bogey, and he made the turn in 33. He got to three under par with a birdie at the 11th, then bogeyed the tough 18th for 68, a two-under 208 total and his first lead in a major since winning the 2003 Open Championship. He was one stroke up on J.B. Holmes and Sweden's Henrik Stenson.

Holmes had a grudging 70. He turned on the power to beat the two par-fives, producing an eagle at the second hole and a birdie at the 12th. But he also made three bogeys, the third at the 18th. "One more good round and I'll be in good shape," said Holmes. Stenson posted four birdies in his 68 — including a rare one at the 18th — and when someone reminded him that he could become the first Swede to win a major championship, he shook it off. "I've just got to put that behind me," said Stenson, a six-time winner on the European Tour. "I've got 18 to go, and I'm going to go out there and do my best."

The players faced a somewhat easier Oakland Hills on Sunday. The Saturday rains had softened the course, and then the PGA put extra water on the greens overnight and trimmed some of the rough in the landing areas. "It was a little more comforting," Curtis said, "to know you could actually fly one to the hole instead of trying to bounce it 30 feet short of the pin." So the tough greens were more agreeable.

"I think it is fair to say they will be significantly more receptive,'" said Kerry Haigh, the PGA official in charge of setting up the course.

It didn't help Justin Rose, Curtis's playing companion Sunday morning. Rose started just a stroke off Curtis's lead, then saw his dreams disappear in a 74 that included seven at the par-four 11th hole. "Every shot, I had a bad lie on, off the tee," Rose said. "And whenever you make a hash of a hole, you invariably miss from four feet." He double-bogeyed the 16th. "I played it short of the hole to give myself a chance to make a par and three-putted there," he said. The promise of the kid in the 1998 Open Championship once again would go unfulfilled. ("Overall, I felt like things are still not clicking," Rose would say. "I'm not hitting enough quality shots.")

Harrington got in nine holes before the suspension, and he had shown no signs of the golfer who won the Open Championship three weeks earlier. He birdied the second, bogeyed the fifth and birdied the sixth for a one-under 34 on the first nine — solid work, but not the stuff to quicken pulses. He would quicken pulses the next morning, though, when he came out for the final nine of his third round. He ran off four straight birdies from the 13th, then bogeyed the 18th for 66. How good was it? "Right at this moment, disappointing," the disarming Harrington said. "Bogeyed the last."

Harrington finished the third round at three-over 211, three strokes behind Ben Curtis. But how far back is too far back? "It depends on how many people there are," he said. "I caught six up in the Open in 2007. As long as there are not too many bodies ahead of you, you can make up a big amount in the last round of a major."

As time would soon tell, later that Sunday, Harrington was not at all too far back.

Third-Round Leaders: Ben Curtis 68–208, J.B. Holmes 70–209, Henrik Stenson 68–209, Padraig Harrington 66–211, Sergio Garcia 69–211, Charlie Wi 71–211, Andres Romero 65–212, Jeev Milkha Singh 70–212, Camilo Villegas 67–213, Steve Flesch 70–213, Aaron Baddeley 71–213, David Toms 72–213

Fourth Round

If it was destiny that Padraig Harrington win this PGA Championship, then he kept destiny waiting. He really didn't get into the chase until the final home stretch, and even then, he willed his way in.

"The only thing from experience that I know is that in a major, nobody goes without making some mistakes," Harrington would say. "So as long as I could hang in there, I knew I would get my opportunity, and if it was going to be my day, I would take that opportunity."

Until those closing holes, it seemed Harrington was sliding quietly into the also-ran pile, along with, for example, Phil Mickelson, who was never really a threat. Three quick birdies from the second hole got him revved up. Then he sputtered from there to three bogeys for 70 and a tie for seventh place. "I let a lot of shots slide around the greens," Mickelson said. He had now gone 11 majors, since the 2006 Masters, without winning one. J.B. Holmes, one shot behind going into the final round, removed himself from the race in a hurry. He hit his opening tee shot under a tree and triple-bogeyed the first hole. "It just wasn't my day," Holmes said. It surely wasn't. He struggled on from there to an 81.

Others made futile moves as well. Anders Romero finished bogey-double bogey for 72 and tied for seventh, his fourth top-10 finish in his eight majors. Colombia's Camilo Villegas staked an early claim with two birdies and made six over all, but he also had four bogeys for 68 and a tie for fourth, his best finish ever in a major.

This underlined an interesting view of the spread of talent in the world. Three Americans finished in the top 12 — Ben Curtis, tied for second, Steve Flesch, tied for sixth, and Mickelson, tied for seventh. The other nine were from nine different countries.

As the PGA Championship slipped into the fourth round, Padraig Harrington — the gutsy Irishman who took the last two Open Championships in Britain — still hadn't shown up. That 66 in the third round only served to get him to within three of Curtis at the start of the fourth round.

The PGA came down to a three-man race, down the final nine holes — Curtis, Garcia and Harrington.

Curtis started the last round leading by a stroke, and though he couldn't hold on to win, he did hold on well enough to tie for second with Sergio Garcia, two strokes behind Harrington. It was his best finish in a major since he won the 2003 Open Championship.

Curtis got to four under par with birdies at the first and sixth, but bogeyed the eighth and ninth for 35 on the first nine, trailing Garcia by one stroke.

Garcia made his big leap with a birdie-eagle start, the eagle coming off a nine iron from 184 yards to a stunning four feet. He got to three under with a birdie at the sixth, but it would be his last birdie.

Harrington, meanwhile, plodded to 34 on the first nine. "I was patient in the sense that even though I was two, three shots behind in the middle of the round, through the turn I started playing golf," Harrington said. Then he birdied the 10th from 15 feet. At the par-five 12th, where Garcia chipped poorly and parred, Harrington hit a great five wood from a dangerous lie — "There was no backing off," he said — and birdied. He also birdied the 13th, but missed the green at the par-three 14th and bogeyed. Garcia went for a close-cut pin at the 16th and watered his approach and bogeyed. "The opportunity I was looking for," Harrington said. And he holed a curling 20-foot putt for par. They were tied.

Now came the decisive moment. At the 238-yard, par-three 17th, Harrington put his tee shot to 10 feet, and Garcia stuck his sensationally to four feet. Said Harrington, "I knew if I holed this, I probably would win the PGA. If I missed, Sergio would probably win the PGA. So it was down to that. And I hit a lovely putt."

Harrington again showed his guts under pressure. He holed his 10-footer for a birdie. Garcia burned the hole with high short try. Harrington led the PGA for the first time.

Garcia had one last chance. He needed a birdie at the 18th, the formidable 18th. He had already bogeyed it twice. Of course, most everybody else did, too. He drove into the right rough, then caught a bunker with his second and came out to 10 feet. Then he missed the par and bogeyed.

Harrington reached the green in three, 15 feet from the cup. Again, he rolled in the putt, this for his par and another 66. He finished at three-under 277, two ahead of Garcia.

Curtis, in the group behind, had bogeyed the 17th and now needed an eagle at the 18th to tie Harrington. That's just arithmetic talking. An eagle on the 498-yard par-four would be a miracle. Curtis parred for a one-over 71 and joined Garcia at 279, the only other players under par.

Harrington had just won his first major championship in the United States, his second major in a row and his third in 13 months.

Garcia was now 0-for-37 in majors. "Are you thinking you'll ever get your first?" someone wondered. "Next question, please," Garcia told the media. "Let's try to keep this as positive as we can, please."

Said Curtis: "You have to look at the big picture — hats off to Padraig for the way he played."

"It looked like (Sergio's) day," Harrington said. "I had to convince myself that, 'No, it's going to be my day, and I deserved to win three majors.' You've got to be very selfish in this situation when you're on the golf course. Off the golf course, you can look at it in a different light. But on the golf course, you've got to be hard. You can't be soft."

The Final Leaders: Padraig Harrington 66–277, Sergio Garcia 68–279, Ben Curtis 71–279, Camilo Villegas 68–281, Henrik Stenson 72–281, Steve Flesch 69–282, Phil Mickelson 70–284, Andres Romero 72–284, Alastair Forysth 70–285, Justin Rose 71–285, Jeev Milkha Singh 73–285, Charlie Wi 74–285

6. The Ryder Cup

It had been just nine years since the United States last won the Ryder Cup, but victory seemed a long time coming — much longer than those nine years and three unsuccessful Ryder Cup competitions. The last two European victories had been by the wide margin of 18½ points to 9½ points, and the American rally to win on Sunday afternoon at Brookline in 1999 was a faded memory.

The American and European teams met this year in September just outside Louisville, Kentucky, most often associated in sports with the Kentucky Derby and Louisville Slugger baseball bats. The residents are known to be avid fans of other sports as well. Kentucky's largest city is the home of the University of Louisville, which has a strong sports program, and Valhalla Golf Club, host to the 1996 and 2000 PGA Championships, and a facility owned by the PGA of America.

When this Ryder Cup was over, United States captain Paul Azinger could be seen springing to his feet, but his scream was drowned out, just one voice in a multitude that blended into the huge roar across the 17th green as Jim Furyk's par putt in the eighth of the 12 singles matches was conceded by Miguel Angel Jimenez to provide the 14½ points needed for the victory, and the United States team went on to defeat Europe 16½ to 11½.

The favored Europeans lost because of a determined and enthusiastic group of motivated newcomers, newly energized veterans like Furyk and a creative captain in Azinger. "I poured my heart and soul into this for two years, and my players poured their hearts into it for this past week," said Azinger, his voice cracking with emotion. "The golf was spectacular on both sides, and our guys just came out on top."

As Azinger knew, "in the end it comes down to heart and putting." Captain Nick Faldo's European team also showed great heart, but not the same putting as their opponents. It was closer than the score suggests, but the home team always held the upper hand. European stalwarts Padraig Harrington, Sergio Garcia and Lee Westwood failed to win a match. Ian Poulter, a captain's pick for the team, led Europe with four points out of five.

It was a stunning team effort by the United States, and Azinger clearly was the architect. He used team-building strategies and brought in experienced past captains Dave Stockton and Raymond Floyd. "But the players had to buy into the concept, and that's what they did," Azinger said. "They embraced the pressure and they embraced the crowd. They are the ones who did it, not me."

Phil Mickelson pointed out that past American teams had as much fun off the course, but Azinger also kept them loose on the course. It did not hurt that there were characters on the team, such as Boo Weekley, who galloped off the first tee on Sunday with a driver between his legs. He was an inspired performer, as were Anthony Kim, Hunter Mahan, who was the team's top scorer with three and a half points out of five, and J.B. Holmes, a big-hitting Kentuckian who thrilled the home crowd. They combined for 11 of the team's 16½ points.

Rookies comprised half of the United States team, but Azinger knew they would perform. Furyk said: "There was a lot of new talent on this team and they made a big difference. They brought enthusiasm and fired up the crowd, but they also brought a lot of points."

It was Azinger's plan to involve the crowd, and it worked perfectly, headed by Kentuckians Holmes and Kenny Perry, and adopted son Weekley. "I'm real proud of these people," Azinger said of the Valhalla galleries. "They made a big difference and kept our guys energized."

First Day

On Thursday evening captain Paul Azinger intended for his American team to have an early night while he quietly set off to downtown Louisville for a happening called Fourth Street Live. But as Azinger was leaving the hotel, the entire team appeared with their wives, all in "13th Man!" tee shirts. They went on stage to boisterous cheers and chants of "USA! USA!" They exhorted the estimated 4,000 people and threw "13th Man!" tee shirts and hats into the gathering. The enthusiasm carried over.

"Have you ever seen anything like this?" Azinger asked Friday morning, and that was on the first tee before a point had gone on the board.

Cheered on by the raucous crowds, Azinger's men were enjoying themselves and, it was said, the United States team rediscovered its passion for the Ryder Cup. A 3-matches-to-1 win in the opening foursomes was followed by a 2½-to-1½ victory in the fourballs for an overall advantage of 5½ to 2½ at the end of the first day. It was the first time since 2004 that the U.S. had won any session, the first time since 1991 they had been ahead after the morning session, and the first time since 1995 they had led after the opening day.

Justin Leonard, one of the Sunday heroes of Brookline in 1999, was making his first appearance since then and recorded his first-ever Ryder Cup match victory, then added another win in the afternoon. He and partner Hunter Mahan, a Ryder Cup rookie, were the first Americans to win twice on the opening day since Lanny Wadkins and Corey Pavin in 1993.

Phil Mickelson, who had a total of one match win in the last two Ryder Cups, won a point and a half with another rookie, Anthony Kim, after they battled back from three down in both matches.

As the home captain was permitted to do, Azinger had reversed the format of the first two days, playing the foursomes in the mornings and the fourballs in the afternoons, because in recent Ryder Cups the Americans had played better in the foursomes, or alternate shot matches. Nevertheless, Europe won the first hole in three of the foursomes and led in all four matches in the early stages.

First off, Mickelson and Kim halved their match with Padraig Harrington and Robert Karlsson after being three down with six holes to play. The Americans won the next three holes, squaring the match when Mickelson rolled in a birdie putt on the 15th from 15 feet.

Paul Casey and Henrik Stenson won the first two holes against Leonard and Mahan, then the Americans birdied three holes in a row from the third to go in front for good, winning 3 and 2. Americans Stewart Cink and Chad Campbell were three down against Justin Rose and Ian Poulter. Campbell struck the decisive blow in their comeback at the 18th, a five iron from 186 yards to within 12 feet of the hole. Cink just missed the eagle putt, then the Europeans conceded the birdie and a 1-up American victory.

Jim Furyk and Kenny Perry were two up with two to play against Sergio Garcia and Lee Westwood, then made two bogeys to secure only a halve.

For the afternoon fourballs, European captain Nick Faldo substituted Graeme McDowell, replacing Karlsson, to play alongside Harrington. Mickelson and Kim found themselves three down after only four holes. Still, they had recovered before and they did again. Mickelson holed a crucial putt from 18 feet at the 17th to take the lead, and the Americans won 2-up.

Europe managed only one win all day, and it came from Poulter and Rose, the only team maintained by Faldo for both sessions. The English pair won 4 and 2 over Steve Stricker and Ben Curtis.

Leonard and Mahan led from the first hole against Garcia and Miguel Angel Jimenez. When Leonard chipped in at the 15th and then both Spaniards missed their birdie putts, the Americans had a 4-and-3 victory.

The one match left out on the course turned into a real thriller as Westwood and Soren Hansen battled Boo Weekley and J.B. Holmes to a halve, with the Europeans securing the score when both of the Americans found the water off the 18th tee. "We may be down in points, but we are up in spirit," Faldo said.

"We are really happy with where we are, but we aren't even halfway yet," Azinger said. "They guys played really well, produced some great comebacks and kept going. But we know what they are capable of. We still need to go and play well."

First Day Morning Foursomes: Phil Mickelson and Anthony Kim (USA) halved with Padraig Harrington and Robert Karlsson, Justin Leonard and Hunter Mahan (USA) won 3 and 2 over Henrik Stenson and Paul Casey, Stewart Cink and Chad Campbell (USA) won 1-up over Justin Rose and Ian Poulter, Kenny Perry and Jim Furyk (USA) halved with Lee Westwood and Sergio Garcia

First Day Afternoon Fourballs: Phil Mickelson and Anthony Kim (USA) won 2-up over Padraig Harrington and Graeme McDowell, Ian Poulter and Justin Rose (Eur) won 4 and 2 over Steve Stricker and Ben Curtis, Justin Leonard and Hunter Mahan (USA) won 4 and 3 over Sergio Garcia and Miguel Angel Jimenez, J.B. Holmes and Boo Weekley (USA) halved with Lee Westwood and Soren Hansen

Second Day

Three points behind on Saturday morning, the European team was on the verge of being overwhelmed by the red paint of the Americans' points on the scoreboard. Ian Poulter knew what they must do. "We need to get some blue paint up there and let everybody see it," he said. Then Poulter went out and helped Europe accomplish just that.

The Europeans won the morning foursomes 2½ to 1½, then tied in the afternoon fourballs 2 to 2 to take back one point overall from the Americans. They prevented the United States from taking a commanding position, although the Americans still led 9 to 7 entering the final-day singles competition.

Many were surprised when European captain Nick Faldo left out Sergio Garcia and Lee Westwood from the morning matches. Garcia was on antibiotics after being ill the previous week and needed a rest. Although wanting to play, Westwood had blisters. But Faldo had decided to save as many of his players as possible from having to play all five matches.

"The physical and mental toll is so great," Faldo said, "I was looking for fresh legs, both this morning and this afternoon."

Poulter and Justin Rose, the only European partners to win on Friday, led the way. Poulter almost holed his approach shot at the first and the tone was set. Stewart Cink and Chad Campbell were demolished 4 and 3. In the second match, the Europeans' Miguel Angel Jimenez and Graeme McDowell got two up on the double winners from Friday, Justin Leonard and Hunter Mahan, but the Americans clawed back and the Europeans needed a birdie at the last for a halve.

European rookie Oliver Wilson was the only player on either side to sit out both sessions on Friday, but he played Saturday morning with Henrik Stenson and they secured an unlikely win by 2 and 1 over Phil Mickelson and Anthony Kim. The Americans were four up after six holes, then the Europeans squared the match on the 12th, and won the 15th and 17th holes, the latter when Wilson rolled in a birdie putt from 25 feet.

Americans Jim Furyk and Kenny Perry took care of the victory in the bottom foursomes match, winning 3 and 1 over Padraig Harrington and Robert Karlsson.

On a thrilling afternoon, either team could have won three points. Three of the four matches went all the way to the 18th hole. Even in the other match, where Boo Weekley and J.B. Holmes were ahead against Westwood and Soren Hansen, the Americans were relieved to claim a 2-and-1 outcome. The result meant the end of Westwood's unbeaten streak in Ryder Cup matches, his 12 wins leaving him tied for the record with Arnold Palmer.

In the second match, there were 16 halves, with each side winning only one hole. Americans Ben Curtis and Steve Stricker were facing Garcia and Paul Casey. Garcia leveled the match with a birdie at the 10th and they played all-square the rest of the way. At the 18th, Stricker holed for an unlikely birdie from 15 feet, then Casey matched him from seven feet for the halve.

Inevitably, Poulter was involved in the only afternoon match in which Europe was ahead. He and Rose won 1-up over Perry and Furyk as Poulter hit a superb chip shot to three feet at the 18th, then holed out to seal the victory.

In the last fourball match, Mickelson and Mahan were two up after 11 holes. The Swedish pairing of Stenson and Karlsson won the 12th and 13th to draw even. They were all-square the rest of the way for the halve, despite the play of Karlsson, who birdied seven of the last 10 holes and four in a row from the 12th.

So America led for the first time after two days since 1995 at Oak Hill, and with an identical score of 9 to 7, although that year was remembered for Europe's 14½-to-13½ comeback victory. "We took some punches today," captain Paul Azinger said, "but we are happy to be two points ahead."

Second Day Morning Foursomes: Ian Poulter and Justin Rose (Eur) won 4 and 3 over Stewart Cink and Chad Campbell, Justin Leonard and Hunter Mahan (USA) halved with Miguel Angel Jimenez and Graeme McDowell, Henrik Stenson and Oliver Wilson (Eur) won 2 and 1 over Phil Mickelson and Anthony Kim, Jim Furyk and Kenny Perry (USA) won 3 and 1 over Padraig Harrington and Robert Karlsson

Second Day Afternoon Fourballs: Boo Weekley and J.B. Holmes (USA) won 2 and 1 over Lee Westwood and Soren Hansen, Ben Curtis and Steve Stricker (USA) halved with Sergio Garcia and Paul Casey, Ian Poulter and Graeme McDowell (Eur) won 1-up over Kenny Perry and Jim Furyk, Phil Mickelson and Hunter Mahan (USA) halved with Henrik Stenson and Robert Karlsson

Third Day

Captain Paul Azinger's plan in the singles was to split his American team into three parts. He led off with his three most aggressive players: Anthony Kim, Hunter Mahan, Justin Leonard and Phil Mickelson. Then he placed the crowd favorites: Kenny Perry, Boo Weekley and J.B. Holmes, along with Jim Furyk, a Pennsylvanian, who said: "I was trying to be as southern as I could this week." At the end were his steady guys: Stewart Cink, Steve Stricker, Ben Curtis and Chad Campbell.

Nick Faldo, Europe's captain, needed to put points on the board early but also to keep strength in reserve. At the top of the order, Faldo placed Sergio Garcia, Paul Casey, Robert Karlsson and Justin Rose. At the end, he had Graeme McDowell, Ian Poulter, Lee Westwood and Padraig Harrington. The question was whether Faldo had kept too much too late. It was asked when the draw came out on Saturday evening and again in the post-match analysis.

"We are the one who hold the clubs and hit the shots, not the captain," Westwood said on Sunday night. "The buck stops with us."

At the beginning of the week, it would have been hard to imagine that Westwood, Garcia and Harrington would all fail to win a match. Garcia said afterwards: "If I had played better and could have won my match, it might have been a different story for the guys coming down the stretch."

It was Garcia versus Kim in the lead-off match. Kim hit his approach shot to the first hole to two feet, then Garcia matched him. A halve in birdies was assured, but Garcia appeared to be upset when Kim asked him to putt out. He holed, and picked up Kim's marker. The American kept hitting the ball close to the hole, winning the second, the sixth and the seventh, where Garcia put two balls in the water. By the 13th Kim was five up and the match ended 5 and 4. That was one point to the Americans, who led 10 to 7.

"This has been the experience of a lifetime," Kim said. "I wouldn't trade it for $10 million."

By the time Harrington teed off in the final match, the Americans led in eight matches, but at the top the Europeans had begun striking back. Karlsson defeated Leonard 5 and 3, and Rose claimed a 3-and-2 win over Mickelson. Europe was just one point behind.

Poulter and McDowell were making good starts, and Casey was engaged in a duel against Mahan. At the 17th Mahan holed a fast-rolling 40-foot putt for an unlikely birdie to take the lead, and the gallery roared, but Mahan was unable to hold it and finished with a halve.

"I really thought that if I could turn my match around, it would be huge for the team," Casey said. "But then Hunter dropped that bomb on me."

The score was then 10½ to 9½ in favor of the Americans, who were four points from regaining the Ryder Cup. Europe still had strength at the bottom of the order, but the American middle order swept to the victory by taking the next four matches.

Henrik Stenson, who scored the winning European point in 2006, could not stop Perry, as the inspired Kentuckian rolled to a 3-and-2 verdict as the crowd went wild. "When my dad came up and hugged me, and for my wife and three kids to be able to experience this — I couldn't hold back the tears," Perry said. "I told everybody this was going to define my career, and now I look at it, and it made my career."

Next came the galloping Weekley, who was eight under par in defeating Oliver Wilson 4 and 2.

Holmes, another electrifying personality for the Kentucky crowds, was in a tight match against Soren Hansen. Just when Europe seemed to be starting a late rally, Holmes let loose on the 16th and 17th holes. He hit his approach to four feet on the 16th for a rare birdie there to go one up, then he rocketed a drive on the 17th tee and flicked a sand wedge to two feet. Hansen almost holed his chip shot, then Holmes claimed the 2-and-1 decision to put America on the verge of reclaiming the Ryder Cup.

"This is unbelievable," Holmes said. "This was a once-in-a-lifetime opportunity and I'm glad I got here and glad I was able to come through for the team."

Victory in the Ryder Cup came moments later on the same 17th green. Miguel Angel Jimenez missed from 20 feet and Furyk was conceded his tap-in for a 2-and-1 win. "I must apologize to J.B.," Furyk said, "because I could have finished off my match at the previous hole and then he would have got the winning point."

Furyk was Paul McGinley's opponent when McGinley claimed victory for Europe in 2002 at The Belfry. "But I know what it is like to stand on your own when the winning putt goes in for the other team and you are listening to all the cheers," Furyk said. "It is a pretty miserable feeling. It's nice to have it flip. Of course, you dream of holing a 10-footer to win the Ryder Cup and have the place go bananas, whereas mine was a conceded two-footer, but I'll take it. I'll take it."

Third Day Singles: Anthony Kim (USA) won 5 and 4 over Sergio Garcia, Hunter Mahan (USA) halved with Paul Casey, Robert Karlsson (Eur) won 5 and 3 over Justin Leonard, Justin Rose (Eur) won 3 and 2 over Phil Mickelson, Kenny Perry (USA) won 3 and 2 over Henrik Stenson, Boo Weekley (USA) won 4 and 2 over Oliver Wilson, J.B. Holmes (USA) won 2 and 1 over Soren Hansen, Jim Furyk (USA) won 2 and 1 over Miguel Angel Jimenez, Graeme McDowell (Eur) won 2 and 1 over Stewart Cink, Ian Poulter (Eur) won 3 and 2 over Steve Stricker, Ben Curtis (USA) won 2 and 1 over Lee Westwood, Chad Campbell (USA) won 2 and 1 over Padraig Harrington

7. Women's Major Championships

Kraft Nabisco Championship

It was Amy Alcott who began the celebratory jump into Poppie's Pond when she won the Nabisco Dinah Shore in 1988. Historians should further note that it was Lorena Ochoa who turned the celebration into a combination family affair and neighborhood block party when she won that LPGA major event — now the Kraft Nabisco Championship — in April 2008.

It looked like a day at a California beach at Mission Hills in Rancho Mirage after Ochoa finished off a tidy five-shot victory for her second straight Kraft Nabisco Championship title. Some two dozen people came jumping into the water with her, including her parents, her brother and some friends from back home. "We promised each other that we would jump in the lake," a delighted Ochoa said. "It was going to be all of us."

What Ochoa couldn't explain was the killer grip she had taken on the LPGA Tour. This was also her second straight victory and her third in four consecutive tournaments. She won her first outing, the HSBC Women's Champions in Singapore, by 11 strokes, and two weeks later won the Safeway International by seven, and now the Kraft Nabisco Championship by five. She played the Mission Hills course in rounds of 68-71-71-67–277, 11 under par.

Possibly the theme to this championship was the surprising power of the Mexican sprite. "They gave me a hard time about that," said Ochoa, talking about the ribbing she gets from the other golfers. "How can I be so little and hit it so far?"

Morgan Pressel, the defending champion and one of the bright young newcomers, played with Ochoa in the first round and put the subject into practical terms. "It's tough to compete when you're hitting three wood into the greens," she said. She was pretty consistently 40 yards behind Ochoa much of the time.

Then there was that object lesson at No. 13, for example. Pressel hit a fairway wood and rolled over the green. Ochoa hit a nine iron from 130 yards and stuck the ball five feet from the hole. Pressel had her first bogey in 27 holes at Mission Hills, dating back to the third round in 2007. Ochoa, on the other hand, had her first birdie. There was another side to the Ochoa power, and that was the Ochoa putter. It taunted her for most of the tournament. If she could have putted, there's no telling how big her margin would have been.

Ochoa opened with a four-under 68, one stroke off Karen Stupples's lead. Ochoa, starting on the second nine, got that first birdie at her fourth hole (No. 13), starting a six-birdie, two-bogey round. She raced off to three straight birdies from her 10th (No. 1) and would have tied Stupples except for a three-putt bogey from 35 feet at her 17th (the par-three eighth).

Stupples was first out and logged five birdies on a tap-in, two five-footers and two 15-footers for a flawless 67. Ai Miyazato tied Ochoa at 68 on a wedge shot to tap-in range at her last hole. Annika Sorenstam, enjoying a revival from a year of injury, shot her 15th consecutive round under par, a score of 71 that was nevertheless disappointing because so many birdie chances got away. "It's a long way to go," she said. "You just have to go out and battle it day by day, stroke by stroke."

Ochoa was asked if she watches for Sorenstam's name on the leaderboard. "All the time," Ochoa said.

It was a different Sorenstam in the second round. It wasn't the golf that got to her, it was a stomach virus. She first thought it was the heat. While talking to reporters, she was hit by sharp pang that bent her over. "This course is tough enough," she said. "You don't need a stomach ache on top of it." She had fought through it. She birdied the first two holes and was only a stroke behind Ochoa until she three-putted the 12th for a bogey. The 70 and 141 total left her two strokes behind Ochoa at the halfway point, and she chided herself.

Yes, the course was tough enough. At the halfway point, only 15 players were still under par and the cut came in at a hefty five-over 149. Among those missing the cut were Louise Friberg, winner of the MasterCard Classic two weeks earlier, Christina Kim and Amy Alcott, now 52, the original lake-jumper when she won in 1988, making her last appearance. "This is not an easy thing to do," said Alcott, "because I have so much of my personal golf history tied in with this tournament." She'd won three times, in 1981, 1988 and 1991, and the last was her final LPGA victory.

Heather Young was one surprised golfer. She had no reason to expect much from her game. First, she had been in struggling for a year, she said. And then she got off to a poor start. She had a three-putt bogey at her second hole, then double-bogeyed her third from rough and sand. But she was bogey-free the rest of the way and played her last 11 holes in five under par for 70 and a 139 total. She would head into the third round tied with Ochoa for the lead. Did she have any expectations this time?

"Loud — I expect it to be loud," Young said, laughing at the thought of Ochoa's entourage. "I expect her to play well. And I expect her to out-drive me on every hole." And for herself? Said Young: "The one thing I expect out of myself is to keep my head on straight."

Ochoa had an off-and-on 71 in the second round. Not that 10-footers are automatic, but she had the unusual experience of missing four birdie putts from inside 10 feet. But she did cash in on her power. Of her three birdies, two came on the par-fives. At No. 2, she hit a three wood from 245 yards to 20 feet, and at the 11th, she hit a five wood from 218 to 35 feet, and two-putted both. But she bogeyed the 12th after hitting a tree, trying to fade a shot around it, and she bogeyed the 15th, two-putting from 10 feet for the 71.

"I can't complain," Ochoa said. "I left a few putts out there that hurt, but that's the way it is. I'm in a good position. It's where I like to be." But then there was the matter of the eight-foot birdie putt at the 18th that lipped out. "I was done," she said, "and ready to go home."

For Annika Sorenstam, a Hall of Fame member and winner of 10 major championships, the third round of the Kraft Nabisco Championship was more than simply trying to catch Lorena Ochoa. It was a time of seeking sweet relief from the pain that was wracking her. She at first thought it was the heat, but it was a stomach virus, and the pain was so severe that she considered quitting. At the 11th, she had to lie down in the grass, on her back. Between shots, she would sit in a folding chair her fiancé Mike McGee carried along. She laid down on a bench at the 17th. She wore an ice pack around her neck.

"I just wanted to finish," Sorenstam said. "I didn't have a score in mind. Just get it done with and see if I can finish. The birdies kept me going." Somehow, through the pain, Sorenstam made four birdies on the last nine and shot a one-over 73 for a 214 total and trailed Ochoa by four. "I still have a chance," she said. "If I feel good, then I'm going to charge."

For Cristie Kerr, it wasn't pain, it was the message in a fortune cookie from dinner the night before. "'A great day ahead,' it said," according to Kerr, and she made the message come true. She shot 66 that carried her to within two strokes of the lead. "I played beautiful golf today," Kerr said. "I mean, it was really beautiful to watch, if I do say so myself."

Suzann Pettersen joined Sorenstam at 214 with a tournament-best 65 that included a hole-out eagle at the par-four No. 7.

It wasn't as neat and simple for some. For Kerr, golf was beautiful Saturday, when she shot herself back into the tournament with 66. Golf showed its other face on Sunday. She shot 80 and tied for 21st.

Ochoa, once again, was on the verge of pulling away, but late mistakes brought her back.

The challenger this time was Hee-Won Han. She birdied Nos. 2, 10 and 11. She also bogeyed the 14th, but it was Ochoa herself who closed the gap. After an early birdie-bogey exchange, Ochoa ran off three straight birdies. She wedged to 15 feet at the 10th, two-putted the 11th after a five iron from 170 yards to 45 feet, and wedged to 15 feet at the 12th. Then came the fall: A three-putt bogey from 20 feet at the 15th and another from 35 feet at the 17th. She shot 71 and ended up just one stroke ahead of Han going into the final round.

"I'm okay," said Ochoa. "I'm not one to be upset. I'm really happy ... that I have a chance to win a major, and that's what I am going to do."

But not quite as decisively as it would seem. And while some golfers, as they approach victory, begin to compose their acceptance speech, with Ochoa, it was something else entirely. "For some reason," she said, "I couldn't stop thinking of that jump in the lake. It was something I've been waiting for, for a long time."

Ochoa needed a little more patience. In the final round, the championship still hung in the balance through the first nine. Ochoa birdied the first two holes, but Han kept her within a stroke with a birdie at the par-four sixth. And then, abruptly, it was over. Ochoa struck for three straight birdies. She put a six-iron shot to 12 feet at the par-three eighth, lofted a wedge to 12 feet at the par-five ninth, then rolled in a 40-footer at the par-four 10th.

"The birdie at No. 8 — that really put me ahead, a couple shots ahead," Ochoa said.

And a little talking-to by her caddie at the turn helped. "Dave came to me and said we have nine holes to go," Ochoa said. "And just try and concentrate 100 percent more than ever. Keep your head down. A lot of people are going to say things to you, and (speaking) Spanish or being funny, or shouting your name, so just try to be focused on what we're doing. That's what we did."

Sorenstam, who had played such a heroic tournament with the stomach virus, closed with 68, as did Pettersen, and they tied for second, five strokes behind Ochoa.

Sorenstam had just played the round of her life. "I mean, it's the worst I've felt, that's for sure," she said. "It was just a matter of come on, one more, one more, just try and finish this round. I'm glad that I fought it through, but it was one of those rounds where you just counted the holes and you wished it was over."

Pettersen just had to deal with the sense of futility, chasing Ochoa. "After I made the cut, I just tried to do the best out of the situation," she said. "But I made one bogey in 36 holes and 11 under, I'm very happy. I just wish I played better on the first two days. Then I could have given Lorena a little more challenge. But next time ..."

When Ochoa had put the formal finishing touches on this championship, it was to a mariachi band serenading her with "Canta y no llores" ("Sing and don't cry"). And then Ochoa joined hands with her parents and sister-in-law and ran toward the water, and they jumped. Her brother Alejandro, her coach Rafael Alcaron and her caddie Dave Brooke jumped in from the bridge, and others soon followed. By Ochoa's reckoning, 25 people jumped in with her.

McDonald's LPGA Championship

Yani Tseng, age 19 and a rookie, knew all she needed to know about the LPGA when she reached this point of the McDonald's LPGA Championship. In the fourth round, she had an imposing playing partner, Lorena Ochoa, No. 1 in the world. This would be a little like being on the edge of the eye of a hurricane. Ochoa does have her followers, to say the least. Tseng had heard them in other tournaments.

"Before I just heard 'Lorena, Lorena,'" said Tseng. "And today it's 'Yani, Yani,' So it's very exciting."

So Tseng heard the cheers. This was the theater surrounding the Taiwanese teenager and she made her way through the class of the LPGA with the aplomb of a veteran to win the championship. Tseng was the fourth rookie to win her first career LPGA victory at a major championship and the first since South Korea's Se Ri Pak won the McDonald's LPGA in 1998. This one came down to a playoff between Tseng and Sweden's Maria Hjorth, and it was Tseng winning on the fourth extra hole.

"This," she said, "is my dream. I can't believe it. I'm a rookie. And everything just came so fast."

Tseng herself came fast. Only a few years earlier she was the top amateur in Taiwan. During this time she had four victories in the United States, beating some of the best youth in the land. In the 2004 U.S. Women's Amateur Public Links, she beat Michelle Wie, and in the 2005 North & South Women's Amateur, she beat Morgan Pressel, now one of the prominent young players on the LPGA.

And indeed, Tseng's victory came fast. She was just one of a small crowd in the final round. Coming down the back nine, all six players in the last two groups had a chance to win — Tseng, Hjorth, Ochoa, Laura Diaz, Annika Sorenstam and Seon Hwa Lee. Of the group, Hjorth was the playoff runner-up, Ochoa and Sorenstam tied for third, Diaz was solo fifth and Seon would finish farthest out, a tie for 10th and five strokes behind the leaders. It was that close. It was a fitting finish to a tight battle in the June heat at rain-soaked Bulle Rock Golf Club at Havre de Grace, Maryland.

In the first round, Tseng opened with a one-over-par 73, as did Pressel, Lee and Natalie Gulbis, a hardly noticeable group with Ochoa and Sorenstam in the field. Ochoa had won six times and Sorenstam three times already this season.

Ochoa opened the tournament seeking to become the fourth woman to win three successive majors, but she didn't get off to a promising start. Four holes into her round, she found herself eight shots behind. She started on the back nine, and at her fourth hole (the par-four 13th), she drove into tall weeds to the left, weeds so high that she had to retreat 50 yards to near the 11th fairway to take her unplayable lie. From there, she hit a three wood from the adjoining No. 11 fairway to 40 yards. She chipped on and two-putted for a six.

"For sure I had to fight hard and catch up," Ochoa said. "And I did it." She almost did it. She fought back for a three-under-par 69 and was three behind Lorie Kane of Canada and Emily Bastel.

Bastel, a fourth-year pro who spent 2007 on the Futures Tour, rang up a bogey-free 66, sparked by a six iron from 115 yards to a foot at No. 1 for the first of her six birdies. She credited the lift-clean-place provision for the generally lower scoring. "If you can keep it in the fairway with us playing lift, clean and place, you can still find good lies out there and be hitting a clean ball into the greens," she said. "And with it being so moist, the greens are receptive." And as to being in such a lofty position in a major: "It's exciting to have this happen," she said. "Early in the week — just try to enjoy it and keep it going."

Kane, a 13-year veteran from Canada, hadn't won in seven years and was perplexed. Then the putts started to fall. She made four in the 10-foot range in her 66.

Sorenstam was having putting problems of her own. She missed a number of birdie putts from 12 feet or less. "Hit the ball beautifully," she said. "Just didn't make some putts today, unfortunately. But I'm very, very happy with my game."

In the second round, Tseng got better. This time she shot 70 for a 143 total, a stroke inside the cut, which came in at par 144. There were some surprises among those who missed: Natalie Gulbis, Laura Davies and Christina Kim. Of the first-round leaders: Lori Kane made the cut easily with 70, and Emily Bastel made it with 76 but withdrew after the second round. In all, 82 players made the cut and 61 were under par.

To no one's surprise, Ochoa asserted herself with a seven-under 65 and took the halfway lead at 10-under 134. And it seemed she shot the 65 from her rocking chair for the one-stroke edge.

"It was a great day, just easy," Ochoa said, and rarely does a golfer admit something like that. "I had 17 birdie chances. I enjoyed it a lot. It was stress-free." In fact, it was a lark. She missed just one fairway, and the field was still playing under lift-clean-place, so she had excellent lies each time. Five of her birdies were from three feet or under, and the toughest came at the 18th, a 20-footer downhill that just made it into the cup. "It was one of those days I could have shot 10 or 11 under par," she said. "I think that was my best round of the season."

"She's obviously the one to beat," said Lindsey Wright, who posted 68–135 and was one behind Ochoa. "When you see her up there, you know she's not going to make too many mistakes. It keeps me focused. I have to make birdies."

Sorenstam had a bogey on her front nine, and then she saw that Ochoa was in at 10 under. It seemed to inspire her. She made three birdies coming in for 68 and was at 138, four off Ochoa's lead and unruffled.

"We have a long way to go," Sorenstam said. "This is a major. Anything can happen. After four days are over, you add up your scores."

With an Ochoa-Sorenstam shootout looming in the third round, few noticed that Yani Tseng, the teenager who had yet to win, shot 65 and crept up into contention after 54 holes. She was in a group at 208, eight under par and four strokes behind the leader, Korea's Jee Young Lee, who also had 65. And this on a day when the temperature climbed over 100 and the humidity was heavy.

Ochoa, stress-free a day earlier, got a little stress at the start in the third round. She had gone 30 holes without a bogey, and then broke the spell with a three-putt at No. 1. But bigger trouble lay ahead. At the par-three seventh, she pulled her tee shot into messy rough to the left of the green. She tried to float a flop shot to the green, but somehow missed the shot and hit the ball only a few inches. She double-bogeyed the hole. She birdied two of her last three holes for 72–206, to tie with Sorenstam, who was now through 30 holes without a bogey, shooting another 68.

"The key in majors is not how it's done — you've got to get it done," said Sorenstam, aiming for the fourth LPGA Championship in her career.

Jee Young Lee, a third-year pro, holed a 25-foot putt for birdie at the 18th, wrapping up a stretch of four under in her last four holes for a 65 and the lead at 12-under 204. "I've been waiting to win the tournament ever since I came to the United States," Lee said through an interpreter. She led by three over Ochoa, Sorenstam and Maria Hjorth, who also shot 65–204.

Hjorth held the lead briefly. She made four birdies at the turn, took the lead at the 12th, and saved par at the 18th after her tee shot bounced off a cart path and into heavy rough. She would be playing in the final round, with Lee and Sorenstam.

"As long as I don't occupy my mind with thinking, 'Oh, this is the last group in a major,' hopefully I can handle it well," Hjorth said. "And I'm looking forward to it."

"Everybody is looking forward to tomorrow, and everyone wants it badly," Sorenstam said. "The one that wins is the one that stays cool, stays patient and makes less mistakes. So that's going to be my plan."

Ochoa said she'd hoped to play with Sorenstam, but officials, anticipating heavy fog, decided to send the field out in threesomes instead of twosomes, and this precluded an Ochoa-Sorenstam pairing. Instead, she would be in the next-to-last threesome. So she saw it as an advantage to finish before the leaders.

"It's better when they know what I have done,' Ochoa said, indicating she expected to shoot a low score. "That will be important, to get a good start and to put my name up there. And they can stay with the pressure in the last group."

While third-round leader Jee Young Lee was in the process of blowing to 78 in the final round, Yani Tseng and Maria Hjorth both held up under the pressure of the marquee pairings they were in. Sorenstam and Ochoa both shot 71 to tie for third, a stroke short.

"I played very well today," said Sorenstam, leaving her final LPGA Championship empty-handed and admitting to a little sadness as she left the final green. "I thought this was going to be my week. So close, and not being able to finish. But it's been a great championship."

Was there a shot she would want back? someone asked. "A dozen or two would do it," she said.

Ochoa started with promise, a birdie from six feet at No. 1. But she couldn't get anything going. She bogeyed the 12th and 13th, then birdied the 16th on a chip that hit the pin and stopped a foot away, and birdied the 18th from 12 feet. "It wasn't my time," Ochoa said. "Now I move on and try to win the next few tournaments."

Tseng opened her 68 with a wedge to 35 feet and the putt for the birdie at the first. She had three other one-putts, from 12, 27 and nine feet, and she two-putted the par-five eighth. She had only one bogey on her final card, the par-four 13th, where so many stumbled, including Ochoa to a double bogey in the first round.

Hjorth had an erratic 71. A birdie-bogey exchange at Nos. 4 and 5 typified her day, with a wedge to six feet for the birdie, then missing the green short and pitching over it for the bogey. She crashed at the 13th, making a double bogey after losing her first tee shot in the tall weeds. She got a break at the par-five 15th when her second shot bounced off some rocks in the creek and ended up near the green. She chipped to a foot and made birdie. Then she chipped in for birdie at the 16th, but two-putted for bogey from four feet at the 18th.

They tied in pars through the first three holes of the playoff. Then on the fourth extra hole, at No. 18, Tseng choked down on a six iron and punched her approach out of the rough to within five feet of the cup, and holed the putt for the win.

Said Hjorth: "I don't think it's really hit me, but I'm sure I'm going to be very, very tired pretty soon."

For Tseng, it was a question of nerves. It seemed she had none. Maybe her position at the start had a lot to do with it. "I was four shots behind and I didn't think I would win the tournament," she said. "I wasn't that nervous when I teed off."

And then standing over that last five-footer? "I just tell myself, just make this putt and win a major championship," she said. And so she did.

U.S. Women's Open

A number of interesting storylines had emerged late in June at the U.S. Women's Open at Interlachen, the noted Donald Ross course near Minneapolis, Minnesota. For example, would an American win the national championship? This was akin to those other celebrated questions such as would a British player win their Open, a European win the Masters, the Americans win the Ryder Cup? There is, of course, only one real answer, and that is — the golf ball speaks all tongues. But it was of interest that Americans had won only six of the past 30 women's major championships.

Could Annika Sorenstam, the great dominator of recent note, find enough game for one last hurrah? She had won three U.S. Women's Opens, and this would be her last try. She was departing from competition at the end of the 2008 season. Would Stacy Lewis, who turned professional the day she qualified for the Open, become the first player to win a women's major title in her first start as a pro? And would Lorena Ochoa, No. 1 in the world, come back to life at Interlachen? She had won six of the first 12 tournaments and then had seemed to be treading water.

Then at the end, when the tournament had run its course, there was one final question: Who was Inbee Park and where did she come from?

That answer, at least, was simple. Inbee Park was a 19-year-old South Korean, just two weeks from her 20th birthday, in her second season on the LPGA Tour, and the only player to break Interlachen's par of 73 for all four days (72-69-71-71–283), who didn't lead until the final round and then won by four strokes. Park was the third player in the last six years to make the U.S. Women's Open her first victory on the LPGA Tour.

"Really, I can't believe I just did this, especially with all these big names on the trophy," she said, looking at the trophy that would bear her name along with that of her hero of 10 years ago, Hall of Fame member Se Ri Pak, 1998, whom she had just replaced as the youngest U.S. Women's Open champion. "Hopefully, I'll put a couple of my names on there," Park said.

Coming into the tournament, Park was probably best known for being No. 1 on the LPGA Tour in putts per green in regulation, at an average of 1.74, and second in birdies made, 203, behind Ochoa's 206. So there would be little or no notice of her shooting a one-under 72 in the first round, with four birdies and three bogeys. She was tied with, among others, defending champion Cristie Kerr, five behind co-leaders Ji Young Oh and Pat Hurst, both at 67.

Hurst, who hadn't made a cut since the last week of May, was miffed at herself for missing short putts early in the first round. "I was whining — I was being a golfer," she said. Then she dropped a 35-foot putt, and went six under par in a stretch of seven holes on her way to the 67, her lowest round ever in the Open. Oh, playing in the morning, before the moist greens could dry out, got all seven of her birdies from within 10 feet, and four of them were of two feet or less, for her 67. "I love hitting my drivers and short irons," she said. "And for that, I think this golf course suits my game pretty well."

A total of 32 players broke par in the first round, the most since 1999, but Sorenstam wasn't among them. She twice made back-to-back bogeys and shot three-over 75, her highest first-round score in the championship since the 76 she shot at Oakmont as a 22-year-old amateur in 1992. "A few putts go in, it would have been a different story," she said. "I've just got to be patient. I know I've got the game, and I love the golf course. Long way to go."

Ochoa puzzled herself. She shot par 73 and couldn't understand why. "Because it was playing fairly easy in the morning," she said. "For sure I could have finished two or three under par … But I think it will come back. The U.S. Open is always tough, and I'm okay where I am."

Michelle Wie was also okay, for the first eight holes. Then came a disaster at the par-four No. 9, the anatomy of which was pure weekender. She was short of the green in two, hit a wedge over the green, chunked a chip shot, putted from the back down and off the front of the green, hit a weak chip that rolled back down to her, finally got on, and two-putted for a quintuple-bogey nine. She shot 81. It was the second straight year that she failed to break 80 in the first round. (She would shoot 75 in the second and miss the cut by six shots and say, "I'm feeling very confident over my shots — I just take it as a bad week and move on from here.")

Inbee Park still was back in the pack after the second round, with 69–141, five under. She eagled the par-five second, bogeyed the fifth and sixth, and played the last 12 holes in four under. But another South Korean named Park — Angela — took the lead with 67 and a six-under 140 total. (She was born in Brazil of Korean parents, came to the U.S. as a little girl, and became an American citizen.) Park broke from the gate early with a bunch of birdies and an eagle at the par-five second off a five wood to 30 feet. She had fulfilled her belief that anything under par would be good on this day. "Just get me back up in the tournament," she said.

The world's No. 1 and 2 golfers could not say the same. Lorena Ochoa, who went 13 holes without a birdie in her opening 73, went 12 holes without one to start the second round. She missed three birdie putts on her last four holes and shot 74–147 and was seven strokes behind. "It was a tough day for me today," Ochoa said, and she was pleased by a storm that delayed play for two and a half hours. "I needed some time to relax," she said. "I came back strong."

Annika Sorenstam's putting was floundering badly. She needed 33 putts for the second day, and nothing showed her troubles more clearly than her stumble at her final hole. She hit a brilliant three wood across water to five feet, but her eagle putt didn't even touch the hole. "It has to do with tempo," she said. "It has to do with the length of my backswing. It just takes awhile to get that."

Cristie Kerr might have tied Angela Park for the lead, or at least have gotten to within a stroke, but for a fly, it seems. Kerr was a stroke off the lead coming to her final hole. She was all set to hit her tee shot when a fly bothered her and she interrupted her swing. Then restarting, she drove into the woods and ended up with a bogey for 70–142 and was two off the lead.

Stacy Lewis, a new pro and a great success story just for playing golf, birdied the last hole for 70 and was just three strokes off the lead.

Lewis was diagnosed with scoliosis (a lateral curvature of the spine) at age 11, and some eight years later surgeons inserted a steel rod and screws into her back. She had an outstanding collegiate and amateur career, and by the third round at Interlachen had been a professional for only 19 days. She shot a day's-best, bogey-free 67 for a three-round 210 total and was the leader by a stroke over Paula Creamer (69) and by two over Helen Alfredsson (71) and Inbee Park (71).

"I'm not really that surprised," said Lewis, who needed just 23 putts. "I felt I could play at this level and compete at this level."

Creamer, a six-time winner on the LPGA Tour and seeking her first major title, birdied four of the five par-fives en route to her 69. "I couldn't ask for any better position," she said. "If someone had said, 'You want to be at eight under par going into Sunday?' I would take it in a heartbeat. I'm there."

Ochoa shot herself out of it with 76–223 that put her 13 off the lead going into the final round. Sorenstam shot 72–217 and was still clinging to hope, seven behind. But clinging. "I'm about to cry," she said. "When you do everything you can and then it just doesn't happen ... I'm not giving up. I'm going to tell you that."

Alfredsson and Inbee Park both shot 71 and were two off the lead. Alfredsson started strong, with birdies at the second and third, but made two birdies and two bogeys from the sixth. Park started birdie-bogey, then made three straight birdies from the ninth before cooling down to a birdie and two bogeys coming in.

In the final round, Sorenstam didn't give up, but the results didn't get much better. She shot 41 on the first nine, and at the 18th she drove to the right and seemed headed for 80 or worse. But she finished her final U.S. Women's Open spectacularly — a six iron from 199 yards that holed out for an eagle, a score of 78–295 and a tie for 24th place. "Leaving with another great memory, that's for sure," Sorenstam said. "Maybe not the one I had in mind, but I'll take it."

Ochoa likewise didn't want her finish. Never in sync, she closed with 74–297 and tied for 31st.

Lewis started the round with a one-stroke lead over Creamer, and both double-bogeyed the easy par-five second. They both bogeyed the eighth, and at the ninth both hit over the green. Lewis bogeyed and Creamer had her second double bogey of the day. Both closed with 78s, Lewis tying for third, Creamer for sixth.

For Alfredsson, 43, the final round was a chance to make up for her collapse in the 1994 Women's Open. But it was just beyond her grasp. She birdied No. 2, to stay within a stroke of Park, then fell away with four bogeys over the next six holes and was out in 39. Coming in she more than offset two bogeys with an eagle at the par-five 13th and a birdie at the 18th for a two-over 75 and a 287 total, four behind Park.

"It was a grinding day, just fighting on every single shot," Alfredsson said. "It's nice that it's over. I'm getting too old for this."

Inbee Park chipped in for birdie at the first hole, then took the lead with a birdie at the second, which Lewis and Creamer had double-bogeyed. Park then holed a 10-footer for a birdie at the 11th, saved par from a bunker at the 12th with an eight-footer, and birdied the 13th with another 10-footer. She made bogey at the 17th, her third of the day, but got the stroke back with a birdie at the 18th. Not that she needed it. She was winning by four.

"Everything happened so fast," Park said. "It's scary. I really tried to stay calm, but it was so exciting, I couldn't do it. This is my day."

Park recalled the night 10 years earlier, as a nine-year-old back home in Korea, when she joined her parents in the living room at three o'clock in the morning to watch Se Ri Pak become the first South Korean to win the U.S. Open.

"It was very impressive for a little girl," Park said. "I just thought that I could do it, too."

Ricoh Women's British Open

Is there no end to the supply of Koreans inspired by Se Ri Pak? Just to prove Inbee Park's victory at the U.S. Women's Open was not a one-off, another young Korean who was inspired to take up the game by watching Pak win the U.S. Open in 1998 went on to triumph at the Ricoh Women's British Open, played at Sunningdale Golf Club in Berkshire, England. Ji-Yai Shin was only 11 when Pak broke through to the top of the women's game. "Before, I never know golf," she said. "I'm watching her then; now I'm watching her and still she's my hero."

At the age of only 20, Shin is now the youngest winner of the Women's British Open. This victory was even more remarkable than those of Yani Tseng at the McDonald's LPGA Championship or Park at the U.S. Open. Before winning, Shin did not hold a card for either the LPGA or the Ladies European Tour. She had won in Japan and earned her card for that circuit, where she intended to go and play. "Now, I think I change my plans," Shin said.

But do not suppose that Shin was unproven as a winner, something she confirmed with a flawless round of 66 over the Old Course at Sunningdale, with six birdies and no bogeys, to win by three strokes over Tseng at 18-under-par 270. Shin, the only non-LPGA based player in the top 10 of the Rolex Rankings, has dominated the Korean LPGA circuit in recent years, already having won three times in her 2008 season to date, as well as 12 times since the start of 2007.

Her nickname in Korea translates as "Final Queen." Simply put, it means she dominates on Sunday, one of her rare near-misses coming at the Australian Women's Open earlier in 2008 when she lost a playoff to Karrie Webb. "Actually, last night I can't sleep because I was very nervous, and then today I was still nervous," Shin admitted. You could not tell, for the bespectacled Korean smiles serenely at all times. "Today my driver and my irons, putting, everything was very good, and so that gave me confidence. I felt comfortable. My whole life, I've been waiting for this time and my dream comes true now."

So there was no 11th, and last, major victory for Annika Sorenstam, or even a second major of the year for world No. 1 Lorena Ochoa, the defending champion. But it was a significant year in the majors. While Sorenstam dominated the game, there was the odd year when no American won any of the four majors, but this was the first year ever that no American nor any European won one of them.

Ochoa was at the height of her domination when the Mexican won her second major in a row at the Kraft Nabisco Championship, but since then Asians won the three remaining majors. And to further highlight the shift in the women's game to the east, the leading five positions at Sunningdale were all taken by Asians: after Shin and Tseng came Yuri Fudoh of Japan and Korea's Eun-Hee Ji sharing third place, and Japanese star Ai Miyazato in fifth. Cristie Kerr finished in sixth place, with Ochoa tying for seventh.

"I think what we're seeing is going to continue for a little while," said Sorenstam. "It's totally a global sport and the players are younger. I think the growth of Asian golf is going to continue. If you watch the KLPGA, there is some tremendous talent and they all want to be out here, so the next five years will probably be about the same."

Sorenstam singled out Taiwan's Tseng as a possible future world No. 1, and if anyone is going to appreciate the effort put in by many of the Asian players, practicing for eight to 10 hours a day, every day, it is the hardworking Swede. "Well, that's what it takes," she said. "If you want to be the best, you've got to do it. That's what my dad always told me, there are no shortcuts to success. It shouldn't matter what country you're from. If you want it badly, you should go get it."

As Sorenstam always did. But will no longer. It was impossible to get away from the fact that it was Sorenstam's last major championship. And, quite rightly. She arrived with much anticipation and hoping to add to her victory at Royal Lytham in 2003. After all, her 10 major titles included multiple wins at all the others. But early on Thursday morning she opened with two bogeys in the first three holes and never got into the running. After an even-par 72 she was asked if there were any special emotions. "No, at 7:30 on the morning, I just wanted to have a good round," she replied.

Another 72 followed on Friday and the 37-year-old Swede made the cut, but only with a shot to spare. After an injury-hit 2007, Sorenstam began the 2008 season in fine form with three victories by May. But then she announced that she was "stepping away" from competition at the end of the year, intending to get married and start a family and concentrate on her many golf-related businesses.

Here she never looked quite her old self, but it would have been a travesty had she not qualified for the weekend. "You just have to keep fighting," she said. "That's what I've been doing since I came out here and I'm not going to change until my last day. I have pride and I know what I'm capable of. I know I'm stepping away, but in my mind, I'm as good as I've ever been.

"I feel I'm playing good enough, but I'm throwing shots away. You can't do that in these tough conditions. It's pretty much been like this since I made my announcement. I have not been able to get anything going. I'm not really sure what it is. I'm not deflated, I'm as happy as I can be. It was my decision. On the contrary, you'd think I'd be relieved knowing I've shared my thoughts with everybody. My caddie and I have analyzed the last two and a half months to death, trying to figure out what's happening. For some reason, I am having a hard time scoring."

She got under par with 70 on Saturday, and although she would have liked to have been finishing later on Sunday, it was a champion's finale with 68 for six-under-par 282. She eagled the 14th and walked up the 18th hole to a great reception, despite the heavy rain shower at the time. On the scoreboard was the message: "Annika, you will be missed, XXX." Here her six-iron approach was not quite as good as on the 72nd hole at the U.S. Open, which she holed, but it was a pretty fine one, and then, inevitably, she rolled in the 12-footer for the birdie.

"To finish with a birdie was extra special," Sorenstam said, "and it seemed there wasn't any doubt it was going to go in." Fittingly, she signed off with 18 greens hit in regulation. "What can you say, it's an ironic game.

"I didn't care about the rain. I just enjoyed the moment walking up the 18th. The message on the board was very special and then everyone was cheering and clapping. It makes you feel so good when you get that type of applause. I'm usually so focused inside the ropes, but the game has meant so much to me that it would be weird if I didn't feel anything. I've been out here for 15 years and I've experienced the joy, a few setbacks, but overall it's been great. All of a sudden you reflect on everything and you're just so grateful."

It was somewhat ironic that Juli Inkster should be the first-round leader after a seven-under 65. At age 48 and with seven majors and two teenage daughters, Inkster has demonstrated that it is possible to be a mother and continue a golf career. "But there are times when you have to settle for 12th place as the best you can do and I was happy to do that — I don't think Annika is," Inkster said.

Inkster is a role model to many mothers on tour, including England's Karen Stupples, who won the Women's British Open the last time it was at Sunningdale in 2004. Then she had started memorably with an eagle and an albatross at the opening two holes, which are both par-fives. This time she started par-birdie, but then nothing would have compared. Still Stupples came in with 67 and was able to savor the memories of coming up the last with a winning lead.

But the leading home player was Johanna Head, born in nearby Ascot. She opened with 66, while her twin sister, Sam, had to withdraw after a few holes with tonsillitis. Among others at 66 were Japan's Yuri Fudoh and Korea's Ji-Yai Shin, both of whom added 68s on Friday to share the halfway lead and equal the best 36-hole score for the championship of 134.

Yet Friday's best score, on a windier day than the first round, was 65 by Cristie Kerr, who was four under for the par-fives. "This is a course where you have to play the tough holes well and take advantage of the holes where you can take advantage," said the 2007 U.S. Open champion.

That is exactly what Laura Diaz did, becoming the third player in LPGA history to have three eagles in a round. The first was Alice Richmond, also at Sunningdale, in the 1979 Colgate European Open. Diaz hit her rescue club, called "Mazie Girl" after her parents' dog, to three feet at the first, holed from 30 feet on the 10th green and pitched in from 56 yards at the par-four 11th. She still had the 14th to come, but three-putted for a par. "I had never had two eagles in a round, so I knew it was a record for me, but I was hoping it was an LPGA record," Diaz said.

Inkster retook the lead briefly on Saturday by starting eagle-birdie, but it was Fudoh, with 69 to Shin's 70, who finished one in front with a round to play. Fudoh was being guided by her English caddie, Peter Coleman, who worked for Bernhard Langer for many years. Fudoh speaks very little English and Coleman absolutely no Japanese, but the player was happy to be handed a club and to then get on with it. "I think 50 percent of what I have done is because of the caddie," she said through an interpreter.

Ochoa was on the fringe of contention all week but always just off the pace after two late bogeys meant she had to settle for an opening 69. She finished with rounds of 68, 71 and 69 to reach the clubhouse seven strokes behind the champion. A year that had started so brilliantly, even with thoughts of a Grand Slam after winning at the Kraft Nabisco Championship, ended slightly tamely but, as Tiger Woods always says, any year with one major victory is a great year.

"You cannot win all of them," Ochoa said. "I always like to be in contention and another top 10 is always good. You have to be patient and wait for the right times to win. But in the majors, it can always be better. I'm always trying to win more than one, but this is what happened this year, and I'm really disappointed. I think I played pretty good in all of them. The U.S. Open was the one that hurt me the most, but you know, hopefully we win a few more next year."

Shin credits her father with training her to reach the level she has. In 2004 the family suffered a tragedy when her mother died in a car crash. Her younger brother and sister were also involved in the accident and were so severely injured that they spent almost a year in the hospital. Shin used to sleep in the hospital so she was on hand to help take care of them. Perhaps this explains a maturity that belies her age.

Playing in the final pairing, both Fudoh and Shin birdied the first hole, but then Shin caught the overnight leader with a birdie at the fifth. Then she birdied the short par-four ninth while Fudoh bogeyed, and Shin never looked back. Miyazato was challenging until her double bogey at the last, but by then Shin had walked away with it. She birdied the par-five 10th, holed a long putt at the short 13th, and added another birdie-four at the 14th. The last four holes at Sunningdale are particularly fearsome, but Shin calmly parred in, recovering from a bunker at the last to leave a tap-in for victory.

"So many tough holes, only until the 18th did I think I had won," she said.

8. American Tours

Fully 104 on the PGA Tour topped $1 million in winnings in 2008, from Vijay Singh, No. 1 at $6,601,094, down to No. 104 Bill Haas, $1,000,939. (No. 105 did all right, too — Lucas Glover at $998,491.) And they didn't have to win a tournament to join the club. This bounty was possible, of course, because of the rich purses.

But the riches couldn't disguise the fact that the PGA Tour took two big hits in 2008. Tiger Woods pulled up lame, and after winning the U.S. Open courageously on one good leg. He missed the rest of the season to rehabilitate from a surgically reconstructed anterior cruciate ligament. It was no surprise that television ratings dropped in his absence. He was not expected to reappear until sometime in 2009.

The other hit could be more severe, depending on how the future went. This was the economic crisis that developed in the latter half of the year and swept around the world. Before long, the federal government was providing billions upon billions in aid to bail out automakers, financial houses and other businesses. Various sports were hurt quickly — auto racing, women's professional basketball, and others. The severity wasn't apparent in golf.

Said PGA Tour Commissioner Tim Finchem in December: "Thus far, we have not suffered any major damage. But clearly, if the instability were to continue for a sustained period of time, we will have real challenges."

The tour was protected by its long-term contracts with sponsors and tournaments, running through 2010 and beyond, by which time the economy might be turned around.

Even in hard times, businesses still have to sell their wares, and to do that, they would have to advertise and promote. And golf still had the demographics that appeal to its principal backers — auto makers, financial institutions and the like.

Meanwhile, out on the golf course, Vijay Singh, spinning his wheels much of the year, found new life in the belly putter, the longer one the golfer anchors at his belly. He won three times in six weeks, topped the money list, and took the $10 million FedExCup payoff. He vowed his love for the belly putter forever more. "If you see me with a short one," he said, "that means something is wrong with me."

Woods won four times on the PGA Tour, including the U.S. Open, before his season ended in mid-June. His painful victory in the U.S. Open at Torrey Pines was easily the most dramatic episode of the season. The second-most might have been Rocco Mediate, hugely the underdog, fighting Woods through an 18-hole playoff and even to the first hole of sudden death.

In the hall of heroes, there was Padraig Harrington, who owned Ireland after winning his second straight Open Championship in Britain and then the PGA Championship as well.

It was the year of the 20-somethings, with 13 of them winning on the tour, the most prominent of which was Anthony Kim, age 23, once noted more for his partying than his putting. He finally got serious and won the

Wachovia Championship and the AT&T National, and then was a standout in the Ryder Cup. Spain's Sergio Garcia, age 28, won The Players Championship, tied for second in the PGA Championship, and had 11 other top-10 finishes. When he won the HSBC Championship in Shanghai, he rose to No. 2 on the World Ranking. Colombia's Camilo Villegas, age 24, broke through late in the season with wins at the BMW Championship and The Tour Championship. South Africa's Trevor Immelman, age 27, was the surprise winner of the Masters. Just four months earlier, fearful of having cancer, he had what proved to be a benign tumor removed from under his rib cage.

There was muscle and skill at the other end of the age spectrum, as well. Kenny Perry, age 48, won three times in five starts, trying to play his way onto the Ryder Cup team. Which he did. Vijay Singh, age 45, kept telling himself, "I'm the best putter in the world," and if he wasn't, he was good enough to win three times. And Davis Love, age 44, was the feel-good story of the season. He had struggled for a couple of years, and then he had ankle surgery, and 2008 was looking like a bust until he bounced back and won the season finale, the Children's Miracle Network Classic.

U.S. PGA Tour

Mercedes-Benz Championship
Maui, Hawaii
Winner: Daniel Chopra

The Mercedes-Benz Championship, the winners-only party opening the 2008 PGA Tour season, began with a touch of the bizarre. Brandt Snedeker, leading for most of the first round, finished with a double bogey and a bogey, and discovered it was a cracked driver that cost him the bad tee shots. "It's a stinky way to end a round of golf," said Snedeker, settling for 71. Scott Verplank was penalized when his ball moved a smidgen in the strong wind. He argued that he hadn't addressed the ball, but officials decided otherwise, and he was stuck with a par 73. A good time was not had by all. Boo Weekley, inactive the past month, thought he would shoot closer to 82 than to 72. He shot 80. "I was close," he cracked. Paul Goydos shot the day's-high 81.

It was in this setting that Daniel Chopra, age 34, the man with the spiked white hair and a most unusual heritage, made his debut among the winners. "My thinking might be a little bit more Indian ... the physical side of me a little bit more Swedish," Chopra said. It was the golfer side of him that took the lead in the final round and that then beat Steve Stricker on the fourth hole of a playoff for the second win of his career.

For openers, though, Nick Watney, untouched by the ills that are supposed to plague newcomers to the Plantation course at Kapalua, Hawaii, shot 68 for the first-round lead over Chopra, who got into the exclusive 31-man field with his first PGA Tour victory in the Ginn sur Mer Classic late in 2007.

Chopra said he always believed he would win some day. "But sometimes you think, 'Wow ... I might never be there,'" he said.

A 72 in the second round put Chopra three behind Mike Weir (67–138), and he got within two in the third round with 67, behind Weir's 68–206. Then came the running shootout between Chopra and Steve Stricker. Chopra went into the final round trailing by two, Stricker by four. Stricker had seven birdies and an eagle, that on a 109-yard hole-out wedge at the par-four 12th, for 64. Chopra had seven birdies and could have won outright, but his birdie putt at the 18th hung on the lip of the hole. He shot 66 and tied Stricker at 18-under 274. They tied through the first three playoff holes. At the fourth, the par-five No. 9, Chopra was on in two, 23 feet from the cup. His eagle putt stopped on the lip. He nudged it in for a birdie. Stricker missed the green and chipped to 15 feet, but missed his birdie try.

"It's a little bittersweet," said Stricker. "I guess I can't be too disappointed. Well," he added, "I guess I can be disappointed."

Said Chopra: "Unbelievable. It's the best round I ever played to win a tournament. And I get to go to Augusta, my lifelong dream."

Sony Open
Honolulu, Hawaii
Winner: K.J. Choi

Steve Marino was talking about chasing K.J. Choi in the final round of the Sony Open. "I think I can catch him," Marino was saying, "but I'll need some help from him." Actually, Marino was speaking for all challengers at Waialae Country Club in Hawaii. The ambition was commendable, but futile. This wasn't the same Choi who finished nearly last in the Mercedes-Benz Championship the week before. When Choi clicks into his zone, everyone else is on his own, and he certainly was clicked in this time.

Choi, age 37, led wire-to-wire, 64-65-66-71, a 14-under-par 266 total for a three-stroke victory over Rory Sabbatini, the last of a host of challengers. It was Choi's seventh PGA Tour victory.

Choi launched his bid with a 20-foot birdie putt at No. 1 and turned in a bogey-free 64 for a one-stroke lead. He used to trip over the second round at Waialae, but this time he birdied four of his last five holes for a 65–129 and a two-stroke lead on Kevin Na (64). Campbell was making a strong move in the second round, but bogeyed three of his last five holes and shot 69. Then he failed to cash in on a hugely promising third round. He hit all 14 driving fairways and all 18 greens, but managed only four birdies and shot 66.

Even so, Choi was turning back all comers. New Zealander Tim Wilkinson, in only his third PGA Tour event, birdied seven of his first 11 holes and shot 62 in the third round. Unflustered, Choi put up 66 highlighted by an up-and-down out of a bunker at the par-five 18th. Choi shot 66 and was at 15-under 195, with Wilkinson second at 199. Na fell behind with 69 and was at 10 under with Marino (68).

It was a wind-beaten final round. "I can't remember having such a difficult round," Choi said. "I told myself, 'Try not to lose focus.'" Only eight players broke par, among them Sabbatini, who double-bogeyed No. 8 out of a hazard, then birdied two of the next three holes and shot 68 to finish second by three. Choi saved par with 12-foot putts on the first two holes, bogeyed the fourth, and three-putted the 13th for a bogey.

"That woke me up, and I said, 'I have to hang in there — not fall apart,'" Choi said. "It motivated me." He parred in to the 18th and there got his only birdie for a 71 and the three-stroke win.

"You just can't get too greedy," Choi said. "You have to accept the conditions as they are."

The Sony Open, first full-field tournament on the schedule, was the introduction of the PGA Tour's new cut policy designed to limit the size of the field on the weekend. It allows for the top 70 professionals and ties, but if that exceeds 78 players, then the closest number of players to 70 can play the last two rounds. It was not received warmly.

Bob Hope Chrysler Classic
Palm Desert and La Quinta, California
Winner: D.J. Trahan

D.J. Trahan, age 27, a one-time winner on the PGA Tour, contemplated having to face Justin Leonard, owner of 11 victories and — at that moment — a four-stroke lead going into the final round of the Bob Hope Chrysler Classic. Said Trahan: "You certainly don't feel particularly optimistic about it ... I wasn't playing against a rookie who was in the lead for the first time."

The final observation came from Leonard: "To have a four-shot lead and come out and play as well as I did the first eight holes, and lose, is disappointing."

And that was the story in late January. Leonard made three birdies on the first nine, but sank himself with three bogeys coming in, while Trahan went racing past with an eight-birdie, one-bogey 65 for a three-stroke victory.

Moving through the four par-72 courses near Palm Desert, Trahan shot 67-64-68-70-65 for a 26-under-par 334 total. He set his stage in the windy second round, breaking from the gate with four straight birdies. The 64 tied him with Robert Gamez for the lead at 13-under 131. Gamez (67) held the solo lead in the third round, when the tournament got a preview of the finale with Leonard (67) and Trahan (68) tied for second. Boo Weekley rocketed into contention with a 10-under 62 that included six birdies on the back nine (he would go on to tie for eighth).

Leonard, playing with more confidence now that he had quit tinkering with his swing, took the lead in the fourth round with a birdie from five feet at the 13th. Then he added an eagle at the par-five 14th, hitting a four wood from 247 yards to six feet. Some prophetic words came out of the fourth round, after Leonard took a four-stroke lead with a 66. Not from Trahan, but from Anthony Kim, the 22-year-old whiz, who tied for second: "Four shots is a lot of shots. You never know what can happen, though."

It did happen in the final round. Leonard made three birdies on the front, but Trahan gained ground, answering with four at Nos. 1, 3, 5 and 6. He bogeyed the seventh, then birdied the ninth. Trahan birdied the 10th on a 40-footer from the fringe and parred the 11th while Leonard bogeyed both. Trahan went ahead for good at No. 14, dropping an eight-foot birdie, then added his eighth and final birdie at the 18th on a five-footer while Leonard bogeyed again, and Trahan had his 65 and a three-stroke win.

Leonard did find some consolation in his improved play from a year ago. "Still, it only takes a little bit of the sting out of it — not all of it," he said.

Trahan, who won his first in 2006, learned that he was the best putter in the event, averaging 26 putts per round. "Pardon me for smiling," he said, "but I've never heard anybody tell me that before."

Buick Invitational
San Diego, California
Winner: Tiger Woods

The Buick Invitational, played at Torrey Pines Golf Course, was distinctive in a number of respects. Among them, Tiger Woods, ranked No. 1 in the world, came face-to-face with No. 1,354 in the person of Kevin Streelman in the second round. Streelman, 29, a rookie on the PGA Tour, got into the tournament as an alternate, and looked up from his practice putts before the first round and "Boom — he was right there in front of me." Thus did Streelman first see Woods. "I was kind of awestruck for a second," he said. But he didn't really meet him. "I was too scared to do that," Streelman said.

Still, Streelman shot 69 for 136 and was second to Woods at the halfway point. The figure didn't really matter — the margin was only four strokes at the time — because Woods, making his first appearance of 2008, simply ran away from everyone to win the tournament for the fourth straight year. It got to the point where writers were conceding the tournament to Woods and wondering who might win the "B Flight," and that happened to be, finally, Ryuji Imada, by a distant eight strokes.

You could chart Woods's progress by his comments in each round:

• "It wasn't pretty off the tee, but I hung in there," Woods said after the first round. "Shooting 67 is always going to feel pretty good on the South Course." The 67, by the way, left Woods two behind Troy Matteson.

• "If they handed out the trophy today, then it would be over, and no big deal," Woods said after the second round. "But since we have so many more holes to play ... as you've seen on tour, anything can happen." This was after he shot another 67 and took that four-shot lead over Streelman.

• "If it was over, they'd be handing out the trophy," Woods said, responding to comments that the tournament was over after the third round. He'd shot 66 and was at 18-under-par 198 and was leading by nine strokes over Stewart Cink.

• "Yeah," Woods said. The question was whether he had room for improvement. He'd just closed with a 71, for a 19-under 269 total, and won by eight strokes.

Imada shot 67 and finished second, eight behind Woods. "My goal going into today was to finish second," Imada said. "That's almost like winning the golf tournament to me."

As part of his closing salute to the fans, Woods escaped from the trampled grass behind the ninth green with a wonderful flop shot to save par. Perhaps his final margin, eight strokes, became more impressive when one realizes that he made three straight bogeys on the last nine.

At any rate, this was Woods's 62nd career victory, which tied him with Arnold Palmer for fourth place on the PGA Tour's all-time victory list. Said Palmer: "I'm sure that there are many, many more coming in the future."

FBR Open
Scottsdale, Arizona
Winner: J.B. Holmes

It was as though the TPC Scottsdale had a mind of its own and considered itself Phil Mickelson country, and it wouldn't let an interloper pass. It will be recalled that Mickelson, a San Diego native, was the adopted son of Arizona golf. He played college golf at Arizona State University, then won the old Tucson Open three times (the first as an amateur in 1991) and then won the FBR Open twice. So with Mickelson playing well through the final round, the golf gods of the desert sent J.B. Holmes squandering a four-stroke lead through the middle of the final round.

Holmes, who shared the lead in the second round and led from the third, did get one last chance. In order to tie Mickelson, Holmes would have to birdie the 18th hole, which he hadn't birdied in any of the three rounds so far. He proceeded to do so, slugging a huge drive some 350 yards, but to the left near a temporary fence. He got a free drop in the rough and hit the next out to within 13 feet of the cup, and he holed the putt for a birdie and a 71 to tie Mickelson at 14-under 270. Then a few minutes later, Holmes birdied the 18th again, on the first hole of the playoff, this time with a drive into the fairway and an approach to the green. After Mickelson missed his birdie try from 28 feet, Holmes sank his eight-footer for the winning putt.

"I can play under pressure, I guess," Holmes said.

Said Mickelson: "Starting the day, I would have gladly taken getting into a playoff, but I've got to give J.B. a lot of credit ... That's pretty impressive golf."

Mickelson hung in contention for the first three rounds before he broke away in the fourth, birdieing the 13th, 15th and 17th holes for 67 and the clubhouse lead. Then suddenly Mickelson, who had finished about a half hour before Holmes, was on the verge of winning his third FBR title. Holmes had gone 23 holes without a bogey, then began to fold. He bogeyed Nos. 7, 8 and 10 and slipped to 13 under. He birdied the 13th, but bogeyed the 15th and was back at 13 under and out of the lead. It was then, Holmes said, that the word "choke" popped into his mind.

"But I fought through it," he said. This he did first at the 18th, getting the birdie to tie Mickelson, then again with a birdie to win.

AT&T Pebble Beach National Pro-Am
Pebble Beach, California
Winner: Steve Lowery

To adapt a cliché, a funny thing happened to Vijay Singh on the way to winning the AT&T Pebble Beach National Pro-Am. He didn't get there. His wonderful swing went astray. And Steve Lowery, a veteran who hadn't won since 2000, came from behind to tie him and then beat him in a playoff. And then Lowery gave a strange explanation for his victory.

"I told my family if I win this tournament," Lowery said, "it's because of the bounce-backs after the double bogeys."

Lowery had a good point. If a guy didn't fold after those doubles, he had winner stamped all over him. In the third round at Poppy Hills, one of three courses used for the famous February tournament on the California coast, Lowery had a wild back nine: After a bogey-birdie exchange heading into the turn, he double-bogeyed the 10th, birdied the 11th, doubled the 12th, then birdied Nos. 13, 14, 15, 17 and 18 for probably the toughest two-under 70 he ever shot. It was the jewel in a card of 69-71-70-68–278, 10 under par. Singh tied Dudley Hart for the lead in the third round, and after shooting 70-70-67, he stumbled on the final nine and birdied just in time — at the 18th — for a 71 to tie Lowery.

Singh was just the last surprise. Defending champion Phil Mickelson provided one earlier. Mickelson opened with 71-72 and still had hope in the third round until he crashed to a whopping 11 on Pebble Beach's par-five 14th. He finished with 78 and missed the third-round cut.

Singh, meanwhile, creaky with his putter, settled for a 67 and a share of the third-round lead with Dudley Hart (68) at 207. Lowery, with a 70–210, was three behind going into the final round.

It was like a sprint to the finish. Lowery burned up the first nine with birdies at Nos. 1, 4, 7, 8 and 9, but gained only one stroke because Singh had answered with birdies at Nos. 2, 4, 6 and 9. Singh was leading by two through the turn, then his troubles started. A bogey at the 10th was just a warm-up. He then bogeyed Nos. 14, 15 and 16. Lowery bogeyed the 11th and 14th, then birdied the 17th for 68. Singh birdied the 18th for 71 to tie and force the playoff. It lasted one hole. At Pebble Beach's 18th, with the Pacific Ocean for its backdrop, Lowery had a perfect drive, a lay-up, then put his approach close to the cup and made the birdie for the win.

"I let this one slip away," Singh said. "I was in control, but those (bogeys) took a little air out of me. There's no excuse for that."

Said Lowery: "After seven years, and winning on this course against Vijay, it's probably the most special."

Northern Trust Open
Pacific Palisades, California
Winner: Phil Mickelson

Phil Mickelson came to Los Angeles carrying heavy baggage. A week earlier, he ran up an 11 and missed the cut, and the week before that he lost in a playoff. If he was troubled, he showed no signs. He kept his head and made the Northern Trust Open, finally, his first victory at historic Riviera Country Club, which he had first visited 20 years earlier, joining Nelson, Snead, Hogan and others who won the tournament under its various names.

"The fact it has taken me so long to win (here) makes it that much more special," Mickelson said. Add this baggage: In the 2007 tournament, Mickelson bogeyed the last hole, fell into a playoff and lost to Charles Howell.

This time he got a big lift from Jeff Quinney, 29, looking for his first PGA Tour victory. Quinney was putting beautifully in the final round, making four consecutive putts of more than 10 feet, and then his putter went cold. He made three straight bogeys on makeable putts from the 13th. "I just put a little too much pressure on the putter in the back nine," Quinney said. He did birdie the last hole from 25 feet, but that just cut Mickelson's winning margin to two. Mickelson shot 68-64-70-70–272, 12 under par.

K.J. Choi solved the chilly February winds for a six-under 65 in the first round, one ahead of Kevin Na. It was encouraging. In seven previous visits to Riviera, he had just one top-20 finish. He tied for seventh this time.

Mickelson, who opened the second round three behind, took the halfway lead with a 64–132, four ahead of Quinney (67) and Robert Allenby (66). "I've made lots of birdies before," Allenby said, "so there's no reason why I can't do it again." But he faded.

Mickelson clearly had his game under control in the second round. He birdied four of five holes from No. 7, and at the par-three 16th, he was long with his tee shot, chipped 12 feet past, but holed the putt for his par and a 64–132 total. In the third round, Quinney made up ground with 67 highlighted by an ace at the par-three No. 6 (he used a seven iron) to close within to one of Mickelson (70–202).

Quinney sampled the lead in the final round. After a birdie from 15 feet at No. 8, he took the lead at No. 9 with a birdie from 12 feet while Mickelson bogeyed. But Mickelson caught up at the 10th with an elegant flop shot to six feet, setting up a birdie. Leading by one at the par-three 14th, Mickelson made par from a bunker with a seven-foot putt while Quinney two-putted from six feet for a bogey. Mickelson was up by two, and went on to win by that margin.

"I didn't understand the nuances of this golf course — where you can hit it and where you can't," Mickelson said. "Last year was when I started to put it together, and I'm fortunate to break through this year."

WGC - Accenture Match Play Championship
Marana, Arizona
Winner: Tiger Woods

The game is Monopoly, but it's not played on a board, and you don't deal with Park Place and such. This game is Tiger Woods and the World Golf Championships. Ho-hum. Another WGC victory, another $1.35 million in prize money.

This was the WGC - Accenture Match Play Championship at the Gallery Golf Club in Arizona, in late February. It was Woods's third straight WGC victory, following the American Express Championship and the Bridgestone Invitational in 2007. He was the first to hold three of the jewels at the same time. It was also his 15th win in 26 WGC events and raised his total winnings in the series to $19.8 million.

Then there was this: It was his 63rd PGA Tour victory, moving him past Arnold Palmer and one behind Ben Hogan on the career list. It was also his fourth straight victory on the PGA Tour and his fifth straight worldwide, counting the win at Dubai three weeks earlier.

"I think this is the best stretch I've ever played," Woods said.

Woods's victory this time was a walk in the park. He made 14 birdies in 29 holes in a crushing 8-and-7 exercise over Stewart Cink in the 36-hole final. It was the biggest margin in the 10-year history of the tournament. But getting to that final through four matches was a different matter. Woods had to rally from three down with five holes to play to beat J.B. Holmes, 1 up, in the first round. Woods won four straight holes with three birdies and an eagle from 35 feet. After ousting Arron Oberholser 3 and 2, Woods had to go 20 holes to beat Aaron Baddeley, and then beat K.J. Choi, 3 and 2, and went 18 holes against Henrik Stenson in the semi-finals. Cink made his way to the final with less trouble, beating Miguel Angel Jimenez, 4 and 3; Padraig Harrington, 2 up; Colin Montgomerie, 4 and 2; Angel Cabrera, 2 and 1, and Justin Leonard, 4 and 2.

In the final, Woods led 4 up after the morning round, and that was as close as Cink would get. Cink didn't win a hole until the 12th, and the only hole he won in the afternoon was the par-five 10th, and this on a 36-foot eagle putt when Woods's try from 35 feet lipped out. Said Cink: "I thought, 'Hey, come on. At least give me a moment to shine here.' And he said, 'Sorry.'" Woods was eight up at the time.

Later, Cink thought it might be nice to know what made Woods tick, suggesting that opening him up might reveal something interesting. What would they find? "Maybe nuts and bolts," Cink said.

Mayakoba Golf Classic
Riviera Maya, Mexico
Winner: Brian Gay

The kids were at the pool Saturday afternoon, not long after Brian Gay shot his career-low 62 in the third round of the Mayakoba Golf Classic. And kids will talk. Thus Taylor Funk, son of Fred, told Makinley Gay, eight, that his dad said that her dad was going to win the tournament the next day. But Brian Gay didn't hear about it. His wife thought it best not to add to the pressure on him. After all, he was going after his first victory.

And so Gay, 36, went out in the final round, drew on the experience of winning nine mini-tour events in 1995, and wrapped up the Mayakoba, the PGA Tour's second annual stop in Mexico, played opposite the WGC - Accenture Match Play.

Gay, an average hitter but a strong putter, is a study in determination. Since joining the tour in 1999, his best finishes were second twice, but not since 2002, and third once, in 2005. This was his 293rd start. Only 12 players still on tour had entered more events and not won.

"It has been a long time," said Gay. "Obviously, a lot of hard work. I was doing really well on the mini-tours and had my chances through the years and wasn't able to get it done. So this is really a big, big relief to finally do it."

Gay played the par-70 El Camaleon (The Chameleon) course in 66-67-62-69–264, 16 under par. Gay emerged in the second round, chasing John Merrick on a windy day that saw only 16 able to break par against the 30 mile-per-hour winds off the Caribbean. Guy shot 67 for a seven-under 133 total, closing to within a stroke of Merrick. Gay then sprinted to a five-stroke lead in the third round, birdieing his last three holes and five of the last six for 62 and a 15-under 195 total.

"I've never had a five-shot lead," Gay said. "I'll try to play my game as best I can, and just play smart." The five-shot cushion served him well in the final round. He was at even par through the 10th with two birdies and two bogeys. Fortunately, no one was making a move. He birdied the 11th and 13th to get back under par, going four ahead. He survived a small crisis at the 16th. He bunkered his tee shot and came out poorly 30 feet short of the cup. But he holed the putt to save his par. Marino birdied the 11th, 13th, 14th and 18th holes, but two shots was as close as he could get.

Then Gay's little daughter could say, "I told you so." Gay not only had his first win, he had probably the heaviest trophy in golf, a hefty carved limestone chameleon.

Honda Classic
Palm Beach Gardens, Florida
Winner: Ernie Els

Truth be known, Ernie Els might have been counting the hours, too. But just years and days would do. When Els stepped off the final green at the Honda Classic on March 2, 2008, it had been three years, four months and 29 days since his last PGA Tour win. He remembered the heady feeling back when he was one of the best in the world.

"I guess we get addicted to that feeling," Els said, "and when you don't get your rush, you miss it."

This one came as a surprise. When Els left that final green, a number of pieces had to fall into place before he could know that rush again.

First, Els had to do his part, and this he did by playing the tough Champion course at PGA National in Florida in 67-70-70-67–274, six under par. He trailed by two in the first round, then by five, and then he started the final round three strokes behind a three-way tie for the lead — Luke Donald, Mark Calcavecchia and Matt Jones, a rookie out of Australia, all at 204. What were the odds that all three would stumble in the last round?

Els made four birdies in the first seven holes. He bogeyed the 17th and parred the 18th for the 67–274 total. The leaders were still on the course. Els needed help, and they gave it to him.

Back at the 15th, Calcavecchia blasted out of a greenside bunker, but his ball rolled off the green and into the water hazard. "I thought it was a pretty good bunker shot, and the thing didn't grab," Calcavecchia said. It cost him a double bogey. He shot 73 and tied for fourth. Jones double-bogeyed the 17th and also shot 73 and tied for fourth. "I can only build from this experience," the rookie said. Donald bogeyed the 12th and 13th after good drives and was short on the chip-in birdie he needed at the 18th. "These are good steps toward proving that I'm getting better," a disappointed Donald said.

And so Ernie Els had his first PGA Tour victory since the 2004 Memorial Tournament. This would help heal some severe wounds. A month earlier, in the Dubai Desert Classic, he was leading by four, then missed two par putts from inside five feet, then hit a shot in the water at the final hole and lost to Tiger Woods. At the 2007 Alfred Dunhill Championship in South Africa, Els led by two going into the last hole, then hit into the water twice, made eight, and lost by a stroke. At the 2007 Verizon Heritage, Els was within reach of the victory, but Boo Weekley chipped in twice from long range on the last two holes. And finally, his victory in the Honda.

"It feels even sweeter," Els said. "Losing so many tournaments — and now one going my way."

PODS Championship
Tampa Bay, Florida
Winner: Sean O'Hair

Sean O'Hair remembered it as the highlight of his career and a thrilling moment in his rookie season in 2005 — how he broke through to win the John Deere Classic and also qualify for the Open Championship the next week, and then the frantic chase through the arrangements to get to St. Andrews.

O'Hair had another sip of that heady wine, winning again three years later when he passed a sagging Stewart Cink in the final round to take the PODS Championship as March winds battered the Florida coast. After rounds of 69-71-71, O'Hair entered the final round trailing Cink by three strokes, and he didn't have the lead until late in the round. He closed with 69 at the tough, par-71 Innisbrook Copperhead Course for a four-under 280 total and two-stroke win over six players, including the frustrated Cink, who closed with 74. The win left O'Hair in tears, thinking of the disappointment in the years afterward.

"When I won, it just kind of happened," said O'Hair, wiping his eyes. "I didn't really appreciate it, because I was like, 'Hey, I'll do this every year.' It's been such a struggle to get to this point again."

It's been even more of a struggle for Cink. He had won four times on the PGA Tour, but he was now 0-for-9 when he either led or shared the lead after three rounds.

"I think it's not a coincidence," Cink said, with brutal honesty. "It's like I'm a little bit tentative. Against Tiger, I was a little bit tentative. I told myself I wasn't going to do that any more." He was referring to his crushing 8-and-7 loss to Tiger Woods in the recent Accenture Match Play.

With rounds overlapping because of weather delays, Cink had to play 28 holes on Saturday, and he played beautifully in the strong winds. He leaped from four shots behind to a two-stroke lead over five holes in 30 mile-an-hour winds and chilling temperatures. Darkness was falling when he left the course Saturday. "I've got to keep pushing," he said. "My goal is to give no one a chance tomorrow."

He went ahead by four with birdies on the first two holes Sunday, and then the day turned sour. He played the next 14 holes in a scattering of four bogeys and a double bogey at the 16th, where he drove into the water.

O'Hair pulled to within a stroke of Cink at the 11th, chipping tight to set up a birdie. He made the last of his four birdies at the 15th, on a 30-foot putt, and a bogey at the 18th merely cut his winning margin to two strokes. His outlook wasn't as bold this time.

"Obviously, I'm good enough to win," O'Hair said. "I definitely work hard enough, and this isn't going to hurt my confidence."

Arnold Palmer Invitational
Orlando, Florida
Winner: Tiger Woods

Tiger Woods opened the Arnold Palmer Invitational with rounds of 70 and 68. He trailed Fred Couples by five strokes after the first round and Vijay Singh by seven after the second. Then when he was walking into the Bay Hill Club locker room Saturday morning, he got his marching orders from none other than the tournament namesake.

"He told me to get off my butt and play a good round," Woods said. And so Woods responded with a four-under-par 66 in the third round and a share of a five-way tie for the lead with Bart Bryant (68), Bubba Watson (68), Sean O'Hair (63) and Vijay Singh (73). The deadlock wouldn't have materialized if Singh hadn't gone five over par on four holes on his first nine.

Woods barged in with the help of two great birdies. At the 15th, he curved a four iron around the trees to about two feet from the cup, and at the 16th he hit a seven iron into a brisk wind to within three feet. "I've played my way back into the tournament," Woods said.

So 16 players were within three strokes of each other going into the final round. Arithmetically, it was anyone's game. Bryant sought to correct that notion. "It's pretty much Tiger's game," said Bryant, age 45, a three-time winner. The record bears him out. Woods had a 42-3 record when he had at least a share of the 54-hole lead.

Ironically, Bryant became a self-fulfilling prophet. He battled Woods pretty much even in the fourth round. Woods took the lead at No. 2, holing a 15-foot putt for a birdie. The touch deserted him at the 10th where, from six feet, he had his first three-putt of the tournament. The bogey dropped him into a tie with Bryant, who handed the lead right back at the 11th, two-putting from two feet for bogey. Bryant, who was the only player in the field to break par in all four rounds, was sitting in the scoring trailer going over his 67 when Woods fired his approach to 24 feet at the 18th.

"There was no television," Bryant said. "So I told the rules official that I'll just sit here and listen. I'll know by the roar."

Soon enough, the roar came and Bryant knew he had finished second. The long birdie putt gave Woods another 66 and a 10-under 270 total.

It was Woods's fifth straight win on the PGA Tour and his 64th career victory, tying him with Ben Hogan at No. 3 on the all-time list. And it had come down to that decisive putt at the 18th. Woods likened it to a classic basketball situation.

"It's like having the ball with a few seconds to go," Woods said. "Do you want it or not want it? I would much rather have it in my hands than anyone else's."

WGC - CA Championship
Miami, Florida
Winner: Geoff Ogilvy

It was a bit too much to get on your average hero poster, but here's what was at stake for Tiger Woods at the World Golf Championships CA Championship in Miami: His sixth straight PGA Tour victory, 65th overall, seventh win in the CA Championship, 16th in a WGC tournament and his fourth straight victory at the Doral Resort's famed Blue Monster course.

The stakes for Australian Geoff Ogilvy paled by comparison. He was merely seeking his second WGC title, his fourth PGA Tour victory and his first since the 2006 U.S. Open.

Ogilvy was off to a sluggish start to the season, so there was no reason to expect much from him in the exclusive field of 79 players. When he took the first-round lead with a seven-under-par 65, about all it meant to anybody was that it was quite an accomplishment on the Blue Monster. What got more attention was Woods's three-putt bogey at the 18th, after a fat bunker shot left him 72 feet from the cup. "You three-putt 18, you're not going to be real happy," said Woods, who was two behind at 67. Woods went on to shoot 66-72-68–273 and finished fifth, two behind Ogilvy.

Ogilvy's big challenges came from a classy triumvirate — Retief Goosen, Jim Furyk and Vijay Singh — and they came on Monday morning, after storms interrupted Sunday's play. All three shot 68s and fell a stroke short and tied for second at 272. Singh was one behind at the 10th, then bogeyed the 13th and 14th, and birdied the 16th and 17th. Furyk was two behind at the turn, bogeyed the 14th, then birdied the 15th and 17th. Goosen was three behind, then birdied the 14th and 16th. Woods also finished Monday morning. He narrowed his five-stroke deficit to two with birdies at the 12th, 15th and 17th, but could get no closer.

Ogilvy ground out 11 straight pars (from No. 8), but the stretch included an echo. Ogilvy missed the green at the par-three 13th, was short with his first chip, and his second hit the flagstick and dropped into the hole for a par, raising memories of the 17th at Winged Foot, where he chipped in for par and won the 2006 U.S. Open. It should be noted that Ogilvy confounded the statisticians. How can anyone hit only 25 of 56 fairways and yet make only one bogey in 72 holes? It came at No. 7 in the final round, and he made 11 straight pars after that.

"Holding off the group is pretty nice," Ogilvy said. "It's pretty nice to come in in front of them, ending the (Woods's) streak. It was going to end at some point. I'm very glad I did it."

Not only that, Ogilvy had wearied of hearing of Woods's invincibility in the media. "He's such a special player that it doesn't frustrate you when he gets on a streak," Ogilvy said. "It's the chit-chat about is he going to win every golf tournament this year — that's the frustrating thing to hear."

Puerto Rico Open
Rio Grande, Puerto Rico
Winner: Greg Kraft

It's not often that golf and justice are mentioned in the same breath. Actually, Greg Kraft meant "poetic justice," but who's to quibble? It's the thought that counts.

Kraft swept past the failing Bo Van Pelt to take a one-shot victory over him and Jerry Kelly in the inaugural Puerto Rico Open, at Trump International, to brighten his tropical March day. It was Kraft's first win since the 1993 Magnolia Classic 15 years earlier. But the Magnolia Classic wasn't an "official" PGA Tour event because it was played the same week as the Masters, meaning that he got none of the blessings that go with winning an official event. But this time, the Puerto Rico Open was official, playing opposite the main tour event, the exclusive WGC - CA Championship in Florida. Which raised the question — how did he feel about winning the small event this time?

"I wish I could describe how I feel," Kraft said. "Maybe justice."

The win gave Kraft playing privileges on the tour for two years, financial security and playing flexibility.

"I enjoyed it (the Magnolia), don't get me wrong," Kraft said. "But it doesn't compare to the way I feel now. I don't have to play the Nationwide Tour to get my card back. That's no fun — go out there and starve."

It was an unlikely story, however. Bo Van Pelt birdied three of his last four holes for 64 and a two-stroke lead. Van Pelt stayed in front with 68-71 and led by one over Kraft (69) and Briny Baird (69) going into the final round. It looked like a life-changing finish for someone. Van Pelt and Baird had never won, and Kraft had just that unofficial Magnolia title on his resume.

Van Pelt held the lead for much of the final round, and he took a big step when he eagled the par-five fifth to go up by two. Kraft stayed on his heels with a birdie there. Then Van Pelt bogeyed Nos. 8 and 9 and fell into a tie with Kraft and Baird. Kraft and Van Pelt pulled away with birdies at the 12th and stayed tied at 14 under. Then at the 14th, Van Pelt bogeyed and Kraft was in the lead to stay.

Baird ran into a wild patch. He bogeyed four straight, then rebounded with three straight birdies, but his chances were gone. And so were Van Pelt's. Kraft locked it up with a birdie at the 17th and led by three with one to play. He bogeyed the 18th, ending a string of 29 holes without one. It wrapped up a card of 69-66-69-70, for a 14-under 274 total and a one-stroke win over Van Pelt (72) and Jerry Kelly (70). Baird (72) was another shot back.

It was a deliverance for Kraft. He contracted a respiratory ailment that wasted him and crippled his career. Said Kraft: "I never thought I'd make it back."

Zurich Classic
Avondale, Louisiana
Winner: Andres Romero

The toughest part of the Zurich Classic for Andres Romero was the last two hours and 50 minutes. It was that long between his own final putt for the clubhouse lead and the end of the procession of all the men who could beat him.

"I didn't know if I was going to win," Romero had said, "but I'm finished, and that's the most important thing. The score was there and they had to catch it."

Nobody could, and Romero, age 26, the bold Argentine, had his first PGA Tour victory in only his 12th tour event. Romero played the TPC Louisiana in 73-69-65-68–275, 13 under par, winning by one stroke over Australia's Peter Lonard.

Lonard was the one with the best chance. He birdied the 11th, 13th and 16th holes to tie the waiting Romero. "I figured I'd par 17 and birdie 18, then happy days," Lonard said. But he missed the green at the par-three 17th and bogeyed. He needed a birdie at the 18th, but a stray tee shot left him in a bunker nearly 200 yards from the green. He shot 69 and finished second by a stroke.

Woody Austin also had a chance to tie. He needed a birdie at the 18th, but he hit his third shot in the water and double-bogeyed. "I'm not afraid to admit when I choke," Austin said, "and I choked." Nicholas Thompson had a slim chance, needing at least one birdie, but a bogey-bogey finish did him in.

Romero gave them a hefty job to do. Because of the storms that forced the suspension of the third round on Saturday, Romero had to complete his round on Sunday morning. He finished birdie-birdie to close within a stroke of the lead. In the final round, he bogeyed No. 6, making his first bogey since the eighth hole of the second round. Then he birdied Nos. 7,

11, 12 and 16. He posted his 68–275 and went off to the players' lounge to wait to see whether anyone could catch him.

Romero's victory surprised no one who had been paying attention. He'd taken the world stage as an unknown in the 2007 Open Championship when he raced through Carnoustie in the last round with 10 birdies, only to fall short, the victim of an overly bold move. But he looked like anything but a winner at the start. He opened with a one-over 73, fully seven behind Dean Wilson, leading at 66. A 69 in the second round got him safely inside the cut by two strokes, but he was six behind Briny Baird (69–136).

Actually, Romero came through the trauma of the Open Championship unscathed, and if anything, stronger. "I learned much from that experience," he said.

He learned fast, too. He'd won the following week on the European Tour, and still by playing bold golf. "But I've always been aggressive," Romero said. "That's my way of playing. That's the way I got here."

Shell Houston Open
Humble, Texas
Winner: Johnson Wagner

The Shell Houston Open, rich with over $1 million to the winner, offered a huge extra prize. The winner, if not otherwise qualified, would get that last berth in the Masters the following week. And Johnson Wagner wasn't otherwise qualified — not by a long shot.

In nine starts, he tied for 38th in the first, tied for 78th and 64th in the last two, and in between missed six straight cuts. If ever a golfer figured not to win, Wagner was it. So he took the Shell Houston Open, his first PGA Tour victory, and thus grabbed that last berth for his first Masters.

"I'm just thrilled, and not shocked, but just — I just can't believe it," Wagner said.

Wagner came to the top furiously in the first round, going five under par on his last five holes, including an eagle at the par-five No. 8 off a 260-yard second shot to a tap-in, for a nine-under 63 that tied defending champion Adam Scott for the lead. Scott withdrew after the second round with strep throat, and Wagner went on to lead the rest of the way. He shot 69-69-71 for a total 272, 16 under at Redstone Golf Club, and won by two over Geoff Ogilvy and Chad Campbell.

Storms forced a suspension of play in the second round, but Wagner was already in with his 69 and a 12-under 132. He got up-and-down out of a bunker at the par-five fourth, holed a six-foot putt at the fifth, and birdied the par-five eighth. He led by three over Charley Hoffman (70) and Mathew Goggin, who shot 64, making his pitch to become the eighth Australian to win the Shell Houston Open. Others were giving mixed reviews. Phil Mickelson, preparing for the Masters, shot 68 and was eight behind. Fred Couples shot 29 on his second nine, tying the course's nine-hole record, and had 67.

Wagner kept the lead in the third round, thanks in part to two great breaks off errant tee shots. He hit a spectator at the 13th and a tree at the 15th and escaped with pars and didn't blush. "I've had enough bad breaks not to feel bad about the good ones," Wagner said. Another 69 left him one up on Campbell going into the final round, and that's where he passed his toughest tests. First, Campbell backslid with a 39 on the front and Wagner went ahead by five with a birdie at No. 4. He was leading by four through the turn, and that's when the pressure came thick and fast from Billy Mayfair, Bob Estes and Ogilvy and Campbell.

And finally, Wagner had to save himself with two tough pars. At the 17th he holed an 11-foot putt for one and scrambled from a fairway bunker for the other at the 18th, and he was on his way to the Masters.

"I don't care if I shoot 90 both days and miss the cut," Wagner said. "I'm so excited to be there."

Masters Tournament
Augusta, Georgia
Winner: Trevor Immelman

See Chapter 2.

Verizon Heritage
Hilton Head Island, South Carolina
Winner: Boo Weekley

A leader coming down the 18th might be rehearsing his acceptance speech. Not Boo Weekley at the Verizon Heritage. The homespun Weekley, the defending champion, was coming down the final yards trying to decide on his victory celebration. He was thinking of a golf equivalent of a touchdown dance in the National Football League.

"I wanted to do the moonwalk," Weekley said, a not likely thing in golf spikes, soft or not. "Or the belly-roll," he said. He had been deprived when he won in 2007, when he chipped in at the two final holes and there was no time for theatrics. This time, he had time. He came strolling up the final fairway of the Harbour Town Golf Links, on the South Carolina coast, holed his last putt, then simply doffed his golf cap and bowed from the waist to the gallery, setting a new standard for gentlemanly conduct. Not bad for a rough-hewn tobacco-chewer from the Florida Panhandle.

Weekley began the tournament with a three-stroke deficit on his two-under-par 69. Justin Leonard, Lucas Glover and an old friend who had been struggling, Davis Love, a five-time winner of the tournament, shared the first-round lead at 66. Love, age 44, was still recovering from tearing ligaments in his left ankle the previous September. "It's getting close," said Love, who birdied four of his first seven holes. That tied him with Leonard, who fired his approach to within four feet of the cup at the 15th, and Glover, who birdied five holes over an eight-hole span.

Glover shot another 66 and took the halfway lead at 132 by a stroke over Weekley (64), while Anthony Kim shot another 67 and was third at 134. Weekley finally came to the top in the third round with 65 for 15-under

198 and a three-shot lead over Kim (67). Weekley started a stroke behind Glover and fell two behind with a par out of the sand at No. 2 to Glover's birdie. Then Weekley took off. He chipped in for a birdie at the par-three fourth, then two-putted the par-five fifth, then tied Glover with an approach to seven feet for a third straight birdie at the sixth. He wasn't done. Next came a 10-foot birdie at No. 7, then a 20-footer at No. 8 — five straight birdies for 65 and a two-shot lead.

Weekley moved methodically through the final round, staying out of trouble while others labored to catch him. Kim lost his chance when he double-bogeyed No. 9. Jim Furyk, six behind at the start, birdied three of the first five holes but sagged on a bogey at No. 11. Weekley caused himself some uneasy moments. He bogeyed No. 8 on a bad chip and escaped a tight spot at No. 10, chipping in for a birdie that put him five ahead. And finally came the 18th, and a bow as graceful as Weekley could make it.

EDS Byron Nelson Championship
Irving, Texas
Winner: Adam Scott

In a sense, Adam Scott was merely picking up where he left off. Two weeks earlier, he started the Shell Houston Open with 63, then had to withdraw after the second round with a strep throat. Now it was the EDS Byron Nelson Championship near Dallas, and Scott, after flirting with failure, beat Ryan Palmer in a playoff for his sixth PGA Tour victory.

Scott took the lead by a stroke in the second round, expanded his margin to three in the third, then had to go three extra holes for the win.

"I got away with one today — a bit lucky," said Scott, the highest ranked player in the tournament at No. 10. Scott had to rally down the stretch to tie Palmer at seven-under-par 273 at the wind-whipped TPC Four Seasons Las Colinas.

Following a so-so performance in the Masters — he finished 25th — Scott went home to Australia for some R&R. Then it dawned on him. "I felt like I was still playing well," he said, "and I should waste that at home." He rushed back.

Scott was one off the lead in the first round, then in the second, starting at No. 10, he ran off four straight birdies on his way to a second 67, and a remarkable 67 at that. He hit only five fairways. "It was just a matter of hanging in there," he said, as if it were that simple. And there he was, leading by one at the halfway point. Mathew Goggin (69), Mark Hensby (67) and Scott McCarron (66) were tied for second a stroke behind.

Scott continued to flirt with failure in the third round. He started to slide, and bogeyed twice on the front nine but recovered on the back. He birdied the 16th with a six-foot putt after recovering from the rough, and dropped a three-footer for a birdie at the 18th. His 67 gave him a three-stroke lead over a crowd — Kevin Sutherland (67), Bart Bryant (67), Charley Hoffman (65) and Ryan Moore (68), all at 205.

In the final round, Scott was nothing if not spectacular, in more ways than one. First, he squandered a three-stroke lead, with a bogey at No. 1

from the rough and double bogey out of the water at the par-three fifth. His lead was down to one over Moore. From there, Scott and Moore batted the lead back and forth. Moore inched ahead at the par-three 17th, holing a curling 12-foot birdie putt. Scott answered with his last chance, at the 18th, dropping a nine-foot putt for 71 to tie Moore (68) at 273. On the third playoff hole, Scott holed a 48-foot putt for a birdie and had the victory when Moore missed his try from the fringe.

Wachovia Championship
Charlotte, North Carolina
Winner: Anthony Kim

It was said that Anthony Kim had the right stuff and that it was just a question of time — and attitude — before he made good on his considerable promise. And that time came in the first week of May in the Wachovia Championship against a field loaded with stars and missing only Tiger Woods, recuperating from arthroscopic surgery on his left knee.

Kim was 22 years, 10 months and 15 days old — the first under-23 player to win on the PGA Tour since 2005. Would this be the seed of a new era?

Kim opened with a two-under-par 70 and trailed David Toms by five strokes, then shot 67 and trailed Jason Bohn by two. Then he ran away from the field, closing with 66-69 and a 16-under 272 total, winning by five over Ben Curtis at the tough Quail Hollow Club in Charlotte, North Carolina. To put his victory in perspective: Jim Furyk finished seventh, Adam Scott and Stewart Cink in a group at eighth, Phil Mickelson tied for 12th and Vijay Singh tied for 17th.

"It was a long ride, but it is worth it," Kim said, revealing a youthful impatience. His "long ride" consisted of just 38 starts since he joined the PGA Tour about a year and a half earlier. Odd to say, but given his youth, it was a new Anthony Kim who took this tournament. He'd readily admitted to immature behavior in 2007 — practicing little, partying much. "How can you not hit balls before a tournament and say you want to win?" he chided himself rhetorically.

"He's 22, and sometimes he's 22 off the course," said Adam Schriber, Kim's swing coach. "But on the course, he's a veteran with a very high golf IQ."

Kim started his breakthrough at No. 9 in the third round, dropping a nine-foot birdie putt to take the lead. He birdied the 14th and got up-and-down to par the 17th, then closed spectacularly. He slugged a 324-yard drive, put his approach to seven feet, and made the birdie putt for a 65.

"I played with somebody who played ... almost Tigeresque," said Jason Bohn.

Said Kim: "I feel like I'm ready, but you never know."

It's almost guaranteed that a player of Kim's youth and inexperience will crack under the pressure of a fourth-round lead. Kim's answer to that bit of golf lore was to flip a wedge to five feet at No. 1 and open the final round with a birdie. He shot 32 on the first nine, with only 11 putts, and was up by seven at the turn.

Kim bogeyed the 13th and birdied the next two for 18 under. Two late bogeys brought him back to 69, the runaway victory and, it seems, maturity.

"I'm a little bit numb right now," Kim said, "but that walk up 18 was the best feeling of my life ... I want to re-create that ... so I'm really going to work hard."

The Players Championship
Ponte Vedra Beach, Florida
Winner: Sergio Garcia

Sometimes Sergio Garcia's putter is like a magic wand and sometimes it's like a live wire in his hands. At The Players Championship, it was both for the 28-year-old Spaniard, but it was magic when he needed it most, and he made the prestigious Players his first PGA Tour victory since 2005.

And, as usual, the tournament was pretty much decided by Devil's Island, the par-three 17th in the lake at the TPC Sawgrass. With the heavy May winds battering Ponte Vedra Beach, Florida, the 17th was nastier than usual. This time, in the final round, it was a feast for Garcia but famine for Goydos. It was a mere 128 yards, but in 30 mile-an-hour gusts, every tee shot was a coin toss. Goydos hit first and his ball came down short, in the water. Garcia braced himself, and he did reach the green. His ball trickled down to within four feet of the cup. He missed the birdie putt, but he got the par and with it his first championship in three years and 53 tour starts.

But speaking for his frustrations, Garcia said, cryptically: "I felt I putted nicely. Unfortunately the putts didn't want to drop."

Goydos, a former substitute math and science teacher, had no alibis, only compliments. "I got beat," he said. "I played good golf. That doesn't mean you win. You have to accept that the guy beat me."

Garcia shot 66-73-73-71, tying Goydos (68-71-70-74) at five-under 283. There might have been others, but the 17th intervened. In the first round, for example, Ernie Els was two under coming to the 17th tee. He put his tee shot in the water and triple-bogeyed, shot 72 and didn't threaten thereafter. "I think they should blow it up," he said. Garcia was about to take the second-round lead, but his tee shot ended up on the footpath and he double-bogeyed without hitting the water.

Goydos, with a 70–209, took his first-ever 54-hole lead, and found himself under heavy pressure, with Kenny Perry at 210, Garcia at 212, and Mickelson, Bernhard Langer and Jeff Quinney at 214. The wind was ripping and quickly shrank the field. Mickelson shot 78, Langer 77 and Perry 81. It was down to Garcia and Goydos.

Goydos led by three with five holes to play. Then everything changed. Garcia, playing just ahead, holed a 45-foot putt for birdie at the 14th, and Goydos bogeyed, two-putting from 10 feet. Then Goydos bogeyed the next, two-putting from seven feet. He retook the lead at the 16th, two-putting from 60. Garcia then holed a seven-footer to par the 18th, but Goydos two-putted from 15 feet and bogeyed and they were tied. For the first time in

Players history, since 1987, the playoff would begin at the 17th. Goydos, hitting first in the heavy winds, put his tee shot in the water. Garcia hit the green and stuck, and two-putted for the par and the victory.

"It's been a lot of work," Garcia said. "It felt like everything was so hard. I'm just thrilled the week is over and I managed to finish on top."

AT&T Classic
Duluth, Georgia
Winner: Ryuji Imada

It was an ironic twist of fate. Ryuji Imada had come back to the scene not of his success but of his failure. It was the AT&T Classic in mid-May at the TPC Sugarloaf near Atlanta. Imada stood on the ridge looking down on the 18th green. A year ago, from about the same place, he went for the green in two and his approach came down short in the fronting pond and he lost the playoff to Zach Johnson. Now here he was again, again in a playoff, this time against Kenny Perry.

"I never believed in destiny," Imada said. "But I'm starting to believe it."

Destiny — or whatever it was — took a different path this time. This time, it was Perry who hit into the water, but in the weirdest possible way. His five-wood second cleared the pond but hit a big pine tree to the right of the green, and the ball bounced backward across the green and ended up in the water.

With Perry in the water, Imada chose to lay up with an iron, and he got up-and-down for a par and his first victory in his fourth year on the PGA Tour, leaving Perry perplexed by that approach shot going past the green and hitting the tree. "I hit a beautiful five wood," said Perry. "I must have been pumped up."

Imada shot 71-69-66-67 and Perry 66-69-69-69, tying at 15-under 273. Imada didn't surface until the third round, and then only tied for third place. He seemed set for just another good finish. He was runner-up twice already, in the Buick Invitational and the PODS Championship.

The fourth round had to sort itself out. Camilo Villegas played the last seven holes in five under par, but missed the playoff when he missed an eagle putt at the 18th and shot 66 and finished third. Parker McLachlin holed a bunker shot for an eagle at the 13th and led by three, but he bogeyed three of the last five holes for 67, three out of the playoff. Howell, the third-round leader, shot 74. Imada, playing in front of Perry, needed a birdie at the 18th to tie him. His three-wood approach was to the right of the green, and he chipped to four feet and holed the putt for the birdie and 67–273. Perry needed a birdie at the last for the outright win, but he misread a 25-foot putt and shot 69 and tied Imada. It was back to the 18th tee for the playoff, and time for the irony to kick in for Imada. He won $990,000, but a different prize was on his mind, redeemable in 2009.

"I know I get invited to the Masters now," Imada said. "I always dreamed of playing there since I was a kid. I can't wait to see what it's like."

Crowne Plaza Invitational
Fort Worth, Texas
Winner: Phil Mickelson

Leave it to Phil Mickelson to miss the obvious. With the tournament hanging by a thread, Mickelson had bashed his final tee shot at the 18th hole far left into thick rough and under some trees. The smart way out would be to pitch back to the fairway. True, it would waste a shot, but it might save a lot of others. "I didn't see that option," Mickelson said. Accordingly, he followed the path that he wanted to see — a daring 141-yard wedge shot out of the rough, under one tree and over another. Observers were stunned. Mickelson threaded the needle, and the ball dropped on the green, nine feet from the flag. Mickelson holed the putt and took the Crowne Plaza Invitational at Colonial Country Club by a stroke over Tim Clark and Rod Pampling. It was his 34th PGA Tour victory.

"If there is at all a chance, I'm going for it," he said. "You have to take some risks to win." And so Mickelson, with rounds of 65-68-65-68–266, 14 under par, led after 54 holes and won for the 20th time in 27 tries.

Mickelson had started the final round with the lead, but Pampling raced two strokes ahead of him on the front nine with birdies at No. 6 on a 48-foot putt, then No. 7 from seven feet and No. 9 from four.

"He looked like he was in control," Mickelson said. "I was obviously very fortunate to come out on top."

Mickelson gained a stroke at the par-five 11th with a birdie on two putts from 33 feet. At the 17th, Pampling drove into a ditch on the right and had to take a penalty drop and bogeyed. "It was a really bad swing," he said. "It was the only one I was disappointed in."

Then it came down to the 18th. Mickelson hit one of his wild drives, this one into a clearly dead situation. Dead except by Mickelson's definition. From his lie in the trees, Mickelson couldn't see the shot he hit. He had to trot to a nearby opening and got there in time to see the ball drop to the green. "It came off perfectly," Mickelson said. And he said he was as "surprised as anybody" that he had pulled it off and made a birdie from there. As to the shot itself: "Probably top five" of all the shots in his career.

Although Pampling was harpooned by that shot, that didn't dull his appreciation of it. "That's what No. 2's in the world do," he said. "Those guys make those kinds of shots."

For Mickelson, it was more than just another victory. "I felt like before I came here that this tournament needed to be the start of my run to the U.S. Open," Mickelson said. As a tune-up, this one had a sweet sound.

Memorial Tournament
Dublin, Ohio
Winner: Kenny Perry

They had just handed Kenny Perry a $1.08 million check for winning the Memorial Tournament. "Oh, sweet," Perry said. But he wasn't talking about the money. He was talking about the Ryder Cup points that went with the victory, which lifted him to fifth on the points list. It was a huge step toward his dream of making the Ryder Cup team.

Not that this hurt the feelings of Jack Nicklaus, tournament founder and host. Perry, age 47, had made no secret that his goal in all the 2008 tournaments was to make the U.S. Ryder Cup team, and recognizing this, Nicklaus grinned and said, "You're going to get there."

"Magic always happens for me here," said Perry, who joined Tiger Woods as a three-time winner of the Memorial. But it was a late-developing magic. The Muirfield Village course was playing fast and hard, with greens that were bringing muffled howls from the golfers. Perry shot 66-71-74-69, for an eight-under total of 280, to win by two strokes with the Memorial's highest winning score in 23 years.

In the first round, Australian Mathew Goggin needed only nine putts over his last nine holes — "Is that possible?" he asked — and shot a seven-under-par 65 for a one-stroke lead over Jack Kelly and Perry. Perry holed an eight-footer for birdie at No. 11, and his next five came from 18 feet or more. It was pretty much the Goggin show from there. Perry tied him with a 71 in the wind-beaten second round, when only three players broke 70 and 20 couldn't break 80. Goggin had seven birdies overall and only managed a par 72. Perry bogeyed three of his first five holes and eagled the par-five 15th. "Hit the shot of my life to keep the ship from sinking," he said. Phil Mickelson shot 75 and was 10 behind, and Ernie Els shot 78 and missed the cut.

Rain rolled in for the third round, and through it Goggin shot 71 and stretched his lead to three strokes over Mike Weir (68) and Perry (74). Goggin conceded that expectations were rising, including his own. "Three shots in front — I expect to win," Goggin said. Perry all but conceded the tournament to him, but then turned prophet. "If he shoots 75, then the door's wide open," Perry said. And Goggin, after bogeying two of his first four holes, shot 74.

Perry put on quite a closing show. He hit 13 of the 14 driving fairways and was equally sharp making putts, among them a par save from 10 feet at the 12th and another from four feet at the 14th. He shot a three-under 69 for the two-stroke win over Goggin, Weir, Jerry Kelly and Justin Rose. And he was closer to the Ryder Cup.

"My time is running out," Perry said. "It's getting close to September. And to be able to get the win here is huge."

Stanford St. Jude Championship
Memphis, Tennessee
Winner: Justin Leonard

It seemed to Justin Leonard that all people wanted to talk about was his 45-foot putt that clinched the 1999 Ryder Cup — the last one the United States won. Now it was Ryder Cup time again, 2008, and the Ryder Cup was about all that was on his mind, too. So upon winning the playoff for the Stanford St. Jude Championship in June, his thoughts turned toward September.

"I don't know how much of a lock I am," said Leonard, on this big harvest of Ryder Cup points, "but I feel pretty good about making it. I'm looking forward to being on that team."

But from the start of the tournament, in the heat at TPC Southwind at Memphis, making the cut was about the only thing Leonard had locked up. This was a classic example of woulda-coulda's. Tommy Armour was an early victim. Armour was tied for the lead, then bogeyed the 16th about the time Boo Weekley was birdieing the 18th. Weekley shot five-under 65, and Armour was a stroke behind. (Leonard was three behind with 68.) Armour was about to take the second-round lead but double-bogeyed the 18th and dropped into a six-way tie for the lead at 137. (Leonard slipped a stroke further back with 73–141.)

South Africa's Tim Clark broke through the traffic jam in the third round, burning up the last five holes with three birdies and an eagle for 64 and a two-stroke lead at 205. Clark had finished solo or joint second six times but never won. (Leonard still had not made a ripple in the field. A 67 left him three behind going into the final round.)

The woulda-coulda's struck hard in the final round. Clark's dreams died fast, in a triple bogey at No. 1. Australian Gavin Coles was the last to have a chance to win outright. A birdie at the 18th would do the trick. But he hit rough, bunker and more rough, and double-bogeyed. "It was like a train wreck," Coles said. Leonard was one of 10 who shared the lead at one time or another, and he had a chance to win outright, leading by one stroke with two to play. But at the 17th, he missed the fairway and bogeyed, then just missed a birdie putt at the 18th. He closed with 68 and tied four-under 276 with Robert Allenby (65) and Masters champion Trevor Immelman (69).

They parred the first playoff hole, No. 18, and went to the par-three 11th. Allenby, who was 10-0 in playoffs worldwide, putted first from 20 feet and missed his birdie try a foot to the right. Leonard holed his 19-footer, but only just. "I don't think the ball would've rolled another half inch," he said. Then Immelman tried from 11 feet. When he missed, Leonard had his victory and, he hoped, a date with the Europeans for September.

U.S. Open Championship
San Diego, California
Winner: Tiger Woods

See Chapter 3.

Travelers Championship
Cromwell, Connecticut
Winner: Stewart Cink

Stewart Cink had come into the Travelers Championship with the harsh reputation as a folder. He had the ignominious distinction of being one-for-nine when he led or shared the lead after 54 holes. And so at the Travelers he had to face the reality that he had been a marked man.

"I know there has been some talk that I have not been a closer," said Cink, in what was, frankly, a huge understatement. His latest fold was in the PODS Championship in March. "They had every right to say that because I felt the same way myself," Cink admitted. "So I felt that I had something to prove to myself."

And this he proved in the Travelers Championship in mid-June. Shooting 66-64-65-67, he grabbed the lead in the second round and held off all comers the rest of the way. The last of them were Tommy Armour and defending champion Hunter Mahan. Both closed with 65s, finishing a stroke behind Cink's 18-under-par 262 total at the par-70 TPC River Highlands, in Cromwell, Connecticut. Cink also turned away Heath Slocum, matching his birdies at Nos. 6, 9, 13 and 15. Slocum closed with a 67 and finished fourth.

After sitting two strokes out of a four-way tie for the lead on 64s in the first round, Cink shot a 64 of his own in the second and inched into a one-stroke lead. The question then wasn't a final-round collapse, but whether he might finally win after six top-10 finishes this season. "I hope it's just a matter of about two days," said Cink. But the signs were mixed. He'd bogeyed his first two holes, then made two long eagle putts, a 26-footer at the sixth and a 49-footer at the 13th, for his 64 and the lead. Mahan (63), Ken Duke (66) and Lucas Glover (66) were just a stroke behind. Cink expanded that to two strokes in the third round with 65 when 24 golfers shot 66 or better and 17 ended up within five strokes of Cink's 195, his best 54-hole score ever.

They put on a rousing finish in the final round. Armour birdied the 17th after an approach to four feet, and he needed a 37-footer at the 18th but just missed. Mahan birdied the last two holes, on an 18-footer at No. 17, then flipped a brilliant wedge to three feet at the 18th. Next came a real test for Cink. His lead hanging by a stroke at the 18th, he hit his tee shot into the gallery on the right, then he hit his approach shot just over the green. Then he putted neatly to two feet and dropped the next for the par and the win.

"Sometimes (when) you have to go through a few extra trials," said the liberated Cink, "it seems a little bit sweeter."

Buick Open
Grand Blanc, Michigan
Winner: Kenny Perry

They were calling him the hottest player on the PGA Tour not named Tiger Woods. But with Woods sidelined after season-ending knee surgery, Kenny Perry was simply the hottest player on the tour. Add to his collection the Buick Open, which belonged to just about anybody until Perry smelled the finish line. But it was just the kind of finish for people who like the lump-in-the-throat feeling.

"I still can't believe it," Perry said, posting his second win of the season after the Memorial Tournament a few weeks earlier. "I feel like I need to go make a birdie out there to win this tournament."

What Perry couldn't believe was not that he'd won, but how he won. After rounds of 69-67-67, he closed with a six-under-par 66, then had to wait out the leaders. He needed their help, and got it. The stage, at Warwick Hills Golf and Country Club at Grand Blanc, Michigan, was set by a dramatist. Perry had started the final round at 203, 13 under par and three strokes out of the lead.

First to fall back was the leader himself, Daniel Chopra, who was 16 under par and up by two going into the final round. Chopra slid out of the picture with 75 and dropped to a tie for 17th. Next came a trio who had started the final round tied, two strokes behind Chopra. They also obliged Perry, as needed.

Dudley Hart, who missed most of the 2007 season because of his wife's illness, bogeyed three of the last four holes and tied for ninth. Bubba Watson, playing in the last two groups, needed a birdie at the 18th to tie Perry. Watson drove into the trees to the left of the fairway, but still reached the green, 12 feet from the cup. But he missed the birdie putt, shot 68, and tied for second with the frustrated Woody Austin, who was kicking himself. Austin suffered from poor approaches. He left himself 40 feet from the flag at the 17th and 63 feet at the 18th, and three-putted both for bogeys. "I threw it away," Austin said. "I didn't hit the ball close enough to counteract my yips."

Perry had birdied Nos. 1, 4, 6, 7 and 10, then had a bumpy ride. He bogeyed the 13th, holed out from a bunker for an eagle at the 14th, bogeyed the 15th and birdied the 16th for his 66–269, and when the others slipped, he had his 11th career win and, better yet, almost certainly a berth in the Ryder Cup. But first — would he change his mind and play in the Open Championship in Britain next week?

"No — I'm going to play Milwaukee," Perry said. "I committed to all these tournaments before, when I was ranked 100th in the world. I'm already committed to Milwaukee, and I'm not going to back out on them."

AT&T National
Bethesda, Maryland
Winner: Anthony Kim

Anthony Kim's cell phone rang. The setting is important here. Kim was just off Congressional Country Club's 18th green. The call wasn't recorded, but it almost certainly went something like this: "Hey, Anthony, this is Tiger Woods — Congratulations..."

Kim, 23, regarded as the next new whiz kid — maybe even the next challenger to Tiger Woods — justified that lofty tag with the second victory of his career and second of the season in the AT&T National with a closing rush for 65 and a two-stroke margin over Fredrik Jacobson.

"This means the world to me," said Kim, marveling at the call from the world's No. 1 player. Woods was the tournament host, but he was at home recuperating from season-ending knee surgery. "I get chills down my back when I think of it," Kim said.

While Kim was hanging just on the edge of the competition, others were making their bid and falling back. Steve Marino took the first-round lead with a five-under-par 65, then eventually slipped back. Tom Pernice tied the course record with a 63 in the second round and shared the halfway lead with Jeff Overton (65) at nine-under 131. Pernice moved into the third-round lead with 69–200, and it was at this time that Kim came crashing into the picture with six wild holes in the middle of his round — six holes without a par.

He started with a 35-foot putt for birdie at the sixth, Congressional's toughest hole. He bogeyed the seventh when his tee shot spun back off the green. Next on the roller coaster, he birdied the eighth and ninth, then bogeyed the 10th from a bunker, and bogeyed the 11th from the heavy collar. Kim settled into a run of pars the rest of the way and capped them off with a birdie at the last.

"I've got some positive things to look forward to," said Kim, whose career-first victory came in the Wachovia Championship two months earlier.

Positive and then some. He entered the final round trailing by three strokes, and erased that deficit with aggressive playing, shooting at the pins on every opportunity. Kim broke away with a birdie at No. 10, hitting a five-iron tee shot to 18 feet behind the cup. He played like a seasoned vet coming in. At the 14th, he saved par after a bunker shot to seven feet, and got his final birdie at the 16th off a wedge to five feet. He'd played the last 22 holes without a bogey, and his lead, never in real danger, shrank from four to two when Jacobson birdied four straight. Kim played Congressional in 67-67-69-65 for a 12-under 268 total, showing the kind of game that stamped him as a real comer. He was the first American under 25 to win at least twice in the same year. Would he be challenging Tiger Woods?

Said Kim: "I've got to win about 13 majors to worry him..."

John Deere Classic
Silvis, Illinois
Winner: Kenny Perry

You wouldn't know Kenny Perry if you ran into him on the street, and that would suit him just fine. "I don't want to live in a fishbowl," the pleasant guy-next-door from Kentucky said. "I don't want Tiger Woods status."

Fair enough, but he's got to quit winning like this. He'd just made the John Deere Classic his third victory in five starts. Even so, he was still getting criticized for passing up the Open Championship in Britain, trying to run up Ryder Cup points. "I'm getting hammered for it," said Perry. He had said early on that his goal for 2008 was to play in the Ryder Cup in September in his home state, Kentucky.

Well, if the criticism affected his play, it wasn't apparent. He shot 65-66-67-70–268, and was tied at 16 under par with Jay Williamson and the PGA Tour's oldest rookie, Brad Adamonis, 35. Perry won the playoff with a par on the first extra hole.

Perry had his nose in or near the lead all the way. He was one behind Ken Duke and Charlie Wi, who led the first round with 64s. "I feel very comfortable here," Perry said, and this after the fire alarm in his hotel went off at 3:30 a.m. and he couldn't get back to sleep. It didn't seem to bother his putting eye. Starting at No. 10, he birdied his first three holes from 18, 11 and 10 feet. In the second round, he birdied six of his last 10 holes. Now other golfers were touching him, hoping whatever it was would rub off. "In my 22 years out there, that's never happened," Perry said.

He tied in the third round with Adamonis (66) and Eric Axley (67) at 15-under 198, but he wasn't perfect. He bogeyed the par-four 15th, two-putting from nine feet. But at No. 18, he holed a six-footer for birdie after hitting the flag with his approach.

"It's been awesome how well I've played this year," he said.

Perry had his toughest time in the final round, if a one-under 70 can be called tough. He took the lead with a birdie at the 14th, then at the 16th, after an awful chip, holed from 16 feet to save par. He chipped all the way across the green at the 18th, but this time bogeyed and fell into the tie. In the playoff, Adamonis and Williamson both hit their approaches into the pond. Perry was on and two-putted from 24 feet for the par and the victory.

Okay, the guys said, what's your secret? "If I knew the answer," Perry said, "I'd have done this 20 years ago."

The Open Championship
Southport, Lancashire, England
Winner: Padraig Harrington

See Chapter 4.

U.S. Bank Championship
Milwaukee, Wisconsin
Winner: Richard S. Johnson

You really did need a program at the U.S. Bank Championship. The field was thick with Johnsons — four of them. Brown Deer Park Golf Course in Milwaukee, Wisconsin, a par-70 venue, sorted things out. Two of the Johnsons — Mike, an American, and one of two Richards, a Welshman — missed the cut. That left two in a field thinned out by the attraction of the Open Championship in Britain that same mid-July week. Dustin Johnson, American, tied for 19th. The other Richard Johnson, a Swede, who mercifully uses his middle initial S, established his identity by winning.

"It all started that first day," said Johnson, and he meant his hole-in-one in the first round. "All of a sudden I felt like I could make some birdies. I haven't had that feeling for a while."

Johnson, the sixth Swede to win on the PGA Tour and the seventh first-time winner of the season, had made the cut in only three of his 10 previous starts. He led most of the way, shooting 63-67-70-64—264, 16 under par, winning by a stroke over Ken Duke.

Johnson was two under, then birdied three straight from No. 11. Next came the par-three 14th. "I drew a seven iron straight up in the wind,"

Johnson said. "It looked perfect, but you never think it's going to go in when it's this windy." He birdied the 18th for the 63, blocking Brenden and Deane Pappas, both with 64s, from becoming the first brothers to share the lead in a PGA Tour event. Johnson lipped out birdie putts on his last two holes in the second round and shot 67, tying for the halfway lead with Australia's Nick Flanagan (63). Fellow Aussie Gavin Coles raced up to third place with 62.

Kenny Perry, the hottest man on the tour with three wins in five starts, never was really in contention. But he was reaping Ryder Cup points. He closed with a 64 and tied for sixth. "I said, if I can just have a good top-10, I've accomplished my mission," he said.

The tournament came down to Johnson and Duke, who both trailed by one going into the final round. Johnson bogeyed two of his first four holes, then got turned around with an unlikely birdie at the par-five sixth, where he drove into the rough, hit a tree and stayed in the rough, then reached the green and holed a 15-footer.

"Then all of a sudden," Johnson said, "I just said, 'Okay, I can do this.' From there, I played unbelievably." He birdied Nos. 7, 10 and 11 and edged into the lead at the par-four 17th, holing a 12-foot birdie putt. That was his winning edge when both he and Duke birdied the 18th.

RBC Canadian Open
Oakville, Ontario, Canada
Winner: Chez Reavie

It seems that Anthony Kim, the 23-year-old whiz kid, already a two-time winner this season, was getting up some serious steam in the final round of the RBC Canadian Open. He coolly holed a 15-footer for a birdie at the par-four ninth. But Chez Reavie matched him from nine feet.

"When I made it right on top of him, I killed his momentum," Reavie said. And so he had. Reavie then poured in a 30-footer at the 10th and was on his way to his first PGA Tour title, winning by three strokes over veteran Billy Mayfair, who had cruised past a fading Kim. And an interesting victory it was for the little-known Reavie, age 26, 5-foot-9 and 160 pounds, a former U.S. Amateur Public Links champion and a PGA Tour rookie. He made a great case for a long-running debate.

Do wet grounds favor the big hitter, who can carry the ball farther, and hurt the short hitter, who gets little roll? The answer generally is yes. But Reavie proved the flip side of the argument at Glen Abbey, in Oakville, Ontario, which got hit with some eight inches of rain through that late-July week. His accuracy topped anyone else's length.

"It was crucial to hit the fairways so you could lift and clean your ball and place it in a good lie," Reavie said, "especially when you don't hit it as far as some of the other guys do."

That was the key to Reavie's success. In a wire-to-wire victory, Reavie played the par-72 Glen Abbey course in 65-64-68-70–267, 17 under, despite a series of rain delays that forced carryover play. Reavie, for example, had to play 33 holes on Friday. The stage was set on Saturday. Kim made nine birdies and an eagle in 21 holes to tie Reavie during the suspended third round. But when the round ended, Reavie was leading Kim, a big hitter, by a stroke.

A victory would have carried Kim into the top 10 in the World Ranking, but he sputtered to 75 and tied for eighth. The ever-present Mayfair was there to take up the chase. He was the only one in the field to shoot four rounds in the 60s, the last an unsatisfying 68. "I played terrible," said Mayfair, after hitting only two greens on the front nine. He finished second by three.

After Reavie made that key 30-footer at the 10th, he got out of a fairway bunker neatly at the 11th, despite an awkward stance, then chipped to a foot and saved par. He bogeyed the 13th, three-putting, but parred the next four holes, then birdied the 18th, holing a 12-foot putt for his 70 and the three-stroke win.

Reavie had hit 44 of 56 fairways, and of 18 greens he missed in regulation, he got up-and-down at 15 of them. His game had paid off.

WGC - Bridgestone Invitational
Akron, Ohio
Winner: Vijay Singh

Happiness is a belly putter to Vijay Singh.

Singh came to Firestone South, at Akron, Ohio, saying he'd sworn off those conventional putters forever. Give him one of those long ones, the kind the golfer tucks into his belly. The payoff was a victory for Singh in the WGC - Bridgestone Invitational early in August. The win ended an 0-for-34 drought for Singh on the PGA Tour.

"I was really confident, and although I hadn't won, I was confident I was going to win." Singh said. "I told everybody that knows me that it's just a matter of time."

Singh got some timely help when Phil Mickelson folded down the stretch. Singh shot the long, par-70 Firestone South course in 67-66-69-68–270, 10 under par, winning by one over Stuart Appleby (68) and Lee Westwood (69).

The most notable aspect of this WGC was that Tiger Woods, who had won six WGCs at Firestone, was off recuperating from reconstructive knee surgery. It his absence, the tournament had become something of a summit meeting, with the rest of the top golfers in a chase. Retief Goosen held the first-round lead with a four-under-par 66, followed by Singh (67), Mickelson (68) and Ernie Els (69).

In the second round, Singh broke into the lead for the first time in more than four months with 66–133 that lifted him a stroke ahead of Mickelson (66–134).

The third round was a veritable stage-setter. Mickelson adjusted his alignment and made three straight birdies and a 68, his third round in the 60s, which happened to equal his number of times under par at Firestone in the past four years. Westwood missed only two fairways and shot 67. Singh missed two putts from about 40 inches, but made two straight birdies from 12 feet and shot 69. The three tied for the lead at eight-under 202, moving Mickelson to note, "I think it will be a fun shootout."

Actually, it looked more like hard work. Westwood pretty well killed his chances when he left a shot in the bunker and double-bogeyed the par-three seventh. Mickelson was bogey-free through the 14th and took a one-stroke lead, then made three bogeys over the final four holes for 70. Singh broke out of the tie with four birdies across five holes, beginning with a two-putt at the par-five second and ending with a tap-in at the sixth.

Then the touch deserted him. "I started missing five- and six-footers," Singh said. He missed a four-footer for birdie at the 16th, but he got down in two putts from 25 feet at the 17th, the second a four-footer. In all, Singh missed three putts inside eight feet on the back nine, then dropped the 40-incher that gave him a one-stroke victory over Westwood and Stuart Appleby.

"What a relief," Singh said. "I didn't think I would finish it there at the end." And he swore his allegiance to the belly putter. "If you see me with a short one," he said, "that means something is wrong with me."

Legends Reno-Tahoe Open
Reno, Nevada
Winner: Parker McLachlin

The Legends Reno-Tahoe Open went for the billboard power and invited Michelle Wie, the former girl phenom, now 18, to try to become the first female since 1945 to make the cut on the PGA Tour. This was her eighth try. She shot 73 in the first round and was eight strokes out of the lead. She shot 80 in the second round. She was, in baseball parlance, 0-for-8. Wie said she wasn't playing enough PGA Tour events. "I think if I played a couple in a row, it would be a different story," she said.

Meanwhile, Parker McLachlin, 29, a little-known second-year man on the tour, shocked the tournament with a 10-under-par 62 to take the second-round lead. His resume to date included five top-25 finishes this season, and he was in 98th place on the money list. He birdied seven of his last 10 holes and had 10 birdies overall on his way to a four-stroke lead. McLachlin was deadly with his wedge. He got to within seven feet of the flag seven times and twice got to two feet and once to four inches.

"Nothing really crazy — it was just pretty solid," said McLachlin. And the man who had won on the Hooters Tour, the Tight Lies Tour, the Gateway Tour and the Spanos Tour was on his way to his first victory in the big time. It looked ridiculously easy. He'd opened three off the lead, with a 68, then shot 62-66-74 and led by four in the second round, six in the third, and he won by seven with an 18-under 270 total at Montreux Golf and Country Club.

Yes, he was playing against a weakened field, with the world's top 50 at the WGC - Bridgestone Invitational. Still, he did what he had to do in this tournament. His 66 in the third round put him six shots ahead of Brian Davis (68) and 10 ahead of John Rollins (70). But they weren't giving up.

"Parker's never won before, so you never know...," Davis said.

McLachlin had blown a seven-stroke lead in the final round of the Nationwide Tour's Pete Dye Classic in 2007. And he wasn't exactly steady this time. McLachlin hit only one of his first 10 greens and only five for the round. But his wedge saved par at least 10 times, including at the par-three 12th, where he sank a 15-foot putt after a 20-yard miss. His lead shrank to four with seven holes to play. "Brian was putting the heat on and I was feeling it," McLachlin admitted. But then Davis suffered a double bogey and two bogeys down the final stretch and shot 75. McLachlin got his only birdie, on a 15-footer at the 18th, for a nice bit of theatrics, a 74 and a seven-stroke win.

"This is a new thing for me, to be leading on Friday, Saturday and Sunday...," McLachlin said. "I just never felt comfortable out there."

Funny. He seemed to be right at home.

PGA Championship
Bloomfield Township, Michigan
Winner: Padraig Harrington

See Chapter 5.

Wyndham Championship
Greensboro, North Carolina
Winner: Carl Pettersson

Carl Pettersson, a transplanted Swede, had favored moving the Wyndham Championship from Forest Oaks Country Club back to its old home, Sedgefield Country Club in Greensboro, North Carolina. It turned out this was like ordering up a big helping of homecooking. Pettersson had come to the area as a teenager, went to high school there, played his college golf at North Carolina State, and then he was put on the committee to find a new home for the Wyndham Championship. He liked Sedgefield the minute he set foot on it and recommended it as the tournament's new/old home. So it was hardly a surprise that he would do well. But 61?

"The courses (on the PGA Tour) have been set up hard, so it's a nice change to be really aggressive, and (Sedgefield) kind of suits my style," Pettersson said.

"This is like his retirement fund," defending champion Brandt Snedeker said.

Pettersson admitted he was nervous starting out. "This is a home game for me," he said, but he settled down for 64. He shot the nine-under-par 61 in the second round and took a three-stroke lead over Garrett Willis (64). He began with three straight birdies and made six of his 11 on the first nine. By the par-five 15th, he admitted he was daydreaming about shooting 59, then promptly bogeyed. He snapped out of it and dropped a 40-foot putt on the 16th, then birdied the 17th as well.

"I was glad Carl ran out of holes," Willis said. "Every time I made a birdie, it seemed like he made one too."

Pettersson posted a sparkling 21-under-par 259 total on rounds of 64-61-66-68 and won by two over Scott McCarron. It was Pettersson's third tour victory and his first after a two-year drought.

Once he took the lead in the second round, he slipped out of it briefly when he bogeyed the 10th and 11th in the fourth. He was especially angry with himself over the failed up-and-down at the 11th. "It kind of ticked me off," Pettersson said. "I told myself, I'm letting the tournament get away from me again. That's where the tournament was won for me." He bounced back with three birdies over the next four holes.

McCarron popped into the lead when Pettersson bogeyed the 11th. But then he three-putted the 12th for a bogey and Pettersson birdied from 15 feet. "Making that putt was the key to the whole tournament," Pettersson said.

McCarron birdied the 18th for 68 to lock up second place, his best finish since 2005. It also locked up his tour playing card after an 18-month absence with elbow surgery. "Second place is tough to swallow right now," McCarron said. "But I'll probably be pretty happy here when I realize I've got a job for the rest of the year."

Pettersson bogeyed the 18th to win by two, and true to his subdued nature, merely raised his hands over his head. "Yeah, I'm thrilled," he said. "I'm just not one to jump around and high-five everybody."

PGA Tour Playoffs for the FedExCup

The Barclays
Paramus, New Jersey
Winner: Vijay Singh

Good putting, Vijay Singh will tell you, is in the eye of the beholder doing the putting. And that was the secret to his win in The Barclays, the first of the PGA Tour's FedExCup Playoffs, at the par-71 Ridgewood Country Club in Paramus, New Jersey, where the tournament moved after 41 years at Westchester Country Club in New York.

Singh tapped in for a birdie to beat Sergio Garcia on the second hole of a playoff, taking The Barclays for a record fourth time and turning a drab season into a smash success. He had won the WGC - Bridgestone Invitational just a few weeks earlier, and the next week blamed a missed cut at the PGA Championship on Oakland Hills' "ugly greens."

Kevin Sutherland also made the playoff, but bowed out on the first extra hole when Singh and Garcia rocked the gallery with a pair of birdies. Garcia holed from 27 feet, and Singh followed him in from 26 feet. At the next, the par-five 17th, Garcia put a new twist on the "burrowing animal" rule. He drove into the left rough, then put his second behind a big tree in the right rough and watched in astonishment as the ground began moving. An animal underneath — probably a mole — was burrowing along. Garcia got a free drop, missed the green with his third, and got up-and-down for par. Meantime, Singh hit a 267-yard second to 20 feet and two-putted for a birdie and the win.

Sometimes, Singh said, bad thoughts about putting creep into a golfer's head. "So I made a point after last week that I'm going to ... believe that I'm the best putter ... and I putted great this week." The figures said as much. He led the tournament with an average of four feet, four inches in putts made, and he didn't have a three-putt. Garcia also had a rebirth on the greens. He led in putts in greens hit in regulation, averaging 1.625, and he one-putted six of the last 11 greens on Sunday.

Singh and Garcia trailed through the first three rounds, both by eight in the first round on 70s, behind Hunter Mahan's hot nine-under 62. Singh was still eight back at the halfway point, behind Steve Stricker's 64–132. When Stricker blew to a 77 in the third round, tour rookie Kevin Streelman, with a 68, took the lead at eight-under 205. Singh (66) and Garcia (69) were a stroke behind.

In the final round, the three-way playoff narrowly missed becoming a small logjam. Ben Curtis one-putted 10 of his first 15 holes, but failed to birdie the par-five 17th. Mike Weir took a share of the lead early, but bogeyed the 12th and 13th. If the fans were disappointed, the Singh-Garcia finish more than made up for it. The roar for the birdie-birdie on the first playoff hole could be heard at Westchester.

"I think he was surprised to make his," Singh said. "I was surprised to see it go in, and he was even more surprised to see mine go in."

Deutsche Bank Championship
Norton, Massachusetts
Winner: Vijay Singh

It was in the running for the understatement of the year: "I'm not a great putter, but I'm not a bad putter." That was Vijay Singh, when he was winning the Bridgestone Invitational. But in the Deutsche Bank Championship a few weeks later, if he wasn't a great putter, he was the next thing to it. He made 130 feet of clutch birdie putts — 35 feet, 60 feet, 35 feet — on three holes in the final round for an eight-under-par 63 and a five-stroke victory.

It was his second straight win and his third of the season. It moved him to No. 3 in the World Ranking and also put him atop the money list, over the rehabilitating Tiger Woods, with $6.4 million. And with the tournament the second in the FedExCup Playoffs, after his win in The Barclays the week before, he also had a huge lead in that race.

Singh played the TPC Boston course in 64-66-69-63–262, 22 under par, beating Mike Weir by five strokes and breaking Adam Scott's 2003 tournament record by two strokes.

But the Deutsche Bank Championship didn't come automatically. Singh seemed to be in great shape in the first round, but along came Weir, former Masters champion, to tie the course record with a 10-under 61, the lowest round of his PGA Tour career. It put him three up on Singh and three others. "Just one of those days where I made a 15-footer on the first hole, another on the second hole," Weir said. "I just kind of built on that momentum." Only three of his birdie putts were inside 10 feet.

Tim Clark took over the momentum in the second round. He made two eagles over three holes and shot 62 for a one-stroke lead on Weir. Singh birdied three of his last four for a 66 and was two off the lead. Then the pendulum swing back to Weir in the third round. In the blustery weather, he hit only half of the fairways and half of the greens, but birdied three of the last five holes for 67–196 and a one-stroke lead on Camilo Villegas (63). Singh (69) and Sergio Garcia (68) were three back. With 10 players separated by only five strokes, Garcia was asked what it would take to win. He grinned. "One less than the guy who came in second," he said.

That man was Singh, the one with the red-hot belly putter. Weir double-bogeyed the ninth, and Singh moved ahead and went from there. He birdied the 11th from eight feet, the 13th from 35, but got into a jam at the 16th, where he put a poor approach 60 feet from the flag. He kept telling his caddie, "I'm the best putter in the world." And the caddie said, "You're damn right you are, now go ahead and knock it in." And so he did.

BMW Championship
St. Louis, Missouri
Winner: Camilo Villegas

Camilo Villegas, the 26-year-old Colombian in this third year on the PGA Tour, had it all — a strong game, good looks, personality — everything he needed to see his name up on the marquee. Everything but a victory, and that he took care of in the storm-battered BMW Championship in September. Actually, he did more than just win. If a golfer needs to prove himself in the flames, then Villegas was tested in the fire a number of times in the final round.

First, he could have been rattled right out of contention when he four-putted No. 9 in the second round for a double bogey. The last three were inside four feet. He answered with two straight birdies. He could easily have fallen apart under the pressure in the final round, when he made back-to-back bogeys on the front nine and handed the lead to Jim Furyk. But he held himself together and re-took the lead. Then he was in trouble at the par-four 12th. He had put his tee shot into a bunker and ended up needing a 12-footer to save par. He rolled it in and kept the lead.

Villegas came through again at the par-three 13th, this time not escaping trouble but grabbing his opportunity. Furyk had bunkered his tee shot and Villegas rammed home a 10-foot putt for birdie and a three-stroke lead. Then at the 14th, he holed a 35-footer. He would complete a card of 65-66-66-68, posting a 15-under-par 265 at Bellerive Country Club in St. Louis, Missouri, and winning by two. Dudley Hart closed strong with a 65 to finish second in the 68-man field. Furyk closed with a 70 and tied for third with Anthony Kim (67) at 12 under.

"They kept asking me when am I going to win," Villegas said. "I guess they've got it now. I finally did it, not only for me but for everybody back home."

This was Villegas's 86th start in his three seasons on the PGA Tour. He had raised expectations early with his powerful game and finishing second three times. This season alone, he threatened in the Open Championship going into the weekend. Then he rallied late and finished fourth at the PGA Championship, and just a week ago, in the Deutsche Bank Championship, he faltered after starting the final round a stroke off the lead.

This BMW Championship had a subplot — Vijay Singh and the $10 million FedExCup. With victories in the first two Playoffs, Singh could wrap up the rich prize in the BMW. But he finished 44th and so would head to The Tour Championship in a month needing only to play four rounds — never mind the score — to win it all.

Villegas headed home to Colombia where, he said, "it's all about soccer." But where, he was sure, they'd be doing a little street dancing for the native son who plays golf.

The Tour Championship
Atlanta, Georgia
Winner: Camilo Villegas

It was a little like trying to thread a needle from long range. That was the shot Camilo Villegas faced in the final round of The Tour Championship with the victory hanging in the balance.

Villegas had come from five strokes behind with six birdies over his last 11 holes, and at the par-four 17th was facing a scary 184-yard approach shot from the first cut of rough that could make or break him. In fact, it made him, and he went on to take his second straight victory, though a month after his first PGA Tour win in the BMW Championship.

"Probably the shot of the tournament there," Villegas said. "There's a great chance the ball is going to plug if it comes up short in that bunker, and a yard long and it's in the water. So it's just hit and beg. It happened to be just fine."

"Fine" as in a seven iron to 12 feet. He made the birdie, the last of the clutch six, to tie Sergio Garcia for the lead. Then he two-putted the par-three 18th from 45 feet for par and a four-under 66. Garcia missed his 20-foot birdie putt for the win in regulation, and it was back to No. 18 for the playoff. Garcia was 30 yards short with his four-iron tee shot, then failed to get his flop shot to the green. Next, he was short with a chip for a par. Villegas had hit the green and two-putted from 45 feet for a par and the victory.

Anthony Kim and Phil Mickelson closed with 69s and had chances to get into the playoff. But Kim missed a birdie try from 30 feet, and Mickelson missed from 20. Vijay Singh closed with 70, completing the formality of playing four rounds, and won the FedExCup and the $10 million prize.

For the puzzled Garcia, it was the third straight time when he led by at least three going into the final round and wasted it. This time: "I doubted myself too much early on, and it cost me," Garcia said.

Villegas could credit this win at least partly to a couple of pep talks by his caddie. Villegas started the final round five strokes off the lead, and after two encouraging birdies he watered his tee shot at the par-three sixth and bogeyed the seventh. Then up stepped his caddie, Gary Matthews.

"My caddie looked at me straight in the eyes, and he goes, 'You ain't going to give up on me. We can still do it,'" Villegas said. "He was probably the only one believing at that point." Then he got a second pep talk, this at the crucial 17th, over the 184-yard approach from the first cut of rough to that dangerous pin. The plan had been to aim safely for the center of the green. "I wasn't sure if was going to jump or not," Villegas said. "But ... my caddie goes, 'Trust it — it's not going to jump.' I changed my target, looked straight at the pin, and went at it."

The Ryder Cup
Louisville, Kentucky
Winners: United States

See Chapter 6.

Viking Classic
Madison, Mississippi
Winner: Will MacKenzie

Will MacKenzie, a former kayaker, snowboarder and rock climber, didn't leave the adventures at the gate when he stepped out on the golf course. Take the Viking Classic, kicking off the PGA Tour's Fall Series in September. There were, among other things, the terrific putting, the absent-minded error costing a two-stroke penalty and the playoff victory over the good friend he was rooting for to win, Marc Turnesa.

"There was a time today I wanted him to win," MacKenzie said. "When I was so far behind, I really wanted Marc to win." But then MacKenzie got within reach and decided he'd like the victory himself, to go with his other win, the 2006 Reno-Tahoe Open.

Turnesa was leading coming to the 17th hole in the final round, then double-bogeyed it. "I played well most of the day, until the 17th hole," said Turnesa, a 30-year-old rookie from the famed golfing family. "I made a mistake there, and it cost me the tournament."

Turnesa was a putting whiz in the first round, one-putting 12 times and needing just 22 putts overall in a 65 for a one-stroke lead. "I'm surprised I shot seven under," Turnesa said. "I didn't really feel like I was hitting it great. But putting is a great equalizer." Turnesa led by a stroke over a field that was having a great time at Annandale Golf Club, at Madison, Mississippi. MacKenzie was five behind, at 70.

MacKenzie picked up the chase in the second round, shooting an eight-birdie 64 for a 10-under 134 total, tied for second, a stroke behind Turnesa (68–133).

A careless error cost MacKenzie a share of the lead in the third round. At the par-five 18th, he brushed away a few blades of grass near his ball in a hazard. Under the rules, this was removing loose impediments, and on reporting this to a rules official, it cost him a two-stroke penalty, a triple-bogey eight and 67, and left him tied with Brian Gay (67), two behind Turnesa (66–199).

It was at No. 11 in the final round that MacKenzie found himself six behind Turnesa and wishing him success. Then he had a change of heart. He birdied three of the last four holes for 68 and tied Turnesa, who double-bogeyed the 17th for 70, and Gay (68) at 19-under 269.

Gay left the playoff at the first hole when MacKenzie two-putted for a birdie from 59 feet and Turnesa matched him from 11. At the second, also No. 18, Turnesa was on in three and missed his birdie putt from 18 feet. MacKenzie hit the green in two and two-putted from 63 feet for the winning birdie.

MacKenzie credited his putting. And he was back to the claw grip. "I won my only tournament with a claw, but I actually switched back for some reason," he said. "That's the way I am."

PGA Tour Fall Series

Turning Stone Resort Championship
Verona, New York
Winner: Dustin Johnson

The Turning Stone Resort Championship might well have been named the First Win Open. When the final round got under way, six players had a chance to notch that coveted first PGA Tour victory. Dustin Johnson, age 24, whose rookie year turned sour after a promising start, was one of them. A number of things would have to fall into place for him. The chances of all of them happening in the same round was a mathematical exercise. But much to Johnson's delight, they did.

"It's kind of hard to explain," Johnson said. "I haven't grasped everything yet."

Johnson did his part, closing with a three-under-par 69 and a nine-under 279 total at the Atunyote Golf Club at Turning Stone in Verona, New York. Then it was up to everybody else, chief among them:

• Tag Ridings had missed 12 cuts this season, six of them in a row, and entered the final round tied with Charles Howell at eight under. Then Ridings blew sky-high with a triple bogey, a double bogey and three singles across eight holes and shot 79.

• Jay Overton, who slipped back after leading the first two rounds, flirted with success all through the final round. He eagled No. 5 to tie Robert Allenby for the lead. Then he bogeyed the seventh on a three-putt, bogeyed the eighth on a lip-out. He rallied and tied Allenby with a birdie at the 14th, then missed five-foot par putts at the 16th and 17th.

• Allenby was within reach of his fifth tour victory, and his first since

2001, and playing steadily. But at No. 15, he put his tee shot into the trees on the right and hit his second into a greenside bunker. He blasted out to nine feet, but two-putted for a bogey.

Through all this, Johnson was grinding away, but not without difficulty. He started the day two shots off the lead and got within a stroke of Allenby with a birdie at the par-five 12th, then bogeyed the 13th after driving into the water. "Coming down 17, I knew I had to go birdie-birdie," Johnson said. And he did. At the 17th, he hit a drive 328 yards and birdied from six feet and tied Allenby at eight under. At the 18th, he bombed a drive 357 yards, and with 256 yards left to the green, he hit his second nearly 40 feet past. But he chipped back and dropped the eight-foot putt for the final birdie. Allenby had one last chance to tie, a 12-foot birdie putt at the 18th. But he left it short.

Johnson had started the year with two top-10 finishes in his first four starts, then missed nine cuts and withdrew twice. Then he went off for a session with his coach.

"I practiced hard and tried to get my game back," Johnson said. It seems it worked.

Valero Texas Open
San Antonio, Texas
Winner: Zach Johnson

Zach Johnson entered the Valero Texas Open with two goals, one of which was to have no goals.

"I had two things in my mind this week, as far as going into the week," he said, "and one was no expectations. So, no, I did not expect to be here. But I guess that's a good thing. The second was just to, you know, I made some commitments to my fundamentals, to my golf swing, and (they are) starting to pay off. So it's very encouraging."

Johnson, former Masters champion, hadn't won since the 2007 AT&T Classic, nearly 17 months earlier, and he arrived at LaCantera Golf Club in San Antonio, Texas, with just one top-10 finish in 21 starts. And so apart from his Masters credentials, he was hardly given threat status at the Valero Texas Open. Until, that is, he shot 62 in the third round. A 64 in the fourth round got him a two-stroke victory and set off the celebrating in his hometown, Cedar Rapids, Iowa.

It was Johnson's first tour victory outside the state of Georgia. He had won the Masters, the 2004 BellSouth Classic and 2007 AT&T Classic.

The early October tournament got off to a rousing start when Australia's Nathan Green, winless in three seasons on the PGA Tour, shot an eight-under-par 62 in the first round, much to his surprise. "I didn't feel really good before the round started, and then on the first hole I snapped my drive," he said. "It hit a rock and bounced back in the fairway. From there, everything went pretty well."

But he didn't last, and neither did Chris Stroud, the halfway leader with 64–130, nor did third-round leader Rory Sabbatini (63–196). Sabbatini led by a stroke over Johnson, who shot the front nine in five-under 30 on his way to the 62. "Some of my best rounds have come with limited confidence," said Johnson. "I didn't have high expectations coming in, but when I've played well, I've putted well, and that was the case today."

Johnson swept into the lead in the final round with a trio of birdies from the sixth and another at the 10th. He added another birdie at the 14th and finished the round with a five-footer at No. 18 for a closing 64 and a two-stroke lead that held up under some hot finishes. Charlie Wi, who matched Steve Elkington for the day's-low 61, tied for second with Mark Wilson (63) and Tim Wilkinson (64).

"I was pretty far back starting today, so I knew that I needed to make some birdies out there," Wi said.

Johnson also appreciated the return of the birdies. "I guess I take it for granted," he said, of his putting. "I've always been a pretty good putter, but for some reason, early on this year, it kind of left me." Then came the hard work. "I don't want to say I tried doing different things, but...," he said, "I didn't anticipate it hitting me this quick, but it certainly helped."

Justin Timberlake Shriners Hospitals for Children Open
Las Vegas, Nevada
Winner: Marc Turnesa

That was Will MacKenzie wishing that his old pal Marc Turnesa would finally win. That was in the Viking Classic, and of course that was before MacKenzie realized he himself could win it, which he did. But the sentiment was real. It was just a month early.

Turnesa, age 30, of the famous golfing family, who had been grinding at golf in a number of places, finally chalked up that first victory, leading wire-to-wire in the Justin Timberlake Shriners Hospitals for Children Open at Las Vegas.

This was the former Las Vegas tour stop that underwent a total change in character. The old pro-am format was scrapped, and the event was played at just one course, TPC Summerlin. And Timberlake, the music star, got on board as title celebrity to attract attention to the tournament.

Turnesa came into Las Vegas ranked 138th on the PGA Tour money list and was running out of chances to crack the coveted top 125, meaning exempt for the next year. So he had already mailed in his application for the 2008 qualifying tournament. It wasn't that long ago that he thought of quitting. So the Las Vegas stop opened up a new world to him.

"To be honest (earning a tour card) has been weighing on me more than anything," Turnesa said. "... not having a job out here and the uncertainty. It's just nice to have a little bit of a cushion, because it's something I've never had before."

Turnesa played the par-72 Summerlin course in 62-64-69-68–263, 25 under par, for a one-stroke win over Matt Kuchar. The breakthrough wasn't without pain, though. In the second round, Turnesa double-bogeyed the 17th. But he bounced right back at the 18th, coolly hitting a nine-iron approach from 159 yards that found the cup for 64 and a share of the lead with Kuchar.

Turnesa was in trouble in the final round. He started with a one-stroke lead but was running pars while others were making birdies. He was about to let a chance slip away at the par-five ninth, chunking a chip shot, leaving himself 23 feet from the cup. Then he holed the putt for a birdie. He followed with birdies at the 11th and 12th, and tapped in at the par-three 14th after nearly holing his tee shot. Then came the eight iron to 10 feet at the 17th, setting up the birdie for a two-stroke lead. The cushion spared him when he bogeyed the 18th after missing the fairway off the tee. It merely cut his winning margin to one. The latest Turnesa had made his contribution to the family name.

"I guess I am (carrying on the tradition) without even thinking about it," Turnesa said. "I'm just trying to play golf as best I can, and that's all I can really do."

Frys.com Open
Scottsdale, Arizona
Winner: Cameron Beckman

"I just had a calmness about me this week, and it just happened," Cameron Beckman was saying, just after winning the Frys.com Open. "It's just like the last time I won. It just kind of happened. It's strange. I don't know what it is."

Well, it's a fact of golf that peace is known to come from an amicable putter. Beckman needed just 11 putts over his last nine holes of regulation, including five straight one-putts. Maybe that had something to do with it. The putting stretch gave Beckman 63 that tied Kevin Sutherland (66) at 17-under-par 263, then he beat him with a tap-in par on the second playoff hole.

Beckman was a certified surprise winner. Consider that he had missed the cut in his last three starts and missed 11 cuts overall.

The victory came just in time for Beckman, age 38, who was on the verge of losing his PGA Tour playing card and possibly even quitting the game. A bad back was a great concern. He had missed eight weeks of the season because of the back, and when he arrived at Grayhawk Golf Club at Scottsdale, Arizona, he was 176th on the money list and 447th in the World Ranking, both figures not encouraging for a man hoping to continue on the tour.

"I sat down with my wife and said, 'What do you think?'" Beckman said. "I honestly was just trying to finish in the top 150 so I'd get to the (qualifying tournament) finals."

It was the second playoff loss for Sutherland this season. He and Sergio Garcia lost to Vijay Singh at The Barclays in August. "A second-place finish is nothing to sneeze at," said Sutherland, "but right now it's a little hard to see that through the disappointment."

Beckman showed his first signs that he was playing well in the third round, when he shot 64 and was in a group at 11 under, three strokes behind Sutherland, who had taken the lead with 63–196. "I got off to a pretty good start," Beckman said. "All week long, I've been hitting a lot of greens. Played real solid all day."

Sutherland seemed to be in good shape until Beckman caught fire on the second nine. Beckman made the final turn at 13 under and trailing Sutherland by four, then birdied Nos. 10, 11, 14, 15 and 16. They tied when Sutherland missed a six-footer for par at the 18th. On the second playoff hole, Sutherland hit his second shot far to the right into dirt, then hit his third over the green and down a hill. Beckman hit his second to six feet, just missed the birdie putt, and tapped in for the win.

"It's been a tough year," Beckman said. "I honestly was thinking about quitting the game. That's how bad I felt. I can't explain to you how good I feel right now."

Ginn sur Mer Classic
Palm Coast, Florida
Winner: Ryan Palmer

Ryan Palmer had enough errors and misfortunes in the Ginn sur Mer Classic to deflate most men. There were, for example, the driver off the deck that went bad, the snap hook into the water and the moving ball penalty. And somewhere in the course of such events he was trying to compose his winner's remarks. The marvel was that, even though he lost the lead, he was convinced he was going to win, and he didn't win until his last shot — a birdie putt on the final hole that broke a six-way tie and left him the last man standing.

"I kept getting ahead of myself," Palmer said. "I always get ahead of myself, thinking what am I going to say in my interview, what am I going to say on TV?" So much for staying in the moment and playing 'em one shot at a time.

Palmer's status on the PGA Tour for 2009 was hanging by a thread in this next-to-last tournament of the year, at the Ginn Hammond Beach Resort in Florida. He was 143rd on the money list. To gain exempt-from-qualifying status, he had to crack the top 125 or, better yet, win.

Palmer was on his way with three birdies in the first five holes, shooting a five-under-par 67, two behind co-leaders Kent Jones and rookie Michael Letzig. Palmer took the lead with a 71 in the second round, and he had never led a tour event after the second or third round. His only victory came on a final-round 64. This time he played himself out of the lead when he decided to hit his driver off the deck — the ground — on his second shot at the par-five 18th and ended up in the water. "I've hit that shot a bunch," he said. "I can hit that driver off the ground from anywhere..." He had just bogeyed three of the last four holes.

Then things got dicier. Seven players had at least a share of the lead at one point, and six were tied during the first rain delay. Then the others were getting out of his way. John Huston watered a tee shot, Mark Wilson needed two to get out of a bunker, Robert Allenby put his wedge into a back bunker at the 18th.

Palmer was leading by two at the 10th, and as he addressed his 30-foot birdie putt, he noticed the ball move slightly and called a penalty on himself. Then he slipped out of the lead at the 11th with a double bogey after pulling his tee shot into the water. But eventually, at the 18th, he prudently laid up this time, lofted a wedge shot to 10 feet, and holed the birdie putt for 67 and a seven-under 281 total and a one-stroke win.

And he thought back to the penalty he called on himself at the 10th. "I kind of laughed," he said. "I told myself, now I'll win by one less."

Children's Miracle Network Classic
Lake Buena Vista, Florida
Winner: Davis Love

The Walt Disney Resort is the feel-good capital of the world, and the Children's Miracle Network Classic there in November was the feel-good tournament of the year. Davis Love, one of the nicest nice guys on the PGA Tour, coming back from ankle surgery, put his game back together again and won the Children's, the final tournament of the 2008 schedule. It was his 20th career tour win, giving him a lifetime exemption from qualifying.

"I'm not worried about the exemption," Love said, heading into the final round. "I just want to win."

There were times when Love, 44, had his doubts about continuing. "I always questioned, 'Am I doing the right thing? Why am I still doing this?'" said Love, who tore two ankle ligaments when he stepped into a hole during a recreational round a year earlier. "I didn't doubt my desire, or that I could still compete. It was just the little things I had to do."

Tommy Gainey, best known as a winner on the Golf Channel's "Big Break VII: Reunion," also eased his doubt. In a closing rush, Gainey (64) finished second to Love by a stroke, making his finest appearance of the year. "I played terrible, horrible this year," Gainey said. "I had one week, and this was the week. I definitely assured myself of a place to play next year." Gainey made his biggest paycheck by far, $496,800, vaulting to 148th on the money list and gaining conditional exemption status for 2009.

Love shot 66-69-64-64—263, a whopping 25 under par for the one-stroke win over Gainey. But he was plugging away in the first two rounds. He trailed Troy Matteson (63) by three in the first round. Scott Verplank shot 64 with a reborn putter. "Today, I felt like a kid again," he said. The kid touch stayed with him for another 64 and the second-round lead at 128. Love (69) was seven behind, and with a 64 in the third round closed to within two of Steve Marino (66) and Verplank (69).

In the final round, Marino was tied with Love for the lead until the 13th, when he made his first bogey of the tournament. Love was leading by two with two to play when his tee shot at the 17th caught the deep rough, forcing him to lay up 100 yards short of the green. Then a wedge to seven feet set up a par. At the 18th, he scrambled from rough into a back bunker, blasted out to three feet, and made the putt. Gainey, known as "Two Gloves" because he wears two, was warming up for a playoff. Then he heard the roar from the crowd at the 18th.

"I took my gloves off," Gainey said, "and put them back in the bag."

Special Events

Tavistock Cup
Orlando, Florida
Winner: Isleworth

In what amounts to golf's version of a neighborhood feud — actually a battle of high-profile Orlando country clubs — Tiger Woods and his Isleworth pals retook the Tavistock Cup from Ernie Els's Lake Nona team late in March. It was something of a romp.

Isleworth ran up a 7-3 lead in the first day of the two-day competition, then ran off with an 19½-to-11½ victory. In the second round, a bookkeeper's carnival, each player in a group plays an 18-hole stroke play singles match against each of the two players on the other side. Woods beat both Retief Goosen and Justin Rose for two points, and Woods's partner, Charles Howell, also took two points. Isleworth's J.B. Holmes ran off with medalist honors. "It's been a pretty good two days for me," Holmes said. "It's been a lot of fun for my first time out here."

CVS/Caremark Charity Classic
Barrington, Rhode Island
Winners: Bubba Watson and Camilo Villegas

The CVS/Caremark Charity Classic, hit by a tremendous late-June storm in the second and final round, was cut to 28 holes, and then had to be decided by a three-hole playoff for four teams tied for the lead at 15 under par.

Camilo Villegas and Bubba Watson, a pair of long hitters who led the first round, birdied all three holes to win the better-ball event. Villegas tapped in a two-foot putt at the par-four 16th and holed a 15-footer from the fringe at the par-three 17th, and Watson locked it up with a three-footer at the par-four 18th, shutting the door on Paul Goydos/Tim Herron, Rocco Mediate/Brandt Snedeker and Davis Love and co-host Billy Andrade.

"We came in and made par on the last three holes (in the first round)," said Villegas, "and I told Bubba, 'Let's make three birds (in the playoff).'"

Peter Jacobsen, in his first competition since having his right knee replaced in mid-March, and co-host Brad Faxon, also recovering from major knee surgery, finished 10th and last.

PGA Grand Slam of Golf
Tucker's Town, Bermuda
Winner: Jim Furyk

Jim Furyk figured 2008 wasn't exactly a vintage year for him, but it took a big turn for the better when he was asked to fill in for Tiger Woods in the PGA Grand Slam of Golf in October. He didn't have the credentials. This was a meeting of the winners of the four majors at the Mid-Ocean Club in Bermuda. But he had the game when he needed it, and that was when he came to the final hole of regulation needing a birdie to tie Padraig Harrington. He got the birdie. Then he dropped an eight-footer for eagle on the first playoff hole for the title.

Furyk shot 68-68–136, matching Harrington, who won both the Open Championship and the PGA Championship. Retief Goosen, former U.S. Open champion, filling a spot for Harrington's double win, shot 70-71–141, and Masters champion Trevor Immelman shot 76-69–145.

"It's kind of a wonder that I'm even in the event to start with, so I kind of treated the week like I had nothing to lose," Furyk said. "Rarely do I kind of go in just thinking about having fun. I'm usually all business and maybe it's something to learn."

Callaway Golf Pebble Beach Invitational
Pebble Beach, California
Winner: Tommy Armour

It was golf in a nutshell: "I hit some shots that were close to being really good," Tommy Armour said. "They just didn't turn out to be that good. But that's part of the inner battle of winning a golf tournament."

It all translated to winning the championship the hard way in the Callaway Golf Pebble Beach Invitational. Armour, the defending champion, scrambled back from blowing the final-round lead to win in a three-way playoff. Armour started the final round with a five-stroke lead, but then shot up to 76. He missed a 24-foot birdie putt for the win in regulation, then holed a four-foot par putt for a 10-under 278 total. Simpson, in the same group as Armour, was tied with him at 11 under par through the 15th hole. Simpson fell a stroke behind with bogeys at the 16th and 17th, then holed a 12-foot birdie putt at the 18th to tie Armour. Brock MacKenzie, a former Nationwide Tour player, had shot 67 and was already in with his 278.

Then Armour, age 49, a two-time winner on the PGA Tour, rolled in a 36-foot putt for birdie on the first playoff hole to become the first repeat winner in the 37 years of the tournament. Armour last won on the PGA Tour in the 2003 Valero Texas Open. Armour's four-over 76 in the final round included four bogeys, a double bogey and two birdies.

Del Webb Father/Son Challenge
Orlando, Florida
Winner: Larry and Drew Nelson

Same tournament, same winners, different cast.

Enter the Nelsons: Larry and — this time — son Drew, striking for a late birdie to take the Del Webb Father/Son Challenge, the Nelsons' second straight victory in the event. In 2007 it was Larry and son Josh. And Larry and Drew won it four years ago. It was starting to look like the Nelson

Member-Guest, just as the Raymond Floyd family had dominated before them.

Larry Nelson made a 20-foot birdie putt on the 17th hole to pull away for a 10-under-par 62 and a 123 total to beat Davis Love and son Dru by two shots at the ChampionsGate Golf Club near Orlando in December. The Nelsons had opened the two-round scramble tied at 61 with Tom and David Kite, who finished third in the 18-team event. The finish worked out the way Nelson had hoped. "We really felt like 17 was going to be the pivotal hole," Nelson said. "We didn't want to have to make eagle on the last hole, but we felt like we could make birdie if we needed to. We felt when we made that, we pretty much had won the tournament." And so they had.

The tournament is restricted to major champions and their sons, but some exceptions are made. Arnold Palmer, who has two daughters, again played with his grandson Sam Saunders. They tied for seventh. Fuzzy Zoeller played with his daughter Gretchen, and they tied for 12th with Paul Azinger and Aaron Stewart, son of the late Payne Stewart.

Merrill Lynch Shootout
Naples, Florida
Winners: Scott Hoch and Kenny Perry

"Kenny is probably the best player right now playing," Boo Weekley was saying. "Granted, he was here with us, but if he was in a regular tournament, he'd have been hard to handle this week." And that was Weekley's tip of the hat to Kenny Perry, who had just run in an eagle for the second straight day at No. 17 to give him and Scott Hoch the 20th playing of the Merrill Lynch Shootout.

Perry made the eagle just after he dropped an eight-foot putt for birdie, following Hoch's miss, which kept them four ahead with one hole to play in the scramble format. The teams played modified alternate shot in the first round and better-ball in the second round.

"Obviously, that was big," Hoch said. "That pretty much took any chance unless we just fell on our face." Weekley and Holmes trailed by four starting the final round of the $2.9 million, 54-hole event at Tiburon Golf Club in Naples, Florida, in December. They got to three back on birdies at the 12th and 13th and an eagle on the 14th.

On Saturday, Perry and Hoch birdied Nos. 16 and 18 and eagled No. 17 to build a four-shot lead. Perry made eight birdies and an eagle on his own ball in the better-ball format, and followed it up with another strong round while Hoch was hampered by a bad left wrist.

Tournament founder Greg Norman and Camilo Villegas shot the lowest round of the tournament, a 15-under 57, and finished third at 25 under.

Chevron World Challenge
Thousand Oaks, California
Winner: Vijay Singh

When the third round ended, Vijay Singh was in third place, two shots behind Anthony Kim, the whiz kid who had taken an abrupt and exciting place on the PGA Tour in 2008, and one behind the veteran Jim Furyk. It was as if on cue that the two cleared out of his way to let him wrap up his richest year in the game in the Chevron World Challenge, Tiger Woods's charity event at Sherwood Country Club in Thousand Oaks, California, late in December. Woods, recuperating from knee surgery, was not in the 16-man field.

"Very unexpected," Singh said. "I was just hanging in there. I figured if I shot 67 or 68, I would be right there with a chance."

Singh figured right. He did shoot 67, and the chance was provided by others. Kim made double bogeys at the 15th and 16th, and Furyk dropped five shots over the last five holes, leaving Singh with the $1.35 million first prize to add to his $6.6 million in PGA Tour winnings and the $10 million FedExCup bonus.

Singh shot 71-72-67-67–277 for a one-stroke victory over Steve Stricker. Singh got into contention with three straight birdies early on the last nine and then won by holing a 10-foot birdie putt on the last hole. The win ended a remarkable season for Singh at age 45. "When I show up and I know I can't win the golf tournament, I'm going to quit," Singh said. "But as long as I show up and know that I can win, I'm going to keep playing."

Nationwide Tour

The Nationwide Tour Class of 2008 sent 25 of its graduates on in pursuit of the American dream in golf, which is to say, on to the PGA Tour. Among them were Colt Knost, who had the audacity to pass up an invitation to the Masters as an amateur in order to turn professional; India's Arjun Atwal, returning after a couple of years; Matt Bettencourt, the No. 1 graduate, thanks to a new putter he had come to know and love, and England's Greg Owen, a returnee who led the tour in nearly every statistical category. But nobody typifies the pursuit of the American dream like Rick Price.

Price was 40 when he got his diploma in 2008, and he would be the oldest rookie on the PGA Tour in 2009. How does it feel to be the oldest? Price wouldn't know.

"I certain don't feel like I'm 40," Price said. "This is how it was supposed to work for me."

But age wasn't the real story behind Price. Persistence was. As Bettencourt was to say, after finally breaking through, "Don't give up. Don't quit on your dreams." Bettencourt must have got the idea from Price.

Price spent 10 years on the mini tours, 10 years on the Nationwide Tour, and he took 19 cracks at the qualifying tournament. He finally reached the tour by winning the Nationwide Tour Players Cup in July. Price squandered a one-shot lead on the final hole with a bogey, then beat Chris Anderson with a bogey on the first playoff hole. The $180,000 first prize pretty well locked up a spot for him on the PGA Tour, and Price was one relieved guy.

"Just being able to hang in there this long and finally get through is persistence," Price said. And then some.

Bettencourt, age 33, a self-taught golfer, was another study in persistence. Bettencourt was dreaming of a baseball career until a shoulder injury in high school ended it. He took up golf as a recreation, played on a junior college team, and didn't turn pro until he was 27. Then his game took a turn for the lively in September, when he found that magic putter. He won the Oregon Classic and had a second place and a fifth and came to the season-ending Nationwide Tour Championship as a new golfer.

But he came within a whisker of withdrawing from the Nationwide Tour Championship. A severe backache sent him to the hospital the night before the first round. It turned out to be a kidney stone, which he passed, but he was still in pain in the third round. He won on a six-foot birdie putt at the final hole. The $180,000 first prize carried him to the top of the Nationwide Tour money list with $447,863, just about $10,000 ahead of Brendon de Jonge.

De Jonge, 28, from Zimbabwe, who played the PGA Tour in 2007, turned a hot putter into the Xerox Classic title in August. He was only 29th in hitting greens in regulation, 48 of 72, but led the tournament in putting, needing just over 26 per round. "This is the best it's been over the course of a full week," he said. "I just had one of those weeks." He was about to claim the top spot on the money list until Bettencourt drew the hot hand in the finale. So de Jonge settled for second with $437,035, about $10,000 less than he won on the PGA Tour in 2007.

Colt Knost is almost certain to get the question again — how could you possibly pass up the Masters to turn pro? He had the invitation as the reigning U.S. Amateur and the U.S. Public Links champion. Knost received a lot of criticism and answered it then as he probably will answer it on the tour. "I basically would have been putting off my career for a whole year," Knost had said. "I would have had nothing to do. I would have had to play amateur golf again, which just would cost me and my family money." The next question would be: Does he regret having passed up the Masters? His answer would be victories in the Fort Smith Classic and the Price Cutter Charity Championship, and sixth place on the money list at $329,509.

Scott Gutschewski, who played the PGA Tour for two years, returned as a golfer who was doing really well when he wasn't doing really badly. He won the Rex Hospital Open, had four other top-10 finishes, but made only 14 cuts in 26 starts. "I think I've proved I belong out there," Gutschewski said. "I've had a couple of chances already, and I'm glad to have another shot at it." When he won the Rex Hospital, he was the Nationwide's 14th different winner in 14 events, tying the third-longest such streak to start a season. The record is 22, in 1996.

If golf is a matter of attitude, then a huge change of same carried Bill

Lunde, 32, to the big tour. He had quit golf in disgust 18 months ago and worked for a company that stages golf tournaments, and then for a mortgage title company.

"I appreciate it a lot more than I used to," Lunde said, on winning the Children's Hospital Invitational. "Before, it was just something I'd been doing for so long. From being behind a desk to going out and playing golf every day, it's a big difference."

In other words, golf beats working for a living.

Canadian Tour

The year 2008 on the Canadian Tour was pretty much the story of a Big Man on Campus, a hot freshman and an old graduate.

The BMOC was John Ellis, former University of Oregon star out of San Jose, California, a three-time winner who ran off with both the Rolex Player of the Year and the Order of Merit honors.

There's nothing like a grand entrance, and that's what Daniel Im made. Im, age 23, a Canadian Tour freshman out of UCLA, won the Rookie of the Year title and seemed bent on taking the Player of the Year award as well, with his two victories.

But first came Spencer Levin, the old graduate, Class of 2007, who had a week off and dropped by at the Spring International. Levin was trailing by eight shots with nine holes to play and caught a floundering Andrew Parr, then beat him with a par on the second playoff hole. "I've never won a tournament when I thought I had no chance of winning — especially with nine holes left," Levin said.

Ellis had three victories, two ties for seconds, and nothing worse than ninth to win the Rolex Player of the Year award and top the Order of Merit with C$113,315.

The Stockton Sports Commission Classic was a steeplechase in the final round, with 24 players within four strokes of each other. Ellis blew a late lead and rookie Tommy Barber went ahead with a birdie at the 17th, then was up by two when Ellis bogeyed the 16th. Then Barber bogeyed the 18th out of the rough, and Ellis tied him with a five-footer for birdie. On the first playoff hole, Barber found rough again, and Ellis hit a six iron to 35 feet and two-putted for the win. "I'm really enjoying this," Ellis said, "but now I want to go to Mazatlan next week and win again."

Which he did, in the Corona Mazatlan Mexican PGA Championship, but not before wasting a four-stroke lead going into the final round. Wes Heffernan made a charge, but bogeyed the 18th from the trees, and Ellis went from fairway to green and dropped a seven-foot birdie putt, wrapping up a wire-to-wire win.

At the Telus Edmonton Open, Ellis underlined his entire season with a dynamite start to the final round. He eagled the first hole from a foot, aced the third and birdied the fourth and fifth, and was six under par in the first five holes. He finished with 67 and a three-stroke win over Andrew Parr. "The first one, in Stockton, seemed so tough," Ellis said, "and after I won the second one, I was thinking, 'Oh, this is kind of nice.' But winning three times? I can't say I expected that."

Daniel Im had a debut like few have ever had. Making his first start in the Iberostar Riviera Maya Open, he told a friend he was going to be "dangerous," and when the friend wondered what he meant, he said, "Just watch me." Im started the final round leading by one, and at the 18th he holed a scary downhill 10-footer for a birdie and a one-stroke win. Im then won the Times Colonist Open, but it wasn't pretty. Im struggled to a bogey on the first playoff hole to beat James Lepp, who bounced his second shot off the clubhouse and out of bounds. "I'm still a bit stunned," Im said, but he could have been speaking of his entire rookie season — two wins, two ties for second and a tie for eighth in his 10 starts, worth C$82,954, third in winnings.

Heffernan won the Canadian Tour Players Cup and had six other top-10s and was a solid second on the money list with C$96,154. Dustin Risdon shot 62 in the second round and beat George Bradford in a playoff for the ATB Financial Classic, his second tour title. Two popular players scored their career-first victories. "I don't even remember what I did when the final putt dropped," said an ecstatic Adam Speirs after winning the Greater Vancouver Charity Classic. And Tom Stankowski closed with 69 to take the season-ending Tour Championship. "I proved to myself that I can win at this level," said Stankowski.

There were some truly odd performances in 2008, the kind that leave fans and golfers alike shaking their heads.

There was New Zealand's Josh Geary, who made only five cuts in his 10 starts and only one top-10 finish — a victory in the Saskatchewan Open. Chasing George Bradford in the final round, he two-putted the last hole for a birdie, 66 and the win. "It's hard to describe what I'm feeling right now," Geary said.

Graham DeLaet had 12 starts and made only six cuts, but he had three top-three finishes — one a win in the Desjardins Montreal Open. He birdied the last hole to tie George Bradford and Daniel Im, then got up and down at the first playoff hole for his first Canadian Tour victory. "I'm speechless, emotional, numb and everything else," DeLaet said.

Russell Surber made only four cuts in 12 starts, and in the last three he tied for 52nd, 55th and 56th. But in the first one, he won the San Luis Potosi Open in Mexico, hitting a four iron to 15 feet for a winning par at the 18th. "I still felt nervous after I won," he said.

On the business side, the Canadian Tour joined with the Tour de las Americas in co-sanctioning three tournaments late in 2008 — the Sports Frances Open in Chile in November, and two in December, the Torneo de Maestros in Argentina and the Costa Rica Golf Classic. Winners of the events will be granted full membership on both tours.

Tour de las Americas (South America)

It's not often that a rookie starts at the top, but that was the case in 2008 for Tour de las America sensation Estanislao Goya, a mere 20-year-old from Argentina. He scored an unprecedented triple play, becoming Rookie of the Year and Player of the Year, and also topping the Order of Merit. It took a remarkable accomplishment like that to top the three-win season by Argentina's Rafael Gomez.

Goya and Gomez headlined a sparkling 2008 for the TLA, whose 15 events led off with three co-sanctioned European Challenge Tour tournaments and closed with, for the first time, three co-sanctioned Canadian Tour tournaments.

Goya led off the season by winning the qualifying tournament. Goya, a professional for only four months, didn't merely win it, he won by nine strokes with a closing 61. The victory got him a berth in the Abierto Visa del Centro, the season-opener in May and the first of the three co-sanctioned Challenge Tour events, and what a debut. Goya birdied four of the last seven holes for 66 and England's Gary Boyd birdied six of the last for 65 to tie at 12-under-par 272. Goya then birdied the first extra hole to win. In the other two co-sanctioned events, Finland's Antti Ahokas won the Abierto Visa de Argentina and Goya finished third, and the Netherlands' Wil Besseling won the Club Colombia Masters and Goya tied for fifth. Later, Goya also finished fifth in the Argentina Torneo de Maestros and finished at the top of the TLA's Order of Merit with US$58,104.

Goya finished the European Challenge Tour season as spectacularly as he began it. In the season-ending Apulia San Domenico Grand Final, he birdied four of the last five holes for a one-stroke victory, finishing fifth on the Order of Merit and locking up his European Tour card for 2009. "I would have been happy to finish in the top 20, so to finish in the top 10 is fantastic," Goya said. Obviously, Goya figured to be a closely watched young man on the 2009 European Tour.

Until Goya returned to the TLA Tour, Rafael Gomez was poised to wrap up the Order of Merit. At age 40, twice as old as of Goya, Gomez became the winningest player in TLA Tour history when he took the inaugural Sport Frances Open late in November. It was his third win of the season and his record eighth tour win, topping countryman Angel Cabrera, whom he had tied at seven when he won the Abierto de San Luis three weeks earlier. Gomez started the final round of the Sport Frances three strokes off the lead, shot a three-under-par 68, and with his seven-under 277 total won by a stroke when Canadian Tour Rookie of the Year Daniel Im bogeyed two of the last three holes. "I just kind of lost it, I guess," Im said.

Gomez withstood a late challenge to lock up the TLA Players Championship in May, the first of his three victories of the season, his sixth TLA Players title and the 20th win of his career. "I lost my focus, especially on eight, nine and 10," Gomez said, when his lead was cut to two, "and I felt the pressure of those hunting me, and that fired me up." He birdied the 11th then went on to a 70 for a 10-under 270 to win by three. For his second victory, in the Abierto de San Luis in June, Gomez closed with a nine-under 62 to tie countryman Walter Rodriguez at eight-under 276, then beat him in a playoff.

"It has been a great year for me," Gomez said, "and this one means a lot because now I'm first (on Order of Merit)." Which he was, until Goya passed him up.

Argentines won all three events co-sanctioned by the Canadian Tour at the end of the season — Rafael Gomez in the Sport Frances Open, Fabian Gomez in the Torneo de Maestros and Mauricio Molina in the Costa Rica Golf Classic.

"From top to bottom this was a very successful season for the Tour de las Americas," said Commissioner Henrique Lavie. "Our ties with the European Challenge Tour remain as strong as ever. The Europeans have co-sanctioned events with us for six consecutive seasons, allowing many of our top players to advance to the European Tour over the past few years. However, in our search to reach for new horizons we established a new partnership with the Canadian Tour, which joined us for a first series of joint sanctioned events over the last three weeks of the season."

The tour, meanwhile, also celebrated the accomplishments of its "graduates." Argentina's Andres Romero, on the U.S. PGA Tour, claimed his first victory in the Zurich Classic and went on to win the Rookie of the Year award. He did stop by on the TLA Tour to take the Abierto del Litoral. Chile's Felipe Aguilar won the European Tour's Indonesia Open, and Argentina's Eduardo Romero, 54, enjoyed a brilliant season on the U.S. Champions Tour, winning the U.S. Senior Open Championship as well as the Dick's Sporting Goods Open and the SAS Championship.

The TLA took an ethnic pride in two other golfers who, though they didn't play on the tour, were from Latin America — Colombia's Camilo Villegas, who won two straight PGA Tour titles in September, the BMW Championship and The Tour Championship, and Mexico's Lorena Ochoa, who dominated the LPGA Tour and won its Rolex Player of the Year honors for the third time.

9. European Tours

Not even Padraig Harrington seemed to be able to take in the scale of his achievements in 2008. It was not his most consistent year, but that was the least of his worries after two historic weeks in the heart of the summer. First the Irishman successfully defended his title at the Open Championship — and kept the claret jug in its rightful place on the Harringtons' breakfast table — and then he became the first European in living memory to win the U.S. PGA Championship. No European had ever won the two championships in the same year.

Both victories were earned the hard way, which is the only way Harrington would want it. He almost could not play at the Open because of a wrist injury caused by doing what he enjoys most — practicing. Yet he mastered the treacherous Royal Birkdale course, the awful weather and the nostalgic challenge of Greg Norman. Three weeks later Harrington was exhausted at Oakland Hills. Yet on the final day he holed putt after vital putt and again got the better of Sergio Garcia, as he did at Carnoustie in 2007.

After his first Open win, Harrington was determined not to fall into the trap of resting on his laurels — he wanted to win majors, not a major. But bringing his tally up to three major titles almost dumbfounded the Irishman. Suddenly he was in the same bracket as Phil Mickelson, Ernie Els and Vijay Singh, but more pertinently, the only living Europeans with more majors are Nick Faldo (with six) and Seve Ballesteros (five). In that summer whirlwind he had left behind the likes of Bernard Langer, a particular hero, Sandy Lyle and Jose Maria Olazabal (all two majors) and Ian Woosnam (one).

"The toughest thing to get to grips with is that I am now more successful than guys who were heroes of mine," Harrington admitted. "There are guys who I put up on a pedestal when I was growing up as a junior golfer and an amateur, and now I have more majors than them and that shocks me a bit. It is amazing to me, and trying to put yourself in that sort of bracket takes a bit of getting used to. If I were to catch Seve or Nick, that's something I'll have to get my head around, to believe it and then go ahead and try to do it."

After lurking on the leaderboard at the Masters, Harrington knew he was on the right path when he came away from the U.S. Open thoroughly disappointed with a 36th-place finish. "I do try to peak for the majors. I'm going to play my very best golf," he said. "I know if I stay patient and disciplined and wait my turn, come Sunday afternoon I'll be there, or thereabouts. It's easier to win majors than tournaments. Patience is what it takes to win and patience is one of my strong points." Yet he remains endearingly modest of his own presence. "The strangest thing is I have never played very well with confidence and definitely haven't walked away from three majors and brought more confidence onto the golf course. It's something I would like to develop — but I don't feel I walk onto the first tee and have that presence that makes you play better."

Harrington's twin triumphs were the undoubted highlight of the European year. How often had Ryder Cup victories come around without a major championship to cherish. This year was the opposite, with Nick Faldo's team losing to the newly inspired Americans at Valhalla. It was a shock after three successive wins, as was how little was contributed to the cause, in points anyway, by such stars as Harrington, Garcia and Lee Westwood. But the result guaranteed one thing — that anticipation for the match at Celtic Manor in 2010 will be as high as ever.

If Harrington was not as consistent as is usually expected — he flopped in the PGA Tour's FedExCup series in the aftermath of his major highs — then you only had to turn to Robert Karlsson. The Swede enjoyed an amazing summer. From April to October he was outside of the top 20 only once. From the Masters to the Open Championship he was only once outside the top eight. He was eighth at the Masters, fourth at the U.S. Open and seventh at the Open Championship. He followed a run of three successive third places in May with a second place at the Celtic Manor Wales Open. The wins finally came in the autumn. He claimed the Mercedes-Benz Championship in Germany and then the Alfred Dunhill Links Championship at St. Andrews.

Karlsson has tried many things over the years, from the sane to the eccentric, but at the age of 39 he improved his statistics in every category but one, his driving being long enough already. After a nervy performance at the Volvo Masters, Karlsson nevertheless held on to become the first Swede to win the Order of Merit ahead of Harrington and Westwood. He admitted it was still Harrington's year, but the Vardon Trophy was a deserved reward for the talented Swede.

That Westwood still had a chance to claim the Order of Merit at Valderrama was all due to his own consistency. What let the Englishman down was not finding the right putts at the right time to give himself a victory celebration. There was much to applaud as he was third at the U.S. Open, second at the WGC - Bridgestone Invitational and lost a playoff at the Quinn Direct British Masters, but he was always inches from victory. Not so Garcia, whose putting enjoyed a welcome renaissance. The Spaniard claimed the biggest victory of his career to date at The Players Championship, and at the end of the year won on his own course at Castellon as well as at the HSBC Champions in China to become the No. 2 player on the World Ranking.

Other European stars had mixed years. Luke Donald, like Tiger Woods, was missing from the game after the U.S. Open, in his case with a wrist injury. Paul Casey did not quite get going and nor did Justin Rose, while Ian Poulter had two great highlights with second place at the Open Championship and then leading the point scoring at the Ryder Cup. Darren Clarke had two emotional comeback wins, while Colin Montgomerie remarried but missed out on the Ryder Cup or a victory.

The talent coming through continued to impress. Martin Kaymer followed up his rookie of the year award from 2007 with two victories. Graeme McDowell established himself by also winning twice. Ross Fisher claimed the European Open by blowing away Garcia, Harrington, Montgomerie and the rest. Pablo Larrazabal, another potential Spanish superstar, did the same at the French Open and was the rookie of the year.

For 21 years Valderrama marked the end of the European season, but this was the last Volvo Masters. Beginning in 2009 the season will conclude with the $10 million Dubai World Championship and the Order of Merit has been restyled as the "Race to Dubai" with a $10 million bonus pool. In a time of global economic crisis, it was good timing to find such a strong backer as Leisurecorp, a Dubai investment company. But in golfing terms it should ensure more of Europe's leading players play more often on the circuit and even some of the PGA Tour's finest have signed up. The talent drain may not always be westward these days.

Joburg Open
Johannesburg, South Africa
Winner: Richard Sterne

See African Tours chapter.

Abu Dhabi Golf Championship
Abu Dhabi, United Arab Emirates
Winner: Martin Kaymer

Martin Kaymer was doubly impressive in the way he claimed his first title on the European Tour at the Abu Dhabi Golf Championship. First, Kaymer swept away from a strong field of challengers to lead by six strokes after the second and third rounds. Then, as his advantage was whittled down on the final afternoon, Kaymer steadied himself on the last nine and eventually secured a four-stroke victory over Henrik Stenson and Lee Westwood.

Kaymer, at 23 years and 24 days, became the youngest German ever to win on the European Tour, being 14 days younger than when Bernhard Langer claimed his first title. The win confirmed the remarkable rise of Kaymer, from Dusseldorf. In 2006 he won five times and shot 59 on the EPD satellite tour. In the same summer he graduated to the Challenge Tour where he finished in the top five in six out of his eight events, including two victories, and finished fourth on the rankings. Promoted to the main tour in 2007, Kaymer became the first German to earn the Sir Henry Cotton Salver as rookie of the year.

A couple of chances of victories went begging in 2007, but not on the National Course at the Abu Dhabi Golf Club. He opened with 66 to be one ahead of Stenson. A 65 on day two was even better, giving him a six-shot lead over the Swede.

There was no let-up on Saturday as Kaymer added a 68 to be six ahead of Anthony Wall, with Stenson seven adrift and Westwood eight behind. But when Kaymer dropped three shots in a row from the fourth hole, the two Ryder Cup men sensed an opportunity. Both were out in 35, compared to the German's 39, but Kaymer birdied the 10th before dropping another shot at the 12th. Westwood appeared to be the biggest threat, but his run faltered with five pars in a row from the 13th. Although he got within two shots of the lead, he bogeyed the last, where Kaymer birdied to finish with 74 and 15-under-par 273.

"This is an unbelievable feeling," Kaymer said. "The back nine was tough, especially with players like Stenson and Westwood chasing me. I was struggling a bit on the front nine, but I really tried to stay patient and just try to make pars."

Commercialbank Qatar Masters
Doha, Qatar
Winner: Adam Scott

How good was Adam Scott in winning the Commercialbank Qatar Masters? Look at it this way: Henrik Stenson scored 65 in the final round to lose by three strokes and finish runner-up for the second successive week. Charl Schwartzel scored 67 to lose by five. And Johan Edfors, the leader after the second and third rounds, scored 70 to lose by six shots.

Scott simply blitzed the final round at Doha with his lowest-ever score and a new course record by two strokes. His closing 61, 11 under par, was the lowest final round by a winner since Jamie Spence scored 60 to win the European Masters in 1992 at Crans-sur-Sierre. After rounds of 69-73, Scott was two under par and seven behind Edfors. He got going with 65 on day three, which put him three behind the leader and set up a weekend tally of 18 under par, equaling another record from Crans set by Colin Montgomerie in 1996. Scott finished at 20 under par with a total of 268.

Scott, a 27-year-old Australian, rarely looks at himself on video, but caught some tape-delayed coverage of his second round later on Friday afternoon. He soon went to the practice range to work on the flaw he picked up and the results were dramatic. On Sunday he birdied the first five holes and then the seventh to be out in 30. He then birdied the next three holes, plus the 15th where he holed from 15 feet. At this point he looked in range of 59, but at the drivable par-four 16th he missed a four-foot putt. An eight iron to eight feet at the par-three 17th gave him an 11th birdie and a par-five to come, but with water in play, he tacked safely up to the green and took his par. It was his sixth European Tour win and the 14th of his career. It was also his second victory at the Qatar Masters in only two starts, the other coming in 2002.

"I just came out of the gates firing this afternoon," Scott said. "To string off five birdies in a row was ideal, kept me right in the tournament from there, and to keep it going, it put pressure on those guys who were leading. Suddenly they were chasing."

Dubai Desert Classic
Dubai, United Arab Emirates
Winner: Tiger Woods

Tiger Woods arrived in Dubai from halfway round the world, having just won his opening event of the year by eight strokes at the Buick Invitational. After an opening 65 at the Emirates course, for a two-shot lead, it looked like another procession was about to unfold. Winning the Dubai

Desert Classic for the second time in three years looked inevitable, but in fact, after a series of unlikely events, it took a moment of brilliance from the world No. 1, holing a curling, rapid, downhill putt at the last hole to claim a one-stroke victory.

Woods's difficulties began in the pro-am where he snapped the shaft of his driver. He was never as comfortable with the back-up as the original and when the wind got up on Friday his 71 left him only one ahead of the field. Worse was to follow the next day, when he still appeared unsettled after playing in the wind and was disturbed after having to back off a short birdie putt at the first hole, which he then missed. His 73 was his first over-par round in five visits to Dubai and his first anywhere since the first round of the Deutsche Bank Championship the previous September. He was outscored by the 72 of his playing partner Damian McGrane, ranked 318 places lower in the world.

Ernie Els, in his first event of the season, turned in 65 on Saturday to take the lead by one from Henrik Stenson, with Woods, who had ballooned his second shot into the water at the 18th hole, four behind. Tiger was still four adrift at the turn in the final round, but with Els not finding the going as easy as the previous day, the tournament was still wide open. Another South African, Louis Oosthuizen, led briefly before a bogey at the last, while Martin Kaymer, the winner in Abu Dhabi, came in with 66 to set the target at 13 under par after a birdie-birdie-eagle finish.

Woods came home in 31, starting with a birdie at the 10th. But what really got him going was chipping in for a three at the 12th. Two more birdies followed at the next two holes and the roars that rang out unsettled Els to the point where he bogeyed the 11th and 12th. Woods was not finished as he birdied the final two holes for 65 and 14 under par. The four at the last, however, was only secured after he found the bank of the back bunker with his second shot and fluffed the recovery barely onto the green. The putt, though, was outrageously brilliant. Els could still catch him with a birdie at the 18th, but just like Woods the day before, his second shot was knocked down by the wind into the lake in front of the green.

"It was a pretty exciting final round," Woods said. "On 18 I'm thinking I could easily chip the ball in the water. You have to make your mistake short. At least I got it to the green, and the putt went in."

Emaar-MGF Indian Masters
New Delhi, India
Winner: S.S.P. Chowrasia

See Asia/Japan Tours chapter.

Enjoy Jakarta Astro Indonesia Open
Jakarta, Indonesia
Winner: Felipe Aguilar

See Asia/Japan Tours chapter.

Johnnie Walker Classic
New Delhi, India
Winner: Mark Brown

See Asia/Japan Tours chapter.

Maybank Malaysian Open
Kuala Lumpur, Malaysia
Winner: Arjun Atwal

See Asia/Japan Tours chapter.

Ballantine's Championship
Jeju Island, South Korea
Winner: Graeme McDowell

See Asia/Japan Tours chapter.

Madeira Islands Open BPI - Portugal
Madeira, Portugal
Winner: Alastair Forsyth

Alastair Forsyth twice birdied the 18th hole at Santo da Serra to win the Madeira Islands Open. The 32-year-old Scot required an extra hole to defeat South African Hennie Otto in a playoff, but the action was wrapped up rather quicker than the last time they tied for a championship. In 1996, Forsyth and Otto went into a playoff for the Scottish Amateur Strokeplay and it took the Scot nine holes before securing the title. Twelve years later, Forsyth claimed his second victory on the European Tour, the previous one also coming with a playoff at the Malaysian Open in 2002.

Forsyth had missed the cut in his first five events of the season, but after a practice session with his coach, Bob Torrance, he knew his game was coming around. With the weather at home turning stormy, Forsyth made a late decision to play in Madeira in order to test himself under tournament conditions. He opened with two rounds of 70 before adding 66 on Saturday, but that still left the Scot five behind leader Otto, who was a model of consistency with three rounds of 67 to stand at 15 under par with one round to play.

But Forsyth was playing alongside the South African and was able to exert some pressure with an approach to six inches at the fifth for a birdie. Otto bogeyed the hole for a two-shot swing, and Forsyth followed up with a string of birdies, taking the lead outright at the 14th. A three-putt at the 17th led to a bogey that dropped Forsyth down into a tie with Otto, but then both men birdied the 18th. Forsyth closed with 67 for a total of 15-under-par 272, while Otto returned 72. Englishman Gary Clark also birdied the 18th for 70 to take third place on his own, four strokes outside the playoff but one ahead of Sven Struver.

In the playoff, Otto's approach almost found the cup but spun eight feet past and he could not hole for the birdie. In contrast, Forsyth rolled in his seven-footer, an almost identical putt to the one he holed in regulation play. "It was the worst start to a year I've ever had, but it was just a wee bit of winter rust," Forsyth said. "I always had faith in my game and so did Bob. It took three swings for him to sort me out and after that I just wanted to get back out on the course in tournament conditions."

MAPFRE Open de Andalucia
Marbella, Spain
Winner: Thomas Levet

When Lee Westwood opened up with 65 at Aloha Golf Club, in Marbella on the Costa del Sol, the Englishman looked in a good position to defend his title at the MAPFRE Open de Andalucia. A silly three-putt at the 18th on Friday was careless but still left him only two behind. A 66 in the third round put that right as he retook the lead, and four birdies in the first six holes on Sunday kept his momentum going. But then he ran into a brick wall. He bogeyed the eighth and ninth and no more birdies arrived on the last nine. Instead, it was 19-year-old Oliver Fisher, from Essex in England, who charged ahead.

Fisher was the youngest player to appear in the Walker Cup and the youngest to earn his tour card at the qualifying tournament. Now in his second full season on tour, Fisher was contending for a title for the first time but doing a good job. A 67 in the third round alongside Westwood had put him only one behind overnight, and as the leader suddenly struggled, Fisher went ahead by three strokes. Bogeys at the 13th and 14th holes did not throw him off his stride and he hit his approach at the 15th to three feet, then got the second shot back at the par-five 16th.

If Fisher bested his more illustrious countryman over the weekend, the third player in the final group could not be discounted. France's Thomas Levet also birdied the 16th to stay two behind Fisher and then holed from 25 feet for a birdie at the 17th. At the last hole, Fisher went with a three iron off the tee but, with the adrenaline flowing, smashed it around 280 yards into the lake on the left. He scrambled well for a bogey, but it meant 67 and a total of 16-under 272. Levet, from the front greenside bunker, got up and down for another 67 and a playoff. At the same hole again, Fisher now took a four iron and went in the bunker on the right. Levet won the hole with a par. A professional almost as long as Fisher has been alive, it was a fourth European Tour win for Levet and his first for four years. In 2006 he was struck down with vertigo and could hardly stand at times, only returning to the circuit in mid-2007.

"After everything I've been through this is a great feeling," said Levet. "Oliver was playing super golf, but the finishing holes here are very difficult. It is very tough on him though. But I think he is going to be the next Nick Faldo, his game is that good."

Estoril Open de Portugal
Estoril, Portugal
Winner: Gregory Bourdy

Even with Gregory Bourdy four strokes ahead, the final round of the Estoril Open de Portugal turned into a dramatic finale at Oitavos Dunes. It took three holes of a playoff for the 25-year-old Frenchman to join his compatriot from the week before, Thomas Levet, in the winner's circle. It was his second title on the European Tour, after he won the Mallorca Classic late in 2007. Bourdy shared the course record of 63 on the first day with defending champion Pablo Martin, but then took hold of the event with rounds of 65 and 68.

Admitting to nerves early on the last day, Bourdy bogeyed three of the first six holes and went to the turn in 39. At that stage he was two behind Miles Tunnicliff, who birdied four of the first eight holes, and a host of players were back in contention. Bourdy rallied superbly, coming home in 31 strokes with birdies at the 10th, 11th, 13th and 16th holes, the last two both par-fives. But David Howell and Alastair Forsyth also came home in 31s to set up the playoff. Howell made three birdies in a row on the first nine and added four more on the inward half. He got up and down at the last hole for 64 just two weeks after starting work with a new coach, Jamie Gough, the brother of former Scottish football international Richard Gough. He set the target at 266, 18 under.

Forsyth, who won the Madeira Islands Open a fortnight earlier, birdied the last two holes. But after all three parred the 18th in the playoff, the Scot pulled his drive into a bush playing the 18th again and dropped out. Howell was looking to end a period where he had dropped to 247th in the world — he had been top 10 after winning the BMW PGA Championship in 2006 — after a series of shoulder and back injuries.

At the 17th for the third extra hole, Howell hit his approach left and his chip came up 20 feet short. He missed for par and Bourdy two-putted from 30 feet. "It was very hard at the start of the day," said Bourdy. "I didn't look at the leaderboards but I knew that the other players were making birdies. Then I was quite nervous because it was my first playoff on the tour, so to win against players like Alastair Forsyth and David Howell was amazing."

Volvo China Open
Beijing, China
Winner: Damien McGrane

See Asia/Japan Tours chapter.

BMW Asian Open
Shanghai, China
Winner: Darren Clarke

See Asia/Japan Tours chapter.

Open de Espana
Seville, Spain
Winner: Peter Lawrie

After victories for Damien McGrane at the Volvo China Open and for Darren Clarke at the BMW Asian Open, Peter Lawrie made it a hat-trick of Irish triumphs with his maiden win at the Open de Espana at Real Club de Golf at Seville. It was a brilliant charge on the last nine and an impressive performance in a dramatic playoff that helped Lawrie to match his usual roommate McGrane from only a fortnight earlier.

Lawrie started the final round five strokes behind Ignacio Garrido and still trailed at the turn. But a run of four birdies in five holes from the 13th meant the 34-year-old set the clubhouse target at 15-under-par 273 after rounds of 68, 70, 68 and 67.

Garrido had taken the halfway lead by four strokes with a course record of 63 in the second round. He still led by three after 72 on Saturday but went to the turn in 39 on the final day. In seven holes from the second to the eighth he had five bogeys and two birdies. Birdies at the 10th and 12th kept the Spaniard in contention, but at the 18th he needed to hole from 30 feet for a closing 72 to keep alive his hopes of winning his national championship.

Although he is one of three pairs of fathers and sons to have won on the European Tour, none has done it in the same event. Antonio Garrido won the Spanish Open in 1972, just 19 days after Ignacio was born. The younger Garrido had twice been runner-up in 1995 and 1999 and now made it an unwanted hat-trick. At the first extra hole he put his second shot to six feet, but Lawrie holed from 25 feet, which meant the home player had to hole his just to stay alive.

Garrido did so, but again at the 18th his approach spun off the green into the water while Lawrie's second with an eight iron from a fairway bunker safely found the green. "I thought I'd already won the tournament once because I didn't think Ignacio would hole that putt at 18 in regulation," admitted Lawrie.

"So I had to regroup for the playoff and ended up hitting one of the best putts of my life to keep myself in contention. It was a one-in-a-hundred chance, and luckily it dropped in. I've been playing quite well lately, without really getting my rewards, so maybe it was just my turn today. It was nice to add another trophy for the Irish contingent."

Methorios Capital Italian Open
Milan, Italy
Winner: Hennie Otto

Just six weeks after seeing a large lead disappear and then losing the Madeira Islands Open in a playoff, Hennie Otto secured his first title on the European Tour at the Methorios Capital Italian Open. It was a low-scoring week at Castello di Tolscinasco with the South African's total of 263, 25 under par, a new record for the tournament.

Sweden's Robert Karlsson scored a course-record 61 in the second round, but weekend scores of 69 and 67 meant a third-place finish, two strokes behind Otto. England's Oliver Wilson, a runner-up for the third time in the season, closed with rounds of 65 and 64 for 24 under par and gave Otto quite a fright. Otto was four ahead with rounds of 65, 66 and 63 before finishing with 69.

Wilson birdied four holes in a row from the 11th, so that by the time Otto got to the 12th, where he dropped a shot, he was now only tied for the lead. But he immediately birdied the 13th and added five pars, at the 18th finding the green despite an awkward stance when his tee shot finished by the edge fairway bunker. "It's great to win at last," Otto said. "I don't think I've ever holed so many long putts."

Otto, the feisty 31-year-old with seven wins on the Sunshine Tour, admits that he has become mellower since the birth of his son Boeta two years ago. A colorful past includes a story about his golf bag ending up in a river at the Nashua Masters at Wild Coast seven years ago. "There's been several versions of that incident, but here's the real story," Otto explained. "I shot 63 in the pro-am that year, then opened with 70 before blowing out in the second round to miss the cut. I was so mad. I went straight to the car park and smashed holes in my bag with an iron.

"Then I broke every single shaft before piling them into the bag. Liezel (Otto's wife) was driving and as we headed towards Durban over the bridge I told her to stop the car. I opened the boot, picked up the bag and tossed it into the Umtamvuna River below. I felt much better after that. I wanted to change my clubs anyway."

Irish Open
Co. Limerick, Ireland
Winner: Richard Finch

For a man who only just saved his card last year at the final event of the season, a dip in the River Maigue was nothing to get excited about on the way to winning the Irish Open. But it will be a moment that will linger long in the memory. Richard Finch had a comfortable lead coming up the 18th hole at Adare Manor, but after a poor drive his second shot only just stopped on the bank of the river on the left of the fairway. A chip-out lay-up seemed on the cards, but instead Finch went for the green with disastrous consequences — for his dignity but not the ball which landed safely on the putting surface.

"When I was walking down there I had a little feeling that I might have hit it just too hard with my second shot," said Finch, "but when I got there, I thought, well, it looks fine, I've got room to swing and I can get my stance. I never really gave falling in a thought to be honest.

"As I hit the shot, I knew straight away I had made decent contact. I don't know whether I slipped or went round with momentum. And then the next thing I know I was gradually falling down the bank. I kept trying to follow the ball, but then I looked up and saw it on the green, and I was in a bit of shock of thinking, my God, what have I done!"

Finch allowed himself a smile as he was fished out by his caddie and despite three-putting for a bogey still won by two strokes over Felipe Aguilar. It was the second win of the season for the 30-year-old from Hull after his victory at the New Zealand Open at the end of 2007. A 65 in the third round put Finch one stroke behind Bradley Dredge, the man who lost a playoff at Adare Manor the year before but failed to contend this time after a closing 76.

Finch closed with 70 for a 10-under-par total of 278, while Aguilar finished at eight under after a double bogey at the 16th. A group of four players were a further stroke behind including Robert Karlsson and Lee Westwood. "Winning in New Zealand was absolutely superb, and to follow that up with another win in Europe with such a strong field is brilliant," Finch said. "I'll probably have to sit down when things have calmed down, but I'm delighted to have won."

BMW PGA Championship
Virginia Water, Surrey, England
Winner: Miguel Angel Jimenez

A beaming Miguel Angel Jimenez, cigar in its rightful place, gave the BMW PGA Championship a stirring climax with his victory at the second extra hole against England's Oliver Wilson at Wentworth. For Wilson it was his third second-place finish in five weeks and the seventh of his career — no one has had more without winning — but his impressive game should soon reward him with a victory. Jimenez certainly thought so but was happy to grab the biggest title of his career, which also capped a BMW hat-trick after he won in Munich and at the Asian Open in 2004. A hole-in-one at the fifth hole, with a four iron, propelled the veteran Spaniard into the lead, but it took another 15 holes to shake off Wilson.

Both Jimenez and Wilson closed with 68s, to tie at 11-under-par 277, compared to the 74 of overnight leader Robert Karlsson, who tied for third place two strokes behind alongside Luke Donald, who finished off with 65. Karlsson three-putted from three feet at the last to fall out of the playoff, while a two-shot swing at the 15th brought Wilson even when Jimenez missed from a foot. In the playoff both parred the 18th the first time, but Jimenez two-putted for a birdie the next time around while Wilson missed from 12 feet for his four.

"It feels great," said Jimenez. "I have won all three BMW events and this is my 20th season on the tour, so to win the most important tournament on my 20th anniversary is fantastic."

But it was strange week for the tour's flagship event with Padraig Harrington and Ian Poulter missing and Ernie Els, Justin Rose, Darren Clarke, Jose Maria Olazabal and, for the first time in 19 years in the event, Colin Montgomerie all missing the cut. For two days Paul McGinley loved the hard and fast conditions and led with rounds of 65 and 66, only to slump to 79 on day three.

The up-and-down nature of the week was emphasized by Robert Dinwiddie's scores: 78, 63, 79, 79 for 67th place. "Usually I'm quite consistent, but not at the moment," he said. The 63 was a new course record for the Els-redesigned course and tied the lowest ever on the West course by Nick Job and Wayne Riley.

But the quality of the greens on the West course came in for severe criticism with different grasses seeding at different times and growing at different speeds. It was later announced that all the greens on the West course would be dug up and relaid after the 2009 championship.

Celtic Manor Wales Open
Newport, Wales
Winner: Scott Strange

A strange way to introduce the new Twenty Ten course at Celtic Manor, the venue for the Ryder Cup in, you guessed it, 2010. Scott Strange, a 31-year-old Australian, claimed his maiden win on the European Tour at the Celtic Manor Wales Open. Strange led from wire-to-wire to win by four strokes over Robert Karlsson. With a second place following three successive third-place finishes, the Swede's chances of making the Ryder Cup team for Valhalla got a big boost. But Strange played some terrific golf and his closing 64 contained seven birdies and no bogeys. Even when Karlsson threw six consecutive birdies at him the Australian hardly blinked.

Strange, who opened with 63, finished at 22-under-par 262, with Karlsson four back and Raphael Jacquelin eight behind the winner in third place. Strange, in his first full season on the European Tour, overcame a dizzy spell on the course in the third round and a topped drive at the 14th in the final round. Without elaborating he said it would be a special win for his family back home in Perth.

But an Australian and the Ryder Cup course? "I'm not sure I can comment about that," Strange joked. "It could create some interesting matches. It requires some quality iron play. There are certain holes where you've got to put it in the fairway to have a go at the pins and some pins you don't even bother with. It's pretty generous off the tee, but if you're not hitting your irons well you could struggle."

Although the weather did not help, the course got a good reception. But for the 2010 Ryder Cup, Colin Montgomerie was worried about possible fog delays in the Usk Valley, as occurred twice during the Wales Open, and raised the old specter of a four-day Ryder Cup.

Padraig Harrington, the headline act, struggled with his alignment and decision making and missed the cut, not the start he wanted to his preparations for the U.S. Open. But at the other end of the career spectrum, the Wales Open marked the professional debut of Danny Willett, formerly the No. 1 amateur in the world. Willett showed some class by powering over the lake with his second shot at the par-five 18th and then chipping in for an eagle to make the cut on the mark. He ended the week with his first check after tying for 61st.

Bank Austria GolfOpen
Vienna, Austria
Winner: Jeev Milkha Singh

When Jeev Milkha Singh holed his eagle putt at the last hole of the second round, the Indian stood at 15 under par. With the first day being totally washed out, the tournament was reduced to 54 holes, and after rounds of 64 and 63 Singh had a four-stroke lead. He went on to win the Bank Austria GolfOpen, but after the electric scoring of his first two rounds he went into Nick Faldo mode. Faldo won the 1987 Open at Muirfield with 18 pars on the final day and Singh did the same here in his closing 71 for 198 total.

Singh was never less than two ahead until the final hole and eventually won by just one over Simon Wakefield, whose 68 left the Englishman at 14 under after a fine late charge. He left five players sharing third place, two further back, including Iain Pyman, Pelle Edberg and Martin Erlandsson, who all had 65s.

It was Singh's third win on the European Tour and his first since taking the Volvo Masters in 2006. It also came after two second-place finishes on the 2008 tour. "I feel very fortunate to win with 18 pars," said Singh. "Shooting even par on the last day, it's tough to win, and Simon put up a great fight. I think the golfing gods were looking out for me. They did not want a playoff with the bad weather forecast. I didn't hit my last putt hard enough, but it caught the edge of the hole and went in.

"I had no idea about matching Nick Faldo. I was trying to make birdies but they just weren't going in. When you have a lead you don't want to be too aggressive or too defensive, you just play 'mediocre' golf and hit fairways and greens. It's great to win, it's always a feather in your cap. I've knocked on the door a few times this season and at last the door has opened for me. I'm pretty excited about that."

Saint-Omer Open
Lumbres, France
Winner: David Dixon

Seven years after being the leading amateur at the 2001 Open Championship at Royal Lytham, England's David Dixon captured his first European Tour title at the 108th attempt at the Saint-Omer Open. Dixon secured a one-stroke victory despite opening the tournament at Aa St. Omer in northern France with 77, which left him nine strokes off the lead.

Dixon fought his way back into the tournament with rounds of 67, 69 and a flawless 66 to win at five-under-par 279, just ahead of overnight leader Christian Nilsson, who closed with 71. A round of 68 from Steven O'Hara was good enough to secure third place for the Scot on three under par. But it was the 31-year-old Dixon who collected the trophy, in the process taking the number of European Tour wins by Challenge Tour players to 200, ironically in a tournament that has dual ranking with the Challenge Tour. Dixon's three previous seasons on the European Tour ended with him losing his card, and he got back on tour for the first time since 2006 by coming through the qualifying tournament at the end of 2007. He will not have to go back for at least another year.

"I don't really know what to say. I guess I'll get home, speak to my family and manager, and try to make some sense of it all," Dixon said. "It's unbelievable really. It's everyone's dream to win a European Tour event. It's my first win, so it's massive, an awesome feeling."

Dixon took advantage of the three par-fives, the seventh, ninth and 14th, but it was his run of four birdies in a row from the seventh that propelled him to the top of the leaderboard. "The biggest bonus today was that I didn't think too much about what might happen if I won," he said. "I just blocked everything out of my mind and concentrated on the job in hand. I felt quite calm really. I holed some really good putts on the last few holes to hold it together, and it worked out perfectly.

"I took a bit of a gamble on the 14th, hitting a driver off the tee then a three wood into the green. But they were two great shots, so it paid off handsomely. After that I just hung on a little bit. So it's been tough to get my first win on the board, but now I have, I hope for many more."

BMW International Open
Munich, Germany
Winner: Martin Kaymer

Martin Kaymer achieved something not even Bernhard Langer managed by becoming the first German to win the BMW International in the 20th year of the tournament at Munchen Eichenried. The 23-year-old, who was the rookie of the year in 2007, claimed his second title of the season after winning in Abu Dhabi at the start of the year. And the circumstances were remarkably similar on home soil. On both occasions Kaymer went into the final round having built a six-stroke lead only to struggle on the final day. In Abu Dhabi he was never quite caught, but in Munich he eventually won the title in a playoff against Anders Hansen at the first extra hole.

Kaymer's 63 on the second day put him five strokes in front and he followed up with 67 to go six ahead of Charl Schwartzel and seven ahead of a group including Paul Casey. John Bickerton was 10 behind and put in a great charge, but his 67 in the final round left him two adrift, tying for third place with Casey and Mark Foster. Hansen was eight behind starting the final day and he also scored 67 to set the clubhouse target at 15-under-par 273.

It was all in Kaymer's hands, but by the time he had gone to the turn in 38 his huge lead had disappeared. Things got worse with a triple-bogey eight at the 11th where he found the water and then began to get frustrated with himself. But the youngster regrouped and two birdies put him one behind coming to the par-five 18th. He was 40 feet away in two and almost holed the putt for a winning eagle but was simply relieved to be in the playoff.

Playing the 18th again, Hansen found two bunkers while Kaymer hit a superb six iron to seven feet and, with the Dane taking six, two-putted for the winning birdie. Kaymer dedicated the victory to his seriously ill mother and admitted he struggled again with the large lead. "I struggled a little bit and made a big mistake on the 11th," he said.

"I thought I would make it easy with a five iron, but got a little loft on the ball. I didn't keep my patience but I will know for next time and I kept fighting. It was very exciting today and to be the first German to win this tournament is very special for me. It was a great support out there today, and I can't wait to play next year."

Open de France ALSTOM
Paris, France
Winner: Pablo Larrazabal

A new Spanish star arrived at the National Club in Paris as Pablo Larrazabal won the Open de France ALSTOM ahead of stars such as Colin Montgomerie and Lee Westwood. The 25-year-old rookie from Barcelona was only playing after winning the 36-hole qualifier at Chantilly because his ranking from the qualifying tournament was not high enough to gain direct entry. Ranked 481st in the world at the start of the week, his life changed from the moment he took the first-day lead with a six-under 65. A 70 on Friday left him still tied for the lead, but two rounds of 67 over the weekend gave him 269 and the win by four over Montgomerie.

It was not just the amazing story that was unfolding that caught the imagination but the panache with which Larrazabal went about winning the huge prize of €666,660. Although he went without a driver on the firm and fast fairways, the Spaniard went for his shots in spectacular style. He started the final round with three birdies in the first five holes, and even after a double-bogey seven at the ninth, he responded with birdies at the next two holes. Nor did he twitch after a bogey at the par-five 14th.

Both the 15th and 16th holes feature dangerous water hazards, but with a four-stroke lead, Larrazabal took on the perilous pin locations on the basis that even if he found the water he would "still be leading by one or two strokes." Two more birdies resulted and the only time he hit the water was when he was pushed into the lake at the 18th by his brother, Alejandro, and some fellow Spanish professionals. Montgomerie holed from 40 feet for an unlikely birdie at the last to take second place, one ahead of Soren Hansen, with Richard Green in fourth and a late collapse dropping Westwood to a tie for fifth.

Larrazabal caddied in the French Open in 2003, as he had at the Masters that year, for his brother, following Alejandro's victory at the British Amateur in 2002. The younger brother's professional career was delayed because his father wanted him to work at the family fish farm. "I worked there for seven months and it was really hard work," said Larrazabal. "My dad wanted me to see how normal people work for a living before I turned pro and I am glad that I did it.

"Today and yesterday was probably the best golf of my life. I played great golf at the qualifying tournament as well. Montgomerie is probably one of the greatest players in the history of the European Tour and I was watching Lee Westwood finish third at the U.S. Open on TV two weeks ago. I feel great. Right now I know that I can play like those guys, so this is amazing."

European Open
Ash, Kent, England
Winner: Ross Fisher

The last time Ross Fisher had not played a course before the tournament he almost won it. It was at the HSBC Champions in China late in 2007, but he slipped up at the last and lost in a playoff to Phil Mickelson. Tired after a long run of tournaments and qualifying for the Open at Sunningdale at the start of the week, Fisher arrived at the London Club for the European Open without having seen the Jack Nicklaus layout, yet promptly shot a course-record 63.

A brilliant wire-to-wire victory followed as he left a quality field behind, runner-up Sergio Garcia coming in seven strokes adrift. Hard as he tried, Garcia could not make it a Spanish double with his friend Rafael Nadal winning Wimbledon on the same Sunday.

Garcia finished with one of his best-ever putting rounds on the perfect greens — he had only 21 putts — for 66 in foul weather with both rain and strong winds. But nothing seemed to disturb Fisher as he holed from 50 feet for an eagle at the fifth and holed out of a bunker at the last to finish at 20-under-par 268. After the opening 63 he followed up with scores of 68, 69 and 68. Garcia had 64 on Friday but lost ground with 74 on Saturday, while Graeme McDowell's weekend scores of 71 and 73, as the Northern Irishman finished in third place just behind Garcia, showed that scoring was not exactly straightforward at the new venue next to the famous Brands Hatch race track.

Fisher was guided round by his caddie on the first day, but it helped to hole a bunker shot, his first of two for the week, when at the 448-yard ninth hole his driver came up only 20 yards short of the green. The 27-year-old from Wentworth is known as one of longest hitters on the tour, but the improvement in his short game came recently after work with former tour player Mark Roe.

This was Fisher's second win after his KLM victory in 2007, but if things have not always gone right when he has got in contention, they certainly did here. "I might have made it look easy but it wasn't," he said. "It was really tricky out there, but to get my second win this way ahead of a quality field is really special. Perhaps I should give up on practice rounds!"

Barclays Scottish Open
Glasgow, Scotland
Winner: Graeme McDowell

Graeme McDowell could not keep up with the pace of Ross Fisher at the European Open, but the following week at Loch Lomond the Northern

Irishman capitalized on his fine form by winning his second title of the season and the biggest of his career at the Barclays Scottish Open.

McDowell came from two behind with seven holes to play with some stunning approach play. He birdied the 13th, 14th and 15th holes and, after a bogey at the 17th, almost hit the pin at the 18th. The 28-year-old won by two over James Kingston as Simon Khan dropped five strokes in six holes to fall to fifth place, although the Englishman still claimed a place in the Open Championship by getting up and down at the last.

McDowell compiled rounds of 67, 70, 66 and 68 to be at 13-under-par 271. Kingston closed with 66 to take second place, while Richard Green and Miguel Angel Jimenez tied for third. "I've never had a two-shot lead up the last. Before it's been playoffs and the like, and it was great to have a lot less stress and drama. But this was great, especially against a field as stacked as this and on one of the toughest finishing stretches on the tour," he said after consolidating a strong place in the Ryder Cup standings.

"I desperately want to be on the team. I refused to be measured up for my clothing last week at the European Open. Maybe I'll accept that invitation next time I get it." This was McDowell's fourth victory, but it was the first time his father, Kenny, who introduced his son to the game, had seen him win, having just retired that week. "My dad first put a club in my hand aged seven and he's been with me and my golf for 20 years, through thick and thin. He just retired last Friday. This is my retirement present to him. He's an emotional man and I'm sure there'll be a few tears tonight."

The Open Championship
Southport, Lancashire, England
Winner: Padraig Harrington

See Chapter 4.

Inteco Russian Open Golf Championship
Moscow, Russia
Winner: Mikael Lundberg

Sweden's Mikael Lundberg feels quite at home at Le Meridien Moscow Country Club as he proved in winning the Inteco Russian Open Golf Championship for the second time in four years. Since winning the title in 2005 Lundberg lost his card in 2006 and returned to the European Tour in 2008 after a year on the Challenge Tour. But the 34-year-old had not enjoyed a top-10 finish all season before returning to Moscow and returning scores of 67, 64, 68 and 68 for a 21-under-par total of 267.

Lundberg won by two strokes over Spain's Jose Manuel Lara, who charged into contention with a closing 64. Lara was six behind going into the last day, but eight birdies in the first 14 holes brought him into a tie for the lead. Lara immediately bogeyed the 15th, but then birdied the 17th before signing for 269.

Lundberg might have been in more trouble if he had not saved par at the 15th after driving into the trees. His second shot hit the woodwork and he could only hack down the fairway for his third shot. But a good pitch to seven feet and a fine putt meant a par, and then Lundberg birdied the 16th from 25 feet and the 17th from five feet to give himself some breathing room again.

"This is my absolute favorite place, everything is great here," said Lundberg. "The worst part is you come here and it feels like I always play well and I should do well, so you put a lot of pressure on yourself and you wonder when you are going to screw up. Today I didn't want to make any mistakes and just tried to play it safe until Lara went in front and I then loosened up a bit. On 15 I hit a terrible drive in the trees but managed to save par somehow, and I holed two great putts on 16 and 17. The save on 15 turned everything around."

SAS Masters
Stockholm, Sweden
Winner: Peter Hanson

Not since Jesper Parnevik won for the second time in 1998 had a home player won the renamed SAS Masters. But on a cold, wet and windy afternoon at Arlandastad in Stockholm, Peter Hanson joined Parnevik and Joakim Haeggman as Swedish champions on home soil. After a four-day battle with Nick Dougherty, Hanson triumphed by one stroke over the Englishman and another Swede, Pelle Edberg.

Both Hanson and Dougherty opened with two rounds of 66 before the Swede went in front with 68 to a 70. On Sunday morning Dougherty woke up with a back injury, which only got worse when he went to the gym to warm up. Although he decided to go ahead and play, capitalizing on his best form of the summer following the death of his mother in May, Hanson stretched his lead to four with eight holes to play. But then he came back to the field in a hurry.

A double bogey at the 11th was the first sign Hanson was in trouble. Then bogeys followed at the 16th and 17th, but he was still one in front going to the last. After Edberg's long range effort at the 18th just missed, Hanson put his approach safely onto the green and claimed the victory, which kept him in with an outside chance of making the Ryder Cup team. Hanson closed with 71 for nine-under-par 271 total, while Dougherty and Edberg both had 70s.

This was Hanson's second win on the European Tour following victory at the Spanish Open in 2005. "It feels great, of course," he said. "It's been a long wait for me. I started pretty well, but then struggled on the back nine the same as yesterday."

Dougherty was runner-up in the event for the second year running. "What a day. If my chiropractor had been here he might have told me to pull out, so I'm glad he wasn't," said the 26-year-old. "After all I've been through, I was going to finish no matter what."

KLM Open
Zandvoort, Netherlands
Winner: Darren Clarke

One week after celebrating his 40th birthday Darren Clarke proved he could still be a contender for the Ryder Cup team with his second win of the season at the KLM Open at Kennemer Golf Club. Clarke put together superb rounds of 68, 64, 66 and 66 again for a 16-under-par 264 total and a four-stroke victory over Paul McGinley. A 64 in the final round from McGinley hauled the Irishman up the leaderboard, but the man who really frightened Clarke was Henrik Stenson, who finished in third place after 68.

Clarke led Stenson by three shots going into the final round, but was soon behind after bogeying the second while the tall Swede opened with three birdies. But Clarke responded by birdieing three of the next four holes, and Stenson lost ground with a bogey at the seventh and a double bogey at the eighth. Clarke gave himself more breathing room with three birdies in a row from the 10th.

Although Clarke was still adrift in terms of qualifying automatically for the Ryder Cup team, he hoped the win would impress captain Nick Faldo when it came to making his wild card selections the following week. "It's nice to win knowing that I had to play well and then actually doing it," said Clarke. "I had two weeks to try to impress Nick. The first is out of the way and I seem to have done that.

"I don't know if I have done enough, but I'm going to Gleneagles in better shape and hopefully he will take notice. It's his call, and if he thinks there are other guys more deserving of a pick, then I have no problem with that whatsoever. Whoever is on the plane will be part of a really strong team going there."

Of Stenson's early charge, Clarke added: "I am 40 years old, six feet two inches and a little bit overweight. Not much frightens me I have to say. But he is a great player and he was always going to come at me at some stage. I got caught between clubs on the second and made a mistake by getting too aggressive with my pitch, but it's 18 holes, not a sprint from the start, and I knew that I was going to have some chances because I was feeling so good swinging the club."

Johnnie Walker Championship
Perthshire, Scotland
Winner: Gregory Havret

For the first time the Johnnie Walker Championship at Gleneagles was filling the role as the last qualifying event for the European Ryder Cup team and, as always, there was as much attention on who made Nick Faldo's team as on the victory of Gregory Havret. For the 31-year-old Frenchman, it was a third win on the European Tour and his second in Scotland in just over a year after he won the Scottish Open at Loch Lomond in 2007. But Havret was not in with a chance of making the Ryder Cup team, so there were plenty of others with their own tournament-within-a-tournament.

These did not include Ian Poulter, however. The Englishman had been due to return from America, but at the last moment decided to stay on the PGA Tour where he wanted to try to qualify for the third leg of the FedExCup. But it was a futile gesture as he missed the cut, although he stated he had been distracted by the media attention that had accompanied his decision.

By finishing in the top five at Gleneagles, Poulter would have been in with a chance of getting into the top 10 automatic qualifying spots. Justin Rose, in eighth place and almost certain of his spot on the team, remained after Holland and made absolutely sure after finishing tied for fifth. Likewise, ninth-placed Soren Hansen and 10th-placed Oliver Wilson held onto their positions by tying for 10th place. They were helped by Poulter's absence and by Martin Kaymer, in 11th spot, missing the cut. Ross Fisher and Nick Dougherty challenged hard, but needed to do even better than their tie for 10th and tie for seventh finishes respectively. Wilson, in particular, deserved credit after opening with 76 and then, at six over, conjuring two birdies and an eagle in the last 10 holes on Friday to make the cut on the mark. His weekend scores of 68 and 69 then confirmed his Ryder Cup debut.

After his victory in Holland the week before, Darren Clarke could not hole any putts on saturated greens that were severely criticized by many players, Lee Westwood among them. Clarke finished tied for 44th, but his two wins in 2008 were not enough to claim one of Faldo's wild cards. Instead, at the conclusion of the tournament, Faldo announced he was adding Paul Casey, as expected, but also Poulter, to the player's evident relief and to the dismay of Clarke's supporters.

Meanwhile, Havret led the tournament after every round with scores of 68, 71, 69 and 70 for a 14-under-par 278 total. By getting up and down from a bunker at the last for a par he stayed one ahead of Graeme Storm, who came home in 32 to put the frighteners on the Frenchman. "It was definitely a tough day," said Havret. "I remember last year at Loch Lomond, I was up and down from the trap also."

Storm had birdied the 15th and 16th, but slipped up at the short 17th, before a four at the par-five last. Peter Hanson, after his win in Sweden, and David Howell shared third place three strokes behind the winner.

Omega European Masters
Crans Montana, Switzerland
Winner: Jean-Francois Lucquin

More French celebrations on the 18th green, but what was a "dream" for Jean-Francois Lucquin as he notched up his maiden victory on the European Tour in the Omega European Masters was a nightmare for Rory McIlroy. The 19-year-old rookie from Northern Ireland had come off three successive missed cuts but was apparently about to win for the first time and become the third youngest champion on the European Tour. Seve Ballesteros was five days younger when he won the Dutch Open in 1976, while Dale Hayes was 18 when he won the Spanish Open in 1971.

McIlroy opened with 63 at Crans-sur-Sierre, then added an even-par 71 before a 66 in the third round gave him the lead. But bogeys at the second and third holes in the final round let everyone else back in. Lucquin played steadily, picking up birdies at the first, eighth, 10th and 11th. A par at the last for 67 and he had posted the target at 13-under-par 271. McIlroy recovered from his early stumble and was one ahead after birdieing the 15th. He then got up and down for pars at the 16th and 17th holes, but then went over the back of the 18th green. He chipped to five feet but missed the putt for victory, closing with 71.

At the same hole in the playoff, McIlroy had a chance from 15 feet but two-putted. Staying on the 18th for the second extra hole, McIlroy putted up to a foot and then, trying to finish off, missed the tap in. Everyone around the 18th was shocked, but Lucquin kept his composure. Needing only two putts from 12 feet to win, he holed for a birdie and the title.

"I have no words to explain what I am feeling. I don't know what happened to Rory on the second playoff hole," Lucquin said. "He asked if he could finish, I said that was okay and he missed it. That made it easier for me.

"When I saw my wife and little boy, it was a dream," he added. "At the beginning of the season I was not happy with my game. I was 129th on the Order of Merit, but didn't want to go back to the qualifying school."

McIlroy said: "Obviously I am very disappointed. I got very unlucky on the 18th in regulation, where it got a pretty big bounce for a sand wedge. I hit a good chip, but not a very good putt. Then second time around in the playoff it didn't really matter as he holed his. That made me feel a bit better after missing that putt. C'est la vie."

Mercedes-Benz Championship
Cologne, Germany
Winner: Robert Karlsson

After taking three weeks off due to a slight neck injury, Robert Karlsson proved his form and fitness perfectly by winning the Mercedes-Benz Championship at Gut Larchenhof in Cologne. Karlsson was able to fly off to the Ryder Cup the following day having collected his eighth win on the European Tour and with a morale-boosting victory for the European team heading for Valhalla.

It was also a reward for Karlsson's fine form all season, with nine top-10 finishes having enabled the 39-year-old Swede to qualify for the Ryder Cup team for the second match running. This was his first win since two victories in 2006. "It's very nice to win, a great relief, and it would have felt a bit strange not to win this season because I've been playing so well," Karlsson said. "Hopefully Nick (Faldo, the European captain) will be delighted. It was a pretty good result for all of us."

Karlsson took the halfway lead after rounds of 67 and 69 and then went three ahead with 68 on Saturday. He would have been even further ahead but for a one-stroke penalty, assessed after watching television footage after his round, for the ball moving after he had grounded his putter while tapping in on the second green.

But the Swede was hardly affected overnight as his lead expanded to six strokes without him having to work too hard. But then everything changed as Italy's Francesco Molinari rolled in four birdies in a row from the 12th, his long attempt at the 15th just missing for an eagle. Molinari only just missed his fifth birdie in a row at the short 16th, but there Karlsson dropped a shot after finding a bunker, so the lead was now only two.

It proved enough over the closing holes as 71 gave Karlsson a total of 13-under-par 275, with Molinari at 11 under and Ross Fisher, Michael Campbell and Miguel Angel Jimenez tying for third four shots back. "It was really good," Karlsson said. "It got closer than necessary maybe, but I felt there was not much more I could do. All credit to Francesco, he played fantastic the last eight or nine holes. I just tried to do my own thing, but it's not easy when he is holing putts from 40 feet, but in the end it was enough."

The Ryder Cup
Louisville, Kentucky
Winner: United States

See Chapter 6.

Quinn Insurance British Masters
Sutton Coldfield, West Midlands, England
Winner: Gonzalo Fernandez-Castano

As one of only two players from the Ryder Cup to turn up for action at The Belfry, Lee Westwood would have wished for an easier week as he tried to defend his title at the Quinn Insurance British Masters. The Englishman from Worksop, playing in the closest tournament to his home, admitted to jet lag and exhaustion, and although he did not use it as an excuse, it perhaps caught up with him on a final day that required him to play 28 holes as Spain's Gonzalo Fernandez-Castano claimed the biggest victory of his career.

Fog was the big problem throughout the week, with rounds delayed and having to be finished the next day. On Sunday morning Westwood completed a 68 to tie for the third-round lead with Michael Campbell, Fernandez-Castano lagging three shots behind. The Spaniard was still three back after Westwood birdied the sixth and seventh holes but then the gap began to close.

Fernandez-Castano birdied the 10th, while Westwood drove the green at the short par-three and then three-putted. Fernandez-Castano then chipped in for a par at the short 12th, after his tee shot finished in a stream, before birdieing the 13th to tie for the lead. While Campbell would finish two shots adrift, Fernandez-Castano, after a bogey-free 67, and Westwood, with 70, tied at 12 under par.

The Spaniard had got up and down for a par at the last while Westwood, on the top tier where the pin was located, had missed his birdie chance for the win. They would play the daunting 18th three more times. At the first extra hole, Fernandez-Castano had a birdie chance but Westwood got up and down. They both chipped and putted the next time around, but on the third occasion, while Fernandez-Castano did it again, this time Westwood could not chip close enough and bogeyed.

"I just struggled with my swing all day and didn't feel under control at any point," said Westwood. "I was pleased to be in a playoff as I felt I really hung in there. Playing 28 holes today was no excuse. I just couldn't feel my swing. I hit a lot of poor iron shots and when Gonzo chipped in on the par-three 12th I think the writing was on the wall."

"I have to say it's probably the best victory of the four," said Fernandez-Castano, wearing a towel after ending up in the water following the win. He had started the week 105th on the Order of Merit, but kept up a streak of winning for the fourth year in succession. "I'm really happy, and of course my main goal was to get into the last Volvo Masters at Valderrama, and I think I've done that."

Alfred Dunhill Links Championship
St. Andrews & Fife, Scotland
Winner: Robert Karlsson

There might have been the small matter of the Ryder Cup in between, but Robert Karlsson won his second individual event in a row at the Alfred Dunhill Links Championship. The 39-year-old Swede also went to the top of the Order of Merit ahead of Padraig Harrington.

Karlsson only triumphed in a playoff after tying at 10-under-par 278 with Ross Fisher and Martin Kaymer in the event played over three courses. All the leading contenders played at Kingsbarns on the first day in relatively calm weather, then in the freezing cold at St. Andrews on Friday and the wind and rain of Carnoustie in the third round.

Having slumped to 76 in that third round to fall three strokes off the pace, Karlsson described his eventual win as: "Unexpected! I played a really bad round yesterday, but today it was good, and all of a sudden I am in a playoff."

On the Old Course, Karlsson closed with 65, as did Fisher, who had set the clubhouse target in the group ahead. On the best day of the week, calm and with even some warmth, Karlsson did not drop a shot as he birdied three of the first four holes and collected seven in all. Fisher's highlight was his eagle at the par-five 14th, where he chipped in from 35 feet.

Both made good par saves at the 17th but missed birdie chances at the 18th. Kaymer, in the last group, went into the lead at 11 under with his fifth birdie of the day at the 16th, but then dropped a shot at the next. He, too, had a chance at the last but missed. In the playoff, at the first hole, Fisher put himself out of contention by driving into the Swilcan Burn. Kaymer had a 10-footer for a three but just missed again. Karlsson, birdieing the hole for the third time out of three for the week, hit a three wood and a gap wedge to two and a half feet, which he tapped in for his ninth career win.

"It felt easier today with the win in Germany under my belt," Karlsson said. "I felt really comfortable in the playoff having birdied the hole before and I had the perfect yardage for the approach. Leading the Order of Merit is a bonus. It's not my goal, I still think Padraig has had the better season, but it will be an exciting finish."

Karlsson and his pro-am partner Dermot Desmond, the Irish financier whose great friend J.P. McManus has won the event twice with Harrington, finished second in the team competition at 26 under, one behind John Bickerton and South African businessman Bruce Watson. Nick Dougherty, who won the individual title in 2007, and Peter Dawson, chief executive of The R&A, tied for fourth place.

Madrid Masters
Madrid, Spain
Winner: Charl Schwartzel

Charl Schwartzel's second victory in Madrid was overshadowed by the distressing news from the city's hospital where Seve Ballesteros was diagnosed with a brain tumor after collapsing at Madrid airport at the start of the week. After tests during the week, Ballesteros issued a statement on the Sunday night, saying: "Throughout my entire career I have been one of the best at overcoming obstacles on the golf course. And now I want to be the best, facing the most difficult game of my life, using all my strength and also counting on those who have been sending me get-well messages. I have always sympathized with those people who face illnesses. Therefore, I want to remind them that with bravery, faith, serenity, confidence and a lot of mental strength, we have to face any situation no matter how difficult it may be."

A frequent visitor to Ballesteros's bedside during the week was his old Ryder Cup partner Jose Maria Olazabal, himself playing in his first tournament for three months after suffering again from rheumatoid arthritis. Rounds of 70, 72, 71 and 73 gave him a tie for 65th place, but the former double Masters champion was simply delighted to be back on the course.

Schwartzel's play at Club de Campo was dazzling as he finished at 19-under-par 265 with rounds of 69, 64, 66 and 66. He won by three strokes over Argentina's Ricardo Gonzalez, whose 62 in the third round had put him into contention. But he could only get within one of Schwartzel before there was a two-shot swing at the 13th. The 24-year-old South African, having gone back to a conventional putting grip after experimenting with the claw grip, was flawless in the final round, with neither a bogey nor a five on a card containing five birdies. He followed one at the 13th with another at the next and one more at the 17th.

Yet Schwartzel, with his third European Tour title but his second in the city after winning the Spanish Open in 2007, had his own ailments. His father, George, had to talk him into continuing on Friday morning and a seven-under 64 followed. "I spoke to my Dad and he told me to tee off and see how I feel," said Schwartzel. "I'm very happy I took his advice now and I felt like I ground it out nicely all week. I haven't felt great. I had a shoulder problem and some sort of flu bug which has been going around. I've been waking up in the mornings feeling achy and sore and not having any energy, but this morning I actually felt a bit better."

Portugal Masters
Vilamoura, Portugal
Winner: Alvaro Quiros

With Seve Ballesteros recovering in a Madrid hospital after two operations to remove a tumor from his brain, Spain's Alvaro Quiros was inspired to win his second title on the European Tour at the Portugal Masters. Quiros finished three clear of Paul Lawrie at the Oceanico Victoria course in Vilamoura, with Order of Merit leader Robert Karlsson finishing tied for third place.

"My caddie told me that Seve always wanted to beat everybody and today I drew inspiration from thinking about the way he played his golf," said Quiros. "Seve was and still is a personal inspiration for all of the Spaniards and we wish him well. Today was a tough day for me with the long game. But with the short game, I kind of stopped and remembered him, you know, when he made chip and putts and wonderful recoveries.

"Seve played in a different way to the rest of the world. He was something special. He was playing more with the heart than the real game, and today was one of those days for me."

One shot ahead going into the final round after completing the last five holes of his third round — held over after a thunderstorm on Saturday afternoon — Quiros, age 25 from Cadiz, holed from 50 feet for a birdie at the first hole. But then he bogeyed the next and England's Ross Fisher took the lead before Karlsson's three birdies in a row put him at the top of the leaderboard.

But on the second nine the big-hitting Quiros emerged triumphant after Fisher made three bogeys in a row while Karlsson faltered when he found water at the 17th. In contrast, Quiros birdied both the 17th and 18th, where he holed from five feet. Rounds of 66, 68, 67 and 68 gave Quiros a total of 19-under-par 269. It came almost two years after his maiden win in his first event on the European Tour at the Alfred Dunhill Championship in South Africa and came after he missed five months in 2007 with a wrist injury.

Lawrie, the 1999 Open champion, recorded his highest finish for three years when he holed from 30 feet at the last, but Karlsson, who tied for third place with Fisher and defending champion Steve Webster, still extended his lead over Padraig Harrington at the top of the Order of Merit.

Castello Masters Costa Azahar
Castellon, Spain
Winner: Sergio Garcia

Sergio Garcia held off a strong challenge from Peter Hedblom to achieve a fairy-tale victory on his home course at Castellon, near Valencia. It was the course where the Spaniard played as a youngster and still returns to, since his father, Victor, remains the club professional. To bring a tournament to the club was a dream in itself, but for Garcia to win the Castello Masters Costa Azahar was even better. Yet the 28-year-old immediately dedicated the victory to Seve Ballesteros, who during the week underwent a third operation to remove a brain tumor.

"I couldn't help but think about Seve," Garcia said. "I'm sending all my love to him and his family and hope he recovers soon. I hope this victory helps him to get a little better."

Rounds of 66, 65 and 66 gave Garcia a four-stroke lead over Hedblom, Soren Kjeldsen, Simon Dyson and David Lynn. Garcia birdied the first hole but Hedblom birdied the first four, and when the Spaniard bogeyed the sixth they were tied for the lead. But Garcia, using all his local knowledge, responded by birdieing the next two holes to go out in 34.

Both contenders birdied the 13th and 16th holes, and when Hedblom dropped a shot at the 17th the margin was up to three strokes. Garcia's closing 67 left him at 20-under-par 264 total, with Hedblom's 66 leaving the Swede two ahead of compatriot Alexander Noren in third place.

"It feels absolutely awesome," said Garcia. "I didn't play amazing and when Peter had such a great start I thought these guys were not making it easy for me. On the back nine I felt I had it under control and had a lot of chances and putts but didn't make that many. It just feels very special and means so much. Just getting the tournament here was special for me and my family, but to play the way I did and win it is awesome."

At the wrong end of the Order of Merit, Sweden's Patrik Sjoland missed the cut and failed to retain his position in 118th place, the last to gain a full card for 2009, with France's Francois Delamontagne going ahead by just £240 despite a closing 74.

Volvo Masters
Sotegrande, Cadiz, Spain
Winner: Soren Kjeldsen

Soren Kjeldsen's wire-to-wire victory at the 21st and last Volvo Masters was good news not just for the diminutive 33-year-old Dane, who won for only the second time in his career, but for the tall 39-year-old Swede Robert Karlsson. Kjeldsen produced the best performance of his life to triumph over the tricky fairways of Valderrama, but it was the achievement of Karlsson's career to claim the Vardon Trophy as winner of the Order of Merit.

Karlsson finished tied for 32nd place, a surprising slump given that from April to October he finished outside the top 20 only once. His amazing consistency, with 12 top-10 finishes, was capped by a powerful finish with two victories and a third place, but going into Valderrama he could still have been surpassed by three other players. In a week of difficult weather, with interruptions on both Friday and Saturday, Karlsson was always off the pace, as were Padraig Harrington and Miguel Angel Jimenez, who had an 80 in the second round.

But Lee Westwood was right in contention for the title until two bogeys late on the first nine of the final round. Westwood went on to tie for fourth place with Sergio Garcia, and with Harrington tied for 13th and Jimenez 24th, it was enough for Karlsson to top the Order of Merit. "It was the hardest week of my career, but also my greatest achievement," Karlsson said. "It was sort of in my hands, but also out of it, and I was glad to see Kjeldsen and Kaymer up on the leaderboard today."

It was Martin Kaymer who challenged Kjeldsen in the final round, drawing even with four birdies in five holes. Kjeldsen, three ahead at the start of the last round, had parred the first 10 holes, but seeing Kaymer at eight under par alongside him, birdied the par-five 11th and then the par-three 12th to give himself some breathing room. Kaymer dropped shots at two of the last three holes, as did Kjeldsen. But a closing 71, after rounds of 65 — a superb effort in difficult, windy conditions on the opening day — 71 and 69, left Kjeldsen at eight-under 276 and two ahead of Kaymer, with 68, and Anthony Wall, whose 69 included an inward 34.

Kjeldsen had lost in a playoff to Justin Rose the year before at Valderrama, but now added to his lone victory at the Diageo Championship at Gleneagles in 2003. "I have good memories from last year and I felt comfortable in the lead," the Dane said. "My little boy said when Tiger Woods got injured that now it was my turn to win, and now I have."

HSBC Champions
Shanghai, China
Winner: Sergio Garcia

See Asia/Japan Tours chapter.

UBS Hong Kong Open
Fanling, Hong Kong
Winner: Lin Wen-tang

See Asia/Japan Tours chapter.

Sportsbet Australian Masters
Melbourne, Victoria, Australia
Winner: Rod Pampling

See Australasian Tour chapter.

Alfred Dunhill Championship
Malelane, South Africa
Winner: Richard Sterne

See African Tours chapter.

South African Open Championship
Paarl, Western Cape, South Africa
Winner: Richard Sterne

See African Tours chapter.

Challenge Tour

What better time to graduate to the European Tour than with the start of the Race to Dubai for the 2009 season. David Horsey not only confirmed his place in the race but gave himself the best possible chance by qualifying for events like the HSBC Champions and the BMW PGA Championship as the No. 1 player on the Challenge Tour. The 23-year-old from Cheshire, England, won twice in his rookie season and sealed the top spot with his ninth top-10 finish of the year at the Apulia San Domenico Grand Final.

Horsey did not turn professional until after playing in the Walker Cup in Northern Ireland in 2007. His first win came at the Telenet Trophy, where he birdied three of the last four holes, and then two weeks later Horsey won the AGF-Allianz EurOpen de Lyon with a last round of 65. Although the wins ensured he would be among the top 20 on the money list who gain their cards on the European Tour, his consistency was the key to finishing No. 1.

"I'm just so excited because it is a fantastic time to be joining the European Tour, what with the Race to Dubai starting this year," Horsey said. "It's going to be great to be a part of it. I obviously dreamed of playing alongside some of the best players in the world when I was growing up and now it's a reality."

Horsey finished ahead of Gary Lockerbie, the Kazakhstan Open champion, and Taco Remkes, the Dutch three-time champion and an ECCO Performance Award winner. Remkes, who only took up golf seriously six years ago, was also in his rookie season on the Challenge Tour but triumphed at the Scottish Challenge, the Dutch Futures event on home soil and at the Margara Diehl-Ako Platinum Open in Italy.

Argentina's Estanisloa Goya won the Apulia San Domenico Grand Final with four birdies in the last five holes to defeat Richard Bland and John E. Morgan. It was Goya's second win of the season, but it was Morgan, the Englishman who has played on the PGA Tour but suffered from epilepsy, who dramatically jumped into the top 20.

Other players to win twice during the season were Finland's Antti Ahokas, Scotland's Richie Ramsay, the former U.S. Amateur champion, and

England's Seve Benson, so named because his father was a fan of Seve Ballesteros.

Benson has a big name to live up to and, introducing himself on the first tee — "Hi, I'm Seve" — has often been told: "Yeah, right, and I'm Tiger." Benson said of meeting the great man a few years ago: "I don't think he realized my name was really Seve. I introduced myself and he just smiled. He said, 'No, your name can't be Seve.' It was a bit strange. But I don't feel I have anything to live up to. My ambition has always been to be the best, but if I don't make it, I'm going to give it my best effort."

Other players to earn their cards were Gareth Maybin, from Northern Ireland, Italy's Alessandro Tadini, Steve O'Hara of Scotland, Denmark's Jeppe Huldahl, England's Richard Bland, Marcus Higley and Stuart Davis, Alexandre Rocha of Brazil, Sweden's Klas Eriksson and Christian Nilsson, Rafael Cabrera Bello of Spain and Holland's Wil Besseling.

Oskar Henningsson, of Sweden, who only played in four Challenge Tour events, became the first player to come through all three stages of qualifying to win the finals in Spain. Daniel Willett, formerly the world's No. 1 amateur, and Chris Wood, who finished fifth as an amateur at the Open Championship, also made it through all three stages to earn their cards, while Ryder Cup players Andrew Coltart and Joakim Haeggman regained their status on the main tour.

10. Asia/Japan Tours

"Move over, Shingo Katayama. Here I come." Imagine that as something that 17-year-old Ryo Ishikawa could have said as the 2008 Japan Tour season was drawing to a close. But he wouldn't have, considering his modest demeanor, even though the teenaged star had brought his first professional campaign to a sparkling finish in its final months.

"Wait a minute. I'm far from ready to leave center stage." Imagine that as the 35-year-old Katayama's likely response after he ran away with his fourth money title in the last five years (five in all) and won both the Japan Open and PGA Championship in the process, each for a second time. Katayama also took the rich Taiheiyo Masters, his 26th career win, as he put himself in position to jump from fourth to second behind Masashi Ozaki on the all-time Japan Tour money list with one more comparable season of success.

Meanwhile, Ishikawa continued to set new "youngest" records, was designated the male athlete of the year in Japan, and gained international attention. Ishikawa, who startled the golf world in 2007 when he won the tour's Munsingwear KSB Cup as a 15-year-old schoolboy amateur, took his first tournament as a professional — the 2008 mynavi ABC Championship — amid a strong run in the fall that carried him to fifth place on the money list. He had two seconds (one in the Japan Open), a third and two fifth-place finishes in that flurry.

Only three overseas players won in Japan in 2008. Thailand's Prayad Marksaeng matched Katayama's three-victory total, his first wins in Japan, and South Korea's S.K. Ho and India's Jeev Milkha Singh each snagged a pair of titles. Unless you count Ishikawa, the tour's rookies went winless and only three older players picked up their first victories in 2008. Azuma Yano, the money list runner-up who had never placed higher than 18th before, and Hideto Tanihara, second in 2006, were the other double winners.

Youth came to the Asian Tour as well, in the person of Korea's Noh Seung-yul, age 17, who took the Midea China Classic in October. Noh did it in veteran style, too, holding up under the pressure in the final round. He fought off the threat by Australian veteran Terry Pilkadaris with a three-under-par 68 to win by one with a 17-under 267 total. Noh finally permitted himself a smile at the end. "I always try to control my emotions when I play, as I tend to focus solely on my game," he said. "Maybe I should learn to relax more now and enjoy my game." Noh is the third youngest tour winner after Thailand's Chinnarat Phadungsil and Korea's Kim Dae-sub.

The Asian Tour opened the season with the unexpected in February, with New Zealander Mark Brown scoring his first two wins. Brown, 33, now in his second season on the tour, also withstood the pressure to score his first win in the SAIL Open. "I was nervous when I started," said Brown, uncomfortable with a one-stroke lead. But rather than fold, as some might expect of a player going for his first win, Brown just got tougher and won by four. Then he won again the following week, taking the Johnnie Walker Classic, coming from behind with five birdies over the last nine holes to win by three.

If the season began with the unexpected, it ended with the expected. Thailand's Thongchai Jaidee, long a fixture on the tour, ended his two-year absence from the winner's circle with a playoff victory in the Hana Bank Vietnam Masters the first week of December. His five-foot par putt brought him his ninth Asian Tour title. Thongchai made it two in a row in the Johnnie Walker Cambodian Open the following week, though this one was — no pun intended — in a walk, by six strokes. Thongchai sprinted away with three successive birdies from No. 10, and it was over. "I played really well all week — I only had four bogeys throughout the four rounds, and I know that my game is all coming back now," said Thongchai. The victory tied him with fellow Thai Thaworn Wiratchant with a record 10 tour victories.

Two Asian Tour veterans from Indian now also plying the world stage stopped by to pick off victories in tournaments co-sanctioned with the European Tour. Arjun Atwal beat Sweden's Peter Hedblom in a playoff for the Maybank Malaysian Open in March. Then Jeev Milkha Singh held off Padraig Harrington and Ernie Els for a one-stroke win in the Barclays Singapore Open.

Asian Tour

Emaar-MGF Indian Masters
New Delhi, India
Winner: S.S.P. Chowrasia

India's S.S.P. Chowrasia made up his game plan, modest by most standards, but it suited him perfectly.

"My plan was not to bogey," Chowrasia said, "and I knew if I got pars, I would get my birdie chances." And thus did Chowrasia, 29, former caddie and son of a greenskeeper, make the leap from the deep ranks to full membership on the Asian and European Tours with his first victory, an upset win in the Emaar-MGF Indian Masters at Delhi Golf Club.

And the birdies did come. Chowrasia, shooting 70-71-71, trailed through the first three rounds but was never far from sight of the lead. He entered the final round trailing by two and proceeded to post four birdies on the first nine, including a chip-in from 25 feet at the third hole and a 25-foot putt at the seventh that broke him out of a tie with Ireland's Damien McGrane. Chowrasia got his fifth and final birdie at the 11th and rolled on to a five-under-par 67 — with no bogeys. His nine-under 279 total gave him a two-stroke victory over McGrane in India's biggest tournament.

Chowrasia had the added pleasure of realizing his dream against some intimidating competition. The field included Ernie Els and Thomas Bjorn (in a tie for sixth), Mark O'Meara and Indian standouts Jyoti Randhawa, who ballooned after leading the first round with 65, and Arjun Atwal, who finished nine strokes off the lead.

Chowrasia had stuck to his game plan. "I wasn't thinking too much about the win," he said. "All I wanted to do was to score pars and to keep it going, and I did." The celebration had to wait awhile. "Right now, my mind is totally blocked," he said. "I'm not able to think about anything."

Enjoy Jakarta Astro Indonesia Open
Jakarta, Indonesia
Winner: Felipe Aguilar

So now they're quoting Yogi Berra even in Chile.

Felipe Aguilar, an unknown from Chile, was discussing an uncertain moment on the way to his surprise victory in the Enjoy Jakarta Astro Indonesia Open. Said Aguilar: "...but you never know how golf is — it's not over till it's over." Aguilar's grammar was better, but that was Yogi's immortal line: "It ain't over till it's over."

Whatever the language, the point was that Aguilar, age 33, started the final round leading by two. He bogeyed the second hole, but birdied three straight from No. 9. But Jeev Milkha Singh was hot on his trail. He had eagled the sixth and birdied the eighth and then eagled the par-four 11th. Aguilar was hoping he could hold on for a playoff. "After Jeev made bogey on the 16th, I realized I was still in the game," Aguilar said. "I knew I had to make a three on the 18th for a playoff."

But he didn't need that. The usually sharp Singh bogeyed the 18th, and that's when Aguilar uttered Berra's immortal words — with a sigh of relief.

Aguilar, playing Cengkareng Golf Club in 65-62-67-68–262, 18 under par, led from the second round. Singh trailed by four strokes at worst, that in the second round, and was poised to win in the fourth until he bogeyed two of the last three holes. "It was Aguilar's day and not mine today," Singh said. "It was disappointing for me, but I guess that's golf."

Aguilar, a graduate of the European Challenge Tour, opened a huge door for himself. The tournament was co-sanctioned by the Asian and European Tours, and so the win elevated him to full eligibility. "It feels awesome," he said. "This is life-changing for me. I can play whatever I want to play."

SAIL Open
Noida, India
Winner: Mark Brown

New Zealander Mark Brown finally found his comfort zone. A four-stroke lead would do, thank you. One stroke felt too tight when he started the final round. "I was nervous when I started," said Brown. "A one-shot lead made me feel everybody was chasing me."

Brown, age 33, once a discouraged professional but now in his second full season on the Asian Tour, held up nicely and ended up taking his first Asian Tour victory by four shots in the SAIL Open. Interestingly enough, he surfaced in the third round while the others were being bounced around by the blustery February weather hitting the Jaypee Greens Golf Resort near New Delhi. In the calm first round, Australia's Tony Carolan and Scotland's Ross Bain tied for the lead with six-under-par 66s. The second round started with frost, and India's Jyoti Randhawa warmed up coming home with four birdies for 68 and a share of the lead with Carolan (69). Brown (69-69) trailed by three strokes in each round.

The blustery winds in the third round were homecooking to Brown. "It was quite like Wellington, where I have played a lot of my golf," he said, after 67 left him an uncomfortable one stroke up on Scott Hend (69) and Rhys Davies (67).

Brown actually was tougher than he thought, and he proved it under the final-round pressure. He was one under at the turn, then birdied the 12th and holed a 10-foot birdie putt at the 18th. But his four-shot margin was deceptive. It didn't materialize until Randhawa bogeyed the 16th and 17th, and Hend double-bogeyed the 18th, both falling into a tie for second with Korea's Noh Seung-yul.

"It was so emotional," Brown said. "I was remembering my father. I wish he were here to see me win."

Johnnie Walker Classic
New Delhi, India
Winner: Mark Brown

Nothing succeeds like success, the honored cliché holds. New Zealand's Mark Brown, who had scored his first victory just a week earlier, underlined the old saw by picking off the Johnnie Walker Classic in March. And he did it with a flourish, bursting to the front with five birdies on the final nine to win by three strokes at the DLF Golf Club at New Delhi, India.

Brown tagged along for three and a half rounds and came to the final nine trailing Japan's Taichiro Kiyota by four huge strokes. "I played terribly on the front side," Brown said. "I don't think I hit a fairway or green, and got to the 10th and said to myself, let's have a solid nine holes. The rest is a dream."

This was the stuff of dreams: Of those five birdies, he ran off four in succession from the 12th and then found himself leading by two when Kiyota three-putted the 17th. Brown then barely escaped trouble at the 18th when he mis-hit his second shot and seemed doomed for a watery finish. But the ball caught the edge of the green, and he two-putted for his fifth birdie and the three-stroke win that told him again he'd been smart to give up his teaching and return to competition.

Brown had become so discouraged that he left the tournament trail and spent three years on the lesson tee. But he repaired his flaws and came back, and proved himself by taking the SAIL Open the week before and now the Johnnie Walker Classic, shooting 71-68-64-67–270, 18 under par, for a comfortable three-stroke win over Kiyota and Aussies Greg Chalmers and Scott Strange. Even Brown didn't expect a second straight win.

"The last two weeks," he said, "have been a blur."

Maybank Malaysian Open
Kuala Lumpur, Malaysia
Winner: Arjun Atwal

Beauty had to be in the eye of the winner in the Maybank Malaysian Open. "The playoff wasn't pretty," India's Arjun Atwal conceded, but there was no way he would love it less. Especially not after trailing Sweden's Peter Hedblom, the defending champion, by seven shots entering the final round.

The playoff for the co-sanctioned Asian-European Tour event was a bit sloppy. Hedblom narrowly missed a winning birdie putt on the 72nd hole, leaving them tied at 18-under-par 270. Hedblom then hit his tee shot into the water on the first extra hole, but scrambled to a par. Atwal also parred. On the second extra hole, the par-three 17th, Hedblom put his tee shot 40 feet from the flag. Atwal missed the green. Hedblom three-putted for a bogey, and Atwal got up and down for a par and the win.

"Playoffs are not my thing," Hedblom said. "I've played three on the European Tour now, and lost them all."

"A win is a win," said Atwal, getting his seventh on the Asian Tour. "It's been five years, and I'm glad I got it done."

Atwal, taking a break from the American PGA Tour, wasn't part of the picture for the first three rounds. A first-round 70 left him eight behind England's Nick Dougherty, who shot a career-low 62, 10 under at Kota Permai Golf and Country Club. A 68 in the second round left Atwal six behind halfway leader Danny Chia (67–132). Then it seemed the door closed. Hedblom (65) took the lead at 17-under 199, two ahead of Australian Daniel Vancsik (64), while Atwal lost ground with another 68, falling seven behind. Then came the 64 and the dramatic finish.

"It hasn't sunk in yet," Atwal said. "Right now, I'm in a different world."

Ballentine's Championship
Jeju Island, South Korea
Winner: Graeme McDonald

The inaugural Ballentine's Championship meant more than just a victory to Northern Ireland's Graeme McDowell. It was a coming-of-age, a rite of passage. For him, it had no less than "Ryder Cup" written all over it.

"The ultimate goal is to make (captain) Nick Faldo's team in September," McDowell said. "At The K Club (in 2006), I realized I should have been on the team. And I was disappointed not to be there."

McDowell was drawing his strength along with his conclusions from his playoff victory over India's Jeev Milkha Singh at the Pinx Golf Club on South Korea's Jeju Island in mid-March. The showdown was building from the start, McDowell shooting 68-64-66-66 and Singh 68-66-64-66, whipping the course for 24-under 264s. Ireland's Paul McGinley, a former Ryder Cup hero, finished third but a distant seven shots back in the co-sanctioned event (Asian, European and Korean PGA Tours).

The final round was a stunner. Singh sprinted ahead with three birdies in his first four holes, but bogeyed the seventh. McDowell, after three birdies and a bogey, eagled the 10th against Singh's birdie. The clinchers came toward the end. McDowell birdied the 15th, Singh birdied the 16th but bogeyed the 17th. They played off at the par-four 18th and tied the first two times. On the third visit, Singh hit his approach to five feet, but McDowell fired his seven-iron second to 18 inches. Singh missed his birdie, and McDowell holed his for the win and a hungry look at the Ryder Cup.

"I feel I've arrived now as a three-time winner on the European Tour," McDowell said. "This is the year for me."

But would Nick Faldo agree?

Asian Tour International
Chonburi, Thailand
Winner: Lin Wen-tang

Taiwan's Lin Wen-tang was hoisting the trophy with one hand and hoping someone would put a telephone in the other. "Last night I told my wife that I will win it, but she said not to be overconfident," Lin said. "Now I can't wait to call her."

Confident? Lin trailed through the first three rounds, then fired a sizzling eight-under-par 64 to run off with the inaugural Asian Tour International at Pattana Golf Resort in Thailand. Lin's third Asian Tour win came from some impressive numbers: 65-68-68-64–265, a whopping 23 under par for an easy five-stroke margin over South Korea's Noh Seung-yul, a mere 16, who turned pro in 2007. Noh wasn't playing like a teenager — he was tied for the lead through the first three rounds.

Lin, trailing Noh and Scotland's Ross Bain by two going into the final round, exploded out of the starting gate and kept on going. He birdied the first and eagled the par-five second, and rang up five more birdies through the 15th and was leading Noh by three when lightning brought a suspension of play.

"I came back out and I kept my game steady and pulled through," Lin said. Someone was going to have to catch him. He played carefully coming in for a trouble-free win. Lin got a bigger cushion when Noh came back from the suspension and double-bogeyed the 16th hole.

Noh opened with 64 that included eagles at the par-five second and 11th, both on 15-foot putts. A cool customer, he needed a birdie at the 18th for 68 to stay tied for the lead in the third round, and he got it.

"I'm happy with my performance this week," Noh said. "Overall, it has been a great experience, and two second-place finishes from two events is not a bad feat."

Philippine Open
Manila, Philippines
Winner: Angelo Que

It seems golf became this basic for Angelo Que: A seed planted in the Open Championship qualifier bore fruit in the Philippine Open just a week later.

"Making it through the Open qualifier has definitely given me a boost and helped lift my game," Que said. Thus the newly confident Que came from eight strokes behind after 36 holes, then nursed a one-stroke lead all the way home for his second Asian Tour victory and his first since 2004. Que opened with no great promise (73-71) and trailed Japanese rookie Kodai Ichihara (66-70) by seven strokes, then eight. Then Ichihara faded, and Que closed with 66-73 for a five-under-par 283 total on Manila's short, tight Wack Wack golf course for a one-stroke win over Malaysia's Danny Chia.

Que bolted from the gates in the third round, going five under for the first five holes, including a tap-in eagle at No. 4. "I was hitting it close, and considering the very tough conditions, I'm glad to end the day at six under," Que said. Ichihara faded, but up popped Chia to challenge Que in the final round.

"I woke up feeling lucky," Chia said. He enjoyed a bit of luck at the par-five No. 4, where he hit his four-iron second shot over the green, then chipped in for an eagle. He posted his 66 and 284 total early.

Que was one over through the 13th hole, birdied the 14th, then bogeyed the 17th and was back to a one-stroke lead. Coming down the 18th, he could see Chia's score on the leaderboard and knew what he had to do.

"I needed to par the 18th," Que said. "So I focused on my breathing exercise." He put his approach off the edge of the green, chipped back 20 feet to tap-in range, and got the win.

Volvo China Open
Beijing, China
Winner: Damien McGrane

The amazing thing about Damien McGrane's victory in the Volvo China Open wasn't so much that he won by a whopping nine strokes, and not so much that he finally got his first victory. The amazing thing was that he managed to keep his head above the water.

A powerful late-April storm hit Beijing CBD International in the final round, lifting scores in the Asian and European Tour co-sanctioned event. But McGrane, who started the day ahead by three strokes, shot a steady one-over-par 73 for a 10-under 278 total. Tied for a distant second were French rookie Michael Lorenzo-Vera (79) and England's Simon Griffiths (74) and Oliver Wilson (79).

"I have been thinking about winning one tournament for so long, and this week, everything went my way," said McGrane, age 37.

Lorenzo-Vera, age 23, a European Tour rookie, led through the first two rounds on 67-69, and confessed to a case of nerves. "I always look super-relaxed, but the hands are always shaking," Lorenzo-Vera said. He shot 72 in the third round, but the rains got to him in the fourth. He shot 79.

McGrane, runner-up in the Indian Masters in February, barged ahead in the third round. He birdied the last two holes for 68 to go three ahead of Lorenzo-Vera (72) and Wilson (70). But he wasn't comfortable. "I finished third the last time I was leading going into the third round," McGrane said.

Nobody could break par in the downpour the last day. McGrane started shakily, bogeying twice in the first eight holes. Then he settled down, birdied two out of three, and was home free.

"I've won once, so the world is my oyster," McGrane said. "My first win — it's what I've worked for since I was a little boy."

BMW Asian Open
Shanghai, China
Winner: Darren Clarke

If you can't get the death of your wife out of your mind, if you're trying to raise two young sons, and if you let the lead slip away and you're facing a 40-footer on the last hole, well, your chances of winning aren't all that promising.

It was yes to all of the above for Darren Clarke, but the Northern Irishman rolled in that 40-footer for birdie to take the BMW Asian Open by one stroke over the Netherlands' Robert-Jan Derksen at Tomson Shanghai Pudong Golf Club in the co-sanctioned Asian and European Tour event. It was his 11th European Tour win but his first since 2003.

"This is the toughest one of them all," he said. "This win is for Tyrone and Conot."

Clarke led by a stroke going into the final round, but bogeyed three of four holes from the par-three 14th. Fortunately for him, Derksen took a watery double bogey at the 14th, falling two behind. "I had a bad lie," Derksen said.

Clarke, with 71, was four behind Australian Peter O'Malley (67) in the first round. The nearly retired Greg Norman, age 53, also shot 71 but was never a threat.

Derksen, a two-time European Tour winner, surfaced in the second round on 69–139 and tied for the lead with China's Zhang Lian-wei. Clarke took the third-round lead with 67–207. "It's been awhile since I led," he said. "I just hope I can continue doing what I've been doing." And Clarke did, in a way. He had that rocky stretch in the final round, but got the gift double bogey from Derksen, who would then pull even with four holes to play. Clarke's last chance was the 40-footer at the final hole.

"I wasn't going to lag it up," Clarke said. "I wanted to give myself a chance. It was tracking six feet out. Sometimes it's meant to go in."

GS Caltex Maekyung Open
Seoul, Korea
Winner: Hwang Inn-choon

It could be called the "Noh-Watch," named after Korea's Noh Seung-yul. Noh, a rookie on the Asian Tour, came to the GS Caltex Maekyung Open in early May just under a month from his 17th birthday. Observers were waiting for him to become the youngest winner ever on the tour. He had that kind of talent.

Noh came within a playoff of making the Maekyung Open his first. Korea's Hwang Inn-choon beat him with a par on the first extra hole, after they tied at nine-under 279 at Nam Seoul Country Club. But Noh, who won his playing card at the qualifying tournament the previous December, still was having an outstanding rookie year. This was his third runner-up finish in five starts, and the nearly $67,000 he had won lifted him to 11th on the Order of Merit.

Hwang, after starting with 71-67-73, was four off Noh's lead going into the final round and closed with four-under 68 to clinch a tie. Noh (69-70-68) shot par 72 in the final round. In the playoff at the par-four 18th, Noh's approach missed the green while Hwang was on in two. Noh chipped short and bogeyed. Hwang then two-putted for the victory.

"I am very happy as I didn't expect to win," Hwang said. "Before the last round, I was four shots behind. I wasn't even thinking of winning. I was playing my own game."

The lead was batted about. Kang Ji-man posted a seven-birdie 67 for the first-round lead, and Jun Tae-hyun shot 68 to tie with Hwang (67) at 138 in the second. In the third, Noh made three birdies and an eagle for 68 and a two-stroke lead. "I'm feeling better about my game after every round," Noh said. And so the Noh-Watch goes on.

Pine Valley Beijing Open
Beijing, China
Winner: Hiroyuki Fujita

Japanese veteran Hiroyuki Fujita was just trying to have some fun — as the modern expression goes — when he took the lead at the halfway point of the Pine Valley Beijing Open. Before long, he was having a party, wrapping up the first tournament ever co-sanctioned by the Asian and Japan Tours and the China Golf Association.

Fujita warmed up with 67 in the first round, two behind Thailand's Chinnarat Phadungsil and Malaysia's Iain Steel, who shared first with seven-under-par 65s. Chinnarat, age 19, a two-time winner on the Asian Tour, ran off three closing birdies for his 65. At No. 7, he converted a bad lie in a divot hole into a birdie and noted, "China is a lucky place for me." But his luck ran out the next day, when Fujita racked up nine birdies against two bogeys for 65 and a two-stroke lead.

Fujita separated himself from the field in the third round with a strong par 72 in heavy winds that carried him six strokes ahead of the field. "The wind was extremely strong and I tried to stay even par," Fujita said. And he planned the same strategy for the finish. "It is expected to rain tomorrow, so I will adopt a safe approach," he said.

The weather forecast was more than accurate. Cold, wind and rain hit the final round. Fujita was one over after nine holes, but stretched his lead to four with a birdie at the 13th and was delighted to walk away with 72 and a 276 total and the three-stroke win over countryman Shintaro Kai (68).

"It was a tough, tough day," said Fujita, who was solid in the miserable conditions with two birdies and two bogeys in his 72. "I had a six-stroke lead coming in," Fujita said, "but I felt the pressure."

Bangkok Airways Open
Koh Samui, Thailand
Winner: Thaworn Wiratchant

Among golf's great axioms is this one: The golf ball doesn't know how old you are. Well, neither does the golf course, as Thai veteran Thaworn Wiratchant discovered to his immense satisfaction in the Bangkok Airways Open.

"I thought I was getting too old to play on this golf course, but I guess age is just a number," said Thaworn, age 41, after making the tournament a record 10th Asian Tour victory, and by a comfortable three strokes. The course he respected so much was the demanding par-71 Santiburi Samui Country Club course, where he shared the first-round lead, dropped back, then rallied in the final round, posting rounds of 66-69-68-68–271, 13 under par.

This was after a running battle with the bold Filipino, Antonio Lascuna, who rode a new cross-handed putting grip to a five-under 66 for a share of the first-round lead. "I usually chalk up 34 putts, but today I had 25, so I'm thrilled with this change," Lascuna said. A second 66 gave him the solo lead in the second round, then he started to fade and Taiwan's Lien Lu-sen stepped up with 66, leaving Thaworn tied for second, three behind. Then came the big break in the fourth round.

While the challengers were fading, Thaworn bounced back from an opening bogey with three birdies on the front nine, then ran into trouble. His second shot at the 15th ended up unplayable and he bogeyed. "But when I sank the birdie putt on the 17th," he said, "I knew the title was mine."

The great irony was that Thaworn's biggest challenge might have come from countryman Prayad Marksaeng. Prayad was on the fringe all the way, then finished four strokes behind — the four he wasted in a quadruple bogey-eight at the 16th.

Singha Thailand PGA Championship
Chiang Rai, Thailand
Winner: Mo Joong-kyung

It had been awhile since Korea's Mo Joong-kyung knew what it felt like to win. Twelve years, in fact, and then it was just once. He picked a good time to win again.

This was the debut of the Singha Thailand PGA Championship, so a few introductory fireworks were in order. First came native son Prayad Marksaeng conquering all four par-fives at the Santiburi Country Club for birdies, for five-under 67 and the first-round lead. Next, the Philippines' Juvic Pagunsan vaulted into the lead by a stroke over Prayad with an electrifying 63. He made seven birdies in a row, 10 overall. "I was in a zone," Pagunsan said, in understatement.

Next came Mo, age 36, in the third round with a different kind of fireworks — an eagle, three birdies and two bogeys on the last nine, but it was enough for 69 to tie Pagunsan (71) for the lead at 14-under 202. Now he was in strange territory. He had won once, the 1996 Guam Open.

"If I'd made one mistake, I would have been gone," Mo said. "I was just trying to keep the ball on the fairways and greens and make putts. Luckily, I did that all day." Mo broke into a two-stroke lead with 33 on the first nine, and after a bogey at the 10th, he and Pagunsan matched three straight birdies from the 11th. Mo birdied the 15th from 10 feet, going two ahead. He stayed there until the par-five 18th when Pagunsan, desperately trying to catch him, ran a 25-foot eagle putt well past the hole. Mo birdied for 65 and a 21-under 267 total, and won by three.

Worldwide Selangor Masters
Kuala Lumpur, Malaysia
Winner: Ben Leong

The Worldwide Selangor Masters, new on the Asian Tour, was so battered by rain it was difficult to tell who was doing what. But when things finally got sorted out, the tour had a rising young star on its hands when Malaysia's Ben Leong, age 22, held off Thai star Thongchai Jaidee for his first victory. And what did it mean to the young new champion? Fame? Fortune? Not quite.

"Finally," Leong said, "I don't have to go back to Q school now."

The tournament, played at the Seri Selangor Golf Club, Malaysia's first public course, was added to the Asian Tour schedule in June, backed by the Selangor State Government of Malaysia. It lifted the tour to a record 29 tournaments and US$38 million in prize money.

Leong played the par-71 course in 71-65-64-69–269, 15 under par, to beat Thongchai by one. Malaysia's Iain Steel was a distant third, nine back. Leong wasn't the only young force in the field. Thailand's Chinnarat Phadungsil, age 19, shot a course-record 64 for the first-round lead. He would finish tied for 11th, but he had made his presence known.

In the final round, Leong was breathing easier when Thongchai took back-to-back bogeys after the turn. But quality tells. Thongchai bounced back with three straight birdies from the 12th.

"That's what great players do," Leong said. "I was telling myself to stay in the present and don't get ahead of myself." He did, saving par at the 16th from five feet and at the 17th from eight feet. The crisis came at the par-four 18th: Leong faced a five-footer for bogey. After Thongchai missed a birdie from 20 feet, Leong rolled in his bogey putt for the victory.

"I was pretty confident with the putt," Leong said, "but I was just trying to keep the devil out of the head."

Brunei Open
Jerudong, Brunei
Winner: Rick Kulacz

The arrival of a new star is usually preceded by some kind of fanfare, but that wasn't the case with Australian rookie Rick Kulacz, unless you count a modest amateur record and some local events. So Kulacz was largely dismissed when he took the third-round lead in the Brunei Open at the Empire Hotel and Country Club. He was, after all, only 23 years old and a rookie on the Asian Tour. It was after the third round that he said: "If I play well and win, so be it. If someone else plays better than I do, good on him."

But no one did, and Kulacz holed a sensational bunker shot on the first playoff hole for his first win.

Korea's Young Nam took the first-round lead with 64, but fell out with a triple bogey on the last hole in the second round. Ted Oh, another Korean, took the halfway lead on 66–131, and in the third round, he birdied three of his first five holes then unraveled when he got too aggressive in the heavy winds. "I tried to go for the shots in tough conditions, and it backfired," he said.

Kulacz, meanwhile, holed five-foot putts for birdies on the second and eighth holes, a 10-footer at the 13th and a 30-footer at the 16th for a 67 and 12-under 201 total. In the final round, he shook off a double bogey at the first, missed a 15-foot birdie putt at the 18th, and shot 70 and was tied by Taiwan's Lu Wen-teh (67). The playoff ended at the first extra hole, with Kulacz holing out from a bunker for a birdie.

"I've been hitting into bunkers all week," Kulacz said. "I finally found one that was sitting up perfectly."

Pertamina Indonesia President Invitational
Jakarta, Indonesia
Winner: Scott Hend

There had been a lot of jockeying for position for three rounds, and then the Pertamina Indonesia President Invitational came down to Taiwan's Lin Wen-tang and Malaysia's Iain Steel. Steel was posting his second consecutive 66 in the third round, and Lin had run off six straight birdies and shot a seven-under-par 65, and they tied at 15-under 201 going into the final round. Scott Hend, the big-hitting Australian and former U.S. PGA Tour player, was trailing by five. That first victory he had been seeking seemed out of reach.

But then things took a strange turn. Steel ran into one of those days and shot 76 at the Damai Indah Golf and Country Club in Jakarta. "It was my real chance to win without having to do anything spectacular," said Steel, who had finished in the top 10 in his last two Asian Tour events. Lin, who won the Asian Tour International in March, hit his tee shot into the water at the par-three 15th and double-bogeyed. "I was too fast off the tee," he said.

Hend, second at the SAIL Open earlier, eagled the par-five 13th to close to within one of Lin, then took the lead with a par at the 15th to Lin's double bogey. "I was thinking that if I shot a six under today, I'll be happy no matter what the outcome," Hend said. "There was no real pressure." He got a final birdie at the 17th.

The pressure was on Steel and Lin. Steel slipped to 76 and finished sixth. Lin shot 74 and finished solo second, three strokes behind Hend, who hit his six-under 66 on the nose for a 16-under 272 total and that first victory by three.

"I had a few runner-up finishes, which is nice, financially," Hend said. "But there is nothing like winning a tournament."

Mercuries Taiwan Masters
Taipei, Taiwan
Winner: Lu Wen-teh

Taiwan's Lu Wen-teh made an amazing discovery as the Asian Tour moved through September — the Fountain of Youth, or what serves the same for him. At age 45 now, Lu survived a late-round wobble to take the Mercuries Taiwan Masters for the second straight year and the fourth time overall.

"The win has made me feel young again," Lu said beaming. "It's a great feeling." Yes, the Taiwan Golf and Country Club is Lu's home course, but his age might negate some of the home course advantage. So it could be argued that sheer ability and determination are what pulled him through when three straight bogeys plus Thaworn Wiratchant's birdie at the 13th cut his lush five-stroke lead to a mere one. Thaworn bogeyed the 17th and Lu rolled home a tricky three-foot par putt at the 18th.

Lu opened with 70-67 and was three off the halfway lead after Taiwan's Lin Wen-hong shot a course-record 63, then uttered a fateful observation. "I've matched the course record before," he said, "but I collapsed under the pressure in the following round." It seemed he crumbled again. He shot 78 in the third round while Lu was posting 69 for a one-stroke lead over his old Thai friend, Thaworn.

Said Thaworn: "Even after my bogey on the 17th, I was telling myself I could still do it. Well, there will always be another day."

Lu went ahead by five through the 11th, then stumbled to the three con-secutive bogeys. "I was being too aggressive and trying to push myself even more," he said. "I told myself to relax." And he did, for a one-under 71, a 277 total and the two-stroke victory.

"It shows," Lu said, "there is still a lot left in me."

Asia-Pacific Panasonic Open
Ibaraki, Osaka
Winner: Hideto Tanihara

See Japan Tour section.

Kolon-Hana Bank Korea Open
Cheonan, South Korea
Winner: Bae Sang-moon

It was a kind of replay of the recent Ryder Cup, what with the two key heroes in the Kolon-Hana Bank Korea Open at Seoul's Woo Jeong Hills Country Club — the Americans' Anthony Kim and Europe's Ian Poulter.

"I'll be playing with some famous golfers tomorrow," said Korea's Kim Wi-joong, the leader going into the final round. "So I'll try to focus on my game."

Alas, he couldn't. The glare was too much for some, but one man shrugged it off — Korea's Bae Sang-moon. He was close for three rounds, shooting 67-70-67. In the fourth round, as Anthony Kim couldn't get going and Poulter stumbled late, Bae kept his head and plucked the championship with a steady hand. Bae was one under on the front, birdied No. 10 and parred in for 69, an 11-under 273 total and a one-stroke win over Poulter. Kim shot 71 and was two back.

"The birdie on the 10th gave me the confidence I needed to keep it going in the closing holes," Bae said.

Anthony Kim started out like a winner, taking the first-round lead with 64. "I'm satisfied as I did a lot of good things out there," Kim said. Poulter bogeyed the 16th and shot 69. "If I keep playing as steady as I did today, I'll stand a strong chance," he said.

Kim's satisfaction was short-lived, and he finished tied for third. "But I'll be back and I'll be a much better player when I return," he promised.

Poulter was leading down the home stretch until he bogeyed the 16th and 18th and shot 70. "I came here to win but I'm going home second, so I'm not very happy," he said.

Then there was Bae's view. "I don't think I've realized the magnitude of my win," he said. "I've very proud of myself."

Hero Honda Indian Open
New Delhi, India
Winner: Liang Wen-chong

"I feel good about my game," China's Liang Wen-chong was saying — unconvincingly, it seemed — "but this is the first time I've been in this position for so long, so it's new to me." Those were the words of a golfer bending under the pressure. But he didn't crack, and he walked away with the Hero Honda Indian Open by the grace of birdies on the last two holes.

It was a just reward for a golfer who opened with a stunning 12-under-par 60 at the Delhi Golf Club, in New Delhi. "Everything worked well today," said Liang, in the understatement of the season.

It was a little different the next day. "I lost my concentration on the back nine," Liang said. Even so, he managed a six-birdie 71 for a 131 total and kept his five-stroke lead, this time over Daniel Chopra (70), who birdied four of his last nine holes and noted, "Frankly, I played much better than what the score suggests."

The pressure got to Liang in the third round, and he wasted four birdies with a bogey out of a bunker at the 14th, and he double-bogeyed the 15th for 71–202. His lead was down to one behind Australian rookie Darren Beck. Could Liang hold on in the final round?

Beck himself was wondering. He'd finished with a seven-birdie 65 and was on the practice green, expecting a playoff. Liang tied him with a birdie at the 17th, then at the 18th he chipped to three feet. He would win with a birdie. Then Beck got his answer — a roar from the 18th green.

"This is an important win for me," said Liang, who finished with a 16-under 272 total. "It proves I'm heading in the right direction."

Midea China Classic
Guangzhou, China
Winner: Noh Seung-yul

It's not often that a 17-year-old can keep a straight face on a golf course. But then, it's not often that a 17-year-old is chasing a victory in a professional tournament. Meet Korea's Noh Seung-yul, coming of age in a hurry at the Midea China Classic, the third-youngest winner on the Asian Tour, who held off Australian veteran Terry Pilkadaris, age 34, for a one-stroke victory.

Why no smile? "I always try to control my emotions when I play, as I tend to focus solely on my game," Noh said. "Maybe I should learn to relax more now and enjoy my game."

Noh trailed just once, when his opening 66 left him two behind Taiwan's Lu Wei-chih. Then Noh took charge, adding 66-67-68 for a 17-under-par 267 total, one better than Pilkadaris's four 67s at Royal Orchid International at Guangzhou.

"Playing with the more experienced players on the Asian Tour has really made me a better player," said Noh, taking the halfway lead by two strokes. He went up in the third by three over Korea's Park Jun-won (66) and Pilkadaris (67), who made a loud start with an eagle at the first.

"I did not let this distract me in any way," Noh said. "I continued to play my own game, which was to attack the pins and not make bogeys."

Noh's big test came in the final round, when he bogeyed the third and was tied by Park. At his age, Noh could have folded, and to cheers. But he just got tougher. He birdied the fourth and sixth and was back up by two. Park slipped, but Pilkadaris made three birdies after the turn and it was head-to-head from there. When Pilkadaris missed a birdie at the 18th, Noh was free to break into a smile.

Macau Open
Macau
Winner: David Gleeson

Sometimes good things happen to one who goes after them. As Australia's David Gleeson was telling his caddie, "I wanted to win this week by as many shots as possible. I also told myself that if I don't go for it, I won't have a chance, so I'm happy that I went for it."

Gleeson turned that resolve into a wire-to-wire victory in the Macau Open, his second win on the Asian Tour and six grinding years in the making.

Gleeson opened with 64-64, which announced his intentions all across Macau Country Club. The 128 gave him a five-stroke lead at the halfway point. "A 14 under after two days is a good score," Gleeson said. But his lead shrank to two in the third round when he shot 69 and Taiwan's Kao Bo-song closed in with 65. "Leading the round made me stressful and I had to think of a game plan out there while taking the wind into consideration," said Gleeson. He bogeyed the 16th but birdied the last two and then braced himself for the final round.

"I hope to recall my past success and manage the demons by not allowing the negative thoughts to creep in," Gleeson said. "I'm confident that if I do the right job, I can win it."

Gleeson started the final round with a bogey at the first hole and fell into a tie with Kao when he birdied the second. Then Gleeson rallied for five birdies, against two bogeys, and left himself a one-foot putt at the 18th for the win.

"I reached the little goals that I had set all day, which proved to be the key," Gleeson said. "On the 18th, I just had to avoid the water, and I knew I had it once the ball landed on the green."

Iskandar Johor Open
Johor, Malaysia
Winner: Retief Goosen

Retief Goosen, figuratively, tiptoed right up to the brink before rallying in time to keep alive his record of at least one individual or team victory a year since 1995. The odds, however, weren't encouraging in the Iskandar Johor Open in Malaysia late in October. He trailed by seven in the first round, by five in the second round and by four going into the final. Then a superb four-under-par 66 at the Royal Johor Country Club to sprint to a two-stroke victory.

"It means a lot," said Goosen, two-time U.S. Open champion. "It's been a drought. Coming down the stretch, you haven't won for a while — it's nice to finish it off with some good shots." It was Goosen's fourth international title and his first since the 2007 Qatar Masters.

Goosen started the final round four behind Sweden's Niclas Fasth, and got off and running with a birdie at the par-five second. Then he eagled the par-five fourth, holing out his third shot from 69 yards with a 60-degree wedge. "That," said Goosen, "was a good hole."

He dropped a 15-foot putt for a birdie at the 10th to tie Thailand's Thaworn Wiratchant and took the lead when Thaworn bogeyed it. Goosen pulled ahead by three with two more birdies — from 15 feet at No. 14 and six feet at No. 15. Thaworn, looking for his career 11th win, got within two of Goosen with a birdie at No. 14. But that was as close as he would get.

Goosen finished with a bogey-free 66 and a 12-under 276 total, and so his record was safe for another year.

HSBC Champions
Shanghai, China
Winner: Sergio Garcia

Spain's Sergio Garcia had just won the rain-delayed HSBC Champions and hadn't yet settled into his digs as the new No. 2 in the World Ranking, and someone asked what was he going to do for an encore. What could he say at a time like this?

"I think my next goal is to win a major," Garcia said, after his playoff victory over England's Oliver Wilson, his Ryder Cup teammate of two months earlier. "I've been trying for quite a while, but winning a major would be the next goal."

Garcia entered the HSBC Champions picture in the second round with an eagle at the par-four 14th and birdies at the 16th and 18th for a four-under-par 68. He was on his way to the trophy against a strong international field at — fittingly enough — Shanghai's Sheshan International Golf Club for the Asian-European Tour co-sanctioned event.

Garcia then started the final round of the weather-battered tournament two strokes behind Wilson and closed with 68 to tie him at 274. They parred the first playoff hole. On the second, Wilson missed his birdie try, but Garcia, often troubled with the putter, dropped his seven-footer for the win.

There was, inevitably, another question for Garcia. Now that you're No. 2, can you get to No. 1, past the recuperating Tiger Woods?

"Taking over Tiger ... depends a little bit on how much Tiger takes off, and if I keep playing well," Garcia said. "It's possible, mainly because he's been injured."

The HSBC Champions marked the start of the 2009 Race for Dubai, the European Tour's $10 million season-ending bonus pool for the top 15 on the money list, with $2 million going to No. 1. The pot of gold was stirring interest in a number of U.S. PGA Tour players.

Barclays Singapore Open
Singapore
Winner: Jeev Milkha Singh

A golfer makes a name for himself by, one, going out into the world of competition, and two, by handling the world competition when it comes to him. That's the thumbnail description of India's Jeev Milkha Singh, the

Asian Tour star who has also made his mark on the world stage and who underlined it when he turned back both Ireland's Padraig Harrington and South Africa's Ernie Els to win the Barclays Singapore Open in November. And an impressive performance it was.

Singh, who had won in Europe and Japan earlier in the season, started the final round five strokes off the lead and raced into contention with 33 on the first nine. He birdied the 11th to take what seemed a safe lead, but bogeys at Nos. 13 and 16 put him in the fire. With a one-stroke edge coming to the 18th, it was time to get cautious.

"I wasn't hitting my driver that well, so I took a three wood," said Singh. "At least be sure of a five, and if you make a four, great. I was fortunate the other guys didn't make a four."

Harrington, Singh's playing companion, matched his outward 33 but double-bogeyed the 16th after an approach shot in the water. At the 18th, he missed a five-foot birdie chance that would have forced a playoff. Els holed a 20-footer for birdie at the 16th, then had a 15-footer for birdie at the 18th, but missed. Thailand's Chapchai Nirat led by three going into the final round, but blew to a 78. Phil Mickelson closed with 75 and finished 11th.

"I couldn't have asked for more," said Singh. "I think I am a very fortunate man to win. Those boys put on a good effort out there."

UBS Hong Kong Open
Fanling, Hong Kong
Winner: Lin Wen-tang

Taiwan's Lin Wen-tang was four feet away from winning the UBS Hong Kong Open on the final hole of the last round and missed that putt. But thanks, he thought, to a bit of divine intervention in the playoff he ended up only a few inches away. He couldn't miss this one. He tapped in for a birdie to pluck the title away from Northern Ireland's Rory McIlroy and Italy's Francesco Molinari.

McIlroy and Molinari each closed with 65 to catch Lin, who two-putted the 18th for 67 and a 265 total at the Hong Kong Golf Club. They had outrun a classy field that included Oliver Wilson, Bernhard Langer and Jeev Milkha Singh at 268, and Colin Montgomerie at 270.

The playoff turned into a question of who would survive the mistakes. At the first extra hole, Lin hooked his tee shot into the trees, but he lofted a great recovery shot to within four feet and made the birdie putt. McIlroy got there conventionally and followed him in from three feet. Molinari ended up needing a 15-footer to stay alive, but he missed and was out of the running.

On the second extra hole, it was McIlroy's turn to make the mistake. He also hit into the trees on the left and made a spectacular escape, hooking a gap wedge 40 yards around the trees to the back of the green. Lin, however, had hit a good drive and flipped a pitch next to the hole.

"It was like help from the gods," Lin said. "It cannot be described, how I feel. All I can do is use my smile to say thank you to you all."

Omega Mission Hills World Cup
Shenzhen, China
Winners: Sweden (Robert Karlsson and Henrik Stenson)

Sweden's Robert Karlsson and Henrik Stenson, the pre-tournament favorites in the 28-team field at the Omega Mission Hills World Cup, weren't looking too convincing. They hadn't led, and worse, they started the fourth round four strokes behind Spain. Then five birdies on the front nine caught the Spaniards, Miguel Angel Jimenez and Pablo Larrazabal.

Then the Swedes birdied Nos. 11, 12, 14 and 15, sprinting four ahead of the Spaniards and finishing with a nine-under 63, turning the tournament into something of a rout and Sweden's first World Cup victory since 1991. They finished at 261, beating Spain by three strokes, and they were a distant 11 strokes ahead of Australia's Brendan Jones and Richard Green and Japan's Ryuji Imada and Toru Taniguchi, tied for third.

"I thought it was our turn today," said Stenson, who had yet to win this season in individual play and it was now November. "I'm starting to run out of tournaments. But winning for Sweden is nice. It's been awhile." The win wrapped up a fine season for Karlsson, a two-time winner and leading money winner on the European Tour.

The World Cup, played at fourballs (better ball) in the first and third rounds and at foursomes (alternate shot) in the second and fourth, was held at Mission Hills, at Shenzhen, China, and it was anybody's tournament from the start:

• First Round: Martin Kaymer and Alex Cejka gave Germany the lead with a 10-under-par 62 in fourballs.

• Second Round: Miguel Angel Jimenez and Pablo Larrazabal combined in foursomes for a nine-under 63, giving Spain a four-stroke lead at 127.

• Third Round: Richard Green dropped a four-footer for birdie on the last hole, joining Brendan Jones to give Australia a 63 in fourballs and a tie with Spain at 22-under 194.

Then, as Stenson said, it was Sweden's turn in the final round.

Hana Bank Vietnam Masters
Ho Chi Minh City, Vietnam
Winner: Thongchai Jaidee

It was a great time for birthday gifts — literally. Gift No. 1: Thongchai Jaidee's son, Kittiuch, was born on December 5. That was the gift to Thongchai. Gift No. 2: Thongchai then won the Hana Bank Vietnam Masters, and that was his gift to his son.

Someday Thongchai will sit down with the lad and tell him how it all happened, how dad had to battle from behind to forge a tie, and then win in a three-way playoff. It was his ninth Asian Tour victory, ending a two-year drought.

"This win is dedicated to my family, especially my two-day-old son," said the Thai veteran. "He has given me inspiration and the drive to win."

And the inspiration showed in Thongchai's charge at the finish. He had started the final round tied for the lead with Korea's Pyo Suk-min and Japan's Kodai Ichihara. They faded, but up stepped Wales' Rhys Davies and Australia's Andrew Dodt, and Thongchai suddenly was in danger of falling short. Both had already finished with birdies at the 18th, Davies for 66 and Dodt for 63, to tie at 15-under-par 273. That left Thongchai having to tie them to stay alive for a chance at the victory. Which he did, with 67.

Davies missed the best chance to win on the first playoff hole when his three-foot birdie putt didn't find the hole. Dodt bowed out with a par on the second hole, and then there were two. On the third extra hole, Davies drove into a bunker and Thongchai found the fairway, and when he chipped on, he faced a five-foot putt for a par and the victory. It was time to sing "Happy Birthday."

Johnnie Walker Cambodian Open
Siem Reap, Cambodia
Winner: Thongchai Jaidee

Thongchai Jaidee was turning the Asian Tour into one long birthday party. He had won the Vietnam Masters in early December and dedicated it to his newborn son. Then came the Johnnie Walker Cambodian Open the following week, and after the proud papa ran away with it by six strokes, here came another gift.

"I'm really happy," he said, "and this win goes out to my son."

And it was a historic win. Thongchai had now matched countryman Thaworn Wiratchant's record of 10 Asian Tour victories. He won the Vietnam Masters in a playoff, but this one was a breeze. Thongchai posted four rounds in the 60s — 68-66-64-66 for a 24-under-par 264 total at the Phokeethra Country Club.

Thongchai entered the final round leading by five and suffered a slight attack of nerves and bogeyed the first hole. He settled down quickly and birdied Nos. 3 and 4, then four straight from No. 9, and added the Nos. 14 and 16.

"I played really well all week," Thongchai said. "I only had four bogeys throughout the four rounds, and I know my game is all coming back now."

With the tournament pretty much decided by Thongchai's romp, eyes turned to two other competitions.

One was who would finish second. The race came down to Singapore's Lam Chih Bing and America's Anthony Kang. Lam was zeroed in. He shot the front nine in a four-birdie, two-bogey 34, then birdied four of the last six holes for 65 to Kang's 71.

The other competition was the Race to 65 — the 65th place on the Order of Merit, the last spot on the tour's exempt list. India's Gaganjeet Bhullar started the round three behind but swept ahead with a day's-best 64. His secret: "I did a lot of yoga," he said.

Volvo Masters of Asia
Bangkok, Thailand
Winner: Lam Chih Bing

Singapore's Lam Chih Bing figured it was finally his time to win, and he was so sure of it that he put it in writing. Well, in a text message, anyway. "I felt really good," Lam said, "and I texted my coach (Andrew Welsford) and told him I felt I was ready to win." And so he did, taking his first Asian Tour victory by two strokes.

"I have won a bunch of small ones before, but this is just unbelievable," Lam said.

Lam had been denied enough. He was second in the Johnnie Walker Cambodian Open the previous week, and earlier he'd challenged in the Barclays Singapore Open. He neglected to mention that he'd be cutting it close. It came down to the Volvo Masters of Asia — the final event on the 2008 Asian Tour, and then the final round.

The third round had ended in gridlock traffic atop the leaderboard, with Lam and five others tied for the lead. In the final round, Lam edged ahead with a 34 on the front nine, then broke free on the back, turning some shining iron play into four birdies, three of them down the stretch, the 15th, 16th and 18th, for a bogey-free 67 and a two-stroke win at 14-under 274 at Thai Country Club in Bangkok.

"It was such a jam-packed leaderboard," Lam said. "I'm just so glad I went out and finished the job."

He didn't exactly coast home, though. Thailand's Chapchai Nirat shot 31 on the back for 67 to finish second. Australia's Terry Pilkadaris had a run of four birdies coming home for 66 and finished third.

But anybody privy to Lam's text messages would know this was a fight for second place from the beginning. Said Lam: "It just felt like it was my week."

Omega China Tour

If any one episode in the 2008 season showed how far Chinese golf has come, it would be in the Omega China Tour's Sofitel Championship in May. In fact, it was in the finish that three "generations" of Chinese golf came face-to-face. These were Zhang Lian-wei, the father of Chinese golf, now age 42, clearly the class of the land; Liao Gui-ming, 28, reaching his prime, and the future, represented by James Su Dong, an 18-year-old amateur.

The Sofitel Championship seemed to be Su's for the taking. He was leading down the home stretch, but then made a kid's mistake at the par-four 16th, pulling out the driver when caution was called for. He hit his tee shot into the water and triple-bogeyed. Zhang and Liao came to the 18th tied for the lead, and Su had a four-foot birdie putt to join them. But he missed it. "I don't know what I'm feeling," Su said.

Liao closed with 74, Zhang had 71 and they tied at 10-under 278. Liao then beat Zhang in the playoff for his first tour victory. "The pressure has been building up," Liao said. "It has been a long time coming." And Zhang had already won the season-opening Guangzhou Championship.

For a while, it seemed the Guangzhou was going to have the Omega China Tour's first winner who wasn't from Mainland China. Taiwan's Chan Yih-shin and Hsu Mong-nan, both making their tour debuts, were also making good moves. Then Zhang, the 2007 champion, restored order at the Dragon Lake Golf Club. He started the final round leading by two, and went on to win by four as Chan crumbled to 75 and Hsu shot 73. "I was really nervous, I was too urgent," Chan said. The seasoned Zhang shot 73 for a three-under 285 total and won by four strokes. "I was always confident," Zhang said. "I believe in myself and play my game."

Zhang was bent on making it two in a row in the Dell Championship at the Orient (Xiamen) Club. But Li Chao, age 27, a former soccer goalie, had other ideas. Li, playing just ahead of Zhang in the final round, turned for home and took the lead with three birdies in the next four holes. But it was his par at the 17th that saved his round. He was leading by a stroke when he left a long birdie putt 10 feet short. Then he dropped that one for the save. "My putt on 17 was the winning shot," Li said. "I was in danger of a bogey." Li closed with a four-under 66 and a six-under 274 total to win by three, taking his eighth victory in 20 events.

Taiwan's Tsai Chi-huang gave the tour the third back-to-back winner in its short history, taking the inaugural Luxehills Championship (rescheduled from May because of the Sichuan earthquake) and the Tianjin Championship in successive starts in September. Tsai, co-leader going into the final round at Luxehills, pulled away with four birdies in the first seven holes and came home with 68 for an 18-under 270 total and a three-stroke win. "This is a great achievement for me," said Tsai. "I know I'm getting old."

So a few weeks later, he gave himself a great birthday gift when he wrapped up the Tianjin Championship the day before he turned 40. Ironically, the Tianjin became a test of age vs. youth. James Su Dong, the teenage amateur who challenged at the recent Sofitel Championship, blew the lead in the fourth round, dropping three strokes over the eighth and ninth holes, then bogeyed the 12th and 13th. Tsai held steady and shot a one-over 289 total for a one-stroke win over Su. "I think I won because I stayed with my philosophy of playing one shot at a time and being patient," Tsai said.

Said Su: "At the end of the day, I was one stroke from winning, and I can tell myself that I can beat the best in China."

At the Kunming Championship, Taiwan's Lu Wen-teh, age 45, a standout on the Asian Tour, scored his first Omega China Tour win in a seven-stroke runaway. Fans also got a glimpse of the future there, with two young amateurs taking the next two spots — Benny Ye Jian-feng, age 16, finishing second, and Su Dong third.

The Shanghai Championship in mid-May brought the tour its first woman ever to make the cut. She was Yang Tao-li, age 25. "I'm not worried by the fact that it's a men's event," she said. "I just see it as an opportunity to play with golfers at a higher level." She shot 77-72-72-75–296, eight over par, tying for 19th place. Yang's accomplishment nearly overshadowed the fact that Hsu Mong-nan survived the howling winds for a two-under 70 and a 285 total for a two-stroke victory.

For a storybook finish, the season-ending Omega Championship at the Beijing Longxi Hotspring Golf Club had it all. Zhou Jun, out of Tianjin, turned on the high drama by going wire-to-wire to score his first victory and also, at age 24, to give the tournament its youngest winner. He closed with 71 for a 282 total and won by seven strokes. Li Chao, the Dell Championship winner, finished fourth and clinched the Order of Merit with RMB375,125 (about US$55,000).

If the Omega China Tour gave a Quote of the Year Award, it would go to the kid, James Su Dong, for his reaction to the disappointment of missing a four-footer that cost him a spot in the playoff at the Sofitel Championship. Said Su: "After all, this is not the end of my career, it's just the beginning."

Japan Tour

Token Homemate Cup
Nagoya, Mie
Winner: Katsumasa Miyamoto

All eyes were on Ryo Ishikawa, the Japan Tour's answer to Michele Wie, as the 16-year-old made his professional debut in the season-opening Token Homemate Cup. The Japanese teenager, who startled the golfing world in 2007 when he was invited to play in the Munsingwear Open and defied all logic by winning, came close to doing it again at Token Tado Country Club.

As the players and officials battled winds and heavy rains just to get the tournament in, Ishikawa, now being called "the Shy Prince," was seemingly unfazed by the conditions. He trailed Taichi Teshima (67) by a single shot when the interrupted first round was completed Friday morning and was the leader with 68-67–135 when everybody had finished 36 holes Saturday morning. With a third-round 72–207, Ishikawa shared first place with Teshima, who had posted a pair of 70s.

However, it was not to be another miracle. While he didn't exactly collapse, Ishikawa bogeyed his first three holes and managed just a 74 Sunday, dropping into a final tie for fifth place. The title was claimed by veteran Katsumasa Miyamoto, who birdied the last two holes and, with his 66–276, nipped Teshima by a stroke. It was the 34-year-old Miyamoto's seventh victory on the Japan Tour.

Tsuruya Open
Kawanishi, Hyogo
Winner: S.K. Ho

Brendan Jones's domination of the Tsuruya Open ended at the 2008 renewal. Although he rallied in the final round to finish in a fourth-place tie, the Australian failed in his bid for a third straight victory and fourth in the last five years at Yamanohara Golf Club. The win instead went to S.K. Ho, one of South Korea's stalwarts on the tour who scored five victories over the previous four seasons but was winless in 2007.

Ho came from a stroke off the pace in the final round, shooting a 68 for 272 and a one-shot win over Hiroshi Iwata, who led after the second and third days. Ho had moved within a stroke of Iwata with a sparkling 65 Saturday for 204. Iwata slipped to 203 with his 73 after opening a three-shot lead with a brilliant, eight-under-par 63 for 130. Kiyoshi Miyazato matched that 63 Friday for 133 and was the only man within five shots of the leader after 36 holes.

Iwata had begun the tournament with 67, sharing second place with Shingo Katayama and Hirofumi Miyase, two behind Hiroyuki Fujita, who ultimately faded to a 12th-place finish.

The Crowns
Togo, Aichi
Winner: Tomohiro Kondo

Tomohiro Kondo scored his fourth victory on the Japan Tour in the venerable Crowns tournament and, like the earlier three, it did not come easily. After squeezing out the three earlier wins in 2006 and 2007 via a one-hole playoff and two one-stroke margins, Kondo had to go two extra holes to land the 2008 title in one of the circuit's founding events. He birdied his 74th hole of the week to defeat veteran Hiroyuki Fujita.

A strong weekend performance carried Kondo into contention after he sat in a tie for 36th place (72-68) following Friday's round at Nagoya Golf Club's Wago course. Ryoken (Ricky) Kawagishi occupied the halfway lead at 134 after firing one of the day's four 65s and, seeking his first win in nearly a decade, was still in front by two Saturday night after 68–202. Kondo jumped all the way into a second-place tie with Fujita, though, carving out a tournament-best 64. Tour star Shingo Katayama, twice before a Crowns champion, also was in contention another shot back, tied with Toru Suzuki and Jeev Milkha Singh.

Kawagishi faltered again Sunday and fell back with three bogeys on the first four holes, leaving the battle to Kondo, Fujita and Katayama. When Katayama bogeyed the 14th, he slipped a shot behind Kondo, and it remained that way until the 38-year-old Fujita, a five-time winner during his 17 seasons, birdied the 18th hole to forge the final deadlock with Kondo as all three players finished with 67s.

Pine Valley Beijing Open
Beijing, China
Winner: Hiroyuki Fujita

See Asian Tour section.

Japan PGA Championship
Annaka, Gunma
Winner: Shingo Katayama

Fortunately for him, two bad dreams didn't come true in the light of the next day and Shingo Katayama coasted to a six-stroke victory in the Japan PGA Championship, the Japan Tour season's first major, which he won for a second time. "I had a dream twice last night and lost each time," recalled a smiling Katayama after posting the 24th victory of his superb career.

His first win of the season was nearly a wire-to-wire rout. Only Toshinori Muto's eight-under-par 64 in the opening round marred his entire weekend. He put up a 66 Friday to go with his opening 67 (tied for second with Daisuke Maruyama) and moved ahead to stay, three strokes in front of Maruyama (69). He racked up five birdies on the first seven holes.

His margin went to seven Saturday as he chopped another shot off par with a 65 for 198. To show how commanding his lead was, Kazuhiko Hosokawa had to shoot 64 just to get that close. Katayama rang up seven more birdies, finishing 54 holes without a bogey on his cards. Interestingly, Katayama defeated Hosokawa in a playoff 10 years earlier to win his first tournament.

Sunday was a picnic. Katayama, now Japan's fourth-leading all-time money winner behind Masashi Ozaki, Tsuneyuki Nakajima and Naomichi Ozaki, ran the margin to nine on the front nine as Hosokawa fired and fell back early. China's Liang Wen-chong chipped three shots off the lead with an eagle and birdie in the stretch. Katayama finished with 67–265 and Liang shot 65 for 271.

Munsingwear Open KSB Cup
Tamano, Okayama
Winner: Hideto Tanihara

There was nothing historic or out of the ordinary about the outcome of the Munsingwear Open KSB Cup this time. A year after the odds-defying and record-setting 2007 victory of Ryo Ishikawa, a 15-year-old amateur invitee, the Munsingwear title went to one of the Japan Tour's most successful players. Nothing surprising when Hideto Tanihara, who had scored three victories in the two previous seasons after an unsuccessful year in America in 2005, swept to a three-stroke victory at Tojigaoka Marine Hills Golf Club.

The 29-year-old Tanihara was nearly as dominant as Shingo Katayama was when he won by six strokes the previous week in the Japan PGA. Tanihara began the tournament in a tie for the lead at 65 with Nobuhito Sato as Ishikawa shot himself out of it with a 78. The co-leader, who would pick off his seventh title, had a bogey-free, seven-birdie round. Tanihara then took command Friday with seven more birdies for 67 (two bogeys) and 132. That moved him two shots in front of Sato and Toru Taniguchi.

Tanihara duplicated his opening-round 65 Saturday, this time with eight birdies and an eagle to go with a single bogey. His 197 practically sewed things up, jumping him six strokes ahead of runners-up Sato (69) and Masaya Tomida (67). An unimpressive 73 Sunday only narrowed the victory margin, his 270 total leaving him three strokes in front of runners-up Katayama (69), Sato (70) and Katsunori Kuwabara, who closed with 64, the week's lowest round. Of note, Ishikawa, though still missing the cut by two, came back gamely with 67 in the second round.

Mitsubishi Diamond Cup
Kobe, Hyogo
Winner: Prayad Marksaeng

Despite his successes — six victories — during 13 years on the Asian Tour and several close calls in Japan, Thailand's Prayad Marksaeng had played through seven seasons in the Land of the Rising Sun without chalking up a victory. The drought ended the first day of June when the 42-year-old birdied the par-five 18th hole to capture the Mitsubishi Diamond Cup tournament by a single stroke with his 10-under-par 274. He thus became just the second Thai to win on the Japan Tour, the other being Chawalit Plaphol, the ANA Open winner in 2004.

Prayad progressed up the leaderboard throughout the tournament as Hidemasa Hoshino led the way for three rounds. Hoshino opened with a six-under-par 65 at Higashi Hirono Golf Club near Kobe, taking a three-stroke lead over Ryoken Kawagishi, Takashi Kanemoto, Michio Matsumura and Eddie Lee. Prayad shot 70 and was tied for 13th place. He advanced into a tie for fifth with another 70 Friday as Hoshino, seeking his third tour victory and first in two seasons, wobbled with 72 but maintained a one-shot lead over Hideto Tanihara and Australia's Paul Sheehan.

Prayad nearly became the third-round leader Saturday. He was six under par for the round until he plunked his second shot into a water hazard on the final hole. The subsequent bogey gave him a 66–206 and Hoshino retained his one-stroke lead with a closing birdie for 68–205. Sheehan had a 68 that tied him with Prayad. Hoshino established a three-shot lead early Sunday, but Prayad whittled it away on the back nine and clinched the triumph with the final-hole birdie for his 68–274. Shintaro Kai snatched the runner-up slot with 68–275. Hoshino (71), Shingo Katayama (68) and Hiroshi Iwata (69) finished at 276.

Gateway to the Open Mizuno Open Yomiuri Classic
Nishinomiya, Hyogo
Winner: Prayad Marksaeng

The two-week gap in the slimmed-down summer schedule didn't slow Prayad Marksaeng nor take any luster off his game. After winning the Mitsubishi Diamond Cup, the Thailand pro filled in the time by finishing third in the Bangkok Airways event back home on the Asian Tour, then returned to Japan and picked off the jaw-breaking title in the Gateway to the Open Mizuno Open Yomiuri Classic. That made him the season's first double winner.

Just as at the Mitsubishi event, Prayad squeezed out the victory by a single stroke, coming from two strokes off the pace in the final round with a six-under-par 65 for 269 to edge Azumo Yano, who also closed with 65. Those two, along with third-place finishers Michio Matsumura and Yoshinobu Tsukada, qualified for the Open Championship in Britain; hence the front half of the cumbersome tournament name. (The Mizuno and Yomiuri Opens joined forces in 2007.)

The outcome was a bitter disappointment for Lee Dong-hwan. The South Korean had taken a one-stroke lead into the final round at the West course of the Osaka Yomiuri Country Club, shot 69, and not only lost by two strokes but also lost an Open invitation to the other 271-shooters because Tsukada shot 68 and Matsumura 67.

His third-round 71 short-circuited Yano, who started in a four-way tie for the lead at 67 with Kazuhiro Yamashita, Norio Shinozaki and Frankie

Minoza and took over solo first with another 67 Friday as bad weather led to a Saturday finish of the second round. With a 66–202, Lee seized first place Saturday by a stroke over Matsumura (64), Steven Conran (66) and Kiyoshi Murota (65) as Prayad moved into position for his Sunday surge with 69–204.

UBS Japan Golf Tour Championship
Kasama, Ibaraki
Winner: Hidemasa Hoshino

Hidemasa Hoshino, who failed to reel in a title he had on the hook a month earlier, did not let a big one get away. Still smarting from his failure to close out a victory in the Mitsubishi Diamond Cup on the final holes, Hoshino hammered out an impressive, five-stroke win in the UBS Japan Golf Tour Championship, the second major championship of the 2008 season.

Hoshino, scoring the third win of his circuit career and first since 2006, shrugged off a pair of mid-round bogeys to close out the victory with a one-under-par 70 and 12-under 272 total on the demanding Shishido Hills Country Club course in Ibaraki. "Winning at a difficult course like this makes me feel like I've finally come on top," he said afterward.

A pair of mid-tournament 66s set up Hoshino's victory. The first one moved him into second place, a stroke behind Kenichi Kuboya, who led through the Friday round. Kuboya, 36, winless on the tour since a 2002 victory, opened with 67-68 for 135, seven under par. Hoshino's second 66 advanced him into a three-stroke lead over Kuboya (70) and Hiroshi Iwata (69). He needed just a 70 Sunday to wrap up the decisive victory as Kuboya shot 73 and Iwata 75, offsetting three bogeys — two in the middle of the round and the other on the 18th — with four birdies. Takao Nogami (68) and Australia's Brendan Jones (70) tied for second place at 277.

Nagashima Shigeo Invitational Sega Sammy Cup
Chitose, Hokkaido
Winner: Jeev Milkha Singh

Busy enjoying a highly successful international season elsewhere in the world, India's Jeev Milkha Singh had been to Japan just once earlier in the year before coming for the Sega Sammy Cup tournament in late July. Able to pick his spots because of his pair of victories on the Japan Tour in 2006, Singh chose the right one as he staged a brilliant final-round comeback and snagged a two-stroke victory.

The win came at the expense of Sushi Ishigaki, a former Asian Tour player who had experienced a feeble season in Japan before reaching the North Country Club in Hokkaido's Chitose, missing seven cuts in his nine previous starts. Ishigaki shared the second-round lead with Tatsuhiko Takahashi at 136 with rounds of 69-67 and surged three shots in front Saturday with a wild 69 for 205. The three-under-par round was the product of an eagle, five birdies, two bogeys and a double bogey. The runners-up then were Koumei Oda, who was the first-round leader with 65, and Fiji's Dinesh Chand. Singh, with 68, came into the picture at 209.

The Indian star dominated the final round. He birdied four of the first 11 holes, then three of the final four for a six-under 66 and the winning 275. Ishigaki's final chance failed when he bogeyed the par-five 18th and had to settle for a par 72 and 277 total. Teenager Ryo Ishikawa shot 67 Sunday and tied for third, the best professional finish for the 16-year-old.

Sun Chlorella Classic
Otaru, Hokkaido
Winner: Takuya Taniguchi

It had been a long dry spell for the other Taniguchi. While the eminently successful Toru Taniguchi was ringing up half of his career 14 victories on the Japan Tour, Takuya Taniguchi spent those last four years trying to add to his lone triumph in the now-defunct Aiful Cup in 2004. Takuya had given little indication that it might happen in the Sun Chlorella Classic, having made only four cuts when he arrived in Hokkaido for the tournament, but he finally landed his second win, chalking up a final-hole birdie to edge old friend Hideto Tanihara by a stroke.

The victory was hard-earned in another way as well. The Otaru Country Club course was again the most difficult of the season, ultimately yielding only three sub-par 72-hole scores, Taniguchi's winning four-under-par 284, Tanihara's 285 and Lee Dong-hwan's 286.

Yui Ueda had the week's best score — the only 66 — to lead the first day, but he followed with 81-77 as Taniguchi (70-72) and Tetsuya Haraguchi (71-71) went in front Friday. Only one player broke par on a gusty Saturday, and Lee took over first place despite a double-bogey start. The 21-year-old South Korean, a third-season pro with a lone victory on his record, shot 72 for 215 to inch a shot in front of Taniguchi (74) and Tanihara (73).

That trio battled it out all day Sunday, Taniguchi holing a seven-foot birdie putt on the 18th for 68 and the 284 total. Tanihara, his college teammate, had 69 and Lee 71.

Vana H Cup KBC Augusta
Shima, Fukuoka
Winner: Shintaro Kai

It took until the end of August for the Japan Tour to produce its first-time career victor of the season. Shintaro Kai, who had knocked at the door a couple of times earlier in the year, broke the ice for the non-winners in the Vana H Cup KBC Augusta tournament on the last day of the month. Actually, the 27-year-old Kai was the second man to land an initial Japan Tour title in 2008, but the other, Prayad Marksaeng, had logged six Asian Tour wins before picking up his first two in Japan in June.

It had been feast or famine this year for Kai, a five-year veteran, who finished second in the Mitsubishi Diamond Cup and Pine Valley Beijing

Open but missed six cuts in eight other starts, including his most recent four.

Kai lingered a stroke off the lead the first two days at Keya Golf Club in Shima with rounds of 69 and 70, he and Tatsuhiko Takahashi trailing Japan Tour Championship winner Hidemasa Hoshino (69-69) going into the weekend. After a three-hour storm delay Saturday morning, Kai converted five birdies and three bogeys into a 70–209 and a one-shot lead over little-known Shinichi Akiba, with Hoshino, Australian Steven Conran and Azuma Yano another stroke back.

Kai was solid Sunday. He packed 15 pars around three birdies in the middle of the round for 69–278, just enough when Hoshino bogeyed the par-three 17th hole for 68–279.

Fujisankei Classic
Fujikawaguchiko, Yamanashi
Winner: Toyokazu Fujishima

Playoffs had been a rarity on the 2008 Japan Tour, but it took the season's second one to decide which of two players would be become the freshest of the circuit's first-time winners at the Fujisankei Classic. Perhaps deservedly so, Toyokazu Fujishima won the overtime test against Hiroshi Iwata on the first extra hole to get that initial career title, a week after Shintaro Kai became the first new career victor of the season. Neither playoff contestant had won before.

Fujishima was impressive throughout the tournament at Fujizakura Country Club. The fifth-year pro came out blazing Thursday with a seven-under-par, seven-birdie 64, his lowest round ever, and took a two-stroke lead over South Korea's Lee Dong-hwan and Azuma Yano. He maintained that margin over Lee as both men shot 68s Friday. Money leader Shingo Katayama was just another stroke back (68-67) with Taichi Teshima.

Fujishima slipped to 71 Saturday and dropped into a tie with Kenichi Kuboya, one shot behind Katayama — 67–202 — who was trying to build on his PGA Championship, his lone win of the season. Iwata charged into the picture Sunday. He birdied five of his first six holes and rang up a 65 to match Fujishima's 68–271 and force the playoff. Both players missed the green on the par-four 18th in the playoff, but Fujishima blasted to three feet from the right bunker and saved par for the win after Iwata missed his par putt after coming up 10 feet short with his chip from the rough. Katayama bogeyed the 18th for 70 to miss the playoff by a stroke, as did China's Liang Wen-chong (66) and Kuboya (69).

ANA Open
Kitahiroshima, Hokkaido
Winner: Azuma Yano

Persistence finally paid off for Azuma Yano at the ANA Open. With a runner-up finish in the Mizuno Yomiuri tournament and several other not-quites behind him in 2008, Yano pieced together four solid rounds in the 60s on the Wattsu course of Sapporo Golf Club in mid-September and rolled to a four-stroke victory with a 15-under-par 273 total, the second of his Japan Tour career. The first came back in 2005.

The 31-year-old trailed only after the first round, when rookie Kim Kyung-tae, the leading money winner on the domestic South Korean Tour, hammered out a 65 and took a one-stroke lead over veterans Kazuhiko Hosokawa and Tsuneyuki (Tommy) Nakajima, who is still talented enough to have won the prestigious 2006 Taiheiyo Club Masters at age 52, his 46th career title. He later won on the Japan Senior Tour.

With a pair of 68s, Yano overtook Kim when the young South Korean shot 71 Friday. He had seven birdies and three bogeys, then followed Saturday with a rather wild 69 that included an eagle, four birdies and three more bogeys. The 205 spurted Yano three shots in front of Shingo Katayama, who already had a win and three top-three finishes on his 2008 record.

Katayama took an early run of the title Sunday, but Yano was equal to the challenge. Back-to-back birdies at the 14th and 15th holes restored a lead that had dwindled to a single stroke, and he finished with a third 68 for the 273 total, four in front of Nakajima (67) and Toshinori Muto (68).

Asia-Pacific Panasonic Open
Ibaraki, Osaka
Winner: Hideto Tanihara

In one way, the Japan Tour went two up on the Asian Tour when Hideto Tanihara bagged the Asia-Pacific Panasonic Open title in late September in the second of two 2008 co-sanctioned tournaments. Another Japan Tour regular — Hiroyuki Fujita — won the first one, the Pine Valley Beijing Open in China in May.

In landing his second victory of the season and eighth in his six-year career, Tanihara fended off Azuma Yano, the previous week's winner in Japan, and two of the top players on the Asian Tour — Mark Brown of New Zealand, the Order of Merit leader, and China's Liang Wen-chong, the 2007 circuit champion. Tanihara closed with a 66 and a 16-under-par 264, to edge good friend Yano by a stroke. Liang fell two shots short despite a 65 and tied Kenichi Kuboya for third place, two ahead of Brown (67) and Kaname Yokoo (69).

Yokoo was a contender from the word go, conjuring up a brilliant 62 in the opening round on the West course of Ibaraki Country Club to lead Liang and Australia's Marcus Both by two shots. He remained on top when he finished his 69–131 in the rain-delayed second round on Saturday morning before yielding first place to Tanihara and Yano by a stroke later in the day. Tanihara shot 64 and Yano 65 for 198s, Yokoo 68–199.

Although he never trailed Sunday as he moved to the top of the money list, the 29-year-old Tanihara needed a crucial par save from a greenside bunker at the 15th hole to hold off Yano, who birdied the last two holes.

Coca-Cola Tokai Classic
Miyoshi, Aichi
Winner: Toshinori Muto

The biggest surprise about the outcome of the Coca-Cola Tokai Classic was not who won the tournament but rather who didn't. The table was all set for either Shingo Katayama or Toru Taniguchi, Japan's two most successful players in recent years — five of the last seven money titles — to make off with the win. They entered the final round just a shot behind Toshimori Muto, whose lone Japan Tour victory was in 2006, and winless Yuta Ikeda, who wasn't even in the field until the Monday qualifier.

So, what happened? Katayama shot 73 and Taniguchi 74 Sunday on Miyoshi Country Club's West course, while Muto was nailing his second victory with a 69 for 277 total, 11 under par, and the unheralded Ikeda gave it a good try with 71–279 to finish second.

The lead bounced around in the early rounds. Keiichiro Fukabori, an eight-time winner but without a victory for three years, opened with 65, two strokes ahead of Australia's Brendan Jones, who won three times in 2007. Things jammed up Friday when five players, including Ikeda and Fukabori, finished with 138s. The others were Fiji's Dinesh Chand, Shinichi Yokota and Akio Sadakata, fighting just to keep his tour privileges. Muto was one back with 69-70–139 with Taniguchi and Masaya Tomida.

Katayama, moving up the money list with constant high finishes but winless since May, shot 67 Saturday to position himself with Taniguchi (70) at 209, as Muto (69) and Ikeda (70) took over first place at 208. Ikeda fought Muto evenly through 17 holes Sunday, but dumped his approach into the water in front of the 18th green and his bogey, coupled with a closing birdie by Muto, established the final margin.

Canon Open
Yokohama, Kanagawa
Winner: Makoto Inoue

Things finally turned around for Makoto Inoue. "I hadn't even come close for a long time," he remarked after staging the season's biggest final-round rally to win the initial Canon Open at Totsuka Country Club near Yokohama. It had been four years, in fact, since he posted his lone victory on the Japan Tour in the 2004 ABC Championship.

Inoue did not appear to have a chance after Hiroyuki Fujita carved out a strong 66 and established a two-stroke lead over Yusaka Miyazato and at least four over the rest of the field going into the final round. The 33-year-old Inoue, with rounds of 70-71-69 for 210, was six strokes behind Fujita, who already had a 2008 victory in the Pine Valley Beijing Open.

"I never imagined that I'd win," Inoue observed after his seven-birdie 65 Sunday carried him to the triumph — by a stroke over Fujita (72), Miyazato (70), Yasuharu Imano (66) and Taichi Teshima (68). Starting with a chip-in birdie on the first hole, Inoue ripped off four more birdies in a nine-putt 31 on the front nine and added a final two on back side.

Hideto Tanihara and Shingo Katayama, battling for the money lead, both started well with 68 and 69, respectively, behind little-known leader Tetsuya Haraguchi, but faded from contention later in the week. So did veteran Katsunori Kuwabara, the second-round leader at 69-68–137, seeking to end a much-longer dry spell than Inoue — 10 years since winning the old Japan Match Play Championship.

Japan Open
Koga, Fukuoka
Winner: Shingo Katayama

It had been considered just a matter of time before Shingo Katayama officially joined the truly elite in the history of Japanese golf, but when he did so in mid-October he did it in appropriate, first-class fashion. On the verge for several months, Katayama scored his landmark 25th victory on the Japan Tour with a highly impressive triumph in the Japan Open, the country's oldest and most prestigious tournament.

The colorful 35-year-old star broke from a first-round leadership tie to dominate on an unyielding Koga Golf Club course that nobody else could battle on even terms. He chalked up four steady rounds on a layout called "one of the most treacherous courses used in Japan's major tournament history." Winning by four shots, he was the only man to finish below par with his one-under 283 total.

The next player to follow Katayama into the stratosphere of 25-tournament winners may well be the Open runner-up — 17-year-old Ryo Ishikawa — who posted a final-round 69 for 287, edging Australian Brendan Jones, an eight-time winner in Japan, by a stroke. He matched Katayama's opening 68, fell just one back with 73 to Katayama's 72 Friday, but dropped too far behind when he shot 76 Saturday as Katayama registered another 72 and established what proved to be his ultimate four-stroke margin at 212.

Katayama was never threatened as he skillfully crafted his par round Sunday, Jones once getting within three before falling behind Ishikawa. Impressively, Katayama's earlier 2008 victory was in the tour's other long-standing major, the Japan PGA Championship. He joined Isao Aoki, Masashi and Naomichi Ozaki, Tsuneyuki Nakajima, Masahiro Kuramoto and Teruo Sugihara in the exclusive 25-win club and became exempt lifetime on the circuit.

Bridgestone Open
Chiba
Winner: Azuma Yano

Azuma Yano's consistent season continued when he pulled in his second victory of the year in the Bridgestone Open. Following four consecutive top-10 finishes after the first win in the ANA Open in September, Yano rolled to a four-stroke victory and into first place on the money list. He became the season's fourth double winner, joining Shingo Katayama, Hideto Tanihara and Prayad Marksaeng.

Except for Katsumasa Miyamoto's sensational, nine-under-par 63 in the first round, Yano would have had total 72-hole control at Sodegaura Country Club. As it was, he started in second place with a potent 65, stepped in front by three with a 66 for 131 after 36 holes, and wound up with the four-shot margin with his 21-under-par 267 total.

He couldn't relax at any point, though, with the ever-present Shingo Katayama among others hovering in contention. Kaname Yokoo was at 134 and Shegeki Maruyama, back trying to recoup a poor season in America, at 136. Katayama, attempting to win two in a row, made his presence felt Saturday when he shot 64 and jumped into second place at 202, two behind Yano, who shot 69 for his 200.

Yano was solid Sunday, clicking off six birdies and taking a single bogey for 67 and 267. Takao Nogami snatched second place with 66–271, his second runner-up finish of the year, and Maruyama took third with 68–273 as Katayama surprisingly faded with a 73.

mynavi ABC Championship
Kato, Hyogo
Winner: Ryo Ishikawa

No doubt about it. Ryo Ishikawa is for real. There had to be a few skeptics in 2007 when the 15-year-old high school freshman made world golf history by winning the Munsingwear Open, wondering if it might have been a fluke happening. Perhaps a naysayer or two remained after the young man turned pro and produced some solid performances, particularly when he finished second to Shingo Katayama in the Japan Open in October. Who can argue the point now that Ishikawa has backed up that Munsingwear victory with his first professional win in the mynavi ABC Championship under the spotlight of media attention that has followed him throughout the 2008 season?

Ishikawa snatched the victory away from veteran Keiichiro Fukabori, who led for two days at the ABC Golf Club at Kato and carried a one-stroke margin into the final round with his 67-68-72–207 total. Fukabori, an eight-time winner but without a victory since 2005, eagled the 18th hole and grabbed a three-shot lead with the 135 Friday. He was three in front of Ishikawa Saturday night after Ishikawa, now 17, was stuck on 70s for three rounds and settled into third place, two back of runner-up Saturo Hirota.

As Fukabori gave ground Sunday, Ishikawa worked his way to the fore. His birdies at the 15th and 16th holes moved him a stroke in front and he finished "a tough round" with a fine two-putt par after his second shot to the 18th green spun back to the edge of the fronting water hazard. That gave him a 69–279 while Fukabori had 73 for his 280. Nobody else was within three strokes.

The Championship by Lexus
Bando, Ibaraki
Winner: S.K. Ho

Golfers from South Korea have been making a major impact on many of the tours around the world in recent years. In Japan, S.K. Ho has been his country's standout representative during the current decade, and he added luster to his reputation in early November when he picked up his second victory of the season and eighth of his career in Japan. He won The Championship by Lexus, one of two new events in the series of rich fall tournaments, by a resounding five-stroke margin in contrast to his come-from-behind, one-shot win in April in the Tsuruya Open.

It was a commanding performance almost from the start. American Brandt Jobe, a six-time winner on the circuit in the mid-1990s who had played his first tournament in Japan in four years the week before, came out of the gate fast at Otone Country Club at Bando with a seven-under-par 64. Ho was right on his heels, though, sharing second place with Toshinori Muto at 66, then followed with 68 Friday. That tied him for the lead with Australian Steven Conran (68-66), as Jobe slipped to 135 with a 71.

The South Korean soared Saturday. Ho ran off three consecutive early birdies and three more in the middle of the round. His bogey-free 65 jumped him five shots in front of Conran, who mustered just 70, and Ho needed only a 70 himself Sunday to maintain that five-stroke margin at the end. Kiyoshi Miyazato shot 68 to pick off second place, two ahead of Jobe and Australian Wayne Perske.

Mitsui Sumitomo Visa Taiheiyo Masters
Gotemba, Shizuoka
Winner: Shingo Katayama

Shingo Katayama moved closer to his fifth money title when he captured one of the few big ones that had eluded him earlier in his illustrious career. Two consecutive birdies on the par-five 18th hole, the latter in a playoff, gave Katayama the title in the Mitsui Sumitomo Visa Taiheiyo Masters, one of the oldest of the circuit's more lucrative tournaments.

His 26th victory fit nicely among his collection of major and other coveted events and propelled him past Azuma Yano into a commanding lead in the money race on both the domestic and all-inclusive lists. At just age 35, Katayama trails only Masashi and Naomichi Ozaki and Tsuneyuki Nakajima in career earnings with his nearly ¥1.5 billion.

Katayama was in and out of the lead throughout the week on the Taiheiyo Club's Gotemba course in Shizuoka Prefecture before becoming the season's first three-time winner. He started a stroke off the lead behind teen sensation Ryo Ishikawa, who bounced back from a missed cut in the Lexus and fired a six-under-par 66. The youthful star fell back with a 72 Friday as Katayama and Yasuharu Imano, the eventual playoff participants, moved into the top two positions, Katayama with 67-68–135 and Imano with 67-69–136.

Imano, a five-time career titlist but winless since 2005, ran off five back-nine birdies for 65 Saturday and took a two-stroke lead on Katayama. Katayama fought back Sunday with 69 to Imano's 71 for the tying 272s that brought about the year's third playoff.

Dunlop Phoenix
Miyazaki
Winner: Prayad Marksaeng

The Dunlop Phoenix, which invariably attracts the strongest international field of the season, has a victory list spangled with the names of many of the game's greatest players from home and abroad. Missing was an Asian winner from anywhere besides Japan — until Prayad Marksaeng filled that void in the 2008 tournament. The 42-year-old veteran from Thailand embellished his finest season with his third victory in 15 starts in Japan, standing off a stretch charge by rookie flash Ryo Ishikawa.

The name visitors, led this time by Ernie Els, Henrik Stenson and defending champion Ian Poulter, had little impact at Phoenix Country Club. With a four-under-par 67 in the opening round, Paul Sheehan of Australia, whose three past wins in Japan included the Japan Open in 2006, eked out a one-stroke lead over seven others, among them Prayad.

Tomohiro Kondo, one of those 68 shooters, went in front with 69–137 Friday. Prayad remained a shot behind with a 70 and was joined at 138 by Stenson, Spain's Gonzalo Fernandez-Castano and Michio Matsumura. Prayad birdied two of his last three holes Saturday, shot 67 for 205 and a two-stroke lead over Kondo (70).

Prayad turned an easy win into a tight one Sunday. He stretched his margin to five shots on the front nine, but, as Ishikawa came on strong, he lost strokes and wound up with 71–276 and the one-shot triumph. With the win, he joined Shingo Katayama as the year's only three-time victors.

Casio World Open
Geisei, Kochi
Winner: Koumei Oda

By normal standards, it was slim pickings in 2008 for the many players on the Japan Tour who were searching for a first victory. Other than Prayad Marksaeng, a winner on the Asian Tour before accumulating his first three Japan titles during the season, only three Japanese players scored maiden triumphs during the 25-event campaign. Koumei Oda was the last of that trio to do so, running off with an impressive, three-stroke victory in the Casio World Open, the final full-field tournament of the year.

With only two top-10 finishes all year, Oda was hardly highly regarded when the field teed off at Kochi Kuroshio Country Club in Geisei. However, he had placed eighth the week before in the Dunlop Phoenix with a strong 67 in the final round and carried that momentum to a wire-to-wire victory in the Casio.

At the site of a window-shattering bombing just a week past and unfounded phone threats of planted mines, the 30-year-old exploded a six-under-par 66 Thursday, taking a one-stroke lead over Achi Sato, another unlikely contender. Oda widened the gap on Sato to four shots, packing an eagle and five birdies with two bogeys for 67–133 as Sato posted a 70–137. He still had the four-stroke advantage after an erratic par 72 for 205, offsetting five birdies with five bogeys. At 209 were Yusaku Miyazato, Kenichi Kuboya and Hirofumi Miyase.

With the scoring generally high in tough playing conditions, Oda eased to the three-shot win with another 72 Sunday for his winning 11-under 277 total. Kuboya held onto second place with 71–280. Ryo Ishikawa's tie for 13th took him over the ¥100 million mark in earnings for the season, at 17 the youngest ever to do that in Japan.

Golf Nippon Series JT Cup
Tokyo
Winner: Jeev Milkha Singh

Jeev Milkha Singh's victory in the season-ending Golf Nippon Series JT Cup was not the joyous affair that it should have been. Singh bore a heavy heart as he hoisted the JT Cup aloft after his charging, two-stroke win and dedicated the victory to his hospitalized wife, Kudrat. She was recuperating in Tokyo following the stillborn delivery of their first child earlier in the week.

The golfing star of India teed it up in the select-field tournament only because Kudrat urged him to play and he seemed motivated by her insistence. Singh, who won his third Japan Tour title earlier in the season at the Sega Sammy Cup, was never worse than third at the end of any round at Tokyo's Yomiuri Country Club in the 26-man field of 2008 winners and top 25 on the money list. He finished it off Sunday with a sparkling, four-under-par 66 and won by two strokes with his 268 total. He had also landed that title in 2006.

Singh banged out a 64 Thursday, but he and three others — multiple winners Prayad Marksaeng and Azuma Yano and Katsumasa Miyamoto — trailed Kaname Yokoo by a stroke. Scoring rose in the rain Friday, and Singh's 70–134 was enough to nudge him a shot into the lead ahead of Toshinori Muto (70) and Miyamoto (71) as Yokoo slipped to 73.

Things bunched up Saturday. Prayad, seeking his fourth 2008 victory, shot 63 and Muto 66 for 201s, a stroke in front of Singh (68), Taichi Teshima (65) and the exciting Ryo Ishikawa (66). Singh then capped an excellent season that also was highlighted by his November victory over Ernie Els and Padraig Harrington in the Barclays Singapore Open that clinched his second Asian Tour money title and his June triumph in the Bank Austria Open on the European Tour. The runners-up were Australian Brendan Jones (64), the defending champion; New Zealand's David Smail (66) and Teshima (68).

Shingo Katayama, who tied for 10th, eight shots behind Singh, officially wrapped up his fifth money title, fourth in five years. His ¥180,094,895 left Yano far behind in second place.

11. Australasian Tour

There was a blast from the past in Australian golf when the closest anyone from Down Under came to winning a major championship was ... Greg Norman. The 53-year-old businessman spends more time playing tennis than golf these days, but for a few days at Royal Birkdale the Great White Shark again revealed himself as one of the most fearsome predators in the world game. It was nostalgic and sentimental, but there was Norman interrupting his honeymoon after marrying Chris Evert, the former tennis superstar, and enjoying the thrill of competition once again.

While many of the game's finest struggled with the wild conditions of the British summer, Norman very nearly added a third Open Championship victory to those of 1986 and 1993. Just like in the 1980s and 1990s, Norman led going into the last round of a major championship. His age and his history of last day disasters had little to do with what happened next. It was simply unrealistic for a player unused to regular competition, who admitted his body and other priorities limited his practice, to hold off a man in his prime such as Padraig Harrington. Ultimately Harrington clung onto the claret jug, but it was also a triumph and a glorious one at that.

Of the younger generation, Geoff Ogilvy led the way, finishing the year as the 12th best player in the world. At Doral in March he won his second World Golf Championship event at the CA Championship. At the end of the year he returned home and won in Australia for the first time at the Cadburys Schweppes Australian PGA Championship. Ogilvy's victory was one of the highlights of Australia's brief season at the end of the year. Rod Pampling won the Sportsbet Australian Masters, while South Africa's Tim Clark, on his first visit to the country, took the Australian Open. There was disappointment for Matthew Goggin as he finished runner-up to both Ogilvy and Clark.

That the Australian Open had no main sponsor highlights the problems for the Australasian Tour, which merged with the Australian PGA during the year. The Australian Masters, after 30 years at Huntingdale, moves to a new venue in Melbourne in 2009 but was likely to lose its co-sanction status with the European Tour. The New Zealand Open has already decided to move to the start of the year and link up with the Nationwide Tour in the United States. An attempt to join together all the tours in Asia, promoted by the Australasian and Japanese tours, also appears to have floundered as the Asian Tour goes from strength to strength.

Forced to ply their trade around the globe, their golfers, however, continue to find success wherever they go. Adam Scott won both on the European Tour at the Qatar Masters and at the Byron Nelson Championship in America. Scott Strange won the Wales Open. Jarrod Lyle finished fourth on the Nationwide Tour in the United States, and there were wins in Asia for Rick Kulacz, Scott Hend, David Gleason and New Zealander Mark Brown, who finished third on the Asian Tour Order of Merit. In fact Brown won twice in India, at the SAIL Open and then the Johnnie Walker Classic, a tri-sanctioned event which gave him an exemption on the European Tour and also propelled him to victory on the Australasian Tour Order of Merit. Brown, age 33, turned professional in 1996 and played all around the world. But for three years he became a development officer for the Wellington Golf Association before rediscovering the bug to try tournament golf once again. At the other end of the spectrum to Norman there was Danny Lee, who won the U.S. Amateur Championship and showed himself one to keep an eye on for the future.

HSBC New Zealand PGA Championship
Christchurch, New Zealand
Winner: Darron Stiles

After two days were washed out at the Clearwater Resort in Christchurch, there was still a thrilling finish to the HSBC New Zealand PGA Championship as Darron Stiles holed a six-footer for a par on the final green to win by one stroke. The 34-year-old American from Pinehurst, North Carolina, claimed his fifth Nationwide Tour title in the co-sanctioned event.

Stiles was one of three co-leaders after a six-under 66 in the first round. The second day's play was cancelled due to torrential rain, while only 90 minutes was possible on day three. Those scores were wiped out as the event was reduced to a 36-hole affair with the second and final round on Sunday. Stiles started as if it was an even shorter sprint with five birdies in the first six holes to take a four-stroke lead. But from then on his advantage was whittled away as David Smail, the New Zealander who finished second on the Australasian Tour Order of Merit in 2007, birdied the 14th and 15th holes and came in with a best-of-the-day 66.

Smail found the clubhouse at nine-under-par 134 and then had to wait for 40 minutes for the leaders to finish. By saving par at the last, Stiles also closed at 10 under after 66. "It was a pressure putt," said Stiles, who lost his card after playing on the PGA Tour in 2007. "Even though it was only the second round today, it felt every bit as pressure packed as a normal fourth round Sunday one. That's how I approached going into today, and to make that putt when that's been the area and length that I've been struggling with is awesome."

Moonah Classic
Fingal, Victoria
Winner: Ewan Porter

Ewan Porter found the strong winds of the final round to his liking as the 25-year-old Australian clinched his first professional title by the comfortable margin of seven strokes at the inaugural Moonah Classic, the second of two events co-sanctioned with the Nationwide Tour. Porter's closing 66, in which he never looked back after three birdies in a row from the second hole, was three strokes better than anyone else achieved on the last day at Moonah Links.

Porter led from the start of the tournament after an opening 67 and then added two rounds of 71 before finishing with 275, 13 under par. But Porter nearly did not make it to the first tee on Saturday for the third round. An early morning workout session in the gym caused an old shoulder injury to flare up and he spent the next few hours immobile. After taking anti-inflammatories and having manipulation from a physiotherapist, Porter decided to play less than 20 minutes before his tee time. Once on the course he kept his game together and ended the day with a one-stroke lead.

On the final day some terrific recovery shots and fine putting kept any mistakes off Porter's card while others piled up the bogeys. Americans Daniel Brigman and Tee McCabe shared second place, with Australian Terry Price alone in fourth. "It was definitely the round of my life under the circumstances," Porter said. "I hit a couple of wayward drives, that's for sure, but for the most part I was thrilled to bits with the last two days. I felt this week like I was ready to win, like it was my tournament this week, my turn. I'm definitely way more ready for it now than I ever was."

Johnnie Walker Classic
New Delhi, India
Winner: Mark Brown

See Asia/Japan Tours chapter.

Sportsbet Australian Masters
Melbourne, Victoria
Winner: Rod Pampling

For the sixth time in the last seven Sportsbet Australian Masters, the victor was decided by a playoff, with Queenslander Rod Pampling defeating compatriot Marcus Fraser on the third extra hole. It was the 30th tournament at Huntingdale, but the last for a while, with the event rotating around the Melbourne sandbelt, while the status of the event's co-sanctioning with the European Tour was also in doubt.

Pampling started the day at seven under, three shots behind overnight leaders Robert Allenby and Michael Sim, and shot a closing 67 which included five birdies and an eagle. Fraser, five shots off the pace after 54 holes, hit the lead with six birdies on the front nine and held it together in the run home for a round of 65. The pair finished tied at 12-under-par 276, while Allenby was alone in third place.

Both players parred the 18th twice in the playoff, but at the third time of asking it came down to a six-foot putt for par that Fraser missed and a three-footer that Pampling made. "Playoffs are never fun to be in," said Pampling, who had not won in his homeland since 1999. "You work so hard for 72 holes and then you have to go out again. Thankfully, I came out on the right end. Marcus played great golf today to shoot seven under.

"It's great to win at home and to win such a great event," added Pampling. "The Masters anywhere has had some unbelievable names on the trophy, it's a very special tournament and I am glad that I am going to be a part of its history."

Fraser's performance was amazing considering his pregnant wife Carlie was in and out of the hospital during the day. But Allenby had revealed he wanted to win the title for his dying mother, Sylvie, who came out to watch at the 15th hole. As she arrived Allenby took three from the sand and the double bogey ended his hopes. He left the green in tears. "On 15 I pretty well lost the plot," he said. "I could not hold my emotions in any more. I think my emotions on that green showed you everything. I think you can put two and two together without me even saying it."

Cadbury Schweppes Australian PGA Championship
Coolum Beach, Queensland
Winner: Geoff Ogilvy

Geoff Ogilvy won the U.S. Open in 2006 and his second World Golf Championship at the CA Championship at Doral early in 2008. But the 31-year-old could not have been more delighted to end the year by winning for the first time on home soil at the Cadbury Schweppes Australian PGA Championship.

Ogilvy lifted the Joe Kirkwood Cup by defeating Matthew Goggin, the overnight leader, by two strokes at Coolum. Ogilvy closed with 69 to finish at 14-under-par 274, while Goggin, runner-up for the second time in three years at the PGA, scored 72.

"It feels pretty good," said Ogilvy. "It's been a long time coming in Australia. Historically it means a lot. It's a pretty nice trophy and there's some pretty solid names on this one. I've hardly played in the last two or three months, but I played in China and I knew I was playing quite well and felt really good about it all week. I think when you sit down at the end of it all, its nice to have an Australian PGA Championship now as opposed to a sponsor sponsor Open."

Goggin opened up a three-stroke lead on the front nine, but dropped a couple of shots around the turn to let Ogilvy back into it. Ogilvy birdied the 12th to draw even, but Goggin found the water at the 15th, only for Ogilvy to go two ahead with another birdie at the 16th. Goggin kept it interesting with a birdie at the 17th, but then dropped a shot at the last.

Australian Open
Sydney, New South Wales
Winner: Tim Clark

South Africa's Tim Clark claimed the Australian Open, defeating Mathew Goggin on the first hole of a playoff at Royal Sydney. After a brilliant closing 67 to force the playoff, Clark claimed the Stonehaven Cup with a miraculous sand save on the first extra hole, forcing Goggin to make a testing three-foot putt to stay alive. But Goggin's par-saving effort was unsuccessful, leaving the Tasmanian to settle for runner-up honors for the second week running.

Overnight leader David Smail appeared to be heading for victory when he was leading by three shots late in the day, before consecutive double bogeys derailed his campaign and opened the door for Goggin and Clark. The South African produced seven birdies in the first 12 holes, but his campaign appeared over when he dropped three shots in consecutive holes starting with a double bogey from the greenside bunker at the 13th.

But the 32-year-old steadied himself, posting two closing birdies to set a competitive target at nine-under-par 279. Goggin went almost unnoticed for much of the final round, but his closing three-under 69 was enough to force extra holes. Robert Allenby finished his round in style with a birdie at the 18th, but it wasn't enough to force his way into the playoff and he tied with Smail and Stephen Dartnell.

Clark, on his first trip to Australia, became the first South African to win the Australian Open since Gary Player won his record seventh title in 1974. "I've had a great three weeks here, been made to feel right at home, and to get the win is a bonus," Clark said. "It was a bonus to get into the playoff. I didn't even consider there would be a playoff until half an hour after I'd finished. I was clearing out my locker, but thought it was tough out there and I'd better hang around."

12. African Tours

Trevor Immelman's victory at the Masters Tournament signaled that a new generation of South African golfers is ready to win on the world stage. It was an unlikely victory. After winning the Nedbank Golf Challenge late in 2007, it was discovered Immelman had a tumor the size of a golf ball next to his diaphragm. The recovery after the operation was slow, at least when Immelman could get a golf club in his hands. Of the few tournaments he had played before arriving at Augusta, Immelman had missed the cut in most of them. "And here I am, the Masters champion. It's the craziest thing I've ever heard of," he said once clothed in a green jacket. His display at Augusta was superb and there was never any doubting his talent. Certainly Gary Player, the only other South African to have won the Masters, had never doubted it. Player had been a mentor to Immelman and, with a round to play, left an inspiring voicemail message for the youngster.

"I think he realized even at a young age how much passion for the game I have," Immelman said. "He has been kind of another type of father for me, and to have somebody with that much experience on your side, giving you advice, is just incredible."

Immelman, perhaps not surprisingly, struggled slightly to live up to his new billing for the rest of the year, but his victory was clearly the highlight of the season in Africa. Indeed, its other two stars, Ernie Els and Retief Goosen, could not reach such heights. Both were going through swing changes, Els switching to Butch Harmon as his swing coach. Els also had to deal with going public about his son Ben's autism, which has led to the family moving to Florida. There was, however, a first victory in the United States for almost four years when he won the Honda Classic.

But elsewhere the younger generation was following Immelman's lead. Charl Schwartzel won his third European Tour title at the Madrid Masters, while Hennie Otto claimed his first at the Italian Open. Meanwhile, Tim Clark won the Australian Open, the first South African to do so since Player won for a record seventh time in 1974.

At home there were some stunning performances. If Henrik Stenson's domination of the Nedbank Golf Challenge at Sun City was some of the best golf ever played in the event, then Louis Oosthuizen produced something similar in claiming the Telkom PGA Championship by a massive 14 strokes with a winning score of 28 under par. But the man of the season was clearly Richard Sterne. He started the year by winning the Joburg Open and made it a hat-trick of European Tour co-sanctioned events by ending the year with the double of the Alfred Dunhill Championship and the South African Open. He won the Order of Merit with a tournament to spare, but still had work to do at Pearl Valley. He needed that second successive win to get himself into the top 50 in the world and claim a place in the Masters and the World Golf Championship events.

"I was 109th in the world two weeks ago and knew I had to win two in a row to get back into the top 50, and that was just dream talk then. But here it's happened," Sterne explained. A superb bunker shot at the 72nd hole at the South African Open, which helped get him into a playoff, was just an example of how his confidence has increased. "Fortunately, every time the big shots are on, I've put it in the right place. I have no idea why. Luck, maybe. I've been fortunate to always do that throughout my career. I know that when I'm in that position I can pull it off."

Joburg Open
Johannesburg, South Africa
Winner: Richard Sterne

Of all the 204 competitors who teed up in the Joburg Open, Richard Sterne was the highest ranked in the world and started as the favorite. The South African lived up to his billing, but only after a dramatic final day at Royal Johannesburg and Kensington when Sterne emerged as the champion on the second hole of a playoff. With the event being co-sanctioned, Sterne recorded his third title on the European Tour, where his win in the 2007 Wales Open lifted him to 14th on the Order of Merit.

Joining Sterne with a 13-under-par total of 271 were Garth Mulroy and Sweden's Magnus A. Carlsson, who was seventh on the Challenge Tour in 2007. Carlsson set the target after birdies at the 17th and 18th holes for 66. Sterne repeated the feat, missing a good eagle chance at the last, with 65, the best score of the day. Mulroy claimed a two at the 16th to draw even, but could not birdie either of the last two holes.

In the playoff at the 18th hole, Sterne set up another eagle chance when he hit a six iron from a fairway bunker to 25 feet. But the putt stopped on the lip and all three players managed a birdie. At the same hole the next time around, however, Sterne was the only one to make his four after an even better second shot to 12 feet, although again he could not convert for the eagle. Carlsson could not get up and down from a greenside bunker, and though Mulroy chipped to eight feet, his putt to stay alive horseshoed out.

"It was a tough day and it took a lot out of me," said Sterne. "I haven't felt great the last couple of days and I surprised myself today. It was close and it needed some special things. Any time you're the favorite to win or anything like that, I think it's a little bit more pressure. I didn't get off to a good start at all. I think I was three over at some stage early in the week, but I came back strong and that's what it's about."

Darren Clarke finished in fourth place, two strokes behind, in a welcome return to form for the Irish Ryder Cup star. He scored 65 in the second round and five birdies from the seventh promised better times after a loss of form in 2007.

Dimension Data Pro-Am
Sun City, South Africa
Winner: James Kamte

James Kamte created history by becoming the first black South African to win on the summer swing of the Sunshine Tour. Kamte roared back from two behind at the turn in the final round with five birdies to beat South African Open champion James Kingston by three strokes at the Gary Player Country Club at Sun City.

A rising star, Kamte won his first title on the winter section of the Sunshine Tour in 2007. The 25-year-old from Queenstown, dressed colorfully in orange trousers, red shirt and red cap, birdied the 10th and 12th, went in front with another at the 14th, then set up four-footers at the 15th and 17th. His 70 left Kamte at 11 under par, while Kingston closed with 74. Peter Karmis was a stroke further back, while among those tied for fourth place was Thomas Aiken, who was challenging for the title until an eight at the 17th.

"Coming up the ninth, I hit a great five iron in, but messed up the hole," said Kamte, who is deeply religious. "I looked at the leaderboard and saw I was only two behind. I prayed all the way to the 10th and when I got out of the cart, I turned to my caddie Stanley (Moeng) and said to him 'We are going to win this.' I just heard God talking to me so clearly. From there, He did all the work. I had a great birdie at the 10th and 12th, and walking up the 13th fairway, I could just make out that I was lying second. That was the kick I needed. Even after that bogey, I just told myself, 'you only need two birdies, James.'"

Nashua Masters
Port Edward, Natal
Winner: Marc Cayeux

Zimbabwe's Marc Cayeux claimed his ninth Sunshine Tour title and dedicated his victory to his baby son Ross after collecting the Nashua Masters at the Wild Coast Sun Country Club. Cayeux came from three behind Bradford Vaughan with a closing 68. A couple of early birdies brought Cayeux to one behind, but then the wind picked up and Vaughan stumbled with a double bogey at the fifth followed by two more bogeys.

Vaughan was attempting to overcome a bout of encephalitis and fought back on the last nine with a chance of a playoff only slipping away when his birdie putt at the last lipped out. "I felt flat over the first four holes," said Vaughan. "I couldn't feel my legs and it really threw me. But I'll take the result. At least I'm out there playing. And Marc deserves a well-fought for victory."

Vaughan closed with 73 to finish two behind Cayeux's 12-under-par 268 total. Warren Abery placed third after a final round of 65, while Justin Walters finished a further stroke behind.

"The wind turned three days of 'Mild Coast Sun' into the Wild Coast Sun. That's how it earned its reputation and I am really thrilled to have won under these conditions," said Cayeux. "It's also great to have my name on the same trophy as my idol, Mark McNulty. It's a special thing for me to be up there with Mark."

Africa Open
Port Alfred, South Africa
Winner: Shaun Norris

In fierce winds that blew away the rest of the field, Shaun Norris stood firm to record his first victory on the Sunshine Tour in the inaugural Africa Open at the Gary Player layout at Fish River Sun Country Club in the Eastern Cape. Having taken a one-stroke lead after rounds of 68, 69 and 70, Norris's final effort of 68, the best of the day, stretched his winning margin to six strokes over Nic Henning.

With winds gusting up to 60 miles per hour on the coastal course, Norris started brilliantly with a birdie at the first and an eagle at the par-five second. The Pretoria professional dropped a couple of shots, but then birdied the seventh and was in total command of the tournament by the turn. Birdies at the 14th, 16th and 17th holes meant a bogey at the last was immaterial.

Norris credited his father, Patrick, for teaching him how to play in the wind. "My dad was a member at Humewood in Port Elizabeth in the 1970s and '80s. He taught me all I know about playing in the wind and is hugely responsible for this victory today."

Norris earned R190,200 for the victory, more than in any of his six seasons on the Sunshine Tour, but in 2007 had tasted victory on a satellite tour in America at the Southern Open in Charlotte, North Carolina. "I set myself a goal at the beginning of the week to stay calm and collected and to stick to a well-laid game plan," he said. Norris finished at 13-under-par 275, while Henning came through the pack with a 69 to finish two clear of Marc Cayeux, Jean Hugo and Grant Muller.

Vodacom Championship
Pretoria, South Africa
Winner: James Kingston

James Kingston's wonderful summer continued as the 40-year-old added to the South African Airways Open he won in December 2007 with the Vodacom Championship two months later. Kingston rallied from a four-stroke deficit with a round to play by closing with a best-of-the-day 65 to beat long-time leader Adilson da Silva by two strokes. Da Silva, who was on top of the leaderboard for 52 holes after going ahead during the second round, faltered with 71, while Kingston triumphed with 17-under-par 271 at Pretoria Country Club.

It was a pair of bogeys at the 13th and 14th holes from the Brazilian that gave encouragement to the fast-charging Kingston. A birdie from 25 feet at the tricky par-three 16th brought Kingston even with da Silva, and he then went on to birdie both the 17th and the par-five 18th, chipping up from short of the green to two feet, while his opponent was unable to respond.

"This is obviously a fairytale ending for me," said Kingston, "but I do feel for Adilson, having been in the same position too many times myself. I always thought I had a chance, that Adilson having led for two days could affect him today and that two or three behind would always have a chance on this layout. You would expect to have a chance of birdie at 17 and 18, but a birdie at that tough par-three 16th, that's something special."

Kingston's win qualified him for the WGC - Bridgestone Invitational in August, while Hennie Otto picked up a R100,000 bonus for winning the Vodacom Swing, including events from the 2007 winter schedule and the 2008 Vodacom Championship.

Telkom PGA Championship
Johannesburg, South Africa
Winner: Louis Oosthuizen

Louis Oosthuizen continued his love affair with the Woodmead course at the Country Club in Johannesburg by defending his title at the Telkom PGA Championship with an astonishing 14-stroke victory. This set a record for the largest winning margin in a 72-hole event on the Sunshine Tour, which was founded in 1967.

Oosthuizen, who won in 2007 on the same course with a score of 22 under par, this time upped that to 28 under par with a total of 260. This was one stroke outside Mark McNulty's record of 29 under par (259) when winning the Royal Swazi Sun Pro-Am in 1987, a total matched by David Frost at the 1994 Lexington PGA Championship at Wanderers, which equated to 21 under par.

Oosthuizen's fourth win in 12 months in South Africa began with a round of 66 that left him two strokes off the lead. On the second day he set a course record of 63 to take a five-stroke lead. He extended the margin to nine strokes after another 66 in the third round, and while everyone else was playing for second place, he talked openly about trying to beat McNulty's record. Five birdies in the first six holes had him on course and another at the 10th got him to 27 under. But he then bogeyed, and although he picked up another couple of birdies, he could not take advantage of the par-fives at the 16th and 18th holes. The closing 65 left the runner-up, Hennie Otto, far adrift at 14 under, with Jake Roos in third place and Charl Schwartzel in fourth.

Oosthuizen was perturbed that the final group was put on the clock, but it was still a grand way to end the summer season in South Africa. "To manage to par the last four holes was disappointing because I wanted that McNulty record," he said. "Still, this was by far the best four rounds of my career and I'll take a lot of confidence onto the European Tour, knowing I can go so low. I haven't won there yet, but I'm sure it'll come."

Mount Edgecombe Trophy
Kwazulu Natal, South Africa
Winner: Mark Murless

Mark Murless did not have a lot going for him on the last day of the Mount Edgecombe Trophy. He was seven strokes behind leader Darren Fichardt and on the third hole realized his driver was cracked. "After my tee shot there, I realized something was very wrong," Murless explained. "I had been hitting the driver poorly for two days, but this time the ball went nowhere near where I aimed. I checked the driver and saw that the graphite was cracked at the back of the head. Nothing for it but to carry on. In a sense it helped, because it took the stress off knowing it wasn't me hitting the ball so badly."

Four birdies on the first nine put Murless right in contention as Fichardt, who enjoyed eight birdies in a row from the 10th to the 17th in the third round to take a two-stroke lead over Adilson da Silva, faltered. Birdies at the 11th, 14th and 16th holes put Murless into the lead at 15 under par, but back down the course Fichardt birdied the 13th and 14th holes to get back to his overnight position of 15 under.

But both men dropped two shots on the closing holes. Murless drove into the hazard at the par-five 17th and took six before three-putting at the par-three 18th. Although Fichardt had bogeyed the 16th, Murless assumed he had lost the tournament and headed for the showers. But Fichardt also had a bogey at the last, so they went back to the 18th.

Again, both men finished on the right edge of the green, with the flag on the extreme left, and while Fichardt took three to get down, Murless hit a superb lag-putt up to a foot and holed that for his fourth victory on the Sunshine Tour and his second of the summer after winning the Nedbank Affinity Cup in the previous November. Murless had closed with 67 for 13-under-275 total, while Fichardt had 74. "I wasn't expecting anything today, so this is a great feeling," Murless said.

Chainama Hills Zambia Open
Lusaka, Zambia
Winner: Tyrone Ferreira

It is not often the leader going into the final round of a tournament can afford to score 10 strokes worse than the previous day and still win, but that is exactly what happened to Tyrone Ferreira at the Chainama Hills Zambia Open. After two sunny and calm days in Lusaka, Ferreira was at 11 under par with rounds of 68 and 65. He led by two strokes over Johan Etsebeth and by three over Jean Hugo. But for the final day, a strong southeasterly wind played havoc with the field. Ferreira shot 75 and, at eight-under 208 total, still won by two strokes over Charl Coetzee and Divan van den Heever, who scored rounds of 69 and 70 respectively. Hugo and Etsebeth were among those tied for fourth place after rounds of 75 and 76.

Ferreira, age 19 from Alberton, won four times on the South African amateur circuit in 2007 and then earned his card for the Sunshine Tour at the December qualifying tournament. He finished ninth at the Joburg Open, and then his rookie season got even better here with his maiden victory. Three bogeys in the first nine left him tied with Hugo, but a couple of birdies after the turn and a double bogey from Hugo at the 14th put Ferreira clear. He had three shots in hand at the last, and after driving into the trees, chipped back to the fairway and settled for a bogey.

"It's not exactly the way I would have liked to finish, but a win is a win. Actually it's a little unreal still; maybe it will sink in when I hold the trophy. It's great, just great. I'll always remember this day," Ferreira said. "When I teed off, I was nervous as hell. I tried not to think about winning, but rather to focus on keeping the lead."

Vodacom Origins of Golf Free State
Bloemfontein, South Africa
Winner: Dion Fourie

A wrist injury that prevented him from practicing helped Dion Fourie to his first victory for five years at the Vodacom Origins of Golf Free State in Bloemfontein. Fourie was forced to sit out much of the summer season in South Africa with the left wrist injury, which he now felt would not improve. The only answer had been to rest it as much as possible and so Fourie had cut back on practicing as much as he used to. "I have to rest my wrist quite a bit, which means I only seriously practice when something in my game goes out of whack," he said. "Kind of ironic how not practicing has actually paid off for me."

Fourie, a former South African motor cross champion, began the final round one stroke behind John Bele, but left the rest of the grid trailing in his wake as he sped away on the front nine. Fourie eagled the third hole, had three birdies in a row from the fifth, and also birdied the ninth to be out in 29.

At the turn Fourie was six ahead, and although he leaked shots coming home, including a double bogey at the short 16th, he still coasted home to win by two strokes over Jean Hugo and Chris Swanepoel. Both the runners-up finished with 70s, but Fourie had 69 to get to a 15-under-par total of 201. Bele, after a closing 73, shared fourth place with Chris Williams and Merrick Bremner.

Fourie's previous win came at the 2003 Bearing Man Highveld Classic. "This win feels better than the first because I feel I have improved in many areas," said Fourie. "I wouldn't call it the perfect victory, because there are a lot of areas where I can improve; but in terms of managing my game, my pace and patience, I would say it is probably the best tournament I've had in years."

Vodacom Origins of Golf Gauteng
Pretoria, South Africa
Winner: Tyrone van Aswegen

Tyrone van Aswegen produced a strong finish with five birdies in a row on the final nine to claim his maiden victory as a professional in the Vodacom Origins of Golf Gauteng at Pretoria Country Club. The 26-year-old from Johannesburg came from three shots behind at the start of the round and posted 65 to win by a commanding four strokes at 15-under-par 201.

Darren Fichardt and Neil Schietekat shared second place at 11-under-par 205 with respective final rounds of 68 and 72, while Chris Swanepoel finished third at 10 under with a closing 69. Schietekat initially maintained his overnight lead to be two ahead of van Aswegen after nine holes, but van Aswegen rallied with a last nine of 31 to take the title.

"I'm absolutely delighted," he said. "I was proud of the way I finished off, with that really good back nine. It was a really strong field this week but I always knew I had a chance."

While admitting to being a bit nervous going into the last nine, van Aswegen holed a 20-foot putt for par on the 10th to settle himself before his final charge. "That helped a lot and really kick-started my back nine," he said, referring to the five birdies he made thereafter, the most impressive of which came on the par-four 13th. "That's a difficult hole. When I made that 15-footer for birdie I went one ahead of the field. And then I just finished strong."

He hit a superb second shot into the 17th green for a tap-in birdie there, and then birdied the 18th as well. Van Aswegen's victory went some way towards easing the disappointment of losing in a playoff to Alan McLean for the 2006 Dimension Data Pro-Am.

Samsung Royal Swazi Sun Open
Mbabane, Swaziland
Winner: Jean Hugo

After steaming to a nearly unassailable lead on the opening day, Jean Hugo almost strolled to the finish line to win the Samsung Royal Swazi Sun Open. The 32-year-old Stellenbosch professional signed off on a final round of 73 at the Royal Swazi Sun Country Club, which was worth just a single point under the modified-Stableford format. Hugo walked away with the top prize of R110,950 for his sixth Sunshine Tour victory, celebrating a six-point triumph over Kwazulu Natal's Neil Schietekat with a winning total of 56 points.

Schietekat added nine points to take his total to 50 points and edge out first-round leader Desvonde Botes for sole second place. Trevor Fisher, Jr. picked up 14 points to finish fourth with 45 points.

After a string of top-10 finishes, it was no surprise to see Hugo race into contention with first-day scores of 16 and 26 points, before adding 13 points in the third round.

"It's a different kind of stress when you are leading by such a margin.

You know under this format the guys can catch you, especially if they start making eagles," said Hugo. "I kept my eye on the leaderboard and I could see some guys starting to make a move. It was only after that second birdie at the 15th that I knew I would be okay. Winning is great, but to tell you the truth, right now it's more of a relief after the pressure of staying ahead today."

Nashua Golf Challenge
Sun City, South Africa
Winner: Keith Horne

Keith Horne surprised himself by ending up in a playoff, but took advantage of his luck to win the Nashua Golf Challenge at the Gary Player Country Club at Sun City. It was the 36-year-old's third victory on the Sunshine Tour and came at the expense of Nic Henning, who only four days earlier had been involved in a serious car crash.

Both players benefited from the collapse of overnight leader Desvonde Botes, who squandered a five-stroke lead with a closing 78 to finish tied for third place. Horne got himself into contention with two birdies and a bogey on the front nine. He then got into a tie for the lead with another birdie at the 14th, not that he was aware of the situation.

"It was a tough day. I thought I was still three behind because there were no leaderboards," said Horne. "I only realized I was in contention when Nic told me walking down the 17th fairway."

At the par-five 18th, which plays as the ninth for the Nedbank Golf Challenge later in the year, Horne blocked his tee shot into the trees. His third barely escaped and he was left with a four iron to the green, which just climbed over the water hazard. "I've been in that water hazard more times than I care to remember. One foot shorter and it would have gotten very wet," he said.

Horne signed for 70 and Henning for 72 to tie at six-under-par 210. Both men birdied the 18th at the first extra hole, but playing the hole again Henning drove offline and had to lay up. Horne went for the green and made it home to two-putt for victory.

"It was a great feeling when that last putt dropped. This has been the toughest victory of my three wins. It felt like I was swimming against the current all day and Nic is a tough competitor. It's a nice feeling to walk away from it all with this accomplishment," said Horne.

Vodacom Origins of Golf Kwazulu Natal
Kwazulu Natal, South Africa
Winner: Jean Hugo

Jean Hugo claimed his second victory in three starts when he won the Vodacom Origins of Golf Kwazulu Natal at Selborne. Hugo started the final round two strokes off the lead and closed with 68 to win by two strokes with 13-under-par 203 total. Bradford Vaughan finished second at 11 under with a final round of 68, while Steve van Vuuren, Prinavin Nelson, P.H. McIntyre and Desvonde Botes all finished at 10 under par.

Hugo's fine form had seen him collect eight top-10s in 13 events and finish no worse than sixth in his last six tournaments. "I've been working hard and it's very pleasing to see it pay off," said Hugo.

He started the round two strokes behind leader Vaughn Groenewald and made an immediate impact on the leaderboard with birdies at his first two holes. As Groenewald stumbled to a 79, including a back nine of 42, Hugo dropped only one shot in a round where he had to grind out some vital pars.

"It was difficult out there, particularly on the back nine where I just tried to hang in there," said Hugo. "I made a very good par on 17. It was a bit lucky actually, but I guess the bounces just went my way on that back nine."

Lombard Insurance Classic
Mbabane, Swaziland
Winner: Merrick Bremner

Despite oversleeping that morning, Merrick Bremner held his nerve down the stretch to upstage some of the biggest names on the Sunshine Tour and lift the Lombard Insurance Classic trophy for his maiden title. Showing maturity beyond his 22 years, Bremner held off the combined challenges of Kevin Stone and Bradford Vaughan and kept his overnight advantage going with a six-under 66. His winning total of 18-under 198 was three shots better than Stone, who matched his 66 for second place on his own, and four clear of Vaughan (69) and former South African Amateur Strokeplay winner Josh Cunliffe, who carded 67.

Bremner birdied the first hole, gave it back at the fourth, but forged ahead again with a birdie at the fifth. After birdies at the seventh and ninth, he romped home in style with six straight pars after a birdie on the 11th and an eagle at the 13th. "It was the perfect finish, the kind of result you dream of," said Bremner. "It was an unbelievable round. After the start I had this morning, who would have thought it."

Bremner had booked a wake-up call for seven o'clock but fell asleep again, only to wake up an hour and a half later. "I had to rush to get ready, rush to the driving range and rush to the course. This left me very little time to think about things and that was probably my saving grace."

Although thankful for the support of his parents, the emotional Bremner dedicated his maiden victory to his grandmother, Pamela, the person he says gave him the biggest incentive to win. "My grandma used to walk with me as a junior, when I was an amateur and when I won Q School in 2005. Every time I see her, she tells me that she wants to see me win a pro event before she passes away. I'm glad I could have done that for her."

SAA Pro-Am Invitational
Paarl, Western Cape, South Africa
Winner: George Coetzee

A former leading South African amateur, George Coetzee won his second title on the Sunshine Tour when he claimed the SAA Pro-Am Invitational at Paarl. The 22-year-old registered rounds of 72, 66 and 69 for nine-under-par total of 207 to finish three ahead of the experienced Warren Abery and Doug McGuigan in soaking rain. Grant Muller, Jaco Van Zyl and Bradford Vaughan all tied for fourth place a further stroke behind, while Richard Sterne settled for seventh with his final-round 72.

"The questions just kept going and going through my head on the front nine," said Coetzee, who earned R79,250 for his winning effort. "After the birdie at the ninth, I told myself to concentrate on the job at hand. It was the only thing I could control and that calmed me down a lot."

The gap between Coetzee and his experienced challengers widened to two shots when both Abery and McGuigan, who birdied the 11th but dropped a stroke again at the 12th, dropped shots and the youngster rolled in a seven-footer for a birdie. "I knew it was important to be patient over the last two holes," said Coetzee. "That's where I nearly blew it the last time I was in contention. I started thinking ahead about the closing holes and almost gave it away."

Vodacom Origins of Golf Western Cape
Hermanus, South Africa
Winner: Garth Mulroy

All it took was one moment of brilliance at the first hole for Garth Mulroy to seal his victory in the Vodacom Origins of Golf Western Cape at Arabella. Mulroy went into the final round with a three-stroke lead and then surged further ahead when he holed out with a seven iron for an eagle-two on the first. He went on to close with a round of 69 to win by four strokes with six-under-par 210 total.

"The weather wasn't great the last few days and it was tough, so I'm certainly happy to have won," said Mulroy. Richard Sterne finished second at two-under-par 214 with a final round of 69, while Steve van Vuuren and Gerhard Trytsman shared third place at even par.

After the wind and rain of the previous day, the final round dawned with much more benign conditions. But it was Mulroy's even-par 72 in the stormy second round which really laid the platform for his victory. "That second round was pretty tough and a lot of the guys went backwards," he said. "I played well the first day and then shot even par the second day because I was determined not to go backwards."

Determined not to play defensively on the last day, Mulroy's eagle-two at the first effectively ended any hopes the rest of the field had of making a charge. "A few guys around me made bogey at the first, so that was a three-shot swing right there. It kind of relaxed me, but at the same time you've got to keep going. You can't just keep playing safe all day because

Major Champions

Padraig Harrington defended at the Open Championship, then added the PGA Championship trophy.

Trevor Immelman, Masters Tournament

Tiger Woods, U.S. Open Championship

Masters Tournament

Trevor Immelman, following Gary Player, became the second South African to win the Masters.

His 72 left Tiger Woods second, three shots back.

Brandt Snedeker was second after 54 holes.

Stewart Cink climbed into a tie for third place.

U.S. Open

Doug Pensinger/Getty Images

It took 91 holes before Tiger Woods could claim his third U.S. Open Championship trophy.

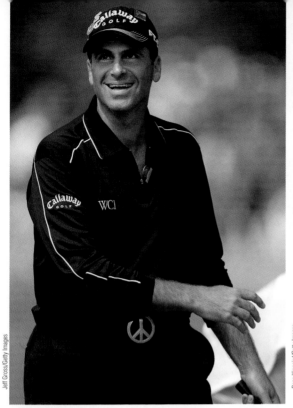

Rocco Mediate became a crowd favorite.

Lee Westwood contended late.

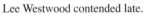

D.J. Trahan (left) and Robert Karlsson were tied for third place on 286.

Ross Kinnaird/Getty Images

Unsure whether he would be able to play, Padraig Harrington surprised even himself.

Turning back the years, Greg Norman led the Open with but nine holes to play.

Henrik Stenson, with 71, joined Norman on 289.

Ian Poulter tied for the lead.

PGA Championship

David Cannon/Getty Images

Padraig Harrington posted a pair of 66s on the weekend to win the PGA Championship by two.

Stuart Franklin/Getty Images

Sergio Garcia shot 279 to tie for second, having 69 in the third round and 68 in the fourth.

With spiderman-like technique in studying putts, Camilo Villegas shared fourth place.

Henrik Stenson tied for fourth place.

Ben Curtis led after 54 holes.

There was champagne spray over Valhalla as the United States won the Ryder Cup.

Ian Poulter topped Europe with 4 points.

Hunter Mahan led the U.S. with 3½ points.

Boo Weekley was inspiring and entertaining.

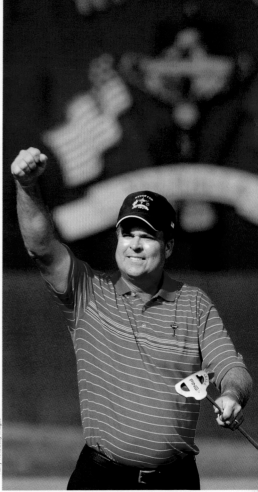

Rival captains Paul Azinger and Nick Faldo.

Kenny Perry was a Kentucky favorite son.

A large, vocal gallery gathered in anticipation of the first shots in the Ryder Cup singles matches.

Around The World

Vijay Singh easily claimed the FedExCup championship after winning the first two events.

While not winning, Phil Mickelson was close at the WGC - Bridgestone Invitational.

Sergio Garcia claimed his biggest victory yet at The Players and was a runner-up four times.

Geoff Ogilvy was a winner in the Australian PGA.

Swede Robert Karlsson led Europe.

Rising star Camilo Villegas made his mark.

Ernie Els had his first U.S. win in four years.

Lee Westwood was third in Europe.

Jim Furyk had a rare year without winning.

Steve Stricker had two second-place finishes.

K.J. Choi won the Sony Open in Hawaii.

Anthony Kim had two PGA Tour victories.

Adam Scott took the Byron Nelson title.

Ryuji Imada won the AT&T Classic.

Miguel Angel Jimenez celebrated his PGA win.

Ryo Ishikawa turned pro and won.

Shigeki Katayama won three in Japan.

that's when you make mistakes and the next thing they're right on top of you."

Telkom PGA Pro-Am
Pretoria, South Africa
Winner: Merrick Bremner

Merrick Bremner made a brilliant birdie at the final hole to steal his second title of the season by one stroke at the Telkom PGA Pro-Am at Centurion Country Club in Pretoria. Two off the pace at the start of the day, Bremner held off a spirited challenge from both Dean Lambert and Jaco Van Zyl. With Van Zyl and Lambert in the clubhouse at 15-under-par 201, the 22-year-old from Cullinan holed a pressure 12-foot putt at the 18th for the winning birdie to deny the seasoned campaigners a shot at a playoff.

Bremner's five-under-par 67 saw him wrap up his second Sunshine Tour title with a 16-under 200 winning total. Lambert, who twice held a share of the lead in the final round, finished with 66, which was matched by Van Zyl to share second place, while defending champion Michiel Bothma signed for 71 to finish alone in fourth at 14 under.

Bothma, the overnight leader, stayed clear of the field through the first four holes, but a bogey at the fifth opened the door to let in Van Zyl, Lambert and Bremner. The lead changed hands frequently, and ironically, although Bremner never held the outright lead, the young man's tenacity saw him gain the upper hand. He made eight birdies, including crucially three in the last four holes.

"The first victory was sweet but this one is even sweeter," said Bremner, who opened with 63 before falling back with a 70 in the second round. "Not only do I qualify for the co-sanctioned events at the end of the year, but to win at home is really special, and to win twice in one season is proof to me of just how far I have come this year."

SunCoast Classic
Durban, South Africa
Winner: Jake Roos

It was a little more work than he wanted, but Jake Roos two-putted the third hole of a playoff for a birdie to beat Omar Sandys and claim his first title at the SunCoast Classic at Durban Country Club. Sandys, who took a three-stroke lead into the final round after a blistering 63 on Friday, limped home in 78 strokes, while Roos signed for a slightly healthier 74 on a day of strong winds.

The 27-year-old from Cape Town turned the tables in his favor when he rolled in a five-foot birdie putt at the final hole of regulation to tie the overnight leader at six-under-par 210 and force the extra play. At the third extra hole, Roos found the fringe of the 18th green with a four iron at the short par-four which was playing downwind. Sandys missed the green, and as Roos two-putted, Sandys missed from 20 feet to stay alive.

The wind had been at its worst on the opening holes, which played into the elements. Roos lost a ball at the second hole, but birdied the next two to regain some momentum. Sandys, however, remained ahead until he bogeyed the 16th and 17th holes to open the door to Roos. The expected challenge from Marc Cayeux, in second place after round two, failed to materialize, and the Zimbabwean finished where he started, three off the pace and in third place with three-under 213.

Roos had spent several months in the United States during the year with the International Athlete Management program and reaped the benefit of playing on the Nationwide Tour. "I definitely learned how to compete, how to keep my composure and fight until the last ball drops. I've learned how to stay positive and believe I can do it, even if the odds are against me."

Vodacom Origins of Golf Eastern Cape
Port Elizabeth, South Africa
Winner: George Coetzee

Pretoria's George Coetzee claimed the third victory of his career when he won the Vodacom Origins of Golf Eastern Cape at a wet and windy Humewood. Coetzee started the final round with a two-stroke lead and weathered a disastrous opening few holes as well as the rain and wind on his way to a one-stroke victory over Jean Hugo.

A final round of 73 for a total of four-under-par 212 was good enough to earn Coetzee the title and his second victory in five tournaments. Hugo took second place at 213 with a closing 72 in which he threw away a chance for a playoff with a three-putt for bogey on the 18th. Chris Williams finished third at 214 with a final round of 73.

"This was really nerve-wracking," said Coetzee. "This was close to the worst weather I've played in, and there were a lot of players in contention. It's nice to win when there are so many players fighting for it."

Coetzee hardly enjoyed the perfect start and was four over par through the first four holes thanks to two bogeys and a double bogey from the second hole. "I was kicking myself after that," he said. "I thought, 'Here we go again.' I think the problem was that I haven't led a tournament going into the final round in quite a while, and I'm still learning how to do that."

The turning point proved to be when Coetzee holed a putt from off the green at the ninth. He added birdies at the 11th, 12th and 15th holes. Hugo birdied the 15th and 16th to get back to even, but then three-putted from 40 feet at the last to hand victory to Coetzee.

Seekers Travel Pro-Am
Johannesburg, South Africa
Winner: Trevor Fisher, Jr.

It took three extra holes to find a winner of the Seekers Travel Pro Am at Dainfern, but Trevor Fisher, Jr. eventually prevailed over a valiant Desvonde

Botes for his third Sunshine Tour title. Fisher had a 30-foot putt for eagle to win the tournament at the 18th in regulation play of the 54-hole event, but only managed a birdie to tie with Botes at 10 under par for a 206 total. Moments earlier, Botes had missed a five-foot birdie putt on the same green which would have moved him to 11 under and given him the title.

Both played the first two playoff holes in par. Botes let Fisher off the hook, first when he missed a five-footer, then a 10-foot putt for birdie with Fisher putting for par at the second hole. Fisher took full advantage of his lifeline at the third extra hole. His tee shot found the left-hand rough behind a few saplings, and with no clear shot the 29-year-old executed a terrific hook to land five feet from the pin. "It was a great shot," said the Modderfontein Golf Club professional. "I had 191 meters to the flag, into the wind, and I hit a six iron."

Botes's second shot found the right greenside bunker. He, too, played an exquisite shot out of the bunker to within five feet of the hole, but Fisher was not about to let a third chance slip away and duly drained his eagle putt.

Earlier in his round, Fisher was 11 under through eight holes, but a disastrous triple bogey on the par-three 11th quashed his momentum. "I let a lot of guys in there with that score," he said. "I told myself to be patient and got back nicely with a birdie on the 14th, missed a short putt for birdie on the 17th, and then the birdie on the 18th to force the playoff."

BMG Classic
Johannesburg, South Africa
Winner: Doug McGuigan

Doug McGuigan ended a two-year title drought with a narrow one-shot defeat over Jaco Van Zyl at the inaugural BMG Classic at Ebotse Golf and Country Estate. McGuigan put the seal on a flawless round when he holed a monster 28-yard putt for eagle at the 18th to take the clubhouse lead with a final-round 68. After an unexpected bogey at the 15th, the pressure was on tournament leader Van Zyl to birdie at least one of the finishing holes to tie McGuigan and force a playoff.

Having failed to take advantage at the 16th and 17th, Van Zyl faced a 20-yard birdie putt at the last, but again the putter failed to cooperate. He had to settle for the runner-up spot, one shot shy of the winner's 10-under total of 206. Cape Town's Christiaan Basson carded 69 to finish alone in third, one shot behind Van Zyl, while Jbe' Kruger (71), Ulrich van den Berg (69), SunCoast Classic winner Jake Roos (68) and Brazil's Adilson da Silva (71) shared fourth at seven under.

McGuigan, who had not won since the 2007 Telkom PGA Pro-Am, described this triumph as the best of his three Sunshine Tour victories. But da Silva ran into trouble at the ninth after leading the tournament at nine under. The Brazilian and his playing partner, Lindani Ndwandwe, played each other's balls and incurred a two-stroke penalty each. Both returned to the area where the infringement occurred, but played from incorrect lies and were penalized a further two shots each. Having signed for eights at the par-four ninth, da Silva did well to recover for a third-place tie.

Metmar Highveld Classic
Witbank, South Africa
Winner: James Kamte

James Kamte added his name to an illustrious list of former winners when he stormed to victory at the 29th Metmar Highveld Classic, the Sunshine Tour's longest running Pro-Am, at Witbank. Among the past winners are Ernie Els, Retief Goosen, Marc McNulty, John Bland and David Frost. Recent winners include Darren Fichardt, Bradford Vaughn and Marc Cayeux.

Kamte, a 26-year-old from Queenstown, produced a scintillating final-round eight-under-par 64 to come from behind to claim his third professional title with a winning total of 20-under-par 196. Five shots back, overnight leader Brandon Pieters (71), Desvonde Botes (68) and BMG Classic winner Doug McGuigan (65) tied for second place. Four players, including Seekers Travel Pro-Am winner Trevor Fisher, Jr. (70), tied for fourth at 14 under.

Over the first two rounds, Kamte had gone about his business quietly and efficiently before emerging from the chasing pack on the final day to steal victory. Two off the pace at the start of the round, he pushed his way to the lead with three successive birdies from the first hole. Kamte cancelled his first bogey with a birdie at the fifth and inched ahead with birdie number five at the par-four seventh to turn in four under.

After the turn and a birdie-bogey combination at the 10th and 11th, Kamte turned a blind eye to the battle for second unfolding behind him. A scintillating finish included birdies at the 15th and 16th holes before an eagle at the 17th.

"This year has been a really special one," said Kamte, who had returned from his first campaign in Europe. "I played a lot of tough courses in Europe this year and learned so much. Unfortunately I didn't keep my card, but this win changes a lot of things for me. I will go back to Tour School at the end of the month carrying a lot more confidence. I'm very happy with my victory, coming home with a target and achieving it."

Vodacom Origins of Golf Final
St. Francis Bay, South Africa
Winner: Jaco Van Zyl

Jaco Van Zyl broke a three-year title drought with a spirited challenge to capture the Vodacom Origins of Golf Final on a windy and wet day at St. Francis Links. After weeks of coming close, the overnight leader grinded his way to his second Sunshine Tour title. A final round of 76 in the stormy conditions at the Links, leaving him two under par, was enough to beat Bradford Vaughan (72) by one stroke. The leading pair were the only players to complete the tournament with sub-par scores.

Following five top-10 finishes in his last seven starts, it was a case of "about time" for the winner. "I've been knocking on the door for a couple of weeks now, and I've been asking myself when the next victory is going to be. Today was obviously the day," said the 2005 Platinum Classic winner. "The second one is definitely a lot sweeter than the first."

Van Zyl was three clear of first-round leader Mark Murless at the start of the day and immediately upped the ante to six after Murless walked off the first hole with a triple bogey. "After Mark's triple at the first, it hit me again that this is the kind of course where something like that could happen to anyone, especially in the conditions out there today. It doesn't take much to make a triple or double, so I stuck to playing safe. I didn't take any unnecessary risks. I tried to just take it shot for shot and not to get ahead of myself."

Murless rattled off three birdies before the turn to get back in the contest, and Vaughan steadily brought himself into the fight. After eight straight pars Van Zyl looked a shoo-in for victory until a double bogey at the ninth and a bogey at the 10th. But Murless come home in 44, including a quadruple bogey, and although Vaughan finished with a birdie, Van Zyl kept himself ahead to the finish.

Platinum Classic
Rustenburg, South Africa
Winner: Thomas Aiken

Two years after his agonizing loss to Vaughn Groenewald at Mooinooi Golf Club, Thomas Aiken claimed the Platinum Classic with an impressive five-stroke victory. The long-hitting Aiken reeled in four birdies and two eagles at the par-72 layout for a final round of 64 and secured the first-place check worth R111,743 with a winning total of 19-under-par 197.

Former winner Desvonde Botes blasted through the field with a flawless 65 to tie for second at 14-under 202 with Nashua Golf Challenge champion Keith Horne (65) and Nic Henning, who returned a blemish-free 66. David Hewan secured sole fifth place with a 67, while overnight leader Jbe' Kruger (72) tied for sixth at 12 under. Kruger performed well on the front stretch, but three unfortunate bogeys on the back nine saw the 22-year-old sign for a 72.

Aiken, who spent the season campaigning on the European Tour, said the victory was well-timed with the launch of the Summer Swing less than a month away. "I wasn't hitting the ball great the whole week, but today it turned in my favor and I got my swing working when it mattered most," said Aiken. "I am very pleased with this win. I haven't played that much here in Mooinooi, so to win this tournament is an absolute honor. The whole year in Europe I was hitting the ball great and not putting well and it seems the opposite has happened here. Golf is such a funny game. I guess today, it all went my way."

MTC Namibia PGA Championship
Windhoek, Namibia
Winner: T.C. Charamba

It might have taken four extra holes, but T.C. Charamba kept up his fine record in playoffs to defeat Merrick Bremner and win the MTC Namibia

PGA Championship at Windhoek Country Club. "I looked back to my junior golf days and I've never lost a playoff," said Charamba, "and I went to do my best and beat the other guy, which is what happened."

Charamba and Bremner each recorded five-under-par 66s in the final round to draw even with third-round leader Nic Henning, who fell out of the playoff at the second extra hole. Charamba, a 26-year-old Zimbabwean, pushed his drive to the left of the fairway on the par-five 10th after the first three holes of the playoff had failed to produce a winner. Bremner, who was long all weekend, was slap in the middle and seemed to hold the aces.

But Charamba hit a long iron onto the edge of the green, leaving himself with a 35-foot putt for eagle and putting all the pressure on Bremner. The 22-year-old Cullinan professional dropped his approach short of a green-side bunker and flopped his attempted chip into the sand. He got up and down, but Charamba made no mistake with his three-foot birdie putt and celebrated his second tour victory jubilantly.

"My putting has been letting me down all year long, and I got to a stage when I was missing two-footers," he said, "but this week I seem to have made my putter work for me and hope to keep it that way ahead of the summer."

Hassan II Trophy
Rabat, Morocco
Winner: Ernie Els

At the other end of the African continent from the Sunshine Tour, Ernie Els made a winning debut on his first trip to Morocco. Els was victorious at the unofficial Hassan II Trophy at Royal Dar-es-Salam in Rabat. Els closed with a five-under 68 on the Red Course, after scores of 69, 67 and 71, to finish two strokes ahead of Simon Dyson of England and Sweden's Johan Edfors with a winning total of 17-under-par 275.

"I suppose of all my 64 professional career wins around the world this one might, from an international perspective, slip under the radar a bit, but having experienced this tournament for the first time I can tell you it is a huge event in Morocco, boosted obviously by the King's support and involvement," Els reflected. "I must say I really enjoyed the whole experience. I loved the area, too, and had been made aware of its natural beauty from our golf course design team who have for a while been looking at this region and researching potential new golf course design projects.

"Having had a month off, this was a pretty solid effort in my first week back at work and it shows that the hard work is paying off. I'm swinging it well and hitting the ball nicely. And I feel as fit and healthy as I've ever been. I just need to keep working hard, keep playing well and keep building momentum. That's one key element that has been lacking in my game this year and, to be honest, it mainly comes down to a lack of confidence. This win in Morocco won't cure that, but it's a small step in the right direction."

Coca-Cola Championship
George, South Africa
Winner: Garth Mulroy

There was a touch of nerves for about six holes of the final round of the Coca-Cola Championship hosted by Gary Player, but Garth Mulroy settled down and pulled away for a big seven-shot victory. "It took a little while to get going," he admitted after he had bogeyed the third hole and let Neil Schietekat and Chris Williams back into the hunt, "but I had the same control as I had throughout the tournament, so I wasn't too worried."

Mulroy started a superb run of birdies from the eighth, getting four in a row, and added three more on Nos. 13, 15 and 17 to nail down the win with some ease. He led after the second round with a pair of 66s, and then his final round of 65 on a cool day at The Outeniqua at Fancourt was too hot for the rest of the field as he finished at 19-under-par 197. James Kamte and Williams had a pair of 69s to finished tied for second, but with both seeming unable to really kick-start a scoring spree, it was never enough to halt Mulroy.

Schietekat shot an edgy 71 to slip to a share of fourth with Merrick Bremner and Warren Abery. "I was doing the exact opposite of what Garth was doing," lamented Schietekat. "My putting was really not very good." Mulroy, on the other hand, felt he putted "very nicely." "I had a good week on the green," he said after closing the gap between himself and Richard Sterne at the top the Order of Merit.

Gary Player Invitational
George, South Africa
Winners: Bobby Lincoln and Garth Mulroy

Just a few days after winning the Coca-Cola Championship at Fancourt, Garth Mulroy enjoyed another winning performance on one of the resort's other courses, The Links, when he partner Bobby Lincoln to victory in the unofficial Gary Player Invitational. The pair won the better-ball competition with two rounds of 64 for a total of 18 under par. They won by three strokes over Retief Goosen and Costantino Rocca. Ironically, the veteran Lincoln had previously won the title with Goosen in 2006. On his first outing on The Links, Mulroy produced three birdies and an eagle on the back nine of the second round to confirm the victory. "It was great fun. It was a pretty nice course to play. I'll take a few days off now and then start practicing again for the upcoming summer on the Sunshine Tour," he said.

Goosen and Rocca did have something to celebrate as they combined with their amateur partners, Ines Sastre, the Spanish model and actress, and businessman Alan Pearson, to claim an eight-stroke victory with 35 under par in the four-ball team event. "It's been pleasing for me to see the swing changes starting to pay off, and my putting this weekend is back to where I want it," said Goosen.

Nedbank Affinity Cup
Sun City, South Africa
Winner: Tyrone van Aswegen

Tyrone van Aswegen won the Nedbank Affinity Cup, the warm-up event for
the Nedbank Golf Challenge, also at Sun City. Van Aswegen claimed his
second victory of the season with a four-under 68, a round which included
six birdies, to hold off a charge from Andrew Curlewis (70), Chris Williams (74) and Desvonde Botes (68) at Lost City County Club. Aswegen
finished at 12-under-par 204 to win by one over Curlewis. Overnight leader
Williams struggled after two solid rounds and only managed two birdies
with four bogeys in the final round to tie for third with Botes, two behind
the winner.

"I feel great with my second win this year, and I am absolutely happy as
I never thought it would end this way at the start of my final round, and I
just went out to play without noticing what everyone else was doing," said
van Aswegen. "I was quite surprised that 12 under was a winning target,
but I went out there today and made a few good putts."

Curlewis found himself heading the leaderboard for a while, after carding
four birdies and three bogeys on what was the hottest of the three days in
North West Province. Botes made a charge too and headed the scoreboard
after an eagle on the 11th, but a double bogey on the 16th cost the 35-
year-old the lead and a possible playoff.

Bradford Vaughn (65) turned in 35, but a late charge proved too little,
too late. He got impressive birdies on the 15th, 16th and 17th, topped with
an eagle on the 18th to tie with George Coetzee (67) and Warren Abery
(68). Van Aswegen moved from 45th to 34th on the Order of Merit with his
second victory this season after winning the Vodacom Origins in Pretoria.

Nedbank Golf Challenge
Sun City, South Africa
Winner: Henrik Stenson

Henrik Stenson had waited all year for a win and then two came in successive weeks. While the tall Swede had watched his compatriot Robert
Karlsson become the European No. 1, he finally got to share in the glory
when the pair combined to win the World Cup for Sweden in China. A
week later and Stenson could not be stopped as he ran away with the
Nedbank Golf Challenge at the Gary Player Country Club at Sun City.
Stenson led by five after an opening 63, slipped back to four ahead after
a second round of 71, but went eight clear with 65 in the third round, and
closed with 68 to win by nine strokes over American Kenny Perry with
21-under-par 267 total.

It was the largest margin in the tournament since Nick Price won by 12
strokes in 1993. Stenson was six under for his last 10 holes in the third
round and never looked like being stopped on the final day after birdieing
the second hole. Perry's 65 took him into second place, three ahead of
Karlsson, with Rory Sabbatini a further stroke behind. Stenson's total was

four strokes outside Ernie Els's record in 1999, but the course has been lengthened and strengthened significantly since then.

Not even the loss of his favored three wood — the shaft snapped while he was scuffing up a grass tee — failed to distract Stenson. The 32-year-old simply geared down to the four wood or a long iron, kept hitting the ball in the fairway and putting confidently to continue his relentless progress. Stenson revealed afterwards that he had spent a lot of time in practice working out the exact distances he was able to hit his irons in the rarefied air, and it certainly paid off as his distance control was superb — an important aspect given the horrendously thick collars of unkempt kikuyu grass around every green.

Alfred Dunhill Championship
Malelane, South Africa
Winner: Richard Sterne

Richard Sterne overcame his 18th-hole jitters at Leopard Creek to win the Alfred Dunhill Championship and confirm his position as 2008 Sunshine Tour Order of Merit winner. He parred the difficult par-five after a triple-bogey eight in the second round and a double-bogey seven in the third, and after a 69 finished at 17-under 271 total, one ahead of Johan Edfors and Robert Rock.

Sterne's mind was racing as he stood on the 18th tee. "I was thinking I've got to make par, that's all I have to do," he said. "Obviously, I wasn't feeling too comfortable on that hole. But I played it exactly how I wanted to. I would have liked to have hit the putt a little closer, but I had to knock in that final putt, which I did."

His birdie on the par-five 15th took him into the outright lead, after overnight leader Thomas Aiken was unable to reproduce his third-round heroics when he scored a course-record 11-under-par 61. Instead, he bogeyed the ninth and 10th, and then a double-bogey six on the 11th saw him relinquish the lead. He had a final opportunity to force his way to the top of the leaderboard on the 18th, but he dumped his approach into the water short of the island green. Aiken eventually bogeyed the final hole and finished the day with a 75 to tie for fourth place with Rafael Cabrera Bello.

Sterne's eight on No. 18 on the second day prompted him to say of his six-under 66 that he had yet to see such a good round with an eight in it. "I get confused with the yardage. It's not Johannesburg and it's not the coast, so it's sort of in between, and that five or six yards is what makes the difference," he said.

American Len Mattiace, who was just one stroke behind Aiken going into the final round, seemed to lose all the steadiness which had taken him to the brink of a win. A double-bogey seven on the 14th and a triple-bogey eight on the 18th saw him slide to a share of 14th place. Lee Westwood had a steady week, his final 71 giving him a share of 16th, while Rory Sabbatini didn't enjoy his golf in the bush too much. A pair of concluding 73s saw him way down in a tie for 49th place in the event co-sanctioned with the European Tour.

South African Open Championship
Paarl, Western Cape, South Africa
Winner: Richard Sterne

It took what he thought was the best bunker shot of his life to take Richard Sterne to the South African Open Championship title on a Sunday which he eventually won on the first playoff hole against Gareth Maybin. Sterne pulled his approach slightly left at the par-five 18th hole at Pearl Valley in regulation play and it landed in the bunker with very little green for him to work with. "I don't even remember hitting that bunker shot," he said. "I was trying to hit it to 15 feet, to be honest, to give myself a chance there, and it just came out perfect. It came out to three feet, way better than I could have hoped."

The birdie took Sterne to 14-under-par 274 with his final-round 66, the clubhouse lead and a chance at a second title in two weeks. He spent an anxious time in the players' lounge, reading but not absorbing a newspaper, while the 28-year-old Maybin from Belfast went about his final round with the calm of a veteran rather than someone about to play his first year on the European Tour. But Maybin couldn't buy a birdie on the homeward nine. However, he set himself up for a tournament-winning birdie on the 18th, but the eight-footer agonizingly lipped out, and the pair had to walk back down the fairway to do it all over again.

Maybin pushed his drive into a bunker on the right of the fairway, while Sterne was as long and as straight down the middle as he had been all week. Sterne made a cast-iron birdie, but Maybin could not match him, leaving the South African not just as the first man to do the double of the South African Open and the Alfred Dunhill Championship, but winner of all three co-sanctioned events on the European Tour after he had won the Joburg Open at the start of the year. He was already confirmed as the winner of the Order of Merit.

After England's Lee Westwood had held the third-round lead at 14 under, it seemed unlikely that it would also be the winning score. Ernie Els made the biggest move with a closing 64, already having had a chance of 62 before three-putting the 18th. He finished one back alongside Westwood and Rory McIlroy, who, like Sterne, confirmed his place in the world's top 50 and earned an invitation to the Masters.

"The South African Open is so prestigious and the names on this trophy are unbelievable. To have my name among those has always been a dream and a goal. I'll have to set new goals now," Sterne said. "I knew I needed to at least get to 14 under to have a chance. That last shot was probably the best bunker shot I've hit."

13. Women's Tours

The U.S. LPGA Tour's 2008 was a little like a round of golf at a strange course. You get your birdie here and there, and you get your bogeys, and then sometimes you fall in a hole.

The season started with Annika Sorenstam, after an injury-plagued 2007, winning the opener, the SBS Open. That was a big birdie. Then Lorena Ochoa, World No. 1, came out playing like gangbusters, and that was another birdie. Then followed a patchwork season.

Sorenstam won her third title in May and announced she was hanging up her clubs. Then came a debacle — the tour's new language policy, seeking to compel South Koreans to learn to speak English. The economic crisis hit, turning gloomy all over the world and leaving golf wondering. And then, finally, along came Michelle Wie. She made it through the LPGA qualifying and would join the tour in 2009.

The season looked like a Standing Room Only. Sorenstam won the SBS Open, the season starter, and then Ochoa came out in the third event, winning the HSBC Women's Champions by 11 shots. It looked like an Ochoa-Sorenstam Shootout Year. Except that Ochoa ran away from everyone, winning, all told, five of her first six starts and three of them in succession, including the first major, the Kraft Nabisco Championship. Then she cooled off and won only two more. In between, Sorenstam won two more, and then at the Sybase Classic in mid-May announced that this would be her last year. But would it?

"I know what it's like to play at the top, and you know, I don't want to do anything else," said Sorenstam, age 38. "So it's either on or it's not." Then a touch of the soap opera began to creep in. "If it's forever, I'm not really sure," she said. "But it's definitely for now." Sorenstam made similar statements during the year, indicating that it was over. Then in October she said she never used the "R-word" (retire) and that the door was open for her return. Then in November, when she missed the cut in the season-ending ADT Championship, she slammed the flag into the cup and said, "It's over." So that was it — Sorenstam was done with the LPGA Tour, possibly.

The tour fell into a big hole with its new language policy. The tour in August announced to South Korean member-players that they would have to be learn to speak English, the better to make pro-ams more fun for the amateurs who put up all that money to play with the pros. Learn to speak English, that is, or be suspended. The backlash rocked tour headquarters. There were even denouncements on editorial pages and allegations of bigotry. Some sponsors recoiled, including State Farm, which indicated it might reconsider its sponsorship unless the tour reconsidered its policy. Commissioner Carolyn Bivens quickly announced that the language policy would not include any penalties.

There were 17 new winners and six multiple winners, led by Ochoa with seven victories, including a major, the Kraft Nabisco Championship. She also led the money list with $2.7 million. Paula Creamer won four times and was No. 2 at $1.8 million. Annika Sorenstam won three, and Angela Stanford, Seon Hwa Lee and Helen Alfredsson, at 43 the senior citizen of the group, won two each.

The other majors were parceled out. Two 19-year-olds scored their first wins in majors — Taiwan's Yani Tseng, a rookie, in the McDonald's LPGA Championship, and South Korea's Inbee Park, a second-year player, in the U.S. Women's Open. Then the Ricoh Women's British Open went to the mystery golfer of the year, Korea's Ji-Yai Shin, not even a member of the LPGA. She then added the Mizuno Classic and the season-ending, million-dollar ADT Championship. She had won 21 times around the world since 2007. Which left the golf world wondering what would happen when Shin joined the tour in 2009.

The tour enjoyed a landmark event, holding its first-ever tournament in China, the Grand China Air LPGA. It was yet another example of not only the global spread of the LPGA Tour, but also the growth of the game in China. Helen Alfredsson is in the books as winner of that historic event.

The global economic crisis that hit in the fall of 2008 had an immediate impact on the LPGA's 2009 schedule. Bivens announced that four events would be lost — the ADT Championship, the Fields Open, the Ginn Tribute and the SemGroup Championship, and one event in Thailand was added. "Like many businesses and individuals, the economic crisis we are all facing has resulted in a slightly different tournament landscape for 2009," she said.

The season ended on the highest possible note for Wie, now age 19, who won her LPGA Tour playing card in the qualifying tournament in December. "I can play whenever I want now, not when I have to play ... I can pick and choose," said Wie, who in the 62 tournaments she played over the previous seven years received 53 exemptions or invitations. She drew international fame for playing in PGA Tour events as a young teen. She did not make the cut in eight tries. Wie said she would return to Stanford University for the winter quarter of classes, and planned a full LPGA schedule in 2009.

The battle for the No. 1 position on the money list of the Japan LPGA Tour came down to the final stroke of the season. When Yuri Fudoh missed a two-foot putt in the season-ending LPGA Tour Championship, the tournament victory and the money title went to Miho Koga for the first time. Koga and Fudoh, who was No. 1 six times in the past and is the all-time money winner with more than a billion yen, each won four times during the 37-event season.

Besides the victory in the Mizuno Open, the joint U.S.-Japan LPGA sanctioned tournament, South Korea's sensational Ji-Yai Shin won an early season event and finished second in her other three starts in Japan.

U.S. LPGA Tour

Women's World Cup of Golf
Sun City, South Africa
Winners: Philippines (Jennifer Rosales and Dorothy Delasin)

See Ladies African Tour section.

SBS Open
Oahu, Hawaii
Winner: Annika Sorenstam

The LPGA Tour season for 2008 got under way with the SBS Open at Turtle Bay in Hawaii in mid-February, and they might as well have hung out a sign saying, "Open for (Usual) Business."

Welcome back, Annika.

Annika Sorenstam, the smiling Swede who dominated the tour for years, fought off a host of challengers down the stretch to win by two strokes. She wrapped it up in typical Sorenstam style, with two late birdies on a four-foot putt at the 16th and a 24-footer at the 17th.

"It was huge," Sorenstam said, speaking of that putt, but she might have said the same about the victory itself. This was vintage Sorenstam. She hadn't won since 2006, and she spent 2007 in an injury limbo. This was her 70th career victory, third behind Mickey Wright (82) and Kathy Whitworth (88).

Sorenstam led off with 70, tied for 10th. In the second round, she rebounded from a double bogey at No. 4 to post a five-under 67. The tournament turned into a scramble in the final round. Going down the stretch, she was atop the leaderboard, but not alone. She was tied at one time or another with Jane Park and Momoko Ueda, and she was chased by Laura Diaz and Russy Gulyanamitta.

"It's nice to have a one-stroke lead going into 18," Sorenstam said, "but to have two — especially when it's a par-five — it's nice to have a little extra cushion." Diaz and Gulyanamitta also solved the 18th for birdies from long range, Diaz from 20 feet for a 70 and Guliyanamitta from 48 feet for a 68, giving both their career-bests, a tie for second with Jane Park (70) at eight-under 208.

"I could not have asked for a better start," Sorenstam said. "It's very gratifying to see that the preparation I've done paid off, and now I really want to put 2007 behind me and say, 'Hey, I'm a contender,' and I intend to be that all year."

Fields Open
Honolulu, Hawaii
Winner: Paula Creamer

Apart from the fact that Paula Creamer was wearing her trademark pink and Korea's Jeong Jang was not, they were perfectly matched in the Fields Open at Ko Olina Golf Club in Hawaii. Through the 54 holes of the Fields Open, they both hit 37 fairways, both hit 42 greens in regulation and both had 81 putts. But there was a crucial difference.

At the 54th and final hole, Jang was short of the green and parred. Creamer put her approach to five feet and birdied, and that was the winner.

"I went out and won the tournament over the last three holes," Creamer said. "I knew I had to make some birdies down the stretch, and those were three good holes to make birdie on."

Three closing birdies — but actually four birdies over the last five holes — that's a clutch performance. Creamer shot 66-68-66 for a 16-under-par 200 total and the one-stroke win over Jang.

Actually, it looked like Jang's tournament until that final hole. She led the first two rounds with 64-68. That one last par gave her 69 and left her one stroke short. Annika Sorenstam, who won the season-opening SBS Open the week before, was within reach in the final round until she double-bogeyed the 10th and finished fourth. Lindsey Wright birdied three of the last five holes for 67 and fell two strokes short to finish third, her career-best finish.

Creamer started the final round two behind Jang, and they played tag until Jang went back to two ahead with a birdie at the 15th. It came down to Creamer's closing magic — a 12-foot birdie putt at the par-three 16th, a 20-footer at the 17th, and at the par-four 18th, where Jang came down short and two-putted for par, Creamer hit a brilliant six iron from 164 yards to within five feet.

"I knew, coming down the stretch — just that pressure and knowing if you want to win this golf tournament — you have to make this putt," Creamer said. "I was nervous, but I was confident."

HSBC Women's Champions
Singapore
Winner: Lorena Ochoa

Annika Sorenstam, former No. 1 on the Rolex Rankings, said that putting was the difference between her and Lorena Ochoa, current No. 1, in the inaugural HSBC Women's Champions tournament in Singapore. Then there was this other difference — 11 strokes.

Ochoa, making her 2008 debut after skipping the first two tournaments in Hawaii, won the HSBC title by 11 strokes.

"It was a fantastic week," said Ochoa, who won eight times in 2007. "Starting on Thursday, the first two days (were) pretty low rounds, and on the weekend I wasn't as good with the putter, but I managed to shoot under par every day."

Ochoa's figures were 66-65-69-68–268, 20 under par at Singapore's Tanah Merah Country Club. She made 23 birdies and only three bogeys, notching her 18th career victory. Sorenstam was second at nine-under 279 and Paula Creamer was third at 281.

"She's playing well, but it's nothing I don't think that's not achievable by any means," Sorenstam said. "I think I'm playing as good from tee to green ... I just didn't make a single thing. It's really frustrating."

Said Creamer: "Lorena played awesome — what are you going to do? This was her tournament, her golf course, and it was nice to have played with her."

Ochoa began the final round leading by eight. She would have to fold completely for anyone to have a chance. But she was better than steady, shooting a bogey-free 68. She birdied the second from 20 feet and the third from five feet, both after nine irons from 130 yards. At the par-five ninth, she hit a rescue club to 30 feet and two-putted for another birdie, and made her fourth at the par-four 16th, blasting to seven feet from a greenside bunker.

"It was just great because I also had pressure," Ochoa said. "I wanted to keep the pace. I didn't want to make mistakes. I wanted to win by more than eight, which was my lead yesterday. It was good today."

MasterCard Classic Honoring Alejo Peralta
Mexico City, Mexico
Winner: Louise Friberg

Sweden's Louise Friberg, a rookie making just her third start, had a game plan. But it didn't include winning — not just yet. "I didn't think it would take me just three times to win," she said. That explains her surprise when she found herself with the MasterCard Classic trophy. If winning was the toughest part, the wait was no picnic. It was about two hours between her last putt and the good news. She'd started the final round so far behind — 10 strokes — that winning was hardly an ambition.

"I wasn't expecting to win at six under," said Friberg, who decided to wait around with the leaders still out on the course. "A lot of things went through my mind, but to be honest, I don't remember what. I don't know if I was hungry, thirsty, what. I was just waiting."

Friberg missed the cut in her first start, the season opener, and next tied for seventh place. She opened the MasterCard Classic with 72 and 73, a 145 total that left her 10 behind the leader, Ji Young Oh. And then there was Lorena Ochoa, native daughter, hoping to reward her adoring Mexican fans. But she couldn't overcome her opening 76 and tied for eighth. She was now one-for-seven in her native land.

The final round belonged to Friberg. She birdied the third, fifth and ninth holes and made the turn in two under par, then birdied the par-three 11th. At the par-five 12th, she hit a five-wood second shot from 215 yards to 20 feet and made the eagle, and now she was getting some serious attention. She birdied the 14th on a nine-foot putt and the 15th from five feet and was seven under. A bogey at the 16th left her with a six-under 210 and a long wait.

When the leaders fizzled, Friberg's tournament-low 65 gave her a one-stroke win over fellow rookie Yani Tseng (74–211). It was worth the wait. "A lot of times I played good in the last round, and I did today," Friberg said. "I guess Sundays are my day."

Safeway International
Superstition Mountain, Arizona
Winner: Lorena Ochoa

Angela Stanford, whose only LPGA Tour win came in 2006, opened the Safeway International with a 10-under-par 62 and a three-stroke lead. This was, unfortunately, the first step on her way to becoming a footnote. In fact, everyone became a footnote.

Lorena Ochoa, the defending champion, turned this one into a seven-stroke romp. She played the Prospector Course at Superstition Mountain in Arizona in 65-67-68-66–266, a whopping 22 under par. For the record, the runner-up was South Korea's Jee Young Lee. Stanford closed with a two-over 74 and tied for fourth.

"I like how I'm playing, how I feel playing on Sunday in the last group," Ochoa said. "I like to win."

The victory was her second win in three starts this season, beginning with her first, in Singapore, by a ridiculous 11 strokes. It was also the 16th win in her last 48 starts.

But this seven-stroke romp didn't turn into a romp until the final nine holes. Stanford trailed Ochoa by one entering the final round and tied her with a birdie at No. 1. Then Stanford bogeyed the 12th and triple-bogeyed the 13th. "Whether it's me or golf, I don't know," she said.

Lee bogeyed the 11th and 12th, and then was battling just to hang onto second place, which she did with 72 on a clutch putt at the 18th. "Last birdie putt, so nervous," Lee said. "It's big money."

Ochoa turned the tournament into a romp with an electrifying finish. She played her last 11 holes in six under, including three straight birdies — a 12-foot putt at the par-five 13th, and then she drove the green at the 310-yard 14th and two-putted, and hit a pitching wedge to two feet at the 15th. Then at the par-five 18th, she two-putted from 30 feet for her eighth and final birdie.

"Once I enter the tournament," Ochoa said, "I know I can win and I play to win."

Kraft Nabisco Championship
Rancho Mirage, California
Winner: Lorena Ochoa

See Chapter 7.

Corona Championship
Morelia, Michoacan, Mexico
Winner: Lorena Ochoa

This was getting ridiculous. Lorena Ochoa was reducing the LPGA Tour to the Theater of the Absurd. Another week, another win, another runaway. This time it was the Corona Championship by 11 strokes, back among the homefolks at the Tres Marias course in western Mexico. Not that geography makes any difference to Ochoa. This was her third win in succession, the fourth in her five starts and by margins of 11, seven, five and 11 strokes. Geography? She won first in Singapore, then twice in the United States, and now the Corona Championship in Mexico. This is how she did it:

• Ochoa opened with 66 at the par-73 course, tying for the lead with South Korea's Song-Hee Kim. She eagled two par-fives, holing a 25-foot putt at No. 5 and a 22-footer at No. 8. The tie was as close as anyone would get to her.

• Another 66 in the second round gave her a 14-under-par 132 total and a one-stroke lead over Inbee Park (64). Ochoa's eagle output fell to one, at the par-five 10th. "It was a great day," she said. "No bogeys."

• A third straight 66 gave Ochoa a seven-stroke lead over Park (72). Ochoa relentlessly birdied Nos. 5, 8, 9, 10, 11, 13 and 16. The home fans were getting delirious. "Every time I hit the ball, they cheer and scream," said Ochoa, now a national hero. "It's just great."

• Ochoa finally cooled off. In the final round, she managed only a four-under 69. After birdies at Nos. 1, 6 and 8, she triple-bogeyed the 11th. It never fazed her. She bounced right back and birdied Nos. 13, 14, 16 and 18 for a 25-under 267 total and an 11-stroke win over Kim.

"It was an amazing week," Ochoa said. More than she realized at first. The win, the 21st of her career, qualified her for the LPGA Tour Hall of Fame, the second youngest at age 26 years, four months, 29 days. But LPGA rules also require a player to be a member for 10 years, and she won't reach that point until 2012. No problem. She preaches patience.

Ginn Open
Reunion, Florida
Winner: Lorena Ochoa

Lorena Ochoa didn't run away with this one. This time, she won by only three strokes.

But the Mexican beat goes on (with a mariachi band in the background?). A leg-weary Ochoa didn't get to the lead until the third round, but the result was the same. Ochoa shot 68-67-65-69–269, 19-under-par 269 at the Ginn Reunion Resort near Orlando, Florida, and calmly took the Ginn Open by three strokes over Yani Tseng, age 19, a rookie out of Taiwan who was runner-up in the MasterCard Classic a month earlier.

The report card: This was Ochoa's fifth win in six starts and her fourth in succession, making her the first LPGA Tour player in 45 years to win four tournaments in four consecutive weeks. But that's as far as the consecutive-week streak would go. A worn-out Ochoa would take the next week off.

"I didn't have many legs in the end," she said. "I kept thinking — a few more minutes and I will be done. For sure, it was the toughest back nine ..."

Ochoa was leading by one starting the final round, but quickly found herself trailing when Tseng got hot and birdied three of the first five holes. Tseng holed a short putt at No. 1, then a 24-footer at No. 2 for a one-stroke lead, then a 40-footer at the par-three No. 5. Then Tseng went sour and three-putted No. 6, the first of three three-putt bogeys in the round.

Ochoa's putter failed on three consecutive birdie chances from No. 5, but she bounced right back with three straight birdies — on a 12-foot putt at the eighth, two putts from 35 feet at the par-five ninth, and a chip to two feet at the par-five 10th. Tseng eagled the 10th to get back within a stroke, but stumbled to three bogeys over the final eight holes.

Ochoa's winning margins were 11, seven, five, 11 and now three strokes. Ochoa watchers had already realized how tired she was when she didn't take her half-hour run after the third round.

"You have to make sure you don't overdo it," Ochoa said. As far as her pursuers were concerned, she already had.

Stanford International Pro-Am
Adventura, Florida
Winner: Annika Sorenstam

The inaugural Stanford International Pro-Am would come down to the great Annika Sorenstam beating future-great Paula Creamer in a playoff. But the new tournament, with its new format, would open more to rages than raves, thanks to the set-up of the two courses at Turnberry Isle and the Florida winds that whipped them. Only 21 of the 111 players broke par the first day, only 13 broke par for the week, and most rounds took nearly six hours.

"Silly tough," Sorenstam said. "It was way too tough."

It was also a scoring workout. The play alternated between the par-71 Soffer Course and the par-70 Miller Course the first two days, then went to the Soffer for the last two. The best-ball pro-am was played for the first three rounds.

And horror stories abounded. Christina Kim was leading the first round until the par-five 18th, where she triple-bogeyed off cart path, water and sand, leaving the lead to Creamer, Momoko Ueda and Young Kim at 68. (Then there was Christina Kim's nine at the 18th in the third round.) In the final round, Moira Dunn made seven at the par-three seventh and eight at the 18th and finished at 13 over par. Brittany Lincicome shot 80-80. And so it went.

Sorenstam (70) took the lead by one over Creamer (67) in the third round. In the final round, Creamer went ahead with two birdies in the first three holes, and Sorenstam caught her with a birdie at No. 6. Creamer slipped behind on a bogey out of a hazard at No. 7, then tied with a birdie at

No. 8. Then Creamer re-took the lead when Sorenstam missed a four-foot par putt at the 13th. At the par-three 17th, Creamer bogeyed off a short nine-iron tee shot and a chunked chip, and they were tied.

In the playoff, both laid up at the 18th, and both had birdie putts. Sorenstam missed, but Creamer missed worse, sending her downhiller six feet past. She missed coming back, and Sorenstam had her second win of the season, her 71st career victory and 16th in 22 playoffs.

"That's what I love, that's why I do this," Sorenstam said. "Not to say I want to have playoffs every week."

SemGroup Championship
Broken Arrow, Oklahoma
Winner: Paula Creamer

Paula Creamer had a couple of goals at the SemGroup Championship. First, there was that nagging problem of the late blow-up again. She lost the Stanford International the week before after a late stumble. Now she blew the lead again and was facing a playoff against Juli Inkster. And then there was the matter of stopping Lorena Ochoa, who was going for her fifth consecutive victory. So this was a determined Creamer at Cedar Ridge Country Club near Tulsa, Oklahoma.

"I was not going to lose this week," Creamer said. "I was going to win. This was my turn this time."

Creamer (70-71-69-72–282, two under par) did take her turn. She beat Inkster on the second extra hole and met all goals with her second win of the season and the sixth of her young career. Actually, Creamer didn't stop Ochoa single-handed. Ochoa just never got her game revved up. She tied for fifth place. "It's done," Ochoa said.

Creamer started to take control in the second round despite bogeying two of the last three holes for 71, but at one-under 141 she was the only player still under par in the strong winds that whipped across the Oklahoma flatlands. The cut came in at 10-over 152, the highest on the LPGA Tour since 2003.

Inkster got back into contention with 67 in the third round and trailed Creamer by two. The final round was not a smooth cruise. Inkster shot a comparatively quiet one-under 70 with three birdies and two bogeys. Creamer shot an erratic one-over 72, with three birdies and four bogeys. At the par-four 18th in regulation, Creamer hit her five-iron approach over the green, chipped back to 10 feet, and two-putted for a bogey. Inkster holed an 18-footer for a birdie and a two-shot swing for the tie. After a tie in pars at the first playoff hole, No. 18, Creamer holed an eight-foot putt at the second, No. 10, for a birdie and the win.

"I'm done," Creamer said. "I'm mentally done right now."

Michelob Ultra Open
Williamsburg, Virginia
Winner: Annika Sorenstam

The Michelob Ultra Open was billed as a showdown between Lorena Ochoa and Annika Sorenstam, between No. 1 and No. 2 in the world, but the shootout never materialized. Ochoa just couldn't get up steam, and Sorenstam was a runaway train, taking her third victory in eight starts by seven strokes. The other two came in tournaments Ochoa didn't play, hence the heightened anticipation for this one.

"I'm feeling it — it's turning around," said Sorenstam, who spent most of 2007 trying to get healthy. "I can't wait for the next month or so to come to the big tournaments, and I'm excited."

Ochoa, who won five of the first 10 events of the season by early May, struggled on the greens. She was within striking distance in the first two rounds, shooting 65-68, but tailed off (74-70) and tied for 12th, 12 strokes behind Sorenstam. "But I'm not upset," Ochoa said. "We know she's a great player and wants to become No. 1 again. It will be a fun year."

The Sorenstam-Ochoa show was upstaged at the start when Mhairi McKay opened with a course-record, eight-under 63 at the River Course in Williamsburg, Virginia. But she followed with 77 and finished tied for 50th. Sorenstam took over in the second round with 66 for a three-stroke edge and led from there. She was solid in the third round and stretched her bogey-free string to 53 holes before having to salvage a bogey at the 18th after hooking her drive into the water. "I saved everything today," she said. "Even the last hole."

Sorenstam sprinted home in the fourth round, making four birdies over a five-hole stretch. Nine-iron approaches set her up at the 13th from seven feet and the 14th from six. A sand wedge left her five feet at the 15th, and a six iron put her only two feet away at the 17th. A three-putt bogey at the 18th merely cut into her lush lead. She finished with 19-under 265, winning by seven over Jeong Jang, Allison Fouch, Karen Stupples and Christina King. This earned her a beer shower.

Michelle Wie, with a sponsor's exemption, made her first appearance since February, missed the cut on 75-71, and said, "I'm not far off."

Sybase Classic
Clifton, New Jersey
Winner: Lorena Ochoa

It was ironic that Lorena Ochoa returned to the spotlight just when Annika Sorenstam said she was leaving. Two days after Sorenstam won the Michelob Ultra Open in mid-May, and shortly before the Sybase Classic, she announced that this would be her last season on the LPGA Tour.

"I know what it's like to play at the top, and ... I don't want to do anything else," said Sorenstam, who had won three times so far this season. "So it's either on or it's not."

As for Ochoa, it was as though she had paused to catch her breath. She hadn't won for three weeks, including a week off. So she went back to her old ways and made the Sybase, at Upper Montclair Country Club in New Jersey, her sixth victory of the season. But this one wasn't quite a lark like the other five. Ochoa slipped by for a one-stroke win over a crowd tied for second. The tournament was reduced to three rounds when rain washed out the second.

Sorenstam opened pitching for her fourth win of the season, shooting 67 and tying with South Korea's Song-Hee Kim for the first-round lead. "This is the way I enjoy the game," Sorenstam said. "It's fairways and greens." But not for long. In the second round, Sorenstam double-bogeyed the par-five 18th and shot a one-over-par 73, and Ochoa took a two-stroke lead on Sophie Gustafson (68), who had two eagles, and Teresa Lu (69), who had one. Ochoa birdied three of the four par-fives in a five-under 67–135. "I'm going to play tomorrow like I am three shots behind," Ochoa said.

But a balky putter stopped any dreams of a runaway. Ochoa moved ahead by four early, then started missing birdie putts — 10 of them from 20 feet or less. Gustafson got to within a stroke with her birdie at the 16th and Ochoa's bogey out of a bunker at the 17th. Both reached the par five 18th in three. Gustafson missed her 12-foot birdie putt to tie, and Ochoa had only to two-putt from eight feet for a par for a 71, a 10-under 206 and her third straight Sybase victory.

Maybe Sorenstam's stunning announcement motivated her. Said Ochoa: "I don't need any more motivation."

LPGA Corning Classic
Corning, New York
Winner: Leta Lindley

The LPGA Corning Classic seemed to be the time for overdue rewards for hard work and persistence. It started with Dina Ammaccapane. A 69-69 start carried her to the 36-hole lead, and it seemed that, at age 40, after two decades and 330 starts, her first LPGA Tour win was on the horizon. Then she slipped to a 76-76 finish. Janice Moodie, 35, who won her second title six years earlier, was a stroke behind going into the third round, then disappeared with 77.

Nobody saw Leta Lindley coming, not even Lindley herself. For Lindley, 35 and the mother of two, it was 13 years, 296 starts and finally 73 holes. It came with a birdie on the first playoff hole against South Korea's Jeong Jang.

"I can hardly believe it," said Lindley, whose previous best was two runner-up finishes. "I've been dreaming about this day forever." Lindley started 73-67, but wasn't really noticed until a third-round 70 pulled her within a shot of co-leaders Jang and Erica Blasberg.

Lindley shot 73-67-70-67 and Jang tied her with 71-69-69-68, both strong 11-under-par 277 performances at the par-72 Corning (New York) Country Club, hit by March-like chill and winds late in May.

Lindley, with her husband caddying, came to the final hole tied with Jang at 11 under and two-putted for par. Jang, in the group behind, survived rough and bunker and holed a six-foot putt for par to tie Lindley. On the first extra hole, the 18th, Jang again went from rough to sand. A brilliant sand shot left her a tap-in for par, but it was meaningless. Lindley drove down the right side of the fairway, hit a seven iron to six feet, and holed the putt for a winning birdie, thus answering her own question.

Back at No. 5 in regulation, Lindley missed a three-footer for birdie and was miffed at herself. "When it comes down to it," she said, "am I going to be good enough to make those clutch putts coming down the stretch, or to win on 18?" And 14 holes later, she had her answer.

Ginn Tribute Hosted by Annika
Mt. Pleasant, South Carolina
Winner: Seon Hwa Lee

What's Korean for "getting all the breaks"? Because that's what Seon Hwa Lee, a 22-year-old South Korean, was saying after — much to the surprise of everyone, including herself — she made the Ginn Tribute Hosted by Annika her third LPGA victory. And she had started the final round nine shots out of the lead.

The first break was Lorena Ochoa withdrawing because of illness in the family. Life is always easier with No. 1 out of the way. Lee's next break was beyond belief. Sophie Gustafson, leading the field by six strokes at the start of the fourth round, self-destructed and shot a crushing 79. Lee got her last break when Karrie Webb missed a short par putt in their playoff.

"She has a lot of experience and she is a Hall of Famer," Lee said. "So I didn't expect she was going to miss it."

Gustafson had played outstanding golf for three rounds — 66-65-67 at the par-72 River Towne Country Club at Mt. Pleasant, South Carolina — and was leading by six. Then came the 79, and the questions.

Anything you weren't hitting good? "Everything."

And what happened? "I don't know."

In the final round, Lee — who had shot 68-70-69 — chipped in from 40 yards for a birdie at the 13th and realized she had a chance to win. She was within a stroke of the lead. She bogeyed the 16th and fell into a tie for the lead, then retook the lead when she curled in a 20-footer for birdie on the last hole for 67 and a 274 total, 14 under. Webb, playing behind her, birdied from 12 feet for 70 to tie.

In the playoff, at No. 18, Lee two-putted from 40 feet for a par. Webb, putting from 25, missed her birdie putt by three feet. Then she missed that, and Lee was a winner. "There's lots of luck," Lee said. In this case, tons of it.

McDonald's LPGA Championship
Havre de Grace, Maryland
Winner: Yani Tseng

See Chapter 7.

Wegmans LPGA
Pittsford, New York
Winner: Eun-Hee Ji

How does victory feel? South Korea's Eun-Hee Ji found a new way to express it. "I'm like a fly in the sky," she said. The notion is fanciful but as good a way as any to describe the indescribable feeling of coming from way behind and beating Norway's Suzann Pettersen in the Wegmans LPGA in June at Locust Hill, near Rochester, New York.

Pettersen, who won five times in 2007, was on the verge of getting her first victory of 2008. She had opened the fourth round at 14 under par and leading Ji by three strokes. Her lead evaporated over the first three holes, but she went back in front at the 12th. Then the issue was settled over the last six holes on a nearly matched set of three Ji birdies against three Pettersen bogeys.

Ji birdied the 13th while Pettersen bogeyed it. Then Ji took the lead for good on another two-stroke swing at No. 15, holing a seven-footer for birdie against Pettersen's bogey on missing a five-footer. Ji then birdied the 17th, and Pettersen bogeyed the 18th.

"I just got out-raced," said Pettersen, who closed with 72–274 and finished two behind Ji. "There's so many good young players. They just stay in there … You just got to keep knocking on that door. Hopefully, it will open."

Ji's previous best was second place behind Pettersen in the Kolon Championship in South Korea the previous October.

"I cannot describe what I feel right now," said Ji. "Last year, Suzann beat me, and today I beat Suzann, so now I have a confidence."

Elsewhere in the tournament, Lorena Ochoa, frustrated in the LPGA McDonald's Championship the week before, couldn't get up steam this time and tied for sixth. Annika Sorenstam, who made the cut by a stroke, tied for 33rd.

Michelle Wie, playing on a sponsor's exemption, continued looking better. After qualifying for the U.S. Open and tying for sixth at the Ladies European Tour's German Open, she shot 71-71-73-69–284, four under, and tied for 24th. "This is my comeback tour," Wie said.

U.S. Women's Open
Edina, Minnesota
Winner: Inbee Park

See Chapter 7.

P&G Beauty NW Arkansas Championship
Rogers, Arkansas
Winner: Seon Hwa Lee

If anyone still had any doubts about the rise of Asian women's golf, a check of the immediate LPGA Tour charts should have wiped them away. With

Seon Hwa Lee's victory in the P&G Beauty NW Arkansas Championship in July, five straight tournaments had been won by Asian women, including two majors on the LPGA schedule, the McDonald's LPGA Championship by Taiwan's Yani Tseng and the U.S. Women's Open by South Korea's Inbee Park.

At Pinnacle Country Club in Rogers, Arkansas, South Korea's Seon Hwa Lee made it five in a row when she dropped a three-foot birdie putt at the final hole to pluck a one-stroke victory from South Korean Meena Lee and Jane Park, an American of South Korean parents. Interestingly enough, Seon Hwa had started the string June 1 with her victory in the Ginn Tribute.

"It was really a tough day — the weather was really hard," Lee said of that final round. The temperatures had hit the 90s, and many players — Lee included — had to come out early Sunday to complete their storm-interrupted second round. "The weather was really hard, but I felt good about my game. And every single shot was what I wanted today."

The tournament came to a crucial point when Meena Lee, leading by a stroke down the final stretch, was short of the green at the par-three 17th. She chipped 10 feet long and missed the par putt coming back and bogeyed. The door was now open to Seon Hwa. She had eagled the par-five seventh, holing out a 45-yard wedge shot, then made 10 straight pars. She came to the 18th hoping to force a playoff, and to this end hit a fine approach to three feet.

"When I was on the green, I saw the scoreboard," Lee said. "I didn't know how (Meena) made bogey on 17." Lee sank her three-footer to complete a 68–201 total, 15 under par, that held up for a one-stroke victory over Meena and Jane Park, who closed with 10-under 62.

Jamie Farr Owens Corning Classic
Sylvania, Ohio
Winner: Paula Creamer

"After you shoot 60, I swear it's the hardest thing to come back out," Paula Creamer was saying. "Anything after that, you feel like you're shooting 85." Especially if the 60 was in the first round and everyone was yelling congratulations.

Creamer kept her wits and wrapped up a wire-to-wire victory at Highland Meadows Golf Club near Toledo, Ohio, her third win of the year and the seventh of her career, but she was shaky again in the final round. She fell out of contention with a 74 in the final round of the tournament the previous week, and the week before that she lost her chances in the U.S. Women's Open with 78. In the Jamie Farr event, shooting 60-65-70, she led by five, then six with a tournament-record 125 at the halfway point, and then by four going into the final round.

And then Creamer bogeyed the first hole from a bad lie. After seven pars, she hit her approach to the ninth over the green, but scrambled to a par. "That was probably the biggest moment of the day," Creamer said.

Then rookie Shanshan Feng, the first exempt player from China, after 64 in the third round, birdied five of her first 11 holes in the fourth, cutting

Creamer's lead to one. Feng said her dad had called her from China to tell her not to pay attention to what others were doing. "So I didn't let it bother me at all," she said. Still, she made three straight bogeys down the stretch and shot 69 for her best finish, a solo fourth place.

Nicole Castrale was next to apply pressure, aiming "to post a number and let her see it." It was 64. But Creamer held steady and closed with six straight pars for a 73 and a two-stroke win on a 16-under 268 total. And she marched up the 18th fairway to a huge ovation.

"You try to soak it up," Creamer said, "because you don't know when the next one is going to be."

LPGA State Farm Classic
Springfield, Illinois
Winner: Ji Young Oh

The 2008 LPGA State Farm Classic goes into the books known for what didn't happen as much as for what did. And what didn't happen was that Michelle Wie, now 18 and playing her best in a long time, forgot to sign her scorecard and so was disqualified. It was just the latest chapter in the tormented tale of the Girl Who Would Be Queen.

And what did happen was that Ji Young Oh, age 20, in her second year on the tour, calmly got up and down like a seasoned veteran at the first playoff hole to beat Yani Tseng for her first victory.

Wie (67-65-67) finished the third round a stroke off the lead, but then was disqualified after officials learned of her rules violation of the day before. She had left the scoring area without signing, and though she did return and sign after scoring officials discovered her lapse, it was too late. In effect, she had already turned in an unsigned card, a disqualifying violation.

"I don't know why or how it happened," said Wie, for whom golf had become a case of one thing or another. "But I just forgot to sign it."

Someone suggested that Wie's departure cheapened Oh's victory. Oh shrugged off the notion. "Nobody knows how well she would have played," Oh noted gracefully.

Oh shot 66-66-69-69, tying with rookie Yani Tseng (66-66-66-72) at 18-under par at Panther Creek Country Club in Springfield, Illinois. Tseng, who won the McDonald's LPGA Championship in June, squandered her third-round lead with three bogeys on the front nine. She had regained the lead, then bogeyed the 18th and slipped back into a tie. On the first playoff hole, Oh chipped to six inches for her winning par while Tseng two-putted from five feet.

"It's hard to explain how happy I am right now," Oh said. "I would love to do this interview in English, but my mind is just a total blank right now."

Where Wie stumbled again, Chinese rookie Shanshan Feng, age 19, rocketed to a tie for fourth with a career-low 63. After two birdies on the first nine, she shot 27 coming in with an eagle at the par-five 13th from six feet and five birdies on putts of three, three, five, five and 10 feet. Said Shanshan: "It's a pretty awesome round."

Evian Masters
Evians-les-Bains, France
Winner: Helen Alfredsson

See Ladies European Tour section.

Ricoh Women's British Open
Berkshire, England
Winner: Ji-Yai Shin

See Chapter 7.

CN Canadian Women's Open
Ottawa, Ontario, Canada
Winner: Katherine Hull

Katherine Hull felt that 2008 would be her breakthrough year. But not in the CN Canadian Women's Open, not with only one round to go. "At six shots back, I didn't think much about it," she said. But the way things developed in that final round, Hull had to rethink things.

The key development was the meltdown of Taiwanese rookie Yani Tseng, winner of the McDonald's LPGA Championship in June. She was leading by four going into the fourth and final round, and she shot 77. Se Ri Pak, who had trailed by four, finished with a wildly erratic par 72. She went bogey-bogey-double bogey from No. 4, then birdied three out of the next four holes, and finished bogey-birdie-birdie.

Hull closed with a one-bogey 69, three under par at the Ottawa Hunt & Golf Club. She birdied the third on a four-foot putt and the par-three eighth with a 15-footer. She birdied the ninth, as well, chipping in from 20 feet. After a three-putt bogey at the 10th, she got her last birdie at the 14th, set up by a six iron to five feet. She shot 71-65-72-69–277, 11 under, to edge Pak by a stroke. The shattered Tseng finished third, her sixth top-three finish of the season.

Lorena Ochoa, the World No. 1, took the first-round lead, shooting 66. "I probably hit 18 greens, and I don't remember chipping," Ochoa said. But she couldn't quite keep up that pace and finished joint fourth. Michelle Wie, using the last of her six sponsor's exemptions for the year, bounced back from an opening 75 and tied for 12th.

And Annika Sorenstam, who would be leaving the tour at the end of the season, started 67-71 and was tight in the race, then finished 76-74 and tied for 21st, after which she left open the possibility she would return. "I never used the R-word (retire)," she said. "If I will come back in the future, time will tell. In my announcement, I said I was stepping away."

Safeway Classic
Portland, Oregon
Winner: Cristie Kerr

The question to Cristie Kerr was whether it's possible to have a good season without winning. The question was pertinent inasmuch as she felt she was playing better in 2008 but hadn't won.

"I was starting to think you could," Kerr said, grinning. "But now I don't have to answer that question."

The whole thing was rendered moot when Kerr birdied the first playoff hole to take the Safeway Classic, beating Sophie Gustafson and the revitalized Helen Alfredsson. It was her first victory of the year, the 11th of her career.

Kerr made her move in the final round. After trailing on rounds of 71 and 67, she charged to a tournament-low 65 for a 203 total, 13 under at the par-72 Columbia Edgewater course in Portland, Oregon. She streaked to four straight birdies from No. 5, two-putting there from 14 feet, then dropping an eight-footer, a tap-in and a 15-footer. Kerr took her only bogey, at the 11th after chunking her second shot, then got four birdies — at the 12th from 10 feet, the 14th from two, the 17th from five and the 18th from 12.

But Kerr needed help, and she got it from Alfredsson and Gustafson, playing behind her. Alfredsson, shooting 69, had five birdies but two bogeys, both after stray tee shots. Gustafson had an erratic 68, with seven birdies but three bogeys, all on three-putts. They helped Kerr by bogeying the 17th, Gustafson three-putting and Alfredsson bunkering her tee shot. Then they birdied the 18th, Gustafson on a wedge to 15 feet and Alfredsson on an eight iron to five, tying Kerr.

In the playoff, at the 18th, Alfredsson hit a tree with her second, and Gustafson two-putted from 20 feet for a par. Kerr hit an eight iron to 20 feet and holed the putt for the winning birdie.

In the post-mortems:

Said Gustafson: "I'm happy. I played well, and I can't ask for more than that."

Said Alfredsson: "It's late in my career. I'm just very happy to be playing well."

Said Kerr: "When you smell blood in the water, go for it."

Bell Micro LPGA Classic
Mobile, Alabama
Winner: Angela Stanford

The champagne shower came as a great relief to Angela Stanford, eight-year veteran of the LPGA Tour. "It felt great," Stanford said, after winning the inaugural Bell Micro LPGA Classic in September. "I didn't get that my first time, the first win in 2003. The final hole was a little more drama than I would have wanted, so it was a welcome treat to be greeted by my friends."

Stanford had entered the final round with a four-shot lead after a pair of

67s in the preceding two rounds. But she double-bogeyed No. 2 and her lead was down to two. The drama at the 18th was created by Shanshan Feng, a rookie from China, who birdied the last hole of The Crossings course near Mobile, Alabama, for a final-round 68. This put the burden squarely on Stanford, in the form of a four-foot putt for par. Coolly, she sank the putt for a one-over-par 73 — her only over-par round — and a one-stroke victory on 11-under 277. Said Feng, on posting her career-best performance: "Actually, I was very nervous. I shot 68, and I felt like I was shooting 60."

"I honestly believe the second (win) is harder," said Stanford, "because the first time, you don't really know it's happening when it happens. You try to duplicate it, and I've been trying — and probably too hard. I'm just relieved that I did it again."

Stanford was relieved, in part, because the win helped make up for two tournaments that got away in 2006, which she'd led by four strokes. Both were won by Cristie Kerr.

"Regardless of how much you really try to forget it, you can't," she said.

Stacy Lewis, the new pro, found her race for an LPGA Tour card set back by a two-stroke penalty for slow play. Lewis two-putted for par from 60 feet in the second round, and was informed by a rules official that she took 19 seconds too long. Her appeal failed and she tied for 28th.

Navistar LPGA Classic
Prattville, Alabama
Winner: Lorena Ochoa

If Lorena Ochoa, the World No. 1, hadn't started the season so hot, perhaps no one would have wondered what was wrong with her when she cooled off and started playing like a mortal again. But she did start off hot — six victories in the first 12 tournaments, three of them in succession, including the season's first major, the Kraft Nabisco Championship. Then she finally cooled down, which gave rise to all the questions.

Well, whatever was wrong was nothing a little rest couldn't heal, and so after about a month off, Ochoa came back in September and notched victory No. 7 for the year in the Navistar LPGA Classic in Prattville, Alabama. But she didn't merely snap her fingers and make it happen. She had to go to a playoff to do it.

"It wasn't easy," Ochoa said. "If you look at the leaderboard, a lot of players were up there one and two shots behind..."

Ochoa eagled the par-five No. 8 on a five-foot putt, had a birdie and a bogey, and closed with six straight pars for a two-under-par 70 to tie with Candie Kung (67) and former U.S. Women's Open champion Cristie Kerr (66) at 273, 15 under par on the Capitol Hill Senator Course.

Kerr left on the first extra hole with a three-putt bogey. "It's very disappointing because all I had to do was two-putt," said Kerr, who holed a 25-foot birdie putt at the 18th to get into the playoff.

Kung birdied from 22 feet at the 18th to get into the playoff. "All day

I was focused," she said. "I was happy that I got myself to the playoff. And it's been a solid four days — or three and a half at least." The last part ending with three putts from 30 feet on the second playoff hole, while Ochoa two-putted from the back fringe for the winning par.

"It's been a little slow in the last few months," Ochoa said. "I'm glad I did it this week, and hopefully get in a good rhythm to keep it going."

Samsung World Championship
Half Moon Bay, California
Winner: Paula Creamer

How can a golfer make a putt from only five feet and not see it drop? Well, one way would be to keep her eyes shut because she's too afraid to look.

"Honestly, I didn't see it go in," Paula Creamer said. "I heard the people. It was like the longest two seconds of my life, having it roll into the hole."

It was the last hole of the last round, and when that ball rolled around the right edge of the cup and dropped, it touched off the roars. Creamer had won the Samsung World Championship. It was Creamer's fourth victory of the season, making her the first American to win at least four times in a season since Juli Inkster won five in 1999.

It was an especially satisfying victory since it came in an elite 20-player field on the Ocean Course at Half Moon Bay, California, and with the final day basking in sunlight, without the wind, fog, rain and chill of the first three rounds. With all this as a background, Creamer played the last 37 holes without a bogey.

It was looking like a playoff. Song-Hee Kim caught up with Creamer with a chip-in birdie from 20 feet at the 14th. It was the first time in the round that Creamer wasn't the solo leader. And it didn't last long. Creamer holed a 25-footer for birdie at No. 15. "I tried just saying, 'C'mon, keep playing your own game,'" Creamer said. "Today I knew I couldn't be too aggressive, but I needed to shoot three or four under and everybody else would have to shoot six or seven under to beat me."

But no one could. Kim came closest with the 68. Lorena Ochoa, who won the past two Samsungs, shot 69 and tied for third with Juli Inkster (68), Suzann Pettersen (68) and Angela Stanford (70).

Annika Sorenstam, a five-time winner, finished her final Samsung World Championship with 70 and a three-over 291 total, and tossed her ball into the crowd in farewell.

Longs Drugs Challenge
Danville, California
Winner: In-Kyung Kim

In-Kyung Kim played the course at least 10 times. That was in her mind the night before the final round, when she tossed and turned. The next day, Kim, a second-year player on the LPGA Tour, survived another attack down the final nine to win the Longs Drugs Challenge, but pulled herself together for her first victory, a three-stroke decision over Angela Stanford.

"Yeah, I was nervous — it was excitement, everything," Kim said. "But par putts, a lot of par putts on the front nine was more stressful than anything." Next on her list was some joyful venting following a 25-foot putt that dropped into the final hole, putting the official stamp on her first victory. She began to cry. "I was overwhelmed," she said. "It was a happy cry."

After shooting 67-69-69 at Blackhawk Country Club in Danville, California, she closed with a one-over-par 73 for a 10-under 278 total and a three-stroke win. Stanford, winner of the recent Bell Micro Classic, might have been even more nervous. She trailed Kim by a stroke going into the final round, then bogeyed three times on the front nine, missing a two-foot par putt at the first, three-putting the par-three third from 35 feet, and missing a 12-footer at the ninth. She was three behind, but was spared another stroke of deficit when Kim bogeyed No. 2 after a stray drive. Stanford's chances evaporated on the back nine when she sandwiched two bogeys by two birdies from the 10th through the 17th.

Kim also stumbled to two bogeys. She three-putted the 14th from 20 feet and missed the green at the par-three 16th. But at the 17th, she came out of a bunker to eight feet and birdied, and at the 18th, she hit a nine iron from 144 yards to 25 feet and made that one before a cheering gallery, fulfilling the belief she'd had back on Thursday.

"For myself, I just kind of knew I was going to win," she said. "I tried not to say it too loud."

Kapalua LPGA Classic
Maui, Hawaii
Winner: Morgan Pressel

Morgan Pressel, one of the promising young players on tour, decided she needed a swing doctor to fix her game. So she switched instructors early in the year and went through the long, demanding retooling process. If the inaugural Kapalua LPGA Classic was any indication, the fix had taken. She birdied the last hole to edge out the frustrated Suzann Pettersen by a stroke.

It was her first victory of the season. "We worked really hard to simplify the swing so we could make it more powerful and more reliable," Pressel said. Her scores showed as much at the par-72 Kapalua resort course — 72-72-67-69–280, eight under par.

Pettersen, trailing by one stroke going into the final round, caught fire at No. 5 and made four birdies through five holes. She had birdied the 18th for 69 and held the clubhouse lead at 281. Pressel caught up with a birdie off a seven-foot putt at the 16th. She saved par out of a bunker at the 17th, then won the tournament when she holed a 15-foot putt from the fringe at the 18th. It was a great relief. Pressel had taken a big gamble, wanting to change the swing that won her the Kraft Nabisco Championship in 2007. Then came the predictable erratic play during the changeover. She missed three straight cuts in the spring and didn't finish in the top 30 in the last five tournaments.

Pettersen had to be wondering what she had to do to get that sixth victory. She was leading at Kapalua after the first two rounds, and she led partway on Saturday morning and then much of the final round on Sunday, only to be turned back again.

"Last year I played great, and when I had a chance, I got it," she said. "This year, I had a chance, but I haven't got it. It's such a fine line of what defines a great year, a good year, an average year."

Grand China Air LPGA
Hainen Island, China
Winner: Helen Alfredsson

Helen Alfredsson uttered the statement that would have fit the occasion anywhere, but this one happened to fit perfectly in, of all places, China.

"It's great to be on 18," she said, "and have a four-shot lead."

And with that, Alfredsson, the veteran Swede, added another star to her strong career with a three-shot victory in the inaugural Grand China Air LPGA in late October, the LPGA's first tournament in China. It was a publicity vehicle for a Chinese airline, but it also served to underline the growth of the game in China.

Alfredsson, one of 63 in the field, opened with 70 and trailed the leader, Laura Diaz (63) by seven. A 69 in the second round left her five behind Karen Stupples (67–134), and then she took the lead with some remarkable iron play across the par-72 Hainan West Golf Club. Playing three groups behind her, Diaz and Stupples opened the door by stumbling badly on the final nine, Diaz making three bogeys and Stupples four. Diaz closed with a 72–208 and finished third, and Stupples fourth with 75–209. Annika Sorenstam, her career winding down, was not a factor, shooting 72-70-72–214, tying for 17th. Lorena Ochoa, the world's No. 1, didn't play.

Alfredsson, 43, was on a roll reminiscent of the early days of her career. She birdied seven of 15 holes starting from the third. Her longest putts were a 10-footer at the fourth and a nine-footer at the 17th, and the other five were from three to seven feet. A poor chip shot at the 18th cost her her only bogey. "It was not a great shot," she said. But by then, she was comfortably there with a four-stroke lead, as she noted.

Taiwan's Yani Tseng, 19, who won the McDonald's LPGA Championship in June, closed with 68 to take second place, three behind. Alfredsson said she enjoyed beating the younger players. "They don't want to get beat by us because we are so old," Alfredsson said, "and we still want to beat them because they are so young."

Hana Bank-Kolon Championship
Incheon, Korea
Winner: Candie Kung

Candie Kung hadn't won since her three-victory 2003 and now the last thing she needed, with the Hana Bank-Kolon Championship on the line in the final round, was a pulled hamstring muscle. How does a golfer pull a hamstring, anyway?

Start out with cold that hit the Sky 72 Golf Club at Incheon, Korea, that early November week, and then the golfers having to brace themselves against the strong winds. That's two parts of the recipe.

"It was my second shot, out of the rough," Kung was saying. She was playing the par-five ninth. "I hit a five wood and it just happened to pull one of the muscles, and from there on I just said, keep saying, 'We have nine more holes left.' The physio(therapist) came out to look at it. Just asking for some stretches to get me through nine holes."

The five-wood shot left her 76 yards from the hole, and she took a lob wedge and floated the ball up there, and it ended up in the hole for an eagle — the decisive shot of the tournament.

Kung rolled from there and added a closing three-under-par 69 to her 70-71 start for a six-under-par 210 total and a one-stroke victory over Australia's Katherine Hull (69–211). But that final day, eight players were hovering in the four-under range. Kung's eagle was the separating blow. She birdied No. 1 from 15 feet and No. 6 from four. She bogeyed No. 8 out of a bunker, then eagled No. 9, and birdied No. 16 from 12 feet. A three-putt bogey from 40 feet at the 17th nearly cost her the tournament.

Hull, who started 66-76, was two under for the tournament through the 12th. Then she birdied the 13th from 30 feet, the 14th from six and the 16th from a foot, and she was five under. Her try for a tying birdie at the 18th just lipped out, and Kung had her victory. Her golf course, too. Club officials decided to rename the Ocean Course the Candie Kung Course for a year.

Mizuno Classic
Shima, Mie, Japan
Winner: Ji-Yai Shin

See Japan LPGA Tour section.

Lorena Ochoa Invitational
Guadalajara, Mexico
Winner: Angela Stanford

"Wish I'd been in contention," Lorena Ochoa was saying, "but this has been a week where I've learned a lot, both as a player and a tournament hostess." She tied for 14th, but she was a winner anyway, staging the first Lorena Ochoa Invitational for charity at home in Mexico.

It was almost a grand sign-off for Annika Sorenstam, in her next-to-last start before leaving the LPGA Tour. She holed a bunker shot for birdie at the par-three 16th. And at the par-five 18th, she nearly holed another, this for eagle, and then lipped out her nine-foot birdie try, leaving Angela Stanford with her second victory of the season and the third of her career. Stanford closed with a three-under-par 69 at Guadalajara Country Club and a 13-under 275 total. Sorenstam, parring the last two holes, shot 69 for 276, tying for second with Brittany Lang, who closed with a course-record 65.

Stanford had blocked out thoughts of winning. "I had done such a good job all day of staying in the moment and kind of prepared myself for the playoff," she said. "I would have been a little nervous in that playoff just because it's Annika. There was a moment there where I thought, 'Hmmm, I'd rather not have a playoff.'"

Stanford was facing great pressure. Lang was already in at 12 under par, and Stanford and Sorenstam were riding the edge. Stanford's crucial shot was a par-saving 10-foot putt at the 17th.

"That putt — now that I won at 13 under — that putt won the tournament," Stanford said. "Because I think if I would have missed there, the momentum would have shifted to Annika, and Brittany was already in at 12 (under). So that would have put three of us at 12."

It was a performance to build on for Stanford. "It continues to give me confidence," she said, "and going into next year, hopefully this will push me into the top 10 in the world — I hope."

ADT Championship
West Palm Beach, Florida
Winner: Ji-Yai Shin

There was the young reign of Mexico's Lorena Ochoa, No. 1 in the world, replacing the outgoing Annika Sorenstam. There were the rising young stars — Paula Creamer, Morgan Pressel, Natalie Gulbis, names known to all. Then who was this Ji-Yai Shin?

Shin, a 20-year-old South Korean, had been playing elsewhere and surfaced in winning the Ricoh Women's British Open in August. She added the Mizuno Classic in early November, and then in late November, in the rich and season-ending ADT Championship, she beat out a super-restricted field and won the $1 million top prize. And she wasn't even a member of the LPGA Tour.

"A really special year for me," said Shin, who had won 21 times worldwide since 2007 and obviously stamped herself as someone to watch in the LPGA's 2009 season.

The ADT Championship, at Trump International in West Palm Beach, Florida, had a field of 32 players that was reduced to 16 for the third round, with new scorecards, then to eight for the finale, and with new scorecards. Shin shot a final-round two-under-par 70, turning back Karrie Webb (71). Paula Creamer played despite an inflamed abdominal wall all week and had to be hospitalized the night before the final and ordered her own release early Sunday.

Creamer made two birdies in a three-hole stretch on the back nine, but her chances for a fifth victory and the LPGA money title just about ended in a three-putt bogey at the par-five 15th. Creamer tied for third with Seon Hwa Lee at 74. Eun-Hee Ji was fifth at 75, Angela Stanford sixth at 78, and Suzann Pettersen and Jeon Jang tied for seventh at 79.

Shin, who didn't shoot over par in the tournament, started the final round with two birdies in the first three holes, then scrambled for a par after watering a shot at the sixth. She took the lead when Webb suffered three straight bogeys from the 11th. Webb birdied the 18th, and Shin two-putted for the win.

"I think," said Webb, paying Shin the ultimate compliment, "out of all the Koreans that have come up, she's got the most potential."

Lexus Cup
Singapore
Winners: International Team

It was a kind of farewell gift to Annika Sorenstam. The Lexus Cup was the next-to-last event before the end of the season and the announced end of her competitive career. Sorenstam was the playing captain of the International Team, meeting the Asia Team at Singapore Island Country Club. And what better send-off than a victory from the women she had competed against in her Hall of Fame career. And they gave it to her.

Sorenstam did her part, beating Se Ri Pak, the Asian captain, 3 and 2, in the first singles match. Christina Kim, a few hours later, birdied the par-five 18th against Namika Omata for the half-point that gave Sorenstam's Internationals a 12½-11½ victory, ending their two-year losing streak to even the series at 2-2.

"It's one thing to be inside the ropes in control, but when you're cheering for everyone, you want to help them however you can," said Sorenstam. "I kept getting goose bumps after goose bumps out there. I'm really proud of this team ... I could not have asked for a better ending."

"I'm amazed it came down to my match," Kim said. "This is such a thrill. To be here and to win for Annika is the greatest feeling. To have it come down to me — I was scared."

Sorenstam's farewell match started easy but turned into a fight. She took a quick three-up lead when Pak bogeyed three of the first five holes. Pak got two back, then Sorenstam went to two up with a par at the 12th. Both birdied the next two holes, and then Sorenstam added a third to return to three up, then won when they halved the 16th in pars.

Angela Stanford, Katherine Hull, Helen Alfredsson and Natalie Gulbis also earned full points for the International Team, while Suzann Pettersen and Karen Stupples halved their matches.

The teams were tied after each of the first two days, splitting the opening alternate-shot matches and Saturday best-ball matches.

With the Lexus Cup in hand, Sorenstam headed off to end her career the following week in the Ladies European Tour's Dubai Ladies Masters.

Ladies European Tour

Women's World Cup of Golf
Sun City, South Africa
Winners: Philippines (Jennifer Rosales and Dorothy Delasin)

See Ladies African Tour section.

MFS Women's Australian Open
Melbourne, Victoria, Australia
Winner: Karrie Webb

See Australian Ladies Tour section.

ANZ Ladies Masters
Ashmore, Queensland, Australia
Winner: Lisa Hall

See Australian Ladies Tour section.

VCI European Ladies Golf Cup
Alicante, Spain
Winners: England (Trish Johnson and Rebecca Hudson)

The English pairing of Trish Johnson and Rebecca Hudson won the inaugural VCI European Ladies Cup at La Sella Golf Resort, an unofficial team event marking the start of the European season. Johnson and Hudson led every day and finished five clear of Belgium and Germany with a total of 270, 18 under par. Under the format for the event, four-ball better-ball was played in rounds one and three, while the "Valencian Cup" format was used in rounds two and four. This is a variation on greensomes: on par-threes, each player hits a tee shot and then they pick one ball; on par-fours, after the tee shots, each player hits their partner's ball on the second shots and then they pick one ball; on par-fives, they alternate for three shots and then pick a ball.

Johnson and Hudson opened with 64, and then rounds of 70 and 65 put them five ahead of Belgium's Lara Tadiotto and Ellen Smets. Johnson and Hudson had an early bogey in the final round but added three birdies on the back nine, including at the 15th and 17th holes. It was the German pairing of Martina Eberl and Anja Monke who made the biggest move on the last day with 65, but they lost out on second place on their own by bogeying the last hole. The Netherlands finished in fourth place, with Italy fifth, Russia sixth, and host Spain in seventh place.

"We gelled perfectly," said Johnson. "The two Belgian girls were absolutely fantastic. They deserve better than what they got actually in the end, but they played great and they pushed us all the way." Both players offered best wishes to Kirsty Taylor, who was replaced by Hudson after undergoing brain surgery.

Catalonia Ladies
Gualta, Girona, Spain
Winner: Lotta Wahlin

Sweden's Lotta Wahlin enjoyed the perfect pre-season boost as the 24-year-old won the unofficial Catalonia Ladies, this year a non-Order of Merit pro-am event for 20 professionals played over 36 holes. Wahlin, about to start her fourth season on the Ladies European Tour but without a victory to date, recorded rounds of 68 and 65 for a nine-under-par total of 133 at Emporda Golf Hotel, near Girona. A stroke behind Spain's Tania Elosegui going into the second and final round, Wahlin won by a comfortable six shots. Elosegui, after 72, shared second place with compatriot Paula Marti, who had 67, and Rebecca Hudson, who closed with 66.

A two-shot swing at the seventh hole gave Wahlin the lead and she never looked back. On the back nine she produced birdies at the 12th, 14th and 15th holes before finishing in style with an eagle at the last after hitting her seven-iron approach from 150 yards stone dead.

"A perfect distance to finish it," Wahlin said. "I like this kind of course. It's open and it's a very good layout because the bunkers are in play and you have to be careful with your tee shots. The greens are great because they are really huge, but there are some small spots where you can put the pin and it makes a big difference in how you play the hole, so it's a fun course to play."

Open de Espana Femenino
San Jordi, Castellon, Spain
Winner: Emma Zackrisson

In her first tournament since recovering her playing card, Sweden's Emma Zackrisson secured her first win on the Ladies European Tour at the Open de Espana Femenino in Castellon. Zackrisson, who led after the second and third rounds, posted a final round of 71 to finish with a four-round total of seven-under-par 281. After three days of strong winds at Panoramica Golf and Country Club, the 29-year-old Swede began the day with a four-stroke cushion and finished four ahead of three players, including defending champion Nikki Garrett, Joanne Mills and Italian Diana Luna (69).

Zackrisson had never previously led an LET event, but turned in nine steady pars before a weather delay of over an hour. Returning to the course she bogeyed the 13th, but holed from almost 40 feet for a birdie at the 15th, and after narrowly avoiding a water hazard at the 17th, closed with a birdie at the last.

"This win means everything to me," said Zackrisson. "I was thinking about quitting after this year because I've been having a really hard time out here for the last three years. This has changed that. I did not expect this coming in. But I played so well and it felt so easy for me. Everything just worked. I'd been struggling for so long and finally it all came together."

Aberdeen Asset Management Ladies Scottish Open
The Carrick on Loch Lomond, Scotland
Winner: Gwladys Nocera

France's Gwladys Nocera claimed her sixth title in two years with a two-stroke victory over Sweden's Maria Boden at De Vere Cameron House. Nocera, a 32-year-old from Biarritz who now lives in Lausanne in Switzerland, won three times in 2006 and twice in 2007 to establish herself as one of the best players on the circuit.

Nocera and Boden shared the first-round lead with opening 69s, and then the Frenchwoman added 70 to lead Amy Yang by one. Three birdies on the first nine in the final round was followed by a three-putt bogey at the ninth which left her three ahead of five players. In difficult conditions, Nocera added a birdie at the 10th before bogeying the 12th and 14th. Coming to the last hole one ahead, Nocera made certain with a drive of 317 yards and then she holed from 20 feet for a birdie. She closed with 69 to have a five-under-par 208 total.

Boden, who also had 69 on the last day with compatriot Emma Zackrisson, the Spanish Open winner, caddieing for her after missing the cut, birdied the last to claim second place at three under par, one ahead of Rebecca Hudson, who bogeyed the last for 68, and Austria's Nicole Gergely.

"It's great. Winning is one of the best things in life, I think. I'm really happy. I had a really good day," said Nocera. After finishing in second and third place on the money rankings in the previous two seasons, Nocera added: "My goal when I started the season was to win the money list because I haven't won it yet. That's the plan this year."

Garanti American Express Turkish Open
Belek, Antalya, Turkey
Winner: Lotta Wahlin

Sweden's Lotta Wahlin cruised to her first official Ladies European Tour victory at the inaugural Garanti American Express Turkish Open. The 24-year-old from Linkoping carded rounds of 71, 71, 73 and 70 at the punishing National Golf Club in Antalya to win by 12 shots with a total of seven-under-par 285.

Her winning margin was the second largest in the tour's 30-year history, trailing only Laura Davies's victory the 1995 Irish Open by 16 shots. Another Swede, Johanna Westerberg (71), shared second place with South African Stacy Lee Bregman (72) and Spaniard Paula Marti (74). Both Westerberg and Bregman recovered from having a round of 80 early in the tournament.

Wahlin, who was the only player to finish below par for the tournament, led from start to finish and never faltered on a course featuring narrow fairways, numerous red pine trees and extremely hard greens. She extended her lead each day from two after the first round to seven and then eight strokes.

"It's fantastic. I only understood I'd won on the 18th green because I didn't think about it before," said Wahlin. "I was just enjoying it. I wanted to finish well. My goal for today was to shoot in the 60s, so I had to make a birdie on the last, but I didn't. The four days have just been so good. It's the best moment in my career."

Wahlin, in her fourth year on tour, gave up her job as a secretary at a large computer firm to play professionally. A key part of this victory was winning the unofficial Catalonia Ladies a month earlier. "It was important because I knew that I can win. I finished with 65 in the last round, so I knew I could shoot a low round."

Deutsche Bank Ladies Swiss Open
Ticino, Switzerland
Winner: Suzann Pettersen

Suzann Pettersen won the Deutsche Bank Ladies Swiss Open after the final round had to be cancelled with the fairways and greens at Golf Gerre Losone under water. Pettersen was well in front, but was prevented from trying to break the LET scoring record for four rounds. The 27-year-old from Oslo did, however, set a new record for 54-hole events with her 22-under-par total of 194. Pettersen opened with 67, but then equaled the then-course record with 63 to go five clear.

A 64 in the third round put her six ahead of South Korean teenager Amy Yang, whose 65 on day three included her first hole-in-one at the 145-yard seventh with a seven iron. Gwladys Nocera was a further stroke behind after breaking her own, and Pettersen's, course record with 62 in the third round.

Pettersen broke the record of 17 under for a 54-hole tournament set by Karine Icher at the 2004 Catalonia Masters. But the world No. 3 had Laura Davies's mark of 25 under at the 1995 Irish Open in her sights going into the final day.

"I was going to try to get to 30," said Pettersen after claiming her third tour title and the eighth of her career. "I would have had to have played really well today if that was the case, but I think it was possible. But if it's not playable, it's not playable. I was kind of looking forward to keeping going, throwing some birdies on the board and seeing how low I could go."

HypoVereinsbank Ladies German Open
Munich, Germany
Winner: Amy Yang

On winning the HypoVereinsbank Ladies German Open by four shots at Golfpark Gut Hausern, South Korea's Amy Yang announced that she would donate the €37,500 first-prize money to the victims of the Chinese earthquake. Yang, 18, began the final round with a five-shot lead after rounds of 71, 66 and 63 and then shot a five-under 67 for a 21-under-par 267 total. Sweden's Louise Stahle, the 2007 rookie of the year, finished in second place at 17-under 271, with Gwladys Nocera one stroke further back.

The victory was the first in Yang's professional career but her second on the Ladies European Tour after she won the ANZ Ladies Masters in Australia as a 16-year-old amateur. At that time she was the youngest ever winner on the tour. She turned professional in October 2006 and was granted a three-year exemption to play, but was unable to commit to full-time golf until she finished her school exams in Australia at the end of 2007.

"I'm so happy now," said Yang, the runner-up in the Swiss Open the previous week. "I practiced really hard to get this, but I need to work harder. I just found last week after playing with Suzann (Pettersen) that I needed to practice more to be like her."

Another teenager, American Michelle Wie, 18, came in sixth at 14 under par, which marked her first sub-par tournament total in 14 appearances since she tied for second at the 2006 Evian Masters in France.

Wie chipped in for eagle at the first hole and then birdied the third, but couldn't keep the momentum going. Her final round of 67 was her best score in three tournaments this year. "I'm glad that I shot under par, it feels good," said Wie, whose presence helped to attract almost 17,000 spectators to the remote course over the tournament week.

ABN AMRO Ladies Open
Valkenswaard, Netherlands
Winner: Gwladys Nocera

Gwladys Nocera successfully defended the ABN AMRO Ladies Open at Eindhovensche Golf Club in the Netherlands, but only after winning by one shot with a birdie at the last hole. The 33-year-old Frenchwoman held a four-stroke lead overnight and closed with a one-under-par 71 to secure her second title of the year and the seventh of her career.

Nocera posted a 13-under-par total of 203, but it was a lot closer than in 2007 when she won by seven shots at the same course. She rolled in a perfectly judged 18-footer at the last to edge ahead of English rookie Melissa Reid, who had three rounds of 68.

"I don't think Melissa did anything wrong," said Nocera. "It's just the experience to hole the putt on 18 even when you have not been playing well. I had some really ugly shots. I had to fight to make pars, and then when I didn't make pars, I made bogeys. It was just not really nice golf. I just told myself, 'It doesn't matter how you play, it only matters if you lift the cup or not,' so I tried to win anyway."

As Nocera found trouble on the front nine she watched her lead narrow as Reid gradually caught up. The 20-year-old was just one shot behind Nocera after six holes and drew even with a birdie at the 11th. The players were still tied after 17 holes, but Reid's hopes of a first title disappeared when she missed her 20-foot birdie chance at the 18th.

"I definitely feel I can win now," said Reid. "I felt I gave a couple of shots away on the golf course, but Gwladys had a great birdie on the last. She won it."

Ladies Open de Portugal
Algarve, Portugal
Winner: Anne-Lise Caudal

Gwladys Nocera could not win the Ladies Open de Portugal, but the next best thing was to have a French one-two with her compatriot Anne-Lise Caudal claiming her maiden title at Quinta de Cima in the Algarve. Caudal led all three rounds after opening up with a course-record 64. The 24-year-old from Ciboure, near Biarritz, added rounds of 69 and 70 for 203 total to win by one stroke over Nocera, who charged into contention with a 66, and England's Georgina Simpson, who closed with a 68. Early in the final round it was Louise Stahle who overtook Caudal with four birdies in the first six holes, but the Swede faded to finish tied for fourth place with Martina Eberl.

Caudal came to the last hole needing a birdie to win and put her second shot to 20 feet to set up an eagle chance. She left the putt three feet short, but rolled in the next one for the victory, only to be sprayed in champagne by her compatriots.

Nocera, who was rooming with Caudal during the week, said: "Anne-Lise is like a little sister on tour and I'm really happy for her. She lost her card last year and now she wins a tournament. I think it's good. It's good for us because it's good motivation to have the new ones kicking our butts."

Caudal said: "When we arrived at the golf course today, Gwladys said to me, 'Okay, one and two, first and second.' I said, 'Okay, why not.' When I saw her on the leaderboard I thought, 'Unbelievable.' She is unbelievable. She is a great player."

Tenerife Ladies Open
Tenerife, Spain
Winner: Rebecca Hudson

England's Rebecca Hudson birdied the third hole of a playoff against Anne-Lise Caudal to capture the Tenerife Ladies Open at Golf Costa Adeje. Hudson, a 29-year-old from Doncaster, began the final round one shot behind Caudal and posted a final-round 69 in regulation play to finish at 10-under-par 278 total.

Caudal, who won the previous week's tournament in Portugal, was a shot ahead with one hole to play, but bogeyed the par-five 18th after hitting her second shot into a greenside bunker, from where she took four shots to get down. She signed for a final-round 70. Gwladys Nocera finished three shots behind, tying for third place at 281 with Spanish amateur Carlotta Ciganda, who was the halfway leader. Another Spanish amateur, Marta Silva, finished tied for fifth with Melissa Reid and Russia's Maria Verchenova.

Hudson holed from 12 feet for a birdie at the 18th on the first playoff hole, but Caudal matched her from four feet. Both then parred the 18th before they moved to the 17th. Caudal took four, but Hudson put her second shot to three feet and holed the putt for her second tour victory and first in two years. She was also part of England's European Cup winning team earlier in the season.

"I didn't expect Anne-Lise to bogey the last in regulation play, so to actually get into the playoff and then win it, I'm thrilled," said Hudson. "When she did it was a bit of a shock, but I managed to hole that 12-footer on the first extra hole and that was crucial. I'll definitely have a nice bottle of something tonight."

Oxfordshire Ladies English Open
Thame, Oxfordshire, England
Winner: Rebecca Hudson

Rebecca Hudson captured her second title in the space of three weeks with a final-round 64 at the Oxfordshire Ladies English Open. Hudson came from four shots behind the overnight leader Melissa Reid to capture the title by a stroke on a wet and windy day at the Oxfordshire Golf Club. The 29-year-old from Doncaster produced eight birdies, with four on the front nine and four on the back, for a 10-under-par 206 total.

After a week off following her victory in Tenerife, Hudson claimed her third tour title after waiting two years for the second. "Back-to-back wins, I can't believe it," she said. "To win in your home country is just fantastic. At the beginning of the day I knew that someone would have to shoot low to catch Mel, but I didn't think this would happen."

As in Tenerife, Hudson employed her good friend and fellow tour professional Kirsty Fisher as her caddie for the final round. "Kirsty and I lined up the putts well. We worked well together. We didn't fight the wind, we worked with it."

Playing in the final pairing, one group behind Hudson, Reid closed with 69 and finished at nine under, three ahead of Joanne Mills. She missed a 10-foot birdie putt to catch Hudson on the par-five 17th and then had to settle for a regulation par at the last hole after pulling her approach shot into the rough. "To be honest, I can't take anything away from Rebecca's 64," Reid said. "In these conditions it was phenomenal. She won the tournament. I'm pretty gutted right now, but I've got to stay patient and maybe the win will come pretty soon."

AIB Ladies Irish Open
Portmarnock, Co. Dublin, Ireland
Winner: Suzann Pettersen

Suzann Pettersen secured her second victory of the season with a five-shot win at the AIB Ladies Irish Open. After two rounds of 69, the Norwegian produced a final-round five-under-par 67 to finish with an 11-under-par 205 total after three rounds at Portmarnock Links in Dublin. Compatriot Marianne Skarpnord was second at six-under-par 210, which was her career-best finish in four seasons on the tour.

Pettersen began the final round one stroke ahead of New Zealand's Lynn Brooky, but a birdie to the Kiwi's bogey at the second hole extended her lead to three. The 27-year-old from Oslo collected six birdies in all, four on the four par-fives, and dropped only one shot in the difficult conditions.

"It was windy and challenging, so I'm very happy with my performance," said Pettersen, who collected a first prize of €67,500 for her ninth career title, following her recent victory in May's Deutsche Bank Ladies Swiss Open. "The wind was different today, which made the course play totally different. It made some of the holes a little harder and the other way round, so the par-fives were very reachable. I tried to be patient and get my score on the par-fives."

Skarpnord got within one stroke of Pettersen after an eagle at the 460-yard, par-five 12th hole, where she played her approach shot to within 18 inches of the cup. She birdied the third and fourth holes going out, but bogeyed the 17th and 18th for a closing 70. "Suzann is a great player. She plays so well it's difficult to beat her. I tried but I didn't make it," said Skarpnord. Brooky finished in third place after 73.

BMW Ladies Italian Open
Porto Ercole, Tuscany, Italy
Winner: Martina Eberl

Ignorance was bliss for Martina Eberl as she claimed her second title on the LET with a five-stroke victory at the BMW Ladies Italian Open at Argentario in Tuscany. Eberl went into the final round two ahead of the field, but avoided looking at any leaderboard until she walked up to the 18th green. It was good news. She tapped in for her fourth birdie in a round of 69 which, following scores of 65, 74 and 67, gave her a nine-under total of 275.

None of Eberl's closest rivals prospered in the final round, and it was Spain's Carmen Alonso who took second place at four-under 280. After 77 in the third round, the longest hitter on tour rallied with 66, including five birdies in a row from the 10th hole. Maria Hjorth, Becky Brewerton and Lisa Holm Sorensen, none of whom did better than 72, all tied for third place.

Eberl dropped an early shot at the second hole, but birdied the seventh and eighth to go three clear. She picked up another shot at the 10th, only to give it back at the 13th, but was not challenged on the way home.

"I'm so happy right now," said the 26-year-old from Munich, whose first win came 10 months earlier in Madrid. "It was very hard out there and the wind was very difficult all week. I didn't know I was leading until I hit my second shot into the 18th hole and looked over to the leaderboard. I ignored every scoreboard all day because it doesn't help me and I figured that out a long time ago."

Evian Masters
Evians-les-Bains, France
Winner: Helen Alfredsson

A year after taking on the responsibility of being the European Solheim Cup captain, Helen Alfredsson returned to winning ways by claiming her third victory at the Evian Masters, the second biggest event in Europe and co-sanctioned with the LPGA. Alfredsson won the inaugural event in 1994 and then collected the title again in 1998. Ten years later the 43-year-old Swede surprised even herself with a stunning victory against two young stars. Alfredsson defeated 19-year-old Brazilian Angela Park and 20-year-old South Korean Na Yeon Choi at the third extra hole.

Despite a course-record 63 in the second round, after 72 and to be followed by 71, Alfredsson trailed Park by four going into the last round. After she three-putted the 13th she was five behind Choi, who had blitzed into the lead but then bogeyed the 15th and 16th holes. Alfredsson had 67 and Choi 66 to tie with 15-under-par 273s, alongside Park, who closed with a 71. Jin Joo Hong finished two shots behind, while Lorena Ochoa took fifth place.

Alfredsson birdied the 18th all three times in the playoff. Park departed at the first extra hole, but while the Swede kept holing crucial putts, Choi missed from six feet on the third extra hole. "I really am too old for this. I keep saying that, but this is really too far to go," Alfredsson said. "I can't even describe it in words. Like I said so many times this week, this tournament is so special for me. I've had nothing but great memories here. I just love this place. Somebody's looking after me for this to be my next win."

Alfredsson won $487,500 for her 20th career victory. "At this point the satisfaction of winning and making your putt or making some putts that I made today, there is nothing, there is no money in the world that can pay for that. I worked so hard last winter. I started getting my feeling back in my right arm. Then I had to figure out the swing to work with that. You never know if you're going to win, especially when time is running out a little bit. But I knew I was playing really well."

Ricoh Women's British Open
Berkshire, England
Winner: Ji-Yai Shin

See Chapter 7.

Scandinavian TPC Hosted by Annika
Vasteras, Sweden
Winner: Amy Yang

Annika Sorenstam, twice a winner of her own tournament, made the perfect start to her last event on home soil with an opening 66 to take the lead at the Scandinavian TPC at Frosaker Golf Club, near Stockholm. But the second day's play was completely washed out and over the weekend Sorenstam could not keep her challenge going. Instead, Amy Yang, a player with whom she played for the first two days, was inspired to a closing 63 and a six-stroke victory.

Yang, the 18-year-old South Korean who had already won in Germany earlier in the season, finished the 54-hole event with 14-under-par 202, leading Lill Saether, of Norway and the 36-hole leader, Maria Hjorth, Melodie Bourdy and Finland's Minea Blomqvist, who also closed with 63.

Yang, who after three years living in Australia has moved to Florida, produced 10 birdies in her final round, including at the last three holes. "I never thought I would win this tournament," Yang said. "Of course, all the Korean golfers like Se Ri Pak because she is like Annika is in Sweden. I like Annika too. I like the routine and the way she plays. I think I was 10 or 11 and I watched Annika's game on the TV. I didn't think I would play with her when I grew up! It is very exciting."

Sorenstam finished tied for sixth place, her challenge fading after finding water at the 15th. "I didn't finish on a very high note, so it takes the life out of you a little bit," she said. "But the support has been great and it's been nice to have all the family and friends here."

S4/C Wales Ladies Championship of Europe
Llanelli, Carmarthenshire, Wales
Winner: Lotta Wahlin

Sweden's Lotta Wahlin claimed her third title of the season at the S4/C Wales Ladies Championship of Europe by defeating Germany's Martina Eberl at the second hole of a playoff. The 24-year-old birdied the par-five 18th hole twice in the playoff at Machynys Peninsula Golf Club. Eberl, who led after the first and second rounds, birdied the first extra hole but bogeyed the second after her ball twice found the sand near the green.

Wahlin, who won by 12 shots in Turkey three months earlier, had a chance to win the tournament at the 18th green in regulation but missed a three-footer for par and dropped a shot, falling back into a tie with Eberl. "I did everything for the crowd, to make it more exciting," she said.

Wahlin battled through wind and light showers to sign for a final round of one-under 71 and a seven-under-par 209 total after 54 holes, Saturday's play having been cancelled due to unplayable conditions. The Swede began the final round in fifth place, two shots behind overnight leader Eberl. She carded an eagle and three bogeys on the front nine for an outward total of one-over 37 and was three behind Eberl at the turn, but then produced birdies at the 11th, 13th and 15th holes.

"I'm just so happy," she said. "When I won the last time I was leading every day and it was quite obvious that I was going to win. This time I came from fifth place, but I'm just so happy. Now I have proved to myself that I'm one of the best players on this tour and I'm really proud of that."

SAS Masters
Oslo, Norway
Winner: Gwladys Nocera

Gwladys Nocera notched her eighth tour victory at the SAS Ladies Masters at Haga in Oslo. Starting the third and final round a shot behind Diana Luna, the 33-year-old from France closed with a four-under 68 to finish with 13-under-par 203. She won by three over Spaniard Tania Elosegui, who had 67, and England's Samantha Head, who had 68, with a further eight players, including Luna, in a share of third place at eight under par.

As she achieved in 2006, the victory was Nocera's third of the season and underlined her dominance on the tour this year after wins in Scotland and the Netherlands. But she was still lying in second place on the New Star Money List behind Sweden's Helen Alfredsson, who won the lucrative Evian Masters.

"My aim is still to win the New Star Money List, so I knew I had to win at least this week and a couple more. I'm getting closer to my goal, but I still have a lot of work to do," she said. "I really played well today, the best round of the week."

Nocera was tied for the lead with Luna at the turn, but after both birdied the 10th, the Italian bogeyed the 12th to give Nocera the advantage. An eagle at the 14th, where she holed from 23 feet, was followed by birdies at Nos. 16 and 17. Nocera found the water on the right with her tee shot at the last, but maintained her composure to take a bogey. "I didn't see it until I got there, but I knew I had a four-stroke lead, so it was alright. I just had to make a five and go with it," she explained.

Finnair Masters
Tali, Finland
Winner: Minea Blomqvist

Minea Blomqvist won a dramatic victory on home soil after a tense duel with compatriot Ursula Wikstrom at the Helsinki Golf Club. In front of ecstatic home supporters, Blomqvist countered Wikstrom's birdie at the last to claim her second title. Her first came as a 19-year-old at the Central European Open in 2004, the year she took the rookie honors on tour.

The two Finns shared the lead with a round to go with Italy's Diana Luna. Blomqvist closed with 65 to finish at 11-under-par 202 after previous rounds of 69 and 68. Wikstrom had 66, while Beatriz Recari, the first-round leader, finished third after 67 alongside Martina Eberl at seven under. Luna finished fifth after a closing 70.

Blomqvist, a 23-year-old from Espoo, took control early on to lead by two at the turn. Wikstrom, who lives 15 minutes from the course and was runner-up in the event in 2005, was three behind after Blomqvist birdied the 12th, but finished superbly, birdieing four of the last five holes.

Blomqvist matched her birdie at the par-five 17th to stay one ahead and hit her approach at the 18th to 10 feet. But after Wikstrom holed from 30 feet, Blomqvist had to hole out to win. "Winning in front of your home crowd is very special, but for Ursula and me to play really well and for it to be a great match makes it even more special," Blomqvist said. "After the 17th, I was thinking, it's okay if Urski wins, but when she holed on the 18th I didn't notice at all. I was just thinking about making my putt."

Nykredit Masters
Humlebaek, Denmark
Winner: Martina Eberl

Germany's Martina Eberl overcame a six-stroke deficit to win the Nykredit Masters at the Simon's Golf Club near Helsingor, Denmark. The 27-year-old from Munich was chasing England's Melissa Reid and caught her with six birdies in the first 15 holes. Eberl then birdied the 16th and 17th holes to go two clear before, after a long wait on the 18th tee, driving into the trees at the 18th.

At that point her caddie, Paul Vincent-Fernie, intervened and advised chipping out to the fairway rather than going for glory and the green. She found the green in four and two-putted for a bogey, but Reid missed from five feet for a birdie, so Eberl finished one clear. "I'm glad I have a great caddie who tells me that a bogey is enough," said Eberl. "I am really happy that Paul kept his head cool because mine was a little bit too hot in that moment. It was a great day and I enjoyed playing with Annika for three rounds."

Annika Sorenstam was playing for the last time in Europe and finished in third place. Eberl claimed her third title within a year, having won the Madrid Masters in 2007 and the Italian Open in July. Her closing 66 was her second of the week, having opened with the same score and then having a even-par 73 in the second round, for a total of 205. Reid, the 20-year-old rookie, was runner-up for the third time in 2008. It was a dazzling finish to her second round that gave her the huge lead. She finished birdie, eagle, eagle to go six clear, but the magic was missing on Sunday as 73 left her at 13-under 206.

UNIQA Ladies Golf Open
Wiener Neustadt, Austria
Winner: Laura Davies

Laura Davies's record at Golf Club Fohrenwald in Wiener Neustadt, Austria, simply gets better and better. The 44-year-old former major champion was third on her first appearance there in 2005, then was second the following year before winning in 2007. The only way for the progression to continue was for Davies to successfully defend her title and she did so by winning the UNIQA Ladies Golf Open by three strokes over Lisa Hall.

"Four times I've been here and four times I've been in the presentation. Twice a winner now, it's good," said Davies. "The first year I came here I knew I liked the course and I knew I could win, and sure enough the last two years I have."

Davies posted rounds of 71, 67, 67 and 68 for a total of 15-under-par 273 to claim her 37th European Tour win and the first of the year, other than a victory on the ALPG circuit in Australia in January. "I love winning and that is what I do this for. It is just fantastic to have won," she added.

It was a run of five birdies in the last seven holes to complete her third round that put Davies into a tie for the lead alongside Sweden's Emma Zackrisson. In the final round, at the 291-yard 12th hole, Davies utilized her power to hit a superb drive to four feet and holed the putt for an eagle. "It was probably one of the best shots I've ever hit," Davies said. "That was pretty much the time when I really felt comfortable to win."

Italy's Diana Luna briefly closed within one with a hole-in-one at the 16th, but Davies birdied the 16th and 18th to secure her win, while Luna slipped back to third place.

Goteborg Masters
Gothenburg, Sweden
Winner: Gwladys Nocera

Gwladys Nocera not only achieved her fourth win of the year but became the new low-scoring queen of the Ladies European Tour. The 33-year-old Frenchwoman produced brilliant rounds of 66, 62, 65 and 66 to win the Goteborg Masters by 11 strokes at Lycke Golf Club in the Swedish city.

But Nocera also set new records for the lowest ever total of 259, eight strokes inside the previous best 72-hole score on the tour, and with her score to par of 29 under. The previous best was 25 under achieved by Laura Davies when she won the Guardian Irish Holidays Open in 1995. In that event she also equaled her own then-record total of 267 that she had achieved at the 1988 Biarritz Open and also matched by Juli Inkster at the 2004 Evian Masters.

"It feels so good," Nocera said. "I really didn't think I could shoot that low when I came here. It's probably much better than I expected." Ahead by eight shots overnight, Nocera went out in 34 and then came home with four birdies, just missing another at the last to reach 30 under. Nevertheless, she had plenty of time to ready herself for the traditional French celebration of being soaked in champagne on the 18th green, this time for her ninth career win.

It took another record round to get even as close as 11 strokes to Nocera, with Sweden's Nina Reis, from a nearby town, shooting a 61 to match the tour's best single-round effort set by Kirsty Taylor at the 2005 Wales Championship of Europe. Reis had three eagles and a 59 was a possibility until she drove into a bunker at the 18th and finished with a bogey.

Vediorbis Open de France Dames
Nord-Pas de Calais, France
Winner: Anja Monke

Five years after deciding to quit her job in a hospital laboratory, Anja Monke proved it was the right decision by winning her maiden title at the

Vediorbis Open de France Dames near Arras. Monke, a 31-year-old German, spent four years working as a medical technologist before qualifying in 2003 and seeing how she enjoyed life on tour. "I know how real life is and real work, so that makes my life even more enjoyable," Monke said.

Monke shared the first-round lead after 67, but seemed to have wrecked her chances with 78 in the second round. But she responded with 65 on the third day to lie four behind Stefania Croce.

While the Italian stumbled with a closing 75, Spain's Tania Elosegui took over the lead with an eagle at the sixth after holing her second shot from 110 yards. Monke parred the entire front nine but then picked up birdies at the 10th and 13th before she holed from 10 feet at the 16th for a three, while Elosegui bogeyed to fall out of the lead. Monke also holed from 10 feet at the 17th to go two ahead. Her closing 68 put her at 10-under-par 278 and she won by two over Elosegui and Nina Reis.

"I can't believe it," said Monke. "I've worked for this moment for the last five years and so it's nice to see it happen. I was in a pretty good mood today because I didn't have anything to lose, that's how I felt this morning. If I lost it, then I lost it on Friday for sure. The other three days I won it."

Madrid Ladies Masters
Madrid, Spain
Winner: Gwladys Nocera

Not even a double-bogey six at the opening hole of the final round could prevent Gwladys Nocera compiling her fifth victory of the season and the 10th of her career at the Madrid Ladies Masters. After opening with 72, Nocera took the lead in the 54-hole event on day two after a 69, and then sprinted clear with a closing 67 for an 11-under-par 208 and a four-stroke win over Spain's Paula Marti.

Nocera had trouble in the sand on the opening hole and ended up making a good putt for her six. But after that point she dropped only one more shot but collected nine birdies. Marti closed with 70 to take second place, one ahead of Scotland's Catriona Matthew, who also finished with 70. Tania Elosegui and Rebecca Hudson shared fourth place a further shot back.

The €100,000 first prize took Nocera €62,500 clear of Evian Masters winner Helen Alfredsson at the top of the New Star Money List. "I knew this week was important for the money list and it's big for me because that was the plan at the beginning of the year. It is a big thing for me and I'm just happy I did it," said the 33-year-old Frenchwoman, who has had 12 top-10 finishes this year. "I think it is just a good year for me. Golf is a funny sport. It is up and down. This year is up and you never know what will happen now. I want to enjoy it because you don't know what will happen tomorrow."

Suzhou Taihu Ladies Open
Taihu, Suzhou, China
Winner: Annika Sorenstam

As October turned into November, Annika Sorenstam had not won since the Swede declared in May that she would be "stepping away from competition" at the end of the season. Finally she put that right. The 38-year-old started the week by winning the Japanese Skins Game and then moved on to claim the Suzhou Taihu Ladies Open in China. It was her 17th victory on the Ladies European Tour and the 89th of her career.

Sorenstam started the final round tied for second place but five strokes behind Li Ying Ye, who led after each of the first two rounds. But the former world No. 1 was swiftly into her stride with four birdies in the first five holes. Sorenstam kept up the pressure with another birdie at the 14th and drew even with Ye at the next. She went one in front with another birdie at the 16th, but Ye matched her at the 17th before both birdied the 18th. Sorenstam closed with a 65, after two rounds of 69, for a 13-under-par 203 total, while Ye scored 65, 68 and 70.

Both players birdied the 18th on the first playoff hole, and Sorenstam did again at the second extra hole, making five birdies out of five at the par-five for the week, but Ye missed a short putt to keep the playoff going. "I had a good start and that's what I wanted to do. Ye played well and it was difficult to play catch-up. I tried my best to apply the pressure on her, but she never succumbed to it, and I thought anything could happen in the playoff. This is my 89th career win and I'm so happy," Sorenstam said.

Saint Four Ladies Masters
Jeju Island, Korea
Winner: Hee Kyung Seo

Sun Ju Ahn led the Saint Four Ladies Masters for 70 holes, but it was a brilliant finish of four birdies in the last four holes that brought victory to Hee Kyung Seo in the Korean LPGA co-sanctioned event on Jeju Island. Seo had rounds of 69, 67 and 66 for 14-under-par 202 and finished two ahead of Ahn, who was at 12 under after scores of 65, 70 and 69. The 22-year-old Seo earned a three-year exemption on the LET, while it was also her fifth win on the KLPGA to take her to second on the local money list behind British Open champion Ji-Yai Shin.

One behind going into the final round, Seo trailed Ahn by four strokes at the turn before firing six birdies over the back nine for an inward half of 30. After tapping in for birdie at the tricky par-five 15th, Seo eventually caught Ahn when she sank a curling 20-foot birdie putt at the par-three 16th. She pulled a shot clear at the par-four 17th and sealed the win with an eight-foot birdie putt at the last hole.

"From the very beginning of the event, I thought I could win," said Seo, whose game has improved since she started to practice with Shin. "I achieved quite good scores yesterday, which improved my confidence."

Dubai Ladies Masters
Dubai, United Arab Emirates
Winner: Anja Monke

Just as Annika Sorenstam herself would have done, Anja Monke blocked out all the distractions and concentrated on claiming her second title of the season at the Dubai Ladies Masters. But circumstances dictated that Monke was on the 16th green, which is close to the final green, as Sorenstam played her last hole before stepping away from competition to get married. Although the Swede's challenge for a 90th career title had faltered over the weekend after taking the halfway lead, fittingly she finished with a birdie at the 18th in front of a large gallery, including many of her fellow players at greenside.

Sorenstam holed from eight feet for 71 to tie for seventh place. "It means a lot," Sorenstam said of the finale. "When you get that kind of respect from the players it breaks your heart. I felt it today and it was very special."

Monke began the final round with a two-stroke lead after Veronica Zorzi was penalized two strokes for not replacing her ball after it moved at address during the third round. The Italian fought her way back into contention on the last day, but Monke took control with three birdies in a row from the 10th. A three-putt at the 15th was erased with another birdie at the next as the 31-year-old from Hanover closed with 68 for 13-under-par 275 total and a four-stroke win over Zorzi, with Laura Davies a further stroke back.

"I'm feeling very happy," said Monke. "I had to play my game no matter what or where the focus is. I just tried to focus on my game, and of course I heard the big applause when Annika was hitting her shot into the 18th green. And then we saw her actually finishing it off on 18. We had hit our tee shots on 17 by that time and so I could at least see a little bit."

Gwladys Nocera was confirmed as the winner of the New Star Money List following her five victories and after finishes of fourth, second and third on the ranking in the previous three years. England's Melissa Reid won the Bill Johnson Trophy as the Ryder Cup Wales Rookie of the Year.

Japan LPGA Tour

Daikin Orchid Ladies
Nanjo, Okinawa
Winner: Bo-Bae Song

A decade-long run of homeland victories in the season-launching Daikin Orchid Ladies tournament on the Japan LPGA Tour ended in 2008. Bo-Bae Song, one of the more successful members of the sizeable South Korean contingent who was starting just her second season in Japan, emerged from a tightly packed group of contenders and registered a four-stroke victory, her first on the circuit. It was the first win in the Daikin Orchid for a non-Japanese player since other South Koreans ran off three consecutive triumphs in the late 1990s.

Miho Koga, who was to end the season as the leading money winner, began it with a nine-under-par 63 and a three-stroke lead over Saiki Fujita, only to fall from contention with a 75 Saturday as Song, Michie Ohba and Orie Fujino posted matching 70-67s and took over first place.

Two eagles decorated Song's 65 Sunday, but she received unintentional help from Sakura Yokomine. The highly regarded Yokomine had surged into the lead with six birdies on the first 12 holes, but two late bogeys led to a 68 and second place, four strokes behind the 22-year-old. Song had four birdies to go with the pair of eagles, one a chip-in, and a bogey.

Accordia Golf Ladies
Miyazaki
Winner: Yuri Fudoh

Yuri Fudoh wasted little time in ensuring that her impressive record of consecutive seasons with at least one victory stretched to 10 years. Although it required three holes of a playoff to achieve it, Fudoh landed the Accordia Golf Ladies title in the Japan LPGA Tour season's second tournament, the 43rd victory for clearly one the country's finest players ever. Beginning with a lone win in 1999, the 31-year-old Fudoh has been a multiple winner every year since.

A non-winner led the first day at Aoshima Golf Club in Miyazaki. Yui Kawahara shot 67, one better than Taiwan's Yun-Jye Wei and Bo-Bae Song, who was riding the momentum of her win the week before in the Daikin Orchid. Fudoh, who started with a 70, was still four off the pace after another 70 in Saturday's round, as Wei duplicated her 68 for 136 and led Hiroko Yamaguchi by four shots.

Fudoh came alive Sunday with a sparkling 65 for 205 total, 11 under par, to bring about the tie when Wei shot 69, and led to the three-hole playoff victory.

Yokohama Tire PRGR Cup
Konan, Kochi
Winner: Ji-Yai Shin

Japan golf fans got their first up-close look at Ji-Yai Shin, the young South Korean sensation, and what an eyeful it was. Just 20 and already twice the leading money winner on the South Korean Tour with 18 victories, Shin captured the Yokohama Tire PRGR Cup in her first start on the Japan LPGA Tour. She ground out a playoff win over Sakura Yokomine, another young Asian star who was No. 2 on the 2007 money list. It was a harbinger of a most impressive season to come for Shin, one that brought her international recognition.

Those two players were in contention from the beginning. Shin was among a group of five players at two-under-par 70, two strokes behind leader Akiko Fukushima, for years Japan's most recognized international player, and Yokomine was part of another larger bunch at 71.

Yokomine fashioned 67 on Saturday, the week's best round, and moved a stroke in front of Shin (69) atop the standings with her 138. Sunday came up beastly with strong winds and steady rain at Tosa Country Club in Kochi. Both players incurred double bogeys as they fought it out down the stretch. The South Korean hit her tee shot out of bounds at the 16th and Yokomine blew her two-shot lead on the last hole. The playoff ended when Shin sank a 30-foot birdie putt on the fourth extra hole.

Yamaha Ladies Open
Fukuroi, Shizuoka
Winner: Hiroko Yamaguchi

Hiroko Yamaguchi encountered both extremes as unusually high scores were the order of the week in the Yamaha Ladies Open at Katsuragi Golf Club in Shizuoka. Yamaguchi shot 69, the only sub-70 score posted throughout the tournament, on opening day, never trailed the rest of the way, but had to make a birdie on the 54th hole to manage a five-over-par 77 and win by two shots over Ayako Uehara and Hyun-Ju Shin, who both had 75s.

Her final score was 217, one over par and the highest winning total by far throughout the season in the 54-hole events. It was Yamaguchi's first win since the 2001 Sankyo Open in her rookie season.

Yamaguchi carried a four-stroke lead into the final round, expanding on her one-shot edge on Uehara the first day with 71 for 140. Uehara shot 73 and was joined at 144 by Akiko Fukushima and Shin, who both had 71-73 cards. Yamaguchi struggled a bit midway through Sunday's round, her lead dwindling to one at one point, before the birdie finish polished off the victory.

Studio Alice Ladies Open
Miki, Hyogo
Winner: Hyun-Ju Shin

Hyun-Ju Shin obviously liked what she saw, if not the outcome, when she finished second to Hiroko Yamaguchi at the Yamaha Ladies Open, and she proceeded to duplicate the feat when she headed into the Studio Alice Ladies Open. Just as Yamaguchi did, Shin seized the lead the first day at Hanayashiki Golf Club at Miki, Hyogo Prefecture, and toted it to victory.

The win, Shin's third in her fourth season on tour, came with a six-under-par 210 total, one stroke ahead of Miho Koga, from whom much more would be heard later in the season. The 27-year-old South Korean had had another disappointing second-place finish earlier in the year when she missed a little putt on the final hole of the Air New Zealand Women's Masters.

Scoring was again nearly as high in the Studio Alice as it had been in the Yamaha. The best scores all week were 68s. The first one gave Shin her permanent lead Friday, by two strokes over Esther Lee and Eriko Moriyama. The second one Saturday pulled Koga within a stroke of Shin, who followed with a 71. She repeated the 71 Sunday and that was just enough to fend off Koga and her matching 71.

Life Card Ladies
Kikuyo, Kumamoto
Winner: Yukari Baba

Although the score sheet doesn't indicate it, Yukari Baba put on a rather spectacular performance when she won the Life Card Ladies in mid-April. With rounds of 70, 69 and 68 at Kumamoto Airport Country Club, Baba won by three strokes with her 207. But consider what helped her shoot those scores. After starting the tournament two strokes behind leader Shinobu Moromizato, Baba was sliding back Saturday, two over par for the round after 10 holes. Then she caught fire with three birdies and capped the 69 and took a one-shot lead when she eagled the par-five 18th hole. Midori Yoneyama was second with 69-71–140, and Moromizato dropped back to 142 with a 74, tied for third with Yuko Mitsuka.

Baba had another eagle Sunday, this time a hole-in-one at the 13th, where she sank her five-iron tee shot on the 188-yard hole. Moromizato shot 68 and Yoneyama 70 Sunday to share second place. The victory was Baba's second, the earlier one coming in the 2004 Yonex.

Fujisankei Ladies Classic
Ito, Shizuoka
Winner: Ayako Uehara

Ayako Uehara accomplished at the end of April what she barely failed to do at the beginning of the month. "I finally got a win," she said after landing the first title of her six-year career.

A final-round 75 three weeks earlier left her in second place in the Yamaha Open. Things didn't look any brighter for her in the Fujisankei Ladies Classic. She teed off in the final round five strokes off the pace of Erina Hara, another tour non-winner, and trailing five others. This time, instead of 75, Uehara produced a brilliant, six-under-par 66 and edged Hara by a stroke with her eight-under-par 208 total.

Hara, who opened with 73, five off Kayo Yamada's lead, had staked her bid Saturday with a sterling 64, by four strokes the best score shot by anybody the first two days. It jumped her two strokes ahead of Keiko Sasaki (72-67). Uehara had a 70-72 start, but revved it up Sunday, virtually wrapping up the win with three consecutive birdies from the 14th hole, giving her seven against a lone bogey in the round. A late birdie for 72 salvaged Hara's second-place finish, one ahead of Miki Saiki.

Crystal Geyser Ladies
Chiba
Winner: Miho Koga

On the cusp of success during the first two months of the season, Miho Koga broke through with her first victory of the year in the Crystal Geyser Ladies tournament, though it wasn't easy. Koga had to rally on the final nine holes to overtake teenager Maiko Wakabayashi and go three extra holes to gather in her eighth career title.

Koga entered the last round four strokes behind Wakabayashi and Ritsuko Ryu, another youngster shooting for her first win in her third season on tour. That wasn't known until Sunday morning when the second round was completed. A three-hour rain delay Saturday morning forced the runover at Keiyo Country Club. The 20-year-old Ryu, the first-round leader with 65, added a 70, and Wakabayashi matched her nine-under-par 135 with rounds of 66 and 69.

Koga (71-68), who shared third place with Sakura Yokomine (70-69) and Mihoko Iseri (66-73), still trailed Wakabayashi by three strokes through 14 holes Sunday. Then, she turned up the heat and birdied three of the last four for 67 to catch Wakabayashi, who shot 71 for her 206. The season's third playoff went three holes before Wakabayashi bowed out with a bogey.

World Ladies Championship Salonpas Cup
Tokyo
Winner: Akiko Fukushima

Her playoff victory over South Korean phenom Ji-Yai Shin was particularly gratifying for Akiko Fukushima. Although she has rarely gone through a season without at least one victory, Fukushima had not captured a major on the Japan LPGA Tour in 11 years until that Sunday in the World Ladies Championship Salonpas Cup, designated as the circuit's fourth major for the first time.

"It's been a long while since I got so thrilled at winning a tournament,"

Fukushima gushed after the five-hole playoff that ended rather ingloriously when she three-putted for par and the win as Shin four-putted for bogey. Shin had caught Fukushima with a 71 as Fukushima sputtered to a 73 and her four-under-par 284. It was her 22nd career victory in Japan.

Fukushima took first place away from China's Na Zhang on Saturday with her second 70 and 211. Zhang, a four-time winner in 2007, had led the first two days at Tokyo's Yomiuri Country Club. Playing in just her fifth Japanese event of the season, she opened with 68 and led Miho Koga by a shot. She retained that margin Friday with 72–140, but the runner-up then was Fukushima (71-70). The two traded places Saturday as China's No. 1 player took a 72. Shin moved within two shots with a 68–213, one of only five players who broke par amid the day's difficult conditions.

Vernal Ladies
Asakura, Fukuoka
Winner: Eun-A Lim

South Korea's Eun-A Lim picked up her first victory on the Japan LPGA Tour in impressive fashion, jumping off to a three-stroke lead in the first round and holding on to it to the end. With her one-stroke victory, Lim become her country's fourth different winner in Japan in 2008 and the fourth first-time victor of the season.

The 24-year-old South Korean, in her third season in Japan, rattled off a seven-under-par 65 Friday at Fukuoka Century Golf Club. Closest at 68 was Kayo Yamada with five others, including Yuri Fudoh and Akiko Fukushima, coming off her 22nd victory in the World Ladies Championship the previous Sunday. Lim gave away one stroke of her lead Saturday, shooting 71–136, but Bo-Bae Song (68–138) was the only one within four strokes.

Lim slipped a little more in the final round, taking a 73, but her seven-under-par 209 was just good enough to edge the 34-year-old veteran Fukushima, who closed with 70–210. Yukari Baba, the Life Card winner, and Ji-Hee Lee had 71s for 211.

Chukyo TV Bridgestone Ladies
Toyota, Aichi
Winner: Ji-Hee Lee

Ji-Hee Lee was coming off a rare down year on the Japan LPGA Tour when she teed off in late May in the Chukyo TV Bridgestone Ladies. The 29-year-old South Korean had placed among the top 10 money winners four times since 2001, but had gone without a victory in 2007. Several high finishes earlier in the 2008 season encouraged her and she was playing at Chukyo Golf Club in Toyota, a course where she had scored her ninth victory. The combination jelled.

Lee staged a spirited rally in the final round to overtake Miho Koga, the second-round leader, and Miki Saiki, then defeat them in a playoff. Koga, who had won the Crystal Geyser earlier in May, shot 67 for 138 Saturday and took over first place from veteran Michiko Hattori and Yukari Baba, who had opened with 68s.

Lee was two back with 71-69–140 after 36 holes, but needed five birdies on her last 10 holes Sunday just to get into the playoff, as Koga shot 70 and Saiki 69. Lee wrapped up her 10th title with a 20-foot birdie putt on the first extra hole as Saiki missed the green and Koga a 10-foot birdie putt.

Kosaido Ladies Golf Cup
Ichihara, Chiba
Winner: Akane Iijima

One super round rarely begets another in golf, but in 54-hole tournaments that one is usually enough to gain a victory. Such was the case in the Kosaido Ladies Golf Cup as Akane Iijima joined the lengthening list of different winners on the Japan LPGA Tour.

Iijima, the reigning LPGA champion, tied the tour record in the opening round, blasting out a 10-under-par 62 at Chiba Kosaido Country Club, to take a huge, five-stroke lead. She managed no better than 73 the next day, though, and clicked off a pair of birdies on the final nine Sunday to pull off a two-stroke victory, the fourth of her career.

Deadly putting played a big role in the 10-birdie first round. Iijima had five birdies on each nine and needed only 19 putts in the round, which also tied a tour record. A distant second that Friday were Nahoko Hirao, Esther Lee and Mayumi Nakajima, who pursued Iijima through the weekend and ultimately took the runner-up position.

A cold rain pushed up the scores as Iijima mustered just one birdie in shooting the 73 for 135 and Nakajima moved close with 70–137. Prophetically, the 24-year-old Iijima aimed for a four-stroke improvement Sunday, which would have been good enough, but she went one stroke better with 68 for her winning 203. Nakajima also shot 68 for 205, the only player within six strokes of the winner.

Resort Trust Ladies
Koga, Shiga
Winner: Mi-Jeong Jeon

The South Korean presence continued to permeate the Japan LPGA Tour when Mi-Jeong Jeon snatched the Resort Trust Ladies tournament in early June. Jeon, the most dominant of the South Koreans with seven victories in 2006 and 2007, became the sixth from that country to land a title in the first 13 events of the season with her three-stroke victory over Sakura Yokomine, a second-place finisher for the third time in 2008.

Jeon posted three rounds in the 60s en route to the victory. The first, a 68, put her two strokes behind leader Kaori Higo, briefly reviving the game that brought her 17 titles during her long career, the last in 2004. The second, 67, left her just a shot behind the new leader Miki Saiki (68-66–134) as Higo slipped to 138 with a par round.

The final day Jeon shot 69, which raced her past Saiki, who was headed for 75. Yokomine moved within two strokes with an eagle at the eighth hole, but Jeon eliminated the threat with three birdies over the next four holes, then parred in with a one-bogey interruption. Yokomine matched the 69 for 207. Ji-Hee Lee, Bo-Bae Song, Ji-Yai Shin, Eun-A Lim and Hyun-Ju Shin were the earlier 2008 winners from South Korea.

We Love Kobe Suntory Ladies Open
Kobe, Hyogo
Winner: Momoko Ueda

Momoko Ueda had succumbed to the lure of the prestige and riches of the LPGA Tour in America after her brilliant 2007 season when, at age 21, she won five tournaments and became the youngest player to land the money title in the history of the Japan LPGA Tour. The venture abroad did not pan out very well for her in her first months abroad, but she picked up where she left off when she returned to her native land to play in the We Love Kobe Suntory Ladies Open.

In a final-round duel of leading money winners, Ueda bested Shiho Oyama, the No. 1 of 2006, and landed the sixth title of her young career on her 22nd birthday. Her par 72 gave her a seven-under-par total of 281 and a one-stroke victory over Oyama, the second- and third-round leader, and South Korea's Bo-Bae Song and Eun-A Lim.

Oyama shot a pair of 69s in the first two rounds at Rokko Kokusai Golf Club as she took over the lead from Sakura Yokomine, who had three runner-up finishes on her 2008 record. Yokomine had begun the tournament in front with her 66. Oyama added a third 69 Saturday for 207 as Ueda took over second place at 209 with rounds of 70-69-70. On Sunday, Ueda caught Oyama at the turn as Oyama had three front-nine bogeys. They were still tied going to the 72nd hole, where Oyama missed a short par putt that cost her a 75 and a playoff shot at her first 2008 win.

Nichirei PGM Ladies
Miho, Ibaraki
Winner: Yuko Mitsuka

Yuko Mitsuka generated momentum with a strong finish in the Suntory Open and maintained it in record-setting abundance in the Nichirei PGM Ladies the following week. Mitsuka followed up her final-round 67 in the Suntory with a potent 66 in the first round of the Nichirei and left the rest of the field in her dust over the weekend at Ibaraki's Miho Golf Club. When it cleared, the 23-year-old had a 10-stroke victory with her 16-under-par 200, the lowest total in the tournament's history. It was also the largest winning margin of the season.

Mitsuka's march to the second title of her young career was a display of steady positional improvement. The starting 66 put her a stroke in front, with Ritsuko Ryu in second place and five others tied for third. Although her 69 Saturday was matched or bettered by several players, her 135 total widened her lead to three strokes over Namika Omata and Ji-Hee Lee, who won her ninth title a month earlier and shot 65 that day.

Mitsuka quickly dispelled any doubts in her or any other mind Sunday with an overwhelmingly flawless round — a seven-birdie 65. Four of the birdies came on the front nine as she put it away for all intents and purposes. Her back-nine 33 also was unmatched. Shiho Oyama, with a 71, took second place, her second runner-up finish in a row. Not that it would have mattered if she had played better, but Ji-Hee Lee shot 75 Sunday to finish 13 strokes behind the winner.

Promise Ladies
Kato, Hyogo
Winner: Chie Arimura

Talk about impatient confidence. Although just 20 years old, Chie Arimura had this to say after scoring her initial victory on the Japan LPGA Tour in the Promise Ladies tournament: "My first win has been a long time coming." It was an impressive victory at that. Arimura outplayed two of the circuit's best players — former leading money winners Yuri Fudoh and Shiho Oyama — over the final nine holes at Madame J Golf Club in Kato, Hyogo Prefecture, to secure the title and become the tour's fifth first-time winner of the season.

Arimura had wrested the lead away from Yuko Mitsuka in the second round after Mitsuka, riding the momentum of her victory the previous week in the Nichirei Ladies, had opened with a 65 that Friday. Arimura shot her second straight 67 Saturday and jumped into a three-stroke lead when Mitsuka double-bogeyed her last hole to drop into a second-place tie with Fudoh (68-69) and Esther Lee (71-66).

Oyama, who began the Sunday round five off the pace, birdied three of her first seven holes to climb into contention, and Fudoh birdied the last three holes of the front nine to overtake Arimura. It was all Arimura the rest of the way, though, as Fudoh suffered a double bogey and bogey and Oyama couldn't make up any more ground on the incoming nine. Arimura sailed home with a 68 for a 14-under-par 202 total and a five-shot victory over Oyama (68–207), stuck with her third consecutive runner-up finish and still winless for the season.

Belluna Ladies Cup
Kanra, Gunma
Winner: Hiromi Mogi

Hiromi Mogi put on quite a show for her family and local fans when she returned home to Gunma Prefecture for the Belluna Ladies Cup tournament at Kanra's Obatago Golf Club. Not only did Mogi lead the event from start to finish, but she polished off the victory with a had-to-have birdie on her final hole to win by a stroke.

Picking off the fourth title of her six-season career, Mogi came to the 18th green Sunday knowing that she needed a birdie to avoid a playoff against Akiko Fukushima, the defending champion and current leading money winner. The veteran Fukushima, playing ahead of Mogi, had registered her sixth birdie of the day, posted a 67 for 204 total and was watching as Mogi coolly matched the birdie for 70 and the one-stroke victory at 13-under-par 203.

Mogi's trail to victory began with a seven-under-par 65 Friday and followed with 68 for 133. South Korea's Ji-Woo Lee shared the lead with her Saturday after tacking a 67 onto her starting 66. Fukushima was at 137 and gradually closed the gap Sunday before the dramatics at the final green. Ji-Woo Lee managed just 73 and dropped into a third-place tie at 206 with Ji-Hee Lee.

Meiji Chocolate Cup
Kita-Hiroshima, Hokkaido
Winner: Yuri Fudoh

Not surprisingly, Yuri Fudoh was the one to end the rare streak of 17 consecutive different winners in the Japan LPGA Tour's 2008 season, and the triumph in the Meiji Chocolate Cup tournament was a landmark victory in another way as well. With the ¥12.6 million awarded for her 44th career win, the brilliant 31-year-old shotmaker lifted her career earnings over the billion-yen mark, by far a Japan LPGA Tour record.

Fudoh, who won the Accordia tournament, the second event of the season in mid-March, and had only one strong showing in the interim, carved out a one-stroke victory in the Meiji Chocolate Cup with a final-round 70 for 207 total. It was a day when Chie Arimura came up with a nine-under-par 63, one of the year's hottest rounds with an eagle and six successive birdies starting at the sixth hole, but fell a stroke short of her second victory in three weeks when she bogeyed the 71st hole.

Saori Ikushima, 32, who had made only one cut in seven starts earlier in the season, had her day in the sun Friday when she shot 66 and led Ji-Woo Lee and Saiki Fujita by two strokes, Fudoh and four others by three. Fudoh, six seasons the tour's leading money winner, took over Saturday with 68–137 as Ikushima shot the first of two 78s and plummeted to a 45th-place finish.

Fudoh lost a stroke off her two-shot lead when she bogeyed the 17th hole Sunday, but her par at the final hole gave her the one-shot win over Arimura, Fujita and South Korea's Hyun-Ju Shin, who both equaled Fudoh's closing 70.

Stanley Ladies
Susano, Shizuoka
Winner: Akiko Fukushima

Akiko Fukushima enhanced her hold on the money list when she came out on top as she and South Korea's Ji-Hee Lee, No. 2 on the money list, pursued Ayako Uehara, the second-round leader, to the wire in the Stanley Ladies tournament in mid-July.

The two trailed Uehara by two strokes going into Sunday's round at Tomei Country Club at Susano, Shizuoka Prefecture. Fukushima mustered three back-nine birdies for 67, just enough to nip Uehara, who shot 70 after a pair of 67s had enabled her to slip past Australian Nikki Campbell, the first-round leader whose only victory in six seasons came in the 2006 Suntory Open. Fukushima's winning score was 203, 13 under par.

Uehara, who won the Fujisankei Classic in April, yielded the lead to Fukushima early on the back nine Sunday, and the 34-year-old veteran carried it to her 23rd victory in Japan, her second of the season and 25th of her career, counting her two wins in America during her years on the U.S. LPGA Tour. Lee shot 69 and tied for third place with Mikiyo Nishizuka, who shot 66 Sunday for her 205.

Kagome Philanthropy LPGA Players Championship
Inzai, Chiba
Winner: Mi-Jeong Jeon

South Korea's Mi-Jeong Jeon showed the form in the Kagome Philanthropy LPGA Players Championship that led to successive high finishes on the Japan LPGA Tour's money list the two previous years. Jeon, who was third in 2007 and runner-up in 2006, bolted up the money list again with a five-stroke victory in the Players Championship, which sported the year's third largest purse.

The South Korean nosed in front of compatriot Ji-Woo Lee the second day and was never headed again, although she had to shake off a final-round challenge from Yuko Mitsuka, the Nichirei Classic winner. Lee, playing her second season in Japan, opened with 65, but fell from contention with 76 Friday, as Jeon posted 69–137 to lead Mitsuka (70-69) and Hiromi Mogi (69-70), the Belluna Cup victor, by two.

An even-par 72 preserved Jeon's lead, then by one over Mitsuka (71–210), setting up their brief final-round duel at Narashino Country Club in Inzai, Chiba Prefecture. After five holes Sunday, Jeon and Mitsuka were tied at seven under. Three holes later, on the strength of two birdies and a pair of Mitsuka bogeys, Jeon led by four. She finished with a three-birdie flourish for 67 and 276 total to Mitsuka's 71–281, winning her ninth title in the last three years in Japan.

AXA Ladies
Tomakomai, Hokkaido
Winner: Shinobu Moromizato

Thus far in 2008 Shinobu Moromizato had not fared as well as might be expected of the reigning Japan Women's Open champion and seventh-ranked money winner of 2007. The little 22-year-old, who had endured an unsuccessful fling in America the year before, had only a single runner-up finish as a real positive in the current season and she languished well down the money list. The frustration ended, though, in early August in the AXA Ladies tournament, when she outdueled Miho Koga over the final holes and claimed a two-stroke victory, the third of her career on the Japan LPGA Tour.

Moromizato and Koga were head to head in the final round at Mitsui Kanto Tomakomai Golf Club after completing the first 36 holes as the co-leaders, Moromizato with 69-71–140 and Koga with 71-69–140. They had taken over first place from South Korea's Ji-Woo Lee, who was demoralized for the second week in a row as she faded badly again after starting with 67.

Moromizato basically put the title away on the front nine Sunday. She jumped to a four-stroke lead and finished with a comfortable 70 for 210 as Koga cut that margin in half, closing with a par 72. Visiting American star Natalie Gulbis was never in contention, winding up in a 37th-place tie.

NEC Karuizawa 72
Karuizawa, Nagano
Winner: Erina Hara

When Erina Hara joined the winners' ranks with her first victory in the NEC Karuizawa 72 tournament, she did so with a vengeance. For weeks beforehand, Hara had been making waves on the Japan LPGA Tour, finishing in the top 10 in six of her last seven starts. Finally, she went over the top at the Karuizawa 72 golf complex in Nagano, never out of first place and seven strokes in front of the field at week's end.

Her 21-under-par score of 195 not only was the lowest of the year by far but also was the only total under 200. Only Yuko Mitsuka's 10-stroke victory in the Nichirei Ladies exceeded Hara's margin as she became the sixth first-time winner of the 2008 season.

After sharing first place with Miho Koga, Yumiko Yoshida and Hiroko Fukushima at 67 in the opening round, the second-season pro erupted with a 63 Saturday and leaped to a six-shot lead over Koga. Hara left no doubt about it early Sunday when she birdied four of the first six holes and went on to the 65 that brought about the 195 total. Ji-Hee Lee, in hot pursuit of Akiko Fukushima and the money title, put together a pair of 32s, but still finished the distant seven shots behind the 20-year-old winner in second place.

CAT Ladies
Hakone, Kanagawa
Winner: Miho Koga

Miho Koga is proving to be a master of winning tournaments the hard way. Back in early May, the 26-year-old Koga had to rally on the final nine and go three extra holes to defeat rookie Maiko Wakabayashi. At the CAT Ladies tournament at Hakone, Kanagawa Prefecture, she had to work out a hard par on the last hole to nip Mi-Jeong Jeon and become the fourth double winner of the season.

Koga came off a two-stroke, second-round lead en route to her ninth circuit victory. She was three back of leader Yuko Mitsuka in a three-way tie at 69 with Jeon and Mie Nakata the first day, as Mitsuka racked up a pair of eagles and a 66. Koga seized the lead Saturday with a 68 for 137, two in front of Mitsuka (73) and Saiki Fujita (73-66) on the par-73 Daihakone Country Club course.

She had early problems Sunday with two front-nine bogeys, and with birdies at the par-five 13th hole, Jeon and Mitsuka stood even with Koga at nine under par. With seven straight pars after a birdie at the 10th hole, Koga came to the final hole needing a par to win after Mitsuka bogeyed the 17th and Jeon the 18th. She did it, shooting 73 for her nine-under-par 210 total.

Yonex Ladies
Nagaoka, Niigata
Winner: Rui Kitada

It wasn't destined to spark a repeat or even a resemblance to her brilliant 2004 season as things turned out, but Rui Kitada's victory in the Yonex Ladies tournament at the end of August and her other win late in 2007 surely raised her morale measurably after the lean years in between. Kitada, then 22, registered her other three wins in 2004, when she finished third on the money list behind major stars Yuri Fudoh and Ai Miyazato.

As the first-round co-leaders Yasuko Sato and Woo-Soon Ko (68s) shot themselves in the foot Saturday with 74s, Kitada took over first place with her 70-68–138. She led Erina Hara, the NEC Karuizawa winner, by two, thanks primarily to a pair of 40-foot birdie putts on the front nine. Hara had five birdies on the last 10 holes for her 69–140.

Despite two early birdies, Kitada led Hara by just two shots going down the stretch Sunday, eventually stretching the margin to the concluding three strokes with her 69–207, nine under par at Yonex Country Club at Nagaoka, Niigate Prefecture. Hara shot 70–210, edging Sakura Yokomine by a stroke for second place.

Golf 5 Ladies
Mizunami, Gifu
Winner: Saiki Fujita

Saiki Fujita continued her one-victory-a-season pace when she pulled away from one of the brightest new stars in women's golf and an untested young amateur to win the Golf 5 Ladies tournament. The 22-year-old Fujita, already in her fourth year on the circuit, had picked off the Promise Ladies titles in 2006 and 2007 and had a pair of runner-up finishes in 2008 before landing her third win by two strokes with a closing 67 for 203, 13 under par, at Mizunami Country Club in Gifu Prefecture.

Ji-Yai Shin, the dynamic young South Korean whose tremendous early years were highlighted when she won the Women's British Open, took a one-shot lead into the final round. Playing an international schedule and making just her third start in Japan, Shin already had a win (Yokohama Tire) and a playoff loss (Salonpas Cup) on the record. The 20-year-old phenom had to settle for second place again when Fujita charged Sunday.

Fujita, two back after 36 holes with rounds of 70-66–136, made up that deficit with birdies on the first two holes and went ahead to stay with three more in the middle of the round. Shin negated birdies with bogeys and managed just a 71, winding up in a second-place tie with 19-year-old amateur Kumiko Kaneda, who went out in 31 and finished with 66 for her 205.

Japan LPGA Championship Konica Minolta Cup
Kaga, Ishikawa
Winner: Hyun-Ju Shin

For the first time in six years, the Konica Minolta Cup, symbolic of the Japan LPGA Championship, did not wind up in the hands of one of the homeland stars. South Korea's Hyun-Ju Shin prevailed in a stretch duel against younger countrywoman Ji-Yai Shin under difficult typhoon-threatening conditions on Katayamazu Golf Club's Hakusan course. She became the first non-Japanese winner of the major title since Ok-Hee Ku, another South Korean stalwart, accepted the trophy in 2002.

Hyun-Ju Shin, who won the Studio Alice tournament in April, led the tournament all the way and on the weekend had serious competition only from Ji-Yai Shin, still riding a torrid streak, and young Japanese star Sakura Yokomine, still surprisingly seeking her first 2008 win.

The victor opened with a five-under-par 67, one ahead of Momoko Ueda, the 2007 money leader, and two in front of Erina Hara, the NEC Karuizawa winner. Hyun-Ju stretched the gap to four over the next two rounds, shooting 71-68 for 206. Ji-Yai (68–210) and Yokomine (67–211) were the only players within nine strokes.

Both challengers faltered on the front nine Sunday, and Hyun-Ju seemed headed for a comfortable win only to stumble with three back-nine bogeys to go five over par for the round. But an up-and-down par at last hole for 77–283 was just enough for the one-stroke victory when Ji-Yai (74) bogeyed that final hole and Yokomine (73) missed a tying birdie for 284s. It was Hyun-Ju's fourth win since first playing in Japan in 2005.

Munsingwear Ladies Tokai Classic
Mihama, Aichi
Winner: Yuri Fudoh

In most of the glorious seasons Yuri Fudoh has enjoyed as Japan's No. 1 female player, three victories entrenched her grip on another money title. In 2008, even though she was the first competitor to stow away three wins for the season in the Munsingwear Ladies Tokai Classic, it merely moved her up to ninth place on the cash list, more than ¥30 million behind leader Akiko Fukushima. The reasons? A light playing schedule and a dearth of high finishes (three top 10s) besides the two previous wins.

Victory No. 3 came in one of Fudoh's favorite tournaments, one that she had won twice before, in 2000 and 2003, but she had to beat Momoko Ueda and Yayoi Arasaki in the first playoff in four months.

The unheralded Arasaki, who had not finished better than third in six seasons on the circuit, had taken a two-stroke lead into the final round with 69-67–136 after dislodging Sakura Yokomine and Shinobu Moromizato, the first-round leaders with 68s, at Minami Aichi Country Club.

With Fudoh, who came from five strokes off the pace with a five-under 67, already in with 208, Ueda needed only a par at the last hole to win, but bogeyed for 68–208. Arasaki parred for 72–208. Fudoh then put her 45th career victory into the books by holing a 25-foot birdie putt on the first extra hole.

Miyagi TV Cup Dunlop Ladies Open
Rifu, Miyagi
Winner: Momoko Ueda

One wonders what might have happened had Momoko Ueda not chosen to take a fling at the LPGA Tour in America instead of defending her money title in Japan? Ueda had moderate success in the U.S., finishing 45th on the money list with three top-10 finishes in 19 events, but in just seven starts on the Japan LPGA Tour, Ueda picked up two victories, the second in the Miyagi TV Cup Dunlop Ladies Open a week after losing to Yuri Fudoh in the Munsingwear Tokai Classic playoff.

At the same time, it was another frustrating week for Sakura Yokomine and her fruitless efforts to bag her first 2008 triumph. When all except one of the five unlikely first-round leaders at Rifu Golf Club in Miyagi Prefecture went south Saturday, Yokomine slipped a stroke in front of the other one — Julie Lu — with rounds of 70-69.

Ueda (70-72) and Yuko Mitsuka (71-70) moved up to challenge Yokomine in Sunday's final round. The 16th hole proved pivotal in the three-way battle. Ueda parred there and took her winning, one-stroke lead when both Yokomine and Mitsuka took bogeys, Yokomine's second in a row. Ueda closed with pars for 69–211, five under par, and watched as Mitsuka also parred the 18th for 69–212 to tie Lu (72) and Akane Iijima (69) for second. Yet another bogey dropped Yokomine (74) into a tie for fifth with Miki Saiki. For the 22-year-old Ueda, it was her seventh victory since joining the tour in 2006.

Japan Women's Open
Shibata, Niigata
Winner: Ji-Hee Lee

When Ji-Hee Lee pulled off a stirring victory over the final holes of the Japan Women's Open, it chalked up further evidence of the remarkable talent of a plethora of women golfers from South Korea through much of the world. Lee's victory came just three weeks after compatriot Hyun-Ju Shin won the Japan LPGA Championship, the year's second major. It was the ninth victory of the season for South Koreans in Japan and vaulted Lee past Akiko Fukushima into first place on the money list.

Although Ji-Hee was close by, another South Korean Lee, Esther, was making most of the noise in the early rounds of the Women's Open on testing Shiun Golf Club's Kajigawa course. The 22-year-old from Seoul, winless in her second season in Japan, led by a stroke after her opening 68 and by two when she followed Friday with 73 for 141. Ji-Hee trailed badly after rounds of 73-76, but the 10-time winner since 2001 rebounded nicely Saturday with 68 and climbed within two strokes of then co-leaders Esther Lee (74) and Akane Iijima (69), the 2007 LPGA champion, at 215.

The tightly packed race to the wire Sunday also included Yuri Fudoh and Ai Miyazato, playing in just her second tournament since returning from her season in America. They were factors in the exciting finish, but Fudoh bogeyed the par-five 18th and Miyazato managed only a string of five pars at the end. Ji-Hee won it at the final hole when she played a brilliant recovery hook off a bad tee shot and sank a 15-foot birdie putt for 67–284. Esther Lee (70) tied Miyazato (68) for second and Fudoh finished fourth.

Sankyo Ladies Open
Kiryu, Gunma
Winner: Maiko Wakabayashi

Six previous 2008 tournaments on the Japan LPGA Tour produced first-time winners, all of whom had past-season experience to bring to the table. So Maiko Wakabayashi had the distinction of being the first rookie to break the ice in the season when she rallied from a two-stroke deficit to score a three-shot victory in the Sankyo Ladies Open in mid-October. At age 20, she was the sixth youngest winner in circuit history.

Wakabayashi, who first made a golfing stir when she won the World Junior Championship at age 17, had gone through an up-and-down year, ranging from a three-hole playoff loss in the Crystal Geyser Open in May to upcoming No. 1 Miho Koga to missed cuts.

In the Sankyo Open, Wakabayashi lingered close to leader Hiromi Mogi for two days before charging to victory Sunday. Comfortable playing in front of family and friends on her home Akagi Country Club course, Mogi led by two with 67 Friday and by a stroke over Shinobu Moromizato and two over Wakabayashi with 138 after the Saturday round. When Mogi struggled Sunday, Wakabayashi edged into the lead with her fourth birdie (against two bogeys) at the turn and held off Mogi and Ji-Hee Lee, who tied for second at 211. She finished with 68 and was eight under par at 208.

Fujitsu Ladies
Chiba
Winner: Yuri Fudoh

Only a highly talented and nerveless veteran like Yuri Fudoh likely could have pulled off what she did during the first seven months of the Japan LPGA Tour. Her four victories alone are always an achievement, but the way she won them was remarkable: three playoffs and a one-stroke victory over three other contenders.

The third overtime triumph in the Fujitsu Ladies was truly extraordinary. Not only did the 31-year-old Fudoh have to go five extra holes before notching her 46th career victory, but she had to make up seven strokes on her faltering victim, Yuko Mitsuka, just to get the opportunity.

The tournament of extremes began Friday when Akiko Fukushima, hoping to regain the top spot on the money list that she had held most of the season, fired a blazing, nine-under-par 63, a course-record score at the Tokyu Seven Hundred Club even with a bogey on the card. Fukushima short-circuited with 73 the next day, and Mitsuka, the Friday runner-up with 66, roared to a six-shot lead with 64 for 130.

Mitsuka seemed a sure thing at that point, considering that she had expanded a second-round lead to a 10-stroke victory earlier in the year at the Nichirei Ladies. Not with Fudoh around. Fudoh methodically carved out a 66–203 while Mitsuka was struggling to a 73 for her 13-under total. The two then matched scores for four holes before Mitsuka missed a needed par putt at the fifth.

Masters Golf Club Ladies
Miki, Hyogo
Winner: Shiho Oyama

One of the major surprises through the first seven months of the season was the absence of Shiho Oyama from the victory list. The 2006 money winning champion had not mounted a serious challenge since enduring three consecutive runner-up finishes at mid-season. Oyama turned things around at the end of the year, though, starting with a breakthrough victory in the Masters Golf Club Ladies at Miki, Hyogo Prefecture, in late October and capping it with a fourth-place showing in the U.S. LPGA qualifier in December.

Oyama was a bit erratic until the final holes when two late birdies opened her four-stroke victory margin and seven-under-par 209 score.

The first round actually set up the win. She shot a bogey-free 65, the only player to break 70, the score posted by six other players. Even though she floundered to a 75 Saturday and didn't make a birdie all day, Oyama only slipped a stroke off the lead, then held by money leader Ji-Hee Lee with 70-69–139.

An opening birdie and 14 straight pars Sunday enabled Oyama to move past Lee, crippled by five early bogeys. She still had to contend with rookie Ah-Reum Hwang, who had seven birdies, a bogey and a double bogey to catch her at five under par. However, while the 21-year-old graduate of the developmental Step-Up Tour was bogeying the 16th and 17th holes, Oyama followed with birdies at the 16th and 18th to clinch her 11th circuit victory with a 69. Hwang (70) tied Eun-A Lim (68) for second place.

Hisako Higuchi IDC Otsuka Ladies
Hanno, Saitama
Winner: Mayu Hattori

Another young lady was heard from in the Hisako Higuchi IDC Otsuka tournament. Mayu Hattori joined five other Japan LPGA pros in their early 20s who acquired their first tour victories in 2008, squeezing out a one-stroke victory in the early November tournament at Musashigaoka Golf Club in Hanno, Saitama Prefecture. She was the eighth and final maiden victor of the season.

Hattori credited her win to a 50-foot birdie putt she made at the 53rd hole in Sunday's final round. "It was a miracle," exclaimed the 20-year-old tour sophomore. That birdie, her third on the back nine en route to her 69–210, put her into a first-place tie with Chie Arimura, the second-round leader (72-66–138).

With a playoff looking likely, Arimura, who also was a first-time winner in 2008 at the Promise Cup, incurred a disastrous double bogey at the final hole and dropped into a tie for third with Maiko Wakabayashi, who broke the victory ice three weeks earlier in the Sankyo Open. Arimura, whose game had tailed off after a mid-season splurge to a point where she had missed three straight cuts prior to the IDC Otsuka, shot 74 and Wakabayashi 71 for their 212s. Esther Lee (71–211) grabbed the runner-up spot.

Mizuno Classic
Shima, Mie
Winner: Ji-Yai Shin

Ji-Yai Shin put the icing on her spectacular Japanese cake when she added the Mizuno Classic to her remarkable accomplishments in Nippon and around the world in 2008. Shin's victory in the tournament that is a regular stop on both the U.S. and Japan LPGA tours was her 10th of the season and, with the Women's British Open, second in an American circuit event.

She was close to perfect in her first five starts in Japan with her Mizuno and Yokohama Tire wins, a playoff loss in the Salonpas Cup and ties for second in the Japan LPGA Championship and Golf 5 tournament.

Against the strongest international field of the season in the Mizuno Classic at Kintetsu Kashikojima Country Club at Shima, Shin marched to an eye-popping, six-stroke victory with a 15-under-par 201. She began with a 68, one behind leaders Miki Saiki and Mayu Hattori, maintaining the momentum from her maiden victory the preceding Sunday in the Otsuka event. Shin took charge Saturday with 66, the 134 pushing her two strokes in front of Hattori (69) and three ahead of Shiho Oyama and Jee Young Lee (69-68s).

It was a breeze Sunday. Shin doubled her lead with two birdies and a chip-in eagle on the front nine and saw Hattori and Lee, her closest pursuers, wreck their chances with double bogeys on consecutive holes after the turn. Two more birdies and just her second bogey of the week brought her home with the easy win, by six over Hattori and seven over Eun-A Lim.

Itoen Ladies
Chonan, Chiba
Winner: Miho Koga

Miho Koga took another big step toward her first money title when she acquired her third title of the season with a two-stroke victory in the Itoen Ladies tournament. With the win the eight-year veteran rose to the No. 2 spot on the money list behind Ji-Hee Lee, setting up a tight race to the wire with two events remaining.

Interestingly, the two players, along with first-round leader Shiho Oyama, headed into the final round tied at 136. Both came from well off the pace of Oyama's opening 64, Koga adding 66 to her first-round 70 and Lee following 69 with 67. Oyama ran off five birdies in a row as she fashioned a back-nine 30 for the 64, as she sought her second win in three weeks.

The 26-year-old Koga, winner of nine tour titles since 2003, produced a birdie string of her own — six straight and seven in eight holes — as she took command of the competition Sunday. Koga led a quartet that included Ai Miyazato by four shots after 13 holes and coasted home in 67 strokes for the winning 13-under-par 203. Yuko Mitsuka had another strong tournament, shooting 65 to pair with Miyazato (68) at 205 to take second place.

Daioseishi Elleair Ladies Open
Matsuyama, Ehime
Winner: Sakura Yokomine

Sakura Yokomine deserved — and earned — the four-stroke victory she scored in the Daioseishi Elleair Ladies Open. She had done just about everything short of winning during the season and was running out of chances to snag a victory before the schedule ran out. Eighteen times in her 28 starts, Yokomine placed in the top 10, losing a playoff and finishing second or third six other times. The net result was that, with the Elleair victory, she climbed into second place on the money list, where she finished in 2007 and within range of Ji-Hee Lee, the leader.

Bad weather disrupted play in the Friday round at the Elleair Golf Club in Matsuyama, Ehime Prefecture, and 30 women had to complete their rounds Saturday morning. Yokomine was one of them. She finished with 71, then later in the day tallied 68 for 139 and a one-stroke lead over Kumiko Kaneda, two over six others.

Yokomine left nothing to chance Sunday. The 22-year-old came out firing and virtually ensured her ninth tour victory by ringing up seven birdies on the first 10 holes. She went on to a six-under-par 66 and 205. Midori Yoneyama shot 68 for 209 and second place, a stroke in front of Ai Miyazato, who also had 68 Sunday. Miyazato, now a regular on the U.S. LPGA Tour, failed to add to her Japan LPGA Tour win total of 14 in the five fall tournaments in which she played after returning to the country.

Japan LPGA Tour Championship Ricoh Cup
Sadohara, Miyazaki
Winner: Miho Koga

As the last of the circuit's majors, the Japan LPGA Tour Championship Ricoh Cup brings the long season to a big finish. Only the year's most successful players make the limited field. Rarely does the finale have the added attraction of deciding the season's money title. It did in 2008 though, when, in a rather bizarre turn of events, Miho Koga came from behind not only to win the tournament but also to capture the money winning mantle for the first time.

Although she said afterward that "I am so lucky ... it feels like a miracle," the 26-year-old, eight-season pro made her "luck" with birdies on the final two holes. They produced a splendid 68 and the clubhouse lead at six-under-par 282 after she started the day three shots off the lead and third on the money list. On the other hand, luck was all bad for the two women still on the course who seemed likely, at worst, to overtake her.

Despite a bogey at the 53rd, Mi-Jeong Jeon led by a stroke, but bunkered her approach at the last hole, skulled the sand shot and took a double bogey for 70–283. Then Yuri Fudoh, sitting just four feet above the cup with a birdie putt for her fifth win of the year, shocked everybody with a ghastly three-putt to hand Koga her 11th title and the ¥25 million purse that shot her ahead of leader Ji-Hee Lee and No. 2 Sakura Yokomine, who now has finished second, third twice and fourth on the final money list the last four seasons.

The unlikely finish overshadowed the disappointment of Bo-Bae Song, who led for three rounds at Miyazaki Country Club (69–140–211), but shot 75 Sunday.

Australian Ladies Tour

LG Bing Lee Women's NSW Open
Melbourne, Victoria
Winner: Laura Davies

Laura Davies enjoyed the perfect start to the year by extending her record of winning every season as a professional, barring 2005, with victory at the LG Bing Lee Women's NSW Open. After two rounds of 70 at the Oatlands Golf Club, Davies came from two behind overnight leader 19-year-old Sandra Oh with a closing 67 to finish at nine-under-par 207. She won by two strokes over Oh, playing only her third event as a professional, and by four over Sweden's Lotta Wahlin.

Davies's win in the ALPG event was the 69th of the 44-year-old's career. After three birdies on the first nine, Davies chipped in on the 11th to tie Oh and then hit a seven iron to 15 feet at the par-three 12th. She holed the putt and also birdied the par-five 13th to go three ahead. She bogeyed the 14th, but then parred in, escaping with a par at the 16th despite driving to within 20 yards of the green before finding sand with her second shot.

"This is a big thing for me," said Davies. "There were some really good players in the field this week. The greens were just to my liking and I always look forward to coming to Australia."

MFS Women's Australian Open
Melbourne, Victoria
Winner: Karrie Webb

Karrie Webb retained her title at the MFS Women's Australian Open, winning for the fourth time in all, with a playoff victory at Kingston Heath in Melbourne, a venue that has seen the likes of Greg Norman and Gary Player claim the men's equivalent championship. The 33-year-old Australian and South Korea's Ji-Yai Shin both scored six-under 67s in the final round to tie at eight-under-par 284. Shin, a prolific winner on her home tour, set the target, and Webb was two behind with three to play before she claimed birdies at the 16th and 17th holes.

In the playoff, the first extra hole at the 18th was halved, but the second time around on the same hole Webb holed from 12 feet for a winning birdie. "I guess the old girl still has plenty of petrol in the tank," Webb said after her 45th career victory. "I hadn't seen a leaderboard for a while until the 15th and I knew then I had to go up a gear."

Melissa Reid, the 20-year-old English rookie, led briefly after eagling the eighth and birdieing the ninth, but stalled on the back nine. But a closing 70 left her alone in third place at 288, one ahead of Korea's Amy Yang.

ANZ Ladies Masters
Ashmore, Queensland
Winner: Lisa Hall

After two victories in 2007, her first wins in a decade, Lisa Hall continued her fine run of form by winning the ANZ Ladies Masters at Royal Pines Resort. Due to the course being flooded earlier in the week, the event was cut to 54 holes, with Hall a stroke behind Karrie Webb, Hyun-Ju Shin and Tamie Durdin with a round to play. Webb, hoping for a seventh win in the event and completing a double with the Australian Open as she achieved in 2007, closed with a 70 to fall three behind Hall.

A closing 66 gave Hall a total of 203, 13 under par, and a one-stroke win over Shin, who slipped to 68 after three-putting the 18th green. Hall had drawn even with Shin after holing from 12 feet at the 16th, but Shin faced a 25-foot birdie putt to win on the final green. But she left the putt four feet short and then missed for a par to force a playoff.

"Anything can happen in golf and I was on the lucky end of it today," said the 40-year-old Hall. "I thought I would be in a playoff and then the realization that I had won was shocking."

Ladies African Tour

Women's World Cup of Golf
Sun City, South Africa
Winners: Philippines (Jennifer Rosales and Dorothy Delasin)

After finishing as runners-up in the inaugural Women's World Cup of Golf in 2005, the pairing of Dorothy Delasin and Jennifer Rosales from the Philippines claimed victory in the fourth staging of the championship at the Gary Player Country Club at Sun City. Playing together for the third time, Delasin, age 27, and Rosales, 29, with a combined six LPGA wins between them, finished two strokes ahead of South Korea's Ji-Yai Shin and Eun-Hee Ji. In a breathtaking finale, the Philippines pairing came home in 30, six under par, with Delasin birdieing each of the last four holes.

Under the new format for the event, there were two rounds of fourball, on the first and third days, with foursomes on day two. The winners combined for fourball rounds of 65 on both Friday and Sunday and managed 68 in the foursomes. They finished with a total of 198, 18 under par. South Korea finished at 16-under 200, with Japan's Shinobu Moromizato and Miki Saiki and the Taiwan team of Yun-Jye Wei and Amy Hung tying for third place at 203, and France's Gwladys Nocera and Virginie Lagoutte-Clement in fifth place a further two strokes behind. Host nation South Africa, with Laurette Maritz and Ashleigh Simon, finished in their highest position, tying for sixth with Wales and Canada, while defending champion Paraguay was ninth and Scotland and America joint 10th.

Korea opened up in stunning fashion with a fourball score of 61, 11 under par, but stumbled to a foursomes score of 72. They shared the lead with the Philippines at 11 under going into the last round, and despite going two clear on the front nine, during which Shin holed out of a bunker for an eagle at the fifth, closed with 67. Birdies at the 11th and 12th holes brought the Philippines even with Korea at 14 under, and although Korea birdied the 14th to go one clear, Delasin then took charge in dramatic style. She holed from 10 feet at the 15th, chipped in at the 16th and then holed from 15 feet at both the 17th and 18th holes.

"I had some adrenaline pumping, it was so cool. I felt like Superwoman out there," Delasin said. "Like I said all week, we were ham-and-egging." Rosales added: "We had fun all week. It was really good teamwork today too. I want to thank all the fans who came out here to support women's golf."

WPGA Masters
Johannesburg, South Africa
Winner: Rebecca Hudson

Rebecca Hudson won for the third time in her career and the second time in South Africa by claiming the WPGA Masters, the opening event of the Ladies African Tour. Hudson, the 28-year-old Englishwoman, beat America's Anna Temple by twice birdieing the 18th hole, first to get into a playoff and then to win it at the first extra hole.

Hudson, after rounds of 71 and 66, was one of three leaders going into the third and final round, and four birdies on the first nine put her two clear of the field. But Temple roared home to a closing 64 and set the target at 12-under-par 204. Norway's Lill Kristin Saether also finished off with 64 to take third place one stroke behind, while Hudson's co-leaders overnight, Marianne Skarpnord, also of Norway, and South African amateur Gina Switala, were fourth and fifth after rounds of 71 and 73 respectively.

Hudson hit an eight iron to six feet to birdie the 18th hole in regulation play and then, after a similar drive, hit the same approach shot to eight feet and converted the putt again to win. Hudson also won the South African Women's Open in 2006, the year she won on the European Tour in Hungary.

"I must say it feels as good to win here as it did winning the SA Open two years ago," Hudson said. "I really enjoy playing here. It is great preparation for the year ahead; the weather is great and the standard of competition just keeps getting better and better."

Acer Women's South African Open
Durban, South Africa
Winner: Julie Tvede

Denmark's Julie Tvede was grateful for her six-stroke overnight lead as she battled the wind and the course at the Durban Country Club before clinching victory in the Acer Women's South African Open by just a single shot. Tvede sprinted ahead of the field with rounds of 66 and 69 on the par-73 layout, but then struggled with a closing 74 to win on 209, 10 under par. As her advantage slipped away, Tvede came under pressure from France's Anne-Lisa Caudal, whose closing 69 was the best score on the final day. Norway's Marianne Skarpnord and South African Stacy Bregman finished a further two and four strokes behind Caudal respectively.

Tvede, who had been bogey-free on the second day, dropped a stroke at the first hole after driving into the rough as the wind whipped in off the sea. Another shot went at the seventh, but she birdied the eighth to stay one ahead. Further birdies at the 11th and 14th holes steadied the ship, but then more shots went at the next three holes. Caudal's only bogey of the day came at the 17th and a birdie would have forced a playoff, but she just missed and a relieved Tvede took her first title in South Africa.

Pam Golding Ladies International
Nelspruit, South Africa
Winner: Stacy Bregman

Six years after taking up golf at the age of 15, Stacy Bregman claimed her first professional title at the Pam Golding Ladies International at Nelspruit. Bregman excelled at athletics and karate before switching to golf and was a member of the South Africa's World Amateur Team Championship winning team in 2006. A professional for little more than a year, the 21-year-old Bregman led from start to finish at Nelspruit, an opening 68 followed by rounds of 70 and 71 for a seven-under-par total of 209.

Three strokes ahead going into the last round, Bregman zoomed further ahead with birdies at the first four holes. With two more birdies at the 10th and 15th, she could afford a couple of bogeys on the first nine and another at the 13th before a double bogey at the 16th. Unperturbed, she then parred in to seal a four-stroke victory over South Africa's Morgana Robbertze and Danish player Lisa Holm Sorensen, who both carded final rounds of 71. Maria Boden of Sweden, Bregman's closest pursuer with a round to go, finished with 76 to tie for fourth place with compatriot Johanna Westerberg.

Bregman said: "I've had a really great tour, and with today's win, I'm very excited about next week's Telkom Women's Classic."

Telkom Women's Classic
Johannesburg, South Africa
Winner: Lisa Holm Sorensen

Lisa Holm Sorensen enjoyed the sodden Zwartkop Country Club course to claim victory at the Telkom Women's Classic and top the Ladies African Tour Order of Merit for 2008. "We had rain all night — it was perfect. I must say I did enjoy playing in some European weather today!" said Sorensen. Sharing the lead with compatriot Julie Tvede, the 25-year-old Dane closed with 69 to finish at 13-under-par 203 and win by two strokes over Sweden's Maria Boden, who had 68 in the final round. Tvede closed with 72 to finish a further stroke back, with Stacy Bregman among those tied for fourth place alongside Emma Zackrisson and Norway's Marianne Skarpnord.

Skarpnord opened the week with a brilliant 62 but could not keep up the stunning pace, falling back with rounds of 74 and 72. Sorensen made a great start on the final day with birdies at the second, fourth and seventh holes. She dropped a shot at the 10th, as she had in the previous two rounds, but got it back at the next. With Tvede dropping a shot at the 14th, Sorensen moved into a comfortable lead with another birdie at the 15th. The advantage came in handy at the last, where her second shot finished in the trees. She raced her par putt five feet past the hole, but made the return for a winning bogey.

"My goal at the start of the tour was to be the winner of the Order of Merit, so today's win was in my plan," said Sorensen. Bregman finished second on the money list, with Tvede third and Rebecca Hudson fourth.

Princess Lalla Meryem Cup
Rabat, Morocco
Winner: Laura Davies

Making her debut in the event, Laura Davies claimed a wire-to-wire victory in the 15th Princess Lalla Meryem Cup. The unofficial tournament, played on the par-73 Blue course at Royal Dar-es-Salam in Rabat, takes place alongside the Hassan II Trophy, which was also won on debut by Ernie Els and is the highlight of the golfing season in Morocco.

Davies, adding a 71st career victory, opened with 67 and then added 69 on the second day. She led by three strokes over defending champion Gwladys Nocera, but the Frenchwoman could not challenge and closed with 73. Davies compiled a final round of 70 to win at 13-under-par 206 by three strokes over Spain's Tania Elosegui. Nocera was three further back, while Rebecca Hudson and Patricia Meunier Lebouc shared fourth place, 10 strokes behind of the winner.

14. Senior Tours

For Bernhard Langer, 2008 was of purest vintage. Langer won not only the U.S. Champions Tour Player of the Year Award, but also the Rookie of the Year Award, and was only the third ever to win the unrepeatable double. Lee Trevino did it in 1990, and Bruce Fleisher in 1999. (Langer actually came out in late 2007, but under tour rules, a player competing in fewer than six events after turning age 50 is still considered a rookie in the following year.)

Langer led off with the Toshiba Classic in March, then added the Ginn Championship two weeks later, and repeated in the Administaff Small Business Classic in October. Langer also won the Arnold Palmer Award as the leading money winner ($2,035,073) and the Byron Nelson Award for the lowest scoring average (69.65). He would have won the Penalty of the Year Award, as well, if there was one.

As he was on his way to the Administaff Classic win, he picked up his ball for cleaning after missing a green, forgetting that the lift-clean-place practice was no longer in effect that day.

"It was," Langer said, with a weak smile, "a senior moment."

Argentina's Eduardo Romero also won three times, and eight other players won twice, including sore-kneed Fred Funk, sore-wristed Scott Hoch, sore-hipped Tom Watson (one with Andy North in the Liberty Mutual Legends), and Denis Watson, Jeff Sluman and Jay Haas.

Romero became the first Argentine since Roberto de Vicenzo in 1980 to win the U.S. Senior Open. Which he did after settling himself from a string of four straight bogeys in the final round. Said Romero: "I said to my caddie, 'I have to make a putt, just one putt.'" Which he did, and he won by four. Romero also took the Dick's Sporting Goods Open and the SAS Championship.

Big, affable Andy Bean took two titles. He won the Regions Charity Classic in May, after a 230-yard miracle approach out of trouble to 21 feet at the final hole. "That one was about as good as I've hit it all day, all week, all year," Bean said. Then in the season-ending Charles Schwab Cup Championship, rain delays forced him to play 32 holes the final day, starting just after dawn. He put his second approach shot into a bunker, then holed the bunker shot. "This," he said, "is the way to start a day." And at the end he birdied six of his first nine holes. And that is the way to end a day. He won by nine.

R.W. Eaks won twice despite playing on two knees that creaked and groaned and ached. He repeated in the Greater Hickory Classic after opening with a 61, and earlier won the 3M Championship hurting so badly he could barely get into and out of the cart. But he shot 23 under and won by six. "I never dreamed I could shoot that low," Eaks said.

The Champions Tour had two big surprises. One was Greg Norman, putting in a few rare appearances, and not only did he tie for third in the Open Championship, he also tied for sixth in the Senior PGA Championship, tied for fifth in the Senior British Open and was fourth in the U.S.

Senior Open. The other surprise was Bruce Vaughan, a former Nationwide Tour player, coming from nowhere to take the Senior British Open.

The Puzzle of 2008 was the same as the Puzzle of 2007 — how could a player of Nick Price's caliber not win? And yet he didn't. Among his close calls: In the Constellation Energy Senior Players Championship, he led by four early in the final round, then faded to a tie for third. Said Price, and he could have been speaking about his game in general, "I didn't play well enough — it's that simple."

Champions Tour

MasterCard Championship
Ka'upulehu-Kona, Hawaii
Winner: Fred Funk

When Fred Funk turned a senior-eligible 50 in 2007, he opted to split his time between the PGA Tour and the Champions Tour. He has won on both, and so players on each invited him to go to the other (joking, of course). Funk chuckled. "I'm confused," he cracked when the subject came up, not surprisingly, after he won the Champions Tour's season-opening, winners-only MasterCard Championship in Hawaii in mid-January. And, to complete the picture, this was right after he'd taken a cool $185,571 in two PGA Tour stops in Hawaii just before. He was becoming unwelcome in a hurry.

"We've got to stay in Hawaii," Funk said.

Funk trailed through the first two rounds of the MasterCard Championship, then won with sensational burst at the finish. He chipped in for a birdie from 20 feet at the 17th, then at the 18th hit a dazzling six iron out of a bunker from 149 yards to seven feet and holed the putt for another birdie, adding a seven-under-par 65 to his 67-63 for a 21-under 195 total. He won by two strokes over Allen Doyle, who led by four with 11 holes to play.

Tom Purtzer hit all 18 greens in a 10-under 62 for the first-round lead. Then talk about irony: In the second round, Funk birdied five of his first six holes and eagled No. 7 and had the clubhouse lead with 63. Then Doyle jumped ahead of him with birdies at the 17th and 18th holes. One round later, Funk would return the grand gesture at the 17th and 18th for the win.

Funk, unruffled by winds in the final round, broke loose on the second nine, beginning with a tap-in birdie at the par-five 10th. Doyle parred it, then bogeyed the 11th off a weak chip. It was a battle from there. Funk tied Doyle at the par-three 12th, dropping a 26-foot birdie putt. Both birdied the 13th, Funk with a tap-in, Doyle with a 21-foot putt. Doyle parred the last five holes, but Funk birdied the last two.

"What are you going to do?" Doyle asked. "The chip on 17. The great sand shot on 18. That's the way it goes."

Turtle Bay Championship
Kahuku, Hawaii
Winner: Jerry Pate

The Hawaiian trade winds came up strong and blustery over Turtle Bay, blowing hopes and games hither and yon. Fred Funk, for example, defending champion of the Turtle Bay Championship, closed with 81. Bernhard Langer had 76, and Hale Irwin, who had won six times at Turtle Bay and nine times in Hawaii, shot 77 without a birdie. Jerry Pate, on the other hand, must have been saying, "What wind?"

"The tougher the better," Pate said, taking his second Champions Tour victory by two strokes over Jim Thorpe and tour rookie Fulton Allem. "For me, when you stand out there and see who can hit it best, and when par means something — that plays right into my hands." Pate opened with a one-under-par 71 and trailed Gil Morgan by six strokes in the benign first round, then added 70 in the windy second round and trailed by four.

It was heavy in the second round. "What we tried to do out there was hold on to what you've got," said Thorpe (71). "Making birdies out there was almost out of the question."

The final round was as tough as Pate would want, with winds at 20 to 25 miles an hour and gusting to 30. Morgan was among the victims. He shot 77. Pate and Wayne Grady shot the day's low, two-under 70, and Loren Roberts and Denis Watson, with 71s, were the only others under par.

While the rest of the field was trying to keep their feet, Pate took command with three straight birdies. At No. 8, a burst of wind forced him to step away from his four-foot birdie putt, and then he stepped back in and dropped it to tie for the lead. He took the lead outright at No. 9 with an eight-footer, and he was on his way, thanks in part to a putting tip. Thorpe had told him to shorten his backswing in strong winds. That helped boost Pate to a $240,000 payoff.

Allianz Championship
Boca Raton, Florida
Winner: Scott Hoch

At one point in the final round, you could have thrown a dart at the leaderboard and hit the winner. There were 13 players within two strokes of the lead and another seven three behind. This would take some unscrambling, and Scott Hoch proved to be the man to do it, streaking to five birdies on his last eight holes to pick off the Allianz Championship. He did this with an aching arthritic thumb that had required a shot of cortisone.

Hoch didn't have a hint this win was coming. His game was hardly encouraging. He'd finished 36th in the season-opening MasterCard Championship, and a week ago he tied for 44th in the Turtle Bay Championship.

"I felt great the first few weeks and I played terrible," Hoch said. "I didn't think I could play like that when I felt fine."

Hoch's 67-67 start left him a stroke behind Mark McNulty and Jerry Pate in the first round, then a stroke behind Pate in the second. Then things developed on the final nine. He bogeyed the 10th, then started his birdie surge. He got the 11th after bouncing a shot off a spectator's chair. Hoch birdied the par-four 12th off a four-iron second through the trees to 38 feet. At the 15th, his tee shot glanced off a tree and into the fairway. He then hit a seven iron to 11 feet and birdied. "You need luck to win any tournament," Hoch said. "After that, I didn't miss a shot."

This included a three iron through the wind at the 193-yard 17th to 22 feet for a birdie to tie Brad Bryant at 13 under. At the par-five 18th, he fired a five-iron second shot to 23 feet and two-putted for a birdie for 68 and 202 total and the one-stroke victory.

But there was a bittersweet side to it. Hoch had to call on his old caddie, Damon Green, to take his bag. His regular caddie, Greg Rita, was undergoing treatment for a brain tumor. Hoch dedicated the win to Rita. "Hopefully, he gets to come back and caddie for me again," Hoch said.

ACE Group Classic
Naples, Florida
Winner: Scott Hoch

It took Scott Hoch until the 54th and final hole of the ACE Group Classic before he tasted the lead, and then he found himself sharing it with three others. Heading for the playoff, Hoch had had enough. "I just said, 'Look, let's end it here — I don't want to play anymore,'" Hoch said. And so he did, with a birdie on the first extra hole for his second straight victory.

It was one of the wildest finishes on the Champions Tour. In regulation, Hoch holed an eight-foot putt for a birdie at the par-five 18th for a 68 to tie Tom Jenkins (70), Tom Kite (65) and Brad Bryant (65) at 14-under 202. In the playoff at the 18th, Jenkins and Kite missed the green, Bryant missed a 10-foot birdie putt, and Hoch ended it right there, holing his eight-footer.

"This is something new for me," Hoch said. "I certainly haven't run away with anything ... I wasn't really in this one until right at the very end."

True enough. Talk about your scrambles. Hoch opened with 68, three behind four co-leaders. Hoch followed with 66 to tie for second, two behind Tom Jenkins, who eagled the par-five 13th from 28 feet en route to 64 and a 132 total. Hoch was still trying to catch up in the final round. He took a big step at the par-five ninth, holing out from 65 yards for an eagle. He bogeyed the 10th and birdied the 11th, and finally caught up with the birdie at the 18th.

Hoch, facing an eight-foot putt, remembered Nick Price missing a 15-footer from the same line. "That pin was in such a tough spot, you have to have a fairly short putt there, and luckily, I did," Hoch said. And when the other three had all missed their chances, Hoch made his. Then came a second week of victory parties.

"I'm just glad I wouldn't have to do that every week," Hoch said. "I'd be dead now, having to celebrate that often."

Toshiba Classic
Newport Beach, California
Winner: Bernhard Langer

The Toshiba Classic began as an all-out assault on Newport Beach Country Club. Tim Simpson opened with eight-under-par 63, heading a list of 42 out of the 79 starters shooting in the 60s. But the tournament ended in a grueling shootout, with Bernhard Langer tapping in for a birdie to beat Jay Haas on the seventh extra hole. It was the second Champions Tour victory for Langer, age 50, the two-time Masters champion.

"I'm pretty tired right now," Langer said. "I'm just glad there's something called adrenaline, because that's what kept me going."

Langer (65-65-69) and Haas (65-69-65) tied at 14-under 199, three better than an interesting mix tied for second — former U.S. Open champion Scott Simpson (65), two-time Masters champion Ben Crenshaw (67) and Gary McCord (67), now a television commentator in one of his rare outings.

Langer seemed to be running away with the tournament in the second round. He drained a 50-foot putt for an eagle at the par-five No. 3 to go with five birdies and one lone bogey for the 65 that put him at 130, three ahead of a crowd of four that included Simpson (70). Haas was four back at 134.

In the final round, Langer fell out of the lead, but birdied the 18th to tie Haas at 199. As playoffs go, theirs was a slugfest. They two-putted the first extra hole (the 18th) for birdies and parred the next three (16th, 17th, 18th). Then they matched birdies at the fifth (16th), Langer from 28 feet, and Haas followed him in from 13. "I had a feeling he would make it," Langer said. They parred the sixth (No. 17), and then at the seventh (18th), Langer put his second 42 feet from the pin. Haas missed the green, left his chip four feet from the hole, and two-putted from there. Langer had rolled his long eagle try to inches, then tapped in for the victory.

Almost unnoticed in all this was Sandy Lyle, making his Champions Tour debut. He shot 70-72-71 for a par-213 total and tied for 54th place.

AT&T Champions Classic
Valencia, California
Winner: Denis Watson

Fortunately there are no instant replays on the golf course. Otherwise, Denis Watson might still be out there admiring the shot that won him the AT&T Champions Classic. "I'd like to watch that shot over and over again," Watson said. "That was so pure. That's as good a shot as I've hit in a long time."

The shot was Watson's nine iron from 152 yards to a mere 20 inches at the par-four 10th, the third playoff hole. Watson sank the birdie putt to beat Loren Roberts, who wasn't exactly crushed. "I probably shouldn't have gotten in the playoff," said Roberts, who did get in by holing out from 43 yards at the 18th for an eagle and a 70 to tie with Watson and Brad Bryant at seven-under-par 209 at Valencia Country Club in California. "But once I got in, I wanted to finish it," he said.

Bryant surfaced in the second round, feasting on the four par-fives in five under, including an eagle on a 37-foot putt at the 15th, for 67 and a two-shot edge on Roberts and four others. Watson announced himself in the final round with two eagles and a bogey on the first nine. Coming home, he birdied Nos. 11, 13, 16 and 18 for a seven-under 65 to tie Roberts and Bryant.

All three parred the first extra hole. At the second, Watson and Roberts birdied, and Bryant was out with a par. ("It's three straight seconds," Bryant said. "I thought I would have won one of them.") The third time, Watson lofted that great nine iron to close range and picked up his third Champions Tour victory in two seasons.

Meanwhile, the Nick Price mystery rolled on. The former PGA Tour star was still looking for his first Champions Tour win in 17 starts. He started strong, with 66 and the first-round lead. Then he shot 77.

Ginn Championship Hammock Beach Resort
Palm Coast, Florida
Winner: Bernhard Langer

Lonnie Nielsen was speaking for everyone that nasty Sunday. "When I saw what the weather was going to be," Nielsen said, "I would have bet, with his short game, that he was going to win. He's a magician."

Nielsen was speaking of Bernhard Langer, who worked his magic with club and ball, not with spells. The late-March weather turned uncharacteristically nasty across the Ginn Championship Hammock Beach Resort at Palm Coast, Florida. The winds off the Atlantic were at a knifing 25 miles an hour and the temperatures were in the 50s. While others shivered, Langer warmed up and posted his third victory in 11 Champions Tour starts.

Langer, who started the final round with a two-stroke lead on Nielsen, was off and running in the miserable weather with two early birdies, chipping close at the par-five second and chipping in at the par-five sixth. He rolled in a 22-foot putt to save par at the 18th for a 71 and a 12-under 204 total, and won by a whopping eight strokes over Nielsen and Tim Simpson.

As for his closing 71 in that weather, it didn't feel like magic to him. "It was more like a 65," Langer said. "I stayed aggressive, and I was able to pull most of it off."

Nielsen, a club professional with one victory on the Champions Tour, seemed headed for No. 2 in the first round. He rallied from a double bogey at his third hole, No. 12, and birdied six of his last 10 holes for a six-under 66 and a one-stroke lead over Langer and Fred Funk. "The putter was good and the short game was good," Nielsen said. The next round,

Nielsen fell back after three consecutive birdies while Langer moved from birdies on his first two holes to a steady day that yielded a 66–133 total and the lead by two over Nielsen (69) and Funk (69).

It was the measure of Langer's closing 71 that only two others broke par that day — Fuzzy Zoeller, 69, and Bruce Summerhays, 71. The course played to an average of 76.571, the highest so far this year.

Cap Cana Championship
Cap Cana, Dominican Republic
Winner: Mark Wiebe

If Mark Wiebe could view a replay, he would know when he lost the lead. It was in the second round when Scott Hoch holed out an 85-yard wedge shot for an eagle at the par-four eighth hole. Of course, if Wiebe would check again in 20 minutes, he would see when he got it back — also at No. 8, also on a hole-out eagle, this from 45 yards — and he was on his way to victory in the inaugural Cap Cana Championship at Punta Espada, the first professional tournament ever in the Dominican Republic. He did it on rounds of 67-68-67 for a 14-under-par 202 total for a four-stroke margin over Vicente Fernandez.

Said Wiebe, pocketing his second Champions Tour victory, "I really felt good about my game all week." From the start, actually, when he holed a bunker shot for a birdie at his first hole. Then he chipped in from 20 feet for a birdie at the par-three 13th, and he birdied the par-four 18th, hitting a three iron to three feet for 67 and a two-stroke lead on Fernandez and Fulton Allem.

Hoch, a two-time winner this year, at least tasted the lead in the second round with the eagle sparking 67 and a 138 total, three behind Wiebe. "I would like to see it where the player who shoots two or three under will win," Hoch said. Jay Haas (69) and Eduardo Romero (68) were four behind Wiebe. "I've been four back and won before," said Romero, looking for his first tour win.

The closest thing to pressure on Wiebe in the final round was Fernandez getting within two strokes on five straight birdies from No. 4. If that was pressure, Wiebe shrugged it off with an eagle at the par-five sixth, holing a 10-foot putt to get back to four up. Then he birdied the par-three seventh on a five-foot putt. He did stumble once, making a double bogey at the par-five 15th after hitting the wrong club off the tee. And so he won by only four.

Outback Steakhouse Pro-Am
Lutz, Florida
Winner: Tom Watson

Tom Watson made no bones about it: Thanks to a little luck and a back door, Watson had his second straight Outback Steakhouse Pro-Am victory and his 50th career title.

"I backed in through the back door," said Watson, after getting gifts from both Mark Wiebe and Scott Hoch. But he had done his part. He raced into the first-round lead, slipped a little, and then that back door flew wide open in the final round. Wiebe collapsed down the last four holes and Hoch missed a short putt at the 18th, and there was Watson saying "Thank you very much."

Watson, who played the TPC Tampa Bay in rounds of 63-71-70–204, nine under par, started the final round three strokes off the lead. He even closed with a bogey when his seven-iron approach at the 18th missed the green and trickled back into the water. He holed a five-footer for that bogey. Meanwhile, Wiebe, who led Watson and Hoch by three to start the round, slipped into deep trouble. Wiebe, who had won the week before, birdied the 14th and was 12 under and leading Watson by three with four holes to play. Then he played those last four in six over par. A four-stroke swing suddenly reversed his position. Wiebe drove into the water at the 15th and triple-bogeyed, and Watson, who had birdied the hole moments earlier, led by one. Wiebe proceeded to double-bogey the 17th and bogeyed the 18th and shot 76.

Watson escaped the 18th with a bogey. Hoch needed a par at the 18th to tie Watson. His approach stopped short of the water, and he chipped to two feet, then missed the par putt, and there went the playoff. "I had not been putting all that good," Hoch said, "but I haven't missed anything like that." Hoch shot 71 and tied for second with Jay Haas, who shot 64.

There was some extra zest to Watson's victory. When Watson won his first Outback event in 2007, he broke a weird 0-for-93 career drought in Florida. Now he had his second straight victory there. "I'm on a streak," Watson said. "I've got to buy a house down here."

Liberty Mutual Legends of Golf
Savannah, Georgia
Winners: Tom Watson and Andy North

Andy North and Tom Watson teamed for a blistering 59 in the first round of the Liberty Mutual Legends of Golf, for a three-stroke lead, after which North cautioned, "To win this thing, you'll probably have to shoot about 62 every day." It turned out North came within four-tenths of a stroke of being right.

The Legends, returning to a better-ball team format after six years as an individual tournament, was just what the doctor ordered for Watson and North. They won the team event for the past three years when it was unofficial. Make that No. 4, this time official, as they shot 59-62-64–185, 31 under par at the Westin Savannah Harbor Resort in Georgia. And they averaged 61.6 strokes per round, just four-tenths off North's prediction. They led comfortably through the first two rounds, then had to hang on to beat Jeff Sluman and Craig Stadler by one stroke.

After that opening 59, North noted the extreme need for birdies. "You make three pars," he said, "and eight teams go past you."

They expanded their lead to four strokes with 62 in the second round,

and ran their bogey-free run to 144 straight holes. They ran off four consecutive birdies, the last of them on Watson's chip-in at the 14th. Then
North tacked on the final birdie of the round with a 45-foot putt at the
18th. The others were scrambling. Sluman launched a 240-yard utility club
to an inch for an eagle at the par-five 11th, sparking the 63 that tied him
and Stadler for second.

Sluman and Stadler, playing one hole ahead, caught North and Watson
with birdies at the 13th, 14th and 16th, and each time Watson and North
came along the retook the lead with birdies. The last time was the clincher,
Watson's 18-footer at No. 17.

The official win meant North had his first win — or at least a share
— since the 1985 U.S. Open. And Watson, who won the Outback Steakhouse Pro-Am the week before, had his second straight. And it was a battle
down the stretch.

"To hit quality shots when it counts — that's what makes me tingle,"
Watson said.

FedEx Kinko's Classic
Austin, Texas
Winner: Denis Watson

This was one Denis Watson never expected to win. It was also one Nick
Price, seeking his first Champions Tour victory, didn't expect to lose.
They were two stunned Zimbabweans at the end of the FedEx Kinko's
Classic.

"Never give up," said Watson, who was back in the pack all the way
and trailed Price by five strokes going into the third and final round.

Said Price, the solo leader through the first two rounds and deep into the
third round, "This is such a crazy game. I was hitting it so well today. I
thought I could have closed my eyes on the 15th and made a bogey." A
bogey would have been very nice. Price, who had led with 65-67, stumbled
to a closing 75, three over par at The Hills Country Club at Austin, Texas.
Watson, tagging along at 67-70, birdied the final hole for a 10-under 206
total and a one-stroke win over Price, Scott Hoch (69) and Tim Simpson
(70). It was Watson's second win of the season.

Price had started the final round with a two-stroke lead over Scott Simpson
and Loren Roberts and was still the man to beat with four holes to play.
Then boom.

Price figured he could bogey the par-four 15th with his eyes closed, but
he double-bogeyed with his eyes wide open in disbelief. His seven-iron
approach hit a tree arching over the fairway and caromed into the creek
guarding the green. Then he double-bogeyed the par-three 16th when the
wind shifted and his five-iron tee shot hit the front bank and bounced back
into the water.

Price had one final chance. He needed a birdie at the par-five 18th. His
tee shot was excellent, but his approach caught the greenside bunker. He
blasted out to 19 feet, but missed the birdie putt. "It was pretty much over
for me before then," a dejected Price said. Watson had already finished with

a strong birdie at the 18th. He reached the green in two and two-putted from 50 feet for what proved to be the winning edge.

"This is my first time," Watson said, "as the recipient of a back-in win."

Regions Charity Classic
Hoover, Alabama
Winner: Andy Bean

Just one of those shots would be enough. "That one was about as good as I've hit it all day, all week, all year," Andy Bean was saying. "I wouldn't want to have a bucket of balls and have to hit another one." This was Bean after he drove into deep trouble at the final hole and escaped with a great shot from 230 yards to 21 feet. He two-putted for his par and a one-stroke victory over Loren Roberts in the Regions Charity Classic. It was Bean's second win in five years on the Champions Tour, and his first since October 2006. Maybe a serene attitude helped.

"This week, I've been really just very calm," the big, likeable redhead said. "I never really got excited about anything, and just kept plugging."

Bean shared the first-round lead with Monday qualifier Mike Goodes at 65, seven under par at the Robert Trent Jones Golf Trail at Ross Bridge at Hoover, Alabama. Bean inched ahead in the second round with a 68 for a 133 total, and there was the diminutive Goodes, a slight 5-foot-7, with 69 and just a shot behind. "I just can't shake the little guy," Bean said.

Bean, after the 65-68 start, wrapped it up with a two-under 70 in the final round, but not without some uneasy moments. Roberts, who started the final round two strokes behind, ran off three straight birdies from the 14th and shot 69 for a 204 total and figured he was out of the running. Bean was playing the 18th.

"I was ready to pack it up there, then I saw that he'd bogeyed 17," Roberts said. "We got in and the guy told me, 'He hit it way left on 18,' so I was ready to hit a few balls." But the playoff never materialized. Bean hit his great recovery shot to the green, upstaging a sensational finish by Jeff Sluman. Sluman birdied eight of the first 10 holes and shot 64, his best round in 10 Champions events.

Senior PGA Championship
Rochester, New York
Winner: Jay Haas

If a golfer can get revenge on a golf course — or heal old wounds — Jay Haas did it when he beat the 18th hole at Oak Hill and won the Senior PGA Championship. The memory from the 1995 Ryder Cup singles was still raw — how he anxiously popped up his drive into the trees, lost on a bogey to Philip Walton, and handed the winning point to the Europeans. Now it was 13 years later, and Haas was still smarting when he came to the 18th tee in the final round. Said Haas: "It was like, 'You've been talking about this. Time to put up or shut up. You talked a good game about just getting up there and ripping it.'" Could he beat the 18th in the clutch? "Damn if I didn't do it," Haas said, chuckling. And had his second Senior PGA Championship.

And he did it on a tough course made even tougher by bone-chilling, windy weather, out of place for mid-May in Rochester, New York. Note that the cut came in at a whopping 12-over 152 and that Haas won by a stroke, closing with a four-over 74 for a 287 total.

If Haas could point to any one shot as pivotal, it would be his 162-yard eight iron from the rough that skipped through a slot and rolled into the hole for an eagle at the par-four 17th in the third round. "I won't say that won for me," Haas said, "but it certainly put me in the mix." His 72 tied him with native son Jeff Sluman (70) for second, a stroke behind Langer (70–212).

In the final round, with everyone else slipping, Haas had the title if he could hold on. He took the lead at the par-three fifth with a 10-foot birdie and was up by as many as three strokes. Finally, he holed a two-footer for a par at the 18th, shooting 74 for a seven-over 282 total to win by a stroke over Langer. Then he thought about the 18th again.

"I said on the green I exorcised some demons from 1995," Haas said. "And that's what I'm leaving here with. With the trophy and the thought of doing that under the gun. I feel pretty happy about that."

Principal Charity Classic
West Des Moines, Iowa
Winner: Jay Haas

Going into the final round of the Principal Charity Classic, there were fully 18 players within three shots of the lead. In this setting, Jay Haas was getting restless.

"I didn't really have time to get conservative because I was chasing the whole time, which was probably a good thing," said Haas. Indeed. He raced through the final round to a six-under-par 65 — after a 70-68 start — for a 10-under 203 total and a one-stroke victory over Andy Bean (67). It was a nice dessert after Haas's win in the Senior PGA the week before.

Haas left Glen Oaks Country Club at West Des Moines, Illinois, littered with frustrated golfers. R.W. Eaks, who would need to have both knees replaced one day, shot a one-bogey 66 to tie Lonnie Nielsen for the first-round lead. Nick Price, probably the most frustrated golfer of all, took the second-round lead with 66–136 and was hoping, finally, for that first Champions Tour win in his second season. But it was not to be — again. Price shot a serviceable 69, but it was only good for third. "If I putted well, I could have won by three or four," Price said. Bean climbed into the race with birdies at the 15th and 16th, and needed one more. But he drove into the rough at the 18th, and that was that.

Haas broke from the crowd with four birdies on the back nine, three of them in succession. He holed a 48-foot putt at the 14th and two-footers at the next two for the 65, and after going winless from the start he suddenly had two straight wins.

"A month ago, I had a bunch of good finishes," Haas said, "and now all of a sudden I've had a great year. It was a sweet win, for sure. To do it under pressure when you need to do it, there's nothing like that."

Bank of America Championship
Concord, Massachusetts
Winner: Jeff Sluman

Jeff Sluman walked into the Bank of America Championship feeling ragged and walked out feeling like a million dollars. Well, like $247,500, anyway — the winner's prize.

It was Sluman's first win since joining the Champions Tour nine months earlier, in September 2007, and his first victory since the 2002 Greater Milwaukee Open. It came as a great relief. "I knew when I turned 50 in September, my game needed help," Sluman said. "It was really in tatters."

He didn't say how he stitched it back together, but one thing is for certain — a hot putter helped. Sluman averaged just 26.7 putts for the three rounds and was dazzling with three birdies over the final four holes to beat Loren Roberts by two strokes. Sluman, trailing most of the tournament, shot 68-67-64–199, 17 under par at Nashawtuc Country Club near Boston.

Tom Kite, winless since 2005, got a moment's encouragement when he tied the course record with a nine-under 63 in the first round. "It's nice to have something to get excited about," said Kite, leading by two. (Sluman was five behind.) Roberts took over in the second with a 66 that included a birdie-birdie-eagle stretch from No. 3 and a double bogey at No. 9, and was a stroke up on Mark McNulty (70), Kite (72) and Sluman (67).

The Sluman-Roberts duel began immediately in the third round when Sluman birdied the first hole and tied Roberts. Roberts re-took the lead, and Sluman tied him again with a birdie at the 10th. After a rain delay, they parred the next four holes.

"Then," Roberts said, "he stepped on the gas."

Sluman birdied the 15th from 13 feet (for his first lead of the tournament), the 17th from 30 feet and 18th from 34 feet for 64 against Roberts's 67.

Sluman had finished no better than a tie for 12th since joining the tour, a sluggish show for a rookie. "But I felt I had enough game to win out here," he said. And he proved it.

Commerce Bank Championship
East Meadow, New York
Winner: Loren Roberts

Loren Roberts had a modest ambition going into the final round. "My first goal," he said, after the second round, "is to hit the fairway at No. 1." Which reveals how things had been going for him at No. 1, and then in the final round, sure enough, he missed the fairway again and bogeyed again. But no matter. Roberts wasn't known as the "Boss of the Moss" for nothing, and once again he rode his magic putter to victory, his first of 2008. He went wire-to-wire in the Commerce Bank Championship on Eisenhower Park's Red Course on Long Island.

Roberts stayed a step ahead of the field all the way, playing the par-71 course in 65-68-68–201, for a one-stroke win over Nick Price and Lonnie Nielsen. In the first round, his approaches set him up beautifully. He made two birdie putts totaling five feet at the 15th and 17th, then holed a 45-footer at the 18th for a one-stroke lead over Gene Roberts and Greg Hickman (the latter usually a caddie). In the second round, a bogey at No. 1 and nine straight pars put him three shots out of the lead. Then the putter started perking again. He birdied the 11th, 14th, 15th and 17th, the longest putt from 12 feet, and led by two.

Price, still looking for that first Champions win, and Nielsen were next to get a shot at him. Price closed with 65, Nielsen 66, and Roberts bogeyed No. 1 again. After some jockeying, Roberts took the lead for good with a birdie at the 12th from four feet, and then came his jewel, a double-breaking 29-footer at the par-five 17th. Thus he came to the 18th leading comfortably by two. And then he two-putted for a bogey and 68 to win by a shot.

"It seems when you can make a bogey to win," Robert said sheepishly, "you always do."

Dick's Sporting Goods Open
Endicott, New York
Winner: Eduardo Romero

It was more than just a win to Eduardo Romero — it was national celebration. "For Romero, it's another victory," said the big Argentine, logging his second Champions Tour win in the Dick's Sporting Goods Open. "But this is very important for Latin America, especially Argentina." There had to be a sigh of relief in there, too. Romero won by a shot, with a huge assist from Joey Sindelar.

Romero started the final round with a one-shot lead on Fulton Allem and Sindelar, the homeboy favorite at the En-Joie Golf Course at Endicott, New York. It was a slugfest all the way. Sindelar trailed Romero by a shot going into the final hole, then disaster crushed him. He drove into the trees, nicked a branch with his second and ended up over a wall. He double-bogeyed for 71 and finished fourth, three back. Romero, after a big drive, knocked his second to six feet and two-putted for a par, 69 and a 17-under 199 total, edging Allem (69) and television commentator Gary Koch (65) by one.

The tournament began with a splash, with Japan's Joe Ozaki, needing just 22 putts, shooting a nine-under 63 under lift-clean-place on the rain-soaked course. Then Romero, who opened with 65, shot another in the second round, taking a one-stroke lead over Sindelar and Allem, who also had 65s. "It's a good match tomorrow," Romero said. "I have to make 65 again."

Romero, Sindelar and Allem all played the first nine in two under. Romero birdied the par-four 10th from five feet and Allem from eight inches, and Sindelar parred. Romero and Allem birdied the 12th, and Sindelar birdied the 13th from six feet. Romero opened the door at the par-three 14th, two-putting for bogey from four feet, and Romero and Sindelar birdied the par-four 16th. At the par-three 17th, Sindelar bogeyed, two-putting from four feet. Allem parred, and Romero two-putted from four feet for a bogey, cutting his lead to one with one to play, and he made the best of it.

3M Championship
Blaine, Minnesota
Winner: R.W. Eaks

By the time the 3M Championship had run its course, one big question remained: What would R.W. Eaks be like on two good knees?

Consider that Eaks's knees were aching so badly that he could barely get into and out of the cart he had to ride, and yet he shot 23 under par and won the tournament by six strokes.

"I never dreamed I could shoot that low," said Eaks.

An admiring Bernhard Langer, co-victim with Gary Hallberg at 17 under par, echoed the sentiment. "I didn't think you could go that low," Langer marveled.

This was Eaks's low: 65-63-65–193 at the par-72 TPC Twin Cities, near Minneapolis. But it wasn't that easy. Eaks was up by as much as six shots in the third round, but coming home, Gene Jones made back-to-back birdies to cut Eaks's lead to two. Then Eaks chipped in from 22 feet at the 15th. Jones then went bogey, double bogey.

"The chip-in deflated me a little bit," Jones said.

"Gene just kept putting the pressure on me," Eaks said. "It was a lot of fun being pressed like that. That's the most fun I've had playing golf in a long time."

Dana Quigley opened the assault on the course with a 10-under 62, then Eaks took over in the second round, after a heavy rainstorm softened the course. Eaks went six under in the first 10 holes of the second round. "When I'm playing like this, I don't think about the score," Eaks said. "I just want to get to the next hole."

He led by three going into the final round and clinched it down the closing holes. His 193 was the fourth-lowest score in Champions Tour history. Here's what was under that score: 24 birdies, one eagle and only three bogeys. He hit 89.7 percent of the fairways, 81.5 percent of greens in regulation, averaged 26.7 putts per round, and was not in any bunkers.

Eaks eventually will have both knees replaced. "Even hurt, I love this game," he said. "I don't want to quit."

The Senior Open Championship
Ayrshire, Scotland
Winner: Bruce Vaughan

See European Senior Tour section.

U.S. Senior Open
Colorado Springs, Colorado
Winner: Eduardo Romero

Eduardo Romero was a man in crisis in the final round of the U.S. Senior Open. He no sooner rolled in a 45-foot putt for a birdie at No. 10 than he staggered to four straight bogeys. His mind flashed back to the most infamous collapse in modern golf.

"I remember Greg Norman, when he lost the (1996) Masters and he started to make bogeys and never stopped," the big Argentine said. "I said to my caddie, 'I have to make a putt, just one putt.'"

And so he did, at the 15th, for a calming par. But what was the worry? While Romero was going through that nightmare, Fred Funk, his chief challenger, was going through one of his own. Funk bogeyed the 11th, then drove into deep grass at the 13th and triple-bogeyed, and then bogeyed the 14th. Romero parred the last four holes, completing a card of 67-69-65-73 and a six-under total of 274 for a luxurious four-stroke victory over Funk.

Then it was off to the telephone to call countryman Roberto de Vicenzo, who won the first U.S. Senior Open in 1980. Romero also became a national hero, like Angel Cabrera before him for winning the 2007 U.S. Open.

The tournament, played at the Broadmoor in Colorado Springs, opened with a storm of protests over greens, pin placements and the influence of the nearby mountains on putts. Funk came to terms with all of them for the first-round lead on 65 and a one-stroke lead over John Cook. "I hate to say it — I think I could have shot 61 or 62," Funk said. A 69 the next day gave him a 134 and the halfway lead by two over Romero. Romero then took the lead in the third round, logging seven birdies and two bogeys for 65 and a two-stroke lead on Funk (69).

In the final round, Romero and Funk both played the first nine in par, with one birdie and one bogey. The tournament, then, came down to the final nine — to Romero's fold and Funk's matching fold, and then with Romero strolling off with a four-stroke win. Mark McNulty finished third, five behind, and Greg Norman fourth, six behind.

The victory, Romero said, was a national matter. "This is very important," he said, "because we're working hard for golf in Argentina."

JELD-WEN Tradition
Sunriver, Oregon
Winner: Fred Funk

Fred Funk, leading comfortably through the final round of the JELD-WEN Tradition, turned to a rare if not unprecedented strategy to get him home — reverse psychology. Golfers in this situation generally play defensively. Not Funk. He went on the attack.

The idea, he said, was to pretend he was four shots behind. "Don't protect anything and fire at all the flags," said Funk. Did it work? Well, he got up to six ahead at the 15th, and it took a late stumble to leave him at 19-

under-par 269 for a mere three-stroke win over Mike Goodes at the par-72 Crosswater Club in Sunriver, Oregon. It was his first win in a Champions Tour major, his second win of the season and his fourth since joining the tour in 2006.

"In my mind, I just wanted to get up as far as I could and basically bury the field," said Funk. That being the case, it was time for the funeral services early in the final round. Funk was back in the pack with 69 in the first round, behind a seven-man logjam tied at 67. He moved to within a stroke with 66 in the second round, behind Bernhard Langer (66) and Tim Simpson (67), tied at 10-under 134. Then Funk exploded in the third round, shooting a bogey-free 65 for a one-stroke lead on Jay Haas, who made his first bogey of the tournament at the 18th. "To go 72 holes without bogeying would have been pretty wishful thinking," said Haas, who had won twice this season, including the Senior PGA.

Funk would lead going into the final round of a major for the first time in his career. "I'll be a little nervous," he said. But it didn't slow him down. He birdied the 11th, 14th and 15th to get to 22 under and lead by six. He double-bogeyed the 16th, and after an hour storm delay, he bogeyed the 17th, and the three-shot stumble was a luxury he could well afford.

"He wasn't going to be denied today," said Haas, who tied for third. "He got to six up after 15 and I just took my foot off the gas."

Boeing Classic
Snoqualmie, Washington
Winner: Tom Kite

You never forget what it feels like to win, but Tom Kite, age 58, was wondering whether he'd ever feel that thrill again. His last Champions Tour victory was in the 2006 Boeing Classic, and here he was at the 2008 Boeing Classic and hardly showing any promise through the first two rounds.

"At some point in time, we're going to win our last golf tournament, and when you win it you obviously don't think that's going to be your last one," Kite was saying. "When I won this tournament in 2006, I thought I was just going to light it up. After two years, you start to wonder — am I going to win one?"

His answer came in the third and final round, when he raced to four birdies on the last seven holes to outleg Scott Simpson by two strokes at the TPC Snoqualmie Ridge near Seattle, Washington, for his 10th Champions Tour victory. Kite opened the tournament with 69-67, trailing Mark Wiebe and Simpson by two in the first round, then Simpson alone by three in the second round. Then the tournament came down to the last seven holes.

Kite's charge began, oddly enough, with a bogey. He was looking at heavier damage at No. 11 when he ran in the clutch eight-foot putt for the bogey that kept him only two behind. He bounced back with a birdie at the 12th, then wisely laid up at the tempting 14th and holed a nine-footer to tie Simpson. He ran in a seven-footer for a birdie at the 15th. The three birdies in four holes gave him the lead, and a birdie at the 18th locked up 66 and a two-stroke win on a 14-under 202 total.

Simpson, after starting the final round leading by two, went cold. At No. 8, he took his first bogey in 44 holes, dating back to the JELD-WEN Tradition the week before. His chances finally ended at the 16th, where his two-foot par putt spun out, leaving him two behind and with a two-year drought of his own.

Wal-Mart First Tee Open
Monterey Peninsula, California
Winner: Jeff Sluman

At 5-foot-7 and 140 pounds, Jeff Sluman can't bludgeon a golf course into submission. But he does have the touch to pick it to pieces, which is what he did in breezing through the Wal-Mart First Tee Open, taking his second Champions Tour victory after a winless and frustrating rookie season in 2007.

"I'm happy to finally be playing the kind of golf I knew I could play out here," said Sluman. "It's been a struggle, but I'm glad to be feeling comfortable."

Sluman was more than comfortable; he felt downright at home running off with a five-stroke victory in the Wal-Mart, a pro-am with 78 First Tee juniors held at two courses on California's Monterey Peninsula late in August. The field alternated between Pebble Beach and the Del Monte Golf Club for the first two rounds, then finished at Pebble Beach on Sunday. Sluman, starting at Del Monte, shot 69-66-67–202, 14 under par and five ahead of Fuzzy Zoeller and Craig Stadler, both winless since 2004.

Sluman did his part, but got some big help when challengers essentially eliminated themselves. A five-man logjam ahead of Sluman in the first round fell apart, and in the second his 66 at Pebble tied him with Phil Blackman (68), Loren Roberts (69) and John Harris (66). All three slipped out of range in the final round — Blackmar to 73, Roberts to 76, and Harris to 79. Sluman, meanwhile, shot the day's low, 67, in the finish at Pebble Beach. He took the lead for good with a birdie at the fifth, and saved par with a couple of clutch putts, a 17-footer at the ninth and a 12-footer at the 11th, and then birdied the 15th and 18th for the five-stroke win. Beyond that, the key figures were in his performance chart. He hit 76 percent of the fairways and ranked No. 1 in the field in hitting 83 percent of the greens in regulation.

"Golf is a game of ebbs and flows," Sluman said. "And it's going well now."

Greater Hickory Classic
Conover, North Carolina
Winner: R.W. Eaks

Good signs come in a variety of forms. For R.W. Eaks, the defending champion, it was nothing more than his very first tee shot of the Greater Hickory Classic.

"I hit my first ball down the fairway and thought, 'You know what? This is going to be a great day.'" It was better than that — a 61, 11 under par at Rock Barn, in Conover, North Carolina, good for a three-stroke lead on Tom Jenkins. It was the best score of the year so far on the Champions Tour and just a stroke short of tying the tour record.

Eaks had nine birdies and an eagle to get to 11 under after 15 holes. He missed a five-foot birdie chance at the 16th, then missed from 13 feet at the 17th and 10 feet at the 18th. He was seven under on the first nine, then birdied four of the first five holes on the back.

"I didn't start thinking about the record until I hit my birdie putt on 15," Eaks said. "That's when I knew I had a chance. But I have no complaints about this day at all."

Jenkins wasn't letting up in the second round. "My objective was to try and stay close if I could," he said. He did better than that. With five straight birdies from the seventh keying the round, he shot a 65 that caught Eaks (68) at 15-under 129. Then September winds came up in the third round, sending Jenkins to a double bogey at the sixth and bogeys at the 11th, 12th and 14th. He shot 75 and tied with Tom Kite (67) for second.

"Nobody was really making a run," said Eaks, in the final round. "I felt that if I just stayed out of trouble and played a nice, safe game, things might work out." Which they did, tidily. Eaks had two birdies and a bogey for a workaday 71 and won by four, his second victory of the season and his fourth on the Champions Tour.

SAS Championship
Cary, North Carolina
Winner: Eduardo Romero

By Eduardo Romero's own admission, he allowed himself the luxury of breathing again once he got past the 15th hole in the final round. He was leading the SAS Championship at Prestonwood Country Club in Cary, North Carolina, and he was also conscious of Tom Kite applying the pressure. Then he rolled in a 15-footer for birdie at the 15th and took a deep, satisfying breath. "This tournament," he told himself, "is for me."

The birdie pushed Romero's lead back up to three strokes, and three holes later he had a three-stroke win, his third Champions Tour victory of the year.

But first Romero had to overcome a touch of the flu in the first round. "I told my caddie I had to wake up," said Romero, who was two over after the first four holes. Awake then, he birdied four of the last five holes for 68 and tied for the first-round lead with a traffic jam — Bruce Fleisher, Dana Quigley, Andy Bean, Don Pooley and Chip Beck.

Fleisher overcame some tentative moments in the second round for 66–134 to take a one-stroke lead over Romero (67) and Kite (66). Kite birdied six of the last nine holes, and Romero got the break of the round — maybe of the tournament — at the 17th. He hit his third shot out of a bunker, and the ball was heading for trouble until it hit a chair and bounced back to the fringe of the green. From there, he chipped to three feet and saved par. With 67 safely in hand, he plotted his course for the final round. "If I can make 66," he said, "nobody can get me."

Maybe "Romero" is the Argentine word for "prophet." He hit the 66 on the nose. He started the final round with a birdie at No. 1 to take the lead from Fleisher and was on his way. Next came the pressure from Kite, then the birdie at the 15th, and then the deep breath.

Constellation Energy Senior Players Championship
Timonium, Maryland
Winner: D.A. Weibring

D.A. Weibring has been playing golf long enough to know that sometimes it rewards good play and sometimes it doesn't. This explained what sounded like a contradiction after he won the Constellation Energy Senior Players Championship.

"I didn't play my best golf," Weibring said. "I've played better in the final round and haven't been rewarded." Not that he was complaining. "I'm very proud to have won," he added, having posted his first victory in a major championship in 65 tries. In those coveted majors he was 0-for-39 on the PGA Tour and 0-for-25 on the Champions Tour. It was also his fifth win in six years on the tour.

Weibring did it with a classic literary finish. He trailed Nick Price by four strokes with 14 holes to play. Then when the unfortunate Price began to tail off again, Weibring went whizzing by. It also helped that four of the top seven finishers bogeyed Baltimore Country Club's 18th, but Weibring wasn't among them. Weibring holed a two-foot putt at the last hole for a two-under-par 68 and a nine-under 271 total and a one-stroke victory over Fred Funk (66), the hometown boy anywhere in Maryland.

Price led by a stroke going into the final round and went to four ahead with birdies at the first and fourth, and then another one got away. He bogeyed Nos. 7, 8 and 10, and finally the 18th. "I didn't play well enough — it's that simple," said Price, who tied for third.

But Weibring wasn't out of the woods. Ben Crenshaw birdied three straight to tie Weibring, and Jay Haas joined them with a birdie at the 12th. Then Crenshaw missed a four-foot birdie putt at the 17th and bogeyed the 18th.

Weibring made four birdies in the final round and made two excellent saves — out of a bunker at the 16th and with a nine-foot putt at the 17th.

"I always did believe I could win a major," Weibring said. "Sometimes things happen, and they just fall into place."

Administaff Small Business Classic
The Woodlands, Texas
Winner: Bernhard Langer

There have been an uncounted number of victory speeches down the history of golf, but Bernhard Langer's had to be possibly the first that included the embarrassing words, "It was a senior moment." This was the start of his explanation of how he picked up probably the only penalty of its kind ever on the Champions Tour.

But first, Langer did have a moment to enjoy his victory in the Administaff Small Business Classic at Augusta Pines, at The Woodlands, near Houston. It was his second straight victory in the Administaff event, his third of the year and his fourth on the Champions Tour. But the first with a red face.

His 12-under-par 204 total included an embarrassing penalty. Heavy rains had hit The Woodlands, so players were allowed to lift, clean and place the ball. The course dried out enough by the final round that play went back to the regular rules. And so Langer was at the par-three third, having missed the green with an eight iron. He picked up the ball and handed it to his caddie for cleaning.

"And then I'm going — oh-oh," Langer said sheepishly. He realized he had just picked up a live ball. "It was a senior moment," he said. "I had a great two-putt for a four there." Which included his one-stroke penalty. "I totally forgot we couldn't do that today." Langer said. "But I just thought, it's done. I've got to deal with it and make the best of it and move on."

Langer had started the tournament 68-67 and was tied with Lonnie Nielsen and Brad Bryant going into the final round. He made up the lost ground and then some on the back nine. He birdied the 11th from close in, then the 13th from 12 feet and 14th from 10, and next saved par at the 15th.

"Those three in a row were huge," said Langer. He shot a three-under 69 and won by two over Nielsen (71). Bryant triple-bogeyed No. 13, shot 77 and tied for 20th.

AT&T Championship
San Antonio, Texas
Winner: John Cook

You've got to play hurt, they say. And sometimes you've got to play sick, too, and that was John Cook, with a stomach ache at Oak Hills Country Club in San Antonio, Texas, winning his second straight AT&T Championship and his second Champions Tour win.

"I didn't feel good right from the get-go," said Cook. "Sometimes you have to dig a little deeper when you don't have your best stuff and you don't feel good."

Cook, who won 11 times on the PGA Tour, was no stranger to adversity and disappointment. The latest brush was his playoff loss to Bruce Vaughan in the Senior British Open in July. But in the AT&T event in October, he was starting the final round a stroke behind second-round leader Jeff Sluman and hurting. Cook added to his problems by bogeying the first hole. He had some digging to do, and he started with three birdies over the next four holes. He took the lead at the par-five 10th, rolling in a 25-foot birdie putt. He wasn't home free by any means. There was the ever-present Jay Haas, who had won on Oak Hills three years earlier and had also won the Texas Open twice when it was played there. Haas tied Cook for the lead with an eagle from nine feet, after getting home from 217 yards. But he wasn't celebrating yet.

"I knew John had some birdie holes coming up, so I didn't really feel like I was in the lead," Haas said. "I needed to keep going." Then Haas bogeyed the 13th after hitting his tee shot in the water.

Cook birdied the par-five 15th with two putts from 30 feet, birdied the 17th after a wedge to eight, and he wrapped up a six-under 65 for a three-stroke win over Keith Fergus (65). But first, Cook escaped trouble by saving par at Nos. 11, 12 and 13 and said "Whew!"

"I knew guys were making runs," he said. "After 13, when I got up and down from a tough spot, that's when I knew that I was digging pretty hard."

Charles Schwab Cup Championship
Sonoma, California
Winner: Andy Bean

Andy Bean, facing the last 32 holes of the season-ending Charles Schwab Cup Championship just before dawn on Sunday morning, got chased off the golf course by still another early November rain. When he finally got started, he put his first approach shot into a bunker, 45 feet from the cup. He blasted out, and the ball hurried right into the hole.

"That," said the big, affable Bean, "is the way to start a day."

Bean knew how to finish a day, as well — with a whopping nine-stroke victory over the cream of the Champions Tour. It was the largest winning margin of the season, a tremendous luxury against the exclusive 29-man field at Sonoma (California) Golf Club. (The answer to who finished second is Gene Jones.)

In the final round, Bean birdied six of the first nine holes, shot 66, and finished at 20-under 268.

Rains on Saturday forced the golfers to complete their third round on Sunday morning, hence Bean's early arrival and long day.

"The whole day, I was very comfortable," Bean said. "I was just hitting a lot of shots right at the flag. I didn't really have to scramble too much, except at the first hole that I played. The front nine (final round) was one of those rounds you just wish for. The back nine was an enjoyable walk because all I had to do was keep driving the ball the way I did, and the rest was going to set itself up."

The tournament also decided the Charles Schwab Cup and its $1 million annuity, and it went to Jay Haas for the second time in three years, this time without a fight. Haas finished 16th and got no points for being out of the top 10. But his nearest challengers, Fred Funk and Bernhard Langer, finished behind him and won no points, either.

Theirs wasn't the only frustration, however. There was Brad Bryant, needing a short putt at the 18th to tie Gene Jones for second. But he missed it and finished third. The miss cost him about $200,000.

European Senior Tour

DGM Barbados Open
St. James, Barbados
Winner: Bill Longmuir

With "a bit of a mountain to climb" after starting the DGM Barbados Open six strokes off the lead, Bill Longmuir staged a overwhelming finish on the back nine of Royal Westmoreland Country Club to win the traditional season-opening tournament of the European Senior Tour going away. Coming from three strokes off the pace, the Englishman shot a seven-under-par 65 for his three-shot victory at 10-under-par 206, picking up a seventh title in his sixth season on the circuit.

Delroy Cambridge, comfortable in his native Caribbean setting, led the field for two days. The Jamaican opened with 68, taking a one-stroke lead over Australian newcomer Graham Bannister and American Jerry Bruner. The consistent Bob Cameron joined Cambridge at the top the second day with his 67–138 and Cambridge shot 70.

Longmuir, sitting at 141 (74-67) with Italy's Giuseppe Cali and Ian Woosnam (72-69), straightened out a balky putter in the wet and windy final round. He ran off seven birdies, five of them in a row starting at the 13th hole. When he dropped a long one at the 17th, Longmuir "knew I had the tournament in the bag." Cameron, who has never been outside the top 20 since joining the tour in 2003, placed second at 209.

Longmuir's triumph overshadowed the seniors debut of Woosnam, former Ryder Cup captain and Masters champion. The Welshman finished fifth at 212, a respectable start before moving on to the U.S. Champions Tour.

Azores Senior Open
Ponta Delgado, Portugal
Winner: Stewart Ginn

Stewart Ginn, truly an internationalist who figures he has gone through 20 passports during his long golf career, added another tour to his victory list in the Azores at the end of March. With his two-stroke triumph in the inaugural Azores Senior Open, Ginn now owns titles on six circuits of varying reputations, going back to early victories in his native Australia and New Zealand. Others came on European, Japan and Asian regular circuits and, most recently, the major Senior Players Championship on the U.S. Champions Tour.

The 59-year-old Melbourne native, who switched to the European Senior Tour in 2006 after three seasons in America, did not come into view until the final round at the Batalha Golf Club, trailing leader Martin Gray of Scotland by five strokes after rounds of 72-71 for 143 after 36 holes.

Gray, winless in his previous six seasons on the senior tour, opened with

69 to take a one-stroke lead over Chuck Milne, a little-known American from Washington. He widened his advantage to four shots Saturday with another 69, then over Nick Job (73-69). Ginn was tied for third with American Bob Boyd (72-71) and Luis Carbonetti of Argentina (71-72).

Ginn was on top of his game Sunday, ringing up five birdies and the winning 68–211, five under par, as Gray encountered a flock of bogeys that ran him up to 78 and a tie-for-sixth finish at 216. Job retained the No. 2 spot with 71–213.

Parkridge Polish Seniors Championship
Krakow, Poland
Winner: Ian Woosnam

Not surprisingly, it took Ian Woosnam just two starts to notch his first victory on the European Senior Tour. The erstwhile Welshman, the former Masters champion and Ryder Cup player and captain, did it in sensational fashion. He carved out a final-round, nine-under-par 63 for 202 total in the inaugural Parkridge Polish Seniors Championship, just enough to finish a stroke in front of Spaniard Domingo Hospital, who dueled him to the end and shot 64.

Woosnam, who placed fifth in the Barbados Open in his senior debut in March, had gone nearly 11 years since his last of 29 wins on the regular European Tour in the 1997 Volvo PGA Championship. "It was nice to get the monkey off my back," he said after holding off Hospital with a struggling par to Hospital's birdie at the par-five final hole.

On the other hand, Irishman Eamonn Darcy was not happy. Winless, but with seven second-place finishes since joining the circuit in 2002, Darcy carried a one-shot lead into the final round at Krakow Golf and Country Club with 68-69–137. However, he fell back to 13th place with a closing 78. Japan's Katsuyoshi Tomori, with 70-68, was one back, while Woosnam and Hospital trailed by two at 139 in the company of Luis Carbonetti of Argentina and Englishman Bob Cameron, the first-round leader with 67.

Woosnam trailed Hospital early at Krakow. Then a chip-in birdie at the sixth hole ignited a series of four following birdies. By the 16th hole, he had built a two-shot lead that he needed when he gave that one back at the final hole. Tomori was four back in third place with a closing 69.

Jersey Seniors Classic
Jersey, Channel Isles
Winner: Tony Johnstone

Back in 2004, Tony Johnstone's doctor delivered the shocking news to him that he had multiple sclerosis. "Four years ago when I was diagnosed, I could never have dreamed of standing here," said the teary-eyed 52-year-old native of Zimbabwe after posting a wire-to-wire victory in the Jersey Seniors Classic, one of the founding tournaments on the European Senior Tour. "I didn't even think I would play golf again."

Clearly it was the most emotional and gratifying victory for Johnstone in a career that had included 22 victories in Europe and South Africa. Then living in England, he had ventured onto the European Senior Tour in 2006 after undergoing revolutionary treatment and rebuilding his game to compensate for the illness, had top-10 finishes in 10 of his 31 starts, but had not won until teeing it up at La Moye Golf Club in Jersey.

"This feels so good. It is a massive victory for me," Johnstone said after posting his final-round 74 for three-under-par 213 and a two-stroke victory over Englishmen Ross Drummond and Gordon J. Brand.

Johnstone started the tournament with 69, tied for the lead with Brand and a shot in front of Denis O'Sullivan of Ireland. Then he surged two shots in front of American Steve Stull with 70–139. He nervously endured challenges Sunday from Drummond, Brand, Paraguay's Angel Franco and South Africa's Bertus Smit, establishing the final margin over that quartet when he converted his worst drive of the week into a birdie on the 70th hole.

Ryder Cup Wales Seniors Open
Conwy (Caernarvonshire), Wales
Winner: Peter Mitchell

In a remarkably ironic twist, Peter Mitchell duplicated a feat achieved by Ian Woosnam earlier in the season and did so at Woosnam's expense. Playing in just his second event as a senior, the 50-year-old Englishman scored a two-stroke victory in the Ryder Cup Wales Seniors Open at Conwy Golf Course. And who was that runner-up? None other than Welsh national favorite Woosnam, the man who also had won his second seniors tour start two weeks previously.

Mitchell, a journeyman on the regular European Tour with three victories to his credit, the last one the 1998 Portuguese Open, broke from a 36-hole deadlock with Woosnam, shooting a one-under-par 71 to Woosnam's 73 for the winning 213. He was the third successive first-time victor on the circuit, following Woosnam (Poland) and Tony Johnstone (Jersey).

Devoid of competitive experience for the last five years while running a golf academy in Kent, Mitchell tuned up with a tie-for-11th showing at Jersey before landing the victory at Conwy. He opened comfortably with 72, trailing leader Sandy Lyle by three strokes. Woosnam, who was especially determined to win the Wales Seniors for his home country fans since he had never won the national title on the regular circuit, was two shots further back.

The gallery favorite racked up a 68 Saturday and joined Mitchell (70) in the lead at 142 as Lyle's bid fizzled with a 76 that dropped him into a third-place tie with Jim Rhodes. Mitchell began poorly Sunday with two early bogeys, but birdies at the seventh, ninth and 14th holes and Woosnam's bogey at the 16th gave him the two-shot margin he carried to victory.

Irish Seniors Open
Co. Donegal, Ireland
Winner: Juan Quiros

Golf is one of few sports that doesn't seem to have a home advantage. Unlike major sports teams, which usually do much better at home than on the road, the pressure of trying to win a golf tournament in one's own backyard more often than not proves to be too trying a task for most players.

Such was the case in two successive events on the European Senior Tour, first when Englishman Peter Mitchell nipped favorite son Ian Woosnam in Wales and a week later when Spaniard Juan Quiros edged popular Irishman Des Smyth at the wire on the Emerald Isle.

With the entire final round of the Irish Seniors Open played in fierce wind and rain at Ballyliffin Golf Club in County Donegal, the issue came down to a sensational wedge shot by Quiros to 18 inches and a tap-in birdie on the 54th hole. It gave him a one-over-par 72 and a one-stroke victory over Smyth, a Drogheda native. Quiros's 212 total was the only sub-par total posted and it gave him his third victory in his three seasons on the circuit.

"I can't remember the last time I played in conditions like that," remarked a weary Quiros, who entered the final round at 140 (71-69), tied with Gordon J. Brand (70-70) and one stroke behind Smyth, who shot 68 for 139 Saturday. Meanwhile, first-round leader Alan Tapie monumentally collapsed from 67 to 83.

Smyth built a three-stroke lead in the early going Sunday, but a double bogey at the 13th let the Spaniard back into contention. The two were tied playing the 18th hole when Quiros nearly holed the deciding 132-yard wedge shot.

Russian Seniors Open
Moscow, Russia
Winner: Ian Woosnam

Ian Woosnam probably wished that the 2008 European Senior Tour schedule had included such non-existent tournaments as a Romanian Open and/or a Bulgarian Open, considering the success he enjoyed in Eastern Europe in his first months on the over-50 circuit. Little more than a month after Woosnam scored his maiden victory in Poland he added the Russian Open title to his record.

Playing in an all-day rain, the stocky Welshman yielded an early lead, then bounced back to fashion a two-under-par 70 in Sunday's final round at Moscow's Pestovo Golf and Yacht Club and register a three-stroke victory with his 12-under-par 204. He was the first two-time winner of the 2008 season.

Woosnam had opened with 67 at Pestovo, tied for the lead with England's Jeff Hall and Scotland's Bill Longmuir, the Barbados winner who played with borrowed clubs when his disappeared in transit to Moscow. Woosnam repeated the 67 Saturday and moved two strokes ahead of Longmuir, who continued his victory bid when he overtook Woosnam with two birdies on the first three holes Sunday. Woosnam regained command with three birdies on the next nine holes and wrapped up the victory with a final birdie at the 17th.

Angel Franco of Paraguay slipped into second place with 68–207, a shot in front of Longmuir. The win was the 46th of Woosnam's illustrious career.

The Senior Open Championship
Ayrshire, Scotland
Winner: Bruce Vaughan

Over its 20-year history, the Senior Open Championship has had its share of surprise winners, and the circumstance resumed in 2008 at Royal Troon Golf Club. Just when the championship seemed back on track in that regard with Tom Watson (twice) and Loren Roberts winning the previous three years, up pops Bruce Vaughan, not exactly a household name in his native Kansas.

The unheralded Vaughan, never before a winner on any tour, joined the ranks of unlikely Senior Open champions like Pete Oakley (2004), Noboru Sugai (2002), Bob Verwey (1991) and John Fourie (1992) with his stunning playoff victory over well-known fellow American John Cook, 50, who already had won as a senior late in the 2007 Champions Tour season.

Cook, an 11-time victor on the regular U.S. Tour, appeared on the verge of bagging his first major title before frittering away most of a three-stroke lead on Troon's final nine holes. He dropped into a tie with Vaughan at six-under-par 278 when he bogeyed the final hole with three putts from off the front of the green for 71 to Vaughan's 70. Vaughan then holed a 15-foot birdie putt when they replayed the 18th in the playoff, the win for the one-time fireman climaxing tough recent times that included six operations on his left knee and the loss of his mother in an auto accident in America.

The two men were contenders from the first. Vaughan shared first place with Eduardo Romero at 68 Thursday, with Cook just one back, and led by himself with 71–139 Friday. Cook also shot 71 for 140, then followed Saturday with 67 to Vaughan's 69 to move into a one-shot lead going into the final round, only to falter at the end as he did 16 years earlier in the Open Championship when he lost to Nick Faldo. Romero, who has had five top-10s in the Senior Open since 2003, missed an eight-footer at the last hole and a spot in the playoff, finishing third.

Bad Ragaz PGA Seniors Open
Zurich, Switzerland
Winner: Carl Mason

It took him longer than usual this year, but Carl Mason, the European Senior Tour's most dominant player of the 2000s, kept his successful record in order with his 20th victory in the senior realm. With his successful defense of the Bad Ragaz PGA Seniors Open in early August, Mason made it six successive seasons in which he has posted at least one win since turning 50 in 2003.

In his back-to-back victories at Bad Ragaz Golf Club in Switzerland, Mason laid waste to the golf course. In 2007, he shot 194 and won by six shots; in 2008, 195 and a two-stroke margin over Bill Longmuir. His total was by six shots the best of the season.

Mason's second-round 61 was critical to the victory. He trailed first-day leader Bob Boyd by six when he opened in a 15th-place tie at 69, but jumped a stroke into the lead with the nine-under-par follow-up. Longmuir, with 65-66, was the runner-up, with Spain's Domingo Hospital another shot back. America's Boyd slipped back to 134 with 71.

Longmuir, the Scot who won his seventh European Senior Tour title in the season-opening Barbados Open, gave Mason a battle Sunday, but two bad holes — a bogey at the ninth and a double bogey at the 11th — crippled his bid. Mason birdied the 10th and 11th to open a five-stroke lead, and Longmuir's late rally fell short as Mason registered a 65 for the 195 and the two-shot win.

With his win, Mason became just the second 20-win player in the history of the tour and moved within three victories of Tommy Horton, the all-time leader.

De Vere Collection PGA Seniors Championship
Northumberland, England
Winner: Gordon J. Brand

Gordon Brand Jr., an eight-time winner on the regular European Tour, turned 50 just in time to play in the major De Vere Collection PGA Seniors Championship and Gordon Brand wound up with the important title. Gordon J. Brand, the other Brand that is. The unrelated twosome with virtually the same names went through a grueling six-hole playoff before the older Brand, a 53-year-old Englishman, took the victory from the rookie Scot at De Vere Slaley Hall.

Actually, Gordon J. gave Gordon Jr. a chance for a rare first-start victory when he bogeyed the 54th hole to drop into a tie with him at four-over-par 292 on Slaley Hall's Hunting Course. He carried a two-stroke lead into the final round after shooting 68, the week's lowest round, thanks to some putting advice from his golf-wise wife, but his closing 75 opened the door for Gordon Jr., who posted a 70 for his 292 total.

After matching scores on the par-four 18th five times in the overtime session, the two were sent to the par-three 17th and the issue was decided with a routine par when Brand Jr. overshot the green into a nearly unplayable lie. It was Gordon J. Brand's fourth victory in his three-season career on the European Senior Tour.

"It's a shame it had to end that way," he said. "But Gordon's a great player and will be a fantastic asset to the Senior Tour."

Sam Torrance, still without a 2008 victory, jumped into a tie for third when he exceeded Brand's third-round 68 with a 67. He, Eamonn Darcy and Juan Quiros, the Irish Seniors winner, finished just a shot out of the playoff. Quiros had shared the second-round lead with Ross Drummond at 144. Drummond and Italy's Giuseppe Cali were the first-round leaders.

Travis Perkins plc Senior Masters
Milton Keynes, England
Winner: Gordon J. Brand

Gordon J. Brand rode a hot August streak to his second straight victory in the Travis Perkins plc Senior Masters. The win at Woburn Golf Club came much more easily than the six-hole-playoff victory the previous Sunday in the PGA Senior Championship as Brand came from a stroke off the pace and posted a two-shot victory, his fifth on the circuit.

Although he never led until the final round, Brand was on the heels of the early leaders the first two days. He, Horacio Carbonetti and Juan Quiros trailed Paraguay's Angel Franco (66) by two strokes after the opening round and Quiros by a shot going into Sunday's finale. Quiros had 68, Brand 69 on Saturday.

Brand jumped ahead immediately on Sunday when he birdied the first hole and the Spaniard hit his opening tee shot out of bounds for a double bogey. Although Quiros maintained his composure after the first-hole disaster, he never overtook Brand, who followed with four more birdies and finished with 70–207. Quiros won the runner-up duel with defending champion Carl Mason, who shot 71 for 210, placing third behind Quiros's 73–209.

Brand was the first back-to-back victor of the 2008 season and he joined Ian Woosnam as the only multiple winners of the year.

Casa Serena Open
Prague, Czech Republic
Winner: Bernhard Langer

Bernhard Langer accomplished a rare feat when he landed the Casa Serena Open title in the Czech Republic in early September. That victory made him a winner in senior golf on both sides of the Atlantic Ocean in 2008, a double only John Bland (1995) and Des Smyth (2005) have also pulled off. In Langer's case, though, it thrust him into strong contention for seasonal titles on both the Champions and European Senior Tours.

The 51-year-old German star emerged from a head-to-head battle with Order of Merit-leading Ian Woosnam with a three-stroke victory, thanks to his near-perfect, third consecutive 67 at Prague's Casa Serena Golf Club, to add his initial senior victory in Europe to his pair of 2008 wins in America. Interestingly, Langer also had a victory in 1997 on the regular European Tour in the Czech Republic, where his father was born. Further along family lines, his brother Erwin's company managed the tournament. "It was pretty cool," said the low-key international champion.

Langer and England's Peter Mitchell overtook Woosnam with 67s for

134 after the Welshman jumped off to a one-stroke lead over Tony Allen and Pete Oakley with an opening-round 65 in his bid to widen his lead in the Order of Merit standings with a third victory of the season in Eastern Europe (following Poland and Russia). Woosnam shot 69 Saturday to join Langer and Mitchell, the Wales Open winner in June, at the top.

Langer went in front early in the final round with a one-under-par front nine as Woosnam slipped to one over through the 11th and Mitchell began a slide back to a final one-over 72. Langer built the three-stroke final margin by the 13th hole and matched birdies with Woosnam on the 14th and 18th for the 67 and 201 total, 12 under par.

Gordon J. Brand, in his failed shot at three in a row, tied for third at 205 with American Bob Boyd.

Weston Homes PGA International Seniors
Suffolk, England
Winner: Nick Job

Nick Job hoped that he hadn't just become a defending champion with nothing to defend after his two-stroke victory in the Weston Homes PGA International Seniors. Precedent was ruling against him. The 59-year-old Englishman had four previous victories on the European Senior Tour and "Every time I've won, we've never gone back to the place again."

Job, who hadn't won since May 2007 in the defunct Gloria Classic in Turkey, fended off the late challenge of Carl Mason to complete a wire-to-wire victory at the Stoke by Nayland Club in Suffolk in mid-September. He finished with a 69 for 202 total and a two-shot margin over the reigning circuit champion. No overtime on this Job.

The march to victory began with a four-under-par 68 Friday that put him in an all-England tie with Jeff Hall and Mason, who won the PGA Seniors Championship at Stoke by Nayland in 2007. Job broke free and opened a three-stroke lead over Mason with a 67 Saturday, racking up three of his eight birdies on the final trio of holes after a rather mundane front nine.

Sunday became a duel between Job and Mason, although Job built a five-stroke lead early, only to have Mason gradually close the gap. The outcome came down to the final hole, where Job, leading by just a stroke, tacked on his final birdie for his fifth tour victory and first-ever wire-to-wire win.

Scottish Seniors Open
Edinburgh, Scotland
Winner: Peter Mitchell

You could say that it was "out with the old, in with the new" at the Scottish Seniors Open in late November. Tommy Horton, the all-time leading light on the European Senior Tour, declared an end to his exemplary regular playing career on the circuit at the same time as Peter Mitchell moved into its upper strata with his second victory of the season.

Mitchell, who broke the ice in the Wales Seniors Open in just his second start on the circuit, held off Sam Torrance at the Marriott Dalmahoy Hotel and Country Club in Edinburgh, Scotland, and finished two strokes ahead of him with his nine-under-par 207. He joined Ian Woosnam and Gordon J. Brand as the year's only double victors.

The 50-year-old Englishman, a three-time winner on the regular European Tour, had slipped a shot ahead of first-round leader Des Smyth with a tournament-best 67 for 138 in Saturday's second round after opening with 71. Smyth had come out with 68 Friday and had six birdies in a wild second round, winding up with a 71.

Torrance forged a shot in front on the front nine Sunday, but Mitchell birdied three of the next four holes to establish a lead he held the rest of the way. Both he and Torrance, who was winless in 2008, had 69s, while Smyth dropped to third place with 71–210.

Horton, now 67, wound up a brilliant 17 seasons of senior golf with 23 victories and five Order of Merit titles, both records. "It's been great fun," he remarked. "I'm just grateful to have gotten a second bite of the cherry."

Lake Garda Italian Seniors Open
Lake Garda, Italy
Winner: Peter Mitchell

As the Lake Garda Italian Seniors Open was drawing to a close, the only three players with a pair of 2008 victories on their European Senior Tour records locked up in a tight battle to decide which one would be the first of the season to bag a third title. It turned out to be Peter Mitchell, who was on a roll after winning the Scottish Seniors Open, the previous event two weeks earlier.

The tour rookie Englishman fought off the challenges of Ian Woosnam, the Order of Merit leader, and Gordon J. Brand, who also had back-to-back victories in August. Mitchell edged them by a stroke with his final-round 68 and 13-under-par 203 at the Palazzo Arzaga Hotel and Golf Resort, moving into fourth place in the standings behind Woosnam, Bernhard Langer and Brand.

In contrast to the big names finish, the tournament began with lesser lights David Merriman of Australia and Chuck Milne of the United States showing the way with 66s. The ultimate protagonists moved into the picture Saturday. Mitchell shot 67 and shared the lead at 135 with Guillermo Encina, while Brand and Woosnam both fired 65s, Brand moving just a stroke off the pace with Emilio Rodriguez and Woosnam sitting another shot back with home country favorite Costantino Rocca.

Although Brand had the lead briefly Sunday when he eagled the eighth hole from 30 feet and Woosnam ran off a string of four birdies starting at that hole, they couldn't catch Mitchell, who had five birdies and a bogey, dropping a tricky three-foot par putt on the 54th hole for the win. Brand shot 68 and Woosnam 67 for their 204s.

OKI Castellon Open Espana – Senior Tour Championship
Castellon, Spain
Winner: Sam Torrance

A victory in an important tournament at the end of a season has a way of erasing memories of a year fraught with futility. So it was for Sam Torrance, whose 2008 campaign ended on a high note in the OKI Castellon Open Espana, otherwise known as the Senior Tour Championship.

After winning nine tournaments and two Order of Merit titles (2005 and 2006) in his first four full years on the European Senior Tour, Torrance went winless through a 2008 season that had him 20th in the rankings when he teed off in the year-ending championship in Spain in early November. Three days later, the elated Scot had win No. 10 in the bag and jumped to eighth place on the money list with his two-stroke victory. A final-round 69 gave him a final 13-under-par 203 and the win over runners-up Angel Fernandez of Chile and Katsuyoshi Tomori of Japan.

"It's a lovely way to spend four months now reflecting," said the relieved Torrance. "It was last chance saloon to keep that run (all five senior seasons with at least one victory) going."

Even though he had to drop out during the final round at Club de Campo del Mediterrraneo in Castellon, Ian Woosnam waltzed to the Order of Merit title in his rookie season on the European Senior Tour.

Englishmen Gordon J. Brand and Peter Mitchell, the year's two other multiple winners, finished a distant two-three in the standings.

Fernandez and defending champion Costantino Rocca led with 66s the first day at Castellon before Torrance took charge. Torrance, who played the first 36 holes without a bogey, matched the 66s Saturday for 134 and a two-shot lead over Bob Cameron (69-67), Jose Rivero (70-66) and Fernandez (66-70).

Torrance's only scare Sunday came at the 10th hole, when his lone bogey enabled Fernandez to catch him, but subsequent birdies at the 11th and 16th and Fernandez's bogey at the 17th secured the victory.

Japan Senior Tour

Starts Senior Golf Tournament
Narita, Chiba
Winner: Hajime Meshiai

Hajime Meshiai launched his run to the Order of Merit championship of the Japan PGA Senior Tour with a three-stroke victory in the Starts Senior Golf Tournament, a new event opening the season in June. Meshiai, a 14-tournament victor and 1993 leading money winner on the regular Japan Tour, played internationally in senior competition, including a middling season in America in 2005, when he picked off his only previous Japan Senior Tour victory after returning to Japan in the fall.

The 54-year-old trailed just off the pace the first two days of the Starts at Narita Golf Club in Chiba. Takashi Miyoshi, a five-time winner on the circuit, and Katuji Hasegawa led the first day with 69, a shot ahead of Meshiai and four others. One of those others — Katsunari Takahashi, the tour's all-time victory leader with 12 spread over eight seasons — shot 66 and took the lead Saturday, two ahead of Meshiai (68) and Miyoshi (69). Meshiai then rolled to the decisive win with a 65 Sunday for a 13-under-par 203 total. Takahashi finished second with 70–206.

Fancl Classic
Susono, Shizuoka
Winner: Tateo Ozaki

Tateo (Jet) Ozaki, a solid player in his younger days but not quite as successful as his high-flying brothers Masashi (Jumbo) and Naomichi (Joe), has made a mark on the Japan PGA Senior Tour. Ozaki, 54, playing in his fifth season on the circuit, landed his third title in August when he pulled out a one-stroke victory in the Fancl Classic.

The defending Senior PGA champion shot a one-under-par 71 in the final round to edge Tsukasa Watanabe by a stroke on a tough final day when that 71 and two others were the low scores of the round. His total was 207, nine under par.

Watanabe held the lead for two days at Susono Country Club in Shizuoka Prefecture. He opened with 67 and led five players at 68. Ozaki was at 69, then took sole possession of second place Saturday when Watanabe produced a 68 for 135 and he shot 67 for 136.

Five players were tied for third at 138, but none factored into the final outcome. Tsuneyuki (Tommy) Nakajima, the highly successful all-time No. 2 money winner, had another of those 71s Sunday and tied for third at 210 with Tomohiro Maruyama.

Komatsu Open
Komatsu, Ishikawa
Winner: Hisashi Nakase

The season's only first-time winner emerged at the Komatsu Open. Hisashi Nakase, who had no previous track record on Japan's pro tours, came up with three solid rounds at Komatsu Country Club and nipped two of the tour's strongest players by a stroke in the early September tournament.

Tsukasa Watanabe, in contention again, began the week with 66 and led Nakase, South Korea's Lim Jin-han and Hajime Meshiai, the Starts winner, by a stroke. Nakase slipped past Watanabe into first place Saturday, shooting 68 for 135. His victory chances did not look favorable, though, considering that right on his heels were multiple seniors winners Meshiai (69), Katsunari Takahashi (71-65) and Watanabe (70) at 136 and Takashi Miyoshi (69-68) at 137. But Nakase crafted a fine 68 Sunday for 203, 13 under par, one stroke better than the 204s of Meshiai (68) and Miyoshi (67).

Akira Kobayashi Invitational Sanko Senior
Sakakibaraonsen, Mie
Winner: Hajime Meshiai

Hajime Meshiai had a short week's work in winning his second title of the season. The Akira Kobayashi Invitational Sanko Senior was the only sanctioned 36-hole event on the circuit's nine-tournament schedule, and Meshiai, who won the year-opening Starts in the spring, made things rather easy when he blistered the Sakakibaraonsen Golf Club course with a nine-under-par 63 in the first round.

That potent score gave him a three-stroke lead on Tsukasa Watanabe and five over the next-best shooters — Yutaka Hagawa, Somei Sudo and Seiji Ebihara. The scoring was generally high Sunday and Meshiai went 12 strokes higher to 75. However, none of the closest pursuers could take advantage of his lapse, and his 138 total was just good enough to nip Tomohiro Maruyama and his 69-70–139.

Japan PGA Senior Championship
Hitachiomiya, Ibaraki
Winner: Tsukasa Watanabe

During his long career on the Japan Tour, Tsukasa Watanabe made many ill-fated runs at victory before, at age 36, he won his first of two victories. It didn't take him nearly as long on the PGA Senior Tour and the first one was a big one — the PGA Senior Championship — in his second season among the over-50 set.

Watanabe, a strong contender in several of the earlier tournaments of the season, was inconsistent in the first three rounds of the Senior PGA. After sharing the first-round lead with Lim Jin-han with 68s, Watanabe slipped to 74 Friday and dropped three strokes behind the South Korean and his

68-71–139. Nobumitsu Yuhara was second at 69-71–140 and Katsunari Takahashi next at 73-68–141.

Lim blinked with 75 Saturday, and Watanabe bounced back with 69 and rebounded into a tie for the lead with Nichito Hashimoto (73-70-68), a shot ahead of Takahashi (71) and Akira Yabe (73-70-69). Watanabe polished off the victory with a 70 Sunday for 281 total, two strokes better than Takahashi.

Fujifilm Senior Championship
Hirakawa, Chiba
Winner: Tsukasa Watanabe

The Japan PGA Senior Tour schedule, with nine tournaments scattered across six months, rarely has tournaments back to back. Much to Tsukasa Watanabe's pleasure, though, that was the case with the Fujifilm Senior Championship immediately following the Senior PGA Championship the first week of October. Riding the momentum of his first victory in that major, Watanabe rolled to a runaway triumph in wire-to-wire fashion in the new event.

Watanabe opened with 69 at Hirakawa Country Club and took a one-stroke lead over Hajime Meshiai, Takashi Miyoshi, Katsumi Nanjyo and Naomichi (Joe) Ozaki, playing in his first senior event of the year. The margin went to three when Watanabe followed with 64. Kyoshi Murota nearly matched that score and, with 65, took over second place at 136, a shot in front of Meshiai (67). Watanabe went one way and the other two went the other Sunday. He fired a steady 69 for 202 total and won by eight strokes when Murota bumbled to 74 and Meshiai to 73 for 210s. Ozaki (70) also finished with 210.

Japan Senior Open Championship
Sayama, Saitama
Winner: Tsuneyuki Nakajima

The Japan Senior Open Championship has become almost the exclusive province of Tsuneyuki Nakajima and properly so. The best players are supposed to win any tour's most prestigious tournaments and that premise fits Nakajima, one of Japan's all-time greats, perfectly. The 2008 Open victory was Nakajima's fourth win as a senior — three Opens in his four seasons on the circuit and a Senior PGA Championship. It would seem appropriate that Isao Aoki was the one to interrupt his Open streak when, at age 65, he won the national senior championship for the fifth time in 2007.

Nakajima was in total control of his game and the tournament in 2008. It went his way: First round: Nakajima shot 66, six under par at Sayama Golf Club in Saitama Prefecture, and led Noboru Fujiike and Chen Tzeming by two. Second round: Nakajima shot 68 for 134, led Chen (70) and Nobumitsu Yuhara (70-68) by four. Third round: Nakajima shot 67, led Yuhara (69) by six.

Nakajima closed it out with 72 Sunday for 273 and retained the six-stroke margin as Kiyoshi Murota closed with 68–279.

Kinojo Senior Open
Kinojo, Okayama
Winner: Isao Aoki

Absent the prestige, the irrepressible Isao Aoki came up with a near duplicate of his 2007 triumph in the Japan Senior Open by again shooting his age — 66 — in the final round and winning the Kinojo Senior Open. The difference was that the 66 merely gained Aoki a tie with Tsukasa Watanabe, one of the season's hottest players, and forced him to go four more holes before winning the playoff.

Japan's first and only male Hall-of-Fame golfer had gone into the third round tied at 69-67–136 with Minoru Hatsumi, the first-round leader, who added a 70 to his opening 66, and Seiji Ebihara (68-68), the country's other senior who has enjoyed success on the world front.

Watanabe brewed up a 63, the week's finest round, to overtake Aoki at 202, 14 under par at Kinojo Golf Club in Okayama Prefecture, and brought about the playoff. Nobody else was within four strokes. Aoki's birdie on the fourth extra hole gave him his eighth title on the Japan PGA Senior Tour, including five Japan Opens, to go with his extensive array of victories in all parts of the world.

PGA Handa Cup Philanthropy Senior Open
Ohmurasaki, Saitama
Winner: Takashi Miyoshi

Takashi Miyoshi resurrected memories of his big 2005 Japan PGA Senior Tour season when he captured the title in 2008's final event. Miyoshi, who won three of 2005's eight tournaments, deprived Hajime Meshiai of his third 2008 win when he defeated him in a four-hole playoff.

Miyoshi appeared to have kicked away his chances of nailing his sixth Senior Tour win in the third round of the 72-hole event. He had jumped into a share of the second-round lead with Meshiai (67-69) when he drilled an eight-under-par 64 for his 136, but skied to 77 Saturday. That dropped him three strokes behind Meshiai, who shot 74 for 210. Meshiai led Masahiro Kuramoto (72-67-73) by two and, besides Miyoshi, Hiroshi Makino (70-70-73) and Australian Terry Gale (65-73-75), the first-round leader, by three.

With 68, the day's best round, Miyoshi forced the playoff when Meshiai managed only a 71 for his 281 total, seven under par at Ohmurasaki Golf Club in Saitama Prefecture. For the second event in a row, the overtime went four holes and was decided by a birdie.

Despite the loss, though, Meshiai collected a large enough runner-up check — ¥13.8 million — to edge Tsukasa Watanabe for the season's Order of Merit title by less than ¥2 million with his ¥46,275,833.

APPENDIXES

American Tours

Mercedes-Benz Championship

Plantation Course at Kapalua, Maui, Hawaii
Par 36-37–73; 7,411 yards

January 3-6
purse, $5,500,000

	SCORES				TOTAL	MONEY
Daniel Chopra	69	72	67	66	274	$1,100,000
Steve Stricker	73	69	68	64	274	630,000
(Chopra defeated Stricker on fourth playoff hole.)						
Stephen Ames	72	67	70	66	275	410,000
Mike Weir	71	67	68	70	276	310,000
Jim Furyk	74	70	66	68	278	218,000
Hunter Mahan	73	72	69	64	278	218,000
Nick Watney	68	72	67	71	278	218,000
Charles Howell	74	70	68	67	279	175,000
Justin Leonard	73	68	69	69	279	175,000
Mark Calcavecchia	75	66	71	68	280	155,000
Brandt Snedeker	71	69	70	70	280	155,000
Aaron Baddeley	70	71	73	67	281	130,000
Chad Campbell	75	68	68	70	281	130,000
Vijay Singh	74	70	67	70	281	130,000
Jonathan Byrd	70	69	69	74	282	105,000
Angel Cabrera	70	71	70	71	282	105,000
Rory Sabbatini	72	74	69	69	284	90,000
Woody Austin	73	74	69	70	286	86,000
Scott Verplank	73	70	72	71	286	86,000
Steve Flesch	72	70	71	74	287	81,000
Charley Hoffman	75	72	70	70	287	81,000
Zach Johnson	76	67	71	73	287	81,000
Brian Bateman	76	70	72	70	288	76,000
Boo Weekley	80	74	68	66	288	76,000
Fred Funk	75	71	72	72	290	72,000
George McNeill	74	69	72	75	290	72,000
Mark Wilson	74	72	73	72	291	69,000
K.J. Choi	79	75	69	69	292	67,500
Henrik Stenson	76	75	73	68	292	67,500
Paul Goydos	81	73	67	73	294	66,000
Joe Ogilvie	75	73	74	74	296	65,000

Sony Open

Waialae Country Club, Honolulu, Hawaii
Par 35-35–70; 7,060 yards

January 10-13
purse, $5,300,000

	SCORES				TOTAL	MONEY
K.J. Choi	64	65	66	71	266	$954,000
Rory Sabbatini	66	69	66	68	269	572,400
Jerry Kelly	67	67	69	67	270	360,400
Steve Marino	65	67	68	72	272	208,687.50
Kevin Na	67	64	69	72	272	208,687.50
Pat Perez	69	66	67	70	272	208,687.50
Steve Stricker	71	65	66	70	272	208,687.50
Troy Matteson	69	67	65	72	273	159,000

	SCORES				TOTAL	MONEY
Tom Pernice, Jr.	70	67	66	70	273	159,000
Stephen Ames	70	68	65	71	274	113,571.43
Fred Funk	69	64	69	72	274	113,571.43
Dustin Johnson	68	68	67	71	274	113,571.43
Doug LaBelle	67	69	66	72	274	113,571.43
Parker McLachlin	73	66	65	70	274	113,571.43
Heath Slocum	65	69	69	71	274	113,571.43
Chad Campbell	66	69	66	73	274	113,571.42
J.B. Holmes	68	70	64	73	275	79,500
Matt Jones	68	69	68	70	275	79,500
George McNeill	68	71	70	66	275	79,500
James Driscoll	66	69	73	68	276	59,572
Jim Furyk	68	70	69	69	276	59,572
Steve Lowery	66	72	71	67	276	59,572
Jay Williamson	67	68	66	75	276	59,572
Y.E. Yang	69	68	69	70	276	59,572
Chad Collins	67	70	73	67	277	39,598.58
Jeff Maggert	69	69	68	71	277	39,598.57
Shigeki Maruyama	68	68	68	73	277	39,598.57
Carl Pettersson	67	68	69	73	277	39,598.57
Vaughn Taylor	67	70	69	71	277	39,598.57
Tim Wilkinson	68	69	62	78	277	39,598.57
Mark Wilson	72	65	66	74	277	39,598.57
Brad Adamonis	66	68	70	74	278	28,090
Paul Azinger	70	68	69	71	278	28,090
Cameron Beckman	67	71	70	70	278	28,090
Daniel Chopra	66	71	68	73	278	28,090
Zach Johnson	67	70	69	72	278	28,090
John Merrick	69	69	69	71	278	28,090
Jesper Parnevik	69	70	66	73	278	28,090
Chez Reavie	68	66	69	75	278	28,090
Shane Bertsch	71	66	72	70	279	20,670
Alejandro Canizares	67	67	71	74	279	20,670
Brian Gay	67	67	70	75	279	20,670
J.P. Hayes	66	70	71	72	279	20,670
Yusaku Miyazato	68	69	69	73	279	20,670
Jason Allred	69	69	74	68	280	15,518.40
Spencer Levin	67	68	73	72	280	15,518.40
Vijay Singh	70	68	69	73	280	15,518.40
Scott Sterling	70	69	69	72	280	15,518.40
Liang Wen-chong	70	66	70	74	280	15,518.40
Robert Gamez	67	70	73	71	281	12,783.60
Sean O'Hair	69	70	71	71	281	12,783.60
Patrick Sheehan	71	68	69	73	281	12,783.60
Kevin Streelman	68	69	72	72	281	12,783.60
Bubba Watson	70	69	67	75	281	12,783.60
Bob Estes	69	66	71	76	282	11,925
Martin Laird	69	70	70	73	282	11,925
Tom Lehman	70	68	68	76	282	11,925
John Mallinger	67	72	71	72	282	11,925
Jim McGovern	71	65	70	76	282	11,925
Kiyoshi Miyazato	69	70	70	73	282	11,925
Briny Baird	68	68	73	74	283	11,448
Mitsuhiro Tateyama	66	70	75	72	283	11,448
Jimmy Walker	65	68	73	77	283	11,448
Daisuke Maruyama	68	69	71	76	284	11,236
Matt Kuchar	70	67	73	75	285	11,130
Dudley Hart	68	69	74	75	286	10,971
John Riegger	67	69	74	76	286	10,971
Mark Calcavecchia	68	71	73	75	287	10,812

Bob Hope Chrysler Classic

The Classic Club: Par 36-36–72; 7,305 yards
PGA West, Palmer Course: Par 36-36–72; 6,950 yards
La Quinta CC: Par 36-36–72; 7,060 yards
SilverRock Resort: Par 36-36–72; 7,578 yards
Palm Desert and La Quinta, California

January 16-20
purse, $5,100,000

	SCORES					TOTAL	MONEY
D.J. Trahan	67	64	68	70	65	334	$918,000
Justin Leonard	68	64	67	66	72	337	550,800
Anthony Kim	69	67	67	66	69	338	295,800
Kenny Perry	66	72	65	66	69	338	295,800
Steve Elkington	66	68	69	67	69	339	186,150
Ryan Moore	75	64	67	67	66	339	186,150
Chez Reavie	69	68	67	70	65	339	186,150
Charley Hoffman	68	72	71	63	67	341	142,800
Brett Rumford	67	68	69	67	70	341	142,800
Vaughn Taylor	70	68	68	69	66	341	142,800
Boo Weekley	69	70	62	69	71	341	142,800
Robert Allenby	73	69	68	64	68	342	103,275
Ben Crane	66	69	69	67	71	342	103,275
Dustin Johnson	67	69	72	63	71	342	103,275
Nicholas Thompson	68	70	68	66	70	342	103,275
Shane Bertsch	70	71	64	66	72	343	73,950
Bart Bryant	71	69	68	67	68	343	73,950
Robert Gamez	66	65	67	71	74	343	73,950
Bill Haas	69	68	69	68	69	343	73,950
Ryuji Imada	71	68	67	67	70	343	73,950
John Merrick	73	65	67	68	70	343	73,950
Jason Bohn	66	74	66	69	69	344	51,000
John Senden	68	73	66	68	69	344	51,000
Scott Verplank	70	65	70	68	71	344	51,000
Charlie Wi	68	68	74	67	67	344	51,000
Stewart Cink	68	71	66	71	69	345	39,270
Brian Davis	72	69	69	67	68	345	39,270
Bubba Watson	70	71	66	72	66	345	39,270
Olin Browne	68	68	75	68	67	346	32,427.50
Matt Jones	70	70	68	66	72	346	32,427.50
Steve Marino	72	71	68	66	69	346	32,427.50
Jesper Parnevik	67	74	66	68	71	346	32,427.50
Charles Warren	74	69	65	67	71	346	32,427.50
Y.E. Yang	71	70	67	69	69	346	32,427.50
Michael Allen	69	71	70	69	68	347	26,265
Mathew Goggin	65	73	69	69	71	347	26,265
Frank Lickliter	72	69	68	69	69	347	26,265
Tommy Armour	70	71	70	68	69	348	21,420
Rich Beem	72	72	68	66	70	348	21,420
Joe Durant	65	73	71	69	70	348	21,420
Brian Gay	71	67	71	68	71	348	21,420
Jin Park	69	74	66	70	69	348	21,420
Johnson Wagner	67	71	73	65	72	348	21,420
Ryan Armour	70	75	68	67	69	349	15,419
Steve Flesch	72	69	69	65	74	349	15,419
Jeff Maggert	70	71	70	66	72	349	15,419
Rod Pampling	71	70	67	69	72	349	15,419
Tim Petrovic	65	70	68	72	74	349	15,419
Heath Slocum	69	70	72	65	73	349	15,419
Brad Adamonis	68	70	69	72	71	350	12,206
Chad Campbell	76	68	69	68	69	350	12,206
J.J. Henry	71	72	69	69	69	350	12,206
Jeff Quinney	66	69	73	72	70	350	12,206
Tom Scherrer	71	70	66	69	74	350	12,206

	SCORES					TOTAL	MONEY
Kyle Thompson	68	67	72	72	71	350	12,206
Paul Claxton	70	73	68	69	71	351	11,373
Fred Couples	69	73	71	68	70	351	11,373
Martin Laird	71	69	71	70	70	351	11,373
Joe Ogilvie	71	70	67	73	70	351	11,373
Kevin Sutherland	70	71	71	68	71	351	11,373
Mike Weir	70	70	68	70	73	351	11,373
Lucas Glover	70	71	69	71	71	352	10,863
Shaun Micheel	72	71	67	70	72	352	10,863
Patrick Sheehan	73	71	72	65	71	352	10,863
Chris Stroud	70	71	69	70	72	352	10,863
Justin Bolli	72	71	69	67	74	353	10,455
Michael Letzig	68	75	67	71	72	353	10,455
Kevin Na	69	69	70	69	76	353	10,455
Brett Wetterich	71	71	67	72	72	353	10,455
Woody Austin	68	72	73	67	74	354	9,996
Mark Brooks	71	70	70	70	73	354	9,996
Jason Gore	71	72	69	68	74	354	9,996
Paul Goydos	72	70	71	68	73	354	9,996
Scott McCarron	68	74	70	69	73	354	9,996
Ken Duke	67	70	69	74	75	355	9,639
Kevin Stadler	72	69	68	71	75	355	9,639

Buick Invitational

Torrey Pines Golf Course, San Diego, California
South Course: Par 36-36–72; 7,569 yards
North Course: Par 36-36–72; 6,874 yards

January 24-27
purse, $5,200,000

	SCORES				TOTAL	MONEY
Tiger Woods	67	65	66	71	269	$936,000
Ryuji Imada	69	72	69	67	277	561,600
Stewart Cink	68	69	69	73	279	301,600
Rory Sabbatini	67	75	70	67	279	301,600
Justin Leonard	76	68	65	72	281	208,000
Joe Durant	70	70	67	75	282	180,700
Phil Mickelson	70	73	68	71	282	180,700
Stuart Appleby	67	72	71	73	283	150,800
Fred Couples	71	69	71	72	283	150,800
John Senden	70	69	72	72	283	150,800
Nathan Green	68	72	72	72	284	124,800
Troy Matteson	65	75	73	71	284	124,800
Steve Elkington	71	71	69	74	285	91,866.67
Kenneth Ferrie	73	67	71	74	285	91,866.67
Charles Howell	68	72	71	74	285	91,866.67
Kevin Sutherland	73	68	70	74	285	91,866.67
Aaron Baddeley	71	67	71	76	285	91,866.66
Camilo Villegas	69	72	70	74	285	91,866.66
Doug LaBelle	68	72	69	77	286	65,260
Frank Lickliter	72	70	73	71	286	65,260
Carl Pettersson	70	72	70	74	286	65,260
Boo Weekley	72	66	71	77	286	65,260
Carlos Franco	71	69	71	76	287	44,980
Matt Jones	72	70	70	75	287	44,980
Matt Kuchar	71	72	71	73	287	44,980
John Mallinger	74	66	72	75	287	44,980
Steve Marino	74	70	71	72	287	44,980
Vijay Singh	73	68	74	72	287	44,980
Bill Haas	72	68	73	75	288	33,063.34
Dean Wilson	69	71	73	75	288	33,063.34

	SCORES				TOTAL	MONEY
Hunter Mahan	71	69	73	75	288	33,063.33
Parker McLachlin	69	73	73	73	288	33,063.33
Jeff Quinney	69	71	70	78	288	33,063.33
Kevin Streelman	67	69	75	77	288	33,063.33
Robert Allenby	70	70	72	77	289	27,430
Roland Thatcher	73	71	73	72	289	27,430
Jim Furyk	73	68	73	76	290	22,360
Dustin Johnson	72	70	75	73	290	22,360
Shigeki Maruyama	71	71	73	75	290	22,360
Rod Pampling	70	72	74	74	290	22,360
Kevin Stadler	68	74	76	72	290	22,360
Marc Turnesa	73	70	76	71	290	22,360
Brett Wetterich	72	72	74	72	290	22,360
Briny Baird	71	71	71	78	291	17,160
J.B. Holmes	71	73	72	75	291	17,160
Jon Mills	73	70	73	75	291	17,160
Jin Park	71	73	72	76	292	14,664
Bubba Watson	73	71	75	73	292	14,664
Justin Bolli	74	69	70	80	293	12,506
Jason Day	72	72	75	74	293	12,506
Cliff Kresge	76	67	74	76	293	12,506
Jeff Maggert	71	72	72	78	293	12,506
George McNeill	72	72	75	74	293	12,506
Sean O'Hair	76	68	74	75	293	12,506
Tom Pernice, Jr.	71	73	75	74	293	12,506
Chris Stroud	73	70	73	77	293	12,506
Tim Herron	72	72	73	77	294	11,752
Brad Adamonis	66	72	80	77	295	11,596
Craig Barlow	71	73	75	76	295	11,596
Jason Gore	73	71	73	79	296	11,388
Travis Perkins	76	68	77	75	296	11,388
*Jamie Lovemark	73	71	73	79	296	
Tag Ridings	73	71	70	83	297	11,232
Cody Freeman	70	74	77	80	301	11,128
John Rollins	71	71	78	82	302	11,024
Mark O'Meara	72	72	75	84	303	10,920

FBR Open

TPC Scottsdale, Scottsdale, Arizona
Par 35-36–71; 7,216 yards

January 31-February 3
purse, $6,000,000

	SCORES				TOTAL	MONEY
J.B. Holmes	68	65	66	71	270	$1,080,000
Phil Mickelson	68	68	67	67	270	648,000
(Holmes defeated Mickelson on first playoff hole.)						
Charles Warren	65	69	67	70	271	408,000
Stuart Appleby	69	66	71	66	272	226,200
Ben Crane	70	65	67	70	272	226,200
Steve Elkington	69	66	70	67	272	226,200
Kevin Na	69	67	67	69	272	226,200
Kevin Sutherland	65	72	66	69	272	226,200
Bill Haas	67	68	69	69	273	156,000
Brandt Snedeker	67	69	67	70	273	156,000
Boo Weekley	68	69	69	67	273	156,000
Mark Wilson	68	69	68	68	273	156,000
Briny Baird	71	64	74	65	274	112,500
Jonathan Byrd	69	64	68	73	274	112,500
Nick O'Hern	69	65	68	72	274	112,500
Charlie Wi	66	71	67	70	274	112,500

	SCORES				TOTAL	MONEY
Brian Gay	66	71	69	69	275	90,000
Kenny Perry	67	66	71	71	275	90,000
Jeff Quinney	69	71	69	66	275	90,000
Rich Beem	66	72	66	72	276	67,440
Mark Calcavecchia	70	70	64	72	276	67,440
K.J. Choi	68	68	74	66	276	67,440
Jason Day	71	68	70	67	276	67,440
Tom Pernice, Jr.	70	70	65	71	276	67,440
Robert Allenby	68	67	71	71	277	46,800
Todd Hamilton	70	68	68	71	277	46,800
Charles Howell	67	68	72	70	277	46,800
Fredrik Jacobson	71	66	72	68	277	46,800
Jeff Overton	69	71	66	71	277	46,800
Richard Johnson	68	72	68	70	278	38,100
Anthony Kim	69	70	69	70	278	38,100
Stephen Leaney	69	69	68	72	278	38,100
John Rollins	69	68	70	71	278	38,100
Tommy Armour	67	69	70	73	279	28,400
Woody Austin	68	70	71	70	279	28,400
Jason Gore	71	65	69	74	279	28,400
Frank Lickliter	69	65	71	74	279	28,400
Steve Marino	73	66	69	71	279	28,400
Jon Mills	70	70	69	70	279	28,400
Rory Sabbatini	68	70	70	71	279	28,400
Camilo Villegas	66	67	73	73	279	28,400
Nick Watney	71	66	71	71	279	28,400
Daniel Chopra	69	67	67	77	280	18,720
Cliff Kresge	71	67	67	75	280	18,720
Justin Leonard	70	67	66	77	280	18,720
Billy Mayfair	72	68	70	70	280	18,720
Pat Perez	69	65	75	71	280	18,720
John Senden	68	69	74	69	280	18,720
Mike Weir	70	68	70	72	280	18,720
Nathan Green	70	70	74	67	281	14,610
Rocco Mediate	70	69	70	72	281	14,610
Sean O'Hair	69	70	68	74	281	14,610
Ted Purdy	70	70	72	69	281	14,610
Cameron Beckman	69	70	69	74	282	13,740
Chris DiMarco	68	70	71	73	282	13,740
Fred Funk	69	70	68	75	282	13,740
Troy Matteson	68	72	73	69	282	13,740
Michael Allen	67	71	72	73	283	13,080
Lucas Glover	68	69	74	72	283	13,080
J.J. Henry	68	71	73	71	283	13,080
Doug LaBelle	69	64	75	75	283	13,080
Tom Lehman	69	69	71	74	283	13,080
Chez Reavie	69	70	72	72	283	13,080
Jay Williamson	69	68	72	74	283	13,080
Eric Axley	68	70	74	72	284	12,480
Craig Barlow	70	70	75	69	284	12,480
Ben Curtis	73	67	73	71	284	12,480
Joe Durant	73	66	70	76	285	12,240
John Mallinger	71	69	72	74	286	12,120

AT&T Pebble Beach National Pro-Am

Pebble Beach GL: Par 36-36–72; 6,816 yards
Poppy Hills: Par 36-36–72; 6,833 yards
Spyglass Hill GC: Par 36-36–72; 6,858 yards
Pebble Beach, California

February 7-10
purse, $6,000,000

	SCORES				TOTAL	MONEY
Steve Lowery	69	71	70	68	278	$1,080,000
Vijay Singh	70	70	67	71	278	648,000
(Lowery defeated Singh on first playoff hole.)						
Dudley Hart	69	70	68	72	279	312,000
John Mallinger	67	74	73	65	279	312,000
Corey Pavin	73	69	71	66	279	312,000
Jason Day	69	70	71	70	280	216,000
Dustin Johnson	73	68	68	73	282	193,500
Nicholas Thompson	69	69	74	70	282	193,500
Brent Geiberger	69	73	71	70	283	150,000
Jason Gore	70	74	69	70	283	150,000
Joe Ogilvie	74	69	70	70	283	150,000
Tag Ridings	73	71	68	71	283	150,000
Y.E. Yang	69	73	68	73	283	150,000
Michael Allen	68	70	71	75	284	87,360
Shane Bertsch	77	70	68	69	284	87,360
James Driscoll	72	68	72	72	284	87,360
Jim Furyk	71	75	67	71	284	87,360
Padraig Harrington	72	70	70	72	284	87,360
Fredrik Jacobson	73	67	70	74	284	87,360
Daisuke Maruyama	71	72	71	70	284	87,360
Parker McLachlin	70	70	74	70	284	87,360
D.A. Points	68	73	70	73	284	87,360
Mike Weir	75	69	71	69	284	87,360
Ryan Armour	71	71	68	75	285	44,400
Andrew Buckle	69	73	71	72	285	44,400
Marco Dawson	73	69	72	71	285	44,400
Craig Kanada	72	71	72	70	285	44,400
Davis Love	70	71	72	72	285	44,400
Pat Perez	74	70	69	72	285	44,400
Jeff Quinney	69	70	71	75	285	44,400
Chris Riley	73	68	72	72	285	44,400
Paul Stankowski	74	72	69	70	285	44,400
Bo Van Pelt	74	74	67	70	285	44,400
Robert Damron	71	70	70	75	286	28,400
Tim Herron	68	69	74	75	286	28,400
Lee Janzen	74	69	72	71	286	28,400
Matt Kuchar	74	69	69	74	286	28,400
Jin Park	72	69	74	71	286	28,400
Tom Pernice, Jr.	70	74	70	72	286	28,400
John Riegger	72	70	70	74	286	28,400
Jay Williamson	68	71	72	75	286	28,400
Mark Wilson	68	71	72	75	286	28,400
Olin Browne	68	73	73	73	287	19,800
Alejandro Canizares	70	73	72	72	287	19,800
Mathew Goggin	71	70	72	74	287	19,800
Justin Leonard	70	71	74	72	287	19,800
Kevin Na	71	69	73	74	287	19,800
Robert Floyd	68	70	74	76	288	15,264
Kent Jones	66	74	71	77	288	15,264
Greg Kraft	72	73	70	73	288	15,264
Ryan Moore	71	70	74	73	288	15,264
Tim Petrovic	76	66	73	73	288	15,264
Carlos Franco	71	73	71	74	289	13,824
Jonathan Kaye	70	71	70	78	289	13,824

	SCORES				TOTAL	MONEY
Jeff Maggert	72	73	70	74	289	13,824
Jim McGovern	71	69	71	78	289	13,824
Charlie Wi	73	72	70	74	289	13,824
Alex Cejka	72	72	70	76	290	13,320
Brandt Snedeker	73	72	70	75	290	13,320
Nick Watney	76	71	67	76	290	13,320

Northern Trust Open

Riviera Country Club, Pacific Palisades, California
Par 35-36–71; 7,279 yards

February 14-17
purse, $6,200,000

	SCORES				TOTAL	MONEY
Phil Mickelson	68	64	70	70	272	$1,116,000
Jeff Quinney	69	67	67	71	274	669,600
Luke Donald	68	71	70	68	277	359,600
Padraig Harrington	69	69	71	68	277	359,600
Ryuji Imada	71	69	70	68	278	235,600
Scott Verplank	68	69	71	70	278	235,600
Robert Allenby	70	66	75	68	279	186,775
Stuart Appleby	69	70	69	71	279	186,775
K.J. Choi	65	73	71	70	279	186,775
J.B. Holmes	74	66	69	70	279	186,775
Chad Campbell	67	70	73	70	280	142,600
Steve Stricker	71	69	71	69	280	142,600
Mark Wilson	70	70	69	71	280	142,600
Joe Durant	71	70	69	71	281	96,100
Steve Flesch	71	71	68	71	281	96,100
Jason Gore	71	72	71	67	281	96,100
Matt Kuchar	73	71	70	67	281	96,100
John Rollins	68	70	69	74	281	96,100
Adam Scott	73	69	70	69	281	96,100
Bubba Watson	71	68	71	71	281	96,100
Charlie Wi	70	68	71	72	281	96,100
Paul Casey	73	70	69	70	282	53,044.45
Peter Lonard	69	70	74	69	282	53,044.45
Kevin Sutherland	70	69	73	70	282	53,044.45
Marc Turnesa	75	70	67	70	282	53,044.45
Lucas Glover	72	69	70	71	282	53,044.44
Nathan Green	72	70	70	70	282	53,044.44
Vaughn Taylor	67	70	71	74	282	53,044.44
David Toms	71	68	72	71	282	53,044.44
D.J. Trahan	70	74	66	72	282	53,044.44
Angel Cabrera	68	73	70	72	283	36,766
Fred Couples	70	70	72	71	283	36,766
Brandt Jobe	71	68	71	73	283	36,766
Hunter Mahan	68	74	70	71	283	36,766
Tag Ridings	75	68	70	70	283	36,766
Brad Adamonis	72	71	69	72	284	27,318.75
Bart Bryant	74	69	71	70	284	27,318.75
Alex Cejka	68	72	73	71	284	27,318.75
Bill Haas	72	71	72	69	284	27,318.75
George McNeill	72	69	71	72	284	27,318.75
Jeff Overton	74	69	70	71	284	27,318.75
Pat Perez	69	72	71	72	284	27,318.75
Vijay Singh	71	72	71	70	284	27,318.75
Billy Mayfair	68	69	74	74	285	21,080
Rory Sabbatini	72	67	74	72	285	21,080
Aaron Baddeley	73	70	74	69	286	16,120
Craig Barlow	69	74	69	74	286	16,120

	SCORES				TOTAL	MONEY
Brian Bateman	70	70	76	70	286	16,120
Sergio Garcia	74	71	69	72	286	16,120
Zach Johnson	72	67	71	76	286	16,120
Steve Marino	69	70	71	76	286	16,120
Scott McCarron	72	65	76	73	286	16,120
Tom Pernice, Jr.	72	72	68	74	286	16,120
Toru Taniguchi	72	71	71	72	286	16,120
Ben Crane	70	74	73	70	287	14,074
Charles Howell	71	70	74	72	287	14,074
Fredrik Jacobson	72	73	72	70	287	14,074
Kevin Na	66	76	73	72	287	14,074
Michael Allen	75	70	73	70	288	13,640
Cody Freeman	70	74	72	72	288	13,640
Dustin Johnson	68	73	69	78	288	13,640
Cameron Beckman	74	70	72	73	289	13,082
Ben Curtis	70	71	76	72	289	13,082
Shigeki Maruyama	71	74	74	70	289	13,082
Rocco Mediate	75	70	70	74	289	13,082
Ryan Moore	72	71	71	75	289	13,082
Kenny Perry	72	73	70	74	289	13,082
Mathew Goggin	73	71	72	74	290	12,586
Kevin Streelman	75	69	74	72	290	12,586
Briny Baird	71	74	70	76	291	12,152
Fred Funk	74	70	71	76	291	12,152
Will MacKenzie	71	73	75	72	291	12,152
Bo Van Pelt	71	74	72	74	291	12,152
Dean Wilson	71	72	74	74	291	12,152
Eric Axley	71	72	78	71	292	11,656
John Daly	69	74	73	76	292	11,656
Carl Pettersson	70	74	74	74	292	11,656
Chez Reavie	73	71	71	78	293	11,408

WGC - Accenture Match Play Championship

The Gallery at Dove Mountain, South Course, February 20-24
Marana, Arizona purse, $8,000,000
Par 36-36–72; 7,351 yards

FIRST ROUND

Tiger Woods defeated J.B. Holmes, 1-up.
Arron Oberholser defeated Mike Weir, 3 and 1.
David Toms defeated Zach Johnson, 2 and 1.
Aaron Baddeley defeated Mark Calcavecchia, 4 and 2.
Bradley Dredge defeated Rory Sabbatini, 4 and 3.
Paul Casey defeated Robert Karlsson, 2-up.
K.J. Choi defeated Camilo Villegas, 3 and 2.
Ian Poulter defeated Soren Hansen, 2 and 1.
Jonathan Byrd defeated Ernie Els, 6 and 5.
Andres Romero defeated Retief Goosen, 2 and 1.
Henrik Stenson defeated Robert Allenby, 1-up.
Trevor Immelman defeated Shingo Katayama, 1-up.
Adam Scott defeated Brendan Jones, 2 and 1.
Woody Austin defeated Toru Taniguchi, 6 and 5.
Sergio Garcia defeated John Senden, 3 and 2.
Boo Weekley defeated Martin Kaymer, 2 and 1.
Steve Stricker defeated Daniel Chopra, 20 holes.
Hunter Mahan defeated Richard Sterne, 4 and 3.
Angel Cabrera defeated Anders Hansen, 3 and 2.
Luke Donald defeated Nick Dougherty, 2 and 1.
Colin Montgomerie defeated Jim Furyk, 3 and 2.

Charles Howell defeated Stephen Ames, 19 holes.
Padraig Harrington defeated Jerry Kelly, 4 and 3.
Stewart Cink defeated Miguel Angel Jimenez, 4 and 3.
Phil Mickelson defeated Pat Perez, 1-up.
Stuart Appleby defeated Tim Clark, 3 and 2.
Justin Leonard defeated Geoff Ogilvy, 2 and 1.
Lee Westwood defeated Brandt Snedeker, 3 and 2.
Rod Pampling defeated Justin Rose, 2 and 1.
Nick O'Hern defeated Scott Verplank, 3 and 2.
Vijay Singh defeated Peter Hanson, 19 holes.
Niclas Fasth defeated Richard Green, 6 and 5.

(Each losing player received $40,000.)

SECOND ROUND

Woods defeated Oberholser, 3 and 2.
Baddeley defeated Toms by default.
Casey defeated Dredge, 2 and 1.
Choi defeated Poulter, 19 holes.
Byrd defeated Romero, 6 and 4.
Stenson defeated Immelman, 25 holes.
Austin defeated Scott, 19 holes.
Weekley defeated Garcia, 3 and 1.
Stricker defeated Mahan, 20 holes.
Cabrera defeated Donald, 2 and 1.
Montgomerie defeated Howell, 1-up.
Cink defeated Harrington, 2-up.
Appleby defeated Mickelson, 2 and 1.
Leonard defeated Westwood, 2 and 1.
Pampling defeated O'Hern, 5 and 4.
Singh defeated Fasth, 1-up.

(Each losing player received $90,000.)

THIRD ROUND

Woods defeated Baddeley, 20 holes.
Choi defeated Casey, 2-up.
Stenson defeated Byrd, 1-up.
Austin defeated Weekley, 3 and 2.
Cabrera defeated Stricker, 4 and 3.
Cink defeated Montgomerie, 4 and 2.
Leonard defeated Appleby, 3 and 2.
Singh defeated Pampling, 25 holes.

(Each losing player received $130,000.)

QUARTER-FINALS

Woods defeated Choi, 3 and 2.
Stenson defeated Austin, 2-up.
Cink defeated Cabrera, 3 and 2.
Leonard defeated Singh, 1-up.

(Each losing player received $260,000.)

SEMI-FINALS

Woods defeated Stenson, 2-up.
Cink defeated Leonard, 4 and 2.

PLAYOFF FOR THIRD-FOURTH PLACE

Stenson defeated Leonard, 3 and 2.

(Stenson earned $575,000; Leonard earned $475,000.)

FINAL

Woods defeated Cink, 8 and 7.

(Woods earned $1,350,000; Cink earned $800,000.)

Mayakoba Golf Classic

El Camaleon, Riviera Maya, Mexico
Par 35-35–70; 6,923 yards

February 21-24
purse, $3,500,000

	SCORES				TOTAL	MONEY
Brian Gay	66	67	62	69	264	$630,000
Steve Marino	67	69	64	66	266	378,000
Matt Kuchar	68	69	64	67	268	203,000
John Merrick	64	68	69	67	268	203,000
Cliff Kresge	68	71	64	66	269	140,000
Patrick Sheehan	71	67	67	65	270	126,000
Peter Lonard	68	71	64	68	271	112,875
Tim Petrovic	67	71	67	66	271	112,875
Nick Flanagan	75	66	68	64	273	98,000
Roland Thatcher	71	73	61	68	273	98,000
Esteban Toledo	70	69	63	72	274	87,500
Briny Baird	68	73	68	66	275	64,500
Joe Durant	71	69	66	69	275	64,500
Bob May	69	71	67	68	275	64,500
Joe Ogilvie	70	71	64	70	275	64,500
Corey Pavin	72	68	67	68	275	64,500
Paul Stankowski	71	72	64	68	275	64,500
Chris Stroud	68	71	66	70	275	64,500
Alex Cejka	70	73	68	65	276	45,500
Kenneth Ferrie	65	72	72	67	276	45,500
Greg Kraft	67	72	67	70	276	45,500
Matt Jones	67	72	70	68	277	32,491.67
Larry Mize	65	74	69	69	277	32,491.67
Chris Riley	72	68	69	68	277	32,491.67
Michael Sim	69	69	68	71	277	32,491.67
Robert Damron	65	75	67	70	277	32,491.67
Tim Herron	70	70	64	73	277	32,491.66
Steve Allan	71	72	69	66	278	22,290.63
David Lutterus	65	69	73	71	278	22,290.63
Alvaro Quiros	68	73	68	69	278	22,290.63
Joey Sindelar	70	74	64	70	278	22,290.63
Craig Kanada	67	73	66	72	278	22,290.62
Neal Lancaster	70	70	68	70	278	22,290.62
Kevin Streelman	69	70	67	72	278	22,290.62
Tim Wilkinson	67	76	70	65	278	22,290.62
Brad Adamonis	68	71	72	68	279	16,129.17
Colt Knost	70	70	69	70	279	16,129.17
Jim McGovern	72	72	68	67	279	16,129.17
Dean Wilson	67	75	67	70	279	16,129.17
Scott Sterling	70	69	68	72	279	16,129.16
Ron Whittaker	68	73	67	71	279	16,129.16
Cameron Beckman	67	71	75	67	280	11,900
Marco Dawson	72	71	69	68	280	11,900
Michael Letzig	71	73	71	65	280	11,900

	SCORES				TOTAL	MONEY
Shigeki Maruyama	69	68	71	72	280	11,900
Parker McLachlin	67	74	69	70	280	11,900
Nick Price	70	68	68	74	280	11,900
Justin Bolli	68	74	70	69	281	8,796.67
Richard S. Johnson	70	70	70	71	281	8,796.67
Kevin Stadler	67	73	74	67	281	8,796.67
Jay Williamson	69	74	70	68	281	8,796.67
Alejandro Canizares	71	73	70	67	281	8,796.66
Doug LaBelle	70	71	73	67	281	8,796.66
Glen Day	70	73	70	69	282	8,085
Tommy Gainey	66	74	73	69	282	8,085
Mark Brooks	71	71	70	71	283	7,875
Gavin Coles	70	73	70	70	283	7,875
Len Mattiace	70	74	70	69	283	7,875
Jin Park	69	75	68	71	283	7,875
John Daly	66	73	71	74	284	7,630
Scott Piercy	72	71	71	70	284	7,630
Chez Reavie	70	73	68	73	284	7,630
Brad Elder	69	71	75	70	285	7,420
Fred Funk	73	71	66	75	285	7,420
Jesper Parnevik	72	71	70	72	285	7,420
Harrison Frazar	71	72	73	70	286	7,210
Jon Mills	73	71	70	72	286	7,210
John Morse	71	72	72	71	286	7,210
Jose Coceres	67	74	72	74	287	7,035
Jimmy Walker	72	69	73	73	287	7,035
Jason Dufner	70	73	69	77	289	6,895
Marc Turnesa	72	72	70	75	289	6,895
Brett Rumford	71	73	77	71	292	6,790
Martin Laird	68	73	74	80	295	6,720
Bob Burns	74	70	74	81	299	6,650

Honda Classic

PGA National, Champion Course,
Palm Beach Gardens, Florida
Par 35-35–70; 7,241 yards

February 28-March 2
purse, $5,500,000

	SCORES				TOTAL	MONEY
Ernie Els	67	70	70	67	274	$990,000
Luke Donald	64	74	66	71	275	594,000
Nathan Green	71	70	68	67	276	374,000
Robert Allenby	69	68	70	70	277	227,333.34
Mark Calcavecchia	70	67	67	73	277	227,333.33
Matt Jones	66	67	71	73	277	227,333.33
Alex Cejka	69	71	68	70	278	160,050
Brian Davis	65	67	73	73	278	160,050
Mathew Goggin	71	70	68	69	278	160,050
Michael Letzig	70	69	68	71	278	160,050
John Mallinger	68	67	73	70	278	160,050
Jose Coceres	68	69	68	74	279	115,500
Ben Crane	69	66	71	73	279	115,500
Brett Quigley	67	70	70	72	279	115,500
Shane Bertsch	70	69	71	70	280	88,000
Dudley Hart	68	66	72	74	280	88,000
Cliff Kresge	70	71	66	73	280	88,000
John Merrick	72	69	68	71	280	88,000
Justin Rose	72	70	71	67	280	88,000
Chad Campbell	70	73	67	71	281	64,075
Joe Durant	68	69	73	71	281	64,075

	SCORES				TOTAL	MONEY
Jerry Kelly	68	71	72	70	281	64,075
Kenny Perry	73	67	69	72	281	64,075
Bart Bryant	69	72	70	71	282	44,550
Steve Marino	69	71	72	70	282	44,550
Jesper Parnevik	68	75	69	70	282	44,550
Carl Pettersson	72	66	70	74	282	44,550
Roland Thatcher	68	73	67	74	282	44,550
Camilo Villegas	72	69	72	69	282	44,550
Woody Austin	70	73	69	71	283	31,968.75
Paul Goydos	68	74	70	71	283	31,968.75
J.J. Henry	69	73	70	71	283	31,968.75
Zach Johnson	74	69	68	72	283	31,968.75
Justin Leonard	69	71	69	74	283	31,968.75
Peter Lonard	71	71	69	72	283	31,968.75
Davis Love	70	73	69	71	283	31,968.75
Tim Wilkinson	67	74	67	75	283	31,968.75
Robert Gamez	71	68	73	72	284	23,650
Kevin Sutherland	67	74	71	72	284	23,650
Nicholas Thompson	71	72	72	69	284	23,650
Marc Turnesa	70	71	69	74	284	23,650
Jimmy Walker	67	75	70	72	284	23,650
Sergio Garcia	73	69	70	73	285	17,636.67
Matt Kuchar	73	67	69	76	285	17,636.67
John Senden	77	67	69	72	285	17,636.67
Heath Slocum	73	71	69	72	285	17,636.67
Kenneth Ferrie	69	72	67	77	285	17,636.66
Arron Oberholser	69	75	65	76	285	17,636.66
Brad Adamonis	76	66	69	75	286	12,980
Eric Axley	69	71	72	74	286	12,980
Briny Baird	70	69	76	71	286	12,980
Alejandro Canizares	74	68	70	74	286	12,980
Carlos Franco	72	72	69	73	286	12,980
Robert Garrigus	71	70	71	74	286	12,980
Richard Green	72	71	71	72	286	12,980
Mathias Gronberg	75	69	68	74	286	12,980
Richard S. Johnson	72	69	71	74	286	12,980
Anthony Kim	72	69	70	75	286	12,980
Vaughn Taylor	70	69	74	73	286	12,980
Retief Goosen	73	70	71	73	287	11,880
David Lutterus	74	69	71	73	287	11,880
Jeff Maggert	70	71	71	75	287	11,880
Tag Ridings	69	75	73	70	287	11,880
Kevin Streelman	73	71	69	74	287	11,880
Ben Curtis	73	71	66	78	288	11,385
Scott Hoch	75	69	72	72	288	11,385
Will MacKenzie	69	74	69	76	288	11,385
Patrick Sheehan	70	74	72	72	288	11,385
Frank Lickliter	72	71	72	74	289	11,055
Charlie Wi	72	70	70	77	289	11,055
Glen Day	73	70	74	73	290	10,890
Pete Jordan	75	67	72	77	291	10,725
Y.E. Yang	69	71	80	71	291	10,725
Alan Morin	72	72	75	73	292	10,505
Boo Weekley	70	72	70	80	292	10,505
Tim Herron	69	73	73	78	293	10,340
Jin Park	73	71	71	79	294	10,230

PODS Championship

Innisbrook Resort & Golf Club, Copperhead Course,
Tampa Bay, Florida
Par 36-35–71; 7,340 yards

March 6-9
purse, $5,300,000

	SCORES				TOTAL	MONEY
Sean O'Hair	69	71	71	69	280	$954,000
Ryuji Imada	72	70	72	68	282	294,591.67
Troy Matteson	70	72	71	69	282	294,591.67
George McNeill	70	72	71	69	282	294,591.67
John Senden	67	74	74	67	282	294,591.67
Stewart Cink	66	73	69	74	282	294,591.66
Billy Mayfair	68	71	71	72	282	294,591.66
Rod Pampling	70	71	73	69	283	159,000
Brandt Snedeker	69	68	73	73	283	159,000
Stuart Appleby	66	73	74	71	284	127,200
Lee Janzen	65	74	75	70	284	127,200
Geoff Ogilvy	69	72	69	74	284	127,200
Tom Pernice, Jr.	67	73	71	73	284	127,200
Robert Allenby	70	73	73	69	285	79,617.78
Bart Bryant	65	74	73	73	285	79,617.78
Mathew Goggin	72	72	71	70	285	79,617.78
Steve Marino	70	74	71	70	285	79,617.78
Corey Pavin	75	70	69	71	285	79,617.78
Justin Rose	70	74	71	70	285	79,617.78
Kevin Sutherland	74	68	70	73	285	79,617.78
Mark Calcavecchia	69	70	73	73	285	79,617.77
Steve Stricker	70	74	75	66	285	79,617.77
Ryan Armour	69	73	72	72	286	44,671.43
Rich Beem	69	74	71	72	286	44,671.43
Jeff Maggert	66	72	77	71	286	44,671.43
Hunter Mahan	72	70	73	71	286	44,671.43
Carl Pettersson	67	75	74	70	286	44,671.43
Charlie Wi	69	73	74	70	286	44,671.43
Nick Watney	68	74	77	67	286	44,671.42
Nathan Green	67	77	71	72	287	32,197.50
Bill Haas	70	73	72	72	287	32,197.50
Jerry Kelly	67	75	74	71	287	32,197.50
Michael Letzig	69	71	75	72	287	32,197.50
Kenny Perry	66	75	75	71	287	32,197.50
Heath Slocum	69	71	76	71	287	32,197.50
Shane Bertsch	71	74	73	70	288	24,424.17
Daniel Chopra	70	72	74	72	288	24,424.17
Shigeki Maruyama	69	71	74	74	288	24,424.17
Tim Petrovic	72	68	74	74	288	24,424.17
Jonathan Byrd	67	76	70	75	288	24,424.16
Chez Reavie	70	73	76	69	288	24,424.16
Paul Casey	67	72	75	75	289	18,550
Fred Couples	69	74	73	73	289	18,550
Ben Crane	71	73	73	72	289	18,550
Steve Flesch	72	73	72	72	289	18,550
Robert Garrigus	70	74	75	70	289	18,550
Chad Campbell	71	72	73	74	290	14,013.20
Alex Cejka	69	72	73	76	290	14,013.20
Todd Hamilton	70	74	76	70	290	14,013.20
Patrick Sheehan	69	73	74	74	290	14,013.20
Mark Wilson	72	73	73	72	290	14,013.20
Steve Elkington	73	68	73	77	291	12,235.43
Bob Estes	71	73	74	73	291	12,235.43
Robert Gamez	75	69	74	73	291	12,235.43
Lucas Glover	71	72	74	74	291	12,235.43
Nicholas Thompson	67	75	74	75	291	12,235.43

	SCORES				TOTAL	MONEY
D.J. Trahan	68	74	74	75	291	12,235.43
Stephen Ames	71	74	73	73	291	12,235.42
Matt Jones	72	72	73	75	292	11,713
Peter Lonard	69	75	73	75	292	11,713
Billy Andrade	69	74	74	76	293	11,395
Olin Browne	70	73	75	75	293	11,395
James Driscoll	71	74	73	75	293	11,395
Nick Flanagan	70	75	74	74	293	11,395
Charles Howell	71	74	75	74	294	11,077
Trevor Immelman	72	73	75	74	294	11,077
Ken Duke	70	75	75	75	295	10,865
Tag Ridings	70	70	75	80	295	10,865
Frank Lickliter	68	73	75	80	296	10,653
Jeff Overton	68	73	79	76	296	10,653
Derek Lamely	70	74	73	82	299	10,494

Arnold Palmer Invitational

Bay Hill Club & Lodge, Orlando, Florida
Par 35-35–70; 7,157 yards

March 13-16
purse, $5,800,000

	SCORES				TOTAL	MONEY
Tiger Woods	70	68	66	66	270	$1,044,000
Bart Bryant	68	68	68	67	271	626,400
Cliff Kresge	67	68	71	67	273	301,600
Sean O'Hair	72	69	63	69	273	301,600
Vijay Singh	66	65	73	69	273	301,600
Ken Duke	67	67	72	68	274	201,550
Hunter Mahan	68	72	65	69	274	201,550
Alex Cejka	67	70	71	68	276	150,800
Niclas Fasth	71	66	73	66	276	150,800
Tom Lehman	66	69	71	70	276	150,800
Tom Pernice, Jr.	73	66	68	69	276	150,800
Carl Pettersson	68	65	74	69	276	150,800
Bubba Watson	67	69	68	72	276	150,800
Retief Goosen	70	71	68	68	277	104,400
Geoff Ogilvy	72	69	70	66	277	104,400
Brandt Snedeker	70	70	68	69	277	104,400
Woody Austin	71	67	72	68	278	84,100
Fredrik Jacobson	71	70	67	70	278	84,100
Frank Lickliter	69	71	68	70	278	84,100
Lee Westwood	66	68	72	72	278	84,100
Chad Campbell	68	68	72	71	279	51,620
Brian Gay	70	71	68	70	279	51,620
John Mallinger	69	70	70	70	279	51,620
Steve Marino	75	67	66	71	279	51,620
Pablo Martin	71	71	68	69	279	51,620
Phil Mickelson	72	67	71	69	279	51,620
Dicky Pride	71	70	67	71	279	51,620
Richard Sterne	69	71	70	69	279	51,620
Nick Watney	69	67	70	73	279	51,620
Boo Weekley	71	69	70	69	279	51,620
J.J. Henry	65	70	76	69	280	31,513.34
Billy Mayfair	69	71	71	69	280	31,513.34
D.J. Trahan	70	72	70	68	280	31,513.34
Tim Clark	68	70	72	70	280	31,513.33
Jim Furyk	67	67	73	73	280	31,513.33
Sergio Garcia	70	66	73	71	280	31,513.33
Joe Ogilvie	70	70	70	70	280	31,513.33
Pat Perez	73	65	70	72	280	31,513.33

	SCORES				TOTAL	MONEY
Vaughn Taylor	68	67	72	73	280	31,513.33
*Webb Simpson	71	71	70	68	280	
Lucas Glover	66	75	70	70	281	23,780
D.A. Points	68	68	73	72	281	23,780
John Rollins	70	68	71	72	281	23,780
Brian Bateman	69	70	75	68	282	19,720
Will MacKenzie	70	71	70	71	282	19,720
Bo Van Pelt	69	73	71	69	282	19,720
Camilo Villegas	69	70	73	70	282	19,720
Ian Poulter	72	70	72	69	283	15,099.34
John Senden	70	72	72	69	283	15,099.34
Trevor Immelman	73	64	75	71	283	15,099.33
Matt Jones	70	68	72	73	283	15,099.33
Kenny Perry	69	72	72	70	283	15,099.33
Andres Romero	68	71	73	71	283	15,099.33
Brian Davis	75	64	68	77	284	13,363.20
Dustin Johnson	68	69	75	72	284	13,363.20
Richard Johnson	69	70	70	75	284	13,363.20
Zach Johnson	70	71	72	71	284	13,363.20
Mark Wilson	70	69	71	74	284	13,363.20
Stephen Ames	74	68	72	71	285	12,876
Ben Crane	70	68	75	72	285	12,876
J.B. Holmes	71	67	74	73	285	12,876
Davis Love	72	69	73	72	286	12,586
George McNeill	70	72	71	73	286	12,586
Fred Couples	65	73	78	71	287	12,238
Steve Elkington	74	68	71	74	287	12,238
Paul Goydos	73	67	74	73	287	12,238
Andrew Magee	72	70	75	70	287	12,238
Robert Gamez	72	68	76	73	289	11,890
Marc Turnesa	70	70	77	72	289	11,890
Steve Lowery	68	72	79	73	292	11,716
Heath Slocum	71	70	73	80	294	11,600

WGC - CA Championship

Doral Golf Resort & Spa, Blue Course, Miami, Florida
Par 36-36—72; 7,266 yards
(Event completed on Monday—rain and darkness.)

March 20-24
purse, $8,000,000

	SCORES				TOTAL	MONEY
Geoff Ogilvy	65	67	68	71	271	$1,350,000
Jim Furyk	69	71	64	68	272	530,000
Retief Goosen	71	69	64	68	272	530,000
Vijay Singh	73	68	63	68	272	530,000
Tiger Woods	67	66	72	68	273	285,000
Steve Stricker	71	68	73	63	275	198,333.34
Nick O'Hern	67	75	67	66	275	198,333.33
Graeme Storm	71	70	63	71	275	198,333.33
Zach Johnson	69	72	67	68	276	147,500
Adam Scott	67	68	69	72	276	147,500
Soren Kjeldsen	69	71	71	66	277	125,000
K.J. Choi	70	70	67	71	278	106,166.67
Anders Hansen	67	71	67	73	278	106,166.67
Tim Clark	71	69	66	72	278	106,166.66
Stephen Ames	73	68	68	70	279	86,700
Aaron Baddeley	69	74	70	66	279	86,700
Sergio Garcia	69	73	69	68	279	86,700
Gregory Havret	68	74	68	69	279	86,700
Justin Rose	70	71	70	68	279	86,700

	SCORES				TOTAL	MONEY
Robert Allenby	69	75	66	70	280	75,000
Stewart Cink	66	74	71	69	280	75,000
Luke Donald	68	72	70	70	280	75,000
Phil Mickelson	67	74	70	69	280	75,000
John Rollins	74	71	67	68	280	75,000
Mike Weir	73	69	67	71	280	75,000
Miguel Angel Jimenez	65	74	71	71	281	66,500
Jeev Milkha Singh	68	70	70	73	281	66,500
Toru Taniguchi	68	73	72	68	281	66,500
Camilo Villegas	71	72	68	70	281	66,500
Mark Calcavecchia	68	71	71	72	282	62,500
Robert Karlsson	68	70	70	74	282	62,500
Andres Romero	68	72	73	69	282	62,500
Boo Weekley	72	73	69	68	282	62,500
Stuart Appleby	73	71	68	71	283	57,500
Daniel Chopra	72	70	69	72	283	57,500
Ross Fisher	68	73	70	72	283	57,500
Ryuji Imada	68	73	73	69	283	57,500
Justin Leonard	69	74	70	70	283	57,500
Lee Westwood	71	72	72	68	283	57,500
J.B. Holmes	69	72	75	68	284	52,500
Trevor Immelman	70	74	70	70	284	52,500
Brendan Jones	76	75	66	67	284	52,500
Scott Verplank	71	70	74	69	284	52,500
Woody Austin	70	70	74	71	285	48,875
Niclas Fasth	72	69	70	74	285	48,875
Hunter Mahan	72	72	71	70	285	48,875
Richard Sterne	71	77	67	70	285	48,875
Graeme McDowell	72	71	70	73	286	47,000
Andrew McLardy	74	74	70	68	286	47,000
Brandt Snedeker	74	70	72	70	286	47,000
Paul Casey	72	75	67	73	287	44,750
S.S.P. Chowrasia	74	73	68	72	287	44,750
Nick Dougherty	70	73	71	73	287	44,750
Richard Green	74	72	71	70	287	44,750
Charles Howell	69	76	72	70	287	44,750
Arron Oberholser	72	70	72	73	287	44,750
Martin Kaymer	68	74	73	73	288	42,250
Ian Poulter	71	72	72	73	288	42,250
Henrik Stenson	72	72	76	68	288	42,250
D.J. Trahan	74	73	75	66	288	42,250
Peter Hanson	71	74	73	73	291	40,250
Chapchai Nirat	70	70	74	77	291	40,250
Paul Sheehan	72	73	72	74	291	40,250
Brett Wetterich	70	74	76	71	291	40,250
Jonathan Byrd	74	74	72	72	292	38,500
Anton Haig	72	80	73	67	292	38,500
Colin Montgomerie	75	74	70	73	292	38,500
Louis Oosthuizen	74	72	70	77	293	37,625
Liang Wen-chong	74	74	71	74	293	37,625
Soren Hansen	77	77	68	72	294	37,000
James Kingston	74	75	68	77	294	37,000
Rory Sabbatini	72	74	69	79	294	37,000
Shingo Katayama	75	76	72	72	295	36,375
Craig Parry	73	75	72	75	295	36,375
Ernie Els	74	75	73	74	296	36,000
Mark Brown	73	74	76	74	297	35,750
Heath Slocum	74	72	78	74	298	35,500
Angel Cabrera	75	74	68		WD	
Sean O'Hair	73	75			WD	

Puerto Rico Open

Trump International Golf Club, Rio Grande, Puerto Rico

March 20-23

Par 36-36–72; 7,569 yards

purse, $3,500,000

	SCORES				TOTAL	MONEY
Greg Kraft	69	66	69	70	274	$630,000
Jerry Kelly	67	66	72	70	275	308,000
Bo Van Pelt	64	68	71	72	275	308,000
Briny Baird	67	68	69	72	276	154,000
Kevin Stadler	70	69	70	67	276	154,000
Tommy Armour	72	67	67	71	277	117,250
Marco Dawson	68	69	69	71	277	117,250
Tim Wilkinson	71	67	70	69	277	117,250
Brenden Pappas	67	69	69	73	278	101,500
Steve Allan	70	70	71	69	280	87,500
Larry Mize	71	68	72	69	280	87,500
Ted Purdy	66	68	73	73	280	87,500
John Merrick	68	70	71	72	281	70,000
Jon Mills	73	68	70	70	281	70,000
Ryan Armour	69	74	71	68	282	54,250
Ryan Blaum	69	66	72	75	282	54,250
Gavin Coles	71	69	69	73	282	54,250
Ben Curtis	71	70	70	71	282	54,250
Bill Haas	74	69	70	69	282	54,250
Kyle Thompson	66	72	70	74	282	54,250
Billy Andrade	68	72	72	71	283	33,850
Paul Claxton	70	70	70	73	283	33,850
Carlos Franco	72	68	72	71	283	33,850
Shaun Micheel	71	72	69	71	283	33,850
Chris Riley	70	69	69	75	283	33,850
Nicholas Thompson	67	71	70	75	283	33,850
Bob Tway	71	68	70	74	283	33,850
Andrew Buckle	70	72	73	69	284	22,775
Robert Damron	73	68	71	72	284	22,775
Lee Janzen	73	71	69	71	284	22,775
Neal Lancaster	73	70	69	72	284	22,775
Alvaro Quiros	69	70	74	71	284	22,775
Chris Smith	73	69	68	74	284	22,775
Diego Vanegas	70	70	69	75	284	22,775
Tom Byrum	73	68	73	71	285	17,631.25
Tom Gillis	69	70	73	73	285	17,631.25
Jin Park	69	68	73	75	285	17,631.25
Garrett Willis	71	71	68	75	285	17,631.25
Ronnie Black	71	70	72	73	286	12,294.55
Alejandro Canizares	73	71	69	73	286	12,294.55
Tommy Gainey	72	69	72	73	286	12,294.55
Mathias Gronberg	70	70	71	75	286	12,294.55
Stephen Leaney	71	70	71	74	286	12,294.55
Ryan Palmer	72	68	72	74	286	12,294.55
Eric Axley	69	73	72	72	286	12,294.54
James Driscoll	70	71	70	75	286	12,294.54
Kenneth Ferrie	71	70	70	75	286	12,294.54
Jeff Overton	67	73	74	72	286	12,294.54
Travis Perkins	71	71	73	71	286	12,294.54
Joe Durant	69	73	73	72	287	8,522.50
Pablo Martin	72	70	74	71	287	8,522.50
Jimmy Walker	73	71	73	70	287	8,522.50
Jay Williamson	71	71	69	76	287	8,522.50
Cameron Beckman	71	73	71	73	288	7,910
Brian Gay	69	70	75	74	288	7,910
Skip Kendall	69	72	76	71	288	7,910
Tim Petrovic	74	70	70	74	288	7,910

	SCORES				TOTAL	MONEY
Michael Sim	72	70	75	71	288	7,910
Bob Sowards	68	72	72	76	288	7,910
Esteban Toledo	69	75	71	73	288	7,910
Jason Allred	71	69	72	77	289	7,350
Chad Collins	71	70	75	73	289	7,350
Jason Dufner	68	75	73	73	289	7,350
Dan Forsman	69	72	72	76	289	7,350
Harrison Frazar	73	70	74	72	289	7,350
Tom Scherrer	72	71	70	76	289	7,350
Miguel Suarez	68	72	77	72	289	7,350
Chip Sullivan	73	71	73	72	289	7,350
Duffy Waldorf	70	74	71	74	289	7,350
John Morse	73	71	72	74	290	7,000
Kent Jones	72	72	72	75	291	6,930
John Riegger	71	70	72	79	292	6,860
Patrick Sheehan	72	71	74	76	293	6,790
Dudley Hart	73	69	73	82	297	6,720
Brent Geiberger	74	68	74	84	300	6,650

Zurich Classic

TPC Louisiana, Avondale, Louisiana
Par 36-36–72; 7,341 yards

March 27-30
purse, $6,200,000

	SCORES				TOTAL	MONEY
Andres Romero	73	69	65	68	275	$1,116,000
Peter Lonard	67	70	70	69	276	669,600
Tim Wilkinson	71	68	71	67	277	421,600
Woody Austin	69	71	67	71	278	256,266.67
Padraig Harrington	71	70	68	69	278	256,266.67
Nicholas Thompson	69	71	67	71	278	256,266.66
Tim Petrovic	74	68	66	71	279	193,233.34
Tommy Armour	70	68	75	66	279	193,233.33
John Merrick	72	67	67	73	279	193,233.33
Marco Dawson	71	68	70	71	280	161,200
Steve Elkington	68	71	72	69	280	161,200
Briny Baird	67	69	71	74	281	110,825
Jonathan Byrd	72	71	67	71	281	110,825
James Driscoll	75	67	73	66	281	110,825
Dudley Hart	73	69	68	71	281	110,825
Parker McLachlin	72	67	71	71	281	110,825
Pat Perez	71	70	71	69	281	110,825
John Senden	74	69	66	72	281	110,825
Liang Wen-chong	71	72	69	69	281	110,825
Jason Bohn	74	68	72	68	282	74,813.34
Jon Mills	71	70	69	72	282	74,813.33
Roland Thatcher	70	70	70	72	282	74,813.33
Craig Barlow	72	71	68	72	283	48,670
Cameron Beckman	68	71	75	69	283	48,670
Jose Coceres	75	68	68	72	283	48,670
Steve Flesch	69	72	71	71	283	48,670
Carlos Franco	71	70	72	70	283	48,670
Nathan Green	71	69	71	72	283	48,670
Jeff Maggert	70	70	71	72	283	48,670
Kenny Perry	71	71	69	72	283	48,670
Carl Pettersson	71	70	71	71	283	48,670
Charles Warren	70	74	68	71	283	48,670
Daniel Chopra	71	73	66	74	284	30,724.45
Bob Estes	72	72	68	72	284	30,724.45
Jeff Quinney	71	73	70	70	284	30,724.45

	SCORES				TOTAL	MONEY
Chip Sullivan	76	68	72	68	284	30,724.45
Mark Calcavecchia	71	71	73	69	284	30,724.44
Brian Davis	71	68	73	72	284	30,724.44
Todd Hamilton	70	70	69	75	284	30,724.44
Tom Pernice, Jr.	73	71	71	69	284	30,724.44
Jay Williamson	68	69	72	75	284	30,724.44
John Mallinger	69	73	72	71	285	19,948.50
Jin Park	70	74	72	69	285	19,948.50
Ted Purdy	70	71	72	72	285	19,948.50
Chez Reavie	67	72	74	72	285	19,948.50
Patrick Sheehan	69	73	70	73	285	19,948.50
Kevin Sutherland	71	71	70	73	285	19,948.50
Nick Watney	71	67	76	71	285	19,948.50
Dean Wilson	66	73	75	71	285	19,948.50
Mathew Goggin	73	70	71	72	286	14,738.29
Mathias Gronberg	75	69	72	70	286	14,738.29
Robert Karlsson	70	73	72	71	286	14,738.29
Frank Lickliter	72	71	72	71	286	14,738.29
Brian Bateman	73	70	69	74	286	14,738.28
Shigeki Maruyama	70	68	75	73	286	14,738.28
Rocco Mediate	70	70	73	73	286	14,738.28
Justin Bolli	74	68	73	72	287	13,640
Bubba Dickerson	70	73	75	69	287	13,640
Robert Gamez	70	74	75	68	287	13,640
Retief Goosen	73	71	74	69	287	13,640
J.J. Henry	74	68	69	76	287	13,640
Zach Johnson	72	71	74	70	287	13,640
Scott Sterling	71	73	72	71	287	13,640
Paul Goydos	74	70	71	73	288	12,834
Mark Hensby	74	68	70	76	288	12,834
Matt Jones	74	68	74	72	288	12,834
Troy Matteson	69	73	72	74	288	12,834
Chris Stroud	72	71	73	72	288	12,834
Johnson Wagner	71	72	76	69	288	12,834
Tim Clark	73	66	74	76	289	12,152
Harrison Frazar	69	73	71	76	289	12,152
Cliff Kresge	75	68	70	76	289	12,152
George McNeill	71	73	72	73	289	12,152
Bubba Watson	73	69	75	72	289	12,152
Alex Cejka	72	72	75	71	290	11,656
Joe Durant	69	71	77	73	290	11,656
Jonathan Kaye	74	70	75	71	290	11,656
Rich Beem	73	71	73	74	291	11,408
Brandt Jobe	70	74	76	72	292	11,284
Brett Rumford	72	72	72	77	293	11,160

Shell Houston Open

Redstone Golf Club, Tournament Course, Humble, Texas
Par 36-36–72; 7,457 yards

April 3-6
purse, $5,600,000

	SCORES				TOTAL	MONEY
Johnson Wagner	63	69	69	71	272	$1,008,000
Chad Campbell	73	64	65	72	274	492,800
Geoff Ogilvy	67	73	66	68	274	492,800
Fred Couples	73	69	67	66	275	246,400
Billy Mayfair	72	68	69	66	275	246,400
Bob Estes	71	69	64	72	276	194,600
Charley Hoffman	65	70	69	72	276	194,600
Jason Day	73	71	69	65	278	162,400
Pat Perez	69	73	72	64	278	162,400

		SCORES			TOTAL	MONEY
Kevin Sutherland	70	70	71	67	278	162,400
Bart Bryant	69	74	66	70	279	128,800
K.J. Choi	74	66	69	70	279	128,800
Steve Stricker	66	76	66	71	279	128,800
Ryan Armour	73	69	67	71	280	92,400
Aaron Baddeley	72	72	65	71	280	92,400
Steve Elkington	67	74	69	70	280	92,400
Lucas Glover	69	69	70	72	280	92,400
Jeff Quinney	72	68	70	70	280	92,400
Kevin Streelman	72	69	70	69	280	92,400
Dean Wilson	67	75	70	69	281	67,573.34
Ben Crane	74	65	70	72	281	67,573.33
Mathew Goggin	71	64	72	74	281	67,573.33
Stuart Appleby	70	70	72	70	282	53,760
Phil Mickelson	72	68	71	71	282	53,760
Rod Pampling	70	72	68	72	282	53,760
Padraig Harrington	71	73	71	68	283	38,920
J.J. Henry	69	72	71	71	283	38,920
Davis Love	69	72	69	73	283	38,920
John Merrick	71	69	72	71	283	38,920
Shaun Micheel	71	72	71	69	283	38,920
Kevin Na	76	68	68	71	283	38,920
Joe Ogilvie	74	68	70	71	283	38,920
Jose Maria Olazabal	69	70	73	71	283	38,920
Robert Allenby	75	68	69	72	284	30,240
Anders Hansen	69	71	75	69	284	30,240
Chez Reavie	70	71	70	73	284	30,240
Scott Sterling	70	71	73	71	285	26,880
Nicholas Thompson	69	70	78	68	285	26,880
Kenneth Ferrie	75	69	71	71	286	21,280
Tim Herron	72	70	72	72	286	21,280
Fredrik Jacobson	72	72	72	70	286	21,280
Justin Leonard	68	76	71	71	286	21,280
Frank Lickliter	75	67	72	72	286	21,280
John Riegger	71	70	69	76	286	21,280
Jeev Milkha Singh	73	70	72	71	286	21,280
Omar Uresti	68	76	69	73	286	21,280
Michael Allen	72	71	70	74	287	13,932.80
Briny Baird	67	77	73	70	287	13,932.80
Ben Curtis	69	72	72	74	287	13,932.80
Marco Dawson	72	72	70	73	287	13,932.80
Mark Hensby	70	74	73	70	287	13,932.80
Charles Howell	71	72	71	73	287	13,932.80
Craig Kanada	70	71	73	73	287	13,932.80
J.L. Lewis	72	72	72	71	287	13,932.80
Jeff Overton	71	71	69	76	287	13,932.80
Tim Wilkinson	73	69	71	74	287	13,932.80
Harrison Frazar	72	69	76	71	288	12,432
Martin Laird	69	71	74	74	288	12,432
Stephen Leaney	72	71	73	72	288	12,432
Michael Sim	72	72	70	74	288	12,432
Bubba Watson	68	72	74	74	288	12,432
Craig Barlow	70	74	71	74	289	11,928
Shane Bertsch	72	69	75	73	289	11,928
Robert Garrigus	71	67	75	76	289	11,928
Charlie Wi	71	69	77	72	289	11,928
Nathan Green	74	70	72	74	290	11,480
Steve Marino	71	73	72	74	290	11,480
Brett Quigley	68	72	68	82	290	11,480
Y.E. Yang	71	73	73	73	290	11,480
Brett Wetterich	73	70	72	78	293	11,200
Carl Pettersson	70	74	73	78	295	11,088
Justin Bolli	74	70	75	78	297	10,976

Masters Tournament

Augusta National Golf Club, Augusta, Georgia
Par 36-36–72; 7,445 yards

April 10-13
purse, $7,000,000

	SCORES				TOTAL	MONEY
Trevor Immelman	68	68	69	75	280	$1,350,000
Tiger Woods	72	71	68	72	283	810,000
Stewart Cink	72	69	71	72	284	435,000
Brandt Snedeker	69	68	70	77	284	435,000
Phil Mickelson	71	68	75	72	286	273,750
Padraig Harrington	74	71	69	72	286	273,750
Steve Flesch	72	67	69	78	286	273,750
Miguel Angel Jimenez	77	70	72	68	287	217,500
Robert Karlsson	70	73	71	73	287	217,500
Andres Romero	72	72	70	73	287	217,500
Nick Watney	75	70	72	71	288	172,500
Lee Westwood	69	73	73	73	288	172,500
Paul Casey	71	69	69	79	288	172,500
Stuart Appleby	76	70	72	71	289	135,000
Vijay Singh	72	71	72	74	289	135,000
Sean O'Hair	72	71	71	75	289	135,000
Henrik Stenson	74	72	72	72	290	112,500
Mike Weir	73	68	75	74	290	112,500
Retief Goosen	71	71	72	76	290	112,500
Bubba Watson	74	71	73	73	291	84,300
Justin Leonard	72	74	72	73	291	84,300
Brian Bateman	69	76	72	74	292	84,300
Zach Johnson	70	76	68	77	291	84,300
Boo Weekley	72	74	68	77	291	84,300
Richard Sterne	73	72	73	74	292	54,844
Angel Cabrera	73	72	73	74	292	54,844
Stephen Ames	70	70	77	75	292	54,844
Jeev Milkha Singh	71	74	72	75	292	54,844
J.B. Holmes	73	70	73	76	292	54,844
Adam Scott	75	71	70	76	292	54,844
Arron Oberholser	71	70	74	77	292	54,844
Ian Poulter	70	69	75	78	292	54,844
Heath Slocum	71	76	77	69	293	42,375
Nick Dougherty	74	69	74	76	293	42,375
Jim Furyk	70	73	73	77	293	42,375
Todd Hamilton	74	73	75	73	295	36,875
Justin Rose	68	78	73	76	295	36,875
Johnson Wagner	72	74	74	75	295	36,875
Geoff Ogilvy	75	71	76	74	296	33,000
Niclas Fasth	75	70	76	75	296	33,000
K.J. Choi	72	75	78	73	298	30,750
David Toms	73	74	72	80	299	28,500
Robert Allenby	72	74	72	81	299	28,500
Ian Woosnam	75	71	76	78	300	26,250
Sandy Lyle	72	75	78	77	302	24,750

Out of Final 36 Holes

Sergio Garcia	76	72	148	John Senden	80	71	151
Ernie Els	74	74	148	Bernhard Langer	74	77	151
Aaron Baddeley	75	73	148	*Michael Thompson	73	78	151
Brett Wetterich	73	75	148	Vaughn Taylor	75	76	151
Charles Howell	78	70	148	Jose Maria Olazabal	76	75	151
Michael Campbell	77	71	148	Richard Green	77	75	152
Fred Couples	76	72	148	Tim Clark	77	75	152
Martin Kaymer	76	72	148	Woody Austin	79	73	152
Luke Donald	73	75	148	Shingo Katayama	79	73	152

Toru Taniguchi	76	72	148	Peter Lonard	71	81	152
Craig Stadler	77	72	149	Ben Crenshaw	75	77	152
Jonathan Boyd	75	74	149	Soren Hansen	75	78	153
Mark O'Meara	71	78	149	Mark Calcavecchia	73	80	153
Hunter Mahan	77	72	149	D.J. Trahan	76	77	153
Nick O'Hern	74	75	149	Scott Verplank	77	76	153
Jerry Kelly	72	77	149	Raymond Floyd	80	74	154
Rory Sabbatini	75	74	149	Liang Wen-chong	76	78	154
John Rollins	77	73	150	Anders Hansen	80	75	155
Daniel Chopra	72	78	150	*Drew Weaver	76	80	156
Tom Watson	75	75	150	Steve Lowery	81	76	157
Steve Stricker	73	77	150	Larry Mize	77	81	158
Camilo Villegas	73	77	150	Fuzzy Zoeller	81	79	160
Ben Curtis	75	75	150	Gary Player	83	78	161
Shaun Micheel	76	74	150	Prayad Marksaeng	82		WD
*Trip Kuehne	78	72	150				

(Professionals who did not complete 72 holes received $5,000.)

Verizon Heritage

Harbour Town Golf Links, Hilton Head Island, South Carolina   April 17-20
Par 36-35–71; 6,973 yards   purse, $5,500,000

	SCORES				TOTAL	MONEY
Boo Weekley	69	64	65	71	269	$990,000
Aaron Baddeley	69	67	67	69	272	484,000
Anthony Kim	67	67	67	71	272	484,000
Jim Furyk	68	68	68	69	273	264,000
Cliff Kresge	69	66	68	71	274	220,000
Jason Bohn	70	66	67	72	275	198,000
Stewart Cink	67	68	70	71	276	160,050
Lucas Glover	66	66	73	71	276	160,050
Matt Kuchar	71	70	68	67	276	160,050
Michael Letzig	68	73	70	65	276	160,050
Camilo Villegas	67	71	71	67	276	160,050
Charles Howell	67	71	69	70	277	121,000
Fredrik Jacobson	70	67	73	67	277	121,000
Robert Allenby	70	66	71	71	278	99,000
Billy Andrade	69	72	68	69	278	99,000
John Rollins	67	71	71	69	278	99,000
Briny Baird	68	69	76	66	279	74,433.34
D.J. Trahan	68	70	75	66	279	74,433.34
Shane Bertsch	71	71	66	71	279	74,433.33
Mathew Goggin	70	67	70	72	279	74,433.33
Justin Leonard	66	71	72	70	279	74,433.33
Kevin Na	71	67	73	68	279	74,433.33
Woody Austin	69	72	71	68	280	47,575
Brian Davis	67	74	69	70	280	47,575
Robert Garrigus	70	69	71	70	280	47,575
John Senden	74	67	72	67	280	47,575
Marc Turnesa	69	67	73	71	280	47,575
Dean Wilson	69	71	70	70	280	47,575
Stephen Ames	71	64	74	72	281	34,217.86
Tim Clark	70	70	69	72	281	34,217.86
Ben Crane	69	71	70	71	281	34,217.86
Steve Flesch	70	71	70	70	281	34,217.86
Frank Lickliter	72	69	69	71	281	34,217.86
Ken Duke	68	69	71	73	281	34,217.85
Tim Wilkinson	68	69	71	73	281	34,217.85
Jonathan Byrd	69	67	72	74	282	25,905
Mathias Gronberg	67	74	70	71	282	25,905

	SCORES				TOTAL	MONEY
Davis Love	66	71	69	76	282	25,905
Rocco Mediate	74	65	71	72	282	25,905
Heath Slocum	71	67	73	71	282	25,905
Ben Curtis	69	68	75	71	283	20,350
Nathan Green	74	69	69	71	283	20,350
Lee Janzen	69	70	71	73	283	20,350
Billy Mayfair	70	71	72	70	283	20,350
Bob Tway	71	72	71	69	283	20,350
Ryan Armour	71	69	75	69	284	16,023.34
Michael Allen	68	69	73	74	284	16,023.33
Jesper Parnevik	73	69	72	70	284	16,023.33
John Mallinger	70	69	71	75	285	13,722.50
Corey Pavin	72	71	69	73	285	13,722.50
Jeff Quinney	69	72	71	73	285	13,722.50
Bo Van Pelt	69	73	71	72	285	13,722.50
Parker McLachlin	69	68	74	75	286	12,732.50
Brandt Snedeker	70	70	70	76	286	12,732.50
Scott Verplank	68	71	74	73	286	12,732.50
Mark Wilson	69	72	74	71	286	12,732.50
Daniel Chopra	69	72	74	72	287	12,265
Niclas Fasth	69	73	74	71	287	12,265
Peter Lonard	68	72	74	73	287	12,265
Jonathan Moore	70	72	73	72	287	12,265
Chris DiMarco	73	69	74	72	288	11,880
Brett Quigley	72	68	74	74	288	11,880
David Toms	72	70	73	73	288	11,880
Glen Day	71	70	72	76	289	11,385
Tim Herron	67	74	74	74	289	11,385
J.L. Lewis	71	71	75	72	289	11,385
Patrick Sheehan	69	68	79	73	289	11,385
Richard Sterne	69	73	75	72	289	11,385
Jay Williamson	67	69	73	80	289	11,385
Nick Flanagan	73	70	74	74	291	11,000
Nicholas Thompson	71	72	73	76	292	10,890
Will MacKenzie	74	69	73	77	293	10,780
Matt Jones	74	69	77	75	295	10,615
Greg Kraft	73	70	76	76	295	10,615

EDS Byron Nelson Championship

TPC Four Seasons Resort Las Colinas, Irving, Texas
Par 35-35–70; 7,166 yards

April 24-27
purse, $6,400,000

	SCORES				TOTAL	MONEY
Adam Scott	68	67	67	71	273	$1,152,000
Ryan Moore	67	70	68	68	273	691,200
(Scott defeated Moore on third playoff hole.)						
Bart Bryant	72	66	67	72	277	435,200
Nicholas Thompson	69	72	70	67	278	264,533.34
Mark Hensby	69	67	73	69	278	264,533.33
Carl Pettersson	74	68	67	69	278	264,533.33
Roland Thatcher	69	68	72	70	279	179,733.34
Charlie Wi	71	70	70	68	279	179,733.34
Brian Gay	72	67	68	72	279	179,733.33
Dudley Hart	70	70	66	73	279	179,733.33
Charley Hoffman	69	68	68	74	279	179,733.33
Kevin Sutherland	68	70	67	74	279	179,733.33
Briny Baird	68	72	70	70	280	113,066.67
Jeff Gove	69	71	70	70	280	113,066.67
Frank Lickliter	73	65	72	70	280	113,066.67

	SCORES				TOTAL	MONEY
Scott McCarron	70	66	73	71	280	113,066.67
Eric Axley	67	74	68	71	280	113,066.66
Jesper Parnevik	68	70	68	74	280	113,066.66
Shane Bertsch	74	66	70	71	281	69,600
Luke Donald	72	68	68	73	281	69,600
Nick Flanagan	71	69	72	69	281	69,600
Sergio Garcia	71	70	65	75	281	69,600
Mathew Goggin	67	69	72	73	281	69,600
Tim Herron	74	69	67	71	281	69,600
Anthony Kim	73	70	68	70	281	69,600
Justin Leonard	71	66	74	70	281	69,600
Michael Bradley	69	72	70	71	282	46,400
Shaun Micheel	68	74	72	68	282	46,400
John Senden	73	68	71	70	282	46,400
Johnson Wagner	69	73	70	70	282	46,400
Richard Johnson	72	71	75	65	283	38,800
John Mallinger	73	66	71	73	283	38,800
Jeff Quinney	71	72	68	72	283	38,800
Nick Watney	75	68	68	72	283	38,800
Ian Poulter	68	73	71	72	284	30,217.15
Ted Purdy	72	69	70	73	284	30,217.15
Ken Duke	70	70	68	76	284	30,217.14
Jeff Overton	72	68	76	68	284	30,217.14
Corey Pavin	72	70	68	74	284	30,217.14
Bo Van Pelt	73	70	72	69	284	30,217.14
Jimmy Walker	75	66	69	74	284	30,217.14
Matt Kuchar	71	71	70	73	285	22,400
Hunter Mahan	71	68	72	74	285	22,400
Steve Marino	73	68	70	74	285	22,400
Billy Mayfair	71	71	69	74	285	22,400
Parker McLachlin	68	69	74	74	285	22,400
Cliff Kresge	69	72	71	74	286	17,578.67
John Rollins	74	69	68	75	286	17,578.67
Craig Kanada	69	74	67	76	286	17,578.66
Stuart Deane	70	69	72	76	287	15,213.72
Kevin Na	71	67	73	76	287	15,213.72
Y.E. Yang	70	70	71	76	287	15,213.72
Tommy Armour	69	70	74	74	287	15,213.71
George McNeill	72	70	71	74	287	15,213.71
Tom Pernice, Jr.	71	71	70	75	287	15,213.71
Kenny Perry	72	67	69	79	287	15,213.71
Chad Collins	73	67	74	74	288	14,272
J.J. Henry	72	71	69	76	288	14,272
Brett Quigley	72	71	72	73	288	14,272
Michael Sim	70	71	71	76	288	14,272
Patrick Sheehan	74	68	72	75	289	13,888
Scott Verplank	72	69	73	75	289	13,888
Dustin Johnson	68	73	73	76	290	13,568
Martin Laird	74	69	72	75	290	13,568
Jon Mills	73	68	77	72	290	13,568
Todd Hamilton	71	68	74	78	291	13,248
Stephen Leaney	71	72	75	73	291	13,248
Olin Browne	72	71	71	78	292	12,864
Alejandro Canizares	69	73	74	76	292	12,864
Joe Durant	70	71	75	76	292	12,864
Nathan Green	72	71	74	75	292	12,864
Shigeki Maruyama	70	73	73	77	293	12,544
Joe Ogilvie	70	69	79	76	294	12,416
Omar Uresti	73	70	73	79	295	12,288
Paul Stankowski	71	71	75	80	297	12,160
Brad Elder	71	72	79	77	299	12,032

Wachovia Championship

Quail Hollow Club, Charlotte, North Carolina
Par 36-36–72; 7,442 yards

May 1-4
purse, $6,400,000

		SCORES			TOTAL	MONEY
Anthony Kim	70	67	66	69	272	$1,152,000
Ben Curtis	69	71	72	65	277	691,200
Jason Bohn	68	67	72	71	278	435,200
Robert Allenby	70	70	73	66	279	307,200
Dudley Hart	71	67	70	72	280	243,200
Heath Slocum	71	68	68	73	280	243,200
Jim Furyk	71	67	71	72	281	214,400
Stewart Cink	73	70	65	74	282	179,200
Fred Couples	72	69	69	72	282	179,200
Rod Pampling	71	70	75	66	282	179,200
Adam Scott	72	73	66	71	282	179,200
Hunter Mahan	71	70	71	71	283	125,440
Phil Mickelson	68	74	69	72	283	125,440
Jesper Parnevik	71	74	71	67	283	125,440
Pat Perez	72	73	65	73	283	125,440
Dean Wilson	71	69	74	69	283	125,440
Mathew Goggin	71	72	73	68	284	89,600
J.B. Holmes	71	72	69	72	284	89,600
Ryuji Imada	71	73	70	70	284	89,600
Vijay Singh	70	70	70	74	284	89,600
David Toms	67	75	72	70	284	89,600
Steve Flesch	73	68	71	73	285	66,560
George McNeill	71	67	76	71	285	66,560
Geoff Ogilvy	70	70	69	76	285	66,560
James Driscoll	70	72	74	70	286	45,795.56
Zach Johnson	69	76	71	70	286	45,795.56
Parker McLachlin	73	72	72	69	286	45,795.56
Ian Poulter	71	71	74	70	286	45,795.56
Kevin Stadler	75	70	71	70	286	45,795.56
Brian Davis	74	70	71	71	286	45,795.55
Paul Goydos	71	69	75	71	286	45,795.55
Charles Howell	75	68	70	73	286	45,795.55
John Senden	72	71	71	72	286	45,795.55
Michael Allen	73	70	73	71	287	32,320
Stephen Ames	69	75	74	69	287	32,320
Ken Duke	73	72	71	71	287	32,320
Sergio Garcia	71	72	74	70	287	32,320
Todd Hamilton	72	71	72	72	287	32,320
John Merrick	69	71	73	74	287	32,320
Tommy Armour	74	68	74	72	288	22,428.45
Aaron Baddeley	73	71	74	70	288	22,428.45
Justin Bolli	73	71	73	71	288	22,428.45
Andres Romero	72	71	72	73	288	22,428.45
Brad Adamonis	70	70	74	74	288	22,428.44
Robert Garrigus	74	68	72	74	288	22,428.44
Steve Marino	69	71	74	74	288	22,428.44
Nick O'Hern	71	70	71	76	288	22,428.44
Nick Watney	73	69	71	75	288	22,428.44
Troy Matteson	71	73	74	71	289	15,795.20
Shaun Micheel	76	69	71	73	289	15,795.20
Kenny Perry	74	71	73	71	289	15,795.20
D.J. Trahan	71	73	73	72	289	15,795.20
Boo Weekley	72	70	76	71	289	15,795.20
Jeff Quinney	69	73	73	75	290	14,848
Carlos Franco	72	70	75	74	291	14,336
Billy Mayfair	74	67	76	74	291	14,336
Rocco Mediate	72	72	73	74	291	14,336

		SCORES			TOTAL	MONEY
Carl Pettersson	72	73	74	72	291	14,336
Brandt Snedeker	73	69	76	73	291	14,336
Camilo Villegas	69	70	77	75	291	14,336
Jay Williamson	70	70	77	74	291	14,336
Nathan Green	73	72	70	77	292	13,568
Matt Kuchar	73	72	73	74	292	13,568
Steve Lowery	70	72	77	73	292	13,568
Patrick Sheehan	74	71	73	74	292	13,568
Y.E. Yang	73	69	76	74	292	13,568
Rory Sabbatini	70	72	77	74	293	13,120
Mark Wilson	74	71	71	77	293	13,120
Lucas Glover	73	70	72	80	295	12,928
Rich Beem	72	71	75	78	296	12,736
Nick Flanagan	69	75	74	78	296	12,736
Angel Cabrera	71	74	73	82	300	12,544

The Players Championship

TPC Sawgrass, Ponte Vedra Beach, Florida
Par 36-36–72; 7,215 yards

May 8-11
purse, $9,500,000

		SCORES			TOTAL	MONEY
Sergio Garcia	66	73	73	71	283	$1,710,000
Paul Goydos	68	71	70	74	283	1,026,000
(Garcia defeated Goydos on first playoff hole.)						
Jeff Quinney	71	73	70	70	284	646,000
Briny Baird	71	71	73	72	287	456,000
Stephen Ames	74	68	74	72	288	380,000
Ben Crane	70	72	75	72	289	307,562.50
Ernie Els	72	71	74	72	289	307,562.50
Tom Lehman	73	73	69	74	289	307,562.50
Brett Quigley	70	76	72	71	289	307,562.50
Chad Campbell	73	72	77	68	290	218,500
J.B. Holmes	72	72	71	75	290	218,500
Greg Kraft	75	72	68	75	290	218,500
Henrik Stenson	73	71	75	71	290	218,500
Dean Wilson	74	72	75	69	290	218,500
Stuart Appleby	72	72	71	76	291	147,250
Fred Couples	70	72	77	72	291	147,250
Bernhard Langer	72	67	75	77	291	147,250
Kenny Perry	68	70	72	81	291	147,250
Tim Petrovic	73	73	69	76	291	147,250
Kevin Stadler	70	72	78	71	291	147,250
Woody Austin	71	76	73	72	292	95,000
Stewart Cink	71	75	73	73	292	95,000
Phil Mickelson	70	73	71	78	292	95,000
Ian Poulter	69	74	73	76	292	95,000
Nicholas Thompson	70	77	71	74	292	95,000
Boo Weekley	70	71	74	77	292	95,000
Luke Donald	75	72	74	72	293	67,450
Jim Furyk	74	72	71	76	293	67,450
John Merrick	70	72	77	74	293	67,450
Ryan Moore	72	74	73	74	293	67,450
Rory Sabbatini	73	71	75	74	293	67,450
Aaron Baddeley	71	74	77	72	294	48,260
Jonathan Byrd	76	71	72	75	294	48,260
Steve Elkington	69	76	77	72	294	48,260
Brian Gay	72	74	75	73	294	48,260
Fredrik Jacobson	76	70	70	78	294	48,260
Miguel Angel Jimenez	70	74	76	74	294	48,260

	SCORES				TOTAL	MONEY
Jerry Kelly	74	72	70	78	294	48,260
Nick O'Hern	73	74	75	72	294	48,260
David Toms	77	70	76	71	294	48,260
Mike Weir	71	76	75	72	294	48,260
Robert Allenby	74	71	77	73	295	29,830
Bart Bryant	73	71	79	72	295	29,830
Daniel Chopra	72	72	73	78	295	29,830
Ben Curtis	74	72	71	78	295	29,830
Soren Hansen	71	73	73	78	295	29,830
J.J. Henry	71	73	73	78	295	29,830
Anthony Kim	70	70	79	76	295	29,830
Pat Perez	72	74	72	77	295	29,830
Mark Wilson	76	71	72	76	295	29,830
D.J. Trahan	70	77	75	74	296	22,863.34
Retief Goosen	73	71	77	75	296	22,863.33
Carl Pettersson	74	71	75	76	296	22,863.33
Chris DiMarco	71	73	78	75	297	21,280
Ken Duke	72	75	76	74	297	21,280
Todd Hamilton	69	77	75	76	297	21,280
Davis Love	73	74	70	80	297	21,280
Rocco Mediate	74	72	72	79	297	21,280
Kevin Na	72	75	76	74	297	21,280
Jose Maria Olazabal	70	75	80	72	297	21,280
Adam Scott	75	71	71	80	297	21,280
Johnson Wagner	72	74	77	74	297	21,280
Nick Watney	76	71	74	77	298	20,235
Charlie Wi	74	73	69	82	298	20,235
Cliff Kresge	74	71	77	77	299	19,950
Jose Coceres	72	75	71	82	300	19,570
Richard Sterne	77	70	76	77	300	19,570
Camilo Villegas	74	73	77	76	300	19,570
Jesper Parnevik	72	74	70	85	301	19,095
Heath Slocum	69	76	78	78	301	19,095
Jason Bohn	74	73	79	76	302	18,810
Billy Mayfair	72	73	77	81	303	18,620
Tommy Armour	71	76	80	80	307	18,335
Troy Matteson	70	76	80	81	307	18,335

AT&T Classic

TPC Sugarloaf, Duluth, Georgia
Par 36-36–72; 7,293 yards

May 15-18
purse, $5,500,000

	SCORES				TOTAL	MONEY
Ryuji Imada	71	69	66	67	273	$990,000
Kenny Perry	66	69	69	69	273	594,000
(Imada defeated Perry on first playoff hole.)						
Camilo Villegas	68	69	71	66	274	374,000
Jonathan Byrd	66	66	73	70	275	264,000
Justin Bolli	73	66	68	69	276	200,750
James Driscoll	71	72	66	67	276	200,750
Parker McLachlin	66	70	73	67	276	200,750
Charles Howell	67	69	67	74	277	165,000
Heath Slocum	69	68	69	71	277	165,000
Ryan Palmer	66	69	70	73	278	148,500
Briny Baird	72	69	70	68	279	102,666.67
Stewart Cink	68	71	71	69	279	102,666.67
Bill Haas	69	74	70	66	279	102,666.67
John Huston	70	74	68	67	279	102,666.67
John Rollins	73	67	73	66	279	102,666.67

	SCORES			TOTAL	MONEY
Bob Tway	72	70	69	68	279	102,666.67
Steve Elkington	71	69	68	71	279	102,666.66
Craig Kanada	68	71	69	71	279	102,666.66
Bubba Watson	75	66	68	70	279	102,666.66
Gavin Coles	70	70	70	70	280	61,820
Matt Kuchar	71	69	69	71	280	61,820
Nick O'Hern	69	72	69	70	280	61,820
David Toms	67	69	69	75	280	61,820
Omar Uresti	74	69	65	72	280	61,820
Steve Flesch	68	73	73	67	281	42,900
Brian Gay	71	68	72	70	281	42,900
John Mallinger	68	72	71	70	281	42,900
Brett Quigley	70	70	68	73	281	42,900
D.J. Trahan	70	70	70	71	281	42,900
Dan Forsman	72	70	68	72	282	34,925
Bob Heintz	68	72	70	72	282	34,925
Bob May	68	76	69	69	282	34,925
Ted Purdy	67	73	71	71	282	34,925
Michael Allen	71	71	72	69	283	27,775
Tom Byrum	72	69	70	72	283	27,775
Retief Goosen	73	68	71	71	283	27,775
Zach Johnson	69	70	71	73	283	27,775
Tom Scherrer	69	74	70	70	283	27,775
Kevin Sutherland	70	72	71	70	283	27,775
Brandt Jobe	73	67	72	72	284	22,000
Ian Leggatt	72	72	72	68	284	22,000
Joe Ogilvie	73	70	71	70	284	22,000
Chez Reavie	72	72	69	71	284	22,000
Dustin Johnson	70	73	70	72	285	15,895
Jonathan Kaye	66	78	70	71	285	15,895
Stephen Leaney	70	72	71	72	285	15,895
Troy Matteson	71	70	72	72	285	15,895
Jim McGovern	74	70	67	74	285	15,895
Larry Mize	71	73	70	71	285	15,895
Esteban Toledo	71	72	72	70	285	15,895
Jay Williamson	72	67	75	71	285	15,895
Rich Beem	70	73	68	75	286	12,980
Brian Davis	69	71	75	71	286	12,980
Chris Kirk	69	71	71	75	286	12,980
Guy Boros	68	73	72	74	287	12,485
Len Mattiace	75	69	71	72	287	12,485
Corey Pavin	72	69	72	74	287	12,485
Dean Wilson	73	71	74	69	287	12,485
Nick Flanagan	72	72	70	74	288	12,210
Kenneth Ferrie	76	68	72	73	289	11,990
Jeff Gove	69	75	72	73	289	11,990
Lee Janzen	70	74	73	72	289	11,990
Eric Axley	72	69	75	74	290	11,495
Andrew Buckle	74	70	71	75	290	11,495
Gabriel Hjertstedt	70	71	72	77	290	11,495
John Morse	71	71	76	72	290	11,495
Bob Sowards	67	71	76	76	290	11,495
Kevin Streelman	71	72	79	68	290	11,495
Robert Damron	71	73	70	77	291	10,945
Chris Riley	70	72	75	74	291	10,945
Kyle Thompson	76	68	78	69	291	10,945
Marc Turnesa	74	68	74	75	291	10,945
David Lutterus	75	69	74	74	292	10,670
Shane Bertsch	71	72	76	77	296	10,560
Todd Demsey	72	72	74	80	298	10,450
Reid Edstrom	72	71	84	72	299	10,340

Crowne Plaza Invitational

Colonial Country Club, Fort Worth, Texas
Par 35-35–70; 7,054 yards

May 22-25
purse, $6,100,000

	SCORES				TOTAL	MONEY
Phil Mickelson	65	68	65	68	266	$1,098,000
Tim Clark	68	69	64	66	267	536,800
Rod Pampling	69	67	63	68	267	536,800
Stephen Ames	68	67	64	70	269	292,800
Ben Crane	68	68	67	67	270	244,000
Pat Perez	72	68	67	65	272	219,600
Geoff Ogilvy	72	64	69	68	273	196,725
Jeff Quinney	71	68	66	68	273	196,725
Matt Kuchar	70	64	71	69	274	176,900
Tommy Armour	71	66	68	70	275	140,300
Brian Gay	69	65	69	72	275	140,300
Paul Goydos	68	71	66	70	275	140,300
Steve Marino	68	70	71	66	275	140,300
Mark Wilson	70	67	68	70	275	140,300
Ryan Palmer	70	70	69	67	276	80,409.10
Briny Baird	68	70	67	71	276	80,409.09
Chris DiMarco	72	69	65	70	276	80,409.09
Lucas Glover	70	70	65	71	276	80,409.09
Jerry Kelly	68	71	66	71	276	80,409.09
Corey Pavin	67	69	69	71	276	80,409.09
Ian Poulter	68	70	69	69	276	80,409.09
Brett Quigley	70	69	67	70	276	80,409.09
Kevin Sutherland	67	68	68	73	276	80,409.09
Mike Weir	71	69	66	70	276	80,409.09
Charlie Wi	71	70	67	68	276	80,409.09
Bart Bryant	72	65	69	71	277	43,310
Alex Cejka	67	72	67	71	277	43,310
Nathan Green	71	68	71	67	277	43,310
Sean O'Hair	72	70	66	69	277	43,310
Heath Slocum	74	68	67	68	277	43,310
David Toms	72	69	66	70	277	43,310
Dean Wilson	72	69	66	70	277	43,310
Justin Leonard	70	72	69	67	278	31,545.72
Nick O'Hern	70	70	72	66	278	31,545.72
Carl Pettersson	72	69	70	67	278	31,545.72
Mark Brooks	67	68	70	73	278	31,545.71
Ben Curtis	69	71	67	71	278	31,545.71
Richard Johnson	67	69	72	70	278	31,545.71
George McNeill	69	71	68	70	278	31,545.71
Daniel Chopra	73	68	67	71	279	23,180
Jose Coceres	68	69	69	73	279	23,180
Glen Day	66	74	69	70	279	23,180
Anthony Kim	69	72	70	68	279	23,180
Joe Ogilvie	72	70	67	70	279	23,180
Kevin Stadler	71	70	68	70	279	23,180
Brian Bateman	70	65	70	75	280	16,592
Steve Elkington	73	67	72	68	280	16,592
Mathew Goggin	67	73	69	71	280	16,592
Jon Mills	72	69	69	70	280	16,592
Kenny Perry	70	69	71	70	280	16,592
Johnson Wagner	63	71	73	73	280	16,592
Jason Bohn	73	67	70	71	281	14,082.29
Billy Mayfair	71	69	69	72	281	14,082.29
Ryan Moore	71	68	71	71	281	14,082.29
Brett Wetterich	65	76	72	68	281	14,082.29
Tim Herron	73	67	68	73	281	14,082.28
Vaughn Taylor	67	68	70	76	281	14,082.28

	SCORES				TOTAL	MONEY
Nicholas Thompson	71	69	69	72	281	14,082.28
Brian Davis	68	72	70	72	282	13,298
Parker McLachlin	70	70	70	72	282	13,298
John Merrick	70	70	70	72	282	13,298
Kevin Na	70	71	70	71	282	13,298
Arron Oberholser	70	71	71	70	282	13,298
James Driscoll	69	70	69	75	283	12,688
Robert Garrigus	70	69	67	77	283	12,688
Steve Lowery	68	67	73	75	283	12,688
Chez Reavie	73	68	72	70	283	12,688
Tag Ridings	69	68	72	74	283	12,688
Olin Browne	74	68	71	71	284	12,322
Rocco Mediate	73	68	70	74	285	12,139
Bo Van Pelt	72	70	71	72	285	12,139
Bubba Watson	69	73	69	75	286	11,956
Patrick Sheehan	70	72	67	78	287	11,834

Memorial Tournament

Muirfield Village Golf Club, Dublin, Ohio
Par 36-36–72; 7,265 yards

May 29-June 1
purse, $6,000,000

	SCORES				TOTAL	MONEY
Kenny Perry	66	71	74	69	280	$1,080,000
Mathew Goggin	65	72	71	74	282	396,000
Jerry Kelly	66	72	73	71	282	396,000
Justin Rose	68	73	70	71	282	396,000
Mike Weir	71	72	68	71	282	396,000
Luke Donald	68	71	74	73	286	201,000
Steve Lowery	70	70	75	71	286	201,000
Rocco Mediate	70	73	74	69	286	201,000
Geoff Ogilvy	69	71	73	74	287	174,000
Robert Allenby	69	76	72	71	288	120,666.67
Cliff Kresge	73	73	74	68	288	120,666.67
John Mallinger	71	74	74	69	288	120,666.67
Ryan Moore	73	71	75	69	288	120,666.67
Carl Pettersson	68	75	74	71	288	120,666.67
Brett Quigley	67	78	74	69	288	120,666.67
Matt Kuchar	68	72	71	77	288	120,666.66
Nick O'Hern	70	70	72	76	288	120,666.66
Joe Ogilvie	69	75	71	73	288	120,666.66
Tom Lehman	76	70	72	71	289	84,000
Stuart Appleby	72	76	68	74	290	65,000
Jason Bohn	72	71	74	73	290	65,000
Nathan Green	75	71	73	71	290	65,000
J.B. Holmes	74	69	70	77	290	65,000
Phil Mickelson	72	75	70	73	290	65,000
Rod Pampling	67	74	77	72	290	65,000
Jon Mills	73	76	74	68	291	45,300
Pat Perez	70	73	73	75	291	45,300
Vaughn Taylor	71	73	70	77	291	45,300
Nick Watney	68	80	68	75	291	45,300
Trevor Immelman	72	78	73	69	292	34,133.34
George McNeill	73	73	75	71	292	34,133.34
Jeff Quinney	71	79	71	71	292	34,133.34
Stewart Cink	71	77	69	75	292	34,133.33
Bill Haas	74	72	69	77	292	34,133.33
Dudley Hart	73	73	71	75	292	34,133.33
Bo Van Pelt	71	76	73	72	292	34,133.33
Johnson Wagner	78	67	74	73	292	34,133.33

	SCORES				TOTAL	MONEY
Mark Wilson	73	74	74	71	292	34,133.33
Chris DiMarco	75	72	73	73	293	24,000
Jim Furyk	71	74	73	75	293	24,000
Todd Hamilton	70	76	74	73	293	24,000
Ryuji Imada	75	72	72	74	293	24,000
Sean O'Hair	75	75	69	74	293	24,000
John Rollins	71	76	76	70	293	24,000
Sergio Garcia	72	77	75	70	294	19,800
Richard Green	72	75	77	71	295	16,045.72
Zach Johnson	71	79	72	73	295	16,045.72
Tim Petrovic	73	75	76	71	295	16,045.72
Bart Bryant	76	74	71	74	295	16,045.71
Fred Couples	72	71	77	75	295	16,045.71
Ben Curtis	76	72	71	76	295	16,045.71
Arron Oberholser	77	71	73	74	295	16,045.71
K.J. Choi	76	74	74	72	296	13,824
Daniel Chopra	76	68	76	76	296	13,824
Ken Duke	71	77	75	73	296	13,824
Ian Poulter	75	72	76	73	296	13,824
Tim Wilkinson	72	75	75	74	296	13,824
Aaron Baddeley	74	76	75	72	297	13,380
Paul Casey	76	71	79	71	297	13,380
Davis Love	74	74	77	73	298	13,140
Tom Pernice, Jr.	71	75	82	70	298	13,140
Travis Perkins	76	74	75	74	299	12,900
D.J. Trahan	73	76	78	72	299	12,900
Jin Park	75	75	76	75	301	12,660
Chez Reavie	73	77	76	75	301	12,660
Kevin Na	75	72	73	82	302	12,480
John Senden	71	78	73	81	303	12,360
Dustin Johnson	75	73	77	79	304	12,240
Lee Janzen	74	76	75	80	305	12,000
Shaun Micheel	71	77	78	79	305	12,000
Brett Wetterich	76	73	81	75	305	12,000
Charley Hoffman	74	74	76	82	306	11,760
Woody Austin	71	76	76	84	307	11,580
Dean Wilson	78	72	83	74	307	11,580
Parker McLachlin	73	77	76	82	308	11,400
Anton Haig	71	79	83	78	311	11,280

Stanford St. Jude Championship

TPC Southwind, Memphis, Tennessee   June 5-8
Par 35-35–70; 7,244 yards   purse, $6,000,000

	SCORES				TOTAL	MONEY
Justin Leonard	68	73	67	68	276	$1,080,000
Robert Allenby	71	71	69	65	276	528,000
Trevor Immelman	74	66	67	69	276	528,000
(Leonard defeated Allenby and Immelman on second playoff hole.)						
Alex Cejka	69	69	69	70	277	236,250
Sergio Garcia	68	72	71	66	277	236,250
Padraig Harrington	71	72	66	68	277	236,250
Boo Weekley	65	75	69	68	277	236,250
Gavin Coles	73	64	70	71	278	174,000
Tom Pernice, Jr.	72	72	71	63	278	174,000
Scott Verplank	71	72	67	68	278	174,000
Bob Heintz	73	70	68	68	279	144,000
Vijay Singh	67	71	70	71	279	144,000
Stephen Ames	69	71	68	72	280	109,200

		SCORES			TOTAL	MONEY
Jason Dufner	69	68	72	71	280	109,200
Bob Estes	74	65	70	71	280	109,200
Tim Herron	74	67	69	70	280	109,200
Dean Wilson	69	68	71	72	280	109,200
Tim Clark	72	69	64	76	281	75,600
Dan Forsman	70	70	72	69	281	75,600
Bill Haas	71	69	67	74	281	75,600
J.P. Hayes	70	71	69	71	281	75,600
Michael Letzig	70	68	72	71	281	75,600
Camilo Villegas	71	71	71	68	281	75,600
Stuart Appleby	68	76	68	70	282	43,445.46
Davis Love	68	70	75	69	282	43,445.46
Jeff Maggert	71	70	74	67	282	43,445.46
Brett Rumford	69	73	70	70	282	43,445.46
Heath Slocum	73	67	74	68	282	43,445.46
Tommy Armour	66	71	73	72	282	43,445.45
Bart Bryant	69	76	67	70	282	43,445.45
Glen Day	69	71	71	71	282	43,445.45
Kenny Perry	71	71	69	71	282	43,445.45
Bob Tway	72	71	68	71	282	43,445.45
Omar Uresti	70	69	71	72	282	43,445.45
Jeff Overton	70	71	70	72	283	31,650
Brandt Snedeker	69	71	69	74	283	31,650
Richard S. Johnson	72	73	69	70	284	27,000
Craig Kanada	68	72	74	70	284	27,000
Vaughn Taylor	70	72	71	71	284	27,000
David Toms	72	72	71	69	284	27,000
Marc Turnesa	68	69	70	77	284	27,000
Michael Bradley	69	68	76	72	285	19,834.29
John Huston	71	69	75	70	285	19,834.29
Fredrik Jacobson	73	72	69	71	285	19,834.29
Brandt Jobe	71	74	70	70	285	19,834.29
Rich Beem	71	72	70	72	285	19,834.28
Jeff Gove	70	73	67	75	285	19,834.28
Scott Sterling	70	70	73	72	285	19,834.28
Woody Austin	71	72	73	70	286	14,660
Marco Dawson	71	71	72	72	286	14,660
Ken Duke	72	72	73	69	286	14,660
Lucas Glover	71	71	74	70	286	14,660
Bob May	75	69	70	72	286	14,660
Brenden Pappas	73	70	77	66	286	14,660
Jonathan Byrd	69	75	73	70	287	13,740
Jin Park	73	71	67	76	287	13,740
Todd Demsey	73	72	72	71	288	13,440
Jim McGovern	71	68	72	77	288	13,440
Jimmy Walker	70	74	72	72	288	13,440
David Duval	70	75	72	72	289	13,020
Brian Gay	76	67	70	76	289	13,020
Kevin Streelman	74	69	69	77	289	13,020
Garrett Willis	72	73	69	75	289	13,020
Charley Hoffman	69	75	71	75	290	12,660
Webb Simpson	71	72	75	72	290	12,660
Stephen Leaney	70	74	73	74	291	12,360
Dicky Pride	75	70	75	71	291	12,360
Patrick Sheehan	73	70	72	76	291	12,360
Eric Axley	70	71	78	73	292	11,940
Brad Elder	69	76	73	74	292	11,940
Harrison Frazar	72	70	74	76	292	11,940
Troy Matteson	74	70	71	77	292	11,940
Billy Andrade	76	68	73	76	293	11,640

U.S. Open Championship

Torrey Pines South Golf Course, San Diego, California
Par 35-36–71; 7,643 yards

June 12-16
purse, $7,000,000

	SCORES				TOTAL	MONEY
Tiger Woods	72	68	70	73	283	$1,350,000
Rocco Mediate	69	71	72	71	283	810,000

(Woods and Mediate tied after 72-hole playoff, 71-71; Woods won on first sudden-death playoff hole, 4-5.)

Lee Westwood	70	71	70	73	284	491,995
Robert Karlsson	70	70	75	71	286	307,303
D.J. Trahan	72	69	73	72	286	307,303
Carl Pettersson	71	71	77	68	287	220,686
John Merrick	73	72	71	71	287	220,686
Miguel Angel Jimenez	75	66	74	72	287	220,686
Heath Slocum	75	74	74	65	288	160,769
Eric Axley	69	79	71	69	288	160,769
Brandt Snedeker	76	73	68	71	288	160,769
Camilo Villegas	73	71	71	73	288	160,769
Geoff Ogilvy	69	73	72	74	288	160,769
Stewart Cink	72	73	77	67	289	122,159
Retief Goosen	76	69	77	67	289	122,159
Rod Pampling	74	70	75	70	289	122,159
Ernie Els	70	72	74	73	289	122,159
Phil Mickelson	71	75	76	68	290	87,230
Chad Campbell	77	72	71	70	290	87,230
Ryuji Imada	74	75	70	71	290	87,230
Brandt Jobe	73	75	69	73	290	87,230
Sergio Garcia	76	70	70	74	290	87,230
Mike Weir	73	74	69	74	290	87,230
Robert Allenby	70	72	73	75	290	87,230
Hunter Mahan	72	74	69	75	290	87,230
Adam Scott	73	73	75	70	291	61,252
Boo Weekley	73	76	70	72	291	61,252
Anthony Kim	74	75	70	72	291	61,252
Bart Bryant	75	70	78	69	292	48,482
*Michael Thompson	74	73	73	72	292	
Steve Stricker	73	76	71	72	292	48,482
Patrick Sheehan	71	74	74	73	292	48,482
Jeff Quinney	79	70	70	73	292	48,482
Scott Verplank	72	72	74	74	292	48,482
Aaron Baddeley	74	73	71	74	292	48,482
Pat Perez	75	73	75	70	293	35,709
Daniel Chopra	73	75	75	70	293	35,709
Padraig Harrington	78	67	77	71	293	35,709
Jon Mills	72	75	75	71	293	35,709
Justin Leonard	75	72	75	71	293	35,709
Andres Romero	71	73	77	72	293	35,709
Todd Hamilton	74	74	73	72	293	35,709
Joe Ogilvie	71	76	73	73	293	35,709
Robert Dinwiddie	73	71	75	74	293	35,709
Stuart Appleby	69	70	79	75	293	35,709
Jim Furyk	74	71	73	75	293	35,709
Oliver Wilson	72	71	74	76	293	35,709
Jarrod Lyle	75	74	74	71	294	23,985
John Rollins	75	68	79	72	294	23,985
Matt Kuchar	73	73	76	72	294	23,985
Dustin Johnson	74	72	75	73	294	23,985
Tim Clark	73	72	74	75	294	23,985
Ben Crane	75	72	77	71	295	20,251
Soren Hansen	78	70	76	71	295	20,251
Kevin Streelman	68	77	78	72	295	20,251

	SCORES				TOTAL	MONEY
Martin Kaymer	75	70	73	77	295	20,251
Davis Love	72	69	76	78	295	20,251
Stephen Ames	74	74	77	71	296	18,664
Rory Sabbatini	73	72	75	76	296	18,664
Nick Watney	73	75	77	72	297	17,691
*Rickie Fowler	70	79	76	72	297	
Alastair Forsyth	76	73	74	74	297	17,691
Brett Quigley	73	72	77	75	297	17,691
David Toms	76	72	72	77	297	17,691
John Mallinger	73	75	78	72	298	16,514
Vijay Singh	71	78	76	73	298	16,514
Paul Casey	79	70	76	73	298	16,514
Trevor Immelman	75	73	72	78	298	16,514
*Derek Fathauer	73	73	78	75	299	
D.A. Points	74	71	77	77	299	15,778
Andrew Dresser	76	73	79	72	300	15,189
Andrew Svoboda	77	71	74	78	300	15,189
Woody Austin	72	72	77	79	300	15,189
Jesper Parnevik	77	72	77	75	301	14,306
Ian Leggatt	72	76	76	77	301	14,306
Justin Hicks	68	80	75	78	301	14,306
Ross McGowan	76	72	78	77	303	13,718
Rich Beem	74	74	80	76	304	13,276
Chris Kirk	75	74	78	77	304	13,276
Luke Donald	71	71	77		WD	2,000

Out of Final 36 Holes

Jon Turcott	77	73	150	Nick Dougherty	78	77	155
Scott Sterling	80	70	150	Jason Gore	79	76	155
Zach Johnson	76	74	150	Dean Wilson	76	79	155
Toru Taniguchi	74	76	150	Joey Lamielle	76	79	155
J.B. Holmes	75	75	150	Travis Bertoni	82	73	155
Robert Garrigus	77	73	150	Colin Montgomerie	79	77	156
*Kyle Stanley	72	78	150	Kevin Silva	80	76	156
Casey Wittenberg	72	78	150	Bob Gaus	80	76	156
Hunter Haas	80	70	150	Craig Barlow	80	76	156
Thomas Levet	74	76	150	Brad Bryant	77	79	156
Mathew Goggin	77	73	150	Craig Parry	75	81	156
Rob Rashell	81	70	151	Johan Edfors	79	77	156
Richard Sterne	76	75	151	Jerry Kelly	75	82	157
Ben Curtis	75	76	151	*Jordan Cox	80	77	157
Justin Rose	79	72	151	Sean English	75	82	157
Mark O'Meara	75	76	151	Philip Archer	78	81	159
Ross Fisher	73	78	151	Jay Choi	79	80	159
Steve Marino	73	78	151	*Jeff Wilson	78	81	159
John Ellis	77	74	151	Steve Flesch	78	81	159
Peter Tomasulo	76	75	151	Jeffrey Bors	81	79	160
David Hearn	76	75	151	Chris Stroud	84	77	161
Scott Piercy	78	73	151	Philippe Gasnier	86	75	161
K.J. Choi	74	77	151	Michael Campbell	78	83	161
*Nick Taylor	77	75	152	Yohann Benson	83	78	161
Jonathan Byrd	75	77	152	Bobby Collins	83	78	161
Michael Letzig	77	75	152	Artemio Murakami	79	83	162
Michael Allen	78	75	153	Garrett Chaussard	80	82	162
Charles Howell	75	78	153	Brian Kortan	78	84	162
*Kevin Tway	75	78	153	*Jimmy Henderson	81	82	163
Jason Bohn	76	77	153	Fernando Figueroa	78	85	163
Fredrik Jacobson	74	79	153	Niclas Fasth	78	86	164
Lee Janzen	75	78	153	*Gary Wolstenholme	83	82	165
Shingo Katayama	77	76	153	*Michael Quagliano	86	81	167
D.J. Brigman	79	75	154	Mike Gilmore	86	81	167
Henrik Stenson	78	76	154	Chris Devlin	84	83	167

Bubba Watson	77	77	154
Charlie Beljan	76	79	155
Angel Cabrera	79	76	155

Brian Bergstol	86	81	167
Ian Poulter	78		WD
Mark Calcavecchia			WD

Travelers Championship

TPC River Highlands, Cromwell, Connecticut
Par 35-35–70; 6,820 yards

June 19-22
purse, $6,000,000

	SCORES				TOTAL	MONEY
Stewart Cink	66	64	65	67	262	$1,080,000
Tommy Armour	69	64	65	65	263	528,000
Hunter Mahan	68	63	67	65	263	528,000
Heath Slocum	67	66	64	67	264	288,000
Vijay Singh	66	68	64	68	266	240,000
Brad Adamonis	64	68	68	67	267	194,250
Michael Allen	69	66	68	64	267	194,250
Kenny Perry	66	67	65	69	267	194,250
Bubba Watson	66	68	67	66	267	194,250
Michael Letzig	68	68	63	69	268	150,000
Corey Pavin	68	66	70	64	268	150,000
Kevin Streelman	73	63	62	70	268	150,000
Ben Curtis	68	66	69	66	269	106,000
Brian Davis	64	70	69	66	269	106,000
Chris DiMarco	66	69	64	70	269	106,000
John Huston	65	69	67	68	269	106,000
Tom Pernice, Jr.	65	68	68	68	269	106,000
Tag Ridings	66	70	66	67	269	106,000
Briny Baird	67	70	66	67	270	65,250
Lucas Glover	65	66	71	68	270	65,250
Bill Haas	68	67	69	66	270	65,250
Tim Herron	66	69	67	68	270	65,250
Jon Mills	70	64	65	71	270	65,250
Nick O'Hern	68	69	65	68	270	65,250
Justin Rose	65	72	66	67	270	65,250
D.J. Trahan	67	70	62	71	270	65,250
Chad Campbell	67	70	62	72	271	40,800
Jason Day	67	67	66	71	271	40,800
Ken Duke	65	66	70	70	271	40,800
Steve Elkington	70	64	66	71	271	40,800
Scott McCarron	68	69	68	66	271	40,800
Kevin Sutherland	67	65	72	67	271	40,800
David Toms	67	69	64	71	271	40,800
Bob Estes	69	68	64	71	272	32,400
Dustin Johnson	66	70	67	69	272	32,400
Nicholas Thompson	67	69	68	68	272	32,400
Fred Funk	66	68	65	74	273	25,800
Craig Kanada	67	68	70	68	273	25,800
Greg Kraft	69	67	66	71	273	25,800
Peter Lonard	66	70	70	67	273	25,800
Joe Ogilvie	70	67	68	68	273	25,800
Carl Pettersson	70	65	70	68	273	25,800
Webb Simpson	67	70	67	69	273	25,800
Larry Mize	67	70	67	70	274	21,000
Bob Sowards	67	70	66	72	275	16,817.15
Johnson Wagner	64	71	67	73	275	16,817.15
Stuart Appleby	68	66	72	69	275	16,817.14
Jason Gore	71	66	69	69	275	16,817.14
Kent Jones	66	70	73	66	275	16,817.14
Steve Lowery	64	73	69	69	275	16,817.14
Brenden Pappas	69	65	65	76	275	16,817.14
Jason Allred	68	67	68	73	276	13,851.43

	SCORES				TOTAL	MONEY
Olin Browne	68	69	69	70	276	13,851.43
Andrew Buckle	68	68	72	68	276	13,851.43
Matt Kuchar	67	70	66	73	276	13,851.43
Kevin Na	69	66	69	72	276	13,851.43
John Rollins	70	64	68	74	276	13,851.43
John Mallinger	67	67	74	68	276	13,851.42
J.J. Henry	66	70	68	73	277	13,320
*Michael Thompson	65	67	72	73	277	
Brett Rumford	68	66	72	72	278	13,200
Notah Begay	66	71	70	72	279	12,900
Harrison Frazar	69	68	71	71	279	12,900
Steve Marino	67	70	72	70	279	12,900
Billy Mayfair	66	70	71	72	279	12,900
Billy Andrade	69	68	69	74	280	12,480
Dudley Hart	68	68	72	72	280	12,480
Charlie Wi	68	68	72	72	280	12,480
Vaughn Taylor	67	68	78	69	282	12,240
Chris Stroud	67	69	75	72	283	12,120
Peter Karmis	65	70	72	77	284	11,940
Jim McGovern	67	69	75	73	284	11,940

Buick Open

Warwick Hills Golf & Country Club, Grand Blanc, Michigan
Par 36-36–72; 7,127 yards

June 26-29
purse, $5,000,000

	SCORES				TOTAL	MONEY
Kenny Perry	69	67	67	66	269	$900,000
Woody Austin	66	67	69	68	270	440,000
Bubba Watson	67	67	68	68	270	440,000
Ken Duke	69	66	69	67	271	206,666.67
Bob Tway	68	71	67	65	271	206,666.67
Matt Jones	70	63	71	67	271	206,666.66
Brian Gay	69	68	70	65	272	161,250
Lucas Glover	70	66	69	67	272	161,250
Dudley Hart	64	68	70	71	273	135,000
Fredrik Jacobson	68	66	72	67	273	135,000
John Rollins	72	64	72	65	273	135,000
Briny Baird	65	71	68	70	274	98,000
Michael Letzig	69	67	69	69	274	98,000
Corey Pavin	64	74	67	69	274	98,000
Brett Rumford	70	69	67	68	274	98,000
Kevin Streelman	70	68	70	66	274	98,000
Daniel Chopra	65	67	68	75	275	63,250
Glen Day	72	69	66	68	275	63,250
Robert Garrigus	69	69	72	65	275	63,250
Charles Howell	71	66	71	67	275	63,250
Rod Pampling	71	69	65	70	275	63,250
Bo Van Pelt	64	66	73	72	275	63,250
Scott Verplank	68	72	66	69	275	63,250
Charles Warren	67	68	69	71	275	63,250
Ben Crane	68	73	68	67	276	40,833.34
Jason Gore	68	68	71	69	276	40,833.33
Charlie Wi	72	65	69	70	276	40,833.33
Paul Goydos	71	70	65	71	277	34,750
Tom Lehman	71	67	70	69	277	34,750
Rocco Mediate	71	69	67	70	277	34,750
Marc Turnesa	71	69	69	68	277	34,750
Craig Barlow	70	69	67	72	278	28,937.50
Stephen Leaney	67	70	70	71	278	28,937.50

	SCORES				TOTAL	MONEY
Ryan Palmer	70	66	71	71	278	28,937.50
Tag Ridings	67	70	71	70	278	28,937.50
J.P. Hayes	71	68	74	66	279	21,527.78
Charley Hoffman	70	70	72	67	279	21,527.78
Lee Janzen	67	73	70	69	279	21,527.78
Shigeki Maruyama	66	75	69	69	279	21,527.78
Chris Riley	71	69	72	67	279	21,527.78
Jimmy Walker	72	65	72	70	279	21,527.78
Nick Watney	69	66	76	68	279	21,527.78
Jim Furyk	68	72	68	71	279	21,527.77
Todd Hamilton	70	66	70	73	279	21,527.77
Todd Demsey	68	67	71	74	280	15,500
Peter Lonard	70	68	73	69	280	15,500
Billy Mayfair	69	70	69	72	280	15,500
Cameron Beckman	74	67	71	69	281	12,428.58
Shane Bertsch	71	69	70	71	281	12,428.57
Tom Byrum	67	69	72	73	281	12,428.57
Brad Elder	67	71	72	71	281	12,428.57
Mark Hensby	71	68	69	73	281	12,428.57
Jon Mills	66	69	73	73	281	12,428.57
Nick O'Hern	68	72	70	71	281	12,428.57
Michael Bradley	73	68	70	71	282	11,350
Harrison Frazar	68	69	73	72	282	11,350
Justin Leonard	71	68	72	71	282	11,350
Tim Wilkinson	71	70	71	70	282	11,350
Gavin Coles	71	69	68	75	283	10,950
Kenneth Ferrie	66	73	74	70	283	10,950
Heath Slocum	72	69	71	71	283	10,950
Kyle Thompson	71	70	72	70	283	10,950
Bob Estes	70	71	71	72	284	10,600
Mathew Goggin	68	72	73	71	284	10,600
Kevin Stadler	70	70	68	76	284	10,600
Mark Brooks	70	71	72	72	285	10,250
James Driscoll	72	68	71	74	285	10,250
Dustin Johnson	68	70	72	75	285	10,250
Jay Williamson	68	73	70	74	285	10,250
Billy Andrade	71	70	71	74	286	9,950
Chris DiMarco	70	68	74	74	286	9,950
Justin Bolli	70	70	71	76	287	9,800
Paul Claxton	69	70	74	75	288	9,650
Dicky Pride	69	71	73	75	288	9,650
John Huston	71	70	71	77	289	9,500

AT&T National

Congressional Country Club, Bethesda, Maryland
Par 35-35–70; 7,255 yards

July 3-6
purse, $6,000,000

	SCORES				TOTAL	MONEY
Anthony Kim	67	67	69	65	268	$1,080,000
Fredrik Jacobson	67	72	66	65	270	648,000
Robert Allenby	68	69	67	67	271	256,500
Tommy Armour	67	69	66	69	271	256,500
Jim Furyk	70	68	67	66	271	256,500
Nick O'Hern	70	65	67	69	271	256,500
Rod Pampling	66	69	71	65	271	256,500
Dean Wilson	69	70	65	67	271	256,500
Alex Cejka	67	71	68	66	272	162,000
Jeff Overton	66	65	71	70	272	162,000
Tom Pernice, Jr.	68	63	69	72	272	162,000

	SCORES				TOTAL	MONEY
Tim Herron	68	70	65	70	273	114,000
Peter Lonard	74	69	67	63	273	114,000
Hunter Mahan	69	72	64	68	273	114,000
Pat Perez	71	67	67	68	273	114,000
Patrick Sheehan	69	67	69	68	273	114,000
Bo Van Pelt	70	69	68	66	273	114,000
Cliff Kresge	69	65	69	71	274	81,000
Rocco Mediate	73	68	67	66	274	81,000
John Senden	70	69	67	68	274	81,000
Steve Stricker	71	64	66	73	274	81,000
Charles Howell	70	70	68	67	275	64,800
D.J. Trahan	71	68	72	64	275	64,800
Michael Allen	70	68	70	68	276	52,800
Steve Marino	65	70	72	69	276	52,800
Billy Mayfair	67	68	72	69	276	52,800
Fred Couples	71	68	67	71	277	39,100
Robert Garrigus	68	70	70	69	277	39,100
Davis Love	70	73	69	65	277	39,100
Parker McLachlin	71	66	70	70	277	39,100
John Merrick	71	64	72	70	277	39,100
Kevin Streelman	69	70	71	67	277	39,100
Kevin Sutherland	69	71	70	67	277	39,100
Johnson Wagner	70	68	71	68	277	39,100
Charles Warren	69	72	68	68	277	39,100
Brad Adamonis	68	71	70	69	278	26,437.50
Tim Clark	73	69	67	69	278	26,437.50
Jose Coceres	69	68	73	68	278	26,437.50
Bill Haas	70	70	69	69	278	26,437.50
Todd Hamilton	70	67	74	67	278	26,437.50
Jeff Maggert	70	65	72	71	278	26,437.50
Camilo Villegas	71	70	69	68	278	26,437.50
Nick Watney	69	72	67	70	278	26,437.50
Rich Beem	71	68	69	71	279	18,648
Todd Demsey	70	70	68	71	279	18,648
Bob Estes	66	73	67	73	279	18,648
Andres Romero	71	71	70	67	279	18,648
Mark Wilson	70	73	67	69	279	18,648
Olin Browne	69	70	72	69	280	14,808
K.J. Choi	68	71	71	70	280	14,808
J.B. Holmes	70	71	68	71	280	14,808
George McNeill	68	74	68	70	280	14,808
Vaughn Taylor	70	73	64	73	280	14,808
Billy Andrade	70	73	66	72	281	13,620
Shane Bertsch	72	69	67	73	281	13,620
Jonathan Byrd	70	71	70	70	281	13,620
Lucas Glover	71	71	70	69	281	13,620
J.J. Henry	73	67	67	74	281	13,620
Tim Wilkinson	71	72	68	70	281	13,620
Stuart Appleby	67	74	70	71	282	13,080
Ryan Armour	72	71	67	72	282	13,080
Jesper Parnevik	68	71	74	69	282	13,080
Gavin Coles	69	71	72	71	283	12,600
Ben Crane	71	70	72	70	283	12,600
Fred Funk	70	69	68	76	283	12,600
Stephen Leaney	71	71	71	70	283	12,600
John Rollins	68	70	73	72	283	12,600
Justin Bolli	74	68	71	72	285	12,180
Corey Pavin	73	67	73	72	285	12,180
Frank Lickliter	66	74	70	76	286	11,940
Jim McGovern	68	73	70	75	286	11,940

John Deere Classic

TPC Deere Run, Silvis, Illinois
Par 35-36–71; 7,257 yards

July 10-13
purse, $4,200,000

	SCORES				TOTAL	MONEY
Kenny Perry	65	66	67	70	268	$756,000
Brad Adamonis	66	66	66	70	268	369,600
Jay Williamson	69	68	62	69	268	369,600
(Perry defeated Adamonis and Williamson on first playoff hole.)						
Eric Axley	65	66	67	71	269	173,600
Will MacKenzie	65	64	70	70	269	173,600
Charlie Wi	64	67	69	69	269	173,600
Chad Campbell	67	67	67	69	270	140,700
Kevin Sutherland	68	68	67	68	271	130,200
Woody Austin	66	71	66	69	272	113,400
Jeff Gove	66	68	70	68	272	113,400
J.P. Hayes	67	68	65	72	272	113,400
Cameron Beckman	66	73	69	65	273	79,800
Brian Gay	72	66	69	66	273	79,800
Craig Kanada	74	65	65	69	273	79,800
Scott Sterling	67	67	67	72	273	79,800
Vaughn Taylor	68	67	69	69	273	79,800
Bob Tway	73	64	67	69	273	79,800
Tim Clark	70	67	64	73	274	52,920
Ken Duke	64	72	73	65	274	52,920
Jerry Kelly	67	72	64	71	274	52,920
Jin Park	70	69	66	69	274	52,920
Tim Petrovic	69	66	70	69	274	52,920
John Riegger	68	67	68	71	274	52,920
Harrison Frazar	69	65	69	72	275	34,860
David Lutterus	68	70	68	69	275	34,860
Jeff Overton	67	68	68	72	275	34,860
Nicholas Thompson	67	68	70	70	275	34,860
Garrett Willis	65	70	70	70	275	34,860
Aaron Baddeley	71	64	68	73	276	27,300
Shane Bertsch	69	70	69	68	276	27,300
Todd Hamilton	69	68	66	73	276	27,300
Martin Laird	72	65	70	69	276	27,300
Billy Mayfair	70	67	69	70	276	27,300
Rich Beem	68	68	69	72	277	21,210
Paul Claxton	68	69	71	69	277	21,210
Brian Davis	67	66	73	71	277	21,210
Kent Jones	67	72	70	68	277	21,210
Bob Sowards	69	66	73	69	277	21,210
Dean Wilson	68	67	76	66	277	21,210
*Philip Francis	67	71	64	75	277	
Jonathan Byrd	67	68	71	72	278	14,718.67
Gavin Coles	68	70	71	69	278	14,718.67
Jason Day	71	67	67	73	278	14,718.67
Steve Marino	69	70	70	69	278	14,718.67
Ted Purdy	70	67	73	68	278	14,718.67
Heath Slocum	69	69	73	67	278	14,718.67
Jesper Parnevik	69	69	67	73	278	14,718.66
Chez Reavie	67	68	68	75	278	14,718.66
Bubba Watson	70	68	65	75	278	14,718.66
Ryan Armour	66	72	74	67	279	10,176
Andrew Buckle	72	66	69	72	279	10,176
Chad Collins	69	70	71	69	279	10,176
Nick Flanagan	69	68	71	71	279	10,176
Jim McGovern	70	69	70	70	279	10,176
Joe Ogilvie	69	68	70	72	279	10,176
Kirk Triplett	68	67	69	75	279	10,176

	SCORES				TOTAL	MONEY
Marco Dawson	68	70	72	70	280	9,408
Glen Day	70	69	72	69	280	9,408
Lee Janzen	72	67	66	75	280	9,408
Jon Mills	68	70	71	71	280	9,408
Ron Whittaker	70	69	71	70	280	9,408
Parker McLachlin	72	67	73	69	281	9,030
Tag Ridings	70	68	74	69	281	9,030
Patrick Sheehan	66	68	73	74	281	9,030
Chris Stroud	69	70	69	73	281	9,030
Bart Bryant	69	70	67	76	282	8,736
Nathan Green	71	66	69	76	282	8,736
Pat Perez	67	68	72	75	282	8,736
Zach Johnson	69	68	75	71	283	8,484
Michael Letzig	70	68	70	75	283	8,484
Mark Wilson	71	68	73	71	283	8,484
Dan Forsman	69	69	74	73	285	8,274
Scott McCarron	71	68	73	73	285	8,274
Ryan Moore	68	71	74	73	286	8,106
Chris Riley	66	71	71	78	286	8,106
*Jamie Lovemark	70	66	73	77	286	

The Open Championship

See European Tours chapter.

U.S. Bank Championship

Brown Deer Park Golf Course, Milwaukee, Wisconsin
Par 35-35–70; 6,759 yards

July 17-20
purse, $4,000,000

	SCORES				TOTAL	MONEY
Richard S. Johnson	63	67	70	64	264	$720,000
Ken Duke	67	65	68	65	265	432,000
Chad Campbell	67	67	68	65	267	208,000
Chris Riley	68	66	67	66	267	208,000
Dean Wilson	65	73	64	65	267	208,000
Troy Matteson	67	65	70	66	268	125,200
George McNeill	67	67	66	68	268	125,200
Joe Ogilvie	66	67	68	67	268	125,200
Kenny Perry	67	68	69	64	268	125,200
Patrick Sheehan	65	68	68	67	268	125,200
Gavin Coles	69	62	68	70	269	77,000
Chad Collins	69	66	68	66	269	77,000
Jason Dufner	70	63	69	67	269	77,000
Nick Flanagan	67	63	69	70	269	77,000
Jason Gore	67	66	68	68	269	77,000
Brandt Jobe	68	65	68	68	269	77,000
Ryan Palmer	69	67	67	66	269	77,000
Omar Uresti	69	67	69	64	269	77,000
Brian Davis	68	70	67	65	270	42,088.89
Todd Demsey	70	67	68	65	270	42,088.89
Steve Flesch	66	67	70	67	270	42,088.89
Bill Haas	67	67	68	68	270	42,088.89
Dustin Johnson	69	66	70	65	270	42,088.89
Kent Jones	66	65	71	68	270	42,088.89
Jimmy Walker	69	66	67	68	270	42,088.89
Mark Wilson	69	67	68	66	270	42,088.89
Jon Mills	68	68	64	70	270	42,088.88
Ryan Armour	70	63	71	67	271	24,933.34

	SCORES				TOTAL	MONEY
Cliff Kresge	66	72	66	67	271	24,933.34
Brenden Pappas	64	70	70	67	271	24,933.34
Jason Allred	70	64	68	69	271	24,933.33
Alejandro Canizares	68	69	69	65	271	24,933.33
Kevin Na	69	68	70	64	271	24,933.33
Brett Rumford	69	67	70	65	271	24,933.33
Bob Tway	67	71	69	64	271	24,933.33
Bo Van Pelt	67	68	68	68	271	24,933.33
Glen Day	68	69	69	66	272	17,200
Carlos Franco	70	66	69	67	272	17,200
Tim Herron	69	67	69	67	272	17,200
John Huston	71	63	68	70	272	17,200
Frank Lickliter	66	68	71	67	272	17,200
John Mallinger	68	69	68	67	272	17,200
Tom Pernice, Jr.	67	70	66	69	272	17,200
Chez Reavie	68	69	67	69	273	12,093.34
Kevin Streelman	66	68	71	68	273	12,093.34
Joe Durant	68	67	68	70	273	12,093.33
Robert Garrigus	65	70	68	70	273	12,093.33
Bob Heintz	71	66	69	67	273	12,093.33
Jin Park	70	68	68	67	273	12,093.33
Eric Axley	67	70	68	69	274	9,573.34
Jim McGovern	66	68	71	69	274	9,573.34
Tom Byrum	69	68	71	66	274	9,573.33
Marco Dawson	66	70	70	68	274	9,573.33
Mathias Gronberg	67	67	68	72	274	9,573.33
Deane Pappas	64	72	70	68	274	9,573.33
Shane Bertsch	71	66	70	68	275	8,960
James Driscoll	67	67	69	72	275	8,960
Nathan Green	68	68	69	70	275	8,960
Steve Marino	66	69	72	68	275	8,960
D.J. Trahan	69	69	70	67	275	8,960
Brad Elder	68	68	69	71	276	8,640
Harrison Frazar	68	70	71	67	276	8,640
Ron Whittaker	71	67	73	65	276	8,640
Neal Lancaster	71	66	72	68	277	8,360
Will MacKenzie	70	67	70	70	277	8,360
Corey Pavin	67	69	71	70	277	8,360
Jon Turcott	71	67	69	70	277	8,360
Brad Adamonis	70	68	71	69	278	8,120
Paul Stankowski	70	68	70	70	278	8,120
Martin Laird	70	68	70	71	279	7,960
David Lutterus	67	67	71	74	279	7,960
Tommy Armour	67	70	70	73	280	7,840
John Merrick	69	67	73	72	281	7,760
Briny Baird	67	71	72	72	282	7,680
Scott Sterling	70	68	75	70	283	7,600
Jim Gallagher, Jr.	67	69	76	72	284	7,520
Paul Claxton	68	69	73	75	285	7,440

RBC Canadian Open

Glen Abbey Golf Club, Oakville, Ontario, Canada

July 24-27

Par 35-36–71; 7,222 yards

purse, $5,000,000

	SCORES				TOTAL	MONEY
Chez Reavie	65	64	68	70	267	$900,000
Billy Mayfair	68	66	68	68	270	540,000
Steve Marino	67	67	67	70	271	290,000
Sean O'Hair	65	71	67	68	271	290,000

	SCORES				TOTAL	MONEY
Scott McCarron	66	72	63	71	272	182,500
Nicholas Thompson	67	66	70	69	272	182,500
Mike Weir	65	70	68	69	272	182,500
Glen Day	71	70	64	68	273	145,000
Anthony Kim	65	69	64	75	273	145,000
Kevin Na	69	66	70	68	273	145,000
Briny Baird	69	65	71	69	274	115,000
Ken Duke	68	67	69	70	274	115,000
Carl Pettersson	68	70	67	69	274	115,000
Mark Calcavecchia	70	66	67	72	275	82,500
Brian Davis	69	64	70	72	275	82,500
Bob Estes	68	73	65	69	275	82,500
Carlos Franco	67	68	69	71	275	82,500
Jim Furyk	70	68	67	70	275	82,500
Charlie Wi	69	69	67	70	275	82,500
Eric Axley	65	67	73	71	276	62,500
Fred Couples	69	69	70	68	276	62,500
Kent Jones	71	70	69	67	277	46,416.67
Ryan Palmer	71	70	68	68	277	46,416.67
Omar Uresti	72	68	69	68	277	46,416.67
Mark Wilson	71	69	69	68	277	46,416.67
John Huston	65	72	68	72	277	46,416.66
Martin Laird	71	67	69	70	277	46,416.66
Charley Hoffman	69	70	71	68	278	36,250
Corey Pavin	71	70	69	68	278	36,250
Shane Bertsch	67	73	68	71	279	29,714.29
Retief Goosen	73	68	65	73	279	29,714.29
Kevin Streelman	68	67	71	73	279	29,714.29
Kevin Sutherland	70	71	69	69	279	29,714.29
Steve Flesch	68	67	69	75	279	29,714.28
Todd Hamilton	69	68	69	73	279	29,714.28
Parker McLachlin	69	69	68	73	279	29,714.28
Steve Allan	68	69	68	75	280	21,500
Todd Demsey	69	70	72	69	280	21,500
Mathias Gronberg	69	68	72	71	280	21,500
Bill Haas	68	68	71	73	280	21,500
Jerry Kelly	67	70	71	72	280	21,500
Tom Pernice, Jr.	71	65	75	69	280	21,500
Y.E. Yang	68	68	73	71	280	21,500
Robert Garrigus	70	71	72	68	281	16,000
J.P. Hayes	67	73	70	71	281	16,000
Tim Petrovic	69	72	72	68	281	16,000
Bob Tway	74	67	70	70	281	16,000
Chad Collins	75	66	70	71	282	12,720
Ben Curtis	70	68	73	71	282	12,720
Jason Day	65	75	69	73	282	12,720
Jason Dufner	72	69	70	71	282	12,720
Joe Durant	71	68	72	71	282	12,720
Ryan Armour	67	73	71	72	283	11,575
Andrew Buckle	69	70	70	74	283	11,575
Frank Lickliter	69	72	72	70	283	11,575
Camilo Villegas	71	68	72	72	283	11,575
*Nick Taylor	70	70	72	71	283	
Alex Cejka	69	69	73	73	284	11,100
Dudley Hart	68	70	70	76	284	11,100
David Hearn	69	72	69	74	284	11,100
Cliff Kresge	69	66	76	73	284	11,100
Ted Purdy	68	71	73	72	284	11,100
Bryan DeCorso	74	67	70	74	285	10,600
Michael Letzig	68	73	71	73	285	10,600
Jeff Quinney	69	71	72	73	285	10,600
Patrick Sheehan	70	68	73	74	285	10,600
Scott Sterling	72	69	72	72	285	10,600

	SCORES			TOTAL	MONEY
Jason Allred	67 72 73 74			286	10,300
Nick Flanagan	73 68 70 76			287	10,200
Jeff Maggert	68 73 71 76			288	10,100
Cameron Beckman	68 70 75 78			291	10,000

WGC - Bridgestone Invitational

Firestone Country Club, South Course, Akron, Ohio   July 31-August 3
Par 35-35–70; 7,400 yards   purse, $8,000,000

	SCORES			TOTAL	MONEY
Vijay Singh	67 66 69 68			270	$1,350,000
Stuart Appleby	70 66 67 68			271	635,000
Lee Westwood	70 65 67 69			271	635,000
Retief Goosen	66 71 68 67			272	310,000
Phil Mickelson	68 66 68 70			272	310,000
Darren Clarke	70 71 65 67			273	220,000
Peter Lonard	69 66 72 66			273	220,000
Paul Casey	70 71 68 65			274	162,500
D.J. Trahan	69 67 70 68			274	162,500
Miguel Angel Jimenez	70 66 70 69			275	133,000
Hunter Mahan	71 66 70 68			275	133,000
Chris DiMarco	68 70 68 70			276	111,000
Sean O'Hair	68 67 73 68			276	111,000
Chad Campbell	68 71 68 70			277	95,500
Daniel Chopra	67 74 66 70			277	95,500
K.J. Choi	73 67 70 68			278	82,625
Zach Johnson	67 68 72 71			278	82,625
Ian Poulter	70 68 69 71			278	82,625
Henrik Stenson	73 70 68 67			278	82,625
Robert Allenby	71 70 70 68			279	71,000
Tim Clark	67 71 71 70			279	71,000
Padraig Harrington	69 75 68 67			279	71,000
Robert Karlsson	71 67 71 70			279	71,000
Justin Leonard	68 70 70 71			279	71,000
Steve Lowery	75 67 70 67			279	71,000
Scott Verplank	71 70 70 68			279	71,000
Ernie Els	69 74 69 68			280	60,000
Jim Furyk	68 69 71 72			280	60,000
Charles Howell	68 70 70 72			280	60,000
Paul McGinley	70 67 72 71			280	60,000
Nick O'Hern	70 68 71 71			280	60,000
Justin Rose	71 70 68 71			280	60,000
Rory Sabbatini	69 67 70 74			280	60,000
Vaughn Taylor	72 67 69 72			280	60,000
Oliver Wilson	71 69 72 68			280	60,000
Angel Cabrera	72 73 68 68			281	52,000
Richard Finch	69 75 70 67			281	52,000
Sergio Garcia	69 72 68 72			281	52,000
J.B. Holmes	69 68 72 72			281	52,000
Trevor Immelman	75 64 68 74			281	52,000
Brendan Jones	69 73 69 70			281	52,000
Anthony Kim	71 72 70 68			281	52,000
Aaron Baddeley	79 69 66 68			282	46,600
Stewart Cink	68 68 74 72			282	46,600
Richard Green	72 73 70 67			282	46,600
Brandt Snedeker	68 76 69 69			282	46,600
Steve Stricker	68 69 75 70			282	46,600
Stephen Ames	69 71 71 72			283	44,250
Steve Flesch	70 70 73 70			283	44,250

	SCORES				TOTAL	MONEY
Hidemasa Hoshino	75	73	65	70	283	44,250
David Toms	72	72	70	69	283	44,250
Woody Austin	71	70	72	71	284	42,250
Niclas Fasth	71	71	72	70	284	42,250
Rocco Mediate	68	73	71	72	284	42,250
Chez Reavie	68	74	70	72	284	42,250
Ross Fisher	69	73	70	73	285	40,000
Fredrik Jacobson	71	71	70	73	285	40,000
Graeme McDowell	70	71	73	71	285	40,000
Rod Pampling	69	71	75	70	285	40,000
Adam Scott	69	76	72	68	285	40,000
Nick Dougherty	72	76	69	69	286	38,250
Steve Webster	68	72	72	74	286	38,250
Lucas Glover	70	75	72	70	287	37,000
Andres Romero	73	71	73	70	287	37,000
Scott Strange	68	74	73	72	287	37,000
Kenny Perry	74	69	73	72	288	35,750
Boo Weekley	72	73	71	72	288	35,750
Martin Kaymer	72	79	68	70	289	34,500
Prayad Marksaeng	70	73	73	73	289	34,500
Geoff Ogilvy	71	67	79	72	289	34,500
Brett Rumford	75	70	76	69	290	33,250
Johnson Wagner	70	74	75	71	290	33,250
Soren Hansen	75	73	70	74	292	32,500
J.J. Henry	69	73	73	77	292	32,500
David Howell	70	75	70	77	292	32,500
Pablo Larrazabal	72	75	71	76	294	32,000
Colin Montgomerie	72	71	76	76	295	31,750
James Kingston	73	72	71	80	296	31,500
Craig Parry	70	75	75	77	297	31,250
Mark Brown	80	75	76	70	301	31,000

Legends Reno-Tahoe Open

Montreux Golf & Country Club, Reno, Nevada
Par 36-36–72; 7,472 yards

July 31-August 3
purse, $3,000,000

	SCORES				TOTAL	MONEY
Parker McLachlin	68	62	66	74	270	$540,000
Brian Davis	67	67	68	75	277	264,000
John Rollins	70	66	70	71	277	264,000
Eric Axley	72	66	71	69	278	118,125
Harrison Frazar	67	68	74	69	278	118,125
Martin Laird	73	70	69	66	278	118,125
Ryan Palmer	71	66	71	70	278	118,125
Jason Gore	68	70	70	71	279	87,000
John Merrick	67	67	73	72	279	87,000
Mark Wilson	74	67	71	67	279	87,000
Bob Heintz	71	69	69	71	280	69,000
Kevin Na	71	69	71	69	280	69,000
Brenden Pappas	74	67	69	70	280	69,000
Andrew Buckle	70	69	68	74	281	48,000
Jonathan Byrd	71	73	70	67	281	48,000
Jay Delsing	68	72	69	72	281	48,000
Steve Elkington	73	69	73	66	281	48,000
Carlos Franco	68	69	72	72	281	48,000
Mathias Gronberg	68	68	74	71	281	48,000
Rob Grube	70	74	69	68	281	48,000
Marco Dawson	67	73	69	73	282	28,162.50
Robert Garrigus	74	69	68	71	282	28,162.50
John Huston	70	66	73	73	282	28,162.50

	SCORES				TOTAL	MONEY
Lee Janzen	71	70	68	73	282	28,162.50
Joe Ogilvie	70	66	72	74	282	28,162.50
John Riegger	72	72	72	66	282	28,162.50
Tim Wilkinson	73	71	69	69	282	28,162.50
Y.E. Yang	72	70	67	73	282	28,162.50
Ben Crane	71	70	70	72	283	19,950
Glen Day	72	70	69	72	283	19,950
Jason Dufner	74	69	69	71	283	19,950
Charley Hoffman	69	69	75	70	283	19,950
Cameron Beckman	68	71	69	76	284	16,575
Ian Leggatt	68	76	71	69	284	16,575
Larry Mize	68	66	79	71	284	16,575
Kevin Streelman	68	73	69	74	284	16,575
Alejandro Canizares	71	67	74	73	285	13,200
Robert Gamez	71	69	70	75	285	13,200
Greg Kraft	72	68	71	74	285	13,200
Jeff Overton	65	75	75	70	285	13,200
Tag Ridings	68	73	71	73	285	13,200
Tom Scherrer	70	68	74	73	285	13,200
Michael Allen	68	71	73	74	286	9,620
Gavin Coles	74	68	72	72	286	9,620
Tim Herron	72	69	71	74	286	9,620
Kent Jones	72	70	71	73	286	9,620
Neal Lancaster	69	73	73	71	286	9,620
Nick Watney	73	70	71	72	286	9,620
Bob Estes	69	66	76	76	287	7,485
Doug LaBelle	72	72	69	74	287	7,485
Len Mattiace	69	73	73	72	287	7,485
Chip Sullivan	72	72	65	78	287	7,485
Notah Begay	69	74	70	75	288	6,980
Patrick Sheehan	72	70	68	78	288	6,980
Omar Uresti	68	70	77	73	288	6,980
Dan Forsman	72	70	74	73	289	6,810
Scott Sterling	72	72	72	73	289	6,810
Ryan Moore	72	68	74	76	290	6,630
Kirk Triplett	71	72	68	79	290	6,630
Jimmy Walker	72	71	72	75	290	6,630
Charles Warren	68	69	74	79	290	6,630
Ryan Armour	76	68	77	70	291	6,420
Dennis Paulson	71	71	73	76	291	6,420
Ted Schulz	69	75	72	75	291	6,420
Jin Park	70	72	71	79	292	6,270
Kevin Stadler	70	70	72	80	292	6,270
Nick Flanagan	69	65	77	82	293	6,150
Spike McRoy	71	72	75	75	293	6,150
Matt Jones	71	72	72	80	295	6,060
Kenneth Ferrie	72	72	75	78	297	6,000
Rick Fehr	70	71	80	81	302	5,940

PGA Championship

Oakland Hills Country Club, South Course,
Bloomfield Township, Michigan
Par 35-35–70; 7,395 yards

August 7-10
purse, $7,500,000

	SCORES				TOTAL	MONEY
Padraig Harrington	71	74	66	66	277	$1,350,000
Sergio Garcia	69	73	69	68	279	660,000
Ben Curtis	73	67	68	71	279	660,000
Camilo Villegas	74	72	67	68	281	330,000
Henrik Stenson	71	70	68	72	281	330,000

	SCORES				TOTAL	MONEY
Steve Flesch	73	70	70	69	282	270,000
Phil Mickelson	70	73	71	70	284	231,250
Andres Romero	69	78	65	72	284	231,250
Alastair Forsyth	73	72	70	70	285	176,725
Justin Rose	73	67	74	71	285	176,725
Jeev Milkha Singh	68	74	70	73	285	176,725
Charlie Wi	70	70	71	74	285	176,725
Ken Duke	69	73	73	71	286	137,250
Aaron Baddeley	71	71	71	73	286	137,250
Paul Casey	72	74	72	69	287	107,060
Stuart Appleby	76	70	69	72	287	107,060
Prayad Marksaeng	76	70	68	73	287	107,060
Graeme McDowell	74	72	68	73	287	107,060
David Toms	72	69	72	74	287	107,060
Brian Gay	70	74	72	72	288	78,900
Robert Karlsson	68	77	71	72	288	78,900
Angel Cabrera	70	72	72	74	288	78,900
Boo Weekley	72	71	79	66	288	78,900
Nicholas Thompson	71	72	73	73	289	57,000
Brandt Snedeker	71	71	74	73	289	57,000
Fredrik Jacobson	75	71	70	73	289	57,000
Mark Brown	77	69	74	69	289	57,000
Retief Goosen	72	74	69	74	289	57,000
Jim Furyk	71	77	70	72	290	47,550
J.B. Holmes	71	68	70	81	290	47,550
Ian Poulter	74	71	73	73	291	38,825
Sean O'Hair	69	73	76	73	291	38,825
Chris Dimarco	75	72	72	72	291	38,825
Paul Goydos	74	69	73	75	291	38,825
D.J. Trahan	72	71	76	72	291	38,825
Robert Allenby	76	72	72	71	291	38,825
Ernie Els	71	75	70	75	291	38,825
Geoff Ogilvy	73	74	74	70	291	38,825
Rory Sabbatini	72	73	73	74	292	30,200
Steve Elkington	71	73	73	75	292	30,200
Steve Stricker	71	75	77	69	292	30,200
Mike Weir	73	75	71	74	293	24,500
Michael Campbell	73	71	75	74	293	24,500
Tom Lehman	74	70	75	74	293	24,500
Briny Baird	71	72	73	77	293	24,500
John Senden	76	72	72	73	293	24,500
Michael Allen	70	75	71	78	294	18,070
Carl Pettersson	71	74	76	73	294	18,070
Billy Mayfair	69	78	75	72	294	18,070
Dean Wilson	73	73	77	71	294	18,070
Charles Howell	72	76	77	69	294	18,070
John Merrick	73	75	70	77	295	16,250
Peter Hanson	71	73	75	76	295	16,250
Charl Schwartzel	77	70	73	75	295	16,250
Anthony Kim	70	75	74	77	296	15,750
Tim Clark	76	72	73	75	296	15,750
James Kingston	72	76	74	74	296	15,750
Justin Leonard	74	71	72	80	297	15,375
Pat Perez	73	73	79	72	297	15,375
Steve Marino	73	74	75	76	298	15,000
John Mallinger	72	75	77	74	298	15,000
Chez Reavie	78	70	78	72	298	15,000
Corey Pavin	75	73	73	78	299	14,500
Niclas Fasth	73	73	75	78	299	14,500
Mark Calcavecchia	71	76	76	76	299	14,500
Paul Azinger	72	76	76	75	299	14,500
Kevin Sutherland	76	71	77	75	299	14,500
Peter Lonard	74	74	74	78	300	14,150

	SCORES	TOTAL	MONEY
Hiroyuki Fujita	77 70 76 77	300	14,150
Bubba Watson	75 73 77 76	301	14,000
Richard Green	71 77 79 76	303	13,900
Rocco Mediate	73 74 72 85	304	13,800
Louis Oosthuizen	76 72 81 77	306	13,700

Out of Final 36 Holes

Brendan Jones	71	78	149	Jerry Kelly	79	74	153
John Daly	74	75	149	Sonny Skinner	78	75	153
Soren Kjeldsen	75	74	149	Tim Weinhart	74	79	153
Bob Tway	75	74	149	Parker McLachlin	76	77	153
Fred Couples	76	73	149	Steve Webster	78	76	154
Tom Pernice, Jr.	75	74	149	Martin Kaymer	75	79	154
Johnson Wagner	78	71	149	Toru Taniguchi	79	75	154
Frank Esposito, Jr.	71	78	149	Sam Arnold	80	74	154
Simon Dyson	73	76	149	Bart Bryant	77	77	154
Zach Johnson	76	73	149	Ryan Benzel	77	78	155
Ryan Moore	70	79	149	Jim Estes	79	76	155
Rich Beem	73	76	149	Scott Verplank	77	78	155
Todd Hamilton	76	73	149	George McNeill	78	77	155
J.J. Henry	76	74	150	Ben Crane	75	80	155
Jay Haas	73	77	150	Cliff Kresge	83	72	155
Mark Brooks	74	76	150	Lee Westwood	77	78	155
Adam Scott	77	73	150	Oliver Wilson	78	77	155
Daniel Chopra	74	76	150	Mathew Goggin	81	75	156
Richard S. Johnson	75	75	150	Jeff Quinney	81	75	156
Nick O'Hern	74	76	150	Scott Hebert	80	76	156
Vaughn Taylor	78	72	150	Peter Hedblom	76	80	156
Heath Slocum	74	77	151	Rick Leibovich	78	78	156
Darren Clarke	75	76	151	Tim Thelen	81	76	157
Anders Hansen	75	76	151	Jonathan Byrd	75	82	157
Scott Strange	73	78	151	Jeff Martin	78	79	157
Don Yrene	75	76	151	Ryuji Imada	80	77	157
K.J. Choi	78	73	151	Greg Kraft	78	79	157
Stewart Cink	75	76	151	Woody Austin	79	79	158
Miguel Angel Jimenez	73	78	151	Kyle Flinton	79	79	158
Rod Pampling	70	81	151	Pablo Larrazabal	80	78	158
Steve Lowery	74	77	151	Brad Martin	77	81	158
Tommy Armour	79	73	152	Curt Sanders	78	80	158
Vijay Singh	76	76	152	Nick Dougherty	77	82	159
Stephen Ames	77	75	152	Colin Montgomerie	76	84	160
Chad Campbell	76	76	152	Hunter Mahan	81	79	160
Jyoti Randhawa	77	75	152	Eric Dugas	87	74	161
Alan Morin	76	76	152	David Long	80	82	162
Davis Love	77	75	152	Vince Jewell	85	78	163
Hennie Otto	76	76	152	Eric Manning	81	88	169
Trevor Immelman	76	77	153	Brad Dean	86	84	170
Soren Hansen	77	76	153	Kenny Perry			WD
Ross Fisher	77	76	153				

Wyndham Championship

Sedgefield Country Club, Greensboro, North Carolina
Par 35-35–70; 7,117 yards

August 14-17
purse, $5,100,000

	SCORES	TOTAL	MONEY
Carl Pettersson	64 61 66 68	259	$918,000
Scott McCarron	65 64 64 68	261	550,800
Rich Beem	70 67 63 63	263	346,800

	SCORES				TOTAL	MONEY
J.J. Henry	70	66	66	62	264	224,400
Martin Laird	63	74	64	63	264	224,400
Tim Clark	64	67	68	66	265	170,850
John Senden	66	66	67	66	265	170,850
Kevin Streelman	66	64	67	68	265	170,850
Briny Baird	67	68	62	69	266	122,400
Shane Bertsch	67	68	67	64	266	122,400
Jerry Kelly	66	65	68	67	266	122,400
Michael Letzig	67	66	67	66	266	122,400
Bob Sowards	65	66	68	67	266	122,400
Mark Wilson	68	67	67	64	266	122,400
Justin Bolli	68	66	68	65	267	81,600
Lee Janzen	67	66	67	67	267	81,600
Scott Sterling	64	71	64	68	267	81,600
Vaughn Taylor	67	67	66	67	267	81,600
Garrett Willis	64	64	69	70	267	81,600
Lucas Glover	66	68	66	68	268	57,324
Kent Jones	66	68	65	69	268	57,324
John Riegger	67	65	67	69	268	57,324
Patrick Sheehan	66	71	65	66	268	57,324
Jay Williamson	67	67	67	67	268	57,324
*Danny Lee	68	66	67	67	268	
Paul Casey	70	66	67	66	269	40,672.50
Jason Dufner	66	69	66	68	269	40,672.50
Zach Johnson	66	70	69	64	269	40,672.50
Tom Pernice, Jr.	68	66	69	66	269	40,672.50
Mark Brooks	68	66	68	68	270	32,427.50
Bob Estes	71	66	67	66	270	32,427.50
Robert Garrigus	66	66	71	67	270	32,427.50
David Lutterus	69	64	72	65	270	32,427.50
Jon Mills	68	69	65	68	270	32,427.50
Y.E. Yang	67	69	66	68	270	32,427.50
Billy Andrade	66	69	67	69	271	25,143
George McNeill	68	67	68	68	271	25,143
Stephen Poole	66	71	69	65	271	25,143
Marc Turnesa	69	68	65	69	271	25,143
Charles Warren	67	66	69	69	271	25,143
Eric Axley	67	69	64	72	272	18,870
Ben Crane	68	66	70	68	272	18,870
Glen Day	66	69	69	68	272	18,870
Charley Hoffman	68	69	66	69	272	18,870
Joe Ogilvie	69	68	68	67	272	18,870
David Toms	68	67	71	66	272	18,870
Bob Tway	70	65	69	68	272	18,870
Mark Calcavecchia	67	69	70	67	273	14,382
Brian Gay	67	68	66	72	273	14,382
Tom Byrum	71	66	68	69	274	12,886
John Daly	70	67	66	71	274	12,886
Nick Flanagan	68	69	70	67	274	12,886
Cody Freeman	70	67	70	68	275	11,773.72
Bob Heintz	63	72	72	68	275	11,773.72
Richard S. Johnson	67	70	71	67	275	11,773.72
Jeff Maggert	66	70	70	69	275	11,773.71
Steve Marino	65	68	71	71	275	11,773.71
Brenden Pappas	69	67	69	70	275	11,773.71
Kyle Thompson	68	67	71	69	275	11,773.71
Todd Demsey	69	68	68	71	276	11,067
Ken Duke	65	71	71	69	276	11,067
Joe Durant	67	69	70	70	276	11,067
Jeff Gove	68	66	73	69	276	11,067
Davis Love	66	70	71	69	276	11,067
Bo Van Pelt	67	66	72	71	276	11,067
Jason Gore	67	69	70	71	277	10,608

	SCORES				TOTAL	MONEY
Mathias Gronberg	71	64	75	67	277	10,608
Mark Hensby	66	66	75	70	277	10,608
Ryuji Imada	68	68	73	69	278	10,149
Doug LaBelle	70	67	70	71	278	10,149
Frank Lickliter	68	68	71	71	278	10,149
Brandt Snedeker	66	68	74	70	278	10,149
Tim Wilkinson	66	69	69	74	278	10,149
Dean Wilson	66	71	71	70	278	10,149
Peter Lonard	66	71	73	69	279	9,690
Troy Matteson	69	67	70	73	279	9,690
Ted Purdy	68	68	71	72	279	9,690
Billy Mayfair	67	68	71	75	281	9,486

PGA Tour Playoffs for the FedExCup

The Barclays

Ridgewood Country Club, Paramus, New Jersey
Par 35-36–71; 7,304 yards

August 21-24
purse, $7,000,000

	SCORES				TOTAL	MONEY
Vijay Singh	70	70	66	70	276	$1,260,000
Sergio Garcia	70	67	69	70	276	616,000
Kevin Sutherland	70	69	69	68	276	616,000
(Singh defeated Sutherland on first and Garcia on second playoff hole.)						
Mathew Goggin	67	74	69	67	277	289,333.34
Ben Curtis	71	68	70	68	277	289,333.33
Kevin Streelman	67	70	68	72	277	289,333.33
Paul Casey	66	71	69	72	278	203,700
Martin Laird	70	69	72	67	278	203,700
Justin Leonard	70	70	71	67	278	203,700
Nicholas Thompson	75	68	68	67	278	203,700
Mike Weir	72	67	67	72	278	203,700
K.J. Choi	74	69	68	68	279	129,000
Ken Duke	72	71	67	69	279	129,000
Jim Furyk	70	71	68	70	279	129,000
Dudley Hart	67	69	73	70	279	129,000
Anthony Kim	70	67	72	70	279	129,000
Scott Verplank	73	70	67	69	279	129,000
Bubba Watson	68	70	71	70	279	129,000
Stuart Appleby	71	70	68	71	280	84,840
Angel Cabrera	69	67	72	72	280	84,840
Jerry Kelly	72	70	71	67	280	84,840
Phil Mickelson	70	70	72	68	280	84,840
Steve Stricker	68	64	77	71	280	84,840
Glen Day	70	71	70	70	281	55,400
Tim Herron	69	71	73	68	281	55,400
J.B. Holmes	71	71	73	66	281	55,400
Jesper Parnevik	68	72	72	69	281	55,400
Rory Sabbatini	70	70	72	69	281	55,400
Patrick Sheehan	69	70	70	72	281	55,400
Mark Wilson	72	70	71	68	281	55,400
Jason Day	74	68	66	74	282	39,700
Hunter Mahan	62	73	74	73	282	39,700
Billy Mayfair	70	70	73	69	282	39,700
George McNeill	68	70	73	71	282	39,700

		SCORES			TOTAL	MONEY
Kevin Na	72	70	68	72	282	39,700
John Senden	71	70	72	69	282	39,700
Jay Williamson	74	68	70	70	282	39,700
Robert Allenby	69	73	66	75	283	26,600
Eric Axley	78	65	68	72	283	26,600
Stewart Cink	73	70	70	70	283	26,600
Tim Clark	70	69	73	71	283	26,600
Brian Davis	69	74	70	70	283	26,600
Charley Hoffman	67	71	74	71	283	26,600
John Merrick	69	71	70	73	283	26,600
Jeff Overton	74	67	68	74	283	26,600
Tim Petrovic	71	72	69	71	283	26,600
Brett Quigley	71	69	71	72	283	26,600
Briny Baird	69	71	69	75	284	17,400
Justin Bolli	71	71	72	70	284	17,400
Lee Janzen	71	69	72	72	284	17,400
John Mallinger	70	73	69	72	284	17,400
Kenny Perry	69	67	72	76	284	17,400
Carl Pettersson	72	70	71	71	284	17,400
Dean Wilson	72	70	67	75	284	17,400
Rich Beem	68	74	71	72	285	15,680
Jonathan Byrd	72	70	73	70	285	15,680
Steve Elkington	71	71	71	72	285	15,680
Lucas Glover	70	70	75	70	285	15,680
Bill Haas	71	68	71	75	285	15,680
J.J. Henry	70	72	74	69	285	15,680
Andres Romero	72	68	77	68	285	15,680
Ryan Palmer	69	69	72	76	286	15,050
Nick Watney	71	69	75	71	286	15,050
Frank Lickliter	71	71	71	74	287	14,840
Michael Allen	73	67	75	73	288	14,560
Chad Campbell	71	72	69	76	288	14,560
Charlie Wi	72	71	72	73	288	14,560
Richard S. Johnson	74	69	74	72	289	14,210
Brandt Snedeker	71	71	73	74	289	14,210
Trevor Immelman	70	71	76	73	290	14,000
Bo Van Pelt	67	74	70	80	291	13,860
Paul Goydos	70	72	77	76	295	13,720

Deutsche Bank Championship

TPC Boston, Norton, Massachusetts
Par 36-35–71; 7,207yards

August 29-September 1
purse, $7,000,000

		SCORES			TOTAL	MONEY
Vijay Singh	64	66	69	63	262	$1,260,000
Mike Weir	61	68	67	71	267	756,000
Ernie Els	66	65	69	70	270	406,000
Camilo Villegas	68	66	63	73	270	406,000
Sergio Garcia	67	64	68	72	271	266,000
Tim Herron	72	67	67	65	271	266,000
Chad Campbell	67	70	69	66	272	218,166.67
Justin Leonard	69	70	66	67	272	218,166.67
Jim Furyk	66	65	69	72	272	218,166.66
Ben Crane	72	65	63	73	273	175,000
Ken Duke	66	67	70	70	273	175,000
Steve Marino	66	66	71	70	273	175,000
Ryuji Imada	69	65	68	72	274	140,000
Steve Stricker	69	67	70	68	274	140,000
Angel Cabrera	67	68	69	71	275	108,500

	SCORES				TOTAL	MONEY
Tim Clark	66	62	73	74	275	108,500
Steve Flesch	68	65	73	69	275	108,500
Hunter Mahan	70	64	72	69	275	108,500
Heath Slocum	64	68	69	74	275	108,500
Johnson Wagner	68	65	74	68	275	108,500
Briny Baird	64	69	68	75	276	70,000
K.J. Choi	69	70	70	67	276	70,000
Richard S. Johnson	67	66	69	74	276	70,000
Pat Perez	69	69	68	70	276	70,000
Carl Pettersson	67	68	68	73	276	70,000
Brett Quigley	69	70	67	70	276	70,000
Michael Allen	71	68	66	72	277	48,650
Ben Curtis	65	65	75	72	277	48,650
J.J. Henry	68	69	71	69	277	48,650
Anthony Kim	66	66	74	71	277	48,650
Brandt Snedeker	67	68	72	70	277	48,650
Boo Weekley	70	67	70	70	277	48,650
Stuart Appleby	70	66	70	72	278	36,200
Jonathan Byrd	67	69	69	73	278	36,200
Stewart Cink	67	69	69	73	278	36,200
Charley Hoffman	67	69	71	71	278	36,200
John Merrick	64	68	76	70	278	36,200
Jesper Parnevik	68	71	66	73	278	36,200
John Senden	69	69	70	70	278	36,200
Woody Austin	72	66	66	75	279	28,000
Tim Petrovic	71	65	72	71	279	28,000
John Rollins	73	66	70	70	279	28,000
Mark Wilson	69	69	67	74	279	28,000
Bo Van Pelt	67	67	74	72	280	21,163.34
Bubba Watson	70	69	71	70	280	21,163.34
Robert Allenby	70	67	71	72	280	21,163.33
Scott McCarron	69	70	69	72	280	21,163.33
Nick O'Hern	69	66	73	72	280	21,163.33
Charlie Wi	66	67	71	76	280	21,163.33
Stephen Ames	71	67	71	72	281	16,100
Bart Bryant	69	70	68	74	281	16,100
Brian Davis	70	66	70	75	281	16,100
Jason Day	70	66	74	71	281	16,100
Brian Gay	68	68	73	72	281	16,100
Lucas Glover	68	71	67	75	281	16,100
Trevor Immelman	71	67	71	72	281	16,100
Martin Laird	70	68	70	73	281	16,100
Ryan Palmer	67	68	74	72	281	16,100
Tom Pernice, Jr.	69	67	69	76	281	16,100
Andres Romero	68	69	72	72	281	16,100
Kevin Streelman	66	65	73	77	281	16,100
Kevin Sutherland	70	67	71	73	281	16,100
John Mallinger	66	67	74	75	282	14,770
Jeff Overton	66	67	72	77	282	14,770
Chez Reavie	69	69	69	75	282	14,770
Scott Verplank	69	68	71	74	282	14,770
Fredrik Jacobson	67	68	74	74	283	14,350
D.J. Trahan	67	66	70	80	283	14,350
Bill Haas	69	70	66	79	284	14,000
Frank Lickliter	73	65	70	76	284	14,000
Rocco Mediate	69	70	71	74	284	14,000
Geoff Ogilvy	67	70	73	76	286	13,720

BMW Championship

Bellerive Country Club, St. Louis, Missouri
Par 35-35–70; 7,456 yards

September 4-7
purse, $7,000,000

	SCORES				TOTAL	MONEY
Camilo Villegas	65	66	66	68	265	$1,260,000
Dudley Hart	67	69	66	65	267	756,000
Jim Furyk	70	62	66	70	268	406,000
Anthony Kim	68	67	66	67	268	406,000
Stephen Ames	68	69	66	66	269	255,500
K.J. Choi	70	68	64	67	269	255,500
D.J. Trahan	71	63	68	67	269	255,500
Tim Clark	67	68	66	69	270	210,000
Hunter Mahan	69	67	68	66	270	210,000
Aaron Baddeley	71	64	67	69	271	175,000
Fredrik Jacobson	67	67	72	65	271	175,000
Steve Stricker	66	71	68	66	271	175,000
Ben Curtis	70	70	68	65	273	131,250
Brian Gay	67	67	67	72	273	131,250
Lucas Glover	68	68	69	68	273	131,250
Trevor Immelman	69	67	70	67	273	131,250
Ernie Els	68	72	66	68	274	105,000
Justin Leonard	69	67	68	70	274	105,000
Phil Mickelson	68	65	71	70	274	105,000
Tommy Armour	71	64	69	71	275	87,500
Sergio Garcia	68	68	69	70	275	87,500
Eric Axley	70	69	70	67	276	64,983.34
Steve Marino	69	69	70	68	276	64,983.34
Angel Cabrera	69	69	66	72	276	64,983.33
Billy Mayfair	73	67	67	69	276	64,983.33
Kevin Streelman	70	68	69	69	276	64,983.33
Dean Wilson	69	71	66	70	276	64,983.33
Bart Bryant	69	68	69	71	277	47,600
Geoff Ogilvy	69	71	67	70	277	47,600
Scott Verplank	73	69	68	67	277	47,600
Bubba Watson	73	73	66	65	277	47,600
Boo Weekley	71	65	71	70	277	47,600
Ben Crane	70	70	69	69	278	37,800
Ken Duke	70	72	67	69	278	37,800
J.B. Holmes	68	73	67	70	278	37,800
Carl Pettersson	72	70	70	66	278	37,800
Chez Reavie	67	70	75	66	278	37,800
Robert Allenby	71	68	68	72	279	29,400
Stuart Appleby	66	73	70	70	279	29,400
Briny Baird	73	66	69	71	279	29,400
Brian Davis	75	67	72	65	279	29,400
Mathew Goggin	70	71	67	71	279	29,400
Tim Herron	66	71	67	75	279	29,400
Kenny Perry	66	72	68	74	280	21,163.34
Andres Romero	66	70	73	71	280	21,163.34
Rory Sabbatini	72	66	67	75	280	21,163.33
Vijay Singh	70	70	71	69	280	21,163.33
Heath Slocum	71	73	70	66	280	21,163.33
Nicholas Thompson	70	73	70	67	280	21,163.33
Adam Scott	69	71	69	72	281	17,430
John Senden	69	73	73	66	281	17,430
Jonathan Byrd	71	68	71	72	282	16,520
Johnson Wagner	72	69	67	74	282	16,520
Jay Williamson	68	69	72	73	282	16,520
Padraig Harrington	69	71	72	71	283	15,820
Martin Laird	69	70	76	68	283	15,820
John Mallinger	71	65	75	72	283	15,820

		SCORES			TOTAL	MONEY
Brandt Snedeker	69	77	67	70	283	15,820
Kevin Sutherland	70	73	68	72	283	15,820
Stewart Cink	73	70	71	70	284	15,190
Charley Hoffman	68	71	68	77	284	15,190
Jerry Kelly	74	66	73	71	284	15,190
John Merrick	76	74	65	69	284	15,190
Woody Austin	69	71	73	72	285	14,700
Charlie Wi	76	71	67	71	285	14,700
Mark Wilson	69	75	71	70	285	14,700
Ryuji Imada	72	70	72	73	287	14,350
Mike Weir	69	72	71	75	287	14,350
Chad Campbell	73				WD	

The Tour Championship

East Lake Golf Club, Atlanta, Georgia
Par 35-35–70; 7,154 yards

September 25-28
purse, $7,000,000

		SCORES			TOTAL	MONEY
Camilo Villegas	72	66	69	66	273	$1,260,000
Sergio Garcia	70	65	67	71	273	756,000
(Villegas defeated Garcia on first playoff hole.)						
Anthony Kim	64	69	72	69	274	409,500
Phil Mickelson	68	68	69	69	274	409,500
Ben Curtis	71	69	68	70	278	280,000
Ernie Els	68	73	70	69	280	238,000
Jim Furyk	72	70	69	69	280	238,000
Mike Weir	70	69	71	70	280	238,000
K.J. Choi	69	70	70	72	281	210,000
Stuart Appleby	72	71	70	69	282	180,040
Dudley Hart	73	69	71	69	282	180,040
Trevor Immelman	68	73	71	70	282	180,040
Justin Leonard	73	69	73	67	282	180,040
Billy Mayfair	72	71	69	70	282	180,040
Kevin Sutherland	71	71	69	72	283	154,000
Robert Allenby	75	66	67	76	284	148,400
Ken Duke	77	69	69	71	286	138,600
Ryuji Imada	75	72	71	68	286	138,600
Hunter Mahan	74	75	68	69	286	138,600
D.J. Trahan	71	72	71	72	286	138,600
Carl Pettersson	76	72	71	68	287	131,600
Chad Campbell	72	73	75	69	289	127,400
Vijay Singh	73	74	72	70	289	127,400
Stewart Cink	75	73	73	69	290	120,400
Kenny Perry	76	75	67	72	290	120,400
Steve Stricker	74	74	70	72	290	120,400
Briny Baird	74	71	70	76	291	115,500
Andres Romero	73	68	78	72	291	115,500
Tim Clark	78	74	71	69	292	113,400
Bubba Watson	71	74	74	76	295	112,000

Final Standings – PGA Tour Playoffs for the FedExCup

RANK	NAME	FEDEXCUP POINTS	BONUS MONEY
1	Vijay Singh	125,101	$10,000,000
2	Camilo Villegas	124,550	3,000,000
3	Sergio Garcia	119,400	2,000,000
4	Anthony Kim	114,419	1,500,000
5	Jim Furyk	113,180	1,000,000
6	Mike Weir	113,118	800,000
7	Phil Mickelson	112,201	700,000
8	Justin Leonard	111,638	600,000
9	Ben Curtis	110,702	550,000
10	K.J. Choi	110,646	500,000
11	Kevin Sutherland	109,378	300,000
12	Dudley Hart	108,931	290,000
13	Ernie Els	108,475	280,000
14	Steve Stricker	108,381	270,000
15	Kenny Perry	108,090	250,000
16	Trevor Immelman	108,028	245,000
17	Stuart Appleby	108,025	240,000
18	Hunter Mahan	107,999	235,000
19	Robert Allenby	107,701	230,000
20	Stewart Cink	107,407	225,000
21	Carl Pettersson	107,394	220,000
22	Ken Duke	107,082	215,000
23	Billy Mayfair	106,689	210,000
24	D.J. Trahan	106,303	205,000
25	Ryuji Imada	106,203	200,000
26	Tim Clark	105,920	195,000
27	Briny Baird	105,609	190,000
28	Andres Romero	105,378	185,000
29	Chad Campbell	105,262	180,000
30	Bubba Watson	105,003	175,000

The Ryder Cup

Valhalla Golf Club, Louisville, Kentucky   September 19-21
Par 443 444 534–35, 534 434 445–36–71; 7,496 yards

FIRST DAY
Morning Foursomes

Phil Mickelson and Anthony Kim (USA) halved with Padraig Harrington and Robert Karlsson.

Mickelson/Kim	4	4	2	3	4	5	5	3	4	5	4	4	4	3	3	4	4	5
Harrington/Karlsson	3	4	4	3	4	4	5	4	4	4	3	3	5	4	4	4	4	5

Justin Leonard and Hunter Mahan (USA) defeated Henrik Stenson and Paul Casey, 3 and 2.

Leonard/Mahan	5	5	2	3	3	5	3	3	4	5	3	4	4	2	4	4	
Stenson/Casey	4	4	3	4	5	4	7	4	4	4	3	4	4	3	5	4	

Stewart Cink and Chad Campbell (USA) defeated Justin Rose and Ian Poulter, 1-up.

Cink/Campbell	4	4	3	3	4	5	6	2	4	3	4	3	3	5	4	4		
Rose/Poulter	4	4	2	3	3	5	3	4	4	4	4	5	4	4	4	6		

Kenny Perry and Jim Furyk (USA) halved with Lee Westwood and Sergio Garcia.

Perry/Furyk	4	4	2	4	4	4	4	3	4	5	3	3	4	3	4	5	5	6
Westwood/Garcia	3	4	3	3	4	5	5	3	4	5	3	4	3	3	6	5	4	4

POINTS: United States 3, Europe 1

FIRST DAY
Afternoon Fourballs

Phil Mickelson and Anthony Kim (USA) defeated Padraig Harrington and Graeme McDowell, 2-up.

Player	1	2	3	4	5	6	7	8	9	10	11	12	13	14	15	16	17	18
Mickelson	3	5	3	4	3			3	3		3	3	3		4		3	4
Kim		5	3	4		3	4	3		4			2		4			
Harrington	3		2		4		4	3	3	4			4	4	5			
McDowell		4		3		4	4	2	4		4	3	3		4			

Ian Poulter and Justin Rose (Europe) defeated Steve Stricker and Ben Curtis, 4 and 2.

Player	1	2	3	4	5	6	7	8	9	10	11	12	13	14	15	16
Stricker	4	4	2	3		5		3	4	3	4		3		4	
Curtis				4		5	3		4		4					
Poulter	4		3	3	4	4	4	3	3	4		4	2		3	
Rose		3					3	4			4					

Justin Leonard and Hunter Mahan (USA) defeated Sergio Garcia and Miguel Angel Jimenez, 4 and 3.

Player	1	2	3	4	5	6	7	8	9	10	11	12	13	14	15
Leonard			2	3	4	4	5		4	3	3		3	3	
Mahan	3	3				3	3		3						
Garcia			3	3	4	4	3		4		4				
Jimenez	4	3			3	4		2		4	3	4			

J.B. Holmes and Boo Weekley (USA) halved with Lee Westwood and Soren Hansen.

Player	1	2	3	4	5	6	7	8	9	10	11	12	13	14	15	16	17	18
Holmes	3			4	4		2	3		3						3		5
Weekley		4	3		4	4		4		3	4	3	4		3			
Westwood		3	3	3	3		2	4	5			3	4	3	3			
Hansen	4			4	4			3	4	4								4

POINTS: United States 5½, Europe 2½

SECOND DAY
Morning Foursomes

Ian Poulter and Justin Rose (Europe) defeated Stewart Cink and Chad Campbell, 4 and 3.

Player	1	2	3	4	5	6	7	8	9	10	11	12	13	14	15
Cink/Campbell	4	6	3	4	5	4	6	3	4	4	3	4	3	4	5
Poulter/Rose	3	4	3	3	3	4	4	3	4	5	3	5	5	3	3

Justin Leonard and Hunter Mahan (USA) halved with Miguel Angel Jimenez and Graeme McDowell.

Player	1	2	3	4	5	6	7	8	9	10	11	12	13	14	15	16	17	18
Leonard/Mahan	4	3	4	4	4	4	6	2	4	5	3	3	4	3	3	4	3	5
Jimenez/McDowell	4	3	3	3	4	5	5	3	4	5	3	5	3	4	3	4	4	4

Henrik Stenson and Oliver Wilson (Europe) defeated Phil Mickelson and Anthony Kim, 2 and 1.

Player	1	2	3	4	5	6	7	8	9	10	11	12	13	14	15	16	17
Mickelson/Kim	4	3	2	3	4	4	6	4	4	5	3	5	4	4	5	4	4
Stenson/Wilson	4	5	3	4	4	5	4	3	4	4	3	4	4	4	3	4	3

Jim Furyk and Kenny Perry (USA) defeated Padraig Harrington and Robert Karlsson, 3 and 1.

Player	1	2	3	4	5	6	7	8	9	10	11	12	13	14	15	16	17
Furyk/Perry	4	3	3	3	3	5	5	3	4	5	3	5	3	2	4	4	3
Harrington/Karlsson	5	4	3	4	5	4	4	3	4	5	3	5	3	3	3	4	4

POINTS: United States 7, Europe 5

SECOND DAY
Afternoon Fourballs

Boo Weekley and J.B. Holmes (USA) defeated Lee Westwood and Soren Hansen, 2 and 1.

Player	1	2	3	4	5	6	7	8	9	10	11	12	13	14	15	16	17
Weekley	3	4	3		4	4		3			3	5		2	3		
Holmes				4			4		4	3		4				4	4
Westwood	3	4	3				3	4	5				3	3	4		
Hansen				4	4	5	5			2	5	3					4

Ben Curtis and Steve Stricker (USA) halved with Sergio Garcia and Paul Casey.

	1	2	3	4	5	6	7	8	9	10	11	12	13	14	15	16	17	18
Curtis	4	3		4		4	5	3	4			3	4					
Stricker			3	3	4		4	2				3				4	4	4
Garcia		4	3		4	4	2	4	4		4	3	3		4			
Casey	4			3	4					3			4			4	4	

Ian Poulter and Graeme McDowell (Europe) defeated Kenny Perry and Jim Furyk, 1-up.

	1	2	3	4	5	6	7	8	9	10	11	12	13	14	15	16	17	18
Perry	4	3				4			4		3			2				
Furyk			3	4	4		5	2		4		4	3		3	4	3	4
Poulter	3	4	3		4		3	4		4						3	4	
McDowell		4	4	4		2		3			3	3	3		4			

Phil Mickelson and Hunter Mahan (USA) halved with Henrik Stenson and Robert Karlsson.

	1	2	3	4	5	6	7	8	9	10	11	12	13	14	15	16	17	18
Mickelson	4	3	2			3	3			4	3	4	4	2		4	4	
Mahan		4	4	4				3					3					4
Stenson	3			3	4		4	4			3					4	4	
Karlsson		4			4			3	3	4		3	3	2	3			4

POINTS: United States 9, Europe 7

THIRD DAY
Singles

Anthony Kim (USA) defeated Sergio Garcia, 5 and 4.

	1	2	3	4	5	6	7	8	9	10	11	12	13
Kim	3	3	3	4	4	3	3	4	5	3	3	3	3
Garcia	3	4	3	4	5	6	3	4	4	4	5	5	3

Hunter Mahan (USA) halved with Paul Casey.

	1	2	3	4	5	6	7	8	9	10	11	12	13	14	15	16	17	18
Hunter Mahan	5	3	3	3	4	4	5	2	4	4	3	4	4	2	5	4	3	5
Casey	4	5	3	4	5	4	4	4	3	4	3	3	5	2	5	3	4	4

Robert Karlsson (Europe) defeated Justin Leonard, 5 and 3.

	1	2	3	4	5	6	7	8	9	10	11	12	13	14	15
Leonard	4	4	3	4	4	4	5	3	4	6	3	4	4	3	4
Karlsson	4	4	3	3	4	3	5	2	4	5	3	4	4	3	3

Justin Rose (Europe) defeated Phil Mickelson, 3 and 2.

	1	2	3	4	5	6	7	8	9	10	11	12	13	14	15	16
Mickelson	4	4	3	3	4	5	5	3	4	5	3	4	3	3	3	3
Rose	4	4	3	3	4	4	4	3	4	4	3	3	3	3	4	3

Kenny Perry (USA) defeated Henrik Stenson, 3 and 2.

	1	2	3	4	5	6	7	8	9	10	11	12	13	14	15	16	17
Perry	3	4	2	3	3	4	3	3	4	6	2	4	3	4	3	4	
Stenson	3	5	3	3	4	3	6	3	4	4	3	4	3	4	3	4	4

Boo Weekley (USA) defeated Oliver Wilson, 4 and 2.

	1	2	3	4	5	6	7	8	9	10	11	12	13	14	15	16
Weekley	4	4	2	3	3	4	3	2	4	4	3	4	4	3	4	3
Wilson	4	3	3	3	4	4	4	3	4	5	3	4	4	3	3	4

J.B. Holmes (USA) defeated Soren Hansen, 2 and 1.

	1	2	3	4	5	6	7	8	9	10	11	12	13	14	15	16	17
Holmes	4	4	2	3	3	4	6	4	4	7	3	4	4	2	4	3	3
Hansen	3	4	3	3	4	5	5	3	4	5	4	4	4	4	3	4	4

Jim Furyk (USA) defeated Miguel Angel Jimenez, 2 and 1.

	1	2	3	4	5	6	7	8	9	10	11	12	13	14	15	16	17
Furyk	3	4	3	3	5	4	4	3	5	4	3	4	3	3	3	5	4
Jimenez	4	4	4	3	4	3	4	4	4	6	4	4	3	3	4	4	

Graeme McDowell (Europe) defeated Stewart Cink, 2 and 1.

	1	2	3	4	5	6	7	8	9	10	11	12	13	14	15	16	17
Cink	4	3	2	3	4	4	6	3	5	4	3	5	4	3	4	4	4
McDowell	4	3	3	3	4	4	3	3	4	4	4	4	3	3	4	4	4

Ian Poulter (Europe) defeated Steve Stricker, 3 and 2.

	1	2	3	4	5	6	7	8	9	10	11	12	13	14	15	16
Stricker	4	3	3	4	4	5	5	3	4	4	3	4	3	3	4	4
Poulter	3	3	3	3	4	4	5	3	3	5	3	3	3	4	4	4

Ben Curtis (USA) defeated LeeWestwood, 2 and 1.

| Curtis | 3 | 4 | 3 | 3 | 5 | 4 | 4 | 3 | 4 | 5 | 3 | 4 | 4 | 2 | 3 | 4 | 3 |
| Westwood | 4 | 3 | 3 | 3 | 4 | 3 | 5 | 3 | 4 | 3 | 4 | 5 | 3 | 3 | 4 | 4 | 4 |

Chad Campbell (USA) defeated Padraig Harrington, 2 and 1.

| Campbell | 5 | 4 | 3 | 3 | 4 | 4 | 6 | 3 | 3 | 5 | 4 | 5 | 4 | 3 | 3 | 5 | 4 |
| Harrington | 3 | 5 | 2 | 4 | 5 | 6 | 5 | 3 | 4 | 5 | 4 | 4 | 4 | 3 | 5 | 5 | 4 |

TOTAL POINTS: United States 16½, Europe 11½

Viking Classic

Annandale Golf Club, Madison, Mississippi
Par 36-36–72; 7,199 yards

September 18-21
purse, $3,600,000

	SCORES				TOTAL	MONEY
Will MacKenzie	70	64	67	68	269	$648,000
Brian Gay	66	68	67	68	269	316,800
Marc Turnesa	65	68	66	70	269	316,800
(MacKenzie defeated Gay on first and Turnesa on second playoff hole.)						
Steve Allan	71	68	67	66	272	148,800
Bill Haas	69	69	66	68	272	148,800
Casey Wittenberg	68	67	68	69	272	148,800
Greg Kraft	68	69	68	68	273	120,600
Woody Austin	69	69	67	69	274	97,200
Brad Elder	68	68	69	69	274	97,200
Jason Gore	71	69	68	66	274	97,200
Dicky Pride	67	67	68	72	274	97,200
David Toms	69	68	71	66	274	97,200
Tom Scherrer	69	72	66	68	275	75,600
Rich Beem	71	68	65	72	276	55,800
Shane Bertsch	69	68	71	68	276	55,800
J.P. Hayes	70	68	70	68	276	55,800
Lee Janzen	67	70	70	69	276	55,800
Doug LaBelle	68	70	70	68	276	55,800
Troy Matteson	69	68	71	68	276	55,800
Joe Ogilvie	71	71	66	68	276	55,800
Rory Sabbatini	69	69	67	71	276	55,800
David Duval	69	69	68	71	277	37,440
Tim Petrovic	68	72	66	71	277	37,440
Bo Van Pelt	68	69	68	72	277	37,440
Brad Adamonis	67	71	72	68	278	26,897.15
Ken Duke	71	71	69	67	278	26,897.15
Dan Forsman	68	70	69	71	278	26,897.14
Nathan Green	67	73	70	68	278	26,897.14
Todd Hamilton	68	70	71	69	278	26,897.14
Brett Quigley	69	70	70	69	278	26,897.14
Paul Stankowski	69	65	71	73	278	26,897.14
Justin Bolli	69	67	72	71	279	19,080
Guy Boros	69	72	68	70	279	19,080
Chris Riley	72	67	72	68	279	19,080
Patrick Sheehan	71	71	69	68	279	19,080
Scott Sterling	68	70	68	73	279	19,080
Bob Tway	71	68	69	71	279	19,080
Jay Williamson	67	73	67	72	279	19,080
Garrett Willis	68	69	75	67	279	19,080
Cameron Beckman	71	70	69	70	280	14,040
John Daly	70	67	70	73	280	14,040
Todd Demsey	69	70	71	70	280	14,040
Dustin Johnson	72	69	66	73	280	14,040
Ron Whittaker	69	70	71	70	280	14,040
Gavin Coles	71	69	71	70	281	9,490.91

	SCORES				TOTAL	MONEY
Marco Dawson	70	68	70	73	281	9,490.91
Cody Freeman	74	68	68	71	281	9,490.91
Jeff Gove	70	72	72	67	281	9,490.91
Charles Howell	71	70	72	68	281	9,490.91
Spike McRoy	71	67	73	70	281	9,490.91
Kevin Na	75	64	73	69	281	9,490.91
Tag Ridings	72	69	71	69	281	9,490.91
John Riegger	70	72	68	71	281	9,490.91
Vaughn Taylor	72	70	67	72	281	9,490.91
John Huston	68	69	68	76	281	9,490.90
Eric Axley	70	69	71	72	282	7,992
Notah Begay	69	69	69	75	282	7,992
Andrew Buckle	67	71	73	71	282	7,992
Robert Gamez	68	73	69	72	282	7,992
Larry Mize	73	69	71	69	282	7,992
Heath Slocum	73	68	73	68	282	7,992
Chris Stroud	74	68	68	72	282	7,992
Mark Brooks	73	68	71	71	283	7,488
Tom Byrum	72	70	67	74	283	7,488
Chad Collins	75	65	76	67	283	7,488
Nick Flanagan	68	74	70	71	283	7,488
Richard Johnson	72	69	70	72	283	7,488
Craig Kanada	70	68	73	72	283	7,488
Len Mattiace	70	69	72	72	283	7,488
Billy Andrade	74	67	68	75	284	7,092
Neal Lancaster	70	71	71	72	284	7,092
Michael Letzig	71	68	69	76	284	7,092
Y.E. Yang	71	71	73	69	284	7,092
Jeff Overton	73	69	69	74	285	6,912
Martin Laird	72	69	73	72	286	6,840
Bart Bryant	72	70	72	73	287	6,696
James Driscoll	70	72	72	73	287	6,696
Kirk Triplett	72	69	73	73	287	6,696

PGA Tour Fall Series

Turning Stone Resort Championship

Atunyote Golf Club, Verona, New York
Par 36-36–72; 7,482 yards

October 2-5
purse, $6,000,000

	SCORES				TOTAL	MONEY
Dustin Johnson	72	68	70	69	279	$1,080,000
Robert Allenby	71	68	71	70	280	648,000
Steve Allan	68	74	70	69	281	244,714.29
Woody Austin	74	69	69	69	281	244,714.29
Mathew Goggin	71	70	71	69	281	244,714.29
Ryuji Imada	72	71	69	69	281	244,714.29
Robert Garrigus	72	72	68	69	281	244,714.29
Charles Howell	71	68	69	73	281	244,714.28
Davis Love	75	70	66	70	281	244,714.28
Nick O'Hern	71	72	71	68	282	138,000
Joe Ogilvie	75	69	68	70	282	138,000
Jeff Overton	67	69	73	73	282	138,000
Pat Perez	71	72	69	70	282	138,000

		SCORES			TOTAL	MONEY
Charles Warren	73	71	67	71	282	138,000
Brian Davis	71	69	69	74	283	99,000
Steve Elkington	73	71	70	69	283	99,000
Mark Hensby	70	69	72	72	283	99,000
Vaughn Taylor	75	69	69	70	283	99,000
Jason Day	69	69	71	75	284	78,000
J.J. Henry	74	72	71	67	284	78,000
Bo Van Pelt	70	73	71	70	284	78,000
James Driscoll	76	71	68	70	285	62,400
Brad Elder	71	69	72	73	285	62,400
George McNeill	73	71	72	69	285	62,400
Ryan Moore	74	74	69	69	286	50,400
Kevin Stadler	71	75	69	71	286	50,400
Michael Allen	68	74	74	71	287	39,100
Carlos Franco	69	78	70	70	287	39,100
Harrison Frazar	72	70	72	73	287	39,100
Brandt Jobe	71	75	71	70	287	39,100
Richard Johnson	76	71	69	71	287	39,100
Troy Matteson	70	73	71	73	287	39,100
Sean O'Hair	73	71	70	73	287	39,100
Tag Ridings	69	68	71	79	287	39,100
John Senden	73	71	73	70	287	39,100
Nathan Green	73	75	70	70	288	27,042.86
Kent Jones	70	74	72	72	288	27,042.86
Steve Marino	75	73	68	72	288	27,042.86
Patrick Sheehan	72	76	68	72	288	27,042.86
Tim Wilkinson	73	71	74	70	288	27,042.86
Briny Baird	70	72	71	75	288	27,042.85
Kyle Thompson	71	69	69	79	288	27,042.85
Olin Browne	72	71	75	71	289	18,720
Chad Collins	72	75	72	70	289	18,720
Todd Demsey	72	71	75	71	289	18,720
Joe Durant	71	75	71	72	289	18,720
Tommy Gainey	71	74	70	74	289	18,720
Scott Sterling	70	76	72	71	289	18,720
Casey Wittenberg	74	74	72	69	289	18,720
Shane Bertsch	75	71	69	75	290	14,472
Michael Bradley	75	73	70	72	290	14,472
Mathias Gronberg	74	74	71	71	290	14,472
Kevin Na	72	71	75	72	290	14,472
Bob Sowards	74	69	72	75	290	14,472
Rich Beem	74	74	69	74	291	13,500
Paul Claxton	70	72	71	78	291	13,500
Bob Estes	72	74	72	73	291	13,500
Peter Lonard	78	67	73	73	291	13,500
Carl Pettersson	73	73	73	72	291	13,500
Y.E. Yang	74	72	72	73	291	13,500
Steve Flesch	74	73	73	72	292	12,840
Cody Freeman	74	72	74	72	292	12,840
Tom Pernice, Jr.	72	73	69	78	292	12,840
Brett Rumford	73	71	74	74	292	12,840
Johnson Wagner	73	73	70	76	292	12,840
Parker McLachlin	73	75	72	73	293	12,420
Nick Watney	77	70	73	73	293	12,420
Brad Adamonis	74	73	72	75	294	12,060
Ryan Armour	74	74	70	76	294	12,060
Dicky Pride	76	71	71	76	294	12,060
Joey Sindelar	77	71	72	74	294	12,060

Valero Texas Open

LaCantera Golf Club, San Antonio, Texas
Par 35-35–70; 6,896 yards

October 9-12
purse, $4,500,000

	SCORES				TOTAL	MONEY
Zach Johnson	69	66	62	64	261	$810,000
Charlie Wi	67	68	67	61	263	336,000
Tim Wilkinson	67	69	63	64	263	336,000
Mark Wilson	68	66	66	63	263	336,000
Jeff Overton	69	64	67	65	265	180,000
Stephen Ames	68	71	66	62	267	156,375
Chris Stroud	66	64	69	68	267	156,375
Tim Herron	65	67	67	69	268	130,500
Pat Perez	71	64	68	65	268	130,500
Rory Sabbatini	67	66	63	72	268	130,500
Harrison Frazar	69	69	65	66	269	99,000
Greg Kraft	65	71	65	68	269	99,000
Justin Leonard	70	69	64	66	269	99,000
Tim Petrovic	67	65	68	69	269	99,000
Shane Bertsch	69	69	66	66	270	74,250
Dustin Johnson	67	69	68	66	270	74,250
Jeff Maggert	73	65	64	68	270	74,250
Bob Tway	66	72	64	68	270	74,250
Steve Allan	66	70	71	64	271	47,350
Chad Collins	65	73	65	68	271	47,350
Chris DiMarco	68	69	70	64	271	47,350
Joe Durant	68	67	72	64	271	47,350
Jason Gore	65	74	66	66	271	47,350
Paul Goydos	66	66	73	66	271	47,350
Bob Sowards	68	70	70	63	271	47,350
Kevin Streelman	70	63	69	69	271	47,350
Jimmy Walker	67	66	69	69	271	47,350
Steve Elkington	68	70	73	61	272	32,625
*Michael Thompson	68	65	67	72	272	
Brian Gay	68	67	69	69	273	27,337.50
Nathan Green	62	75	70	66	273	27,337.50
Mark Hensby	68	66	67	72	273	27,337.50
Troy Matteson	68	70	66	69	273	27,337.50
Joe Ogilvie	66	67	67	73	273	27,337.50
Tag Ridings	66	70	69	68	273	27,337.50
Jason Allred	68	66	74	66	274	19,828.13
Nick O'Hern	65	72	70	67	274	19,828.13
Jhonattan Vegas	69	67	69	69	274	19,828.13
Scott Verplank	68	66	70	70	274	19,828.13
Chad Campbell	71	65	68	70	274	19,828.12
Charles Howell	68	67	68	71	274	19,828.12
Chez Reavie	67	67	69	71	274	19,828.12
David Toms	68	66	70	70	274	19,828.12
Michael Bradley	66	70	67	72	275	12,760
Todd Demsey	66	70	69	70	275	12,760
Bob Estes	68	68	69	70	275	12,760
Carlos Franco	69	70	67	69	275	12,760
Craig Kanada	69	65	70	71	275	12,760
John Riegger	68	69	67	71	275	12,760
Patrick Sheehan	65	71	70	69	275	12,760
Bo Van Pelt	68	70	67	70	275	12,760
Dean Wilson	71	67	69	68	275	12,760
Doug LaBelle	69	69	68	70	276	10,470
Steve Marino	68	69	69	70	276	10,470
Nick Watney	67	71	69	69	276	10,470
Olin Browne	64	69	74	70	277	10,215
Kevin Stadler	67	66	69	75	277	10,215

	SCORES				TOTAL	MONEY
Paul Claxton	64	70	72	72	278	9,855
Robert Gamez	70	68	73	67	278	9,855
J.J. Henry	70	68	70	70	278	9,855
Richard S. Johnson	70	67	70	71	278	9,855
Sean O'Hair	72	66	70	70	278	9,855
Vaughn Taylor	70	68	67	73	278	9,855
Alejandro Canizares	66	73	70	70	279	9,360
Brad Elder	68	69	73	69	279	9,360
Matt Jones	69	64	73	73	279	9,360
Jim McGovern	67	70	66	76	279	9,360
Tom Pernice, Jr.	70	69	68	72	279	9,360
Scott Sterling	69	70	72	69	280	9,090
Charley Hoffman	68	69	71	73	281	8,955
Martin Laird	67	71	71	72	281	8,955
Frank Lickliter	69	66	70	77	282	8,820
J.L. Lewis	68	69	68	78	283	8,685
Nicholas Thompson	72	67	72	72	283	8,685
Kyle Thompson	66	69	71	79	285	8,550

Justin Timberlake Shriners Hospitals for Children Open

TPC Summerlin, Las Vegas, Nevada   October 16-19
Par 36-36–72; 7,243 yards   purse, $4,100,000

	SCORES				TOTAL	MONEY
Marc Turnesa	62	64	69	68	263	$738,000
Matt Kuchar	63	63	71	67	264	442,800
Michael Allen	63	69	64	70	266	213,200
Chad Campbell	65	67	67	67	266	213,200
John Mallinger	64	64	70	68	266	213,200
Tim Herron	72	65	68	62	267	142,475
Davis Love	68	67	65	67	267	142,475
Tom Pernice, Jr.	68	68	67	65	268	123,000
Scott Sterling	69	65	70	64	268	123,000
Brad Adamonis	67	65	66	71	269	94,300
Chris DiMarco	69	64	63	73	269	94,300
Charles Howell	67	67	69	66	269	94,300
Zach Johnson	62	65	70	72	269	94,300
Mike Weir	69	68	66	66	269	94,300
James Driscoll	71	65	68	66	270	57,673.34
Bob Estes	66	68	70	66	270	57,673.34
Ryuji Imada	67	66	71	66	270	57,673.34
Daniel Chopra	69	65	68	68	270	57,673.33
Brian Davis	65	68	66	71	270	57,673.33
Ken Duke	63	66	67	74	270	57,673.33
Charley Hoffman	67	67	68	68	270	57,673.33
George McNeill	67	67	67	69	270	57,673.33
Kevin Na	64	70	67	69	270	57,673.33
Fred Couples	68	64	69	70	271	29,058.75
Jason Day	70	67	68	66	271	29,058.75
Mathew Goggin	68	67	71	65	271	29,058.75
Bill Haas	68	68	65	70	271	29,058.75
Mark Hensby	69	65	68	69	271	29,058.75
Kent Jones	69	69	66	67	271	29,058.75
Hunter Mahan	65	69	72	65	271	29,058.75
Ryan Moore	66	64	68	73	271	29,058.75
Pat Perez	66	63	71	71	271	29,058.75
Chris Stroud	65	65	67	74	271	29,058.75
Kevin Sutherland	69	67	66	69	271	29,058.75
Mark Wilson	70	65	69	67	271	29,058.75

	SCORES				TOTAL	MONEY
Eric Axley	68	69	69	66	272	18,479.29
Jeff Maggert	70	68	69	65	272	18,479.29
Parker McLachlin	67	69	67	69	272	18,479.29
Nick Watney	63	68	73	68	272	18,479.29
Woody Austin	67	67	68	70	272	18,479.28
Robert Garrigus	65	69	68	70	272	18,479.28
Jesper Parnevik	69	65	66	72	272	18,479.28
Joe Durant	65	70	68	70	273	13,940
John Huston	71	63	69	70	273	13,940
Kevin Streelman	68	69	68	68	273	13,940
Tim Wilkinson	72	65	70	66	273	13,940
Martin Laird	67	68	70	69	274	10,673.67
Frank Lickliter	65	69	71	69	274	10,673.67
Brett Quigley	68	67	72	67	274	10,673.67
Dean Wilson	69	63	72	70	274	10,673.67
Steve Marino	71	64	69	70	274	10,673.66
Chez Reavie	64	66	69	75	274	10,673.66
Rich Beem	66	65	72	72	275	9,491.50
Ben Crane	69	69	68	69	275	9,491.50
Bo Van Pelt	67	69	68	71	275	9,491.50
Charlie Wi	69	66	71	69	275	9,491.50
Jason Gore	68	70	68	70	276	9,266
Peter Lonard	66	69	72	70	277	9,143
Steve Lowery	68	70	70	69	277	9,143
Omar Uresti	68	70	70	70	278	8,979
Charles Warren	65	72	67	74	278	8,979
Jason Allred	69	69	70	71	279	8,815
John Riegger	66	68	70	75	279	8,815
Mike Ruiz	67	71	69	73	280	8,692
David Duval	69	68	69	75	281	8,569
Matt Jones	66	71	71	73	281	8,569
Nick Flanagan	64	74	68	76	282	8,405
Patrick Sheehan	68	69	66	79	282	8,405
Kenneth Ferrie	66	70	70	78	284	8,241
Jeff Overton	69	69	70	76	284	8,241
Nicholas Thompson	68	65	75	79	287	8,118

Frys.com Open

Grayhawk Golf Club, Raptor Course, Scottsdale, Arizona   October 23-26
Par 35-35–70; 7,125 yards   purse, $5,000,000

	SCORES				TOTAL	MONEY
Cameron Beckman	69	66	64	63	262	$900,000
Kevin Sutherland	67	66	63	66	262	540,000
(Beckman defeated Sutherland on second playoff hole.)						
Mathew Goggin	69	63	68	63	263	340,000
J.J. Henry	65	69	68	64	266	206,666.67
Mike Weir	66	68	69	63	266	206,666.67
Arron Oberholser	65	64	71	66	266	206,666.66
Steve Allan	67	63	68	69	267	150,625
Paul Goydos	70	62	66	69	267	150,625
Pat Perez	71	66	67	63	267	150,625
Michael Sim	72	63	68	64	267	150,625
Woody Austin	69	65	65	69	268	102,500
Aaron Baddeley	67	70	66	65	268	102,500
Davis Love	69	67	67	65	268	102,500
George McNeill	68	63	66	71	268	102,500
Brenden Pappas	69	69	64	66	268	102,500
Bob Tway	69	67	64	68	268	102,500

	SCORES				TOTAL	MONEY
Steve Elkington	66	67	68	68	269	75,000
Billy Mayfair	69	64	68	68	269	75,000
Sean O'Hair	68	65	69	67	269	75,000
Robert Garrigus	66	66	71	67	270	48,944.45
Charley Hoffman	70	65	69	66	270	48,944.45
Peter Lonard	69	70	64	67	270	48,944.45
Rod Pampling	70	68	65	67	270	48,944.45
Brad Elder	68	63	70	69	270	48,944.44
Bill Haas	66	68	68	68	270	48,944.44
Todd Hamilton	69	69	64	68	270	48,944.44
John Mallinger	63	69	66	72	270	48,944.44
Nick Watney	69	67	66	68	270	48,944.44
Tim Clark	70	64	71	66	271	32,500
Robert Gamez	67	69	69	66	271	32,500
Michael Letzig	69	66	68	68	271	32,500
Rocco Mediate	68	69	66	68	271	32,500
Chris Stroud	65	71	67	68	271	32,500
Mathias Gronberg	65	68	72	67	272	23,666.67
Doug LaBelle	63	72	69	68	272	23,666.67
Jeff Quinney	68	71	65	68	272	23,666.67
Patrick Sheehan	72	64	68	68	272	23,666.67
Omar Uresti	67	70	66	69	272	23,666.67
Bubba Watson	69	66	70	67	272	23,666.67
Martin Laird	73	66	67	66	272	23,666.66
John Merrick	74	65	67	66	272	23,666.66
Y.E. Yang	66	71	64	71	272	23,666.66
Tommy Gainey	68	68	66	71	273	16,500
Tim Herron	72	65	71	65	273	16,500
Steve Lowery	72	64	69	68	273	16,500
John Riegger	70	68	66	69	273	16,500
Rory Sabbatini	72	67	68	66	273	16,500
Bob Estes	71	68	66	69	274	13,350
Ryan Palmer	73	66	69	66	274	13,350
Jonathan Byrd	71	67	67	70	275	11,885.72
Brett Quigley	71	67	68	69	275	11,885.72
Charlie Wi	68	70	67	70	275	11,885.72
Steve Flesch	69	70	67	69	275	11,885.71
Richard Johnson	64	71	72	68	275	11,885.71
Jim McGovern	67	70	71	67	275	11,885.71
Scott Verplank	69	70	67	69	275	11,885.71
Olin Browne	68	71	66	71	276	11,150
John Douma	70	69	65	72	276	11,150
James Driscoll	70	69	68	69	276	11,150
Kevin Streelman	68	67	67	74	276	11,150
Chad Collins	67	68	66	76	277	10,750
Todd Demsey	65	69	72	71	277	10,750
Mark Hensby	69	66	70	72	277	10,750
Tom Pernice, Jr.	67	70	68	72	277	10,750
Nick Flanagan	71	67	69	71	278	10,450
Chris Riley	67	67	73	71	278	10,450
Brian Davis	72	63	71	73	279	10,300
Eric Axley	73	66	69	72	280	10,050
Shane Bertsch	69	69	70	72	280	10,050
Marco Dawson	65	71	69	75	280	10,050
Frank Lickliter	69	67	70	74	280	10,050

Ginn sur Mer Classic

Conservatory Course, Palm Coast, Florida
Par 36-36–72; 7,663 yards

October 30-November 2
purse, $4,600,000

	SCORES				TOTAL	MONEY
Ryan Palmer	67	71	72	71	281	$828,000
Ken Duke	70	69	72	71	282	276,000
Michael Letzig	65	74	70	73	282	276,000
George McNeill	71	71	71	69	282	276,000
Vaughn Taylor	69	74	69	70	282	276,000
Nicholas Thompson	71	70	72	69	282	276,000
Robert Allenby	68	71	73	71	283	133,860
Brian Gay	72	70	72	69	283	133,860
John Huston	70	70	70	73	283	133,860
Troy Matteson	71	74	70	68	283	133,860
Tom Scherrer	68	76	70	69	283	133,860
Chad Collins	74	69	70	71	284	87,400
Bob Estes	75	67	72	70	284	87,400
J.J. Henry	71	72	69	72	284	87,400
Peter Lonard	70	69	76	69	284	87,400
Jesper Parnevik	73	70	71	70	284	87,400
Mark Wilson	73	71	67	73	284	87,400
Todd Hamilton	71	74	70	70	285	52,133.34
Carl Pettersson	72	70	73	70	285	52,133.34
Michael Sim	72	73	70	70	285	52,133.34
Kenneth Ferrie	70	73	67	75	285	52,133.33
Jeff Maggert	73	72	73	67	285	52,133.33
Steve Marino	72	71	71	71	285	52,133.33
Nick O'Hern	69	73	72	71	285	52,133.33
Jeff Overton	71	73	70	71	285	52,133.33
Tim Petrovic	71	72	72	70	285	52,133.33
Cameron Beckman	68	73	72	73	286	32,660
Kent Jones	65	77	74	70	286	32,660
Matt Jones	70	74	71	71	286	32,660
Chris Stroud	69	72	73	72	286	32,660
Bob Tway	70	71	73	72	286	32,660
Alejandro Canizares	72	73	70	72	287	27,216.67
Martin Laird	72	71	72	72	287	27,216.67
Michael Allen	71	71	72	73	287	27,216.66
Gavin Coles	71	71	72	74	288	22,678
David Duval	71	69	74	74	288	22,678
Mathias Gronberg	69	74	74	71	288	22,678
Bob Heintz	72	74	69	73	288	22,678
John Riegger	73	72	70	73	288	22,678
Billy Andrade	75	71	73	70	289	19,320
Joe Durant	72	73	72	72	289	19,320
Robert Gamez	72	74	73	71	290	15,640
Robert Garrigus	70	76	68	76	290	15,640
J.B. Holmes	73	72	73	72	290	15,640
Jerry Kelly	71	72	75	72	290	15,640
Greg Kraft	72	74	75	69	290	15,640
Y.E. Yang	73	71	73	73	290	15,640
Jeff Gove	70	73	73	75	291	11,561.34
Steve Lowery	70	71	76	74	291	11,561.34
Briny Baird	74	72	74	71	291	11,561.33
Todd Demsey	72	72	78	69	291	11,561.33
Chris DiMarco	72	72	77	70	291	11,561.33
Omar Uresti	73	72	73	73	291	11,561.33
Justin Bolli	72	74	72	74	292	10,350
Brian Davis	74	72	74	72	292	10,350
Chip Deason	71	71	75	75	292	10,350
Jason Dufner	70	73	71	78	292	10,350

	SCORES				TOTAL	MONEY
Matt Kuchar	71	75	72	74	292	10,350
John Rollins	74	71	75	72	292	10,350
Kevin Stadler	73	72	74	73	292	10,350
Tim Wilkinson	74	72	73	73	292	10,350
Marco Dawson	71	71	73	78	293	9,936
David Lutterus	74	72	73	75	294	9,798
Brett Quigley	73	73	76	72	294	9,798
Frank Lickliter	72	74	73	76	295	9,660
Eric Axley	71	75	76	74	296	9,476
Olin Browne	72	71	74	79	296	9,476
Will MacKenzie	75	70	79	72	296	9,476
Jason Gore	71	73	77	76	297	9,154
J.P. Hayes	74	72	78	73	297	9,154
Lee Janzen	70	75	74	78	297	9,154
Rod Perry	70	76	77	74	297	9,154
Kyle Thompson	70	76	76	79	301	8,924

Children's Miracle Network Classic

Walt Disney World Resort, Lake Buena Vista, Florida
Magnolia Course: Par 36-36–72; 7,516 yards
Palm Course: Par 36-36–72; 6,957 yards

November 6-9
purse, $4,600,000

	SCORES				TOTAL	MONEY
Davis Love	66	69	64	64	263	$828,000
Tommy Gainey	68	66	66	64	264	496,800
Steve Marino	65	66	66	71	268	266,800
Scott Verplank	64	64	69	71	268	266,800
Joe Durant	68	68	68	65	269	184,000
Troy Matteson	63	68	69	70	270	154,100
Scott Sterling	70	63	66	71	270	154,100
Kevin Streelman	64	69	69	68	270	154,100
Michael Allen	70	67	68	67	272	133,400
Cameron Beckman	68	68	67	70	273	101,966.67
Bob Estes	70	63	71	69	273	101,966.67
Tag Ridings	66	66	71	70	273	101,966.67
Chris Stroud	70	68	66	69	273	101,966.67
Robert Garrigus	65	67	68	73	273	101,966.66
Tim Petrovic	67	67	68	71	273	101,966.66
Jason Day	72	66	70	66	274	69,000
Harrison Frazar	67	68	71	68	274	69,000
Jason Gore	66	67	69	72	274	69,000
Ryan Palmer	71	65	69	69	274	69,000
Kevin Stadler	67	71	68	68	274	69,000
Steve Flesch	67	68	73	67	275	49,680
Martin Laird	68	66	70	71	275	49,680
Jeff Overton	67	68	71	69	275	49,680
Jimmy Walker	64	72	71	68	275	49,680
Rich Beem	65	70	69	72	276	33,637.50
Michael Bradley	70	67	70	69	276	33,637.50
Tim Clark	69	66	69	72	276	33,637.50
Ken Duke	66	67	69	74	276	33,637.50
J.B. Holmes	71	68	69	68	276	33,637.50
Charles Howell	68	68	68	72	276	33,637.50
Brenden Pappas	71	66	67	72	276	33,637.50
Bo Van Pelt	68	66	68	74	276	33,637.50
Robert Allenby	66	72	70	69	277	22,310
Stephen Ames	68	68	69	72	277	22,310
Woody Austin	68	68	69	72	277	22,310
Lee Janzen	69	67	72	69	277	22,310

	SCORES				TOTAL	MONEY
Matt Jones	70	64	72	71	277	22,310
Tom Pernice, Jr.	66	67	72	72	277	22,310
Carl Pettersson	68	68	73	68	277	22,310
John Rollins	68	69	72	68	277	22,310
Nick Watney	69	70	71	67	277	22,310
Tim Wilkinson	68	66	72	71	277	22,310
Stewart Cink	66	70	71	71	278	15,640
J.J. Henry	67	69	72	70	278	15,640
Ted Purdy	69	68	68	73	278	15,640
Vaughn Taylor	68	71	67	72	278	15,640
John Riegger	68	69	74	68	279	13,340
Robert Gamez	65	67	70	78	280	11,868
Bob Sowards	69	68	70	73	280	11,868
Marc Turnesa	71	68	72	69	280	11,868
Omar Uresti	67	72	70	71	280	11,868
Chris DiMarco	68	71	73	69	281	10,568.50
Carlos Franco	69	67	75	70	281	10,568.50
Mathias Gronberg	67	71	77	66	281	10,568.50
Jerry Kelly	71	68	73	69	281	10,568.50
Tom Scherrer	69	68	73	71	281	10,568.50
Patrick Sheehan	68	71	73	69	281	10,568.50
Bob Tway	73	62	75	71	281	10,568.50
Boo Weekley	68	71	71	71	281	10,568.50
Erik Compton	70	68	72	72	282	10,074
Heath Slocum	71	67	73	71	282	10,074
Zach Johnson	66	72	74	71	283	9,890
Will MacKenzie	68	69	73	73	283	9,890
Richard S. Johnson	70	68	76	70	284	9,752
Dudley Hart	70	69	74	72	285	9,614
Y.E. Yang	68	68	75	74	285	9,614
Todd Demsey	67	70	75	74	286	9,430
Frank Lickliter	74	65	76	71	286	9,430
Kirk Triplett	65	70	76	76	287	9,292
Jeff Maggert	73	66	79	80	298	9,200

Omega Mission Hills World Cup

See Asia/Japan Tours chapter.

Special Events

Tavistock Cup

Isleworth Golf & Country Club, Orlando, Florida   March 24-25
Par 36-36–72; 7,544 yards   purse, $3,880,000

FIRST DAY
(Team better ball; 2 points for win, 1 point for tie)

Tiger Woods and John Cook (Isleworth) tied with Graeme McDowell and Henrik Stenson (Lake Nona), 66-66.
Mark O'Meara and Charles Howell (Isle) defeated Trevor Immelman and Mark McNulty (LN), 69-73.
J.B. Holmes and Daniel Chopra (Isle) defeated Ian Poulter and Ben Curtis (LN), 65-66.
Nick O'Hern and Robert Allenby (Isle) defeated Ernie Els and Chris DiMarco (LN) 67-69.
Retief Goosen and Justin Rose (LN) defeated Stuart Appleby and Craig Parry (Isle) 69-70.

POINTS: Isleworth 7, Lake Nona 3

SECOND DAY
(Singles versus both players on other team; 1 point for win, ½ point for tie)

Annika Sorenstam (LN) defeated Paula Creamer (Isle), 69-74.
O'Meara 70 and Cook 73 (Isle) versus McNulty 72 and McDowell 76 (LN).
Holmes 68 and Chopra 75 (Isle) versus Poulter 69 and DiMarco 74 (LN).
Appleby 73 and Allenby 75 (Isle) versus Els 77 and Immelman 72 (LN).
Parry 75 and O'Hern 72 (Isle) versus Curtis 72 and Stenson 73 (LN).
Woods 70 and Howell 71 (Isle) versus Goosen 73 and Rose 73 (LN).

POINTS: Isleworth 12½, Lake Nona 8½
TWO-DAY TOTAL: Isleworth 19½, Lake Nona 11½

(Each member of the Isleworth team received $100,000; each member of the Lake Nona team received $50,000. Holmes received $500,000, Poulter received $300,000, and O'Meara and Woods received $100,000 each for the lowest scores on the second day.)

CVS/Caremark Charity Classic

Rhode Island Country Club, Barrington, Rhode Island   June 23-24
Par 35-36–71; 6,688 yards   purse $1,350,000
(Event shortened to 28 holes—rain.)

	SCORES		TOTAL	MONEY (Team)
Bubba Watson/Camilo Villegas	61	34	95	$300,000
Billy Andrade/Davis Love	62	33	95	173,333.34
Rocco Mediate/Brandt Snedeker	62	33	95	173,333.34
Paul Goydos/Tim Herron	62	33	95	173,333.34
(Watson and Villegas won on third playoff hole.)				
Charles Howell/Nick Price	62	34	96	130,000
Brett Quigley/Dana Quigley	63	34	97	120,000
Nicole Diaz/Nicole Castrale	63	35	98	115,000
Nick Faldo/Justin Rose	66	36	102	110,000
J.J. Henry/Stewart Cink	65	38	103	105,000
Brad Faxon/Peter Jacobsen	70	34	104	100,000

PGA Grand Slam of Golf

Mid-Ocean Club, Tucker's Town, Bermuda
Par 34-36–70; 6,666 yards

October 14-15
purse, $1,350,000

	SCORES		TOTAL	MONEY
Jim Furyk	68	68	136	$600,000
Padraig Harrington	68	68	136	300,000
(Furyk defeated Harrington on first playoff hole)				
Retief Goosen	70	71	141	250,000
Trevor Immelman	76	69	145	200,000

Callaway Golf Pebble Beach Invitational

Pebble Beach GL: Par 36-36–72; 6,828 yards
Spyglass Hills GC: Par 36-36–72; 6,953 yards
Del Monte GC: Par 36-36–72; 6,365 yards
Pebble Beach, California

November 20-23
purse, $300,000

	SCORES				TOTAL	MONEY
Tommy Armour	66	71	65	76	278	$60,000
Brock Mackenzie	70	68	73	67	278	24,600
Scott Simpson	71	71	66	70	278	24,600
(Armour defeated Mackenzie and Simpson on first playoff hole.)						
Tommy Purtzer	68	70	74	67	279	11,500
Rich Beem	70	69	68	73	280	8,200
Arron Oberholser	71	66	72	71	280	8,200
Nicholas Thompson	69	69	72	70	280	8,200
Charley Hoffman	70	75	64	72	281	6,600
Chez Reavie	73	69	68	72	282	6,000
Andrew Hoffer	69	69	72	73	283	5,200
Bryce Molder	71	68	69	75	283	5,200
Rob Oppenheim	73	70	72	68	283	5,200
Brendon de Jonge	67	76	66	75	284	4,450
David Mathis	73	69	73	69	284	4,450
Eric Axley	69	72	73	71	285	3,850
D.A. Points	69	73	70	73	285	3,850
John Cook	62	76	75	73	286	3,200
Dan Forsman	73	69	70	74	286	3,200
Jeff Gove	70	72	75	69	286	3,200
Scott Sterling	74	69	69	74	286	3,200
Jason Gore	73	74	70	70	287	2,700
Colt Knost	68	75	68	76	287	2,700
Cliff Kresge	70	77	71	69	287	2,700
Jay Delsing	72	74	71	71	288	2,370
Vicky Hurst	69	74	72	73	288	2,370
Jeff Quinney	72	70	70	76	288	2,370
Kyle Thompson	75	69	73	71	288	2,370
Kevin Sutherland	78	70	69	72	289	2,200
Bobby Clampett	70	75	68	77	290	2,125
Scott Gutschewski	70	74	72	74	290	2,125
Mark Brown	68	76	74	73	291	2,050
Matt Every	70	77	70	74	291	2,050
Jill McGill	68	77	72	74	291	2,050
Jason Bohn	73	73	72	74	292	2,000
Brad Martin	65	74	74	79	292	2,000
Rick Price	71	73	72	76	292	2,000
Bubba Dickerson	67	76	75	75	293	1,930
Brittany Lincicome	71	79	68	75	293	1,930

	SCORES				TOTAL	MONEY
Steve Lowery	73	78	65	77	293	1,930
Chris Stroud	69	78	65	78	293	1,930
Ryan Hietala	76	72	70	79	297	1,850

Del Webb Father/Son Challenge

ChampionsGate Golf Resort, Orlando, Florida
Par 37-35–72; 7,120 yards

December 6-7
purse, $1,185,000

	SCORES		TOTAL	MONEY
				(Won by professional)
Larry Nelson/Drew Nelson	61	62	123	$210,000
Davis Love/Dru Love	63	62	125	120,000
Tom Kite/David Kite	61	65	126	90,000
Raymond Floyd/Raymond Floyd, Jr.	63	64	127	65,000
Hale Irwin/Steve Irwin	65	62	127	65,000
Bernhard Langer/Stefan Langer	63	64	127	65,000
Nick Faldo/Matthew Faldo	64	64	128	52,000
Mark O'Meara/Shaun O'Meara	64	64	128	52,000
Arnold Palmer/Sam Saunders	64	64	128	52,000
Greg Norman/Gregory Norman	62	67	129	50,000
Vijay Singh/Qass Sing	65	66	131	49,000
Paul Azinger/Aaron Stewart	68	65	133	47,500
Fuzzy Zoeller/Gretchen Zoeller	66	67	133	47,500
Curtis Strange/David Strange	65	69	134	46,000
Jack Nicklaus/Jack Nicklaus II	69	69	138	45,000
Billy Casper/Bob Casper	73	66	139	44,000
Craig Stadler/Chris Stadler	69	71	140	43,000
Lee Trevino/Daniel Trevino	71	71	142	42,000

Merrill Lynch Shootout

Tiburon Golf Course, Naples, Florida
Par 36-36–72; 7,288 yards

December 12-14
purse, $2,900,000

	SCORES			TOTAL	MONEY
					(Each)
Scott Hoch/Kenny Perry	65	60	60	185	$365,000
J.B. Holmes/Boo Weekley	67	62	60	189	230,000
Greg Norman/Camilo Villegas	69	65	57	191	132,500
Nick Price/Jeff Sluman	64	66	62	192	105,000
Zach Johnson/Scott Verplank	68	64	62	194	87,500
Jerry Kelly/Steve Stricker	70	64	60	194	87,500
Stewart Cink/Fred Couples	68	66	61	195	80,000
Paul Azinger/Rocco Mediate	73	62	63	198	77,500
Graeme McDowell/Ian Poulter	70	67	63	200	75,000
Brad Faxon/Scott McCarron	69	69	64	202	72,500
Woody Austin/Mark Calcavecchia	73	71	62	206	70,000
Chris DiMarco/Fred Funk	74	65		WD	67,500

Chevron World Challenge

Sherwood Country Club, Thousand Oaks, California   December 18-21
Par 36-36–72; 7,027 yards   purse, $5,750,000

	SCORES				TOTAL	MONEY
Vijay Singh	71	72	67	67	277	$1,350,000
Steve Stricker	71	71	68	68	278	840,000
Hunter Mahan	71	72	70	68	281	495,000
Anthony Kim	71	70	67	73	281	495,000
Camilo Villegas	74	67	69	73	283	285,000
Jim Furyk	68	71	70	74	283	285,000
Ben Curtis	72	73	72	70	287	240,000
Luke Donald	73	75	74	66	288	230,000
Boo Weekley	70	73	72	75	290	215,000
K.J. Choi	70	71	73	76	290	215,000
Paul Casey	74	72	69	76	291	200,000
Fred Couples	73	69	72	78	292	190,000
Stephen Ames	78	71	73	71	293	185,000
Justin Leonard	75	75	73	72	295	175,000
Kenny Perry	73	72	75	75	295	175,000
Mike Weir	78	71	70	76	295	175,000

Nationwide Tour

Movistar Panama Championship

Panama Golf Club, Panama City, Panama   January 24-27
Par 35-35–70; 7,102 yards   purse, US$600,000

	SCORES				TOTAL	MONEY
Scott Dunlap	65	68	73	71	277	$108,000
Arjun Atwal	70	66	68	74	278	52,800
Jeff Klauk	64	73	72	69	278	52,800
Chris Smith	67	70	68	74	279	28,800
Bill Lunde	68	70	71	71	280	24,000
Jarrod Lyle	74	65	69	73	281	20,850
Grant Waite	72	73	66	70	281	20,850
Craig Bowden	72	71	68	71	282	16,800
Greg Chalmers	72	68	73	69	282	16,800
Brendon de Jonge	66	73	71	72	282	16,800
Scott Parel	71	74	68	69	282	16,800
Matthew Every	67	73	67	76	283	13,800
Tom Carter	71	69	73	71	284	11,250
Glen Day	69	72	71	72	284	11,250
Rick Price	72	71	69	72	284	11,250
Casey Wittenberg	72	73	67	72	284	11,250
Skip Kendall	74	71	68	72	285	9,300
B.J. Staten	69	72	70	74	285	9,300

	SCORES				TOTAL	MONEY
Jeremy Anderson	74	70	72	70	286	7,272
Scott Gutschewski	72	73	69	72	286	7,272
Bob Heintz	69	73	70	74	286	7,272
Jason Schultz	72	72	68	74	286	7,272
Vance Veazey	73	68	73	72	286	7,272
Sebastian Fernandez	69	74	75	69	287	4,626.67
Fabian Gomez	69	75	72	71	287	4,626.67
Bret Guetz	72	71	71	73	287	4,626.67
J.J. Killeen	71	74	68	74	287	4,626.67
Marco Ruiz	73	70	69	75	287	4,626.67
Esteban Toledo	76	69	69	73	287	4,626.67
Benjamin Alvarado	71	69	68	79	287	4,626.66
Ben Bates	66	71	73	77	287	4,626.66
Joe Daley	70	69	72	76	287	4,626.66

Mexico Open

Tres Marias Golf Club, Morelia, Michoacan, Mexico
Par 35-36–71; 7,528 yards

January 31-February 3
purse, US$625,000

	SCORES				TOTAL	MONEY
Jarrod Lyle	68	69	67	63	267	$112,500
Matthew Every	69	65	71	67	272	67,500
Tom Johnson	65	70	70	68	273	42,500
Bubba Dickerson	71	72	65	67	275	30,000
Greg Chalmers	68	65	71	72	276	23,750
Steve Pate	69	69	71	67	276	23,750
Todd Fischer	72	68	68	69	277	19,479.17
Jose de Jesus Rodriguez	69	70	72	66	277	19,479.17
Peter Tomasulo	70	71	67	69	277	19,479.16
Josh Broadaway	75	67	68	68	278	16,875
Jeff Brehaut	76	70	68	66	280	13,750
Bill Lunde	71	73	69	67	280	13,750
Alex Prugh	75	71	68	66	280	13,750
Michael Putnam	68	71	72	69	280	13,750
Dicky Pride	74	68	68	71	281	11,250
Kris Blanks	71	70	74	67	282	10,000
Rafael Gomez	70	73	68	71	282	10,000
Michael Sim	67	74	69	72	282	10,000
Gabriel Hjertstedt	70	71	70	72	283	8,437.50
Casey Wittenberg	68	75	70	70	283	8,437.50
Andrew Buckle	73	71	74	66	284	5,937.50
Scott Gutschewski	72	71	70	71	284	5,937.50
Mike Heinen	78	68	67	71	284	5,937.50
Jeff Klauk	72	73	72	67	284	5,937.50
Colt Knost	71	70	73	70	284	5,937.50
Chris Nallen	72	72	69	71	284	5,937.50
B.J. Staten	67	79	69	69	284	5,937.50
Esteban Toledo	69	72	71	72	284	5,937.50

HSBC New Zealand PGA Championship

See Australasian Tour chapter.

Moonah Classic

See Australasian Tour chapter.

Chitimacha Louisiana Open

Le Triomphe Country Club, Broussard, Louisiana
Par 36-35–71; 7,004 yards

March 27-30
purse, $525,000

	SCORES				TOTAL	MONEY
Gavin Coles	70	66	66	70	272	$94,500
Kyle Thompson	72	67	69	65	273	56,700
Brendon de Jonge	72	67	68	67	274	27,300
Michael Letzig	68	72	70	64	274	27,300
Greg Owen	68	70	68	68	274	27,300
Ryan Palmer	75	66	67	67	275	18,900
Greg Chalmers	71	67	70	68	276	16,931.25
Matthew Every	70	68	67	71	276	16,931.25
Chris Riley	65	68	70	74	277	14,700
B.J. Staten	72	69	63	73	277	14,700
Andrew Dresser	67	72	66	73	278	11,550
Garth Mulroy	72	69	69	68	278	11,550
Travis Perkins	67	71	68	72	278	11,550
Dicky Pride	71	68	68	71	278	11,550
David Branshaw	72	69	70	68	279	8,137.50
Tom Byrum	72	68	65	74	279	8,137.50
Fabian Gomez	69	70	70	70	279	8,137.50
Kyle Reifers	72	67	71	69	279	8,137.50
Geoffrey Sisk	73	67	69	70	279	8,137.50
Daniel Summerhays	73	66	67	73	279	8,137.50
Richard S. Johnson	68	69	71	72	280	6,300
Gary Christian	74	67	67	73	281	4,800
Brent Delahoussaye	73	69	68	71	281	4,800
Jason Dufner	71	70	67	73	281	4,800
Bret Guetz	70	68	73	70	281	4,800
Mike Heinen	73	68	69	71	281	4,800
Tripp Isenhour	72	68	71	70	281	4,800
Garrett Osborn	70	71	71	69	281	4,800

Livermore Valley Wine Country Championship

The Course at Wente Vineyards, Livermore, California
Par 36-36–72; 7,185 yards

April 3-6
purse, $600,000

	SCORES				TOTAL	MONEY
Aron Price	70	69	72	72	283	$108,000
J.J. Killeen	65	69	73	76	283	64,800
(Price defeated Killeen on second playoff hole.)						
Joe Daley	69	70	72	73	284	40,800
Colt Knost	74	72	69	72	287	28,800
Chris Nallen	72	70	73	73	288	22,800
Fran Quinn	68	77	71	72	288	22,800
Tom Gillis	70	72	69	78	289	19,350
Dicky Pride	75	72	71	71	289	19,350
Ricky Barnes	72	72	72	74	290	16,200
Marc Leishman	75	69	72	74	290	16,200
Chris Tidland	69	76	74	71	290	16,200
Henrik Bjornstad	75	69	74	73	291	11,400
Jeff Klauk	72	70	73	76	291	11,400
James Love	67	74	73	77	291	11,400
Paul Stankowski	73	69	79	70	291	11,400
Esteban Toledo	75	72	70	74	291	11,400
Vance Veazey	71	74	73	73	291	11,400
Guy Boros	71	69	80	72	292	8,100

	SCORES				TOTAL	MONEY
Jonathan Fricke	73	72	76	71	292	8,100
Steve Friesen	75	69	74	74	292	8,100
Casey Wittenberg	72	71	76	73	292	8,100
Garth Mulroy	75	70	72	76	293	6,480
Keith Nolan	73	71	74	75	293	6,480
Gary Christian	74	69	77	74	294	5,220
Jeff Gove	73	74	71	76	294	5,220
Bill Lunde	69	74	77	74	294	5,220
David Mathis	75	69	77	73	294	5,220

Athens Regional Foundation Classic

Jennings Mill Country Club, Athens, Georgia
Par 36-36–72; 7,004 yards

April 17-20
purse, $525,000

	SCORES				TOTAL	MONEY
Robert Damron	70	69	72	66	277	$94,500
Greg Owen	66	71	69	71	277	56,700
(Damron defeated Owen on first playoff hole.)						
Casey Wittenberg	69	72	70	67	278	35,700
Roger Tambellini	75	69	68	67	279	23,100
Vance Veazey	72	72	67	68	279	23,100
Bubba Dickerson	72	67	69	72	280	18,900
Jarrod Lyle	70	71	68	72	281	16,931.25
Michael Putnam	66	71	72	72	281	16,931.25
Henrik Bjornstad	71	69	70	72	282	13,650
Joe Daley	70	69	70	73	282	13,650
Tom Johnson	68	74	68	72	282	13,650
Darron Stiles	68	73	67	74	282	13,650
Greg Chalmers	73	68	71	71	283	9,555
Tom Gillis	74	69	68	72	283	9,555
Chad Ginn	73	71	69	70	283	9,555
Ryan Palmer	70	73	71	69	283	9,555
Jason Schultz	70	70	71	72	283	9,555
Sonny Skinner	73	70	75	66	284	7,612.50
Chris Smith	72	71	69	72	284	7,612.50
Brendon de Jonge	74	69	74	68	285	5,901
Skip Kendall	69	71	72	73	285	5,901
Jeff Klauk	74	69	69	73	285	5,901
Geoffrey Sisk	66	74	69	76	285	5,901
Phil Tataurangi	70	72	72	71	285	5,901
Miguel Angel Carballo	68	73	71	74	286	4,005
Paul Gow	69	74	71	72	286	4,005
David Hearn	73	69	70	74	286	4,005
Ryan Hybl	73	71	71	71	286	4,005
Colt Knost	75	69	70	72	286	4,005
David Mathis	72	70	71	73	286	4,005
Brendon Todd	68	68	70	80	286	4,005

Henrico County Open

The Dominion Club, Richmond, Virginia
Par 36-36–72; 7,089 yards

April 24-27
purse, $500,000

	SCORES				TOTAL	MONEY
Greg Chalmers	68	68	68	70	274	$90,000
Henrik Bjornstad	66	68	70	70	274	54,000
(Chalmers defeated Bjornstad on second playoff hole.)						
Neal Lancaster	66	71	67	71	275	34,000
Arjun Atwal	72	70	66	68	276	18,125
Bryan DeCorso	68	68	66	74	276	18,125
Bubba Dickerson	62	68	74	72	276	18,125
Matt Hansen	69	67	66	74	276	18,125
Jeff Klauk	70	68	67	71	276	18,125
Roger Tambellini	65	70	71	70	276	18,125
Tom Gillis	68	71	66	72	277	12,500
Scott Gutschewski	70	66	69	72	277	12,500
Chris Riley	66	70	69	72	277	12,500
Tom Byrum	68	69	67	74	278	9,375
David Mathis	72	67	69	70	278	9,375
Peter Tomasulo	67	70	70	71	278	9,375
Garrett Willis	68	71	67	72	278	9,375
Michael Putnam	69	68	72	70	279	6,766.67
Rick Schuller	70	71	67	71	279	6,766.67
Chris Smith	74	68	68	69	279	6,766.67
Casey Wittenberg	70	70	71	68	279	6,766.67
Gary Christian	69	67	71	72	279	6,766.66
Greg Owen	68	69	68	74	279	6,766.66
John Kimbell	70	68	72	70	280	5,000
Dave Schultz	67	73	68	72	280	5,000
Wade Ormsby	69	67	68	77	281	4,400

South Georgia Classic

Kinderlou Forest Golf Club, Valdosta, Georgia
Par 36-36–72; 7,781 yards

May 1-4
purse, $625,000

	SCORES				TOTAL	MONEY
Bryan DeCorso	68	69	68	69	274	$112,500
Bryce Molder	72	68	69	69	278	55,000
Greg Owen	74	67	65	72	278	55,000
Scott Parel	72	68	69	71	280	30,000
Jeff Brehaut	72	68	69	72	281	25,000
Blake Adams	71	71	69	71	282	20,937.50
Marco Dawson	71	68	72	71	282	20,937.50
David Mathis	71	69	68	74	282	20,937.50
Jason Enloe	71	73	68	71	283	16,250
David K. Miller	69	70	69	75	283	16,250
Daniel Summerhays	72	69	68	74	283	16,250
Brendon Todd	72	70	69	72	283	16,250
Matt Weibring	71	72	71	70	284	12,083.34
Chris Nallen	68	75	69	72	284	12,083.33
Fran Quinn	72	71	69	72	284	12,083.33
Arjun Atwal	74	71	69	71	285	8,484.38
Sebastian Fernandez	71	74	70	70	285	8,484.38
Chad Ginn	70	75	70	70	285	8,484.38
Jeff Klauk	70	75	70	70	285	8,484.38
Ronnie Black	70	71	72	72	285	8,484.37
D.J. Brigman	72	73	72	68	285	8,484.37

	SCORES				TOTAL	MONEY
Garrett Osborn	71	72	70	72	285	8,484.37
Jason Schultz	73	71	69	72	285	8,484.37
Kris Blanks	70	72	73	71	286	4,921.88
Michael Bradley	71	72	73	70	286	4,921.88
Aron Price	73	72	70	71	286	4,921.88
Vance Veazey	69	71	73	73	286	4,921.88
Miguel Angel Carballo	74	69	70	73	286	4,921.87
Stephen Dartnall	70	75	71	70	286	4,921.87
Bob May	72	71	70	73	286	4,921.87
Garth Mulroy	67	74	72	73	286	4,921.87

Fort Smith Classic

Hardscrabble Country Club, Fort Smith, Arkansas
Par 35-35–70; 6,783 yards

May 8-11
purse, $550,000

	SCORES				TOTAL	MONEY
Colt Knost	68	65	70	65	268	$99,000
Darron Stiles	67	63	68	71	269	59,400
David Lutterus	66	68	68	69	271	31,900
Daniel Summerhays	70	67	65	69	271	31,900
Ricky Barnes	68	67	69	68	272	20,075
Rich Morris	67	63	72	70	272	20,075
Matt Weibring	64	67	66	75	272	20,075
Kris Blanks	69	66	66	72	273	15,400
Kris Cox	64	68	70	71	273	15,400
Tee McCabe	68	64	71	70	273	15,400
Jason Schultz	67	67	70	69	273	15,400
David Morland	67	65	70	72	274	12,100
Chris Smith	68	69	67	70	274	12,100
Henrik Bjornstad	68	70	67	71	276	9,350
Craig Lile	70	65	69	72	276	9,350
Steve Schneiter	67	67	71	71	276	9,350
Chris Thompson	68	65	72	71	276	9,350
Jon Turcott	71	66	68	71	276	9,350
Jay Delsing	70	67	71	69	277	5,830
Cody Freeman	73	63	69	72	277	5,830
Tommy Gainey	64	69	72	72	277	5,830
Kelly Grunewald	69	68	71	69	277	5,830
Chris Kamin	71	67	67	72	277	5,830
Skip Kendall	68	68	69	72	277	5,830
Scott Piercy	68	70	67	72	277	5,830
Casey Wittenberg	69	69	67	72	277	5,830
Willie Wood	69	68	72	68	277	5,830

BMW Charity Pro-Am

Thornblade Club, Greer, South Carolina
Par 35-36–71; 6,669 yards
Carolina Country Club, Spartanburg, South Carolina
Par 36-36–76; 6,877 yards
Bright's Creek Golf Club, Mill Spring, North Carolina
Par 36-36–76; 7,435 yards

May 15-18
purse, $675,000

	SCORES				TOTAL	MONEY
David Mathis	65	65	68	68	266	$121,500
Roger Tambellini	69	67	68	65	269	72,900

	SCORES				TOTAL	MONEY
Matt Weibring	66	65	68	71	270	45,900
Bill Lunde	66	69	67	69	271	32,400
Peter Tomasulo	65	69	68	71	273	27,000
Marc Leishman	68	68	67	71	274	23,456.25
Brendon Todd	70	68	65	71	274	23,456.25
Arjun Atwal	69	67	69	70	275	20,250
Kim Felton	66	69	72	68	275	20,250
Ricky Barnes	70	71	69	66	276	16,200
Josh Broadaway	68	72	68	68	276	16,200
Greg Chalmers	67	67	74	68	276	16,200
Lee Won-joon	69	65	72	70	276	16,200
Rob Bradley	71	66	72	68	277	11,812.50
Cameron Percy	67	70	71	69	277	11,812.50
D.A. Points	70	68	69	70	277	11,812.50
Casey Wittenberg	69	66	73	69	277	11,812.50
D.J. Brigman	70	72	63	73	278	8,505
Chris Nallen	71	67	72	68	278	8,505
Jim Rutledge	68	71	69	70	278	8,505
Michael Sim	69	70	69	70	278	8,505
Geoffrey Sisk	67	71	71	69	278	8,505
Daniel Summerhays	68	70	71	69	278	8,505
Matt Bettencourt	68	67	74	70	279	5,315.63
Gary Christian	73	71	65	70	279	5,315.63
Matt Hendrix	65	68	76	70	279	5,315.63
Mark Walker	75	66	68	70	279	5,315.63
Rich Barcelo	69	67	68	75	279	5,315.62
Doug Barron	69	69	70	71	279	5,315.62
Todd Fischer	67	72	72	68	279	5,315.62
Tommy Tolles	69	68	70	72	279	5,315.62

Melwood Prince George's County Open

The Country Club at Woodmore, Mitchellville, Maryland
Par 36-36–72; 7,059 yards

May 22-25
purse $650,000

	SCORES				TOTAL	MONEY
Jeff Klauk	64	70	73	69	276	$117,000
Jeff Brehaut	73	65	72	67	277	57,200
David Mathis	74	67	66	70	277	57,200
Craig Bowden	73	67	69	69	278	26,866.67
Scott Gutschewski	68	70	71	69	278	26,866.67
Greg Chalmers	73	70	65	70	278	26,866.66
Ricky Barnes	75	63	70	71	279	20,962.50
Gary Christian	70	70	68	71	279	20,962.50
Chad Ginn	70	65	72	73	280	16,900
David Hearn	68	69	71	72	280	16,900
Roger Tambellini	74	67	69	70	280	16,900
Matt Weibring	66	70	71	73	280	16,900
Tripp Isenhour	70	69	70	72	281	13,000
Bill Lunde	70	68	71	72	281	13,000
Paul Gow	71	72	70	69	282	11,050
J.J. Killeen	68	71	72	71	282	11,050
Chris Parra	69	73	72	68	282	11,050
Kris Blanks	69	72	71	71	283	7,911.43
Andrew Buckle	71	72	70	70	283	7,911.43
John Kimbell	73	64	78	68	283	7,911.43
Spike McRoy	73	71	69	70	283	7,911.43
Jon Turcott	69	71	71	72	283	7,911.43
Steve Wheatcroft	70	69	72	72	283	7,911.43
Fran Quinn	76	66	68	73	283	7,911.42

	SCORES				TOTAL	MONEY
D.J. Brigman	72	70	74	68	284	4,958.58
Arjun Atwal	72	71	71	70	284	4,958.57
Andy Bare	66	69	75	74	284	4,958.57
Kris Cox	71	73	70	70	284	4,958.57
Bryan DeCorso	68	69	75	72	284	4,958.57
Jim Herman	70	72	72	70	284	4,958.57
Tom Scherrer	73	67	71	73	284	4,958.57

Bank of America Open

The Glen Club, Glenview, Illinois
Par 36-36–72; 7,263 yards

May 29-June 1
purse, $750,000

	SCORES				TOTAL	MONEY
Kris Blanks	65	70	69	68	272	$135,000
Bob May	69	70	70	64	273	81,000
Brendon de Jonge	67	75	64	69	275	43,500
Casey Wittenberg	68	70	69	68	275	43,500
Spencer Levin	68	73	70	65	276	26,343.75
David McKenzie	66	71	67	72	276	26,343.75
Kyle Reifers	63	71	73	69	276	26,343.75
Tommy Tolles	67	70	69	70	276	26,343.75
Matt Hansen	69	69	72	67	277	19,500
Tom Johnson	70	71	68	68	277	19,500
Niklas Lemke	69	70	69	69	277	19,500
Keith Nolan	65	75	69	68	277	19,500
Rob Bradley	68	71	71	68	278	12,083.34
David Mathis	67	74	69	68	278	12,083.34
Aron Price	68	72	71	67	278	12,083.34
Andrew Buckle	66	71	71	70	278	12,083.33
David Lutterus	65	74	70	69	278	12,083.33
D.A. Points	70	71	68	69	278	12,083.33
Darron Stiles	65	76	68	69	278	12,083.33
Daniel Summerhays	70	71	71	66	278	12,083.33
Matt Weibring	67	70	70	71	278	12,083.33
Arjun Atwal	67	72	69	71	279	6,500
Greg Chalmers	68	71	70	70	279	6,500
Stephen Dartnall	68	72	72	67	279	6,500
Glen Day	68	71	70	70	279	6,500
John Kimbell	71	71	68	69	279	6,500
Bryce Molder	73	69	69	68	279	6,500
Greg Owen	68	70	71	70	279	6,500
Chris Smith	69	69	68	73	279	6,500
Steve Wheatcroft	71	70	69	69	279	6,500

Rex Hospital Open

TPC Wakefield Plantation, Raleigh, North Carolina
Par 35-36–71; 7,257 yards

June 5-8
purse, $500,000

	SCORES				TOTAL	MONEY
Scott Gutschewski	67	69	68	66	270	$90,000
Chad Ginn	68	69	64	71	272	44,000
Esteban Toledo	72	67	64	69	272	44,000
Garth Mulroy	68	68	71	67	274	20,666.67
Greg Owen	65	68	71	70	274	20,666.67
Matt Every	69	68	63	74	274	20,666.66

	SCORES				TOTAL	MONEY
Reid Edstrom	70	72	63	70	275	16,750
Jeff Gallagher	67	69	71	69	276	14,000
Garrett Osborn	69	68	68	71	276	14,000
Chris Tidland	71	68	68	69	276	14,000
Brendon Todd	69	69	66	72	276	14,000
Josh Broadaway	67	75	66	69	277	8,666.67
Keoke Cotner	66	72	69	70	277	8,666.67
Ian Leggatt	67	69	71	70	277	8,666.67
David McKenzie	72	68	67	70	277	8,666.67
Brendan Steele	70	71	69	67	277	8,666.67
Chris Thompson	71	70	69	67	277	8,666.67
Dustin Bray	67	74	66	70	277	8,666.66
Brad Fritsch	66	69	69	73	277	8,666.66
Fran Quinn	65	70	65	77	277	8,666.66
David Branshaw	68	68	72	70	278	5,033.34
Aron Price	76	66	68	68	278	5,033.34
Rich Barcelo	71	66	70	71	278	5,033.33
Oskar Bergman	70	70	65	73	278	5,033.33
Jonathan Fricke	68	66	71	73	278	5,033.33
Bret Guetz	68	69	70	71	278	5,033.33

Knoxville Open

Fox Den Country Club, Knoxville, Tennessee
Par 36-36–72; 7,110 yards

June 19-22
purse, $500,000

	SCORES				TOTAL	MONEY
Jarrod Lyle	66	67	67	69	269	$90,000
Chris Kirk	66	70	66	67	269	54,000
(Lyle defeated Kirk on first playoff hole.)						
D.J. Brigman	67	64	70	70	271	29,000
Kyle Reifers	71	69	65	66	271	29,000
Doug Barron	69	67	66	70	272	19,000
Chris Smith	67	67	70	68	272	19,000
Jeff Brehaut	67	71	67	68	273	16,125
Spencer Levin	69	67	68	69	273	16,125
Arjun Atwal	66	70	68	71	275	12,500
Rich Barcelo	69	71	68	67	275	12,500
Greg Chalmers	68	68	73	66	275	12,500
Brad Fritsch	69	67	68	71	275	12,500
Bob May	68	69	70	68	275	12,500
Scott Dunlap	69	71	66	71	277	7,280
Reid Edstrom	68	68	72	69	277	7,280
Sebastian Fernandez	67	70	67	73	277	7,280
Thomas Hagler	71	68	63	75	277	7,280
J.J. Killeen	70	71	67	69	277	7,280
Wade Ormsby	68	67	74	68	277	7,280
Scott Parel	70	69	65	73	277	7,280
B.J. Staten	71	68	67	71	277	7,280
Chris Tidland	72	67	67	71	277	7,280
Matt Weibring	68	67	70	72	277	7,280
Brendan Steele	72	69	70	67	278	4,028.58
Matt Bettencourt	71	70	64	73	278	4,028.57
Keoke Cotner	70	68	66	74	278	4,028.57
Bradley Iles	70	70	71	67	278	4,028.57
Tee McCabe	70	68	72	68	278	4,028.57
Tim O'Neal	70	68	72	68	278	4,028.57
Garrett Osborn	72	68	70	68	278	4,028.57

Ford Wayne Gretzky Classic

Georgian Bay Club, Clarksburg, Ontario
Par 35-36–72; 7,139 yards
Raven Golf Club at Lora Bay, Thornbury, Ontario
Par: 36-35-71; 7,112 yards

June 26-29
purse, $800,099

		SCORES			TOTAL	MONEY
Justin Hicks	70	63	67	69	269	$144,017.82
Casey Wittenberg	66	66	67	70	269	86,410.69
(Hicks defeated Wittenberg on first playoff hole.)						
Garrett Osborn	70	66	72	62	270	46,405.74
Peter Tomasulo	69	69	69	63	270	46,405.74
Hunter Haas	65	71	69	66	271	27,123.36
Greg Owen	69	68	70	64	271	27,123.36
Aron Price	65	67	72	67	271	27,123.36
Matt Every	68	66	67	70	271	27,123.35
Gibby Gilbert	69	63	70	69	271	27,123.35
Bret Guetz	67	69	71	65	272	19,202.38
D.A. Points	69	62	72	69	272	19,202.38
Sebastian Fernandez	67	65	68	72	272	19,202.37
Kyle Reifers	69	65	67	71	272	19,202.37
Jim Herman	69	67	70	67	273	13,601.69
Rich Barcelo	66	70	67	70	273	13,601.68
Bubba Dickerson	66	67	67	73	273	13,601.68
Michael Putnam	68	65	68	72	273	13,601.68
Chris Tidland	67	65	70	71	273	13,601.68
Ricky Barnes	71	66	69	68	274	9,697.20
Keoke Cotner	68	70	66	70	274	9,697.20
Scott Dunlap	67	70	68	69	274	9,697.20
Matt Hansen	69	66	70	69	274	9,697.20
Fran Quinn	68	66	73	67	274	9,697.20
Josh Broadaway	69	67	69	70	275	6,784.84
Tripp Isenhour	67	71	68	69	275	6,784.84
Bryce Molder	71	66	68	70	275	6,784.84
Scott Piercy	66	71	74	64	275	6,784.84
Chris Smith	71	65	71	68	275	6,784.84
Kris Blanks	73	63	72	68	276	5,312.66

Nationwide Tour Players Cup

Pete Dye Golf Club, Bridgeport, West Virginia
Par 36-36–72; 7,309 yards

July 10-13
purse, $1,000,000

		SCORES			TOTAL	MONEY
Rick Price	64	71	66	72	273	$180,000
Chris Anderson	67	69	66	71	273	108,000
(Price defeated Anderson on first playoff hole.)						
David Branshaw	70	68	65	72	275	52,000
David Hearn	67	72	67	69	275	52,000
Peter Tomasulo	67	73	67	68	275	52,000
Oskar Bergman	69	69	71	67	276	34,750
D.J. Brigman	71	69	66	70	276	34,750
Stephen Dartnall	71	69	68	69	277	30,000
Matt Weibring	70	70	67	70	277	30,000
Matt Bettencourt	70	64	71	73	278	24,000
Greg Chalmers	68	68	71	71	278	24,000
Geoffrey Sisk	74	69	69	66	278	24,000
B.J. Staten	70	69	69	70	278	24,000
Brendon de Jonge	71	71	71	66	279	17,500

	SCORES				TOTAL	MONEY
Bret Guetz	72	70	69	68	279	17,500
Kyle Reifers	66	71	75	67	279	17,500
Roger Tambellini	69	73	68	69	279	17,500
Michael Boyd	67	70	72	71	280	14,000
Josh Broadaway	71	65	72	72	280	14,000
James Love	68	68	72	72	280	14,000
Randy Leen	72	68	70	71	281	10,066.67
Garrett Osborn	73	70	68	70	281	10,066.67
Fran Quinn	71	70	71	69	281	10,066.67
Jon Turcott	69	70	73	69	281	10,066.67
Skip Kendall	67	71	77	66	281	10,066.66
Bill Lunde	73	68	68	72	281	10,066.66

Price Cutter Charity Championship

Highland Springs Country Club, Springfield, Missouri
Par 36-36–72; 7,060 yards

July 17-20
purse, $600,000

	SCORES				TOTAL	MONEY
Colt Knost	64	67	69	62	262	$108,000
Webb Simpson	66	68	67	65	266	64,800
Oskar Bergman	68	69	66	65	268	40,800
Josh Broadaway	66	72	67	64	269	26,400
Brendan Steele	68	69	66	66	269	26,400
David Branshaw	71	67	64	68	270	20,850
Vance Veazey	66	68	67	69	270	20,850
Matt Bettencourt	71	68	67	65	271	16,800
Joe Daley	69	68	67	67	271	16,800
Bradley Iles	68	65	72	66	271	16,800
James Love	67	67	67	70	271	16,800
Henrik Bjornstad	69	67	67	69	272	12,600
Andy Choi	72	66	68	66	272	12,600
Matt Weibring	69	69	71	63	272	12,600
Arjun Atwal	66	68	69	70	273	8,715
Camilo Benedetti	66	70	68	69	273	8,715
Brendon de Jonge	68	68	68	69	273	8,715
Jeff Gallagher	70	67	68	68	273	8,715
Chad Ginn	66	72	66	69	273	8,715
Hunter Haas	69	70	65	69	273	8,715
Spencer Levin	67	67	68	71	273	8,715
Darron Stiles	68	65	69	71	273	8,715
Brent Delahoussaye	70	63	70	71	274	5,424
Michael Putnam	66	71	65	72	274	5,424
Mark Walker	67	70	70	67	274	5,424
Tyler Williamson	71	66	68	69	274	5,424
Willie Wood	68	69	67	70	274	5,424

Nationwide Children's Hospital Invitational

The OSU Golf Club, Scarlet Course, Columbus, Ohio
Par 36-35–71; 7,141 yards

July 24-27
purse, $750,000

	SCORES				TOTAL	MONEY
Bill Lunde	67	72	67	73	279	$135,000
Dustin Bray	69	70	72	69	280	81,000
Brendon de Jonge	70	69	69	73	281	39,000
Skip Kendall	72	72	66	71	281	39,000

	SCORES				TOTAL	MONEY
Tommy Tolles	69	70	73	69	281	39,000
Josh Broadaway	74	66	67	75	282	22,687.50
Scott Gardiner	68	71	68	75	282	22,687.50
Garth Mulroy	71	73	67	71	282	22,687.50
Alex Prugh	72	72	68	70	282	22,687.50
Michael Putnam	69	72	71	70	282	22,687.50
Peter Tomasulo	70	67	72	73	282	22,687.50
*Sihwan Kim	72	71	70	69	282	
Oskar Bergman	70	72	70	71	283	15,187.50
Keith Nolan	71	71	72	69	283	15,187.50
Darron Stiles	69	72	69	73	283	15,187.50
Steve Wheatcroft	73	70	69	71	283	15,187.50
Blake Adams	72	72	66	74	284	10,181.25
Rich Barcelo	68	70	75	71	284	10,181.25
Kris Blanks	71	71	70	72	284	10,181.25
Stephen Gangluff	72	71	67	74	284	10,181.25
Bradley Iles	73	66	71	74	284	10,181.25
Jason Schultz	71	68	74	71	284	10,181.25
Geoffrey Sisk	69	72	72	71	284	10,181.25
Matt Weibring	71	71	72	70	284	10,181.25
Jim Herman	74	69	71	71	285	6,200
J.J. Killeen	72	72	70	71	285	6,200
Marc Leishman	68	74	72	71	285	6,200
Bob May	69	73	67	76	285	6,200
David McKenzie	71	73	69	72	285	6,200
Phil Tataurangi	68	71	73	73	285	6,200

Cox Classic

Champions Run, Omaha, Nebraska
Par 35-36–71; 7,145 yards

July 31-August 3
purse, $700,000

	SCORES				TOTAL	MONEY
Ryan Hietala	64	62	70	69	265	$126,000
David Branshaw	64	64	64	73	265	75,600
(Hietala defeated Branshaw on first playoff hole,)						
Skip Kendall	66	70	68	64	268	36,400
Garth Mulroy	64	65	70	69	268	36,400
Alex Prugh	66	64	71	67	268	36,400
Ricky Barnes	70	66	68	65	269	21,175
Gary Christian	66	70	65	68	269	21,175
Jeff Klauk	67	66	70	66	269	21,175
Bill Lunde	68	64	68	69	269	21,175
Vance Veazey	64	66	65	74	269	21,175
Casey Wittenberg	69	67	66	67	269	21,175
Greg Chalmers	69	65	69	67	270	13,300
Nick Malinowski	71	64	69	66	270	13,300
David McKenzie	65	67	73	65	270	13,300
Greg Owen	70	65	66	69	270	13,300
D.A. Points	63	68	70	69	270	13,300
Brendan Steele	68	69	66	67	270	13,300
Blake Adams	69	64	72	66	271	7,964.45
Brendon de Jonge	68	68	69	66	271	7,964.45
Hunter Haas	69	69	67	66	271	7,964.45
Mike Wendling	67	70	69	65	271	7,964.45
Miguel Angel Carballo	70	67	67	67	271	7,964.44
Spencer Levin	66	67	69	69	271	7,964.44
Bryce Molder	66	66	71	68	271	7,964.44
Madalitso Muthiya	69	67	67	68	271	7,964.44
Chris Thompson	66	72	64	69	271	7,964.44

Preferred Health Systems Wichita Open

Crestview Country Club, Wichita, Kansas
Par 35-36–71; 6,886 yards

August 7-10
purse, $525,000

	SCORES				TOTAL	MONEY
Scott Piercy	64	62	65	71	262	$94,500
Daniel Summerhays	65	65	67	67	264	39,200
Hunter Haas	65	65	64	70	264	39,200
Spencer Levin	66	66	65	67	264	39,200
Brendon de Jonge	68	67	63	68	266	21,000
Chris Anderson	64	65	68	70	267	18,900
Brian Smock	65	68	68	67	268	15,816
Fabian Gomez	65	69	67	67	268	15,816
Lee Won-joon	66	69	64	69	268	15,816
Bob May	63	70	67	68	268	15,816
Aaron Watkins	63	68	69	69	269	13,125
D.A. Points	68	67	67	68	270	10,631
Ian Leggatt	68	68	66	68	270	10,631
Blake Adams	68	66	68	68	270	10,631
Josh McCumber	66	68	66	70	270	10,631
Brendon Todd	64	69	70	68	271	7,875
Bryce Molder	66	72	65	68	271	7,875
Anders Hultman	65	69	69	68	271	7,875
Scott Gardiner	64	69	68	70	271	7,875
Scott Gutschewski	67	66	68	70	271	7,875
Aron Price	68	66	69	69	272	6,090
Ben Bates	67	69	65	71	272	6,090
Jim Rutledge	66	71	67	69	273	5,250
Scott Dunlap	68	68	66	71	273	5,250
Ryan Hietala	71	66	68	69	274	4,200
J.J. Killeen	68	70	67	69	274	4,200
Zoran Zorkic	68	69	69	68	274	4,200
Scott Gordon	68	66	72	68	274	4,200
Tommy Tolles	62	73	69	70	274	4,200

Xerox Classic

Irondequoit Country Club, Rochester, New York
Par 35-35–70; 6,720 yards

August 14-17
purse, $600,000

	SCORES				TOTAL	MONEY
Brendon de Jonge	67	64	67	69	267	$108,000
Jarrod Lyle	68	68	66	69	271	64,800
Ricky Barnes	68	67	71	66	272	31,200
Jonathan Fricke	69	69	63	71	272	31,200
Greg Owen	66	68	67	71	272	31,200
Hunter Haas	67	72	68	66	273	18,780
David Hearn	68	66	69	70	273	18,780
Garrett Osborn	68	66	71	68	273	18,780
Scott Piercy	69	67	69	68	273	18,780
Dave Schultz	65	69	70	69	273	18,780
Jeff Gallagher	69	65	73	67	274	13,800
Bill Lunde	72	68	67	67	274	13,800
Bob May	64	69	75	66	274	13,800
Craig Bowden	66	73	67	69	275	11,100
Brendon Todd	66	73	70	66	275	11,100
Jim Herman	68	69	69	70	276	9,600
Anders Hultman	69	69	70	68	276	9,600
Vance Veazey	67	68	71	70	276	9,600

	SCORES				TOTAL	MONEY
Greg Chalmers	66	68	75	68	277	7,272
Marc Leishman	70	68	69	70	277	7,272
Nick Malinowski	68	70	71	68	277	7,272
Scott Parel	68	69	71	69	277	7,272
Alex Prugh	68	69	66	74	277	7,272
Matt Every	71	68	73	66	278	5,088
Bradley Iles	70	67	70	71	278	5,088
Josh McCumber	73	66	70	69	278	5,088
Brian Stuard	67	69	68	74	278	5,088
Esteban Toledo	72	66	68	72	278	5,088

Northeast Pennsylvania Classic

Elmhurst Country Club, Moscow, Pennsylvania
Par 35-35–70; 6,781 yards

August 21-24
purse, $525,000

	SCORES				TOTAL	MONEY
Scott Piercy	66	68	69	64	267	$94,500
Brendon de Jonge	71	67	63	68	269	46,200
Cameron Percy	66	68	69	66	269	46,200
Rich Barcelo	68	68	66	68	270	21,700
Brad Fritsch	67	65	71	67	270	21,700
Jeff Gallagher	69	70	65	66	270	21,700
Mark Brooks	65	72	69	65	271	16,931.25
Rick Price	64	70	69	68	271	16,931.25
Ben Bates	69	68	67	68	272	12,150
Greg Chalmers	63	69	69	71	272	12,150
Jeff Curl	71	63	68	70	272	12,150
Sebastian Fernandez	66	71	68	67	272	12,150
Chris Nallen	67	68	67	70	272	12,150
D.A. Points	68	64	67	73	272	12,150
Brendon Todd	69	66	70	67	272	12,150
Ryan Hietala	71	68	67	67	273	8,925
Craig Bowden	67	70	71	66	274	6,641.25
Joe Daley	69	70	68	67	274	6,641.25
Chris Kirk	68	66	68	72	274	6,641.25
Jeff Klauk	66	69	70	69	274	6,641.25
Keith Nolan	68	67	70	69	274	6,641.25
Garrett Osborn	70	68	66	70	274	6,641.25
Webb Simpson	70	69	67	68	274	6,641.25
Brian Stuard	71	67	69	67	274	6,641.25
Jeff Brehaut	66	71	66	72	275	4,305
Bubba Dickerson	66	69	67	73	275	4,305
Roger Tambellini	69	69	68	69	275	4,305
Chris Tidland	63	72	69	71	275	4,305

Utah Championship

Willow Creek Country Club, Sandy, Utah
Par 35-36–71; 7,104 yards

September 4-7
purse, $550,000

	SCORES				TOTAL	MONEY
Brendon Todd	64	66	65	67	262	$99,000
Jeff Klauk	70	67	66	65	268	30,570.84
Lee Won-joon	68	66	70	64	268	30,570.84
Ryan Hietala	67	68	67	66	268	30,570.83
Marc Leishman	65	63	68	72	268	30,570.83

	SCORES				TOTAL	MONEY
Brian Smock	68	68	66	66	268	30,570.83
Kyle Thompson	64	65	68	71	268	30,570.83
Jonathan Fricke	68	68	64	69	269	14,300
Scott Gardiner	68	68	67	66	269	14,300
Matt Hansen	68	69	65	67	269	14,300
Spencer Levin	67	67	68	67	269	14,300
David Mathis	67	68	69	65	269	14,300
Clay Ogden	68	67	68	66	269	14,300
Mark Brooks	68	66	69	67	270	9,350
Rob Grube	70	68	63	69	270	9,350
Chris Nallen	66	65	72	67	270	9,350
Darron Stiles	71	65	66	68	270	9,350
Roger Tambellini	68	66	68	68	270	9,350
Jeff Curl	66	68	67	70	271	6,666
Bob May	67	70	68	66	271	6,666
Bryce Molder	69	68	68	66	271	6,666
Jimmy Walker	67	69	65	70	271	6,666
Matt Weibring	67	67	69	68	271	6,666
David Branshaw	63	72	68	69	272	4,785
Fran Quinn	73	65	67	67	272	4,785
Peter Tomasulo	67	69	68	68	272	4,785
Jeff Wood	68	67	72	65	272	4,785

Albertsons Boise Open

Hillcrest Country Club, Boise, Idaho
Par 35-36–71; 6,698 yards

September 11-14
purse, $725,000

	SCORES				TOTAL	MONEY
Chris Tidland	69	65	66	64	264	$130,500
Scott Piercy	67	68	72	61	268	78,300
Greg Owen	71	68	65	65	269	49,300
Peter Tomasulo	68	70	66	66	270	34,800
Matt Bettencourt	66	71	66	68	271	29,000
Clay Ogden	71	68	70	63	272	21,180
Tag Ridings	67	66	70	69	272	21,180
Wade Ormsby	67	67	68	70	272	21,180
Spencer Levin	67	66	69	70	272	21,180
Michael Putnam	65	71	66	70	272	21,180
Hunter Haas	68	68	66	70	272	21,180
Bill Lunde	66	65	69	72	272	21,180
Brendan Steele	69	66	70	68	273	14,017
Brendon de Jonge	70	67	67	69	273	14,017
Alex Prugh	69	68	68	68	273	14,017
Brendon Todd	70	66	70	68	274	11,963
Kris Blanks	67	71	66	70	274	11,963
Arjun Atwal	66	68	73	68	275	9,788
Scott Gutschewski	68	70	69	68	275	9,788
Dave Schultz	70	65	70	70	275	9,788
Ricky Barnes	69	69	66	71	275	9,788
Greg Chalmers	69	69	71	67	276	7,250
Jason Enloe	70	68	69	69	276	7,250
Fran Quinn	70	69	68	69	276	7,250
Brian Smock	67	72	67	70	276	7,250

Oregon Classic

Shadow Hills Country Club, Junction City, Oregon
Par 36-36–72; 7,007 yards

September 18-21
purse, $500,000

	SCORES				TOTAL	MONEY
Matt Bettencourt	65	70	65	69	269	$90,000
Bubba Dickerson	67	66	70	68	271	54,000
Spencer Levin	68	70	66	68	272	34,000
Bradley Iles	73	66	68	66	273	22,000
Brian Smock	68	68	68	69	273	22,000
Alex Prugh	70	69	68	67	274	18,000
Brad Fritsch	70	67	71	67	275	16,750
Rich Barcelo	72	68	70	66	276	13,000
Scott Gardiner	68	72	69	67	276	13,000
Scott Gutschewski	68	72	67	69	276	13,000
Hunter Haas	70	67	69	70	276	13,000
Daniel Summerhays	69	70	68	69	276	13,000
Matt Weibring	71	69	68	68	276	13,000
Patrick Damron	68	71	70	68	277	7,511.12
Arjun Atwal	71	69	67	70	277	7,511.11
Gary Christian	70	69	68	70	277	7,511.11
Matt Every	69	71	69	68	277	7,511.11
Lee Won-joon	68	67	72	70	277	7,511.11
Bill Lunde	71	67	69	70	277	7,511.11
Jarrod Lyle	69	68	70	70	277	7,511.11
B.J. Staten	67	70	71	69	277	7,511.11
Darron Stiles	67	67	72	71	277	7,511.11
Brian Guetz	71	70	71	66	278	4,800
Ryan Hietala	65	71	70	72	278	4,800
Jim Rutledge	68	70	71	69	278	4,800

WNB Golf Classic

Midland Country Club, Odessa, Texas
Par 36-36–72; 7,345 yards

October 9-12
purse, $525,000

	SCORES				TOTAL	MONEY
Marc Leishman	67	66	66	68	267	$94,500
Keoke Cotner	70	71	69	68	278	56,700
Aron Price	67	72	68	72	279	35,700
Greg Chalmers	70	72	70	68	280	20,671.88
Darron Stiles	71	69	70	70	280	20,671.88
Lee Won-joon	69	69	71	71	280	20,671.87
Spencer Levin	66	70	72	72	280	20,671.87
Ricky Barnes	69	68	71	73	281	14,175
Brendon de Jonge	71	68	67	75	281	14,175
Fabian Gomez	69	73	68	71	281	14,175
Cameron Percy	72	68	66	75	281	14,175
Brendon Todd	68	68	73	72	281	14,175
Tom Gillis	66	70	74	72	282	10,500
Vance Veazey	72	69	71	70	282	10,500
Michael Boyd	69	67	68	79	283	8,137.50
Mark Brooks	74	70	68	71	283	8,137.50
Brad Fritsch	71	72	68	72	283	8,137.50
Justin Hicks	74	67	68	74	283	8,137.50
Ian Leggatt	72	68	72	71	283	8,137.50
Garrett Osborn	73	68	69	73	283	8,137.50
D.J. Brigman	71	72	69	72	284	5,285
Gary Christian	67	74	69	74	284	5,285

	SCORES			TOTAL	MONEY
Hunter Haas	70	71 69	74	284	5,285
Anders Hultman	72	69 70	73	284	5,285
Chris Smith	72	69 69	74	284	5,285
Roger Tambellini	73	70 69	72	284	5,285

Chattanooga Classic

Black Creek Club, Chattanooga, Tennessee   October 16-19
Par 36-36–72; 7,040 yards   purse, $500,000

	SCORES			TOTAL	MONEY
Arjun Atwal	66	60 66	72	264	$90,000
Webb Simpson	61	64 70	69	264	54,000
(Atwal defeated Simpson on first playoff hole.)					
Kris Blanks	63	68 69	68	268	34,000
Hunter Haas	67	64 67	71	269	24,000
Brendon de Jonge	67	66 67	70	270	20,000
Ricky Barnes	65	68 71	67	271	16,187.50
Lee Won-joon	68	65 68	70	271	16,187.50
Bill Lunde	67	62 68	74	271	16,187.50
Matt Weibring	63	66 70	72	271	16,187.50
Bryce Molder	65	72 69	66	272	13,500
Tom Gillis	66	64 71	72	273	12,000
Skip Kendall	63	67 72	71	273	12,000
Daniel Summerhays	69	67 69	69	274	10,500
Bob Heintz	66	67 68	74	275	8,750
Justin Hicks	71	66 68	70	275	8,750
D.A. Points	69	68 73	65	275	8,750
Scott Stallings	64	62 73	76	275	8,750
Matt Bettencourt	66	68 69	73	276	6,520
Gary Christian	65	70 71	70	276	6,520
Scott Dunlap	67	70 68	71	276	6,520
Spencer Levin	71	66 69	70	276	6,520
Casey Wittenberg	69	69 70	68	276	6,520
Matt Hansen	65	66 74	73	278	4,650
Colt Knost	68	70 67	73	278	4,650
Michael Putnam	69	62 75	72	278	4,650
Chris Tidland	66	70 71	71	278	4,650

Miccosukee Championship

Miccosukee Golf & Country Club, Miami, Florida   October 23-26
Par 35-36–71; 7,200 yards   purse, $625,000

	SCORES			TOTAL	MONEY
D.A. Points	73	70 62	67	272	$112,500
Matt Bettencourt	71	68 66	67	272	67,500
(Points defeated Bettencourt on first playoff hole.)					
Josh Broadaway	69	68 69	68	274	32,500
Gavin Coles	69	69 68	68	274	32,500
Bryce Molder	69	69 69	67	274	32,500
Scott Gardiner	68	71 68	69	276	21,718.75
Matt Hansen	69	70 70	67	276	21,718.75
Chris Nallen	67	71 72	67	277	18,125
Brendon Todd	70	72 68	67	277	18,125
Steve Wheatcroft	73	69 70	65	277	18,125
Chad Ginn	72	67 70	69	278	12,410.72

	SCORES				TOTAL	MONEY
Jim Herman	69	73	69	67	278	12,410.72
Matt Weibring	69	72	71	66	278	12,410.72
Bubba Dickerson	74	68	73	63	278	12,410.71
Scott Dunlap	74	69	66	69	278	12,410.71
Marc Leishman	70	66	70	72	278	12,410.71
Daniel Summerhays	68	72	67	71	278	12,410.71
Ricky Barnes	72	64	74	69	279	9,062.50
Tom Gillis	72	67	72	68	279	9,062.50
Rich Barcelo	72	71	69	68	280	6,012.50
Andrew Bonhomme	70	69	71	70	280	6,012.50
Jay Delsing	72	68	69	71	280	6,012.50
Reid Edstrom	71	69	68	72	280	6,012.50
Matt Every	71	71	70	68	280	6,012.50
Hunter Haas	72	70	69	69	280	6,012.50
Jeff Klauk	73	69	69	69	280	6,012.50
Rick Price	73	71	68	68	280	6,012.50
Geoffrey Sisk	74	70	70	66	280	6,012.50
Peter Tomasulo	71	70	71	68	280	6,012.50

Nationwide Tour Championship

TPC Craig Ranch, McKinney, Texas
Par 36-35–71; 7,438 yards

November 6-9
purse, $1,000,000

	SCORES				TOTAL	MONEY
Matt Bettencourt	68	67	63	69	267	$180,000
Jeff Klauk	65	69	69	65	268	108,000
Colt Knost	67	66	71	65	269	58,000
Bryce Molder	67	67	64	71	269	58,000
Peter Tomasulo	68	70	63	69	270	40,000
Garrett Osborn	66	65	71	69	271	36,000
Oskar Bergman	73	66	67	66	272	32,250
Marc Leishman	67	67	68	70	272	32,250
D.J. Brigman	69	69	67	68	273	28,000
Scott Gutschewski	70	67	67	69	273	28,000
David Branshaw	70	67	69	68	274	21,200
Brendon de Jonge	69	69	67	69	274	21,200
Kyle Reifers	72	64	65	73	274	21,200
Webb Simpson	70	73	67	64	274	21,200
Darron Stiles	64	67	70	73	274	21,200
Josh Broadaway	74	67	68	66	275	15,000
Gavin Coles	68	69	68	70	275	15,000
Spencer Levin	66	69	69	71	275	15,000
Aron Price	70	70	70	65	275	15,000
Alex Prugh	71	67	70	67	275	15,000
Hunter Haas	68	66	70	72	276	10,800
Bill Lunde	67	71	69	69	276	10,800
David Mathis	71	69	69	67	276	10,800
Fran Quinn	71	68	68	69	276	10,800
Greg Chalmers	69	72	69	67	277	8,000
Lee Won-joon	71	70	69	67	277	8,000
Bob May	70	68	71	68	277	8,000
Daniel Summerhays	71	70	66	70	277	8,000
Casey Wittenberg	71	64	70	72	277	8,000

Canadian Tour

Spring International

Del Rio Country Club, Modesto, California
Par 36-36–72; 6,678 yards

April 10-13
purse, US$100,000

	SCORES				TOTAL	MONEY
Spencer Levin	71	67	66	69	273	US$16,000
Andrew Parr	70	68	65	70	273	9,600
(Levin defeated Parr on second playoff hole.)						
Joseph Lanza	68	69	69	69	275	6,000
Brent Schwarzrock	66	67	72	71	276	4,400
Joel Kribel	67	65	72	72	276	4,400
Byron Smith	71	68	71	67	277	3,450
Garrett Frank	72	66	69	70	277	3,450
John Ellis	71	70	68	69	278	2,800
Scott Gibson	72	68	67	71	278	2,800
Steve Conway	69	67	70	72	278	2,800
Troy Kelly	69	68	69	72	278	2,800
Antonio Maldonado	66	69	72	72	279	2,300
James Love	71	72	69	68	280	1,933.33
Jaime Gomez	71	69	69	71	280	1,933.33
Matt Bettencourt	74	65	67	74	280	1,933.33
D.J. Fiese	72	69	71	69	281	1,500
Mark Warman	73	70	68	70	281	1,500
Michael Wilson	72	68	70	71	281	1,500
Adam Speirs	71	70	68	72	281	1,500
Luke Swilor	70	74	63	74	281	1,500
David Bradshaw	72	71	71	68	282	1,150
Jim Rutledge	69	70	72	71	282	1,150
Ryan Carter	69	71	71	71	282	1,150
Justin Itzen	73	70	68	71	282	1,150
Will Mitchell	70	69	70	73	282	1,150

Stockton Sports Commission Classic

Brookside Golf & Country Club, Stockton, California
Par 36-36–72; 6,741 yards

April 17-20
purse, US$100,000

	SCORES				TOTAL	MONEY
John Ellis	68	65	70	69	272	US$16,000
Tommy Barber	73	65	66	68	272	9,600
(Ellis defeated Barber on first playoff hole.)						
Kris Wasylowich	67	70	73	64	274	6,000
Adam Bland	66	64	73	72	275	3,760
Rob Johnson	69	69	71	66	275	3,760
Troy Kelly	70	64	72	69	275	3,760
Dustin Risdon	67	69	73	66	275	3,760
Byron Smith	66	69	70	70	275	3,760
Alex Coe	68	69	71	68	276	2,700
Travis Johnson	68	68	70	70	276	2,700
Marc Peterson	69	66	71	70	276	2,700
Stephen Gangluff	67	69	69	72	277	2,200
Eugene Smith	66	69	70	72	277	2,200
James Hahn	72	66	73	67	278	1,800

	SCORES				TOTAL	MONEY
Adam Short	69	66	72	71	278	1,800
Andy Walker	68	70	72	68	278	1,800
Conway Steve	70	67	75	67	279	1,342.86
Jaime Gomez	69	68	69	73	279	1,342.86
Brad Heaven	69	66	73	71	279	1,342.86
Wes Heffernan	68	69	71	71	279	1,342.86
Mike Nicoletti	67	70	71	71	279	1,342.86
Conner Robbins	68	66	71	74	279	1,342.86
Adam Speirs	70	68	70	71	279	1,342.86
Graham DeLaet	70	68	73	69	280	986.67
Torey Edwards	72	65	75	68	280	986.67
Josh Geary	65	72	74	69	280	986.67
Peter Laws	72	67	67	74	280	986.67
Brent Schwarzrock	69	66	74	71	280	986.67
Mark Warman	68	66	76	70	280	986.67

Corona Mazatlan Mexican PGA Championship

El Cid Golf & Country Club, Mazatlan, Mexico　　　　　　　　　　　　April 24-27
Par 36-36–72; 6,623 yards　　　　　　　　　　　　　　　　　purse, US$125,000

	SCORES				TOTAL	MONEY
John Ellis	62	69	71	71	273	US$20,000
Wes Heffernan	67	67	74	66	274	9,750
Adam Bland	67	73	66	68	274	9,750
Jose Trauwitz	72	69	67	68	276	6,000
Oscar Fraustro	70	71	66	70	277	5,000
Shawn Jasper	72	71	68	68	279	4,167
Jaime Gomez	70	69	71	69	279	4,167
George Bradford	70	70	69	70	279	4,167
Craig Scott	69	73	73	65	280	3,500
Conner Robbins	68	74	66	72	280	3,500
Adam Speirs	68	71	69	73	281	3,000
Tom Stankowski	70	70	67	74	281	3,000
Tim Wood	71	69	72	70	282	2,417
Andrew Johnson	70	70	70	72	282	2,417
Yoon Kwang-soo	73	68	67	74	282	2,417
Eugene Smith	69	70	73	71	283	1,875
Richard Gilkey	67	68	77	71	283	1,875
Oscar Serna	69	72	70	72	283	1,875
Federico Garcia	68	70	72	73	283	1,875
Garrett Sapp	68	68	74	73	283	1,875
James Hahn	76	67	70	71	284	1,406
Torey Edwards	70	73	70	71	284	1,406
Justin Smith	69	68	75	72	284	1,406
Mike Grob	70	74	72	68	284	1,406
Jay Choe	73	70	69	72	284	1,406
Andy Walker	69	72	70	73	284	1,406

Iberostar Riviera Maya Open

Iberostar Playa Paraiso Golf Club, Riviera Maya, Mexico　　　　　　　May 15-18
Par 36-36–72; 6,712 yards　　　　　　　　　　　　　　　　　purse, US$125,000

	SCORES				TOTAL	MONEY
Daniel Im	67	69	72	69	277	US$20,000
Oscar Serna	70	69	71	68	278	9,750

	SCORES				TOTAL	MONEY
Brent Schwarzrock	67	69	73	69	278	9,750
Wil Collins	70	70	74	65	279	6,000
Tom Stankowski	70	68	72	71	281	5,000
Anthony Rodriguez	68	73	72	69	282	4,167
Scott Gibson	73	70	69	70	282	4,167
Ryan Thornberry	73	66	70	73	282	4,167
Ryan Horn	70	70	75	68	283	3,375
John Ellis	69	75	69	70	283	3,375
Ricardo Carrillo	72	70	70	71	283	3,375
Stephen Gangluff	67	74	75	68	284	2,531
Zach Doran	70	72	72	70	284	2,531
Will Dodson	69	72	71	72	284	2,531
James Love	71	69	70	74	284	2,531
Dean Kennedy	71	69	76	69	285	1,875
Dustin Pimm	72	73	71	69	285	1,875
Craig Matthew	69	67	78	71	285	1,875
Taylor Wood	71	70	73	71	285	1,875
Jim Lemon	71	70	72	72	285	1,875
J.C. Deacon	73	72	73	68	286	1,469
Wes Heffernan	73	71	71	71	286	1,469
Josh Habig	72	73	76	65	286	1,469
Jose Trauwitz	73	71	69	73	286	1,469
Steve Conway	70	71	73	73	287	1,254
Jordan Krantz	72	68	73	74	287	1,254
Greg McAuley	73	70	70	74	287	1,254

La Loma San Luis Potosi Open

Nicklaus La Loma Golf Club, San Luis Potosi, Mexico 　　　　May 22-25
Par 36-36–72; 7,477 yards 　　　　purse, US$125,000

	SCORES				TOTAL	MONEY
Russell Surber	67	72	71	72	282	US$20,000
Wil Collins	75	74	69	66	284	9,750
Adam Bland	70	70	71	73	284	9,750
Marc Lawless	67	74	70	74	285	5,500
Brad Heaven	74	65	76	70	285	5,500
Anthony Rodriguez	74	72	73	68	287	4,313
Byron Smith	74	67	72	74	287	4,313
John Ellis	70	75	71	72	288	3,625
Chris Wall	72	72	73	71	288	3,625
Eugene Smith	72	70	72	74	288	3,625
Tommy Barber	70	75	72	72	289	3,000
Steve Conway	71	72	75	71	289	3,000
Garrett Frank	76	70	73	72	291	2,500
Daniel Im	76	70	74	71	291	2,500
Mike Grob	74	75	68	75	292	2,000
Ryan Thornberry	78	71	71	72	292	2,000
Jim Seki	77	71	74	70	292	2,000
Wes Heffernan	75	74	72	71	292	2,000
Adam Speirs	71	71	79	71	292	2,000
Oscar Serna	72	74	72	75	293	1,563
Mike Mezei	81	69	67	76	293	1,563
Barrett Jarosch	75	70	76	72	293	1,563
Eric Wang	76	72	73	73	294	1,315
Mark Warman	79	69	71	75	294	1,315
Alex Quiroz	72	76	77	69	294	1,315
Craig Scott	76	71	72	75	294	1,315
Kyle Monfort	74	70	71	79	294	1,315

Times Colonist Open

Uplands Golf Club, Victoria, British Columbia
Par 35-35–70; 6,315 yards

June 12-15
purse, C$150,000

	SCORES				TOTAL	MONEY
Daniel Im	66	72	62	68	268	C$24,000
James Lepp	68	70	65	65	268	14,400
(Im defeated Lepp on first playoff hole.)						
Jim Rutledge	63	68	68	70	269	9,000
Clayton Ogden	67	73	66	65	271	6,200
John Shin	69	67	66	69	271	6,200
Andrew Johnson	68	70	64	69	271	6,200
Mike Grob	68	68	70	66	272	4,500
Garrett Sapp	66	70	69	67	272	4,500
Wes Heffernan	67	67	69	69	272	4,500
Troy Kelly	68	69	65	70	272	4,500
Andrew Parr	70	68	66	69	273	3,600
Joseph Lanza	70	68	66	69	273	3,600
Hoyt McGarity	70	71	67	66	274	3,600
Dustin Risdon	73	65	69	67	274	2,900
Richard Scott	67	72	66	69	274	2,900
Warren Pineo	75	66	67	67	275	2,250
Mario Tiziani	71	68	68	68	275	2,250
Craig Scott	71	68	67	69	275	2,250
John Cassidy	67	72	67	69	275	2,250
Eric Wang	69	68	68	70	275	2,250
Derek Gillespie	71	65	73	67	276	1,725
Dale Vallely	68	70	70	68	276	1,725
Stephen Dixon	71	70	67	68	276	1,725
Greg Machtaler	69	67	71	69	276	1,725
Andy Walker	70	68	68	70	276	1,725

Greater Vancouver Charity Classic

Hazelmere Golf Club, South Surrey, British Columbia
Par 36-36–72; 6,806 yards

June 19-22
purse, C$100,000

	SCORES				TOTAL	MONEY
Adam Speirs	67	67	69	72	275	C$16,000
Wes Heffernan	73	66	67	70	276	7,800
Byron Smith	72	65	69	70	276	7,800
Ben Fox	71	69	70	68	278	4,800
John Ellis	72	72	66	69	279	4,000
Scott Hawley	71	67	73	69	280	3,333.33
Bryn Parry	73	67	70	70	280	3,333.33
Adam Bland	70	71	67	72	280	3,333.33
Mike Sica	71	68	73	69	281	2,600
Kent Eger	73	68	69	71	281	2,600
Mike Grob	71	67	69	74	281	2,600
Derek Gillespie	72	70	62	79	281	2,600
Joseph Lanza	67	72	68	75	282	2,100
Shawn Jasper	76	68	73	66	283	1,800
Jim Seki	75	67	71	70	283	1,800
Ryan Carter	69	72	69	73	283	1,800
James Lepp	67	71	72	74	284	1,550
Brad Heaven	67	68	73	76	284	1,550
Dong Yi	72	69	75	69	285	1,260
Drew Stoltz	69	72	73	71	285	1,260
Michael Harris	72	70	71	72	285	1,260

	SCORES				TOTAL	MONEY
Brent Schwarzrock	73	72	68	72	285	1,260
Ryan Thornberry	74	69	69	73	285	1,260
Eugene Smith	71	69	75	71	286	986.67
Philip Jonas	71	73	71	71	286	986.67
Andrew Parr	72	73	70	71	286	986.67
Daniel Im	71	73	70	72	286	986.67
Liam Kendregan	75	69	67	75	286	986.67
Graham DeLaet	73	66	71	76	286	986.67

ATB Financial Classic

Cottonwood Golf & Country Club, Calgary, Alberta
Par 36-35–71; 6,963 yards

June 26-29
purse, C$150,000

	SCORES				TOTAL	MONEY
Dustin Risdon	67	62	65	70	264	C$24,000
George Bradford	66	65	70	63	264	14,400
(Risdon defeated Bradford on first playoff hole.)						
Steve Conway	65	67	68	65	265	6,510
Josh Habig	66	68	66	65	265	6,510
Ricky Romano	67	66	67	65	265	6,510
Andy Walker	69	66	65	65	265	6,510
Kris Wasylowich	66	66	65	68	265	6,510
Clint Rice	66	67	69	64	266	4,200
Mike Grob	67	67	66	66	266	4,200
Mike Sica	64	67	66	69	266	4,200
Jordan Krantz	65	67	66	68	266	4,200
Brad Heaven	69	65	71	62	267	3,300
Kent Eger	68	66	68	65	267	3,300
Derek Gillespie	66	65	67	70	268	2,850
Andrew Johnson	63	71	72	63	269	2,325
Marc Peterson	66	67	71	65	269	2,325
Dong Yi	67	67	70	65	269	2,325
Mitch Tasker	69	65	67	68	269	2,325
Chris Wall	67	67	67	68	269	2,325
Jim Seki	65	66	67	71	269	2,325
Tommy Barber	69	67	70	64	270	1,652.14
Ryan Yip	68	68	68	66	270	1,652.14
Luke Hickmott	67	66	70	67	270	1,652.14
John Lieber	68	64	70	68	270	1,652.14
Eugene Smith	63	66	73	68	270	1,652.14
Clayton Ogden	65	68	69	68	270	1,652.14
Barrett Jarosch	67	65	69	69	270	1,652.14

Saskatchewan Open

Dakota Dunes, Saskatoon, Saskatchewan
Par 36-36–72; 7,301 yards

July 3-6
purse, C$150,000

	SCORES				TOTAL	MONEY
Josh Geary	67	67	71	66	271	C$24,000
George Bradford	68	66	66	72	272	14,400
James Love	68	66	72	67	273	9,000
Clayton Rask	70	69	72	63	274	5,425
Luke Swilor	66	73	72	63	274	5,425
Dale Vallely	62	69	75	68	274	5,425
Stuart Anderson	68	68	70	68	274	5,425

	SCORES				TOTAL	MONEY
J.C. Deacon	70	63	71	70	274	5,425
Rob Grube	63	68	72	71	274	5,425
Derek Gillespie	67	69	74	65	275	3,600
Andres Gonzales	69	69	72	65	275	3,600
Scott Hawley	68	70	71	66	275	3,600
Dustin Risdon	66	69	73	67	275	3,600
Brad Heaven	69	68	77	62	276	2,400
Garrett Frank	70	65	75	66	276	2,400
Brent Schwarzrock	73	66	71	66	276	2,400
Wes Heffernan	74	65	68	69	276	2,400
Ryan Thornberry	68	68	71	69	276	2,400
Michael Harris	68	71	68	69	276	2,400
Clayton Ogden	69	65	71	71	276	2,400
Mike Mezei	66	70	74	67	277	1,763
Mike Grob	67	68	74	68	277	1,763
Ryan Carter	63	68	76	70	277	1,763
Graham DeLaet	65	66	73	73	277	1,763
Eugene Smith	65	71	75	67	278	1,474
Jordan Krantz	70	67	73	68	278	1,474
Jim Lemon	66	68	75	69	278	1,474
Troy Kelly	68	68	72	70	278	1,474

Telus Edmonton Open

Windermere Golf Club, Edmonton, Alberta
Par 36-35–71

July 10-13
purse, C$150,000

	SCORES				TOTAL	MONEY
John Ellis	66	68	65	67	266	C$24,000
Andrew Parr	71	67	64	67	269	14,400
Justin Itzen	67	67	70	67	271	8,100
Adam Bland	63	70	66	72	271	8,100
Richard Scott	68	72	68	64	272	5,450
Brent Schwarzrock	67	74	67	64	272	5,450
Mike Grob	69	71	66	66	272	5,450
Conner Robbins	69	69	69	67	274	4,350
John Cassidy	74	67	64	69	274	4,350
James Hahn	68	70	67	69	274	4,350
Scott Gibson	68	71	68	68	275	3,450
Wes Heffernan	67	73	67	68	275	3,450
Jim Seki	72	69	65	69	275	3,450
Ryan Carter	69	73	70	64	276	2,475
Alan McLean	74	65	71	66	276	2,475
*Jordan Irwin	69	73	67	67	276	2,475
John Lieber	68	73	67	68	276	2,475
Dale Vallely	68	66	73	69	276	2,475
Luke Hickmott	67	70	69	70	276	2,475
Scott Ford	69	72	65	70	276	2,475
Zack Shriver	69	70	70	68	277	1,837.50
Kevin Kim	69	71	69	68	277	1,837.50
Steve Conway	69	69	70	69	277	1,837.50
Brian Unk	69	70	68	70	277	1,837.50
Michael Walton	66	71	75	66	278	1,480
Drew Stoltz	73	69	70	66	278	1,480
Garrett Frank	70	68	71	69	278	1,480
Troy Kelly	70	69	69	70	278	1,480
Eugene Smith	70	70	68	70	278	1,480
Jay Choe	68	69	69	72	278	1,480

Canadian Tour Players Cup

Pine Ridge Golf Club, Winnipeg, Manitoba
Par 37-35–72; 6,622 yards

July 17-20
purse, C$200,000

	SCORES				TOTAL	MONEY
Wes Heffernan	69	67	68	66	270	C$32,000
Dustin Risdon	69	70	70	62	271	15,600
John Ellis	66	68	71	66	271	15,600
Mark Leon	70	68	71	63	272	9,600
Rob Grube	69	65	71	68	273	7,600
Richard Scott	69	69	66	69	273	7,600
Joseph Lanza	70	68	68	68	274	6,400
Michael Walton	71	62	70	71	274	6,400
Josh Habig	69	70	70	66	275	5,200
Rob McMillan	69	69	69	68	275	5,200
Marc Lawless	73	66	69	67	275	5,200
Alex Coe	68	69	69	69	275	5,200
Rob Oppenheim	66	70	70	70	276	4,000
Kris Wasylowich	68	71	67	70	276	4,000
Eugene Smith	68	70	68	71	277	3,600
Brent Schwarzrock	70	69	71	68	278	3,200
Brian Unk	70	69	70	69	278	3,200
Drew Stoltz	71	69	67	71	278	3,200
Richard Gilkey	66	73	71	69	279	2,466.67
George Bradford	66	73	71	69	279	2,466.67
Scott Hawley	69	71	70	69	279	2,466.67
Jordan Krantz	70	71	69	69	279	2,466.67
Mike Grob	70	69	69	71	279	2,466.67
Andy Walker	72	69	68	70	279	2,466.67
Ryan Horn	68	70	72	70	280	2,100

RBC Canadian Open

See U.S. PGA Tour section.

Desjardins Montreal Open

Saint-Raphael Golf Club, Montreal, Quebec
Par 36-36–72; 7,050 yards

August 14-17
purse, C$200,000

	SCORES				TOTAL	MONEY
Graham DeLaet	70	69	68	67	274	C$32,000
Daniel Im	63	73	68	70	274	15,600
George Bradford	65	68	70	71	274	15,600
(DeLaet defeated Im and Bradford on first playoff hole.)						
Barrett Jarosch	69	64	70	72	275	9,600
Wes Heffernan	70	66	72	68	276	7,600
Lee Williamson	66	71	69	70	276	7,600
Will Dodson	71	67	72	67	277	6,000
Mitch Tasker	70	71	66	70	277	6,000
Andrew Parr	70	68	68	71	277	6,000
Michael Walton	70	66	69	72	277	6,000
Wil Collins	69	71	68	70	278	5,000
Jason Moon	69	68	71	71	279	4,200
Jay Choe	68	71	69	71	279	4,200
Rob Johnson	68	71	68	72	279	4,200
D.J. Fiese	71	69	72	68	280	3,200
Scott Gibson	73	68	71	68	280	3,200

	SCORES				TOTAL	MONEY
Alex Coe	70	67	73	70	280	3,200
Mike Grob	68	68	72	72	280	3,200
Adam Short	71	69	68	72	280	3,200
Jim Lemon	72	68	70	71	281	2,400
Clayton Rask	67	68	74	72	281	2,400
Josh Habig	69	69	70	73	281	2,400
Rob Grube	69	68	70	74	281	2,400
Taylor Wood	74	66	67	74	281	2,400
John Cassidy	71	68	76	67	282	1,827.50
Dong Yi	68	68	78	68	282	1,827.50
Will Mitchell	68	69	76	69	282	1,827.50
Andres Gonzales	69	69	72	72	282	1,827.50
Robert Hamilton	74	67	69	72	282	1,827.50
Dustin Risdon	70	70	70	72	282	1,827.50
Ryan Thornberry	66	67	74	75	282	1,827.50
Mike Mezei	68	66	73	75	282	1,827.50

Jane Rogers Championship of Mississauga

Lakeview Golf Club, Mississauga, Ontario
Par 35-35–70; 6,404 yards

August 21-24
purse, C$125,000

	SCORES				TOTAL	MONEY
Alex Coe	67	65	65	68	265	C$20,000
Graham DeLaet	65	70	64	69	268	12,000
George Bradford	65	66	75	64	270	7,500
Dave Levesque	74	68	66	63	271	7,500
Richard Scott	69	70	65	67	271	7,500
Liam Kendregan	69	67	67	68	271	7,500
Jim Seki	67	68	69	68	272	4,000
Tim Wood	67	66	68	71	272	4,000
Clayton Rask	71	68	66	68	273	3,375
Michael Gligic	66	69	69	69	273	3,375
John Ellis	68	70	66	69	273	3,375
Lee Williamson	68	67	75	64	274	2,625
Ben Bunny	71	69	68	66	274	2,625
James Love	69	67	70	68	274	2,625
Craig Scott	75	66	68	66	275	1,938
Adam Short	67	72	69	67	275	1,938
Luke Hickmott	67	71	69	68	275	1,938
John Lieber	68	69	69	69	275	1,938
Clint Rice	69	72	65	69	275	1,938
D.J. Fiese	68	66	70	71	275	1,938
Dustin Risdon	71	68	70	67	276	1,469
Andrew Parr	72	70	67	67	276	1,469
Manuel Villegas	68	70	70	68	276	1,469
Mark Leon	68	70	68	70	276	1,469
Wes Heffernan	67	72	71	67	277	1,163
Byron Smith	70	70	70	67	277	1,163
Andy Walker	67	72	69	69	277	1,163
Yoon Kwang-soo	70	70	68	69	277	1,163
Josh Geary	64	71	71	71	277	1,163
K. Fortin-Simard	70	68	68	71	277	1,163
Jim Lemon	74	67	65	71	277	1,163

Seaforth Country Classic

Seaforth Golf Club, Seaforth, Ontario
Par 71

August 28-31
purse, C$150,000

	SCORES				TOTAL	MONEY
Kent Eger	65	64	65	64	258	C$24,000
Wil Collins	65	63	70	62	260	10,200
John Ellis	66	65	66	63	260	10,200
Daniel Im	64	66	67	63	260	10,200
Derek Gillespie	68	64	66	64	262	6,000
Andrew Parr	65	63	69	66	263	5,000
Dong Yi	67	67	64	65	263	5,000
Adam Bland	63	70	61	69	263	5,000
Wes Heffernan	66	67	68	63	264	4,350
Ryan Yip	70	66	66	63	265	3,750
Scott Gibson	68	67	66	64	265	3,750
Jim Lemon	67	69	64	65	265	3,750
Eric Couture	65	66	68	67	266	3,000
Josh Geary	67	65	67	67	266	3,000
Stuart Anderson	66	68	68	65	267	2,400
Danny Sahl	68	65	68	66	267	2,400
Justin Smith	69	64	68	66	267	2,400
Joseph Lanza	67	63	69	68	267	2,400
Mitchell Gillis	67	64	65	71	267	2,400
Ben Ferguson	71	66	65	66	268	1,913
Mark Warman	66	63	68	71	268	1,913
Tom Stankowski	69	66	71	63	269	1,763
Ryan Horn	69	65	67	68	269	1,763
Luke Hickmott	66	70	69	65	270	1,509
James Hahn	70	66	68	66	270	1,509
Alan McLean	66	70	68	66	270	1,509
Barrett Jarosch	66	69	68	67	270	1,509
Brian Unk	67	69	67	67	270	1,509

Canadian Tour Championship

National Pines Golf Club, Barrie, Ontario
Par 36-36–72; 7,013 yards

September 4-7
purse, C$235,000

	SCORES				TOTAL	MONEY
Tom Stankowski	66	70	67	69	272	C$37,600
Graham DeLaet	66	68	71	69	274	18,330
Wes Heffernan	68	68	67	71	274	18,330
Steve Friesen	74	70	65	68	277	10,340
John Ellis	65	73	67	72	277	10,340
Barrett Jarosch	68	73	69	69	279	8,108
Dale Vallely	68	71	70	70	279	8,108
Dustin Risdon	67	71	70	73	281	7,050
Daniel Im	64	68	72	77	281	7,050
Wil Collins	70	71	72	70	283	5,875
J.C. Deacon	71	71	70	71	283	5,875
D.J. Fiese	71	72	67	73	283	5,875
Michael Walton	74	66	72	72	284	4,700
Scott Gibson	67	69	75	73	284	4,700
James Love	71	74	71	69	285	3,878
Marc Lawless	70	63	79	73	285	3,878
Jim Lemon	69	71	72	73	285	3,878
Adam Bland	72	69	70	74	285	3,878
Byron Smith	74	70	70	72	286	3,094

	SCORES			TOTAL	MONEY
Tim Wood	69	74	67	76	286	3,094
Mike Grob	68	71	69	78	286	3,094
Adam Speirs	70	71	74	72	287	2,644
Brian Unk	71	74	69	73	287	2,644
Hoyt McGarity	67	76	70	74	287	2,644
Lee Williamson	68	75	69	75	287	2,644

Sport Frances Open

See Tour de las Americas section.

Torneo de Maestros

See Tour de las Americas section.

Costa Rica Golf Classic

See Tour de las Americas section.

Tour de las Americas (South America)

Abierto Visa del Centro

Cordoba Golf Club, Cordoba, Argentina
Par 35-36–71; 6,824 yards

March 27-30
purse, US$200,000

	SCORES				TOTAL	MONEY
Estanislao Goya	71	67	68	66	272	US$32,000
Gary Boyd	67	71	69	65	272	22,000
(Goya defeated Boyd on first playoff hole.)						
James Heath	70	73	69	62	274	14,000
Taco Remkes	66	71	67	72	276	12,000
Inder Van Weerelt	71	67	71	68	277	10,000
Bernd Wiesberger	68	74	70	66	278	6,200
Angel Cabrera	67	73	71	67	278	6,200
David Horsey	67	73	70	68	278	6,200
Johan Skold	73	66	70	69	278	6,200
Christophe Hanell	67	77	68	67	279	4,200
Carlos Cardeza	70	69	67	73	279	4,200
Anthony Snobeck	71	68	71	70	280	3,700
Jeppe Huldhal	72	72	66	70	280	3,700
Jordi Garcia	69	74	72	66	281	2,900
Anders Hansen	74	69	69	69	281	2,900
Diego Vanegas	72	70	69	70	281	2,900
Carlos Del Moral	74	69	67	71	281	2,900
Tim Milford	69	69	71	72	281	2,900
Daniel Altamirano	65	71	72	73	281	2,900
Edward Rush	69	71	75	67	282	2,045

	SCORES				TOTAL	MONEY
Gustavo Acosta	73	69	72	68	282	2,045
Pablo Acuna	69	71	71	71	282	2,045
Wilhelm Schauman	75	68	68	71	282	2,045
Roberto Coceres	73	71	72	67	283	1,740
Philippe Gasnier	73	70	72	68	283	1,740
Roope Kakko	71	71	72	69	283	1,740
Gareth Maybin	73	71	69	70	283	1,740
Toni Karjalainen	72	72	69	70	283	1,740
Ramiro Goti	70	71	71	71	283	1,740
Joakim Haeggman	69	69	72	73	283	1,740
Sebastian Saavedra	70	73	67	73	283	1,740

Abierto Visa de Argentina

Hurlingham Club, Buenos Aires, Argentina
Par 35-35–70; 6,505 yards

April 3-6
purse, US$200,000

	SCORES				TOTAL	MONEY
Antii Ahokas	67	66	66	71	270	US$32,000
Martin Monguzzi	64	68	70	71	273	22,000
Estanislao Goya	69	65	70	70	274	14,000
Rodolfo Gonzalez	66	72	67	70	275	12,000
Eric Ramsay	70	70	69	67	276	7,500
Edward Rush	70	72	65	69	276	7,500
David Horsey	69	68	67	72	276	7,500
Stephen Browne	65	65	73	73	276	7,500
Rafael Gomez	68	71	72	66	277	4,120
Daniel Vancsik	65	71	71	70	277	4,120
Wil Besseling	68	69	70	70	277	4,120
Marco Soffietti	70	68	69	70	277	4,120
Fredrik Widmark	67	73	66	71	277	4,120
Alexandre Rocha	71	72	68	67	278	3,100
Gareth Maybin	69	69	70	70	278	3,100
Wilhelm Schauman	71	69	68	70	278	3,100
James Morrison	69	68	69	72	278	3,100
Lorenzo Gagli	71	69	71	69	280	2,433.33
Inder Van Weerelt	73	68	70	69	280	2,433.33
Roberto Coceres	72	70	69	69	280	2,433.33
Christophe Hanell	73	66	75	67	281	1,860
Jeppe Huldhal	72	70	70	69	281	1,860
Johan Skold	72	67	72	70	281	1,860
Tino Schuster	70	70	71	70	281	1,860
Gary Boyd	71	66	73	71	281	1,860
Klas Eriksson	69	71	70	71	281	1,860
Anders Hansen	69	70	70	72	281	1,860
Sergio Acevedo	73	69	67	72	281	1,860

Club Colombia Masters

Country Club de Bogota, Bogota, Colombia
Par 35-36–71; 7,099 yards

April 10-13
purse, US$180,000

	SCORES				TOTAL	MONEY
Wil Besseling	67	66	69	66	268	US$28,800
Mark Haastrup	69	64	71	71	275	16,200
Antii Ahokas	68	66	70	71	275	16,200
Alexandre Rocha	71	69	69	67	276	10,800

	SCORES				TOTAL	MONEY
Juan Hoyos	72	67	70	68	277	6,750
Estanislao Goya	68	68	72	69	277	6,750
Seve Benson	68	73	65	71	277	6,750
Alvaro Pinedo	70	68	67	72	277	6,750
Benjamin Alvarado	69	72	70	68	279	3,825
Richard McEvoy	68	72	72	67	279	3,825
Jesus Amaya	72	70	66	71	279	3,825
Toni Karjalainen	72	67	68	72	279	3,825
Gustavo Acosta	69	70	72	69	280	2,790
Marco Ruiz	67	70	73	70	280	2,790
Daniel De Leon	69	68	72	71	280	2,790
Pablo Acuna	70	66	72	72	280	2,790
Inder Van Weerelt	67	69	71	73	280	2,790
Klas Eriksson	69	67	70	74	280	2,790
James Morrison	67	72	72	70	281	1,838.57
Paulo Pinto	74	67	70	70	281	1,838.57
Jamie Little	71	67	72	71	281	1,838.57
Carlos Del Moral	73	68	68	72	281	1,838.57
Miguel Rodriguez	70	70	73	68	281	1,838.57
Daniel Barbetti	68	70	70	73	281	1,838.57
Rodrigo Castaneda	71	68	69	73	281	1,838.57

Abierto de Chile Visa

Hacienda de Chicureo, Santiago, Chile
Par 36-36–72; 7,297 yards

April 17-20
purse, US$70,000

	SCORES				TOTAL	MONEY
Felipe Aguilar	65	67	65	68	265	US$12,600
Sebastian Saavedra	68	70	71	67	276	7,980
Nilson Cabrera	68	72	69	71	280	5,600
Fernando Figueroa	72	71	67	71	281	4,480
Francisco Cerda	75	69	70	69	283	2,376
Paulo Pinto	67	77	70	69	283	2,376
Fabiano Dos Santos	74	69	69	71	283	2,376
Alejandro Villavicencio	67	71	73	72	283	2,376
Julio Noguera	72	71	68	72	283	2,376
Clodomiro Carranza	71	75	65	72	283	2,376
Francisco Valdes	73	71	66	73	283	2,376
Rafael Ponce	74	69	73	68	284	1,533
Carlos Baquedano	67	70	74	73	284	1,533
Angel Franco	72	71	70	72	285	1,428
Mark Tullo	71	75	68	72	286	1,358
Santiago Russi	70	76	72	69	287	1,183
Guillermo Encina	71	74	70	72	287	1,183
Jesus Amaya	70	72	71	74	287	1,183
Roberto Coceres	69	71	71	76	287	1,183
Ronaldo Francisco	66	76	73	73	288	973
Cesar Costilla	66	70	76	76	288	973

Copa 3 Diamantes

Barquisimeto Golf Club, Barquisimeto, Venezuela
Par 36-35–71; 6,644 yards
(Fourth round cancelled—rain.)

May 14-17
purse, US$50,000

	SCORES			TOTAL	MONEY
Sebastian Saavedra	69	67	70	206	US$9,000
Daniel Barbetti	71	71	67	209	5,700
Mario Hurtado	71	70	69	210	4,000
Jesus Amaya	73	71	69	213	2,900
Miguel Martinez	71	71	71	213	2,900
*Jose Daniel Ortega	72	72	70	214	
Fernando Figueroa	74	69	71	214	1,773.33
Diego Vanegas	72	71	71	214	1,773.33
Rafael Ponce	72	71	71	214	1,773.33
Ramon Bescansa	73	71	71	215	1,370
Alejandro Rauhut	73	68	74	215	1,370
Gustavo Sosa	68	76	72	216	1,220
Juan Nutt	75	74	68	217	1,070
Richard Rojas	74	70	73	217	1,070
Otto Solis	79	72	66	217	1,070
Rodrigo Castaneda	70	76	73	219	945
Juan Martin Hoyos	72	71	76	219	945
*Oscar Zapata	74	73	73	220	
Ricardo Lyon	78	72	70	220	845
Carlos Larrain	79	71	70	220	845

TLA Players Championship

The Fairmont Acapulco Princess, Acapulco, Mexico
Par 35-35–71; 6,355 yards

May 23-25
purse, US$70,000

	SCORES			TOTAL	MONEY
Rafael Gomez	64	66	70	200	US$12,600
Raul Sanz	72	66	65	203	7,980
Sergio Acevedo	73	69	62	204	4,165
Fernando Figueroa	71	66	67	204	4,165
Alan Wagner	67	69	68	204	4,165
Juan Ignacio Gil	65	69	70	204	4,165
Walter Miranda	70	68	67	205	2,170
Alfredo Adrian	67	70	68	205	2,170
Ricardo Aranda	69	70	67	206	1,820
Alejandro Villavicencio	70	68	69	207	1,680
Eduardo Herrera	73	67	68	208	1,423.33
Warren Jurkowitz	73	66	69	208	1,423.33
Julio Noguera	65	68	75	208	1,423.33
Jose Gonzalez	70	71	68	209	1,225
Juan Berastegui	72	68	69	209	1,225
Clark Burroughs	73	71	66	210	1,078
Alejandro Rauhut	67	75	68	210	1,078
Alessandro Fabbietti	70	70	70	210	1,078
Diego Larrazabal	69	69	72	210	1,078
Martin Stanovich	69	72	70	211	910

Canal i Abierto de Venezuela

Lagunita Country Club, Caracas, Venezuela
Par 35-35–70; 6,909 yards

September 11-14
purse, US$70,000

	SCORES				TOTAL	MONEY
Angel Romero	69	68	70	66	273	US$12,600
Diego Vanegas	68	71	68	67	274	7,980
Clodomiro Carranza	69	67	71	68	275	5,600
Cipriano Castro	70	69	68	69	276	3,360
Mauricio Molina	73	64	69	70	276	3,360
Rafael Gomez	69	68	67	72	276	3,360
Jesus Amaya	68	70	66	72	276	3,360
Otto Solis	72	66	72	67	277	1,750
Benjamin Alvarado	67	69	72	69	277	1,750
Luciano Giometti	71	65	71	70	277	1,750
Raul Sanz	67	69	71	70	277	1,750
Juan Martin Hoyos	69	66	73	70	278	1,330
Rafael Romero	64	70	72	72	278	1,330
Alan Wagner	66	69	71	72	278	1,330
Alejandro Villavicencio	68	68	74	69	279	1,147.33
Alfredo Adrian	72	68	68	71	279	1,147.33
Alvaro Pinedo	71	72	65	71	279	1,147.33
Julio Noguera	71	69	71	69	281	1,060
Rodrigo Castaneda	67	70	73	71	282	1,000
Rafael Ponce	68	71	73	70	283	844
Peter Horrobin	70	70	72	70	283	844
Paulo Pinto	68	72	71	71	283	844
Miguel Martinez	72	67	69	74	283	844
Jaime Clavijo	68	70	69	75	283	844

Taurus Abierto de Peru

Los Incas Country Club, Lima, Peru
Par 36-36–72; 6,924 yards

September 18-21
purse, US$70,000

	SCORES				TOTAL	MONEY
Alan Wagner	65	70	74	66	275	US$12,600
Juan Echeverry	72	69	65	71	277	7,980
Benjamin Alvarado	69	73	69	67	278	5,600
Clodomiro Carranza	68	71	68	72	279	4,480
Rafael Ponce	70	68	70	72	280	3,640
Sebastian Salem	68	71	73	69	281	2,275
Rafael Romero	74	72	66	69	281	2,275
Mauricio Molina	68	74	69	70	281	2,275
Paulo Pinto	64	70	74	73	281	2,275
Luis Graf	68	75	69	70	282	1,680
Raul Sanz	69	75	69	70	283	1,540
Diego Vanegas	70	77	69	69	285	1,400
Eric West	72	70	75	70	287	1,233
Santiago Russi	73	72	70	72	287	1,233
Hoyt McGarity	72	70	72	73	287	1,233
Juan Ignacio Gil	72	68	71	76	287	1,233
Julio Noguera	74	73	69	72	288	1,017.50
Shawn Jasper	68	74	73	73	288	1,017.50
Luciano Giometti	69	74	72	73	288	1,017.50
Hugo Leon	71	73	71	73	288	1,017.50

Carlos Franco Invitational

Carlos Franco Country Club, Asuncion, Paraguay

October 23-26

Par 36-36–72; 7,100 yards

purse, US$40,000

		SCORES			TOTAL	MONEY
Clodomiro Carranza	70	71	71	68	280	US$6,234
Cesar Monasterio	70	68	73	69	280	3,734
(Carranza defeated Monasterio on first playoff hole.)						
Carlos Franco	73	73	69	68	283	2,200.50
Sebastian Saavedra	74	69	70	70	283	2,200.50
Mauricio Molina	73	72	70	69	284	1,550.50
Fabrizio Zanotti	67	72	72	73	284	1,550.50
Carlos Cardeza	69	71	73	73	286	1,317
Nilson Cabrera	72	75	70	70	287	1,200
Ian Leggatt	68	74	73	74	289	1,023.50
Angel Franco	72	71	68	78	289	1,023.50
Daniel Altamirano	74	73	73	72	292	860
Hector Cespedes	74	70	75	73	292	860
Alejandro Martinez	78	71	70	73	292	860
Matias Anselmo	76	73	70	73	292	860
Rafael Gomez	73	73	71	75	292	860
Rodolfo Gonzalez	73	72	77	71	293	721.75
Mario Acosta	69	74	77	73	293	721.75
Matias O'Curry	70	76	73	74	293	721.75
Ramon Franco	72	66	80	75	293	721.75
Luciano Dodda	74	73	73	74	294	661.50
Claudio Machado	71	74	72	77	294	661.50

Abierto de San Luis

Villa Mercedes Golf Club, San Luis, Argentina

November 6-9

Par 35-36–71; 6,851 yards

purse, US$50,000

		SCORES			TOTAL	MONEY
Rafael Gomez	71	72	71	62	276	US$9,486
Walter Rodriguez	76	69	67	64	276	5,522
(Gomez defeated Rodriguez on first playoff hole.)						
Juan Ignacio Gil	69	66	70	72	277	3,583
Walter Miranda	72	71	67	68	278	2,848
Sebastian Salem	71	67	73	68	279	2,408
Jaime Clavijo	70	71	71	68	280	1,738.60
Daniel Barbetti	69	73	70	68	280	1,738.60
Miguel Fernandez	72	71	68	69	280	1,738.60
Luciano Giometti	70	68	72	70	280	1,738.60
Cesar Costilla	71	70	65	74	280	1,738.60
Hector Cespedes	70	72	72	68	282	1,220
Felix Cordoba	77	68	71	67	283	1,056
Alan Wagner	74	69	71	69	283	1,056
Marcos Figueroa	72	71	71	69	283	1,056
Eduardo Argiro	72	74	70	68	284	916
Sergio Vera	72	70	73	69	284	916
Rafael Ponce	72	69	71	72	284	916
Miguel Guzman	67	72	71	74	284	916
Ramiro Goti	74	69	74	68	285	815
Eduardo Romero	75	71	71	68	285	815
Lucas Juncos	69	70	77	69	285	815

Abierto del Litoral

Rosario Golf Club, Rosario, Argentina
Par 35-35–70; 6,539 yards

November 13-16
purse, US$45,000

	SCORES				TOTAL	MONEY
Andres Romero	62	71	67	68	268	US$7,113
Mauricio Molina	68	64	72	67	271	4,182
Jose Buezas	73	70	70	65	278	2,374
Luciano Giometti	69	71	70	68	278	2,374
Franco Barrera	71	69	74	65	279	1,630.50
Ramiro Goti	70	69	73	67	279	1,630.50
Julio Nunez	68	71	74	68	281	1,185.50
Gustavo Acosta	70	71	70	70	281	1,185.50
Daniel Altamirano	68	67	73	73	281	1,185.50
Sergio Acevedo	67	66	74	74	281	1,185.50
Ricardo Gonzalez	69	70	73	70	282	953.50
Diego Ortiz	70	72	70	70	282	953.50
Miguel Fernandez	71	67	73	72	283	892
Gonzalo Ruiz	69	73	73	69	284	838
Francisco Cerda	69	71	72	72	284	838
Claudio Machado	75	69	73	68	285	725.28
Jose Correa	70	74	73	68	285	725.28
Martin Monguzzi	67	73	75	70	285	725.28
Tomas Argonz	71	72	72	70	285	725.28
Sergio Vera	71	70	73	71	285	725.28
Rodolfo Gonzalez	69	71	73	72	285	725.28
Lucas Juncos	70	73	69	73	285	725.28

De Vicenzo Classic

San Eliseo Golf & Country Club, Buenos Aires, Argentina
Par 36-36–72

November 20-23
purse, US$45,000

	SCORES				TOTAL	MONEY
Paulo Pinto	70	73	72	69	284	US$6,426
Sebastian Fernandez	69	69	74	72	284	3,778
(Pinto defeated Fernandez on first playoff hole.)						
Ramiro Goti	69	71	73	72	285	2,553
Rodolfo Gonzalez	70	75	69	72	286	1,832
Javier Brunel	71	70	73	72	286	1,832
Jesus Amaya	71	71	77	68	287	1,502
Matias Anselmo	73	74	72	69	288	1,291
Miguel Carballo	68	73	72	75	288	1,291
Sergio Acevedo	72	76	71	71	290	1,022
Gustavo Rojas	71	72	75	72	290	1,022
Mauricio Molina	72	69	73	76	290	1,022
Tomas Argonz	72	74	72	73	291	880
Jose Garrido	75	73	74	70	292	810
Omar Solis	73	76	70	73	292	810
Elvio Ruiz	68	75	77	73	293	741
Vicente Fernandez	71	79	69	74	293	741
Jose Buezas	71	74	72	76	293	741
Martin Velazquez	71	78	74	71	294	670
Daniel Altamirano	69	80	73	72	294	670
Walter Rodriguez	71	79	72	72	294	670
Gustavo Acosta	79	71	69	75	294	670

Sport Frances Open

Sport Frances Golf Club, Santiago, Chile
Par 36-35–71; 6,857 yards

November 27-30
purse, US$160,000

	SCORES				TOTAL	MONEY
Rafael Gomez	69	69	71	68	277	US$25,600
Daniel Im	73	67	67	71	278	15,360
Clodomiro Carranza	73	67	71	68	279	9,600
Hugo Leon	65	75	69	71	280	7,040
Christoph Guenther	69	66	70	75	280	7,040
Martin Ureta	73	69	66	73	281	5,760
Francisco Valdes	71	73	71	68	283	5,280
Guillermo Encina	71	69	74	70	284	4,960
Ramon Bescansa	68	73	73	71	285	4,160
Angel Fernandez	74	70	70	71	285	4,160
Benjamin Alvarado	69	73	71	72	285	4,160
Raul Fretes	70	69	72	74	285	4,160
Pierre Relecom	73	72	73	68	286	2,912
Stuart Anderson	75	73	68	70	286	2,912
Luis Moreno	72	69	73	72	286	2,912
Rafael Ponce	71	73	70	72	286	2,912
Mike Meizi	70	70	72	74	286	2,912
Scott Ford	72	76	70	69	287	1,990
Luis Berrios	75	74	69	69	287	1,990
Walter Rodriguez	68	71	77	71	287	1,990
Cristian Leon	73	70	73	71	287	1,990
Alex Coe	70	70	75	72	287	1,990
Jose Garrido	72	72	71	72	287	1,990
Rob Grube	69	72	73	73	287	1,990
Julio Noguera	71	69	71	76	287	1,990

Torneo de Maestros

Olivos Golf Club, Buenos Aires, Argentina
Par 36-35–71; 6,740 yards

December 4-7
purse, US$141,000

	SCORES				TOTAL	MONEY
Fabian Gomez	69	71	64	67	271	US$22,545
Andres Romero	71	68	70	64	273	13,527
Jesus Amaya	72	71	68	63	274	8,455
Eduardo Romero	68	68	69	72	277	6,764
Estanislao Goya	65	75	73	65	278	5,354.50
Stuart Anderson	68	69	68	73	278	5,354.50
Rafael Ponce	68	76	66	69	279	4,368
Mike Meizi	72	69	67	71	279	4,368
Josh McCumber	67	70	70	72	279	4,368
Daniel Vancsik	68	76	68	68	280	3,664
Rodolfo Gonzalez	71	67	70	72	280	3,664
Miguel Carballo	73	74	70	64	281	2,959
Kris Wasylowich	69	72	69	71	281	2,959
Miguel Rodriguez	75	69	66	71	281	2,959
Vicente Fernandez	72	70	70	70	282	2,395.33
Julio Zapata	69	67	74	72	282	2,395.33
Sebastian Fernandez	72	71	67	72	282	2,395.33
Mario Hurtado	69	72	74	68	283	1,874.20
Mike Grob	68	74	72	69	283	1,874.20
Clodomiro Carranza	72	71	70	70	283	1,874.20
Eduardo Argiro	71	72	68	72	283	1,874.20
Russ Cochran	69	75	67	72	283	1,874.20

Costa Rica Golf Classic

Reserva Conchal Golf Club, Guanacaste, Costa Rica

December 11-14
purse, US$125,000

Par 36-35–71; 6,956 yards

	SCORES				TOTAL	MONEY
Mauricio Molina	71	65	71	68	275	US$20,000
Rob Grube	66	74	66	72	278	12,000
Robert Gates	69	71	70	69	279	7,500
Sebastian Saavedra	67	72	75	66	280	6,000
Chris Baryla	67	74	70	70	281	4,541.66
Paulo Pinto	73	68	70	70	281	4,541.66
Byron Smith	72	69	69	71	281	4,541.66
Clark Burroughs	69	70	74	69	282	3,750
Hugo Leon	71	70	69	72	282	3,750
Josh McCumber	69	74	71	70	284	3,250
Diego Larrazabal	69	69	71	75	284	3,250
John McLean	75	71	70	69	285	2,625
Stuart Anderson	72	70	73	70	285	2,625
Ramon Bescansa	71	71	73	70	285	2,625
Juan Ignacio Gil	68	75	69	74	286	2,250
Erik Compton	73	76	70	69	288	2,125
Lucas Lee	70	71	76	72	289	1,937.50
Matt Johnston	72	70	75	72	289	1,937.50
Kris Wasylowich	68	74	78	70	290	1,609.25
Rafael Ponce	71	71	76	72	290	1,609.25
Brian Benedcitson	77	67	72	74	290	1,609.25
Victor Ciesielski	72	74	69	75	290	1,609.25

European Tours

Joburg Open

See African Tours chapter.

Abu Dhabi Golf Championship

Abu Dhabi Golf Club, Abu Dhabi, United Arab Emirates
Par 36-36–72; 7,500 yards

January 17-20
purse, €1,347,504

	SCORES				TOTAL	MONEY
Martin Kaymer	66	65	68	74	273	€225,421.38
Henrik Stenson	67	70	69	71	277	117,475.02
Lee Westwood	69	73	65	70	277	117,475.02
Richard Finch	71	70	69	68	278	57,437.94
Ignacio Garrido	69	70	70	69	278	57,437.94
Peter Hedblom	69	70	69	70	278	57,437.94
James Kingston	71	68	72	68	279	37,194.90
Scott Strange	72	71	66	70	279	37,194.90
Paul McGinley	72	71	66	71	280	28,673.89
Ian Poulter	70	70	73	67	280	28,673.89
Luke Donald	71	73	67	70	281	21,595.58
Oliver Fisher	72	71	69	69	281	21,595.58
Padraig Harrington	72	72	69	68	281	21,595.58
Robert Karlsson	68	72	70	71	281	21,595.58
Rory McIlroy	73	71	69	68	281	21,595.58
Alexander Noren	70	72	69	70	281	21,595.58
Ricardo Gonzalez	71	70	72	69	282	16,613.72
Richard Green	75	68	73	66	282	16,613.72
Peter Lawrie	73	70	70	69	282	16,613.72
Alvaro Quiros	73	69	68	72	282	16,613.72
Anthony Wall	71	69	65	77	282	16,613.72
Steve Webster	70	68	71	73	282	16,613.72
Jamie Donaldson	70	71	71	71	283	13,660.67
Simon Dyson	73	71	68	71	283	13,660.67
Maarten Lafeber	74	69	68	72	283	13,660.67
Thomas Levet	70	72	68	73	283	13,660.67
Andrew McLardy	71	72	69	71	283	13,660.67
Colin Montgomerie	72	72	68	71	283	13,660.67
Adam Scott	68	74	71	70	283	13,660.67
Phillip Archer	71	68	73	72	284	11,428.98
Paul Lawrie	70	73	71	70	284	11,428.98
Daniel Vancsik	71	71	73	69	284	11,428.98
Leif Westerberg	72	73	69	70	284	11,428.98
Mark Foster	70	70	69	76	285	9,873.56
Soren Hansen	71	71	74	69	285	9,873.56
Thongchai Jaidee	71	74	68	72	285	9,873.56
Charl Schwartzel	70	70	72	73	285	9,873.56
Paul Sheehan	73	72	70	70	285	9,873.56
John Bickerton	71	70	71	74	286	8,656.27
Rhys Davies	73	71	72	70	286	8,656.27
Mikko Ilonen	70	74	70	72	286	8,656.27
Francesco Molinari	73	71	71	71	286	8,656.27
Fredrik Andersson Hed	71	72	73	71	287	7,168.47
Paul Broadhurst	72	72	68	75	287	7,168.47
Johan Edfors	73	71	70	73	287	7,168.47
Gonzalo Fernandez-Castano	70	68	76	73	287	7,168.47

	SCORES				TOTAL	MONEY
Peter Hanson	74	70	69	74	287	7,168.47
Miguel Angel Jimenez	74	69	73	71	287	7,168.47
Sam Little	75	69	71	72	287	7,168.47
Nick Dougherty	72	71	69	76	288	5,545.42
Jean-Francois Lucquin	71	72	71	74	288	5,545.42
David Lynn	74	70	73	71	288	5,545.42
Chapchai Nirat	73	72	73	70	288	5,545.42
Henrik Nystrom	73	71	73	71	288	5,545.42
Thomas Aiken	70	75	69	75	289	4,463.39
Michael Lorenzo-Vera	71	73	73	72	289	4,463.39
Matt Weibring	74	70	75	70	289	4,463.39
Martin Erlandsson	75	70	70	75	290	3,922.37
Jean-Baptiste Gonnet	74	71	70	75	290	3,922.37
Damien McGrane	70	72	73	75	290	3,922.37
Darren Clarke	72	72	74	73	291	3,584.24
Simon Wakefield	72	71	73	75	291	3,584.24
Benn Barham	74	71	75	72	292	3,313.73
Jose-Filipe Lima	71	73	74	74	292	3,313.73
Louis Oosthuizen	72	73	73	76	294	3,043.22
Phillip Price	73	71	75	75	294	3,043.22
Thomas Bjorn	73	70	72	80	295	2,772.71
Rafa Echenique	75	68	76	76	295	2,772.71

Commercialbank Qatar Masters

Doha Golf Club, Doha, Qatar
Par 36-36–72; 7,388 yards

January 24-27
purse, €1,713,022

	SCORES				TOTAL	MONEY
Adam Scott	69	73	65	61	268	€285,071.48
Henrik Stenson	69	70	67	65	271	190,045.37
Charl Schwartzel	70	67	69	67	273	107,074.56
Johan Edfors	69	66	69	70	274	85,522.81
Lee Westwood	67	70	73	65	275	72,523.34
Colin Montgomerie	71	68	69	69	277	59,865.97
Christian Cevaer	71	69	68	70	278	37,915.11
Nick Dougherty	72	67	70	69	278	37,915.11
Sergio Garcia	69	75	67	67	278	37,915.11
Anton Haig	67	71	69	71	278	37,915.11
David Howell	70	68	71	69	278	37,915.11
Jyoti Randhawa	70	70	72	66	278	37,915.11
Emanuele Canonica	73	68	70	68	279	24,190.74
Andrew Coltart	70	70	65	74	279	24,190.74
Jean-Baptiste Gonnet	71	72	68	68	279	24,190.74
Ross McGowan	70	68	69	72	279	24,190.74
Alexander Noren	69	69	72	69	279	24,190.74
Marc Warren	74	70	67	68	279	24,190.74
Steve Webster	72	70	67	70	279	24,190.74
Raphael Jacquelin	71	72	69	68	280	19,362.36
Soren Kjeldsen	70	72	69	69	280	19,362.36
Jose Manuel Lara	71	72	68	69	280	19,362.36
Graeme McDowell	70	71	70	69	280	19,362.36
Oliver Wilson	72	68	70	70	280	19,362.36
Luke Donald	70	72	68	71	281	15,992.77
Oliver Fisher	72	73	67	69	281	15,992.77
Ross Fisher	74	71	68	68	281	15,992.77
Thongchai Jaidee	71	71	70	69	281	15,992.77
Paul Lawrie	73	70	66	72	281	15,992.77
Francesco Molinari	71	70	70	70	281	15,992.77
Louis Oosthuizen	72	70	71	68	281	15,992.77

	SCORES				TOTAL	MONEY
Anthony Wall	71	69	70	71	281	15,992.77
Phillip Archer	71	70	69	72	282	12,163.24
Thomas Bjorn	72	72	68	70	282	12,163.24
Gregory Bourdy	70	71	68	73	282	12,163.24
Gonzalo Fernandez-Castano	70	70	74	68	282	12,163.24
Gregory Havret	73	70	68	71	282	12,163.24
Barry Lane	73	71	69	69	282	12,163.24
Damien McGrane	72	71	66	73	282	12,163.24
Rory McIlroy	71	71	66	74	282	12,163.24
Scott Strange	71	73	69	69	282	12,163.24
Simon Dyson	72	70	71	70	283	9,749.60
Richard Finch	72	73	71	67	283	9,749.60
Soren Hansen	72	69	73	69	283	9,749.60
Peter O'Malley	72	70	74	67	283	9,749.60
Marcel Siem	69	72	71	71	283	9,749.60
Niclas Fasth	74	71	72	67	284	8,210.19
Shiv Kapur	73	68	74	69	284	8,210.19
Jean-Francois Lucquin	71	71	71	71	284	8,210.19
Rolf Muntz	73	71	72	68	284	8,210.19
Bradley Dredge	73	72	71	69	285	6,670.78
Martin Erlandsson	72	72	73	68	285	6,670.78
Peter Hanson	75	70	69	71	285	6,670.78
Thomas Levet	74	67	71	73	285	6,670.78
Phillip Price	73	72	70	70	285	6,670.78
Robert-Jan Derksen	74	70	72	70	286	5,259.65
Jose-Filipe Lima	73	71	73	69	286	5,259.65
Jeev Milkha Singh	74	71	73	68	286	5,259.65
Sam Walker	70	73	70	73	286	5,259.65
Richard Green	75	70	71	71	287	4,532.71
Robert Karlsson	71	74	70	72	287	4,532.71
Simon Khan	73	72	71	71	287	4,532.71
Carlos Rodiles	74	70	70	73	287	4,532.71
Seve Benson	72	70	74	72	288	3,934.05
Peter Lawrie	73	72	74	69	288	3,934.05
Miles Tunnicliff	73	71	72	72	288	3,934.05
Pelle Edberg	71	73	76	69	289	3,420.91
Ricardo Gonzalez	74	71	73	71	289	3,420.91
Miguel Angel Jimenez	74	71	69	75	289	3,420.91
Michael Campbell	73	71	74	72	290	3,126.71
Jean-Francois Remesy	72	73	76	75	296	2,566

Dubai Desert Classic

Emirates Golf Club, Dubai, United Arab Emirates
Par 35-37–72; 7,301 yards

January 31-February 3
purse, €1,700,703

	SCORES				TOTAL	MONEY
Tiger Woods	65	71	73	65	274	€283,965.09
Martin Kaymer	67	73	69	66	275	189,307.79
Ernie Els	68	72	65	71	276	95,924.94
Louis Oosthuizen	73	69	69	65	276	95,924.94
Graeme McDowell	67	72	69	70	278	72,241.87
Ricardo Gonzalez	72	71	72	65	280	47,877.28
Soren Hansen	68	72	70	70	280	47,877.28
Peter Hedblom	69	70	70	71	280	47,877.28
Henrik Stenson	68	70	68	74	280	47,877.28
Niclas Fasth	72	71	70	68	281	30,540.93
Ross Fisher	69	70	71	71	281	30,540.93
Thomas Levet	67	71	72	71	281	30,540.93
Lee Westwood	69	71	68	73	281	30,540.93

	SCORES				TOTAL	MONEY
Bradley Dredge	73	72	68	69	282	24,023.83
Jean-Baptiste Gonnet	72	68	72	70	282	24,023.83
Scott Hend	67	72	72	71	282	24,023.83
Paul McGinley	71	72	69	70	282	24,023.83
Gary Murphy	67	72	71	72	282	24,023.83
Sergio Garcia	68	71	70	74	283	19,593.90
Thongchai Jaidee	69	73	70	71	283	19,593.90
Robert Karlsson	70	70	73	70	283	19,593.90
Hennie Otto	69	70	72	72	283	19,593.90
Jeev Milkha Singh	67	76	69	71	283	19,593.90
Anthony Wall	73	72	68	70	283	19,593.90
Paul Broadhurst	70	71	69	74	284	16,697.41
Simon Dyson	67	77	67	73	284	16,697.41
David Frost	72	69	69	74	284	16,697.41
Brendan Jones	71	71	74	68	284	16,697.41
Shiv Kapur	68	72	69	75	284	16,697.41
Ariel Canete	68	75	72	70	285	14,652.83
Gonzalo Fernandez-Castano	73	71	72	69	285	14,652.83
Peter O'Malley	68	73	70	74	285	14,652.83
Johan Edfors	71	70	73	72	286	12,636.65
Marcus Fraser	69	75	70	72	286	12,636.65
Soren Kjeldsen	69	74	71	72	286	12,636.65
Jyoti Randhawa	67	74	75	70	286	12,636.65
Richard Sterne	69	75	71	71	286	12,636.65
Miles Tunnicliff	69	74	70	73	286	12,636.65
Phillip Archer	72	72	74	69	287	10,734.05
Andrew McLardy	67	74	73	73	287	10,734.05
Mark O'Meara	70	74	73	70	287	10,734.05
Ian Poulter	70	71	70	76	287	10,734.05
Jean Van de Velde	73	72	72	70	287	10,734.05
Thomas Bjorn	74	70	73	71	288	8,178.33
Pelle Edberg	67	74	71	76	288	8,178.33
Stephen Gallacher	70	73	71	74	288	8,178.33
Gregory Havret	72	71	72	73	288	8,178.33
David Howell	68	75	72	73	288	8,178.33
Mikko Ilonen	74	71	68	75	288	8,178.33
James Kamte	74	71	71	72	288	8,178.33
James Kingston	68	74	75	71	288	8,178.33
Maarten Lafeber	71	72	71	74	288	8,178.33
Damien McGrane	68	69	72	79	288	8,178.33
Robert-Jan Derksen	68	75	71	75	289	5,427.88
Martin Erlandsson	72	72	71	74	289	5,427.88
Miguel Angel Jimenez	67	74	73	75	289	5,427.88
Simon Khan	72	73	70	74	289	5,427.88
Jose Manuel Lara	70	74	73	72	289	5,427.88
Alexander Noren	71	71	71	76	289	5,427.88
Steve Webster	73	71	71	74	289	5,427.88
Anders Hansen	70	74	72	74	290	4,600.31
Benn Barham	68	74	74	75	291	4,259.54
Per-Ulrik Johansson	71	74	74	72	291	4,259.54
Graeme Storm	69	72	75	75	291	4,259.54
Andrew Coltart	69	71	72	80	292	3,833.59
Colin Montgomerie	72	72	73	75	292	3,833.59
Stephen Dodd	73	72	73	77	295	3,578.02
Garry Houston	68	77	78	73	296	3,407.64
Daniel Vancsik	68	77	75	79	299	3,237.25

Emaar-MGF Indian Masters

See Asia/Japan Tours chapter.

Enjoy Jakarta Astro Indonesia Open

See Asia/Japan Tours chapter.

Johnnie Walker Classic

See Asia/Japan Tours chapter.

Maybank Malaysian Open

See Asia/Japan Tours chapter.

Ballantine's Championship

See Asia/Japan Tours chapter.

Madeira Islands Open BPI - Portugal

Santo da Serra Golf Club, Madeira, Portugal
Par 36-36–72; 6,826 yards

March 20-23
purse, €700,000

	SCORES				TOTAL	MONEY
Alastair Forsyth	70	70	66	67	273	€116,660
Hennie Otto	67	67	67	72	273	77,770
(Forsyth defeated Otto on first playoff hole.)						
Gary Clark	72	71	64	70	277	43,820
Sven Struver	66	72	71	69	278	35,000
John Bickerton	69	72	68	70	279	25,060
Alvaro Velasco	73	70	68	68	279	25,060
Fredrik Widmark	68	70	70	71	279	25,060
Gary Orr	72	70	67	71	280	17,500
Martin Wiegele	73	71	68	69	281	15,680
Sebastien Delagrange	71	75	67	69	282	12,180
Ben Evans	74	72	70	66	282	12,180
Peter Gustafsson	68	73	73	68	282	12,180
Peter Lawrie	75	69	69	69	282	12,180
Matthew Millar	75	70	68	69	282	12,180
Benn Barham	74	72	68	69	283	8,827.78
Sion E. Bebb	71	74	68	70	283	8,827.78
Markus Brier	71	74	71	67	283	8,827.78
Adilson da Silva	71	68	70	74	283	8,827.78
Bradley Dredge	70	75	69	69	283	8,827.78
Raphael Eyraud	70	71	74	68	283	8,827.78
Pablo Larrazabal	73	70	71	69	283	8,827.78
Gareth Paddison	70	75	69	69	283	8,827.78
Miles Tunnicliff	71	69	71	72	283	8,827.78
Michael Lorenzo-Vera	68	71	69	76	284	7,280
Santiago Luna	73	74	68	69	284	7,280
Peter Whiteford	70	75	71	68	284	7,280
Gregory Bourdy	68	76	71	70	285	6,650
Mattias Eliasson	70	72	70	73	285	6,650
*Pedro Figueiredo	74	72	69	70	285	
Alexander Noren	71	73	70	71	285	6,650
Joakim Backstrom	72	70	72	72	286	6,020
Andrew Coltart	74	71	72	69	286	6,020
Hugo Santos	72	71	71	72	286	6,020
Francois Delamontagne	72	72	70	73	287	5,337.50
George Murray	73	74	68	72	287	5,337.50
Andrew Oldcorn	71	71	69	76	287	5,337.50
Paul Waring	75	73	70	69	287	5,337.50
Jesus Maria Arruti	72	74	72	70	288	4,760

	SCORES				TOTAL	MONEY
Jose-Filipe Lima	74	71	73	70	288	4,760
Gary Lockerbie	71	74	69	74	288	4,760
Wade Ormsby	73	73	73	69	288	4,760
Ariel Canete	74	73	70	72	289	3,850
Marcus Higley	74	72	74	69	289	3,850
Steven Jeppesen	79	68	70	72	289	3,850
Pedro Linhart	71	73	74	71	289	3,850
Edoardo Molinari	72	76	70	71	289	3,850
Christian Nilsson	76	70	70	73	289	3,850
Iain Pyman	76	72	69	72	289	3,850
Nicolas Vanhootegem	70	76	67	76	289	3,850
Tom Whitehouse	72	76	73	68	289	3,850
Steve Alker	76	70	75	69	290	2,940
Robert Coles	76	70	70	74	290	2,940
Ben Mason	73	74	73	70	290	2,940
Henrik Nystrom	76	71	72	71	290	2,940
Gabriel Canizares	73	72	72	74	291	2,380
Ian Garbutt	75	73	71	72	291	2,380
Andrew McArthur	75	72	72	72	291	2,380
Ulrich van den Berg	72	75	70	74	291	2,380
Juan Abbate	74	70	75	73	292	2,100
Nuno Campino	75	70	71	77	293	1,890
Tim Dykes	72	74	74	73	293	1,890
Alan McLean	72	72	73	76	293	1,890
Manuel Quiros	71	77	74	71	293	1,890
Simon Wakefield	74	73	71	75	293	1,890
Notah Begay	71	74	73	76	294	1,610
Philip Golding	75	73	73	73	294	1,610
Lee Slattery	74	73	72	75	294	1,610
Liam Bond	72	71	76	76	295	1,470
Jamie McLeary	72	74	70	80	296	1,400
Ricardo Santos	73	75	77	72	297	1,330
Matthew King	77	69	76	79	301	1,290

MAPFRE Open de Andalucia

Aloha Golf Club, Marbella, Spain
Par 36-36–72; 6,881 yards

March 27-30
purse, €996,270

	SCORES				TOTAL	MONEY
Thomas Levet	69	68	68	67	272	€166,660
Oliver Fisher	70	68	67	67	272	111,110
(Levet defeated Fisher on first playoff hole.)						
Lee Westwood	65	73	66	71	275	62,600
Alexander Noren	69	70	68	69	276	46,200
Patrik Sjoland	70	69	68	69	276	46,200
Robert Dinwiddie	72	65	75	66	278	32,500
Michael Jonzon	69	69	69	71	278	32,500
Markus Brier	71	72	66	70	279	23,700
David Lynn	70	67	68	74	279	23,700
Manuel Quiros	72	72	71	65	280	19,200
Alvaro Velasco	73	69	70	68	280	19,200
Anders Hansen	71	72	70	68	281	15,825
Peter Hedblom	69	67	70	75	281	15,825
Matthew Millar	67	69	72	73	281	15,825
Marcel Siem	70	69	71	71	281	15,825
Ariel Canete	70	73	72	67	282	13,500
Emanuele Canonica	68	72	71	71	282	13,500
Maarten Lafeber	68	70	76	68	282	13,500
Pelle Edberg	70	68	69	76	283	11,660

	SCORES				TOTAL	MONEY
Ricardo Gonzalez	72	72	70	69	283	11,660
Miguel Angel Jimenez	74	67	69	73	283	11,660
Peter Lawrie	72	72	70	69	283	11,660
Joost Luiten	74	65	72	72	283	11,660
*Danny Willett	66	75	72	70	283	
Christian Cevaer	68	71	74	71	284	9,800
Bradley Dredge	70	68	71	75	284	9,800
Simon Dyson	71	68	74	71	284	9,800
Alastair Forsyth	70	70	70	74	284	9,800
David Frost	72	70	68	74	284	9,800
Peter Gustafsson	73	71	71	69	284	9,800
Pablo Martin	70	70	74	70	284	9,800
Eduardo De La Riva	71	71	71	72	285	7,785.71
Stephen Gallacher	74	68	74	69	285	7,785.71
Pablo Larrazabal	74	69	70	72	285	7,785.71
Paul Lawrie	78	66	73	68	285	7,785.71
Damien McGrane	68	72	71	74	285	7,785.71
Jarmo Sandelin	70	74	68	73	285	7,785.71
Anthony Wall	72	71	74	68	285	7,785.71
Richard Bland	70	71	72	73	286	6,300
Robert-Jan Derksen	73	69	72	72	286	6,300
Johan Edfors	71	71	70	74	286	6,300
Martin Kaymer	71	73	71	71	286	6,300
Mikael Lundberg	72	70	74	70	286	6,300
Rory McIlroy	68	73	71	74	286	6,300
Gareth Paddison	71	73	73	69	286	6,300
David Griffiths	71	71	69	76	287	5,300
Garry Houston	75	69	75	68	287	5,300
Lee Slattery	72	68	72	75	287	5,300
John Bickerton	72	71	73	72	288	4,500
Gregory Bourdy	69	74	72	73	288	4,500
Jan-Are Larsen	66	72	76	74	288	4,500
Henrik Nystrom	69	72	74	73	288	4,500
Peter Whiteford	73	69	75	71	288	4,500
Phillip Archer	72	72	72	73	289	3,342.86
Sion E. Bebb	73	69	76	71	289	3,342.86
Jamie Donaldson	70	70	75	74	289	3,342.86
Martin Erlandsson	71	71	69	78	289	3,342.86
Peter Hanson	72	71	72	74	289	3,342.86
Per-Ulrik Johansson	73	71	74	71	289	3,342.86
Francesco Molinari	74	68	75	72	289	3,342.86
Pedro Linhart	73	69	72	76	290	2,700
Jose Maria Olazabal	71	72	71	76	290	2,700
Gary Orr	71	72	76	71	290	2,700
Gonzalo Fernandez-Castano	74	69	74	74	291	2,500
Florian Praegant	69	73	72	78	292	2,350
Carl Suneson	69	70	76	77	292	2,350
Sebastien Delagrange	74	70	80	70	294	2,200
Carlos Rodiles	74	70	69	83	296	2,100
Birgir Hafthorsson	73	71	76	77	297	2,000

Estoril Open de Portugal

Oitavos Dunes, Estoril, Portugal
Par 36-35–71; 6,894 yards

April 3-6
purse, €1,259,345

	SCORES				TOTAL	MONEY
Gregory Bourdy	63	65	68	70	266	€208,330
Alastair Forsyth	65	69	66	66	266	108,565
David Howell	67	68	67	64	266	108,565

(Bourdy defeated Forsyth on second and Howell on third playoff hole.)

	SCORES				TOTAL	MONEY
Miles Tunnicliff	69	69	63	66	267	62,500
Gonzalo Fernandez-Castano	64	66	72	66	268	53,000
Damien McGrane	67	69	67	66	269	43,750
Paul McGinley	69	68	67	67	271	34,375
Charl Schwartzel	65	70	66	70	271	34,375
Peter Baker	67	69	69	67	272	22,791.67
Johan Edfors	68	68	69	67	272	22,791.67
Simon Khan	65	67	72	68	272	22,791.67
Jose Lara Manuel	64	70	70	68	272	22,791.67
Andrew McLardy	66	68	72	66	272	22,791.67
Steve Webster	67	66	70	69	272	22,791.67
David Drysdale	71	67	66	69	273	16,900
Oliver Fisher	68	65	74	66	273	16,900
Soren Kjeldsen	69	65	68	71	273	16,900
Pablo Martin	63	71	69	70	273	16,900
Rory McIlroy	69	67	66	71	273	16,900
Felipe Aguilar	68	68	71	67	274	14,343.75
Lee Slattery	66	68	68	72	274	14,343.75
Ulrich van den Berg	69	71	69	65	274	14,343.75
Mads Vibe-Hastrup	69	71	67	67	274	14,343.75
Darren Clarke	68	70	69	68	275	12,437.50
David Dixon	68	68	70	69	275	12,437.50
Martin Erlandsson	69	66	71	69	275	12,437.50
Jan-Are Larsen	68	72	66	69	275	12,437.50
Thomas Levet	67	64	72	72	275	12,437.50
Gareth Paddison	68	68	68	71	275	12,437.50
Brian Davis	71	68	69	68	276	10,053.57
Pelle Edberg	69	68	72	67	276	10,053.57
Stephen Gallacher	71	63	74	68	276	10,053.57
Mikko Ilonen	68	70	66	72	276	10,053.57
James Kamte	65	72	69	70	276	10,053.57
Sam Little	69	68	68	71	276	10,053.57
Jean-Francois Remesy	70	63	74	69	276	10,053.57
Fredrik Andersson Hed	72	68	70	67	277	8,125
Francois Delamontagne	65	75	71	66	277	8,125
Michael Jonzon	64	70	71	72	277	8,125
Zane Scotland	69	65	75	68	277	8,125
Patrik Sjoland	70	70	68	69	277	8,125
Anthony Wall	69	70	67	71	277	8,125
Marc Warren	71	69	69	68	277	8,125
Robert-Jan Derksen	70	69	66	73	278	6,625
Simon Dyson	67	66	70	75	278	6,625
Ricardo Gonzalez	69	70	68	71	278	6,625
David Park	72	67	68	71	278	6,625
Marius Thorp	67	73	71	67	278	6,625
Ben Evans	67	71	72	69	279	5,750
Jean-Baptiste Gonnet	71	68	70	70	279	5,750
John Bickerton	71	68	70	71	280	4,750
Robert Dinwiddie	70	70	71	69	280	4,750
Steven Jeppesen	71	68	69	72	280	4,750
Jarmo Sandelin	70	68	74	68	280	4,750
Sam Walker	69	68	76	67	280	4,750
Fabrizio Zanotti	68	70	72	70	280	4,750
Jamie Donaldson	70	67	73	71	281	3,750
Barry Lane	67	71	76	67	281	3,750
Ross McGowan	70	70	68	73	281	3,750
Nuno Campino	67	69	73	73	282	3,187.50
Birgir Hafthorsson	69	70	66	77	282	3,187.50
*Matt Haines	72	68	73	69	282	
Santiago Luna	66	71	75	70	282	3,187.50
Stuart Manley	67	68	76	71	282	3,187.50
Matthew Millar	68	69	74	71	282	3,187.50
Simon Wakefield	68	71	71	72	282	3,187.50

	SCORES				TOTAL	MONEY
Benoit Teilleria	70	70	68	75	283	2,750
Marcel Siem	71	66	74	73	284	2,562.50
Sven Struver	74	66	69	75	284	2,562.50
Emanuele Canonica	70	70	76	70	286	2,375
*Pedro Figueiredo	72	66	78	71	287	
Steven O'Hara	70	70	77	70	287	2,012.33
Paolo Terreni	71	67	73	76	287	2,012.33
Peter Whiteford	74	64	75	74	287	2,012.33
Ian Garbutt	71	69	75	73	288	1,867.50
Peter Gustafsson	68	71	74	75	288	1,867.50
Henrik Nystrom	71	65	80	74	290	1,863

Volvo China Open

See Asia/Japan Tours chapter.

BMW Asian Open

See Asia/Japan Tours chapter.

Open de Espana

Real Club de Golf, Seville, Spain
Par 36-36–72; 7,140 yards

May 1-4
purse, €2,011,982

	SCORES				TOTAL	MONEY
Peter Lawrie	68	70	68	67	273	€333,330
Ignacio Garrido	66	63	72	72	273	222,220
(Lawrie defeated Garrido on second playoff hole.)						
Soren Hansen	68	70	67	69	274	125,200
Alfredo Garcia-Heredia	69	69	69	68	275	84,933.33
Miguel Angel Jimenez	70	67	67	71	275	84,933.33
David Lynn	70	66	73	66	275	84,933.33
Richard Finch	72	69	67	68	276	60,000
Martin Erlandsson	65	68	73	71	277	47,400
Peter Hanson	74	67	69	67	277	47,400
Robert-Jan Derksen	71	68	69	70	278	35,850
Niclas Fasth	72	69	71	66	278	35,850
Andrew McLardy	72	65	69	72	278	35,850
Alexander Noren	74	64	70	70	278	35,850
*Danny Willett	73	70	64	71	278	
Pablo Martin	72	70	67	70	279	29,400
Hennie Otto	72	66	71	70	279	29,400
Marco Ruiz	70	66	69	74	279	29,400
Eduardo De La Riva	74	65	71	70	280	25,400
Michael Jonzon	72	68	69	71	280	25,400
Gareth Paddison	73	69	67	71	280	25,400
Iain Pyman	71	68	71	70	280	25,400
Alejandro Canizares	70	69	71	71	281	20,500
Darren Clarke	72	69	67	73	281	20,500
Mark Foster	70	67	68	76	281	20,500
Peter Fowler	70	66	70	75	281	20,500
Ricardo Gonzalez	70	71	72	68	281	20,500
Gary Lockerbie	72	71	70	68	281	20,500
Edoardo Molinari	71	71	70	69	281	20,500
Steven O'Hara	68	70	75	68	281	20,500
Carlos Rodiles	68	68	70	75	281	20,500
Fabrizio Zanotti	71	69	68	73	281	20,500
Felipe Aguilar	72	71	70	69	282	16,040

	SCORES				TOTAL	MONEY
Liam Bond	76	65	71	70	282	16,040
Jose Manuel Lara	71	66	70	75	282	16,040
Henrik Nystrom	68	69	71	74	282	16,040
Manuel Quiros	69	70	70	73	282	16,040
Fredrik Andersson Hed	70	69	70	74	283	12,800
Per-Ulrik Johansson	74	67	70	72	283	12,800
Pedro Linhart	70	70	73	70	283	12,800
Paul McGinley	74	68	70	71	283	12,800
Gary Orr	71	68	75	69	283	12,800
Alvaro Quiros	73	70	71	69	283	12,800
Simon Wakefield	73	70	71	69	283	12,800
Anthony Wall	71	66	73	73	283	12,800
Peter Whiteford	68	72	72	71	283	12,800
Julio Zapata	72	71	68	72	283	12,800
Thomas Aiken	72	70	69	73	284	10,000
Gary Clark	67	74	70	73	284	10,000
Francis Valera	71	68	72	73	284	10,000
Mads Vibe-Hastrup	71	71	72	70	284	10,000
Miles Tunnicliff	72	68	70	75	285	9,000
Francois Delamontagne	69	71	73	73	286	8,400
Garry Houston	75	68	74	69	286	8,400
Magnus A. Carlsson	73	69	72	73	287	7,200
Gregory Havret	71	71	73	72	287	7,200
Matthew Millar	70	72	76	69	287	7,200
Robert Rock	69	71	73	74	287	7,200
Stephen Gallacher	70	69	77	72	288	5,600
Ian Garbutt	72	71	70	75	288	5,600
Jan-Are Larsen	73	70	77	68	288	5,600
Jean-Francois Lucquin	70	71	70	77	288	5,600
Santiago Luna	74	69	72	73	288	5,600
Alan McLean	72	71	72	73	288	5,600
Florian Praegant	70	72	75	71	288	5,600
Peter Baker	69	74	73	73	289	4,700
Sion E. Bebb	75	67	74	73	289	4,700
Pelle Edberg	73	70	71	76	290	4,300
Carl Suneson	76	67	75	72	290	4,300
Klas Eriksson	71	69	75	76	291	4,000
Gary Boyd	75	68	72	77	292	3,725
Colin Montgomerie	70	73	74	75	292	3,725
Rafael Cabrera Bello	74	69	74	76	293	2,998.50
Jamie Donaldson	72	70	78	73	293	2,998.50
Jordi Garcia	66	76	77	76	295	2,994
Jose Manuel Carriles	70	72	76	78	296	2,991

Methorios Capital Italian Open

Castello di Tolcinasco Golf & Country Club, Milan, Italy
Par 36-36–72; 7,286 yards

May 8-11
purse, €1,707,641

	SCORES				TOTAL	MONEY
Hennie Otto	65	66	63	69	263	€283,330
Oliver Wilson	66	69	65	64	264	188,880
Robert Karlsson	68	61	69	67	265	106,420
Phillip Archer	70	64	65	68	267	78,540
Marcel Siem	70	66	65	66	267	78,540
Ross McGowan	64	71	64	69	268	59,500
Gregory Havret	70	67	63	70	270	43,860
Christian Nilsson	67	67	64	72	270	43,860
Alvaro Velasco	70	64	64	72	270	43,860
Nick Dougherty	71	66	67	67	271	32,640

	SCORES				TOTAL	MONEY
Marco Soffietti	72	66	63	70	271	32,640
Paul Broadhurst	69	67	67	70	273	26,316
Mark Foster	65	66	72	70	273	26,316
Estanislao Goya	66	67	68	72	273	26,316
Jarmo Sandelin	71	66	67	69	273	26,316
Fabrizio Zanotti	66	72	66	69	273	26,316
Marcus Fraser	67	67	69	71	274	20,881.67
Anders Hansen	68	65	68	73	274	20,881.67
Per-Ulrik Johansson	66	73	66	69	274	20,881.67
Shiv Kapur	70	65	70	69	274	20,881.67
Edoardo Molinari	67	69	69	69	274	20,881.67
Paul Waring	70	67	67	70	274	20,881.67
Scott Barr	70	69	65	71	275	17,170
John Daly	67	73	68	67	275	17,170
Maarten Lafeber	68	66	69	72	275	17,170
Santiago Luna	71	68	68	68	275	17,170
Henrik Nystrom	68	70	69	68	275	17,170
David Park	70	70	67	68	275	17,170
Steve Webster	66	69	71	69	275	17,170
Peter Baker	69	71	68	68	276	13,472.50
Gregory Bourdy	66	73	69	68	276	13,472.50
Bradley Dredge	69	65	70	72	276	13,472.50
David Frost	71	68	65	72	276	13,472.50
Ignacio Garrido	68	70	67	71	276	13,472.50
Matthew Millar	68	70	69	69	276	13,472.50
Lee Slattery	71	68	66	71	276	13,472.50
Miles Tunnicliff	69	68	68	71	276	13,472.50
Michael Jonzon	69	70	72	66	277	11,050
Soren Kjeldsen	66	71	71	69	277	11,050
Thomas Levet	69	70	67	71	277	11,050
Alexandre Rocha	69	68	66	74	277	11,050
Marco Ruiz	64	70	70	73	277	11,050
Emanuele Canonica	68	70	68	72	278	8,840
Stephen Dodd	72	68	71	67	278	8,840
Jose Manuel Lara	69	70	70	69	278	8,840
David Lynn	68	67	73	70	278	8,840
Ben Mason	68	68	69	73	278	8,840
Doug McGuigan	68	68	70	72	278	8,840
Alexander Noren	66	71	70	71	278	8,840
Mark Pilkington	74	64	71	69	278	8,840
Richard Bland	68	71	72	69	280	6,141.25
Rafael Cabrera Bello	67	71	69	73	280	6,141.25
Gary Clark	71	69	71	69	280	6,141.25
Sam Little	69	66	74	71	280	6,141.25
Robert Rock	71	69	74	66	280	6,141.25
Charl Schwartzel	67	73	72	68	280	6,141.25
Alessandro Tadini	71	67	71	71	280	6,141.25
Martin Wiegele	71	69	72	68	280	6,141.25
*Federico Colombo	69	70	67	75	281	
Lorenzo Gagli	71	66	73	71	281	4,675
James Kamte	69	70	72	70	281	4,675
Gareth Paddison	67	72	74	68	281	4,675
Ulrich van den Berg	70	68	71	72	281	4,675
Jean-Francois Remesy	67	72	70	73	282	4,250
Christian Cevaer	71	69	70	73	283	3,740
Alastair Forsyth	74	66	72	71	283	3,740
Pedro Linhart	70	70	71	72	283	3,740
Gary Orr	69	69	73	72	283	3,740
Marc Warren	65	70	72	76	283	3,740
Jose-Filipe Lima	67	70	70	80	287	3,230
Raphael Jacquelin	67	71	72	78	288	3,110
Ian Garbutt	73	67	73	77	290	2,550
Jan-Are Larsen	69	70	82	70	291	2,547

	SCORES				TOTAL	MONEY
*Nunzio Lombardi	68	71	76	77	292	
Renaud Guillard	72	67	75	81	295	2,544
*Claudio Vigano	75	65	78	78	296	

Irish Open

Adare Manor Hotel & Golf Resort, Co. Limerick, Ireland
Par 36-36—72; 7,453 yards

May 15-18
purse, €2,490,680

	SCORES				TOTAL	MONEY
Richard Finch	71	72	65	70	278	€416,660
Felipe Aguilar	71	72	67	70	280	277,770
Robert Karlsson	71	70	69	71	281	118,750
Maarten Lafeber	71	71	72	67	281	118,750
Gary Murphy	74	70	68	69	281	118,750
Lee Westwood	75	70	64	72	281	118,750
Rory McIlroy	70	72	70	70	282	75,000
Bradley Dredge	68	73	66	76	283	59,250
Alvaro Quiros	72	72	68	71	283	59,250
Martin Kaymer	77	68	70	69	284	46,333.33
James Kingston	75	68	69	72	284	46,333.33
Anthony Wall	72	70	70	72	284	46,333.33
Johan Edfors	68	73	73	71	285	38,416.67
David Frost	74	70	66	75	285	38,416.67
Alvaro Velasco	69	72	72	72	285	38,416.67
Darren Clarke	72	69	72	73	286	31,875
Mikko Ilonen	77	66	68	75	286	31,875
Lee S. James	69	73	70	74	286	31,875
Pablo Larrazabal	70	70	73	73	286	31,875
Paul McGinley	73	69	73	71	286	31,875
Jarmo Sandelin	76	66	71	73	286	31,875
Oliver Fisher	72	75	69	71	287	27,875
Peter Lawrie	71	75	72	69	287	27,875
Paul Broadhurst	73	74	68	73	288	24,500
Ross Fisher	74	68	69	77	288	24,500
Stephen Gallacher	73	71	68	76	288	24,500
Gregory Havret	77	70	65	76	288	24,500
Peter Hedblom	77	69	71	71	288	24,500
Steven O'Hara	74	68	72	74	288	24,500
Peter O'Malley	70	73	71	74	288	24,500
Martin Erlandsson	73	73	70	73	289	20,375
Padraig Harrington	72	71	70	76	289	20,375
Michael Lorenzo-Vera	68	70	75	76	289	20,375
Stuart Manley	71	72	76	70	289	20,375
Thomas Aiken	75	69	73	73	290	17,750
John Bickerton	72	70	77	71	290	17,750
Soren Kjeldsen	70	77	74	69	290	17,750
Scott Strange	71	74	74	71	290	17,750
Oliver Wilson	74	73	71	72	290	17,750
Richard Green	66	74	75	76	291	15,250
Simon Khan	71	74	75	71	291	15,250
Edoardo Molinari	70	73	72	76	291	15,250
Gary Orr	71	73	73	74	291	15,250
Jeev Milkha Singh	66	76	75	74	291	15,250
Peter Baker	72	69	76	75	292	13,250
Alejandro Canizares	72	72	73	75	292	13,250
Julio Zapata	72	73	72	75	292	13,250
Francois Delamontagne	73	72	72	76	293	11,250
Steven Jeppesen	74	72	73	74	293	11,250
Colin Montgomerie	75	69	73	76	293	11,250

	SCORES				TOTAL	MONEY
Jean Van de Velde	74	70	72	77	293	11,250
Ulrich van den Berg	71	75	75	72	293	11,250
Louis Oosthuizen	72	73	72	77	294	9,750
Barry Lane	73	72	73	77	295	9,000
Marcel Siem	68	71	75	81	295	9,000
Stephen Dodd	74	71	75	76	296	8,000
Alastair Forsyth	71	72	75	78	296	8,000
Peter Hanson	74	73	75	75	297	7,375
Jose Manuel Lara	71	74	75	77	297	7,375
Emanuele Canonica	72	74	77	75	298	6,750
Mikael Lundberg	73	74	76	75	298	6,750
Ross McGowan	74	71	75	78	298	6,750
David Drysdale	74	72	79	74	299	6,125
Pedro Linhart	71	76	74	78	299	6,125
Matthew Millar	73	73	79	76	301	5,750
Paul Waring	76	70	75	81	302	5,500
Luis Claverie	73	73	73	85	304	5,250
Benoit Teilleria	75	72	77	82	306	5,000

BMW PGA Championship

Wentworth Club, Virginia Water, Surrey, England
Par 35-37–72; 7,320 yards

May 22-25
purse, €4,500,000

	SCORES				TOTAL	MONEY
Miguel Angel Jimenez	70	67	72	68	277	€750,000
Oliver Wilson	70	66	73	68	277	500,000
(Jimenez defeated Wilson on second playoff hole.)						
Luke Donald	72	69	73	65	279	253,350
Robert Karlsson	66	69	70	74	279	253,350
Jyoti Randhawa	73	68	69	70	280	190,800
Retief Goosen	76	69	70	66	281	126,450
Richard Green	70	69	73	69	281	126,450
Alexander Noren	75	68	71	67	281	126,450
Andres Romero	72	69	73	67	281	126,450
Alejandro Canizares	72	66	74	70	282	76,275
Paul Casey	71	68	73	70	282	76,275
Simon Khan	71	71	71	69	282	76,275
Soren Kjeldsen	71	65	76	70	282	76,275
Paul McGinley	65	66	79	72	282	76,275
Steve Webster	71	70	72	69	282	76,275
Felipe Aguilar	71	67	74	71	283	57,375
Oliver Fisher	71	73	69	70	283	57,375
Peter Hanson	72	71	70	70	283	57,375
Martin Kaymer	71	70	71	71	283	57,375
Gary Orr	70	68	73	72	283	57,375
Daniel Vancsik	68	70	72	73	283	57,375
Paul Lawrie	72	73	70	69	284	49,500
Charl Schwartzel	68	71	73	72	284	49,500
Marc Warren	69	70	75	70	284	49,500
Robert-Jan Derksen	70	70	76	69	285	44,100
Simon Dyson	75	67	73	70	285	44,100
Jean-Baptiste Gonnet	75	69	73	68	285	44,100
James Kingston	72	71	71	71	285	44,100
Carlos Rodiles	72	71	70	72	285	44,100
Alastair Forsyth	72	70	72	72	286	38,025
Thongchai Jaidee	72	69	74	71	286	38,025
Sam Little	74	68	73	71	286	38,025
Miles Tunnicliff	70	65	77	74	286	38,025
Rafa Echenique	70	73	68	76	287	33,300

	SCORES				TOTAL	MONEY
Marcus Fraser	67	69	76	75	287	33,300
Soren Hansen	76	66	73	72	287	33,300
Peter Lawrie	73	72	70	72	287	33,300
Gregory Bourdy	72	71	71	74	288	30,600
Gregory Havret	70	74	73	71	288	30,600
Anders Hansen	75	69	77	68	289	27,000
Damien McGrane	72	66	77	74	289	27,000
Louis Oosthuizen	67	76	74	72	289	27,000
Hennie Otto	71	69	75	74	289	27,000
Henrik Stenson	74	70	74	71	289	27,000
Simon Wakefield	68	71	77	73	289	27,000
Angel Cabrera	73	72	72	73	290	21,150
Ricardo Gonzalez	73	70	74	73	290	21,150
Garry Houston	68	74	75	73	290	21,150
Henrik Nystrom	72	72	70	76	290	21,150
Peter O'Malley	71	72	74	73	290	21,150
Alvaro Velasco	69	76	71	74	290	21,150
Sam Walker	75	68	72	75	290	21,150
Paul Broadhurst	72	71	74	74	291	16,200
Ariel Canete	74	71	71	75	291	16,200
Jamie Donaldson	72	72	74	73	291	16,200
Nick Dougherty	70	73	76	72	291	16,200
Graeme McDowell	70	73	75	74	292	13,950
Johan Edfors	71	74	73	75	293	12,825
Mark Foster	72	70	73	78	293	12,825
Thomas Levet	74	71	73	75	293	12,825
Michael Lorenzo-Vera	69	76	75	73	293	12,825
Anton Haig	70	75	75	74	294	11,700
Ignacio Garrido	73	68	74	82	297	11,025
David Howell	70	71	77	79	297	11,025
Magnus A. Carlsson	70	72	79	77	298	10,125
Marcel Siem	71	73	78	76	298	10,125
Robert Dinwiddie	78	63	79	79	299	9,450
Ross Fisher	72	73	80	75	300	8,775
Matthew Morris	71	74	76	79	300	8,775
Ross McGowan	73	72	74	83	302	8,200

Celtic Manor Wales Open

Celtic Manor Resort, Newport, Wales
Par 36-35–71; 7,352 yards

May 29-June 1
purse, €2,270,187

	SCORES				TOTAL	MONEY
Scott Strange	63	66	69	64	262	€376,671.02
Robert Karlsson	67	67	68	64	266	251,114.01
Raphael Jacquelin	66	68	68	68	270	141,477.63
Benn Barham	69	64	70	68	271	82,445.75
Darren Clarke	70	68	67	66	271	82,445.75
Nick Dougherty	67	69	67	68	271	82,445.75
Rafa Echenique	67	67	69	68	271	82,445.75
Francesco Molinari	72	66	69	64	271	82,445.75
Gonzalo Fernandez-Castano	67	68	70	67	272	50,624.58
Robert Dinwiddie	68	65	70	70	273	39,324.45
Ross Fisher	67	70	67	69	273	39,324.45
Ross McGowan	66	68	69	70	273	39,324.45
Jeev Milkha Singh	65	68	69	71	273	39,324.45
Alvaro Velasco	65	68	68	72	273	39,324.45
Jamie Donaldson	72	66	67	69	274	29,983.01
Mikko Ilonen	69	70	66	69	274	29,983.01
Pablo Larrazabal	69	67	67	71	274	29,983.01

	SCORES				TOTAL	MONEY
Thomas Levet	69	69	65	71	274	29,983.01
Hennie Otto	67	68	71	68	274	29,983.01
Marcel Siem	71	69	68	66	274	29,983.01
Thomas Bjorn	71	68	70	66	275	24,182.28
Gregory Bourdy	70	67	69	69	275	24,182.28
Magnus A. Carlsson	66	73	71	65	275	24,182.28
Martin Kaymer	71	66	68	70	275	24,182.28
Sam Little	68	70	67	70	275	24,182.28
Michael Lorenzo-Vera	70	70	68	67	275	24,182.28
Gary Orr	70	67	72	66	275	24,182.28
Fredrik Andersson Hed	71	67	71	67	276	20,792.24
Mark Foster	69	71	68	68	276	20,792.24
Charl Schwartzel	69	68	72	67	276	20,792.24
Garry Houston	71	68	68	70	277	18,419.21
Per-Ulrik Johansson	69	70	67	71	277	18,419.21
Maarten Lafeber	71	68	71	67	277	18,419.21
Edoardo Molinari	64	70	72	71	277	18,419.21
Soren Hansen	68	68	69	73	278	16,272.19
David Howell	75	66	68	69	278	16,272.19
Simon Wakefield	71	66	72	69	278	16,272.19
Julio Zapata	69	69	72	68	278	16,272.19
Christian Cevaer	69	70	69	71	279	13,560.16
Johan Edfors	69	70	69	71	279	13,560.16
Thongchai Jaidee	70	69	75	65	279	13,560.16
Barry Lane	71	69	69	70	279	13,560.16
Mikael Lundberg	69	69	71	70	279	13,560.16
Graeme McDowell	69	72	68	70	279	13,560.16
Rory McIlroy	68	71	68	72	279	13,560.16
Paul Waring	66	72	69	72	279	13,560.16
Ricardo Gonzalez	66	70	77	67	280	11,074.13
David Lynn	72	68	71	69	280	11,074.13
Peter Whiteford	68	67	72	73	280	11,074.13
Ariel Canete	72	69	70	70	281	8,588.10
Emanuele Canonica	73	68	73	67	281	8,588.10
Luis Claverie	70	71	69	71	281	8,588.10
David Frost	69	71	70	71	281	8,588.10
Gareth Paddison	73	68	71	69	281	8,588.10
Phillip Price	68	71	70	72	281	8,588.10
Kyron Sullivan	70	68	72	71	281	8,588.10
Tom Whitehouse	73	68	69	71	281	8,588.10
Stephen Gallacher	69	69	71	73	282	6,554.08
Colin Montgomerie	69	68	73	72	282	6,554.08
Chapchai Nirat	71	68	73	70	282	6,554.08
Soren Kjeldsen	72	68	72	71	283	5,537.06
Jose Manuel Lara	69	70	74	70	283	5,537.06
Jean-Francois Lucquin	74	66	73	70	283	5,537.06
Peter O'Malley	69	72	71	71	283	5,537.06
Lee Slattery	70	71	70	72	283	5,537.06
Danny Willett	70	71	69	73	283	5,537.06
Niclas Fasth	70	71	73	72	286	4,633.05
Carlos Rodiles	71	68	75	72	286	4,633.05
Peter Baker	70	70	75	72	287	4,294.05
Rafael Cabrera Bello	71	69	73	75	288	3,754.13
Alastair Forsyth	67	73	72	76	288	3,754.13
Jarmo Sandelin	70	71	75	75	291	3,387
Francois Delamontagne	70	70	77	76	293	3,384

Bank Austria GolfOpen

Fontana Golf Club, Vienna, Austria
Par 35-36–71; 7,065 yards
(Event shortened to 54 holes—rain.)

June 5-8
purse, €1,300,000

	SCORES			TOTAL	MONEY
Jeev Milkha Singh	64	63	71	198	€216,660
Simon Wakefield	66	65	68	199	144,440
Pelle Edberg	64	72	65	201	57,200
Martin Erlandsson	67	69	65	201	57,200
Peter Fowler	65	67	69	201	57,200
Michael Jonzon	70	64	67	201	57,200
Iain Pyman	69	67	65	201	57,200
Francois Delamontagne	69	68	65	202	26,780
Soren Hansen	68	65	69	202	26,780
Sam Little	68	67	67	202	26,780
Graeme McDowell	67	67	68	202	26,780
Robert Rock	68	69	65	202	26,780
Mark Brown	69	63	71	203	18,763.33
Thongchai Jaidee	71	68	64	203	18,763.33
Steven Jeppesen	67	71	65	203	18,763.33
Francesco Molinari	68	67	68	203	18,763.33
Kyron Sullivan	71	67	65	203	18,763.33
Paul Waring	68	68	67	203	18,763.33
Richard Bland	66	67	71	204	14,950
Emanuele Canonica	65	69	70	204	14,950
Darren Clarke	70	69	65	204	14,950
Stephen Gallacher	67	70	67	204	14,950
James Morrison	70	67	67	204	14,950
Graeme Storm	69	69	66	204	14,950
Sion E. Bebb	74	63	68	205	11,765
Markus Brier	68	70	67	205	11,765
David Higgins	71	66	68	205	11,765
Garry Houston	68	67	70	205	11,765
Andrew Marshall	70	69	66	205	11,765
Christian Nilsson	64	71	70	205	11,765
Steven O'Hara	67	70	68	205	11,765
Lee Slattery	69	70	66	205	11,765
Alessandro Tadini	67	70	68	205	11,765
Julio Zapata	70	65	70	205	11,765
Juan Abbate	70	65	71	206	9,490
Anthony Wall	67	71	68	206	9,490
Fabrizio Zanotti	67	68	71	206	9,490
Adilson da Silva	69	68	70	207	8,190
Chris Gane	68	68	71	207	8,190
Pablo Larrazabal	68	68	71	207	8,190
Jan-Are Larsen	71	66	70	207	8,190
Paul Lawrie	68	69	70	207	8,190
Edoardo Molinari	69	69	69	207	8,190
Gary Murphy	64	69	74	207	8,190
Kariem Baraka	69	68	71	208	6,760
Adam Gee	66	71	71	208	6,760
Jean-Francois Lucquin	70	70	68	208	6,760
Andrew Tampion	70	69	69	208	6,760
Thomas Aiken	66	71	72	209	4,845.45
Joakim Backstrom	68	71	70	209	4,845.45
Peter Baker	70	68	71	209	4,845.45
Scott Barr	64	73	72	209	4,845.45
Andrew Coltart	71	65	73	209	4,845.45
Ian Garbutt	66	71	72	209	4,845.45
Maarten Lafeber	67	70	72	209	4,845.45
Santiago Luna	72	68	69	209	4,845.45

	SCORES			TOTAL	MONEY
Terry Pilkadaris	67	72	70	209	4,845.45
Scott Strange	69	67	73	209	4,845.45
Martin Wiegele	64	71	74	209	4,845.45
Louis Oosthuizen	73	64	73	210	3,640
Liam Bond	66	70	75	211	3,315
Stuart Manley	69	71	71	211	3,315
Zane Scotland	70	70	71	211	3,315
Sven Struver	70	65	76	211	3,315
Alejandro Canizares	70	68	74	212	2,925
Tim Dykes	67	73	72	212	2,925
Steve Alker	76	64	73	213	2,665
Craig Lee	71	69	73	213	2,665
Robert McGuirk	74	66	75	215	2,470
Toni Karjalainen	70	70	78	218	2,380

Saint-Omer Open

Aa Saint-Omer Golf Club, Lumbres, France
Par 36-35–71; 6,845 yards

June 12-15
purse, €604,470

	SCORES				TOTAL	MONEY
David Dixon	77	67	69	66	279	€100,000
Christian Nilsson	75	64	70	71	280	66,660
Steven O'Hara	74	69	70	68	281	37,560
Seve Benson	71	72	72	67	282	25,480
Richard Bland	78	69	67	68	282	25,480
Francois Delamontagne	72	72	67	71	282	25,480
Robert Coles	74	71	66	72	283	15,480
David Drysdale	78	66	72	67	283	15,480
Roope Kakko	68	74	72	69	283	15,480
Mikko Korhonen	69	73	73	69	284	11,520
John E. Morgan	69	72	73	70	284	11,520
Jan-Are Larsen	70	73	72	70	285	9,990
Marco Ruiz	74	68	75	68	285	9,990
Alessandro Tadini	73	72	72	69	286	9,000
Nicolas Vanhootegem	74	69	69	74	286	9,000
Michael Hoey	73	72	72	70	287	7,935
Cesar Monasterio	71	73	70	73	287	7,935
Gareth Paddison	71	75	69	72	287	7,935
Robert Rock	75	70	71	71	287	7,935
Matthew Cort	75	70	76	67	288	7,080
Eric Ramsay	70	73	74	71	288	7,080
Chris Gane	74	71	73	71	289	6,330
David Griffiths	72	73	74	70	289	6,330
Benjamin Miarka	75	72	70	72	289	6,330
Iain Pyman	74	72	71	72	289	6,330
Gustavo Rojas	76	71	72	70	289	6,330
Benoit Teilleria	73	73	72	71	289	6,330
Juan Abbate	76	71	70	73	290	5,160
Wil Besseling	78	68	70	74	290	5,160
Sebastien Delagrange	75	72	68	75	290	5,160
Richard McEvoy	76	70	73	71	290	5,160
Terry Pilkadaris	73	70	75	72	290	5,160
Marco Soffietti	72	70	75	73	290	5,160
Richard Treis	73	71	70	76	290	5,160
Scott Barr	73	71	72	75	291	4,200
Liam Bond	73	69	70	79	291	4,200
Andrew Coltart	73	73	75	70	291	4,200
Mark Haastrup	74	69	75	73	291	4,200
Ben Mason	71	74	72	74	291	4,200

	SCORES			TOTAL	MONEY
Edward Rush	74	72	73	72	291	4,200
Steve Alker	74	72	72	74	292	3,540
Christophe Brazillier	72	71	80	69	292	3,540
Lawrence Dodd	71	74	74	73	292	3,540
Marcus Higley	69	75	71	77	292	3,540
Steven Jeppesen	70	76	71	75	292	3,540
David Bransdon	72	73	75	73	293	2,880
Klas Eriksson	73	72	76	72	293	2,880
Andreas Hogberg	75	72	74	72	293	2,880
Gareth Maybin	70	72	77	74	293	2,880
Alvaro Salto	71	74	74	74	293	2,880
Anthony Snobeck	75	69	75	74	293	2,880
Tim Dykes	77	69	78	70	294	2,280
Ian Garbutt	74	71	72	77	294	2,280
Anders Schmidt Hansen	73	74	73	74	294	2,280
Colm Moriarty	75	72	74	73	294	2,280
Thomas Aiken	77	70	73	75	295	1,686.67
Sion E. Bebb	73	70	73	79	295	1,686.67
Olivier David	76	69	75	75	295	1,686.67
Jordi Garcia	76	70	78	71	295	1,686.67
Jeppe Huldahl	76	68	73	78	295	1,686.67
Rikard Karlberg	72	75	76	72	295	1,686.67
Julien Quesne	71	75	71	78	295	1,686.67
Fredrik Widmark	74	71	76	74	295	1,686.67
Julien Xanthopoulos	75	70	75	75	295	1,686.67
Thomas Feyrsinger	71	74	75	77	297	1,260
Rodolfo Gonzalez	75	71	74	77	297	1,260
Toni Karjalainen	73	74	73	77	297	1,260
Matthew King	73	74	75	75	297	1,260
Kyron Sullivan	72	73	73	79	297	1,260
Alessio Bruschi	76	71	75	76	298	947.75
David Higgins	74	73	76	75	298	947.75
James Morrison	75	72	74	77	298	947.75
Alexandre Rocha	75	67	78	78	298	947.75
Joakim Backstrom	75	71	74	79	299	891
Francois Calmels	81	66	76	78	301	888

BMW International Open

Golfclub Munchen Eichenreid, Munich, Germany
Par 36-36–72; 6,956 yards

June 19-22
purse, €1,979,950

	SCORES			TOTAL	MONEY
Martin Kaymer	68	63	67	75	273	€333,330
Anders Hansen	69	70	67	67	273	222,220
(Kaymer defeated Hansen on first playoff hole.)						
John Bickerton	70	70	68	67	275	103,333.33
Paul Casey	70	68	67	70	275	103,333.33
Mark Foster	67	72	68	68	275	103,333.33
Francois Delamontagne	70	66	70	71	277	50,266.67
Robert-Jan Derksen	74	69	69	65	277	50,266.67
Martin Erlandsson	70	70	71	66	277	50,266.67
Thomas Levet	69	69	67	72	277	50,266.67
Charl Schwartzel	69	69	66	73	277	50,266.67
Henrik Stenson	69	68	72	68	277	50,266.67
Ross Fisher	70	68	67	73	278	34,400
Retief Goosen	69	69	69	72	279	30,733.33
Soren Kjeldsen	68	73	68	70	279	30,733.33
Andrew McLardy	68	75	73	63	279	30,733.33
Alex Cejka	74	67	71	68	280	24,700

	SCORES				TOTAL	MONEY
David Lynn	67	73	66	74	280	24,700
Mardan Mamat	66	71	74	69	280	24,700
Colin Montgomerie	70	71	68	71	280	24,700
Alexander Noren	68	73	72	67	280	24,700
Iain Pyman	69	74	64	73	280	24,700
Tino Schuster	69	68	69	74	280	24,700
Graeme Storm	68	69	70	73	280	24,700
Benn Barham	68	68	69	76	281	19,900
Alastair Forsyth	74	68	71	68	281	19,900
David Frost	74	69	68	70	281	19,900
Gary Murphy	71	70	68	72	281	19,900
Peter O'Malley	66	75	68	72	281	19,900
Joel Sjoholm	71	71	65	74	281	19,900
Ariel Canete	73	65	70	74	282	16,600
*Stephan Gross, Jr.	71	68	71	72	282	
Peter Hanson	72	70	69	71	282	16,600
Peter Hedblom	69	72	71	70	282	16,600
Simon Khan	75	65	71	71	282	16,600
Mikael Lundberg	72	68	74	68	282	16,600
Oliver Fisher	71	70	71	71	283	15,000
Barry Lane	70	70	72	72	284	14,200
Bernhard Langer	70	72	71	71	284	14,200
Daniel Vancsik	67	74	69	74	284	14,200
Gregory Bourdy	70	72	70	73	285	13,000
Rafa Echenique	66	73	71	75	285	13,000
Shiv Kapur	71	72	71	71	285	13,000
Jean-Baptiste Gonnet	67	72	75	72	286	11,400
David Howell	69	69	71	77	286	11,400
Peter Lawrie	73	68	71	74	286	11,400
Francesco Molinari	71	72	72	71	286	11,400
Jyoti Randhawa	71	69	75	71	286	11,400
Thomas Bjorn	71	67	76	73	287	9,600
Pelle Edberg	70	68	73	76	287	9,600
Maarten Lafeber	70	68	75	74	287	9,600
Gareth Paddison	70	70	74	73	287	9,600
Markus Brier	71	70	74	73	288	8,400
Peter Fowler	71	70	74	73	288	8,400
Carl Suneson	69	73	75	73	290	7,800
Bradley Dredge	73	65	72	81	291	6,800
Richard Finch	69	68	73	81	291	6,800
Florian Praegant	74	67	79	71	291	6,800
Jarmo Sandelin	71	69	79	72	291	6,800
Niclas Fasth	70	72	81	69	292	5,900
Jean-Francois Lucquin	73	70	75	74	292	5,900
Anton Haig	66	73	79	76	294	5,400
Pablo Larrazabal	69	69	74	82	294	5,400
Pedro Linhart	70	73	73	78	294	5,400
Mark Brown	72	71	80	73	296	5,000
Hennie Otto	73	68	77	80	298	4,800
Tom Whitehouse	72	71	79	77	299	4,600

Open de France ALSTOM

Le Golf National, Paris, France
Par 36-35–71; 7,225 yards

June 26-29
purse, €3,985,100

	SCORES				TOTAL	MONEY
Pablo Larrazabal	65	70	67	67	269	€666,660
Colin Montgomerie	69	68	68	68	273	444,440
Soren Hansen	69	69	67	69	274	250,400

	SCORES				TOTAL	MONEY
Richard Green	73	71	65	67	276	200,000
Markus Brier	70	71	66	70	277	154,800
Lee Westwood	69	68	69	71	277	154,800
John Bickerton	72	69	68	70	279	88,666.67
Oliver Fisher	66	73	69	71	279	88,666.67
Soren Kjeldsen	72	71	66	70	279	88,666.67
Paul McGinley	71	73	70	65	279	88,666.67
Hennie Otto	70	69	75	65	279	88,666.67
Charl Schwartzel	73	70	66	70	279	88,666.67
Angel Cabrera	67	70	74	69	280	55,500
Rafa Echenique	69	71	69	71	280	55,500
Ignacio Garrido	68	69	73	70	280	55,500
Robert Karlsson	72	71	68	69	280	55,500
Graeme McDowell	69	73	67	71	280	55,500
Francesco Molinari	68	75	69	68	280	55,500
Peter O'Malley	71	72	67	70	280	55,500
Danny Willett	74	70	67	69	280	55,500
Jamie Donaldson	68	73	72	68	281	44,000
Shiv Kapur	75	63	76	67	281	44,000
Jeev Milkha Singh	68	74	70	69	281	44,000
Graeme Storm	68	70	72	71	281	44,000
Miles Tunnicliff	68	71	71	71	281	44,000
Martin Erlandsson	68	73	71	70	282	38,600
Peter Lawrie	66	71	74	71	282	38,600
David Lynn	70	65	71	76	282	38,600
Louis Oosthuizen	70	73	67	72	282	38,600
Scott Barr	75	69	68	71	283	32,666.67
Paul Broadhurst	69	69	72	73	283	32,666.67
Alejandro Canizares	71	69	70	73	283	32,666.67
David Frost	69	74	70	70	283	32,666.67
Thomas Levet	75	69	69	70	283	32,666.67
Ian Poulter	72	72	71	68	283	32,666.67
Thongchai Jaidee	70	73	72	69	284	28,400
Michael Jonzon	68	72	73	71	284	28,400
Carl Suneson	72	67	76	69	284	28,400
Gregory Bourdy	70	72	71	72	285	26,000
Simon Dyson	70	70	72	73	285	26,000
Jarmo Sandelin	74	70	73	68	285	26,000
Peter Hanson	71	73	74	68	286	23,600
Maarten Lafeber	73	67	73	73	286	23,600
Tom Whitehouse	71	70	69	76	286	23,600
Jose Manuel Lara	68	73	72	74	287	21,200
Steve Webster	73	68	69	77	287	21,200
Martin Wiegele	68	76	69	74	287	21,200
Phillip Archer	69	74	74	71	288	18,000
Gonzalo Fernandez-Castano	74	69	77	68	288	18,000
Barry Lane	68	76	71	73	288	18,000
Paul Lawrie	73	71	70	74	288	18,000
Mikael Lundberg	71	71	75	71	288	18,000
Nick Dougherty	71	71	74	73	289	13,371.43
Ricardo Gonzalez	72	72	70	75	289	13,371.43
Gregory Havret	73	70	70	76	289	13,371.43
Mikko Ilonen	71	71	74	73	289	13,371.43
Raphael Jacquelin	71	73	70	75	289	13,371.43
Rick Kulacz	72	71	70	76	289	13,371.43
Jean Van de Velde	71	72	70	76	289	13,371.43
Felipe Aguilar	74	69	74	73	290	11,000
Andrew McLardy	72	71	72	75	290	11,000
Andrew Coltart	68	76	73	74	291	10,400
Daniel Vancsik	69	75	75	73	292	10,000
Ross Fisher	73	71	73	76	293	9,400
Alvaro Quiros	70	74	70	79	293	9,400
Miguel Angel Jimenez	72	71	75	76	294	8,600

	SCORES				TOTAL	MONEY
Jyoti Randhawa	70	74	81	69	294	8,600
Sebastien Delagrange	72	72	77	75	296	8,000

European Open

London Golf Club, Ash, Kent, England
Par 36-36–72; 7,257 yards

July 3-6
purse, €3,032,807

	SCORES				TOTAL	MONEY
Ross Fisher	63	68	69	68	268	€506,392
Sergio Garcia	71	64	74	66	275	337,586.23
Graeme McDowell	65	67	71	73	276	190,200.84
David Frost	65	72	69	71	277	151,917.60
Soren Hansen	69	67	72	73	281	128,826.13
Peter Hanson	68	71	71	72	282	98,746.44
Robert Karlsson	74	66	73	69	282	98,746.44
Markus Brier	71	71	71	70	283	72,008.94
Stephen Gallacher	70	68	71	74	283	72,008.94
Sion E. Bebb	74	67	71	72	284	54,462.46
Jamie Donaldson	73	70	73	68	284	54,462.46
Rory McIlroy	67	71	72	74	284	54,462.46
Jeev Milkha Singh	68	72	69	75	284	54,462.46
Mikko Ilonen	69	73	73	70	285	44,663.77
Michael Jonzon	69	68	71	77	285	44,663.77
Maarten Lafeber	71	71	70	73	285	44,663.77
Simon Dyson	73	69	76	68	286	36,764.06
Ignacio Garrido	72	71	67	76	286	36,764.06
Padraig Harrington	72	70	69	75	286	36,764.06
David Howell	71	72	73	70	286	36,764.06
Thomas Levet	72	70	72	72	286	36,764.06
Paul McGinley	69	68	71	78	286	36,764.06
Anthony Wall	70	70	75	71	286	36,764.06
Oliver Fisher	72	70	74	71	287	31,598.86
Colin Montgomerie	70	67	73	77	287	31,598.86
Gary Orr	73	67	72	75	287	31,598.86
Mark Brown	75	68	72	73	288	27,497.09
Robert Coles	76	66	72	74	288	27,497.09
Rafa Echenique	70	69	74	75	288	27,497.09
Jean-Baptiste Gonnet	71	70	72	75	288	27,497.09
James Kingston	69	69	74	76	288	27,497.09
Robert Rock	68	71	73	76	288	27,497.09
Pelle Edberg	71	72	74	72	289	22,848.41
Gregory Havret	73	68	73	75	289	22,848.41
David Lynn	68	72	77	72	289	22,848.41
Andrew Oldcorn	73	70	73	73	289	22,848.41
Jean Van de Velde	75	67	70	77	289	22,848.41
Jean-Francois Lucquin	69	73	73	75	290	19,749.29
Justin Rose	69	73	77	71	290	19,749.29
Carl Suneson	72	69	72	77	290	19,749.29
Alvaro Velasco	73	70	73	74	290	19,749.29
Steve Webster	73	70	71	76	290	19,749.29
Fredrik Andersson Hed	72	69	74	76	291	16,710.94
Francesco Molinari	70	73	73	75	291	16,710.94
Gary Murphy	72	71	73	75	291	16,710.94
Chapchai Nirat	74	69	72	76	291	16,710.94
Patrik Sjoland	76	66	73	76	291	16,710.94
David Griffiths	71	72	75	74	292	13,672.58
Simon Khan	70	72	77	73	292	13,672.58
Jose Manuel Lara	68	75	76	73	292	13,672.58
Stuart Manley	70	70	76	76	292	13,672.58

	SCORES				TOTAL	MONEY
Ian Poulter	70	67	77	78	292	13,672.58
Benn Barham	70	72	74	77	293	10,381.04
Gregory Bourdy	73	70	77	73	293	10,381.04
Francois Delamontagne	73	69	72	79	293	10,381.04
Bradley Dredge	75	66	75	77	293	10,381.04
Peter Hedblom	68	73	79	73	293	10,381.04
Graeme Storm	76	66	73	78	293	10,381.04
Gonzalo Fernandez-Castano	68	75	73	78	294	8,507.39
Hennie Otto	72	70	78	74	294	8,507.39
Martin Wiegele	71	68	72	83	294	8,507.39
Garry Houston	72	70	74	79	295	7,595.88
Michael Lorenzo-Vera	74	66	80	75	295	7,595.88
Santiago Luna	70	71	74	80	295	7,595.88
Richard Green	73	69	72	83	297	6,836.29
Paul Lawrie	73	68	79	77	297	6,836.29
Paul Broadhurst	72	71	78	77	298	6,228.62
Raphael Jacquelin	71	71	77	79	298	6,228.62
Emanuele Canonica	72	70	77	80	299	5,772.87
Thomas Bjorn	72	70	76		WD	

Barclays Scottish Open

Loch Lomond Golf Club, Glasgow, Scotland
Par 36-35–71; 7,149 yards

July 10-13
purse, €3,748,319

	SCORES				TOTAL	MONEY
Graeme McDowell	67	70	66	68	271	€631,044.98
James Kingston	70	70	67	66	273	420,692.45
Richard Green	67	68	70	69	274	213,167
Miguel Angel Jimenez	68	69	68	69	274	213,167
Simon Khan	69	66	68	72	275	160,537.84
Robert Dinwiddie	68	68	71	69	276	113,588.10
Stephen Gallacher	72	68	72	64	276	113,588.10
Francesco Molinari	69	68	72	67	276	113,588.10
Ernie Els	72	66	70	69	277	71,257.60
Paul Lawrie	68	67	72	70	277	71,257.60
Alvaro Quiros	69	70	74	64	277	71,257.60
Jeev Milkha Singh	68	68	69	72	277	71,257.60
Oliver Wilson	71	66	71	69	277	71,257.60
Christian Cevaer	70	67	70	71	278	53,386.41
Oliver Fisher	68	69	70	71	278	53,386.41
Peter Hedblom	70	68	72	68	278	53,386.41
Andrew McLardy	70	70	69	69	278	53,386.41
Patrik Sjoland	67	71	71	69	278	53,386.41
Fredrik Andersson Hed	70	67	69	73	279	43,542.10
Damien McGrane	68	66	76	69	279	43,542.10
Rory McIlroy	70	69	68	72	279	43,542.10
Gary Murphy	68	70	72	69	279	43,542.10
Anthony Wall	70	70	69	70	279	43,542.10
Lee Westwood	67	69	70	73	279	43,542.10
John Bickerton	66	71	72	71	280	35,401.62
Ross Fisher	68	69	68	75	280	35,401.62
Gregory Havret	69	70	72	69	280	35,401.62
Thongchai Jaidee	64	71	71	74	280	35,401.62
Jean-Francois Lucquin	72	65	71	72	280	35,401.62
David Lynn	69	67	70	74	280	35,401.62
Ian Poulter	69	69	68	74	280	35,401.62
Adam Scott	72	66	68	74	280	35,401.62
Pelle Edberg	68	70	74	69	281	28,472.75
Martin Erlandsson	67	70	77	67	281	28,472.75

	SCORES				TOTAL	MONEY
Hennie Otto	71	69	71	70	281	28,472.75
Henrik Stenson	67	69	72	73	281	28,472.75
Simon Wakefield	71	68	72	70	281	28,472.75
Mark Brown	73	66	71	72	282	24,232.13
Angel Cabrera	65	68	78	71	282	24,232.13
David Howell	69	70	70	73	282	24,232.13
Soren Kjeldsen	73	66	74	69	282	24,232.13
Phil Mickelson	71	67	71	73	282	24,232.13
Alexander Noren	64	73	71	74	282	24,232.13
Thomas Bjorn	67	68	75	73	283	20,067.23
Alejandro Canizares	73	67	71	72	283	20,067.23
Johan Edfors	67	71	76	69	283	20,067.23
Mark Foster	68	70	73	72	283	20,067.23
Mardan Mamat	69	70	73	71	283	20,067.23
Maarten Lafeber	67	70	76	71	284	17,416.84
Andres Romero	68	71	75	70	284	17,416.84
Gregory Bourdy	70	68	72	75	285	14,009.20
Alastair Forsyth	73	67	72	73	285	14,009.20
Garry Houston	66	71	74	74	285	14,009.20
Paul McGinley	70	70	72	73	285	14,009.20
Ross McGowan	69	70	74	72	285	14,009.20
Matthew Millar	72	64	77	72	285	14,009.20
Andrew Oldcorn	71	69	72	73	285	14,009.20
David Dixon	68	70	75	74	287	10,980.18
Peter Lawrie	71	68	77	71	287	10,980.18
Tom Whitehouse	68	71	75	73	287	10,980.18
David Drysdale	68	71	74	75	288	10,033.62
Scott Strange	70	68	77	73	288	10,033.62
Iain Pyman	69	71	76	73	289	9,276.36
Carlos Rodiles	69	70	75	75	289	9,276.36
Jean-Francois Remesy	70	68	75	79	292	8,708.42

The Open Championship

Royal Birkdale, Southport, Lancashire, England
Par 34-36–70; 7,173 yards

July 17-20
purse, €5,335,867

	SCORES				TOTAL	MONEY
Padraig Harrington	74	68	72	69	283	€938,565
Ian Poulter	72	71	75	69	287	563,139
Greg Norman	70	70	72	77	289	319,112.10
Henrik Stenson	76	72	70	71	289	319,112.10
Jim Furyk	71	71	77	71	290	225,255.60
*Chris Wood	75	70	73	72	290	
Robert Allenby	69	73	76	74	292	121,318.22
Stephen Ames	73	70	78	71	292	121,318.22
Paul Casey	78	71	73	70	292	121,318.22
Ben Curtis	78	69	70	75	292	121,318.22
Ernie Els	80	69	74	69	292	121,318.22
David Howell	76	71	78	67	292	121,318.22
Robert Karlsson	75	73	75	69	292	121,318.22
Anthony Kim	72	74	71	75	292	121,318.22
Steve Stricker	77	71	71	73	292	121,318.22
K.J. Choi	72	67	75	79	293	66,533.83
Justin Leonard	77	70	73	73	293	66,533.83
Adam Scott	70	74	77	72	293	66,533.83
Anders Hansen	78	68	74	74	294	47,267.18
Gregory Havret	71	75	77	71	294	47,267.18
Trevor Immelman	74	74	73	73	294	47,267.18
Fredrik Jacobson	71	72	79	72	294	47,267.18

Chris Turvey

Lorena Ochoa was in full swing early, winning five of six, and a total of seven victories overall.

By May, Annika Sorenstam had won her third tournament of the year.

Yani Tseng, from Taiwan, was the Rolex Rookie of the Year.

South Korea's Ji-Yai Shin won a block of money at the ADT Championship.

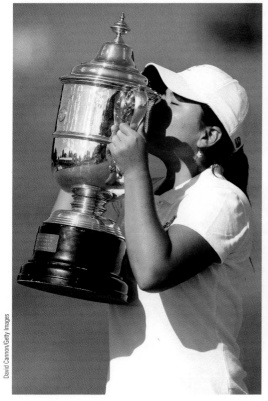

Inbee Park won the U.S. Women's Open.

Paula Creamer had four victories.

Andrew Redington/Getty Images

Helen Alfredsson won the Evian Masters.

Ross Kinnaird/Getty Images

Karrie Webb was second in the ADT.

Chris Turvey

Suzann Pettersen finished No. 5.

Max Morse/Getty Images

Angela Stanford posted two LPGA victories.

Travis Lindquist/Getty Images

Cristie Kerr won the Safeway Classic.

Yuri Fudoh had four victories in Japan.

Seon Hwa Lee won twice on the LPGA Tour.

Jeong Jang placed second three times.

Momoko Ueda won twice in Japan.

Maria Hjorth was top-10 in two majors.

Jee Young Lee had eight top-10 finishes.

Senior Tours

Another outstanding year for Jay Haas resulted in a victory in the Senior PGA Championship.

Eduardo Romero took the U.S. Senior Open.

Bernhard Langer led the money list.

Bruce Vaughn won the Senior British Open.

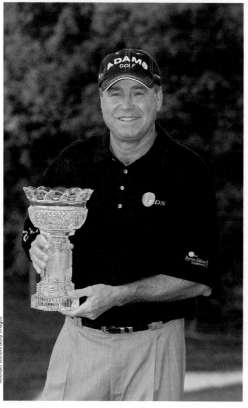

D.A. Weibring was the Senior Players champion.

Fred Funk was the Tradition winner.

Jeff Sluman won over $1.7 million.

Andy Bean won the Charles Schwab event.

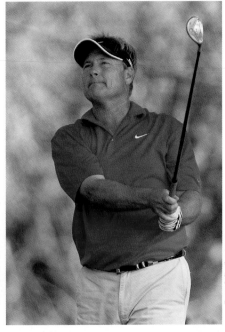

Scott Hoch posted a pair of victories.

John Cook took the AT&T Championship.

	SCORES				TOTAL	MONEY
Davis Love	75	74	70	75	294	47,267.18
Graeme McDowell	69	73	80	72	294	47,267.18
Rocco Mediate	69	73	76	76	294	47,267.18
Phil Mickelson	79	68	76	71	294	47,267.18
Alexander Noren	72	70	75	77	294	47,267.18
*Thomas Sherreard	77	69	76	72	294	
Jean Van de Velde	73	71	80	70	294	47,267.18
Simon Wakefield	71	74	70	79	294	47,267.18
Paul Waring	73	74	76	71	294	47,267.18
Retief Goosen	71	75	73	76	295	31,330.19
Richard Green	76	72	76	71	295	31,330.19
Todd Hamilton	74	74	72	75	295	31,330.19
Tom Lehman	74	73	73	75	295	31,330.19
Nick O'Hern	74	75	74	72	295	31,330.19
Andres Romero	77	72	74	72	295	31,330.19
Heath Slocum	73	76	74	72	295	31,330.19
Thomas Aiken	75	71	82	68	296	20,830.93
Woody Austin	76	72	74	74	296	20,830.93
Gregory Bourdy	74	74	75	73	296	20,830.93
Bart Bryant	70	78	74	74	296	20,830.93
Ariel Canete	78	71	76	71	296	20,830.93
David Duval	73	69	83	71	296	20,830.93
Ross Fisher	72	74	71	79	296	20,830.93
Simon Khan	77	72	71	76	296	20,830.93
Graeme Storm	76	70	72	78	296	20,830.93
Camilo Villegas	76	65	79	76	296	20,830.93
Mike Weir	71	76	74	75	296	20,830.93
Jay Williamson	73	72	77	74	296	20,830.93
Stuart Appleby	72	71	79	75	297	14,748.88
Michael Campbell	75	74	74	74	297	14,748.88
David Frost	75	73	73	76	297	14,748.88
Sergio Garcia	72	73	74	78	297	14,748.88
Zach Johnson	73	72	76	76	297	14,748.88
Douglas Labelle	78	70	74	75	297	14,748.88
Anthony Wall	71	73	81	72	297	14,748.88
Richard Finch	75	73	78	72	298	13,327.62
Tom Gillis	74	72	79	73	298	13,327.62
Peter Hanson	71	72	78	77	298	13,327.62
Colin Montgomerie	73	75	74	76	298	13,327.62
Kevin Stadler	72	75	78	73	298	13,327.62
Scott Verplank	77	67	78	76	298	13,327.62
Soren Hansen	75	69	77	78	299	12,764.48
Liang Wen-chong	77	71	77	74	299	12,764.48
Jonathan Lomas	75	73	76	75	299	12,764.48
Jean-Baptiste Gonnet	75	72	73	80	300	12,389.06
David Horsey	74	70	79	77	300	12,389.06
Lee Westwood	75	74	78	73	300	12,389.06
Brendan Jones	74	73	83	71	301	11,700.78
Pablo Larrazabal	75	74	73	79	301	11,700.78
Jose-Filipe Lima	73	76	75	77	301	11,700.78
Jeff Overton	72	75	75	79	301	11,700.78
Craig Parry	77	70	77	77	301	11,700.78
John Rollins	73	75	77	76	301	11,700.78
Justin Rose	74	72	82	73	301	11,700.78
Martin Wiegele	75	74	78	74	301	11,700.78
Nick Dougherty	75	71	79	77	302	11,075.07
Lucas Glover	78	71	77	76	302	11,075.07
Martin Kaymer	75	72	79	77	303	10,887.35
Phillip Archer	75	74	78	77	304	10,762.21
Sean O'Hair	75	73	80	78	306	10,637.07
Lam Chih Bing	72	75	83	81	311	10,511.93

Out of Final 36 Holes

Peter Appleyard	74	76	150	4,004.54
Aaron Baddeley	75	75	150	4,004.54
Peter Baker	75	75	150	4,004.54
Jon Bevan	78	72	150	4,004.54
Alex Cejka	76	74	150	4,004.54
Stewart Cink	75	75	150	4,004.54
Josh Cunliffe	79	71	150	4,004.54
Pelle Edberg	76	74	150	4,004.54
James Kingston	77	73	150	4,004.54
Paul Lawrie	77	73	150	4,004.54
Prayad Marksaeng	77	73	150	4,004.54
Scott McCarron	75	75	150	4,004.54
Damien McGrane	79	71	150	4,004.54
Pat Perez	82	68	150	4,004.54
Richard Sterne	78	72	150	4,004.54
Yoshinobu Tsukada	75	75	150	4,004.54
Tom Watson	74	76	150	4,004.54
Azuma Yano	74	76	150	4,004.54
Craig Barlow	79	72	151	3,316.26
Mark Calcavecchia	76	75	151	3,316.26
Charles Howell	76	75	151	3,316.26
Ryuji Imada	77	74	151	3,316.26
Soren Kjeldsen	81	70	151	3,316.26
Geoff Ogilvy	77	74	151	3,316.26
Mark O'Meara	74	77	151	3,316.26
Vijay Singh	80	71	151	3,316.26
Brandt Snedeker	72	79	151	3,316.26
Andrew Tampion	78	73	151	3,316.26
Hideto Tanihara	76	75	151	3,316.26
Oliver Wilson	77	74	151	3,316.26
Simon Dyson	82	70	152	3,316.26
Johan Edfors	78	74	152	3,316.26
Niclas Fasth	79	73	152	3,316.26
Paul Goydos	77	75	152	3,316.26
*Benjamin Hebert	79	73	152	
Barry Hume	76	76	152	3,316.26
Matt Kuchar	79	73	152	3,316.26
Michael Letzig	78	74	152	3,316.26
Hunter Mahan	80	72	152	3,316.26
David Smail	76	76	152	3,316.26
Gary Boyd	77	76	153	2,972.13
Tim Clark	76	77	153	2,972.13
Boo Weekley	80	73	153	2,972.13
Angel Cabrera	77	77	154	2,972.13
Miguel Angel Jimenez	72	82	154	2,972.13
Doug McGuigan	79	75	154	2,972.13
Rod Pampling	77	77	154	2,972.13
Angelo Que	76	78	154	2,972.13
Jeff Quinney	79	75	154	2,972.13
Rory Sabbatini	79	75	154	2,972.13
*Rohan Blizard	78	77	155	
Ewan Porter	76	79	155	2,972.13
Jamie Elson	78	78	156	2,972.13
J.B. Holmes	79	77	156	2,972.13
Hennie Otto	79	77	156	2,972.13
Scott Strange	84	72	156	2,972.13
Hiroshi Iwata	73	84	157	2,972.13
*Reinier Saxton	80	77	157	
Adam Blyth	81	77	158	2,972.13
Michio Matsumura	82	76	158	2,972.13
Tim Petrovic	82	76	158	2,972.13
Brad Lamb	85	74	159	2,972.13
Philip Walton	77	82	159	2,972.13

	SCORES				TOTAL	MONEY
Steve Webster	79	80			159	2,972.13
Darren Fichardt	82	78			160	2,627.98
Jerry Kelly	83	77			160	2,627.98
Shintaro Kai	80	81			161	2,627.98
Danny Chia	76	87			163	2,627.98
Peter Fowler	82	82			164	2,627.98
John Daly	80	89			169	2,627.98
Jamie Howarth	85	84			169	2,627.98
Rich Beem					WD	
Sandy Lyle					WD	

Inteco Russian Open Golf Championship

Le Meridien Moscow Country Club, Moscow, Russia
Par 36-36–72; 7,154 yards

July 24-27
purse, €1,265,217

	SCORES				TOTAL	MONEY
Mikael Lundberg	67	64	68	68	267	€210,237.24
Jose Manuel Lara	67	68	70	64	269	140,158.16
Benn Barham	69	68	65	68	270	78,965.90
Jan-Are Larsen	68	65	72	66	271	63,071.80
David Drysdale	68	71	69	64	272	53,484.89
Darren Fichardt	66	71	66	70	273	37,843.08
Jamie Moul	68	68	64	73	273	37,843.08
Lloyd Saltman	69	70	66	68	273	37,843.08
Soren Juul	69	68	69	68	274	25,565.10
Sam Little	70	69	70	65	274	25,565.10
Robert Rock	68	64	71	71	274	25,565.10
Michiel Bothma	68	68	66	73	275	19,527.03
Robert-Jan Derksen	68	73	68	66	275	19,527.03
Gareth Paddison	68	71	69	67	275	19,527.03
Alessandro Tadini	70	68	68	69	275	19,527.03
Danny Willett	69	66	69	71	275	19,527.03
Jamie Donaldson	70	68	72	66	276	15,494.64
Craig Lee	71	67	69	69	276	15,494.64
Jean-Francois Lucquin	73	64	71	68	276	15,494.64
Lee Slattery	70	67	68	71	276	15,494.64
Carl Suneson	67	68	71	70	276	15,494.64
Paul Waring	69	72	69	66	276	15,494.64
Markus Brier	71	69	70	67	277	13,118.93
Stephen Gallacher	69	72	66	70	277	13,118.93
Per-Ulrik Johansson	69	68	71	69	277	13,118.93
Shiv Kapur	67	70	69	71	277	13,118.93
Marcel Siem	69	71	69	68	277	13,118.93
Fredrik Andersson Hed	68	69	72	69	278	11,794.43
Patrik Sjoland	71	67	70	70	278	11,794.43
Luis Claverie	67	68	73	71	279	9,713.06
Francois Delamontagne	67	67	74	71	279	9,713.06
Robert Dinwiddie	70	67	72	70	279	9,713.06
David Higgins	72	70	68	69	279	9,713.06
Garry Houston	67	71	71	70	279	9,713.06
James Kamte	71	69	68	71	279	9,713.06
Andrew Marshall	67	69	72	71	279	9,713.06
Henrik Nystrom	70	70	69	70	279	9,713.06
Jarmo Sandelin	67	64	72	76	279	9,713.06
Tom Whitehouse	72	70	71	66	279	9,713.06
Mark Foster	71	68	69	72	280	7,947.05
Christian Nilsson	72	67	70	71	280	7,947.05
Ignacio Sanchez-Palencia	68	66	73	73	280	7,947.05
Steve Alker	73	67	71	70	281	6,685.61

	SCORES				TOTAL	MONEY
Richard Bland	69	69	71	72	281	6,685.61
David Carter	65	73	76	67	281	6,685.61
Adilson da Silva	69	73	68	71	281	6,685.61
Rafa Echenique	72	69	68	72	281	6,685.61
Philip Golding	70	72	70	69	281	6,685.61
Rob Harris	73	69	70	69	281	6,685.61
*Steven Uzzell	74	68	68	71	281	
Ben Mason	68	69	72	73	282	5,424.17
Guido van der Valk	70	72	65	75	282	5,424.17
Mads Vibe-Hastrup	74	68	69	71	282	5,424.17
Joakim Backstrom	65	73	76	69	283	4,415.03
Maarten Lafeber	72	70	67	74	283	4,415.03
Stuart Manley	72	68	72	71	283	4,415.03
Steven O'Hara	71	71	71	70	283	4,415.03
Kyron Sullivan	71	71	70	71	283	4,415.03
Juan Abbate	68	71	75	70	284	3,595.09
Magnus A. Carlsson	70	70	70	74	284	3,595.09
Gary Orr	71	67	75	71	284	3,595.09
Peter Whiteford	68	74	72	70	284	3,595.09
Christopher Hanell	71	71	71	72	285	3,279.73
Sebastien Delagrange	71	71	69	75	286	3,090.52
Gary Murphy	69	72	73	72	286	3,090.52
Andre Bossert	70	68	76	73	287	2,838.23
Johan Skold	68	72	73	74	287	2,838.23
Roope Kakko	65	73	72	78	288	2,649.02
Phil Worthington	70	71	72	76	289	2,522.87
Peter Baker	71	71	72	77	291	2,396.73
Gareth Davies	68	74	77	73	292	2,027.71
Gonzalo Fernandez-Castano	74	68	75	75	292	2,027.71
Fredrik Henge	65	77	71	79	292	2,027.71

SAS Masters

Arlandastad Golf Club, Stockholm, Sweden
Par 34-36–70; 6,845 yards

August 14-17
purse, €1,602,400

	SCORES				TOTAL	MONEY
Peter Hanson	66	66	68	71	271	€266,660
Nick Dougherty	66	66	70	70	272	138,965
Pelle Edberg	69	67	66	70	272	138,965
Paul Broadhurst	67	68	70	68	273	67,946.67
Gary Orr	67	68	67	71	273	67,946.67
Sam Walker	72	68	64	69	273	67,946.67
Soren Kjeldsen	69	65	68	72	274	48,000
Daniel Chopra	71	64	67	73	275	31,760
Jamie Donaldson	68	68	71	68	275	31,760
Bradley Dredge	71	69	66	69	275	31,760
Oliver Fisher	69	69	68	69	275	31,760
Raphael Jacquelin	73	68	65	69	275	31,760
Paul McGinley	69	70	67	69	275	31,760
Martin Kaymer	69	70	68	69	276	23,040
David Lynn	70	69	68	69	276	23,040
Ross McGowan	70	70	65	71	276	23,040
Jarmo Sandelin	72	68	68	68	276	23,040
Damien McGrane	71	69	68	69	277	20,240
Chris Wood	70	67	68	72	277	20,240
Christian Cevaer	72	67	69	70	278	17,866.67
Niclas Fasth	70	68	70	70	278	17,866.67
Ignacio Garrido	69	70	66	73	278	17,866.67
Mikko Ilonen	70	70	69	69	278	17,866.67

	SCORES				TOTAL	MONEY
Craig Lee	72	65	73	68	278	17,866.67
Graeme Storm	70	66	71	71	278	17,866.67
Peter Baker	67	68	73	71	279	15,440
Robert Dinwiddie	69	69	68	73	279	15,440
Carlos Rodiles	71	70	69	69	279	15,440
Fabrizio Zanotti	74	67	65	73	279	15,440
Thomas Aiken	69	69	70	72	280	12,497.78
Markus Brier	70	70	70	70	280	12,497.78
Magnus A. Carlsson	68	70	69	73	280	12,497.78
Michael Jonzon	70	70	68	72	280	12,497.78
Maarten Lafeber	69	70	71	70	280	12,497.78
Alexander Noren	72	68	71	69	280	12,497.78
Patrik Sjoland	68	66	70	76	280	12,497.78
Anthony Wall	72	69	70	69	280	12,497.78
Marc Warren	68	71	69	72	280	12,497.78
Fredrik Andersson Hed	74	66	70	71	281	9,760
Henrik Bjornstad	70	68	72	71	281	9,760
Robert-Jan Derksen	67	71	72	71	281	9,760
Jean-Baptiste Gonnet	69	69	70	73	281	9,760
Andreas Hogberg	70	67	68	76	281	9,760
Lee S. James	72	68	67	74	281	9,760
Barry Lane	71	69	69	72	281	9,760
Felipe Aguilar	68	70	72	72	282	7,360
Martin Erlandsson	67	74	72	69	282	7,360
Anders Hansen	72	69	72	69	282	7,360
Thomas Levet	73	68	67	74	282	7,360
Gary Murphy	72	67	69	74	282	7,360
Jesper Parnevik	68	69	71	74	282	7,360
Paul Waring	72	69	69	72	282	7,360
Peter Whiteford	70	69	71	72	282	7,360
Johan Edfors	74	66	71	72	283	5,600
Miles Tunnicliff	72	69	72	70	283	5,600
Martin Wiegele	71	66	71	75	283	5,600
Phillip Archer	71	69	71	73	284	4,720
Alejandro Canizares	71	66	72	75	284	4,720
Manuel Quiros	71	66	73	74	284	4,720
Carl Suneson	70	71	71	72	284	4,720
Mattias Eliasson	71	70	71	73	285	4,000
Peter Hedblom	69	71	69	76	285	4,000
Matthew Millar	71	67	71	76	285	4,000
Peter O'Malley	74	67	67	77	285	4,000
Phillip Price	71	69	69	76	285	4,000
Anton Haig	69	72	72	73	286	3,440
*David Palm	79	62	73	72	286	
Robert Rock	72	69	78	67	286	3,440
Pedro Linhart	66	74	72	75	287	3,120
Simon Wakefield	71	68	73	75	287	3,120
Johan Bjerhag	72	68	73	75	288	2,930
Gareth Paddison	68	72	75	74	289	2,400

KLM Open

Kennemer Golf & Country Club, Zandvoort, Netherlands
Par 36-34–70; 6,626 yards

August 21-24
purse, €1,793,300

	SCORES				TOTAL	MONEY
Darren Clarke	68	64	66	66	264	€300,000
Paul McGinley	69	68	67	64	268	200,000
Henrik Stenson	68	65	68	68	269	112,680
Lee Slattery	70	69	67	65	271	83,160

	SCORES				TOTAL	MONEY
Marc Warren	72	64	67	68	271	83,160
Soren Hansen	65	69	70	68	272	58,500
Ross McGowan	69	64	72	67	272	58,500
Gregory Bourdy	69	67	68	69	273	38,610
Michael Campbell	68	66	69	70	273	38,610
Gary Orr	68	67	71	67	273	38,610
Anthony Wall	67	68	69	69	273	38,610
Peter Baker	71	67	72	64	274	26,145
John Bickerton	65	71	66	72	274	26,145
Simon Dyson	70	64	70	70	274	26,145
Anders Hansen	69	66	70	69	274	26,145
David Lynn	70	66	71	67	274	26,145
Alexander Noren	66	66	72	70	274	26,145
Patrik Sjoland	72	66	67	69	274	26,145
Paul Waring	70	68	70	66	274	26,145
Fredrik Andersson Hed	71	67	68	69	275	20,100
Jamie Donaldson	71	65	71	68	275	20,100
Ross Fisher	70	70	69	66	275	20,100
Thongchai Jaidee	70	69	71	65	275	20,100
Damien McGrane	67	69	69	70	275	20,100
Oliver Wilson	69	70	66	70	275	20,100
Felipe Aguilar	70	64	73	69	276	16,830
Peter Fowler	71	67	69	69	276	16,830
David Howell	72	67	71	66	276	16,830
Raphael Jacquelin	67	72	73	64	276	16,830
Matthew Millar	71	69	69	67	276	16,830
Chapchai Nirat	71	69	66	70	276	16,830
Paul Lawrie	71	66	70	70	277	14,670
Edoardo Molinari	72	68	69	68	277	14,670
Alastair Forsyth	68	71	70	69	278	12,960
Jean-Baptiste Gonnet	67	70	69	72	278	12,960
Mathias Gronberg	68	71	68	71	278	12,960
Jan-Are Larsen	69	67	73	69	278	12,960
Rolf Muntz	64	72	69	73	278	12,960
Justin Rose	67	69	71	71	278	12,960
Mark Foster	68	71	69	71	279	10,980
Simon Khan	67	70	72	70	279	10,980
Jean-Francois Lucquin	70	68	74	67	279	10,980
Alvaro Velasco	68	68	70	73	279	10,980
Sam Walker	72	67	69	71	279	10,980
Alejandro Canizares	74	65	70	71	280	9,180
Robert Rock	68	64	80	68	280	9,180
Graeme Storm	71	64	73	72	280	9,180
Peter Whiteford	72	65	74	69	280	9,180
Fabrizio Zanotti	72	66	71	71	280	9,180
Carlos Franco	68	72	68	73	281	7,380
David Frost	72	68	72	69	281	7,380
Santiago Luna	69	69	72	71	281	7,380
Mikael Lundberg	71	69	73	68	281	7,380
Phillip Price	67	73	70	71	281	7,380
Martin Kaymer	72	66	74	70	282	6,120
Jose-Filipe Lima	68	70	69	75	282	6,120
Iain Pyman	69	71	72	71	283	5,580
Joakim Backstrom	69	70	73	73	285	5,040
Peter O'Malley	71	69	70	75	285	5,040
Sven Struver	71	69	72	73	285	5,040
Daniel Vancsik	69	68	76	72	285	5,040
Danny Willett	74	66	74	71	285	5,040
Magnus A. Carlsson	74	65	70	77	286	4,410
Ignacio Garrido	70	69	76	71	286	4,410
Martin Wiegele	69	70	74	74	287	4,140
Jean Van de Velde	70	70	76	72	288	3,960
Rafa Echenique	67	71	75	76	289	3,690

Johnnie Walker Championship

Gleneagles Hotel, Perthshire, Scotland
Par 36-37–73; 7,320 yards

August 28-31
purse, €1,747,617

	SCORES				TOTAL	MONEY
Gregory Havret	68	71	69	70	278	€292,355.49
Graeme Storm	74	69	68	68	279	194,899.48
Peter Hanson	74	72	66	69	281	98,759.09
David Howell	75	67	68	71	281	98,759.09
Justin Rose	73	71	67	71	282	67,885.91
Marcel Siem	74	70	66	72	282	67,885.91
Nick Dougherty	73	72	69	70	284	45,257.28
Bradley Dredge	71	70	70	73	284	45,257.28
Anthony Wall	71	73	65	75	284	45,257.28
Michael Campbell	73	69	71	72	285	28,351.58
Rafa Echenique	76	68	70	71	285	28,351.58
Ross Fisher	72	74	73	66	285	28,351.58
Mark Foster	73	75	70	67	285	28,351.58
Stephen Gallacher	75	72	65	73	285	28,351.58
Soren Hansen	71	71	68	75	285	28,351.58
Lee Westwood	72	72	66	75	285	28,351.58
Oliver Wilson	76	72	68	69	285	28,351.58
Simon Dyson	73	72	69	72	286	22,628.64
Benn Barham	77	70	68	72	287	19,897.16
Pelle Edberg	73	75	70	69	287	19,897.16
Johan Edfors	73	73	71	70	287	19,897.16
Ignacio Garrido	74	71	73	69	287	19,897.16
Paul McGinley	76	69	70	72	287	19,897.16
Francesco Molinari	73	70	69	75	287	19,897.16
Paul Waring	73	71	69	74	287	19,897.16
Louis Oosthuizen	75	71	68	74	288	17,190.75
Gareth Paddison	72	73	71	72	288	17,190.75
Alvaro Velasco	74	73	71	70	288	17,190.75
Anton Haig	75	70	71	73	289	15,612.01
Gary Orr	70	72	72	75	289	15,612.01
Robert Rock	70	70	76	73	289	15,612.01
Gregory Bourdy	71	77	74	68	290	13,419.31
Paul Broadhurst	70	74	72	74	290	13,419.31
Ricardo Gonzalez	76	67	67	80	290	13,419.31
Thongchai Jaidee	73	73	72	72	290	13,419.31
Jose Manuel Lara	75	70	75	70	290	13,419.31
Martin Wiegele	71	74	70	75	290	13,419.31
Christian Cevaer	70	75	73	73	291	11,226.61
Luis Claverie	75	72	70	74	291	11,226.61
Colin Montgomerie	74	70	76	71	291	11,226.61
Lee Slattery	77	71	70	73	291	11,226.61
Benoit Teilleria	71	75	74	71	291	11,226.61
Peter Whiteford	73	68	75	75	291	11,226.61
Darren Clarke	72	73	73	74	292	9,297.04
Lee S. James	72	73	72	75	292	9,297.04
David Lynn	73	71	75	73	292	9,297.04
Paul McKechnie	75	73	75	69	292	9,297.04
Peter O'Malley	78	69	72	73	292	9,297.04
Mark Brown	78	70	69	76	293	7,893.71
Gonzalo Fernandez-Castano	75	73	69	76	293	7,893.71
Patrik Sjoland	72	74	73	74	293	7,893.71
Juan Abbate	72	76	72	74	294	6,665.80
Jamie Donaldson	75	71	76	72	294	6,665.80
Gary Murphy	75	73	71	75	294	6,665.80
Chris Wood	75	69	75	75	294	6,665.80
Peter Fowler	75	73	73	74	295	5,496.36
Marcus Fraser	75	70	71	79	295	5,496.36

	SCORES				TOTAL	MONEY
Matthew Millar	74	74	73	74	295	5,496.36
Peter Baker	75	70	74	77	296	4,823.93
Francois Delamontagne	75	68	73	80	296	4,823.93
Michael Jonzon	78	70	75	73	296	4,823.93
Sam Walker	76	72	72	76	296	4,823.93
Emanuele Canonica	72	75	78	73	298	4,122.27
Robert Dinwiddie	82	66	73	77	298	4,122.27
Jonathan Lomas	72	74	73	79	298	4,122.27
Alvaro Quiros	74	74	75	75	298	4,122.27
*Steven McEwan	78	70	76	75	299	
Stephen Gray	75	72	79	82	308	3,683.73
Robert Arnott	76	72	88	75	311	3,508.32

Omega European Masters

Crans-sur-Sierre Golf Club, Crans Montana, Switzerland   September 4-7
Par 36-35–71; 6,857 yards   purse, €2,008,991

	SCORES				TOTAL	MONEY
Jean-Francois Lucquin	68	67	69	67	271	€333,330
Rory McIlroy	63	71	66	71	271	222,220
(Lucquin defeated McIlroy on second playoff hole.)						
Christian Cevaer	68	71	65	68	272	95,000
Julien Clement	69	68	67	68	272	95,000
Miguel Angel Jimenez	68	69	68	67	272	95,000
Gary Orr	67	71	67	67	272	95,000
Juan Abbate	68	67	69	69	273	48,700
Robert Dinwiddie	76	64	64	69	273	48,700
Rafa Echenique	69	70	66	68	273	48,700
Ross McGowan	67	73	66	67	273	48,700
Alejandro Canizares	67	68	69	70	274	34,466.67
Francesco Molinari	69	70	69	66	274	34,466.67
Julio Zapata	66	72	67	69	274	34,466.67
Barry Lane	71	70	65	69	275	29,400
Michael Lorenzo-Vera	70	69	71	65	275	29,400
Richard Sterne	69	70	68	68	275	29,400
Mark Foster	72	66	68	70	276	26,400
Louis Oosthuizen	69	68	71	68	276	26,400
Mattias Eliasson	70	72	68	67	277	24,400
Ricardo Gonzalez	73	68	70	66	277	24,400
Gonzalo Fernandez-Castano	68	71	75	64	278	22,900
Thongchai Jaidee	70	71	68	69	278	22,900
Fredrik Andersson Hed	69	67	72	71	279	19,600
Michael Campbell	69	71	68	71	279	19,600
Niclas Fasth	68	73	72	66	279	19,600
David Griffiths	70	69	68	72	279	19,600
Peter Hedblom	70	70	70	69	279	19,600
Peter Lawrie	67	69	72	71	279	19,600
Robert Rock	72	68	70	69	279	19,600
Brett Rumford	67	67	73	72	279	19,600
Sven Struver	72	69	66	72	279	19,600
Thomas Aiken	72	70	65	73	280	14,460
Peter Baker	70	70	69	71	280	14,460
Emanuele Canonica	67	70	68	75	280	14,460
Simon Dyson	69	67	72	72	280	14,460
Mikko Ilonen	67	70	70	73	280	14,460
Jan-Are Larsen	71	71	67	71	280	14,460
Andrew Marshall	70	70	71	69	280	14,460
Andrew McLardy	70	72	71	67	280	14,460
Charl Schwartzel	70	72	66	72	280	14,460

	SCORES				TOTAL	MONEY
Paul Waring	71	71	66	72	280	14,460
Francois Delamontagne	67	72	74	68	281	12,000
Santiago Luna	70	71	69	71	281	12,000
Scott Barr	69	68	76	69	282	11,000
Martin Erlandsson	68	72	71	71	282	11,000
Zhang Lian-wei	71	71	71	69	282	11,000
Felipe Aguilar	70	69	72	72	283	8,800
Garry Houston	66	73	70	74	283	8,800
Carlos Rodiles	71	66	70	76	283	8,800
Miles Tunnicliff	71	69	71	72	283	8,800
Daniel Vancsik	71	71	70	71	283	8,800
Mads Vibe-Hastrup	72	70	70	71	283	8,800
Tom Whitehouse	72	68	68	75	283	8,800
Fabrizio Zanotti	71	68	72	72	283	8,800
Bradley Dredge	69	70	72	73	284	6,450
Ignacio Garrido	70	72	67	75	284	6,450
Hennie Otto	69	73	72	70	284	6,450
Jarmo Sandelin	71	66	71	76	284	6,450
Steve Alker	71	70	71	73	285	5,400
Ariel Canete	69	72	70	74	285	5,400
Florian Praegant	72	70	73	70	285	5,400
Eduardo Romero	71	68	75	71	285	5,400
Patrik Sjoland	69	68	73	75	285	5,400
Raphael Jacquelin	73	69	70	74	286	4,700
Matthew Millar	70	72	70	74	286	4,700
Robert-Jan Derksen	69	70	76	72	287	4,010
Marcus Fraser	74	68	74	71	287	4,010
Michael Jonzon	71	69	74	73	287	4,010
Benoit Teilleria	71	69	76	71	287	4,010
Francis Valera	73	67	77	70	287	4,010
Simon Griffiths	76	66	71	76	289	3,000
*Ken Benz	68	74	73	75	290	
Pablo Martin	71	71	74	74	290	2,997
Craig Lee	73	69	74	75	291	2,994

Mercedes-Benz Championship

Gut Larchenhof, Cologne, Germany
Par 36-36–72; 7,289 yards

September 11-14
purse, €2,000,000

	SCORES				TOTAL	MONEY
Robert Karlsson	67	69	68	71	275	€320,000
Francesco Molinari	71	71	65	70	277	220,000
Michael Campbell	71	70	68	70	279	101,516.67
Ross Fisher	68	73	68	70	279	101,516.67
Miguel Angel Jimenez	72	73	68	66	279	101,516.67
Richard Finch	66	73	70	72	281	64,000
Jose Manuel Lara	73	69	67	72	281	64,000
Soren Hansen	73	67	73	69	282	44,666.67
Martin Kaymer	74	70	68	70	282	44,666.67
Marcel Siem	72	68	72	70	282	44,666.67
David Dixon	72	71	71	70	284	34,466.67
Jeev Milkha Singh	73	70	73	68	284	34,466.67
Marc Warren	72	69	72	71	284	34,466.67
Peter Hanson	69	69	73	74	285	30,000
Steve Webster	73	72	68	72	285	30,000
Stuart Appleby	74	75	68	69	286	25,500
Gregory Havret	73	74	67	72	286	25,500
Mikko Ilonen	72	70	67	77	286	25,500
Soren Kjeldsen	73	70	73	70	286	25,500

	SCORES				TOTAL	MONEY
Jean-Francois Lucquin	66	71	70	79	286	25,500
Graeme McDowell	72	73	70	71	286	25,500
Richard Green	72	72	72	71	287	22,000
Paul Lawrie	70	72	71	74	287	22,000
David Lynn	73	75	69	70	287	22,000
Gregory Bourdy	76	72	71	69	288	19,900
Darren Clarke	76	74	69	69	288	19,900
Gonzalo Fernandez-Castano	80	66	73	69	288	19,900
Peter Hedblom	73	70	72	73	288	19,900
Markus Brier	72	74	72	71	289	17,500
Johan Edfors	74	67	73	75	289	17,500
Chapchai Nirat	70	76	71	72	289	17,500
Alexander Noren	71	71	72	75	289	17,500
Maarten Lafeber	71	77	72	70	290	15,700
Richard Sterne	70	73	70	77	290	15,700
Fred Couples	75	70	74	72	291	14,800
James Kingston	69	73	72	77	291	14,800
Ariel Canete	73	72	73	74	292	13,200
Ignacio Garrido	75	75	70	72	292	13,200
David Howell	76	74	68	74	292	13,200
Thomas Levet	75	75	70	72	292	13,200
Paul McGinley	73	74	71	74	292	13,200
Damien McGrane	70	75	75	72	292	13,200
Felipe Aguilar	71	77	70	75	293	11,800
Niclas Fasth	80	72	72	70	294	10,600
David Frost	71	72	77	74	294	10,600
Anders Hansen	76	76	70	72	294	10,600
Raphael Jacquelin	74	71	75	74	294	10,600
Alvaro Quiros	71	73	74	76	294	10,600
John Daly	73	71	74	77	295	9,400
Prayad Marksaeng	71	73	80	72	296	8,800
Mads Vibe-Hastrup	72	75	74	75	296	8,800
Peter Lawrie	72	76	74	75	297	7,800
Phillip Price	71	76	74	76	297	7,800
Scott Strange	74	74	79	70	297	7,800
Daniel Chopra	78	76	72	72	298	6,600
Robert-Jan Derksen	75	77	75	71	298	6,600
Charl Schwartzel	73	75	74	76	298	6,600
Simon Dyson	76	74	76	74	300	5,800
Per-Ulrik Johansson	73	74	72	81	300	5,800
Bernhard Langer	70	76	81	73	300	5,800
Alastair Forsyth	74	78	76	73	301	5,200
Mikael Lundberg	80	75	70	76	301	5,200
Sven Struver	72	76	75	78	301	5,200
Graeme Storm	75	71	73	83	302	4,800
Pablo Larrazabal	76	75	80	72	303	4,500
Mardan Mamat	76	76	74	77	303	4,500
Mark Brown	76	78	76	76	306	4,100
Stephen Dodd	73	76	78	79	306	4,100
Retief Goosen	76	76	78	77	307	3,650
Anton Haig	74	78	81	74	307	3,650
Hennie Otto	77	78	79	73	307	3,650
Oliver Fisher	75	74	80	81	310	3,350
John Bickerton	80	76	74	83	313	3,050
S.S.P. Chowrasia	79	76	79	79	313	3,050
Pablo Martin	77	79	80	77	313	3,050
Scott Drummond	84	74	81	78	317	2,750
Jyoti Randhawa	77	83	79	81	320	2,600
Daniel Vancsik	81				WD	2,450

The Ryder Cup

See American Tours chapter.

Quinn Insurance British Masters

The Belfry, Sutton Coldfield, West Midlands, England
Par 36-36–72; 7,230 yards

September 25-28
purse, €2,296,537

	SCORES				TOTAL	MONEY
Gonzalo Fernandez-Castano	71	70	68	67	276	€381,612
Lee Westwood	68	70	68	70	276	254,408
(Fernandez-Castano defeated Westwood on third playoff hole.)						
Michael Campbell	69	72	65	72	278	143,333.47
Mikael Lundberg	67	75	68	70	280	114,483.60
Charl Schwartzel	72	72	66	72	282	88,610.31
Jeev Milkha Singh	69	71	69	73	282	88,610.31
Magnus A. Carlsson	73	70	68	72	283	59,073.54
Ross Fisher	71	68	71	73	283	59,073.54
Louis Oosthuizen	71	71	75	66	283	59,073.54
Alejandro Canizares	71	68	72	73	284	42,435.25
Michael Jonzon	70	71	72	71	284	42,435.25
Pablo Larrazabal	74	71	69	70	284	42,435.25
Thomas Bjorn	69	73	72	71	285	35,184.63
Alexander Noren	72	66	75	72	285	35,184.63
Anthony Wall	71	74	70	70	285	35,184.63
Marcus Fraser	67	73	77	69	286	30,280.91
David Howell	71	71	77	67	286	30,280.91
Paul Lawrie	69	71	74	72	286	30,280.91
Jean Van de Velde	72	74	66	74	286	30,280.91
Phillip Archer	73	68	77	69	287	25,568
Bradley Dredge	72	74	71	70	287	25,568
Rafa Echenique	68	77	72	70	287	25,568
Mark Foster	72	72	73	70	287	25,568
James Kamte	76	66	73	72	287	25,568
Sam Little	73	72	70	72	287	25,568
Thongchai Jaidee	71	68	76	73	288	22,095.34
Phillip Price	71	71	72	74	288	22,095.34
Simon Wakefield	70	74	73	71	288	22,095.34
Sam Walker	68	72	78	70	288	22,095.34
Markus Brier	71	71	74	73	289	17,884.88
David Dixon	69	72	76	72	289	17,884.88
David Drysdale	75	71	69	74	289	17,884.88
Ricardo Gonzalez	77	70	73	69	289	17,884.88
Anders Hansen	68	78	69	74	289	17,884.88
Peter Hanson	75	68	75	71	289	17,884.88
Soren Kjeldsen	73	69	74	73	289	17,884.88
Greg Owen	69	76	71	73	289	17,884.88
Graeme Storm	70	73	73	73	289	17,884.88
Paul Broadhurst	70	73	72	75	290	14,195.97
Maarten Lafeber	75	72	71	72	290	14,195.97
David Lynn	71	71	77	71	290	14,195.97
Graeme McDowell	72	75	72	71	290	14,195.97
Rory McIlroy	72	73	69	76	290	14,195.97
Henrik Nystrom	76	69	71	74	290	14,195.97
Juan Abbate	73	71	78	69	291	11,677.33
Christian Cevaer	73	73	72	73	291	11,677.33
Johan Edfors	73	74	74	70	291	11,677.33
Martin Erlandsson	74	70	72	75	291	11,677.33
Alvaro Quiros	75	72	75	69	291	11,677.33
Fredrik Andersson Hed	70	73	75	74	292	10,074.56
Jean-Francois Lucquin	71	72	71	78	292	10,074.56

	SCORES				TOTAL	MONEY
Peter Hedblom	75	72	76	70	293	8,700.75
Paul McGinley	73	73	70	77	293	8,700.75
Francesco Molinari	70	76	71	76	293	8,700.75
Peter Whiteford	71	75	75	72	293	8,700.75
Gregory Bourdy	71	76	72	75	294	7,174.31
Mikko Ilonen	69	76	74	75	294	7,174.31
Marc Warren	68	71	77	78	294	7,174.31
Robert-Jan Derksen	70	75	73	77	295	6,411.08
Shiv Kapur	72	71	78	74	295	6,411.08
Patrik Sjoland	73	72	74	76	295	6,411.08
Julien Clement	72	74	77	73	296	5,609.70
Alastair Forsyth	74	71	79	72	296	5,609.70
Robert Giles	71	75	76	74	296	5,609.70
Peter Lawrie	74	72	77	73	296	5,609.70
Jamie Donaldson	76	71	77	73	297	4,922.79
David Horsey	72	75	79	71	297	4,922.79
Simon Dyson	72	75	77	75	299	4,579.34
Marcel Siem	75	72	75	80	302	4,350.38
Niclas Fasth	72	72	82	77	303	3,803.15
Gregory Havret	71	76	81	75	303	3,803.15

Alfred Dunhill Links Championship

St. Andrews Old Course: Par 36-36–72; 7,279 yards
Carnoustie Championship Course: Par 36-36–72; 7,102 yards
Kingsbarns Golf Links: Par 36-36–72; 7,059 yards
St. Andrews & Fife, Scotland

October 2-5
purse, €3,284,691

	SCORES				TOTAL	MONEY
Robert Karlsson	67	70	76	65	278	€545,811.55
Ross Fisher	64	76	73	65	278	284,439.46
Martin Kaymer	65	72	73	68	278	284,439.46
(Karlsson defeated Fisher and Kaymer on first playoff hole.)						
Jarmo Sandelin	66	72	72	70	280	163,743.46
Magnus A. Carlsson	70	68	73	70	281	117,240.32
Jose-Filipe Lima	67	71	75	68	281	117,240.32
Anthony Wall	66	76	71	68	281	117,240.32
Paul Casey	72	70	72	68	282	67,462.31
Jamie Donaldson	70	70	75	67	282	67,462.31
Soren Hansen	64	73	77	68	282	67,462.31
Rory McIlroy	68	69	78	67	282	67,462.31
Lee Westwood	68	70	76	68	282	67,462.31
Thomas Aiken	66	74	76	67	283	47,267.28
Michael Campbell	68	70	77	68	283	47,267.28
Robert-Jan Derksen	72	73	72	66	283	47,267.28
Padraig Harrington	67	71	74	71	283	47,267.28
Charl Schwartzel	68	72	75	68	283	47,267.28
Marc Warren	66	73	75	69	283	47,267.28
John Bickerton	71	72	70	71	284	38,184.98
Gregory Bourdy	66	74	76	68	284	38,184.98
Markus Brier	66	70	76	72	284	38,184.98
Nick Dougherty	74	71	74	65	284	38,184.98
Thongchai Jaidee	69	71	72	72	284	38,184.98
Marcus Fraser	66	77	71	71	285	32,093.72
Stephen Gallacher	70	76	74	65	285	32,093.72
Peter Hedblom	69	71	77	68	285	32,093.72
Charley Hoffman	69	72	75	69	285	32,093.72
Raphael Jacquelin	68	70	77	70	285	32,093.72
Damien McGrane	71	74	73	67	285	32,093.72
Jeev Milkha Singh	71	75	72	67	285	32,093.72

	SCORES				TOTAL	MONEY
Peter Fowler	68	76	77	65	286	26,264.45
Ricardo Gonzalez	70	72	77	67	286	26,264.45
Graeme McDowell	68	75	75	68	286	26,264.45
Gary Orr	66	72	77	71	286	26,264.45
Miles Tunnicliff	68	74	77	67	286	26,264.45
Thomas Bjorn	70	73	76	68	287	22,924.09
Gonzalo Fernandez-Castano	68	73	75	71	287	22,924.09
James Kingston	72	75	72	68	287	22,924.09
Peter Lawrie	70	71	73	73	287	22,924.09
Martin Erlandsson	72	74	73	69	288	18,994.24
Garry Houston	69	74	75	70	288	18,994.24
Mikko Ilonen	68	76	73	71	288	18,994.24
Thomas Levet	67	74	78	69	288	18,994.24
Joost Luiten	73	73	75	67	288	18,994.24
Louis Oosthuizen	70	71	76	71	288	18,994.24
Alvaro Quiros	68	74	76	70	288	18,994.24
Oliver Wilson	69	76	75	68	288	18,994.24
Darren Clarke	72	74	72	71	289	15,064.40
Robert Dinwiddie	75	74	72	68	289	15,064.40
Jose Manuel Lara	68	75	76	70	289	15,064.40
Alexander Noren	73	73	73	70	289	15,064.40
Paul Broadhurst	76	69	75	70	290	11,257.36
Retief Goosen	67	76	76	71	290	11,257.36
Peter Hanson	75	71	75	69	290	11,257.36
Andrew McLardy	69	74	73	74	290	11,257.36
Matthew Millar	72	77	71	70	290	11,257.36
Henrik Nystrom	73	75	73	69	290	11,257.36
Richard Sterne	70	75	76	69	290	11,257.36
Carl Suneson	69	73	78	70	290	11,257.36
Alejandro Canizares	70	73	76	72	291	8,514.66
Emanuele Canonica	70	79	71	71	291	8,514.66
Bradley Dredge	71	73	77	70	291	8,514.66
David Howell	66	73	80	72	291	8,514.66
Francesco Molinari	68	75	78	70	291	8,514.66
Lee Slattery	68	75	77	72	292	7,532.20
Felipe Aguilar	68	76	75	74	293	6,564.75
Greg Chalmers	70	75	76	72	293	6,564.75
Alastair Forsyth	70	77	74	72	293	6,564.75
Justin Rose	71	74	74	74	293	6,564.75
Steve Webster	70	76	75	72	293	6,564.75
Ignacio Garrido	74	72	75	73	294	4,911
Sam Little	72	77	72	73	294	4,911

Madrid Masters

Club de Campo Ville de Madrid, Madrid, Spain
Par 36-35–71; 6,970 yards

October 9-12
purse, €1,000,000

	SCORES				TOTAL	MONEY
Charl Schwartzel	69	64	66	66	265	€166,660
Ricardo Gonzalez	69	69	62	68	268	111,110
Pablo Larrazabal	68	72	62	67	269	62,600
Alvaro Quiros	74	66	66	64	270	46,200
Robert Rock	70	65	71	64	270	46,200
Paul Waring	69	67	67	69	272	35,000
Carlos Del Moral	69	67	67	70	273	30,000
Thongchai Jaidee	69	69	67	69	274	23,700
Damien McGrane	69	68	68	69	274	23,700
Jesus Maria Arruti	72	67	70	66	275	18,533.33
Rafael Cabrera Bello	74	68	66	67	275	18,533.33

	SCORES				TOTAL	MONEY
Ignacio Garrido	70	68	67	70	275	18,533.33
Sion E. Bebb	69	68	68	71	276	15,366.67
Andrew Tampion	75	63	65	73	276	15,366.67
Steve Webster	68	69	71	68	276	15,366.67
Fredrik Andersson Hed	72	69	71	65	277	12,980
James Kamte	68	70	72	67	277	12,980
Martin Kaymer	71	69	67	70	277	12,980
Kyron Sullivan	71	68	68	70	277	12,980
Tom Whitehouse	71	70	66	70	277	12,980
Joakim Backstrom	70	69	71	68	278	10,550
Angel Cabrera	71	69	70	68	278	10,550
Magnus A. Carlsson	67	70	73	68	278	10,550
Pelle Edberg	72	70	67	69	278	10,550
Marcus Fraser	67	66	74	71	278	10,550
Steven Jeppesen	68	67	71	72	278	10,550
Sam Little	71	70	71	66	278	10,550
Patrik Sjoland	70	69	70	69	278	10,550
Steve Alker	73	66	71	69	279	8,187.50
Paul Broadhurst	67	72	69	71	279	8,187.50
Eduardo De La Riva	71	71	65	72	279	8,187.50
Miguel Angel Jimenez	69	71	72	67	279	8,187.50
Jose Manuel Lara	69	69	72	69	279	8,187.50
Paul Lawrie	72	68	72	67	279	8,187.50
Francis Valera	69	70	71	69	279	8,187.50
Leif Westerberg	75	66	72	66	279	8,187.50
Phillip Archer	71	69	69	71	280	6,600
Francois Delamontagne	70	72	71	67	280	6,600
Bradley Dredge	73	66	70	71	280	6,600
Mattias Eliasson	72	69	70	69	280	6,600
Stephen Gallacher	71	65	71	73	280	6,600
Lee Slattery	73	66	69	72	280	6,600
Emanuele Canonica	71	70	74	66	281	5,200
Rafa Echenique	72	70	68	71	281	5,200
Jean-Baptiste Gonnet	69	68	73	71	281	5,200
Santiago Luna	68	68	71	74	281	5,200
Jarmo Sandelin	75	67	73	66	281	5,200
Joel Sjoholm	71	68	75	67	281	5,200
Benoit Teilleria	71	71	69	70	281	5,200
Miles Tunnicliff	74	66	71	70	281	5,200
Ariel Canete	69	71	70	72	282	4,200
Gabriel Canizares	71	71	73	67	282	4,200
Lee S. James	73	69	75	66	283	3,600
Pedro Linhart	71	70	74	68	283	3,600
Peter O'Malley	70	71	72	70	283	3,600
Richard Sterne	72	67	73	71	283	3,600
Miguel Angel Martin	71	70	70	73	284	3,000
Edoardo Molinari	75	67	68	74	284	3,000
Simon Wakefield	72	69	71	72	284	3,000
Alfredo Garcia-Heredia	72	70	70	73	285	2,600
Jean-Francois Lucquin	70	72	76	67	285	2,600
Stuart Manley	71	70	70	74	285	2,600
Gary Murphy	70	71	72	72	285	2,600
Julio Zapata	70	69	74	72	285	2,600
Carlos Balmaseda	71	71	73	71	286	2,250
Jose Maria Olazabal	70	72	71	73	286	2,250
Peter Fowler	72	70	76	72	290	2,050
Paolo Terreni	71	65	72	82	290	2,050
Peter Baker	69	73	76	73	291	1,865
Pablo Martin	73	67	80	71	291	1,865

Portugal Masters

Oceanico Victoria Golf Course, Vilamoura, Portugal
Par 35-37–72; 7,231 yards

October 16-19
purse, €3,000,000

	SCORES				TOTAL	MONEY
Alvaro Quiros	66	68	67	68	269	€500,000
Paul Lawrie	70	65	70	67	272	333,330
Ross Fisher	67	70	65	71	273	155,000
Robert Karlsson	69	67	66	71	273	155,000
Steve Webster	72	67	66	68	273	155,000
James Kingston	69	71	64	70	274	105,000
Gregory Bourdy	69	67	68	71	275	77,400
Simon Dyson	71	69	67	68	275	77,400
Soren Hansen	73	65	65	72	275	77,400
Rory McIlroy	69	69	69	69	276	55,600
Anthony Wall	72	66	70	68	276	55,600
Chris Wood	73	70	68	65	276	55,600
Andrew McLardy	67	75	66	69	277	48,300
David Lynn	70	69	68	71	278	45,000
Stuart Manley	65	68	73	72	278	45,000
Robert-Jan Derksen	71	68	67	73	279	38,940
Bradley Dredge	70	70	67	72	279	38,940
Soren Kjeldsen	67	74	72	66	279	38,940
Alexander Noren	71	69	67	72	279	38,940
Lee Westwood	72	67	72	68	279	38,940
Garry Houston	73	66	73	68	280	34,350
Sam Walker	67	73	69	71	280	34,350
Felipe Aguilar	68	68	72	73	281	30,300
Angel Cabrera	73	69	66	73	281	30,300
Darren Clarke	72	69	74	66	281	30,300
Martin Erlandsson	67	73	73	68	281	30,300
Mark Foster	66	71	73	71	281	30,300
Peter Lawrie	72	69	71	69	281	30,300
Gary Orr	74	68	68	71	281	30,300
Magnus A. Carlsson	69	66	72	75	282	23,775
David Dixon	72	69	72	69	282	23,775
David Howell	74	70	67	71	282	23,775
Martin Kaymer	72	65	73	72	282	23,775
Jean-Francois Lucquin	67	69	73	73	282	23,775
Jyoti Randhawa	66	70	74	72	282	23,775
Paul Waring	71	71	68	72	282	23,775
Marc Warren	68	73	70	71	282	23,775
Jamie Donaldson	69	70	74	70	283	19,800
Oliver Fisher	73	71	71	68	283	19,800
Miguel Angel Jimenez	73	71	69	70	283	19,800
Francesco Molinari	72	72	71	68	283	19,800
Richard Green	71	69	72	72	284	17,700
Graeme McDowell	67	74	73	70	284	17,700
Phillip Price	69	70	74	71	284	17,700
Jesus Maria Arruti	69	72	72	72	285	15,900
Johan Edfors	70	71	72	72	285	15,900
Peter Hanson	73	69	70	73	285	15,900
John Bickerton	71	73	69	73	286	13,500
Stephen Gallacher	69	71	72	74	286	13,500
Ricardo Gonzalez	72	70	72	72	286	13,500
Maarten Lafeber	74	68	73	71	286	13,500
Gary Murphy	69	74	68	75	286	13,500
Thomas Levet	71	73	73	70	287	11,100
Robert Rock	72	72	72	71	287	11,100
Patrik Sjoland	72	72	69	74	287	11,100
David Frost	69	72	73	74	288	9,400
Henrik Nystrom	70	73	73	72	288	9,400

	SCORES				TOTAL	MONEY
Alvaro Velasco	73	71	73	71	288	9,400
Gregory Havret	71	71	71	77	290	8,400
Marcel Siem	68	71	73	78	290	8,400
Antonio Sobrinho	70	73	73	74	290	8,400
Rafa Echenique	72	71	71	77	291	7,800
Nick Dougherty	70	70	73	79	292	7,350
Jean-Baptiste Gonnet	73	71	74	74	292	7,350
Sion E. Bebb	68	74	72	79	293	6,600
Robert Dinwiddie	72	68	72	81	293	6,600
Jarmo Sandelin	73	69	74	77	293	6,600
Graeme Storm	69	69	72	85	295	6,000
Raphael Jacquelin	72	69	73	83	297	5,585
Barry Lane	68	70	78	81	297	5,585

Castello Masters Costa Azahar

Club de Campo del Mediterraneo, Castellon, Spain
Par 36-35–71; 7,111 yards

October 23-26
purse, €1,984,350

	SCORES				TOTAL	MONEY
Sergio Garcia	66	65	66	67	264	€333,330
Peter Hedblom	68	65	68	66	267	222,220
Alexander Noren	68	68	68	65	269	125,200
Simon Dyson	66	67	68	69	270	84,933.33
Soren Kjeldsen	64	67	70	69	270	84,933.33
David Lynn	67	66	68	69	270	84,933.33
Richard Finch	65	66	71	69	271	55,000
Peter Hanson	65	73	67	66	271	55,000
Paul Casey	69	67	69	67	272	39,000
Stephen Gallacher	67	70	65	70	272	39,000
Mikael Lundberg	67	68	68	69	272	39,000
Rory McIlroy	68	67	69	68	272	39,000
Alvaro Quiros	67	66	76	64	273	31,400
Jeev Milkha Singh	71	66	69	67	273	31,400
Angel Cabrera	65	72	69	68	274	27,040
Ignacio Garrido	65	70	69	70	274	27,040
Sam Little	72	69	66	67	274	27,040
Jose Maria Olazabal	66	72	67	69	274	27,040
Alvaro Velasco	66	71	69	68	274	27,040
Phillip Archer	67	68	70	70	275	22,950
Maarten Lafeber	70	66	69	70	275	22,950
Thomas Levet	66	68	73	68	275	22,950
Jarmo Sandelin	69	67	67	72	275	22,950
Felipe Aguilar	71	67	68	70	276	20,200
Jesus Maria Arruti	70	68	67	71	276	20,200
Thomas Bjorn	69	68	68	71	276	20,200
Gary Orr	70	67	69	70	276	20,200
Camilo Villegas	70	66	71	69	276	20,200
Nick Dougherty	68	69	72	68	277	17,200
Gonzalo Fernandez-Castano	69	68	68	72	277	17,200
Jose-Filipe Lima	70	70	67	70	277	17,200
Francesco Molinari	72	65	70	70	277	17,200
Chris Wood	68	72	69	68	277	17,200
John Bickerton	66	70	73	69	278	14,400
Bradley Dredge	71	68	68	71	278	14,400
Martin Erlandsson	71	69	67	71	278	14,400
Mark Foster	72	70	68	68	278	14,400
Justin Rose	67	70	70	71	278	14,400
Jean Van de Velde	68	70	68	72	278	14,400
Markus Brier	74	67	76	62	279	11,800

	SCORES				TOTAL	MONEY
Christian Cevaer	72	68	69	70	279	11,800
Alastair Forsyth	68	70	73	68	279	11,800
David Griffiths	67	71	70	71	279	11,800
Paul Lawrie	71	70	71	67	279	11,800
Stuart Manley	69	68	73	69	279	11,800
Ross McGowan	72	69	70	68	279	11,800
Francois Delamontagne	66	67	73	74	280	9,600
Barry Lane	71	69	72	68	280	9,600
Richard Sterne	71	69	71	69	280	9,600
Anthony Wall	71	69	67	73	280	9,600
Gregory Bourdy	68	70	67	76	281	8,200
Pablo Larrazabal	71	68	71	71	281	8,200
Pedro Linhart	68	72	70	71	281	8,200
Magnus A. Carlsson	71	68	70	73	282	6,800
Ricardo Gonzalez	67	71	73	71	282	6,800
Garry Houston	67	71	71	73	282	6,800
Jean-Francois Remesy	73	69	71	69	282	6,800
Fredrik Andersson Hed	69	73	71	70	283	5,600
Benn Barham	68	72	75	68	283	5,600
Johan Edfors	70	71	72	70	283	5,600
David Howell	69	73	72	69	283	5,600
Simon Wakefield	72	68	73	70	283	5,600
Shiv Kapur	72	70	73	70	285	4,900
Lee Slattery	71	71	69	74	285	4,900
Peter O'Malley	72	70	75	70	287	4,600
Pelle Edberg	70	72	74	77	293	4,400

Volvo Masters

Club de Golf Valderrama, Sotegrande, Cadiz, Spain
Par 35-36–71; 6,988 yards

October 30-November 2
purse, €4,190,600

	SCORES				TOTAL	MONEY
Soren Kjeldsen	65	71	69	71	276	€708,000
Martin Kaymer	73	70	67	68	278	369,000
Anthony Wall	69	69	71	69	278	369,000
Sergio Garcia	68	70	70	72	280	196,000
Lee Westwood	70	68	70	72	280	196,000
David Lynn	69	73	70	69	281	148,400
Richard Green	73	70	72	67	282	127,000
Anders Hansen	74	69	69	71	283	100,500
Graeme McDowell	72	70	74	67	283	100,500
Peter Hedblom	71	74	72	67	284	85,000
Darren Clarke	71	69	72	73	285	76,350
Ross Fisher	76	70	70	69	285	76,350
Markus Brier	72	69	74	71	286	61,285.71
Robert-Jan Derksen	72	70	72	72	286	61,285.71
Soren Hansen	74	71	70	71	286	61,285.71
Peter Hanson	72	69	73	72	286	61,285.71
Padraig Harrington	76	71	71	68	286	61,285.71
Andres Romero	74	72	68	72	286	61,285.71
Steve Webster	72	71	73	70	286	61,285.71
Francesco Molinari	74	73	74	66	287	53,600
Alexander Noren	74	74	73	67	288	52,200
Gonzalo Fernandez-Castano	73	74	67	75	289	50,100
Colin Montgomerie	73	76	68	72	289	50,100
Miguel Angel Jimenez	73	80	70	67	290	48,000
Gregory Bourdy	73	75	71	72	291	44,500
Oliver Fisher	73	71	73	74	291	44,500
David Howell	73	71	75	72	291	44,500

	SCORES				TOTAL	MONEY
Thomas Levet	71	68	75	77	291	44,500
Felipe Aguilar	74	72	70	76	292	40,000
Paul Casey	73	68	73	78	292	40,000
Ian Poulter	76	76	67	73	292	40,000
Robert Karlsson	73	73	72	75	293	37,500
Paul Lawrie	76	72	75	70	293	37,500
Nick Dougherty	78	73	70	73	294	34,000
Simon Dyson	72	68	81	73	294	34,000
Ignacio Garrido	74	75	73	72	294	34,000
Jean-Francois Lucquin	77	74	70	73	294	34,000
Alvaro Quiros	78	76	71	69	294	34,000
Pablo Larrazabal	73	79	73	70	295	29,500
Peter Lawrie	75	79	69	72	295	29,500
Rory McIlroy	74	73	75	73	295	29,500
Hennie Otto	70	77	74	74	295	29,500
Gregory Havret	76	75	67	78	296	27,000
Mark Brown	75	77	71	74	297	26,000
Henrik Stenson	74	75	72	77	298	25,000
Oliver Wilson	75	77	75	72	299	24,000
John Bickerton	74	73	75	78	300	22,550
Paul McGinley	76	78	76	70	300	22,550
Damien McGrane	74	75	73	79	301	21,200
James Kingston	76	78	75	73	302	19,850
Scott Strange	76	74	73	79	302	19,850
Richard Finch	74	77	76	76	303	18,500
Jose Manuel Lara	77	76	77	75	305	17,900
Charl Schwartzel	77	76	76	79	308	16,700
Jeev Milkha Singh	74	77	75	82	308	16,700
Graeme Storm	77	79	71	81	308	16,700
Justin Rose	80	81			WD	

HSBC Champions

See Asia/Japan Tours chapter.

UBS Hong Kong Open

See Asia/Japan Tours chapter.

Sportsbet Australian Masters

See Australasian Tour chapter.

Alfred Dunhill Championship

See African Tours chapter.

South African Open Championship

See African Tours chapter.

Challenge Tour

Tusker Kenya Open

Karen Golf Club, Nairobi, Kenya
Par 35-36–71; 6,969 yards

March 6-9
purse, €185,616

	SCORES				TOTAL	MONEY
Iain Pyman	71	63	70	68	272	€28,800
Thomas Feyrsinger	72	66	67	70	275	19,800
Rafael Cabrera Bello	74	69	67	67	277	11,700
Alexandre Rocha	72	68	70	67	277	11,700
Daniel Barbetti	65	69	69	75	278	6,264
Gary Boyd	69	71	68	70	278	6,264
Gary Clark	70	69	65	74	278	6,264
Scott Henderson	67	70	68	73	278	6,264
Greig Hutcheon	67	70	75	66	278	6,264
Michiel Bothma	69	72	68	70	279	3,555
Carlos Del Moral	68	72	70	69	279	3,555
Dismas Indiza	68	70	67	74	279	3,555
Johan Skold	72	66	72	69	279	3,555
Liam Bond	71	68	67	74	280	2,970
Marcus Higley	70	71	69	70	280	2,970
Dale Marmion	70	74	70	67	281	2,610
Ashok Shah Anil	72	69	68	72	281	2,610
Adrien Bernadet	73	70	71	68	282	2,190
Christopher Hanell	73	67	70	72	282	2,190
Inder Van Weerelt	69	75	69	69	282	2,190
Philip Golding	70	70	74	69	283	1,746
David Horsey	72	74	69	68	283	1,746
Jeppe Huldahl	71	72	70	70	283	1,746
Ben Mason	69	72	69	73	283	1,746
Gareth Davies	75	66	72	71	284	1,566
Philippe Gasnier	72	68	71	73	284	1,566
James Hepworth	69	75	66	74	284	1,566
Steve Lewton	70	66	72	76	284	1,566
Wilhelm Schauman	71	71	71	71	284	1,566
Oliver Whiteley	72	71	72	69	284	1,566

Abierto Visa del Centro
See American Tours chapter.

Abierto Visa de Argentina
See American Tours chapter.

Club Colombia Masters
See American Tours chapter.

AGF-Allianz Open Cotes d'Armor Bretagne

Golf Blue Green, Pleneuf Val Andre, France
Par 35-35–70; 6,435 yards

April 23-26
purse, €143,276

	SCORES				TOTAL	MONEY
Joakim Haeggman	66	74	67	68	275	€22,400
Marcus Higley	72	66	71	67	276	15,400
Stuart Davis	69	70	68	71	278	7,700
Andreas Hogberg	68	68	70	72	278	7,700
Gareth Maybin	72	68	70	68	278	7,700
Alessandro Tadini	72	68	68	70	278	7,700
Gary Clark	65	76	68	70	279	3,710
Adam Gee	70	70	70	69	279	3,710
Jamie McLeary	68	70	71	70	279	3,710
Taco Remkes	73	69	67	70	279	3,710
Andrew Butterfield	68	68	71	73	280	2,800
Robert Coles	72	70	70	69	281	2,520
Richie Ramsay	70	70	70	71	281	2,520
Robert Rock	68	69	70	74	281	2,520
Nicolas Colsaerts	69	65	74	74	282	2,030
David Horsey	68	69	70	75	282	2,030
Mark Pilkington	70	71	69	72	282	2,030
Eric Ramsay	73	70	70	69	282	2,030
Jean-Nicolas Billot	71	71	69	72	283	1,430
Gary Boyd	71	69	72	71	283	1,430
Colm Moriarty	68	74	69	72	283	1,430
David Park	71	70	72	70	283	1,430
Kyron Sullivan	74	69	70	70	283	1,430
Nicolas Vanhootegem	73	67	71	72	283	1,430
Matthew Zions	67	75	68	73	283	1,430

Banque Populaire Moroccan Classic

El Jadida Sofitel Golf Resort, El Jadida, Morocco
Par 36-36–72; 6,738 yards

May 1-4
purse, €154,680

	SCORES				TOTAL	MONEY
Michael Hoey	67	70	71	68	276	€24,000
Greig Hutcheon	65	72	70	70	277	13,500
Julien Quesne	73	68	69	67	277	13,500
Ricardo Santos	68	74	68	68	278	9,000
Branden Grace	69	70	70	71	280	6,100
Gregory Molteni	71	71	68	70	280	6,100
Andrew Tampion	73	70	68	69	280	6,100
Wil Besseling	67	70	72	72	281	3,525
Mark Haastrup	68	68	75	70	281	3,525
Amine Joudar	74	70	68	69	281	3,525
John E. Morgan	69	72	67	73	281	3,525
Eric Ramsay	71	69	72	70	282	2,775
Nicolas Vanhootegem	69	73	71	69	282	2,775
Peter Kaensche	70	70	72	71	283	2,400
David Park	73	68	70	72	283	2,400
Matthew Zions	67	73	73	70	283	2,400
Stephen Browne	71	70	73	70	284	1,674.38
Sebastien Delagrange	72	68	70	74	284	1,674.38
Renaud Guillard	69	73	73	69	284	1,674.38
Andreas Hogberg	69	73	74	68	284	1,674.38
Mikko Korhonen	73	71	73	67	284	1,674.38
Richard McEvoy	75	65	72	72	284	1,674.38

	SCORES				TOTAL	MONEY
Richard Treis	72	72	71	69	284	1,674.38
Julien Xanthopoulos	68	75	72	69	284	1,674.38
Matthew Cort	67	76	71	71	285	1,350
Raphael Eyraud	76	68	71	70	285	1,350
Adam Gee	67	78	76	64	285	1,350

Piemonte Open

Circolo Golf Torino & Royal Park Golf & Country Club,
Torino, Italy
Par 36-36–72; 7,180 yards

May 14-17
purse, €151,710

	SCORES				TOTAL	MONEY
Seve Benson	67	70	62	70	269	€24,000
Raphael De Sousa	70	67	66	69	272	16,500
Bjorn Pettersson	67	70	70	68	275	10,500
Gary Lockerbie	69	69	68	70	276	9,000
Rafael Cabrera Bello	69	70	69	69	277	5,625
James Morrison	64	74	65	74	277	5,625
Damian Ulrich	73	65	68	71	277	5,625
Matthew Zions	72	68	70	67	277	5,625
Mikko Korhonen	72	69	69	68	278	3,600
Francois Calmels	74	68	68	69	279	3,150
Mark Tullo	67	73	70	69	279	3,150
Adrien Bernadet	70	70	70	71	281	2,400
Mickael Dieu	72	71	70	68	281	2,400
Mark Haastrup	72	70	69	70	281	2,400
Gregory Molteni	70	74	68	69	281	2,400
Alessandro Napoleoni	69	71	70	71	281	2,400
Alexandre Rocha	72	72	64	73	281	2,400
Alessandro Tadini	69	74	68	70	281	2,400
Simone Brizzolari	72	72	67	71	282	1,557.50
Alessio Bruschi	74	68	66	74	282	1,557.50
Alex Haindl	75	69	69	69	282	1,557.50
Rikard Karlberg	74	69	66	73	282	1,557.50
Andrew Marshall	66	71	72	73	282	1,557.50
Charles-Edouard Russo	69	73	72	68	282	1,557.50
Julien Clement	64	73	76	70	283	1,290
Jeppe Huldahl	70	73	71	69	283	1,290
Roope Kakko	72	69	71	71	283	1,290
Ally Mellor	70	69	72	72	283	1,290
John E. Morgan	71	73	69	70	283	1,290
Edward Rush	70	72	69	72	283	1,290
Julien Xanthopoulos	73	70	69	71	283	1,290

DHL Wroclaw Open

Toya Golf & Country Club, Wroclaw, Poland
Par 35-35–70; 6,903 yards

May 22-25
purse, €151,710

	SCORES				TOTAL	MONEY
Gary Clark	66	67	63	66	262	€24,000
Gary Boyd	66	68	67	63	264	16,500
Richie Ramsay	67	69	66	64	266	9,750
Richard Treis	67	69	63	67	266	9,750
Klas Eriksson	71	66	67	63	267	6,100
Kasper Linnet Jorgensen	64	70	63	70	267	6,100

	SCORES				TOTAL	MONEY
Andrew Willey	66	64	67	70	267	6,100
Wil Besseling	62	69	70	67	268	3,525
Oscar Floren	66	67	66	69	268	3,525
Andrew McArthur	66	67	68	67	268	3,525
Anthony Snobeck	66	68	65	69	268	3,525
Olivier David	67	66	69	67	269	2,550
Joakim Haeggman	68	68	67	66	269	2,550
Bjorn Pettersson	66	70	66	67	269	2,550
Manuel Quiros	69	67	67	66	269	2,550
Marco Ruiz	66	67	70	66	269	2,550
Christophe Brazillier	67	71	64	68	270	1,893.75
Ben Mason	68	68	67	67	270	1,893.75
Sebastian Saavedra	71	65	66	68	270	1,893.75
Inder Van Weerelt	67	68	68	67	270	1,893.75
Andreas Andersson	69	66	66	70	271	1,440
Andreas Hogberg	69	66	68	68	271	1,440
John E. Morgan	70	67	66	68	271	1,440
Alexandre Rocha	70	66	68	67	271	1,440
Mark Tullo	67	66	70	68	271	1,440

Oceanico Group Pro-Am Challenge

Marriott Worsley Park Hotel & Country Club,
Greater Manchester, England
Par 35-35–70; 6,791 yards

May 29-June 1
purse, €150,000

	SCORES				TOTAL	MONEY
Alessandro Tadini	64	64	67	69	264	€24,000
Raphael De Sousa	63	64	67	71	265	16,500
Klas Eriksson	65	69	66	66	266	10,500
Graeme Clark	66	66	68	67	267	6,300
Gareth Maybin	68	65	67	67	267	6,300
John E. Morgan	66	68	64	69	267	6,300
Robert Rock	63	69	66	69	267	6,300
Ricardo Santos	69	65	66	67	267	6,300
Andrew Coltart	65	68	66	69	268	3,300
Andrew McArthur	66	66	71	65	268	3,300
Richie Ramsay	63	69	67	69	268	3,300
Francois Calmels	65	68	64	72	269	2,775
Tim Milford	69	64	68	68	269	2,775
Tyrone Ferreira	65	68	68	69	270	2,400
Roope Kakko	67	67	67	69	270	2,400
Lorne Kelly	69	66	65	70	270	2,400
Matthew Cort	64	71	66	70	271	1,893.75
Ian Garbutt	67	69	66	69	271	1,893.75
Jan-Are Larsen	64	71	70	66	271	1,893.75
Jamie McLeary	66	70	67	68	271	1,893.75
Gabriel Canizares	68	66	67	71	272	1,410
Branden Grace	71	65	66	70	272	1,410
Joakim Haeggman	70	66	66	70	272	1,410
David Horsey	64	68	71	69	272	1,410
John Mellor	68	66	67	71	272	1,410
Benjamin Miarka	66	66	74	66	272	1,410
Steven O'Hara	69	67	67	69	272	1,410

Reale Challenge de Espana

Casino Club de Golf Retamares, Madrid, Spain
Par 36-36–72; 6,857 yards

June 5-8
purse, €141,596

	SCORES				TOTAL	MONEY
Andrew McArthur	69	65	72	74	280	€22,400
Alfredo Garcia-Heredia	70	71	67	73	281	12,600
Lloyd Saltman	66	75	69	71	281	12,600
Rikard Karlberg	69	71	67	76	283	7,700
Gregory Molteni	67	70	67	79	283	7,700
Richie Ramsay	70	73	71	70	284	5,040
Mark Tullo	70	69	68	77	284	5,040
Wil Besseling	70	68	73	74	285	2,960
Vicente Blazquez	67	74	69	75	285	2,960
Estanislao Goya	72	70	71	72	285	2,960
Gareth Maybin	71	68	73	73	285	2,960
Fredrik Ohlsson	68	72	73	72	285	2,960
Oliver Whiteley	69	71	71	74	285	2,960
Phil Worthington	74	70	69	72	285	2,960
Eduardo De La Riva	68	71	71	76	286	2,170
Rodolfo Gonzalez	72	70	73	71	286	2,170
Jamie McLeary	65	72	74	76	287	1,767.50
Peter O'Keeffe	71	74	72	70	287	1,767.50
Michele Reale	71	72	72	72	287	1,767.50
Marco Ruiz	67	71	75	74	287	1,767.50
Francois Calmels	71	72	72	73	288	1,330
Carlos Garcia	73	71	74	70	288	1,330
Elliot Saltman	72	67	74	75	288	1,330
Mark Searle	72	70	70	76	288	1,330
Johan Skold	71	72	70	75	288	1,330
Matthew Zions	70	76	69	73	288	1,330

Saint-Omer Open

See European Tour section.

SK Golf Challenge

St. Laurence Golf, Finland
Par 35-36–71; 7,053 yards

June 12-15
purse, €152,835

	SCORES				TOTAL	MONEY
Simon Robinson	73	66	69	63	271	€24,000
John Wade	71	70	69	67	277	13,500
Andrew Willey	74	67	66	70	277	13,500
Sebastian Garcia-Grout	70	69	71	68	278	8,250
Mikko Ilonen	71	67	68	72	278	8,250
Joakim Rask	68	68	72	71	279	5,400
Sebastian Saavedra	72	69	70	68	279	5,400
Tyrone Ferreira	73	67	68	72	280	3,900
Kasper Linnet Jorgensen	74	68	68	70	280	3,900
Jamie Moul	69	73	70	69	281	3,150
Georges Plumet	72	67	71	71	281	3,150
*Henri Satama	69	73	66	73	281	
Kariem Baraka	71	73	72	66	282	2,700
Matthew Bliss	73	68	67	74	282	2,700
Rob Harris	70	73	69	70	282	2,700
Oscar Floren	69	70	73	71	283	2,037.50

	SCORES				TOTAL	MONEY
Jaakko Makitalo	74	68	71	70	283	2,037.50
Paulo Pinto	72	69	71	71	283	2,037.50
Pasi Purhonen	70	73	72	68	283	2,037.50
Joel Sjoholm	72	65	73	73	283	2,037.50
Damian Ulrich	70	69	72	72	283	2,037.50
Gareth Davies	72	72	70	70	284	1,410
Matt Ford	72	70	72	70	284	1,410
Fredrik Henge	76	68	71	69	284	1,410
Soren Juul	68	71	73	72	284	1,410
Taco Remkes	76	65	69	74	284	1,410
Antti Ulvio	74	70	69	71	284	1,410
Daniel Wardrop	72	70	72	70	284	1,410

Telenet Trophy

Limburg Golf & Country Club, Houthalen, Belgium
Par 36-36–72; 6,742 yards

June 19-22
purse, €140,000

	SCORES				TOTAL	MONEY
David Horsey	67	66	68	68	269	€22,400
Wil Besseling	69	66	68	67	270	12,600
Soren Juul	72	66	69	63	270	12,600
Michele Reale	67	72	65	68	272	7,700
Inder Van Weerelt	71	69	65	67	272	7,700
Adrien Bernadet	70	68	68	67	273	4,340
Raphael De Sousa	73	67	63	70	273	4,340
Gerald Gresse	68	70	69	66	273	4,340
Charles-Edouard Russo	70	68	69	66	273	4,340
Jean-Nicolas Billot	73	67	65	69	274	2,467.50
Christophe Brazillier	70	67	69	68	274	2,467.50
Francois Calmels	71	66	67	70	274	2,467.50
Jean Pierre Cixous	66	68	70	70	274	2,467.50
Tiago Cruz	69	70	70	65	274	2,467.50
Tim Dykes	71	69	67	67	274	2,467.50
Michael McGeady	70	68	69	67	274	2,467.50
John E. Morgan	70	71	68	65	274	2,467.50
Tyrone Ferreira	70	70	69	67	276	1,703.33
Jeppe Huldahl	71	70	67	68	276	1,703.33
Anthony Snobeck	70	68	71	67	276	1,703.33
Rob Harris	73	69	68	67	277	1,386
Daniel Wardrop	71	71	66	69	277	1,386
Andrew Butterfield	67	71	70	70	278	1,274
Robert Coles	69	73	68	68	278	1,274
Ben Evans	69	70	69	70	278	1,274
Cesar Monasterio	71	71	71	65	278	1,274
Simon Robinson	70	66	70	72	278	1,274
Alexandre Rocha	69	69	64	76	278	1,274

Scottish Challenge

Macdonald Cardrona Hotel Golf & Country Club,
Cardrona, Scotland
Par 36-35–71; 6,937 yards

June 26-29
purse, €221,298

	SCORES				TOTAL	MONEY
Taco Remkes	68	70	67	66	271	€35,200
Seve Benson	68	68	72	68	276	19,800

	SCORES				TOTAL	MONEY
Jeppe Huldahl	71	65	68	72	276	19,800
Matthew Morris	67	68	71	71	277	13,200
Andrew Willey	72	68	69	69	278	11,000
Anders Schmidt Hansen	71	68	69	71	279	6,820
Greig Hutcheon	67	69	73	70	279	6,820
Jan-Are Larsen	70	69	74	66	279	6,820
Bernd Wiesberger	74	65	71	69	279	6,820
David Higgins	71	68	70	71	280	4,473.33
Marcus Higley	75	67	70	68	280	4,473.33
Edward Rush	72	69	71	68	280	4,473.33
Jean-Nicolas Billot	71	72	70	68	281	3,850
Klas Eriksson	67	69	71	74	281	3,850
Robert Coles	70	73	70	69	282	3,190
Tyrone Ferreira	69	66	74	73	282	3,190
Estanislao Goya	68	72	71	71	282	3,190
*Scott Henry	70	72	67	73	282	
James Morrison	74	68	68	72	282	3,190
Jordi Garcia	73	70	71	69	283	2,284.33
Mark Haastrup	71	69	72	71	283	2,284.33
David Horsey	69	70	73	71	283	2,284.33
Craig Lee	70	70	74	69	283	2,284.33
Michele Reale	70	70	72	71	283	2,284.33
Alessandro Tadini	69	74	70	70	283	2,284.33

AGF-Allianz EurOpen de Lyon

Golf du Gouverneur, Monthieux, France
Par 36-36–72; 7,084 yards

July 3-6
purse, €203,300

	SCORES				TOTAL	MONEY
David Horsey	65	68	68	65	266	€32,000
Marcus Higley	68	66	65	68	267	22,000
Carlos Del Moral	67	64	71	66	268	13,000
Bernd Wiesberger	65	69	68	66	268	13,000
Raphael De Sousa	66	69	64	70	269	9,000
John E. Morgan	67	65	66	71	269	9,000
Gary Clark	70	66	64	70	270	5,300
Julien Clement	69	68	66	67	270	5,300
Chris Gane	63	66	71	70	270	5,300
Gareth Maybin	69	64	70	67	270	5,300
Matthew Cort	71	67	64	69	271	3,800
Klas Eriksson	67	71	66	67	271	3,800
Jamie Little	66	73	65	67	271	3,800
Andrew Butterfield	64	70	68	70	272	3,100
Colm Moriarty	66	66	71	69	272	3,100
Alexandre Rocha	70	68	68	66	272	3,100
Alessandro Tadini	66	66	69	71	272	3,100
Nicolas Colsaerts	70	67	66	70	273	2,325
Thomas Feyrsinger	67	70	68	68	273	2,325
Estanislao Goya	69	68	64	72	273	2,325
Jan-Are Larsen	65	69	67	72	273	2,325
Liam Bond	73	64	66	71	274	1,880
Gary Boyd	68	67	71	68	274	1,880
Adam Gee	68	69	65	72	274	1,880
Matthew Morris	67	69	68	70	274	1,880
Richard Treis	67	71	68	68	274	1,880

Credit Suisse Challenge

Wylihof Golf Club, Luterbach, Switzerland
Par 36-37–73; 7,202 yards

July 10-13
purse, €142,968

		SCORES			TOTAL	MONEY
Rafael Cabrera Bello	67	64	68	68	267	€22,400
Gary Lockerbie	69	67	65	68	269	15,400
Lorenzo Gagli	70	69	65	69	273	9,100
Santiago Luna	68	66	69	70	273	9,100
Julien Clement	67	69	69	69	274	6,300
Chris Gane	69	68	69	68	274	6,300
Joel Sjoholm	65	70	70	70	275	4,480
Eirik Tage Johansen	71	69	69	67	276	3,920
Richard Bland	68	67	69	74	278	3,220
Alexandre Rocha	73	69	68	68	278	3,220
Carlos Del Moral	69	73	67	70	279	2,590
Peter Gustafsson	69	74	68	68	279	2,590
Michele Reale	71	69	68	71	279	2,590
Simon Robinson	72	66	72	69	279	2,590
Scott Jamieson	67	72	74	67	280	2,030
Mikko Korhonen	68	71	70	71	280	2,030
Roland Steiner	70	71	67	72	280	2,030
Alan Wagner	71	67	68	74	280	2,030
Johan Axgren	70	70	71	70	281	1,481.20
Christophe Brazillier	69	71	72	69	281	1,481.20
Francois Calmels	70	73	67	71	281	1,481.20
Andrew McArthur	69	73	70	69	281	1,481.20
Steen Ottosen	73	67	71	70	281	1,481.20
Gary Clark	72	70	70	70	282	1,260
Rolf Muntz	72	69	71	70	282	1,260
David Park	69	67	69	77	282	1,260
Christian Reimbold	77	64	70	71	282	1,260
Bernd Wiesberger	70	69	71	72	282	1,260

MAN NO Open

Golfclub Adamstal, Ramsau, Austria
Par 36-34–70; 6,476 yards

July 17-20
purse, €142,310

		SCORES			TOTAL	MONEY
Andre Bossert	65	65	69	66	265	€22,400
Markus Brier	65	68	66	66	265	15,400
(Bossert defeated Brier on first playoff hole.)						
Klas Eriksson	66	70	63	67	266	9,800
Thomas Feyrsinger	70	63	70	66	269	6,370
Taco Remkes	68	70	66	65	269	6,370
Alessandro Tadini	68	66	67	68	269	6,370
Mark Tullo	68	68	69	64	269	6,370
Jamie Little	66	66	73	65	270	3,640
Andrew Marshall	69	67	65	69	270	3,640
Tiago Cruz	67	69	68	67	271	2,940
Tim Dykes	68	67	69	67	271	2,940
Anders Schmidt Hansen	67	65	70	70	272	2,450
Greig Hutcheon	72	65	67	68	272	2,450
Julien Quesne	69	67	69	67	272	2,450
Bernd Wiesberger	69	66	68	69	272	2,450
Christophe Brazillier	71	69	68	65	273	2,030
Joonas Granberg	67	66	67	73	273	2,030
Stuart Davis	70	68	67	69	274	1,576.40

	SCORES				TOTAL	MONEY
Bruno-Teva Lecuona	72	65	69	68	274	1,576.40
Andrew McArthur	72	66	72	64	274	1,576.40
George Murray	69	65	69	71	274	1,576.40
Michele Reale	68	68	69	69	274	1,576.40
Joakim Haeggman	69	66	72	68	275	1,330
Joel Sjoholm	71	68	69	67	275	1,330
Niels Kraaij	66	70	69	71	276	1,232
Ally Mellor	66	71	73	66	276	1,232
Christian Reimbold	69	66	70	71	276	1,232
Roland Steiner	67	71	68	70	276	1,232
Neil Walker	66	68	75	67	276	1,232

SWALEC Wales Challenge

Vale Hotel Golf & Spa Resort, Cardiff,
Vale of Glamorgan, Wales
Par 36-36–72; 7,266 yards

July 24-27
purse, €144,116

	SCORES				TOTAL	MONEY
Michael McGeady	71	74	71	68	284	€22,400
Joel Sjoholm	70	71	71	72	284	15,400
(McGeady defeated Sjoholm on second playoff hole.)						
Gareth Maybin	74	71	71	69	285	9,100
Bjorn Pettersson	69	73	73	70	285	9,100
Ian Garbutt	71	71	71	73	286	5,693.33
Greig Hutcheon	71	70	74	71	286	5,693.33
James Morrison	74	71	74	67	286	5,693.33
Olivier David	78	69	73	67	287	3,453.33
John Mellor	70	70	72	75	287	3,453.33
Marco Soffietti	71	73	73	70	287	3,453.33
Johan Axgren	76	69	72	71	288	2,380
Rafael Cabrera Bello	71	74	72	71	288	2,380
Daniel Gaunt	74	70	71	73	288	2,380
Joakim Haeggman	75	72	72	69	288	2,380
Jeppe Huldahl	75	72	71	70	288	2,380
Steven Jeppesen	71	73	75	69	288	2,380
Inder Van Weerelt	71	75	72	70	288	2,380
Barry Austin	73	71	74	71	289	1,537.67
Gary Clark	73	70	73	73	289	1,537.67
Marcus Higley	70	76	75	68	289	1,537.67
Tim Milford	74	73	71	71	289	1,537.67
George Murray	71	74	73	71	289	1,537.67
Marius Thorp	71	71	74	73	289	1,537.67
Mark Haastrup	75	69	76	70	290	1,288
Eirik Tage Johansen	72	73	74	71	290	1,288
Bernd Wiesberger	74	73	73	70	290	1,288

Challenge of Ireland

Glasson Golf Hotel & Country Club, Athlone, Ireland
Par 36-36–72; 7,159 yards

July 31-August 3
purse, €154,125

	SCORES				TOTAL	MONEY
Andrew Tampion	71	71	71	67	280	€24,000
Richard Bland	68	69	72	72	281	13,500
David Drysdale	67	74	69	71	281	13,500
Jonas Blixt	70	75	66	71	282	6,300

	SCORES				TOTAL	MONEY
Carlos Del Moral	70	71	71	70	282	6,300
Marcus Higley	71	72	66	73	282	6,300
Richie Ramsay	66	70	72	74	282	6,300
Gareth Shaw	69	71	73	69	282	6,300
Rhys Davies	70	75	71	67	283	3,300
Estanislao Goya	65	75	74	69	283	3,300
Gareth Maybin	70	73	73	67	283	3,300
Tiago Cruz	67	72	77	68	284	2,400
Ian Garbutt	74	70	71	69	284	2,400
Craig Lee	67	72	75	70	284	2,400
Gary Lockerbie	69	75	72	68	284	2,400
Andrew McArthur	72	71	72	69	284	2,400
Richard McEvoy	71	73	71	69	284	2,400
Mark D. Smith	70	72	72	70	284	2,400
David Carter	74	68	75	68	285	1,587
Raphael De Sousa	69	74	73	69	285	1,587
Peter Gustafsson	75	68	66	76	285	1,587
Steven Jeppesen	67	73	73	72	285	1,587
Mark Tullo	72	71	72	70	285	1,587
Mark Haastrup	69	72	73	72	286	1,380
Colm Moriarty	67	70	74	75	286	1,380
Simon Thornton	71	73	68	74	286	1,380

Lexus Open

Moss & Rygge Golf Club, Dilling, Norway
Par 37-35–72; 7,050 yards

August 7-10
purse, €152,475

	SCORES				TOTAL	MONEY
Jeppe Huldahl	66	68	68	69	271	€24,000
Steven O'Hara	68	69	68	68	273	16,500
Richard Bland	68	70	64	72	274	9,750
Alessandro Tadini	69	67	69	69	274	9,750
Jaakko Makitalo	70	67	68	70	275	7,500
Gary Boyd	69	70	71	66	276	5,000
Peter Gustafsson	68	68	73	67	276	5,000
Johan Skold	69	70	68	69	276	5,000
Tiago Cruz	69	69	72	68	278	3,090
*Anders Kristiansen	66	71	70	71	278	
George Murray	69	68	72	69	278	3,090
Paul Nilbrink	68	67	72	71	278	3,090
Gareth Shaw	68	71	67	72	278	3,090
Mark Tullo	67	70	69	72	278	3,090
Raphael De Sousa	68	69	71	71	279	2,400
Adam Gee	64	73	72	70	279	2,400
Branden Grace	68	71	71	69	279	2,400
Matthew Bliss	69	68	70	73	280	1,950
*Knut Borsheim	71	68	70	71	280	
Fredrik Henge	68	69	71	72	280	1,950
Benjamin Miarka	70	67	72	71	280	1,950
Ally Mellor	70	69	71	71	281	1,612.50
Johan Wahlqvist	70	67	71	73	281	1,612.50
Gareth Davies	69	68	77	68	282	1,395
Rob Harris	69	69	71	73	282	1,395
Oskar Henningsson	66	69	74	73	282	1,395
Lasse Jensen	69	70	70	73	282	1,395
Christian Nilsson	67	71	74	70	282	1,395
Ben St. John	70	71	70	71	282	1,395

Trophee du Golf Club de Geneve

Golf Club de Geneve, Geneva, Switzerland   August 14-17
Par 36-36–72; 6,727 yards   purse, €178,000

	SCORES				TOTAL	MONEY
Klas Eriksson	68	70	73	63	274	€24,400
Wil Besseling	68	64	67	75	274	15,050
Alexandre Rocha	72	66	66	70	274	15,050
(Eriksson defeated Rocha on third and Besseling on fourth playoff hole.)						
Steven O'Hara	68	66	72	70	276	10,000
Gary Lockerbie	68	70	69	70	277	7,900
Marco Ruiz	70	67	71	69	277	7,900
Richard Bland	65	70	69	74	278	6,300
Gareth Maybin	72	68	71	67	278	6,300
Greig Hutcheon	72	67	71	69	279	5,250
Andrew Tampion	66	69	72	72	279	5,250
Rafael Cabrera Bello	66	70	69	75	280	4,475
David Horsey	72	70	69	69	280	4,475
Simon Robinson	71	70	69	71	281	4,150
Joakim Haeggman	74	66	71	71	282	3,750
Michael Hoey	69	73	69	71	282	3,750
Inder Van Weerelt	70	70	69	73	282	3,750
Marcus Higley	69	69	72	74	284	3,350
Seve Benson	67	73	70	75	285	3,150

Vodafone Challenge

Golf Club An der Elfrather Muhle, Dusseldorf, Germany   August 14-17
Par 36-36–72; 6,859 yards   purse, €142,968

	SCORES				TOTAL	MONEY
Richie Ramsay	65	70	69	68	272	€22,400
*Stephan Gross, Jr.	68	66	69	70	273	
George Murray	67	69	68	69	273	15,400
Lars Brovold	70	69	65	71	275	9,800
Jesus Maria Arruti	69	69	71	68	277	7,700
Chris Gane	68	69	69	71	277	7,700
Liam Bond	72	71	66	69	278	4,088
Michiel Bothma	70	69	66	73	278	4,088
Branden Grace	71	69	69	69	278	4,088
Jaakko Makitalo	69	72	68	69	278	4,088
Paul Nilbrink	70	71	69	68	278	4,088
Pablo Del Grosso	69	74	66	70	279	2,660
Colm Moriarty	69	71	70	69	279	2,660
Anthony Snobeck	69	68	69	73	279	2,660
Julien Clement	69	70	73	68	280	2,100
Carlos Del Moral	65	73	71	71	280	2,100
Fredrik Henge	70	70	73	67	280	2,100
*Maximilian Kieffer	73	68	67	72	280	
Andrew Marshall	73	70	69	68	280	2,100
Eric Ramsay	72	72	69	67	280	2,100
Tiago Cruz	72	67	73	69	281	1,645
Soren Juul	68	68	72	73	281	1,645
Andrew Butterfield	69	75	69	69	282	1,344
Andrew Coltart	71	74	68	69	282	1,344
Anders Schmidt Hansen	70	71	67	74	282	1,344
Jurgen Maurer	75	70	69	68	282	1,344
John Mellor	75	70	70	67	282	1,344

Ypsilon Golf Challenge

Ypsilon Golf Resort, Liberec, Czech Republic
Par 35-36–71; 6,521 yards

August 21-24
purse, €184,212

	SCORES				TOTAL	MONEY
Seve Benson	67	66	65	70	268	€28,800
Rafael Cabrera Bello	67	64	65	72	268	16,200
Branden Grace	68	69	67	64	268	16,200
(Benson defeated Grace on second and Cabrera Bello on third playoff hole.)						
Gareth Maybin	66	66	67	70	269	9,900
Ricardo Santos	67	64	71	67	269	9,900
Robert Coles	68	67	68	67	270	6,480
Mikko Korhonen	66	68	70	66	270	6,480
Richard Bland	67	65	67	72	271	4,680
David Horsey	68	68	67	68	271	4,680
Lorenzo Gagli	66	66	73	67	272	3,555
Marcus Higley	65	71	66	70	272	3,555
Colm Moriarty	70	65	66	71	272	3,555
Taco Remkes	67	69	70	66	272	3,555
Antti Ahokas	67	69	67	70	273	2,610
David Carter	70	69	67	67	273	2,610
Thomas Feyrsinger	66	67	68	72	273	2,610
Peter Kaensche	68	70	68	67	273	2,610
John E. Morgan	68	70	67	68	273	2,610
Alexandre Rocha	66	68	72	67	273	2,610
Jaakko Makitalo	71	63	69	71	274	1,935
Joel Sjoholm	68	68	71	67	274	1,935
Adam Gee	67	69	71	68	275	1,692
Andrew Marshall	69	67	71	68	275	1,692
Marco Ruiz	71	68	69	67	275	1,692
Anthony Snobeck	68	65	67	75	275	1,692
Mark Tullo	69	68	69	69	275	1,692

ECCO Tour Championship

Kokkedal Golf Club, Copenhagen, Denmark
Par 36-36–72; 6,494 yards

August 28-31
purse, €186,966

	SCORES				TOTAL	MONEY
Antti Ahokas	67	69	65	70	271	€28,800
Wil Besseling	72	67	65	68	272	13,050
Eirik Tage Johansen	68	69	71	64	272	13,050
Roope Kakko	67	71	65	69	272	13,050
Taco Remkes	72	68	66	66	272	13,050
Steven Jeppesen	70	68	70	65	273	7,200
Mikko Korhonen	70	69	69	66	274	5,760
Liam Bond	70	68	67	70	275	4,440
Richard McEvoy	69	68	66	72	275	4,440
Julien Quesne	72	67	69	67	275	4,440
Gustav Adell	69	70	67	70	276	3,240
Raphael De Sousa	69	72	67	68	276	3,240
Anders Schmidt Hansen	70	67	70	69	276	3,240
Kasper Linnet Jorgensen	72	70	65	69	276	3,240
Mark Tullo	72	68	67	69	276	3,240
Fredrik Henge	66	70	70	71	277	2,430
Colm Moriarty	72	71	66	68	277	2,430
Christian Nilsson	73	69	67	68	277	2,430
Daniel Wardrop	72	68	68	69	277	2,430
Richie Ramsay	73	71	65	69	278	1,878

	SCORES				TOTAL	MONEY
Alexandre Rocha	69	72	64	73	278	1,878
Roland Steiner	69	72	68	69	278	1,878
Richard Bland	73	69	68	69	279	1,620
Rafael Cabrera Bello	73	68	67	71	279	1,620
Mark Haastrup	72	71	69	67	279	1,620
Joakim Haeggman	72	70	68	69	279	1,620
John E. Morgan	74	67	69	69	279	1,620
Magnus Persson	70	74	64	71	279	1,620
Mark D. Smith	73	71	69	66	279	1,620

The Dubliner Challenge

Hills Golf Club, Gothenburg, Sweden
Par 36-35–71; 7,169 yards
(Fourth round cancelled—rain.)

September 4-7
purse, €141,960

	SCORES			TOTAL	MONEY
Mark Haastrup	70	68	68	206	€22,400
Benjamin Miarka	70	70	67	207	15,400
Gustav Andersson	70	72	68	210	9,800
Nicolas Vanhootegem	70	74	68	212	7,000
Fredrik Ohlsson	73	69	70	212	7,000
Rob Harris	68	70	74	212	7,000
Andreas Hogberg	73	71	69	213	3,710
Daniel Wardrop	71	72	70	213	3,710
Peter O'Keeffe	70	72	71	213	3,710
Pablo Del Grosso	73	67	73	213	3,710
Sebastien Delagrange	71	75	68	214	2,660
Peter Gustafsson	72	73	69	214	2,660
Fredrik Orest	69	73	72	214	2,660
Seve Benson	79	70	66	215	2,030
Gustavo Rojas	72	74	69	215	2,030
Johan Skold	71	73	71	215	2,030
Krister Eriksson	72	71	72	215	2,030
Ally Mellor	72	71	72	215	2,030
Erik Algulin	70	69	76	215	2,030
Robert Eriksson	74	73	69	216	1,388.33
Fredrik Henge	75	70	71	216	1,388.33
Dennis Edlund	72	72	72	216	1,388.33
Jens Fahrbring	72	72	72	216	1,388.33
Jonas Enander-Hedin	75	69	72	216	1,388.33
Toni Karjalainen	73	69	74	216	1,388.33

Qingdao Golf Open

Qingdao Huashan Golf & Resort, Qingdao, China
Par 36-36–72; 7,098 yards

September 11-14
purse, €355,215

	SCORES				TOTAL	MONEY
Gareth Maybin	62	67	72	68	269	€56,049.75
Klas Eriksson	71	70	69	65	275	23,120.52
David Horsey	67	69	69	70	275	23,120.52
Gary Lockerbie	71	68	66	70	275	23,120.52
Richie Ramsay	67	69	70	69	275	23,120.52
Roland Steiner	70	71	69	65	275	23,120.52
Lars Brovold	65	71	71	69	276	9,808.71
Michael McGeady	71	70	68	67	276	9,808.71

	SCORES				TOTAL	MONEY
Julien Quesne	68	66	71	71	276	9,808.71
Alfredo Garcia-Heredia	70	71	67	69	277	7,356.53
John E. Morgan	69	71	71	66	277	7,356.53
Estanislao Goya	70	68	72	68	278	6,480.75
Joel Sjoholm	69	72	70	67	278	6,480.75
Rafael Cabrera Bello	68	73	71	67	279	5,429.82
Francois Calmels	67	70	72	70	279	5,429.82
David Drysdale	70	71	69	69	279	5,429.82
Andrew McArthur	71	70	69	69	279	5,429.82
Richard Bland	71	68	74	67	280	4,262.12
Gary Clark	70	73	68	69	280	4,262.12
Cesar Monasterio	68	68	71	73	280	4,262.12
Raphael De Sousa	68	73	70	70	281	3,362.99
Carlos Del Moral	76	67	68	70	281	3,362.99
Mark Haastrup	70	68	72	71	281	3,362.99
Kasper Linnet Jorgensen	70	71	69	71	281	3,362.99
Gregory Molteni	67	68	72	74	281	3,362.99

Kazakhstan Open

Nurtau Golf Club, Almaty, Kazakhstan
Par 36-36–72; 7,319 yards

September 18-21
purse, €438,127

	SCORES				TOTAL	MONEY
Gary Lockerbie	68	69	66	70	273	€68,800
Stuart Davis	68	71	69	67	275	47,300
Steven O'Hara	66	68	70	72	276	27,950
Alessandro Tadini	69	66	74	67	276	27,950
Chris Gane	72	65	71	70	278	17,486.67
David Horsey	69	65	72	72	278	17,486.67
Alexandre Rocha	67	70	72	69	278	17,486.67
Matthew Morris	68	72	69	70	279	12,040
David Drysdale	68	71	70	71	280	10,320
Alfredo Garcia-Heredia	72	68	72	69	281	8,492.50
Adam Gee	67	71	74	69	281	8,492.50
Gregory Molteni	67	70	71	73	281	8,492.50
Colm Moriarty	67	72	71	71	281	8,492.50
Robert Coles	70	72	71	69	282	7,095
Nicolas Vanhootegem	67	69	72	74	282	7,095
Jonas Blixt	69	68	73	73	283	6,020
Liam Bond	68	71	69	75	283	6,020
Ricardo Santos	71	71	71	70	283	6,020
Wil Besseling	69	71	75	69	284	4,392.14
Peter Kaensche	69	73	72	70	284	4,392.14
Jan-Are Larsen	69	70	73	72	284	4,392.14
Richard McEvoy	68	70	75	71	284	4,392.14
Julien Quesne	72	69	70	73	284	4,392.14
Marco Ruiz	70	69	74	71	284	4,392.14
Richard Treis	71	68	68	77	284	4,392.14

The Dutch Futures

Golfclub Houtrak, Netherlands
Par 36-36–72; 6,996 yards

September 25-28
purse, €142,646

		SCORES			TOTAL	MONEY
Taco Remkes	72	68	69	66	275	€22,400
Jeppe Huldahl	73	69	68	65	275	15,400
(Remkes defeated Huldahl on first playoff hole.)						
Marcus Higley	71	68	71	66	276	9,800
Chris Gane	71	66	70	70	277	7,700
Matthew Morris	71	69	68	69	277	7,700
Andrew Butterfield	74	68	69	67	278	4,088
Michael Hoey	69	69	68	72	278	4,088
Richard McEvoy	75	68	66	69	278	4,088
Ralph Miller	68	72	69	69	278	4,088
Andrew Tampion	71	66	71	70	278	4,088
Ryan Blaum	73	68	68	70	279	2,450
Robert Coles	71	74	66	68	279	2,450
Stuart Davis	70	70	68	71	279	2,450
Ben Evans	69	72	67	71	279	2,450
Roland Steiner	70	69	71	69	279	2,450
Inder Van Weerelt	72	69	69	69	279	2,450
Christophe Brazillier	75	65	70	70	280	1,820
Sebastien Delagrange	70	70	69	71	280	1,820
Andrew McArthur	73	67	73	67	280	1,820
Christian Aronsen	73	69	67	72	281	1,370
Adrien Bernadet	72	73	67	69	281	1,370
Wil Besseling	70	73	66	72	281	1,370
Chris Doak	70	71	70	70	281	1,370
Joakim Haeggman	72	71	70	68	281	1,370
Richie Ramsay	71	72	74	64	281	1,370
Marco Soffietti	73	69	71	68	281	1,370

AGF-Allianz Golf Open Grand Toulouse

Golf de Toulouse-Seilh, Seilh, France
Par 36-36–72; 6,924 yards

October 2-5
purse, €142,968

		SCORES			TOTAL	MONEY
Richie Ramsay	67	70	64	68	269	€22,400
Richard McEvoy	69	70	65	67	271	15,400
Eirik Tage Johansen	68	71	66	68	273	9,800
Taco Remkes	67	69	70	68	274	8,400
Marcus Higley	69	69	70	67	275	4,573.33
Michael Hoey	71	71	68	65	275	4,573.33
Andrew McArthur	69	68	69	69	275	4,573.33
Steven O'Hara	65	70	70	70	275	4,573.33
Miguel Rodriguez	70	65	69	71	275	4,573.33
Roland Steiner	68	70	67	70	275	4,573.33
Marco Ruiz	66	69	71	70	276	2,730
Marco Soffietti	69	65	70	72	276	2,730
Christophe Brazillier	68	73	69	67	277	2,450
Matthew Morris	67	71	67	72	277	2,450
Michael McGeady	70	73	67	68	278	2,170
George Murray	65	72	75	66	278	2,170
Francois Calmels	69	69	69	72	279	1,598
Robert Coles	64	72	72	71	279	1,598
Gareth Davies	71	71	68	69	279	1,598
Chris Gane	72	68	68	71	279	1,598

	SCORES				TOTAL	MONEY
Ian Garbutt	70	69	68	72	279	1,598
Mikko Korhonen	71	68	69	71	279	1,598
Benjamin Miarka	70	71	70	68	279	1,598
Graeme Clark	71	70	68	71	280	1,246
David Horsey	71	69	70	70	280	1,246
Roope Kakko	69	73	65	73	280	1,246
John E. Morgan	66	73	70	71	280	1,246
Bjorn Pettersson	70	73	68	69	280	1,246
Andrew Tampion	73	70	69	68	280	1,246

Margara Diehl-Ako Platinum Open

Golf Club Margara, Margara, Italy
Par 36-36–72

October 15-18
purse, €163,024

	SCORES				TOTAL	MONEY
Taco Remkes	69	63	65	73	270	€25,600
Roope Kakko	66	68	65	71	270	17,600
(Remkes defeated Kakko on first playoff hole.)						
Christian Nilsson	65	66	70	70	271	11,200
Liam Bond	66	67	68	71	272	8,800
David Horsey	71	63	66	72	272	8,800
Marco Crespi	71	67	66	69	273	5,333.33
Matteo Delpodio	65	71	71	66	273	5,333.33
Estanislao Goya	69	70	65	69	273	5,333.33
Rafael Cabrera Bello	70	71	69	64	274	3,680
Alessandro Tadini	69	69	66	70	274	3,680
Klas Eriksson	70	70	68	67	275	3,040
Ben Mason	68	70	68	69	275	3,040
Richard McEvoy	71	65	68	71	275	3,040
Alessio Bruschi	68	67	72	69	276	2,720
Steve Alker	69	72	67	69	277	2,400
Nicola Maestroni	70	69	66	72	277	2,400
Steven O'Hara	70	67	69	71	277	2,400
Chris Gane	71	69	68	70	278	1,721.14
Adam Gee	71	67	69	71	278	1,721.14
Mikko Korhonen	70	69	69	70	278	1,721.14
Jan-Are Larsen	69	69	69	71	278	1,721.14
James Morrison	70	68	72	68	278	1,721.14
Marco Ruiz	67	72	67	72	278	1,721.14
Inder Van Weerelt	69	68	68	73	278	1,721.14
Andre Bossert	72	65	67	75	279	1,360
Gary Clark	71	70	68	70	279	1,360
Olivier David	70	67	71	71	279	1,360
Branden Grace	71	68	70	70	279	1,360
Peter Kaensche	71	65	72	71	279	1,360
Gary Lockerbie	68	68	71	72	279	1,360
Richie Ramsay	72	69	71	67	279	1,360
Lloyd Saltman	68	69	74	68	279	1,360

Apulia San Domenico Grand Final

San Domenico Golf Club, Puglia, Italy   October 22-25
Par 34-37–71; 7,031 yards   purse, €280,000

	SCORES				TOTAL	MONEY
Estanislao Goya	67	69	65	66	267	€48,000
Richard Bland	67	66	67	68	268	24,950
John E. Morgan	66	73	61	68	268	24,950
Rafael Cabrera Bello	66	66	69	68	269	14,350
Alexandre Rocha	68	65	68	69	270	12,200
Jeppe Huldahl	70	66	66	69	271	11,180
David Horsey	69	67	68	68	272	10,270
Gary Clark	67	66	72	68	273	9,115
Marco Ruiz	71	67	67	68	273	9,115
Mikko Korhonen	69	66	69	70	274	7,750
Andrew McArthur	67	65	69	73	274	7,750
Gary Lockerbie	70	68	69	68	275	6,490
Julien Quesne	68	67	68	72	275	6,490
Chris Gane	68	71	66	71	276	5,600
Antti Ahokas	70	70	67	70	277	4,322.50
Marcus Higley	71	70	69	67	277	4,322.50
Taco Remkes	70	69	68	70	277	4,322.50
Bernd Wiesberger	66	68	70	73	277	4,322.50
Robert Coles	72	70	68	68	278	3,337.50
Branden Grace	65	73	70	70	278	3,337.50
Gareth Maybin	67	70	68	73	278	3,337.50
Steven O'Hara	70	68	69	71	278	3,337.50
Liam Bond	70	70	70	69	279	3,050
Stuart Davis	71	69	69	71	280	2,900
Klas Eriksson	71	71	69	69	280	2,900

Asian Tour

Emaar-MGF Indian Masters

Delhi Golf Club, New Delhi, India
Par 36-36–72; 7,014 yards

February 7-10
purse, US$2,500,000

	SCORES				TOTAL	MONEY
S.S.P. Chowrasia	70	71	71	67	279	US$416,660
Damien McGrane	67	69	75	70	281	277,770
Jose Manuel Lara	68	72	71	72	283	156,500
Raphael Jacquelin	69	69	72	74	284	115,500
Digvijay Singh	70	70	74	70	284	115,500
Maarten Lafeber	69	71	73	72	285	66,200
Ross McGowan	72	71	70	72	285	66,200
Thomas Bjorn	68	72	74	71	285	66,200
Gaurav Ghei	75	69	70	71	285	66,200
Ernie Els	75	70	69	71	285	66,200
Soren Kjeldsen	74	71	75	66	286	46,000
Graeme McDowell	69	69	73	76	287	40,500
Hendrik Buhrmann	69	69	75	74	287	40,500
Brendan Jones	74	68	76	69	287	40,500
Arjun Atwal	70	70	72	76	288	34,500
Benn Barham	69	71	74	74	288	34,500
Henrik Nystrom	70	71	74	73	288	34,500
Jean-Baptiste Gonnet	71	73	75	69	288	34,500
Mark O'Meara	69	73	74	73	289	30,000
Martin Wiegele	75	68	73	73	289	30,000
Scott Hend	71	74	73	71	289	30,000
Ross Bain	71	71	72	76	290	26,000
Jyoti Randhawa	65	77	75	73	290	26,000
Oliver Fisher	73	71	73	73	290	26,000
David Lynn	69	75	74	72	290	26,000
Peter Baker	73	71	74	72	290	26,000
Robert-Jan Derksen	74	72	73	71	290	26,000
Christian Cevaer	71	75	74	70	290	26,000
Unho Park	71	72	76	72	291	22,250
Sam Little	70	75	74	72	291	22,250
Adam Groom	72	73	74	72	291	22,250
Simon Yates	70	74	72	76	292	20,000
Mikael Lundberg	71	68	79	74	292	20,000
Simon Wakefield	74	68	78	72	292	20,000
Mark Brown	71	75	71	76	293	18,250
Amandeep Johl	73	71	76	73	293	18,250
Prayad Marksaeng	74	73	78	68	293	18,250
Randhir Singh Ghotra	74	73	70	77	294	16,000
Marcus Fraser	73	69	76	76	294	16,000
Alexander Noren	72	74	75	73	294	16,000
Scott Barr	73	73	75	73	294	16,000
Shiv Kapur	68	78	76	72	294	16,000
Keith Horne	70	73	80	71	294	16,000
Simon Khan	70	75	73	77	295	13,500
Prom Meesawat	71	74	76	74	295	13,500
C. Muniyappa	69	77	77	72	295	13,500
Fabrizio Zanotti	71	76	77	71	295	13,500
Joakim Haeggman	74	69	73	80	296	10,750
Stephen Gallacher	71	72	74	79	296	10,750
Phillip Archer	74	69	76	77	296	10,750
Leif Westerberg	73	71	75	77	296	10,750
Jarmo Sandelin	73	70	77	76	296	10,750

	SCORES				TOTAL	MONEY
Magnus A. Carlsson	70	76	75	75	296	10,750
Shamim Khan	73	74	76	73	296	10,750
Andrew Coltart	76	69	71	81	297	8,500
Ashok Kumar	72	73	75	77	297	8,500
Adam Blyth	74	71	71	82	298	7,500
Suk Jong-yul	70	74	80	74	298	7,500
Carlos Rodiles	74	70	81	73	298	7,500
Jose-Filipe Lima	72	71	79	77	299	7,000
Ali Sher	77	70	78	75	300	6,750
Alvaro Quiros	69	75	76	81	301	6,500
Darren Clarke	72	69	79	82	302	6,250
Harmeet Kahlon	70	75	83	75	303	5,875
Richard Finch	67	77	85	74	303	5,875
Airil Rizman	74	72	81	77	304	5,500
Rahul Ganapathy	76	71	78	84	309	5,250
Anthony Kang	72	72	82	84	310	5,000
Lee Sung	75	72	75	89	311	4,750
Emanuele Canonica	72	71	77		WD	

Enjoy Jakarta Astro Indonesia Open

Cengkareng Golf Club, Jakarta, Indonesia
Par 36-34–70; 6,399 yards

February 14-17
purse, US$1,200,000

	SCORES				TOTAL	MONEY
Felipe Aguilar	65	62	67	68	262	US$200,000
Jeev Milkha Singh	65	66	65	67	263	133,330
Prom Meesawat	66	63	68	67	264	67,560
James Kamte	62	67	68	67	264	67,560
Joost Luiten	64	69	66	66	265	46,440
Mark Brown	67	66	66	66	265	46,440
Jyoti Randhawa	68	70	66	62	266	30,960
Wang Ter-chang	69	64	66	67	266	30,960
Liang Wen-chong	65	67	64	70	266	30,960
Chris Rodgers	68	68	67	64	267	22,240
Bae Sang-moon	71	68	63	65	267	22,240
Arjun Atwal	67	67	66	67	267	22,240
Mikael Lundberg	71	68	65	64	268	18,840
Philip Golding	65	70	65	68	268	18,840
Simon Yates	70	68	68	63	269	16,560
Paul McGinley	68	69	66	66	269	16,560
Jason Knutzon	68	68	67	66	269	16,560
Adam Blyth	66	67	67	69	269	16,560
Tony Carolan	71	67	66	66	270	14,640
Gary Simpson	68	68	67	67	270	14,640
Darren Clarke	68	67	70	66	271	13,380
Chinnarat Phadungsil	69	64	68	70	271	13,380
Chapchai Nirat	69	66	66	70	271	13,380
Prayad Marksaeng	65	65	69	72	271	13,380
Chris Gane	68	66	71	67	272	10,860
Jean Van de Velde	67	71	67	67	272	10,860
Peter Whiteford	68	67	69	68	272	10,860
Simon Griffiths	68	68	68	68	272	10,860
Scott Strange	66	72	66	68	272	10,860
Rhys Davies	66	69	68	69	272	10,860
Warren Bennett	68	70	65	69	272	10,860
Oliver Fisher	67	68	67	70	272	10,860
Scott Hend	66	68	68	70	272	10,860
Martin Wiegele	65	65	70	72	272	10,860
Matthew Millar	70	69	68	66	273	8,520

	SCORES				TOTAL	MONEY
Robert Rock	68	68	70	67	273	8,520
Lee Sung	70	66	70	67	273	8,520
Thomas Aiken	66	70	68	69	273	8,520
Robert Dinwiddie	69	66	67	71	273	8,520
David Bransdon	64	74	69	67	274	7,440
Andrew Coltart	67	72	68	67	274	7,440
Edoardo Molinari	66	73	67	68	274	7,440
Gaurav Ghei	71	67	67	69	274	7,440
Gerald Rosales	67	68	72	68	275	6,240
David Horsey	70	68	69	68	275	6,240
Julio Zapata	69	70	67	69	275	6,240
Sion E. Bebb	69	68	68	70	275	6,240
Shiv Kapur	69	67	69	70	275	6,240
Stuart Manley	69	66	69	71	275	6,240
Scott Barr	66	71	71	68	276	4,793
Peter Baker	68	71	69	68	276	4,793
Mikko Ilonen	66	68	71	71	276	4,793
Kyron Sullivan	65	68	72	71	276	4,793
Angelo Que	67	67	70	72	276	4,793
Thaworn Wiratchant	67	67	67	75	276	4,793
Unho Park	67	72	73	65	277	3,435
Luis Claverie	68	69	74	66	277	3,435
Kane Webber	72	67	71	67	277	3,435
Taichiro Kiyota	71	67	71	68	277	3,435
Lu Wen-teh	70	69	69	69	277	3,435
Maan Nasim	68	70	70	69	277	3,435
Fabrizio Zanotti	65	74	66	72	277	3,435
Antonio Lascuna	68	71	64	74	277	3,435
Steven Jeppesen	71	66	71	70	278	2,820
Liam Bond	67	71	71	69	278	2,820
Rafael Cabrera Bello	69	69	73	68	279	2,520
Adam Groom	69	70	71	69	279	2,520
David Dixon	69	68	72	70	279	2,520
Alan McLean	72	67	73	68	280	2,090
Eddie Lee	67	72	70	71	280	2,090
Iain Steel	71	68	68	73	280	2,090
Mitsuhiro Tateyama	70	69	76	66	281	1,793
Richard Bland	69	70	69	73	281	1,793
Marcus Both	66	72	70	74	282	1,787
Airil Rizman	69	70	71	73	283	1,780
Mattias Eliasson	69	69	69	76	283	1,780
Ben Mason	70	68	72	74	284	1,773
*A. Suprapto	67	71	68	78	284	
A. Ilyasyak	71	66	75	73	285	1,769
Denny Supriadi	67	70	77	73	287	1,765

SAIL Open

Jaypee Greens Golf Resort, Noida, India
Par 36-36–72; 7,347 yards

February 20-23
purse, US$400,000

	SCORES				TOTAL	MONEY
Mark Brown	69	69	67	69	274	US$63,400
Noh Seung-yul	68	70	71	69	278	29,173
Jyoti Randhawa	67	68	72	71	278	29,173
Scott Hend	67	70	69	72	278	29,173
Gaganjeet Bhullar	70	68	69	72	279	14,980
Danny Chia	68	70	69	72	279	14,980
Ross Bain	66	71	75	68	280	9,590
Guido van der Valk	72	67	73	68	280	9,590

	SCORES				TOTAL	MONEY
Kane Webber	70	70	68	72	280	9,590
Adam Groom	67	71	69	73	280	9,590
Kodai Ichihara	70	71	72	68	281	6,760
Ashok Kumar	70	69	71	71	281	6,760
Mardan Mamat	71	69	69	72	281	6,760
Lam Chih Bing	67	74	73	69	283	5,760
Tony Carolan	66	69	75	73	283	5,760
Rhys Davies	70	69	67	77	283	5,760
Zaw Moe	72	72	70	70	284	4,880
Lloyd Saltman	70	75	66	73	284	4,880
Angelo Que	68	70	72	74	284	4,880
Wang Ter-chang	69	67	73	75	284	4,880
Richard Lee	72	69	69	74	284	4,880
Atthaphon Prathummanee	72	70	73	70	285	4,080
Mukesh Kumar	72	73	71	69	285	4,080
Yasin Ali	69	72	73	71	285	4,080
Harinder Gupta	69	70	73	73	285	4,080
Adam Blyth	71	71	69	74	285	4,080
Neven Basic	70	69	72	74	285	4,080
Peter Cooke	67	72	71	75	285	4,080

Johnnie Walker Classic

DLF Golf & Country Club, New Delhi, India
Par 36-36–72; 7,156 yards

February 28-March 2
purse, US$2,500,000

	SCORES				TOTAL	MONEY
Mark Brown	71	68	64	67	270	US$409,743
Taichiro Kiyota	68	67	67	71	273	183,325
Greg Chalmers	68	69	68	68	273	183,325
Scott Strange	71	67	68	67	273	183,325
Graeme Storm	70	66	69	69	274	88,014
Shiv Kapur	69	65	72	68	274	88,014
Johan Edfors	71	69	69	65	274	88,014
Jyoti Randhawa	70	65	68	72	275	61,462
Daniel Vancsik	67	71	68	70	276	52,120
Prayad Marksaeng	74	65	70	67	276	52,120
Jeev Milkha Singh	68	70	70	69	277	42,368
Scott Barr	71	70	67	69	277	42,368
Jose Manuel Lara	69	67	73	68	277	42,368
Lin Wen-tang	70	67	72	69	278	36,139
Soren Hansen	69	69	71	69	278	36,139
Marcus Fraser	71	68	71	68	278	36,139
Phillip Archer	72	64	69	74	279	29,317
Vijay Singh	70	68	69	72	279	29,317
Tony Carolan	71	69	68	71	279	29,317
Scott Laycock	72	68	68	71	279	29,317
Arjun Atwal	69	72	67	71	279	29,317
Kane Webber	73	69	66	71	279	29,317
Thaworn Wiratchant	71	70	68	70	279	29,317
Mark Foster	68	74	67	70	279	29,317
Adam Bland	69	68	71	72	280	24,093
Unho Park	68	66	75	71	280	24,093
Chris Rodgers	72	67	70	71	280	24,093
Gregory Havret	72	68	70	70	280	24,093
Miguel Angel Jimenez	75	67	72	66	280	24,093
Paul Sheehan	68	70	70	73	281	20,774
Rahil Gangjee	68	71	70	72	281	20,774
Adam Scott	68	68	74	71	281	20,774
Lee Won-joon	70	69	74	68	281	20,774

	SCORES				TOTAL	MONEY
Raphael Jacquelin	72	68	67	75	282	18,192
James Kamte	68	71	69	74	282	18,192
Simon Dyson	73	69	71	69	282	18,192
Robert Karlsson	71	70	73	68	282	18,192
Anthony Summers	69	71	70	73	283	15,734
Peter Lawrie	72	68	70	73	283	15,734
Simon Yates	71	71	68	73	283	15,734
Liang Wen-chong	69	71	71	72	283	15,734
Joost Luiten	73	67	71	72	283	15,734
Robert-Jan Derksen	68	72	72	71	283	15,734
Mukesh Kumar	73	69	67	75	284	13,275
Anton Haig	71	71	69	73	284	13,275
David Frost	72	69	71	72	284	13,275
Martin Erlandsson	70	72	72	70	284	13,275
Richard Finch	72	65	73	76	286	11,063
Oliver Wilson	72	68	71	75	286	11,063
Iain Steel	70	72	71	73	286	11,063
Adam Blyth	69	72	73	72	286	11,063
Marc Warren	73	69	72	72	286	11,063
Gavin Flint	73	68	68	78	287	8,604
Michael Long	70	69	73	75	287	8,604
Arjun Singh	69	70	73	75	287	8,604
Peter Hedblom	72	70	73	72	287	8,604
Terry Pilkadaris	74	68	73	72	287	8,604
Gaganjeet Bhullar	72	69	73	74	288	7,006
Mikko Ilonen	72	70	72	74	288	7,006
Keith Horne	72	70	72	74	288	7,006
Sam Walker	72	70	72	74	288	7,006
Prom Meesawat	70	72	73	75	290	6,392
Digvijay Singh	70	70	73	78	291	6,146
Rahul Ganapathy	73	69	74	77	293	5,900
Andrew Tampion	72	70	76	85	303	5,654
Gaurav Ghei	70	72			DQ	

Maybank Malaysian Open

Kota Permai Golf & Country Club, Kuala Lumpur, Malaysia
Par 36-36–72; 6,979 yards

March 6-9
purse, US$2,000,000

	SCORES				TOTAL	MONEY
Arjun Atwal	70	68	68	64	270	US$333,330
Peter Hedblom	66	68	65	71	270	222,220
(Atwal defeated Hedblom on second playoff hole.)						
Kane Webber	67	71	68	65	271	112,600
Simon Dyson	64	71	67	69	271	112,600
Francesco Molinari	67	69	71	65	272	84,800
David Lynn	70	68	70	65	273	56,200
Jyoti Randhawa	67	65	70	71	273	56,200
Charl Schwartzel	71	66	67	69	273	56,200
Daniel Vancsik	65	72	64	72	273	56,200
Johan Edfors	72	68	69	65	274	38,400
Darren Clarke	69	68	67	70	274	38,400
Keith Horne	65	72	72	66	275	30,960
Marcus Fraser	64	72	72	67	275	30,960
Graeme Storm	69	68	70	68	275	30,960
Carlos Rodiles	66	69	71	69	275	30,960
Scott Barr	68	68	68	71	275	30,960
Gary Murphy	70	67	73	66	276	25,400
Chinnarat Phadungsil	67	70	70	69	276	25,400
Raphael Jacquelin	68	69	69	70	276	25,400

	SCORES				TOTAL	MONEY
Graeme McDowell	66	68	71	71	276	25,400
Scott Strange	66	71	72	68	277	22,000
Peter Lawrie	69	67	72	69	277	22,000
David Frost	70	67	70	70	277	22,000
Nick Dougherty	62	70	72	73	277	22,000
Soren Kjeldsen	65	68	69	75	277	22,000
Artemio Murakami	69	71	73	65	278	18,400
Jean-Francois Lucquin	71	69	70	68	278	18,400
Scott Drummond	72	66	72	68	278	18,400
Zhang Lian-wei	68	68	74	68	278	18,400
Mark Brown	66	73	70	69	278	18,400
Felipe Aguilar	70	70	67	71	278	18,400
Robert-Jan Derksen	66	69	72	71	278	18,400
Iain Steel	70	69	72	68	279	15,250
Anton Haig	68	71	70	70	279	15,250
Mardan Mamat	72	65	70	72	279	15,250
Richard Lee	70	70	70	69	279	15,250
Thomas Bjorn	72	67	73	68	280	13,600
Gaurav Ghei	67	71	72	70	280	13,600
Sam Little	73	67	68	72	280	13,600
Martin Erlandsson	69	67	71	73	280	13,600
Danny Chia	65	67	80	69	281	11,800
Jean Van de Velde	71	68	72	70	281	11,800
Jose Manuel Lara	68	67	76	70	281	11,800
Hendrik Buhrmann	71	69	69	72	281	11,800
Terry Pilkadaris	69	69	71	72	281	11,800
Gregory Bourdy	70	70	72	70	282	9,600
Wang Ter-chang	70	68	73	71	282	9,600
Angelo Que	69	71	71	71	282	9,600
Prayad Marksaeng	67	73	70	72	282	9,600
Bryan Saltus	67	71	71	73	282	9,600
S.S.P. Chowrasia	66	73	69	74	282	9,600
Young Nam	69	69	75	70	283	7,200
Anthony Kang	70	70	72	71	283	7,200
Mikko Ilonen	68	72	72	71	283	7,200
Shaaban Hussein	69	71	70	73	283	7,200
Oliver Wilson	66	71	73	73	283	7,200
Gregory Havret	70	68	70	75	283	7,200
Simon Wakefield	69	69	72	74	284	6,000
Mads Vibe-Hastrup	71	68	74	72	285	5,700
Oliver Fisher	68	71	72	74	285	5,700
Zane Scotland	69	69	74	74	286	5,300
Zaw Moe	72	68	70	76	286	5,300
Simon Yates	69	71	74	74	288	4,700
Jose-Filipe Lima	69	71	76	72	288	4,700
S. Murthy	71	67	76	74	288	4,700
Ignacio Garrido	70	67	74	77	288	4,700
Marcus Both	67	72	75	76	290	4,100
Rafa Echenique	66	68	78	78	290	4,100
Yasin Ali	73	67	82	76	298	3,800

Ballantine's Championship

Pinx Golf Club, Jeju Island, South Korea
Par 36-36–72; 7,345 yards

March 13-16
purse, US$2,900,000

	SCORES				TOTAL	MONEY
Graeme McDowell	68	64	66	66	264	US$512,028
Jeev Milkha Singh	68	66	64	66	264	341,352

(McDowell defeated Singh on third playoff hole.)

		SCORES			TOTAL	MONEY
Paul McGinley	68	67	67	69	271	192,319
Shingo Katayama	68	70	68	67	273	153,610
Thomas Bjorn	70	66	70	68	274	109,984
Anthony Kim	68	68	69	69	274	109,984
Johan Edfors	69	65	69	71	274	109,984
Oliver Wilson	70	69	67	69	275	76,805
Phillip Archer	71	70	67	68	276	65,130
Kane Webber	71	68	65	72	276	65,130
Zane Scotland	74	69	68	66	277	52,944
Jyoti Randhawa	68	72	70	67	277	52,944
Terry Pilkadaris	71	66	71	69	277	52,944
David Frost	69	71	70	68	278	44,239
Thaworn Wiratchant	69	70	68	71	278	44,239
Kim Hyung-sung	72	70	66	70	278	44,239
Padraig Harrington	71	65	68	74	278	44,239
Adam Blyth	69	72	70	68	279	38,197
Bae Sang-moon	71	71	69	68	279	38,197
Chris DiMarco	70	68	72	69	279	38,197
David Lynn	71	71	68	70	280	34,715
Kim Hyung-tae	69	66	74	71	280	34,715
Ariel Canete	70	68	67	75	280	34,715
Francesco Molinari	69	72	71	69	281	29,646
Lin Wen-tang	72	71	69	69	281	29,646
Maarten Lafeber	71	70	70	70	281	29,646
Prayad Marksaeng	68	71	71	71	281	29,646
Damien McGrane	71	69	70	71	281	29,646
Anthony Kang	70	71	69	71	281	29,646
K.J. Choi	71	69	69	72	281	29,646
Mikko Ilonen	67	70	69	75	281	29,646
Mo Joong-kyung	74	70	70	68	282	23,502
Paul Broadhurst	70	72	70	70	282	23,502
Garry Houston	69	74	69	70	282	23,502
Kang Wook-soon	73	70	68	71	282	23,502
Hwang Inn-choon	68	69	73	72	282	23,502
Park Do-kyu	71	72	67	72	282	23,502
Marcus Both	74	70	71	68	283	21,198
Thomas Levet	71	73	72	68	284	19,662
David Griffiths	69	71	76	68	284	19,662
Jose Manuel Lara	72	71	70	71	284	19,662
Martin Erlandsson	71	73	69	71	284	19,662
Thomas Aiken	71	73	71	70	285	16,897
Y.E. Yang	73	70	70	72	285	16,897
Suk Jong-yul	71	70	71	73	285	16,897
S.K. Ho	74	67	70	74	285	16,897
Emanuele Canonica	71	71	68	75	285	16,897
Gary Simpson	70	70	74	72	286	14,746
Scott Barr	70	70	74	72	286	14,746
Juvic Pagunsan	70	73	73	71	287	11,981
Mardan Mamat	73	71	71	72	287	11,981
Carlos Rodiles	69	71	75	72	287	11,981
David Bransdon	72	70	73	72	287	11,981
Daniel Vancsik	70	73	72	72	287	11,981
Felipe Aguilar	72	72	70	73	287	11,981
Tony Carolan	67	75	72	73	287	11,981
Oliver Fisher	70	74	75	69	288	9,216
Gaurav Ghei	72	72	74	70	288	9,216
Prom Meesawat	71	71	76	70	288	9,216
Frankie Minoza	75	69	76	69	289	8,602
Kim Sang-ki	70	74	70	77	291	8,294
Kim Kyung-tae	74	70	76	72	292	7,680
Gavin Flint	72	72	74	74	292	7,680
Tom Whitehouse	70	70	77	75	292	7,680
Jun Tae-hyun	69	71	78	75	293	6,912

	SCORES				TOTAL	MONEY
Wang Ter-chang	71	73	72	77	293	6,912
Simon Griffiths	68	74	80	73	295	6,451

Asian Tour International

Pattana Golf & Sports Resort, Chonburi, Thailand
Par 36-36–72; 7,245 yards

March 20-23
purse, US$300,000

	SCORES				TOTAL	MONEY
Lin Wen-tang	65	68	68	64	265	US$47,550
Noh Seung-yul	64	67	68	71	270	32,550
Taichiro Kiyota	71	69	68	64	272	12,858
Marcus Both	70	66	70	66	272	12,858
Ben Leong	67	72	66	67	272	12,858
Han Lee	67	69	69	67	272	12,858
Mardan Mamat	67	67	70	68	272	12,858
Adam Blyth	71	66	70	66	273	6,103
Wisut Artjanawat	67	68	69	69	273	6,103
Jason King	70	64	70	69	273	6,103
Sattaya Supupramai	64	67	71	71	273	6,103
David Bransdon	68	69	67	69	273	6,103
Simon Griffiths	65	69	71	69	274	4,518
Chawalit Plaphol	70	66	69	69	274	4,518
Yoshinobu Tsukada	71	68	65	70	274	4,518
Stephen Scahill	70	70	66	69	275	3,960
Thaworn Wiratchant	71	66	68	70	275	3,960
Ross Bain	70	62	67	76	275	3,960
Prayad Marksaeng	70	71	68	67	276	3,570
Scott Hend	69	68	73	66	276	3,570
Juvic Pagunsan	68	66	75	68	277	3,375
Ashley Hall	70	69	69	69	277	3,375
Dinesh Chand	73	65	71	69	278	2,970
Thongchai Jaidee	72	68	69	69	278	2,970
Gavin Flint	68	68	73	69	278	2,970
Yasin Ali	67	67	74	70	278	2,970
Kiradech Aphibarnrat	71	70	66	71	278	2,970
Thepthat Senawong	72	67	69	70	278	2,970
Terry Pilkadaris	70	69	68	71	278	2,970

Philippine Open

Wack Wack Golf & Country Club, Manila, Philippines
Par 36-36–72; 7,053 yards

April 3-6
purse, US$300,000

	SCORES				TOTAL	MONEY
Angelo Que	73	71	66	73	283	US$47,550
Danny Chia	71	71	76	66	284	32,550
Gavin Flint	67	70	75	73	285	18,300
Mitchell Brown	72	73	69	72	286	12,420
Mardan Mamat	73	72	68	73	286	12,420
Antonio Lascuna	71	70	72	73	286	12,420
Young Nam	71	70	72	74	287	8,130
Kodai Ichihara	66	70	75	76	287	8,130
Lin Wen-tang	73	67	80	68	288	5,975
Lu Wen-teh	73	73	72	70	288	5,975
Andrew Dodt	74	72	71	71	288	5,975
Artemio Murakami	71	76	73	69	289	5,061

	SCORES				TOTAL	MONEY
Thaworn Wiratchant	72	75	74	69	290	4,423
Frankie Minoza	76	72	71	71	290	4,423
Wisut Artjanawat	70	75	73	72	290	4,423
Airil Rizman	77	71	69	73	290	4,423
Mo Joong-kyung	77	72	72	70	291	3,660
Brad Kennedy	71	75	75	70	291	3,660
Jay Bayron	73	71	77	70	291	3,660
Chawalit Plaphol	68	76	77	70	291	3,660
Ross Bain	76	69	74	72	291	3,660
Kang Wook-soon	74	72	75	71	292	3,060
Chang Tse-peng	71	78	71	72	292	3,060
Arjun Singh	72	74	73	73	292	3,060
Olle Nordberg	76	74	73	69	292	3,060
Ben Leong	71	77	70	74	292	3,060
Mars Pucay	75	72	70	75	292	3,060
Ashley Hall	68	71	75	78	292	3,060

Volvo China Open

Beijing CBD International Golf Club, Beijing, China
Par 35-37–72; 7,321 yards

April 17-20
purse, US$2,200,000

	SCORES				TOTAL	MONEY
Damien McGrane	68	69	68	73	278	US$366,660
Simon Griffiths	68	72	73	74	287	164,053
Michael Lorenzo-Vera	67	69	72	79	287	164,053
Oliver Wilson	72	66	70	79	287	164,053
Graeme McDowell	73	72	68	75	288	78,760
Markus Brier	71	69	72	76	288	78,760
Mark Brown	71	71	69	77	288	78,760
Noh Seung-yul	71	71	74	73	289	47,190
Peter Whiteford	73	72	71	73	289	47,190
Liang Wen-chong	73	68	73	75	289	47,190
Jason Knutzon	68	72	72	77	289	47,190
John Bickerton	70	76	72	72	290	36,630
Richard Finch	68	69	76	77	290	36,630
Joost Luiten	68	73	74	76	291	31,680
Lu Wen-teh	73	71	71	76	291	31,680
David Bransdon	73	72	68	78	291	31,680
Scott Strange	73	71	66	81	291	31,680
Christian Cevaer	73	74	72	73	292	27,830
Adam Groom	73	70	72	77	292	27,830
Miles Tunnicliff	70	74	74	75	293	25,245
Louis Oosthuizen	74	72	72	75	293	25,245
Paul Lawrie	71	75	72	75	293	25,245
Daniel Vancsik	73	74	69	77	293	25,245
Stuart Manley	72	74	74	74	294	22,550
Simon Yates	72	72	75	75	294	22,550
Marcus Both	73	73	73	75	294	22,550
Mikko Ilonen	75	71	70	78	294	22,550
Ross Bain	73	73	76	73	295	17,800
Scott Barr	73	74	74	74	295	17,800
Gaurav Ghei	76	69	75	75	295	17,800
Phillip Price	74	71	74	76	295	17,800
Li Chao	68	74	76	77	295	17,800
Sam Little	74	73	71	77	295	17,800
Rhys Davies	71	74	71	79	295	17,800
Jean-Francois Lucquin	72	72	72	79	295	17,800
David Howell	72	73	71	79	295	17,800
Zane Scotland	68	72	74	81	295	17,800

	SCORES				TOTAL	MONEY
Fabrizio Zanotti	71	71	70	83	295	17,800
Carlos Rodiles	72	74	72	78	296	14,300
Sam Walker	71	71	73	81	296	14,300
Antonio Lascuna	72	71	72	81	296	14,300
Lu Wei-chih	75	73	72	77	297	13,200
Airil Rizman	69	72	72	84	297	13,200
David Frost	76	72	74	76	298	11,660
Marcel Siem	76	71	73	78	298	11,660
Marcus Fraser	71	76	73	78	298	11,660
Francesco Molinari	75	72	73	78	298	11,660
Gaganjeet Bhullar	69	75	73	81	298	11,660
Mardan Mamat	72	74	74	79	299	9,680
Jean-Baptiste Gonnet	72	74	72	81	299	9,680
Todd Vernon	71	72	74	82	299	9,680
Robert-Jan Derksen	70	71	75	83	299	9,680
Gavin Flint	73	74	76	77	300	8,140
Paul Broadhurst	76	72	73	79	300	8,140
Barry Lane	78	70	71	81	300	8,140
Lin Keng-chi	75	73	77	76	301	6,893
Soren Kjeldsen	75	72	76	78	301	6,893
Ross Fisher	74	72	74	81	301	6,893
Simon Wakefield	72	71	78	81	302	6,270
Lee Sung	73	75	73	81	302	6,270
Wu Kang-chun	70	73	80	80	303	5,830
Prom Meesawat	71	76	74	82	303	5,830
S.S.P. Chowrasia	74	73	76	81	304	5,390
Frankie Minoza	73	72	77	82	304	5,390
Raphael Jacquelin	75	71	79	84	309	4,950
Rafa Echenique	69	76	82	82	309	4,950
*Hu Mu	74	74	77	84	309	
Wu Wei-huang	73	75	77	86	311	4,620
Julio Zapata	70	78	80	84	312	4,400

BMW Asian Open

Tomson Shanghai Pudong Golf Club, Shanghai, China   April 24-27
Par 36-36–72; 7,326 yards   purse, US$2,300,000

	SCORES				TOTAL	MONEY
Darren Clarke	71	69	67	73	280	US$383,330
Robert-Jan Derksen	70	69	69	73	281	255,550
Francesco Molinari	71	75	68	69	283	118,833
Robert Dinwiddie	70	73	66	74	283	118,833
Lin Wen-tang	71	71	69	72	283	118,833
Henrik Stenson	68	76	72	68	284	80,500
Martin Kaymer	72	72	74	67	285	63,250
John Bickerton	71	75	69	70	285	63,250
Peter Lawrie	72	74	70	70	286	48,760
Scott Hend	69	74	71	72	286	48,760
Oliver Wilson	68	74	74	71	287	39,636
Paul Broadhurst	71	73	71	72	287	39,636
Retief Goosen	72	70	72	73	287	39,636
Greg Norman	71	73	73	71	288	33,120
Scott Strange	71	75	70	72	288	33,120
Joost Luiten	71	75	70	72	288	33,120
Liang Wen-chong	71	71	73	73	288	33,120
Simon Wakefield	73	72	75	69	289	27,692
Iain Steel	71	74	71	73	289	27,692
Soren Kjeldsen	74	73	69	73	289	27,692
Miles Tunnicliff	71	70	73	75	289	27,692

	SCORES				TOTAL	MONEY
Michael Lorenzo-Vera	75	69	69	76	289	27,692
Jean-Francois Lucquin	74	70	74	72	290	24,265
Jeev Milkha Singh	68	76	70	76	290	24,265
Peter O'Malley	67	74	72	77	290	24,265
Digvijay Singh	74	72	67	77	290	24,265
Jean-Baptiste Gonnet	75	72	73	71	291	20,125
David Frost	72	75	72	72	291	20,125
Mardan Mamat	73	74	71	73	291	20,125
Paul Lawrie	75	72	71	73	291	20,125
Young Nam	72	73	72	74	291	20,125
Sam Little	71	76	70	74	291	20,125
Chris Rodgers	71	73	71	76	291	20,125
Rory McIlroy	73	73	69	76	291	20,125
Ross McGowan	71	74	75	72	292	16,100
Michael Campbell	71	76	70	75	292	16,100
Jose-Filipe Lima	70	74	72	76	292	16,100
Marcus Fraser	70	73	73	76	292	16,100
Mark Brown	75	67	73	77	292	16,100
David Gleeson	73	73	68	78	292	16,100
*Hu Mu	73	69	71	79	292	
Raphael Jacquelin	73	74	74	72	293	13,800
Ross Fisher	72	73	74	74	293	13,800
Marcus Both	73	74	72	74	293	13,800
Simon Yates	74	73	71	75	293	13,800
Phillip Price	73	73	78	70	294	11,040
Peter Hedblom	72	73	78	71	294	11,040
Shiv Kapur	71	75	74	74	294	11,040
Mikael Lundberg	73	71	75	75	294	11,040
Barry Lane	74	71	73	76	294	11,040
Hendrik Buhrmann	71	75	71	77	294	11,040
Lu Wei-chih	75	71	70	78	294	11,040
Zhang Lian-wei	70	69	76	79	294	11,040
Gary Murphy	74	73	73	75	295	8,970
Adam Blyth	74	70	73	79	296	8,280
S.S.P. Chowrasia	72	73	72	79	296	8,280
Scott Barr	72	74	76	75	297	7,360
Carl Suneson	71	73	75	78	297	7,360
Mikko Ilonen	68	76	77	77	298	6,785
Keith Horne	77	70	75	76	298	6,785
Li Chao	71	72	75	81	299	6,440
Richard Finch	72	75	78	75	300	5,865
Kang Wook-soon	74	72	79	75	300	5,865
Hsu Mong-nan	73	74	77	76	300	5,865
Richard Lee	70	75	74	81	300	5,865
Julio Zapata	73	72	76	84	305	5,290

GS Caltex Maekyung Open

Nam Seoul Country Club, Seoul, Korea
Par 36-36–72; 6,962 yards

May 1-4
purse, US$600,000

	SCORES				TOTAL	MONEY
Hwang Inn-choon	71	67	73	68	279	US$107,142
Noh Seung-yul	69	70	68	72	279	66,964
(Hwang defeated Noh on first playoff hole.)						
Kang Ji-man	67	72	73	68	280	32,142
*Kim Bi-o	72	69	72	67	280	
Bae Sang-moon	71	68	70	72	281	26,785
Lee Jin-won	69	72	72	70	283	15,803
Chris Riley	71	72	69	71	283	15,803

	SCORES				TOTAL	MONEY
Kim Do-hoon	70	70	69	74	283	15,803
Kim Kyung-tae	69	71	69	74	283	15,803
Kim Dae-hyun	70	75	71	68	284	10,312
Kang Sung-hoon	73	68	73	70	284	10,312
Park Jun-won	75	70	70	70	285	8,095
Jun Tae-hyun	70	68	73	74	285	8,095
Park Sung-kook	69	70	72	74	285	8,095
Unho Park	77	70	71	68	286	6,860
Kim Hyung-tae	72	72	71	71	286	6,860
Lu Wei-chih	72	75	68	71	286	6,860
Kim Sang-ki	73	72	70	71	286	6,860
Kang Mo-hoon	77	65	70	74	286	6,860
Kim Wi-joong	72	70	68	76	286	6,860
*Jeong Yeon-jin	73	71	73	70	287	
Jung Ji-ho	75	72	73	67	287	5,982
Ted Oh	76	71	69	71	287	5,982
Lee Boo-young	71	73	71	72	287	5,982
*Song Tae-hoon	68	75	74	71	288	
J.B. Park	73	72	72	71	288	5,535
Choi In-sik	72	73	72	71	288	5,535
Kim Hye-dong	77	69	67	75	288	5,535

Pine Valley Beijing Open

Pine Valley Golf Resort, Beijing, China
Par 36-36–72; 7,299 yards

May 8-11
purse, US$1,000,000

	SCORES				TOTAL	MONEY
Hiroyuki Fujita	67	65	72	72	276	US$158,500
Shintaro Kai	71	68	72	68	279	108,500
Dinesh Chand	73	69	69	69	280	61,000
Tony Carolan	66	72	75	68	281	41,400
Nobuhiro Masuda	70	67	75	69	281	41,400
Shinichi Yokota	71	70	69	71	281	41,400
Thongchai Jaidee	71	66	76	69	282	23,975
Prayad Marksaeng	69	70	72	71	282	23,975
Chinnarat Phadungsil	65	69	76	72	282	23,975
Chapchai Nirat	75	68	68	71	282	23,975
Bae Sang-moon	67	75	73	68	283	17,460
Gary Simpson	72	65	75	71	283	17,460
Taichiro Kiyota	69	75	71	69	284	14,745
Scott Hend	68	68	78	70	284	14,745
Artemio Murakami	71	69	73	71	284	14,745
Gavin Flint	73	70	69	72	284	14,745
Yasumasa Suzuki	74	70	74	67	285	12,400
Katsunori Kuwabara	68	69	75	73	285	12,400
Koumei Oda	70	73	69	73	285	12,400
Simon Griffiths	71	68	72	74	285	12,400
Kane Webber	70	73	76	67	286	10,350
Rahil Gangjee	72	68	78	68	286	10,350
Iain Steel	65	73	79	69	286	10,350
Keith Horne	70	73	74	69	286	10,350
Zaw Moe	72	70	75	69	286	10,350
Lu Wei-chih	69	70	77	70	286	10,350
Kim Kyung-tae	69	69	76	72	286	10,350
Jason Knutzon	71	72	71	72	286	10,350

Bangkok Airways Open

Santiburi Samui Country Club, Koh Samui, Thailand
Par 35-36–71; 6,853 yards

June 5-8
purse, US$300,000

	SCORES			TOTAL	MONEY
Thaworn Wiratchant	66	69	68	68	271	US$47,550
Shintaro Kai	69	65	70	70	274	32,550
Han Lee	70	72	69	64	275	13,890
Chapchai Nirat	67	69	71	68	275	13,890
Chinnarat Phadungsil	70	68	65	72	275	13,890
Prayad Marksaeng	69	67	68	71	275	13,890
Mitchell Brown	67	70	71	68	276	8,130
Lien Lu-sen	69	65	66	76	276	8,130
Juvic Pagunsan	68	66	73	70	277	5,746
Mars Pucay	69	64	73	71	277	5,746
Rick Kulacz	73	66	68	70	277	5,746
Antonio Lascuna	66	66	72	73	277	5,746
Anthony Kang	70	70	70	68	278	4,423
Brad Kennedy	74	70	71	63	278	4,423
Chawalit Plaphol	68	70	70	70	278	4,423
Ben Leong	69	70	67	72	278	4,423
Kiradech Aphibarnrat	70	72	70	67	279	3,870
Adam Blyth	69	69	72	69	279	3,870
Kunihiro Kamii	69	68	75	68	280	3,426
Varut Chomchalam	68	69	74	69	280	3,426
Udorn Duangdecha	67	68	74	71	280	3,426
Lu Wen-teh	73	69	68	70	280	3,426
Lin Chien-bing	69	64	75	72	280	3,426
Ashley Hall	71	70	73	67	281	2,970
Mardan Mamat	72	70	69	70	281	2,970
Arjun Singh	70	68	72	71	281	2,970
Lin Wen-tang	67	71	71	72	281	2,970
David Gleeson	71	66	69	75	281	2,970

Singha Thailand PGA Championship

Santiburi Country Club, Chiang Rai, Thailand
Par 36-36–72; 7,113 yards

June 26-29
purse, US$300,000

	SCORES			TOTAL	MONEY
Mo Joong-kyung	69	64	69	65	267	US$47,550
Juvic Pagunsan	68	63	71	68	270	32,550
David Gleeson	68	72	67	64	271	16,545
Prayad Marksaeng	67	65	73	66	271	16,545
Ben Leong	69	70	66	69	274	12,300
Prom Meesawat	70	70	69	67	276	10,170
Thaworn Wiratchant	70	68	71	68	277	8,730
Han Lee	68	69	68	73	278	7,530
Guido van der Valk	72	69	68	70	279	6,255
Pariya Junhasavasdikul	72	70	65	72	279	6,255
Unho Park	67	70	70	73	280	5,415
Chinnarat Phadungsil	68	71	75	67	281	4,765
Lien Lu-sen	67	71	72	71	281	4,765
Thammanoon Srirot	68	70	72	71	281	4,765
Adam Groom	71	69	71	71	282	3,966
Antonio Lascuna	72	68	70	72	282	3,966
Arjun Singh	68	69	73	72	282	3,966
Terry Pilkadaris	67	73	71	71	282	3,966
Choengchai Panpumpo	70	71	67	74	282	3,966

	SCORES				TOTAL	MONEY
Gaganjeet Bhullar	68	71	74	70	283	3,285
Lin Wen-hong	74	67	73	69	283	3,285
Lu Wei-chih	70	70	71	72	283	3,285
Wisut Artjanawat	68	71	72	72	283	3,285
Chang Tse-peng	68	69	74	72	283	3,285
Piya Swangarunporn	71	74	68	70	283	3,285

Worldwide Selangor Masters

Seri Selangor Golf Club, Kuala Lumpur, Malaysia
Par 36-35–71; 7,002 yards

August 6-9
purse, US$310,000

	SCORES				TOTAL	MONEY
Ben Leong	71	65	64	69	269	US$48,147
Thongchai Jaidee	70	63	68	69	270	32,958
Iain Steel	68	68	69	73	278	18,529
Danny Chia	68	74	71	66	279	11,641
Gaurav Ghei	69	74	69	67	279	11,641
Mars Pucay	69	72	69	69	279	11,641
Neven Basic	68	67	72	72	279	11,641
Chawalit Plaphol	68	68	72	72	280	7,153
Lu Wen-teh	69	72	65	74	280	7,153
Lin Wen-tang	69	70	70	72	281	5,984
Dinesh Chand	67	74	73	68	282	4,854
Chan Yih-shin	75	66	71	70	282	4,854
Adam Blyth	66	70	74	72	282	4,854
Atthaphon Prathummanee	71	71	69	71	282	4,854
Chinnarat Phadungsil	64	72	70	76	282	4,854
Antonio Lascuna	70	73	72	68	283	3,926
Lam Chih Bing	75	66	72	70	283	3,926
Mardan Mamat	75	68	69	71	283	3,926
Wang Ter-chang	70	68	72	73	283	3,926
Andrew Dodt	77	68	69	70	284	3,417
Scott Barr	68	71	73	72	284	3,417
Kim Nam-kang	71	71	70	72	284	3,417
Craig Smith	70	68	71	75	284	3,417
Muhammad Munir	70	73	71	71	285	3,098
Taichiro Kiyota	67	72	73	73	285	3,098
Gavin Flint	73	72	70	70	285	3,098

Brunei Open

Empire Hotel & Country Club, Jerudong, Brunei
Par 35-36–71; 7,013 yards

August 21-24
purse, US$300,000

	SCORES				TOTAL	MONEY
Rick Kulacz	68	66	67	70	271	US$47,550
Lu Wen-teh	70	65	69	67	271	32,550
(Kulacz defeated Lu on first playoff hole.)						
Anthony Kang	68	68	69	67	272	16,545
Somkiat Srisanga	64	70	70	68	272	16,545
Terry Pilkadaris	65	67	74	67	273	10,400
Andrew Dodt	66	72	66	69	273	10,400
Thaworn Wiratchant	67	69	66	71	273	10,400
Iain Steel	69	70	67	68	274	7,530
Jason King	69	69	72	65	275	5,220
Chinnarat Phadungsil	70	69	69	67	275	5,220

		SCORES			TOTAL	MONEY
Simon Dunn	70	69	69	67	275	5,220
David Gleeson	69	70	67	69	275	5,220
Scott Hend	69	65	71	70	275	5,220
Mitchell Brown	69	70	66	70	275	5,220
Ted Oh	65	66	71	73	275	5,220
Marcus Both	68	68	71	69	276	3,681
Atthaphon Prathummanee	69	69	69	69	276	3,681
Wang Ter-chang	69	68	69	70	276	3,681
Adam Blyth	67	74	65	70	276	3,681
Darren Beck	69	70	67	70	276	3,681
Juvic Pagunsan	72	69	65	70	276	3,681
Chang Tse-peng	69	67	69	71	276	3,681
M. Murugiah	68	72	68	69	277	3,240
Thammanoon Srirot	68	69	71	70	278	3,015
Noh Seung-yul	68	70	70	70	278	3,015
Lin Wen-hong	68	71	68	71	278	3,015
Antonio Lascuna	67	70	70	71	278	3,015

Pertamina Indonesia President Invitational

Damai Indah Golf & Country Club, Pantai Indah Kapuk Course,
Jakarta, Indonesia
Par 36-36–72; 7,144 yards

August 28-31
purse, US$400,000

		SCORES			TOTAL	MONEY
Scott Hend	71	69	66	66	272	US$63,400
Lin Wen-tang	64	72	65	74	275	43,400
Udorn Duangdecha	70	71	68	67	276	20,173
Mars Pucay	71	65	71	69	276	20,173
Anthony Kang	67	70	66	73	276	20,173
Iain Steel	69	66	66	76	277	13,560
Thaworn Wiratchant	67	69	71	71	278	11,640
Ted Oh	68	69	71	71	279	9,420
David Gleeson	71	67	69	72	279	9,420
Gavin Flint	72	71	68	69	280	6,832
Simon Dunn	68	74	69	69	280	6,832
Lam Chih Bing	73	69	68	70	280	6,832
Jason King	69	71	67	73	280	6,832
Panuwat Muenlek	69	69	69	73	280	6,832
Andrew Dodt	69	69	74	70	282	5,288
Noh Seung-yul	72	69	71	70	282	5,288
Kwanchai Tannin	69	72	70	71	282	5,288
Ashley Hall	68	70	72	72	282	5,288
Brad Kennedy	67	72	70	73	282	5,288
Choengchai Panpumpo	74	69	70	70	283	4,620
M. Sasidaran	68	72	70	73	283	4,620
Todd Vernon	72	70	73	69	284	4,200
Martin Rominger	74	71	69	70	284	4,200
Zaw Moe	71	69	72	72	284	4,200
S. Siva Chandran	70	69	71	74	284	4,200
Rhys Davies	72	70	66	76	284	4,200

Mercuries Taiwan Masters

Taiwan Golf & Country Club, Taipei, Taiwan
Par 36-36–72; 6,929 yards

September 18-21
purse, US$500,000

		SCORES			TOTAL	MONEY
Lu Wen-teh	70	67	69	71	277	US$100,000
Thaworn Wiratchant	69	71	67	72	279	60,000
Lin Wen-hong	71	63	78	70	282	35,000
Hsu Mong-nan	72	67	74	70	283	25,000
Wisut Artjanawat	68	72	72	73	285	18,750
Anthony Kang	73	70	66	76	285	18,750
Ted Oh	70	73	70	73	286	15,000
Antonio Lascuna	69	76	73	69	287	11,250
Kim Nam-kang	72	68	74	73	287	11,250
Sung Mao-chang	68	73	75	72	288	8,500
Kao Bo-song	69	71	74	74	288	8,500
Chang Tse-peng	75	71	67	75	288	8,500
Richard Moir	72	70	75	72	289	7,500
Gavin Flint	76	69	73	72	290	6,300
Mitchell Brown	69	71	76	74	290	6,300
Marcus Both	72	71	72	75	290	6,300
Chen Tsang-te	75	71	70	74	290	6,300
David Gleeson	71	72	70	77	290	6,300
Juvic Pagunsan	69	75	76	71	291	5,237.50
Neven Basic	69	72	76	74	291	5,237.50
Lien Lu-sen	74	70	72	75	291	5,237.50
Zaw Moe	69	73	70	79	291	5,237.50
Lu Wei-chih	71	72	75	74	292	4,750
Artemio Murakami	70	75	74	73	292	4,750
S. Siva Chandran	71	74	72	75	292	4,750
Yeh Chang-ting	72	74	71	75	292	4,750

Asia-Pacific Panasonic Open

See Japan Tour section.

Kolon-Hana Bank Korea Open

Woo Jeong Hills Country Club, Cheonan, South Korea
Par 36-35–71; 7,185 yards

October 2-5
purse, US$1,000,000

		SCORES			TOTAL	MONEY
Bae Sang-moon	67	70	67	69	273	US$240,384.62
Ian Poulter	69	66	69	70	274	78,525.64
Kim Wi-joong	67	67	69	72	275	40,064.10
Anthony Kim	64	73	67	71	275	40,064.10
Kim Dae-sub	67	68	69	72	276	27,243.59
Lee In-woo	71	72	70	65	278	22,168.80
Jason King	70	67	72	69	278	22,168.80
Kim Hyung-tae	70	70	68	70	278	22,168.80
S.K. Ho	70	71	71	67	279	17,227.56
Noh Seung-yul	70	72	68	69	279	17,227.56
*Song Tae-hoon	70	70	69	70	279	
Bae Sung-chul	71	73	67	69	280	14,663.46
Chung Jae-hoon	70	69	72	70	281	12,019.23
Zaw Moe	69	70	71	71	281	12,019.23
Rhys Davies	70	73	71	69	283	9,615.38
Anthony Kang	71	73	71	69	284	8,060.90

	SCORES				TOTAL	MONEY
Simon Hurd	71	70	73	70	284	8,060.90
Kim Do-hoon₂	72	68	75	69	284	8,060.90
Juvic Pagunsan	68	74	74	68	284	8,060.90
Moon Kyong-jin	72	69	70	73	284	8,060.90
Guido van der Valk	73	72	70	70	285	6,670.67
Kang Wook-soon	73	72	71	69	285	6,670.67
Kodai Ichihara	72	71	70	72	285	6,670.67
Tony Carolan	68	72	73	72	285	6,670.67
Mars Pucay	73	70	70	72	285	6,670.67
Choi In-sik	73	72	72	68	285	6,670.67
Artemio Murakami	70	70	72	73	285	6,670.67
Kim Do-Hoon₁	73	71	66	75	285	6,670.67

Hero Honda Indian Open

Delhi Golf Club, New Delhi, India
Par 36-36–72; 6,932 yards

October 9-12
purse, US$1,000,000

	SCORES				TOTAL	MONEY
Liang Wen-chong	60	71	71	70	272	US$158,500
Darren Beck	70	70	68	65	273	108,500
Adam Blyth	70	67	66	72	275	61,000
Jeev Milkha Singh	65	74	68	69	276	49,300
Guido van der Valk	77	61	70	69	277	41,000
Mukesh Kumar	68	73	68	70	279	31,500
Ashok Kumar	70	67	70	72	279	31,500
Muhammad Munir	69	69	72	70	280	23,550
Mars Pucay	71	67	70	72	280	23,550
Marcus Both	74	69	70	68	281	16,633.33
Sanjay Kumar	66	72	73	70	281	16,633.33
Rhys Davies	70	72	69	70	281	16,633.33
Artemio Murakami	74	67	68	72	281	16,633.33
Mark Brown	71	67	69	74	281	16,633.33
Steven Tiley	72	66	69	74	281	16,633.33
Atthaphon Prathummanee	67	73	71	71	282	12,680
Jaiveer Virk	71	69	71	71	282	12,680
Wu Ashun	72	71	68	71	282	12,680
Lu Wen-teh	66	71	71	74	282	12,680
Unho Park	67	71	66	78	282	12,680
Shamim Khan	73	70	70	70	283	10,800
Gavin Flint	69	71	72	71	283	10,800
Stephen Scahill	72	71	72	68	283	10,800
Antonio Lascuna	71	74	66	72	283	10,800
Himmat Rai	70	71	69	73	283	10,800

Midea China Classic

Royal Orchid International Golf Club, Guangzhou, China
Par 36-35–71; 6,889 yards

October 16-19
purse, US$500,000

	SCORES				TOTAL	MONEY
Noh Seung-yul	66	66	67	68	267	US$79,250
Terry Pilkadaris	67	67	67	67	268	54,250
Mardan Mamat	69	68	68	64	269	25,216.67
Lu Wei-chih	64	72	66	67	269	25,216.67
Park Jun-won	66	69	66	68	269	25,216.67
Andrew Dodt	67	69	69	66	271	14,683.33

	SCORES				TOTAL	MONEY
Chinnarat Phadungsil	69	68	67	67	271	14,683.33
Neven Basic	69	66	69	67	271	14,683.33
Rahil Gangjee	70	69	64	69	272	10,425
Lin Wen-tang	68	70	64	70	272	10,425
Unho Park	73	66	68	66	273	8,010
Mitchell Brown	67	69	70	67	273	8,010
Rhys Davies	67	71	68	67	273	8,010
Anthony Kang	68	71	67	67	273	8,010
David Bransdon	70	69	67	67	273	8,010
Ashley Hall	70	69	70	65	274	6,600
Simon Dunn	66	72	67	69	274	6,600
Liang Wen-chong	68	70	67	69	274	6,600
Thammanoon Srirot	73	67	71	64	275	5,633.33
Artemio Murakami	71	66	73	65	275	5,633.33
Digvijay Singh	68	72	68	67	275	5,633.33
Chen Yuan-chi	67	68	72	68	275	5,633.33
Hsu Mong-nan	65	70	71	69	275	5,633.33
Henry Epstein	67	71	66	71	275	5,633.33
Brad Kennedy	72	69	67	68	276	4,650
Gaganjeet Bhullar	69	67	71	69	276	4,650
Anirban Lahiri	68	70	68	70	276	4,650
Wu Ashun	68	71	67	70	276	4,650
Darren Beck	69	69	67	71	276	4,650
Marcus Both	69	66	69	72	276	4,650
S. Siva Chandhran	67	68	67	74	276	4,650

Macau Open

Macau Golf & Country Club, Macau
Par 35-36–71; 6,624 yards

October 23-26
purse, US$500,000

	SCORES				TOTAL	MONEY
David Gleeson	64	64	69	69	266	US$79,250
Lin Wen-tang	65	68	70	66	269	54,250
Kao Bo-song	66	68	65	71	270	30,500
Mars Pucay	67	70	69	65	271	22,575
Yasin Ali	69	64	70	68	271	22,575
Lu Wei-chih	68	70	69	65	272	14,683.33
Somkiat Srisanga	69	68	69	66	272	14,683.33
Adam Blyth	68	65	71	68	272	14,683.33
Wisut Artjanawat	65	69	68	71	273	10,425
Steven Tiley	70	67	65	71	273	10,425
Wu Ashun	70	68	69	67	274	8,730
Chan Yih-shin	69	67	67	71	274	8,730
Danny Chia	67	68	72	68	275	7,372.50
Chris Rodgers	72	65	70	68	275	7,372.50
Unho Park	67	72	68	68	275	7,372.50
Tony Carolan	67	69	67	72	275	7,372.50
Zhang Lian-wei	72	67	68	69	276	6,450
Wang Ter-chang	66	69	69	72	276	6,450
Udorn Duangdecha	65	72	73	67	277	5,866.67
Neven Basic	70	67	70	70	277	5,866.67
Lin Wen-hong	65	69	72	71	277	5,866.67
Darren Beck	66	69	77	66	278	5,325
Mitchell Brown	70	66	71	71	278	5,325
Richard Moir	67	71	71	69	278	5,325
Anirban Lahiri	68	65	73	72	278	5,325

Iskandar Johor Open

Royal Johor Country Club, Johor, Malaysia
Par 36-36–72; 6,984 yards

October 30-November 2
purse, US$500,000

	SCORES				TOTAL	MONEY
Retief Goosen	72	69	69	66	276	US$79,250
Thaworn Wiratchant	69	69	69	71	278	54,250
Kane Webber	68	71	70	70	279	30,500
Andrew Dodt	71	71	69	70	281	17,840
Richard Moir	69	71	70	71	281	17,840
Iain Steel	70	69	70	72	281	17,840
Niclas Fasth	68	68	70	75	281	17,840
Mitchell Brown	67	69	72	73	281	17,840
Unho Park	73	72	70	67	282	9,240
Mardan Mamat	71	70	73	68	282	9,240
Danny Chia	75	70	69	68	282	9,240
Yasin Ali	73	72	69	68	282	9,240
Thongchai Jaidee	71	66	73	72	282	9,240
Ben Leong	71	71	73	68	283	6,900
Steven Tiley	75	69	71	68	283	6,900
Anthony Kang	71	72	71	69	283	6,900
Mahal Pearce	67	76	69	71	283	6,900
Rick Kulacz	67	73	71	72	283	6,900
Gavin Flint	71	73	70	70	284	5,866.67
Clay Devers	72	70	71	71	284	5,866.67
Neven Basic	72	73	67	72	284	5,866.67
Juvic Pagunsan	72	73	70	70	285	5,325
Artemio Murakami	67	72	74	72	285	5,325
Park Jun-won	72	72	70	71	285	5,325
Chapchai Nirat	73	69	71	72	285	5,325

HSBC Champions

Sheshan International Golf Club, Shanghai, China
Par 36-36–72; 7,199 yards

November 6-9
purse, US$5,000,000

	SCORES				TOTAL	MONEY
Sergio Garcia	66	68	72	68	274	US$416,650
Oliver Wilson	67	68	69	70	274	277,775
(Garcia defeated Wilson on second playoff hole.)						
Geoff Ogilvy	70	65	70	70	275	140,750
Peter Hanson	69	70	70	66	275	140,750
Henrik Stenson	65	69	72	71	277	106,500
Adam Scott	66	71	71	70	278	81,250
Charl Schwartzel	69	72	67	70	278	81,250
Phil Mickelson	66	70	70	73	279	59,250
Prayad Marksaeng	68	70	71	70	279	59,250
Alvaro Quiros	70	67	73	70	280	50,112.50
Paul Casey	71	70	68	72	281	43,195.84
Padraig Harrington	69	70	74	68	281	43,195.84
Peter Lawrie	68	72	73	68	281	43,195.84
Robert Karlsson	69	73	71	70	283	37,612.50
Ian Poulter	68	73	74	68	283	37,612.50
Damien McGrane	68	71	72	73	284	33,175
Graeme McDowell	71	65	76	72	284	33,175
Lin Wen-tang	69	71	75	69	284	33,175
Louis Oosthuizen	74	70	71	69	284	33,175
Richard Sterne	71	69	71	74	285	28,800
Andrew McLardy	69	69	74	73	285	28,800

	SCORES				TOTAL	MONEY
Martin Kaymer	73	70	73	69	285	28,800
Camilo Villegas	73	72	73	67	285	28,800
Liang Wen-chong	71	69	72	74	286	25,737.50
Marc Cayeux	67	70	78	71	286	25,737.50
David Dixon	74	72	71	69	286	25,737.50
Mikael Lundberg	71	74	73	68	286	25,737.50
Jeev Milkha Singh	70	71	74	72	287	23,112.50
Noh Seung-yul	70	72	73	72	287	23,112.50
Trevor Immelman	72	72	74	69	287	23,112.50
Andrew Bonhomme	73	69	71	75	288	21,237.50
Chapchai Nirat	73	76	72	67	288	21,237.50
Scott Strange	69	68	77	75	289	19,737.50
Wu Ashun	73	71	70	75	289	19,737.50
K.J. Choi	71	74	73	72	290	18,237.50
Hennie Otto	70	73	76	71	290	18,237.50
Soren Hansen	71	70	71	79	291	16,612.50
Richard Finch	71	72	74	74	291	16,612.50
Thomas Levet	68	75	75	73	291	16,612.50
Pablo Larrazabal	78	72	70	71	291	16,612.50
Soren Kjeldsen	72	76	72	72	292	15,112.50
Rick Kulacz	73	76	72	71	292	15,112.50
Ross Fisher	69	74	76	74	293	13,362.50
James Kingston	73	71	75	74	293	13,362.50
David Horsey	75	71	73	74	293	13,362.50
Zhang Lian-wei	71	74	75	73	293	13,362.50
Gonzalo Fernandez-Castano	73	73	74	73	293	13,362.50
Ben Leong	69	72	79	74	294	11,362.50
Jean-Francois Lucquin	73	74	74	73	294	11,362.50
Scott Hend	76	75	70	73	294	11,362.50
Gregory Bourdy	68	73	79	75	295	10,112.50
John Bickerton	77	71	74	73	295	10,112.50
Mark Brown	71	74	78	73	296	9,362.50
Jean Hugo	73	70	76	78	297	8,612.50
Felipe Aguilar	69	75	75	78	297	8,612.50
David Gleeson	76	73	72	77	298	7,612.50
Wu Wei-huang	73	78	73	74	298	7,612.50
Darren Clarke	72	71	77	79	299	6,612.50
David Howell	79	74	73	73	299	6,612.50
Gregory Havret	76	70	77	77	300	5,612.50
Hwang In-choon	77	77	71	75	300	5,612.50
Shang Lei	71	72	80	78	301	4,862.50
Lu Wen-teh	73	75	75	78	301	4,862.50
Thaworn Wiratchant	75	77	74	75	301	4,862.50
Bae Sang-moon	73	70	86	73	302	4,362.50
Alastair Forsyth	73	78	77	75	303	3,987.50
Mo Joong-kyung	72	78	79	74	303	3,987.50
S.S.P. Chowrasia	76	72	76	82	306	3,675
Yuan Hao	75	76	82	73	306	3,675
Li Chao	76	79	81	71	307	3,487.50
James Kamte	77	73	76	82	308	3,362.50
Bryan Saltus	78	75	76	80	309	3,175
Angelo Que	74	79	81	75	309	3,175
Wu Kang-chun	77	80	78	80	315	3,012.50
Shaun Norris	88	77	76	81	322	2,912.50
Anthony Kim	66	73			DQ	
Liao Gui-ming	72				WD	

Barclays Singapore Open

Sentosa Golf Club, Singapore
Par 36-35–71; 7,300 yards

November 13-16
purse, US$5,000,000

	SCORES				TOTAL	MONEY
Jeev Milkha Singh	73	68	67	69	277	US$792,500
Padraig Harrington	72	70	66	70	278	423,750
Ernie Els	66	70	71	71	278	423,750
David Gleeson	72	67	71	69	279	225,750
Rory McIlroy	70	68	72	69	279	225,750
Charlie Wi	70	71	67	72	280	169,500
Thomas Bjorn	72	67	68	74	281	135,500
Chapchai Nirat	70	68	65	78	281	135,500
Phil Mickelson	73	68	66	75	282	110,000
Mitchell Brown	70	70	71	72	283	90,833.33
Somkiat Srisanga	71	71	70	71	283	90,833.33
Simon Dyson	69	67	71	76	283	90,833.33
Ted Oh	76	68	69	71	284	72,100
Thongchai Jaidee	76	67	70	71	284	72,100
Kim Kyung-tae	69	75	67	73	284	72,100
Scott Strange	71	71	69	73	284	72,100
Charl Schwartzel	71	69	69	75	284	72,100
Darren Clarke	73	71	71	70	285	60,666.67
James Kingston	72	71	71	71	285	60,666.67
Lam Chih Bing	67	71	68	79	285	60,666.67
Shigeki Maruyama	72	68	71	75	286	57,000
Prayad Marksaeng	73	69	73	72	287	50,250
Gonzalo Fernandez-Castano	72	70	74	71	287	50,250
Ben Leong	71	70	75	71	287	50,250
Dinesh Chand	74	71	71	71	287	50,250
Adam Blyth	72	70	71	74	287	50,250
Kodai Ichihara	73	73	71	70	287	50,250
Thaworn Wiratchant	71	68	73	75	287	50,250
Gaurav Ghei	74	71	66	76	287	50,250

UBS Hong Kong Open

Hong Kong Golf Club, Fanling, Hong Kong
Par 34-36–70; 6,702 yards

November 20-23
purse, US$2,500,000

	SCORES				TOTAL	MONEY
Lin Wen-tang	65	69	64	67	265	US$416,660
Francesco Molinari	66	67	67	65	265	217,135
Rory McIlroy	70	64	66	65	265	217,135
(Lin defeated Molinari on first and McIlroy on second playoff hole.)						
Chawalit Plaphol	66	66	70	65	267	115,500
Pablo Larrazabal	69	67	64	67	267	115,500
Iain Steel	68	68	66	66	268	66,200
Richard Sterne	64	69	69	66	268	66,200
David Gleeson	72	65	65	66	268	66,200
Oliver Wilson	66	66	65	71	268	66,200
Bernhard Langer	69	67	63	69	268	66,200
Oliver Fisher	67	65	73	64	269	41,875
Graeme McDowell	71	68	65	65	269	41,875
Angelo Que	68	68	67	66	269	41,875
Jeev Milkha Singh	71	63	66	69	269	41,875
Liang Wen-chong	64	71	69	66	270	36,000
Colin Montgomerie	68	65	68	69	270	36,000
John Daly	68	68	73	62	271	33,000

	SCORES				TOTAL	MONEY
Lu Wei-chih	70	69	64	68	271	33,000
Johan Edfors	68	65	73	66	272	29,150
Thongchai Jaidee	70	70	66	66	272	29,150
Jyoti Randhawa	71	68	66	67	272	29,150
Bradley Dredge	69	70	65	68	272	29,150
Kim Kyung-tae	70	67	66	69	272	29,150
Miguel Angel Jimenez	71	69	71	62	273	25,250
Peter Hanson	67	70	69	67	273	25,250
Gareth Maybin	71	67	68	67	273	25,250
David Frost	69	68	67	69	273	25,250
Ben Leong	69	70	65	69	273	25,250
Jose Manuel Lara	71	69	70	64	274	21,500
Taichiro Kiyota	72	67	70	65	274	21,500
Paul Lawrie	69	70	69	66	274	21,500
Rory Sabbatini	71	69	68	66	274	21,500
David Lynn	71	67	65	71	274	21,500
Gavin Flint	68	70	69	68	275	17,500
Darren Beck	68	69	69	69	275	17,500
Paul Waring	72	68	66	69	275	17,500
Louis Oosthuizen	70	62	73	70	275	17,500
Mark Brown	70	70	66	69	275	17,500
Antonio Lascuna	70	70	66	69	275	17,500
Jean-Baptiste Gonnet	69	66	68	72	275	17,500
Marcus Fraser	67	66	70	72	275	17,500
Sattaya Supupramai	71	69	70	66	276	14,000
Tony Carolan	70	67	72	67	276	14,000
Pelle Edberg	69	68	71	68	276	14,000
Thaworn Wiratchant	70	66	70	70	276	14,000
Mikko Ilonen	67	72	67	70	276	14,000
Mardan Mamat	70	67	67	72	276	14,000
Jarmo Sandelin	70	67	73	67	277	11,250
Taco Remkes	69	70	69	69	277	11,250
Gaurav Ghei	71	69	67	70	277	11,250
Daniel Vancsik	69	70	68	70	277	11,250
Soren Kjeldsen	68	68	70	71	277	11,250
Lu Wen-teh	68	69	71	70	278	7,875
David Horsey	70	70	71	67	278	7,875
Jamie Donaldson	75	63	72	68	278	7,875
Jean Van de Velde	73	67	70	68	278	7,875
Zaw Moe	72	68	70	68	278	7,875
Frankie Minoza	65	72	72	69	278	7,875
Anders Hansen	71	68	70	69	278	7,875
Paul McGinley	71	69	67	71	278	7,875
Unho Park	71	68	67	72	278	7,875
Wang Ter-chang	66	71	69	72	278	7,875
Anthony Wall	72	68	72	67	279	5,500
Phillip Archer	72	67	71	69	279	5,500
Scott Strange	71	68	71	69	279	5,500
Artemio Murakami	67	70	72	70	279	5,500
David Bransdon	70	68	70	71	279	5,500
Chinnarat Phadungsil	67	71	70	71	279	5,500
Martin Rominger	71	66	68	74	279	5,500
Jose Maria Olazabal	69	68	74	69	280	3,908.91
Mo Joong-kyung	69	71	71	69	280	3,908.91
Juvic Pagunsan	70	70	70	70	280	3,908.91
David Dixon	68	69	72	71	280	3,908.91
Anthony Kang	70	70	67	73	280	3,908.91
Martin Erlandsson	70	70	74	67	281	3,734.09
*Shun Yat Jason Hak	70	70	73	68	281	
Marcus Both	68	72	73	69	282	3,726.45
Suk Jong-yul	70	69	74	69	282	3,726.45
Kang Wook-soon	69	69	69	75	282	3,726.45
Niclas Fasth	71	69	71	72	283	3,718.82

	SCORES				TOTAL	MONEY
Gregory Bourdy	71	69	71	73	284	3,715
Scott Drummond	68	70	76	74	288	3,711.18

Omega Mission Hills World Cup

Mission Hills GC, Olazabal Course, Shenzhen, China November 27-30
Par 36-36–72; 7,251 yards purse, $5,500,000

	INDIVIDUAL SCORES				TOTAL
SWEDEN—$1,700,000					
Robert Karlsson/Henrik Stenson	65	67	66	63	261
SPAIN—$900,000					
Miguel Angel Jimenez/Pablo Larrazabal	64	63	67	70	264
AUSTRALIA—$429,000					
Brendan Jones/Richard Green	63	68	63	76	270
JAPAN—$429,000					
Ryuji Imada/Toru Taniguchi	66	68	68	68	270
GERMANY—$230,000					
Martin Kaymer/Alex Cejka	62	69	68	73	272
ENGLAND—$200,000					
Ian Poulter/Ross Fisher	69	74	63	67	273
THAILAND—$155,000					
Prayad Marksaeng/Thongchai Jaidee	69	73	64	68	274
SOUTH AFRICA—$155,000					
Rory Sabbatini/Richard Sterne	70	70	67	67	274
UNITED STATES—$125,000					
Ben Curtis/Brandt Snedeker	64	69	69	73	275
FRANCE—$96,667					
Gregory Bourdy/Gregory Havret	68	75	62	71	276
PHILIPPINES—$96,667					
Mars Pucay/Angelo Que	67	72	65	72	276
CHILE—$96,667					
Felipe Aguilar/Mark Tullo	67	76	66	67	276
DENMARK—$70,333					
Soren Hansen/Anders Hansen	65	75	64	73	277
CANADA—$70,333					
Wes Heffernan/Graham DeLaet	64	71	69	73	277
PORTUGAL—$70,333					
Tiago Cruz/Ricardo Santos	67	73	67	70	277
IRELAND—$64,000					
Graeme McDowell/Paul McGinley	65	68	68	77	278
INDIA—$61,000					
Jyoti Randhawa/Jeev Milkha Singh	67	72	70	71	280

	INDIVIDUAL SCORES				TOTAL
CHINA—$61,000 Liang Wen-chong/Zhang Lian-wei	69	75	64	72	280
ITALY—$57,000 Edoardo Molinari/Francesco Molinari	70	73	64	74	281
SCOTLAND—$57,000 Colin Montgomerie/Alastair Forsyth	68	73	68	72	281
FINLAND—$54,000 Mikko Korhonen/Roope Kakko	69	70	68	75	282
NEW ZEALAND—$51,000 David Smail/Mark Brown	65	75	68	75	283
GUATEMALA—$51,000 Pablo Acuna/Alejandro Villavicencio	69	76	66	72	283
TAIWAN—$48,000 Lu Wen-teh/Lin Wen-tang	68	74	69	72	284
WALES—$46,000 Bradley Dredge/Richard Johnson	69	77	68	71	285
SOUTH KOREA—$44,000 Kim Hyung-tae/Bae Sang-moon	68	70	71	78	287
MEXICO—$42,000 Oscar Serna/Daniel DeLeon	66	77	71	74	288
VENEZUELA—$40,000 Miguel Martinez/Raul Sanz	71	74	75	74	294

Hana Bank Vietnam Masters

Vietnam Golf & Country Club, Ho Chi Minh City, Vietnam
Par 36-36–72; 6,950 yards

December 4-7
purse, US$500,000

	SCORES				TOTAL	MONEY
Thongchai Jaidee	67	69	70	67	273	US$79,250
Andrew Dodt	70	71	69	63	273	42,375
Rhys Davies	67	70	70	66	273	42,375
(Thongchai defeated Dodt on second and Davies on third playoff hole.)						
Thaworn Wiratchant	72	65	71	68	276	24,650
Kodai Ichihara	65	69	72	71	277	20,500
Scott Barr	66	72	74	66	278	13,762.50
Chawalit Plaphol	71	70	68	69	278	13,762.50
Sattaya Supupramai	69	70	70	69	278	13,762.50
Lam Chih Bing	73	69	67	69	278	13,762.50
Artemio Murakami	67	69	71	72	279	9,437.50
Young Nam	67	70	70	72	279	9,437.50
Joo Hewng-chul	74	69	71	66	280	7,941.67
Wang Ter-chang	66	70	73	71	280	7,941.67
Pijit Petchkasem	69	70	69	72	280	7,941.67
S. Siva Chandhran	71	70	69	71	281	6,900
Frankie Minoza	69	72	69	71	281	6,900
Pyo Suk-min	66	67	73	75	281	6,900
Corey Harris	73	71	71	67	282	5,890
Hong Chang-kyu	73	71	70	68	282	5,890
Neven Basic	72	69	72	69	282	5,890

	SCORES				TOTAL	MONEY
Simon Griffiths	72	71	69	70	282	5,890
Jason King	71	68	72	71	282	5,890
Amandeep Johl	71	71	73	68	283	5,025
Digvijay Singh	67	74	73	69	283	5,025
Unho Park	71	70	72	70	283	5,025
Anthony Kang	67	76	69	71	283	5,025
Kwanchai Tannin	73	72	67	71	283	5,025
Pornsakon Tipsanit	73	69	68	73	283	5,025

Johnnie Walker Cambodian Open

Phokeethra Country Club, Siem Reap, Cambodia
Par 36-36–72; 7,226 yards

December 11-14
purse, US$300,000

	SCORES				TOTAL	MONEY
Thongchai Jaidee	68	66	64	66	264	US$47,550
Lam Chih Bing	73	65	67	65	270	32,550
Chawalit Plaphol	67	66	72	67	272	18,300
Anthony Kang	65	69	69	71	274	13,545
Rhys Davies	64	75	67	68	274	13,545
J.B. Park	68	67	71	69	275	9,450
Juvic Pagunsan	70	69	68	68	275	9,450
Steven Tiley	70	66	69	71	276	6,680
Thaworn Wiratchant	68	70	69	69	276	6,680
Iain Steel	74	65	68	69	276	6,680
Guido van der Valk	71	67	68	71	277	5,070
Jason King	69	71	70	67	277	5,070
Gaganjeet Bhullar	71	72	70	64	277	5,070
Corey Harris	69	65	69	75	278	4,230
Unho Park	72	67	69	70	278	4,230
Baaz Mann	72	65	72	69	278	4,230
Gavin Flint	68	71	72	67	278	4,230
Rory Hidayat Hie	66	71	69	73	279	3,534
Mars Pucay	70	67	71	71	279	3,534
Artemio Murakami	71	70	67	71	279	3,534
Chang Tse-peng	69	70	70	70	279	3,534
Airil Rizman	68	69	73	69	279	3,534
Prom Meesawat	69	70	67	74	280	3,150
Thammanoon Srirot	69	72	69	70	280	3,150
Sung Mao-chang	71	68	72	69	280	3,150

Volvo Masters of Asia

Thai Country Club, Bangkok, Thailand
Par 36-36–72; 7,082 yards

December 18-21
purse, US$750,000

	SCORES				TOTAL	MONEY
Lam Chih Bing	69	66	72	67	274	US$135,000
Chapchai Nirat	71	66	70	69	276	81,645
Terry Pilkadaris	71	72	68	66	277	46,020
Andrew Dodt	70	72	71	65	278	34,132.50
David Gleeson	72	72	63	71	278	34,132.50
Lin Wen-tang	68	70	72	69	279	23,895
Adam Blyth	68	72	70	69	279	23,895
Mitchell Brown	70	67	74	69	280	17,932.50
Chawalit Plaphol	71	67	69	73	280	17,932.50
Mo Joong-kyung	73	71	67	70	281	14,426.25

	SCORES				TOTAL	MONEY
Shiv Kapur	71	73	67	70	281	14,426.25
Prayad Marksaeng	74	65	72	71	282	12,513.75
Marcus Both	69	68	70	75	282	12,513.75
Thongchai Jaidee	73	74	69	67	283	10,407.50
Mark Brown	72	70	71	70	283	10,407.50
Rhys Davies	72	68	73	70	283	10,407.50
Bae Sang-moon	74	72	66	71	283	10,407.50
Simon Griffiths	72	68	71	72	283	10,407.50
Antonio Lascuna	70	67	71	75	283	10,407.50
Kim Kyung-tae	72	68	73	71	284	8,932.50
Rick Kulacz	72	69	68	75	284	8,932.50
Jyoti Randhawa	73	70	69	73	285	8,370
Gaganjeet Bhullar	72	72	69	72	285	8,370
Chinnarat Phadungsil	72	72	68	73	285	8,370
*Ye Jian-feng	75	72	72	67	286	
Neven Basic	66	74	77	69	286	7,470
Hendrik Buhrmann	69	71	75	71	286	7,470
Mardan Mamat	70	73	72	71	286	7,470
Lu Wei-chih	72	71	72	71	286	7,470
Tony Carolan	69	75	68	74	286	7,470

Omega China Tour

Guangzhou Championship

Dragon Lake Golf Club, Huado, Guangzhou
Par 36-36–72; 6,995 yards

March 13-16
purse, US$100,000

	SCORES				TOTAL	MONEY
Zhang Lian-wei	72	72	68	73	285	RMB150,000
Hsu Mong-nan	70	72	74	73	289	70,000
Chan Yih-shin	67	74	73	75	289	70,000
Li Chao	78	72	68	72	290	22,000
Liao Gui-ming	70	76	72	75	293	17,500
Gao Hui	73	76	74	71	294	14,500
Zhou Xun-shu	71	77	72	74	294	14,500
Yuan Hao	74	78	73	70	295	13,180
Qiu Zhi-feng	76	73	76	70	295	13,180
Huang Ming-jie	74	71	80	70	295	13,180
Wu Wei-huang	76	73	74	72	295	13,180
Wang Xian-feng	71	78	72	74	295	13,180
*Su Dong	75	74	71	75	295	
Zheng Wen-gen	74	73	77	72	296	12,200
Hao Chun-xi	75	73	74	74	296	12,200
Wang Lei	73	73	74	76	296	12,200
Fan Zhi-peng	77	74	74	73	298	11,700
Yang Jin-biao	72	76	76	74	298	11,700
*Hu Mu	81	74	75	69	299	
Huang Yong-huan	76	74	78	72	300	11,100
Zhou Zhen-bin	75	75	77	73	300	11,100

	SCORES				TOTAL	MONEY
Andrew Good	75	75	76	74	300	11,100
Yang Wen-zhang	73	79	72	76	300	11,100

Dell Championship

Orient Golf & Country Club, Xiamen
Par 35-35–70

March 27-30
purse, US$100,000

	SCORES				TOTAL	MONEY
Li Chao	69	70	69	66	274	RMB150,000
Zhang Lian-wei	73	70	65	69	277	90,000
Chan Yih-shin	70	71	68	70	279	50,000
Wu Wei-huang	70	68	70	72	280	22,000
*Hu Mu	70	65	72	74	281	
Hsu Mong-nan	69	71	70	71	281	16,250
Kong Wei-hai	69	71	72	69	281	16,250
Yuan Hao	69	68	69	76	282	13,750
Zhou Xun-shu	72	68	70	72	282	13,750
Liu Guo-jie	64	75	73	70	282	13,750
Wu Li-gui	72	70	74	66	282	13,750
Chen Xiao-ma	73	66	74	71	284	12,800
Zheng Wen-gen	72	69	71	73	285	12,300
Wu Kang-chun	74	72	67	72	285	12,300
Fan Zhi-peng	71	73	71	70	285	12,300
Shang Lei	74	72	70	69	285	12,300
Wu Ashun	72	73	73	68	286	11,800
Xu Qin	72	73	72	70	287	11,400
Liu Anda	73	69	75	70	287	11,400
Yu Gen-dong	67	75	75	70	287	11,400

Kunming Championship

Lakeview Golf Club, Kunming, Yunnan
Par 36-36–72; 7,222 yards

April 10-13
purse, US$100,000

	SCORES				TOTAL	MONEY
Lu Wen-teh	71	72	67	73	283	RMB150,000
*Ye Jian-feng	74	74	66	76	290	
*Su Dong	74	74	73	72	293	
Liu An-lin	70	74	75	75	294	54,000
Chen Ding-gen	70	73	77	74	294	54,000
Jim Johnson	79	73	71	71	294	54,000
*Hung Chien-yao	71	77	74	73	295	
Wu Kang-chun	74	77	73	71	295	16,250
Wu Wei-huang	74	78	74	69	295	16,250
Wu Hong-fu	74	76	71	75	296	14,250
Sha Ke	79	74	72	71	296	14,250
Gao Lei	73	71	75	78	297	13,250
*Hu Mu	76	75	70	76	297	
Liao Gui-ming	72	72	77	76	297	13,250
Yuan Hao	80	74	68	77	299	12,500
Yu Gen-dong	72	70	80	77	299	12,500
Tuo Wen-tao	77	73	75	74	299	12,500
Wu Li-gui	79	72	76	72	299	12,500
Zhang Meng	78	71	73	78	300	11,800
Zheng Wen-gen	78	79	67	76	300	11,800
Liu Guo-jie	75	76	75	74	300	11,800

Shanghai Championship

Orient Golf & Country Club, Shanghai
Par 36-36–72; 7,118 yards

May 15-18
purse, US$100,000

	SCORES				TOTAL	MONEY
Hsu Mong-nan	72	71	72	70	285	RMB150,000
Chen Xiao-ma	66	71	74	76	287	70,000
Liao Gui-ming	74	70	70	73	287	70,000
Fan Zhi-peng	73	66	72	77	288	22,000
Wu Kang-chun	75	70	71	74	290	15,667
Zheng Wen-gen	75	71	71	73	290	15,667
Fu Xin	75	73	72	70	290	15,667
Li Chao	70	73	75	73	291	14,000
Yuan Tian	77	71	76	68	292	13,500
Wu Ashun	74	70	71	78	293	12,900
Lu Wen-teh	75	72	70	76	293	12,900
Deng Yu-chao	72	70	78	74	294	12,400
Yang Wen-zhang	69	79	73	73	294	12,400
Wu Wei-huang	76	76	71	71	294	12,400
*Yuan Hao	69	76	74	76	295	
Gu Shu-tao	73	76	73	73	295	11,700
Kong Wei-hai	76	74	73	72	295	11,700
Nick Redfern	84	70	70	71	295	11,700
Cai Nan	75	73	73	75	296	11,000
Yang Tao-li	77	72	72	75	296	11,000
Liu Anda	76	73	73	74	296	11,000

Sofitel Golf Championship

Zhongshan International Golf Club, Nanjing
Par 36-36–72; 7,189 yards

May 22-25
purse, US$100,000

	SCORES				TOTAL	MONEY
Liao Gui-ming	66	69	69	74	278	RMB150,000
Zhang Lian-wei	72	68	67	71	278	90,000
(Liao defeated Zhang on first playoff hole.)						
*Su Dong	68	67	73	71	279	
Tsai Chi-huang	72	67	74	72	285	29,834
He Shao-cai	73	72	69	71	285	29,834
Huang Yong-huan	72	73	70	70	285	29,834
Shang Lei	73	70	72	71	286	14,750
Li Chao	68	76	72	70	286	14,750
Liu Jun-feng	72	69	74	72	287	14,000
Qiu Zhi-feng	71	73	70	74	288	13,500
Xu Qin	69	77	74	69	289	13,000
Deng Yong-hong	72	76	69	73	290	12,700
Nick Redfern	69	74	74	73	290	12,700
Yuan Zheng	73	69	75	74	291	12,400
Ye Xiong-hui	67	75	73	77	292	11,800
Dominique Boulet	77	67	72	76	292	11,800
Jason Robertson	70	76	72	74	292	11,800
Wu Ashun	73	73	72	74	292	11,800
Gu Shu-tao	72	71	76	73	292	11,800
*Zhang Xin-jun	74	72	73	73	292	

Luxehills Golf Championship

Luxehills International Country Club, Nanjing
Par 36-36–72; 7,335 yards

September 4-7
purse, US$100,000

	SCORES				TOTAL	MONEY
Tsai Chi-huang	68	68	66	68	270	RMB150,000
Liao Gui-ming	72	68	65	68	273	90,000
Yuan Hao	66	69	70	69	274	50,000
*Zhang Xin-jun	67	66	69	75	277	
*Ye Jian-feng	68	69	71	71	279	
*Huang Wen-yi	72	71	70	71	284	
Wang Lei	72	72	70	72	286	19,750
Wu Wei-huang	73	73	71	69	286	19,750
Wu Hong-fu	69	69	73	76	287	14,500
*Wei Wei	71	70	73	73	287	
Chou Huang-nan	71	74	71	71	287	14,500
Xiao Zhi-jin	73	71	74	69	287	14,500
Zhong Yong-guang	75	70	69	74	288	13,100
Chen Xiao-ma	71	73	71	73	288	13,100
Xing Xiao-xuan	73	77	67	71	288	13,100
*Huo Wei	71	70	76	71	288	
Liu Xin	69	77	69	74	289	12,100
Zhou Xun-shu	69	71	75	74	289	12,100
Li Zheng-fang	75	71	71	72	289	12,100
Jim Johnson	73	75	70	71	289	12,100
Zhou Jun	77	70	72	70	289	12,100
Wu Li-gui	76	69	74	70	289	12,100

Tianjin Championship

Tianjin Yangliuqing Golf Club, Tianjin
Par 36-36–72; 7,345 yards

September 25-28
purse, US$100,000

	SCORES				TOTAL	MONEY
Tsai Chi-huang	73	74	69	73	289	RMB150,000
*Su Dong	70	70	74	76	290	
Hsu Mong-nan	73	74	72	73	292	90,000
Zhou Jun	79	74	69	74	296	36,000
Yuan Tian	79	73	69	75	296	36,000
*Zhang Xin-jun	75	75	71	76	297	
Gao Hui	80	75	71	72	298	17,500
Wu Wei-huang	78	72	77	73	300	14,750
Li Chao	73	75	73	79	300	14,750
Wu Ashun	81	72	78	70	301	13,750
Shang Lei	74	78	72	77	301	13,750
Liu Guo-jie	77	76	76	73	302	12,800
*Huo Wei	74	79	75	74	302	
Xiao Zhi-jin	73	75	78	76	302	12,800
Kong Wei-hai	74	73	75	80	302	12,800
*Wei Wei	72	75	82	74	303	
Nick Redfern	74	84	70	75	303	12,400
Hao Chun-xi	73	74	78	79	304	12,100
Chen Ding-gen	76	76	72	80	304	12,100
Chen Xiao-ma	80	74	72	79	305	11,800

Omega Championship

Beijing Longxi Hotspring Golf Club, Beijing
Par 36-36–72; 7,367 yards

October 9-12
purse, US$146,000

	SCORES				TOTAL	MONEY
Zhou Jun	69	72	70	71	282	RMB187,500
Wu Kang-chun	72	70	76	71	289	112,500
Chan Yih-shin	72	71	70	77	290	62,500
Li Chao	72	74	73	72	291	27,500
Fu Xin	72	75	73	73	293	19,583
Chen Xiao-ma	71	77	72	73	293	19,583
He Shao-cai	75	77	75	66	293	19,583
Xiao Zhi-jin	73	74	74	73	294	17,188
Xing Xiao-xuan	73	68	77	76	294	17,188
Liu Anda	76	76	73	70	295	16,250
Liu Guo-jie	75	75	71	75	296	16,000
Liu Xin	76	75	76	70	297	15,250
Hao Chun-xi	75	77	74	71	297	15,250
Fan Zhi-peng	74	76	74	73	297	15,250
Chen Jian	72	74	77	74	297	15,250
Gu Cuilin	73	76	74	74	297	15,250
Liao Gui-ming	72	72	81	73	298	14,375
Jason Robertson	76	73	76	73	298	14,375
Yuan Hao	74	74	76	75	299	13,625
Nick Redfern	70	76	76	77	299	13,625
Sun Peng	73	73	75	78	299	13,625
Deng Yong-hong	75	77	75	72	299	13,625

Japan Tour

Token Homemate Cup

Token Tado Country Club, Nagoya, Mie
Par 35-36–71; 7,062 yards

April 17-20
purse, ¥110,000,000

	SCORES				TOTAL	MONEY
Katsumasa Miyamoto	71	66	73	66	276	¥22,000,000
Taichi Teshima	67	70	70	70	277	11,000,000
Steven Conran	69	67	75	67	278	7,480,000
Lee Dong-hwan	70	67	72	71	280	5,280,000
Ryuichi Oda	68	71	75	67	281	3,996,666
S.K. Ho	68	71	72	70	281	3,996,666
Ryo Ishikawa	68	67	72	74	281	3,996,666
Tomohiro Kondo	69	71	73	69	282	3,355,000
David Smail	68	73	73	69	283	2,992,000
Hidemasa Hoshino	68	70	75	70	283	2,992,000
Masaya Tomida	70	71	75	68	284	2,442,000
Hideto Tanihara	74	70	72	68	284	2,442,000
Yui Ueda	70	69	76	69	284	2,442,000

	SCORES				TOTAL	MONEY
Yeh Wei-tze	69	69	72	75	285	1,947,000
Shuji Ito	72	69	74	70	285	1,947,000
Tatsuhiko Takahashi	73	72	73	68	286	1,529,000
Masafumi Kawase	70	72	76	68	286	1,529,000
Shoichi Yamamoto	72	74	71	69	286	1,529,000
Kazuhiko Hosokawa	74	70	72	70	286	1,529,000
Koumei Oda	68	70	77	71	286	1,529,000
Brendan Jones	71	72	72	71	286	1,529,000
Han Lee	73	69	77	68	287	1,060,400
Keiichiro Fukabori	73	70	75	69	287	1,060,400
Shingo Katayama	71	71	75	70	287	1,060,400
Kiyotaka Inoue	75	67	75	70	287	1,060,400
Takao Nogami	74	68	73	72	287	1,060,400

Tsuruya Open

Yamanohara Golf Club, Kawanishi, Hyogo
Par 35-36–71; 6,770 yards

April 24-27
purse, ¥120,000,000

	SCORES				TOTAL	MONEY
S.K. Ho	70	69	65	68	272	¥24,000,000
Kim Kyung-tae	69	68	70	66	273	12,000,000
Hiroshi Iwata	67	63	73	71	274	8,160,000
Brendan Jones	68	69	71	68	276	4,960,000
Tadahiro Takayama	69	71	67	69	276	4,960,000
Keiichiro Fukabori	70	70	67	69	276	4,960,000
Shingo Katayama	67	68	72	70	277	3,810,000
Toru Taniguchi	71	66	69	71	277	3,810,000
Dinesh Chand	71	72	68	67	278	3,144,000
Taichiro Kiyota	73	69	68	68	278	3,144,000
Tetsuya Haraguchi	72	67	70	69	278	3,144,000
Park Jun-won	72	70	71	66	279	2,424,000
Taichi Teshima	69	70	71	69	279	2,424,000
Hiroyuki Fujita	65	72	71	71	279	2,424,000
Achi Sato	71	70	71	68	280	1,944,000
Tadashi Ezure	70	66	74	70	280	1,944,000
Tomohiro Kondo	72	69	69	70	280	1,944,000
Ryoken Kawagishi	70	71	69	71	281	1,560,000
David Smail	72	67	71	71	281	1,560,000
Shigeru Nonaka	72	69	68	72	281	1,560,000
Kiyoshi Miyazato	70	63	72	76	281	1,560,000
Takashi Kanemoto	72	71	70	69	282	1,224,000
Hirofumi Miyase	67	70	73	72	282	1,224,000
Katsumasa Miyamoto	72	65	70	75	282	1,224,000
Fumihiro Ebine	68	68	74	73	283	1,032,000
Kim Jong-duck	71	69	71	72	283	1,032,000
Keizo Yoshida	71	66	73	73	283	1,032,000

The Crowns

Nagoya Golf Club, Wago Course, Togo, Aichi
Par 35-35–70; 6,514 yards

May 1-4
purse, ¥120,000,000

	SCORES				TOTAL	MONEY
Tomohiro Kondo	72	68	64	67	271	¥24,000,000
Hiroyuki Fujita	71	65	68	67	271	12,000,000
(Kondo defeated Fujita on second playoff hole.)						

	SCORES				TOTAL	MONEY
Shingo Katayama	70	66	69	67	272	8,160,000
Toru Suzuki	73	65	67	68	273	5,280,000
Ryoken Kawagishi	69	65	68	71	273	5,280,000
Steven Conran	68	66	72	68	274	4,140,000
Jeev Milkha Singh	68	67	70	69	274	4,140,000
Tetsuya Haraguchi	73	69	67	66	275	3,522,000
Brendan Jones	70	68	69	68	275	3,522,000
Kaname Yokoo	70	69	69	68	276	3,024,000
Liang Wen-chong	67	68	70	71	276	3,024,000
Hirofumi Miyase	73	69	68	67	277	2,115,428
Tatsuhiko Takahashi	66	70	72	69	277	2,115,428
Naomi Ohta	72	67	69	69	277	2,115,428
David Smail	72	69	67	69	277	2,115,428
Koumei Oda	70	68	69	70	277	2,115,428
Prayad Marksaeng	68	70	69	70	277	2,115,428
Hideto Tanihara	68	68	70	71	277	2,115,428
Katsumasa Miyamoto	76	67	71	64	278	1,512,000
Tsuneyuki Nakajima	67	71	70	70	278	1,512,000
Azuma Yano	72	65	70	71	278	1,512,000
Nobuhiro Masuda	69	66	77	67	279	1,224,000
Kiyoshi Murota	70	68	72	69	279	1,224,000
Hideki Kase	70	72	68	69	279	1,224,000
Chawalit Plaphol	67	72	70	71	280	1,056,000
Michio Matsumura	71	66	71	72	280	1,056,000

Pine Valley Beijing Open

See Asian Tour section.

Japan PGA Championship

Raysum Golf & Spa Resort, Annaka, Gunma
Par 36-36–72; 7,127 yards

May 15-18
purse, ¥130,000,000

	SCORES				TOTAL	MONEY
Shingo Katayama	67	66	65	67	265	¥26,000,000
Liang Wen-chong	69	70	67	65	271	13,000,000
Brendan Jones	73	68	69	66	276	6,240,000
Tadahiro Takayama	71	68	69	68	276	6,240,000
Daisuke Maruyama	67	69	71	69	276	6,240,000
Kazuhiko Hosokawa	71	70	64	71	276	6,240,000
Naoya Takemoto	69	70	73	67	279	3,973,666
Hideto Tanihara	72	69	68	70	279	3,973,666
Azuma Yano	73	69	68	69	279	3,973,666
Hiroshi Iwata	69	73	69	69	280	3,406,000
Scott Laycock	73	67	75	66	281	2,756,000
Toru Taniguchi	73	68	71	69	281	2,756,000
Keiichiro Fukabori	70	72	69	70	281	2,756,000
Toshinori Muto	64	74	70	73	281	2,756,000
Tetsuya Haraguchi	75	70	70	67	282	2,106,000
Kiyoshi Miyazato	72	73	70	67	282	2,106,000
Kaname Yokoo	73	70	69	70	282	2,106,000
Sushi Ishigaki	73	69	72	69	283	1,586,000
Chip Sullivan	73	72	67	71	283	1,586,000
Satoshi Tomiyama	72	73	67	71	283	1,586,000
Katsumasa Miyamoto	74	71	66	72	283	1,586,000
Paul Sheehan	73	72	66	72	283	1,586,000
Masaya Tomida	74	65	71	73	283	1,586,000
Yasuji Kanai	71	71	71	71	284	1,170,000

	SCORES				TOTAL	MONEY
Masao Nakajima	71	71	70	72	284	1,170,000
Fumihiro Ebine	73	70	74	67	284	1,170,000

Munsingwear Open KSB Cup

Tojigaoka Marine Hills Golf Club, Tamano, Okayama
Par 36-36–72; 7,072 yards

May 22-25
purse, ¥100,000,000

	SCORES				TOTAL	MONEY
Hideto Tanihara	65	67	65	73	270	¥20,000,000
Katsunori Kuwabara	70	73	66	64	273	7,200,000
Shingo Katayama	68	68	68	69	273	7,200,000
Nobuhito Sato	65	69	69	70	273	7,200,000
Takashi Kanemoto	73	67	67	68	275	3,354,000
Masao Nakajima	66	70	70	69	275	3,354,000
Steven Conran	69	67	68	71	275	3,354,000
Toru Taniguchi	68	66	71	70	275	3,354,000
Masaya Tomida	68	68	67	72	275	3,354,000
Craig Parry	70	71	66	69	276	2,520,000
Hiroyuki Fujita	69	71	67	69	276	2,520,000
Hiromichi Kubo	73	69	67	68	277	2,120,000
Takuya Saito	72	66	70	69	277	2,120,000
Liang Wen-chong	74	68	70	67	279	1,770,000
Toru Morita	69	70	70	70	279	1,770,000
Yuudai Maeda	71	68	70	71	280	1,570,000
Paul Sheehan	69	71	69	71	280	1,570,000
Shinichi Akiba	67	76	67	71	281	1,380,000
Jung Ji-ho	72	67	69	73	281	1,380,000
Keiichiro Fukabori	69	74	69	70	282	1,037,142
Katsumasa Miyamoto	67	69	75	71	282	1,037,142
Prayad Marksaeng	72	69	73	68	282	1,037,142
Taichiro Kiyota	66	73	71	72	282	1,037,142
Kazuhiro Yamashita	73	70	71	68	282	1,037,142
Tatsuhiko Takahashi	73	66	70	73	282	1,037,142
Kiyoshi Miyazato	70	69	69	74	282	1,037,142

Mitsubishi Diamond Cup

Higashi Hirono Golf Club, Kobe, Hyogo
Par 35-36–71; 7,102 yards

May 29-June 1
purse, ¥110,000,000

	SCORES				TOTAL	MONEY
Prayad Marksaeng	70	70	66	68	274	¥22,000,000
Shintaro Kai	71	70	66	68	275	11,000,000
Hiroshi Iwata	74	66	67	69	276	5,720,000
Shingo Katayama	69	71	68	68	276	5,720,000
Hidemasa Hoshino	65	72	68	71	276	5,720,000
Hideto Tanihara	71	67	73	67	278	3,648,333
Tadahiro Takayama	72	68	69	69	278	3,648,333
Toshinori Muto	72	71	67	68	278	3,648,333
Nobuhiro Masuda	69	73	70	67	279	2,992,000
Kunihiro Kamii	69	71	68	71	279	2,992,000
Tsuneyuki Nakajima	72	71	71	66	280	2,442,000
David Smail	72	73	68	67	280	2,442,000
Toru Taniguchi	69	73	69	69	280	2,442,000
Steven Conran	71	70	71	69	281	1,892,000
Koumei Oda	74	69	69	69	281	1,892,000

	SCORES				TOTAL	MONEY
Kazuhiko Hosokawa	72	67	70	72	281	1,892,000
Tomohiro Kondo	73	70	70	69	282	1,478,400
Keiichiro Fukabori	73	72	67	70	282	1,478,400
Shinichi Yokota	71	70	71	70	282	1,478,400
Lee Seung-ho	70	71	71	70	282	1,478,400
Paul Sheehan	70	68	68	76	282	1,478,400
Makoto Inoue	71	69	72	71	283	1,089,000
I.J. Chang	74	67	71	71	283	1,089,000
Brendan Jones	77	67	68	71	283	1,089,000
Mamo Osanai	75	67	69	72	283	1,089,000

Gateway to the Open Mizuno Open Yomiuri Classic

Yomiuri Country Club, West Course, Nishinomiya, Hyogo
Par 35-36–71; 7,142 yards

June 19-22
purse, ¥130,000,000

	SCORES				TOTAL	MONEY
Prayad Marksaeng	69	66	69	65	269	¥26,000,000
Azuma Yano	67	67	71	65	270	13,000,000
Michio Matsumura	71	68	64	68	271	6,760,000
Yoshinobu Tsukada	69	67	68	67	271	6,760,000
Lee Dong-hwan	69	67	66	69	271	6,760,000
Hiroshi Iwata	72	69	66	66	273	4,485,000
Hidemasa Hoshino	73	70	65	65	273	4,485,000
Kaname Yokoo	73	68	68	65	274	3,679,000
Daisuke Maruyama	70	70	66	68	274	3,679,000
Toshinori Muto	74	68	68	64	274	3,679,000
Hidezumi Shirakata	71	70	68	66	275	2,756,000
Koumei Oda	68	73	68	66	275	2,756,000
Steven Conran	68	69	66	72	275	2,756,000
Kyoji Hirota	69	68	68	70	275	2,756,000
Katsumasa Miyamoto	71	67	66	72	276	2,106,000
Kiyoshi Murota	71	67	65	73	276	2,106,000
Tomohiro Kondo	68	68	69	71	276	2,106,000
Kazuhiro Yamashita	67	69	68	73	277	1,794,000
Achi Sato	69	67	69	72	277	1,794,000
Nobuyuki Okuwa	70	70	72	66	278	1,313,000
Hirofumi Miyase	70	71	66	71	278	1,313,000
S.K. Ho	70	71	69	68	278	1,313,000
Kim Jong-duck	73	68	68	69	278	1,313,000
Katsunori Kuwabara	69	71	69	69	278	1,313,000
Kosei Maeda	72	67	70	69	278	1,313,000
Cho Min-gyu	72	67	70	69	278	1,313,000
Yui Ueda	68	69	71	70	278	1,313,000

UBS Japan Golf Tour Championship

Shishido Hills Country Club, Kasama, Ibaraki
Par 36-35–71; 7,280 yards

July 3-6
purse, ¥150,000,000

	SCORES				TOTAL	MONEY
Hidemasa Hoshino	70	66	66	70	272	¥30,000,000
Brendan Jones	70	67	70	70	277	12,600,000
Takao Nogami	74	68	67	68	277	12,600,000
Daisuke Maruyama	71	71	70	66	278	6,600,000
Kenichi Kuboya	67	68	70	73	278	6,600,000
Lee Dong-hwan	68	70	72	69	279	5,400,000

	SCORES				TOTAL	MONEY
Hiroshi Iwata	68	68	69	75	280	4,950,000
Toshinori Muto	72	68	69	72	281	4,575,000
David Smail	73	66	73	70	282	4,080,000
S.K. Ho	69	68	72	73	282	4,080,000
Kaname Yokoo	70	71	71	72	284	3,480,000
Satoru Hirota	69	71	70	74	284	3,480,000
Yuudai Maeda	77	66	72	70	285	2,880,000
Azuma Yano	70	70	70	75	285	2,880,000
Mamo Osanai	73	75	68	70	286	2,430,000
Shingo Katayama	73	66	74	73	286	2,430,000
Keiichiro Fukabori	75	72	68	71	286	2,430,000
Toru Taniguchi	74	70	73	70	287	1,890,000
Takuya Taniguchi	74	71	71	71	287	1,890,000
Nobuhito Sato	72	70	71	74	287	1,890,000
Prayad Marksaeng	70	71	70	76	287	1,890,000
Tetsuji Hiratsuka	71	71	66	79	287	1,890,000
Scott Laycock	72	75	75	66	288	1,430,000
Koumei Oda	71	72	70	75	288	1,430,000
Shinichi Yokota	71	67	72	78	288	1,430,000

Nagashima Shigeo Invitational Sega Sammy Cup

North Country Golf Club, Chitose, Hokkaido
Par 36-36–72; 7,115 yards

July 24-27
purse, ¥150,000,000

	SCORES				TOTAL	MONEY
Jeev Milkha Singh	67	74	68	66	275	¥30,000,000
Sushi Ishigaki	69	67	69	72	277	15,000,000
Ryo Ishikawa	72	70	70	67	279	7,200,000
Taigen Tsumagari	71	72	68	68	279	7,200,000
Akio Sadakata	70	69	71	69	279	7,200,000
David Smail	72	70	68	69	279	7,200,000
Mamo Osanai	73	66	73	68	280	4,762,500
Nobuhito Sato	67	72	70	71	280	4,762,500
Dinesh Chand	70	69	69	73	281	4,230,000
Yui Ueda	68	72	72	70	282	3,480,000
Ryoken Kawagishi	67	71	71	73	282	3,480,000
Toru Taniguchi	66	75	69	72	282	3,480,000
Michio Matsumura	70	71	68	73	282	3,480,000
Eddie Lee	70	73	70	70	283	2,360,000
Hidemasa Hoshino	71	72	69	71	283	2,360,000
Craig Jones	67	71	73	72	283	2,360,000
Tateo Ozaki	72	70	69	72	283	2,360,000
Kazuhiro Yamashita	71	70	69	73	283	2,360,000
Koumei Oda	65	74	69	75	283	2,360,000
Kaname Yokoo	70	73	70	71	284	1,476,666
Han Lee	67	71	75	71	284	1,476,666
Katsumasa Miyamoto	70	72	70	72	284	1,476,666
S.K. Ho	67	73	72	72	284	1,476,666
Tadahisa Inoue	73	70	72	69	284	1,476,666
Paul Sheehan	72	68	75	69	284	1,476,666
Naoya Sugiyama	68	72	71	73	284	1,476,666
Keiichiro Fukabori	68	69	73	74	284	1,476,666
Mitsuhiro Tateyama	70	72	68	74	284	1,476,666

Sun Chlorella Classic

Otaru Country Club, Otaru, Hokkaido
Par 36-36–72; 7,535 yards

July 31-August 3
purse, ¥150,000,000

	SCORES				TOTAL	MONEY
Takuya Taniguchi	70	72	74	68	284	¥30,000,000
Hideto Tanihara	70	73	73	69	285	15,000,000
Lee Dong-hwan	73	70	72	71	286	10,200,000
David Smail	77	72	74	66	289	5,887,500
Takashi Kanemoto	72	75	74	68	289	5,887,500
Toshinori Muto	70	77	73	69	289	5,887,500
Tetsuya Haraguchi	71	71	75	72	289	5,887,500
Chawalit Plaphol	76	69	74	71	290	4,575,000
Katsumasa Miyamoto	70	74	77	70	291	4,080,000
Akio Sadakata	69	75	73	74	291	4,080,000
Daisuke Maruyama	73	77	75	67	292	3,480,000
Yuudai Maeda	74	72	74	72	292	3,480,000
Yui Ueda	66	81	77	69	293	2,692,500
Kenichi Kuboya	72	75	77	69	293	2,692,500
Takao Nogami	72	76	73	72	293	2,692,500
Satoshi Tomiyama	73	76	70	74	293	2,692,500
Satoru Hirota	72	76	77	69	294	2,016,000
Shingo Katayama	71	76	75	72	294	2,016,000
Kazuhiko Hosokawa	77	73	72	72	294	2,016,000
S.K. Ho	73	73	75	73	294	2,016,000
Yeh Wei-tze	74	69	77	74	294	2,016,000
Mitsuhiro Tateyama	77	73	76	69	295	1,485,000
Taigen Tsumagari	71	77	77	70	295	1,485,000
Eddie Lee	78	71	76	70	295	1,485,000
Ryuichi Oda	75	72	74	74	295	1,485,000

Vana H Cup KBC Augusta

Keya Golf Club, Shima, Fukuoka
Par 36-36–72; 7,173 yards

August 28-31
purse, ¥100,000,000

	SCORES				TOTAL	MONEY
Shintaro Kai	69	70	70	69	278	¥20,000,000
Hidemasa Hoshino	69	69	73	68	279	10,000,000
Toshinori Muto	72	74	70	64	280	4,800,000
Eddie Lee	74	69	72	65	280	4,800,000
Yusaku Miyazato	70	72	71	67	280	4,800,000
Yasuharu Imano	73	67	72	68	280	4,800,000
Steven Conran	70	70	71	70	281	3,175,000
Azuma Yano	74	68	69	70	281	3,175,000
Takao Nogami	72	72	69	69	282	2,720,000
Shinichi Akiba	70	70	70	72	282	2,720,000
Takamasa Yamamoto	74	69	74	66	283	2,120,000
Hideto Tanihara	71	74	71	67	283	2,120,000
Mitsuhiro Tateyama	68	76	70	69	283	2,120,000
S.K. Ho	74	66	72	71	283	2,120,000
Tatsuhiko Takahashi	70	69	77	68	284	1,620,000
Kenichi Kuboya	73	69	73	69	284	1,620,000
Makoto Inoue	68	73	73	70	284	1,620,000
Shinichi Yokota	76	71	70	68	285	1,220,000
Jiho Jung	77	68	71	69	285	1,220,000
Toyokazu Fujishima	72	73	71	69	285	1,220,000
Norio Shinozaki	69	74	72	70	285	1,220,000
Ryoken Kawagishi	72	72	71	70	285	1,220,000

	SCORES				TOTAL	MONEY
Toshimitsu Izawa	68	75	70	72	285	1,220,000
Kim Jong-duck	72	71	74	69	286	920,000
Prayad Marksaeng	76	68	72	70	286	920,000

Fujisankei Classic

Fujizakura Country Club, Fujikawaguchiko, Yamanashi
Par 35-36–71; 7,397 yards
(Event shortened to 54 holes — rain.)

September 4-7
purse, ¥150,000,000

	SCORES				TOTAL	MONEY
Toyokazu Fujishima	64	68	71	68	271	¥30,000,000
Hiroshi Iwata	69	68	69	65	271	15,000,000
(Fujishima defeated Iwata on first playoff hole.)						
Liang Wen-chong	71	71	64	66	272	7,800,000
Shingo Katayama	68	67	67	70	272	7,800,000
Kenichi Kuboya	70	66	67	69	272	7,800,000
Katsumasa Miyamoto	72	69	64	69	274	5,400,000
Lee Dong-hwan	66	68	70	71	275	4,950,000
Hideto Tanihara	68	73	65	70	276	4,575,000
Koumei Oda	71	69	70	68	278	3,630,000
Y.E. Yang	71	69	69	69	278	3,630,000
Yasuharu Imano	73	69	66	70	278	3,630,000
Toru Taniguchi	71	67	69	71	278	3,630,000
Azuma Yano	66	72	67	73	278	3,630,000
Kazuhiro Yamashita	68	69	72	71	280	2,730,000
Keiichiro Fukabori	71	70	70	70	281	2,505,000
Taichi Teshima	67	68	72	74	281	2,505,000
Shintaro Kai	72	69	72	69	282	2,140,000
Makoto Inoue	70	69	72	71	282	2,140,000
Ryo Ishikawa	70	71	69	72	282	2,140,000
Sushi Ishigaki	74	71	69	69	283	1,600,000
Prayad Marksaeng	73	68	72	70	283	1,600,000
Naoya Takemoto	67	69	75	72	283	1,600,000
Tetsuji Hiratsuka	72	68	71	72	283	1,600,000
Yusaku Miyazato	73	67	71	72	283	1,600,000
Frankie Minoza	68	71	77	67	283	1,600,000

ANA Open

Sapporo Golf Club, Wattsu Course, Kitahiroshima, Hokkaido
Par 36-35–71; 7,063 yards

September 18-21
purse, ¥130,000,000

	SCORES				TOTAL	MONEY
Azuma Yano	68	68	69	68	273	¥26,000,000
Tsuneyuki Nakajima	66	71	73	67	277	10,920,000
Toshinori Muto	68	71	70	68	277	10,920,000
Kenichi Kuboya	69	72	69	68	278	5,373,333
Hiroyuki Fujita	67	69	74	68	278	5,373,333
Shingo Katayama	67	72	69	70	278	5,373,333
David Smail	73	67	69	70	279	4,290,000
Masaya Tomida	69	70	75	66	280	3,815,500
Daisuke Maruyama	72	73	67	68	280	3,815,500
Shigeki Maruyama	70	72	73	66	281	3,016,000
Yusaku Miyazato	71	67	73	70	281	3,016,000
Tetsuji Hiratsuka	74	68	69	70	281	3,016,000
Lee Dong-hwan	68	73	69	71	281	3,016,000

	SCORES				TOTAL	MONEY
Hidezumi Shirakata	73	70	70	69	282	2,236,000
Hideto Tanihara	68	71	72	71	282	2,236,000
Kim Kyung-tae	65	71	74	72	282	2,236,000
Craig Parry	69	70	75	69	283	1,800,500
Tateo Ozaki	72	72	72	67	283	1,800,500
Paul Sheehan	68	71	72	72	283	1,800,500
Nobuhiro Masuda	68	71	72	72	283	1,800,500
Tadahisa Inoue	71	74	69	70	284	1,266,571
Mamo Osanai	73	68	73	70	284	1,266,571
Keiichiro Fukabori	71	75	67	71	284	1,266,571
Kazuhiko Hosokawa	66	72	75	71	284	1,266,571
Masafumi Kawase	72	72	68	72	284	1,266,571
Kazuhiro Yamashita	69	73	70	72	284	1,266,571
Naomi Ohta	71	69	69	75	284	1,266,571

Asia-Pacific Panasonic Open

Ibaraki Country Club, West Course, Ibaraki, Osaka
Par 35-35–70; 7,040 yards

September 25-28
purse, ¥200,000,000

	SCORES				TOTAL	MONEY
Hideto Tanihara	66	68	64	66	264	¥40,000,000
Azuma Yano	67	66	65	67	265	20,000,000
Liang Wen-chong	64	70	67	65	266	12,700,000
Kenichi Kuboya	67	69	64	66	266	12,700,000
Mark Brown	66	68	67	67	268	7,700,000
Kaname Yokoo	62	69	68	69	268	7,700,000
Shintaro Kai	71	66	66	66	269	5,600,000
Bae Sang-moon	69	65	67	68	269	5,600,000
S.K. Ho	68	67	68	67	270	4,400,000
Norio Shinozaki	65	68	71	67	271	3,800,000
Taichi Teshima	67	70	67	68	272	3,500,000
Brendan Jones	66	69	72	66	273	2,513,333
Keiichiro Fukabori	66	70	70	67	273	2,513,333
Chinnarat Phadungsil	73	63	70	67	273	2,513,333
Prayad Marksaeng	70	66	69	68	273	2,513,333
Yui Ueda	70	67	74	62	273	2,513,333
Katsumasa Miyamoto	67	68	68	70	273	2,513,333
Toru Suzuki	66	68	72	68	274	1,900,000
Angel Cabrera	68	68	69	69	274	1,900,000
Nobuhito Sato	70	66	67	71	274	1,900,000
Tetsuji Hiratsuka	70	66	69	70	275	1,686,666
Masao Nakajima	67	70	68	70	275	1,686,666
Juvic Pagunsan	68	65	70	72	275	1,686,666
Anthony Kang	67	69	71	69	276	1,540,000
Kazuhiro Yamashita	68	70	70	68	276	1,540,000
Frankie Minoza	69	69	68	70	276	1,540,000
Masaya Tomida	68	69	68	71	276	1,540,000

Coca-Cola Tokai Classic

Miyoshi Country Club, West Course, Miyoshi, Aichi
Par 36-36–72; 7,310 yards

October 2-5
purse, ¥120,000,000

	SCORES				TOTAL	MONEY
Toshinori Muto	69	70	69	69	277	¥24,000,000
Yuta Ikeda	69	69	70	71	279	12,000,000
Makoto Inoue	71	70	69	70	280	8,160,000
Kunihiro Kamii	71	71	70	69	281	5,280,000
Azuma Yano	71	71	68	71	281	5,280,000
Akio Sadakata	71	67	74	70	282	4,140,000
Shingo Katayama	71	71	67	73	282	4,140,000
David Smail	73	71	68	71	283	3,396,000
Brendan Jones	67	73	71	72	283	3,396,000
Toru Taniguchi	68	71	70	74	283	3,396,000
Steven Conran	72	73	71	69	285	2,448,000
Hidezumi Shirakata	73	73	68	71	285	2,448,000
Shinichi Yokota	70	68	74	73	285	2,448,000
Dinesh Chand	69	69	74	73	285	2,448,000
Keiichiro Fukabori	65	73	72	75	285	2,448,000
Chris Campbell	71	71	73	71	286	1,824,000
Jun Kikuchi	71	72	71	72	286	1,824,000
Scott Laycock	74	70	69	73	286	1,824,000
Shinichi Akiba	72	73	72	70	287	1,256,000
Hidemasa Hoshino	71	72	72	72	287	1,256,000
Kiyoshi Miyazato	71	74	70	72	287	1,256,000
Michio Matsumura	72	74	68	73	287	1,256,000
Daisuke Maruyama	76	70	72	69	287	1,256,000
Kazuhiro Yamashita	70	72	72	73	287	1,256,000
Kenichi Kuboya	75	71	72	69	287	1,256,000
Yoshinobu Tsukada	72	71	70	74	287	1,256,000
Tomohiro Kondo	76	70	66	75	287	1,256,000

Canon Open

Totsuka Country Club, Yokohama, Kanagawa
Par 36-36–72; 7,167 yards

October 9-12
purse, ¥200,000,000

	SCORES				TOTAL	MONEY
Makoto Inoue	70	71	69	65	275	¥40,000,000
Yasuharu Imano	74	70	66	66	276	12,800,000
Taichi Teshima	70	69	69	68	276	12,800,000
Hiroyuki Fujita	69	69	66	72	276	12,800,000
Yusaku Miyazato	71	70	65	70	276	12,800,000
Brendan Jones	73	71	70	64	278	6,633,333
Chawalit Plaphol	70	72	69	67	278	6,633,333
Kaname Yokoo	71	68	70	69	278	6,633,333
Toru Suzuki	71	70	70	68	279	5,040,000
Yui Ueda	72	70	69	68	279	5,040,000
Michio Matsumura	74	70	67	68	279	5,040,000
Azuma Yano	71	69	69	70	279	5,040,000
Takao Nogami	73	70	70	67	280	3,180,000
Koumei Oda	72	72	68	68	280	3,180,000
David Smail	73	69	70	68	280	3,180,000
Steven Conran	73	69	69	69	280	3,180,000
Frankie Minoza	69	69	71	71	280	3,180,000
Tetsuya Haraguchi	67	71	71	71	280	3,180,000
Kazuhiko Hosokawa	70	73	66	71	280	3,180,000
Katsunori Kuwabara	69	68	71	72	280	3,180,000

	SCORES				TOTAL	MONEY
Shigeki Maruyama	72	68	74	67	281	2,120,000
Ryo Ishikawa	72	71	68	70	281	2,120,000
Lee Seung-ho	71	70	68	72	281	2,120,000
Taichiro Kiyota	70	68	70	73	281	2,120,000
Craig Parry	71	72	71	68	282	1,640,000
Tomohiro Kondo	71	70	72	69	282	1,640,000
Toyokazu Fujishima	71	71	70	70	282	1,640,000
Masafumi Kawase	72	72	71	67	282	1,640,000
Shinichi Yokota	75	70	72	65	282	1,640,000

Japan Open

Koga Golf Club, Koga, Fukuoka
Par 36-35–71; 6,797 yards

October 16-19
purse, ¥200,000,000

	SCORES				TOTAL	MONEY
Shingo Katayama	68	72	72	71	283	¥40,000,000
Ryo Ishikawa	70	72	76	69	287	22,000,000
Brendan Jones	68	73	76	71	288	15,400,000
Lee Dong-hwan	72	71	77	71	291	10,000,000
Kunihiro Kamii	71	72	73	76	292	8,400,000
Han Lee	74	74	71	75	294	7,000,000
Taichi Teshima	76	72	75	72	295	6,000,000
Michio Matsumura	76	75	75	70	296	4,800,000
Azuma Yano	77	74	72	73	296	4,800,000
S.K. Ho	75	76	77	69	297	3,144,000
Hiroyuki Fujita	74	76	74	73	297	3,144,000
Sushi Ishigaki	71	75	77	74	297	3,144,000
Steven Conran	73	74	76	74	297	3,144,000
Tetsuji Hiratsuka	71	76	75	75	297	3,144,000
Katsumasa Miyamoto	72	75	81	70	298	2,112,000
David Smail	81	73	74	70	298	2,112,000
Toyokazu Fujishima	74	74	78	72	298	2,112,000
Yuta Ikeda	72	76	77	73	298	2,112,000
Mamo Osanai	72	76	76	74	298	2,112,000
Ryuichi Oda	78	73	77	71	299	1,740,000
Kazuhiro Yamashita	74	79	72	74	299	1,740,000
Jun Kikuchi	77	75	70	77	299	1,740,000
Toru Morita	74	78	75	73	300	1,580,000
Frankie Minoza	73	76	77	74	300	1,580,000
Craig Parry	75	73	74	78	300	1,580,000
Hiroshi Iwata	75	73	72	80	300	1,580,000

Bridgestone Open

Sodegaura Country Club, Chiba
Par 36-36–72; 7,138 yards

October 23-26
purse, ¥150,000,000

	SCORES				TOTAL	MONEY
Azuma Yano	65	66	69	67	267	¥30,000,000
Takao Nogami	69	70	66	66	271	15,000,000
Shigeki Maruyama	66	70	69	68	273	10,200,000
Tomohiro Kondo	70	70	65	69	274	6,600,000
Katsumasa Miyamoto	63	76	65	70	274	6,600,000
Hiroyuki Fujita	68	73	67	67	275	4,975,000
Norio Shinozaki	71	69	67	68	275	4,975,000
Shingo Katayama	69	69	64	73	275	4,975,000

	SCORES				TOTAL	MONEY
Yui Ueda	70	72	68	66	276	3,930,000
Shintaro Kai	69	69	68	70	276	3,930,000
Yuta Ikeda	66	71	68	71	276	3,930,000
Lee Dong-hwan	71	71	69	66	277	2,820,000
Ryo Ishikawa	72	71	67	67	277	2,820,000
Taichi Teshima	69	69	69	70	277	2,820,000
Kiyoshi Miyazato	71	70	66	70	277	2,820,000
Kaname Yokoo	68	66	72	71	277	2,820,000
Akio Sadakata	71	72	70	65	278	2,205,000
Daisuke Maruyama	71	71	67	69	278	2,205,000
Han Lee	71	68	72	68	279	1,890,000
Achi Sato	72	70	69	68	279	1,890,000
Sushi Ishigaki	70	70	70	69	279	1,890,000
Lee Seung-ho	71	72	69	68	280	1,650,000
Tatsuhiko Ichihara	70	71	71	69	281	1,362,000
Toru Taniguchi	71	68	71	71	281	1,362,000
Yasuharu Imano	71	74	70	66	281	1,362,000
Koumei Oda	71	70	69	71	281	1,362,000
Yoshikazu Haku	72	69	68	72	281	1,362,000

mynavi ABC Championship

ABC Golf Club, Kato, Hyogo
Par 36-36–72; 7,217 yards

October 30-November 2
purse, ¥150,000,000

	SCORES				TOTAL	MONEY
Ryo Ishikawa	70	70	70	69	279	¥30,000,000
Keiichiro Fukabori	67	68	72	73	280	15,000,000
Satoru Hirota	70	71	67	75	283	10,200,000
Mamo Osanai	70	68	75	71	284	6,200,000
Prayad Marksaeng	70	72	72	70	284	6,200,000
Takao Nogami	69	70	73	72	284	6,200,000
Akio Sadakata	71	71	73	70	285	4,762,500
Tadahiro Takayama	72	70	70	73	285	4,762,500
Michio Matsumura	71	73	72	70	286	4,230,000
Naoya Takemoto	71	73	74	69	287	3,205,000
Kiyoshi Miyazato	74	74	69	70	287	3,205,000
Taichi Teshima	72	74	71	70	287	3,205,000
Chawalit Plaphol	72	76	68	71	287	3,205,000
Yusaku Miyazato	69	70	76	72	287	3,205,000
Azuma Yano	70	74	69	74	287	3,205,000
Tomohiro Kondo	73	74	70	71	288	1,961,250
Katsumasa Miyamoto	68	73	79	68	288	1,961,250
Masaya Tomida	75	71	70	72	288	1,961,250
Koumei Oda	78	69	69	72	288	1,961,250
Hiroyuki Fujita	71	70	73	74	288	1,961,250
S.K. Ho	68	74	72	74	288	1,961,250
Kaname Yokoo	73	70	71	74	288	1,961,250
Sushi Ishigaki	70	69	74	75	288	1,961,250
Ryoken Kawagishi	71	74	72	72	289	1,380,000
Kazuhiro Yamashita	70	71	72	76	289	1,380,000

The Championship by Lexus

Otone Country Club, Bando, Ibaraki
Par 36-35–71; 7,011 yards

November 6-9
purse, ¥200,000,000

	SCORES				TOTAL	MONEY
S.K. Ho	66	68	65	70	269	¥40,000,000
Kiyoshi Miyazato	73	68	65	68	274	20,000,000
Wayne Perske	72	70	66	68	276	11,600,000
Brandt Jobe	64	71	70	71	276	11,600,000
Shintaro Kai	70	71	70	66	277	8,000,000
Daisuke Maruyama	71	65	73	69	278	7,200,000
Shingo Katayama	70	72	70	67	279	6,600,000
Norio Shinozaki	71	73	68	68	280	5,252,000
Azuma Yano	71	70	74	65	280	5,252,000
David Smail	70	69	72	69	280	5,252,000
Toru Suzuki	68	70	71	71	280	5,252,000
Kaname Yokoo	70	69	69	72	280	5,252,000
Shigeki Maruyama	71	70	72	68	281	3,590,000
Kazuhiro Yamashita	67	73	71	70	281	3,590,000
Eddie Lee	71	70	67	73	281	3,590,000
Steven Conran	68	66	70	77	281	3,590,000
Akio Sadakata	70	73	70	69	282	2,688,000
Yuudai Maeda	68	73	72	69	282	2,688,000
Hiroshi Iwata	74	70	68	70	282	2,688,000
Hirofumi Miyase	69	72	69	72	282	2,688,000
Toshinori Muto	66	69	73	74	282	2,688,000
Nobuhito Sato	73	70	69	71	283	2,040,000
Makoto Inoue	71	70	70	72	283	2,040,000
Satoru Hirota	68	72	70	73	283	2,040,000
Gregory Meyer	71	70	72	71	284	1,640,000
Lee Dong-hwan	70	73	69	72	284	1,640,000
Kiyoshi Murota	73	70	72	69	284	1,640,000
Tomohiro Kondo	72	71	69	72	284	1,640,000
Craig Parry	72	72	67	73	284	1,640,000

Mitsui Sumitomo Visa Taiheiyo Masters

Taiheiyo Club, Gotemba Course, Gotemba, Shizuoka
Par 36-36–72; 7,246 yards

November 13-16
purse, ¥200,000,000

	SCORES				TOTAL	MONEY
Shingo Katayama	67	68	68	69	272	¥40,000,000
Yasuharu Imano	67	69	65	71	272	20,000,000
(Katayama defeated Imano on first playoff hole.)						
Shintaro Kai	74	67	68	65	274	13,600,000
Michio Matsumura	68	69	70	68	275	9,600,000
Ryo Ishikawa	66	72	69	69	276	7,600,000
Trevor Immelman	69	71	67	69	276	7,600,000
Satoru Hirota	74	68	70	65	277	5,895,000
Ryuji Imada	71	66	71	69	277	5,895,000
Brendan Jones	70	69	69	69	277	5,895,000
Toshinori Muto	71	69	67	70	277	5,895,000
Mamo Osanai	73	67	70	68	278	4,080,000
Kenichi Kuboya	72	65	73	68	278	4,080,000
Hiroshi Iwata	72	65	72	69	278	4,080,000
Koumei Oda	68	70	71	69	278	4,080,000
Kaname Yokoo	70	72	67	69	278	4,080,000
Steven Conran	71	72	68	68	279	3,040,000
S.K. Ho	68	69	70	72	279	3,040,000

	SCORES				TOTAL	MONEY
Masaya Tomida	71	67	67	74	279	3,040,000
Tetsuji Hiratsuka	69	72	69	70	280	2,600,000
Brandt Jobe	71	70	69	70	280	2,600,000
Daisuke Maruyama	70	69	74	68	281	2,056,000
Sushi Ishigaki	71	69	73	68	281	2,056,000
David Smail	71	74	67	69	281	2,056,000
Tomohiro Kondo	69	70	72	70	281	2,056,000
Hideto Tanihara	69	69	71	72	281	2,056,000

Dunlop Phoenix

Phoenix Country Club, Miyazaki
Par 36-35–71; 7,010 yards

November 20-23
purse, ¥200,000,000

	SCORES				TOTAL	MONEY
Prayad Marksaeng	68	70	67	71	276	¥40,000,000
Ryo Ishikawa	72	67	70	68	277	20,000,000
Gonzalo Fernandez-Castano	68	70	73	67	278	10,400,000
Shigeki Maruyama	71	68	71	68	278	10,400,000
Hiroyuki Fujita	72	69	69	68	278	10,400,000
Masaya Tomida	71	69	69	70	279	7,200,000
Toru Taniguchi	70	69	71	70	280	6,600,000
Koumei Oda	72	70	72	67	281	5,050,000
Ian Poulter	73	73	66	69	281	5,050,000
Yasuharu Imano	71	73	67	70	281	5,050,000
Brandt Snedeker	68	71	70	72	281	5,050,000
Hideto Tanihara	72	70	68	71	281	5,050,000
Tomohiro Kondo	68	69	70	74	281	5,050,000
Daisuke Maruyama	73	73	67	69	282	3,640,000
Ernie Els	72	73	70	68	283	3,240,000
Taichi Teshima	73	66	73	71	283	3,240,000
Kim Hyung-sung	70	74	68	71	283	3,240,000
Yusaku Miyazato	70	73	71	70	284	2,680,000
Steve Marino	71	70	71	72	284	2,680,000
Hirofumi Miyase	69	73	69	73	284	2,680,000
Steven Conran	71	68	76	70	285	2,120,000
I.J. Chang	69	75	71	70	285	2,120,000
Brendan Jones	71	71	71	72	285	2,120,000
Azuma Yano	70	70	70	75	285	2,120,000
Brandt Jobe	74	68	74	70	286	1,522,500
Paul Sheehan	67	73	75	71	286	1,522,500
S.K. Ho	69	70	76	71	286	1,522,500
Martin Kaymer	76	69	70	71	286	1,522,500
Kenichi Kuboya	73	73	69	71	286	1,522,500
Toru Suzuki	68	71	75	72	286	1,522,500
Lee Dong-hwan	69	76	74	67	286	1,522,500
Takao Nogami	72	72	69	73	286	1,522,500

Casio World Open

Kochi Kuroshio Country Club, Geisei, Kochi
Par 36-36–72; 7,300 yards

November 27-30
purse, ¥140,000,000

	SCORES				TOTAL	MONEY
Koumei Oda	66	67	72	72	277	¥28,000,000
Kenichi Kuboya	68	70	71	71	280	14,000,000
Shintaro Kai	69	74	70	68	281	7,280,000

	SCORES				TOTAL	MONEY
Toru Suzuki	73	70	68	70	281	7,280,000
Hirofumi Miyase	70	69	70	72	281	7,280,000
Yusaku Miyazato	70	69	70	73	282	5,040,000
Mamo Osanai	73	72	69	69	283	4,126,500
Tomohiro Kondo	70	71	71	71	283	4,126,500
Azuma Yano	70	73	68	72	283	4,126,500
Tetsuya Haraguchi	72	70	68	73	283	4,126,500
Kazuhiro Yamashita	69	74	71	70	284	3,248,000
Achi Sato	67	70	75	72	284	3,248,000
Gregory Meyer	72	71	70	72	285	2,688,000
Ryo Ishikawa	70	71	71	73	285	2,688,000
I.J. Chang	71	72	72	71	286	2,072,000
Nobuhito Sato	69	74	71	72	286	2,072,000
Kiyoshi Miyazato	69	71	76	70	286	2,072,000
Sushi Ishigaki	71	69	72	74	286	2,072,000
Kim Kyung-tae	69	72	71	74	286	2,072,000
Shingo Katayama	69	70	72	75	286	2,072,000
Taigen Tsumagari	75	70	70	72	287	1,364,000
Toshinori Muto	69	77	68	73	287	1,364,000
Shinichi Yokota	72	73	69	73	287	1,364,000
Hideki Kase	69	75	70	73	287	1,364,000
Daisuke Maruyama	72	74	66	75	287	1,364,000
Masafumi Kawase	69	71	72	75	287	1,364,000
Michio Matsumura	70	70	71	76	287	1,364,000

Golf Nippon Series JT Cup

Tokyo Yomiuri Country Club, Tokyo
Par 35-35–70; 7,016 yards

December 4-7
purse, ¥100,000,000

	SCORES				TOTAL	MONEY
Jeev Milkha Singh	64	70	68	66	268	¥30,000,000
Brendan Jones	67	71	68	64	270	8,683,333
David Smail	68	68	68	66	270	8,683,333
Taichi Teshima	67	70	65	68	270	8,683,333
Ryo Ishikawa	67	69	66	70	272	3,900,000
Toshinori Muto	65	70	66	71	272	3,900,000
Kenichi Kuboya	70	68	68	69	275	3,033,333
Makoto Inoue	68	70	67	70	275	3,033,333
Prayad Marksaeng	64	74	63	74	275	3,033,333
Katsumasa Miyamoto	64	71	71	70	276	2,150,000
Shingo Katayama	67	70	69	70	276	2,150,000
Keiichiro Fukabori	70	67	68	71	276	2,150,000
Koumei Oda	71	68	65	72	276	2,150,000
Hiroyuki Fujita	68	69	67	72	276	2,150,000
Kaname Yokoo	63	73	67	73	276	2,150,000
Takuya Taniguchi	68	71	67	72	278	1,650,000
Hideto Tanihara	68	76	68	68	280	1,450,000
Lee Dong-hwan	67	72	72	69	280	1,450,000
Yasuharu Imano	70	73	68	69	280	1,450,000
Hidemasa Hoshino	69	75	67	71	282	1,250,000
Daisuke Maruyama	69	70	73	71	283	1,100,000
Shintaro Kai	68	75	66	74	283	1,100,000
Tomohiro Kondo	73	70	72	69	284	960,000
Takao Nogami	68	74	71	71	284	960,000
Azuma Yano	64	76	71	73	284	960,000
Toyokazu Fujishima	69	77	70	69	285	920,000

Australasian Tour

HSBC New Zealand PGA Championship

Clearwater Resort, Christchurch, New Zealand
Par 36-36–72; 7,137 yards
(Event reduced to 36 holes — rain.)

February 14-17
purse, US$650,000

	SCORES		TOTAL	MONEY
Darron Stiles	66	68	134	A$128,808
David Smail	69	66	135	72,991.20
Rick Price	67	69	136	48,303
Adam Crawford	69	68	137	34,348.80
Sebastian Fernandez	69	69	138	24,509.30
Kris Blanks	68	70	138	24,509.30
Dave Schultz	67	71	138	24,509.30
D.A. Points	67	71	138	24,509.30
Jason Enloe	70	69	139	15,385.40
Anthony Brown	70	69	139	15,385.40
Cameron Percy	71	68	139	15,385.40
Kim Felton	71	68	139	15,385.40
Ashley Hall	68	71	139	15,385.40
David McKenzie	68	71	139	15,385.40
Miguel Angel Carballo	73	67	140	7,868.84
Spencer Levin	70	70	140	7,868.84
Joe Daley	70	70	140	7,868.84
David Diaz	70	70	140	7,868.84
Peter O'Malley	70	70	140	7,868.84
Scott Dunlap	71	69	140	7,868.84
D.H. Lee	71	69	140	7,868.84
Terry Pilkadaris	71	69	140	7,868.84
Chris Kirk	69	71	140	7,868.84
Jarrod Lyle	71	69	140	7,868.84
Peter Tomasulo	71	69	140	7,868.84
Hunter Haas	68	72	140	7,868.84
Kelly Grunewald	72	68	140	7,868.84

Moonah Classic

Moonah Links, Fingal, Victoria
Par 36-36–72; 7,241 yards

February 21-24
purse, A$850,000

	SCORES				TOTAL	MONEY
Ewan Porter	67	71	71	66	275	A$153,000
D.J. Brigman	74	70	68	70	282	72,037.50
Tee McCabe	70	72	69	71	282	72,037.50
Terry Price	70	70	70	74	284	40,800
Jarrod Lyle	73	73	68	71	285	32,300
Fabian Gomez	69	76	68	72	285	32,300
D.A. Points	75	71	71	70	287	24,933.33
Scott Gutschewski	73	74	69	71	287	24,933.33
Alistair Presnell	71	72	70	74	287	24,933.33
Wade Ormsby	72	72	74	70	288	17,340
Ricky Barnes	71	72	72	73	288	17,340
Bret Guetz	72	71	71	74	288	17,340
Bryan DeCorso	72	72	70	74	288	17,340

	SCORES				TOTAL	MONEY
Wayne Perske	71	67	72	78	288	17,340
Miguel Angel Carballo	72	72	74	71	289	10,667.50
Aron Price	75	70	72	72	289	10,667.50
Paul Sheehan	70	76	71	72	289	10,667.50
Jarrod Moseley	71	75	71	72	289	10,667.50
Bryce Molder	74	69	73	73	289	10,667.50
Adam Crawford	75	72	68	74	289	10,667.50
Fran Quinn	68	73	71	77	289	10,667.50
Josh Geary	72	73	76	69	290	8,245
Jim Herman	75	70	73	72	290	8,245
Peter Fowler	77	71	69	73	290	8,245
Brendon de Jonge	75	70	71	74	290	8,245

Johnnie Walker Classic

See Asia/Japan Tours chapter.

Sportsbet Australian Masters

Huntingdale Golf Club, Melbourne, Victoria
Par 36-36–72; 6,980 yards

November 27-30
purse, A$1,500,000

	SCORES				TOTAL	MONEY
Rod Pampling	71	68	70	67	276	A$270,000
Marcus Fraser	73	67	71	65	276	153,000
(Pampling defeated Fraser on third playoff hole.)						
Robert Allenby	73	66	67	73	279	101,250
Tim Clark	67	70	76	67	280	62,000
Alexander Noren	73	71	68	68	280	62,000
Nathan Green	72	68	70	70	280	62,000
David McKenzie	72	70	71	68	281	48,000
Marc Leishman	71	70	74	67	282	40,500
Martin Erlandsson	74	71	70	67	282	40,500
Anthony Summers	70	68	71	73	282	40,500
Peter Senior	70	72	70	71	283	27,900
Tim Wilkinson	72	72	68	71	283	27,900
*Danny Lee	71	69	71	72	283	
Steve Webster	71	68	70	74	283	27,900
Ashley Hall	73	67	68	75	283	27,900
Michael Sim	72	66	68	77	283	27,900
Andre Stolz	73	70	71	70	284	18,435
Jamie Donaldson	72	67	73	72	284	18,435
Craig Scott	72	72	67	73	284	18,435
Aaron Townsend	75	64	71	74	284	18,435
David Horsey	71	68	71	74	284	18,435
Rob Harris	72	72	73	68	285	15,000
Wade Ormsby	72	71	73	69	285	15,000
Daniel Chopra	70	72	72	71	285	15,000
Mahal Pearce	75	70	74	67	286	12,300
Andrew Tschudin	74	70	71	71	286	12,300
Brad Lamb	73	72	68	73	286	12,300
Michael Wright	69	70	72	75	286	12,300
Daniel Wardrop	69	71	71	75	286	12,300
Scott Hend	67	73	71	75	286	12,300
Ryan Haller	76	69	72	70	287	8,887.50
Tony Carolan	74	68	74	71	287	8,887.50
Brett Rumford	71	70	73	73	287	8,887.50
Marcus Higley	72	71	71	73	287	8,887.50
Phillip Archer	73	71	70	73	287	8,887.50

	SCORES				TOTAL	MONEY
Johan Skold	72	68	73	74	287	8,887.50
Simon Griffiths	70	74	69	74	287	8,887.50
Scott Laycock	73	67	72	75	287	8,887.50
Bradley Hughes	72	71	74	71	288	6,300
Craig Spence	72	72	72	72	288	6,300
Michael Long	72	71	72	73	288	6,300
Alexandre Rocha	77	68	70	73	288	6,300
Peter Lonard	72	71	71	74	288	6,300
Michael Curtain	72	71	71	74	288	6,300
Adam Crawford	71	71	71	75	288	6,300
Greg Chalmers	72	70	71	75	288	6,300
Steve Alker	75	68	70	75	288	6,300
Oliver Fisher	72	73	75	69	289	4,500
Antti Ahokas	74	71	71	73	289	4,500
Steven Bowditch	72	70	73	74	289	4,500
Ewan Porter	70	71	77	72	290	3,300
Matthew Griffin	74	71	73	72	290	3,300
Cameron Percy	74	71	72	73	290	3,300
Lee Slattery	78	67	72	73	290	3,300
James McLean	75	69	72	74	290	3,300
Steve Jones	74	70	75	72	291	2,550
Wilhelm Schauman	76	69	73	73	291	2,550
Scott Draper	73	71	73	74	291	2,550
Anthony Brown	69	76	75	72	292	2,430
Martin Rominger	76	68	72	76	292	2,430
James Morrison	73	69	74	77	293	2,355
Dale Marmion	76	69	71	77	293	2,355
Steven Jeppesen	74	70	71	78	293	2,355
Vernon Sexton-Finck	70	74	74	76	294	2,280
Aaron Black	70	74	73	77	294	2,280
Scott Strange	75	68	78	74	295	2,205
Joel Sjoholm	74	68	77	76	295	2,205
Martin Wiegele	73	71	74	77	295	2,205
Daniel Vancsik	74	70	80	73	297	2,115
Tim Wise	71	73	78	77	299	2,070

Cadbury Schweppes Australian PGA Championship

Hyatt Regency Resort, Coolum Beach, Queensland
Par 36-36–72; 6,852 yards

December 4-7
purse, A$1,500,000

	SCORES				TOTAL	MONEY
Geoff Ogilvy	67	71	67	69	274	A$270,000
Mathew Goggin	67	68	69	72	276	153,000
Peter Senior	70	67	71	69	277	77,750
Scott Strange	70	69	69	69	277	77,750
Rod Pampling	70	67	68	72	277	77,750
Wayne Perske	71	66	73	68	278	44,700
John Senden	69	70	71	68	278	44,700
Brett Rumford	69	72	69	68	278	44,700
Wade Ormsby	70	70	69	69	278	44,700
Chris Gaunt	71	68	68	71	278	44,700
Paul Sheehan	66	70	74	69	279	30,000
Tim Clark	68	73	69	69	279	30,000
Peter O'Malley	72	67	67	73	279	30,000
Peter Wilson	68	69	72	71	280	24,750
Tim Wilkinson	66	72	69	73	280	24,750
Michael Brennan	71	70	71	69	281	20,550
Jarrod Lyle	72	63	71	75	281	20,550
Craig Parry	71	71	72	68	282	17,025

	SCORES				TOTAL	MONEY
Nathan Green	70	68	72	72	282	17,025
Steven Conran	71	70	69	72	282	17,025
Robert Allenby	71	71	72	69	283	15,300
David Lutterus	70	67	74	72	283	15,300
Paul Goydos	72	67	72	72	283	15,300
Ashley Hall	72	71	73	68	284	13,087.50
Heath Reed	69	74	71	70	284	13,087.50
Brad Kennedy	71	70	73	70	284	13,087.50
Stuart Appleby	71	70	73	70	284	13,087.50

Australian Open

Royal Sydney Golf Club, Sydney, New South Wales
Par 36-36–72; 6,941 yards

December 11-14
purse, A$1,500,000

	SCORES				TOTAL	MONEY
Tim Clark	70	73	69	67	279	A$270,000
Mathew Goggin	65	70	75	69	279	153,000
(Clark defeated Goggin on first playoff hole.)						
Robert Allenby	71	67	71	71	280	77,750
Stephen Dartnall	65	68	75	72	280	77,750
David Smail	67	68	70	75	280	77,750
Geoff Ogilvy	72	71	70	68	281	46,500
Steven Conran	70	66	75	70	281	46,500
Chris Gaunt	70	65	74	72	281	46,500
Andre Stolz	69	71	66	75	281	46,500
Richard Green	71	72	71	68	282	37,500
Stuart Bouvier	70	69	73	71	283	27,900
Adam Bland	71	69	71	72	283	27,900
Brendan Jones	70	71	70	72	283	27,900
Tim Wood	70	74	66	73	283	27,900
Ewan Porter	65	71	72	75	283	27,900
Rod Pampling	67	71	74	72	284	20,550
Paul Goydos	71	71	70	72	284	20,550
John Senden	69	72	73	71	285	17,025
Gareth Paddison	70	72	71	72	285	17,025
Andrew Bonhomme	69	72	69	75	285	17,025
Michael Sim	72	67	74	73	286	15,300
Simon Griffiths	71	68	73	74	286	15,300
Mark Brown	67	72	72	75	286	15,300
Josh Geary	73	70	72	72	287	12,350
Ashley Hall	72	71	71	73	287	12,350
Kurt Barnes	71	70	72	74	287	12,350
Matt Jones	71	67	74	75	287	12,350
*Danny Lee	68	75	69	75	287	
Rohan Blizard	70	69	70	78	287	12,350
Steven Bowditch	72	71	66	78	287	12,350

African Tours

Joburg Open

Royal Johannesburg & Kensington Golf Club,
Johannesburg, South Africa
Par 36-35–71; 7,590 yards

January 10-13
purse, €1,100,000

		SCORES			TOTAL	MONEY
Richard Sterne	71	68	67	65	271	R1,726,056
Magnus A. Carlsson	70	66	69	66	271	1,002,964
Garth Mulroy	67	72	66	66	271	1,002,964
(Sterne defeated Carlsson and Mulroy on second playoff hole.)						
Darren Clarke	73	65	67	68	273	534,696
Louis Moolman	68	69	69	69	275	385,504
Chris Williams	73	65	67	70	275	385,504
Mark Murless	65	68	69	73	275	385,504
Tyrone Ferreira	65	70	69	72	276	267,893
Ariel Canete	70	70	70	67	277	199,286
Ian Garbutt	71	69	68	69	277	199,286
Dawie Van der Walt	74	65	68	70	277	199,286
Paul Waring	69	67	69	72	277	199,286
Sven Struver	67	71	66	73	277	199,286
Iain Pyman	68	68	73	69	278	143,902.57
Charl Schwartzel	70	69	70	69	278	143,902.57
Justin Walters	73	67	69	69	278	143,902.57
Jake Roos	71	71	67	69	278	143,902.57
Andrew McLardy	68	73	67	70	278	143,902.57
Warren Abery	70	65	71	72	278	143,902.57
Ross McGowan	66	75	64	73	278	143,902.57
Chris Gane	73	69	70	67	279	119,244.50
James Kamte	68	71	70	70	279	119,244.50
Lee S. James	72	68	68	71	279	119,244.50
Pablo Larrazabal	66	68	70	75	279	119,244.50
Trevor Fisher, Jr.	68	73	71	68	280	101,432
Liam Bond	70	71	70	69	280	101,432
Stephen Gallacher	70	70	70	70	280	101,432
Dave Horsey	72	69	69	70	280	101,432
Craig Lee	74	68	68	70	280	101,432
Gary Lockerbie	67	71	70	72	280	101,432
Kyron Sullivan	74	67	67	72	280	101,432
Klas Eriksson	70	72	71	68	281	81,675
Louis Oosthuizen	68	74	69	70	281	81,675
Martin Wiegele	71	68	71	71	281	81,675
Raphael Jacquelin	72	70	68	71	281	81,675
Marcel Siem	68	71	70	72	281	81,675
John Mellor	69	71	69	72	281	81,675
Hendrik Buhrmann	70	71	68	72	281	81,675
Gary Boyd	68	69	70	74	281	81,675
Robert Rock	74	65	68	74	281	81,675
James Kingston	68	73	72	69	282	66,429
Oliver Bekker	67	74	69	72	282	66,429
Jbe' Kruger	72	70	68	72	282	66,429
Andre Cruse	69	68	72	73	282	66,429
Charl Coetzee	68	67	72	75	282	66,429
Jeppe Huldahl	71	71	72	69	283	51,183
Craig Lile	70	72	71	70	283	51,183
Alex Haindl	68	68	76	71	283	51,183
Ben Mason	70	72	69	72	283	51,183

	SCORES				TOTAL	MONEY
Andrew McArthur	73	69	68	73	283	51,183
Richard Bland	68	74	68	73	283	51,183
Marcus Higley	68	72	69	74	283	51,183
Joakim Backstrom	68	68	72	75	283	51,183
Brandon Pieters	70	68	69	76	283	51,183
Jaco Van Zyl	70	72	74	68	284	37,298.25
Florian Praegant	74	65	74	71	284	37,298.25
Marco Soffietti	70	72	71	71	284	37,298.25
Edward Rush	70	69	73	72	284	37,298.25
Juan Abbate	76	66	73	70	285	32,125.50
Marco Ruiz	67	71	76	71	285	32,125.50
Sion E. Bebb	66	73	73	73	285	32,125.50
Benoit Teilleria	71	70	69	75	285	32,125.50
Francois Delamontagne	70	71	73	72	286	27,769.50
Deane Pappas	72	69	73	72	286	27,769.50
David Drysdale	67	73	73	73	286	27,769.50
Branden Grace	76	65	71	74	286	27,769.50
Prinavin Nelson	68	72	77	70	287	23,958
Brett Liddle	74	66	74	73	287	23,958
Edoardo Molinari	70	72	72	73	287	23,958
Werner Geyer	70	72	72	74	288	18,140
Ryan Reid	67	75	71	75	288	18,140
Jan-Are Larsen	73	69	70	76	288	18,140
Doug McGuigan	71	71	72	75	289	16,261
Jamie Donaldson	70	71	72	76	289	16,261
Warren Bennett	69	72	73	76	290	16,216
Teboho Sefatsa	68	74	77	72	291	16,156.66
Patrik Sjoland	75	67	75	74	291	16,156.66
Henk Alberts	71	71	74	75	291	16,156.66
Bobby Lincoln	71	71	78	72	292	16,097
Gary Emerson	69	72	74	78	293	16,068

Dimension Data Pro-Am

Gary Player Country Club: Par 36-36–72; 7,831 yards
Lost City Golf Course: Par 36-36–72; 6,983 yards
Sun City, South Africa

January 24-27
purse, R1,800,000

	SCORES				TOTAL	MONEY
James Kamte	67	69	71	70	277	R285,300
James Kingston	65	69	72	74	280	207,000
Peter Karmis	70	69	71	71	281	124,560
Thomas Aiken	66	77	69	70	282	75,480
Peter Kaensche	70	70	71	71	282	75,480
Alan McLean	68	69	67	78	282	75,480
Hendrik Buhrmann	69	68	75	72	284	53,100
Jean Hugo	74	71	71	69	285	41,580
Keith Horne	68	75	75	67	285	41,580
Ulrich van den Berg	71	71	73	71	286	32,520
Justin Walters	69	70	76	71	286	32,520
Omar Sandys	71	70	71	74	286	32,520
Grant Muller	69	70	79	69	287	26,760
Oliver Bekker	68	74	75	70	287	26,760
Deane Pappas	66	76	69	76	287	26,760
Hennie Otto	74	67	77	70	288	22,140
Jaco Ahlers	68	79	70	71	288	22,140
Jbe' Kruger	72	72	71	73	288	22,140
Andre Cruse	70	72	72	74	288	22,140
Craig Lile	72	69	71	76	288	22,140
George Coetzee	75	72	73	68	288	22,140

	SCORES				TOTAL	MONEY
Steve Basson	67	69	77	75	288	22,140
Louis Moolman	72	72	74	71	289	18,630
Martin Maritz	80	66	71	72	289	18,630
Christiaan Basson	69	74	76	70	289	18,630
Neil Cheetham	72	67	73	77	289	18,630

Nashua Masters

Wild Coast Sun Country Club, Port Edward, Natal
Par 35-35–70; 6,351 yards

January 31-February 3
purse, R1,200,000

	SCORES				TOTAL	MONEY
Marc Cayeux	66	67	67	68	268	R190,200
Bradford Vaughan	67	66	64	73	270	138,000
Warren Abery	68	71	67	65	271	83,040
Justin Walters	65	68	69	70	272	58,920
Andre Cruse	70	70	67	66	273	36,576
Chris Williams	69	67	69	68	273	36,576
Adilson da Silva	70	68	67	68	273	36,576
Wallie Coetsee	67	67	70	69	273	36,576
Mark Murless	64	69	67	73	273	36,576
Doug McGuigan	68	70	70	67	275	19,760
Ulrich van den Berg	70	69	68	68	275	19,760
Deane Pappas	70	66	68	71	275	19,760
Grant Muller	65	67	69	74	275	19,760
Euan Little	67	68	66	74	275	19,760
Teboho Sefatsa	68	67	64	76	275	19,760
Christiaan Basson	72	69	69	66	276	16,140
Tyrone van Aswegen	69	68	67	72	276	16,140
Grant Veenstra	68	70	70	69	277	14,430
Martin Maritz	66	69	72	70	277	14,430
Ryan Tipping	69	67	70	71	277	14,430
Branden Grace	71	67	67	72	277	14,430
Stuart Clark	70	71	68	69	278	12,600
Omar Sandys	67	70	70	71	278	12,600
Alan McLean	72	66	72	68	278	12,600
Gary Thain	68	71	67	72	278	12,600
Michael du Toit	68	70	73	67	278	12,600

Africa Open

Fish River Sun Country Club, Port Alfred, South Africa
Par 36-36–72; 6,889 yards

February 7-10
purse, R1,200,000

	SCORES				TOTAL	MONEY
Shaun Norris	68	69	70	68	275	R190,200
Nic Henning	69	68	75	69	281	138,000
Grant Muller	67	70	75	70	282	63,840
Jean Hugo	70	66	74	72	282	63,840
Marc Cayeux	65	72	71	74	282	63,840
Jeremy Kavanagh	70	75	69	69	283	33,330
Warren Abery	70	70	72	71	283	33,330
Hennie Otto	75	67	68	73	283	33,330
Jake Roos	65	69	75	74	283	33,330
Bradford Vaughan	75	69	70	70	284	21,680
Brett Liddle	67	73	72	72	284	21,680
James Kamte	72	69	71	72	284	21,680

	SCORES				TOTAL	MONEY
Mark Murless	70	76	70	70	286	17,490
Titch Moore	71	66	76	73	286	17,490
Alan Michell	71	68	73	74	286	17,490
Bafana Hlophe	70	73	67	76	286	17,490
Grant Veenstra	69	74	72	72	287	15,240
Ulrich van den Berg	70	70	73	74	287	15,240
Charl Coetzee	71	70	71	75	287	15,240
Justin Walters	74	69	72	73	288	14,160
Andre Bossert	73	71	76	69	289	12,420
Dawie Van der Walt	70	69	78	72	289	12,420
Jbe' Kruger	68	73	75	73	289	12,420
Adilson da Silva	71	70	73	75	289	12,420
Oliver Bekker	74	72	68	75	289	12,420
Deane Pappas	67	68	78	76	289	12,420
Branden Grace	71	70	69	79	289	12,420
Merrick Bremner	69	68	72	80	289	12,420

Vodacom Championship

Pretoria Country Club, Pretoria, South Africa
Par 36-36–72; 7,063 yards

February 14-17
purse, R2,400,000

	SCORES				TOTAL	MONEY
James Kingston	71	67	68	65	271	R380,400
Adilson da Silva	67	67	68	71	273	276,000
Andre Cruse	70	68	69	67	274	141,960
Brandon Pieters	69	67	70	68	274	141,960
Charl Schwartzel	68	68	72	67	275	99,120
David Hewan	72	69	67	68	276	77,880
Mark Murless	67	68	70	71	276	77,880
Bobby Lincoln	70	72	67	69	278	50,220
Louis Oosthuizen	68	68	72	70	278	50,220
Jean Hugo	69	68	70	71	278	50,220
Warren Abery	71	69	67	71	278	50,220
Chris Williams	76	68	70	66	280	36,780
Shaun Norris	72	70	70	68	280	36,780
Chris Swanepoel	71	67	72	70	280	36,780
Ryan Tipping	70	70	70	70	280	36,780
Trevor Fisher, Jr.	75	71	65	70	281	31,680
Tyrone Ferreira	68	69	69	75	281	31,680
George Coetzee	70	67	68	76	281	31,680
Darren Fichardt	72	73	69	68	282	28,800
Louis Moolman	67	71	73	71	282	28,800
Lars Brovold	73	73	71	66	283	25,920
Desvonde Botes	72	72	72	67	283	25,920
Clinton Whitelaw	67	72	75	69	283	25,920
Johan Etsebeth	72	70	71	70	283	25,920
Martin Maritz	71	73	68	71	283	25,920

Telkom PGA Championship

The Country Club, Johannesburg, South Africa
Par 36-36–72; 7,533 yards

February 21-24
purse, R2,500,000

	SCORES				TOTAL	MONEY
Louis Oosthuizen	66	63	66	65	260	R396,250
Hennie Otto	69	69	66	70	274	287,500

	SCORES				TOTAL	MONEY
Jake Roos	67	69	69	70	275	173,000
Charl Schwartzel	69	74	66	67	276	122,750
Thabang Simon	73	64	72	68	277	103,250
Adilson da Silva	70	70	70	68	278	69,437.50
Ross Wellington	71	66	71	70	278	69,437.50
Alan McLean	72	65	69	72	278	69,437.50
Warren Abery	68	66	71	73	278	69,437.50
Anton Haig	70	66	72	71	279	46,875
Christiaan Basson	71	66	69	73	279	46,875
Craig Lile	69	74	71	66	280	40,500
Louis Moolman	70	74	68	68	280	40,500
Chris Swanepoel	70	70	73	68	281	33,625
Martin Maritz	74	70	68	69	281	33,625
Jean Hugo	69	69	73	70	281	33,625
Marc Cayeux	67	71	73	70	281	33,625
Neil Schietekat	71	69	70	71	281	33,625
David Hewan	65	73	70	73	281	33,625
Thomas Aiken	71	68	77	66	282	28,583.33
James Kamte	70	74	69	69	282	28,583.33
Tyrone van Aswegen	64	72	76	70	282	28,583.33
Justin Walters	72	70	72	69	283	25,875
Dawie Van der Walt	68	71	73	71	283	25,875
Shaun Norris	70	70	72	71	283	25,875
Ryan Cairns	67	73	71	72	283	25,875

Mount Edgecombe Trophy

Mount Edgecombe Country Club, Kwazulu Natal, South Africa
Par 36-36–72; 6,825 yards

February 28-March 2
purse, R500,000

	SCORES				TOTAL	MONEY
Mark Murless	71	69	68	67	275	R79,250
Darren Fichardt	67	68	66	74	275	57,500
(Murless defeated Fichardt on first playoff hole.)						
Michiel Bothma	67	74	70	67	278	31,666.66
Trevor Fisher, Jr.	67	69	73	69	278	31,666.66
Jaco Van Zyl	70	67	69	72	278	31,666.66
Oliver Bekker	71	66	71	71	279	17,375
Adilson da Silva	69	63	71	76	279	17,375
Chris Swanepoel	71	68	73	69	281	11,550
Ryan Cairns	69	71	70	71	281	11,550
Chris Williams	68	66	75	72	281	11,550
Tyrone van Aswegen	71	68	70	72	281	11,550
Grant Muller	72	68	69	72	281	11,550
Doug McGuigan	73	67	73	69	282	9,016.66
Neil Schietekat	69	72	71	70	282	9,016.66
Ryan Tipping	70	71	70	71	282	9,016.66
Jake Roos	67	70	72	74	283	7,816.66
George Coetzee	68	73	67	75	283	7,816.66
Jeff Inglis	68	64	74	77	283	7,816.66
Bradford Vaughan	68	71	75	70	284	6,575
Peter Karmis	75	67	72	70	284	6,575
Toto Thimba	68	73	72	71	284	6,575
Warren Abery	71	69	72	72	284	6,575
Justin Walters	70	70	72	72	284	6,575
Jaco Ahlers	73	68	71	72	284	6,575
Josh Cunliffe	71	71	73	70	285	5,650
Ross Wellington	69	69	73	74	285	5,650

Chainama Hills Zambia Open

Chainama Golf Club, Lusaka, Zambia
Par 36-36–72; 7,196 yards

March 28-30
purse, R750,000

	SCORES			TOTAL	MONEY
Tyrone Ferreira	68	65	75	208	R118,875
Charl Coetzee	74	67	69	210	69,075
Divan van den Heever	70	70	70	210	69,075
T.C. Charamba	67	71	73	211	29,118.75
Andrew Odoh	67	71	73	211	29,118.75
Jean Hugo	67	69	75	211	29,118.75
Johan Etsebeth	65	70	76	211	29,118.75
Grant Muller	72	69	71	212	18,450
Bafana Hlophe	71	72	70	213	14,775
Johary Raveloarison	73	66	74	213	14,775
Jbe' Kruger	69	70	74	213	14,775
Dismas Indiza	71	74	69	214	10,603.12
Theunis Spangenberg	71	73	70	214	10,603.12
George Coetzee	70	73	71	214	10,603.12
Andre Cruse	72	71	71	214	10,603.12
Vaughn Groenewald	74	68	72	214	10,603.12
Adilson da Silva	72	70	72	214	10,603.12
Branden Grace	69	72	73	214	10,603.12
Louis Moolman	70	70	74	214	10,603.12
Oliver Bekker	70	74	71	215	8,850
Brett Liddle	74	71	71	216	8,437.50
Steve van Vuuren	71	72	73	216	8,437.50
Marc Cayeux	74	72	71	217	7,875
Andrew Curlewis	71	71	75	217	7,875
Pelop Panagopoulos	73	66	78	217	7,875

Vodacom Origins of Golf Free State

Bloemfontein Golf Club, Bloemfontein, South Africa
Par 36-36–72; 7,302 yards

April 3-5
purse, R440,000

	SCORES			TOTAL	MONEY
Dion Fourie	66	66	69	201	R69,740
Jean Hugo	69	64	70	203	42,900
Chris Swanepoel	64	69	70	203	42,900
Chris Williams	67	69	68	204	21,706.66
Merrick Bremner	67	67	70	204	21,706.66
John Bele	65	66	73	204	21,706.66
Albert Pistorius	68	70	67	205	12,980
Jaco Van Zyl	70	67	68	205	12,980
Steve Basson	70	68	68	206	8,932
Johary Raveloarison	68	70	68	206	8,932
Alex Haindl	70	67	69	206	8,932
Dean Lambert	68	69	69	206	8,932
Oliver Bekker	66	71	69	206	8,932
Neil Schietekat	69	67	70	206	8,932
Darren Fichardt	69	66	71	206	8,932
Doug McGuigan	68	71	68	207	6,380
Alan Michell	69	70	68	207	6,380
Warren Abery	68	69	70	207	6,380
Jaco Ahlers	69	68	70	207	6,380
Titch Moore	71	66	70	207	6,380
Heinrich Bruiners	69	67	71	207	6,380
Desvonde Botes	68	66	73	207	6,380

	SCORES			TOTAL	MONEY
Trevor Fisher, Jr.	68	70	70	208	5,346
Steve van Vuuren	69	68	71	208	5,346
Des Terblanche	70	70	69	209	4,627.33
Mohamed Tayob	71	68	70	209	4,627.33
Toto Thimba	72	65	72	209	4,627.33
Marc Cayeux	69	68	72	209	4,627.33
Tyrone van Aswegen	66	70	73	209	4,627.33
Brett Liddle	66	70	73	209	4,627.33

Vodacom Origins of Golf Gauteng

Pretoria Country Club, Pretoria, South Africa
Par 36-36–72; 7,063 yards

April 23-25
purse, R440,000

	SCORES			TOTAL	MONEY
Tyrone van Aswegen	67	69	65	201	R69,740
Darren Fichardt	68	69	68	205	42,900
Neil Schietekat	70	63	72	205	42,900
Chris Swanepoel	72	65	69	206	27,720
Vaughn Groenewald	66	69	73	208	20,680
Titch Moore	72	69	68	209	13,365
Thomas Aiken	70	70	69	209	13,365
Jean Hugo	68	71	70	209	13,365
Marc Cayeux	71	63	75	209	13,365
Trevor Fisher, Jr.	65	75	70	210	9,570
Chris Williams	66	73	71	210	9,570
Doug McGuigan	74	70	67	211	8,580
Grant Muller	71	67	73	211	8,580
Alan Michell	72	73	67	212	7,722
T.C. Charamba	72	70	70	212	7,722
Reggie Adams	75	70	68	213	6,497.33
Brandon Pieters	75	69	69	213	6,497.33
George Coetzee	73	71	69	213	6,497.33
James Kamte	72	72	69	213	6,497.33
Desvonde Botes	75	66	72	213	6,497.33
Jbe' Kruger	70	71	72	213	6,497.33
Steve van Vuuren	71	73	70	214	5,456
Bradford Vaughan	71	72	71	214	5,456
Kevin Stone	71	71	72	214	5,456
Grant Veenstra	72	73	70	215	4,884
Andre Cruse	72	72	71	215	4,884
Hennie Otto	74	69	72	215	4,884

Samsung Royal Swazi Sun Open

Royal Swazi Sun Country Club, Mbabane, Swaziland
Par 36-36–72; 6,715 yards

May 7-10
purse, R700,000

	POINTS				TOTAL	MONEY
Jean Hugo	16	26	13	1	56	R110,950
Neil Schietekat	8	13	20	9	50	80,500
Desvonde Botes	21	5	13	10	49	56,000
Trevor Fisher, Jr.	10	12	9	14	45	44,100
Christiaan Basson	13	14	3	14	44	32,900
Peter Karmis	5	14	15	9	43	26,600
Adilson da Silva	7	6	9	19	41	22,050
Warren Abery	9	10	11	10	40	19,250

	POINTS				TOTAL	MONEY
Chris Williams	9	0	18	8	35	16,450
Steve Basson	4	11	7	13	35	16,450
Tyrone van Aswegen	5	10	4	14	33	14,350
Tyrone Ferreira	10	12	7	4	33	14,350
Thabang Simon	10	7	4	11	32	12,623
Nic Henning	9	2	6	15	32	12,623
Louis de Jager	16	5	7	4	32	12,623
Wallie Coetsee	7	4	7	13	31	11,410
Josh Cunliffe	11	10	0	8	29	10,920
Michiel Bothma	5	5	7	11	28	10,290
Mark Murless	10	7	8	3	28	10,290
David Hewan	8	0	3	16	27	9,205
Brandon Pieters	4	11	5	7	27	9,205
Mohamed Tayob	2	10	7	8	27	9,205
Heinrich Bruiners	4	6	9	8	27	9,205
Bradford Vaughan	1	7	3	15	26	7,910
Gerlou Roux	0	10	9	7	26	7,910
Jbe' Kruger	11	4	2	9	26	7,910
T.C. Charamba	4	11	9	2	26	7,910

Nashua Golf Challenge

Gary Player Country Club: Par 36-36–72; 7,831 yards
Lost City Golf Course: Par 36-36–72; 6,983 yards
Sun City, South Africa

May 15-17
purse, R500,000

	SCORES			TOTAL	MONEY
Keith Horne	72	68	70	210	R79,250
Nic Henning	71	67	72	210	57,500
(Horne defeated Henning on second playoff hole.)					
Trevor Fisher, Jr.	72	68	71	211	31,666.66
Jean Hugo	72	68	71	211	31,666.66
Desvonde Botes	68	65	78	211	31,666.66
Kevin Stone	72	70	70	212	19,000
Divan van den Heever	71	69	73	213	15,750
Adilson da Silva	73	71	71	215	12,416.66
Louis Moolman	72	71	72	215	12,416.66
Hendrik Buhrmann	72	70	73	215	12,416.66
Brandon Pieters	71	72	73	216	10,000
Mark Murless	75	68	73	216	10,000
Chris Williams	72	68	76	216	10,000
Jbe' Kruger	73	71	73	217	8,375
Jaco Van Zyl	73	69	75	217	8,375
Louis de Jager	71	71	75	217	8,375
Oliver Bekker	81	67	69	217	8,375
Omar Sandys	73	72	73	218	7,350
Darren Holder	71	70	77	218	7,350
Lindani Ndwandwe	73	72	74	219	6,575
Rossouw Loubser	72	74	73	219	6,575
Neil Schietekat	73	74	72	219	6,575
Theunis Spangenberg	77	71	71	219	6,575
Steve van Vuuren	73	71	76	220	5,750
Jaco Ahlers	72	72	76	220	5,750
P.H. McIntyre	68	75	77	220	5,750

Vodacom Origins of Golf Kwazulu Natal

Selborne Hotel Spa & Golf Estate, Kwazulu Natal, South Africa
Par 36-36–72; 6,607 yards

May 28-30
purse, R440,000

	SCORES			TOTAL	MONEY
Jean Hugo	69	66	68	203	R69,740
Bradford Vaughan	69	68	68	205	50,600
Steve van Vuuren	68	69	69	206	25,080
Prinavin Nelson	69	68	69	206	25,080
P.H. McIntyre	67	69	70	206	25,080
Desvonde Botes	68	67	71	206	25,080
Keith Horne	69	69	69	207	12,246.66
Trevor Fisher, Jr.	65	72	70	207	12,246.66
Nic Henning	70	65	72	207	12,246.66
Louis Moolman	72	69	67	208	9,075
Mark Murless	70	69	69	208	9,075
Marc Cayeux	69	68	71	208	9,075
Christiaan Basson	67	69	72	208	9,075
Warren Abery	69	72	68	209	7,722
Toto Thimba	70	70	69	209	7,722
Neil Schietekat	70	71	69	210	6,878.66
Heinrich Bruiners	68	72	70	210	6,878.66
Grant Muller	67	69	74	210	6,878.66
Andre Cruse	70	72	69	211	6,006
Hendrik Buhrmann	66	73	72	211	6,006
Johan Etsebeth	68	70	73	211	6,006
Adilson da Silva	71	67	73	211	6,006
Doug McGuigan	73	69	70	212	5,068.80
Darren Fichardt	71	70	71	212	5,068.80
Pelop Panagopoulos	68	73	71	212	5,068.80
Omar Sandys	69	67	76	212	5,068.80
Vaughn Groenewald	67	66	79	212	5,068.80

Lombard Insurance Classic

Royal Swazi Sun Country Club, Mbabane, Swaziland
Par 36-36–72; 6,715 yards

June 6-8
purse, R400,000

	SCORES			TOTAL	MONEY
Merrick Bremner	67	65	66	198	R63,400
Kevin Stone	68	67	66	201	46,000
Josh Cunliffe	66	69	67	202	28,600
Bradford Vaughan	68	65	69	202	28,600
Albert Pistorius	65	70	68	203	17,000
Warren Abery	70	65	68	203	17,000
Desvonde Botes	68	70	66	204	9,485.71
Mark Murless	67	70	67	204	9,485.71
Johan Etsebeth	68	69	67	204	9,485.71
Chris Williams	65	71	68	204	9,485.71
Neil Cheetham	70	65	69	204	9,485.71
Johary Raveloarison	69	65	70	204	9,485.71
Jean Hugo	65	69	70	204	9,485.71
Prinavin Nelson	71	68	66	205	6,700
Jbe' Kruger	67	71	67	205	6,700
Clifford Howes	67	70	68	205	6,700
Bafana Hlophe	65	70	70	205	6,700
Ryan Tipping	68	71	67	206	5,773.33
T.C. Charamba	67	71	68	206	5,773.33
Vaughn Groenewald	67	67	72	206	5,773.33

	SCORES			TOTAL	MONEY
Attie Schwartzel	72	69	66	207	4,880
Heinrich Bruiners	72	67	68	207	4,880
Keith Horne	68	71	68	207	4,880
Theunis Spangenberg	72	66	69	207	4,880
Lindani Ndwandwe	67	70	70	207	4,880
Hendrik Buhrmann	71	65	71	207	4,880

SAA Pro-Am Invitational

Paarl Golf Club, Paarl, Western Cape, South Africa

Par 36-36–72; 6,880 yards

August 21-23

purse, R500,000

	SCORES			TOTAL	MONEY
George Coetzee	72	66	69	207	R79,250
Warren Abery	69	69	72	210	46,600
Doug McGuigan	71	66	73	210	46,600
Jaco Van Zyl	72	70	69	211	21,533.33
Grant Muller	69	72	70	210	46,600
Bradford Vaughan	73	67	71	210	46,600
Grant Veenstra	74	68	70	212	11,580.60
Richard Sterne	71	69	72	212	11,580.60
Willie van der Merwe	71	68	73	212	11,580.60
Mark Murless	70	69	73	212	11,580.60
Charl Coetzee	68	71	73	212	11,580.60
Josh Cunliffe	77	68	68	213	8,153
Jbe' Kruger	73	71	69	213	8,153
Merrick Bremner	71	69	73	213	8,153
Jake Roos	71	72	71	214	7,028
Louis de Jager	73	69	72	214	7,028
Trevor Fisher, Jr.	73	68	73	214	7,028
Omar Sandys	70	70	74	214	7,028
Ulrich van den Berg	74	72	69	215	6,165.50
Alan Michell	72	72	71	215	6,165.50
Adilson da Silva	75	69	71	215	6,165.50
Neil Schietekat	72	70	73	215	6,165.50
Theunis Spangenberg	75	70	71	216	5,228
Chris Williams	75	70	71	216	5,228
T.C. Charamba	68	77	71	216	5,228
Gerhard Trytsman	71	73	72	216	5,228
Alex Haindl	71	73	72	216	5,228
Heinrich Bruiners	72	71	73	216	5,228
Wynand Dingle	73	70	73	216	5,228
Lindani Ndwandwe	77	66	73	216	5,228

Vodacom Origins of Golf Western Cape

Arabella Golf Club, Hermanus, South Africa

Par 36-36–72; 6,976 yards

August 27-29

purse, R440,000

	SCORES			TOTAL	MONEY
Garth Mulroy	69	72	69	210	R69,740
Richard Sterne	71	74	69	214	50,600
Steve van Vuuren	69	78	69	216	31,460
Gerhard Trytsman	71	73	72	216	
Jbe' Kruger	73	74	70	217	18,700
Callie Burger	72	73	72	217	18,700
Jaco Van Zyl	72	74	72	218	13,860

	SCORES			TOTAL	MONEY
Mark Murless	73	74	72	219	10,164
Trevor Fisher, Jr.	69	77	73	219	10,164
Merrick Bremner	72	74	73	219	10,164
Chris Williams	76	74	69	219	10,164
Neil Schietekat	71	79	69	219	10,164
Divan van den Heever	73	75	72	220	7,744
Grant Veenstra	74	72	74	220	7,744
Jake Roos	75	70	75	220	7,744
T.C. Charamba	73	77	70	220	7,744
Adilson da Silva	73	75	73	221	6,362.40
Christiaan Basson	72	77	72	221	6,362.40
Tyrone Ferreira	71	74	76	221	6,362.40
Gerlou Roux	72	73	76	221	6,362.40
Jean Hugo	69	76	76	221	6,362.40
Brett Liddle	75	72	75	222	5,456
Doug McGuigan	75	76	71	222	5,456
Prinavin Nelson	72	79	71	222	5,456
Omar Sandys	75	71	77	223	4,972
George Coetzee	69	82	72	223	4,972

Telkom PGA Pro-Am

Centurion Country Club, Pretoria, South Africa
Par 36-36–72; 7,328 yards

September 3-5
purse, R400,000

	SCORES			TOTAL	MONEY
Merrick Bremner	63	70	67	200	R66,570
Dean Lambert	66	69	66	201	40,950
Jaco Van Zyl	66	69	66	201	40,950
Michiel Bothma	66	65	71	202	26,460
Marc Cayeux	70	68	69	207	15,120
Alex Haindl	69	68	70	207	15,120
Garth Mulroy	63	72	72	207	15,120
Tyrone Ferreira	67	66	74	207	15,120
Warren Abery	72	70	66	208	8,526
Omar Sandys	69	71	68	208	8,526
Louis de Jager	67	73	68	208	8,526
Chris Williams	67	72	69	208	8,526
Jbe' Kruger	72	67	69	208	8,526
Kevin Stone	70	69	69	208	8,526
Grant Muller	67	70	71	208	8,526
Jean Hugo	72	68	69	209	6,566
George Coetzee	71	68	70	209	6,566
Keith Horne	68	70	71	209	6,566
Mark Murless	72	71	67	210	5,733
Desvonde Botes	70	72	68	210	5,733
Theunis Spangenberg	72	66	72	210	5,733
Charl Coetzee	68	68	74	210	5,733
Alan Michell	70	72	69	211	4,753
Ryan Tipping	70	72	69	211	4,753
Jake Roos	67	74	70	211	4,753
Albert Pistorius	70	71	70	211	4,753
Trevor Fisher, Jr.	67	71	73	211	4,753
Des Terblanche	66	71	74	211	4,753

SunCoast Classic

Durban Country Club, Durban, South Africa
Par 36-36–72; 6,732 yards

September 11-13
purse, R500,000

	SCORES			TOTAL	MONEY
Jake Roos	68	68	74	210	R79,250
Omar Sandys	69	63	78	210	57,500
(Roos defeated Sandys on third playoff hole.)					
Marc Cayeux	70	65	78	213	35,700
Michiel Bothma	74	68	72	214	25,250
Gerlou Roux	71	72	73	216	18,150
Jaco Van Zyl	69	71	76	216	18,150
Neil Schietekat	68	69	79	216	18,150
Henk Alberts	77	68	72	217	10,291.20
Divan van den Heever	75	70	72	217	10,291.20
Mark Murless	73	72	72	217	10,291.20
Christiaan Basson	71	74	72	217	10,291.20
Michael du Toit	70	70	77	217	10,291.20
Reggie Adams	79	68	72	219	7,078
Doug McGuigan	72	73	74	219	7,078
Jean Hugo	73	71	75	219	7,078
Alex Haindl	73	71	75	219	7,078
Johan Etsebeth	71	72	76	219	7,078
Jaco Ahlers	72	70	77	219	7,078
Hendrik Buhrmann	73	69	77	219	7,078
Neil Cheetham	67	69	83	219	7,078
Bafana Hlophe	77	72	71	220	5,903
Desvonde Botes	72	73	75	220	5,903
Mike Curtis	69	76	75	220	5,903
Dale Burraston	73	74	74	221	5,453
Adilson da Silva	70	75	76	221	5,453
Jbe' Kruger	70	70	81	221	5,453

Vodacom Origins of Golf Eastern Cape

Humewood Golf Club, Port Elizabeth, South Africa
Par 35-37–72; 6,963 yards

September 17-19
purse, R440,000

	SCORES			TOTAL	MONEY
George Coetzee	71	68	73	212	R71,325
Jean Hugo	71	70	72	213	51,750
Chris Williams	70	71	73	214	32,130
Christiaan Basson	73	70	72	215	22,725
Juan Langeveld	69	77	70	216	17,707.50
Neil Schietekat	68	77	71	216	17,707.50
Jbe' Kruger	71	71	75	217	12,442.50
Nico van Rensburg	69	72	76	217	12,442.50
Adilson da Silva	72	73	73	218	8,207
Darren Fichardt	69	74	75	218	8,207
James Kamte	71	72	75	218	8,207
Titch Moore	72	70	76	218	8,207
Omar Sandys	73	69	76	218	8,207
Dean Lambert	73	69	76	218	8,207
Jaco Van Zyl	74	73	72	219	6,438
Johan Etsebeth	72	71	76	219	6,438
Theunis Spangenberg	71	72	76	219	6,438
Lindani Ndwandwe	71	75	74	220	5,988
Divan van den Heever	72	75	74	221	5,718
Brett Liddle	70	75	76	221	5,718

	SCORES			TOTAL	MONEY
Gerlou Roux	76	72	74	222	5,313
Steve van Vuuren	70	78	74	222	5,313
Heinrich Bruiners	73	74	75	222	5,313
Steve Basson	74	73	76	223	4,908
Henk Alberts	71	73	79	223	4,908
Bradford Vaughan	74	77	72	223	4,908

Seekers Travel Pro-Am

Dainfern Country Club, Johannesburg, South Africa
Par 36-36–72; 7,308 yards

October 2-4
purse, R440,000

	SCORES			TOTAL	MONEY
Trevor Fisher, Jr.	68	67	71	206	R69,740
Desvonde Botes	65	73	68	206	50,600
(Fisher defeated Botes on third playoff hole.)					
Albert Pistorius	68	69	70	207	31,460
Louis de Jager	68	67	72	207	31,460
Toto Thimba	71	72	65	208	20,680
Jaco Ahlers	69	71	69	209	15,290
George Coetzee	68	70	71	209	15,290
Steve Basson	71	69	70	210	10,926.66
Greg Upneck	70	68	72	210	10,926.66
Ryan Cairns	66	70	74	210	10,926.66
Ulrich van den Berg	71	72	68	211	8,169.33
Jaco Van Zyl	68	74	69	211	8,169.33
Brandon Pieters	67	74	70	211	8,169.33
Merrick Bremner	71	70	70	211	8,169.33
Jbe' Kruger	67	74	70	211	8,169.33
Doug McGuigan	68	70	73	211	8,169.33
Grant Muller	70	71	71	212	6,479
Teboho Sefatsa	69	72	71	212	6,479
Henk Alberts	72	67	73	212	6,479
Darren Fichardt	68	70	74	212	6,479
Neil Cheetham	71	73	69	213	5,464.80
Kevin Stone	74	70	69	213	5,464.80
Prinavin Nelson	68	75	70	213	5,464.80
Omar Sandys	68	73	72	213	5,464.80
Heinrich Bruiners	67	73	73	213	5,464.80

BMG Classic

Ebotse Golf & Country Estate, Johannesburg, South Africa
Par 36-36–72; 7,522 yards

October 10-12
purse, R500,000

	SCORES			TOTAL	MONEY
Doug McGuigan	68	70	68	206	R79,250
Jaco Van Zyl	67	70	70	207	57,500
Christiaan Basson	70	69	69	208	34,600
Jake Roos	68	73	68	209	19,412.50
Ulrich van den Berg	69	71	69	209	19,412.50
Adilson da Silva	71	67	71	209	19,412.50
Jbe' Kruger	67	71	71	209	19,412.50
Brandon Pieters	72	68	70	210	11,550
Titch Moore	70	67	73	210	11,550
George Coetzee	74	70	67	211	9,033.33
Louis de Jager	72	70	69	211	9,033.33

	SCORES			TOTAL	MONEY
Dean Lambert	74	66	71	211	9,033.33
Chris Williams	68	75	69	212	7,287.50
Prinavin Nelson	75	66	71	212	7,287.50
Lindani Ndwandwe	71	68	73	212	7,287.50
Richard Kemp	69	69	74	212	7,287.50
Wynand Dingle	71	72	70	213	5,942.85
Gerlou Roux	68	75	70	213	5,942.85
Darren Fichardt	68	73	72	213	5,942.85
Tyrone Ferreira	72	68	73	213	5,942.85
T.C. Charamba	73	73	67	213	5,942.85
Omar Sandys	67	73	73	213	5,942.85
Divan van den Heever	70	65	78	213	5,942.85
Bradford Vaughan	69	74	71	214	4,875
Alan Michell	69	75	70	214	4,875
Thabang Simon	69	75	70	214	4,875
Henk Alberts	71	71	72	214	4,875
Jaco Ahlers	73	69	72	214	4,875
Bradley Davison	76	65	73	214	4,875

Metmar Highveld Classic

Witbank Golf Club, Witbank, South Africa
Par 36-36–72; 6,772 yards

October 17-19
purse, R600,000

	SCORES			TOTAL	MONEY
James Kamte	69	63	64	196	R95,100
Doug McGuigan	68	68	65	201	51,600
Desvonde Botes	69	64	68	201	51,600
Brandon Pieters	65	65	71	201	51,600
Ryan Cairns	69	66	67	202	21,600
Neil Schietekat	69	66	67	202	21,600
Michiel Bothma	68	67	67	202	21,600
Trevor Fisher, Jr.	69	63	70	202	21,600
Louis de Jager	67	69	67	203	13,600
Jake Roos	66	69	68	203	13,600
Jaco Ahlers	65	66	72	203	13,600
George Coetzee	68	69	67	204	10,848
Jbe' Kruger	66	71	67	204	10,848
Steve Basson	69	68	67	204	10,848
Prinavin Nelson	69	69	66	204	10,848
Divan van den Heever	70	68	66	204	10,848
Chris Williams	69	68	68	205	9,000
Ryan Tipping	68	68	69	205	9,000
Louis Moolman	67	74	64	205	9,000
Nic Henning	69	69	68	206	7,890
John Bele	71	68	67	206	7,890
Toto Thimba, Jr.	68	68	70	206	7,890
Marc Cayeux	68	72	66	206	7,890
Ulrich van den Berg	66	72	69	207	6,900
Vaughn Groenewald	66	67	74	207	6,900
Grant Muller	70	71	66	207	6,900

Vodacom Origins of Golf Final

St. Francis Links, St. Francis Bay, South Africa
Par 36-36–72; 7,366 yards

October 22-24
purse, R440,000

	SCORES			TOTAL	MONEY
Jaco Van Zyl	70	68	76	214	R69,740
Bradford Vaughan	73	70	72	215	50,600
Andrew Curlewis	74	74	71	219	35,200
Brett Liddle	73	74	74	221	24,200
Mark Murless	68	73	80	221	24,200
Doug McGuigan	73	74	76	223	15,290
Titch Moore	73	71	79	223	15,290
Christiaan Basson	73	75	76	224	11,440
Desvonde Botes	73	72	79	224	11,440
Roberto Lupini	75	76	75	226	8,844
Grant Muller	77	72	77	226	8,844
Ulrich van den Berg	74	73	79	226	8,844
Jean Hugo	76	70	80	226	8,844
Nic Henning	71	73	82	226	8,844
Reggie Adams	79	74	74	227	7,186.66
Heinrich Bruiners	77	71	79	227	7,186.66
Shaun Norris	74	73	80	227	7,186.66
Adilson da Silva	75	73	80	228	6,600
Callie Burger	76	75	78	229	6,116
Ryan Cairns	76	73	80	229	6,116
Brandon Pieters	73	73	83	229	6,116
John Bele	76	74	80	230	5,078.85
Jbe' Kruger	78	72	80	230	5,078.85
Theunis Spangenberg	75	75	80	230	5,078.85
Mike Curtis	74	76	80	230	5,078.85
Thabang Simon	75	74	81	230	5,078.85
P.H. McIntyre	75	72	83	230	5,078.85
James Kamte	75	73	82	230	5,078.85

Platinum Classic

Mooinooi Golf Club, Rustenburg, South Africa
Par 36-36–72; 6,835 yards

October 30-November 1
purse, R705,000

	SCORES			TOTAL	MONEY
Thomas Aiken	65	68	64	197	R111,743
Desvonde Botes	68	69	65	202	60,630
Nic Henning	67	70	65	202	60,630
Keith Horne	66	70	66	202	60,630
David Hewan	70	66	67	203	33,135
James Kamte	69	68	67	204	21,414.75
Bradford Vaughan	68	65	71	204	21,414.75
Neil Schietekat	66	67	71	204	21,414.75
Jbe' Kruger	67	65	72	204	21,414.75
Darren Fichardt	70	71	64	205	14,540.75
Tyrone Ferreira	66	70	69	205	14,540.75
Chris Williams	66	70	69	205	14,540.75
Andrew Curlewis	67	68	70	205	14,540.75
Warren Abery	69	70	67	206	11,809
Marc Cayeux	70	68	68	206	11,809
Mark Murless	66	70	70	206	11,809
Ross Wellington	69	67	70	206	11,809
Ryan Cairns	69	72	66	207	10,175.66
Henk Alberts	68	70	69	207	10,175.66

	SCORES			TOTAL	MONEY
Merrick Bremner	64	71	72	207	10,175.66
Divan van den Heever	73	68	67	208	8,918.50
Omar Sandys	71	70	67	208	8,918.50
T.C. Charamba	71	68	69	208	8,918.50
Bradley Davison	71	66	71	208	8,918.50
Jaco Van Zyl	72	69	68	209	7,826
Trevor Fisher, Jr.	72	68	69	209	7,826
Dean Lambert	71	68	70	209	7,826

MTC Namibia PGA Championship

Windhoek Country Club, Windhoek, Namibia
Par 35-36–71; 7,106 yards

November 6-9
purse, R1,000,000

	SCORES				TOTAL	MONEY
T.C. Charamba	68	67	69	66	270	R158,500
Merrick Bremner	68	69	67	66	270	92,100
Nic Henning	67	65	68	70	270	92,100
(Charamba defeated Henning on second and Bremner on fourth playoff hole.)						
Titch Moore	67	71	68	65	271	45,200
Henk Alberts	68	69	66	68	271	45,200
Desvonde Botes	66	68	70	68	272	35,400
Mark Murless	70	69	66	68	273	27,050
Dion Fourie	70	67	67	69	273	27,050
Christiaan Basson	68	68	67	71	274	21,600
Jeff Inglis	73	69	64	69	275	18,750
Divan van den Heever	70	67	68	70	275	18,750
Brandon Pieters	67	70	70	69	276	16,200
Grant Muller	67	70	67	72	276	16,200
Jbe' Kruger	70	72	67	68	277	12,580
Toto Thimba, Jr.	74	69	66	68	277	12,580
Warren Abery	64	70	74	69	277	12,580
Johan Etsebeth	71	66	71	69	277	12,580
Albert Pistorius	70	69	69	69	277	12,580
Callie Swart	72	70	66	69	277	12,580
Vaughn Groenewald	69	69	69	70	277	12,580
Ulrich van den Berg	72	68	67	70	277	12,580
Steve Basson	69	67	70	71	277	12,580
Ross Wellington	67	71	68	71	277	12,580
Jaco Ahlers	71	72	67	68	278	10,350
Nemanja Savic	68	66	71	73	278	10,350

Hassan II Trophy

Dar-es-Salam Golf Club, Red Course, Rabat, Morocco
Par 36-37–73; 7,307 yards

November 6-9
purse, US$600,000

	SCORES				TOTAL	MONEY
Ernie Els	69	67	71	68	275	US$150,000
Simon Dyson	67	71	65	74	277	67,500
Johan Edfors	68	70	69	70	277	67,500
Paul McGinley	66	69	70	74	279	33,500
Michael Hoey	74	69	70	66	279	33,500
Mark Foster	67	70	73	71	281	21,750
Miguel Angel Martin	73	69	69	70	281	21,750
Mikko Ilonen	70	70	73	71	284	16,250
Joakim Haeggman	71	71	73	69	284	16,250

	SCORES				TOTAL	MONEY
Ross Bain	69	69	70	77	285	13,750
Raphael Jacquelin	71	77	68	69	285	13,750
Greig Hutcheon	71	69	72	74	286	12,750
Robert Coles	70	73	72	71	286	12,750
Thomas Bjorn	73	72	71	73	289	12,000
Younes El Hassani	72	75	74	71	292	11,750
Roger Chapman	71	71	74	77	293	11,375
Carl Suneson	74	74	74	71	293	11,375
Mark O'Meara	71	74	75	74	294	10,875
Marcel Siem	76	76	71	71	294	10,875
Faycal Serghini	74	73	76	75	298	10,375
Barry Lane	73	75	75	75	298	10,375
Simon Wakefield	71	80	76	73	300	10,000
Bobby Casper	75	75	76	76	302	10,000
Amine Joudar	72	76	79	75	302	10,000

Coca-Cola Championship

The Outeniqua, Fancourt, George, South Africa   November 25-27
Par 36-36–72; 6,911 yards   purse, R550,000

	SCORES			TOTAL	MONEY
Garth Mulroy	66	66	65	197	R89,870
James Kamte	67	68	69	204	51,397.50
Chris Williams	68	67	69	204	51,397.50
Merrick Bremner	69	67	69	205	23,778.33
Thomas Aiken	67	69	69	205	23,778.33
Neil Schietekat	64	70	71	205	23,778.33
Warren Abery	67	73	66	206	18,975
Tyrone Ferreira	71	68	68	207	17,820
Jean Hugo	67	70	71	208	16,252.50
Keith Horne	69	67	72	208	16,252.50
Desvonde Botes	71	70	69	210	14,318.33
Mark Murless	70	70	70	210	14,318.33
Darren Fichardt	64	74	72	210	14,318.33
Adilson da Silva	72	73	67	212	12,301.66
Bradford Vaughan	72	69	71	212	12,301.66
Christiaan Basson	68	73	71	212	12,301.66
Nic Henning	70	74	69	213	11,330
Jake Roos	74	71	69	214	10,670
Jaco Van Zyl	71	72	71	214	10,670
Louis Moolman	69	72	73	214	10,670
Jbe' Kruger	70	67	78	215	10,175
Grant Muller	71	77	70	218	9,845
George Coetzee	71	73	74	218	9,845
Brandon Pieters	70	75	74	219	9,515
Marc Cayeux	73	73	75	221	9,295

Gary Player Invitational

The Links, Fancourt, George, South Africa   November 28-30
Par 36-37–73; 7,579 yards   purse, R250,000

	SCORES		TOTAL	MONEY (Team)
Bobby Lincoln/Garth Mulroy	64	64	128	R62,500
Retief Goosen/Costantino Rocca	64	67	131	37,500
John Bland/Adilson da Silva	66	67	133	25,000

	SCORES		TOTAL	MONEY (Team)
Thomas Aiken/Vincent Tshabalala	68	66	134	
Peter Mitchell/Omar Sandys	68	66	134	
Rodger Davis/Carin Koch	69	68	137	
Gary Player/Maria Verchenova	73	70	143	
Sally Little/Ronan Rafferty	72	73	145	

Nedbank Affinity Cup

Lost City Golf Course, Sun City, South Africa
Par 36-36–72; 7,637 yards

December 1-3
purse, R550,000

	SCORES			TOTAL	MONEY
Tyrone van Aswegen	65	71	68	204	R87,175
Andrew Curlewis	67	68	70	205	63,250
Desvonde Botes	69	69	68	206	39,325
Chris Williams	67	65	74	206	39,325
Bradford Vaughan	69	73	65	207	21,358.33
George Coetzee	65	75	67	207	21,358.33
Warren Abery	71	68	68	207	21,358.33
Tyrone Ferreira	69	67	72	208	14,300
Jake Roos	67	67	74	208	14,300
David Hewan	69	73	67	209	11,343.75
Titch Moore	72	68	69	209	11,343.75
Jaco Van Zyl	73	65	71	209	11,343.75
Jean Hugo	68	66	75	209	11,343.75
Neil Schietekat	71	72	67	210	9,652.50
Johan Etsebeth	71	71	68	210	9,652.50
Darren Fichardt	72	67	72	211	8,598.33
Louis Moolman	67	71	73	211	8,598.33
Mark Murless	67	68	76	211	8,598.33
Lindani Ndwandwe	73	71	68	212	7,102.85
Gerlou Roux	71	72	69	212	7,102.85
Alan Michell	67	75	70	212	7,102.85
Marc Cayeux	70	72	70	212	7,102.85
Grant Muller	69	73	70	212	7,102.85
Dean Lambert	68	72	72	212	7,102.85
Ross Wellington	70	70	72	212	7,102.85

Nedbank Golf Challenge

Gary Player Country Club, Sun City, South Africa
Par 36-36–72; 7,831 yards

December 4-7
purse, US$4,385,000

	SCORES				TOTAL	MONEY
Henrik Stenson	63	71	65	68	267	$1,200,000
Kenny Perry	73	70	68	65	276	600,000
Robert Karlsson	72	68	67	72	279	400,000
Rory Sabbatini	68	70	72	70	280	300,000
Sergio Garcia	72	70	72	70	284	267,500
Lee Westwood	70	72	70	72	284	267,500
James Kingston	72	77	70	67	286	245,000
K.J. Choi	72	67	73	74	286	245,000
Justin Rose	73	73	72	72	290	230,000
Trevor Immelman	72	73	69	77	291	220,000
Luke Donald	72	74	71	75	292	210,000
Miguel Angel Jimenez	75	76	73	69	293	200,000

Alfred Dunhill Championship

Leopard Creek Country Club, Malelane, South Africa
Par 35-37–72; 7,249 yards

December 11-14
purse, €1,000,000

	SCORES				TOTAL	MONEY
Richard Sterne	68	66	68	69	271	R2,063,353
Johan Edfors	66	69	71	66	272	1,198,957.80
Robert Rock	66	67	69	70	272	1,198,957.80
Rafael Cabrera Bello	66	71	68	68	273	588,413.60
Thomas Aiken	72	65	61	75	273	588,413.60
Alan McLean	68	74	66	66	274	422,434.10
Keith Horne	70	69	65	70	274	422,434.10
Michael Jonzon	65	72	70	68	275	251,898.30
Robert Dinwiddie	69	70	68	68	275	251,898.30
Alvaro Velasco	68	69	67	71	275	251,898.30
Tyrone Mordt	68	67	68	72	275	251,898.30
Oskar Henningsson	69	64	69	73	275	251,898.30
David Lynn	68	68	66	73	275	251,898.30
Charl Schwartzel	68	67	71	70	276	188,110.10
Len Mattiace	65	68	66	77	276	188,110.10
Chris Wood	69	70	70	68	277	165,588.96
Marc Cayeux	68	67	72	70	277	165,588.96
David Dixon	70	70	67	70	277	165,588.96
Lee Westwood	66	70	70	71	277	165,588.96
John E. Morgan	67	68	68	74	277	165,588.96
Pelle Edberg	68	70	73	67	278	138,641.70
Jean Hugo	73	69	68	68	278	138,641.70
Dave Horsey	72	70	68	68	278	138,641.70
T.C. Charamba	70	68	70	70	278	138,641.70
Garry Houston	72	69	67	70	278	138,641.70
Garth Mulroy	68	69	68	73	278	138,641.70
Andrew Coltart	70	70	69	70	279	123,020.10
Gareth Maybin	72	69	66	72	279	123,020.10
Simon Dyson	71	71	70	68	280	106,910.32
Hennie Otto	69	69	73	69	280	106,910.32
Alfredo Garcia-Heredia	67	70	71	72	280	106,910.32
Sam Walker	71	68	69	72	280	106,910.32
Mark Murless	70	70	68	72	280	106,910.32
David Drysdale	71	71	66	72	280	106,910.32
Damien McGrane	71	66	70	73	280	106,910.32
Gary Lockerbie	68	71	67	74	280	106,910.32
James Kingston	73	69	73	66	281	89,824.20
Callum Macaulay	72	69	71	69	281	89,824.20
Fredrik Andersson Hed	71	69	70	71	281	89,824.20
Michiel Bothma	69	71	68	73	281	89,824.20
Danny Willett	72	70	66	73	281	89,824.20
Darren Fichardt	71	69	69	73	282	79,409.80
Trevor Fisher, Jr.	72	70	66	74	282	79,409.80
Fabrizio Zanotti	70	67	69	76	282	79,409.80
Albert Pistorius	71	71	74	67	283	70,297.20
Deane Pappas	75	66	70	72	283	70,297.20
George Coetzee	70	70	68	75	283	70,297.20
Jaco Van Zyl	70	67	70	76	283	70,297.20
Bradford Vaughan	71	71	72	70	284	59,882.80
Taco Remkes	72	70	72	70	284	59,882.80
Rory Sabbatini	69	69	73	73	284	59,882.80
Ross McGowan	70	72	69	73	284	59,882.80
Branden Grace	70	69	74	72	285	49,468.40
Alexandre Rocha	71	71	69	74	285	49,468.40
Jacques Blaauw	73	67	69	76	285	49,468.40
Magnus A. Carlsson	69	68	71	77	285	49,468.40
Justin Walters	72	70	76	68	286	40,355.80

	SCORES				TOTAL	MONEY
Estanislao Goya	70	68	75	73	286	40,355.80
Adilson da Silva	70	68	73	75	286	40,355.80
Neil Cheetham	68	69	73	76	286	40,355.80
Jonathan Caldwell	70	67	72	77	286	40,355.80
Jake Roos	72	69	76	70	287	35,148.60
Marcus Higley	71	70	73	73	287	35,148.60
Warren Abery	68	68	77	74	287	35,148.60
Seve Benson	68	74	76	70	288	30,592.30
Carlos Del Moral	71	71	76	70	288	30,592.30
Iain Pyman	71	69	73	75	288	30,592.30
Bernd Wiesberger	68	74	71	75	288	30,592.30
Jamie Little	72	69	75	74	290	27,337.80
Tyrone van Aswegen	70	68	78	76	292	26,036

South African Open Championship

Pearl Valley Golf Estate, Paarl, Western Cape, South Africa   December 18-21
Par 36-36–72; 7,391 yards   purse, €1,000,000

	SCORES				TOTAL	MONEY
Richard Sterne	72	69	67	66	274	R2,147,675
Gareth Maybin	66	69	69	70	274	1,558,250
(Stern defeated Maybin on first playoff hole.)						
Ernie Els	67	67	77	64	275	720,860
Rory McIlroy	70	68	67	70	275	720,860
Lee Westwood	66	68	68	73	275	720,860
Richard Finch	69	70	71	66	276	376,351.25
Branden Grace	69	67	73	67	276	376,351.25
Chris Wood	68	69	71	68	276	376,351.25
Retief Goosen	70	66	69	71	276	376,351.25
Trevor Immelman	69	71	70	67	277	265,580
Rory Sabbatini	66	71	74	67	278	227,188.33
Michael Hoey	70	66	73	69	278	227,188.33
Fabrizio Zanotti	64	72	73	69	278	227,188.33
David Frost	68	72	71	68	279	185,635
Ake Nilsson	66	72	72	69	279	185,635
Ross McGowan	66	70	71	72	279	185,635
Damien McGrane	70	64	72	73	279	185,635
Michael Lorenzo-Vera	67	65	72	75	279	185,635
Peter Hanson	74	68	70	68	280	150,985.71
Dave Horsey	70	65	76	69	280	150,985.71
Martin Wiegele	69	68	74	69	280	150,985.71
Oskar Henningsson	65	74	71	70	280	150,985.71
Jarmo Sandelin	72	70	68	70	280	150,985.71
Gary Murphy	72	71	67	70	280	150,985.71
George Coetzee	69	68	68	75	280	150,985.71
Richie Ramsay	66	72	75	68	281	126,015
Thomas Aiken	71	64	75	71	281	126,015
Garth Mulroy	70	71	69	71	281	126,015
John Mellor	70	68	71	72	281	126,015
Len Mattiace	70	66	71	74	281	126,015
Charl Schwartzel	69	65	78	70	282	112,465
Darren Fichardt	67	74	71	70	282	112,465
Jaco Van Zyl	66	71	71	74	282	112,465
Callum Macaulay	71	69	74	69	283	104,335
David Drysdale	74	68	70	71	283	104,335
Henrik Stenson	70	71	69	73	283	104,335
Carlos Del Moral	69	68	77	70	284	86,729
Michael Jonzon	70	70	73	71	284	86,729
Christiaan Basson	73	69	71	71	284	86,729

	SCORES				TOTAL	MONEY
Magnus A. Carlsson	70	70	72	72	284	86,729
Hennie Otto	68	72	72	72	284	86,729
Adilson da Silva	70	68	72	74	284	86,729
Tim Clark	67	73	70	74	284	86,729
Gary Lockerbie	72	69	69	74	284	86,729
Simon Dyson	67	73	68	76	284	86,729
Alessandro Tadini	68	74	66	76	284	86,729
Estanislao Goya	70	72	74	69	285	67,750
Martin Erlandsson	74	69	68	74	285	67,750
Trevor Fisher, Jr.	72	67	71	75	285	67,750
Bernd Wiesberger	72	69	65	79	285	67,750
Rafael Cabrera Bello	69	74	71	72	286	54,200
Tyrone van Aswegen	72	71	70	73	286	54,200
Johan Edfors	72	70	70	74	286	54,200
Lee Slattery	68	72	71	75	286	54,200
Keith Horne	66	70	74	76	286	54,200
Darren Clarke	74	67	67	78	286	54,200
Alan McLean	71	72	73	71	287	43,360
Peter Karmis	69	71	74	73	287	43,360
Dion Fourie	70	71	70	76	287	43,360
Patrik Sjoland	72	69	73	74	288	39,972.50
Justin Rose	69	74	71	74	288	39,972.50
*Adrian Ford	70	71	75	73	289	
Ariel Canete	73	70	72	74	289	37,262.50
Andrew Coltart	71	72	67	79	289	37,262.50
Antti Ahokas	71	69	79	71	290	29,810
Birgir Hafthorsson	71	72	74	73	290	29,810
Wil Besseling	75	68	73	74	290	29,810
Tyrone Ferreira	74	69	73	74	290	29,810
Marco Ruiz	69	73	73	75	290	29,810
Jake Roos	70	70	74	76	290	29,810
Pelle Edberg	71	71	69	79	290	29,810
Louis Oosthuizen	69	73	67	81	290	29,810
Steve Basson	72	71	74	74	291	20,284.35
Jeppe Huldahl	69	71	73	79	292	20,243.70
Albert Pistorius	68	75	76	74	293	20,203.05
Merrick Bremner	71	69	71	83	294	20,162.40

Women's Tours

Women's World Cup of Golf

See Ladies African Tour section.

SBS Open

Turtle Bay Resort, Palmer Course, Oahu, Hawaii
Par 36-36–72; 6,582 yards

February 14-16
purse, $1,100,000

	SCORES			TOTAL	MONEY
Annika Sorenstam	70	67	69	206	$165,000
Russy Gulyanamitta	71	69	68	208	75,867
Laura Diaz	70	68	70	208	75,867
Jane Park	70	68	70	208	75,867
Angela Park	75	65	69	209	40,872
Momoko Ueda	71	67	71	209	40,872
Ji-Yai Shin	71	69	70	210	30,790
Yani Tseng	70	72	69	211	23,432
In-Kyung Kim	70	70	71	211	23,432
Cristie Kerr	69	69	73	211	23,432
Erica Blasberg	69	68	74	211	23,432
Kelli Kuehne	67	79	66	212	17,384
Paula Creamer	70	73	69	212	17,384
Seon Hwa Lee	74	68	70	212	17,384
Hee-Won Han	72	70	70	212	17,384
Karen Stupples	73	72	68	213	12,655
Brittany Lang	73	71	69	213	12,655
Suzann Pettersen	74	69	70	213	12,655
Angela Stanford	71	72	70	213	12,655
Meg Mallon	70	72	71	213	12,655
Jeong Jang	72	69	72	213	12,655
Wendy Ward	69	72	72	213	12,655
Na On Min	73	67	73	213	12,655
Lindsey Wright	69	70	74	213	12,655
Candie Kung	73	71	70	214	9,287
Dina Ammaccapane	71	72	71	214	9,287
Ji Young Oh	69	74	71	214	9,287
Pat Hurst	72	70	72	214	9,287
Mikaela Parmlid	70	72	72	214	9,287
Meena Lee	69	73	72	214	9,287
Sherri Steinhauer	69	71	74	214	9,287

Fields Open

Ko Olina Golf Club, Honolulu, Hawaii
Par 36-36–72; 6,519 yards

February 21-23
purse, $1,300,000

	SCORES			TOTAL	MONEY
Paula Creamer	66	68	66	200	$195,000
Jeong Jang	64	68	69	201	119,590
Lindsey Wright	69	66	67	202	86,755
Annika Sorenstam	70	66	68	204	67,112
Karen Stupples	69	70	66	205	49,107

	SCORES			TOTAL	MONEY
Minea Blomqvist	71	65	69	205	49,107
Louise Friberg	73	68	65	206	32,847
Hee-Won Han	68	69	69	206	32,847
Angela Stanford	67	69	70	206	32,847
Christina Kim	72	67	68	207	23,866
Nancy Scranton	71	68	68	207	23,866
Teresa Lu	69	70	68	207	23,866
Dina Ammaccapane	68	70	69	207	23,866
Johanna Head	69	74	65	208	20,166
Suzann Pettersen	72	71	66	209	16,173
Morgan Pressel	70	73	66	209	16,173
Cristie Kerr	73	68	68	209	16,173
Miki Saiki	69	72	68	209	16,173
Birdie Kim	69	70	70	209	16,173
Nicole Castrale	70	68	71	209	16,173
Moira Dunn	68	70	71	209	16,173
Song-Hee Kim	69	64	76	209	16,173
Erica Blasberg	70	70	70	210	13,226
Maria Hjorth	68	69	73	210	13,226
Angela Park	69	75	67	211	10,542
Leta Lindley	73	70	68	211	10,542
Momoko Ueda	72	69	70	211	10,542
Meg Mallon	71	70	70	211	10,542
Rachel Hetherington	71	68	72	211	10,542
Jimin Kang	69	70	72	211	10,542
Yani Tseng	68	71	72	211	10,542
Sandra Gal	72	66	73	211	10,542
Dorothy Delasin	68	70	73	211	10,542
Kelli Kuehne	67	69	75	211	10,542

HSBC Women's Champions

Tanah Merah Country Club, Garden Course, Singapore
Par 36-36–72; 6,547 yards

February 28-March 2
purse, $2,000,000

	SCORES				TOTAL	MONEY
Lorena Ochoa	66	65	69	68	268	$300,000
Annika Sorenstam	71	67	70	71	279	183,533
Paula Creamer	67	71	70	73	281	133,140
Laura Diaz	70	71	70	71	282	102,995
Stacy Prammanasudh	70	69	73	71	283	75,363
Karrie Webb	69	70	70	74	283	75,363
Ji-Yai Shin	73	69	70	72	284	56,773
Christina Kim	73	71	73	68	285	45,050
Morgan Pressel	70	71	73	71	285	45,050
In-Kyung Kim	68	70	74	73	285	45,050
Lindsey Wright	76	70	74	66	286	37,681
Seon Hwa Lee	73	75	69	70	287	34,064
Angela Stanford	73	69	72	73	287	34,064
Na Yeon Choi	73	72	74	69	288	28,437
Na Zhang	70	74	75	69	288	28,437
Natalie Gulbis	72	68	75	73	288	28,437
Birdie Kim	72	71	71	74	288	28,437
Diana D'Alessio	72	71	76	70	289	23,151
Jimin Kang	73	69	76	71	289	23,151
Ai Miyazato	67	74	77	71	289	23,151
Catriona Matthew	74	72	69	74	289	23,151
Pat Hurst	70	71	73	75	289	23,151
Jeong Jang	73	72	76	69	290	20,298
Katherine Hull	73	70	78	69	290	20,298
Juli Inkster	74	74	74	69	291	17,786

	SCORES			TOTAL	MONEY
Jin Joo Hong	74	74 73	70	291	17,786
Alena Sharp	75	74 69	73	291	17,786
Sarah Lee	70	71 76	74	291	17,786
Jee Young Lee	68	72 75	76	291	17,786
Janice Moodie	74	76 71	71	292	14,872
Meaghan Francella	71	74 75	72	292	14,872
Maria Hjorth	73	70 75	74	292	14,872
Suzann Pettersen	72	71 75	74	292	14,872

MasterCard Classic Honoring Alejo Peralta

Bosque Real Country Club, Mexico City, Mexico   March 14-16
Par 36-36–72; 6,911 yards   purse, $1,300,000

	SCORES			TOTAL	MONEY
Louise Friberg	72	73	65	210	$195,000
Yani Tseng	68	69	74	211	118,722
Jane Park	72	70	70	212	76,375
Jill McGill	67	73	72	212	76,375
Pat Hurst	70	71	72	213	44,742
Na Yeon Choi	74	66	73	213	44,742
Eva Dahllof	69	70	74	213	44,742
Lorena Ochoa	76	70	68	214	30,550
Ji Young Oh	68	67	79	214	30,550
Il Mi Chung	72	74	69	215	24,483
Irene Cho	72	74	69	215	24,483
Kim Hall	74	69	72	215	24,483
Louise Stahle	72	74	70	216	19,500
Leta Lindley	74	73	69	216	19,500
Jeong Jang	71	72	73	216	19,500
Amy Yang	69	73	74	216	19,500
Brandie Burton	72	74	71	217	15,860
Na On Min	73	71	73	217	15,860
Hee-Won Han	78	66	73	217	15,860
Seon Hwa Lee	74	70	73	217	15,860
Allison Fouch	73	73	72	218	13,163
Kristy McPherson	74	72	72	218	13,163
Carolina Llano	74	74	70	218	13,163
A.J. Eathorne	74	70	74	218	13,163
Teresa Lu	72	76	70	218	13,163
Gloria Park	70	71	77	218	13,163
Alena Sharp	71	75	73	219	10,634
Becky Lucidi	74	73	72	219	10,634
Hee Young Park	77	69	73	219	10,634
Virada Nirapathpongporn	73	71	75	219	10,634
Anja Monke	73	71	75	219	10,634

Safeway International

Superstition Mountain Golf & Country Club, Prospector Course   March 27-30
Superstition Mountain, Arizona   purse, $1,500,000
Par 36-36–72; 6,662 yards

	SCORES				TOTAL	MONEY
Lorena Ochoa	65	67	68	66	266	$225,000
Jee Young Lee	67	67	67	72	273	135,135
Minea Blomqvist	70	68	69	67	274	98,031

	SCORES				TOTAL	MONEY
Eun-Hee Ji	70	72	68	65	275	68,436
Angela Stanford	62	69	70	74	275	68,436
Brittany Lang	71	70	68	67	276	42,789
Maria Hjorth	70	71	67	68	276	42,789
Christina Kim	69	68	68	71	276	42,789
Laura Davies	71	71	68	67	277	28,158
Hee Young Park	71	69	67	70	277	28,158
Annika Sorenstam	69	67	71	70	277	28,158
Inbee Park	73	66	65	73	277	28,158
Lindsey Wright	71	67	66	73	277	28,158
Yani Tseng	67	73	69	69	278	22,788
Juli Inkster	74	70	70	65	279	19,384
Sophie Gustafson	68	72	69	70	279	19,384
Katie Futcher	69	70	70	70	279	19,384
Karen Stupples	67	70	71	71	279	19,384
Sarah Kemp	70	69	68	72	279	19,384
Charlotte Mayorkas	73	69	71	67	280	16,721
Jeong Jang	69	70	69	72	280	16,721
Leta Lindley	73	69	71	68	281	14,163
Na Yeon Choi	68	74	69	70	281	14,163
Suzann Pettersen	71	68	69	73	281	14,163
Hee-Won Han	70	69	69	73	281	14,163
Michele Redman	68	68	72	73	281	14,163
Sun Young Yoo	73	67	67	74	281	14,163
Ji Young Oh	71	67	68	75	281	14,163
Nicole Castrale	71	70	72	69	282	10,739
Candie Kung	71	71	70	70	282	10,739
Wendy Doolan	70	71	70	71	282	10,739
Carin Koch	73	67	71	71	282	10,739
Cristie Kerr	74	64	73	71	282	10,739
Natalie Gulbis	71	72	67	72	282	10,739
Grace Park	73	71	65	73	282	10,739

Kraft Nabisco Championship

Mission Hills Country Club, Dinah Shore Course,
Rancho Mirage, California
Par 36-36–72; 6,673 yards

April 3-6
purse, $2,000,000

	SCORES				TOTAL	MONEY
Lorena Ochoa	68	71	71	67	277	$300,000
Suzann Pettersen	74	75	65	68	282	160,369
Annika Sorenstam	71	70	73	68	282	160,369
Maria Hjorth	70	70	72	71	283	104,317
Seon Hwa Lee	73	71	68	72	284	83,963
Mi Hyun Kim	70	70	76	69	285	58,859
Na Yeon Choi	74	72	69	70	285	58,859
Hee-Won Han	72	69	70	74	285	58,859
Inbee Park	73	70	70	73	286	45,289
Se Ri Pak	72	70	73	72	287	39,692
Heather Young	69	70	74	74	287	39,692
Karen Stupples	67	75	74	72	288	35,621
Natalie Gulbis	69	74	73	73	289	32,364
Karrie Webb	76	70	69	74	289	32,364
Angela Stanford	75	73	71	71	290	27,275
Meg Mallon	73	73	72	72	290	27,275
Diana D'Alessio	74	69	72	75	290	27,275
Liselotte Neumann	70	72	71	77	290	27,275
Sakura Yokomine	76	73	72	70	291	23,815
Janice Moodie	73	73	74	71	291	23,815

	SCORES				TOTAL	MONEY
Candie Kung	73	74	75	70	292	19,506
Angela Park	77	71	73	71	292	19,506
Helen Alfredsson	75	72	73	72	292	19,506
Jee Young Lee	73	71	75	73	292	19,506
Michele Redman	71	72	76	73	292	19,506
Paula Creamer	71	74	73	74	292	19,506
Yani Tseng	72	71	75	74	292	19,506
Brittany Lang	75	70	72	75	292	19,506
Cristie Kerr	74	72	66	80	292	19,506
*Amanda Blumenherst	73	73	73	74	293	
Ji Young Oh	77	72	71	74	294	14,190
Jeong Jang	73	73	74	74	294	14,190
Ji-Yai Shin	73	71	76	74	294	14,190
Shiho Oyama	72	72	76	74	294	14,190
Heather Daly-Donofrio	75	71	73	75	294	14,190
Rachel Hetherington	76	69	74	75	294	14,190
Ai Miyazato	68	74	77	75	294	14,190
Giulia Sergas	74	75	77	69	295	11,271
Hee Young Park	75	72	74	74	295	11,271
Katherine Hull	76	70	74	75	295	11,271
Morgan Pressel	71	74	75	75	295	11,271
Lindsey Wright	73	73	76	74	296	9,383
Mhairi McKay	78	71	72	75	296	9,383
Sophie Gustafson	74	71	76	75	296	9,383
Shi Hyun Ahn	74	72	74	76	296	9,383
H.J. Choi	72	74	74	76	296	9,383
Minea Blomqvist	75	74	76	72	297	7,887
Beth Bader	76	71	75	75	297	7,887
Momoko Ueda	71	75	76	75	297	7,887
Marisa Baena	73	72	76	76	297	7,887
Russy Gulyanamitta	78	70	74	76	298	6,819
Soo-Yun Kang	72	76	74	76	298	6,819
Becky Morgan	72	77	72	77	298	6,819
Silvia Cavalleri	76	72	71	79	298	6,819
Laura Davies	76	71	75	77	299	6,106
Pat Hurst	73	72	77	77	299	6,106
Reilley Rankin	72	77	70	80	299	6,106
Juli Inkster	74	75	76	75	300	5,394
Wendy Ward	75	71	78	76	300	5,394
Teresa Lu	72	76	75	77	300	5,394
Il Mi Chung	71	77	75	77	300	5,394
*Maria Jose Uribe	70	74	78	78	300	
Carin Koch	72	76	75	78	301	4,783
Moira Dunn	76	68	78	79	301	4,783
Julieta Granada	74	73	74	80	301	4,783
Meena Lee	71	75	75	80	301	4,783
Sarah Lee	74	74	72	81	301	4,783
Alena Sharp	75	72	78	77	302	4,478
*Mallory Blackwelder	71	76	76	79	302	
Meaghan Francella	75	73	79	76	303	4,376.71
Sung Ah Yim	76	73	80	83	312	4,274

Corona Championship

Tres Marias Golf Club, Morelia, Michoacan, Mexico   April 10-13
Par 36-37–73; 6,539 yards   purse, $1,300,000

	SCORES				TOTAL	MONEY
Lorena Ochoa	66	66	66	69	267	$195,000
Song-Hee Kim	66	69	71	72	278	120,196

	SCORES				TOTAL	MONEY
Karine Icher	75	66	66	72	279	77,323
Inbee Park	69	64	72	74	279	77,323
Carin Koch	69	73	72	66	280	49,356
Na Yeon Choi	69	68	71	72	280	49,356
Kristy McPherson	75	71	71	66	283	37,181
Sun Young Yoo	73	65	76	72	286	32,574
Nina Reis	78	70	71	68	287	27,968
Carolina Llano	76	68	70	73	287	27,968
Sophie Gustafson	70	73	71	74	288	23,855
Sophie Giquel	71	69	72	76	288	23,855
Johanna Head	73	71	75	70	289	20,927
Kris Tamulis	75	69	73	72	289	20,927
Brittany Lincicome	72	72	76	70	290	17,241
Nicole Perrot	75	76	68	71	290	17,241
Amie Cochran	76	69	74	71	290	17,241
Audra Burks	69	76	74	71	290	17,241
Alena Sharp	70	74	73	73	290	17,241
Hee-Won Han	74	71	74	72	291	14,609
Candy Hannemann	71	72	76	72	291	14,609
Soo-Yun Kang	72	72	74	73	291	14,609
Paige Mackenzie	79	71	73	69	292	12,350
Giulia Sergas	71	75	76	70	292	12,350
Dina Ammaccapane	74	69	78	71	292	12,350
Sophia Sheridan	73	74	73	72	292	12,350
Allison Fouch	72	73	75	72	292	12,350
Hee Young Park	69	70	80	73	292	12,350
Silvia Cavalleri	75	73	76	69	293	10,332
Eunjung Yi	76	73	74	70	293	10,332
Jill McGill	72	73	71	77	293	10,332

Ginn Open

Ginn Reunion Resort, Reunion, Florida
Par 36-36–72; 6,505 yards

April 17-20
purse, $2,600,000

	SCORES				TOTAL	MONEY
Lorena Ochoa	68	67	65	69	269	$390,000
Yani Tseng	68	64	69	71	272	233,732
Suzann Pettersen	68	66	72	71	277	150,362
Teresa Lu	67	69	69	72	277	150,362
Song-Hee Kim	71	70	69	68	278	95,976
Candie Kung	74	67	68	69	278	95,976
Carin Koch	67	69	70	73	279	72,301
Stacy Prammanasudh	71	69	71	69	280	57,371
Karen Stupples	70	69	71	70	280	57,371
Minea Blomqvist	69	66	73	72	280	57,371
Young Kim	69	69	74	69	281	46,388
Inbee Park	73	68	68	72	281	46,388
Kate Golden	75	69	70	68	282	38,390
Jeong Jang	71	71	70	70	282	38,390
Becky Lucidi	76	68	67	71	282	38,390
Hee-Won Han	72	71	67	72	282	38,390
Russy Gulyanamitta	71	74	71	67	283	29,048
Jee Young Lee	74	66	72	71	283	29,048
Wendy Ward	71	69	72	71	283	29,048
Sun Young Yoo	69	71	72	71	283	29,048
Na Yeon Choi	72	69	70	72	283	29,048
Brittany Lang	69	71	71	72	283	29,048
Lindsey Wright	69	71	70	73	283	29,048
Angela Stanford	70	68	72	73	283	29,048

	SCORES				TOTAL	MONEY
Gloria Park	73	70	73	68	284	20,603
Morgan Pressel	72	70	74	68	284	20,603
Allison Fouch	68	72	76	68	284	20,603
Ai Miyazato	70	73	71	70	284	20,603
Karin Sjodin	72	71	70	71	284	20,603
Amy Hung	70	73	70	71	284	20,603
Seon Hwa Lee	72	70	71	71	284	20,603
Janice Moodie	71	71	71	71	284	20,603
Eun-Hee Ji	72	68	72	72	284	20,603
Michele Redman	71	69	71	73	284	20,603

Stanford International Pro-Am

Fairmont Turnberry Isle Resort & Club, Aventura, Florida   April 24-27
Soffer Course: Par 36-35–71; 6,244 yards   purse, $2,000,000
Miller Course: Par 35-35–70; 6,133 yards

	SCORES				TOTAL	MONEY
Annika Sorenstam	68	67	70	70	275	$300,000
Paula Creamer	68	71	67	69	275	182,220
(Sorenstam defeated Creamer on first playoff hole.)						
Karrie Webb	73	69	70	64	276	117,224
Young Kim	67	67	73	69	276	117,224
Momoko Ueda	68	72	67	71	278	82,306
Angela Park	71	72	68	69	280	57,697
Seon Hwa Lee	74	68	69	69	280	57,697
Cristie Kerr	69	72	67	72	280	57,697
Lindsey Wright	70	71	75	65	281	40,737
Eun-Hee Ji	75	69	69	68	281	40,737
Hee Young Park	69	73	71	68	281	40,737
Jane Park	73	73	70	66	282	33,821
Meena Lee	69	71	73	69	282	33,821
Mollie Fankhauser	70	72	75	66	283	26,904
Sun Young Yoo	73	69	73	68	283	26,904
Laura Diaz	73	73	68	69	283	26,904
Nicole Castrale	72	72	69	70	283	26,904
Hee-Won Han	71	72	70	70	283	26,904
Teresa Lu	71	72	69	71	283	26,904
Suzann Pettersen	70	76	70	68	284	21,749
Taylor Leon	71	74	69	70	284	21,749
Grace Park	72	69	73	70	284	21,749
Leta Lindley	69	73	70	72	284	21,749
Brittany Lang	71	74	69	71	285	18,706
Rachel Hetherington	70	73	71	71	285	18,706
Mi Hyun Kim	69	72	71	73	285	18,706
Ji Young Oh	72	71	68	74	285	18,706
Catriona Matthew	74	71	70	71	286	16,611
Yani Tseng	68	77	69	72	286	16,611
Erica Blasberg	76	70	74	67	287	14,183
Alena Sharp	72	71	75	69	287	14,183
Pat Hurst	73	72	72	70	287	14,183
Juli Inkster	70	71	76	70	287	14,183
Silvia Cavalleri	73	72	71	71	287	14,183
Angela Stanford	69	70	76	72	287	14,183

SemGroup Championship

Cedar Ridge Country Club, Broken Arrow, Oklahoma May 2-4
Par 36-35–71; 6,602 yards purse, $1,800,000

	SCORES				TOTAL	MONEY
Paula Creamer	70	71	69	72	282	$270,000
Juli Inkster	72	73	67	70	282	166,426
(Creamer defeated Inkster on second playoff hole.)						
Jeong Jang	73	72	73	68	286	107,063
Angela Stanford	73	71	71	71	286	107,063
Dorothy Delasin	78	72	69	68	287	62,719
Lorena Ochoa	73	74	71	69	287	62,719
Brittany Lang	72	71	71	73	287	62,719
Jimin Kang	82	70	69	67	288	45,103
Carin Koch	72	73	74	70	289	37,206
Jee Young Lee	75	69	74	71	289	37,206
Leta Lindley	71	72	72	74	289	37,206
Jin Joo Hong	74	73	75	68	290	30,889
Ji Young Oh	70	72	76	72	290	30,889
Julieta Granada	76	74	72	69	291	24,055
Taylor Leon	73	75	72	71	291	24,055
Johanna Head	74	73	73	71	291	24,055
Danielle Downey	74	71	75	71	291	24,055
Catriona Matthew	73	75	71	72	291	24,055
Ai Miyazato	71	73	75	72	291	24,055
Jamie Hullett	74	71	73	73	291	24,055
Linda Wessberg	75	73	73	71	292	19,864
Vicky Hurst	71	75	73	73	292	19,864
Inbee Park	77	73	74	69	293	17,100
Cristie Kerr	72	78	73	70	293	17,100
Laura Diaz	76	75	71	71	293	17,100
Meaghan Francella	76	74	72	71	293	17,100
Su A. Kim	73	72	76	72	293	17,100
Jane Park	74	74	72	73	293	17,100
Candie Kung	77	72	77	68	294	13,759
Seon Hwa Lee	74	77	72	71	294	13,759
Diana D'Alessio	74	71	77	72	294	13,759
Na Yeon Choi	75	70	75	74	294	13,759
Pat Hurst	74	72	73	75	294	13,759

Michelob Ultra Open

Kingsmill Resort & Spa, River Course, Williamsburg, Virginia May 8-11
Par 36-35–71; 6,315 yards purse, $2,200,000

	SCORES				TOTAL	MONEY
Annika Sorenstam	64	66	69	66	265	$330,000
Allison Fouch	69	71	68	64	272	138,548
Karen Stupples	67	69	70	66	272	138,548
Christina Kim	70	67	66	69	272	138,548
Jeong Jang	67	66	69	70	272	138,548
Katherine Hull	70	69	70	64	273	74,793
Sophie Gustafson	71	71	66	66	274	58,727
Candie Kung	66	74	66	68	274	58,727
Stacy Prammanasudh	66	72	69	69	276	45,245
Jee Young Lee	68	71	67	70	276	45,245
Maria Hjorth	68	71	66	71	276	45,245
Shi Hyun Ahn	71	71	72	63	277	35,347
Hee Young Park	66	72	70	69	277	35,347

	SCORES				TOTAL	MONEY
Meena Lee	67	68	73	69	277	35,347
Lorena Ochoa	65	68	74	70	277	35,347
Yani Tseng	70	69	72	67	278	27,184
Paula Creamer	71	69	70	68	278	27,184
Sun Young Yoo	64	75	71	68	278	27,184
Suzann Pettersen	71	71	65	71	278	27,184
Song-Hee Kim	66	71	70	71	278	27,184
Inbee Park	67	72	67	72	278	27,184
Laura Davies	71	71	70	67	279	22,410
Marisa Baena	69	73	69	68	279	22,410
Kris Tamulis	68	71	69	71	279	22,410
Ji Young Oh	69	69	68	73	279	22,410
Teresa Lu	70	70	69	71	280	19,612
Laura Diaz	70	69	68	73	280	19,612
Jimin Kang	67	69	71	73	280	19,612
Dina Ammaccapane	68	72	74	67	281	16,731
Juli Inkster	68	70	74	69	281	16,731
Sandra Gal	68	70	73	70	281	16,731
Na Yeon Choi	69	73	68	71	281	16,731
Becky Morgan	67	69	74	71	281	16,731

Sybase Classic

Upper Montclair Country Club, Clifton, New Jersey
Par 36-36–72; 6,413 yards
(Second round cancelled—rain.)

May 15-18
purse, $2,000,000

	SCORES			TOTAL	MONEY
Lorena Ochoa	68	67	71	206	$300,000
Morgan Pressel	70	71	66	207	114,360
Catriona Matthew	68	72	67	207	114,360
Brittany Lang	68	71	68	207	114,360
Na Yeon Choi	70	68	69	207	114,360
Sophie Gustafson	69	68	70	207	114,360
Christina Kim	69	72	67	208	56,913
H.J. Choi	70	68	71	209	49,862
Nicole Castrale	71	72	67	210	42,811
Jimin Kang	73	69	68	210	42,811
Becky Morgan	70	72	69	211	34,274
Momoko Ueda	73	68	70	211	34,274
Annika Sorenstam	67	73	71	211	34,274
Teresa Lu	68	69	74	211	34,274
Yani Tseng	71	72	69	212	27,667
Wendy Ward	71	71	70	212	27,667
Kristy McPherson	71	69	72	212	27,667
Inbee Park	72	73	68	213	22,391
Cristie Kerr	69	76	68	213	22,391
Sandra Gal	72	71	70	213	22,391
Minea Blomqvist	71	72	70	213	22,391
Song-Hee Kim	67	75	71	213	22,391
Taylor Leon	72	69	72	213	22,391
Helen Alfredsson	70	71	72	213	22,391
Brandie Burton	71	73	70	214	17,494
Michele Redman	71	73	70	214	17,494
Kyeong Bae	72	70	72	214	17,494
Eunjung Yi	70	72	72	214	17,494
Carolina Llano	68	74	72	214	17,494
Pat Hurst	68	74	72	214	17,494

LPGA Corning Classic

Corning Country Club, Corning, New York
Par 36-36–72; 6,223 yards

May 22-25
purse, $1,500,000

		SCORES			TOTAL	MONEY
Leta Lindley	73	67	70	67	277	$225,000
Jeong Jang	71	69	69	68	277	138,335
(Lindley defeated Jang on first playoff hole.)						
Mi Hyun Kim	71	73	68	66	278	88,992
Sun Young Yoo	74	67	71	66	278	88,992
Meredith Duncan	73	68	71	68	280	62,484
Becky Morgan	70	70	74	67	281	46,958
Song-Hee Kim	71	70	70	70	281	46,958
Diana D'Alessio	73	73	68	68	282	33,956
Hee-Won Han	72	74	67	69	282	33,956
Linda Wessberg	72	72	69	69	282	33,956
In-Kyung Kim	72	72	72	67	283	25,770
Giulia Sergas	70	72	72	69	283	25,770
Jimin Kang	68	73	72	70	283	25,770
Katherine Hull	70	72	68	73	283	25,770
Paula Creamer	70	74	71	69	284	19,440
Anna Rawson	69	75	70	70	284	19,440
Emily Bastel	71	75	67	71	284	19,440
Na Yeon Choi	68	74	71	71	284	19,440
Karine Icher	67	74	72	71	284	19,440
Seo-Jae Lee	72	69	71	72	284	19,440
Laura Diaz	70	73	74	68	285	15,061
Sandra Gal	68	72	76	69	285	15,061
Janice Moodie	71	68	77	69	285	15,061
Meena Lee	75	71	69	70	285	15,061
Kyeong Bae	72	72	71	70	285	15,061
Eva Dahllof	69	73	71	72	285	15,061
Katie Futcher	70	69	74	72	285	15,061
Ji Young Oh	71	72	74	69	286	12,370
Na On Min	67	74	74	71	286	12,370
Jamie Hullett	70	73	70	73	286	12,370

Ginn Tribute Hosted by Annika

RiverTowne Country Club, Mt. Pleasant, South Carolina
Par 36-36–72; 6,459 yards

May 29-June 1
purse, $2,600,000

		SCORES			TOTAL	MONEY
Seon Hwa Lee	68	70	69	67	274	$390,000
Karrie Webb	65	66	73	70	274	237,445
(Lee defeated Webb on first playoff hole.)						
Song-Hee Kim	68	71	67	69	275	172,250
Jane Park	68	70	67	72	277	120,250
Sophie Gustafson	66	65	67	79	277	120,250
Sun Young Yoo	70	68	70	70	278	75,183
Inbee Park	67	68	73	70	278	75,183
Na Yeon Choi	69	67	68	74	278	75,183
Suzann Pettersen	71	65	73	70	279	55,250
Se Ri Pak	73	67	68	71	279	55,250
Jee Young Lee	70	71	69	70	280	45,630
Natalie Gulbis	71	68	71	70	280	45,630
Karen Stupples	69	73	67	71	280	45,630
Sandra Gal	71	73	67	70	281	35,057
Minea Blomqvist	69	69	73	70	281	35,057

	SCORES				TOTAL	MONEY
Juli Inkster	69	70	71	71	281	35,057
Yani Tseng	69	71	69	72	281	35,057
Giulia Sergas	67	71	71	72	281	35,057
Teresa Lu	68	67	72	74	281	35,057
Cristie Kerr	67	73	75	67	282	27,820
Allison Fouch	67	77	69	69	282	27,820
Ai Miyazato	70	71	72	69	282	27,820
Angela Park	72	69	70	71	282	27,820
Candie Kung	71	68	72	71	282	27,820
Stacy Prammanasudh	71	69	74	69	283	22,156
Christina Kim	73	67	73	70	283	22,156
Soo-Yun Kang	71	68	74	70	283	22,156
Il Mi Chung	71	68	73	71	283	22,156
Morgan Pressel	70	69	73	71	283	22,156
Meena Lee	69	70	73	71	283	22,156
Karin Sjodin	74	67	69	73	283	22,156

McDonald's LPGA Championship

Bulle Rock Golf Course, Havre de Grace, Maryland
Par 36-36–72; 6,641 yards

June 5-8
purse, $2,000,000

	SCORES				TOTAL	MONEY
Yani Tseng	73	70	65	68	276	$300,000
Maria Hjorth	68	72	65	71	276	180,180
(Tseng defeated Hjorth on fourth playoff hole.)						
Annika Sorenstam	70	68	68	71	277	115,911
Lorena Ochoa	69	65	72	71	277	115,911
Laura Diaz	71	68	69	70	278	81,385
Morgan Pressel	73	69	70	68	280	53,763
Shi Hyun Ahn	73	69	69	69	280	53,763
Kelli Kuehne	69	70	71	70	280	53,763
Irene Cho	72	68	69	71	280	53,763
Seon Hwa Lee	73	71	70	67	281	31,938
Mi Hyun Kim	72	70	71	68	281	31,938
Candie Kung	70	72	70	69	281	31,938
Paula Creamer	71	70	71	69	281	31,938
Cristie Kerr	71	70	71	69	281	31,938
Giulia Sergas	71	71	69	70	281	31,938
Nicole Castrale	68	72	71	70	281	31,938
Jimin Jeong	73	68	69	71	281	31,938
Jill McGill	72	70	72	68	282	21,929
Jeong Jang	72	72	68	70	282	21,929
Na Yeon Choi	75	67	69	71	282	21,929
Marisa Baena	68	70	71	73	282	21,929
Brittany Lang	70	67	71	74	282	21,929
Lindsey Wright	67	68	73	74	282	21,929
Jee Young Lee	70	69	65	78	282	21,929
Kristy McPherson	73	70	72	68	283	17,806
Angela Stanford	72	71	67	73	283	17,806
Jimin Kang	72	68	70	73	283	17,806
Momoko Ueda	72	67	71	73	283	17,806
H.J. Choi	69	74	71	70	284	14,896
Eun-Hee Ji	72	70	72	70	284	14,896
Liselotte Neumann	70	72	71	71	284	14,896
Karrie Webb	71	71	69	73	284	14,896
Ji Young Oh	69	68	72	75	284	14,896
Louise Friberg	70	73	73	69	285	11,887
Sophie Giquel	70	72	72	71	285	11,887
Brittany Lincicome	75	68	70	72	285	11,887

	SCORES				TOTAL	MONEY
Suzann Pettersen	71	68	74	72	285	11,887
Young Kim	69	73	69	74	285	11,887
Jane Park	72	69	70	74	285	11,887
Amy Hung	71	71	75	69	286	9,289
Il Mi Chung	71	71	72	72	286	9,289
Michelle Ellis	71	67	76	72	286	9,289
Hee-Won Han	69	71	73	73	286	9,289
Lorie Kane	66	70	76	74	286	9,289
Gloria Park	70	69	71	76	286	9,289
Stacy Prammanasudh	75	69	73	70	287	6,905
Sherri Steinhauer	73	71	73	70	287	6,905
Inbee Park	69	74	74	70	287	6,905
Se Ri Pak	70	72	73	72	287	6,905
Jennifer Rosales	70	74	70	73	287	6,905
Karine Icher	70	74	69	74	287	6,905
Kyeong Bae	71	71	70	75	287	6,905
Rachel Hetherington	68	69	75	75	287	6,905
Su A. Kim	70	70	71	76	287	6,905
Carolina Llano	75	67	68	77	287	6,905
Sandra Gal	70	70	75	73	288	5,623
Wendy Doolan	69	75	70	74	288	5,623
Candy Hannemann	75	68	76	70	289	4,876
Karen Stupples	71	71	76	71	289	4,876
Silvia Cavalleri	72	72	73	72	289	4,876
Shanshan Feng	72	72	73	72	289	4,876
Nancy Scranton	71	69	74	75	289	4,876
Jin Joo Hong	68	70	76	75	289	4,876
Michele Redman	71	69	73	76	289	4,876
Mhairi McKay	75	69	77	69	290	4,242
Leta Lindley	72	72	73	73	290	4,242
Julieta Granada	70	69	77	74	290	4,242
Becky Lucidi	73	71	71	75	290	4,242
Linda Wessberg	72	72	71	75	290	4,242
Angela Park	74	70	69	78	291	3,946
Charlotte Mayorkas	73	71	76	72	292	3,872
Young-A Yang	74	68	77	73	292	3,872
Tracy Hanson	70	73	75	75	293	3,725
Alena Sharp	74	70	73	76	293	3,725
Moira Dunn	72	72	72	77	293	3,725
Soo-Yun Kang	69	74	72	78	293	3,725
Meaghan Francella	70	72	77	75	294	3,584
Sun Young Yoo	71	73	73	77	294	3,584
Danielle Downey	71	73	73	78	295	3,514
Jamie Hullett	70	74	79	74	297	3,469
Allison Fouch	72	72	79	76	299	3,425

Wegmans LPGA

Locust Hill Country Club, Pittsford, New York
Par 35-37–72; 6,328 yards

June 19-22
purse, $2,000,000

	SCORES				TOTAL	MONEY
Eun-Hee Ji	70	71	64	67	272	$300,000
Suzann Pettersen	70	65	67	72	274	183,986
Jeong Jang	68	71	69	68	276	118,360
Hee-Won Han	69	74	64	69	276	118,360
Cristie Kerr	68	70	70	69	277	83,103
Christina Kim	71	67	73	68	279	54,899
Lorena Ochoa	72	70	68	69	279	54,899
Ai Miyazato	68	68	71	72	279	54,899

	SCORES				TOTAL	MONEY
Inbee Park	68	68	69	74	279	54,899
Paula Creamer	74	69	68	69	280	39,285
Morgan Pressel	69	65	71	75	280	39,285
Giulia Sergas	75	68	72	66	281	32,133
Laura Diaz	70	73	70	68	281	32,133
Soo-Yun Kang	68	74	70	69	281	32,133
Michele Redman	72	70	69	70	281	32,133
Yani Tseng	72	69	73	68	282	26,257
Kyeong Bae	69	73	71	69	282	26,257
Meena Lee	74	65	73	70	282	26,257
Shi Hyun Ahn	76	66	73	68	283	22,362
Leta Lindley	71	72	70	70	283	22,362
Maria Hjorth	73	72	66	72	283	22,362
Seon Hwa Lee	74	69	67	73	283	22,362
Helen Alfredsson	69	73	67	74	283	22,362
Mi Hyun Kim	73	71	72	68	284	18,887
Ashli Bunch	72	70	74	68	284	18,887
Michelle Wie	71	71	73	69	284	18,887
Jennifer Rosales	71	74	69	70	284	18,887
Stacy Prammanasudh	72	71	73	69	285	15,835
Paige Mackenzie	73	70	70	72	285	15,835
Moira Dunn	71	71	71	72	285	15,835
Candie Kung	71	69	73	72	285	15,835
Jimin Jeong	68	72	72	73	285	15,835

U.S. Women's Open

Interlachen Country Club, Edina, Minnesota — June 26-29
Par 36-37–73; 6,789 yards — purse, $3,250,000

	SCORES				TOTAL	MONEY
Inbee Park	72	69	71	71	283	$585,000
Helen Alfredsson	70	71	71	75	287	350,000
Angela Park	73	67	75	73	288	162,487
In-Kyung Kim	71	73	69	75	288	162,487
Stacy Lewis	73	70	67	78	288	162,487
Giulia Sergas	73	74	72	70	289	94,117
Nicole Castrale	74	70	74	71	289	94,117
Mi Hyun Kim	72	72	70	75	289	94,117
Paula Creamer	70	72	69	78	289	94,117
Teresa Lu	71	72	73	74	290	75,734
*Maria Jose Uribe	69	74	72	75	290	
Stacy Prammanasudh	75	72	71	73	291	71,002
Suzann Pettersen	77	71	73	71	292	60,878
Jee Young Lee	71	75	74	72	292	60,878
Cristie Kerr	72	70	75	75	292	60,878
Momoko Ueda	72	71	73	76	292	60,878
Morgan Pressel	74	74	72	73	293	51,380
Catriona Matthew	70	77	73	73	293	51,380
*Jessica Korda	72	78	75	69	294	
Ji-Yai Shin	69	74	79	72	294	43,376
Candie Kung	72	70	79	73	294	43,376
Na Yeon Choi	76	71	71	76	294	43,376
Jeong Jang	73	69	74	78	294	43,376
Pat Hurst	67	78	77	73	295	35,276
Song-Hee Kim	68	76	75	76	295	35,276
Annika Sorenstam	75	70	72	78	295	35,276
Laura Diaz	77	70	73	76	296	28,210
Ai Miyazato	71	72	76	77	296	28,210
Seon Hwa Lee	75	70	73	78	296	28,210

	SCORES				TOTAL	MONEY
Minea Blomqvist	72	69	76	79	296	28,210
Sun-Ju Ahn	76	71	78	72	297	21,567
Lorena Ochoa	73	74	76	74	297	21,567
Karen Stupples	74	73	75	75	297	21,567
*Alison Walshe	73	74	73	77	297	
Brittany Lang	71	75	74	77	297	21,567
Ji Young Oh	67	76	76	78	297	21,567
Young Kim	74	71	71	81	297	21,567
Jennifer Rosales	74	72	77	75	298	18,690
Karrie Webb	75	75	72	76	298	18,690
Sherri Steinhauer	75	75	71	77	298	18,690
*Amanda Blumenherst	72	78	71	77	298	
Reilley Rankin	72	75	79	73	299	15,261
Eun-Hee Ji	76	72	77	74	299	15,261
Lindsey Wright	78	72	74	75	299	15,261
Jane Park	78	71	75	75	299	15,261
*Paola Moreno	73	76	75	75	299	
Rachel Hetherington	71	75	78	75	299	15,261
Na On Min	77	73	73	76	299	15,261
Katherine Hull	72	72	77	78	299	15,261
Yani Tseng	71	74	75	79	299	15,261
Maria Hjorth	76	74	73	77	300	12,153
Sakura Yokomine	71	75	77	77	300	12,153
Sherri Turner	76	70	81	74	301	10,376
Leta Lindley	77	73	76	75	301	10,376
Christina Kim	73	76	75	77	301	10,376
Louise Friberg	69	74	79	79	301	10,376
Linda Wessberg	70	79	79	74	302	9,463
Meg Mallon	75	72	82	74	303	8,697
Marcy Hart	78	72	78	75	303	8,697
Brittany Lincicome	74	73	78	78	303	8,697
Whitney Wade	77	73	74	79	303	8,697
Karin Sjodin	74	76	74	79	303	8,697
Angela Stanford	76	73	73	81	303	8,697
Janice Moodie	78	71	80	75	304	7,935
Na Ri Kim	76	71	79	78	304	7,935
*Sydnee Michaels	71	76	76	81	304	
Shi Hyun Ahn	73	73	77	81	304	7,935
Jimin Kang	73	72	77	83	305	7,673
Kim Hall	74	76	76	80	306	7,542
Michele Redman	74	76	80	77	307	7,411
*Tiffany Lua	72	75	80	81	308	
Il Mi Chung	76	74	75	83	308	7,215
Hee-Won Han	74	76	74	84	308	7,215
Meena Lee	75	74	80	82	311	7,019

P&G Beauty NW Arkansas Championship

Pinnacle Country Club, Rogers, Arkansas
Par 36-36–72; 6,238 yards

July 4-6
purse, $1,700,000

	SCORES			TOTAL	MONEY
Seon Hwa Lee	64	69	68	201	$255,000
Jane Park	71	69	62	202	133,624
Meena Lee	67	65	70	202	133,624
Karen Stupples	68	69	66	203	65,508
Ai Miyazato	67	68	68	203	65,508
Kristy McPherson	64	69	70	203	65,508
Angela Park	71	62	70	203	65,508
Na Yeon Choi	71	65	68	204	39,856

	SCORES			TOTAL	MONEY
Eun-Hee Ji	67	65	72	204	39,856
Inbee Park	70	65	70	205	34,344
Katherine Hull	70	70	66	206	28,853
Hee-Won Han	72	66	68	206	28,853
Cristie Kerr	72	65	69	206	28,853
Jeong Jang	66	69	71	206	28,853
Soo-Yun Kang	68	70	69	207	23,914
Giulia Sergas	69	69	69	207	23,914
Reilley Rankin	74	66	68	208	20,318
Christina Kim	71	68	69	208	20,318
Morgan Pressel	69	69	70	208	20,318
Jee Young Lee	66	69	73	208	20,318
H.J. Choi	66	69	73	208	20,318
Gloria Park	70	70	69	209	16,233
Catriona Matthew	72	68	69	209	16,233
Paige Mackenzie	70	69	70	209	16,233
Song-Hee Kim	73	68	68	209	16,233
Michelle Ellis	71	67	71	209	16,233
Katie Futcher	73	69	67	209	16,233
Louise Friberg	70	66	73	209	16,233
Karine Icher	70	70	70	210	12,550
Brittany Lincicome	72	68	70	210	12,550
Kelli Kuehne	68	72	70	210	12,550
Lindsey Wright	75	66	69	210	12,550
Dina Ammaccapane	71	70	69	210	12,550
Helen Alfredsson	65	72	73	210	12,550

Jamie Farr Owens Corning Classic

Highland Meadows Golf Club, Sylvania, Ohio   July 10-13
Par 34-37–71; 6,428 yards   purse, $1,300,000

	SCORES				TOTAL	MONEY
Paula Creamer	60	65	70	73	268	$195,000
Nicole Castrale	70	69	67	64	270	118,169
Eun-Hee Ji	65	66	68	72	271	85,723
Shanshan Feng	69	70	64	69	272	66,314
Karrie Webb	70	71	62	70	273	53,375
Katherine Hull	69	68	70	67	274	43,671
Kristy McPherson	74	66	64	71	275	34,290
Brittany Lincicome	70	67	67	71	275	34,290
Angela Stanford	69	70	67	70	276	28,790
Catriona Matthew	68	70	70	69	277	24,369
Ji Young Oh	70	68	67	72	277	24,369
H.J. Choi	67	68	70	72	277	24,369
Karen Stupples	70	68	69	71	278	19,409
Jennifer Rosales	70	67	69	72	278	19,409
Katie Futcher	69	69	67	73	278	19,409
Janice Moodie	69	67	69	73	278	19,409
Heather Young	70	68	71	70	279	15,501
Se Ri Pak	68	69	72	70	279	15,501
Na Ri Kim	68	72	68	71	279	15,501
Young Kim	66	70	71	72	279	15,501
Stacy Lewis	70	66	69	74	279	15,501
Jin Joo Hong	70	69	68	73	280	13,085
Moira Dunn	67	70	69	74	280	13,085
Momoko Ueda	68	70	67	75	280	13,085
Rachel Hetherington	68	67	67	78	280	13,085
Grace Park	72	69	71	69	281	11,225
Mi Hyun Kim	69	70	73	69	281	11,225

	SCORES				TOTAL	MONEY
Stacy Prammanasudh	69	70	71	71	281	11,225
Eunjung Yi	69	70	67	75	281	11,225
Sherri Steinhauer	71	69	73	69	282	8,508
Brandie Burton	71	68	73	70	282	8,508
Nancy Scranton	73	69	69	71	282	8,508
Charlotte Mayorkas	72	70	68	72	282	8,508
Yu Ping Lin	70	71	69	72	282	8,508
Diana D'Alessio	67	72	71	72	282	8,508
Sarah Lee	70	70	69	73	282	8,508
Meena Lee	69	69	71	73	282	8,508
Gloria Park	65	73	71	73	282	8,508
Alena Sharp	69	67	68	78	282	8,508

LPGA State Farm Classic

Panther Creek Country Club, Springfield, Illinois
Par 36-36–72; 6,608 yards

July 17-20
purse, $1,700,000

	SCORES				TOTAL	MONEY
Ji Young Oh	66	66	69	69	270	$255,000
Yani Tseng	66	66	66	72	270	156,002
(Oh defeated Tseng on first playoff hole.)						
Na Yeon Choi	67	67	69	68	271	113,169
Shanshan Feng	70	70	69	63	272	71,887
Stacy Prammanasudh	69	66	68	69	272	71,887
Hee-Won Han	69	71	61	71	272	71,887
Kristy McPherson	65	71	70	67	273	45,268
Kyeong Bae	68	67	69	69	273	45,268
Wendy Ward	73	66	69	66	274	34,876
Christina Kim	63	68	73	70	274	34,876
Katie Futcher	70	64	66	74	274	34,876
Jimin Kang	67	70	69	69	275	27,246
Erica Blasberg	70	66	70	69	275	27,246
Sun Young Yoo	64	69	72	70	275	27,246
Wendy Doolan	67	68	69	71	275	27,246
Anna Grzebien	69	70	67	70	276	22,264
Carri Wood	70	66	70	70	276	22,264
Jane Park	70	66	70	70	276	22,264
Michelle Ellis	73	66	73	65	277	18,620
Jill McGill	68	70	71	68	277	18,620
Marisa Baena	67	69	73	68	277	18,620
Mikaela Parmlid	73	66	68	70	277	18,620
Ai Miyazato	67	72	68	70	277	18,620
Jee Young Lee	65	70	70	72	277	18,620
Hannah Jun	71	70	71	66	278	14,017
Katherine Hull	68	70	73	67	278	14,017
Young-A Yang	68	69	73	68	278	14,017
Diana D'Alessio	69	70	70	69	278	14,017
Becky Morgan	70	69	68	71	278	14,017
Hee Young Park	72	66	68	72	278	14,017
Kris Tamulis	67	69	70	72	278	14,017
Beth Bader	70	66	69	73	278	14,017
Sherri Turner	66	66	73	73	278	14,017

Evian Masters

See Ladies European Tour section.

Ricoh Women's British Open

See Ladies European Tour section.

CN Canadian Women's Open

Ottawa Hunt & Golf Club, Ottawa, Ontario, Canada
Par 36-36–72; 6,510 yards

August 14-17
purse, $2,250,000

	SCORES				TOTAL	MONEY
Katherine Hull	71	65	72	69	277	$337,500
Se Ri Pak	68	70	68	72	278	202,703
Yani Tseng	70	64	68	77	279	147,046
Sun Young Yoo	71	72	69	69	281	93,406
Song-Hee Kim	69	71	71	70	281	93,406
Lorena Ochoa	66	68	74	73	281	93,406
Suzann Pettersen	69	75	70	68	282	62,703
Hee-Won Han	68	72	72	71	283	52,159
Paula Creamer	71	70	70	72	283	52,159
Meena Lee	68	74	70	72	284	43,281
Laura Diaz	70	70	72	72	284	43,281
Michelle Wie	75	70	69	71	285	36,475
Nicole Castrale	68	69	77	71	285	36,475
Jennifer Rosales	72	68	73	72	285	36,475
Wendy Ward	71	72	73	70	286	31,296
Jee Young Lee	71	72	69	74	286	31,296
Angela Stanford	71	77	71	68	287	27,079
Karrie Webb	73	73	72	69	287	27,079
Catriona Matthew	69	74	75	69	287	27,079
In-Kyung Kim	69	73	75	70	287	27,079
Moira Dunn	73	72	72	71	288	23,305
Cristie Kerr	74	71	71	72	288	23,305
Annika Sorenstam	67	71	76	74	288	23,305
Inbee Park	70	72	71	75	288	23,305
Hee Young Park	75	73	74	67	289	20,032
Meaghan Francella	71	74	72	72	289	20,032
Angela Park	72	73	70	74	289	20,032
H.J. Choi	73	67	75	74	289	20,032
Janice Moodie	76	72	73	69	290	17,423
Eva Dahllof	71	74	72	73	290	17,423
Eun-Hee Ji	71	73	72	74	290	17,423

Safeway Classic

Columbia Edgewater Country Club, Portland, Oregon
Par 36-36–72; 6,397 yards

August 22-24
purse, $1,700,000

	SCORES			TOTAL	MONEY
Cristie Kerr	71	67	65	203	$255,000
Sophie Gustafson	67	68	68	203	133,624
Helen Alfredsson	67	67	69	203	133,624
(Kerr defeated Gustafson and Alfredsson on first playoff hole.)					
Katherine Hull	71	67	67	205	86,920
Hee-Won Han	68	72	66	206	69,960
Annika Sorenstam	72	68	69	209	43,842
Catriona Matthew	69	70	70	209	43,842
Lorena Ochoa	69	70	70	209	43,842
Angela Park	66	73	70	209	43,842
Paula Creamer	69	68	72	209	43,842

	SCORES			TOTAL	MONEY
Allison Fouch	71	71	68	210	27,207
Eunjung Yi	71	71	68	210	27,207
Laura Diaz	69	73	68	210	27,207
Karrie Webb	70	69	71	210	27,207
Hee Young Park	67	72	71	210	27,207
Jee Young Lee	70	68	72	210	27,207
Michele Redman	73	69	69	211	19,601
Maria Hjorth	70	72	69	211	19,601
Lindsey Wright	69	73	69	211	19,601
Suzann Pettersen	69	73	69	211	19,601
Na Yeon Choi	71	69	71	211	19,601
Song-Hee Kim	67	72	72	211	19,601
Karen Stupples	67	71	73	211	19,601
Candie Kung	76	68	68	212	13,681
Linda Wessberg	70	74	68	212	13,681
Meaghan Francella	74	68	70	212	13,681
Minea Blomqvist	73	69	70	212	13,681
Rachel Hetherington	70	71	71	212	13,681
Dorothy Delasin	70	71	71	212	13,681
Louise Friberg	73	67	72	212	13,681
Alena Sharp	72	68	72	212	13,681
Gloria Park	72	68	72	212	13,681
Paige Mackenzie	69	70	73	212	13,681
Leta Lindley	69	69	74	212	13,681
Becky Morgan	68	70	74	212	13,681

Bell Micro LPGA Classic

Robert Trent Jones Golf Trail, Magnolia Grove,
Mobile, Alabama
Par 36-36–72; 6,253 yards

September 11-14
purse, $1,400,000

	SCORES				TOTAL	MONEY
Angela Stanford	70	67	67	73	277	$210,000
Shanshan Feng	67	73	70	68	278	127,855
Kim Hall	70	74	67	69	280	92,750
Danielle Downey	69	78	64	70	281	58,917
Hee Young Park	71	70	70	70	281	58,917
Katherine Hull	71	69	68	73	281	58,917
In-Kyung Kim	74	70	68	70	282	35,117
Mollie Fankhauser	71	69	72	70	282	35,117
Kristy McPherson	70	74	67	71	282	35,117
Suzann Pettersen	73	71	72	68	284	23,987
Nicole Castrale	68	76	72	68	284	23,987
Anna Rawson	67	73	75	69	284	23,987
H.J. Choi	71	73	67	73	284	23,987
Reilley Rankin	70	69	72	73	284	23,987
Cristie Kerr	69	66	76	73	284	23,987
Paula Creamer	78	69	67	71	285	17,500
Irene Cho	68	72	74	71	285	17,500
Sarah Jane Kenyon	73	69	71	72	285	17,500
Brittany Lang	72	73	67	73	285	17,500
Angela Park	68	73	69	75	285	17,500
Na On Min	73	74	70	69	286	14,700
Jeong Jang	69	72	72	73	286	14,700
Seon Hwa Lee	73	71	68	74	286	14,700
Heather Daly-Donofrio	72	69	71	74	286	14,700
Song-Hee Kim	69	73	76	69	287	12,880
Jamie Hullett	73	70	73	71	287	12,880
Michelle Ellis	68	70	75	74	287	12,880

		SCORES			TOTAL	MONEY
Sun Young Yoo	70	75	73	70	288	11,004
Louise Friberg	74	73	70	71	288	11,004
Maria Hjorth	70	75	72	71	288	11,004
Brandie Burton	75	71	68	74	288	11,004
Stacy Lewis	70	76	67	75	288	11,004

Navistar LPGA Classic

Robert Trent Jones Golf Trail, Senator Course,
Prattville, Alabama
Par 36-36–72; 6,571 yards

September 25-28
purse, $1,400,000

		SCORES			TOTAL	MONEY
Lorena Ochoa	67	67	69	70	273	$210,000
Cristie Kerr	66	71	70	66	273	108,577
Candie Kung	69	72	65	67	273	108,577
(Ochoa defeated Kerr on first and Kung on second playoff hole.)						
Shanshan Feng	68	70	70	66	274	63,737
Song-Hee Kim	68	68	69	69	274	63,737
Wendy Doolan	68	73	66	68	275	35,624
Sarah Jane Kenyon	70	69	67	69	275	35,624
Jill McGill	65	69	72	69	275	35,624
Yani Tseng	71	66	68	70	275	35,624
Louise Friberg	67	71	65	72	275	35,624
Ji Young Oh	67	70	72	67	276	23,444
Maria Hjorth	76	68	63	69	276	23,444
Katherine Hull	70	70	67	69	276	23,444
Sherri Turner	69	71	67	69	276	23,444
In-Kyung Kim	72	67	71	67	277	18,053
Heather Daly-Donofrio	72	70	66	69	277	18,053
Christina Kim	70	66	69	72	277	18,053
Michele Redman	70	65	70	72	277	18,053
Janice Moodie	66	67	72	72	277	18,053
Karrie Webb	72	68	69	69	278	15,572
Jane Park	65	74	69	70	278	15,572
Jee Young Lee	74	70	69	66	279	13,191
Giulia Sergas	72	70	70	67	279	13,191
Mi Hyun Kim	69	72	69	69	279	13,191
Mikaela Parmlid	69	69	72	69	279	13,191
Shi Hyun Ahn	73	70	65	71	279	13,191
Gloria Park	70	70	68	71	279	13,191
Na On Min	71	67	70	71	279	13,191
Stacy Prammanasudh	73	72	69	66	280	10,405
Hee Young Park	72	69	71	68	280	10,405
Angela Park	71	69	71	69	280	10,405
Carri Wood	73	71	66	70	280	10,405
Karen Stupples	70	72	68	70	280	10,405

Samsung World Championship

Half Moon Bay Golf Links, Ocean Course,
Half Moon Bay, California
Par 35-37–72; 6,450 yards

October 2-5
purse, $1,000,000

		SCORES			TOTAL	MONEY
Paula Creamer	68	74	68	69	279	$250,000
Song-Hee Kim	69	73	70	68	280	156,250

	SCORES				TOTAL	MONEY
Juli Inkster	73	72	68	68	281	64,063
Suzann Pettersen	74	70	69	68	281	64,063
Lorena Ochoa	69	73	70	69	281	64,063
Angela Stanford	69	73	69	70	281	64,063
Katherine Hull	70	73	69	70	282	31,249
Eun-Hee Ji	73	73	70	67	283	27,500
Ji-Yai Shin	67	76	70	70	283	27,500
Cristie Kerr	73	73	68	71	285	23,751
Jeong Jang	72	76	68	70	286	21,249
Seon Hwa Lee	75	69	72	71	287	20,000
Hee-Won Han	75	71	72	71	289	18,126
Yani Tseng	69	74	74	72	289	18,126
Annika Sorenstam	69	77	75	70	291	16,249
Karrie Webb	74	76	73	70	293	15,000
Helen Alfredsson	75	73	76	70	294	14,063
Na Yeon Choi	69	71	75	79	294	14,063
Inbee Park	77	71	74	74	296	13,125
Angela Park	76	76	75	73	300	12,499

Longs Drugs Challenge

Blackhawk Country Club, Danville, California
Par 37-35–72; 6,185 yards

October 9-12
purse, $1,200,000

	SCORES				TOTAL	MONEY
In-Kyung Kim	67	69	69	73	278	$180,000
Angela Stanford	70	69	67	75	281	108,830
Yani Tseng	68	72	70	72	282	78,948
Lorena Ochoa	70	68	74	72	284	61,073
Karen Stupples	71	73	71	70	285	38,134
Silvia Cavalleri	71	73	70	71	285	38,134
Brittany Lang	72	72	69	72	285	38,134
Kristy McPherson	70	70	71	74	285	38,134
Mikaela Parmlid	67	74	75	70	286	25,323
Wendy Ward	68	76	71	71	286	25,323
Mollie Fankhauser	69	68	73	77	287	22,344
Julieta Granada	69	73	75	71	288	20,854
Pat Hurst	70	72	74	73	289	17,398
Meaghan Francella	68	74	74	73	289	17,398
Irene Cho	71	72	72	74	289	17,398
Michele Redman	66	75	74	74	289	17,398
Sarah Kemp	68	73	71	77	289	17,398
Becky Lucidi	75	70	73	72	290	14,777
Paula Creamer	74	70	76	71	291	13,466
Jeong Jang	72	74	73	72	291	13,466
Suzann Pettersen	68	72	79	72	291	13,466
Charlotte Mayorkas	69	71	74	77	291	13,466
Amy Hung	74	74	73	71	292	11,182
Candie Kung	73	74	74	71	292	11,182
Wendy Doolan	75	73	71	73	292	11,182
Juli Inkster	70	77	71	74	292	11,182
Maria Hjorth	66	80	72	74	292	11,182
Teresa Lu	75	70	69	78	292	11,182
Sarah Lee	68	76	74	75	293	9,355
Il Mi Chung	72	69	77	75	293	9,355
Reilley Rankin	68	73	76	76	293	9,355

Kapalua LPGA Classic

Kapalua Resort, Bay Course, Maui, Hawaii
Par 35-37–72; 6,273 yards

October 16-19
purse, $1,500,000

	SCORES				TOTAL	MONEY
Morgan Pressel	72	72	67	69	280	$225,000
Suzann Pettersen	68	72	72	69	281	138,687
Laura Diaz	70	71	71	70	282	100,608
Angela Stanford	71	73	70	70	284	70,236
Sun Young Yoo	70	71	71	72	284	70,236
Stacy Lewis	73	73	73	66	285	47,077
Carin Koch	72	71	68	74	285	47,077
Linda Wessberg	76	71	68	71	286	30,347
Meena Lee	73	72	70	71	286	30,347
Heather Young	72	74	67	73	286	30,347
Cristie Kerr	71	72	70	73	286	30,347
Jee Young Lee	71	70	70	75	286	30,347
Brittany Lang	69	71	71	75	286	30,347
Maria Hjorth	73	74	69	71	287	22,704
Lorena Ochoa	74	69	73	71	287	22,704
Michele Redman	72	74	73	69	288	18,629
Allison Fouch	72	73	74	69	288	18,629
Katherine Hull	73	73	72	70	288	18,629
Sarah Jane Kenyon	72	74	71	71	288	18,629
Becky Morgan	72	71	72	73	288	18,629
Young-A Yang	73	71	70	74	288	18,629
Ji Young Oh	70	71	76	72	289	15,642
Helen Alfredsson	72	71	72	74	289	15,642
Alena Sharp	74	67	72	76	289	15,642
Annika Sorenstam	77	70	71	72	290	12,225
Momoko Ueda	73	73	71	73	290	12,225
Wendy Ward	73	71	73	73	290	12,225
Eun-Hee Ji	73	71	73	73	290	12,225
Jamie Hullett	72	72	73	73	290	12,225
Rachel Hetherington	77	71	68	74	290	12,225
Anna Rawson	70	75	71	74	290	12,225
Laura Davies	76	71	67	76	290	12,225
Janice Moodie	74	72	68	76	290	12,225
Seon Hwa Lee	73	69	72	76	290	12,225

Grand China Air LPGA

Haikou West Golf Club, Hainen Island, China
Par 36-36–72; 6,422 yards

October 24-26
purse, $1,800,000

	SCORES			TOTAL	MONEY
Helen Alfredsson	70	69	65	204	$270,000
Yani Tseng	72	67	68	207	171,913
Laura Diaz	63	73	72	208	124,711
Karen Stupples	67	67	75	209	96,475
Young Kim	70	69	71	210	77,650
Shanshan Feng	70	73	68	211	63,532
Allison Fouch	70	69	73	212	49,885
Christina Kim	70	68	74	212	49,885
Suzann Pettersen	72	73	68	213	32,648
Lindsey Wright	73	69	71	213	32,648
Brittany Lang	73	69	71	213	32,648
Nicole Castrale	72	69	72	213	32,648
Na Yeon Choi	71	68	74	213	32,648

	SCORES			TOTAL	MONEY
Ji Young Oh	68	71	74	213	32,648
Seon Hwa Lee	66	73	74	213	32,648
Candie Kung	69	69	75	213	32,648
Hong Mei Yang	72	74	68	214	22,150
Meena Lee	72	72	70	214	22,150
Annika Sorenstam	72	70	72	214	22,150
Diana D'Alessio	71	71	72	214	22,150
Teresa Lu	70	70	74	214	22,150
Louise Friberg	68	69	77	214	22,150
In-Kyung Kim	70	75	70	215	17,996
Angela Park	75	68	72	215	17,996
Jill McGill	71	72	72	215	17,996
Katherine Hull	73	69	73	215	17,996
Jeong Jang	71	70	74	215	17,996
Hee Young Park	72	76	68	216	14,511
Leta Lindley	74	72	70	216	14,511
Sophie Gustafson	72	74	70	216	14,511
Mi Hyun Kim	74	70	72	216	14,511
Jane Park	73	70	73	216	14,511
Catriona Matthew	70	70	76	216	14,511

Hana Bank-Kolon Championship

Sky 72 Golf Club, Incheon, Korea
Par 36-36–72; 6,482 yards

October 31-November 2
purse, $1,600,000

	SCORES			TOTAL	MONEY
Candie Kung	70	71	69	210	$240,000
Katherine Hull	66	76	69	211	149,117
Jee Young Lee	74	69	69	212	78,579
Sophie Gustafson	72	70	70	212	78,579
Jeong Jang	70	71	71	212	78,579
Hee-Won Han	71	69	72	212	78,579
Jimin Kang	72	71	70	213	43,270
Christina Kim	70	71	72	213	43,270
Paula Creamer	75	69	70	214	32,146
Carin Koch	72	72	70	214	32,146
Brittany Lang	74	69	71	214	32,146
Amy Yang	68	73	73	214	32,146
Catriona Matthew	74	71	70	215	24,492
Mi Hyun Kim	70	73	72	215	24,492
Karen Stupples	70	70	75	215	24,492
In-Kyung Kim	70	69	76	215	24,492
Ji-Yai Shin	70	75	71	216	19,920
Giulia Sergas	73	71	72	216	19,920
Se Ri Pak	71	72	73	216	19,920
Hee Kyung Seo	71	70	75	216	19,920
Jane Park	73	74	70	217	18,124
Ji Young Oh	75	74	69	218	15,628
Na Yeon Choi	74	75	69	218	15,628
Bo Kyung Kim	75	71	72	218	15,628
Sun Young Yoo	72	74	72	218	15,628
Minea Blomqvist	71	74	73	218	15,628
Ha-Neul Kim	73	71	74	218	15,628
Ji-Na Lim	70	74	74	218	15,628
Anna Rawson	75	75	69	219	12,328
Song-Hee Kim	73	76	70	219	12,328
Jin Joo Kim	71	77	71	219	12,328
Seul-A Yoon	74	73	72	219	12,328
Morgan Pressel	72	71	76	219	12,328

Mizuno Classic

See Japan LPGA Tour section.

Lorena Ochoa Invitational

Guadalajara Country Club, Guadalajara, Mexico
Par 36-36–72; 6,644 yards

November 13-16
purse, $1,000,000

	SCORES				TOTAL	MONEY
Angela Stanford	68	66	72	69	275	$200,000
Brittany Lang	68	74	69	65	276	87,818
Annika Sorenstam	68	72	67	69	276	87,818
Meena Lee	69	69	76	66	280	39,959
Jeong Jang	73	68	71	68	280	39,959
Sun Young Yoo	70	70	70	70	280	39,959
Jee Young Lee	69	71	69	71	280	39,959
Katherine Hull	71	71	66	72	280	39,959
In-Kyung Kim	70	71	70	70	281	24,800
Teresa Lu	72	71	69	70	282	22,571
Seon Hwa Lee	68	72	76	67	283	19,562
Hee-Won Han	68	73	72	70	283	19,562
Cristie Kerr	71	72	69	71	283	19,562
Paula Creamer	75	70	69	70	284	15,772
Lorena Ochoa	73	71	70	70	284	15,772
Ji Young Oh	70	71	73	70	284	15,772
Nicole Castrale	68	72	72	72	284	15,772
Juli Inkster	71	69	74	71	285	13,543
Yani Tseng	68	68	78	71	285	13,543
Eun-Hee Ji	71	72	72	71	286	12,595
Na Yeon Choi	69	74	72	71	286	12,595
Karen Stupples	68	71	75	73	287	11,926
Inbee Park	74	72	73	69	288	11,480
Maria Hjorth	74	70	76	69	289	10,645
Laura Davies	75	70	73	71	289	10,645
Helen Alfredsson	70	74	74	71	289	10,645
Sophia Sheridan	76	71	71	73	291	9,864
Song-Hee Kim	73	74	71	74	292	9,103
Suzann Pettersen	75	71	71	75	292	9,103
Laura Diaz	70	73	71	78	292	9,103

ADT Championship

Trump International Golf Club, West Palm Beach, Florida
Par 36-36–72; 6,523 yards

November 20-23
purse, $1,550,000

	SCORES			ROUND 4	MONEY
Ji-Yai Shin	69	75	71	70	$1,000,000
Karrie Webb	73	74	72	71	100,000
Paula Creamer	71	71	70	74	19,875
Seon Hwa Lee	72	72	70	74	19,875
Eun-Hee Ji	70	75	72	75	18,500
Angela Stanford	73	67	69	78	17,750
Jeong Jang	73	70	71	79	16,625
Suzann Pettersen	72	73	68	79	16,625

Players who did not advance after Round 3

Sun Young Yoo	74	71	72		14,000
Helen Alfredsson	73	72	74		14,000

	SCORES				MONEY
Angela Park	73	70	74		14,000
Jee Young Lee	72	73	77		14,000
Karen Stupples	71	75	77		14,000
Katherine Hull	68	71	79		14,000
Christina Kim	71	71	79		14,000
In-Kyung Kim	69	73	80		14,000

Players who did not advance after Round 2

Na Yeon Choi	70	78	148	8,533
Cristie Kerr	78	71	149	8,533
Laura Diaz	75	74	149	8,533
Lorena Ochoa	75	74	149	8,533
Hee-Won Han	74	75	149	8,533
Annika Sorenstam	74	75	149	8,533
Maria Hjorth	72	77	149	8,533
Candie Kung	72	77	149	8,533
Song-Hee Kim	75	75	150	8,533
Nicole Castrale	73	77	150	8,533
Morgan Pressel	72	78	150	8,533
Yani Tseng	72	79	151	8,533
Meena Lee	78	75	153	8,533
Shanshan Feng	78	78	156	8,533
Ji Young Oh	70	87	157	8,533
Inbee Park			WD	

Lexus Cup

Singapore Island Country Club, Bukit Course, Singapore
Par 35-36–71; 5,757 yards

November 28-30
purse, $1,000,000

FIRST DAY
Alternate Shot

Song-Hee Kim and Inbee Park (Asia) defeated Helen Alfredsson and Christina Kim, 3 and 2.
Cristie Kerr and Karen Stupples (Int'l) defeated Sarah Lee and Na Yeon Choi, 2 and 1.
Yani Tseng and Seon Hwa Lee (Asia) defeated Suzann Pettersen and Natalie Gulbis, 2 and 1.
Paula Creamer and Nicole Castrale (Int'l) defeated Se Ri Pak and Eun-Hee Ji, 1 up.
Jeong Jang and Candie Kung (Asia) defeated Angela Stanford and Annika Sorenstam, 3 and 2.
Katherine Hull and Nikki Campbell (Int'l) defeated Namika Omata and Mayumi
Shimomura, 3 and 1.

POINTS: International 3, Asia 3

SECOND DAY
Best Ball

Pettersen and Sorenstam (Int'l) defeated Ji and Park, 1 up.
Kerr and Alfredsson (Int'l) defeated Pak and Seon Hwa Lee, 2 up.
Jang and Choi (Asia) defeated Creamer and Castrale, 1 up.
Sarah Lee and Song-Hee Kim (Asia) defeated Stupples and Christina Kim, 4 and 2.
Kung and Shimomura (Asia) defeated Gulbis and Stanford, 4 and 3.
Hull and Campbell (Int'l) defeated Tseng and Omata, 1 up.

POINTS: Asia 3, International 3

THIRD DAY
Singles

Sorenstam (Int'l) defeated Pak, 3 and 2.
Sarah Lee (Asia) defeated Castrale, 1 up.
Pettersen (Int'l) halved with Tseng.

Alfredsson (Int'l) defeated Park, 3 and 2.
Choi (Asia) defeated Creamer, 3 and 2.
Song-Hee Kim (Asia) defeated Kerr, 1 up.
Stupples (Int'l) halved with Ji.
Hull (Int'l) defeated Jang, 1 up.
Gulbis (Int'l) defeated Shimomura, 2 and 1.
Christina Kim (Int'l) halved with Omata.
Kung (Asia) defeated Campbell, 3 and 2.
Stanford (Int'l) defeated Seon Hwa Lee, 4 and 3.

POINTS: International 6½, Asia 5½
TOTAL POINTS: International 12½, Asia 11½

(Each member of the International team received $52,083; each member of the Asia team received $31,250.)

Ladies European Tour

Women's World Cup of Golf

See Ladies African Tour section.

MFS Women's Australian Open

See Australian Ladies Tour section.

ANZ Ladies Masters

See Australian Ladies Tour section.

VCI European Ladies Golf Cup

La Sella Golf Resort, Alicante, Spain
Par 36-36–72; 6,283 yards

April 3-6
purse, €300,000

	SCORES				TOTAL
ENGLAND—€70,000					
Trish Johnson/Rebecca Hudson	64	70	65	71	270
GERMANY—€30,000					
Martina Eberl/Anja Monke	66	73	71	65	275
BELGIUM—€30,000					
Lara Tadiotto/Ellen Smets	65	70	69	71	275
NETHERLANDS—€9,000					
Marjet van der Graaff/*Marieke Nivard	70	73	70	69	282
ITALY—€17,000					
Stefania Croce/Veronica Zorzi	68	75	73	67	283

	SCORES	TOTAL

RUSSIA — €16,000
| Anastasia Kostina/Maria Kostina | 73 70 69 72 | 284 |

SPAIN — €15,000
| Paula Marti/Tania Elosegui | 68 73 72 72 | 285 |

SWITZERLAND — €13,500
| Frederique Seeholzer/Nora Angehrn | 69 75 74 68 | 286 |

SWEDEN — €13,500
| Johanna Westerberg/Lotta Wahlin | 73 71 70 72 | 286 |

DENMARK — €12,000
| Iben Tinning/Lisa Holm Sorensen | 66 77 70 74 | 287 |

UNITED STATES — €10,500
| Kris Lindstrom/Laura Terebey | 70 75 72 71 | 288 |

AUSTRIA — €10,500
| Eva Steinberger/Nicole Gergely | 72 72 71 73 | 288 |

IRELAND — €8,500
| Rebecca Coakley/Martina Gillen | 67 76 75 71 | 289 |

SCOTLAND — €8,500
| Clare Queen/Lynn Kenny | 71 74 71 73 | 289 |

AUSTRALIA — €6,500
| Karen Lunn/Joanne Mills | 69 75 73 74 | 291 |

WALES — €6,500
| Eleanor Pilgrim/Lydia Hall | 74 74 67 76 | 291 |

FINLAND — €5,000
| Ursula Wikstrom/Kaisa Ruuttila | 73 74 71 74 | 292 |

FRANCE — €4,000
| Ludivine Kreutz/Stephanie Arricau | 68 79 73 74 | 294 |

NORWAY — €3,000
| Cecilie Lundgreen/Lill Kristin Saether | 70 78 76 74 | 298 |

SLOVAKIA — €1,000
| Zuzana Kamasova/*Lujza Bubanova | 74 79 76 78 | 307 |

Catalonia Ladies

Emporda Golf Hotel & Spa, Gualta, Girona, Spain
Par 35-36–71; 6,211 yards

April 12-13
purse, €60,000

	SCORES		TOTAL	MONEY
Lotta Wahlin	68	65	133	€9,480
Rebecca Hudson	73	66	139	4,040
Paula Marti	72	67	139	4,040
Tania Elosegui	67	72	139	4,040
Beatriz Recari	70	70	140	3,300
Lora Fairclough	73	70	143	3,120
Johanna Westerberg	72	71	143	3,120
Nuria Clau	76	68	144	2,820
Melissa Reid	72	72	144	2,820

	SCORES			TOTAL	MONEY
Karen-Margrethe Juul	72	72		144	2,820
Nikki Garrett	76	70		146	2,400
Laura Cabanillas	74	72		146	2,400
Karen Lunn	73	73		146	2,400
Joanne Mills	70	76		146	2,400
Georgina Simpson	78	69		147	1,980
Elisa Serramia	75	72		147	1,980
Marta Prieto	72	75		147	1,980
Rebecca Coakley	78	72		150	1,740
Iben Tinning	79	73		152	1,620
Marina Arruti	81	74		155	1,500

Open de Espana Femenino

Panoramica Golf & Country Club, San Jordi, Castellon, Spain
Par 36-36–72; 6,252 yards

April 17-20
purse, €275,000

	SCORES				TOTAL	MONEY
Emma Zackrisson	72	67	71	71	281	€41,250
Nikki Garrett	75	70	71	69	285	20,670.83
Diana Luna	75	72	69	69	285	20,670.83
Joanne Mills	74	73	67	71	285	20,670.83
Veronica Zorzi	72	68	74	72	286	11,660
Katharina Schallenberg	71	74	73	69	287	7,727.50
Martina Eberl	70	77	70	70	287	7,727.50
Rebecca Hudson	68	73	75	71	287	7,727.50
Lill Kristin Saether	75	72	67	73	287	7,727.50
Titiya Plucksataporn	69	75	75	69	288	5,096.66
Lotta Wahlin	76	72	70	70	288	5,096.66
Marianne Skarpnord	76	73	69	70	288	5,096.66
Paula Marti	70	79	72	68	289	4,253.33
Iben Tinning	68	79	73	69	289	4,253.33
Laura Cabanillas	72	72	72	73	289	4,253.33
Anja Monke	73	73	74	70	290	3,905
Frances Bondad	72	72	73	73	290	3,905
Lisa Holm Sorensen	70	73	78	70	291	3,427.18
Stephanie Arricau	71	79	71	70	291	3,427.18
Georgina Simpson	76	71	73	71	291	3,427.18
Amy Yang	71	77	72	71	291	3,427.18
Lora Fairclough	74	68	77	72	291	3,427.18
Maria Boden	72	76	71	72	291	3,427.18
Samantha Head	71	71	76	73	291	3,427.18
Dana Lacey	75	75	68	73	291	3,427.18

Aberdeen Asset Management Ladies Scottish Open

De Vere Cameron House, The Carrick on Loch Lomond, Scotland
Par 36-35–71; 6,141 yards

May 1-3
purse, €200,000

	SCORES			TOTAL	MONEY
Gwladys Nocera	69	70	69	208	€30,000
Maria Boden	69	72	69	210	20,300
Rebecca Hudson	72	71	68	211	12,400
Nicole Gergely	70	72	69	211	12,400
Amy Yang	70	70	72	212	8,480
Clare Queen	72	71	70	213	5,620
Kathryn Imrie	73	69	71	213	5,620

	SCORES			TOTAL	MONEY
Stacy Lee Bregman	75	67	71	213	5,620
Tania Elosegui	70	71	72	213	5,620
Melissa Reid	77	71	66	214	3,400
Caroline Afonso	77	70	67	214	3,400
Martina Eberl	74	72	68	214	3,400
Becky Brewerton	74	70	70	214	3,400
Emma Cabrera-Bello	72	72	70	214	3,400
Melodie Bourdy	71	73	70	214	3,400
Sophie Gustafson	75	67	73	215	2,880
Mhairi McKay	74	74	68	216	2,720
Johanna Westerberg	71	73	72	216	2,720
Lee-Anne Pace	75	67	74	216	2,720
Lisa Hall	74	76	67	217	2,430
Samantha Head	73	75	69	217	2,430
Ellen Smets	75	72	70	217	2,430
Marina Arruti	77	70	70	217	2,430
Nikki Garrett	70	75	72	217	2,430
Lotta Wahlin	73	71	73	217	2,430

Garanti American Express Turkish Open

National Golf Club, Belek, Antalya, Turkey
Par 36-37–73; 6,412 yards

May 8-11
purse, €250,000

	SCORES				TOTAL	MONEY
Lotta Wahlin	71	71	73	70	285	€37,500
Johanna Westerberg	80	72	74	71	297	18,791.66
Stacy Lee Bregman	74	80	71	72	297	18,791.66
Paula Marti	73	77	73	74	297	18,791.66
Amy Yang	77	77	72	72	298	9,675
Marianne Skarpnord	79	72	74	73	298	9,675
Trish Johnson	78	77	74	70	299	6,875
Lisa Hall	80	74	74	71	299	6,875
Stephanie Arricau	78	73	78	71	300	5,600
Iben Tinning	77	76	75	73	301	5,000
Gwladys Nocera	77	72	81	72	302	4,308.33
Rachel Bell	76	77	74	75	302	4,308.33
Anna Rawson	79	74	73	76	302	4,308.33
Samantha Head	80	79	73	71	303	3,725
Emma Zackrisson	75	74	81	73	303	3,725
Laura Terebey	77	79	72	75	303	3,725
Becky Brewerton	77	80	77	70	304	3,450
Joanne Morley	80	75	75	74	304	3,450
Christine Hallstrom	75	80	76	74	305	3,187.50
Martina Eberl	79	77	74	75	305	3,187.50
Ana B. Sanchez	74	76	79	76	305	3,187.50
Ludivine Kreutz	79	73	76	77	305	3,187.50

Deutsche Bank Ladies Swiss Open

Golf Gerre Losone, Ticino, Switzerland
Par 35-37–72; 6,185 yards
(Fourth round cancelled—rain.)

May 22-25
purse, €525,000

	SCORES			TOTAL	MONEY
Suzann Pettersen	67	63	64	194	€78,750
Amy Yang	67	68	65	200	53,287.50

	SCORES			TOTAL	MONEY
Gwladys Nocera	70	69	62	201	36,750
Lotta Wahlin	71	67	66	204	28,350
Laura Davies	69	68	68	205	22,260
Marianne Skarpnord	71	66	69	206	15,750
Paula Marti	67	70	69	206	15,750
Ludivine Kreutz	67	70	69	206	15,750
Ursula Wikstrom	68	70	70	208	11,130
Ellen Smets	71	66	71	208	11,130
Maria Verchenova	70	71	68	209	8,610
Veronica Zorzi	69	71	69	209	8,610
Cecilia Ekelundh	72	67	70	209	8,610
Rebecca Coakley	63	74	72	209	8,610
Lisa Hall	67	69	73	209	8,610
Marina Arruti	67	76	67	210	7,560
Becky Brewerton	71	73	67	211	6,961.50
Emma Cabrera-Bello	71	72	68	211	6,961.50
Caroline Afonso	72	71	68	211	6,961.50
Nicole Gergely	68	73	70	211	6,961.50
Marta Prieto	71	70	70	211	6,961.50

HypoVereinsbank Ladies German Open

Golfpark Gut Hausern, Munich, Germany
Par 36-36–72; 6,204 yards

May 29-June 1
purse, €250,000

	SCORES				TOTAL	MONEY
Amy Yang	71	66	63	67	267	€37,500
Louise Stahle	68	69	69	65	271	25,375
Gwladys Nocera	68	70	69	65	272	17,500
Marta Prieto	67	69	72	65	273	12,050
Anne-Lise Caudal	69	69	67	68	273	12,050
Michelle Wie	68	69	70	67	274	8,750
Lynn Brooky	68	71	68	68	275	6,875
Becky Brewerton	69	68	68	70	275	6,875
Titiya Plucksataporn	69	67	73	67	276	5,300
Iben Tinning	72	67	68	69	276	5,300
Lisa Holm Sorensen	71	68	71	67	277	4,100
Anna Rawson	71	70	68	68	277	4,100
Paula Marti	68	68	72	69	277	4,100
Ludivine Kreutz	71	69	68	69	277	4,100
Lora Fairclough	66	68	72	71	277	4,100
Samantha Head	71	70	70	67	278	3,450
Veronica Zorzi	67	68	75	68	278	3,450
Christine Hallstrom	68	71	70	69	278	3,450
Joanne Mills	69	71	66	72	278	3,450
Stacy Lee Bregman	71	67	75	66	279	3,187.50
Nina Reis	64	73	70	72	279	3,187.50

ABN AMRO Ladies Open

Eindhovensche Golf Club, Valkenswaard, Netherlands
Par 36-36–72; 6,228 yards

June 6-8
purse, €250,000

	SCORES			TOTAL	MONEY
Gwladys Nocera	67	65	71	203	€37,500
Melissa Reid	68	68	68	204	25,375
Anne-Lise Caudal	68	69	68	205	17,500

	SCORES			TOTAL	MONEY
Paula Marti	69	70	69	208	10,950
Kirsty S. Taylor	71	67	70	208	10,950
Lisa Holm Sorensen	72	65	71	208	10,950
Maria Boden	71	72	66	209	7,500
Becky Brewerton	72	71	67	210	5,925
Marianne Skarpnord	73	70	67	210	5,925
Leah Hart	71	69	71	211	4,481.25
*Christel Boeljon	70	70	71		
Dana Lacey	73	67	71	211	4,481.25
Veronica Zorzi	70	69	72	211	4,481.25
Sophie Walker	70	69	72	211	4,481.25
Karen Lunn	71	71	70	212	3,668.75
Stefania Croce	70	71	71	212	3,668.75
Jade Schaeffer	67	73	72	212	3,668.75
Lotta Wahlin	70	70	72	212	3,668.75
Laurette Maritz	73	71	69	213	3,115.62
Natascha Fink	72	70	71	213	3,115.62
Titiya Plucksataporn	74	68	71	213	3,115.62
Caroline Afonso	71	71	71	213	3,115.62
Anna Knutsson	71	71	71	213	3,115.62
Rebecca Coakley	68	73	72	213	3,115.62
Lisa Hall	71	70	72	213	3,115.62
Isabella Maconi	70	70	73	213	3,115.62

Ladies Open de Portugal

Quinta de Cima Golf Club, Algarve, Portugal
Par 36-37–73; 6,301 yards

June 13-15
purse, €200,000

	SCORES			TOTAL	MONEY
Anne-Lise Caudal	64	69	70	203	€30,000
Gwladys Nocera	67	71	66	204	17,150
Georgina Simpson	69	67	68	204	17,150
Martina Eberl	71	67	67	205	9,640
Louise Stahle	66	68	71	205	9,640
Martina Gillen	70	70	66	206	7,000
Lotta Wahlin	70	70	67	207	5,500
Lisa Hall	70	68	69	207	5,500
Diana Luna	65	71	72	208	4,480
Titiya Plucksataporn	72	69	68	209	4,000
Johanna Westerberg	74	68	68	210	3,355
Iben Tinning	68	73	69	210	3,355
Stefania Croce	66	73	71	210	3,355
Caroline Afonso	69	70	71	210	3,355
Lynn Brooky	71	70	70	211	2,886.66
Rachel Bell	67	73	71	211	2,886.66
Veronica Zorzi	66	72	73	211	2,886.66
Samantha Head	70	73	69	212	2,615
Lydia Hall	71	72	69	212	2,615
Sophie Sandolo	69	69	74	212	2,615
Anja Monke	73	65	74	212	2,615

Tenerife Ladies Open

Golf Costa Adeje, Adeje, Tenerife, Spain
Par 36-36–72; 6,080 yards

June 19-22
purse, €300,000

	SCORES				TOTAL	MONEY
Rebecca Hudson	70	68	71	69	278	€45,000
Anne-Lise Caudal	70	69	69	70	278	30,450
(Hudson defeated Caudal on third playoff hole.)						
Gwladys Nocera	69	71	73	68	281	21,000
*Carlota Ciganda	69	66	75	71	281	
Maria Verchenova	68	69	73	72	282	14,460
*Marta Silva	71	71	68	72	282	
Melissa Reid	70	71	68	73	282	14,460
Paula Marti	72	71	71	69	283	9,750
Lisa Holm Sorensen	73	66	71	73	283	9,750
Lotta Wahlin	73	70	75	66	284	6,180
Anja Monke	69	74	71	70	284	6,180
Martina Eberl	72	73	69	70	284	6,180
Louise Stahle	69	69	73	73	284	6,180
Ursula Wikstrom	69	68	73	74	284	6,180
Nikki Garrett	72	74	69	70	285	4,725
Tania Elosegui	72	74	68	71	285	4,725
Federica Piovano	71	70	75	70	286	4,267.50
Joanne Mills	72	70	73	71	286	4,267.50
Mianne Bagger	74	73	68	71	286	4,267.50
Felicity Johnson	70	70	73	73	286	4,267.50

Oxfordshire Ladies English Open

Oxfordshire Golf Club, Thame, Oxfordshire, England
Par 36-36–72; 6,123 yards

July 4-6
purse, €165,000

	SCORES			TOTAL	MONEY
Rebecca Hudson	72	70	64	206	€24,750
Melissa Reid	68	70	69	207	16,747.50
Joanne Mills	68	76	66	210	11,550
Marina Arruti	69	71	71	211	8,910
Natascha Fink	72	73	67	212	6,385.50
Iben Tinning	73	72	67	212	6,385.50
Lora Fairclough	72	71	70	213	4,537.50
Becky Brewerton	74	69	70	213	4,537.50
Leah Hart	71	73	70	214	3,696
Martina Gillen	70	76	70	216	3,058
Yuki Sakurai	73	72	71	216	3,058
Kiran Matharu	70	73	73	216	3,058
Emma Zackrisson	68	78	71	217	2,508
Valerie Michaud	76	70	71	217	2,508
Lisa Holm Sorensen	73	71	73	217	2,508
Stephanie Arricau	71	72	74	217	2,508
Lisa Hall	72	75	71	218	2,215.12
Nina Reis	74	72	72	218	2,215.12
Kirsty S. Taylor	70	76	72	218	2,215.12
Ellen Smets	75	69	74	218	2,215.12

AIB Ladies Irish Open

Portmarnock Hotel & Golf Links, Portmarnock, Co. Dublin, Ireland
Par 36-36–72; 6,332 yards

July 11-13
purse, €450,000

	SCORES			TOTAL	MONEY
Suzann Pettersen	69	69	67	205	€67,500
Marianne Skarpnord	71	69	70	210	45,675
Lynn Brooky	73	66	73	212	31,500
Tania Elosegui	76	70	67	213	19,710
Federica Piovano	67	78	68	213	19,710
Martina Eberl	70	72	71	213	19,710
Morgan Pressel	77	71	66	214	10,957.50
Becky Brewerton	70	74	70	214	10,957.50
Emma Cabrera-Bello	72	71	71	214	10,957.50
Maria Hjorth	70	72	72	214	10,957.50
Caroline Afonso	75	72	68	215	7,548.75
Melissa Reid	74	73	68	215	7,548.75
Lisa Holm Sorensen	72	74	69	215	7,548.75
Lisa Hall	73	71	71	215	7,548.75
Carmen Alonso	72	70	74	216	6,705
Melodie Bourdy	76	71	70	217	6,210
Ana Larraneta	71	76	70	217	6,210
Ursula Wikstrom	77	70	70	217	6,210
Kirsty S. Taylor	74	70	73	217	6,210
Eva Steinberger	74	75	69	218	5,400
Virginie Lagoutte-Clement	80	68	70	218	5,400
Georgina Simpson	72	76	70	218	5,400
Gwladys Nocera	75	71	72	218	5,400
Anna Tybring	74	71	73	218	5,400
Kiran Matharu	73	70	75	218	5,400
Dana Lacey	74	69	75	218	5,400

BMW Ladies Italian Open

Argentario Golf Resort & Spa, Porto Ercole, Tuscany, Italy
Par 36-35–71; 5,996 yards

July 17-20
purse, €400,000

	SCORES				TOTAL	MONEY
Martina Eberl	65	74	67	69	275	€60,000
Carmen Alonso	67	70	77	66	280	40,600
Maria Hjorth	64	73	72	72	281	22,186.66
Becky Brewerton	66	71	72	72	281	22,186.66
Lisa Holm Sorensen	68	70	70	73	281	22,186.66
Anne-Lise Caudal	72	76	67	67	282	11,240
Christine Hallstrom	70	71	72	69	282	11,240
Stefania Croce	69	73	71	69	282	11,240
Gwladys Nocera	65	70	73	74	282	11,240
Tania Elosegui	70	78	65	70	283	8,000
Cecilia Ekelundh	73	73	73	65	284	7,120
Lynn Brooky	75	71	68	70	284	7,120
Stacy Lee Bregman	73	71	72	69	285	6,300
Lora Fairclough	70	70	73	72	285	6,300
Beatriz Recari	72	77	71	66	286	5,773.33
Iben Tinning	68	71	76	71	286	5,773.33
Samantha Head	74	70	71	71	286	5,773.33
Denise-Charlotte Becker	77	72	72	66	287	5,360
Georgina Simpson	70	69	71	77	287	5,360
Ursula Wikstrom	78	72	68	70	288	5,100
Natascha Fink	74	72	69	73	288	5,100

Evian Masters

Evian Masters Golf Club, Evians-les-Bains, France
Par 36-36–72; 6,347 yards

July 24-27
purse, €1,940,265

	SCORES				TOTAL	MONEY
Helen Alfredsson	72	63	71	67	273	€316,875
Na Yeon Choi	71	67	69	66	273	182,457.31
Angela Park	66	68	68	71	273	182,457.31
(Alfredsson defeated Park on first and Choi on third playoff hole.)						
Jin Joo Hong	71	69	68	67	275	118,685.45
Lorena Ochoa	65	73	70	68	276	95,527.60
Hee Young Park	70	69	70	68	277	66,965.58
Cristie Kerr	70	66	72	69	277	66,965.58
Shi Hyun Ahn	69	69	69	70	277	66,965.58
Paula Creamer	70	69	69	70	278	49,210.85
Juli Inkster	67	69	69	73	278	49,210.85
In-Kyung Kim	68	68	75	68	279	39,397.82
Sun Young Yoo	74	68	69	68	279	39,397.82
Eun-Hee Ji	71	71	67	70	279	39,397.82
Candie Kung	66	70	67	76	279	39,397.82
Ji-Yai Shin	72	73	68	67	280	32,653.10
Meena Lee	67	69	73	71	280	32,653.10
Giulia Sergas	71	74	70	66	281	28,793.11
Annika Sorenstam	71	69	73	68	281	28,793.11
Natalie Gulbis	69	71	72	69	281	28,793.11
Christina Kim	72	70	73	67	282	25,242.56
Young Kim	68	71	74	69	282	25,242.56
Laura Diaz	67	73	71	71	282	25,242.56
Suzann Pettersen	67	74	69	72	282	25,242.56
Becky Brewerton	72	72	71	68	283	22,926.29
Karrie Webb	72	75	71	66	284	20,900.33
Sun Ju Ahn	66	74	73	71	284	20,900.33
Morgan Pressel	69	72	72	71	284	20,900.33
Yani Tseng	70	70	70	74	284	20,900.33
H.J. Choi	73	73	74	65	285	17,484.33
Song-Hee Kim	69	72	74	70	285	17,484.33
Diana D'Alessio	73	71	71	70	285	17,484.33
Momoko Ueda	70	69	74	72	285	17,484.33
Amy Yang	68	73	70	74	285	17,484.33
Inbee Park	69	72	74	71	286	14,531.80
Maria Hjorth	73	69	72	72	286	14,531.80
Jimin Kang	71	71	72	72	286	14,531.80
Lindsey Wright	72	73	69	72	286	14,531.80
Hee-Won Han	72	74	76	65	287	11,830.06
Katherine Hull	72	72	74	69	287	11,830.06
Angela Stanford	67	72	78	70	287	11,830.06
Sophie Gustafson	73	70	74	70	287	11,830.06
Linda Wessberg	69	71	74	73	287	11,830.06
Teresa Lu	71	71	71	74	287	11,830.06
Seon Hwa Lee	69	75	76	68	288	9,668.57
Wendy Doolan	77	68	74	69	288	9,668.57
Ji Young Oh	70	71	75	72	288	9,668.57
Pat Hurst	74	73	70	71	288	9,668.57
Jeong Jang	74	73	72	70	289	8,307.91
Jane Park	74	74	71	70	289	8,307.91
Trish Johnson	70	75	71	73	289	8,307.91
Se Ri Pak	70	76	70	73	289	8,307.91
Brittany Lang	73	73	73	71	290	7,178.98
Sarah Lee	71	73	74	72	290	7,178.98
Ai Miyazato	74	72	70	74	290	7,178.98
Carin Koch	73	74	69	74	290	7,178.98
Rebecca Hudson	72	72	71	75	290	7,178.98

	SCORES			TOTAL	MONEY
Karine Icher	74	70	72	75	291	6,368.53
Mhairi McKay	72	74	69	76	291	6,368.53
Rachel Hetherington	75	71	75	71	292	5,828.11
Julieta Granada	72	73	75	72	292	5,828.11
Meaghan Francella	70	72	76	74	292	5,828.11
Sherri Steinhauer	72	74	74	73	293	5,500.01
Mi Hyun Kim	71	73	73	76	293	5,500.0
Sophie Giquel	71	76	77	70	294	5,326.52
Nicole Castrale	74	74	74	73	295	5,210.39
Minea Blomqvist	74	69	76	77	296	5,094.97
Emma Zackrisson	72	75	78	72	297	4,978.83
Martina Eberl	75	72	78	73	298	4,863.41
Catrin Nilsmark	70	73	81	75	299	4,747.28
Laura Davies	71	77	73	80	301	4,631.17

Ricoh Women's British Open

Sunningdale Golf Club, Berkshire, England
Par 36-36–72; 6,408 yards

July 31-August 3
purse, €1,462,914

	SCORES			TOTAL	MONEY
Ji-Yai Shin	66	68	70	66	270	€202,336.99
Yani Tseng	70	69	68	66	273	126,460.62
Eun-Hee Ji	68	70	69	67	274	79,037.88
Yuri Fudoh	66	68	69	71	274	79,037.88
Ai Miyazato	68	69	68	70	275	56,907.27
Cristie Kerr	71	65	70	70	276	49,319.64
Momoko Ueda	66	72	70	69	277	22,464.30
Lorena Ochoa	69	68	71	69	277	22,464.30
Paula Creamer	72	69	70	67	278	30,603.46
Hee-Won Han	71	69	71	67	278	30,603.46
In-Kyung Kim	71	68	72	67	278	30,603.46
Karrie Webb	72	69	69	68	278	30,603.46
Natalie Gulbis	69	68	70	71	278	30,603.46
Hee Young Park	69	71	69	70	279	21,709.06
Seon Hwa Lee	71	68	70	70	279	21,709.06
Juli Inkster	65	70	71	73	279	21,709.06
Jee Young Lee	71	72	71	66	280	17,625.44
Minea Blomqvist	68	73	72	67	280	17,625.44
Shi Hyun Ahn	68	72	71	69	280	17,625.44
Ji Young Oh	66	73	71	70	280	17,625.44
Kristy McPherson	67	75	74	65	281	15,175.27
Nicole Castrale	69	72	72	68	281	15,175.27
Na Yeon Choi	69	71	68	73	281	15,175.27
Eun-A Lim	74	71	72	65	282	11,786.12
Meredith Duncan	71	73	71	67	282	11,786.12
Annika Sorenstam	72	72	70	68	282	11,786.12
Sakura Yokomine	71	72	69	70	282	11,786.12
Karen Stupples	67	73	72	70	282	11,786.12
Stacy Prammanasudh	66	74	72	70	282	11,786.12
Jane Park	69	70	73	70	282	11,786.12
Sophie Gustafson	69	69	74	70	282	11,786.12
Suzann Pettersen	70	70	71	71	282	11,786.12
Mi Hyun Kim	70	70	67	75	282	11,786.12
Angela Park	71	74	71	67	283	9,010.31
Laura Diaz	66	72	75	70	283	9,010.31
Anja Monke	73	67	70	73	283	9,010.31
Bo-Bae Song	68	68	74	73	283	9,010.31
Catriona Matthew	68	75	72	69	284	7,745.70
Leta Lindley	71	71	72	70	284	7,745.70

	SCORES				TOTAL	MONEY
Paula Marti	68	72	72	72	284	7,745.70
Ji-Hee Lee	68	75	68	73	284	7,745.70
Reilley Rankin	69	73	72	71	285	6,797.25
Candie Kung	72	67	74	72	285	6,797.25
*Anna Nordqvist	70	73	69	73	285	
Lora Fairclough	70	74	73	69	286	6,006.87
Janice Moodie	69	76	70	71	286	6,006.87
Sun Young Yoo	73	72	69	72	286	6,006.87
Gloria Park	73	72	74	68	287	4,552.57
Karin Sjodin	72	73	71	71	287	4,552.57
Lotta Wahlin	69	76	71	71	287	4,552.57
Jill McGill	75	68	72	72	287	4,552.57
Joanne Mills	70	73	72	72	287	4,552.57
H.J. Choi	72	70	73	72	287	4,552.57
Jin Joo Hong	75	70	69	73	287	4,552.57
Katherine Hull	69	73	69	76	287	4,552.57
Helen Alfredsson	69	76	72	71	288	3,224.74
Il Mi Chung	73	72	71	72	288	3,224.74
Rebecca Hudson	67	76	72	73	288	3,224.74
Jimin Kang	69	76	74	70	289	2,541.85
Becky Morgan	72	72	74	71	289	2,541.85
Kris Tamulis	73	70	74	72	289	2,541.85
Wendy Ward	71	71	74	73	289	2,541.85
Teresa Lu	70	72	73	74	289	2,541.85
Erica Blasberg	75	70	73	72	290	1,732.50
Sherri Steinhauer	67	75	76	72	290	1,732.50
Gwladys Nocera	73	69	75	73	290	1,732.50
Christina Kim	71	73	72	74	290	1,732.50
Marianne Skarpnord	68	72	72	78	290	1,732.50
Tania Elosegui Mayor	70	73	75	73	291	1,264.61
Trish Johnson	72	70	76	73	291	1,264.61
Rachel Hetherington	70	72	74	75	291	1,264.61
Maria Hjorth	69	74	72	76	291	1,264.61
Johanna Head	66	76	73	76	291	1,264.61
Becky Brewerton	70	73	76	73	292	1,264.61
Moira Dunn	74	69	77	74	294	1,264.61
*Maria Jose Uribe	71	73	74	76	294	
Laura Davies	70	75	75	75	295	1,264.61
Mhairi McKay	71	74	73	78	296	1,264.61

Scandinavian TPC Hosted by Annika

Frosaker Golf & Country Club, Vasteras, Sweden   August 7-10
Par 36-36–72; 6,264 yards   purse, €200,000
(Event shortened to 54 holes—rain.)

	SCORES			TOTAL	MONEY
Amy Yang	70	69	63	202	€30,000
Minea Blomqvist	74	71	63	208	13,395
Melodie Bourdy	71	71	66	208	13,395
Maria Hjorth	72	64	72	208	13,395
Lill Kristin Saether	71	64	73	208	13,395
Liselotte Neumann	73	70	66	209	6,000
Louise Friberg	70	70	69	209	6,000
*Anna Nordqvist	71	67	71	209	
Annika Sorenstam	66	71	72	209	6,000
Lisa Holm Sorensen	76	68	66	210	4,240
Ursula Wikstrom	72	71	67	210	4,240
*Pernilla Lindberg	71	67	72	210	
*Caroline Hedwall	73	74	64	211	

	SCORES			TOTAL	MONEY
Anna Knutsson	73	68	70	211	3,280
Nikki Garrett	74	67	70	211	3,280
Jill McGill	69	71	71	211	3,280
Johanna Head	67	70	74	211	3,280
Lora Fairclough	70	66	75	211	3,280
Linda Wessberg	74	72	66	212	2,724
Marta Prieto	71	75	66	212	2,724
Leah Hart	72	70	70	212	2,724
Paula Marti	69	73	70	212	2,724
Jenni Kuosa	71	70	71	212	2,724

S4/C Wales Ladies Championship of Europe

Machynys Peninsula Golf Club, Llanelli, Carmarthenshire, Wales
Par 36-36–72; 6,126 yards
(Event shortened to 54 holes—rain.)

August 14-17
purse, €487,682

	SCORES			TOTAL	MONEY
Lotta Wahlin	71	67	71	209	€66,737
Martina Eberl	65	71	73	209	45,158.70
(Wahlin defeated Eberl on second playoff hole.)					
Georgina Simpson	66	74	70	210	27,584.63
Henrietta Zuel	66	71	73	210	27,584.63
Maria Boden	71	71	69	211	17,218.15
Joanne Mills	70	70	71	211	17,218.15
Samantha Head	74	71	67	212	10,833.64
Veronica Zorzi	72	70	70	212	10,833.64
Ashleigh Simon	70	71	71	212	10,833.64
Paula Marti	68	71	73	212	10,833.64
Felicity Johnson	77	69	67	213	6,488.32
Sophie Walker	69	76	68	213	6,488.32
Nathalie David-Mila	72	72	69	213	6,488.32
Cecilia Ekelundh	73	71	69	213	6,488.32
Anna Rawson	71	72	70	213	6,488.32
Louise Stahle	70	72	71	213	6,488.32
Kiran Matharu	67	75	71	213	6,488.32
Martina Gillen	70	71	72	213	6,488.32
Clare Queen	71	70	72	213	6,488.32
Gwladys Nocera	69	70	74	213	6,488.32
Lisa Hall	70	67	76	213	6,488.32
Becky Brewerton	66	71	76	213	6,488.32

SAS Masters

Haga Golf Course, Oslo, Norway
Par 37-35–72; 6,169 yards

August 22-24
purse, €200,000

	SCORES			TOTAL	MONEY
Gwladys Nocera	69	66	68	203	€30,000
Tania Elosegui	70	69	67	206	17,150
Samantha Head	70	68	68	206	17,150
Emma Zackrisson	73	67	68	208	6,180
Johanna Head	69	71	68	208	6,180
Johanna Westerberg	71	69	68	208	6,180
Nina Reis	68	71	69	208	6,180
Becky Brewerton	72	67	69	208	6,180
Lee-Anne Pace	71	67	70	208	6,180

	SCORES			TOTAL	MONEY
Iben Tinning	69	68	71	208	6,180
Diana Luna	66	68	74	208	6,180
Carmen Alonso	69	71	70	210	3,180
Ashleigh Simon	72	68	70	210	3,180
Kirsty S. Taylor	74	65	71	210	3,180
Beatriz Recari	72	65	73	210	3,180
Lena Tornevall	74	68	69	211	2,760
Anne-Lise Caudal	71	70	70	211	2,760
Marianne Skarpnord	66	75	70	211	2,760
Martina Eberl	72	67	72	211	2,760
Laura Cabanillas	69	71	72	212	2,550
Caroline Afonso	70	68	74	212	2,550

Finnair Masters

Helsinki Golf Club, Tali, Finland
Par 34-37–71; 5,916 yards

August 29-31
purse, €200,000

	SCORES			TOTAL	MONEY
Minea Blomqvist	69	68	65	202	€30,000
Ursula Wikstrom	68	69	66	203	20,300
Beatriz Recari	67	72	67	206	12,400
Martina Eberl	71	67	68	206	12,400
Diana Luna	72	65	70	207	8,480
Anna Rawson	70	71	68	209	7,000
Anja Monke	74	66	70	210	5,500
Becky Brewerton	71	68	71	210	5,500
Gwladys Nocera	70	71	70	211	4,480
Marina Arruti	70	69	73	212	3,840
Karen Lunn	72	66	74	212	3,840
Lill Kristin Saether	73	71	69	213	3,180
Joanne Mills	70	71	72	213	3,180
Ana Larraneta	70	70	73	213	3,180
Nina Reis	69	70	74	213	3,180
Lee-Anne Pace	72	75	67	214	2,800
Georgina Simpson	74	72	68	214	2,800
Samantha Head	71	70	73	214	2,800
Julie Tvede	73	74	68	215	2,580
Beth Allen	73	71	71	215	2,580
*Soojin Yang	70	70	75	215	
Rebecca Hudson	69	70	76	215	2,580

Nykredit Masters

Simon's Golf Club, Humlebaek, Denmark
Par 35-38–73; 7,043 yards

September 5-7
purse, €200,000

	SCORES			TOTAL	MONEY
Martina Eberl	66	73	66	205	€30,000
Melissa Reid	67	66	73	206	20,300
Annika Sorenstam	71	68	71	210	14,000
Iben Tinning	70	70	71	211	10,800
Julie Tvede	75	71	68	214	6,620
Laura Davies	73	72	69	214	6,620
Lotta Wahlin	70	74	70	214	6,620
Beth Allen	72	70	72	214	6,620
Anja Monke	72	74	69	215	3,650

	SCORES			TOTAL	MONEY
Carmen Alonso	73	72	70	215	3,650
Denise-Charlotte Becker	68	76	71	215	3,650
Becky Brewerton	72	72	71	215	3,650
Nina Reis	71	72	72	215	3,650
Johanna Westerberg	72	68	75	215	3,650
Lisa Hall	78	69	69	216	2,766.66
Sofia Renell	72	74	70	216	2,766.66
Titiya Plucksataporn	73	71	72	216	2,766.66
Marianne Skarpnord	72	72	72	216	2,766.66
Miriam Nagl	70	74	72	216	2,766.66
Emma Zackrisson	69	74	73	216	2,766.66

UNIQA Ladies Golf Open

Golfclub Fohrenwald, Wiener Neustadt, Austria
Par 37-35–72; 6,179 yards

September 11-14
purse, €250,000

	SCORES				TOTAL	MONEY
Laura Davies	71	67	67	68	273	€37,500
Lisa Hall	69	69	70	68	276	25,375
Diana Luna	68	70	70	69	277	17,500
Denise-Charlotte Becker	67	71	69	71	278	13,500
Sophie Gustafson	69	70	71	69	279	8,950
Carmen Alonso	73	69	68	69	279	8,950
Emma Zackrisson	67	67	71	74	279	8,950
Caroline Afonso	68	71	71	70	280	5,616.66
Anja Monke	67	70	72	71	280	5,616.66
Anne-Lise Caudal	70	69	69	72	280	5,616.66
Iben Tinning	74	67	71	69	281	4,308.33
Gwladys Nocera	71	69	71	70	281	4,308.33
Martina Gillen	71	71	68	71	281	4,308.33
Anna Rossi	69	75	72	66	282	3,668.75
Lisa Holm Sorensen	69	69	74	70	282	3,668.75
Virginie Lagoutte-Clement	72	68	72	70	282	3,668.75
Veronica Zorzi	70	68	71	73	282	3,668.75
Karen Lunn	66	70	76	71	283	3,350
Georgina Simpson	69	70	73	71	283	3,350
Clare Queen	68	74	72	70	284	3,225

Goteborg Masters

Lycke Golf Club, Gothenburg, Sweden
Par 35-37–72; 6,662 yards

September 18-21
purse, €250,000

	SCORES				TOTAL	MONEY
Gwladys Nocera	66	62	65	66	259	€37,500
Nina Reis	69	67	73	61	270	25,375
Felicity Johnson	62	70	71	68	271	17,500
Amy Yang	69	68	70	65	272	12,050
Paula Marti	64	66	71	71	272	12,050
Marianne Skarpnord	71	69	67	66	273	8,750
Samantha Head	71	69	70	64	274	6,450
Sophie Gustafson	69	71	64	70	274	6,450
Marta Prieto	66	69	68	71	274	6,450
Laura Davies	70	70	71	64	275	4,800
Lisa Hall	69	72	66	68	275	4,800
Johanna Westerberg	68	70	67	71	276	4,162.50

	SCORES				TOTAL	MONEY
Julie Tvede	70	66	68	72	276	4,162.50
Carin Koch	69	72	67	69	277	3,725
Lora Fairclough	67	68	72	70	277	3,725
Georgina Simpson	70	65	71	71	277	3,725
Lotta Wahlin	68	74	72	64	278	3,356.25
Frances Bondad	69	71	72	66	278	3,356.25
Anja Monke	66	74	69	69	278	3,356.25
Jade Schaeffer	68	66	72	72	278	3,356.25

Vediorbis Open de France Dames

Golf d'Arras, Nord-Pas de Calais, France
Par 36-36–72; 6,195 yards

September 25-28
purse, €350,000

	SCORES				TOTAL	MONEY
Anja Monke	67	78	65	68	278	€52,500
Tania Elosegui	74	70	67	69	280	30,012.50
Nina Reis	67	69	72	72	280	30,012.50
Lora Fairclough	74	72	69	66	281	15,330
Paula Marti	69	74	70	68	281	15,330
Stefania Croce	67	68	71	75	281	15,330
Iben Tinning	70	69	75	68	282	10,500
Cecilia Ekelundh	68	73	70	72	283	8,750
Carmen Alonso	70	75	70	69	284	7,420
Georgina Simpson	74	70	68	72	284	7,420
Trish Johnson	73	71	72	69	285	5,871.25
Samantha Head	76	66	72	71	285	5,871.25
Karen Lunn	75	68	71	71	285	5,871.25
Laura Davies	72	73	65	75	285	5,871.25
Federica Piovano	74	72	72	68	286	5,127.50
Lisa Hall	74	69	70	73	286	5,127.50
Dana Lacey	73	74	71	69	287	4,760
Amy Yang	71	71	73	72	287	4,760
Anne-Lise Caudal	67	73	72	75	287	4,760
Marta Prieto	73	74	72	69	288	4,515

Madrid Ladies Masters

Casino Club de Golf Retamare, Madrid, Spain
Par 36-37–73; 6,338 yards

October 2-4
purse, €400,000

	SCORES			TOTAL	MONEY
Gwladys Nocera	72	69	67	208	€100,000
Paula Marti	68	74	70	212	42,440
Catriona Matthew	68	75	70	213	28,000
Tania Elosegui	68	77	69	214	19,280
Rebecca Hudson	72	73	69	214	19,280
Johanna Westerberg	70	77	68	215	11,240
Emma Zackrisson	72	74	69	215	11,240
Marianne Skarpnord	73	72	70	215	11,240
Amy Yang	69	73	73	215	11,240
Iben Tinning	70	74	72	216	8,000
Maria Boden	76	71	70	217	6,893.33
Kirsty S. Taylor	67	78	72	217	6,893.33
Laura Davies	70	75	72	217	6,893.33
Melissa Reid	71	78	69	218	6,060
Marina Arruti	72	76	70	218	6,060

	SCORES			TOTAL	MONEY
Emma Cabrera-Bello	73	75	71	219	5,680
Lisa Holm Sorensen	70	76	73	219	5,680
Laura Cabanillas	73	73	74	220	5,440
Lotta Wahlin	73	76	72	221	5,040
Veronica Zorzi	73	77	71	221	5,040
Samantha Head	73	77	71	221	5,040
Lynn Brooky	76	75	70	221	5,040
Georgina Simpson	76	76	69	221	5,040

Suzhou Taihu Ladies Open

Suzhou Taihu International Golf Club,
Taihu, Suzhou, China
Par 36-36–72; 6,299 yards

October 31-November 2
purse, €200,000

	SCORES			TOTAL	MONEY
Annika Sorenstam	69	69	65	203	€30,000
Li Ying Ye	65	68	70	203	20,300
(Sorenstam defeated Ye on second playoff hole.)					
Chutichai Porani	72	70	68	210	11,093.33
Amanda Moltke-Leth	68	74	68	210	11,093.33
Karen Lunn	72	67	71	210	11,093.33
Yang Tao-Li	75	70	67	212	6,000
Russamee Gulyanamitta	70	70	72	212	6,000
Pornanong Phatlum	70	69	73	212	6,000
Veronica Zorzi	68	76	69	213	3,470
Nontaya Srisawang	70	73	70	213	3,470
Zuzana Kamasova	69	73	71	213	3,470
Carmen Alonso	72	70	71	213	3,470
Eun Kyoung Lee	71	70	72	213	3,470
Laurette Maritz	70	71	72	213	3,470
Yan Pan Pan	69	71	73	213	3,470
Stefanie Michl	68	72	73	213	3,470
Yang Hong Mei	68	75	71	214	2,685
Lim Bing	69	74	71	214	2,685
Pimpadsorn Sangkagaro	72	71	71	214	2,685
Ursula Wikstrom	72	70	72	214	2,685

Saint Four Ladies Masters

Saint Four Golf Club, Jeju Island, Korea
Par 36-36–72; 6,303 yards

November 14-16
purse, €220,000

	SCORES			TOTAL	MONEY
Hee Kyung Seo	69	67	66	202	€47,592.60
Sun Ju Ahn	65	70	69	204	21,416.67
So Yeon Ryu	69	71	65	205	14,277.78
Hye-Yong Choi	71	67	69	207	10,708.33
Da Ye Na	71	66	70	207	10,708.33
Chae A. Oh	68	72	69	209	7,733.80
Bo Kyung Kim	73	67	69	209	7,733.80
*Ha-Na Jang	72	68	69	209	7,733.80
Sun Wook Lim	72	70	68	210	5,145.95
Soo-Yun Kang	70	71	69	210	5,145.95
Ae-Ree Pyun	71	68	71	210	5,145.95
Hei Ji Kim	71	67	72	210	5,145.95
Hyun Hee Moon	74	68	69	211	4,164.35

	SCORES			TOTAL	MONEY
Hye Jung Choi	73	67	71	211	4,164.35
Hyun-Ji Kim	71	72	69	212	3,688.43
Veronica Zorzi	69	69	74	212	3,688.43
So Young Kim	71	72	70	213	2,699.18
Hye Jin Jung	74	69	70	213	2,699.18
Chae Young Yoon	70	71	72	213	2,699.18
Lara Tadiotto	74	71	68	213	2,699.18
Anna Rawson	71	70	72	213	2,699.18
Margherita Rigon	70	70	73	213	2,699.18
Bo-Bea Park	72	68	73	213	2,699.18

Dubai Ladies Masters

Emirates Golf Club, Majlis Course, Dubai, United Arab Emirates   December 11-14
Par 35-37–72; 6,412 yards   purse, €500,000

	SCORES				TOTAL	MONEY
Anja Monke	68	71	68	68	275	€75,000
Veronica Zorzi	69	69	71	69	278	50,750
Laura Davies	70	69	71	69	279	35,000
Sophie Giquel	70	70	71	69	280	27,000
Trish Johnson	70	70	72	69	281	19,350
Iben Tinning	70	69	70	72	281	19,350
Anna Rawson	71	69	74	68	282	11,580
Amy Yang	71	69	74	68	282	11,580
Ashleigh Simon	70	71	72	69	282	11,580
Melissa Reid	71	70	71	70	282	11,580
Annika Sorenstam	70	66	75	71	282	11,580
Katharina Schallenberg	69	71	72	71	283	8,116.66
Catriona Matthew	73	68	71	71	283	8,116.66
Becky Brewerton	73	72	67	71	283	8,116.66
Leah Hart	72	71	73	68	284	7,325
Gwladys Nocera	75	69	71	69	284	7,325
Virginie Lagoutte-Clement	70	73	73	69	285	6,900
Sophie Gustafson	72	72	66	75	285	6,900
Carin Koch	72	68	77	69	286	6,375
Tania Elosegui	71	75	70	70	286	6,375
Titiya Plucksataporn	72	69	73	72	286	6,375
Nikki Garrett	71	66	74	75	286	6,375

Japan LPGA Tour

Daikin Orchid Ladies

Ryukyu Golf Club, Nanjo, Okinawa
Par 36-36–72; 6,384 yards

March 7-9
purse, ¥80,000,000

	SCORES			TOTAL	MONEY
Bo-Bae Song	70	67	65	202	¥14,400,000
Sakura Yokomine	70	68	68	206	7,040,000
Eun-A Lim	69	70	68	207	5,200,000
Miki Saiki	69	69	69	207	5,200,000
Momoko Ueda	68	71	70	209	3,333,333
Miho Koga	63	75	71	209	3,333,333
Mi-Jeong Jeon	71	67	71	209	3,333,333
Nahoko Hirao	68	72	70	210	2,000,000
Shiho Oyama	68	70	72	210	2,000,000
Orie Fujino	70	67	73	210	2,000,000
Yun-Jye Wei	71	68	72	211	1,456,000
Michie Ohba	70	67	74	211	1,456,000
Kaori Higo	70	72	70	212	1,176,000
Ayako Uehara	74	68	70	212	1,176,000
Ya-Huei Lu	68	73	71	212	1,176,000
Pei-Lin Yu	69	70	73	212	1,176,000
Hiroko Yamaguchi	69	69	74	212	1,176,000
Maiko Wakabayashi	74	69	70	213	776,000
Yuriko Ohtsuka	69	74	70	213	776,000
Yasuko Satoh	73	69	71	213	776,000
Toshimi Kimura	71	73	69	213	776,000
Midori Yoneyama	73	72	68	213	776,000
Iyoko Wada	68	71	74	213	776,000
Shinobu Moromizato	69	70	74	213	776,000
Akiko Fukushima	69	69	75	213	776,000

Accordia Golf Ladies

Aoshima Golf Club, Miyazaki
Par 36-36–72; 6,391 yards

March 14-16
purse, ¥60,000,000

	SCORES			TOTAL	MONEY
Yuri Fudoh	70	70	65	205	¥10,800,000
Yun-Jye Wei	68	68	69	205	5,280,000
(Fudoh defeated Wei on third playoff hole.)					
Bo-Bae Song	68	72	68	208	4,200,000
Miki Saiki	70	72	67	209	3,600,000
Sakura Yokomine	71	74	65	210	3,600,000
Hiroko Yamaguchi	70	68	73	211	2,400,000
Shiho Oyama	70	71	71	212	2,100,000
Namika Omata	75	72	66	213	1,500,000
Shinobu Moromizato	71	73	69	213	1,500,000
Eun-A Lim	70	71	72	213	1,500,000
Mi-Jeong Jeon	70	72	72	214	942,000
Eun-Hye Lee	73	69	72	214	942,000
Ayako Uehara	71	72	71	214	942,000

	SCORES			TOTAL	MONEY
Saiki Fujita	72	73	69	214	942,000
Miho Koga	73	71	70	214	942,000
Kaori Higo	71	73	70	214	942,000
Michiko Hattori	73	72	69	214	942,000
Yui Kawahara	67	74	74	215	600,000
Yukari Baba	69	74	72	215	600,000
Mayu Hattori	74	72	69	215	600,000
Yui Mukaiyama	72	71	72	215	600,000
Yuko Mitsuka	70	72	73	215	600,000
Erina Hara	71	74	70	215	600,000

Yokohama Tire PRGR Cup

Tosa Country Club, Konan, Kochi
Par 36-36–72; 6,364 yards

March 21-23
purse, ¥80,000,000

	SCORES			TOTAL	MONEY
Ji-Yai Shin	70	69	73	212	¥14,400,000
Sakura Yokomine	71	67	74	212	7,040,000
(Shin defeated Yokomine on fourth playoff hole.)					
Kaori Higo	73	70	72	215	5,600,000
Miho Koga	73	73	71	217	4,400,000
Ji-Hee Lee	71	69	77	217	4,400,000
Yukari Baba	73	70	75	218	2,800,000
Hiromi Mogi	71	76	71	218	2,800,000
Hiroko Yamaguchi	74	69	75	218	2,800,000
So-Hee Kim	70	73	76	219	1,698,666
Akiko Fukushima	68	77	74	219	1,698,666
Shinobu Moromizato	74	74	71	219	1,698,666
Mayumi Shimomura	73	71	76	220	1,336,000
Midori Yoneyama	74	72	74	220	1,336,000
Yuko Mitsuka	73	71	76	220	1,336,000
Junko Omote	72	71	78	221	976,000
Bo-Bae Song	72	74	75	221	976,000
Yuri Fudoh	78	72	71	221	976,000
Pei-Lin Yu	77	73	71	221	976,000
Yun-Jye Wei	75	74	72	221	976,000
Akane Iijima	73	72	76	221	976,000

Yamaha Ladies Open

Katsuragi Golf Club, Yamana Course, Fukuroi, Shizuoka
Par 36-36–72; 6,523 yards

April 4-6
purse, ¥80,000,000

	SCORES			TOTAL	MONEY
Hiroko Yamaguchi	69	71	77	217	¥14,400,000
Ayako Uehara	70	74	75	219	6,320,000
Hyun-Ju Shin	71	73	75	219	6,320,000
Mie Nakata	74	73	74	221	4,000,000
Ji-Hee Lee	74	72	75	221	4,000,000
Akiko Fukushima	71	73	77	221	4,000,000
Yun-Jye Wei	76	76	71	223	2,600,000
*Rikako Morita	73	76	74	223	
Chie Arimura	72	73	78	223	2,600,000
Shinobu Moromizato	72	78	74	224	1,636,000
Yukari Baba	74	76	74	224	1,636,000
Eun-Hye Lee	77	73	74	224	1,636,000

	SCORES			TOTAL	MONEY
Itsumi Okada	79	70	75	224	1,636,000
Maiko Wakabayashi	79	72	74	225	1,272,000
Pei-Lin Yu	79	71	75	225	1,272,000
Miki Saiki	76	73	76	225	1,272,000
Woo-Soon Ko	77	76	73	226	922,666
Julie Lu	78	73	75	226	922,666
Hiromi Mogi	74	75	77	226	922,666
Miho Koga	72	76	78	226	922,666
Mi-Jeong Jeon	75	74	77	226	922,666
Ai Nishikawa	74	74	78	226	922,666

Studio Alice Ladies Open

Hanayashiki Golf Club, Yokawa Course, Miki, Hyogo
Par 36-36–72; 6,480 yards

April 11-13
purse, ¥60,000,000

	SCORES			TOTAL	MONEY
Hyun-Ju Shin	68	71	71	210	¥10,800,000
Miho Koga	72	68	71	211	5,280,000
Ji-Hee Lee	72	73	68	213	3,900,000
Yuko Saitoh	71	73	69	213	3,900,000
Saiki Fujita	72	72	70	214	3,000,000
Yun-Joo Jeong	72	71	72	215	2,400,000
Shinobu Moromizato	71	75	70	216	1,650,000
So-Hee Kim	73	73	70	216	1,650,000
Eun-A Lim	71	74	71	216	1,650,000
Mi-Jeong Jeon	72	71	73	216	1,650,000
Tomomi Hirose	72	76	69	217	1,074,000
Akane Iijima	72	75	70	217	1,074,000
Kurumi Dohi	72	72	73	217	1,074,000
*Mika Miyazato	74	73	71	218	
Mie Nakata	74	69	75	218	954,000
Ayako Uehara	75	73	71	219	774,000
Yuki Ichinose	77	72	70	219	774,000
Hiromi Mogi	76	71	72	219	774,000
Nozomi Satoh	75	75	69	219	774,000
Nikki Campbell	73	72	74	219	774,000

Life Card Ladies

Kumamoto Airport Country Club, Kikuyo, Kumamoto
Par 36-36–72; 6,468 yards

April 18-20
purse, ¥60,000,000

	SCORES			TOTAL	MONEY
Yukari Baba	70	69	68	207	¥10,800,000
Shinobu Moromizato	68	74	68	210	4,740,000
Midori Yoneyama	69	71	70	210	4,740,000
Yuko Mitsuka	69	73	71	213	3,600,000
So-Hee Kim	74	73	69	216	2,500,000
Ai Ogawa	76	70	70	216	2,500,000
Ji-Hee Lee	74	70	72	216	2,500,000
Ayako Uehara	73	71	73	217	1,650,000
Miho Koga	74	69	74	217	1,650,000
Izumi Narita	74	73	71	218	1,051,200
Bo-Bae Song	76	71	71	218	1,051,200
Chie Arimura	73	73	72	218	1,051,200
Mi-Jeong Jeon	74	72	72	218	1,051,200

	SCORES			TOTAL	MONEY
Akane Iijima	72	72	74	218	1,051,200
Akane Azuma	76	72	71	219	672,000
Ji-Woo Lee	74	72	73	219	672,000
Namika Omata	75	71	73	219	672,000
Miki Saiki	72	78	69	219	672,000
Erina Hara	74	71	74	219	672,000
Yuri Fudoh	74	71	74	219	672,000
Yuki Ichinose	74	70	75	219	672,000
Mihoko Takahashi	73	70	76	219	672,000

Fujisankei Ladies Classic

Kawana Hotel Golf Club, Fuji Course, Ito, Shizuoka
Par 36-36–72; 6,464 yards

April 25-27
purse, ¥80,000,000

	SCORES			TOTAL	MONEY
Ayako Uehara	70	72	66	208	¥14,400,000
Erina Hara	73	64	72	209	7,040,000
Miki Saiki	69	71	70	210	5,600,000
Yukari Baba	69	72	70	211	4,800,000
Michiko Hattori	70	75	67	212	4,000,000
Keiko Sasaki	72	67	74	213	2,800,000
Akane Iijima	71	70	72	213	2,800,000
Yuka Shiroto	71	72	70	213	2,800,000
Sakura Yokomine	69	74	71	214	1,528,000
Mi-Jeong Jeon	73	71	70	214	1,528,000
Shiho Oyama	69	72	73	214	1,528,000
Yuko Mitsuka	69	74	71	214	1,528,000
Hiromi Mogi	71	74	69	214	1,528,000
Nobuko Kizawa	71	71	72	214	1,528,000
Bo-Bae Song	75	69	71	215	1,152,000
Ya-Huei Lu	71	73	71	215	1,152,000
Yuki Ichinose	75	70	71	216	992,000
Yun-Joo Jeong	74	71	71	216	992,000
Yoko Yamagishi	72	73	72	217	760,000
Hiromi Takesue	73	71	73	217	760,000
Ai Ogawa	74	70	73	217	760,000
Eun-A Lim	73	73	71	217	760,000
Yumiko Yoshida	75	70	72	217	760,000
Kaori Higo	74	72	71	217	760,000
Ji-Woo Lee	69	74	74	217	760,000
Yuko Saitoh	76	69	72	217	760,000

Crystal Geyser Ladies

Keiyo Country Club, Chiba
Par 36-36–72; 6,355 yards

May 2-4
purse, ¥70,000,000

	SCORES			TOTAL	MONEY
Miho Koga	71	68	67	206	¥12,600,000
Maiko Wakabayashi	66	69	71	206	6,160,000
(Koga defeated Wakabayashi on third playoff hole.)					
Ritsuko Ryu	65	70	72	207	4,900,000
Akiko Fukushima	72	71	65	208	4,200,000
Midori Yoneyama	69	72	68	209	2,712,500
Akane Iijima	70	71	68	209	2,712,500
Shinobu Moromizato	68	72	69	209	2,712,500

	SCORES			TOTAL	MONEY
Sakura Yokomine	70	69	70	209	2,712,500
Hiromi Mogi	71	72	67	210	1,575,000
Mihoko Iseri	66	73	71	210	1,575,000
Ji-Woo Lee	68	73	70	211	1,302,000
Mie Nakata	70	71	71	212	1,127,000
Mayumi Nakajima	70	71	71	212	1,127,000
Yuko Mitsuka	73	69	70	212	1,127,000
Ikue Asama	70	72	70	212	1,127,000
Namika Omata	68	73	72	213	917,000
Miki Saiki	70	74	69	213	917,000
Ji-Hee Lee	70	71	73	214	742,000
*Rikako Morita	73	73	68	214	
Kuniko Maeda	72	72	70	214	742,000
Hyun-Ju Shin	73	71	70	214	742,000

World Ladies Championship Salonpas Cup

Yomiuri Country Club, Tokyo
Par 36-36–72; 6,523 yards

May 8-11
purse, ¥110,000,000

	SCORES				TOTAL	MONEY
Akiko Fukushima	71	70	70	73	284	¥22,000,000
Ji-Yai Shin	73	72	68	71	284	11,000,000
(Fukushima defeated Shin on fifth playoff hole.)						
Sakura Yokomine	73	69	72	74	288	6,985,000
Na Zhang	68	72	72	76	288	6,985,000
Mi-Jeong Jeon	71	74	71	73	289	5,071,000
Bo-Bae Song	74	70	77	69	290	4,345,000
Rui Kitada	71	74	76	70	291	3,663,000
Yukari Baba	71	72	71	78	292	2,854,500
Miho Koga	69	79	71	73	292	2,854,500
Ji-Hee Lee	70	77	74	72	293	1,762,750
Yuko Mitsuka	72	72	74	75	293	1,762,750
Michiko Hattori	72	73	74	74	293	1,762,750
Mihoko Iseri	72	74	73	74	293	1,762,750
Erina Hara	77	71	73	73	294	1,452,000
Mie Nakata	76	74	72	73	295	1,174,800
Chie Arimura	77	70	73	75	295	1,174,800
Yuki Ichinose	73	70	78	74	295	1,174,800
Mayumi Shimomura	72	74	77	72	295	1,174,800
Esther Lee	77	74	73	71	295	1,174,800
Shiho Oyama	73	73	76	74	296	975,333
Tomomi Hirose	75	77	72	72	296	975,333
Hiromi Mogi	78	74	74	70	296	975,333

Vernal Ladies

Fukuoka Century Golf Club, Asakura, Fukuoka
Par 36-36–72; 6,583 yards

May 16-18
purse, ¥120,000,000

	SCORES			TOTAL	MONEY
Eun-A Lim	65	71	73	209	¥21,600,000
Akiko Fukushima	69	71	70	210	10,560,000
Ji-Hee Lee	70	70	71	211	7,800,000
Yukari Baba	71	69	71	211	7,800,000
Na Zhang	72	70	72	214	5,400,000
Miki Saiki	69	75	70	214	5,400,000

	SCORES			TOTAL	MONEY
Yuko Mitsuka	72	75	68	215	3,300,000
Hiromi Mogi	72	73	70	215	3,300,000
Sakura Yokomine	74	69	72	215	3,300,000
Bo-Bae Song	70	68	77	215	3,300,000
Tamie Durdin	72	73	71	216	2,016,000
Hiroko Yamaguchi	72	70	74	216	2,016,000
Michie Ohba	71	72	73	216	2,016,000
Mayu Hattori	71	70	75	216	2,016,000
Yuri Fudoh	69	73	75	217	1,416,000
Ji-Woo Lee	71	72	74	217	1,416,000
Yuko Saitoh	71	74	72	217	1,416,000
Junko Omote	74	72	71	217	1,416,000
Akane Iijima	73	74	70	217	1,416,000
Miho Koga	73	73	71	217	1,416,000

Chukyo TV Bridgestone Ladies

Chukyo Golf Club, Ishino Course, Toyota, Aichi　　　　　　　　May 23-25
Par 36-36–72; 6,381 yards　　　　　　　　purse, ¥70,000,000

	SCORES			TOTAL	MONEY
Ji-Hee Lee	71	69	68	208	¥12,600,000
Miki Saiki	71	68	69	208	5,530,000
Miho Koga	71	67	70	208	5,530,000
(Lee defeated Saiki and Koga on first playoff hole.)					
Michiko Hattori	68	71	71	210	4,200,000
Ayako Uehara	69	70	72	211	3,150,000
Shiho Oyama	70	70	71	211	3,150,000
Sakura Yokomine	71	71	70	212	2,450,000
Ya-Huei Lu	71	75	67	213	2,100,000
Bo-Bae Song	73	71	70	214	1,373,400
Kaori Higo	72	73	69	214	1,373,400
Yukari Baba	68	72	74	214	1,373,400
Midori Yoneyama	71	70	73	214	1,373,400
Nobuko Kizawa	71	74	69	214	1,373,400
Kuniko Maeda	76	68	71	215	994,000
Hyun-Ju Shin	69	72	74	215	994,000
Esther Lee	71	72	72	215	994,000
Hiroko Yamaguchi	77	71	67	215	994,000
Ikuyo Shiotani	69	73	74	216	689,000
Kaori Harada	74	71	71	216	689,000
Yuriko Ohtsuka	73	70	73	216	689,000
Chie Arimura	72	72	72	216	689,000
Ji-Yeon Han	70	74	72	216	689,000
Mihoko Iseri	74	72	70	216	689,000
Erina Hara	73	74	69	216	689,000

Kosaido Ladies Golf Cup

Chiba Kosaido Country Club, Ichihara, Chiba　　　　　　　　May 30-June 1
Par 36-36–72; 6,337 yards　　　　　　　　purse, ¥60,000,000

	SCORES			TOTAL	MONEY
Akane Iijima	62	73	68	203	¥10,800,000
Mayumi Nakajima	67	70	68	205	5,280,000
Esther Lee	67	75	67	209	4,200,000
Yui Kawahara	73	71	68	212	3,300,000

	SCORES			TOTAL	MONEY
Yasuko Satoh	73	72	67	212	3,300,000
Hyun-Ju Shin	69	76	68	213	2,250,000
Toshimi Kimura	75	71	67	213	2,250,000
Miho Koga	72	73	69	214	1,800,000
Midori Yoneyama	72	72	71	215	1,224,000
Junko Omote	72	72	71	215	1,224,000
Akiko Fukushima	70	77	68	215	1,224,000
Shinobu Moromizato	71	76	68	215	1,224,000
Tomoko Kusakabe	70	74	72	216	858,000
Yayoi Arasaki	71	74	71	216	858,000
Erina Hara	68	75	73	216	858,000
Mikiyo Nishizuka	72	75	69	216	858,000
Yuri Fudoh	73	74	69	216	858,000
Mie Nakata	71	75	70	216	858,000
Kuniko Maeda	70	74	73	217	618,000
Ya-Huei Lu	78	68	71	217	618,000

Resort Trust Ladies

The Country Club, Koga, Shiga
Par 36-36–72; 6,619 yards

June 6-8
purse, ¥70,000,000

	SCORES			TOTAL	MONEY
Mi-Jeong Jeon	68	67	69	204	¥12,600,000
Sakura Yokomine	68	70	69	207	6,300,000
Esther Lee	69	70	69	208	4,550,000
Ji-Hee Lee	70	70	68	208	4,550,000
Miki Saiki	68	66	75	209	3,500,000
Hiromi Mogi	69	68	73	210	2,625,000
Akiko Fukushima	72	71	67	210	2,625,000
Chie Arimura	71	71	69	211	2,100,000
Yuki Ichinose	72	70	70	212	1,575,000
Mie Nakata	72	68	72	212	1,575,000
Eun-A Lim	70	71	72	213	1,197,000
Maiko Wakabayashi	70	71	72	213	1,197,000
Kaori Higo	66	72	75	213	1,197,000
Akane Iijima	70	70	73	213	1,197,000
Julie Lu	72	72	69	213	1,197,000
Ji-Woo Lee	72	71	71	214	882,000
Yukari Baba	72	70	72	214	882,000
Ayako Uehara	70	73	71	214	882,000
Mikiyo Nishizuka	67	72	75	214	882,000
Yuko Mitsuka	71	71	73	215	665,000
Kuniko Maeda	72	72	71	215	665,000
Midori Yoneyama	73	70	72	215	665,000
Miho Koga	71	71	73	215	665,000
Mayumi Shimomura	71	71	73	215	665,000
Shiho Oyama	74	70	71	215	665,000
Shinobu Moromizato	72	74	69	215	665,000

We Love Kobe Suntory Ladies Open

Rokko Kokusai Golf Club, Kobe, Hyogo
Par 36-36–72; 6,457 yards

June 12-15
purse, ¥80,000,000

	SCORES				TOTAL	MONEY
Momoko Ueda	70	69	70	72	281	¥14,400,000
Bo-Bae Song	69	71	72	70	282	5,813,333
Eun-A Lim	68	72	71	71	282	5,813,333
Shiho Oyama	69	69	69	75	282	5,813,333
Yuko Mitsuka	72	70	74	67	283	3,333,333
Ji-Woo Lee	74	70	69	70	283	3,333,333
Sakura Yokomine	66	73	72	72	283	3,333,333
*Asako Fujimoto	71	73	72	68	284	
Chie Arimura	70	73	70	71	284	2,400,000
Hiromi Mogi	72	76	67	70	285	1,800,000
Mie Nakata	75	65	72	73	285	1,800,000
Kuniko Maeda	74	72	72	68	286	1,368,000
Julie Lu	73	69	72	72	286	1,368,000
Erina Hara	69	71	72	74	286	1,368,000
Ji-Hee Lee	71	72	71	73	287	1,208,000
*Mika Miyazato	70	74	73	71	288	
Mihoko Takahashi	74	71	71	72	288	1,048,000
Keiko Sasaki	72	74	69	73	288	1,048,000
Kaori Higo	70	70	74	74	288	1,048,000
Yuka Shiroto	70	72	70	77	289	888,000

Nichirei PGM Ladies

Miho Golf Club, Miho, Ibaraki
Par 36-36–72; 6,402 yards

June 20-22
purse, ¥60,000,000

	SCORES			TOTAL	MONEY
Yuko Mitsuka	66	69	65	200	¥10,800,000
Shiho Oyama	71	68	71	210	5,280,000
Namika Omata	68	70	73	211	4,200,000
Hiromi Mogi	72	71	69	212	3,300,000
Esther Lee	68	73	71	212	3,300,000
Ji-Woo Lee	72	68	73	213	1,950,000
Mayu Hattori	72	71	70	213	1,950,000
Ji-Hee Lee	73	65	75	213	1,950,000
Mi-Jeong Jeon	73	70	70	213	1,950,000
Hiromi Takesue	72	71	71	214	1,096,500
Rui Kitada	74	70	70	214	1,096,500
Ritsuko Ryu	67	72	75	214	1,096,500
Shinobu Moromizato	69	74	71	214	1,096,500
Ayako Uehara	70	72	73	215	912,000
Yui Kawahara	73	69	73	215	912,000
Akane Iijima	72	69	75	216	762,000
Itsumi Okada	68	76	72	216	762,000
Bo-Bae Song	74	68	74	216	762,000
Akiko Fukushima	71	73	73	217	558,000
Erina Hara	73	69	75	217	558,000
Yun-Joo Jeong	68	74	75	217	558,000
Ya-Huei Lu	69	74	74	217	558,000
Yukari Baba	72	72	73	217	558,000
Hyun-Ju Shin	69	72	76	217	558,000
Chie Arimura	73	72	72	217	558,000
Kaori Aoyama	73	72	72	217	558,000

Promise Ladies

Madame J Golf Club, Kato, Hyogo
Par 36-36–72; 6,514 yards

June 27-29
purse, ¥80,000,000

	SCORES			TOTAL	MONEY
Chie Arimura	67	67	68	202	¥14,400,000
Shiho Oyama	70	69	68	207	7,040,000
Yuri Fudoh	68	69	71	208	5,200,000
Esther Lee	71	66	71	208	5,200,000
Erina Hara	70	69	70	209	4,000,000
Ji-Hee Lee	69	72	69	210	2,400,000
Kaori Aoyama	70	72	68	210	2,400,000
Mayumi Shimomura	69	72	69	210	2,400,000
Yuko Mitsuka	65	72	73	210	2,400,000
Yasuko Satoh	73	68	69	210	2,400,000
Yun-Jye Wei	74	70	67	211	1,312,000
Yun-Joo Jeong	74	68	69	211	1,312,000
Tomoko Kusakabe	68	70	73	211	1,312,000
Akane Iijima	70	71	70	211	1,312,000
Iyoko Wada	66	74	71	211	1,312,000
Kuniko Maeda	71	67	74	212	912,000
Yayoi Arasaki	72	68	72	212	912,000
Maiko Wakabayashi	69	69	74	212	912,000
Hiromi Takesue	69	72	71	212	912,000
Miho Koga	73	68	71	212	912,000

Belluna Ladies Cup

Obatago Golf Club, Kanra, Gunma
Par 36-36–72; 6,379 yards

July 4-6
purse, ¥60,000,000

	SCORES			TOTAL	MONEY
Hiromi Mogi	65	68	70	203	¥10,800,000
Akiko Fukushima	71	66	67	204	5,280,000
Ji-Woo Lee	66	67	73	206	3,900,000
Ji-Hee Lee	69	69	68	206	3,900,000
Miho Koga	69	69	70	208	2,500,000
Chie Arimura	69	69	70	208	2,500,000
Hiroko Yamaguchi	69	67	72	208	2,500,000
Yasuko Satoh	70	69	70	209	1,800,000
Yuko Saitoh	71	70	69	210	1,350,000
Mie Nakata	67	73	70	210	1,350,000
Izumi Narita	71	68	72	211	978,000
Kaori Higo	71	71	69	211	978,000
Midori Yoneyama	70	71	70	211	978,000
Keiko Sasaki	72	69	70	211	978,000
Eun-Hye Lee	68	71	72	211	978,000
Yui Kawahara	72	70	70	212	678,000
*Kumiko Kaneda	73	65	74	212	
Mayumi Shimomura	69	71	72	212	678,000
Mayumi Nakajima	71	71	70	212	678,000
Mayu Hattori	73	68	71	212	678,000
Sakura Yokomine	71	69	72	212	678,000

Meiji Chocolate Cup

Sapporo Kokusai Country Club, Kita-Hiroshima, Hokkaido
Par 36-36–72; 6,518 yards

July 11-13
purse, ¥70,000,000

	SCORES			TOTAL	MONEY
Yuri Fudoh	69	68	70	207	¥12,600,000
Chie Arimura	70	75	63	208	5,086,666
Hyun-Ju Shin	69	69	70	208	5,086,666
Saiki Fujita	68	70	70	208	5,086,666
Erina Hara	70	70	69	209	3,500,000
Ji-Woo Lee	68	72	70	210	2,800,000
Mi-Jeong Jeon	74	69	68	211	2,450,000
Tomoko Kusakabe	70	69	73	212	1,925,000
Kuniko Maeda	73	70	69	212	1,925,000
Yuka Shiroto	69	75	70	214	1,340,500
Akiko Fukushima	71	71	72	214	1,340,500
*Makoto Takemura	74	67	74	215	
Nobuko Kizawa	74	69	73	216	1,071,000
Sakura Yokomine	74	71	71	216	1,071,000
Hiromi Takesue	72	70	74	216	1,071,000
Yuko Saitoh	70	74	72	216	1,071,000
Orie Fujino	72	71	73	216	1,071,000
Shiho Oyama	73	72	72	217	653,545
Miki Saiki	71	73	73	217	653,545
Mayu Hattori	69	75	73	217	653,545
Yuko Mitsuka	71	71	75	217	653,545
Nikki Campbell	76	72	69	217	653,545
So-Hee Kim	73	69	75	217	653,545
Yui Kawahara	74	73	70	217	653,545
Yukari Baba	72	73	72	217	653,545
Toshimi Kimura	71	73	73	217	653,545
Sachiko Nagamori	73	73	71	217	653,545
Rui Kitada	74	75	68	217	653,545

Stanley Ladies

Tomei Country Club, Susono, Shizuoka
Par 36-36–72; 6,450 yards

July 18-20
purse, ¥90,000,000

	SCORES			TOTAL	MONEY
Akiko Fukushima	69	67	67	203	¥16,200,000
Ayako Uehara	67	67	70	204	8,100,000
Ji-Hee Lee	66	70	69	205	5,850,000
Mikiyo Nishizuka	68	71	66	205	5,850,000
Mi-Jeong Jeon	72	67	67	206	4,050,000
Shinobu Moromizato	73	65	68	206	4,050,000
Erina Hara	71	67	69	207	3,150,000
Yuri Fudoh	70	70	68	208	2,475,000
Chie Arimura	70	70	68	208	2,475,000
Ji-Woo Lee	69	69	71	209	1,716,000
Mai Arai	72	70	67	209	1,716,000
Yukari Baba	71	72	66	209	1,716,000
Kasumi Fujii	66	73	71	210	1,494,000
Chieko Amanuma	73	69	68	210	1,494,000
Ah-Reum Hwang	69	71	71	211	1,224,000
Nikki Campbell	65	72	74	211	1,224,000
Rui Kitada	68	74	69	211	1,224,000
Kuniko Maeda	72	71	68	211	1,224,000
Akane Iijima	71	70	71	212	873,000

	SCORES			TOTAL	MONEY
Esther Lee	73	68	71	212	873,000
Yuko Saitoh	68	69	75	212	873,000
Eun-A Lim	69	71	72	212	873,000
Junko Omote	68	72	72	212	873,000
Yuki Ichinose	68	72	72	212	873,000
Midori Yoneyama	73	70	69	212	873,000
Hiromi Mogi	72	70	70	212	873,000

Kagome Philanthropy LPGA Players Championship

Narashino Country Club, Inzai, Chiba
Par 36-36–72; 6,416 yards

July 24-27
purse, ¥130,000,000

	SCORES				TOTAL	MONEY
Mi-Jeong Jeon	68	69	72	67	276	¥23,400,000
Yuko Mitsuka	70	69	71	71	281	11,440,000
Akane Iijima	74	70	72	67	283	9,100,000
Shiho Oyama	72	73	71	68	284	6,500,000
Ji-Woo Lee	65	76	72	71	284	6,500,000
Ayako Uehara	69	71	71	73	284	6,500,000
Hyun-Ju Shin	72	72	70	71	285	4,550,000
Mayumi Nakajima	67	75	75	69	286	3,250,000
Erina Hara	72	72	70	72	286	3,250,000
Maiko Wakabayashi	69	75	69	73	286	3,250,000
Miho Koga	71	73	73	70	287	2,119,000
Yasuko Satoh	70	73	73	71	287	2,119,000
Yun-Jye Wei	70	75	71	71	287	2,119,000
Hiromi Mogi	69	70	74	74	287	2,119,000
Shinobu Moromizato	73	72	73	70	288	1,469,000
Orie Fujino	73	75	69	71	288	1,469,000
Ji-Hee Lee	73	70	72	73	288	1,469,000
Hiroko Yamaguchi	72	72	71	73	288	1,469,000
Yukari Baba	71	72	71	74	288	1,469,000
Akiko Fukushima	68	71	73	76	288	1,469,000

AXA Ladies

Mitsui Kanto Tomakomai Golf Club, Tomakomai, Hokkaido
Par 36-36–72; 6,375 yards

August 8-10
purse, ¥80,000,000

	SCORES			TOTAL	MONEY
Shinobu Moromizato	69	71	70	210	¥14,400,000
Miho Koga	71	69	72	212	7,040,000
Akiko Fukushima	68	75	70	213	5,600,000
So-Hee Kim	73	73	68	214	3,700,000
Erina Hara	71	71	72	214	3,700,000
Hyun-Ju Shin	68	75	71	214	3,700,000
Shiho Oyama	68	75	71	214	3,700,000
Hiroko Yamaguchi	70	71	74	215	2,000,000
Pei-Lin Yu	73	73	69	215	2,000,000
Rui Kitada	74	71	70	215	2,000,000
Tamie Durdin	73	71	72	216	1,320,000
Mayumi Shimomura	71	74	71	216	1,320,000
Midori Yoneyama	71	72	73	216	1,320,000
Na Zhang	69	78	69	216	1,320,000
Namika Omata	72	73	71	216	1,320,000
Michie Ohba	74	70	73	217	890,666

	SCORES			TOTAL	MONEY
Jae-Hee Bae	73	74	70	217	890,666
Momoko Ueda	68	76	73	217	890,666
Yuka Irie	72	76	69	217	890,666
Tomoko Kusakabe	71	72	74	217	890,666
Michiko Hattori	69	74	74	217	890,666

NEC Karuizawa 72

Karuizawa 72 Golf Club, Karuizawa, Nagano
Par 36-36–72; 6,583 yards

August 15-17
purse, ¥60,000,000

	SCORES			TOTAL	MONEY
Erina Hara	67	63	65	195	¥10,800,000
Ji-Hee Lee	69	69	64	202	5,400,000
Sakura Yokomine	72	67	65	204	4,200,000
Rui Kitada	68	70	69	207	3,300,000
Hyun-Ju Shin	69	69	69	207	3,300,000
Mi-Jeong Jeon	68	71	69	208	2,100,000
Mayu Hattori	71	68	69	208	2,100,000
Eun-A Lim	68	70	70	208	2,100,000
Akiko Fukushima	69	72	68	209	1,191,600
Ji-Woo Lee	70	69	70	209	1,191,600
Chie Arimura	70	68	71	209	1,191,600
Akane Iijima	69	68	72	209	1,191,600
Miho Koga	67	69	73	209	1,191,600
Toshimi Kimura	74	68	68	210	936,000
Nobuko Kizawa	71	69	70	210	936,000
Kasumi Fujii	69	74	68	211	786,000
Hiroko Fukushima	67	72	72	211	786,000
Saiki Fujita	70	68	73	211	786,000
Hiromi Mogi	72	71	69	212	612,000
Midori Yoneyama	74	67	71	212	612,000
Na Zhang	72	69	71	212	612,000
Bo-Bae Song	69	69	74	212	612,000

CAT Ladies

Daihakone Country Club, Hakone, Kanagawa
Par 36-37–73; 6,648 yards

August 22-24
purse, ¥70,000,000

	SCORES			TOTAL	MONEY
Miho Koga	69	68	73	210	¥12,600,000
Mi-Jeong Jeon	69	71	71	211	6,160,000
Yuko Mitsuka	66	73	73	212	4,900,000
Yasuko Satoh	71	70	72	213	3,850,000
Ji-Hee Lee	73	68	72	213	3,850,000
Hyun-Ju Shin	72	69	73	214	2,450,000
Ji-Woo Lee	68	74	72	214	2,450,000
Yuko Saitoh	72	69	73	214	2,450,000
Mayu Hattori	72	69	74	215	1,493,333
Sakura Yokomine	71	71	73	215	1,493,333
Mumi Ohkubo	72	71	72	215	1,493,333
Esther Lee	73	70	73	216	1,260,000
Hiromi Mogi	75	68	74	217	1,120,000
Bo-Bae Song	76	71	70	217	1,120,000
Midori Yoneyama	71	73	73	217	1,120,000
Mayumi Shimomura	73	69	76	218	910,000

	SCORES			TOTAL	MONEY
Itsumi Okada	72	72	74	218	910,000
Mikiyo Nishizuka	73	68	77	218	910,000
Chie Arimura	72	69	78	219	707,000
Yoko Inoue	70	74	75	219	707,000
Rui Kitada	72	73	74	219	707,000
Mie Nakata	69	72	78	219	707,000

Yonex Ladies

Yonex Country Club, Nagaoka, Niigata
Par 36-36–72; 6,371 yards

August 29-31
purse, ¥60,000,000

	SCORES			TOTAL	MONEY
Rui Kitada	70	68	69	207	¥10,800,000
Erina Hara	71	69	70	210	5,400,000
Sakura Yokomine	70	72	69	211	4,200,000
Ya-Huei Lu	73	71	68	212	3,600,000
Momoyo Kawakubo	73	70	70	213	2,325,000
Hiromi Takesue	73	70	70	213	2,325,000
Yuri Fudoh	70	72	71	213	2,325,000
Jae-Hee Bae	72	70	71	213	2,325,000
Maiko Wakabayashi	71	70	73	214	1,500,000
Saiki Fujita	69	74	72	215	1,114,500
Yun-Joo Jeong	73	69	73	215	1,114,500
Mie Nakata	70	71	74	215	1,114,500
Keiko Sasaki	74	67	74	215	1,114,500
Yoko Yamagishi	73	71	72	216	816,000
Shinobu Moromizato	71	72	73	216	816,000
Tamie Durdin	71	72	73	216	816,000
Yuriko Ohtsuka	71	72	73	216	816,000
Kayo Yamada	70	72	74	216	816,000
Junko Omote	70	72	74	216	816,000
Orie Fujino	74	72	71	217	570,000
Nikki Campbell	71	74	72	217	570,000
Kaori Nakamichi	74	71	72	217	570,000
Rie Murata	72	72	73	217	570,000
Akiko Fukushima	73	71	73	217	570,000
Nachiyo Ohtani	70	73	74	217	570,000
Woo-Soon Ko	68	74	75	217	570,000

Golf 5 Ladies

Mizunami Country Club, Mizunami, Gifu
Par 36-36–72; 6,537 yards

September 5-7
purse, ¥60,000,000

	SCORES			TOTAL	MONEY
Saiki Fujita	70	66	67	203	¥10,800,000
*Kumiko Kaneda	74	65	66	205	
Ji-Yai Shin	70	64	71	205	5,280,000
Erina Hara	66	70	71	207	3,900,000
Midori Yoneyama	69	68	70	207	3,900,000
Eun-Hye Lee	73	68	67	208	2,500,000
Hyun-Ju Shin	73	67	68	208	2,500,000
Mayu Hattori	69	70	69	208	2,500,000
Hiromi Takesue	69	72	68	209	1,800,000
Eun-A Lim	71	64	75	210	1,177,200
Hiromi Mogi	68	71	71	210	1,177,200

	SCORES			TOTAL	MONEY
Shinobu Moromizato	70	70	70	210	1,177,200
Bo-Bae Song	70	70	70	210	1,177,200
Rui Kitada	72	68	70	210	1,177,200
Yui Kawahara	69	71	71	211	882,000
Kuniko Maeda	66	72	73	211	882,000
Ji-Hee Lee	74	68	69	211	882,000
Mayumi Shimomura	72	71	69	212	732,000
Shiho Oyama	70	72	70	212	732,000
Akane Iijima	69	74	70	213	579,600
So-Hee Kim	71	68	74	213	579,600
Tomoko Kusakabe	68	72	73	213	579,600
Nachiyo Ohtani	72	67	74	213	579,600
Yuko Saitoh	72	71	70	213	579,600

Japan LPGA Championship Konica Minolta Cup

Katayamazu Golf Club, Kaga, Ishikawa
Par 36-36–72; 6,545 yards

September 11-14
purse, ¥100,000,000

	SCORES				TOTAL	MONEY
Hyun-Ju Shin	67	71	68	77	283	¥18,000,000
Sakura Yokomine	73	71	67	73	284	7,900,000
Ji-Yai Shin	72	70	68	74	284	7,900,000
Momoko Ueda	68	78	69	74	289	5,500,000
Esther Lee	70	71	77	71	289	5,500,000
Maiko Wakabayashi	73	75	72	70	290	4,000,000
Ji-Woo Lee	73	72	71	75	291	2,556,000
Midori Yoneyama	72	74	72	73	291	2,556,000
Ai Miyazato	74	73	71	73	291	2,556,000
Mi-Jeong Jeon	74	75	70	72	291	2,556,000
Miho Koga	73	75	72	71	291	2,556,000
Kaori Higo	74	76	71	71	292	1,580,000
Mayu Hattori	75	73	70	74	292	1,580,000
Yuriko Ohtsuka	75	72	72	73	292	1,580,000
Erina Hara	69	73	75	76	293	1,280,000
Ayako Uehara	77	70	73	73	293	1,280,000
Akane Iijima	75	72	72	74	293	1,280,000
Yuko Saitoh	76	76	72	70	294	1,080,000
Nikki Campbell	73	72	76	74	295	980,000
Hiroko Yamaguchi	70	74	76	76	296	840,000
Namika Omata	73	71	75	77	296	840,000
Rui Kitada	73	73	78	72	296	840,000
Hiromi Mogi	71	75	77	73	296	840,000
Yuko Mitsuka	72	73	71	80	296	840,000

Munsingwear Ladies Tokai Classic

Minami Aichi Country Club, Mihama, Aichi
Par 36-36–72; 6,428 yards

September 19-21
purse, ¥70,000,000

	SCORES			TOTAL	MONEY
Yuri Fudoh	71	70	67	208	¥12,600,000
Momoko Ueda	70	70	68	208	5,530,000
Yayoi Arasaki	69	67	72	208	5,530,000
(Fudoh defeated Ueda and Arasaki on first playoff hole.)					
Bo-Bae Song	76	65	68	209	4,200,000
Hiroko Yamaguchi	69	72	70	211	2,712,500

	SCORES			TOTAL	MONEY
Yuko Saitoh	72	69	70	211	2,712,500
*Asako Fujimoto	71	69	71	211	
Aki Takamura	71	69	71	211	2,712,500
Shinobu Moromizato	68	71	72	211	2,712,500
Miho Koga	70	71	71	212	1,575,000
Ji-Hee Lee	69	70	73	212	1,575,000
Yoko Inoue	71	72	70	213	1,253,000
Yui Mukaiyama	73	70	70	213	1,253,000
Akane Iijima	73	70	70	213	1,253,000
Ayako Uehara	72	72	70	214	1,078,000
Namika Omata	69	69	76	214	1,078,000
Mi-Jeong Jeon	72	74	69	215	729,909
Nobuko Kizawa	71	73	71	215	729,909
Mie Nakata	72	72	71	215	729,909
Tamie Durdin	74	70	71	215	729,909
Hiromi Mogi	76	67	72	215	729,909
So-Hee Kim	73	70	72	215	729,909
Sakura Yokomine	68	74	73	215	729,909
Yuki Sakurai	72	70	73	215	729,909
Ji-Woo Lee	72	70	73	215	729,909
Yuko Mitsuka	71	70	74	215	729,909
Eun-Hye Lee	73	68	74	215	729,909

Miyagi TV Cup Dunlop Ladies Open

Rifu Golf Club, Rifu, Miyagi
Par 36-36–72; 6,525 yards

September 26-28
purse, ¥60,000,000

	SCORES			TOTAL	MONEY
Momoko Ueda	70	72	69	211	¥10,800,000
Akane Iijima	74	69	69	212	4,360,000
Yuko Mitsuka	71	70	71	212	4,360,000
Julie Lu	69	71	72	212	4,360,000
Sakura Yokomine	70	69	74	213	2,700,000
Miki Saiki	72	70	71	213	2,700,000
Yumiko Yoshida	72	78	65	215	1,950,000
Chieko Amanuma	74	69	72	215	1,950,000
Mie Nakata	70	75	71	216	1,260,000
Shinobu Moromizato	71	76	69	216	1,260,000
So-Hee Kim	71	73	72	216	1,260,000
Akiko Fukushima	71	73	73	217	840,000
Na-Ri Lee	75	73	69	217	840,000
Esther Lee	74	70	73	217	840,000
Nikki Campbell	69	78	70	217	840,000
Hiromi Takesue	73	72	72	217	840,000
Shiho Oyama	74	74	69	217	840,000
Yui Kawahara	73	70	74	217	840,000
Mayu Hattori	70	74	74	218	600,000
Saiki Fujita	72	76	71	219	510,000
Natsu Nagai	74	73	72	219	510,000
Eriko Moriyama	73	71	75	219	510,000
Yuko Saitoh	69	78	72	219	510,000
Megumi Kido	75	71	73	219	510,000
Yui Mukaiyama	73	70	76	219	510,000

Japan Women's Open

Shiun Golf Club, Kajigawa Course, Shibata, Niigata
Par 36-36–72; 6,484 yards

October 2-5
purse, ¥140,000,000

	SCORES				TOTAL	MONEY
Ji-Hee Lee	73	76	68	67	284	¥28,000,000
Ai Miyazato	74	71	72	68	285	13,090,000
Esther Lee	68	73	74	70	285	13,090,000
Yuri Fudoh	76	71	71	68	286	7,000,000
Nikki Campbell	70	74	73	70	287	5,390,000
So-Hee Kim	71	74	71	71	287	5,390,000
Namika Omata	74	75	71	69	289	3,920,000
Sakura Yokomine	77	74	68	70	289	3,920,000
Momoko Ueda	73	74	72	71	290	2,870,000
Midori Yoneyama	76	71	71	72	290	2,870,000
Yui Kawahara	69	78	76	68	291	2,450,000
Shiho Oyama	74	79	72	67	292	1,817,200
Bo-Bae Song	75	74	73	70	292	1,817,200
Ji-Woo Lee	75	73	74	70	292	1,817,200
Ayako Uehara	74	73	73	72	292	1,817,200
Eun-A Lim	74	73	73	72	292	1,817,200
Kurumi Dohi	79	73	72	69	293	1,400,000
Shinobu Moromizato	77	70	76	70	293	1,400,000
Akiko Fukushima	72	73	76	72	293	1,400,000
Hiroko Yamaguchi	76	76	72	70	294	1,200,500
Tomomi Hirose	73	74	76	71	294	1,200,500
Erina Hara	75	73	74	72	294	1,200,500
Yuko Mitsuka	74	75	72	73	294	1,200,500

Sankyo Ladies Open

Akagi Country Club, Kiryu, Gunma
Par 36-36–72; 6,453 yards

October 10-12
purse, ¥90,000,000

	SCORES			TOTAL	MONEY
Maiko Wakabayashi	70	70	68	208	¥16,200,000
Ji-Hee Lee	73	68	70	211	7,110,000
Hiromi Mogi	67	71	73	211	7,110,000
Ayako Uehara	73	72	68	213	4,950,000
Nikki Campbell	74	69	70	213	4,950,000
Miho Koga	72	70	72	214	2,925,000
Mihoko Takahashi	70	72	72	214	2,925,000
Miki Saiki	71	70	73	214	2,925,000
Mihoko Iseri	75	68	71	214	2,925,000
Mie Nakata	69	72	74	215	1,424,000
Orie Fujino	71	72	72	215	1,424,000
Ji-Woo Lee	72	74	69	215	1,424,000
Bo-Bae Song	70	75	70	215	1,424,000
Erina Hara	75	69	71	215	1,424,000
Sakura Yokomine	73	70	72	215	1,424,000
Julie Lu	70	73	72	215	1,424,000
Mayu Hattori	73	71	71	215	1,424,000
Yukiyo Haga	72	70	73	215	1,424,000
Mayumi Nakajima	76	69	71	216	856,285
Eun-A Lim	69	73	74	216	856,285
Na-Ri Lee	71	74	71	216	856,285
Yoko Inoue	72	72	72	216	856,285
Natsu Nagai	71	72	73	216	856,285
Rui Kitada	75	68	73	216	856,285
Shiho Oyama	73	69	74	216	856,285

Fujitsu Ladies

Tokyu Seven Hundred Club, Chiba
Par 36-36–72; 6,588 yards

October 17-19
purse, ¥80,000,000

	SCORES			TOTAL	MONEY
Yuri Fudoh	69	68	66	203	¥14,400,000
Yuko Mitsuka	66	64	73	203	7,040,000
(Fudoh defeated Mitsuka on fifth playoff hole.)					
Keiko Sasaki	70	70	66	206	5,600,000
Miho Koga	69	70	68	207	4,800,000
Shinobu Moromizato	70	71	68	209	3,600,000
Mayu Hattori	70	67	72	209	3,600,000
Shiho Oyama	70	69	71	210	2,800,000
Akiko Fukushima	63	73	75	211	2,000,000
Saiki Fujita	68	72	71	211	2,000,000
Akane Iijima	69	70	72	211	2,000,000
Kaori Higo	70	70	72	212	1,400,000
Hiromi Takesue	73	69	70	212	1,400,000
Hiromi Mogi	72	69	71	212	1,400,000
Nikki Campbell	69	72	71	212	1,400,000
Mikiyo Nishizuka	67	72	74	213	1,120,000
Tamie Durdin	70	68	75	213	1,120,000
Erina Hara	68	75	70	213	1,120,000
Ah-Reum Hwang	69	70	75	214	838,400
Esther Lee	71	74	69	214	838,400
Eun-A Lim	71	69	74	214	838,400
Michiko Hattori	69	72	73	214	838,400
Sakura Yokomine	67	73	74	214	838,400

Masters Golf Club Ladies

Masters Golf Club, Miki, Hyogo
Par 36-36–72; 6,510 yards

October 24-26
purse, ¥123,000,000

	SCORES			TOTAL	MONEY
Shiho Oyama	65	75	69	209	¥22,140,000
Eun-A Lim	74	71	68	213	9,717,000
Ah-Reum Hwang	72	71	70	213	9,717,000
Yuki Sakurai	72	71	71	214	6,150,000
Ji-Hee Lee	70	69	75	214	6,150,000
Sakura Yokomine	70	71	73	214	6,150,000
Miki Saiki	71	72	72	215	3,382,500
Mi-Jeong Jeon	70	72	73	215	3,382,500
Nikki Campbell	70	74	71	215	3,382,500
Ji-Woo Lee	74	70	71	215	3,382,500
Maiko Wakabayashi	73	71	72	216	2,140,200
Bo-Bae Song	70	73	73	216	2,140,200
Yuri Fudoh	73	74	69	216	2,140,200
Paula Creamer	73	71	73	217	1,709,700
Momoko Ueda	76	70	71	217	1,709,700
Shinobu Moromizato	73	71	73	217	1,709,700
Rui Kitada	70	71	76	217	1,709,700
Akiko Fukushima	72	72	74	218	1,402,200
Tamie Durdin	74	71	74	219	1,189,000
Esther Lee	77	69	73	219	1,189,000
Mayu Hattori	76	72	71	219	1,189,000

Hisako Higuchi IDC Otsuka Ladies

Musashigaoka Golf Club, Hanno, Saitama
Par 36-36–72; 6,561 yards

October 31-November 2
purse, ¥70,000,000

	SCORES			TOTAL	MONEY
Mayu Hattori	70	71	69	210	¥12,600,000
Esther Lee	73	67	71	211	6,160,000
Chie Arimura	72	66	74	212	4,550,000
Maiko Wakabayashi	72	69	71	212	4,550,000
Shinobu Moromizato	71	71	71	213	2,520,000
Yayoi Arasaki	70	72	71	213	2,520,000
Sakura Yokomine	71	72	70	213	2,520,000
Natsu Nagai	72	70	71	213	2,520,000
Michie Ohba	71	69	73	213	2,520,000
Yuko Mitsuka	69	75	70	214	1,263,500
Ayako Uehara	72	73	69	214	1,263,500
Ji-Woo Lee	72	69	73	214	1,263,500
Mie Nakata	72	69	73	214	1,263,500
Rui Kitada	71	70	74	215	1,008,000
Ji-Yeon Han	71	74	70	215	1,008,000
Orie Fujino	70	75	70	215	1,008,000
Tomoko Kusakabe	72	74	70	216	798,000
Miho Koga	71	77	68	216	798,000
Ah-Reum Hwang	73	71	72	216	798,000
Ai Nishikawa	73	70	74	217	623,000
Mihoko Iseri	74	72	71	217	623,000
Kuniko Maeda	72	74	71	217	623,000
Nobuko Kizawa	75	71	71	217	623,000
Yun-Jye Wei	71	75	71	217	623,000
Nikki Campbell	73	73	71	217	623,000

Mizuno Classic

Kinetetsu Kashikojima Country Club, Shima, Mie
Par 36-36–72; 6,506 yards

November 7-9
purse, ¥140,000,000

	SCORES			TOTAL	MONEY
Ji-Yai Shin	68	66	67	201	¥20,615,700
Mayu Hattori	67	69	71	207	12,464,448
Eun-A Lim	68	70	70	208	9,042,144
Il Mi Chung	71	69	69	209	5,743,730
Yun-Jye Wei	71	68	70	209	5,743,730
Jee Young Lee	69	68	72	209	5,743,730
Yuri Fudoh	71	70	69	210	3,258,556
Bo-Bae Song	70	71	69	210	3,258,556
Allison Fouch	73	67	70	210	3,258,556
Miki Saiki	67	73	70	210	3,258,556
Candie Kung	73	70	68	211	2,253,394
Jin Joo Hong	69	73	69	211	2,253,394
Ji Young Oh	69	72	70	211	2,253,394
Yuko Mitsuka	69	71	71	211	2,253,394
Erina Hara	71	67	73	211	2,253,394
Sandra Gal	69	77	66	212	1,740,161
Sakura Yokomine	71	71	70	212	1,740,161
Alena Sharp	71	69	72	212	1,740,161
Shanshan Feng	69	71	72	212	1,740,161
Carin Koch	72	71	70	213	1,514,959
Young Kim	71	72	70	213	1,514,959
Jimin Kang	69	70	74	213	1,514,959

	SCORES			TOTAL	MONEY
Shinobu Moromizato	73	76	65	214	1,233,506
Heather Young	72	74	68	214	1,233,506
In-Kyung Kim	72	72	70	214	1,233,506
Teresa Lu	70	74	70	214	1,233,506
Hiromi Mogi	71	72	71	214	1,233,506
Jill McGill	71	71	72	214	1,233,506
Esther Lee	72	69	73	214	1,233,506
Shiho Oyama	69	68	77	214	1,233,506

Itoen Ladies

Great Island Club, Chonan, Chiba
Par 36-36–72; 6,594 yards

November 14-16
purse, ¥70,000,000

	SCORES			TOTAL	MONEY
Miho Koga	70	66	67	203	¥12,600,000
Ai Miyazato	70	67	68	205	5,530,000
Yuko Mitsuka	72	68	65	205	5,530,000
Bo-Bae Song	69	69	68	206	3,500,000
Shiho Oyama	64	72	70	206	3,500,000
Mayu Hattori	66	71	69	206	3,500,000
Yun-Jye Wei	70	68	69	207	2,100,000
Miki Saiki	72	69	66	207	2,100,000
Yuki Ichinose	72	66	69	207	2,100,000
So-Hee Kim	69	69	70	208	1,295,000
Midori Yoneyama	75	66	67	208	1,295,000
Mie Nakata	70	69	69	208	1,295,000
Ji-Hee Lee	69	67	72	208	1,295,000
Kaori Higo	69	71	69	209	980,000
Tomoko Kusakabe	69	68	72	209	980,000
Maiko Wakabayashi	68	72	69	209	980,000
Yuri Fudoh	69	68	72	209	980,000
Momoko Ueda	68	70	71	209	980,000
Rui Kitada	73	64	73	210	697,200
Erina Hara	68	70	72	210	697,200
Ayako Uehara	70	70	70	210	697,200
Sakura Yokomine	68	69	73	210	697,200
Na-Ri Lee	72	68	70	210	697,200

Daioseishi Elleair Ladies Open

Elleair Golf Club, Matsuyama, Ehime
Par 36-36–72; 6,442 yards

November 21-23
purse, ¥90,000,000

	SCORES			TOTAL	MONEY
Sakura Yokomine	71	68	66	205	¥16,200,000
Midori Yoneyama	71	70	68	209	8,100,000
Ai Miyazato	73	69	68	210	6,300,000
Junko Omote	69	72	70	211	3,600,000
Yuko Mitsuka	71	70	70	211	3,600,000
Eun-A Lim	74	70	67	211	3,600,000
Ji-Hee Lee	72	70	69	211	3,600,000
Momoko Ueda	74	71	66	211	3,600,000
Michie Ohba	70	71	70	211	3,600,000
*Kumiko Kaneda	70	70	72	212	
Yun-Jye Wei	69	72	72	213	1,759,500
Miki Saiki	72	70	71	213	1,759,500

	SCORES			TOTAL	MONEY
Akane Iijima	69	72	73	214	1,449,000
Bo-Bae Song	75	71	68	214	1,449,000
Ayako Uehara	71	72	71	214	1,449,000
Tamie Durdin	72	72	70	214	1,449,000
Yun-Joo Jeong	74	71	69	214	1,449,000
Yukari Baba	76	70	69	215	1,134,000
Natsu Nagai	71	71	73	215	1,134,000
Ah-Reum Hwang	74	69	73	216	918,000
Keiko Sasaki	75	69	72	216	918,000
Mumi Ohkubo	72	70	74	216	918,000
Erina Hara	74	72	70	216	918,000

Japan LPGA Tour Championship Ricoh Cup

Miyazaki Country Club, Sadohara, Miyazaki
Par 36-36–72; 6,442 yards

November 27-30
purse, ¥100,000,000

	SCORES				TOTAL	MONEY
Miho Koga	73	71	70	68	282	¥25,000,000
Yuri Fudoh	72	73	68	70	283	12,250,000
Mi-Jeong Jeon	71	71	71	70	283	12,250,000
Shinobu Moromizato	72	70	74	69	285	6,790,000
Akiko Fukushima	72	70	71	72	285	6,790,000
Yuko Mitsuka	71	74	69	71	285	6,790,000
Momoko Ueda	74	69	69	74	286	3,713,333
Ji-Woo Lee	76	73	67	70	286	3,713,333
Bo-Bae Song	69	71	71	75	286	3,713,333
Ji-Hee Lee	71	74	72	70	287	1,790,000
Sakura Yokomine	73	75	68	72	288	1,490,000
Yukari Baba	72	75	73	68	288	1,490,000
Saiki Fujita	77	73	70	69	289	1,190,000
Eun-A Lim	74	74	71	72	291	925,000
Rui Kitada	74	73	72	72	291	925,000
Ji-Yai Shin	71	75	72	74	292	740,000
Erina Hara	72	75	73	73	293	605,000
Midori Yoneyama	74	73	74	72	293	605,000
Hiromi Mogi	73	71	75	75	294	510,000
Akane Iijima	72	76	71	76	295	495,000
Esther Lee	75	72	74	74	295	495,000

Australian Ladies Tour

LG Bing Lee Women's NSW Open

Oatlands Golf Club, Melbourne, Victoria
Par 36-36–72; 6,008 yards

January 25-27
purse, A$125,000

	SCORES			TOTAL	MONEY
Laura Davies	70	70	67	207	A$18,750
Sarah Oh	70	68	71	209	13,125
Lotta Wahlin	70	71	70	211	7,750
Lydia Hall	71	71	70	212	6,500
Melissa Reid	74	71	68	213	4,875
Joanne Mills	69	73	71	213	4,875
Gwladys Nocera	73	70	71	214	3,791.67
*Kristie Smith	71	72	71	214	
Kirsty S. Taylor	70	75	69	214	3,791.67
*Jenny Lee	70	73	71	214	
Katherine Hull	68	71	75	214	3,791.67
*Allyce Watkinson	73	69	73	215	
Cecilia Ekelundh	70	76	69	215	2,406.25
Frances Bondad	74	69	72	215	2,406.25
Georgina Simpson	74	72	69	215	2,406.25
Martina Eberl	68	73	74	215	2,406.25
Lynn Kenny	74	69	73	216	1,706.25
Mi Sun Cho	73	71	72	216	1,706.25
Cherie Byrnes	69	74	73	216	1,706.25
Jane Suckling	68	74	74	216	1,706.25

MFS Women's Australian Open

Kingston Heath Golf Club, Melbourne, Victoria
Par 36-37–73; 6,651 yards

January 31-February 3
purse, A$500,000

	SCORES				TOTAL	MONEY
Karrie Webb	72	72	73	67	284	A$75,000
Ji-Yai Shin	72	71	74	67	284	50,000
(Webb defeated Shin on second playoff hole.)						
Melissa Reid	73	76	69	70	288	35,000
Amy Yang	75	73	72	70	290	25,000
Yuki Sakurai	80	73	69	69	291	15,812.50
Na Yeon Choi	78	73	71	69	291	15,812.50
Joanne Mills	74	79	70	68	291	15,812.50
Lindsey Wright	72	72	72	75	291	15,812.50
*Kristie Smith	72	69	77	73	291	
Ha-Neul Kim	76	74	73	70	293	9,916.67
*Rebecca Flood	75	77	70	71	293	
Rui Yokomine	78	72	71	72	293	9,916.67
Carri Wood	75	70	77	71	293	9,916.67
Samantha Head	83	71	71	69	294	7,083.33
Gwladys Nocera	78	71	73	72	294	7,083.33
Birdie Kim	75	72	75	72	294	7,083.33
Lisa Hall	78	74	73	70	295	6,166.67
Ashleigh Simon	75	73	75	72	295	6,166.67

	SCORES				TOTAL	MONEY
*Clare Choi	74	75	76	70	295	
Katherine Hull	71	75	75	74	295	6,166.67

ANZ Ladies Masters

Royal Pines Resort, Ashmore, Queensland
Par 35-37–72; 6,443 yards

February 7-10
purse, A$600,000

	SCORES			TOTAL	MONEY
Lisa Hall	68	69	66	203	A$90,000
Hyun-Ju Shin	68	68	68	204	60,000
Louise Stahle	71	67	67	205	36,000
Felicity Johnson	70	70	65	205	36,000
Karrie Webb	69	67	70	206	24,600
Karin Sjodin	72	67	68	207	18,150
Ji-Yai Shin	70	69	68	207	18,150
Laura Davies	70	69	69	208	15,000
Sakura Yokomine	70	71	68	209	10,680
Johanna Head	68	72	69	209	10,680
Diana D'Alessio	69	69	71	209	10,680
Gwladys Nocera	70	69	70	209	10,680
Amy Yang	69	71	69	209	10,680
Katherine Hull	72	70	68	210	7,500
Ai Miyazato	70	69	71	210	7,500
Haeji Kang	69	74	67	210	7,500
Carri Wood	69	69	72	210	7,500
Leah Hart	68	72	71	211	6,660
Sophie Giquel	69	71	71	211	6,660
Anna Tybring	70	68	73	211	6,660
Virada Nirapathpongporn	69	69	73	211	6,660
Shani Waugh	68	73	70	211	6,660

Ladies African Tour

Women's World Cup of Golf

Gary Player Country Club, Sun City, South Africa
Par 36-36–72; 6,385 yards

January 18-20
purse, US$1,400,000

	SCORES			TOTAL
PHILIPPINES—$280,000 Jennifer Rosales/Dorothy Delasin	65	68	65	198
SOUTH KOREA—$204,400 Eun-Hee Ji/Ji-Yai Shin	61	72	67	200
JAPAN—$122,500 Shinobu Moromizato/Miki Saiki	66	72	65	203
TAIWAN—$122,500 Yun-Jye Wei/Amy Hung	66	69	68	203
FRANCE—$84,000 Gwladys Nocera/Virginie Lagoutte-Clement	62	76	67	205
CANADA—$63,000 Lorie Kane/Alena Sharp	64	73	69	206
SOUTH AFRICA—$63,000 Laurette Maritz/Ashleigh Simon	68	72	66	206
WALES—$63,000 Becky Brewerton/Becky Morgan	67	71	68	206
PARAGUAY—$49,000 Julieta Granada/Celeste Troche	66	73	68	207
SCOTLAND—$38,500 Catriona Matthew/Mhairi McKay	68	73	67	208
UNITED STATES—$38,500 Juli Inkster/Pat Hurst	65	76	67	208
BRAZIL—$26,600 Candy Hannemann/Angela Park	68	73	69	210
CHINA—$26,600 Na Zhang/Chun Wang	67	75	68	210
SWEDEN—$22,400 Sophie Gustafson/Maria Hjorth	65	77	70	212
ENGLAND—$21,000 Trish Johnson/Danielle Masters	67	76	70	213
ITALY—$18,900 Silvia Cavalleri/Diana Luna	73	76	68	217
SPAIN—$18,900 Paula Marti/Tania Elosegui	69	79	69	217

	SCORES			TOTAL
AUSTRALIA—$16,100				
Lindsey Wright/Nikki Garrett	68	78	72	218
GERMANY—$16,100				
Bettina Hauert/Martina Eberl	69	78	71	218
INDIA—$14,000				
Simi Mehra/Irina Brar	70	84	75	229

WPGA Masters

Parkview Golf Club, Johannesburg
Par 36-36–72

February 20-22
purse, R285,000

	SCORES			TOTAL	MONEY
Rebecca Hudson	71	66	67	204	R42,750
Anna Temple	71	69	64	204	31,350
(Hudson defeated Temple on first playoff hole.)					
Lill Kristin Saether	69	72	64	205	22,800
Marianne Skarpnord	71	66	71	208	17,100
*Gina Switala	71	66	73	210	
Stacy Bregman	72	69	70	211	13,680
Ashleigh Simon	71	67	74	212	9,928
Laurette Maritz	72	69	71	212	9,928
Anne-Lise Caudal	71	70	71	212	9,928
Lee-Anne Pace	69	70	74	213	7,268
*Ashleigh Holmes	71	68	74	213	
Lisa Holm Sorensen	73	70	72	215	6,413
Frederique Seeholzer	70	74	72	216	5,462.67
Anna Becker-Frankel	70	73	73	216	5,462.67
Mandy Adamson	72	70	74	216	5,462.67
*Kim Williams	74	72	71	217	
*Bertine Strauss	73	73	71	217	
Morgana Robbertze	68	71	79	218	4,802.50
Michelle de Vries	75	75	68	218	4,802.50
Julie Tvede	71	74	74	219	4,417.67
*Marne Roos	73	74	72	219	
*Mercia Pretorius	72	69	78	219	
Cecilie Lundgreen	74	74	71	219	4,417.67
Antonella Cvitan	70	75	74	219	4,417.67

Acer Women's South African Open

Durban Country Club, Durban
Par 37-36–73; 6,098 yards

February 28-March 1
purse, R285,000

	SCORES			TOTAL	MONEY
Julie Tvede	66	69	74	209	R42,750
Anne-Lise Caudal	69	72	69	210	31,350
Marianne Skarpnord	73	69	70	212	22,800
Stacy Bregman	72	70	72	214	17,100
Lee-Anne Pace	70	74	71	215	13,680
Rebecca Hudson	68	75	74	217	11,543
Lisa Holm Sorensen	70	77	74	221	9,833
*Pam Hayward	75	70	77	222	
*Monique Smit	73	73	77	223	
Laurette Maritz	74	76	73	223	8,408

	SCORES			TOTAL	MONEY
Antonella Cvitan	74	73	77	224	7,268
Lill Kristin Saether	73	74	78	225	6,128
Emma Lyons	73	76	76	225	6,128
Morgana Robbertze	76	70	81	227	5,272.50
Cecilia Ekelundh	75	79	73	227	5,272.50
*Bertine Strauss	69	76	83	228	
Maria Boden	75	77	76	228	4,802.50
Mandy Adamson	73	74	81	228	4,802.50
Johanna Westerberg	75	76	78	229	4,489
Cecilie Lundgreen	75	78	76	229	4,489

Pam Golding Ladies International

Nelspruit Golf Club, Nelspruit
Par 36-36–72

March 6-8
purse, R300,000

	SCORES			TOTAL	MONEY
Stacy Bregman	68	70	71	209	R45,000
Lisa Holm Sorensen	71	71	71	213	28,500
Morgana Robbertze	70	72	71	213	28,500
Johanna Westerberg	71	72	74	217	16,200
Maria Boden	71	70	76	217	16,200
Julie Tvede	73	75	71	219	9,750
Anna Temple	71	75	73	219	9,750
Emma Lyons	73	73	73	219	9,750
Rebecca Hudson	74	72	73	219	9,750
Marianne Skarpnord	73	75	72	220	6,450
Julie Berton	74	73	73	220	6,450
Mandy Adamson	77	71	73	221	5,700
Emma Zackrisson	74	74	74	222	5,170
Lill Kristin Saether	76	72	74	222	5,170
Lee-Anne Pace	74	73	75	222	5,170
Margherita Rigon	79	74	70	223	4,725
Florence Luscher	76	73	74	223	4,725
*Tandi Cuningham	73	74	76	223	
*Gina Switala	77	72	75	224	
Kaisa Ruuttila	75	75	74	224	4,350
Jo Clingan	73	73	78	224	4,350
Caroline Afonso	77	76	71	224	4,350

Telkom Women's Classic

Zwartkop Country Club, Johannesburg
Par 36-36–72

March 12-14
purse, R350,000

	SCORES			TOTAL	MONEY
Lisa Holm Sorensen	66	68	69	203	R52,500
Maria Boden	71	66	68	205	38,500
Julie Tvede	68	66	72	206	28,000
Emma Zackrisson	69	66	73	208	17,325
Marianne Skarpnord	62	74	72	208	17,325
Stacy Bregman	70	68	70	208	17,325
Johanna Westerberg	71	69	69	209	12,075
Morgana Robbertze	71	68	71	210	9,041.67
Laurette Maritz	72	67	71	210	9,041.67
Rebecca Hudson	69	69	72	210	9,041.67
Hanna-Leena Salonen	73	68	70	211	7,175

	SCORES			TOTAL	MONEY
Tsebo Betty Mokoena	70	69	73	212	6,475
Cecilie Lundgreen	71	73	68	212	6,475
Lee-Anne Pace	74	70	69	213	6,020
*Monique Smit	70	72	72	214	
Kaisa Ruuttila	74	69	71	214	5,512.50
*Marne Roos	69	71	74	214	
Antonella Cvitan	71	69	74	214	5,512.50
Anne-Lise Caudal	68	71	75	214	5,512.50
Carmen Alonso	72	67	75	214	5,512.50

Princess Lalla Meryem Cup

Dar-es-Salam Golf Club, Blue Course, Rabat, Morocco
Par 36-37–73; 6,785 yards

November 7-9
purse, US$100,000

	SCORES			TOTAL	MONEY
Laura Davies	67	69	70	206	US$22,000
Tania Elosegui	68	73	68	209	12,000
Gwladys Nocera	69	70	73	212	10,000
Rebecca Hudson	74	71	71	216	8,250
Patricia Meunier Lebouc	69	72	75	216	8,250
Samantha Head	72	68	77	217	6,750
Maria Verchenova	68	70	79	217	6,750
Paula Marti	72	75	72	217	6,000
Lotta Wahlin	76	76	74	226	5,500
Georgina Simpson	74	78	74	226	5,500
Anne-Lise Caudal	73	77	79	229	5,000
Mounya Amalou Sayeh	76	82	76	234	4,000

Senior Tours

MasterCard Championship

Hualalai Golf Course, Ka'upulehu-Kona, Hawaii
Par 36-36–72; 7,053 yards

January 18-20
purse, $1,800,000

	SCORES			TOTAL	MONEY
Fred Funk	67	63	65	195	$300,000
Allen Doyle	63	66	68	197	188,000
Jay Haas	65	67	67	199	118,000
Bernhard Langer	66	68	65	199	118,000
Tom Purtzer	62	69	69	200	91,750
John Cook	67	68	66	201	80,000
Loren Roberts	68	65	69	202	70,000
Craig Stadler	68	67	68	203	62,500
Tom Watson	66	68	69	203	62,500
Brad Bryant	66	68	70	204	50,000
Bob Gilder	66	69	69	204	50,000
D.A. Weibring	64	69	71	204	50,000
Tom Jenkins	66	71	68	205	34,250
Scott Simpson	69	69	67	205	34,250
Jim Thorpe	63	68	74	205	34,250
Mark Wiebe	65	69	71	205	34,250
Ben Crenshaw	68	69	69	206	28,000
Lonnie Nielsen	68	72	67	207	24,000
Jerry Pate	66	75	66	207	24,000
Mike Reid	67	70	70	207	24,000
Eduardo Romero	65	72	70	207	24,000
Denis Watson	67	66	74	207	24,000
R.W. Eaks	67	67	74	208	18,500
Keith Fergus	72	72	64	208	18,500
John Harris	65	71	72	208	18,500
John Jacobs	66	69	73	208	18,500
Dana Quigley	70	67	71	208	18,500
Lanny Wadkins	67	73	68	208	18,500
Morris Hatalsky	70	68	71	209	15,500
Hale Irwin	72	70	68	210	14,750
Mark McNulty	65	69	76	210	14,750

Turtle Bay Championship

Turtle Bay Resort, Palmer Course, Kahuku, Hawaii
Par 36-36–72; 7,088 yards

January 25-27
purse, $1,600,000

	SCORES			TOTAL	MONEY
Jerry Pate	71	70	70	211	$240,000
Fulton Allem	68	72	73	213	128,000
Jim Thorpe	68	71	74	213	128,000
Wayne Grady	71	73	70	214	73,600
Gil Morgan	65	72	77	214	73,600
Loren Roberts	72	71	71	214	73,600
Robert Thompson	71	71	72	214	73,600
Keith Fergus	71	72	72	215	40,533.34
Denis Watson	70	74	71	215	40,533.34
Morris Hatalsky	67	73	75	215	40,533.33

	SCORES			TOTAL	MONEY
Tom Kite	68	73	74	215	40,533.33
Bernhard Langer	68	71	76	215	40,533.33
James Mason	71	72	72	215	40,533.33
Donnie Hammond	68	74	74	216	28,000
Lonnie Nielsen	70	72	74	216	28,000
Dana Quigley	69	75	72	216	28,000
Scott Simpson	69	72	75	216	28,000
John Cook	68	75	74	217	22,560
Allen Doyle	72	70	75	217	22,560
Tom McKnight	73	70	74	217	22,560
Phil Blackmar	68	72	78	218	19,200
Boonchu Ruangkit	69	76	73	218	19,200
Kenny Knox	73	73	73	219	16,400
Mike McCullough	73	74	72	219	16,400
Jeff Sluman	72	74	73	219	16,400
Curtis Strange	70	73	76	219	16,400
Brad Bryant	75	73	72	220	13,280
David Edwards	71	74	75	220	13,280
David Eger	73	75	72	220	13,280
Tom Jenkins	71	75	74	220	13,280
Joe Ozaki	72	74	74	220	13,280

Allianz Championship

Old Course at Broken Sound, Boca Raton, Florida
Par 36-36–72; 6,807 yards

February 8-10
purse, $1,650,000

	SCORES			TOTAL	MONEY
Scott Hoch	67	67	68	202	$247,500
Brad Bryant	68	69	66	203	132,000
Bruce Lietzke	70	65	68	203	132,000
Eduardo Romero	69	67	68	204	89,100
Bobby Wadkins	67	68	69	204	89,100
John Cook	69	66	70	205	59,400
Keith Fergus	67	70	68	205	59,400
Jay Haas	67	71	67	205	59,400
Tom Kite	68	70	68	206	44,550
Jerry Pate	66	67	73	206	44,550
Mitch Adcock	69	71	67	207	35,062.50
Allen Doyle	68	70	69	207	35,062.50
Donnie Hammond	69	70	68	207	35,062.50
Mark McNulty	66	69	72	207	35,062.50
Joe Ozaki	69	71	68	208	28,875
Tom Purtzer	67	70	71	208	28,875
Loren Roberts	72	66	71	209	26,400
Phil Blackmar	67	72	71	210	20,171.25
R.W. Eaks	69	71	70	210	20,171.25
Hale Irwin	69	68	73	210	20,171.25
Mark James	70	66	74	210	20,171.25
Gil Morgan	67	70	73	210	20,171.25
Don Pooley	74	65	71	210	20,171.25
Jeff Sluman	72	67	71	210	20,171.25
Mark Wiebe	71	69	70	210	20,171.25
Wayne Levi	68	73	70	211	14,355
Boonchu Ruangkit	69	72	70	211	14,355
Des Smyth	70	69	72	211	14,355
Jim Thorpe	69	67	75	211	14,355
Fuzzy Zoeller	73	66	72	211	14,355

ACE Group Classic

Quail West, Naples, Florida
Par 36-36–72; 7,090 yards

February 15-17
purse, $1,600,000

	SCORES			TOTAL	MONEY
Scott Hoch	68	66	68	202	$240,000
Tom Kite	65	72	65	202	117,333.34
Brad Bryant	68	69	65	202	117,333.33
Tom Jenkins	68	64	70	202	117,333.33
(Hoch won on first playoff hole.)					
Nick Price	68	66	69	203	76,800
Loren Roberts	65	70	69	204	60,800
Jeff Sluman	68	68	68	204	60,800
Chip Beck	69	66	70	205	42,240
Bob Gilder	68	70	67	205	42,240
Gene Jones	72	65	68	205	42,240
Gary Koch	67	67	71	205	42,240
Ron Streck	68	66	71	205	42,240
Peter Jacobsen	66	68	72	206	30,400
Lonnie Nielsen	71	69	66	206	30,400
Jeff Roth	68	73	65	206	30,400
Keith Fergus	68	69	70	207	24,096
Graham Marsh	69	67	71	207	24,096
Joe Ozaki	66	70	71	207	24,096
Eduardo Romero	67	73	67	207	24,096
Bobby Wadkins	69	69	69	207	24,096
Gil Morgan	73	69	66	208	18,200
Tim Simpson	71	67	70	208	18,200
Des Smyth	69	71	68	208	18,200
Mark Wiebe	70	69	69	208	18,200
Andy Bean	69	71	69	209	15,600
Bruce Fleisher	65	71	73	209	15,600
Vicente Fernandez	71	67	72	210	13,920
Morris Hatalsky	72	66	72	210	13,920
Denis Watson	73	68	69	210	13,920
Allen Doyle	69	69	73	211	11,552
Wayne Levi	67	70	74	211	11,552
Scott Simpson	67	70	74	211	11,552
Craig Stadler	70	67	74	211	11,552
Curtis Strange	68	72	71	211	11,552

Toshiba Classic

Newport Beach Country Club, Newport Beach, California
Par 35-36–71; 6,584 yards

March 7-9
purse, $1,700,000

	SCORES			TOTAL	MONEY
Bernhard Langer	65	65	69	199	$255,000
Jay Haas	65	69	65	199	149,600
(Langer defeated Haas on seventh playoff hole.)					
Ben Crenshaw	66	69	67	202	102,000
Gary McCord	68	67	67	202	102,000
Scott Simpson	69	68	65	202	102,000
Tim Simpson	63	70	70	203	64,600
Curtis Strange	68	69	66	203	64,600
Keith Fergus	67	67	70	204	44,880
Lonnie Nielsen	67	71	66	204	44,880
Craig Stadler	66	70	68	204	44,880
Leonard Thompson	67	72	65	204	44,880

	SCORES			TOTAL	MONEY
D.A. Weibring	66	68	70	204	44,880
John Cook	71	67	67	205	28,113.75
Fred Funk	69	69	67	205	28,113.75
Bob Gilder	71	66	68	205	28,113.75
Walter Hall	69	69	67	205	28,113.75
Mark Johnson	64	69	72	205	28,113.75
Boonchu Ruangkit	67	70	68	205	28,113.75
Jay Sigel	68	69	68	205	28,113.75
Jeff Sluman	68	65	72	205	28,113.75
Scott Hoch	67	72	67	206	16,459.10
Allen Doyle	67	70	69	206	16,459.09
R.W. Eaks	70	68	68	206	16,459.09
Mike Goodes	65	71	70	206	16,459.09
Wayne Grady	71	68	67	206	16,459.09
John Harris	71	69	66	206	16,459.09
Morris Hatalsky	69	64	73	206	16,459.09
Mark McNulty	72	67	67	206	16,459.09
Tom Purtzer	68	69	69	206	16,459.09
Dana Quigley	69	71	66	206	16,459.09
Loren Roberts	71	67	68	206	16,459.09

AT&T Champions Classic

Valencia Country Club, Valencia, California
Par 36-36–72; 6,973 yards

March 14-16
purse, $1,600,000

	SCORES			TOTAL	MONEY
Denis Watson	73	71	65	209	$240,000
Brad Bryant	70	67	72	209	128,000
Loren Roberts	69	70	70	209	128,000
(Watson defeated Bryant on second and Roberts on third playoff hole.)					
Jay Haas	71	68	71	210	96,000
John Cook	71	69	71	211	62,400
Bernhard Langer	71	68	72	211	62,400
Jerry Pate	70	71	70	211	62,400
Scott Simpson	71	69	71	211	62,400
Don Pooley	71	71	70	212	44,800
Tom Purtzer	67	73	73	213	41,600
Wayne Grady	74	70	70	214	35,200
Tom Jenkins	71	68	75	214	35,200
Nick Price	66	77	71	214	35,200
David Edwards	72	72	71	215	26,426.67
Mike McCullough	73	69	73	215	26,426.67
Tim Simpson	71	74	70	215	26,426.67
Bobby Wadkins	71	75	69	215	26,426.67
R.W. Eaks	71	68	76	215	26,426.66
Fred Funk	70	70	75	215	26,426.66
Gene Jones	73	70	73	216	18,784
Mark O'Meara	71	72	73	216	18,784
Eduardo Romero	71	74	71	216	18,784
Rod Spittle	72	73	71	216	18,784
Leonard Thompson	71	73	72	216	18,784
Andy Bean	70	75	72	217	14,592
Hale Irwin	73	72	72	217	14,592
Graham Marsh	69	71	77	217	14,592
Mark McNulty	73	67	77	217	14,592
Mark Wiebe	76	69	72	217	14,592
Dana Quigley	68	78	72	218	11,800
Jeff Sluman	70	70	78	218	11,800
Dave Stockton	70	76	72	218	11,800
Jim Thorpe	72	72	74	218	11,800

Ginn Championship Hammock Beach Resort

Hammock Beach Golf Club, Ocean Course, Palm Coast, Florida

Par 36-36–72; 7,113 yards

March 28-30

purse, $2,500,000

	SCORES			TOTAL	MONEY
Bernhard Langer	67	66	71	204	$375,000
Lonnie Nielsen	66	69	77	212	200,000
Tim Simpson	69	68	75	212	200,000
Fred Funk	67	69	77	213	135,000
Joe Ozaki	74	65	74	213	135,000
David Eger	73	68	73	214	90,000
Nick Price	72	67	75	214	90,000
Tom Watson	70	70	74	214	90,000
John Cook	72	70	73	215	67,500
Craig Stadler	69	70	76	215	67,500
Ben Crenshaw	71	68	77	216	55,000
Mark McNulty	70	69	77	216	55,000
Loren Roberts	71	70	75	216	55,000
David Edwards	68	76	73	217	43,750
Scott Hoch	72	70	75	217	43,750
Tom Kite	71	70	76	217	43,750
Larry Nelson	73	69	75	217	43,750
Mitch Adcock	71	71	76	218	34,187.50
R.W. Eaks	70	75	73	218	34,187.50
Gene Jones	68	72	78	218	34,187.50
Mark Wiebe	71	70	77	218	34,187.50
Mark O'Meara	72	72	75	219	27,583.34
Brad Bryant	70	70	79	219	27,583.33
Tom Jenkins	74	68	77	219	27,583.33
Dana Quigley	74	72	74	220	22,291.67
John Ross	73	72	75	220	22,291.67
Scott Simpson	75	70	75	220	22,291.67
D.A. Weibring	72	75	73	220	22,291.67
Des Smyth	73	71	76	220	22,291.66
Bruce Vaughan	72	70	78	220	22,291.66

Cap Cana Championship

Punta Espanda Golf Club, Cap Cana, Dominican Republic

Par 36-36–72; 7,260 yards

April 4-6

purse, $2,000,000

	SCORES			TOTAL	MONEY
Mark Wiebe	67	68	67	202	$300,000
Vicente Fernandez	69	72	65	206	176,000
Jay Haas	70	69	68	207	132,000
Craig Stadler	73	67	67	207	132,000
Fulton Allem	69	71	68	208	78,000
Scott Hoch	71	67	70	208	78,000
Nick Price	73	68	67	208	78,000
Denis Watson	73	69	66	208	78,000
Morris Hatalsky	75	68	66	209	52,000
Gene Jones	72	68	69	209	52,000
Eduardo Romero	71	68	70	209	52,000
Brad Bryant	71	71	68	210	40,666.67
Joe Ozaki	77	65	68	210	40,666.67
Bruce Vaughan	71	69	70	210	40,666.66
Bernhard Langer	74	68	69	211	34,000
James Mason	70	71	70	211	34,000
Tom Watson	70	71	70	211	34,000

	SCORES			TOTAL	MONEY
Phil Blackmar	72	70	70	212	26,520
R.W. Eaks	72	71	69	212	26,520
Mark McNulty	73	70	69	212	26,520
Tom Purtzer	75	69	68	212	26,520
Mike Reid	71	69	72	212	26,520
Bob Gilder	74	70	69	213	21,500
Scott Simpson	76	67	70	213	21,500
John Cook	72	71	71	214	18,240
Fred Funk	74	68	72	214	18,240
Tom Jenkins	75	69	70	214	18,240
Sandy Lyle	71	72	71	214	18,240
Jeff Sluman	74	71	69	214	18,240
David Eger	76	71	68	215	14,440
Hale Irwin	76	72	67	215	14,440
Lonnie Nielsen	75	69	71	215	14,440
Don Pooley	76	69	70	215	14,440
D.A. Weibring	73	72	70	215	14,440

Outback Steakhouse Pro-Am

TPC Tampa Bay, Lutz, Florida
Par 35-36–71; 6,783 yards

April 18-20
purse, $1,700,000

	SCORES			TOTAL	MONEY
Tom Watson	63	71	70	204	$255,000
Jay Haas	70	71	64	205	136,850
Scott Hoch	67	67	71	205	136,850
John Cook	70	68	68	206	102,000
Tom Jenkins	70	66	71	207	74,800
Mark Wiebe	66	65	76	207	74,800
David Eger	66	74	68	208	61,200
Vicente Fernandez	67	72	70	209	46,750
Mike Hulbert	69	68	72	209	46,750
Nick Price	73	65	71	209	46,750
Jeff Sluman	70	71	68	209	46,750
Gary Koch	69	69	72	210	34,566.67
D.A. Weibring	72	68	70	210	34,566.67
Mike Reid	68	68	74	210	34,566.66
Keith Fergus	74	66	71	211	25,670
Mark James	67	74	70	211	25,670
Masahiro Kuramoto	70	72	69	211	25,670
Joey Sindelar	74	69	68	211	25,670
Curtis Strange	73	72	66	211	25,670
Bruce Vaughan	70	73	68	211	25,670
Denis Watson	71	72	68	211	25,670
Fulton Allem	72	69	71	212	18,317.50
Bruce Fleisher	72	69	71	212	18,317.50
Gil Morgan	73	71	68	212	18,317.50
Dana Quigley	69	71	72	212	18,317.50
Bob Gilder	73	69	71	213	15,470
Lonnie Nielsen	72	71	70	213	15,470
Loren Roberts	72	72	69	213	15,470
Andy Bean	69	71	74	214	12,852
Tom McKnight	71	72	71	214	12,852
Mark McNulty	72	70	72	214	12,852
Tim Simpson	72	67	75	214	12,852
Dave Stockton	69	72	73	214	12,852

Liberty Mutual Legends of Golf

Westin Savannah Harbor Resort & Spa, Savannah, Georgia   April 25-27
Par 36-36–72; 7,087 yards   purse, $2,600,000

	SCORES			TOTAL	MONEY
Tom Watson/Andy North	59	62	64	185	$225,000
Jeff Sluman/Craig Stadler	62	63	61	186	132,000
Sandy Lyle/Ian Woosnam	64	63	60	187	108,000
John Cook/Joey Sindelar	62	65	62	189	81,000
Andy Bean/Jerry Pate	63	64	62	189	81,000
David Edwards/Bernhard Langer	65	61	66	192	60,000
Morris Hatalsky/Don Pooley	62	67	64	193	47,333.34
Mark O'Meara/Nick Price	65	64	64	193	47,333.33
Larry Nelson/Jim Thorpe	63	64	66	193	47,333.33
David Eger/Mark McNulty	66	64	64	194	38,500
Loren Roberts/Scott Simpson	65	65	65	195	31,375
R.W. Eaks/Bob Gilder	62	67	66	195	31,375
Tom Kite/Gil Morgan	65	64	66	195	31,375
Keith Fergus/Wayne Levi	62	65	68	195	31,375
Dave Eichelberger/Tom Wargo	65	67	64	196	25,750
Brad Bryant/Lonnie Nielsen	65	60	71	196	25,750
Allen Doyle/Dana Quigley	65	67	65	197	22,000
Tom Purtzer/D.A. Weibring	66	63	68	197	22,000
Fred Funk/Scott Hoch	65	69	63	197	22,000
Mark Wiebe/Wayne Grady	67	66	65	198	19,500
John Jacobs/Fuzzy Zoeller	67	65	67	199	18,000
Mark James/Eduardo Romero	69	65	65	199	18,000
Isao Aoki/Joe Ozaki	66	67	67	200	16,000
Jay Haas/Curtis Strange	66	69	65	200	16,000
Des Smyth/Denis Watson	67	69	65	201	14,500
Bruce Fleisher/Tom Jenkins	66	68	68	202	13,750
Ben Crenshaw/Raymond Floyd	69	68	65	202	13,750
Mark McCumber/Leonard Thompson	67	68	68	203	12,750
Bruce Lietzke/Bill Rogers	69	67	67	203	12,750
Gibby Gilbert/J.C. Snead	70	68	68	206	12,000

FedEx Kinko's Classic

The Hills Country Club, Austin, Texas   May 2-4
Par 36-36–72; 6,879 yards   purse, $1,600,000

	SCORES			TOTAL	MONEY
Denis Watson	67	70	69	206	$240,000
Scott Hoch	67	71	69	207	117,333.34
Nick Price	65	67	75	207	117,333.33
Tim Simpson	68	69	70	207	117,333.33
Loren Roberts	68	66	74	208	76,800
John Cook	68	72	69	209	60,800
Mark Wiebe	71	69	69	209	60,800
John Ross	73	70	67	210	48,000
Scott Simpson	68	66	76	210	48,000
Mark James	72	70	69	211	38,400
Lonnie Nielsen	71	74	66	211	38,400
Mark O'Meara	66	75	70	211	38,400
Ben Crenshaw	70	71	71	212	28,800
Fred Funk	67	71	74	212	28,800
Bob Gilder	68	70	74	212	28,800
Tom McKnight	67	75	70	212	28,800
Jeff Sluman	68	73	71	212	28,800

	SCORES			TOTAL	MONEY
Larry Nelson	71	71	71	213	23,280
Boonchu Ruangkit	73	68	72	213	23,280
Ed Dougherty	69	74	71	214	19,280
Kirk Hanefeld	75	74	65	214	19,280
Don Pooley	70	74	70	214	19,280
D.A. Weibring	67	73	74	214	19,280
Fuzzy Zoeller	73	75	67	215	14,628.58
Mike Donald	73	69	73	215	14,628.57
Keith Fergus	69	72	74	215	14,628.57
Hubert Green	73	71	71	215	14,628.57
Jerry Pate	71	72	72	215	14,628.57
Joey Sindelar	72	72	71	215	14,628.57
Jim Thorpe	70	70	75	215	14,628.57

Regions Charity Classic

Robert Trent Jones Golf Trail at Ross Bridge, Hoover, Alabama   May 16-18
Par 36-36–72; 7,473 yards   purse, $1,700,000

	SCORES			TOTAL	MONEY
Andy Bean	65	68	70	203	$255,000
Loren Roberts	69	66	69	204	149,600
Jeff Sluman	69	72	64	205	122,400
Mike Goodes	65	69	72	206	102,000
Bernhard Langer	67	71	69	207	70,266.67
Lonnie Nielsen	73	66	68	207	70,266.67
Denis Watson	69	66	72	207	70,266.66
Walter Hall	68	70	70	208	48,733.34
R.W. Eaks	71	67	70	208	48,733.33
Tom Jenkins	70	68	70	208	48,733.33
Brad Bryant	72	70	67	209	31,185.56
Vicente Fernandez	73	68	68	209	31,185.56
Scott Hoch	70	71	68	209	31,185.56
Gary Koch	71	71	67	209	31,185.56
D.A. Weibring	70	72	67	209	31,185.56
Keith Fergus	72	68	69	209	31,185.55
Mike Hulbert	68	68	73	209	31,185.55
Mike Reid	72	67	70	209	31,185.55
Joey Sindelar	69	68	72	209	31,185.55
David Eger	71	71	68	210	19,465
Bob Gilder	71	70	69	210	19,465
Don Pooley	70	69	71	210	19,465
Dave Rummells	71	70	69	210	19,465
Scott Simpson	69	69	72	210	19,465
Mark Wiebe	70	70	70	210	19,465
Gene Jones	75	66	70	211	15,470
Des Smyth	70	70	71	211	15,470
Ian Woosnam	69	72	70	211	15,470
Bobby Wadkins	72	67	73	212	14,110
Allen Doyle	72	69	72	213	12,537.50
Bruce Fleisher	72	70	71	213	12,537.50
Tim Simpson	70	70	73	213	12,537.50
Bruce Vaughan	69	71	73	213	12,537.50

Senior PGA Championship

Oak Hill Country Club, East Course, Rochester, New York
Par 35-35–70; 7,001 yards

May 22-25
purse, $2,000,000

	SCORES				TOTAL	MONEY
Jay Haas	69	72	72	74	287	$360,000
Bernhard Langer	71	71	70	76	288	216,000
Scott Hoch	71	74	72	72	289	102,667
Joey Sindelar	76	69	72	72	289	102,667
Scott Simpson	76	71	69	73	289	102,667
Don Pooley	75	73	72	70	290	62,000
Ron Streck	76	71	72	71	290	62,000
Greg Norman	72	73	72	73	290	62,000
Vicente Fernandez	74	75	73	69	291	50,000
Gene Jones	76	74	72	69	291	50,000
Jeff Sluman	70	73	70	78	291	50,000
Tom Purtzer	73	67	81	71	292	42,000
Craig Stadler	75	70	76	72	293	36,000
Andy Bean	73	72	74	74	293	36,000
Tom Kite	75	71	71	76	293	36,000
David Eger	72	78	74	70	294	23,375
Tom Watson	78	69	75	72	294	23,375
Bruce Fleisher	78	67	76	73	294	23,375
Tim Simpson	71	73	76	74	294	23,375
Ian Woosnam	71	76	73	74	294	23,375
John Cook	73	75	72	74	294	23,375
Eduardo Romero	71	77	71	75	294	23,375
Bill Britton	70	74	72	78	294	23,375
Kiyoshi Murota	75	72	75	73	295	16,500
Mark O'Meara	76	66	77	76	295	16,500
Bob Cameron	72	73	81	70	296	13,875
James Mason	76	71	78	71	296	13,875
John Harris	72	78	73	73	296	13,875
Denis Watson	72	74	74	76	296	13,875
Joe Ozaki	71	79	77	70	297	11,750
Bruce Vaughan	77	70	76	74	297	11,750
Mark Wiebe	74	72	77	74	297	11,750
Keith Fergus	71	74	75	77	297	11,750
John Ross	75	77	78	68	298	8,700
John Jacobs	71	80	74	73	298	8,700
Des Smyth	74	70	80	74	298	8,700
Bob Gilder	73	73	77	75	298	8,700
Nick Job	72	76	75	75	298	8,700
Sam Torrance	76	74	73	75	298	8,700
Kirk Hanefeld	71	74	77	76	298	8,700
Katsuyoshi Tomori	75	77	70	76	298	8,700
Mike Goodes	72	73	75	78	298	8,700
Sandy Lyle	76	76	74	73	299	6,600
Gil Morgan	78	74	71	76	299	6,600
David Edwards	76	73	73	77	299	6,600
Jim Ahern	83	68	76	73	300	5,700
David Ogrin	75	72	78	75	300	5,700
Jim Woodward	72	74	75	79	300	5,700
Loren Roberts	78	74	76	73	301	4,725
Tom McKnight	76	76	75	74	301	4,725
Perry Arthur	77	73	76	75	301	4,725
Chip Beck	73	75	76	77	301	4,725
Tom Jenkins	75	71	84	72	302	4,225
D.A. Weibring	76	74	80	72	302	4,225
Lonnie Nielsen	81	70	78	73	302	4,225
Mike Hulbert	80	72	76	74	302	4,225
Allen Doyle	76	74	77	75	302	4,225

	SCORES				TOTAL	MONEY
Bobby Wadkins	76	75	73	78	302	4,225
Juan Quiros	77	74	75	77	303	4,000
Robert Thompson	73	76	77	77	303	4,000
Masahiro Kuramoto	73	68	80	82	303	4,000
Wayne Levi	73	76	82	73	304	3,875
Dave Eichelberger	77	74	79	74	304	3,875
Jim Chancey	76	71	82	75	304	3,875
Mark James	79	73	76	76	304	3,875
Gary Robison	75	73	79	77	304	3,875
Walter Hall	73	78	80	74	305	3,763
Rod Spittle	76	74	79	76	305	3,763
David Lundstrom	78	74	77	76	305	3,763
Mike Reid	78	74	77	76	305	3,763
Hajime Meshiai	78	74	80	74	306	3,638
Jim Thorpe	74	77	79	76	306	3,638
Tom Wargo	76	76	78	76	306	3,638
Rick Karbowski	77	72	78	79	306	3,638
Costantino Rocca	75	76	76	79	306	3,638
Darrell Kestner	76	70	79	81	306	3,638
Freddy Gibson	77	75	82	75	309	3,500
Bill Longmuir	76	74	82	77	309	3,500
Roy Vucinich	78	72	82	77	309	3,500
Mike Barge	72	80	80	77	309	3,500
Gordon J. Brand	73	77	79	80	309	3,500
Danny Edwards	77	72	85	77	311	3,425
Bill Loeffler	76	76	85	76	313	3,400
Scott Spence	74	78	82	82	316	3,375

Principal Charity Classic

Glen Oaks Country Club, West Des Moines, Iowa
Par 35-36–71; 6,877 yards

May 30-June 1
purse, $1,725,000

	SCORES			TOTAL	MONEY
Jay Haas	70	68	65	203	$258,750
Andy Bean	69	68	67	204	151,800
Nick Price	70	66	69	205	124,200
Joey Sindelar	67	71	68	206	103,500
John Cook	69	70	68	207	57,664.29
John Morse	69	71	67	207	57,664.29
Loren Roberts	68	72	67	207	57,664.29
Ron Streck	70	70	67	207	57,664.29
Kirk Hanefeld	67	70	70	207	57,664.28
Tom Purtzer	67	71	69	207	57,664.28
Bobby Wadkins	70	67	70	207	57,664.28
David Eger	69	68	71	208	34,068.75
Tom McKnight	71	68	69	208	34,068.75
Eduardo Romero	70	70	68	208	34,068.75
Boonchu Ruangkit	70	70	68	208	34,068.75
Jim Colbert	71	70	68	209	25,213.75
Keith Fergus	69	70	70	209	25,213.75
Mike Hulbert	69	69	71	209	25,213.75
Clarence Rose	68	73	68	209	25,213.75
Scott Simpson	70	70	69	209	25,213.75
D.A. Weibring	74	67	68	209	25,213.75
Bob Gilder	73	66	71	210	16,969.69
Mike Goodes	70	71	69	210	16,969.69
Donnie Hammond	69	70	71	210	16,969.69
Hale Irwin	70	71	69	210	16,969.69
Mike McCullough	71	71	68	210	16,969.69

	SCORES			TOTAL	MONEY
Don Pooley	71	71	68	210	16,969.69
James Mason	71	68	71	210	16,969.68
Lonnie Nielsen	66	71	73	210	16,969.68
Fulton Allem	72	73	66	211	12,190
Brad Bryant	71	70	70	211	12,190
John Harris	75	68	68	211	12,190
Mark James	73	70	68	211	12,190
Tom Kite	73	68	70	211	12,190
Mark O'Meara	72	66	73	211	12,190

Bank of America Championship

Nashawtuc Country Club, Concord, Massachusetts
Par 36-36–72; 6,741 yards

June 20-22
purse, $1,650,000

	SCORES			TOTAL	MONEY
Jeff Sluman	68	67	64	199	$247,500
Loren Roberts	68	66	67	201	145,200
Mark McNulty	65	70	70	205	108,900
Dana Quigley	69	68	68	205	108,900
John Cook	70	68	68	206	79,200
Keith Fergus	71	66	70	207	66,000
Chip Beck	70	69	69	208	50,325
John Morse	67	70	71	208	50,325
Lonnie Nielsen	73	69	66	208	50,325
Bobby Wadkins	69	67	72	208	50,325
Wayne Grady	71	68	70	209	33,990
Tom Jenkins	69	69	71	209	33,990
Scott Simpson	68	72	69	209	33,990
Bruce Summerhays	70	69	70	209	33,990
Mark Wiebe	70	67	72	209	33,990
Gary Hallberg	70	72	68	210	25,616.25
Don Pooley	69	70	71	210	25,616.25
Tom Purtzer	72	69	69	210	25,616.25
Ron Streck	71	68	71	210	25,616.25
Phil Blackmar	68	73	70	211	18,892.50
R.W. Eaks	69	72	70	211	18,892.50
David Eger	65	72	74	211	18,892.50
Kirk Hanefeld	71	69	71	211	18,892.50
Tom Kite	63	72	76	211	18,892.50
Joey Sindelar	70	68	73	211	18,892.50
Hale Irwin	68	72	72	212	14,025
Masahiro Kuramoto	68	69	75	212	14,025
Tom McKnight	69	72	71	212	14,025
Mike Reid	68	71	73	212	14,025
Tim Simpson	73	71	68	212	14,025
D.A. Weibring	73	68	71	212	14,025

Commerce Bank Championship

Eisenhower Park, Red Course, East Meadow, New York
Par 36-35–71; 6,904 yards

June 27-29
purse, $1,600,000

	SCORES			TOTAL	MONEY
Loren Roberts	65	68	68	201	$240,000
Lonnie Nielsen	67	69	66	202	128,000
Nick Price	68	69	65	202	128,000

	SCORES			TOTAL	MONEY
Gene Jones	66	70	67	203	86,400
Jeff Sluman	70	67	66	203	86,400
Mike Goodes	68	68	68	204	57,600
Scott Simpson	68	67	69	204	57,600
Tim Simpson	68	69	67	204	57,600
Fulton Allem	69	67	69	205	40,000
Andy Bean	68	69	68	205	40,000
David Eger	69	66	70	205	40,000
Mark McNulty	67	69	69	205	40,000
Keith Fergus	67	70	69	206	32,000
Joe Ozaki	71	69	67	207	25,668.58
Bruce Fleisher	70	69	68	207	25,668.57
Morris Hatalsky	71	67	69	207	25,668.57
Scott Hoch	71	71	65	207	25,668.57
Masahiro Kuramoto	69	70	68	207	25,668.57
Bruce Vaughan	71	68	68	207	25,668.57
Mark Wiebe	72	68	67	207	25,668.57
John Cook	69	73	66	208	17,760
Bob Gilder	69	68	71	208	17,760
Walter Hall	69	70	69	208	17,760
Dana Quigley	68	69	71	208	17,760
Eduardo Romero	67	71	70	208	17,760
Phil Blackmar	74	69	66	209	14,560
Leonard Thompson	71	73	65	209	14,560
Denis Watson	69	67	73	209	14,560
Chip Beck	69	71	70	210	10,864
Brad Bryant	67	72	71	210	10,864
Jim Chancey	70	67	73	210	10,864
R.W. Eaks	70	69	71	210	10,864
David Edwards	69	72	69	210	10,864
Greg Hickman	66	71	73	210	10,864
Tom Kite	73	65	72	210	10,864
Wayne Levi	73	69	68	210	10,864
Gil Morgan	70	69	71	210	10,864
D.A. Weibring	71	68	71	210	10,864

Dick's Sporting Goods Open

En-Joie Golf Course, Endicott, New York
Par 37-35–72; 6,974 yards

July 4-6
purse, $1,600,000

	SCORES			TOTAL	MONEY
Eduardo Romero	65	65	69	199	$240,000
Fulton Allem	66	65	69	200	128,000
Gary Koch	68	67	65	200	128,000
Joey Sindelar	66	65	71	202	96,000
Joe Ozaki	63	70	70	203	70,400
Bruce Vaughan	67	67	69	203	70,400
Ronnie Black	66	68	70	204	51,200
Bob Gilder	71	67	66	204	51,200
Morris Hatalsky	67	68	69	204	51,200
Phil Blackmar	68	68	69	205	32,400
Keith Fergus	68	71	66	205	32,400
Gary Hallberg	69	72	64	205	32,400
John Harris	67	74	64	205	32,400
Mark McNulty	69	71	65	205	32,400
Bobby Wadkins	67	68	70	205	32,400
Mark Wiebe	69	66	70	205	32,400
Fuzzy Zoeller	71	69	65	205	32,400
Gene Jones	68	68	70	206	23,280

	SCORES			TOTAL	MONEY
Masahiro Kuramoto	72	63	71	206	23,280
Andy Bean	69	66	72	207	18,784
Brad Bryant	69	69	69	207	18,784
Jim Chancey	73	65	69	207	18,784
Mark James	68	73	66	207	18,784
Wayne Levi	70	71	66	207	18,784
Scott Simpson	71	69	68	208	16,000
Mike Goodes	72	70	67	209	13,600
Wayne Grady	69	68	72	209	13,600
Bernhard Langer	73	72	64	209	13,600
Lonnie Nielsen	70	71	68	209	13,600
Craig Stadler	68	70	71	209	13,600
Denis Watson	74	68	67	209	13,600

3M Championship

TPC Twin Cities, Blaine, Minnesota　　　　　　　　　　　　　　July 18-20
Par 36-36–72; 7,100 yards　　　　　　　　　　　　　　purse, $1,750,000

	SCORES			TOTAL	MONEY
R.W. Eaks	65	63	65	193	$262,500
Gary Hallberg	66	68	65	199	140,000
Bernhard Langer	67	66	66	199	140,000
Gene Jones	64	67	69	200	105,000
Ron Streck	70	64	67	201	84,000
Mike Goodes	69	67	66	202	63,000
Tom Kite	68	69	65	202	63,000
Rod Spittle	71	66	65	202	63,000
Dana Quigley	62	70	71	203	45,500
Loren Roberts	66	65	72	203	45,500
Jeff Sluman	65	71	67	203	45,500
Hale Irwin	68	66	70	204	38,500
Peter Jacobsen	67	68	70	205	34,125
D.A. Weibring	68	69	68	205	34,125
Morris Hatalsky	72	67	67	206	24,947.23
Gary Koch	69	73	64	206	24,947.23
Ronnie Black	70	69	67	206	24,947.22
David Edwards	69	66	71	206	24,947.22
Lonnie Nielsen	68	66	72	206	24,947.22
Joe Ozaki	70	68	68	206	24,947.22
Tim Simpson	69	66	71	206	24,947.22
Joey Sindelar	68	69	69	206	24,947.22
Bruce Vaughan	68	67	71	206	24,947.22
Keith Fergus	68	68	71	207	16,362.50
Scott Hoch	69	66	72	207	16,362.50
Gil Morgan	70	68	69	207	16,362.50
Tom Purtzer	68	70	69	207	16,362.50
Mike Reid	69	70	68	207	16,362.50
Fuzzy Zoeller	69	69	69	207	16,362.50
Phil Blackmar	68	72	68	208	12,366.67
Tim Conley	69	72	67	208	12,366.67
John Cook	68	72	68	208	12,366.67
Mike McCullough	68	73	67	208	12,366.67
Steve Thomas	69	69	70	208	12,366.66
Jim Thorpe	71	69	68	208	12,366.66

The Senior Open Championship

See European Seniors Tour section.

U.S. Senior Open

The Broadmoor Resort, Colorado Springs, Colorado
Par 35-35–70; 7,254 yards

July 31-August 3
purse, $2,600,000

	SCORES				TOTAL	MONEY
Eduardo Romero	67	69	65	73	274	$470,000
Fred Funk	65	69	69	75	278	280,000
Mark McNulty	68	70	73	68	279	177,650
Greg Norman	70	72	68	70	280	123,794
John Cook	66	72	66	77	281	100,238
Bernhard Langer	72	70	74	66	282	80,895
David Edwards	72	70	73	67	282	80,895
Joey Sindelar	73	72	68	69	282	80,895
Scott Hoch	76	70	68	69	283	62,814
Jay Haas	72	70	70	71	283	62,814
Jeff Klein	73	73	64	73	283	62,814
Loren Roberts	74	72	71	67	284	53,109
Tom Kite	67	71	71	75	284	53,109
Gary Hallberg	69	76	70	70	285	44,779
Brad Bryant	70	71	73	71	285	44,779
Andy Bean	69	71	73	72	285	44,779
Keith Fergus	73	71	66	75	285	44,779
Jeff Sluman	72	76	71	67	286	34,773
Tom Purtzer	70	74	72	70	286	34,773
Don Pooley	70	74	71	71	286	34,773
R.W. Eaks	72	73	69	72	286	34,773
Morris Hatalsky	67	73	72	74	286	34,773
Gil Morgan	71	77	69	70	287	26,493
Ian Woosnam	74	68	71	74	287	26,493
Tom Watson	69	74	69	75	287	26,493
Scott Simpson	74	73	64	76	287	26,493
David Eger	73	74	72	69	288	21,660
Juan Quiros	67	73	70	78	288	21,660
Jim Thorpe	74	72	74	69	289	18,593
John Harris	72	75	71	71	289	18,593
Mark James	72	71	72	74	289	18,593
Joe Ozaki	74	74	75	67	290	17,209
Mike Reid	76	72	66	76	290	17,209
Doug Lacrosse	70	75	72	74	291	15,917
John Morse	69	71	74	77	291	15,917
D.A. Weibring	71	69	72	79	291	15,917
Lonnie Nielsen	74	72	75	71	292	14,626
*Danny Green	72	72	76	72	292	
Bobby Wadkins	69	78	73	72	292	14,626
Tom Carey	71	71	77	74	293	12,575
Jeff Coston	73	74	72	74	293	12,575
Katsuyoshi Tomori	72	76	71	74	293	12,575
Billy Rosinia	71	73	73	76	293	12,575
Hale Irwin	74	71	72	76	293	12,575
Rod Nuckolls	74	72	71	76	293	12,575
*Rick Cloninger	68	74	72	79	293	
Costantino Rocca	74	72	74	74	294	10,527
Gary Ostrega	71	77	72	74	294	10,527
Fuzzy Zoeller	72	75	77	71	295	9,245
Rick Karbowski	70	74	77	74	295	9,245
Jim Woodward	73	75	73	74	295	9,245
Denis Watson	76	72	73	75	296	8,221

	SCORES				TOTAL	MONEY
*Bert Atkinson	72	75	73	76	296	
Jeff Thomsen	74	73	76	74	297	7,800
Craig Steinberg	74	73	76	74	297	7,800
Tom Jenkins	75	73	72	77	297	7,800
Bob Gilder	71	76	74	77	298	7,413
Steve Bowen	75	71	78	75	299	7,227
*Tom Doughtie	72	73	76	80	301	
*Stan Lee	75	72	81	75	303	
*Bob Stephens	71	76	80	77	304	

JELD-WEN Tradition

Crosswater Club at Sunriver Resort, Sunriver, Oregon   August 14-17
Par 36-36–72; 7,683 yards   purse, $2,600,000

	SCORES				TOTAL	MONEY
Fred Funk	69	66	65	69	269	$392,000
Mike Goodes	68	67	69	68	272	231,000
Jay Haas	67	68	66	73	274	174,000
Tom Watson	72	64	68	70	274	174,000
Scott Hoch	72	66	66	71	275	126,600
Scott Simpson	73	66	67	70	276	106,000
Tom Jenkins	71	68	70	68	277	70,600
Gene Jones	67	70	70	70	277	70,600
Bernhard Langer	68	66	72	71	277	70,600
Lonnie Nielsen	70	71	66	70	277	70,600
Loren Roberts	70	69	69	69	277	70,600
D.A. Weibring	68	72	70	67	277	70,600
Fuzzy Zoeller	74	66	69	68	277	70,600
John Cook	69	72	67	70	278	45,500
David Eger	67	71	73	67	278	45,500
Bob Gilder	71	68	70	69	278	45,500
Joe Ozaki	68	72	64	74	278	45,500
John Harris	73	72	68	67	280	32,611.43
Tom Kite	72	70	68	70	280	32,611.43
Eduardo Romero	74	65	71	70	280	32,611.43
Jim Thorpe	69	71	69	71	280	32,611.43
Bobby Wadkins	71	67	72	70	280	32,611.43
Mark Wiebe	67	70	73	70	280	32,611.43
Tim Simpson	67	67	69	77	280	32,611.42
Brad Bryant	71	73	67	70	281	24,245
R.W. Eaks	68	73	71	69	281	24,245
Mark McNulty	67	72	72	70	281	24,245
Tom Purtzer	71	70	69	71	281	24,245
Gary Hallberg	74	67	72	69	282	21,060
Masahiro Kuramoto	68	71	74	69	282	21,060
Keith Fergus	73	72	70	68	283	17,160
Bruce Fleisher	71	72	69	71	283	17,160
Gil Morgan	70	71	71	71	283	17,160
Mark O'Meara	71	75	65	72	283	17,160
Dana Quigley	72	70	71	70	283	17,160
Joey Sindelar	70	76	69	68	283	17,160
Jeff Sluman	72	73	70	68	283	17,160
Morris Hatalsky	71	71	71	71	284	14,300
Dan Forsman	74	69	70	72	285	13,520
Walter Hall	69	70	74	72	285	13,520
Hale Irwin	68	69	72	77	286	11,700
Gary Koch	75	71	71	69	286	11,700
Mike Reid	74	70	68	74	286	11,700
Craig Stadler	67	74	71	74	286	11,700

	SCORES			TOTAL	MONEY
Bruce Vaughan	71 70 74	71		286	11,700
Don Pooley	70 71 73	73		287	10,140
Des Smyth	71 73 75	69		288	9,620
Andy Bean	72 72 72	73		289	8,580
Ed Dougherty	75 71 71	72		289	8,580
Bruce Lietzke	72 73 69	75		289	8,580
Sandy Lyle	73 74 74	69		290	7,540
Ben Crenshaw	74 78 70	69		291	6,586.67
Denis Watson	69 76 74	72		291	6,586.67
Allen Doyle	69 72 73	77		291	6,586.66
David Edwards	72 75 69	76		292	5,720
Dave Eichelberger	77 75 69	71		292	5,720
Tom McKnight	77 71 73	71		292	5,720
Vicente Fernandez	74 69 72	78		293	5,200
Chip Beck	69 78 76	71		294	4,810
Graham Marsh	72 73 73	76		294	4,810
Ron Streck	73 72 74	76		295	4,420
Mike McCullough	74 75 70	77		296	4,160
Pete Oakley	78 72 75	75		300	3,900
Jim Colbert	72 73 77	79		301	3,640
Wayne Grady	75 75 73	80		303	3,250
Leonard Thompson	76 76 77	74		303	3,250
Wayne Levi	76 76 79	73		304	2,860

Boeing Classic

TPC Snoqualmie Ridge, Snoqualmie, Washington   August 22-24
Par 36-36–72; 7,264 yards   purse, $1,700,000

	SCORES		TOTAL	MONEY
Tom Kite	69 67 66		202	$255,000
Scott Simpson	67 66 71		204	149,600
John Cook	72 66 67		205	122,400
Mark Wiebe	67 69 70		206	102,000
Lonnie Nielsen	73 66 68		207	74,800
Denis Watson	74 67 66		207	74,800
David Edwards	68 67 73		208	49,640
Bruce Fleisher	69 68 71		208	49,640
Walter Hall	70 69 69		208	49,640
Mark McNulty	70 68 70		208	49,640
Nick Price	70 71 67		208	49,640
Dan Forsman	72 73 64		209	35,700
Bruce Vaughan	72 66 71		209	35,700
Ronnie Black	71 68 71		210	30,600
Brad Bryant	72 71 67		210	30,600
Ben Crenshaw	73 67 70		210	30,600
Keith Fergus	71 70 70		211	26,350
D.A. Weibring	73 68 70		211	26,350
Andy Bean	71 70 71		212	20,626.67
David Eger	70 72 70		212	20,626.67
Gary Hallberg	68 72 72		212	20,626.67
Mike Reid	72 70 70		212	20,626.67
R.W. Eaks	71 69 72		212	20,626.66
Tom Purtzer	73 68 71		212	20,626.66
Allen Doyle	72 70 71		213	15,504
Wayne Grady	72 70 71		213	15,504
Gene Jones	73 70 70		213	15,504
James Mason	69 69 75		213	15,504
Fuzzy Zoeller	71 71 71		213	15,504
Fred Funk	77 71 66		214	13,090
Joe Ozaki	74 69 71		214	13,090

Wal-Mart First Tee Open

Pebble Beach Golf Links: Par 35-37–72; 6,822 yards
Del Monte Golf Course: Par 36-36–72; 6,357 yards
Monterey Peninsula, California

August 29-31
purse, $2,100,000

	SCORES			TOTAL	MONEY
Jeff Sluman	69	66	67	202	$315,000
Craig Stadler	70	66	71	207	168,000
Fuzzy Zoeller	66	72	69	207	168,000
Chip Beck	66	74	68	208	96,600
Phil Blackmar	67	68	73	208	96,600
Fred Funk	67	70	71	208	96,600
Mark McNulty	68	71	69	208	96,600
David Eger	70	68	71	209	60,200
Scott Simpson	69	72	68	209	60,200
Steve Thomas	67	70	72	209	60,200
Allen Doyle	69	69	72	210	46,200
Sandy Lyle	71	71	68	210	46,200
Bruce Vaughan	70	69	71	210	46,200
Ronnie Black	71	70	70	211	34,685
Tom Kite	68	70	73	211	34,685
Nick Price	69	72	70	211	34,685
Mike Reid	69	73	69	211	34,685
Loren Roberts	66	69	76	211	34,685
Mark Wiebe	70	72	69	211	34,685
Dan Forsman	75	69	68	212	27,720
Ben Crenshaw	70	69	74	213	23,887.50
Gil Morgan	76	66	71	213	23,887.50
Lonnie Nielsen	74	71	68	213	23,887.50
Jeff Roth	70	71	72	213	23,887.50
Jay Haas	68	71	75	214	19,152
John Harris	69	66	79	214	19,152
Dick Mast	70	70	74	214	19,152
Joey Sindelar	68	77	69	214	19,152
Jim Thorpe	70	71	73	214	19,152
Gary Hallberg	71	70	74	215	14,201.25
Hale Irwin	66	73	76	215	14,201.25
Barry Jaeckel	71	74	70	215	14,201.25
Tom Jenkins	71	71	73	215	14,201.25
Gene Jones	71	71	73	215	14,201.25
Tom Purtzer	73	67	75	215	14,201.25
Tom Watson	71	72	72	215	14,201.25
Jim Woodward	72	72	71	215	14,201.25
R.W. Eaks					

Greater Hickory Classic

Rock Barn Golf & Spa, Conover, North Carolina
Par 35-37–72; 7,046 yards

September 12-14
purse, $1,700,000

	SCORES			TOTAL	MONEY
R.W. Eaks	61	68	71	200	$255,000
Tom Jenkins	64	65	75	204	136,000
Tom Kite	66	71	67	204	136,000
Tom McKnight	66	69	70	205	83,866.67
Mark Wiebe	67	67	71	205	83,866.67
Mark McNulty	67	69	69	205	83,866.66
Bob Gilder	69	68	69	206	54,400
Gil Morgan	67	66	73	206	54,400

	SCORES			TOTAL	MONEY
Bruce Vaughan	66	70	70	206	54,400
Fred Funk	65	71	71	207	40,800
Jay Haas	68	69	70	207	40,800
Gene Jones	68	68	71	207	40,800
Bruce Fleisher	70	68	70	208	33,150
Dan Forsman	66	71	71	208	33,150
Kirk Hanefeld	69	70	70	209	28,900
Lonnie Nielsen	69	71	69	209	28,900
Loren Roberts	71	69	69	209	28,900
Brad Bryant	68	73	69	210	22,542
David Edwards	68	73	69	210	22,542
Dave Eichelberger	70	72	68	210	22,542
Larry Nelson	68	75	67	210	22,542
Dana Quigley	70	71	69	210	22,542
Danny Edwards	71	70	70	211	18,275
Keith Fergus	69	69	73	211	18,275
Andy Bean	73	67	72	212	15,158.34
Mark Johnson	68	76	68	212	15,158.34
Mark James	68	71	73	212	15,158.33
Pat Laverty	71	69	72	212	15,158.33
Nick Price	73	67	72	212	15,158.33
D.A. Weibring	69	69	74	212	15,158.33

SAS Championship

Prestonwood Country Club, Cary, North Carolina
Par 36-36–72; 7,137 yards

September 26-28
purse, $2,100,000

	SCORES			TOTAL	MONEY
Eduardo Romero	68	67	66	201	$315,000
Tom Kite	69	66	69	204	184,800
Andy Bean	68	70	67	205	138,600
Gil Morgan	70	68	67	205	138,600
Bruce Fleisher	68	66	72	206	92,400
Jim Thorpe	70	69	67	206	92,400
Brad Bryant	72	69	66	207	67,200
John Cook	70	66	71	207	67,200
Mark McNulty	73	63	71	207	67,200
Fred Funk	74	66	68	208	46,620
Morris Hatalsky	75	65	68	208	46,620
Scott Hoch	71	66	71	208	46,620
Don Pooley	68	69	71	208	46,620
D.A. Weibring	75	63	70	208	46,620
Nick Price	72	66	71	209	36,750
Jeff Sluman	71	71	67	209	36,750
Phil Blackmar	71	69	70	210	28,805
David Eger	71	70	69	210	28,805
Bob Gilder	73	66	71	210	28,805
Jay Haas	75	67	68	210	28,805
Joe Ozaki	71	67	72	210	28,805
Mark Wiebe	72	72	66	210	28,805
Chip Beck	68	69	74	211	21,525
R.W. Eaks	73	67	71	211	21,525
Tom McKnight	70	69	72	211	21,525
Loren Roberts	69	73	69	211	21,525
Mitch Adams	72	70	70	212	17,045
Fulton Allem	74	68	70	212	17,045
Gary Hallberg	75	70	67	212	17,045
Gene Jones	73	68	71	212	17,045
Larry Mize	70	71	71	212	17,045
Dana Quigley	68	71	73	212	17,045

Constellation Energy Senior Players Championship

Baltimore Country Club, Timonium, Maryland   October 9-12
Par 35-35–70; 7,037 yards   purse, $2,600,000

	SCORES				TOTAL	MONEY
D.A. Weibring	67	70	66	68	271	$390,000
Fred Funk	66	68	72	66	272	228,800
Ben Crenshaw	67	66	74	66	273	156,000
Nick Price	70	66	66	71	273	156,000
Jeff Sluman	70	70	64	69	273	156,000
Jay Haas	67	70	69	68	274	104,000
Brad Bryant	70	71	67	67	275	79,300
John Cook	69	69	70	67	275	79,300
Bernhard Langer	66	70	71	68	275	79,300
Eduardo Romero	66	72	67	70	275	79,300
Andy Bean	68	69	71	68	276	59,800
Tom Jenkins	67	68	71	70	276	59,800
Gil Morgan	69	70	71	67	277	49,400
Lonnie Nielsen	70	68	70	69	277	49,400
Dana Quigley	71	68	70	68	277	49,400
Mike Goodes	69	70	68	71	278	42,900
Scott Hoch	66	71	72	69	278	42,900
Fulton Allem	69	70	70	70	279	36,660
Joe Ozaki	69	70	67	73	279	36,660
Bobby Wadkins	70	70	71	68	279	36,660
Bob Gilder	70	68	71	71	280	28,166.67
Loren Roberts	68	71	72	69	280	28,166.67
Scott Simpson	70	67	72	71	280	28,166.67
Joey Sindelar	68	73	69	70	280	28,166.67
Gene Jones	69	66	69	76	280	28,166.66
Tom Kite	71	69	68	72	280	28,166.66
Bruce Fleisher	65	75	67	74	281	21,580
Hale Irwin	72	71	68	70	281	21,580
Larry Mize	70	72	71	68	281	21,580
Don Pooley	71	73	70	67	281	21,580
Denis Watson	67	71	71	72	281	21,580
Walter Hall	71	69	75	67	282	16,417.15
Mike Hulbert	72	71	70	69	282	16,417.15
David Eger	72	70	69	71	282	16,417.14
Mark James	74	70	68	70	282	16,417.14
Tom McKnight	67	73	71	71	282	16,417.14
Mark O'Meara	69	67	72	74	282	16,417.14
Rod Spittle	69	70	69	74	282	16,417.14
Ronnie Black	71	70	66	76	283	13,520
Larry Nelson	70	70	74	69	283	13,520
Kirk Hanefeld	69	72	72	71	284	12,480
Des Smyth	65	75	72	72	284	12,480
Wayne Levi	70	72	71	72	285	10,920
Tom Purtzer	71	71	74	69	285	10,920
Leonard Thompson	73	72	69	71	285	10,920
Mark Wiebe	74	72	71	68	285	10,920
Chip Beck	71	71	75	69	286	8,580
Phil Blackmar	65	73	75	73	286	8,580
Keith Fergus	73	69	78	66	286	8,580
Morris Hatalsky	76	67	68	75	286	8,580
Jim Thorpe	67	75	73	71	286	8,580
Masahiro Kuramoto	74	70	74	69	287	6,017.15
Gary McCord	70	73	71	73	287	6,017.15
David Edwards	70	72	72	73	287	6,017.14
Dave Eichelberger	68	74	72	73	287	6,017.14
Mark McNulty	69	69	73	76	287	6,017.14
John Morse	68	68	76	75	287	6,017.14

	SCORES				TOTAL	MONEY
Ron Streck	72	73	69	73	287	6,017.14
Allen Doyle	71	73	74	71	289	4,290
Vicente Fernandez	74	71	70	74	289	4,290
Donnie Hammond	75	70	74	70	289	4,290
Gary Koch	71	71	74	73	289	4,290
Mike McCullough	75	74	70	70	289	4,290
Boonchu Ruangkit	75	72	74	68	289	4,290
R.W. Eaks	70	71	73	76	290	2,782
Wayne Grady	75	74	72	69	290	2,782
Sandy Lyle	76	71	74	69	290	2,782
James Mason	71	72	74	73	290	2,782
Mike Reid	75	71	72	72	290	2,782
Fuzzy Zoeller	70	75	73	72	290	2,782
Bruce Lietzke	73	72	71	76	292	2,132
John Harris	73	75	74	71	293	1,976
Gary Hallberg	73	76	70	75	294	1,820
Tim Simpson	76	76	69	74	295	1,716
Danny Edwards	72	77	73	75	297	1,612
Bruce Vaughan	73	81	72	73	299	1,508
Mitch Adcock	78	74	76	76	304	1,404
Craig Stadler	72				WD	

Administaff Small Business Classic

The Woodlands Country Club, The Woodlands, Texas
Par 36-36–72; 7,018 yards

October 17-19
purse, $1,700,000

	SCORES			TOTAL	MONEY
Bernhard Langer	68	67	69	204	$255,000
Lonnie Nielsen	67	68	71	206	149,600
Fred Funk	72	66	69	207	122,400
Dave Stockton	69	69	70	208	91,800
Denis Watson	70	66	72	208	91,800
Andy Bean	65	72	72	209	52,700
Bob Gilder	69	71	69	209	52,700
Jay Haas	66	72	71	209	52,700
Nick Price	70	68	71	209	52,700
Loren Roberts	69	71	69	209	52,700
Tim Simpson	71	68	70	209	52,700
Jeff Sluman	70	72	68	210	37,400
Gene Jones	71	69	71	211	28,924.29
Bruce Lietzke	71	72	68	211	28,924.29
Tom Purtzer	71	70	70	211	28,924.29
Joey Sindelar	66	74	71	211	28,924.29
David Eger	68	70	73	211	28,924.28
Larry Mize	70	68	73	211	28,924.28
Curtis Strange	71	67	73	211	28,924.28
Brad Bryant	67	68	77	212	21,080
Vicente Fernandez	69	72	71	212	21,080
Dan Forsman	69	68	75	212	21,080
Phil Blackmar	74	67	72	213	14,620
Walter Hall	74	70	69	213	14,620
Morris Hatalsky	73	66	74	213	14,620
Scott Hoch	73	67	73	213	14,620
Mark James	71	70	72	213	14,620
Gary Koch	70	68	75	213	14,620
Sandy Lyle	67	71	75	213	14,620
Tom McKnight	70	70	73	213	14,620
Joe Ozaki	70	71	72	213	14,620
Hal Sutton	71	70	72	213	14,620

	SCORES			TOTAL	MONEY
Bobby Wadkins	72	70	71	213	14,620
D.A. Weibring	71	73	69	213	14,620

AT&T Championship

Oak Hills Country Club, San Antonio, Texas
Par 35-36–71; 6,670 yards

October 24-26
purse, $1,650,000

	SCORES			TOTAL	MONEY
John Cook	69	63	65	197	$247,500
Keith Fergus	65	70	65	200	145,200
Jay Haas	67	68	66	201	108,900
John Morse	68	70	63	201	108,900
Bruce Fleisher	68	65	69	202	68,200
Mark James	63	69	70	202	68,200
Jeff Sluman	67	64	71	202	68,200
Dan Forsman	64	69	71	204	45,375
Gene Jones	66	69	69	204	45,375
Scott Simpson	69	67	68	204	45,375
Joey Sindelar	72	69	63	204	45,375
Tom McKnight	69	69	67	205	32,587.50
Lonnie Nielsen	69	68	68	205	32,587.50
Mike Reid	69	69	67	205	32,587.50
Bruce Vaughan	67	70	68	205	32,587.50
Fulton Allem	69	69	68	206	25,616.25
Tom Jenkins	68	69	69	206	25,616.25
Mark McNulty	68	69	69	206	25,616.25
D.A. Weibring	72	67	67	206	25,616.25
Andy Bean	68	69	70	207	17,209.50
David Eger	69	69	69	207	17,209.50
Vicente Fernandez	70	69	68	207	17,209.50
Mike Goodes	70	67	70	207	17,209.50
Gary Hallberg	73	64	70	207	17,209.50
Hale Irwin	72	67	68	207	17,209.50
Larry Mize	68	67	72	207	17,209.50
Larry Nelson	68	70	69	207	17,209.50
Tom Purtzer	67	66	74	207	17,209.50
Jim Thorpe	70	63	74	207	17,209.50
Chip Beck	72	70	66	208	11,660
Bob Gilder	74	68	66	208	11,660
Scott Hoch	70	69	69	208	11,660
Gil Morgan	67	73	68	208	11,660
Loren Roberts	68	68	72	208	11,660
Dave Stockton	66	70	72	208	11,660

Charles Schwab Cup Championship

Sonoma Golf Club, Sonoma, California
Par 36-36–72; 7,111 yards

October 30-November 2
purse, $2,500,000

	SCORES				TOTAL	MONEY
Andy Bean	68	66	68	66	268	$442,000
Gene Jones	69	67	70	71	277	255,000
Brad Bryant	69	68	72	69	278	214,000
Loren Roberts	69	68	72	70	279	177,000
Jeff Sluman	70	70	70	70	280	103,167
Mark McNulty	69	73	71	67	280	103,167

	SCORES				TOTAL	MONEY
D.A. Weibring	70	68	75	67	280	103,167
David Eger	66	71	72	71	280	103,167
Tom Jenkins	72	64	73	71	280	103,167
Nick Price	66	69	71	74	280	103,167
Denis Watson	73	68	73	67	281	68,000
Scott Hoch	70	66	74	71	281	68,000
John Cook	70	68	71	73	282	59,500
Tom Kite	68	70	74	71	283	54,500
Scott Simpson	73	71	69	70	283	54,500
Mike Goodes	67	71	75	71	284	48,500
Jay Haas	69	69	74	72	284	48,500
Bob Gilder	69	71	75	70	285	42,500
Bernhard Langer	71	72	72	70	285	42,500
Bruce Vaughan	69	70	74	73	286	39,000
Lonnie Nielsen	70	70	76	71	287	34,000
Mark Wiebe	71	68	76	72	287	34,000
Joey Sindelar	69	72	75	71	287	34,000
Eduardo Romero	69	74	71	73	287	34,000
Tim Simpson	70	73	72	73	288	28,000
Fred Funk	74	71	72	71	288	28,000
Craig Stadler	73	73	75	69	290	26,000
Keith Fergus	73	71	76	76	296	25,000
R.W. Eaks	71	73	77	77	298	24,500

European Senior Tour

DGM Barbados Open

Royal Westmoreland Resort, St. James, Barbados
Par 36-36–72; 6,854 yards

March 5-7
purse, €181,076

	SCORES			TOTAL	MONEY
Bill Longmuir	74	67	65	206	€28,435.27
Bob Cameron	71	67	71	209	18,956.85
Nick Job	73	69	68	210	13,269.80
Delroy Cambridge	68	70	73	211	10,426.27
Ian Woosnam	72	69	71	212	8,568.49
Giuseppe Cali	70	71	73	214	7,582.74
Denis O'Sullivan	75	70	70	215	6,445.33
Juan Quiros	72	75	68	215	6,445.33
Graham Banister	69	74	73	216	5,118.35
Ross Drummond	71	74	71	216	5,118.35
Horacio Carbonetti	72	73	72	217	4,028.33
John Chillas	74	72	71	217	4,028.33
Guillermo Encina	73	70	74	217	4,028.33
Jose Rivero	76	73	68	217	4,028.33
Jerry Bruner	69	73	76	218	3,412.23
Bob Boyd	72	72	75	219	3,127.88
Pete Oakley	71	71	77	219	3,127.88

	SCORES			TOTAL	MONEY
Doug Johnson	76	69	75	220	2,843.53
Gordon J. Brand	76	75	70	221	2,508.62
Bill Hardwick	76	73	72	221	2,508.62
Jimmy Heggarty	79	71	71	221	2,508.62

Azores Senior Open

Batalha Golf Course, Azores, Ponta Delgada, Portugal
Par 36-36–72; 6,925 yards

March 28-30
purse, €325,000

	SCORES			TOTAL	MONEY
Stewart Ginn	72	71	68	211	€48,750
Nick Job	73	69	71	213	32,500
Luis Carbonetti	71	72	72	215	18,438.33
Domingo Hospital	72	72	71	215	18,438.33
Costantino Rocca	73	73	69	215	18,438.33
Martin Gray	69	69	78	216	12,350
David Merriman	73	73	70	216	12,350
Bob Boyd	72	71	74	217	10,400
Mike Miller	75	73	70	218	8,450
Juan Quiros	71	74	73	218	8,450
Jose Rivero	72	74	72	218	8,450
David Good	74	73	72	219	6,825
Bob Larratt	77	76	66	219	6,825
Graham Banister	76	73	71	220	5,687.50
John Benda	75	75	70	220	5,687.50
Bob Cameron	76	72	72	220	5,687.50
Pete Oakley	74	75	71	220	5,687.50
Angel Fernandez	71	74	76	221	4,582.50
Chuck Milne	70	75	76	221	4,582.50
Kevin Spurgeon	73	74	74	221	4,582.50

Parkridge Polish Seniors Championship

Krakow Valley Golf & Country Club, Krakow, Poland
Par 36-36–72; 6,841 yards

May 30-June 1
purse, €280,000

	SCORES			TOTAL	MONEY
Ian Woosnam	71	68	63	202	€42,000
Domingo Hospital	69	70	64	203	28,000
Katsuyoshi Tomori	70	68	69	207	19,600
John Chillas	75	67	66	208	14,028
Philippe Dugeny	72	69	67	208	14,028
Bob Cameron	67	72	70	209	10,080
Luis Carbonetti	72	67	70	209	10,080
Jose Rivero	73	68	68	209	10,080
Gordon J. Brand	70	70	71	211	7,000
Stewart Ginn	70	72	69	211	7,000
Bobby Lincoln	74	67	70	211	7,000
Carl Mason	70	73	68	211	7,000
Eamonn Darcy	68	69	76	213	5,600
Bob Charles	70	71	73	214	4,900
Bruce Heuchan	75	67	72	214	4,900
Jean Pierre Sallat	76	68	70	214	4,900
Kevin Spurgeon	73	69	72	214	4,900
Maurice Bembridge	76	70	69	215	4,200
Delroy Cambridge	68	76	72	216	3,488.80

	SCORES			TOTAL	MONEY
Tony Johnstone	70	72	74	216	3,488.80
Jim Rhodes	70	74	72	216	3,488.80
Emilio Rodriguez	73	70	73	216	3,488.80
Gery Watine	70	73	73	216	3,488.80

Jersey Seniors Classic

La Moye Golf Club, Jersey, Channel Isles
Par 36-36–72; 6,652 yards

June 6-8
purse, €178,086

	SCORES			TOTAL	MONEY
Tony Johnstone	69	70	74	213	€26,712.84
Gordon J. Brand	69	75	71	215	12,029.68
Ross Drummond	72	71	72	215	12,029.68
Angel Franco	71	73	71	215	12,029.68
Bertus Smit	72	72	71	215	12,029.68
Denis O'Sullivan	70	73	73	216	7,123.42
Bobby Lincoln	72	73	72	217	6,054.91
Katsuyoshi Tomori	71	75	71	217	6,054.91
Mike Miller	73	74	72	219	4,808.31
Steve Stull	73	68	78	219	4,808.31
Jerry Bruner	72	75	73	220	3,561.71
David Good	72	72	76	220	3,561.71
Nick Job	75	74	71	220	3,561.71
Peter Mitchell	73	74	73	220	3,561.71
Pete Oakley	71	74	75	220	3,561.71
Alan Tapie	80	70	70	220	3,561.71
Bob Charles	76	76	69	221	2,677.22
Jean Pierre Sallat	73	72	76	221	2,677.22
Gery Watine	75	72	74	221	2,677.22
Jim Lapsley	75	75	72	222	2,350.73

Ryder Cup Wales Seniors Open

Conwy Golf Club, Conwy (Caernarvonshire), Wales
Par 35-37–72; 6,935 yards

June 13-15
purse, €625,995

	SCORES			TOTAL	MONEY
Peter Mitchell	72	70	71	213	€93,899.25
Ian Woosnam	74	68	73	215	62,599.50
Jerry Bruner	74	76	68	218	43,819.65
Gordon J. Brand	71	76	72	219	26,066.43
Martin Gray	75	74	70	219	26,066.43
Bill Longmuir	76	72	71	219	26,066.43
Simon Owen	76	72	71	219	26,066.43
Costantino Rocca	75	73	71	219	26,066.43
Bob Charles	74	75	71	220	16,901.86
David Merriman	70	77	73	220	16,901.86
Eamonn Darcy	74	75	72	221	13,771.89
Angel Franco	75	74	72	221	13,771.89
Sandy Lyle	69	76	76	221	13,771.89
Luis Carbonetti	76	73	73	222	10,641.91
Horacio Carbonetti	74	79	69	222	10,641.91
John Chillas	78	68	76	222	10,641.91
David J. Russell	77	73	72	222	10,641.91
Des Smyth	72	76	74	222	10,641.91
Delroy Cambridge	78	73	72	223	8,028.39

	SCORES			TOTAL	MONEY
Bob Cameron	75	72	76	223	8,028.39
Ross Drummond	79	71	73	223	8,028.39
Carl Mason	78	75	70	223	8,028.39

Irish Seniors Open

Ballyliffin Golf Club, Co. Donegal, Ireland
Par 35-36–71; 6,867 yards

June 20-22
purse, €450,000

	SCORES			TOTAL	MONEY
Juan Quiros	71	69	72	212	€67,500
Des Smyth	71	68	74	213	45,000
Gordon J. Brand	70	70	76	216	20,865
Giuseppe Cali	69	75	72	216	20,865
Luis Carbonetti	69	76	71	216	20,865
Nick Job	71	73	72	216	20,865
Simon Owen	71	73	72	216	20,865
David J. Russell	72	70	74	216	20,865
Bob Cameron	72	74	71	217	10,425
John Chillas	72	71	74	217	10,425
Guillermo Encina	75	71	71	217	10,425
Denis O'Sullivan	72	70	75	217	10,425
Sam Torrance	71	70	76	217	10,425
Ian Woosnam	76	67	74	217	10,425
Bob Charles	71	75	72	218	7,209
Ross Drummond	73	76	69	218	7,209
Terry Gale	75	71	72	218	7,209
Stewart Ginn	74	77	67	218	7,209
David Good	71	73	74	218	7,209
Tony Allen	74	74	71	219	5,422.50
Seiji Ebihara	75	75	69	219	5,422.50
Angel Fernandez	75	73	71	219	5,422.50
Manuel Pinero	71	74	74	219	5,422.50

Russian Seniors Open

Pestovo Golf & Yacht Club, Moscow, Russia
Par 36-36–72; 6,922 yards

July 4-6
purse, €476,219

	SCORES			TOTAL	MONEY
Ian Woosnam	67	67	70	204	€71,432.82
Angel Franco	70	69	68	207	47,621.88
Bill Longmuir	67	69	72	208	33,335.31
Jeff Hall	67	71	71	209	26,192.03
Pete Oakley	70	71	71	212	21,525.09
David Merriman	70	69	75	214	18,096.31
Jose Rivero	73	69	72	214	18,096.31
Bob Boyd	74	71	70	215	11,250.67
Jerry Bruner	71	68	76	215	11,250.67
Giuseppe Cali	72	71	72	215	11,250.67
John Mashego	71	70	74	215	11,250.67
Carl Mason	73	70	72	215	11,250.67
Denis O'Sullivan	71	70	74	215	11,250.67
Juan Quiros	73	71	71	215	11,250.67
Sam Torrance	73	64	78	215	11,250.67
Gordon J. Brand	72	69	75	216	7,619.50
Horacio Carbonetti	74	67	75	216	7,619.50

	SCORES			TOTAL	MONEY
Noel Ratcliffe	74	70	72	216	7,619.50
Luis Carbonetti	73	71	73	217	6,714.68
John Bland	73	71	74	218	5,452.70
John Chillas	70	75	73	218	5,452.70
Ross Drummond	73	70	75	218	5,452.70
Philippe Dugeny	72	69	77	218	5,452.70
Tony Johnstone	73	74	71	218	5,452.70
Costantino Rocca	73	73	72	218	5,452.70

The Senior Open Championship

Royal Troon Golf Club, Ayrshire, Scotland
Par 36-35–71; 7,064 yards

July 24-27
purse, €1,259,405

	SCORES				TOTAL	MONEY
Bruce Vaughan	68	71	69	70	278	€199,054.60
John Cook	69	71	67	71	278	132,766.14
(Vaughan defeated Cook on first playoff hole.)						
Eduardo Romero	68	73	68	70	279	74,740.08
Bernhard Langer	70	71	71	68	280	59,729
Gene Jones	70	76	68	68	282	42,745.86
Greg Norman	75	72	67	68	282	42,745.86
Tom Watson	70	71	71	70	282	42,745.86
Philip Blackmar	74	72	71	68	285	28,300.32
Costantino Rocca	73	73	72	67	285	28,300.32
Andy Bean	69	75	73	69	286	23,853.76
Gary Hallberg	76	69	73	69	287	21,223.66
Tony Johnstone	71	74	71	71	287	21,223.66
Gary Koch	76	76	70	66	288	18,341.28
Tim Simpson	75	75	71	67	288	18,341.28
Ian Woosnam	75	73	71	69	288	18,341.28
Ronnie Black	74	72	75	68	289	15,515.66
James Chancey	77	73	70	69	289	15,515.66
Mark James	75	73	68	73	289	15,515.66
Tom Kite	76	72	71	70	289	15,515.66
Mark McNulty	70	72	75	72	289	15,515.66
Eamonn Darcy	71	76	74	69	290	13,068.48
David Merriman	74	73	69	74	290	13,068.48
Kiyoshi Murota	75	72	69	74	290	13,068.48
Juan Quiros	74	78	68	70	290	13,068.48
Joey Sindelar	70	77	74	69	290	13,068.48
Jeff Sluman	78	74	70	68	290	13,068.48
John Bland	71	76	71	73	291	10,893.76
Wayne Grady	74	72	73	72	291	10,893.76
Kirk Hanefeld	69	73	72	77	291	10,893.76
Tom McKnight	76	76	68	71	291	10,893.76
Mark Wiebe	74	76	71	70	291	10,893.76
Jerry Bruner	78	72	70	72	292	9,681.52
Mike Reid	73	72	74	73	292	9,681.52
Seiji Ebihara	75	73	74	71	293	8,476.85
Mike Goodes	75	74	73	71	293	8,476.85
Nick Job	69	80	72	72	293	8,476.85
John Morse	70	78	69	76	293	8,476.85
Mark O'Meara	74	75	71	73	293	8,476.85
Clarence Rose	76	73	74	70	293	8,476.85
Scott Simpson	75	77	71	70	293	8,476.85
Luis Carbonetti	72	73	76	73	294	7,429.86
Scott Hoch	79	73	69	73	294	7,429.86
Tim Conley	73	74	75	73	295	6,862.21
Jim Lapsley	76	73	76	70	295	6,862.21

	SCORES				TOTAL	MONEY
Denis O'Sullivan	75	74	71	75	295	6,862.21
Adam Adams	76	71	75	74	296	6,067.51
Angel Franco	76	75	73	72	296	6,067.51
Mike Hulbert	75	76	72	73	296	6,067.51
Katsuyoshi Tomori	78	73	73	72	296	6,067.51
Isao Aoki	75	73	76	73	297	5,499.86
Martin Poxon	75	75	73	75	298	5,045.74
Noel Ratcliffe	76	75	72	75	298	5,045.74
Craig Stadler	74	74	76	74	298	5,045.74
Ross Drummond	72	76	75	76	299	4,377.18
Ken Green	75	71	74	79	299	4,377.18
Andrew Murray	72	76	74	77	299	4,377.18
Bob Boyd	78	72	72	78	300	3,792.72
Terry Gale	78	74	70	78	300	3,792.72
Jim Rhodes	74	75	75	76	300	3,792.72
Jon Chaffee	73	75	75	78	301	3,103.13
Jeff Hall	73	73	79	76	301	3,103.13
John Hoskison	75	77	72	77	301	3,103.13
Peter Mitchell	74	75	73	79	301	3,103.13
Manuel Pinero	78	72	78	73	301	3,103.13
Bertus Smit	76	74	75	76	301	3,103.13
Yutaka Hagawa	75	76	77	74	302	2,604.87
Phil Hinton	77	75	73	77	302	2,604.87
Bill McColl	76	76	76	75	303	2,377.81
Pete Oakley	74	77	75	77	303	2,377.81
Tommy Horton	80	72	72	81	305	2,207.51
Mike Williams	72	79	81	77	309	2,093.98

Bad Ragaz PGA Seniors Open

Golf Club Bad Ragaz, Zurich, Switzerland
Par 35-35–70; 6,152 yards

August 8-10
purse, €260,247

	SCORES			TOTAL	MONEY
Carl Mason	69	61	65	195	€39,000
Bill Longmuir	65	66	66	197	26,000
Angel Fernandez	67	68	65	200	13,663
Juan Quiros	68	67	65	200	13,663
Katsuyoshi Tomori	69	68	63	200	13,663
Gery Watine	72	65	63	200	13,663
Domingo Hospital	65	67	69	201	9,360
Bob Boyd	63	71	68	202	7,453.33
Jim Rhodes	69	68	65	202	7,453.33
Adan Sowa	70	69	63	202	7,453.33
Matt Briggs	70	68	65	203	5,525
Giuseppe Cali	67	67	69	203	5,525
David Good	70	67	66	203	5,525
Nick Job	67	68	68	203	5,525
Bobby Lincoln	71	66	67	204	4,550
Peter Mitchell	69	65	70	204	4,550
Luis Carbonetti	71	69	65	205	4,030
Bob Larratt	70	72	63	205	4,030
John Bland	71	65	70	206	3,666
Gordon J. Brand	69	67	71	207	2,711.80
Delroy Cambridge	67	72	68	207	2,711.80
Bob Cameron	69	67	71	207	2,711.80
David Creamer	71	69	67	207	2,711.80
Seiji Ebihara	73	67	67	207	2,711.80
Angel Franco	68	70	69	207	2,711.80
Martin Gray	68	69	70	207	2,711.80

	SCORES			TOTAL	MONEY
Manuel Pinero	71	67	69	207	2,711.80
Costantino Rocca	68	73	66	207	2,711.80
Emilio Rodriguez	72	67	68	207	2,711.80

De Vere Collection PGA Seniors Championship

De Vere Slaley Hall, Hunting Course, Northumberland, England August 21-24
Par 36-36–72; 7,081 yards purse, €382,254

	SCORES				TOTAL	MONEY
Gordon J. Brand	72	77	68	75	292	€63,460.50
Brand Gordon, Jr.	73	75	74	70	292	40,475.11
(Gordon J. Brand defeated Gordon Brand, Jr. on sixth playoff hole.)						
Eamonn Darcy	74	74	74	71	293	19,291.99
Juan Quiros	73	71	76	73	293	19,291.99
Sam Torrance	76	75	75	67	293	19,291.99
John Chillas	75	74	72	73	294	11,994.03
Ross Drummond	71	73	76	74	294	11,994.03
Tony Johnstone	75	75	71	73	294	11,994.03
Carl Mason	77	73	72	72	294	11,994.03
Andrew Murray	73	76	71	74	294	11,994.03
Domingo Hospital	74	75	70	77	296	8,662.36
Costantino Rocca	75	73	73	75	296	8,662.36
Giuseppe Cali	71	76	74	76	297	7,329.69
Nick Job	76	71	81	70	298	5,806.64
Ian Palmer	77	75	74	72	298	5,806.64
Ian Woosnam	79	76	71	72	298	5,806.64
Graham Banister	77	74	79	69	299	4,306.43
Seiji Ebihara	74	77	72	76	299	4,306.43
David Good	74	74	78	73	299	4,306.43
David Merriman	74	79	77	69	299	4,306.43
Katsuyoshi Tomori	74	76	74	75	299	4,306.43

Travis Perkins plc Senior Masters

Woburn Golf Club, Duke's Course, Milton Keynes, England August 29-31
Par 35-37–72; 6,896 yards purse, €313,242

	SCORES			TOTAL	MONEY
Gordon J. Brand	68	69	70	207	€46,986.37
Juan Quiros	68	68	73	209	31,324.25
Carl Mason	73	66	71	210	21,926.97
Angel Franco	66	74	73	213	17,228.34
Eamonn Darcy	69	71	75	215	13,344.13
Stewart Ginn	75	69	71	215	13,344.13
Nick Job	73	71	72	216	9,553.90
Peter Mitchell	71	70	75	216	9,553.90
Jim Rhodes	69	70	77	216	9,553.90
Costantino Rocca	70	72	74	216	9,553.90
Horacio Carbonetti	68	72	77	217	6,891.33
Seiji Ebihara	73	71	73	217	6,891.33
Ian Woosnam	71	73	73	217	6,891.33
Bob Cameron	70	75	73	218	5,638.36
Luis Carbonetti	73	71	74	218	5,638.36
Mark James	69	75	74	218	5,638.36
Tony Johnstone	75	72	72	219	4,429.25
Andrew Murray	73	74	72	219	4,429.25

	SCORES			TOTAL	MONEY
Pete Oakley	73	76	70	219	4,429.25
Katsuyoshi Tomori	73	74	72	219	4,429.25
Sam Torrance	75	73	71	219	4,429.25

Casa Serena Open

Casa Serena Golf, Prague, Czech Republic
Par 35-36–71; 6,785 yards

September 5-7
purse, €600,000

	SCORES			TOTAL	MONEY
Bernhard Langer	67	67	67	201	€90,000
Ian Woosnam	65	69	70	204	60,000
Bob Boyd	67	68	70	205	37,500
Gordon J. Brand	68	67	70	205	37,500
Domingo Hospital	67	69	70	206	25,560
Peter Mitchell	67	67	72	206	25,560
Ross Drummond	70	65	72	207	19,200
Tony Johnstone	67	70	70	207	19,200
Jose Rivero	69	69	69	207	19,200
John Bland	71	69	68	208	13,800
Delroy Cambridge	70	69	69	208	13,800
Carl Mason	70	66	72	208	13,800
Costantino Rocca	71	67	70	208	13,800
John Chillas	72	68	69	209	11,100
David Good	68	73	68	209	11,100
Tony Allen	66	72	72	210	9,600
Andrew Murray	69	72	69	210	9,600
Pete Oakley	66	73	71	210	9,600
Matt Briggs	72	71	68	211	7,476
Jose Maria Canizares	69	74	68	211	7,476
Angel Franco	72	69	70	211	7,476
Bobby Lincoln	70	71	70	211	7,476
Katsuyoshi Tomori	69	71	71	211	7,476

Weston Homes PGA International Seniors

Stoke by Nayland Golf Club, Suffolk, England
Par 36-36–72; 6,757 yards

September 12-14
purse, €217,932

	SCORES			TOTAL	MONEY
Nick Job	68	65	69	202	€32,528.74
Carl Mason	68	68	68	204	21,685.82
Bill Longmuir	69	69	69	207	15,180.08
Gery Watine	71	67	71	209	11,927.20
Jerry Bruner	69	70	71	210	9,238.16
Ross Drummond	71	68	71	210	9,238.16
Eamonn Darcy	70	71	70	211	6,332.26
Guillermo Encina	70	67	74	211	6,332.26
Domingo Hospital	70	69	72	211	6,332.26
Tony Johnstone	71	70	70	211	6,332.26
Jose Rivero	73	68	70	211	6,332.26
Tony Allen	69	72	71	212	4,554.02
Bruce Heuchan	69	70	73	212	4,554.02
Gordon J. Brand	72	69	72	213	3,795.02
Angel Fernandez	70	70	73	213	3,795.02
Jimmy Heggarty	70	73	70	213	3,795.02
David Merriman	72	71	70	213	3,795.02

	SCORES			TOTAL	MONEY
John Chillas	71	71	72	214	2,875.54
David Good	71	72	71	214	2,875.54
Martin Gray	69	75	70	214	2,875.54
Pete Oakley	72	74	68	214	2,875.54
Steve Stull	75	70	69	214	2,875.54

Scottish Seniors Open

Marriott Dalmahoy Hotel & Country Club, Edinburgh, Scotland
Par 35-37–72; 6,936 yards

September 26-28
purse, €286,200

	SCORES			TOTAL	MONEY
Peter Mitchell	71	67	69	207	€42,931.35
Sam Torrance	71	69	69	209	28,620.90
Des Smyth	68	71	71	210	20,034.63
Eamonn Darcy	72	71	69	212	15,741.50
Jerry Bruner	70	70	73	213	12,192.50
Simon Owen	71	72	70	213	12,192.50
Andrew Murray	73	70	71	214	10,303.52
Ross Drummond	74	69	72	215	8,586.27
Denis O'Sullivan	74	70	71	215	8,586.27
Domingo Hospital	69	71	76	216	6,869.02
Bill Longmuir	70	73	73	216	6,869.02
Costantino Rocca	70	73	73	216	6,869.02
Matt Briggs	75	70	72	217	5,437.97
Angel Fernandez	70	78	69	217	5,437.97
Emilio Rodriguez	75	70	72	217	5,437.97
John Hoskison	73	72	73	218	4,579.34
Carl Mason	71	77	70	218	4,579.34
Pete Oakley	75	73	70	218	4,579.34
Gordon Brand, Jr.	74	72	73	219	3,670.63
Tommy Horton	75	73	71	219	3,670.63
Tony Johnstone	74	73	72	219	3,670.63
David Merriman	75	70	74	219	3,670.63

Lake Garda Italian Seniors Open

Palazzo Arzaga Hotel, Spa & Golf Resort, Lake Garda, Italy
Par 36-36–72; 6,940 yards

October 10-12
purse, €200,000

	SCORES			TOTAL	MONEY
Peter Mitchell	68	67	68	203	€30,000
Gordon J. Brand	71	65	68	204	17,000
Ian Woosnam	72	65	67	204	17,000
Guillermo Encina	67	68	70	205	11,000
Philip Harrison	67	71	68	206	9,040
Jim Lapsley	68	72	68	208	8,000
David Merriman	66	73	70	209	6,800
Costantino Rocca	68	69	72	209	6,800
Carl Mason	72	69	69	210	5,400
Emilio Rodriguez	73	63	74	210	5,400
Domingo Hospital	68	70	73	211	4,400
Bobby Lincoln	73	68	70	211	4,400
Bill Longmuir	76	67	68	211	4,400
Tony Allen	69	69	74	212	3,500
Bob Cameron	72	68	72	212	3,500
Denis O'Sullivan	71	72	69	212	3,500

	SCORES			TOTAL	MONEY
David J. Russell	74	72	66	212	3,500
Ross Drummond	74	68	71	213	2,820
Angel Franco	71	69	73	213	2,820
Sam Torrance	73	69	71	213	2,820

OKI Castellon Open Espana – Senior Tour Championship

Club de Campo del Mediterraneo, Castellon, Spain   November 7-9
Par 36-36–72; 6,818 yards   purse, €400,000

	SCORES			TOTAL	MONEY
Sam Torrance	68	66	69	203	€64,433
Angel Fernandez	66	70	69	205	36,512.03
Katsuyoshi Tomori	69	68	68	205	36,512.03
Jose Rivero	70	66	71	207	21,520.62
Emilio Rodriguez	68	70	69	207	21,520.62
Bill Longmuir	70	70	68	208	16,323.03
Des Smyth	70	71	67	208	16,323.03
Jerry Bruner	68	70	71	209	12,886.60
Bob Cameron	69	67	73	209	12,886.60
Horacio Carbonetti	67	70	73	210	10,309.28
Luis Carbonetti	71	68	71	210	10,309.28
Stewart Ginn	75	67	68	210	10,309.28
Giuseppe Cali	72	72	67	211	7,946.74
Ross Drummond	68	71	72	211	7,946.74
Angel Franco	74	70	67	211	7,946.74
Tony Johnstone	72	71	68	211	7,946.74
Jim Rhodes	71	72	69	212	6,872.85
Costantino Rocca	66	76	71	213	6,443.30
Nick Job	70	72	73	215	6,056.70
John Bland	72	73	71	216	4,918.39
Bob Boyd	71	75	70	216	4,918.39
Delroy Cambridge	75	72	69	216	4,918.39
Carl Mason	70	73	73	216	4,918.39
Denis O'Sullivan	74	69	73	216	4,918.39
Juan Quiros	71	71	74	216	4,918.39

Japan Senior Tour

Starts Senior Golf Tournament

Narita Golf Club, Narita, Chiba
Par 36-36–72; 6,944 yards

June 6-8
purse, ¥60,000,000

	SCORES			TOTAL	MONEY
Hajime Meshiai	70	68	65	203	¥13,500,000
Katsunari Takahashi	70	66	70	206	5,130,000
Tsuneyuki Nakajima	73	66	69	208	3,510,000
Takashi Miyoshi	69	69	71	209	2,106,000
Noboru Fujiike	72	71	66	209	2,106,000
Hiroshi Makino	72	70	68	210	1,674,000
Tateo Ozaki	71	68	72	211	1,390,500
Kiyoshi Murota	71	71	69	211	1,390,500
Hisashi Nakase	70	70	72	212	1,042,200
Gohei Sato	71	69	72	212	1,042,200
Sinji Kuraoka	72	69	71	212	1,042,200
Tomohiro Maruyama	74	67	71	212	1,042,200
Nobumitsu Yuhara	70	73	69	212	1,042,200
Hideto Shigenobu	71	69	73	213	783,000·
Minoru Hatsumi	74	68	71	213	783,000
Tsukasa Watanabe	72	73	68	213	783,000
Toru Nakamura	72	73	68	213	783,000
Dragon Taki	71	69	74	214	574,714
Saburo Fujiki	70	71	73	214	574,714
Toyotake Nakao	73	69	72	214	574,714
Katuji Hasegawa	69	74	71	214	574,714
Takaaki Fukuzawa	72	71	71	214	574,714
Teruo Nakamura	71	73	70	214	574,714
Kimpachi Yoshimura	70	75	69	214	574,714

Fancl Classic

Susono Country Club, Susono, Shizuoka
Par 36-36–72; 6,851 yards

August 22-24
purse, ¥60,000,000

	SCORES			TOTAL	MONEY
Tateo Ozaki	69	67	71	207	¥15,000,000
Tsukasa Watanabe	67	68	73	208	6,900,000
Tsuneyuki Nakajima	70	69	71	210	3,300,000
Tomohiro Maruyama	70	68	72	210	3,300,000
Hajime Meshiai	71	69	71	211	2,250,000
Masami Ito	68	70	73	211	2,250,000
Tsunemi Nakajima	68	72	73	213	1,540,000
Kiyoshi Murota	71	69	73	213	1,540,000
Hiroshi Makino	71	67	75	213	1,540,000
Noboru Fujiike	68	72	74	214	1,149,000
David Ishii	71	69	74	214	1,149,000
Gohei Sato	73	70	72	215	885,500
Yoshinori Ichioka	72	71	72	215	885,500
Takashi Miyoshi	73	70	72	215	885,500
Shuichi Sano	70	72	73	215	885,500

	SCORES			TOTAL	MONEY
Teruo Nakamura	72	68	75	215	885,500
Tokio Kaneko	68	70	77	215	885,500
Yoshio Fumiyama	72	70	74	216	735,000
Kimpachi Yoshimura	73	68	75	216	735,000
Katsunari Takahashi	72	73	72	217	645,000
Hisashi Nakase	74	68	75	217	645,000
Chen Tze-ming	70	71	76	217	645,000
Shinji Kuraoka	68	71	78	217	645,000

Komatsu Open

Komatsu Country Club, Komatsu, Ishikawa
Par 36-36–72; 6,932 yards

September 5-7
purse, ¥60,000,000

	SCORES			TOTAL	MONEY
Hisashi Nakase	67	68	68	203	¥12,000,000
Hajime Meshiai	67	69	68	204	4,860,000
Takashi Miyoshi	69	68	67	204	4,860,000
Toyotake Nakao	73	66	66	205	2,700,000
Katsunari Takahashi	71	65	71	207	2,100,000
Tsukasa Watanabe	66	70	71	207	2,100,000
Tomohiro Maruyama	71	69	68	208	1,680,000
Tateo Ozaki	71	70	68	209	1,518,000
Tsunemi Nakajima	69	69	72	210	1,182,000
Seiji Ebihara	71	67	72	210	1,182,000
Lim Jin-han	68	71	71	210	1,182,000
Gohei Sato	72	68	70	210	1,182,000
Masami Ito	72	68	70	210	1,182,000
Taisei Inagaki	69	72	69	210	1,182,000
Tsuneyuki Nakajima	72	70	68	210	1,182,000
Takeru Shibata	69	70	72	211	867,000
Chen Tze-ming	71	68	72	211	867,000
Takaaki Fukuzawa	71	72	69	212	777,000
Nobumitsu Yuhara	73	71	68	212	777,000
Koji Okuno	70	71	72	213	693,000
Toru Nakamura	71	71	71	213	693,000

Akira Kobayashi Invitational Sanko Senior

Sakakibaraonsen Golf Club, Sakakibaraonsen, Mie
Par 36-36–72; 6,809 yards

September 13-14
purse, ¥20,000,000

	SCORES		TOTAL	MONEY
Hajime Meshiai	63	75	138	¥3,600,000
Tomohiro Maruyama	69	70	139	1,490,000
Taisei Inagaki	71	68	139	1,490,000
Yutaka Hagawa	68	72	140	860,000
Somei Sudo	68	73	141	660,000
Hisashi Nakase	71	70	141	660,000
Hideto Shigenobu	71	70	141	660,000
Tsukasa Watanabe	66	76	142	420,000
Takashi Miyoshi	69	73	142	420,000
Masami Ito	70	72	142	420,000
Kikuo Arai	72	70	142	420,000
Katsunari Takahashi	69	74	143	293,500
Shinji Kuraoka	70	73	143	293,500
Nobumitsu Yuhara	72	71	143	293,500

	SCORES				TOTAL	MONEY
Gohei Sato	73	70			143	293,500
Noboru Fujiike	71	73			144	250,000
Kiyoshi Murota	72	72			144	250,000
Yoshio Fumiyama	72	72			144	250,000
Seiji Ebihara	68	77			145	225,000
Tsunemi Nakajima	71	74			145	225,000
Hiroshi Fujita	74	71			145	225,000
Hisao Inoue	74	71			145	225,000
Yukio Noguchi	74	71			145	225,000

Japan PGA Senior Championship

Shizu Hills Country Club, Hitachiomiya, Ibaraki
Par 36-36–72; 7,013 yards

September 25-28
purse, ¥50,000,000

	SCORES				TOTAL	MONEY
Tsukasa Watanabe	68	74	69	70	281	¥10,000,000
Katsunari Takahashi	73	68	71	71	283	5,000,000
Akira Yabe	73	70	69	72	284	3,500,000
Katsuyoshi Tomori	71	72	72	70	285	2,500,000
Gohei Sato	72	72	74	69	287	1,750,000
Hideto Shigenobu	72	76	71	68	287	1,750,000
Lim Jin-han	68	71	75	74	288	1,250,000
Nobumitsu Yuhara	69	71	75	73	288	1,250,000
Masami Ito	74	71	71	72	288	1,250,000
Nichito Hashimoto	73	70	68	78	289	1,000,000
Noboru Fujiike	74	71	73	71	289	1,000,000
Shuichi Sano	72	71	77	69	289	1,000,000
Seiji Ebihara	72	73	71	74	290	825,000
Kiyoshi Murota	72	75	71	72	290	825,000
Hisashi Nakase	77	73	68	72	290	825,000
Chen Tze-chung	73	74	74	69	290	825,000
Yoshinori Ichioka	73	69	72	77	291	632,500
Yoshio Fumiyama	74	71	71	75	291	632,500
Tomohiro Maruyama	70	74	74	73	291	632,500
Tateo Ozaki	72	73	74	72	291	632,500

Fujifilm Senior Championship

Hirakawa Country Club, Hirakawa, Ibaraki
Par 36-36–72; 6,978 yards

October 2-4
purse, ¥100,000,000

	SCORES			TOTAL	MONEY
Tsukasa Watanabe	69	64	69	202	¥20,000,000
Kiyoshi Murota	71	65	74	210	6,833,333
Hajime Meshiai	70	67	73	210	6,833,333
Naomichi Ozaki	70	70	70	210	6,833,333
Takashi Miyoshi	70	73	68	211	3,600,000
Chen Tze-chung	71	70	71	212	2,850,000
David Ishii	73	69	70	212	2,850,000
Yutaka Hagawa	71	70	73	214	2,100,000
Isao Aoki	72	70	72	214	2,100,000
Katsunari Takahashi	71	71	72	214	2,100,000
Hideto Shigenobu	73	70	71	214	2,100,000
Yoshio Fumiyama	73	73	68	214	2,100,000
Tomohiro Maruyama	74	67	74	215	1,575,000
Katsumi Nanjyo	70	73	72	215	1,575,000

	SCORES			TOTAL	MONEY
Tateo Ozaki	74	72	70	216	1,350,000
Hiroshi Fujita	73	75	68	216	1,350,000
Gohei Sato	73	69	75	217	1,160,000
Kimpachi Yoshimura	73	73	71	217	1,160,000
Hisashi Nakase	74	72	72	218	975,000
Yoshitaka Yamamoto	76	70	72	218	975,000
Toyotake Nakao	75	72	71	218	975,000
Katsuyoshi Tomori	74	75	69	218	975,000

Japan Senior Open Championship

Sayama Golf Club, Sayama, Saitama
Par 36-36–72; 6,985 yards

October 23-26
purse, ¥80,000,000

	SCORES				TOTAL	MONEY
Tsuneyuki Nakajima	66	68	67	72	273	¥16,000,000
Kiyoshi Murota	70	69	72	68	279	8,800,000
Nobumitsu Yuhara	70	68	69	73	280	5,080,000
Seiji Ebihara	72	73	69	66	280	5,080,000
Tateo Ozaki	71	68	73	69	281	3,360,000
Toyotake Nakao	69	71	70	72	282	2,600,000
Yutaka Hagawa	70	69	71	72	282	2,600,000
Katsunari Takahashi	74	70	71	68	283	2,080,000
David Ishii	73	70	70	71	284	1,760,000
Noboru Fujiike	68	76	72	69	285	1,520,000
Nick Job	70	72	73	72	287	1,400,000
Chen Tze-ming	68	70	75	75	288	1,122,666
Yoshitaka Yamamoto	73	70	74	71	288	1,122,666
Isao Aoki	74	71	73	70	288	1,122,666
Gohei Sato	74	70	73	72	289	912,000
Hajime Meshiai	72	74	74	69	289	912,000
Hiroshi Makino	72	74	71	73	290	800,000
Tsukasa Watanabe	72	76	71	71	290	800,000
Tomohiro Maruyama	74	70	77	69	290	800,000
Yoshinori Mizumaki	69	72	74	76	291	659,428
Bob Cameron	71	72	75	73	291	659,428
Yoshinori Ichioka	78	70	71	72	291	659,428
Masami Ito	74	73	73	71	291	659,428
Yasuzo Hagiwara	72	75	73	71	291	659,428
Chen Tze-chung	75	75	70	71	291	659,428
Tsunemi Nakajima	73	73	75	70	291	659,428

Kinojo Senior Open

Kinojo Golf Club, Kinojo, Okayama
Par 36-36–72; 6,869 yards

November 7-9
purse, ¥25,000,000

	SCORES			TOTAL	MONEY
Isao Aoki	69	67	66	202	¥4,500,000
Tsukasa Watanabe	71	68	63	202	2,250,000
(Aoki defeated Watanabe on fourth playoff hole.)					
Minoru Hatsumi	66	70	70	206	1,308,333
Teruo Nakamura	69	68	69	206	1,308,333
Chen Tze-chung	72	68	66	206	1,308,333
Seiji Ebihara	68	68	72	208	975,000
Noboru Fujiike	68	71	70	209	800,000
Yoshitaka Yamamoto	69	72	68	209	800,000

	SCORES			TOTAL	MONEY
Katsunari Takahashi	68	71	71	210	556,250
Toshiaki Sudo	71	69	70	210	556,250
Takashi Miyoshi	67	74	69	210	556,250
Hiroshi Makino	71	70	69	210	556,250
Tadami Ueno	70	69	72	211	450,000
Syuichi Sano	68	71	73	212	387,500
Tsunemi Nakajima	68	72	72	212	387,500
Chen Tze-ming	71	71	70	212	387,500
Teruyasu Hayashi	73	75	64	212	387,500
Tokio Kaneko	68	74	71	213	312,500
Tomohiro Maruyama	73	72	68	213	312,500
Gohei Sato	68	73	73	214	265,000
Yoshinori Ichioka	72	72	70	214	265,000

PGA Handa Cup Philanthropy Senior Open

Ohmurasaki Golf Club, Ohmurasaki, Saitama   November 27-30
Par 36-36–72; 6,853 yards   purse, ¥120,000,000

	SCORES				TOTAL	MONEY
Takashi Miyoshi	72	64	77	68	281	¥30,000,000
Hajime Meshiai	67	69	74	71	281	13,800,000
(Miyoshi defeated Meshiai on fourth playoff hole.)						
Masahiro Kuramoto	72	67	73	70	282	8,400,000
Kiyoshi Murota	74	71	70	71	286	6,000,000
Terry Gale	65	73	75	74	287	3,720,000
Gohei Sato	71	69	78	69	287	3,720,000
Masami Ito	71	70	74	72	287	3,720,000
Hisashi Nakase	72	75	71	69	287	3,720,000
Taisei Inagaki	70	70	78	70	288	2,190,000
Naomichi Ozaki	74	71	69	74	288	2,190,000
Teruo Nakamura	73	71	73	71	288	2,190,000
Koichi Suzuki	77	71	68	72	288	2,190,000
Katsunari Takahashi	72	68	76	73	289	1,500,000
Hiroshi Makino	70	70	73	76	289	1,500,000
Takaaki Fukuzawa	73	71	72	73	289	1,500,000
Tsunemi Nakajima	73	70	75	71	289	1,500,000
Tsukasa Watanabe	72	69	74	74	289	1,500,000
Toshiaki Sudo	71	75	71	72	289	1,500,000
Teruyasu Hayashi	72	68	75	75	290	1,065,600
Tateo Ozaki	70	73	74	73	290	1,065,600
Noboru Fujiike	70	73	74	73	290	1,065,600
Shinji Kuraoka	73	72	72	73	290	1,065,600
Shuichi Sano	74	72	71	73	290	1,065,600